Principles of
MARKETING

Principles of
MARKETING

 **18e GLOBAL EDITION**

Philip Kotler
Northwestern University

Gary Armstrong
University of North Carolina

With
Marc Oliver Opresnik
St. Gallen Management Institute

Pearson

Harlow, England • London • New York • Boston • San Francisco • Toronto • Sydney • Dubai • Singapore • Hong Kong
Tokyo • Seoul • Taipei • New Delhi • Cape Town • Sao Paulo • Mexico City • Madrid • Amsterdam • Munich • Paris • Milan

Please contact https://support.pearson.com/getsupport/s/contactsupport with any queries on this content.

Pearson Education Limited
KAO Two
KAO Park
Hockham Way
Harlow
Essex
CM17 9SR
United Kingdom

and Associated Companies throughout the world

Visit us on the World Wide Web at: www.pearsonglobaleditions.com

Authorized adaptation from the United States edition, entitled Principles of Marketing, *18th Edition, ISBN 978-0-13-576659-0 by Philip Kotler and Gary Armstrong, published by Pearson Education © 2021.*

Acknowledgments of third-party content appear on the appropriate page within the text.

ISBN 10: 1-292-34113-0

ISBN 13: 978-1-292-34113-2

British Library Cataloguing-in-Publication Data

A catalogue record for this book is available from the British Library

1 21

Typeset in Palatino LT Pro-Roman by Integra Software Services

Printed and bound by Vivar in Malaysia

To Kathy, Betty, Mandy, Matt, KC, Keri, Delaney, Molly, Macy, and Ben; and Nancy, Amy, Melissa, and Jessica

Brief Contents

Contents

CHAPTER **8** Products, Services, and Brands: Building Customer Value *232*

CHAPTER **9** Developing New Products and Managing the Product Life Cycle *268*

CHAPTER **10** Pricing: Understanding and Capturing Customer Value *294*

CHAPTER **11** Pricing Strategies: Additional Considerations *316*

12 CONTENTS

Preface

New to This Edition

All That's New in Marketing

The eighteenth edition of *Principles of Marketing* reflects the major trends and shifting forces that impact marketing in this digital age of customer value, engagement, and relationships. Here are just some of the major new and continuing changes you'll find in this edition.

- *Customer engagement framework:* This eighteenth edition continues to build on its *customer engagement* framework—creating direct and continuous customer involvement in shaping brands, brand conversations, brand experiences, brand advocacy, and brand community. New coverage and fresh examples throughout the text address the latest customer engagement tools, practices, and developments.
- *Fast-changing marketing trends and topics:* This edition adds fresh coverage of both traditional marketing areas and fast-changing topics such as digital, mobile, and social media marketing; customer engagement marketing; the customer journey; big data, artificial intelligence, and new marketing analytics; the major digital transformation in marketing research; omni-channel marketing and the massive shifts in today's retailing; direct-to-consumer marketing (DTC); real-time customer listening and marketing; marketing content creation and native advertising; B-to-B social media and social selling; online and dynamic pricing; sustainability; global marketing; and much more.
- *Online, mobile, social media, and other digital marketing technologies:* Keeping up with digital concepts, technologies, and practices has become a top priority and major challenge for today's marketers. The eighteenth edition of *Principles of Marketing* provides thoroughly refreshed, up-to-date coverage of these explosive developments in every chapter—from digital, online, mobile, and social media engagement technologies in Chapters 1, 5, 14, 15, and 17; to "big data," new marketing analytics, the Internet of Things, and artificial intelligence in Chapters 1, 3, and 4; to the massive shift to omni-channel and digital retailing in Chapters 13 and 17; to the increasing use of augmented and virtual reality in Chapters 4 and 13. A Chapter 1 section on *The Digital Age: Online, Mobile, and Social Media Marketing* introduces the exciting new developments in digital and social media marketing. Then a Chapter 17 section on *Direct, Online, Social Media, and Mobile Marketing* digs more deeply into digital marketing tools such as online sites, social media, mobile ads and apps, online video, email, and other digital platforms that engage consumers anywhere, anytime via their computers, smartphones, tablets, and other digital devices.
- *Content marketing and marketing communications:* The eighteenth edition continues to track fast-changing developments in marketing communications and the creation of brand content. Marketers no longer simply create advertising and integrated marketing communications programs; they join with customers and media to curate and share marketing content in paid, owned, earned, and shared media. You won't find fresher coverage of these important topics in any other marketing text.

New Real-World Brand Stories, Highlights, Cases, and In-Text Examples

The eighteenth edition of *Principles of Marketing* is loaded with new brand stories, highlight features, cases, in-text examples, and end-of-chapter exercises and features that illustrate brand strategies and contemporary marketing issues and let students apply what they've learned.

- *Chapter-opening stories, Real Marketing highlights, and in-text examples:* The eighteenth edition brings marketing to life with new or heavily revised chapter-opening vignettes,

Company Case Bayer: Big Data for Customer Insights

Bayer Aktiengesellschaft, or Bayer AG, is a life sciences company and a global leader in healthcare and nutrition. Headquartered in Leverkusen, Germany, Bayer has a strong presence in Europe and more than 150 years of experience. To expand its operations, Bayer carefully examines the size of the market, determines its profitability, and analyzes the entry and exit barriers. Marketing information is vital for decisions on entering new markets and about adapting to existing ones, but Bayer must balance its information gathering against its policy on customers' data privacy as well as alignment with future operational objectives. When it comes to entering new markets, Bayer's analyses are based heavily on customer satisfaction and performance measures.

Reading the Customer's Mind

Bayer bases its various strategies on marketing information. Some of its markets are difficult to operate in; for example, pharmaceuticals involves multiple customers, distribution channels, purchasing arrangements and pricing methodologies, marketing techniques, and cost-control tools or prescription drug reimbursement systems. Gaining useful customer or marketplace insights from these various sources is challenging. Additionally, Bayer conducts research to discover new drugs and tests and validates their effectiveness and safety before introducing them to the market. As such, the company accumulates, analyzes, and stores vast amounts of clinical data from patients as well as healthy volunteers. Marketing information is also collected from laboratories and electronic devices but is automatically anonymized at the point of collection, following the guidelines and regulations created by local drugs administrations. Recently, Bayer deployed a microservices-based architecture for its data platform to enable easier and faster analysis of drug development data for company's researchers.

Bayer operates mainly as a business-to-business (B2B) company, but in the pharmaceuticals market, its focus is on researching, developing, and marketing specialty-focused medicines to businesses as well as individual consumers. Its products are distributed to hospitals and general practitioners, who also deliver useful marketplace insights. But Bayer carefully examines all information gathered even before it distributes to these intermediaries. For example, for distribution of the allergy drug Claritin, Bayer uses third-party analytics to analyze global warming data so that it can model the supply based on weather trends and allergy trends.

Bayer's customer insights and marketplace data are processed based mainly on how specialized products are received within the pharmaceutical market. Healthcare division insights are communicated between Bayer and the brands to which its products are distributed. Coupled with a large geographical footprint, this results in an enormous store of insights and techniques that can be used in marketing mix decision-making, formulation of marketing strategy, as well as daily business operations.

Bayer has market- and customer-specific distribution channels for each segment in which it operates. Through a number of programs, such as its Patient-Focused Transformation of Customer Engagement, the company draws on the experiences and challenges of participants to support business transformation initiatives at the company with the objective of shifting mindsets, implementing new processes, building new skills, or changing target behaviors. This customer engagement model

has transformed information gathering into a single customer-centric and patient-focused model.

The consumer health and pharmaceuticals segments are connected to a global pharmaceutical monitoring system that includes safety management teams and experts across various disciplines. To detect potential safety concerns early on and identify changes in the risk-benefit profile, such teams must evaluate internal benefits, safety data, marketing studies, clinical trials, external databases, and scientific publications. These are all entered into Bayer's pharmacovigilance database, which is used in market research to test the viability of new products and services based on the responses of potential customers. The company is constantly investing in R&D—which generates information—but each product must also comply with the relevant regulatory environment.

Diving Deeper for Insights

At Bayer, internal data is information about customers—current and potential—collected primarily from four major sources: sales, finance, human resources, and marketing. However, gaining trade insights from each segments can be challenging due to legal requirements, especially from sources such as patients. For example, to collect customer satisfaction data, the company must follow different standards for prescription medicines and for non-prescription medicines.

Bayer's marketing activities focus on the local needs of its customers, but these needs can vary significantly. The company's customer-focused marketing activities take this into account. For instance, working together with Kansas City-based Consumer Orbit, Bayer combines the data it generates with the firm's databases, resulting in a total of 63 trillion pieces of data that enable Bayer to build a model of its customer base and deliver tailored messages to its customers through their preferred communications platform.

However, customer messages may differ merely because each country or state has its own set of rules and laws. The company must adhere to laws and regulations dealing with marketing practices; global, regional, and local industry codes; customer privacy and protection of consumer information and data; and recommendation and promotion only of lawful uses (for instance, there should be no off-label promotion for medicinal products). Ongoing dialogues with customers enable the company to take such local and country-specific regulatory frameworks into account and deploy optimization measures.

Bayer analyzes customer satisfaction reports and customer complaints to compare the company's performance in the individual segments, optimize its measures, and safeguard its long-term business strategy. Various marketing research techniques ensure accurate directions for shaping and redefining its marketing strategy. For instance, by using AI-driven diagnostic and treatment support for individual customers in the pharmaceuticals segment, the company accelerates the discovery of new drugs for heart conditions while combining processing power with the large data sets and advanced analytics available for marketing information. This allows Bayer to offer a personalized testing and treatment as well as personalized online medical consulting that examines customers' lifestyles, health, and diet directly through a website.

On June 7, 2018 Bayer acquired 100 percent of the outstanding shares of Monsanto Company. Bayer's strong position

boxed features that highlight relevant companies and marketing issues, and loads of new in-text examples throughout that illustrate contemporary marketing practice.

- *New company cases and end-of-chapter applications and exercises:* The eighteenth edition provides 20 new company cases by which students can apply what they learn to actual company situations. End-of-chapter discussion questions, critical thinking exercises, and other applications features are also new and revised.

Solving Teaching and Learning Challenges

Today's marketing is all about creating customer value and engagement in a fast-changing, increasingly digital and social marketplace. Marketing starts with understanding consumer needs and wants, determining which target markets the organization can serve best, and developing a compelling value proposition by which the organization can attract and grow valued consumers. Then, more than just making a sale, today's marketers want to engage customers and build deep customer relationships that make their brands a meaningful part of consumers' conversations and lives.

In this digital age, to go along with their tried-and-true traditional marketing methods, marketers have a dazzling set of new online, mobile, and social media tools for engaging customers anytime, anyplace to jointly shape brand conversations, experiences, advocacy, and community. If marketers do these things well, they will reap the rewards in terms of market share, profits, and customer equity. In the eighteenth edition of *Principles of Marketing*, students learn how customer value and customer engagement drive every good marketing strategy.

Five Major Customer Value and Engagement Themes

The eighteenth edition of *Principles of Marketing* builds on five major customer value and engagement themes:

- *Creating value* **for** *customers in order to capture value* **from** *customers in return.* Today's marketers must be good at *creating customer value, engaging customers,* and *managing customer relationships.* In return, they capture value from customers in the form of sales, profits, and customer equity. This innovative *customer value and engagement framework* is introduced at the start of Chapter 1 in a unique five-step marketing process model, which details how marketing *creates* customer value and *captures* value in return. The framework is carefully developed in the first two chapters and then fully integrated throughout the remainder of the text.

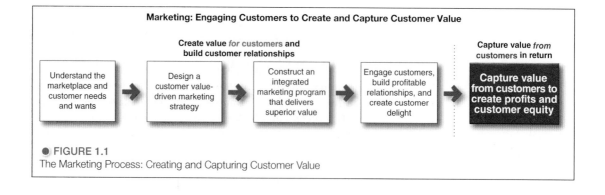

Marketing: Engaging Customers to Create and Capture Customer Value

Create value for customers and build customer relationships | **Capture value from customers in return**

Understand the marketplace and customer needs and wants → Design a customer value-driven marketing strategy → Construct an integrated marketing program that delivers superior value → Engage customers, build profitable relationships, and create customer delight → **Capture value from customers to create profits and customer equity**

● FIGURE 1.1
The Marketing Process: Creating and Capturing Customer Value

- *Customer engagement and today's digital and social media.* Digital and social media have taken today's marketing by storm, dramatically changing how companies and brands engage consumers and how consumers connect and influence each other's brand behaviors. The eighteenth edition thoroughly explores the exciting new digital, mobile, and social media technologies that help brands to engage customers more deeply and interactively. It starts with two major Chapter 1 sections: *Customer Engagement and Today's Digital and Social* Media and *The Digital Age: Online, Mobile, and Social Media*. A refreshed Chapter 17 on *Direct, Online, Social Media, and Mobile Marketing* summarizes the latest developments in digital engagement and relationship-building tools. Everywhere in between, you'll find revised and expanded coverage of the exploding use of digital and social marketing tools.
- *Building and managing strong, value-creating brands.* Well-positioned brands with strong brand equity provide the basis upon which to build customer value and profitable customer relationships. Today's marketers must position their brands powerfully and manage them well to create valued brand experiences. The eighteenth edition provides a deep focus on brands, anchored by a Chapter 8 section on *Branding Strategy: Building Strong Brands*.
- *Measuring and managing return on marketing.* Especially in uneven economic times, marketing managers must ensure that their marketing dollars are being well spent. "Marketing accountability"—measuring and managing marketing return on investment—has now become an important part of strategic marketing decision making. This emphasis on marketing accountability is addressed in Chapter 2, in *Appendix 2: Marketing by the Numbers,* and throughout the eighteenth edition.
- *Sustainable marketing around the globe.* As technological developments make the world an increasingly smaller and more fragile place, marketers must be good at marketing their brands globally and in sustainable ways. New material throughout the eighteenth edition emphasizes the concepts of global marketing and sustainable marketing—meeting the present needs of consumers and businesses while also preserving or enhancing the ability of future generations to meet their needs. The eighteenth edition integrates global marketing and sustainability topics throughout the text. It then provides focused coverage on each topic in Chapters 19 and 20, respectively.

In-Text Teaching and Learning Features

Principles of Marketing provides a wealth of chapter-opening, within-chapter, and end-of-chapter learning features that help students to learn, link, and apply major concepts.

- *Integrated chapter-opening preview sections.* The active and integrative chapter-opening spread in each chapter starts with an *Objectives Outline* that provides a helpful preview of chapter contents and learning objectives, complete with page numbers. Next, a *Chapter Preview* section briefly previews chapter concepts, links them with previous chapter concepts, and introduces the chapter-opening story. Finally, a *chapter-opening vignette*—an engaging, deeply developed, illustrated, and annotated marketing story—introduces the chapter material and sparks student interest.

APPENDIX 2 **Marketing by the Numbers**

Marketing managers are facing increased accountability for the financial implications of their actions. This appendix provides a basic introduction to measuring marketing financial performance. Such financial analysis guides marketers in making sound marketing decisions and in assessing the outcomes of those decisions.

CHAPTER 17 | Direct, Online, Social Media, and Mobile Marketing   **521**

Marketing by the Numbers   Uniqlo's Digital Marketing Campaigns

Uniqlo is a Japanese retail brand that has grown into a global brand in 15 countries thanks to digital marketing campaigns. Founder Tadashi Yanai inherited a chain of men's tailoring retail stores, so he was no stranger to fashion retailing. But he wanted to bring affordable, fashionable, casual clothing to all people, so he created Uniqlo in 1984 to offer casual clothing for all. The philosophy of the brand is "UNIQLO clothes are MADE FOR ALL." The company focuses on its signature innovative clothing lines that have names like HeatTech, UV Cut, LifeWear, and AIRism. In 2007, its pioneering "Uniqlock" viral marketing campaign won dozens of advertising awards, including the coveted Grand Prix award at Cannes. The company continues to run digital marketing campaigns, and while awards are nice, results are better. Marketers measure all sorts of metrics related to digital campaigns, from impressions and click-throughs to purchases.

Consider one of its most recent digital campaigns running in the United States to increase brand awareness and sales of its LifeWear line of clothing:

Measures	Value
Impressions	4,000,000
Click-through to site	150,000
Cost of campaign	$45,000
Number of orders	10,250
Revenue generated	$750,000
Abandoned shopping cart	650
Average cost of goods sold (%)	45%
Shipping and handling costs (per order)	$8.50

Performance Metric	Equation
Click-through rate (CTR)	(Click-throughs ÷ Impressions) × 100
Cost-per-click (CPC)	Cost of campaign ÷ Click-throughs
Conversion ratio	(Number of orders ÷ Click-throughs) × 100
Cost per conversion	Cost of campaign ÷ Number of orders
Average-order-value (AOV)	Revenue generated ÷ Number of orders
Shopping cart abandonment rate	(Abandoned shopping cart ÷ Click-throughs) × 100

Fixed costs
Costs that do not vary with produ
sales level.

17-14 Calculate the performance metrics listed in the preceding table. Based on these metrics, evaluate the campaign. (AACSB: Communication; Analytic Reasoning; Reflective Thinking)

Variable costs
Costs that vary directly with the le
production.

17-15 Calculate the net marketing contribution (NMC), marketing return on sales marketing ROS), and

Total costs
The sum of the fixed and variable
for any given level of production.

marketing return on investment (marketing ROI). Was the campaign successful? Refer to Marketing Profitability Metrics in Appendix 2: Marketing by the Numbers to learn how to do this analysis. (AACSB: Communication; Reflective Thinking; Analytic Reasoning)

Company Case   OfferUp: A Mobile Solution for the Mobile Era

When people think of buying and selling things online locally, most think automatically of Craigslist, the classified ad marketplace that has dominated that business for the past two decades. But as the rest of the world has gone mobile, Craigslist has not. In fact, the familiar but cluttered collection of blue hyperlinks has changed very little over the years. Some critics suggest that Craigslist has taken its monopoly for granted. One industry observer refers to Craigslist as "the cockroach of the internet age—an ugly but effective e-commerce platform that...emerged unscathed from technology shifts that crippled mightier contemporaries like Netscape and Yahoo."

In the new landscape of digital disruption, one thing seems certain: What dominates today could be under threat tomorrow. That tomorrow may already be here for Craigslist as numerous, more user-friendly competitors have emerged to challenge the classified ad market. Enter OfferUp—a relatively new mobile app for buying and selling items that is taking the digital marketplace by storm. OfferUp is not only challenging Craigslist as the go-to platform by which individuals and businesses sell goods and services in local markets, it's also starting to challenge the likes

of eBay and even Amazon by flexing its muscles beyond local market boundaries. Unexpectedly, OfferUp now rivals the most popular social media apps in terms of time spent by users.

About a decade ago, as the mobile device revolution began to explode, Seattle resident Nick Huzar was frustrated as he tried to unload unwanted household items in preparation for his soon-to-be-born daughter's nursery. He didn't have time to post all these items on Craigslist, which required multiple steps that pretty much required a desktop or laptop to complete. Instead, he went to Goodwill, where he always found a line to drop donations. With a smartphone in his hand, he recognized the potential for an online marketplace that made posting, monitoring, and browsing items for sale in a local market as simple as social media interactions. That led to a partnership with friend Arean van Veelen and the ultimate launch of OfferUp in 2011.

A Different Kind of Marketplace
The main thing that differentiates OfferUp from Craigslist and other traditional online marketplace platforms is that it's

- *Author comments and figure annotations.* Throughout each chapter, author comments ease and enhance student learning by introducing and explaining major chapter sections and figures.
- *Reviewing and extending the concepts.* Sections at the end of each chapter summarize key chapter concepts and provide questions and exercises by which students can review and apply what they've learned. The *Objectives Review* section reviews major chapter concepts and links them to chapter objectives. The *Key Terms* section provides a helpful listing of chapter key terms by order of appearance with page numbers that facilitate easy reference. *Discussion Questions* and *Critical Thinking Exercises* sections help students to keep track of and apply what they've learned in the chapter.
- *Applications and Cases.* Completely revised sections at the end of each chapter provide brief *Online, Mobile, and Social Media Marketing; Marketing Ethics;* and *Marketing by the Numbers* applications cases that facilitate discussion of current issues and company situations in areas such as mobile and social marketing, ethics, and financial marketing analysis. All-new end-of-chapter *company cases* in each chapter help students apply major marketing concepts and critical thinking to real company and brand situations.

Developing Employability Skills

Real Marketing features. Each chapter contains two deeply developed Real Marketing highlight features that provide in-depth looks at real brand marketing strategies and contemporary marketing issues. For example, students learn how Uniqlo tries to live up to its philosophy "Made for All"; how Netflix uses big data and advanced marketing analytics to personalize each customer's experience; why Apple's products fly off the shelves despite their premium prices; how Swyp targeted users between the ages of 15 and 29 to craft a brand story; how Instagram has made itself a win-win-win for the company, advertisers, and Instagrammers alike; how Nestlé is integrating marketing communication into its operations; why store retailer Best Buy is thriving in the age of Amazon; how Coca-Cola, long a master of mass market advertising, has now also mastered digital, mobile, and social media marketing; and how Waitrose presents itself as part of the larger movement working toward a more sustainable future. They learn that artificial intelligence in marketing is now "a bigger deal than fire and electricity," how companies are increasingly using augmented and virtual reality to enhance consumer shopping experiences, and how mobile marketing engages consumers in the moments that matter. No other text brings marketing to life like the eighteenth edition of *Principles of Marketing*.

Marketing Plan appendix. Appendix 1 contains a detailed sample marketing plan that helps students to apply important marketing planning concepts.

Marketing by the Numbers appendix. An innovative and freshly revised *Appendix 2* provides students with a comprehensive introduction to the marketing financial analysis that helps guide, assess, and support marketing decisions. A new or revised exercise at the end of each text chapter lets students apply analytical and financial thinking to that chapter's concepts and links the chapter to the *Marketing by the Numbers* appendix.

Careers in Marketing. Appendix 3 helps students to explore marketing career paths and lays out a process for landing a marketing job that best matches their special skills and interests.

For more information and resources, visit www.pearsonglobaleditions.com

---

396 PART 3 | Designing a Customer Value-Driven Strategy and Mix

Real Marketing 13.2 | AR and VR in Retailing: Extending and Enhancing the Shopping Experience

Remodeling a dated kitchen or bathroom can be a Herculean task, and many customers simply throw up their hands and say, "Forget it!" To help solve this customer home-improvement retailer Lo a virtual reality program called I let customers in some stores tools or redo rooms to see ho look without ever knocking dow

Dubbed "Minecraft for Mom let customers use an in-store design their dream room, se nets, countertops, faucets, ap and paint colors in endless cor with Lowe's products, of cours then donned an HTC Vive head themselves standing in the mic designed space in 3D virtual on what they saw, they could design until it looked just rig could export it to YouTube 36 and viewing at home with Goog

Welcome to the fast-growing mented and virtual reality in reta are increasingly using sophis technologies to extend and enh tomer shopping experience, bri world into their stores, and bring the outside world. They are usi reality (AR) and virtual reality (\ artificial intelligence (AI), to cre personalized, and highly engag riences that transcend real-worl

Augmented reality merges mented objects with real-worl can help consumers design, tr ample, Sephora's Virtual Artist scans a customer's face and le ment with different combination and cheek makeup until she likes. It also offers "virtual tutori customers how to apply makeu overlays the results on their fa Sherwin-Williams Color Visualiz "Color It Before You Paint It!" by tual room images and painting And IKEA's AR app, IKEA Place ers place furniture items virtually to see what they look like before

At the NIKEiD Direct Studi augmented video mapping let sign their own one-of-a-kind watch the designs come to li very eyes. Customers start by p white version of the Nike Air Fo NIKEiD Direct configurator—a that serves as the display ar

---

CHAPTER 4 | Managing Marketing Information to Gain Customer Insights **139**

Real Marketing 4.2 | Artificial Intelligence in Marketing: "A Bigger Deal Than Fire or Electricity"

It's early morning, you're headed out to start your day, and you feel the urge for that first jolt of caffeine. As you get in your car, you tap the Starbucks app on your phone and ask for "the usual." Your Starbucks virtual barista replies in her familiar, cheerful voice: "One tall caramel latte!" She then politely suggests a breakfast snack—a Vermont maple nut muffin—not your usual, but it sure sounds good. You agree. "Thanks! Your order will be ready for pickup in five to seven minutes at University and 28th," she confirms. "Would you like to pay for that with your credit card on file?" You step inside the store, bypass the long lines, and grab your order—no fuss, no muss. Welcome to the world of artificial intelligence (AI).

This is just one example of how AI has exploded onto the marketing scene. Starbucks has long been into cutting-edge technology—a full 25 percent of its transactions are already placed through its smartphone apps. But My Starbucks Barista is more than just an ordering app. It uses artificial intelligence to create personalized customer experiences and manage real-time customer interactions, based on everything from customers' past transactions and preferences to demographics, store trends and inventories, and local traffic and weather conditions.

Artificial intelligence is sweeping the world. It involves machines that think and learn in a way that looks and feels human but with a lot more analytical capacity. The engine behind the AI's explosive growth is big data. Raw data is flowing in from everywhere: customer transaction and interaction data, web and social media data, news and environmental data, and data from more than 50 billion connected devices—everything from consumer wearables and GPS technology to household thermostats, washing machines, and cars. Companies need to make sense of all that data for their brands and consumers.

The human mind simply can't grapple with today's glut of big data. But machines can. However, more than just collecting and tabulating mountains of data, AI analyzes it at lightning speed to gain deep insights and apply them to accomplish designated tasks. AI learns as it goes along—the more data it ingests, the smarter and more accurate it gets. "AI is the rocket ship," says one AI expert. "Machine learning is the rocket that's going to get us there. And big data is the fuel."

Marketers use AI to assess, address, service, and sell to customers. In turn, AI can help customers manage their lives and their buying. It might be requesting a ride from Lyft via chat (Facebook Messenger or Slack) or voice (Amazon Echo's Alexa virtual assistant). Lyft's chatbot lets you know the current location of your driver along with a picture of the license plate and car model. Or it might be IBM's Watson supercomputer combining through vast amounts of data to unearth customer and market insights that help marketers sharpen their targeting, personalize customer engagements, design new products, and even craft better ads in real time.

Today's machines are smart and eerily human. IBM's Watson "is loquacious; it can tell jokes, answer questions, and write songs," notes one observer. "Google's AI can now read lips better than a professional and can master video games within hours. MIT's AI can predict action on video two seconds before it begins. Tesla's AI powers [its] innovative self-driving car."

Companies like Amazon have mastered AI, harnessing insights and interactions that let it understand and serve customers. Amazon's Echo brings Alexa's AI magic to nearly 50 million U.S. homes. Beyond serving as a valet for duties such as adjusting household appliances, controlling music, keeping shopping lists, sending text messages, and answering questions on about any subject, Echo and other similar AI devices,

such as Google Home, have become voice-activated personal shopping assistants. Companies ranging from P&G and Clorox to 1-800-Flowers are hard at work perfecting ways to tap into Echo users who voice-shop from the comfort of their own kitchens.

At Amazon's shopping and video sites, AI powers recommendations that help consumers decide what to buy and what to watch. "Increasingly, Amazon will be selling you things you didn't even know you needed because it has learned what you like and are most inclined to buy," says an analyst. Amazon is so good at this that it's even considering what it calls "predictive delivery," sending consumers stuff they haven't even ordered yet. If customers don't want it, they would just keep it for free. Although such deliveries may still be a while off, Amazon uses such AI predictions to keep the right stock in warehouses or even on trucks to support its ever-more-popular one-day or even one-hour delivery promise.

Hosts of retailers are employing AI to improve how they service and sell to their customers. For example, home improvement retailer Lowe's is experimenting with LoweBots—five-foot something, fully mobile, AI-powered robots that roam stores helping customers. The LoweBots detect customers who might need assistance and engage them through voice and touchscreens. The AI robots tap store and external data to answers customer questions, offer solutions,

Artificial intelligence: The My Starbucks Barista uses artificial intelligence to create personalized customer experiences and manage real-time customer interactions, based on everything from customers' past transactions and preferences to local traffic and weather conditions.
Elias Stein Illustration

Acknowledgments

No book is the work only of its authors. We greatly appreciate the valuable contributions of several people who helped make this new edition possible. As always, we owe extra-special thanks to Keri Jean Miksza for her dedicated and valuable contributions to all phases of the project and to her husband Pete and daughters Lucy and Mary for all the support they provide Keri during this very absorbing project.

We owe substantial thanks to Andy Norman of Drake University for his skillful help in developing chapter vignettes and highlights, company cases, and the marketing plan appendix. This and many previous editions have benefited greatly from Andy's assistance. We also thank Christy Ashley of the University of Rhode Island for her dedicated efforts in preparing end-of-chapter materials and Laurie Babin for her updates to the Marketing by the Numbers assignments at the end of each chapter and the Marketing by the Numbers Appendix. Additional thanks go to those who worked to update the Instructor's Manual, PowerPoints, Test Bank, and MyLab Marketing. All of these contributors are greatly appreciated in making the eighteenth edition of *Principles of Marketing* a robust teaching and learning system.

Many reviewers at other colleges and universities provided valuable comments and suggestions for this and previous editions. We are indebted to the following colleagues for their thoughtful input: Timothy W. Aurand, *Northern Illinois University*; Aysen Bakir, *Illinois State University*; Leta Beard, *University of Washington*; Thomas C. Hewett, *Kennesaw State University*; Robert M. McMillen, *James Madison University*; Carlton O'Neal, *University of San Diego*; Rebecca Reczek, *The Ohio State University*; Sandra Robertson, *Thomas Nelson Community College*; Emily Rosenzweig, *Tulane University*; Professor Carol Rowey, *Community College of Rhode Island*; and Aninda Shome, *University of Idaho*.

We also owe a great deal to the people at Pearson Education who helped develop this book. Content Strategy Manager Lynn Huddon provided guidance and support during the revision. Content Producer Yasmita Hota provided valuable assistance and advice in guiding this complex revision project through development, design, and production. We'd also like to thank Director of Content Strategy Lacey Vitetta, Director of Product Management Ellen Geary, Product Manager Krista Mastroianni, Managing Producer Melissa Feimer, and Senior Product Marketer Nayke Heine for their able assistance along the way. We are proud to be associated with the fine professionals at Pearson. We also owe a mighty debt of gratitude to Senior Project Manager Allison Campbell, Design Manager Emily Friel, and the rest of the team at Integra for their fine work on this edition.

Finally, we owe many thanks to our families for all of their support and encouragement along the way—Kathy, Betty, Mandy, Matt, KC, Keri, Delaney, Molly, Macy, and Ben from the Armstrong clan and Nancy, Amy, Melissa, and Jessica from the Kotler family. To them, we dedicate this book.

Philip Kotler
Gary Armstrong

Global Edition Acknowledgments

For their work on the Global Edition, Pearson would like to thank Ayantunji Gbadamosi, *University of East London*; Muneeza Shoaib, *Middlesex University Dubai*; and Mariusz Soltanifar, *Hanze University of Applied Sciences, Groningen*, as well as Hanna van der Stok, *Hanze University of Applied Sciences, Groningen*; Yong Wooi Keong; Michael Grund, *University of Applied Sciences in Business Administration Zurich*; Stephen Tustain, *Glion Institute of Higher Education*; and Jimmy Wong Shiang Yang, *Singapore University of Social Sciences*, for their feedback on the content.

About the Authors

As a team, Philip Kotler and Gary Armstrong provide a blend of skills uniquely suited to writing an introductory marketing text. Professor Kotler is one of the world's leading authorities on marketing. Professor Armstrong is an award-winning teacher of undergraduate business students. Together, they make the complex world of marketing practical, approachable, and enjoyable.

Philip Kotler is S.C. Johnson & Son Distinguished Professor of International Marketing at the Kellogg School of Management, Northwestern University. He received his master's degree at the University of Chicago and his Ph.D. at M.I.T., both in economics. Dr. Kotler is the co-author of *Marketing Management* (Pearson), now in its fifteenth edition and the most widely used marketing textbook in graduate schools of business worldwide. He has authored more than 60 other successful books and has published more than 150 articles in leading journals. He is the only three-time winner of the coveted Alpha Kappa Psi award for the best annual article in the Journal of Marketing.

Professor Kotler was named the first recipient of four major awards: the Distinguished Marketing Educator of the Year Award and the William L. Wilkie "Marketing for a Better World" Award, both given by the American Marketing Association; the Philip Kotler Award for Excellence in Health Care Marketing presented by the Academy for Health Care Services Marketing; and the Sheth Foundation Medal for Exceptional Contribution to Marketing Scholarship and Practice. He is a charter member of the Marketing Hall of Fame, was voted the first Leader in Marketing Thought by the American Marketing Association, and was named the Founder of Modern Marketing Management in the Handbook of Management Thinking. His numerous other major honors include the Sales and Marketing Executives International Marketing Educator of the Year Award; the European Association of Marketing Consultants and Trainers Marketing Excellence Award; the Charles Coolidge Parlin Marketing Research Award; and the Paul D. Converse Award, given by the American Marketing Association to honor "outstanding contributions to science in marketing." A recent *Forbes* survey ranks Professor Kotler in the top 10 of the world's most influential business thinkers. And in a recent *Financial Times* poll of 1,000 senior executives across the world, Professor Kotler was ranked as the fourth "most influential business writer/guru" of the twenty-first century.

Dr. Kotler has served as chairman of the College on Marketing of the Institute of Management Sciences, a director of the American Marketing Association, and a trustee of the Marketing Science Institute. He has consulted with many major U.S. and international companies in the areas of marketing strategy and planning, marketing organization, and international marketing. He has traveled and lectured extensively throughout Europe, Asia, and South America, advising companies and governments about global marketing practices and opportunities.

Gary Armstrong is Blackwell Distinguished Professor Emeritus of Undergraduate Education in the Kenan-Flagler Business School at the University of North Carolina at Chapel Hill. He holds undergraduate and master's degrees in business from Wayne State University in Detroit, and he received his Ph.D. in marketing from Northwestern University. Dr. Armstrong has contributed numerous articles to leading business journals. As a consultant and researcher, he has worked with many companies on marketing research, sales management, and marketing strategy.

But Professor Armstrong's first love has always been teaching. His long-held Blackwell Distinguished Professorship is the only permanent endowed professorship for distinguished undergraduate teaching at the University of North Carolina at Chapel Hill. He has been very active in the teaching and administration of Kenan-Flagler's undergraduate program. His administrative posts have included Chair of Marketing, Associate Director of the Undergraduate Business Program, Director of the Business Honors Program, and many others. Through the years, he has worked closely with business student groups and has received several UNC campuswide and Business School teaching awards. He is the only repeat recipient of the school's highly regarded Award for Excellence in Undergraduate Teaching, which he received three times. Most recently, Professor Armstrong received the UNC Board of Governors Award for Excellence in Teaching, the highest teaching honor bestowed by the 16-campus University of North Carolina system.

Marc Oliver Opresnik is a Professor of Marketing and Management and Member of the Board of Directors at SGMI St. Gallen Management Institute, a leading international business school. In addition, he is Professor of Business Administration at the Technische Hochschule Lübeck as well as a visiting professor to international universities such as the Judge Business School of the University of Cambridge, Regent's University London, and the East China University of Science and Technology (ECUST) in Shanghai. He has 10 years of experience working in senior management and marketing positions for Shell International Petroleum Co. Ltd.

Dr. Opresnik is the author of numerous articles and books. Along with Kevin Keller and Phil Kotler, he is co-author of the German edition of *Marketing Management*, the "Bible of Marketing." In addition, he is co-editor and member of the editorial board of several international journals such as *Transnational Marketing Journal, International Journal of New Technologies in Science and Engineering,* and *International Journal of Management & Social Sciences.*

In March 2014, he was appointed Chief Research Officer at Kotler Impact Inc., the internationally operating company of Phil Kotler. In addition, he was appointed chief executive officer of the Kotler Business Programme, an initiative to enhance marketing education worldwide via online and offline learning with Pearson as global educational partner.

As president of his consulting firm Opresnik Management Consulting, he works for numerous institutions, governments and international corporations, including Google, Coca-Cola, McDonald's, SAP, Shell International Petroleum Co. Ltd., Procter & Gamble, Unilever, L'Oréal, Bayer, BASF, and adidas. More than a quarter of a million people have benefited professionally and personally from his insights and learned from him when he served as a coach in seminars on marketing, sales and negotiation, and as a speaker at conferences all over the world, including locations such as St. Gallen, Berlin, Houston, Moscow, Kuala Lumpur, London, Paris, Dubai, and Tokyo.

Principles of
MARKETING

1 Marketing
Creating Customer Value and Engagement

OBJECTIVES OUTLINE

OBJECTIVE 1-1 Define marketing and outline the steps in the marketing process. **See: What Is Marketing?** *(pp 24–26)*

OBJECTIVE 1-2 Explain the importance of understanding the marketplace and customers and identify the five core marketplace concepts. **See: Understanding the Marketplace and Customer Needs** *(pp 26–30)*

OBJECTIVE 1-3 Identify the key elements of a customer value–driven marketing strategy and discuss the marketing management orientations that guide marketing strategy. **See: Designing a Customer Value–Driven Marketing Strategy and Plan** *(pp 30–34)*

OBJECTIVE 1-4 Discuss customer relationship management and identify strategies for creating value for customers and capturing value from customers in return. **See: Managing Customer Relationships and Capturing Customer Value** *(pp 34–42)*

OBJECTIVE 1-5 Describe the major trends and forces that are changing the marketing landscape in this age of relationships. **See: The Changing Marketing Landscape** *(pp 42–49)*

CHAPTER PREVIEW This first chapter introduces you to the basic concepts of marketing. We start with the question: What is marketing? Simply put, marketing is engaging customers and managing profitable customer relationships. The aim of marketing is to create value for customers in order to capture value from customers in return. Next we discuss the five steps in the marketing process—from understanding customer needs to designing customer value–driven marketing strategies and integrated marketing programs to building customer relationships and capturing value for the firm. Finally, we discuss the major trends and forces affecting marketing in this new age of digital, mobile, and social media. Understanding these basic concepts and forming your own ideas about what they really mean to you will provide a solid foundation for all that follows.

Let's start with a good story about marketing in action at Emirates, the largest international airline in the world and one of the best-known brands on the planet. Emirates' success results from much more than just offering a way to connect people from Point A to Point B. It's based on a customer-focused marketing strategy by which Emirates creates customer value through deep brand–customer engagement and close brand community with and among its customers. You'll see this theme of creating customer value in order to capture value in return repeated throughout this chapter and the remainder of the text.

EMIRATES' CUSTOMER VALUE–DRIVEN MARKETING: Engaging Customers and Building a Brand Community

The Emirates Group operates across six continents and 155 cities with a 103,363-strong team comprising over 160 nationalities. The Emirates airline, headquartered in Dubai, UAE, was founded in 1985. The financial year ending March 31, 2016, saw the Group achieve its 28th consecutive year of profit in a financial year. The company successfully capitalized on its location—a small city-state strategically located to reach three-fourths of the world population in a flight of less than eight hours— to build a fast-growing and profitable hub-based business model, making it the fourth largest international airline in the world.

From the outset, Emirates sought to ensure that it would not only provide high-quality service but also be innovative, modern, and customer-oriented. To that end, the airline has pursued a customer-focused value proposition through a combination of products, services, and experiences, customized for each market at each destination. This approach has led to an array of product offerings such as its onboard Information, Communication, and Entertainment (ICE) system—an all-in-one communications device accommodating customer needs such as surfing the Internet, emailing, or simply calling a land line while in the airplane—as well as exclusive lounges for its clientele.

The Skywards Program, the airlines' frequent traveler loyalty program, is an important part of Emirates' success in building strong customer relationships. Through this program, the first of its kind in the industry, members earn miles using four basic inputs: route, fare type, class, and tier, and a "miles accelerator feature" offers bonus miles on specific flights, thereby boosting turnover on flights that are not full.

Facing increased and fierce competition, Emirates has launched a range of customer service initiatives that support differentiation, including Dubai Connect, an incentive for premium-class passengers that offers free luxury hotel accommodation, including meals, ground transportation, and visa costs in Dubai. Another differentiating element of its customer service is Chauffeur Drive, a service offered to customers flying first-class or business-class. Emirates chauffeurs collect customers from their doorstep or are present to take them to their final destination when they land. This could be the customer's hotel, their next meeting, their favorite restaurant, or even the course for a round of golf. This service is available in over 70 cities worldwide.

Most airlines have had to reduce their fares considerably to remain competitive. Not Emirates. The company has maintained fares while managing healthy yields thanks to its customer value–driven marketing approach and its service proposition, for which customers are still willing to pay a premium. Where competitors emphasized low prices or well-maintained aircraft, Emirates built customer engagement and relationships. Beyond the functional benefit of air travel, Emirates marketed its services as "The Emirates Experience," a genuine passion for comfort and attention to detail. Customers didn't just fly Emirates; they experienced it.

Connecting with customers once required simply outspending competitors on big media ads and celebrity endorsers who talk at rather than to customers. In these digital times, however, Emirates is forging a new kind of

Emirates has emphasized customer engagement and relationships, and customers are willing to pay a premium for "The Emirates Experience."

Iain Masterton/Alamy Stock Photo

customer relationship, a deeper, more personal, more engaging one. Emirates still invests in traditional advertising, but the brand now spends an increasing amount of its marketing budget on cutting-edge digital and social media marketing that interacts with customers to build brand engagement and community.

Emirates uses online, mobile, and social media marketing to connect with their customers. Emirates also creates brand "tribes"—large groups of highly engaged users—with the help of social media platforms such as Facebook, Twitter, Instagram, YouTube, and Pinterest. For example, the main Emirates Facebook page has more than 10 million likes. The Emirates Twitter page adds another 1.17 million; the Emirates Instagram page has 3.8 million subscribers, making it the largest in the industry; and the company's LinkedIn page has 1.1 million followers, also no. 1 in the airline business. Emirates' social media presence engages customers at a high level, gets them talking with each other about the brand, and weaves the brand into their daily lives through cross-media campaigns that integrate digital media with traditional tools to connect with customers. A compelling example is the company's "Hello Tomorrow" campaign. Launched in 2012 and targeted at travelers seeking new experiences and cultures, the campaign sought to position the airline as a lifestyle choice that would connect people with different cultures worldwide, inspiring new conversations on food, fashion, art, and music.

Sir Maurice Flanagan, the founding CEO of Emirates and former executive vice-chairman of The Emirates Group, emphasized that Emirates is not just offering a way to connect people from Point A to Point B but is the catalyst to connect people's dreams, hopes, and aspirations. He also stated that the

> Emirates is not just offering a way to connect people from Point A to Point B but aims to be the catalyst to connect people's dreams, hopes, and aspirations.

company connects people and cultures, creating relevant and meaningful experiences that are shaping the world.

The campaign launch featured print, TV, and digital advertising, including iconic billboards in New York's Times Square and Milan's central train station. Launched in over 80 markets across the world, the new brand platform presented Emirates' new mindset through communication and engagement that celebrate global travel, conveying Emirates' commitment to connecting with people and helping them realize their potential through travel. As it sought to reach a younger audience, the "Hello Tomorrow" campaign debuted with vignettes of the TV spots on Emirates' Facebook channel. Moreover, Emirates collaborated with the BBC to develop a new series called *Collaboration Culture*, which followed 14 celebrities and luminaries who collaborated across their respective fields in music, food, fashion, and art. With CNN, Emirates created *Fusion Journeys*, a concept that took artists to join fellow artists across the world to learn, teach, and even perform with them in their own country. Finally, Emirates' created the "Inspired Culture" channel on Yahoo! Globally,

where globalistas can access recommendations, videos, and content, engaging with other people and drawing inspiration from their creations.

The new global culture reached 43 million viewers across 85 countries through the BBC, CNN, and Yahoo. Awareness of Emirates jumped from 38 percent to 69 percent among viewers and an impressive 84 percent of viewers exposed to the content reportedly believed Emirates was a brand that sought to connect the world and create a "brighter future." Emirates has become the world's 4th most valuable airline brand, with an estimated value of $7 billion, according to the 2018 Brand Finance Global 500 report; it was also the only non-American airline in the top five. As a result of its customer-centric approach and integrated marketing campaigns (such as the Hello Tomorrow initiative), Emirates has demonstrated commitment, authenticity, relevance, and differentiation outside the travel industry. Emirates has successfully changed the way it reaches out to its customers by moving away from the product and creating a discourse of global customer engagement.[1]

TODAY'S SUCCESSFUL COMPANIES have one thing in common: Like Emirates, they are strongly customer focused and heavily committed to marketing. These companies share a passion for satisfying customer needs in well-defined target markets. They motivate everyone in the organization to help build lasting customer relationships based on creating value.

Customer relationships and value are especially important today. Facing dramatic technological advances and deep economic, social, and environmental challenges, today's customers are reassessing how they engage with brands. New digital, mobile, and social media developments have revolutionized how consumers shop and interact, in turn calling for new marketing strategies and tactics. It's now more important than ever to build strong customer engagement, relationships, and advocacy based on real and enduring customer value.

We'll discuss the exciting new challenges facing both customers and marketers later in the chapter. But first, let's introduce the basics of marketing.

| Author Comment | Pause here and think about how you'd answer this question before studying marketing. Then see how your answer changes as you read the chapter. |

What Is Marketing?

OBJECTIVE 1-1 Define marketing and outline the steps in the marketing process.

Marketing, more than any other business function, deals with customers. Although we will soon explore more detailed definitions of marketing, perhaps the simplest definition is this one: Marketing is engaging customers and managing profitable customer relationships. The twofold goal of marketing is to attract new customers by promising superior value and to keep and grow current customers by delivering value and satisfaction.

For example, Amazon dominates the online marketplace by creating a world-class online buying experience that helps customers to "find and discover anything they might want to buy online." Facebook has attracted more than 2 billion monthly active web and mobile users worldwide by helping them to "connect and share with the people in their lives." And Starbucks dominates the U.S. out-of-home coffee market by "creating a culture of warmth and belonging, where everyone is welcome."[2]

Sound marketing is critical to the success of every organization. Large for-profit firms such as Apple, Target, Coca-Cola, Procter & Gamble, and Microsoft use marketing. But so do not-for-profit organizations, such as colleges, hospitals, museums, symphony orchestras, and even churches.

You already know a lot about marketing—it's all around you. Marketing comes to you in the good old traditional forms: You see it in the abundance of products at your nearby shopping mall and the ads that fill your TV screen, spice up your magazines, or stuff your mailbox. ● But in recent years, marketers have assembled a host of new marketing approaches, everything from imaginative websites and smartphone apps to online videos and social media. These new approaches do more than just blast out messages to the masses. They reach you directly, personally, and interactively. Today's marketers want to become a part of your life and enrich your experiences with their brands. They want to help you live their brands.

At home, at school, where you work, and where you play, you see marketing in almost everything you do. Yet there is much more to marketing than meets the consumer's casual eye. Behind it all is a massive network of people, technologies, and activities competing for your attention and purchases. This book will give you a complete introduction to the basic concepts and practices of today's marketing. In this chapter, we begin by defining marketing and the marketing process.

● **Marketing is all around you, in good old traditional forms and in a host of new forms, from websites and mobile apps to online videos and social media.**

Leung Cho Pan/123RF

Marketing Defined

What *is* marketing? Many people think of marketing as only selling and advertising. We are bombarded every day with TV commercials, online pitches, catalogs, and spiels from salespeople. However, selling and advertising are only the tip of the marketing iceberg.

Today, marketing must be understood not in the sense of making a sale—"telling and selling"—but in the sense of satisfying customer needs. If the marketer engages consumers effectively, understands their needs, develops products that provide superior customer value, and prices, distributes, and promotes them well, these products will sell easily. In fact, according to management guru Peter Drucker, "The aim of marketing is to make selling unnecessary."[3] Selling and advertising are only part of a larger marketing mix—a set of marketing tools that work together to engage customers, satisfy customer needs, and build customer relationships.

Broadly defined, marketing is a social and managerial process by which individuals and organizations obtain what they need and want through creating and exchanging value with others. In a narrower business context, marketing involves building profitable, value-laden exchange relationships with customers. Hence, we define **marketing** as the process by which companies engage customers, build strong customer relationships, and create customer value in order to capture value from customers in return.[4]

Marketing
The process by which companies engage customers, build strong customer relationships, and create customer value in order to capture value from customers in return.

The Marketing Process

● **Figure 1.1** presents a simple, five-step model of the marketing process for creating and capturing customer value. In the first four steps, companies work to understand consumers, create customer value, and build strong customer relationships. In the final step,

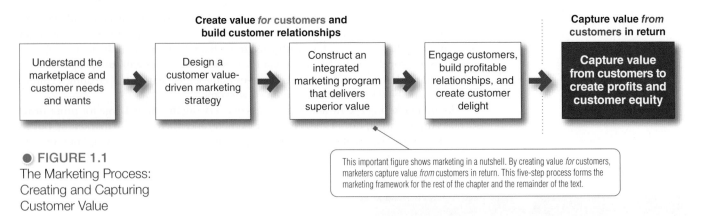

● FIGURE 1.1
The Marketing Process:
Creating and Capturing
Customer Value

companies reap the rewards of creating superior customer value. By creating value for consumers, they in turn capture value from consumers in the form of sales, profits, and long-term customer equity.

In this chapter and the next, we examine the steps of this simple model of marketing. In this chapter, we review each step but focus more on the customer relationship steps—understanding customers, engaging and building relationships with customers, and capturing value from customers. In Chapter 2, we look more deeply into the second and third steps—designing value-creating marketing strategies and constructing marketing programs.

> Author | Marketing is all about
> Comment | creating value for
> customers. So, as the first step in
> the marketing process, the company
> must fully understand customers and
> the marketplace.

Understanding the Marketplace and Customer Needs

OBJECTIVE 1-2 Explain the importance of understanding the marketplace and customers and identify the five core marketplace concepts.

As a first step, marketers need to understand customer needs and wants and the marketplace in which they operate. We examine five core customer and marketplace concepts: (1) needs, wants, and demands; (2) market offerings (products, services, and experiences); (3) value and satisfaction; (4) exchanges and relationships; and (5) markets.

Customer Needs, Wants, and Demands

Needs
States of felt deprivation.

The most basic concept underlying marketing is that of human needs. Human **needs** are states of felt deprivation. They include basic physical needs for food, clothing, warmth, and safety; social needs for belonging and affection; and individual needs for knowledge and self-expression. Marketers did not create these needs; they are a basic part of the human makeup.

Wants are the form human needs take as they are shaped by culture and individual personality. An American needs food but wants a Big Mac, fries, and a soft drink. A person in Papua, New Guinea, needs food but wants taro, rice, yams, and pork. Wants are shaped by one's society and are described in terms of objects that will satisfy those needs. When backed by buying power, wants become **demands**. Given their wants and resources, people demand products and services with benefits that add up to the most value and satisfaction.

Wants
The form human needs take as they are shaped by culture and individual personality.

Demands
Human wants that are backed by buying power.

Companies go to great lengths to learn about and understand customer needs, wants, and demands. They conduct consumer research, analyze mountains of customer data, and observe customers as they shop and interact, offline and online. People at all levels of the company—including top management—stay close to customers. For example, Amazon founder and CEO Jeff Bezos still has a customer-facing email address that helps him to identify customer concerns. "I see most of those emails," says Bezos, "and I forward them, some of them—the ones that catch my eye." ● Similarly, to see up close what their customers experience, Airbnb's CEO Brian Chesky and his co-founder Joe Gebbia regularly stay at the company's host locations. When Airbnb first listed rentals back in 2009, Chesky and Gebbia personally visited all of their New York hosts, staying with them, writing

● **Staying close to customers: Airbnb's CEO Brian Chesky (left) and co-founder Joe Gebbia (center) regularly stay at the company's host locations, helping them shape new customer solutions based on real user experiences.**

Jim Wilson/The New York Times/Redux

Market offerings

Some combination of products, services, information, or experiences offered to a market to satisfy a need or want.

Marketing myopia

The mistake of paying more attention to the specific products a company offers than to the benefits and experiences produced by these products.

reviews, and making sure they lived up to the company's lofty vision. Such personal visits help the pair to shape new customer solutions based on real user experience.[5]

Market Offerings—Products, Services, and Experiences

Consumers' needs and wants are fulfilled through **market offerings**—some combination of products, services, information, or experiences offered to a market to satisfy a need or a want. Market offerings are not limited to physical products. They also include services—activities or benefits offered for sale that are essentially intangible and do not result in the ownership of anything. Examples include banking, airline, hotel, retailing, and home repair services.

More broadly, market offerings also include other entities, such as persons, places, organizations, information, ideas, and causes. For example, to market the cause of suicide prevention, rapper Logic worked with the National Suicide Prevention Lifeline (NSPL) to create a seven-minute online public service video embedded with his song "1-800-273-8255," the NSPL phone number. The results of this lone song and video were staggering. On the day the song and video were released, calls to the Lifeline shot up more than 25 percent, and Google searches for the number doubled. In the following months, visits to the NSPL website increased more than 30 percent.[6]

Many sellers make the mistake of paying more attention to the specific products they offer than to the benefits and experiences produced by these products. These sellers suffer from **marketing myopia**. They are so taken with their products that they focus only on existing wants and lose sight of underlying customer needs.[7] They forget that a product is only a tool to solve a consumer problem. A manufacturer of quarter-inch drill bits may think that the customer needs a drill bit. But what the customer *really* needs is a quarter-inch hole. These sellers will have trouble if a new product comes along that serves the customer's need better or less expensively. The customer will have the same *need* but will *want* the new product.

● **Creating customer experiences: More than just selling products, Apple's highly successful retail stores create engaging life-feels-good brand experiences.**

Maen Zayyad/Shutterstock

Smart marketers look beyond the attributes of the products and services they sell. By orchestrating several services and products, they create brand experiences for consumers. For example, Walt Disney World Resort doesn't offer just amusement park rides, it uses its famed Disney magic to create carefully orchestrated guest experiences that make dreams come true (see Real Marketing 1.1). ● And Apple's highly successful retail stores don't just sell the company's products. They create an engaging Apple brand experience:[8]

Apple's retail stores are very seductive places, where "life-feels-good" experiences abound. The store design is clean, simple, and just oozing with style—much like an Apple iPad or a featherweight MacBook Air. The bustling stores feel more like community centers than retail outlets, with crowds of customers sampling the goods and buzzing excitedly about all things Apple. The stores encourage a lot of purchasing, to be sure. But they also encourage lingering, with tables full of fully functioning Macs, iPads, iPhones, and Apple Watches

Real Marketing 1.1

The Walt Disney World Resort: Making Magical Moments

Each year, more than 50 million people flock to The Walt Disney World Resort, making it the world's number one tourist attraction. On a single busy day, more than 300,000 eager guests might drop by to visit with Mickey and his friends at one of the resort's four major theme parks—the Magic Kingdom, Epcot, Disney's Hollywood Studios, and Disney's Animal Kingdom.

What brings so many people to The Walt Disney World Resort? Part of the answer lies in the resort's many attractions. Disney World is a true fantasyland—more than 40 square miles (as big as San Francisco) brimming with thrill-a-minute attractions such as Expedition Everest, Twilight Zone Tower of Terror, Space Mountain, Soarin', Toy Story Mania, Pirates of the Caribbean, Kilimanjaro Safaris, and Millennium Falcon: Smugglers Run. But Disney World doesn't offer just amusement park rides. The real "Disney Magic" lies in how the resort turns park visits into carefully orchestrated experiences that make dreams come true.

The Walt Disney World Resort is obsessed with making all aspects of every customer's visit memorable. In an increasingly rude, mismanaged, and mundane world, Disney World offers warmth, order, and magical moments. From the moment visitors purchase tickets to the moment they leave the resort, Disney goes to extremes to create experiences that make Disney World "the most magical place on earth."

Each park, attraction, restaurant, and hotel forms part of an enchanted world, with every nuance carefully dreamed up by Disney "Imagineers." On Epcot Center's Test Track, for example, visitors don't just zoom around a track. They become GM test engineers taking a concept vehicle through rigorous testing procedures. At the Be Our Guest dining room in the Magic Kingdom, patrons don't just eat a meal. They experience French-inspired food inside Beast's castle, a place where it's always snowing gently outside, the suits of armor talk, and the magic rose glitters in a corner of the forbidden west wing.

Employees at all levels of Disney World—from executives in the corner office to the person scooping ice cream on Main Street in the Magic Kingdom—are carefully trained in how to do the hard work of helping people have fun. They learn that they are in the entertainment business and that they are "cast members" whose job is to be enthusiastic, knowledgeable, and professional in serving Disney's "guests." Each cast member, they learn, plays a vital role in the Disney World "show," whether it's as a "security host" (police), "transportation host" (driver), "custodial host" (street cleaner), or "food and beverage host" (restaurant worker).

Before they can receive their "theme costumes" and go "on stage," cast members learn how to deal effectively with guests. In a course called "Traditions," they learn the Disney language, history, and culture. They are taught to be enthusiastic, helpful, and *always* friendly. They learn to do good deeds, such as offering to take pictures of guests so that the whole family can be in the picture. They are taught never to say "I don't know" or "It's not my job." When a guest asks a question—whether it's "Where the nearest restroom?" or "What are the names of Snow White's seven dwarves?"—they need to know the answer. If they see a piece of trash on the ground, they must pick it up.

Disney trains cast members to connect with guests on a personal level to make them feel special. Cast members proactively seek out opportunities to turn the mundane into magical. For example, a cast member who notices a child's disappointment might hand out a FastPass ride voucher, confer a coveted special-edition Disney pin, or connect the family to just the right Disney character at just the right moment. One Disney loyalist recalls just such a special personal experience: "I was three and I swear Cinderella was waving [to me] from the castle and my brother yelled, 'Cinderella, my sister wants to meet you!' Minutes later, I was whisked away to meet Cinderella in a private meet and greet."

Cast members now get a lot of help from technology in making personal connections. For example, Disney World guests wear RFID-embedded wristbands called MagicBands that serve as everything from room keys and park passes to payment methods. Combined with the cloud-based MyMagic+ system, these MagicBands also let cast members identify guests individually, greeting them by name and even recognizing celebratory occasions such as birthdays, anniversaries, or reunions. The MagicBands let Disney customize guest experiences in other ways as well. For instance, as guests stroll around the resort, they might see their names appear on a nearby screen with a message like "Samantha! It's a small world after all." Photos on park rides might suddenly pop up on their My Disney Experience apps. The MagicBands even let guests engage with ride experiences while waiting in line, creating details that later become part of displays on the ride itself.

Thus, you don't visit The Walt Disney World Resort just to ride some rides. Instead, you visit to be part of a carefully choreographed

Marketing experiences: You don't just visit Walt Disney World Resort; you immerse yourself in a carefully choreographed experience—a world where dreams come true and things still work the way they should.

Sunshine/Alamy Stock Photo

experience—a magical world of wonder where dreams come true. Disney has become so highly regarded for its ability to deliver customer experiences that many leading corporations have sent managers to Disney Institute to "discover the method behind the magic." As one avid Disney World fan puts it, "Walking down Main Street and seeing Cinderella's castle for the first time always makes my heart jump....No matter what I'm going through...suddenly the world is filled with magic and wonder and possibilities all over again and I feel a wave of happiness flow over me and a smile creep back onto my face easily, not forced or painted on. A real, true smile."[9]

---

sitting out for visitors to try and dozens of laid-back Apple employees close at hand to answer questions and cater to every whim. The stores offer expert technical assistance at the Genius Bar and a full schedule of workshops where customers at all experience levels can learn about their Apple devices and explore their creative sides. You don't just visit an Apple store—you experience it in a way that no other consumer electronics company can match. As one Apple retail executive explains, "I don't want to be sold to when I walk into a store. Don't sell! No! Because that's a turn-off. Build an amazing brand experience, and then [sales] will just naturally happen." And sales certainly do happen at Apple stores. Apples 506 retail stores in 24 countries attract more than 1 million customers daily and generate the highest sales per square foot of any U.S. retailer.

Customer Value and Satisfaction

Consumers usually face a broad array of products and services that might satisfy a given need. How do they choose among these many market offerings? Customers form expectations about the value and satisfaction that various market offerings will deliver and buy accordingly. Satisfied customers buy again and tell others about their good experiences. Dissatisfied customers often switch to competitors and disparage the product to others.

Marketers must be careful to set the right level of expectations. If they set expectations too low, they may satisfy those who buy but fail to attract enough buyers. If they set expectations too high, buyers will be disappointed. Customer value and customer satisfaction are key building blocks for developing and managing customer relationships. We will revisit these core concepts later in the chapter.

Exchanges and Relationships

Exchange

The act of obtaining a desired object from someone by offering something in return.

Marketing occurs when people decide to satisfy their needs and wants through exchange relationships. **Exchange** is the act of obtaining a desired object from someone by offering something in return. In the broadest sense, the marketer tries to bring about a response to some market offering. The response may be more than simply buying or trading products and services. A political candidate, for instance, wants votes; a church wants membership and participation; an orchestra wants an audience; and a social action group wants idea acceptance.

Marketing consists of actions taken to create, maintain, and grow desirable exchange relationships with target audiences involving a product, service, idea, or other object. Companies want to build strong relationships by consistently delivering superior customer value. We will expand on the important concept of managing customer relationships later in the chapter.

Markets

Market

The set of all actual and potential buyers of a product or service.

The concepts of exchange and relationships lead to the concept of a market. A **market** is the set of actual and potential buyers of a product or service. These buyers share a particular need or want that can be satisfied through exchange relationships.

Marketing means managing markets to bring about profitable customer relationships. However, creating these relationships takes work. Sellers must search for and engage buyers, identify their needs, design good market offerings, set prices for them, promote them, and store and deliver them. Activities such as consumer research, product development, communication, distribution, pricing, and service are core marketing activities.

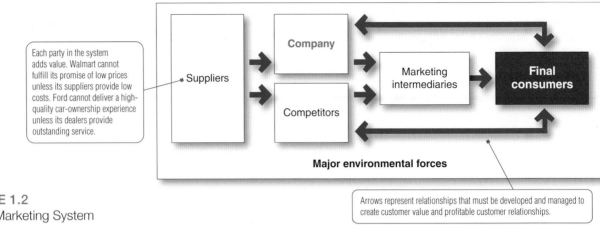

Each party in the system adds value. Walmart cannot fulfill its promise of low prices unless its suppliers provide low costs. Ford cannot deliver a high-quality car-ownership experience unless its dealers provide outstanding service.

Major environmental forces

Arrows represent relationships that must be developed and managed to create customer value and profitable customer relationships.

● FIGURE 1.2
A Modern Marketing System

Although we normally think of marketing as being carried out by sellers, buyers also carry out marketing. Consumers do marketing when they search for products, interact with companies to obtain information, and make their purchases. In fact, today's digital technologies, from websites and smartphone apps to the explosion of social media, have empowered consumers and made marketing a truly two-way affair. Thus, in addition to customer relationship management, today's marketers must also deal effectively with *customer-managed relationships*. Marketers are no longer asking only "How can we influence our customers?" but also "How can our customers influence us?" and even "How can our customers influence each other?"

● Figure 1.2 shows the main elements in a marketing system. Marketing involves serving a market of final consumers in the face of competitors. The company and competitors research the market and interact with consumers to understand their needs. Then they create and exchange market offerings, messages, and other marketing content with consumers, either directly or through marketing intermediaries. Each party in the system is affected by major environmental forces (demographic, economic, natural, technological, political, and social/cultural).

Each party in the system adds value for the next level. The arrows represent relationships that must be developed and managed. Thus, a company's success at engaging customers and building profitable relationships depends not only on its own actions but also on how well the entire system serves the needs of final consumers. Walmart cannot fulfill its promise of low prices unless its suppliers provide merchandise at low costs. And Ford cannot deliver a high-quality car-ownership experience unless its dealers provide outstanding sales and service.

Author Comment | Once a company fully understands its consumers and the marketplace, it must decide which customers it will serve and how it will bring them value.

Designing a Customer Value–Driven Marketing Strategy and Plan

OBJECTIVE 1-3 Identify the key elements of a customer value–driven marketing strategy and discuss the marketing management orientations that guide marketing strategy.

Customer Value–Driven Marketing Strategy

Once it fully understands consumers and the marketplace, marketing management can design a customer value–driven marketing strategy. We define **marketing management** as the art and science of choosing target markets and building profitable relationships with them. The marketing manager's aim is to engage, keep, and grow target customers by creating, delivering, and communicating superior customer value.

To design a winning marketing strategy, the marketing manager must answer two important questions: What customers will we serve (what's our target market)? and How can we serve these customers best (what's our value proposition)? We will discuss these marketing strategy concepts briefly here and then look at them in more detail in Chapters 2 and 7.

Marketing management
The art and science of choosing target markets and building profitable relationships with them.

Selecting Customers to Serve

The company must first decide whom it will serve. It does this by dividing the market into segments of customers (market segmentation) and selecting which segments it will go after (target marketing). Some people think of marketing management as finding as

The Smart Speaker
for Music Lovers

The new Sonos One with Amazon Alexa

SONOS

● **Value propositions:** Sonos positions its
Sonos One with Amazon Alexa as "The smart
speaker for music lovers." It gives you all the
advantages of Alexa but with high-quality Sonos
sound.

The Advertising Archives/Alamy Stock Photo

many customers as possible and increasing demand. But marketing managers know that they cannot serve all customers in every way. By trying to serve all customers, they may not serve any customers well. Instead, the company wants to select only customers that it can serve well and profitably. For example, Nordstrom profitably targets affluent professionals; Dollar General profitably targets families with more modest means.

Ultimately, marketing managers must decide which customers they want to target and the level, timing, and nature of their demand. Simply put, marketing management is customer management and demand management.

Choosing a Value Proposition

The company must also decide how it will serve targeted customers—how it will differentiate and position itself in the marketplace. A brand's value proposition is the set of benefits or values it promises to deliver to consumers to satisfy their needs. JetBlue promises to put "You Above All" by bringing "humanity back to travel." By contrast, Spirit Airlines gives you "Bare Fare" pricing: "Less Money. More Go." Amazon's Echo smart speaker is "Always ready, connected, and fast. Just ask."
● By contrast, the Sonos One with Amazon Alexa is "The smart speaker for music lovers." It gives you all the advantages of Alexa but with high-quality Sonos sound.

Such value propositions differentiate one brand from another. They answer the customer's question: "Why should I buy your brand rather than a competitor's?" Companies must design strong value propositions that give them the greatest advantage in their target markets.

Marketing Management Orientations

Marketing management wants to design strategies that will engage target customers and build profitable relationships with them. But what philosophy should guide these marketing strategies? What weight should be given to the interests of customers, the organization, and society? Very often, these interests conflict.

There are five alternative concepts under which organizations design and carry out their marketing strategies: the production, product, selling, marketing, and societal marketing concepts.

Production concept
The idea that consumers will favor products that are available and highly affordable; therefore, the organization should focus on improving production and distribution efficiency.

The Production Concept. The **production concept** holds that consumers will favor products that are available and highly affordable. Therefore, management should focus on improving production and distribution efficiency. This concept is one of the oldest orientations that guide sellers.

The production concept is still a useful philosophy in some situations. For example, both personal computer maker Lenovo and home appliance maker Haier dominate the highly competitive, price-sensitive Chinese market through low labor costs, high production efficiency, and mass distribution. However, although useful in some situations, the production concept can lead to marketing myopia. Companies adopting this orientation run a major risk of focusing too narrowly on their own operations and losing sight of the real objective—satisfying customer needs and building customer relationships.

Product concept
The idea that consumers will favor products that offer the most quality, performance, and features; therefore, the organization should devote its energy to making continuous product improvements.

The Product Concept. The **product concept** holds that consumers will favor products that offer the most in quality, performance, and innovative features. Under this concept, marketing strategy focuses on making continuous product improvements.

Product quality and improvement are important parts of most marketing strategies. However, focusing only on the company's products can also lead to marketing myopia. For example, some manufacturers believe that if they can "build a better mousetrap, the world will beat a path to their doors." But they are often rudely shocked. Buyers may be looking for a better solution to a mouse problem but not necessarily for a better mousetrap. The better solution might be a chemical spray, an exterminating service, a house cat, or something else that suits their needs even better than a mousetrap. Furthermore, a better mousetrap will not sell unless the manufacturer designs, packages, and prices it attractively; places it in convenient distribution channels; brings it to the attention of people who need it; and convinces buyers that it is a better product.

Selling concept
The idea that consumers will not buy enough of the firm's products unless the firm undertakes a large-scale selling and promotion effort.

The Selling Concept. Many companies follow the **selling concept**, which holds that consumers will not buy enough of the firm's products unless it undertakes a large-scale selling and promotion effort. The selling concept is typically practiced with unsought goods—those that buyers do not normally think of buying, such as life insurance or blood donations. These industries must be good at tracking down prospects and selling them on a product's benefits.

Such aggressive selling, however, carries high risks. It focuses on creating sales transactions rather than on building long-term, profitable customer relationships. The aim often is to sell what the company makes rather than to make what the market wants. It assumes that customers who are coaxed into buying the product will like it. Or, if they don't like it, they will possibly forget their disappointment and buy it again later. These are usually poor assumptions.

Marketing concept

A philosophy in which achieving organizational goals depends on knowing the needs and wants of target markets and delivering the desired satisfactions better than competitors do.

The Marketing Concept. The **marketing concept** holds that achieving organizational goals depends on knowing the needs and wants of target markets and delivering the desired satisfactions better than competitors do. Under the marketing concept, customer focus and value are the paths to sales and profits. Instead of a product-centered make-and-sell philosophy, the marketing concept is a customer-centered sense-and-respond philosophy. The job is not to find the right customers for your product but to find the right products for your customers.

● Figure 1.3 contrasts the selling concept and the marketing concept. The selling concept takes an inside-out perspective. It starts with the factory, focuses on the company's existing products, and calls for heavy selling and promotion to obtain profitable sales. It focuses primarily on customer conquest—getting short-term sales with little concern about who buys or why.

In contrast, the marketing concept takes an outside-in perspective. As Herb Kelleher, the colorful founder of Southwest Airlines, once put it, "We don't have a marketing department; we have a customer department." The marketing concept starts with a well-defined market, focuses on customer needs, and integrates all the marketing activities that affect customers. In turn, it yields profits by creating relationships with the right customers based on customer value and satisfaction.

Implementing the marketing concept often means more than simply responding to customers' stated desires and obvious needs. Customer-driven companies research customers deeply to learn about their desires, gather new product ideas, and test product improvements. Such customer-driven marketing usually works well when a clear need exists and when customers know what they want.

In many cases, however, customers don't know what they want or even what is possible. As Henry Ford supposedly remarked, "If I'd asked people what they wanted, they would have said faster horses." For example, even 20 years ago, how many consumers would have thought to ask for now-commonplace products such as tablet computers, smartphones, digital cameras, 24-hour online buying, digital video and music streaming, and all-electric vehicles? Such situations call for *customer-driving* marketing—understanding customer needs even better than customers themselves do and creating products and services that meet both existing and latent needs, now and in the future. As legendary Apple cofounder Steve Jobs once said, "Our job is to figure out what [consumers are] going to want before they do....Our task is to read things that are not yet on the page."[10]

Societal marketing concept

The idea that a company's marketing decisions should consider consumers' wants, the company's requirements, consumers' long-run interests, and society's long-run interests.

The Societal Marketing Concept. The **societal marketing concept** questions whether the pure marketing concept overlooks possible conflicts between consumer short-run wants and consumer long-run welfare. Is a firm that satisfies the immediate needs and wants of target markets always doing what's best for its consumers in the long run? The

● **FIGURE 1.3**
Selling and Marketing Concepts Contrasted

	Starting point	Focus	Means	Ends
The selling concept	Factory	Existing products	Selling and promoting	Profits through sales volume
The marketing concept	Market	Customer needs	Integrated marketing	Profits through customer satisfaction

The selling concept takes an inside-out view that focuses on existing products and heavy selling. The aim is to sell what the company makes rather than making what the customer wants.

The marketing concept takes an outside-in view that focuses on satisfying customer needs as a path to profits. As Southwest Airlines' colorful founder put it, "We don't have a marketing department, we have a customer department."

● FIGURE 1.4
Three Considerations Underlying the
Societal Marketing Concept

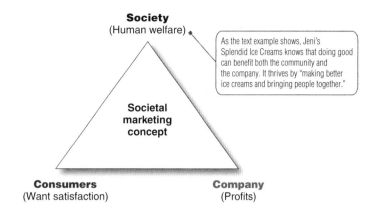

Society
(Human welfare)

As the text example shows, Jeni's
Splendid Ice Creams knows that doing good
can benefit both the community and
the company. It thrives by "making better
ice creams and bringing people together."

Societal
marketing
concept

Consumers
(Want satisfaction)

Company
(Profits)

societal marketing concept holds that marketing strategy should deliver value to customers in a way that maintains or improves both the consumer's and society's well-being. It calls for sustainable marketing, socially and environmentally responsible marketing that meets the present needs of consumers and businesses while also preserving or enhancing the ability of future generations to meet their needs.

Even more broadly, many leading business and marketing thinkers are now preaching the concept of *shared value*, which recognizes that societal needs, not just economic needs, define markets.[11] The concept of shared value focuses on creating economic value in a way that also creates value for society. A growing number of companies known for their hard-nosed approaches to business—such as Google, IBM, Johnson & Johnson, Unilever, and Walmart—are rethinking the interactions between society and corporate performance. They are concerned not just with short-term economic gains but with the well-being of their customers, the depletion of natural resources needed by their businesses, the welfare of key suppliers, and the economic well-being of the communities in which they operate.

As ● **Figure 1.4** shows, companies should balance three considerations in setting their marketing strategies: company profits, consumer wants, and society's interests. Small but fast-growing Jeni's Splendid Ice Creams operates this way:[12]

Jeni's Splendid Ice Creams makes and sells really good artisan ice cream in its own scoop shops, with exotic flavors such as Goat Cheese with Red Cherries, Wildberry Lavender, and Riesling Poached Pear sorbet. But Jeni's does more than just make and sell ice cream. It also dedicates itself to a deeply felt mission of "making better ice creams and bringing people together. That's what gets us out of bed in the morning and keeps us up late at night." Jeni's follows what it calls a "fellowship model"—making great ice creams for communities, by communities. ● Signs in Jeni's shops proudly proclaim: "Ice creams created in fellowship with growers, makers, and producers from around the world all for the love of you."

To achieve this ambitious mission, Jeni's sources its ingredients carefully, using whole fruits and vegetables, milk from local grass-grazed cows, and wildflower honey from nearby farms, along with fair-trade vanilla and bean-to-bar direct trade chocolate. Jeni's believes in "buying directly and paying fairly for the ingredients, in having minimal impact on the environment, and in building and shaping community." It also works to involve its local communities. "Each time we open a store...we spend time in the neighborhoods; we want residents and visitors to be our partners. We think of our company as a community." Thanks to its societal mission, Jeni's is thriving. In 15 years, the business has grown from a pint-sized local operation to 34 scoop shops in 10 cities, all with devoted followings. You'll also find Jeni's in more 3,000 grocery stores, suggesting that doing good can benefit both the community and the company.

● **The societal marketing concept: Jeni's Splendid Ice Cream does more than just make good ice cream. It makes "ice creams created in fellowship with growers, makers, and producers from around the world all for the love of you."**

Jeni's Splendid Ice Creams, LLC

Preparing an Integrated Marketing Plan and Program

The company's marketing strategy outlines which customers it will serve and how it will create value for these customers. Next, the marketer develops an integrated marketing program that will actually deliver the intended value to target customers. The marketing program builds customer relationships by transforming the marketing strategy into action. It consists of the firm's marketing mix, the set of marketing tools the firm uses to implement its marketing strategy.

The major marketing mix tools are classified into four broad groups, called the four Ps of marketing: product, price, place, and promotion. To deliver on its value proposition, the firm must first create a need-satisfying market offering (product). It must then decide how much it will charge for the offering (price) and how it will make the offering available to target consumers (place). Finally, it must engage target consumers, communicate about the offering, and persuade consumers of the offer's merits (promotion). The firm must blend each marketing mix tool into a comprehensive integrated marketing program that communicates and delivers the intended value to chosen customers. We will explore marketing programs and the marketing mix in much more detail in later chapters.

> **Author | Comment |** Doing a good job with the first three steps in the marketing process sets the stage for step four, building and managing customer relationships.

Managing Customer Relationships and Capturing Customer Value

OBJECTIVE 1-4 Discuss customer relationship management and identify strategies for creating value for customers and capturing value from customers in return.

Engaging Customers and Managing Customer Relationships

The first three steps in the marketing process—understanding the marketplace and customer needs, designing a customer value–driven marketing strategy, and constructing a marketing program—all lead up to the fourth and most important step: engaging customers and managing profitable customer relationships. We first discuss the basics of customer relationship management. Then we examine how companies go about engaging customers on a deeper level in this age of digital and social marketing.

Customer Relationship Management

Customer relationship management is perhaps the most important concept of modern marketing. In the broadest sense, **customer relationship management** is the overall process of building and maintaining profitable customer relationships by delivering superior customer value and satisfaction. It deals with all aspects of acquiring, engaging, and growing customers.

Relationship Building Blocks: Customer Value and Satisfaction. The key to building lasting customer relationships is to create superior customer value and satisfaction. Satisfied customers are more likely to be loyal customers and give the company a larger share of their business.

Attracting and retaining customers can be a difficult task. Customers often face a bewildering array of products and services from which to choose. A customer buys from the firm that offers the highest **customer-perceived value**—the customer's evaluation of the difference between all the benefits and all the costs of a market offering relative to those of competing offers. Importantly, customers often do not judge values and costs "accurately" or "objectively." They act on *perceived* value.

To some consumers, value might mean sensible products at affordable prices. To other consumers, however, value might mean paying more to get more. ● For example, a luxurious Patek Philippe costs a small fortune, ranging in price from $20,000 to $500,000. But to those who own one, a Patek is a great value:[13]

● **Perceived value:** Some owners consider a Patek Philippe watch a real bargain, even at prices ranging from $20,000 to $500,000. "You never actually own a Patek Philippe. You merely look after it for the next generation."

Patek Philippe Geneva

Customer relationship management

The overall process of building and maintaining profitable customer relationships by delivering superior customer value and satisfaction.

Customer-perceived value

The customer's evaluation of the difference between all the benefits and all the costs of a marketing offer relative to those of competing offers.

Listen up here, because I'm about to tell you why a certain watch costing $20,000, or even $500,000, isn't actually expensive but is in fact a tremendous value. Every Patek Philippe watch is handmade by Swiss watchmakers from the finest materials and can take more than a year to make. Still not convinced? Beyond keeping precise time, Patek Philippe watches are also good investments. They carry high prices but retain or even increase their value over time. Many models achieve a kind of cult status that makes them the most coveted timepieces on the planet.

But more important than just a means of telling time or a good investment is the sentimental and emotional value of possessing a Patek Philippe. Says the company's president: "This is about passion. I mean—it really is a dream. Nobody needs a Patek." These watches are unique possessions steeped in precious memories, making them treasured family assets. According to the company, "The purchase of a Patek Philippe is often related to a personal event—a professional success, a marriage, or the birth of a child—and offering it as a gift is the most eloquent expression of love or affection." A Patek Philippe watch is made not to last just one lifetime but many. Says one ad: "You never actually own a Patek Philippe. You merely look after it for the next generation." That makes it a real bargain, even at twice the price.

Customer satisfaction

The extent to which a product's perceived performance matches a buyer's expectations.

Customer satisfaction depends on the product's perceived performance relative to a buyer's expectations. If the product's performance falls short of expectations, the customer is dissatisfied. If performance matches expectations, the customer is satisfied. If performance exceeds expectations, the customer is highly satisfied or delighted.

Outstanding marketing companies go out of their way to keep important customers satisfied. Most studies show that higher levels of customer satisfaction lead to greater customer loyalty, which in turn results in better company performance. Companies aim to delight customers by promising only what they can deliver and then delivering more than they promise. Delighted customers not only make repeat purchases but also become willing brand advocates and "customer evangelists" who spread the word about their good experiences to others.

For companies interested in delighting customers, exceptional value and service become part of the overall company culture. For example, L.L.Bean—the iconic American outdoor apparel and equipment retailer—was founded on the principle that keeping customers satisfied is the key to building lasting relationships.[14]

● **Customer satisfaction: Customer service champion L.L.Bean was founded on a philosophy of complete customer satisfaction. "If you are not 100% satisfied with one of our products, you may return it within one year of purchase for a refund."**

Eyal Dayan Photography

Year after year, L.L.Bean lands in the top 10 of virtually every list of top service companies, including J.D. Power's most recent list of "customer service champions." The customer-service culture runs deep at L.L.Bean. More than 100 years ago, Leon Leonwood Bean founded the company on a philosophy of complete customer satisfaction, expressed in the following guarantee: "I do not consider a sale complete until [the] goods are worn out and the customer [is] still satisfied." ● To this day, customers can return any item, no questions asked, up to a year after purchase.

The company's customer-service philosophy is perhaps best summed up in founder L.L.'s answer to the question "What is a customer?" His answer still forms the backbone of the company's values: "A customer is the most important person ever in this company—in person or by mail. A customer is not dependent on us, we are dependent on him. A customer is not an interruption of our work, he is the purpose of it. We are not doing a favor by serving him, he is doing us a favor by giving us the opportunity to do so. A customer is not someone to argue or match wits with. Nobody ever won an argument with a customer. A customer is a person who brings us his wants. It is our job to handle them profitably to him and to ourselves." Adds former L.L.Bean CEO Leon Gorman: "A lot of people have fancy things to say about customer service, but it's just a day-in, day-out, ongoing, never-ending, persevering, compassionate kind of activity."

Other companies that have become legendary for customer delight and their service heroics include Amazon.com, Chick-fil-A, Nordstrom department stores, and JetBlue Airways. However, a company does not necessarily need to have over-the-top service to create customer delight. For example, no-frills grocery chain ALDI has highly satisfied customers, even though they have to bag their own groceries. ALDI's everyday very low pricing on good-quality products delights customers and keeps them coming back. Thus, customers don't need to be wowed. Customer satisfaction comes not just from service heroics but from how well a company delivers on its basic value proposition and helps customers solve their buying problems.

Although a customer-centered firm seeks to deliver high customer satisfaction relative to competitors, it does not attempt to maximize customer satisfaction. A company can always increase customer satisfaction by lowering its prices or increasing its services. But this may result in lower profits. Thus, the purpose of marketing is to generate customer value profitably. This requires a very delicate balance: The marketer must continue to generate more customer value and satisfaction but not "give away the house."

Customer Relationship Levels and Tools. Companies can build customer relationships at many levels, depending on the nature of the target market. At one extreme, a company with many low-margin customers may seek to develop basic relationships with them. For example, P&G's Tide detergent does not phone or call on all of its consumers to get to know them personally. Instead, Tide creates engagement and relationships through product experiences, brand-building advertising, websites, and social media. At the other extreme, in markets with few customers and high margins, sellers want to create full partnerships with key customers. For example, P&G sales representatives work closely with Walmart, Kroger, and other large retailers that sell Tide. In between these two extremes, other levels of customer relationships are appropriate.

Beyond offering consistently high value and satisfaction, marketers can use specific marketing tools to develop stronger bonds with customers. For example, many companies offer frequency marketing programs that reward customers who buy frequently or in large amounts. Airlines offer frequent-flier programs, hotels give room upgrades to frequent guests, and supermarkets give patronage discounts to "very important customers."

Today, almost every brand has a loyalty rewards program. Such programs can enhance and strengthen a customer's brand experience. ● For example, Hilton's HHonors loyalty program allows customers to earn points redeemable for free stays or upgrades. These points can also be converted into miles for flight bookings. In addition, the member-exclusive HHonors smartphone app allows travelers to personalize their stay. It offers options like an eCheck-in or the selection of on-property benefits (such as pillows or snacks) prior to arrival. Travelers can pick their room of choice before their stay, either from a digital floor plan or by choosing their room's view with Google Maps. The app also serves as a digital key, meaning that travelers do not even need to visit the front desk. Additional features include personalized content reflecting the user's forthcoming travels, the option to request Uber rides, as well as restaurant recommendations. For future stays, the app offers the option of marking favorite hotels or hotel rooms."[15]

● Relationship marketing tools: The HHonors smartphone app personalizes and strengthens the customer's brand experience, offering a selection of rooms and on-property benefits.

Halil ERDOĞAN/123rf.com

Significant changes are occurring in the nature of customer-brand relationships. Today's digital technologies—the internet and the surge in online, mobile, and social media—have profoundly changed the ways that people relate to one another. In turn, these events have had a huge impact on how companies and brands connect with customers and how customers connect with and influence each other's brand behaviors.

Customer Engagement and Today's Digital, Mobile, and Social Media

The digital age has spawned a dazzling set of new customer relationship-building tools, from websites, online ads and videos, mobile ads and apps, and blogs to online communities and the major social media, such as Facebook, Twitter, Instagram, YouTube, and Snapchat.

Yesterday's companies focused mostly on mass marketing to broad segments of customers at arm's length. By contrast, today's companies are using online, mobile, and social media to refine their targeting and to engage customers more deeply and interactively. The old marketing involved marketing brands to consumers. The new marketing is **customer-engagement marketing**—fostering direct and continuous customer involvement in shaping brand conversations, brand experiences, and brand community. Customer-engagement marketing goes beyond just selling a brand to consumers. Its goal is to make the brand a meaningful part of consumers' conversations and lives.

Customer-engagement marketing
Making the brand a meaningful part of consumers' conversations and lives by fostering direct and continuous customer involvement in shaping brand conversations, experiences, and community.

The burgeoning internet and social media have given a huge boost to customer-engagement marketing. Today's consumers are better informed, more connected, and more empowered than ever before. Newly empowered consumers have more information about brands, and they have a wealth of digital platforms for airing and sharing their brand views with others. Thus, marketers are now embracing not only customer relationship management but also *customer-managed relationships*, in which customers connect with companies and with each other to help forge and share their own brand experiences. Beyond building brand loyalty and purchasing, marketers want to create **customer brand advocacy**, by which satisfied customers initiate favorable interactions with others about a brand.

Customer brand advocacy
Actions by which satisfied customers initiate favorable interactions with others about a brand.

Greater consumer empowerment means that companies can no longer rely on marketing by *intrusion*. Instead, they must practice marketing by *attraction*—creating market offerings and messages that engage consumers rather than interrupt them. Hence, most marketers now combine their mass-media marketing efforts with a rich mix of online, mobile, and social media marketing that promotes brand-consumer engagement, brand conversations, and brand advocacy among customers.

For example, companies post their latest ads and videos on social media sites, hoping they'll go viral. They maintain an extensive presence on Facebook, Instagram, Twitter, Snapchat, YouTube, LinkedIn and other social media to start conversations with and between customers, address customer service issues, research customer reactions, and drive traffic to relevant articles, web and mobile marketing sites, contests, videos, and other brand activities. They launch their own blogs, mobile apps, brand microsites, and consumer-generated review systems, all with the aim of engaging customers on a more personal, interactive level. Skilled use of social media can get consumers involved with a brand, talking about it, and advocating it to others.

The key to engagement marketing is to find ways to enter targeted consumers' conversations with engaging and relevant brand messages. Simply posting a humorous video, creating a social media page, or hosting a blog isn't enough. Successful engagement marketing means making relevant and genuine contributions to targeted consumers' lives and interactions. Consider Innocent Drinks, the smoothies and juice company:[16]

● **Engaging customers: Rather than using intrusive, hard-sell product pitches, Innocent Drinks interacts with customers in humorous ways, inspiring conversations and fostering relationships.**

AL Robinson/Shutterstock

● Innocent Drinks was established in 1998 with the aim of becoming "Europe's favorite little juice company." The company's timing was crucial; it capitalized on the trend toward healthy eating and living. Rather than using aggressive, hard-sell product pitches, Innocent interacts with customers in a very humorous and informal way. Through engagement marketing, the company fosters a very personal relationship with its customers to make them feel valued and part of the brand. This is reflected in the way that packaging is designed—light-hearted and fun. For example, instead of displaying "use by" on its smoothie bottles, it says "enjoy by." Innocent's social media strategy has a conversational and often irreverent approach; its posts take on relevant topics, keywords, and hashtags with a dry sense of humor but they never hijack these topics to try and sell juice or smoothies. Its shared posts are often reactive; ideas are turned around in about half an hour. For Penguins Awareness Day, for example, the company shared a cartoon of a cute penguin on Twitter with a statement that there were no penguins in any of their products. The text underneath the picture called for action, saying that the company was doing its bit, and asking its customers to tweet about their contribution to this day. Thus, the company creates conversations while keeping the brand's personality in the back of its audience's mind. Innocent's relational approach has engaged a substantial following, with more than a quarter of a million fans on Twitter alone. Innocent, in turn, picks up user-produced content to further deepen the relationship between the brand and its customers.

Consumer-Generated Marketing

Consumer-generated marketing
Brand exchanges created by consumers themselves—both invited and uninvited—by which consumers are playing an increasing role in shaping their own brand experiences and those of other consumers.

One form of customer-engagement marketing is **consumer-generated marketing**, by which consumers themselves play roles in shaping their own brand experiences and those of others. This might happen through uninvited consumer-to-consumer exchanges in social media, blogs, online review sites, and other digital forums. But increasingly, companies themselves are inviting consumers to play a more active role in shaping products and brand content.

Some companies ask consumers for new product and service ideas. For example, Oreo recently ran a #MyOreoCreation contest asking fans to come up with new flavor ideas. Three finalist flavors hit the stores for two months before fans voted online for a winner, who received $500,000. As another example, at the My Starbucks Idea site, Starbucks collects ideas from customers on new products, store changes, and just about anything else that might make their Starbucks experience better. "You know better than anyone else what you want from Starbucks," says the company at the website. "So tell us. What's your Starbucks idea? Revolutionary or simple—we want to hear it." The site invites customers to share their ideas, vote on and discuss the ideas of others, and see which ideas Starbucks has implemented.[17]

Other companies invite consumers to play a role in shaping ads and social media content. For example, all-electric carmaker Tesla held a fan-made ad contest, with three winning "charmingly low-budget" commercials selected from 10 finalists by public voting (via Twitter likes). Tesla posted the finalist ads online simultaneously with the launch of its Model 3 sedan, drawing millions of views and sparking interactions among dedicated Tesla fans. ● One top-three winner: "Sonja's Super Quick Tesla Fan Video" by YouTuber Sonja Jasansky of Minnesota, a super-quick and ultra-quirky video highlighting Tesla specifications and debunking common misconceptions.[18]

● Consumer-generated marketing: "Charmingly low-budget" fan-made Tesla ads drew millions of online views and sparked interactions among dedicated Tesla fans.

Sonja Maria Jasansky

Despite the successes, however, harnessing consumer-generated content can be a time-consuming and costly process, and companies may find it difficult to mine even a little gold from all the content submitted. Moreover, because consumers have so much control over social media content, inviting their input can sometimes backfire. As a classic example, McDonald's famously launched a Twitter campaign using the hashtag #McDStories, hoping that it would inspire heartwarming stories about Happy Meals. Instead, the effort was hijacked by Twitter users, who turned the hashtag into a "bashtag" by posting less-than-appetizing messages about their bad experiences with the fast-food chain. McDonald's pulled the campaign within only two hours, but the hashtag was still churning weeks, even months later.[19]

As consumers become more connected and empowered and as the boom in digital and social media continues, consumer brand engagement—whether invited by marketers or not—will be an increasingly important marketing force. Through a profusion of consumer-generated videos, shared reviews, mobile apps, blogs, and websites, consumers are playing a growing role in shaping their own and other consumers' brand experiences. Brands must embrace this increased consumer empowerment and master the digital and social media relationship tools.

Partner Relationship Management

Partner relationship management
Working closely with partners in other company departments and outside the company to jointly bring greater value to customers.

When it comes to creating customer value and building strong customer relationships, today's marketers know that they can't go it alone. They must work closely with a variety of marketing partners. In addition to being good at customer relationship management, marketers must also be good at **partner relationship management**—working with others inside and outside the company to jointly engage and bring more value to their customers.

Traditionally, marketers have been charged with understanding customers and representing customer needs to different company departments. However, in today's more connected world, every functional area in the organization can interact with customers. Rather than letting each department go its own way, firms must link all departments in the cause of creating customer value.

Marketers must also partner with suppliers, channel partners, and others outside the company. Marketing channels consist of distributors, retailers, and others who connect the company to its buyers. The supply chain describes a longer channel, stretching from raw materials to components to final products that are carried to final buyers. Through supply chain management, companies today are strengthening their connections with partners all along the supply chain. They know that their fortunes rest on how well their entire supply chain performs against competitors' supply chains.

> Author | Look back at Figure 1.1.
> Comment | In the first four steps of the marketing process, the company creates value for target customers and builds engagement and strong relationships with them. If it does that well, it can capture value from customers in return, in the form of loyal customers who buy and advocate for the company's brands.

Capturing Value from Customers

The first four steps in the marketing process outlined in Figure 1.1 involve engaging customers and building customer relationships by creating and delivering superior customer value. The final step involves capturing value in return in the form of sales, market share, advocacy, and profits. By creating superior customer value, the firm creates satisfied customers who stay loyal, buy more, and advocate the brand to others. This, in turn, means greater long-run returns for the firm. Here, we discuss the outcomes of creating customer value: customer loyalty and retention, share of market and share of customer, and customer equity.

Creating Customer Loyalty and Retention

Good customer relationship management creates customer satisfaction. In turn, satisfied customers remain loyal and talk favorably to others about the company and its products. Studies show big differences in the loyalty between satisfied and dissatisfied customers. Even slight dissatisfaction can create an enormous drop in loyalty. Thus, the aim of customer relationship management is to create not only customer satisfaction but also customer delight.

Keeping customers loyal makes good economic sense. Loyal customers spend more and stay around longer. Research also shows that it's five times cheaper to keep an old customer than acquire a new one. Conversely, customer defections can be costly. Losing a customer means losing more than a single sale. It means losing the entire stream of purchases that the customer would make over a lifetime of patronage. For example, here is a classic illustration of **customer lifetime value**:[20]

Customer lifetime value
The value of the entire stream of purchases a customer makes over a lifetime of patronage.

Stew Leonard, who operates a highly profitable seven-store supermarket in Connecticut, New Jersey, and New York, once said that he saw $50,000 flying out of his store every time he saw a sulking customer. Why? Because his average customer spent about $100 a week, shopped 50 weeks a year, and remained in the area for about 10 years. If this customer had an unhappy experience and switched to another supermarket, Stew Leonard's lost $50,000 in lifetime revenue. The loss could be much greater if the disappointed customer shared the bad experience with other customers and caused them to defect.

To keep customers coming back, Stew Leonard's has created what has been called the "Disneyland of Dairy Stores," complete with costumed characters, scheduled entertainment, a petting zoo, and animatronics throughout the store. From its humble beginnings as a small dairy store in 1969, Stew Leonard's has grown at an amazing pace. It's built 30 additions onto the original store, which now serves more than 300,000 customers each week. ● This legion of loyal shoppers is largely a result of the store's passionate approach to customer service. "Rule #1: The customer is always right. Rule #2: If the customer is ever wrong, reread rule #1."

Stew Leonard's is not alone in assessing customer lifetime value. Lexus, for example, estimates that a single satisfied

● Customer lifetime value: To keep customers coming back, Stew Leonard's has created the "Disneyland of dairy stores." Rule #1: The customer is always right. Rule #2: If the customer is ever wrong, reread Rule #1.

Courtesy of Stew Leonard's

and loyal customer is worth more than $600,000 in lifetime sales, and the estimated lifetime value of a Starbucks customer is more than $14,000.[21] In fact, a company can lose money on a specific transaction but still benefit greatly from a long-term relationship. This means that companies must aim high in building customer relationships. Customer delight creates an emotional relationship with a brand, not just a rational preference. And that relationship keeps customers coming back.

Growing Share of Customer

Share of customer

The portion of the customer's purchasing that a company gets in its product categories.

Beyond simply retaining good customers to capture customer lifetime value, good customer relationship management can help marketers increase their **share of customer**—the share they get of the customer's purchasing in their product categories. Thus, banks want to increase "share of wallet." Supermarkets and restaurants want to get more "share of stomach." Car companies want to increase "share of garage," and airlines want greater "share of travel."

To increase share of customer, firms can offer greater variety to current customers. Or they can create programs to cross-sell and up-sell to market more products and services to existing customers. For example, Amazon is highly skilled at leveraging relationships with its more than 310 million customers worldwide to increase its share of each customer's spending budget:[22]

> Once they log onto Amazon.com, customers often buy more than they intend, and Amazon does all it can to help make that happen. The online giant continues to broaden its merchandise assortment, carrying hundreds of millions of products and creating an ideal spot for one-stop shopping. And based on each customer's purchase and search history, the company recommends related products that might be of interest. This recommendation system influences some 35 percent of all sales. Amazon's ingenious Amazon Prime and Amazon Prime Now shipping programs have also helped boost its share of customers' wallets. According to one analyst, the Amazon Prime "converts casual shoppers, who gorge on the gratification of having purchases reliably appear two days [or even two hours] after the order, into Amazon addicts." And that's just online. To dig even deeper into customers' wallets, Amazon is now expanding rapidly to the brick-and-mortar world, opening physical stores to sell everything from groceries to consumer electronics.

Building Customer Equity

We can now see the importance of not only acquiring customers but also keeping and growing them. The value of a company comes from the value of its current and future customers. Customer relationship management takes a long-term view. Companies want to not only create profitable customers but also "own" them for life, earn a greater share of their purchases, and capture their customer lifetime value.

Customer equity

The total combined customer lifetime values of all of the company's customers.

What Is Customer Equity? The ultimate aim of customer relationship management is to produce high customer equity.[23] **Customer equity** is the total combined customer lifetime values of all of the company's current and potential customers. As such, it's a measure of the future value of the company's customer base. Clearly, the more loyal the firm's profitable customers, the higher its customer equity. Customer equity may be a better measure of a firm's performance than current sales or market share. Whereas sales and market share reflect the past and present, customer equity suggests the future. Consider Cadillac:[24]

> In the 1970s and 1980s, Cadillac had some of the most loyal customers in the industry. To an entire generation of car buyers, the name Cadillac defined "The Standard of the World." Cadillac's share of the luxury car market reached a whopping 51 percent in 1976, and based on market share and sales, the brand's future looked rosy. However, measures of customer equity would have painted a bleaker picture. Cadillac customers were getting older (average age 60), and average customer lifetime value was falling. Many Cadillac buyers were on their last cars. Thus, although Cadillac's market share was good, its customer equity was not.
>
> Compare this with BMW. Its more youthful and vigorous image didn't win BMW the early market share war. However, it did win BMW younger customers (average age about 40) with higher customer lifetime values. The result: In the years that followed, BMW's market share and profits soared while Cadillac's fortunes eroded badly. BMW overtook Cadillac in the 1980s. In the years that followed, Cadillac struggled to make the Caddy cool again with

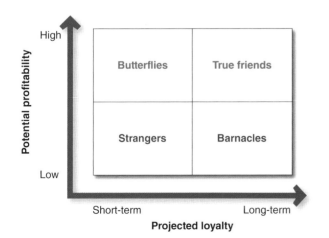

● Managing customer equity: To increase customer equity, Cadillac is making the classic car cool again among younger buyers. For example, says GM, "Cadillac will lead the company to an all-electric future."

General Motors

edgier, high-performance designs that target a younger generation of consumers. More recently, the brand has emphasized marketing pitches based on performance and design, attributes that position it more effectively against the likes of BMW and Audi. ● It is focusing on high-design luxury SUVs and crossovers, and GM recently announced that "Cadillac will lead the company to an all-electric future" with its first fully electric vehicle. As a result, although it still lags other luxury brands, Cadillac's share of the luxury car market has rebounded modestly in recent years. The moral: Marketers should care not just about current sales and market share. Customer lifetime value and customer equity are the name of the game.

Building the Right Relationships with the Right Customers. Companies should manage customer equity carefully. They should view customers as assets that need to be managed and maximized. But not all customers, not even all loyal customers, are good investments. Surprisingly, some loyal customers can be unprofitable, and some disloyal customers can be profitable. Which customers should the company acquire and retain?

The company can classify customers according to their potential profitability and manage its relationships with them accordingly. ● **Figure 1.5** classifies customers into one of four relationship groups, according to their profitability and projected loyalty.[25] Each group requires a different relationship management strategy. *Strangers* show low potential profitability and little projected loyalty. There is little fit between the company's offerings and their needs. The relationship management strategy for these customers is simple: Don't invest anything in them; make money on every transaction.

Butterflies are potentially profitable but not loyal. There is a good fit between the company's offerings and their needs. However, like real butterflies, we can enjoy them for only a short while and then they're gone. An example is stock market investors who trade shares often and in large amounts but who enjoy hunting out the best deals without building a regular relationship with any single brokerage company. Efforts to convert butterflies into loyal customers are rarely successful. Instead, the company should enjoy the butterflies for the moment. It should create satisfying and profitable transactions with them, capturing as much of their business as possible in the short time during which they buy from the company. Then it should move on and cease investing in them until the next time around.

True friends are both profitable and loyal. There is a strong fit between their needs and the company's offerings. The firm wants to make continuous relationship investments to delight these customers and engage, nurture, retain, and grow them. It wants to turn true friends into true believers, who come back regularly and tell others about their good experiences with the company.

Barnacles are highly loyal but not very profitable. There is a limited fit between their needs and the company's offerings. An example is smaller bank customers who bank regularly but do not generate enough returns to cover the costs of maintaining their accounts. Like barnacles on the hull of a ship, they create drag. Barnacles are perhaps the most problematic customers. The company might be able to improve their profitability by selling them more, raising their fees, or reducing service to them. However, if they cannot be made profitable, they should be "fired."

For example, Best Buy offers an attractive returns policy but has found that a small segment of customers abuses this policy. So it uses an outside firm, Retail Equation, to track and score individual customer returns behavior. The system is designed to identify the 1 percent of shoppers whose behavior suggests returns fraud or abuse.

● FIGURE 1.5
Customer Relationship Groups

A shopper who exceeds a certain score is informed that future returns will be denied, even if it means losing the customer. "You could do things that are inside the posted rules, but if you are violating the intent of the rules, like every item you're purchasing you're using and then returning, then at a certain point you become not a profitable customer for [Best Buy]," says a Retail Equation executive.[26]

The point here is an important one: Different types of customers require different engagement and relationship management strategies. The goal is to build the right relationships with the right customers.

The Changing Marketing Landscape

OBJECTIVE 1-5 Describe the major trends and forces that are changing the marketing landscape in this age of relationships.

Every day, dramatic changes are occurring in the marketplace. Richard Love of HP observed, "The pace of change is so rapid that the ability to change has now become a competitive advantage." Yogi Berra, the legendary New York Yankees catcher and manager, summed it up more simply when he said, "The future ain't what it used to be." As the marketplace changes, so must those who serve it.

In this section, we examine the major trends and forces that are changing the marketing landscape and challenging marketing strategy. We look at four major developments: the digital age, the growth of not-for-profit marketing, rapid globalization, and the call for sustainable marketing practices.

The Digital Age: Online, Mobile, and Social Media Marketing

The explosive growth in digital technology has fundamentally changed the way we live—how we communicate, share information, access entertainment, and shop. Welcome to the age of the **Internet of Things (IoT)**, a global environment where everything and everyone is digitally connected to everything and everyone else. More than 4 billion people—55 percent of the world's population—are now online; almost 80 percent of all American adults own smartphones. These numbers will only grow as digital technology rockets into the future.[27]

Most consumers are totally smitten with all things digital. For example, according to one study, 71 percent of Americans keep their mobile phone next to them when they sleep; 3 percent sleep with phone in hand. Six in 10 young adults in the United States use primarily online streaming services to watch TV, and 85 percent of U.S. adults get their news via mobile devices. Importantly to marketers, 79 percent of smartphone users have made a purchase online using a mobile device, and an estimated 80 percent of shoppers have used a phone in stores to look up product reviews or compare prices as they shop.[28]

The consumer love affair with digital and mobile technology makes it fertile ground for marketers trying to engage customers. So it's no surprise that the internet and rapid advances in digital and social media have taken the marketing world by storm. **Digital and social media marketing** involves using digital marketing tools such as websites, social media, mobile ads and apps, online video, email, blogs, and other digital platforms to engage consumers anywhere, anytime via their computers, smartphones, tablets, internet-ready TVs, and other digital devices. These days, almost every company is reaching out to customers with multiple websites, newsy tweets and Facebook pages, Instagram posts and Snapchat stories, viral ads and videos posted on YouTube, rich-media emails, and mobile apps that solve consumer problems and help them shop.

At the most basic level, marketers set up company and brand websites that provide information and promote the company's products. Many companies also set up online brand community sites, where customers can congregate and exchange brand-related interests and information. For example, beauty products retailer Sephora's Beauty Insider Community—"the world's largest beauty forum"—is a thriving online community where customers can ask questions, share ideas and reviews, post photos, and get

Author | Comment | Marketing doesn't take place in a vacuum. Now that we've discussed the five steps in the marketing process, let's look at how the ever-changing marketplace affects both consumers and the marketers who serve them. We'll look more deeply into these and other marketing environment factors in Chapter 3.

Internet of Things (IoT)
A global environment where everything and everyone is digitally connected to everything and everyone else.

Digital and social media marketing
Using digital marketing tools such as websites, social media, mobile apps and ads, online video, email, and blogs to engage consumers anywhere, at any time, via their digital devices.

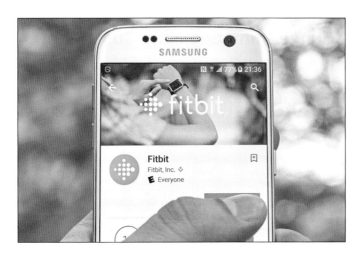

● **Online brand communities: The Fitbit Community serves as a social hub where brand enthusiasts can share inspiration, updates, and milestones with fellow fans.**

dennizn/Shutterstock

beauty advice and inspiration from other enthusiasts. ● And the Fitbit Community section on the Fitbit app serves as a social hub for more 700,000 of the brand's enthusiasts. It's a place where Fitbit fans can share inspiration, updates, and milestones with fellow users; join any of 40 topic-specific groups of like-minded people; learn about local Fitbit events; and read brand-related news and expert content hand-picked for them. "Social engagement has proven to be a key motivator," says Fitbit. The community "makes it easier for you to engage with your friends and meet new people who are passionate about the same things you are."[29]

Beyond brand websites, most companies are also integrating social and mobile media into their marketing mixes.

Social Media Marketing

It's hard to find a brand website, or even a traditional media ad, that doesn't feature links to the brand's Facebook, Instagram, Twitter, YouTube, Snapchat, Pinterest, LinkedIn, or other social media sites. Social media provide exciting opportunities to extend customer engagement and get people talking about a brand.

Some social media are huge—Facebook has more than 2.3 *billion* active monthly users, Instagram more than 1 billion, Twitter more than 326 million, and Snapchat 186 million. Reddit, the online social news community, has 330 million users from 185 countries. But smaller, more focused social media sites are also thriving, such as CafeMom, an online community that reaches 75 million moms monthly who exchange advice, entertainment, and commiseration at the community's online, Facebook, Twitter, Pinterest, YouTube, and mobile sites. Even tiny sites can attract active audiences, such as Newgrounds.com for gamers, programmers, and illustrators or Ravelry.com for knitters and crocheters.[30]

Online social media provide a digital home where people can connect and share important information and moments in their lives. As a result, they offer an ideal platform for real-time marketing, by which marketers can engage consumers in the moment by linking brands to important trending topics, real-world events, causes, personal occasions, or other happenings in consumers' lives. Candy maker Mars did this with its award-winning Snickers Hungerithm social media campaign, which monitored the "mood" of the internet and offered real-time price discounts to consumers when the internet was "angry" (see Real Marketing 1.2).

Using social media might involve something as simple as a contest or promotion to garner Facebook Likes, tweets, Instagram regrams, or YouTube postings. But more often these days, brands create large-scale, carefully integrated social media programs. For example, energy drink maker Red Bull uses a broad mix of social media to connect and inspire its enthusiastic fan base. It now has more than 50 million followers on Facebook, 2 million on Twitter, and 8 million on Instagram. Red Bull's high-energy social media pages hardly mention the company's products at all. Instead, they promote Red Bull's pedal-to-the-metal lifestyle and provide a place where fans can connect with the brand and each other to share their common interests in extreme sports, music, and entertainment. More than just an energy drink maker, "Red Bull is now a top brand for sporting activities and action shots," says an analyst, "and users follow them on social for their adrenaline-filled feed."[32]

Mobile Marketing

Mobile marketing is perhaps the fastest-growing digital marketing platform. Smartphones are ever present, always on, finely targeted, and highly personal. This makes them ideal for engaging customers anytime, anywhere as they move through the buying process. For example, Starbucks customers can use their mobile devices for everything from finding the nearest Starbucks and learning about new products to placing and paying for orders, perhaps through the coffee merchant's artificial intelligence-powered, voice-activated My Starbucks Barista virtual assistant.

Four out of five smartphone users use their phones to shop—browsing product information through apps or the mobile web, making price comparisons, reading online

Real Marketing 1.2 | Snickers Hungerithm: Engaging Customers in Real Time

Mars is the world's number-one candy maker, and its flagship brand—Snickers—is the world's number-one candy brand. Snickers has long been positioned on its "Snickers satisfies" promise—on the stomach-filling, energy-packed properties of the popular chocolate-covered bar crammed with nougat, caramel, and peanuts. For the past several years, Mars has extended the Snickers positioning with its award-winning and fun "You're not you when you're hungry" campaign. The campaign features wacky ads and other executions in which people become someone else and behave badly when they are hungry. Once they eat a Snickers, however, they become themselves again.

The "You're not you when you're hungry" campaign taps into a universal appeal: hunger. The positioning is as powerful for women as for men; for older generations as for younger ones; for office workers, factory workers, or students; in the United States or Australia or even Russia (Snickers' second-largest market). And the appeal is immediate—hunger pops up regularly throughout the day, triggered by needs both physical and emotional.

Candy is an impulse category. On any given purchase occasion, consumers are presented with dozens, even hundreds, of options. So if Snickers wants to be the brand people reach for, it needs to be top-of-mind when the mood strikes. With this in mind, Snickers recently launched an innovative marketing campaign in Australia—called "Hungerithm"—that played off both the immediacy of its "You're not you" hunger appeal and the real-time capabilities of social and mobile media.

Building on the notion that people get cranky when they are hungry, Snickers developed an algorithm—or "Hungerithm"—that gauged the public's general irritability real-time by monitoring social media chatter. Built with the help of MIT and Google, Hungerithm analyzed some 14,000 social media posts a day across platforms such as Twitter, Facebook, and YouTube. It looked at 3,000 commonly used words and phrases, even interpreting slang and sarcasm, to take what one analyst called "a virtual fist-shaking temperature of the internet"—ranging from "Annoyed," "On Edge," or "Irritable" to "Losing It" or even "Full Meltdown." Snickers then linked the public mood in real time with the price of Snickers at 7-Eleven stores. The

angrier the internet got (suggesting the hungrier people were), the lower the price of Snickers at the local 7-Eleven. At the angriest level during the campaign, the price of Snickers dropped by 82 percent.

Mars introduced the Hungerithm campaign with a barrage of TV spots, online videos, and social media posts. "The Internet can be an angry place," said the first Hungerithm promotion. "But what if that's just because we're hungry?" The conclusion: "Angry internet = cheaper Snickers. Now, when the weather's crappy, you'll get cheaper Snickers. Political scandal? Cheaper Snickers. Meteor strike? Definitely cheaper Snickers."

The digital- and mobile-driven Hungerithm campaign targeted people at peak mood-producing moments and places—traffic jams, bad weather, high-profile sports events, or polarizing political shenanigans. It responded in real time with Facebook and Twitter posts addressing breaking political, social, and entertainment news. Mobile-fed coupons let consumers lock in the Snickers price of the moment and directed them to the nearest 7-Eleven.

The real-time design of Hungerithm was for real. The promotion updated every 10 minutes—144 times a day. The Hungerithm website kept a constant posting of the price and mood indicators, and Snickers

partnered with two of Australia's top morning TV shows to give regular price and mood updates. Following the Hungerithm "index" became somewhat of a national pastime in Australia, engaging consumers at a high level.

The Hungerithm campaign produced stunning results. Snickers sales jumped 67 percent during the promotion, with a 1,740 percent increase in Facebook traffic and a 120 percent leap in Snickers mentions on Twitter. The campaign was so successful that Snickers quickly rolled it out in other global markets. In the United States, Hungerithm now runs during the holiday shopping season. "The holidays can be a stressful time for everyone, and the internet reflects the mood of the season," says the brand director for Snickers. "Hungerithm offers a fun way to navigate this time of year with Snickers, offering that moment of satisfaction when you need it most."

Price cutting can be risky. But in the case of Hungerithm, Snickers strategically linked its price discounts to the essence of the brand, creating valuable consumer engagement. According to Mars's chief marketing officer, "Hungerithm hit the exact digital sweet spot we were going for. [It] managed to create a real-life connection to the product that captured everyone's attention and imagination."[31]

Real-time marketing: The Snickers Hungerithm campaigned linked the public mood in real time with the price of Snickers. "Angry internet = cheaper Snickers."

Mars Incorporated

product reviews, and making purchases from home, from work, or in stores. More than 40 percent of all online purchases are now made from mobile devices. As a result, to reach mobile shoppers, mobile advertising is surging and now accounts for more than two-thirds of all digital ad spending.[33]

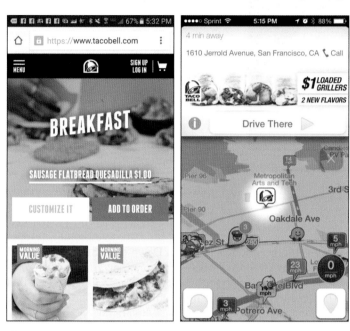

● Mobile marketing: Carefully targeted mobile advertising lets Taco Bell reach breakfast customers at "moments that matter"—such as when they first open their eyes in the morning.

Taco Bell Corp and Google

Marketers use mobile channels to stimulate immediate buying, make shopping easier, enrich the brand experience, reach on-the-go consumers, or all of these. ● For example, Taco Bell uses mobile advertising to reach consumers at what it calls mobile "moments that matter."[34]

As part of its ongoing push to promote Taco Bell for breakfast, the chain uses carefully targeted mobile advertising to reach consumers just as they are starting their day. It targets mobile ads based on specific behaviors such as which apps consumers use first in the morning, their favorite news apps, or what time of day they've looked at a breakfast recipe. "We're weaving into morning behaviors," says a Taco Bell marketer. Taco Bell also targets mobile ads geographically using navigation and traffic apps such as Google's Waze to zero in on specific customer locations, even providing step-by-step directions to nearby stores. In these ways, Taco Bell can customize mobile ads according to each customer's actions, experiences, and environment. In marketing its breakfasts, says the marketer, mobile lets Taco Bell be "present on experiences that consumers turn to when they first open their eyes in the morning."

Online, social media, and mobile marketing are having a huge impact on customer engagement. The key is to blend digital approaches with traditional marketing to create a smoothly integrated marketing strategy and mix. We will examine digital, mobile, and social media marketing throughout the text—they touch almost every area of marketing strategy and tactics. Then, after we've covered the marketing basics, we'll look more deeply into digital and direct marketing in Chapter 17.

Big Data and Artificial Intelligence (AI)

With the explosion in digital technologies, marketers can now amass mountains of data. They are tapping information sources ranging from customer transactions to real-time data flowing from website and social media monitoring, connected Internet of Things (IoT) devices, and many others. Brands can use such *big data* to gain deep customer insights, personalize marketing offers, and improve customer engagements and service.

To make sense of all this big data and use it to benefit their brands and customers, marketers are turning to ever-more-advanced marketing analytics. For example, *artificial intelligence (AI)* has burst onto the marketing scene. AI involves machines that think and learn in a way that looks and feels human but with a lot more analytical capacity. Marketers can use AI to analyze data at lightning speed and apply the insights to engage customers in real time and help them through the buying process.

AI-empowered applications include everything from customer-service chat bots and virtual assistants like Amazon Echo's Alexa or Apple's Siri to IBM's almost-human AI supercomputer Watson. For example, one medicine maker recently used Watson to shape personalized mobile ads to individual allergy medication customers based on real-time weather data and pollen counts in their areas. We will discuss the fascinating developments in big data and artificial intelligence more deeply in Chapter 4.

The Growth of Not-for-Profit Marketing

In recent years, marketing has also become a major part of the strategies of many not-for-profit organizations, such as colleges, hospitals, museums, zoos, symphony orchestras, foundations, and even churches. The nation's not-for-profits face stiff competition for support

● **Not-for-profit marketing:** St. Jude Children's Research Hospital aggressively markets its powerful mission: "Finding cures. Saving children."

ALSAC | St. Jude. St. Jude Children's Research Hospital® and Finding Cures. Saving Children® are registered trademarks of American Lebanese Syrian Associated Charities, Inc. (ALSAC)

and membership. Sound marketing can help them attract membership, funds, and support.

● For example, not-for-profit St. Jude Children's Research Hospital has a special mission: "Finding cures. Saving children." It directly serves some 7,500 patients each year plus countless thousands more through its affiliations and clinical trials in places across the country and around the world. Families never receive a bill from St. Jude, for treatment, travel, housing, or food. To accomplish this mission, St. Jude raises the funds for its $2 million-plus daily operating budget through powerhouse marketing.[35] Fundraising efforts include everything from public service announcements, celebrity endorsements, corporate partnerships, and an extensive online presence to events such as Trike-a-thons, Math-a-thons, an Up 'Til Dawn student challenge, and the St. Jude Dream Home Giveaway. St. Jude works with more than 70 corporate partners such as Target, Domino's, Williams-Sonoma, Regal Cinemas, and Expedia that participate in its annual Thanks and Giving campaign, which asks consumers to "give thanks for the healthy kids in your life, and give to those who are not." The result is a pervasive brand that brings in more than $1.3 billion each year from private donors—ranging from preschoolers and professionals to eighth-graders and 80-year-olds.

Government agencies have also shown an increased interest in marketing. For example, the U.S. military has a marketing plan to attract recruits to its different services, and various government agencies are now designing social marketing campaigns to encourage energy conservation and concern for the environment or discourage smoking, illegal drug use, and obesity. Even the once-stodgy U.S. Postal Service has developed innovative marketing to sell commemorative stamps, promote its Priority Mail services, and lift its image as a contemporary and competitive organization. In all, the U.S. government is the nation's 46th largest advertiser.[36]

Rapid Globalization

Today, almost every company, large or small, is touched in some way by global competition. A neighborhood florist buys its flowers from Mexican nurseries, and a large U.S. electronics manufacturer competes in its home markets with giant Asian rivals. A fledgling internet retailer finds itself receiving orders from all over the world at the same time that an American consumer goods producer introduces new products into emerging markets abroad.

American firms have been challenged at home by the skillful marketing of European and Asian multinationals. Companies such as Toyota, Nestlé, and Samsung have often outperformed their U.S. competitors in American markets. Similarly, U.S. companies in a wide range of industries have developed truly global operations, making and selling their products worldwide. Quintessentially American McDonald's now serves 69 million customers daily in more than 36,000 local restaurants in more than 100 countries worldwide—75 percent of its corporate revenues come from outside the United States. Similarly, Nike markets in 190 countries, with non-U.S. sales accounting for 58 percent of its worldwide sales.[37] Today, companies are not just selling more of their locally produced goods in international markets; they are also sourcing more supplies and components abroad and developing new products for specific markets around the world.

Thus, managers in countries around the world are increasingly taking a global, not just local, view of the company's industry, competitors, and opportunities. They are asking: What is global marketing? How does it differ from domestic marketing? How do global competitors and forces affect our business? To what extent should we "go global"? We will discuss the global marketplace in more detail in Chapter 19.

Sustainable Marketing: The Call for More Environmental and Social Responsibility

Marketers are reexamining their relationships with social values and responsibilities and with the very earth that sustains us. As the worldwide consumerism and environmentalism movements mature, today's marketers are being called on to develop sustainable marketing practices. Corporate ethics and social responsibility have become hot topics for almost every business. And few companies can ignore the renewed and very demanding environmental movement. Every company action can affect customer relationships. Today's customers expect companies to deliver value in a socially and environmentally responsible way.

The social responsibility and environmental movements will place even stricter demands on companies in the future. Some companies resist these movements, budging only when forced by legislation or organized consumer outcries. Most companies, however, readily accept their responsibilities to the world around them. They view sustainable marketing as an opportunity to do well by doing good. They seek ways to profit by serving immediate needs and the best long-run interests of their customers and communities.

Some companies, such as Patagonia, Timberland, Ben & Jerry's, Warby Parker, and others, practice caring capitalism, setting themselves apart by being civic minded and responsible.

● Sustainable marketing: Warby Parker sells eyewear with a purpose. "Companies can do good in the world while still being profitable," says the company's co-founder.

Warby Parker

They build social and environmental responsibility into their company value and mission statements. ● For example, Warby Parker—the highly successful online marketer of low-priced prescription glasses—sells "eyewear with a purpose".[38]

> Warby Parker was founded with a lofty objective: "to offer designer eyewear at a revolutionary price while leading the way for socially conscious businesses." For starters, by cutting out distributors, designing its own glasses in-house, and engaging customers directly online, the company sells high-quality eyewear at very low prices. Buying glasses from Warby Parker "should leave you happy and good-looking, with money in your pocket."
>
> But beyond bringing value to its customers, Warby Parker has a broader social mission. It notes that nearly one billion people worldwide who need glasses lack access to them. To help fix that problem, Warby Parker's Buy a Pair, Give a Pair program promises that for every pair of glasses it sells, another pair will be distributed to someone in need. So far, more than 5 million pairs of glasses have been distributed through the program. "We believe that everyone has the right to see," says the company. Beyond being socially admirable, Warby Parker's Buy a Pair, Give a Pair program also makes good economic sense, for both the company and its customers. After only eight years, the company has grown to more than $320 million in annual sales. "Companies can do good in the world while still being profitable," says Warby Parker co-founder Neil Blumenthal. "Good eyewear, good outcome."

Sustainable marketing presents both opportunities and challenges for marketers. We will revisit the topic of sustainable marketing in greater detail in Chapter 20.

Author Comment | Remember Figure 1.1 outlining the marketing process? Now, based on everything we've discussed in this chapter, we'll expand that figure to provide a road map for learning marketing throughout the remainder of the text.

So, What Is Marketing? Pulling It All Together

At the start of this chapter, Figure 1.1 presented a simple model of the marketing process. Now that we've discussed all the steps in the process,

● **Figure 1.6** presents an expanded model that will help you pull it all together. What is marketing? Simply put, marketing is the process of engaging customers and building profitable customer relationships by creating value for customers and capturing value in return.

● **FIGURE 1.6**
An Expanded Model of the Marketing Process

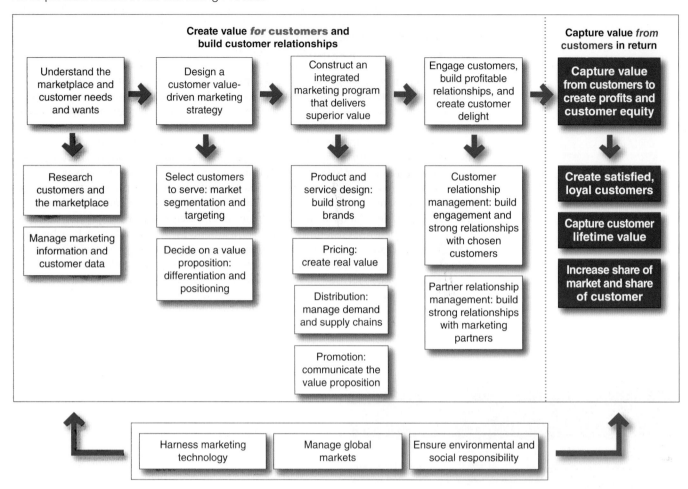

This expanded version of Figure 1.1 at the beginning of the chapter provides a good road map for the rest of the text. The underlying concept of the entire text is that marketing creates value for customers in order to capture value from customers in return.

The first four steps of the marketing process focus on creating value for customers. The company first gains a full understanding of the marketplace by researching customer needs and managing marketing information. It then designs a customer-driven marketing strategy based on the answers to two simple questions. The first question is "What consumers will we serve?" (market segmentation and targeting). Good marketing companies know that they cannot serve all customers in every way. Instead, they need to focus their resources on the customers they can serve best and most profitably. The second marketing strategy question is "How can we best serve targeted customers?" (differentiation and positioning). Here, the marketer outlines a value proposition that spells out what values the company will deliver to win target customers.

With its marketing strategy chosen, the company now constructs an integrated marketing program—consisting of a blend of the four marketing mix elements, the four Ps—that transforms the marketing strategy into real value for customers. The company develops product offers and creates strong brand identities for them. It prices these offers to create real customer value and distributes the offers to make them available to target consumers. Finally, the company designs promotion programs that engage target customers, communicate the value proposition, and persuade customers to act on the market offering.

Perhaps the most important step in the marketing process involves engaging target customers and building value-laden, profitable relationships with them. Throughout the process, marketers practice customer relationship management to create customer satisfaction and delight. They engage customers in the process of creating brand conversations, experiences, and community. In creating customer value and relationships, however, the company cannot go it alone. It must work closely with marketing partners both inside the company and throughout its marketing system. Thus, beyond practicing good customer relationship management and customer-engagement marketing, firms must also practice good partner relationship management.

The first four steps in the marketing process create value for customers. In the final step, the company reaps the rewards of its strong customer relationships by capturing value from customers. Delivering superior customer value creates highly satisfied customers who will buy more, buy again, and advocate for the brand. This helps the company capture customer lifetime value and greater share of customer. The result is increased long-term customer equity for the firm.

Finally, in the face of today's changing marketing landscape, companies must consider three additional factors. In building customer and partner relationships, they must harness marketing technologies in the new digital age, take advantage of global opportunities, and ensure that they act sustainably in an environmentally and socially responsible way.

Figure 1.6 provides a good road map to future chapters of this text. Chapters 1 and 2 introduce the marketing process, with a focus on building customer relationships and capturing value from customers. Chapters 3 through 6 address the first step of the marketing process—understanding the marketing environment, managing marketing information, and understanding consumer and business buyer behavior. In Chapter 7, we look more deeply into the two major marketing strategy decisions: selecting which customers to serve (segmentation and targeting) and determining a value proposition (differentiation and positioning). Chapters 8 through 17 discuss the marketing mix variables one by one. Chapter 18 sums up customer value–driven marketing strategy and creating competitive advantage in the marketplace. The final two chapters examine special marketing considerations: global marketing and sustainable marketing.

Developing Skills for Your Career

Marketing is an exciting, fast-changing discipline that offers a wide range of rewarding careers. See Appendix 3: Careers in Marketing to see if one of these careers is right for you. But even if you're not planning a career in marketing or business, the lessons you learn in this course will help you in whatever career to choose and in your life more generally. You will acquire and apply many of the skills that employers have identified as critical to success in the workplace, which will contribute to your employability.

In studying this text, you'll sharpen your *critical-thinking* and *problem-solving* skills as you learn about and assess marketing strategies and issues. You'll expand your persuasive *communication* skills as you study and report on how marketers create advertising, digital, social media, and other promotional campaigns that engage consumers and create brand relationships. You'll see how *technology and marketing analytics* are dramatically reshaping the marketing world and even apply some of these technologies in completing your own analyses of marketing problems. You'll learn the importance of *collaboration and teamwork* as you see how marketers work closely with others on their marketing teams and with managers in other company areas to develop overall organizational strategies and tactics. And you'll learn more about *business ethics and social responsibility*, from sections in the very first chapter through the final chapter on sustainable marketing.

During the course, your professors will help you to improve your critical thinking, analytical, communication, presentation, and teamwork skills through meaningful assignments, perhaps from the end-of-chapter exercises, cases, or appendixes in this text. Finally, beyond business applications, you'll see that marketing applies to your life more generally. For the rest of your life, you will be marketing yourself to others. In fact, a favorite tactic of some employers during job interviewers is to give you this challenge: "Pretend you are a product and market yourself to me." After taking this course and studying this text, you should have ready answers.

Reviewing and Extending the Concepts

Objectives Review

Today's successful companies—whether large or small, for-profit or not-for-profit, domestic or global—share a strong customer focus and a heavy commitment to marketing. The goal of marketing is to engage customers and manage profitable customer relationships.

OBJECTIVE 1-1 Define marketing and outline the steps in the marketing process. *(pp 24–26)*

Marketing is the process by which companies engage customers, build strong customer relationships, and create customer value in order to capture value from customers in return. The marketing process involves five steps. The first four steps create value *for* customers. First, marketers need to understand the marketplace and customer needs and wants. Next, marketers design a customer value–driven marketing strategy with the goal of getting, engaging, and growing target customers. In the third step, marketers construct a marketing program that actually delivers superior value. All of these steps form the basis for the fourth step: engaging customers, building profitable customer relationships, and creating customer delight. In the final step, the company reaps the rewards of strong customer relationships by capturing value *from* customers.

OBJECTIVE 1-2 Explain the importance of understanding the marketplace and customers and identify the five core marketplace concepts.

(pp 26–30)

Outstanding marketing companies go to great lengths to learn about and understand their customers' needs, wants, and demands. This understanding helps them to design want-satisfying market offerings and build value-laden customer relationships by which they can capture customer lifetime value and greater share of customer. The result is increased long-term customer equity for the firm. The core marketplace concepts are needs, wants, and demands; market offerings (products, services, and experiences); value and satisfaction; exchange and relationships; and markets. Companies address needs, wants, and demands by putting forth a value proposition, a set of benefits that they promise to consumers to satisfy their needs. The value proposition is fulfilled through a market offering, which delivers customer value and satisfaction, resulting in long-term exchange relationships with customers.

OBJECTIVE 1-3 Identify the key elements of a customer value–driven marketing strategy and discuss the marketing management orientations that guide marketing strategy. *(pp 30–34)*

To design a winning marketing strategy, the company must first decide whom it will serve. It does this by dividing the market into segments of customers (*market segmentation*) and selecting which segments it will cultivate (*target marketing*). Next, the company must decide how it will serve targeted customers (how it will *differentiate* and *position* itself in the marketplace).

Marketing management can adopt one of five competing market orientations. The produc*tion concept* holds that management's task is to improve production efficiency and bring down prices. The *product concept* holds that consumers favor products that offer the most in quality, performance, and innovative features; thus, little promotional effort is required. The *selling concept* holds that consumers will not buy enough of an organization's products unless it undertakes a large-scale selling and promotion effort. The *marketing concept* holds that achieving organizational goals depends on determining the needs and wants of target markets and delivering the desired satisfactions more effectively and efficiently than competitors do. The *societal marketing concept* holds that generating customer satisfaction and long-run societal well-being through sustainable marketing strategies is key to both achieving the company's goals and fulfilling its responsibilities.

OBJECTIVE 1-4 Discuss customer relationship management and identify strategies for creating value for customers and capturing value from customers in return. *(pp 34–42)*

Broadly defined, *customer relationship management* is the process of engaging customers and building and maintaining profitable customer relationships by delivering superior customer value and satisfaction. *Customer-engagement marketing* aims to make a brand a meaningful part of consumers' conversations and lives through direct and continuous customer involvement in shaping brand conversations, experiences, and community. The aim of customer relationship management and customer engagement is to produce high *customer equity*, the total combined customer lifetime values of all the company's customers. The key to building lasting relationships is the creation of superior *customer value* and *satisfaction*. In return for creating value *for* targeted customers, the company captures value *from* customers in the form of profits and customer equity.

OBJECTIVE 1-5 Describe the major trends and forces that are changing the marketing landscape in this age of relationships. *(pp 42–49)*

Dramatic changes are occurring in marketing. The digital age has created exciting new ways to learn about, engage, and relate to individual customers. As a result, advances in digital, social, and mobile media have taken the marketing world by storm. Online, mobile, and social media marketing offer exciting opportunities to target customers more selectively and engage them more deeply. And today's big data and improved marketing analytics, such as artificial intelligence, are enhancing how marketers learn about and interact with customers. The key is to blend the new digital technologies and approaches with traditional marketing to create a smoothly integrated marketing strategy and mix.

In recent years, marketing has become a major part of the strategies for many not-for-profit organizations, such as colleges, hospitals, museums, zoos, symphony orchestras, foundations, and even churches. Also, in an increasingly smaller world, many marketers are now connected globally with their customers, marketing partners, and competitors. Finally, today's marketers are also reexamining their sustainability responsibilities. Marketers are being called on to take greater responsibility for the social and environmental impacts of their actions.

Pulling it all together, as discussed throughout the chapter, the major new developments in marketing can be summed up in a single concept: *engaging customers and creating and capturing customer value*. Today, marketers of all kinds are taking advantage of new opportunities for building value-laden relationships with their customers, their marketing partners, and the world around them.

Key Terms

OBJECTIVE 1-1

Marketing (p 25)

OBJECTIVE 1-2

Needs (p 26)
Wants (p 26)
Demands (p 26)
Market offerings (p 27)
Marketing myopia (p 27)
Exchange (p 29)
Market (p 29)

OBJECTIVE 1-3

Marketing management (p 30)

Production concept (p 31)
Product concept (p 31)
Selling concept (p 31)
Marketing concept (p 32)
Societal marketing concept (p 32)

OBJECTIVE 1-4

Customer relationship management (p 34)
Customer-perceived value (p 34)
Customer satisfaction (p 35)
Customer-engagement marketing (p 37)
Customer brand advocacy (p 37)

Consumer-generated marketing (p 38)
Partner relationship management (p 38)
Customer lifetime value (p 39)
Share of customer (p 40)
Customer equity (p 40)

OBJECTIVE 1-5

Internet of Things (IoT) (p 42)
Digital and social media marketing (p 42)

Discussion Questions

1-1 What are the paths to profits under the marketing concept? (AASCB: Written and Oral Communication)

1-2 What is marketing myopia? What are the short- and long-term implications for business in this situation? (AACSB: Communication; Reflective Thinking)

1-3 Describe the five different competing marketing orientations that a business organization can adopt to drive its marketing strategy. (AACSB: Communication; Reflective Thinking)

1-4 Discuss the concept of customer relationship management. Why is it essential that a business incorporate this in its operations? (AACSB: Communication; Reflective Thinking)

1-5 Why is marketing as important for not-for-profit organizations as profit-driven ones? (AACSB: Communication; Reflective Thinking)

1-6 Explain the growing importance of digital and social media marketing. (AACSB: Written and Oral Communication; Reflective Thinking)

Critical Thinking Exercises

1-7 Select an FTSE 100 company. How much did the company spend on marketing activities in the most recent year for which data are available? What percentage of sales does marketing expenditure represent for the company? Have these expenditures increased or decreased over the past five years? Write a brief report of your findings. (AACSB: Communication; Analytic Reasoning)

1-8 Some believe that social marketing is primarily effective only for bigger companies with the time and capacity to manage and update their media content. Choose a local business and evaluate its effectiveness in creating customer engagement. Is the content up-to-date and relevant? How does it manage its content? (AACSB: Communication; Use of IT; Reflective Thinking)

1-9 Use the internet to search for salary information regarding jobs in marketing in your region. What is the national average salary for five different jobs in marketing? How do the averages compare in different areas of the region? Write a brief report on your findings. (AACSB: Communication; Use of IT; Reflective Thinking)

APPLICATIONS AND CASES

Online, Mobile, and Social Media Marketing Fionamania

Fiona, a young hippo who was born prematurely and survived, lives in the Cincinnati Zoo's Africa exhibit. Fiona became a star when the zoo's communication director and her team started posting every move she made from the day she was born prematurely. She became a symbol of resilience and positivity, earning millions of fans and engaging the not-for-profit zoo's visitors and potential donors. Today, videos of Fiona twirling around the internet gain millions of views, she has had her own seven-episode reality show on Facebook, people on Twitter even follow her flatulence, and she has inspired everything from a children's book to beer and ice cream flavors. People are invested in Fiona's story.

1-10 Go to www.facebook.com/cincinnatizoo and find posts that feature Fiona the hippo. How does the zoo's communications team engage with Fiona's fans? (AACSB: Written and Oral Communication; Reflective Thinking)

1-11 What can other not-for-profit marketers learn from the Cincinnati Zoo's use of social media to generate interest in Fiona? How does it fit with the Cincinnati Zoo's overall social media strategy? (AACSB: Written and Oral Communication; Use of IT; Reflective Thinking)

Marketing Ethics Exaggeration and High Pressure

It is a great temptation for manufacturers to exaggerate the benefits of their products on the packaging. Sometimes, the claims are overstated. Businesses want to make bold claims to help them sell more products. Some of the claims are morally wrong; other times they are just "advertising puff." A business might resort to high-pressurized sales techniques. In other cases, they might focus on vulnerable customer groups. Businesses need to make a profit, but is it wrong to try any means to achieve this? Legally, yes, it is.

1-12 How would a business begin to frame an ethical marketing process as a template for their activities now and in the future? (AACSB: Communication; Ethical Reasoning)

1-13 What is likely to motivate a business to adopt ethical marketing? (AACSB: Communication; Ethical Reasoning)

Marketing by the Numbers Be on the First Page

The internet has become a vital marketing medium, and pay-per-click (PPC) is one of the many ways for a business to attract traffic. It is risky, and a business can spend a lot of money, get a lot of visits, but end up with very few actual sales. Search engines allow businesses to buy listings in their search results; they appear next to the non-paid organic search results. These spots are sold by auction. If the business bids the highest, they get a chance, but only the chance to be ranked first.

1-14 If you bid $1.25 on a keyword related to your product and 14,000 people click on your PPC, how much will the search engine charge you? (AACSB: Communication; Analytical Reasoning)

1-15 PPC can be expensive, so why is it popular as a marketing method? (AACSB: Communication; Reflective Thinking)

Company Case Argos: Creating Customer Value amid Change and Turbulence

One of the biggest news items in the UK retail sector recently is the £1.4 billion acquisition in September 2016 of Home Retail Group, the parent company of Argos, by Sainsbury's, one of the leading British supermarkets. Unsurprisingly, the highlights of this business decision are the huge sum involved and the associated risk in the complex marketing environment. Why is this considered a good decision, especially after the British referendum in favor of leaving the European Union and the uncertainty in the business environment that follows?

The key answers to these questions are not hard to find. The deal makers can see the gold in the track record of the organization. Argos was established in July 1973 as the United Kingdom's first catalog retailer with only 17 stores; it now has over 750 stores throughout the United Kingdom and Republic of Ireland. Over 130 million customers, approximately one-third of the UK population, shop in an Argos store annually, buying one thing or another. Even before the agreement on the takeover deal, 10 Argos outlets that opened in Sainsbury's stores already had a record 30 percent sales increase, and the takeover is expected to result in annual savings of £160 million.

As part of its attempts to create value for its customers, Argos has undergone remarkable changes in the 21st century. The design makeover has turned tatty faux wooden floorboards and display cabinets into tiled floors and LED display boards for easy shopping. It is thus not surprising that Argos is valued so highly by Sainsbury's. Ultimately, the plan is to have an Argos center at every Sainsbury's branch to ensure convenience in shopping for customers. While the in-stores catalogs are still in use at Argos stores, the centers have been radically transformed into hi-tech outlets and "digital" stores. The idea behind all these changes is that the customers of today are more informed and deserve the best. Argos's approach is to ensure that value creation for customers permeates every phase of the organization's activities.

Catalog Retailing

Although Argos is noted for a number of things in the British retail sector, its core hallmark is its consistent focus on the satisfaction of the needs and wants of its target customers. This is not only ensured through the thousands of products that it offers its customers both online and across its various stores in the country, but also in all the phases that encapsulate the customers' experience in their transactions, from placing the order to receiving the items. Argos's focus on catalog retailing is based on its quest to satisfy customers through convenience. The shopper checks the catalog, places the order, and receives it shortly afterwards. Its twice-yearly catalog and Internet site support the way the establishment creates value for its customers.

Market Offerings

The assortment of products offered by Argos to its disparate customers across the country illustrates the core value that it offers its target market. The organization is noted for offering a wide range of products, categorized on its website to make shopping easy for its online visitors. For example, customers who are interested in products such as TVs, telephones, or computers simply need to click on the "Technology" link to be ushered into the world of these gadgets. Similarly, there are categorizations for "Home and Garden," "Sports and Leisure," "Clothing," "Health and Beauty," "Toys," and many more.

One critic noted that Argos's focus is on being a "working class" brand, implying that their customers are mainly less well off. However, former CEO John Walden disagrees with this customer stereotype and insists that while this may have been true five years earlier, things have now changed at Argos; the company now targets all demographics. Beyond the rhetoric of who their customers actually are is the issue of keeping those customers satisfied with quality products and excellent customer service. This has been strategically identified by John Rogers, the new CEO of Argos, as the cornerstone of his approach in marketing after taking over the job. The core objective is to ensure not only that the customers are encouraged to shop at Argos but that they are motivated to stay loyal even when the competition tries to draw them away. For example, Tesco has a strong plan in place to price-match best-selling toys by the end of 2019. This is clearly in direct competition with Argos. The retailer's mainstay is the continuous effort to clearly outperform competitors like Tesco and Amazon in meeting customers' needs and addressing their concerns.

Same-Day Delivery

As the retail environment in the UK becomes more competitive, Argos also continues to explore various means of maintaining and improving its market share. To this end, the management has set a long-term goal of having 250 Argos collection points that will be located within Sainsbury's to ensure that customers get their ordered items more quickly than they did before the acquisition of the firm. This, according to Mike Coupe, the CEO of Sainsbury's, is to give customers more choice in their purchasing decisions and make life easier for them.

In 2015, Argos introduced a daring policy—its "Same Day Delivery" service. As the name suggests, a customer could order the desired products and get them immediately in the store or delivered at home on the same day through a "fast tracked" option. This quickly became a very popular strategy and was considered a good gesture by customers. It not only reinforced loyalty among the organization's current clientele but also wooed others happy to see more efficiency in the marketplace. As the company experienced an increase in demand, it also realized that this would require a commensurate increase in resources, hence the recent increase in its delivery vans to about 800 and the 30,000 people employed in different areas of the organization, including customer service, packaging, and order delivery, across its 845 stores. In the run up to Christmas sales in 2016, Argos reportedly added several seasonal staff to the current number.

Digital Retailing

Developments in the world of technology are transforming businesses in various sectors, and retailing is no exception. Based on data from the food and grocery research charity IGD, 5 percent of grocery sales in the United Kingdom are done online. This small figure is due to a variety of challenges associated with this transaction mode, but this is very likely to improve over time. As a key organization in the retail sector in the digital age, Argos is also working toward transforming itself into a "click and collect" business. Toward the end of 2012, Argos announced its mission to rediscover itself as a digital retail leader. John Coombe, the chairman of Home Retail, Argos's parent organization, remarked that Argos is not only an icon of the British high street but also a leading player in the digital transformation of UK retailing business. In June 2016, a report indicated that Argos's Internet sales had gone up by 16 percent, the strongest record in three years. Around the time Argos was being sold to Sainsbury's, John Walden debunked the view that being digital would be like operating a traditional retailing outfit with just one store. According to him, it would still involve hiring people, bringing stock in, expanding, and upgrading. Around 60 percent of Argos's sales are now done as online transactions, which is also closely linked to the fact that the organization is the first retailer in the United Kingdom to make over £1 billion through mobile payments. Its hefty catalogs are being replaced by iPad-style terminals to facilitate order processing. All of this has helped Argos make a seamless entry into the digital world in retail business.

Special Offers

Argos' commitment to delighting its customers is not only evident in the increasing range of products it offers its customers and the sleek distribution system, but also in the various promotional programs it offers. Some of these are offered to existing loyal customers through the Argos loyalty card scheme while others are to attract new customers. Periodically, it sends its customers various promotional offers, money-off vouchers, and other financing offers. When Black Friday hit the UK high street and its public awareness grew, Argos was quick to explore the opportunity through various special price-cut offers that also attracted a response from many new and existing customers. About 12 million customers reportedly visited the company's website on the 2015 Black Friday, resulting in 18 purchases per second. John Rogers also estimates that at least 70 percent of its orders will be taken online on Black Friday while normal trading will account for 50 percent. The Argos gift voucher promotions, which are managed by the company's affiliates, offer its customers something to fall back on during their various subsequent purchases. The periodic product-specific special offers on certain products like furniture, computers, and TVs also constitute part of the package that keeps Argos' stores busy over the years, and with this, it generates customer value profitably.

Argos and Society

It is tempting to conclude that Argos's focus on maximizing customer value is predominantly driven by the profit motive. However, reports suggest that the company does believe in taking responsibility for the environment, improving local communities, and pursing a number of initiatives that revolve around long-run benefits for customers and society. Argos is focused on reducing the amount of resources used in its operations and the CO_2 emissions it produces. It clearly communicates its green credentials on its web pages. Apart from its catalog, which is 100 percent recyclable, it sources the paper it uses from sustainably managed forests and encourages customers to recycle old catalogs in their possession as these have proven useful to newspaper print manufacturers. According to the firm, it has already been able to recycle 91 percent of waste from the business, had a 9 percent reduction in its carbon footprint, ensured a 35 percent reduction in the waste sent to landfill, and has established a goal to reduce its CO_2 emission per square foot by 40 percent by the year 2020. Argos's impacts in the local community are also notable: it supports various charities and other related organizations, and it specifically chose Macmillan Cancer Support as its charity of the year from 2015 to 2017. Argos has shown that it is quite possible to create value for customers and still build relationships with stakeholders.[39]

Questions for Discussion

1-16 To what extent do you think the acquisition of Argos by Sainsbury's resulted in delivering superior value to the customers?

1-17 How is the concept of share of customer illustrated in the case study?

1-18 To what extent would you agree with the claim that Argos's marketing management orientation is a marketing concept? Justify your standpoint with relevant points from the case study.

1-19 What are the key actions taken by Argos which show that the organization is following the changing marketing landscape?

1-20 In view of the stiff competition in the UK retail sector, suggest various ways by which Argos could continue to provide better value to its customers.

2 Company and Marketing Strategy
Partnering to Build Customer Engagement, Value, and Relationships

OBJECTIVES OUTLINE

OBJECTIVE 2-1 Explain company-wide strategic planning and its four steps. **See: Company-Wide Strategic Planning: Defining Marketing's Role** *(pp 58–62)*

OBJECTIVE 2-2 Discuss how to design business portfolios and develop growth strategies. **See: Designing the Business Portfolio** *(pp 62–66)*

OBJECTIVE 2-3 Explain marketing's role in strategic planning and how marketing works with its partners to create and deliver customer value. **See Planning Marketing: Partnering to Build Customer Relationships** *(pp 66–68)*

OBJECTIVE 2-4 Describe the elements of a customer value-driven marketing strategy and mix and the forces that influence them. **See: Marketing Strategy and the Marketing Mix** *(pp 68–73)*

OBJECTIVE 2-5 List the marketing management functions, including the elements of a marketing plan, and discuss the importance of measuring and managing marketing return on investment. **See: Managing the Marketing Effort and Marketing Return on Investment** *(pp 73–78)*

CHAPTER PREVIEW In the first chapter, we explored the marketing process by which companies create value for customers to capture value from them in return. In this chapter, we dig deeper into steps two and three of thatthe marketing process: designing customer value–driven marketing strategies and constructing marketing programs. First, we look at the organization's overall strategic planning, which guides marketing strategy and planning. Next, we discuss how, guided by the strategic plan, marketers partner closely with others inside and outside the firm to engage customers and create value for them. We then examine marketing strategy and planning—how marketers choose target markets, position marketing offers, develop a marketing mix, and manage marketing programs. Finally, we look at the important step of measuring and managing marketing return on investment (marketing ROI).

First, let's look at Rolex, an outstanding company and a good marketing strategy story. Rolex met with enormous instant success by focusing on the customer and on product features that are important to them. The company has pursued this customer-driven marketing strategy since its foundation. Along the way, it discovered that good marketing strategy means more than just growth, sales, and profits. It means skillfully engaging customers and creating value for them. At its core, Rolex doesn't sell just wristwatches; it sells a sentiment of achievement and of belonging to an exclusive club.

ROLEX: Building Brand Equity through a Customer-Driven Marketing Mix

In 1905, in London, Alfred Davis and his brother-in-law Hans Wilsdorf founded Wilsdorf and Davis, the company that would eventually become Rolex SA. Rolex is the single largest luxury watch brand, with estimated 2017 revenues of $4.5 billion. Although its luxury wrist watches are manufactured in Switzerland, the company maintains a network of 4,000 Rolex trained watchmakers in over 100 countries. Rolex has set up and maintained its pole position in the luxury watch market through its customer value–driven marketing strategy and by focusing on features that have been important to its customer base since the company was founded.

Product-wise, Rolex has the distinction of having many new-to-the-world products launched due to its research and development as well as manufacture of unique and timeless watches. In 1910, a Rolex became the world's first wristwatch to receive the Swiss Certificate of Precision, granted by the Official Watch Rating Centre. In 1914, Rolex scored another first when the Kew Observatory in the United Kingdom, which had until then only awarded precision certificates to marine chronometers, gave a Rolex wristwatch a class A certificate. Rolex watches became synonymous with precision all over the world. In 1926, the company took a major step toward developing the world's first waterproof wristwatch, named the "Oyster."

The following year, the watch was worn by Mercedes Gleitze, a young Englishwoman who swam the English Channel. The watch remained in perfect working order after the 10-hour swim, and this event prompted Rolex to use testimonials in their advertising strategy to convey the superiority of the brand. Since then, the Oyster has graced the wrists of personages from Winston Churchill to Che Guevara to Eminem.

Launched in 1953, the "Submariner" was the first watch guaranteed to be waterproof to a depth of 100 meters. In the same year, the expedition led by Sir Edmund Hillary was equipped with the "Oyster Perpetual," and his team became the first to reach the summit of Mount Everest. All of this has made Rolex watches synonymous with precision, achievement, robustness, and reliability. The design of its products have gone through such minor changes that they are recognizable at first sight, setting the brand apart from its rivals. It has become an outward expression of exclusiveness and of the sentiment of belonging to a select club. In this sense, wearers get the feeling of belonging to a special group of achievers.

Distribution-wise, Rolex has a very exclusive network and a limited number of stores in order to make the brand and its products look even more exclusive to customers. A crystal prism indicates that a store is an official Rolex dealer, and the locations selected are all in upscale areas with an established reputation. Its outlets adhere to detailed specifications in terms of geographical location, level of inventory, display patterns, and annual local advertising. This allows Rolex to tightly control its market and closely monitor the brand. Rolex strengthens this positioning strategy by limiting production even as demand increases. For luxury goods, scarcity in the marketplace definitely influences value perception, thus increasing demand and contributing to long-term appreciation in the end. Rolex does not have a retail outlet on the internet. Its website has information on models and dealers in a specific region, but it does not serve as a point of purchase, thus ensuring that it can offer the best possible service and maintain the exclusivity of its brand in terms of its distribution channels.

Rolex endorses sports that reinforce the values of the brand—achievement and exclusivity.
Cal Sport Media/Alamy Stock Photo

Rolex's pricing strategy is distinctive: it pursues a premium pricing policy and sets its prices with little regard to the competition, setting instead the price that others follow. Furthermore, confident that its customers are willing to pay the high prices it sets, it offers no discounts, price reductions, or special sales. After all, the majority of luxury watch shoppers look for a Rolex even during economic downturns.

When it comes to promotion, Rolex uses a number of marketing communication tools to effectively convey its positioning strategy, like print advertising in upmarket publications such as the *Financial Times* and *Vogue*. Sponsorship and testimonials remain central to its marketing communications, for the company chooses people who have achieved something and can reinforce the values of the brand. The sports that the company endorses are also those generally considered upscale, such as golf, equestrianism, yachting, and tennis. By tradition, the brand has been a partner of the famous Wimbledon tennis tournament since 1978, with the Rolex clock prominently placed at the scoreboard on Centre Court. All promotional tools convey a consistent positioning and message—Rolex purchasers are wealthy, attractive, and active and lead interesting lives. A Rolex as a statement of success.

In the future, Rolex will face increasingly fierce competition, particularly in Asia, as competitors search for new ways to gain market share. The large luxury goods conglomerates such as Louis Vuitton Moët Hennessy and Compagnie Financière Richemont enjoy advantages of size and significantly reduced costs from synergies in advertising and marketing. Furthermore, these enterprises are also targeting younger customers to generate further market potential. However, Rolex has successfully managed to build and enhance its brand equity and has effectively generated a distinct perception of the company

> Rolex has established and maintained its pole position as the largest luxury watch brand on the planet. At its core, Rolex doesn't sell just wristwatches, it sells a sentiment of achievement and belonging to an exclusive club.

and its products that is rooted in values such as accuracy, exclusivity, and robustness. This was accomplished by the company's carefully orchestrated customer-driven marketing mix in concert with constant innovation. The company has also successfully reacted to their rival's strategy to target a younger audience by sponsoring more current testimonials in sports, such as young golf pros Ricky Fowler and Martin Kaymer.

With similar goals in mind, Rolex created a fan page on Facebook in 2013 that has earned over 6.9 million likes to date, outperforming rivals like Breitling (690,000) and Cartier (4.5 million). In 2013, after 30 years sponsoring Wimbledon, Rolex added a raft of digital content, including a "scorecard" Facebook app, Twitter hashtags, and video content. In 2012, the brand launched its YouTube channel to launch in-house documentaries on topics that fit the brand and its customers' interests, like deep-sea missions to investigate the polar ice caps and Himalayan expeditions. As to the cost advantage of some of their rivals, Rolex successfully adapted its marketing mix strategy by launching its Tudor brand. Priced significantly lower than the classic Rolex wristwatches, the launch of Tudor has enabled the company to compete with Tag Heuer and other competitors within the accessible luxury market and also to target a younger audience. In this respect, the company ensures a clear distinction between both brands (for example, by not having any reference to the Tudor brand on the official Rolex website) to prevent any dilution of the value of the Rolex brand in the luxury watch market.

In all, its effective and flexible marketing mix strategy, in line with its ability to react to a dynamic environment, has enabled Rolex to not only build brand equity but also successfully repel threats from competitors and stand resilient as one of the world's most powerful and enduring brands.[1]

Author | Comment | Company-wide strategic planning guides marketing strategy and planning. Like marketing strategy, the company's broader strategy must also be customer focused.

Strategic planning
The process of developing and maintaining a strategic fit between the organization's goals and capabilities and its changing marketing opportunities.

Company-Wide Strategic Planning: Defining Marketing's Role

OBJECTIVE 2-1 Explain company-wide strategic planning and its four steps.

Each company must find the game plan for long-run survival and growth that makes the most sense given its specific situation, opportunities, objectives, and resources. This is the focus of **strategic planning**—the process of developing and maintaining a strategic fit between the organization's goals and capabilities and its changing marketing opportunities.

Strategic planning sets the stage for the rest of planning in the firm. Companies usually prepare annual plans, long-range plans, and strategic plans. The annual and long-range plans deal with the company's current businesses and how to keep them going. In contrast, the strategic plan involves adapting the firm to take advantage of opportunities in its constantly changing environment.

At the corporate level, the company starts the strategic planning process by defining its overall purpose and mission (see ● **Figure 2.1**). This mission is then turned into detailed supporting objectives that guide the entire company. Next, headquarters decides what portfolio of businesses and products is best for the company and how much support to give each one. In turn, each business and product develops detailed marketing and other departmental plans that support the company-wide plan. Thus, marketing planning occurs at the business-unit, product, and market levels. It supports company strategic planning with more detailed plans for specific marketing opportunities.

Defining a Market-Oriented Mission

An organization exists to accomplish something, and this purpose should be clearly stated. Forging a sound mission begins with the following questions: What *is* our business? Who is the customer? What do consumers value? What *should* our business be? These simple-sounding questions are among the most difficult the company will ever have to answer. Successful companies continuously raise these questions and answer them carefully and completely.

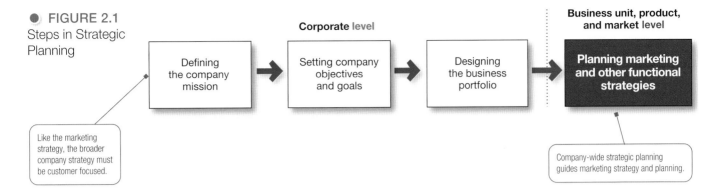

● FIGURE 2.1
Steps in Strategic
Planning

Like the marketing strategy, the broader company strategy must be customer focused.

Company-wide strategic planning guides marketing strategy and planning.

Mission statement

A statement of the organization's purpose—what it wants to accomplish in the larger environment.

Many organizations develop formal mission statements that answer these questions. A **mission statement** is a statement of the organization's purpose—what it wants to accomplish in the larger environment. A clear mission statement acts as an "invisible hand" that guides people in the organization.

Some companies define their missions myopically in product or technology terms ("We make and sell furniture" or "We are a chemical-processing firm"). But mission statements should be *market oriented* and defined in terms of satisfying basic customer needs. Products and technologies eventually become outdated but basic market needs may last forever. For example, social scrapbooking site Pinterest doesn't define itself as just an online place to post pictures. Its mission is to give people a social media platform for collecting, organizing, and sharing things they love. And Sephora's mission isn't to be a beauty products retailer. It's to sell lifestyle and self-expression by helping customers to unlock their beauty potential. ● **Table 2.1** provides several examples of product-oriented versus market-oriented business definitions.

Mission statements should be meaningful and specific yet motivating. Too often, mission statements are written for public relations purposes and lack specific, workable guidelines. Instead, they should emphasize the company's strengths and tell forcefully how it intends to win in the marketplace.

Finally, a company's mission should not be stated as making more sales or profits; profits are only a reward for creating value for customers. Instead, the mission should focus on customers and the customer experience the firm seeks to create. For example, Ritz-Carlton Hotels & Resorts doesn't see itself as just renting out rooms. It's on a mission to create "The Ritz-Carlton Experience," one that "enlivens the senses, instills well-being, and fulfills even the unexpressed wishes and needs of our guests." Ritz-Carlton follows up this mission with specific steps of service by which every employee can help to turn the mission into reality.[2] Similarly, Airbnb doesn't just help people find places to rent. It lets them "Belong Anywhere"—be insiders when they travel and immerse themselves in local cultures and experiences (see Real Marketing 2.1).

Setting Company Objectives and Goals

The company needs to turn its broad mission into detailed supporting objectives for each level of management. Each manager should have objectives and be responsible for reaching them. For example, most Americans know CVS as a chain of retail pharmacies selling prescription and over-the-counter medicines, personal care products, and a host of convenience and other items. But CVS Health has a much broader mission. ● It views itself as a "pharmacy innovation company," one that is "helping people on their path to better health." The company's motto: "Health is everything."[3]

CVS Health's broad mission leads to a hierarchy of objectives, including business objectives and marketing objectives. CVS Health's overall business objective is to increase access, lower costs, and improve the quality of care. It does this through the products it sells at its retail pharmacies and by taking a more active role in overall health-care management through research, consumer outreach and education, and support of health-related programs and organizations.

● **Table 2.1** | **Product- versus Market-Oriented Business Definitions**

Company	Product-Oriented Definition	Market-Oriented Definition
Starbucks	We sell coffee and snacks.	We sell "The Starbucks Experience," one that enriches people's lives one moment, one human being, one extraordinary cup of coffee at a time.
Panera	We sell fast-casual food in our restaurants.	We give customers "Food as it should be": food that tastes good; food that feels good; food that does good things for them and the world around them.
Instagram	We are a social networking app for posting photos and videos.	We help people capture and share the world's moments.
Home Depot	We sell tools and home repair and improvement items.	We empower consumers to achieve the homes of their dreams.
NPR	We are a public radio network.	We create a more informed public—one challenged and invigorated by a deeper understanding and appreciation of events, ideas, and cultures.
Sephora	We are a beauty products retailer.	We sell lifestyle and self-expression by helping customers to unlock their beauty potential.
Ritz-Carlton Hotels & Resorts	We rent rooms.	We create "The Ritz-Carlton experience"—a memorable stay that far exceeds guests' already-high expectations.
Walmart	We run discount stores.	We deliver low prices every day and give ordinary folks the chance to buy the same things as rich people. "Save Money. Live Better."

However, such activities are expensive and must be funded through improved profits, so improving profits becomes another major objective for CVS Health. Profits can be improved by increasing sales or by reducing costs. Sales can be increased by improving customer engagement and raising the company's share of the health-care market.

These goals then become the company's current marketing objectives.

Marketing strategies and programs must be developed to support these marketing objectives. To increase customer engagement, sales, and market share, CVS Health has reshaped and broadened its lines of products and services. For example, it stopped selling tobacco products, items not compatible with its "better health" mission. And it has placed CVS MinuteClinic locations in more than 1,100 of its 9,600 stores, providing walk-in medical care for more than 34 million patient visits since 2000. CVS Health has also broadened its range of customer contact activities to include tailored advising to customers managing chronic and specialty health conditions.

These are CVS Health's broad marketing strategies. Each marketing strategy must then be defined in greater detail. For example, the company's rapidly expanding MinuteClinic services will require more advertising and promotional efforts, and such efforts will need to be spelled out carefully. In this way, CVS Health's broad mission is translated into a set of specific short-term objectives and marketing plans.

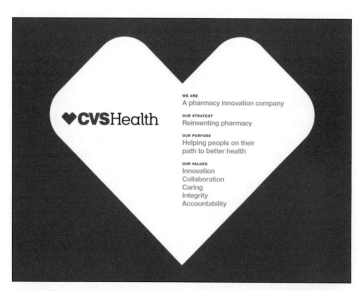

● **CVS Health's overall mission is to be a "pharmacy innovation company," one that is "helping people on their way to better health." Its marketing strategies and programs must support this mission.**

CVS Caremark Corporation

Real Marketing 2.1 | Airbnb's Mission: Belong Anywhere—Don't Stay There. Live There.

Airbnb has revolutionized the hospitality industry. In a little over 10 years, the tech startup that popularized staying at the homes of strangers has built a global network of more than 6 million listings and 400 million guests in 191 countries. That's stunning, especially when compared to the size of the world's largest hotel chain—92-year-old Marriott International—with its 1.25 million rooms across 6,500 properties in 127 countries. In fact, Airbnb boasts more rooms than the six largest global hotel groups combined. Airbnb has become so pervasive that many customers use the brand as a verb—as in "Let's go to Chicago for the weekend. We'll Airbnb a place downtown!"

It all started when Airbnb founders Brian Chesky and Joe Gebbia decided to make some extra income to help pay the rent on their modest San Francisco loft apartment by renting out three air mattresses on the apartment's floor at $40 a night each (hence the "air" in Airbnb). Chesky and Gebbia quickly realized that people who booked their air mattresses got a lot more than just a cheap place to stay. They got an authentic "live-like-the-locals" experience. The idea blossomed into Airbnb, an online lodgings marketplace that matches people who need a place to stay with property owners who have room to spare.

The basic Airbnb model is conceptually simple. It starts with hosts —Airbnb's official term for property owners with space to rent— who register and are vetted for legitimacy. Listings can include anything from a couch, single room, suite of rooms, or apartment to moored yachts, entire houses, or even a castle. Some hosts even rent space in their yards for guests to pitch a tent. Each location is as unique as its owner.

For guests, using Airbnb is like buying or booking almost anything else online. Registered users search by city, room type, price range, amenities, host language, and other options. Most listings provide photos and details that give potential guests a good idea of what their stay will be like. Guests can contact potential hosts with questions before booking. Bookings are made through Airbnb, so money changes hands only through a secure interface. When guests arrive at the property, the host either greets them or arranges for entry.

At first, Airbnb attracted mostly venturesome travelers looking for cheap and cool places to stay. Other potential customers shied away, unwilling to accept the risk or discomfort of staying with strangers. But the concept caught on, and Airbnb grew rapidly. More than the cookie-cutter rooms and impersonal travel experiences offered by conventional hotels, people warmed to Airbnb's authenticity and the unique experiences that Airbnb lodgings offered.

That realization marked a major turning point for Airbnb and its founders. Chesky and Gebbia came to realize that Airbnb provided much more than just spaces to rent. They began a search for the brand's soul, asking difficult but important questions: "We asked ourselves, 'What is our mission? What is the big idea that truly defines Airbnb?'" says Chesky.

To find answers, the Airbnb team interviewed hundreds of guests and hosts around the world. Time and again, they heard guests say that the last thing they wanted was to be tourists. Instead, Airbnb customers wanted to be insiders—to engage with people and immerse themselves in local cultures. According to the company, 86 percent of users picked Airbnb because they wanted to live more like a local. They wanted to belong.

That discovery led Airbnb a new company mission: to help create a world where you can belong anywhere and where people can live in a place instead of just traveling to it. The new mission inspired a new brand tagline—"Belong Anywhere"—and a new brand symbol, the bélo. Carefully conceived to contain the "A" in Airbnb, a heart, and a location pin, Airbnb casts the bélo as "the universal symbol of belonging."

Airbnb's "Belong Anywhere" mission is more than just a plaque on the wall at corporate headquarters or an inspirational statement on the About page of its website. Instead, the mission drives everything the company does, from its travel offerings to its marketing campaigns. Airbnb sees itself not just as a rooms provider but as a curator of unique and authentic "belonging" experiences.

The essence of the Airbnb experience is rooted in the company's hosts, which Airbnb sees as its first-line customers. The company has nurtured a huge global community of lodging providers who are true believers in the Airbnb vision. Airbnb encourages hosts to follow certain guidelines. However, although the guidelines may suggest specific services to guests, such as airport pickup or walking tours, Airbnb gives hosts complete autonomy to shape unique guest experiences. The overriding rule: create belonging.

Shortly after launching the new mission, Chesky addressed a crowd of hosts in Paris at Airbnb's annual host event, called the Airbnb Open. He gave this advice: "What's special in your world isn't just the home you have. It's your whole life." As part of his presentation, Chesky shared pictures relating the experiences of his own parents in Paris as they attended that year's Airbnb Open. On the first day, they did the usual touristy stuff,

Belong Anywhere: Airbnb's mission is to help create a world where you can belong anywhere and where people can live a place instead of just traveling to it. The brand's bélo logo is "the universal symbol of belonging."

M40S Photos/Alamy Stock Photo

hosted by typical tourist guides. "Every year, 30 million people go to Paris," noted Chesky. "They look at everything and they see nothing." Chesky then showed images from his parents' second day in Paris—guided by some of Airbnb's top hosts—where they experienced the city from the perspective of locals. They had coffee at an authentic sidewalk café, took a walk in a garden, and drank and danced at a cozy Parisian nightclub. "Maybe we should not travel *to* Paris," suggested Chesky. "Maybe what we should do is *live* in Paris."

Airbnb is quick to point out that "belonging" doesn't have to be about having tea and cookies with a host. Many hosts don't live in the lodgings they share, and many guests don't actually want to meet the host. More broadly, belonging means hanging out in someone else's space and having a local experience "hosted" by that person, even if the

host is not present. It means venturing into local spots guests might not otherwise see and doing things they might not otherwise do. Airbnb sees the optimal "belonging" experience as a transformational journey.

To broaden its offerings under the new mission, Airbnb introduced Experiences, a platform that lets customers book not just lodging but also one- or two-day excursions with locals, ranging from hiking with wolves in a nature conservatory to singing in a Harlem gospel choir to making a from-scratch pasta meal with two chefs in Florence. "These aren't tours," says Chesky, "You immerse yourself, you join the local communities."

Airbnb has also launched an expanded array of lodging experiences. For example, Airbnb Plus offers a selection of high-quality, well-equipped homes with hosts known for great reviews and attention to detail.

At the upper end, Plus offers premium luxury in extravagant homes with high-end options, such as booking a butler or personal chef.

Airbnb's mission is embodied by the company's "Don't go there. Live there!" ad campaign. Different ads feature people experiencing an artist loft in Tokyo, a quiet Los Angeles retreat, or a cozy Paris apartment. But the ads suggest that guests are getting much more than just a place to stay. The first ad opens with people doing ho-hum standard tours of Paris landmarks like the Eiffel Tower and the Arc de Triomphe, admonishing, "Don't go to Paris. Don't tour Paris, and please don't *do* Paris." Instead, as it cuts to warm scenes of people letting loose and hanging out like locals, the ad urges "*Live* in Paris. Even if it's just for a day." For Airbnb, that's mission accomplished. With Airbnb, you "Belong Anywhere."[4]

Author Comment | Once it sets its mission, a company faces difficult decisions about what businesses and products will make up the company, now and in the future.

Designing the Business Portfolio

OBJECTIVE 2-2 Discuss how to design business portfolios and develop growth strategies.

Guided by the company's mission statement and objectives, management now must plan its business portfolio—the collection of businesses and products that make up the company. The best **business portfolio** is the one that best fits the company's strengths and weaknesses to opportunities in the environment.

Business portfolio
The collection of businesses and products that make up the company.

Most large companies have complex portfolios of businesses and brands. ● For example, you probably know Mars Inc. as the world's number-one candy maker. The giant $35 billion company makes some of the world's best-loved confectionary brands, including M&M's, Snickers, Mars, Twix, Skittles, Starburst, Altoids, and Wrigley and Orbit gums. It also owns the Uncle Ben's rice brand.

But did you know that Mars is also a world-leading pet nutrition and health-care company? Its leading pet food brands include Iams, Royal Canin, Eukanuba, Whiskas, and Pedigree—the world's number-one dog food brand. It also owns several pet hospital, doggie daycare, and veterinary services companies, including Banfield, Blue Pearl, and VCA pet hospitals. Mars even has growing businesses in canine DNA testing and GPS pet tracking and monitoring. In all, Mars sells more pet care products and services than candy. Strategic and marketing planning for such a complex business portfolio can be a daunting but critical task. Through skillful portfolio management, however, Mars profitably manages its broad portfolio under its founding mission of "doing business for the betterment of all" and five guiding principles: "quality, responsibility, mutuality, efficiency, and freedom."[5]

Business portfolio planning involves two steps. First, the company must analyze its *current* business portfolio and determine which businesses should receive more, less, or no investment. Second, it must shape the *future* portfolio by developing strategies for growth and downsizing.

● **Complex business portfolios: You probably know Mars Inc. as the world's number-one candy maker. But did you know that it's also a world-leading pet nutrition and health-care company?**

Randy Duchaine/Alamy Stock Photo

Analyzing the Current Business Portfolio

Portfolio analysis

The process by which management evaluates the products and businesses that make up the company.

The major activity in strategic planning is business **portfolio analysis**, whereby management evaluates the products and businesses that make up the company. The company will want to put strong resources into its more profitable businesses and phase down or drop its weaker ones.

Management's first step is to identify the key businesses that make up the company, called *strategic business units* (SBUs). An SBU can be a company division, a product line within a division, or sometimes a single product or brand. The company next assesses the attractiveness of its various SBUs and decides how much support each deserves. When designing a business portfolio, it's a good idea to add and support products and businesses that fit closely with the firm's core philosophy and competencies.

The purpose of strategic planning is to find ways in which the company can best use its strengths to take advantage of attractive opportunities in the environment. For this reason, most standard portfolio analysis methods evaluate SBUs on two important dimensions: the attractiveness of the SBU's market or industry and the strength of the SBU's position in that market or industry. The best-known portfolio-planning method was developed by the Boston Consulting Group, a leading management consulting firm.[6]

The Boston Consulting Group Approach

Growth-share matrix

A portfolio-planning method that evaluates a company's SBUs in terms of market growth rate and relative market share.

Using the now-classic Boston Consulting Group (BCG) approach, a company classifies all its SBUs according to the **growth-share matrix**, as shown in ● **Figure 2.2**. On the vertical axis, *market growth rate* provides a measure of market attractiveness. On the horizontal axis, *relative market share* serves as a measure of company strength in the market. The growth-share matrix defines four types of SBUs:

1. **Stars.** Stars are high-growth, high-share businesses or products. They often need heavy investments to finance their rapid growth. Eventually their growth will slow down, and they will turn into cash cows.
2. **Cash cows.** Cash cows are low-growth, high-share businesses or products. These established and successful SBUs need less investment to hold their market share. Thus, they produce a lot of the cash that the company uses to pay its bills and support other SBUs that need investment.
3. **Question marks.** Question marks are low-share business units in high-growth markets. They require a lot of cash to hold their share, let alone increase it. Management has to think hard about which question marks it should try to build into stars and which should be phased out.
4. **Dogs.** Dogs are low-growth, low-share businesses and products. They may generate enough cash to maintain themselves but do not promise to be large sources of cash.

● FIGURE 2.2
The BCG Growth-Share Matrix

Under the classic BCG portfolio planning approach, the company invests funds from mature, successful products and businesses (cash cows) to support promising products and businesses in faster-growing markets (stars and question marks), hoping to turn them into future cash cows.

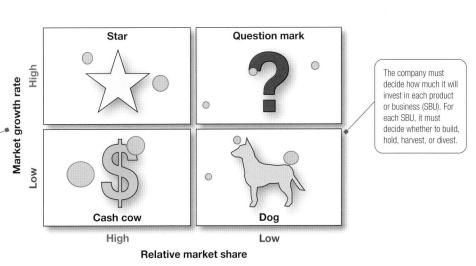

The company must decide how much it will invest in each product or business (SBU). For each SBU, it must decide whether to build, hold, harvest, or divest.

The 10 circles in the growth-share matrix represent the company's 10 current SBUs. The company has two stars, two cash cows, three question marks, and three dogs. The area of each circle is proportional to the SBU's dollar sales. This company is in fair shape, although not in good shape. It wants to invest in the more promising question marks to make them stars and maintain the stars so that they will become cash cows as their markets mature. Fortunately, it has two good-sized cash cows. Income from these cash cows will help finance the company's question marks, stars, and dogs. The company should take some decisive action concerning its dogs and its question marks.

Once it has classified its SBUs, the company must determine what role each will play in the future. It can pursue one of four strategies for each SBU. It can invest more in the business unit to *build* its share. Or it can invest just enough to *hold* the SBU's share at the current level. It can *harvest* the SBU, milking its short-term cash flow regardless of the long-term effect. Finally, it can *divest* the SBU by selling it or phasing it out and using the resources elsewhere.

As time passes, SBUs change their positions in the growth-share matrix. Many SBUs start out as question marks and move into the star category if they succeed. They later become cash cows as market growth falls and then finally die off or turn into dogs toward the end of the life cycle. The company needs to add new products and units continuously so that some of them will become stars and, eventually, cash cows that will help finance other SBUs.

Problems with Matrix Approaches

The BCG and other formal methods revolutionized strategic planning. However, such centralized approaches have limitations: They can be difficult, time-consuming, and costly to implement. Management may find it difficult to define SBUs and measure market share and growth. In addition, these approaches focus on classifying current businesses but provide little advice for future planning.

Because of such problems, many companies have dropped formal matrix methods in favor of more customized approaches that better suit their specific situations. Moreover, unlike former strategic planning efforts that rested mostly in the hands of senior managers at company headquarters, today's strategic planning has been decentralized. Increasingly, companies are placing responsibility for strategic planning in the hands of cross-functional teams of divisional managers who are close to their markets. In this digital age, such managers have rich and current data at their fingertips and can adapt their plans quickly to meet changing conditions and events in their markets.

Portfolio planning can be challenging. For example, when you think about ESPN, you probably think of it as a cable TV network or maybe a website or mobile app. ● But over the years, ESPN has grown to become a huge and complex brand portfolio consisting of more than 50 different entities.[7]

From its original groundbreaking cable network, the ESPN brand has sprouted numerous additional networks, from ESPN2, ESPNU, and ESPN Classic to ESPNEWS, ESPN Deportes (Spanish language), and several collegiate conference networks. The brand has added ESPN Digital Media, composed of 19 U.S. websites—including the flagship ESPN.com, ESPN3 (a multi-screen live 24/7 online sports network), and WatchESPN (an online and mobile destination for major ESPN channels). The ESPN App, with 13 editions in three languages globally, delivers scores, news, highlights, short form video, podcasts, and live audio, plus video streams of ESPN's linear channels.

As if all this weren't enough, ESPN publishes *ESPN The Magazine,* and ESPN Radio is the world's largest sports radio network. The brand also manages events, including the X Games, the ESPYs, college

● **Business portfolio management: Through skillful portfolio management, ESPN has built a cohesive brand, unified powerfully under its mission to serve sports enthusiasts "wherever sports are watched, listened to, discussed, debated, read about, or played."**

dennizn/Shutterstock

bowls, and NCAA basketball games. And it develops ESPN-branded consumer products and services, including video games, apparel, sporting goods, and even golf schools. In turn, ESPN is just one unit in the even more complex portfolio of its parent company, The Walt Disney Company. Through skillful portfolio management, however, ESPN has built a cohesive brand, unified powerfully under its mission to serve sports enthusiasts "wherever sports are watched, listened to, discussed, debated, read about, or played." More than just a haphazard collection of entities, ESPN is an immersive brand experience, inexorably linked with customers' sports memories, realities, and anticipations.

Developing Strategies for Growth and Downsizing

Beyond evaluating current businesses, designing the business portfolio involves finding businesses and products the company should consider in the future. Companies need growth if they are to compete more effectively, satisfy their stakeholders, and attract top talent. At the same time, a firm must be careful not to make growth itself an objective. The company's objective must be to manage "profitable growth."

Marketing has the main responsibility for achieving profitable growth for the company. Marketing needs to identify, evaluate, and select market opportunities and lay down strategies for capturing them. One useful device for identifying growth opportunities is the **product/market expansion grid**, shown in ● Figure 2.3.[8] We apply it here to Starbucks.

In only three decades, Starbucks has grown at an astounding pace from a small Seattle coffee shop to an over $24 billion powerhouse with more than 29,000 retail stores in more than 75 countries. Growth is the engine that keeps Starbucks perking. To maintain its incredible growth in an increasingly overcaffeinated marketplace, Starbucks has brewed up an ambitious, multipronged growth strategy.[9]

First, Starbucks' management might consider whether the company can achieve deeper **market penetration**—making more sales to current customers without changing its original products. It might add new stores in current market areas to make it easier for customers to visit. In fact, Starbucks opened more than 800 new U.S. stores last year. Starbucks can add new features to its mobile app to enhance customer engagement and loyalty. For example, the recently added My Starbucks Barista feature lets customers order via voice commands or messaging to an artificial intelligence-powered virtual barista. And improvements in Starbucks's advertising, prices, service, store design, or menu selection might encourage customers to stop by more often, stay longer, or buy more during each visit. Thanks to an ever-expanding food menu, sales of breakfast items alone have doubled in the past four years, and food sales currently account for 20 percent of Starbucks' total revenue.

Second, Starbucks might consider possibilities for **market development**— identifying and developing new markets for its current products. For instance, managers could review new demographic markets. Perhaps new groups—such as seniors—could be encouraged to visit Starbucks shops for the first time or to buy more from them. Managers could also review new geographic markets. Starbucks is now expanding swiftly in non-U.S. markets, especially Asia. ● For example, the number of Starbucks stores in China has grown from 800 to 3,300 in the past six years, with an average of one new store opening every 15 hours. Starbucks plans to open more than 6,000 stores in China by 2022.

Third, Starbucks could consider **product development**—offering modified or new products to current markets. For example, to capture a piece of the fast-growing

---

Product/market expansion grid
A portfolio-planning tool for identifying company growth opportunities through market penetration, market development, product development, or diversification.

Market penetration
Company growth by increasing sales of current products to current market segments without changing the product.

Market development
Company growth by identifying and developing new market segments for current company products.

Product development
Company growth by offering modified or new products to current market segments.

● **FIGURE 2.3**
The Product/Market Expansion Grid

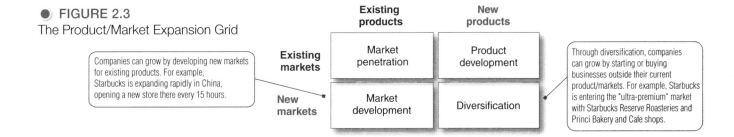

Companies can grow by developing new markets for existing products. For example, Starbucks is expanding rapidly in China, opening a new store there every 15 hours.

	Existing products	New products
Existing markets	Market penetration	Product development
New markets	Market development	Diversification

Through diversification, companies can grow by starting or buying businesses outside their current product/markets. For example, Starbucks is entering the "ultra-premium" market with Starbucks Reserve Roasteries and Princi Bakery and Cafe shops.

● **Strategies for growth: To maintain its incredible growth, Starbucks has brewed up an ambitious, multipronged growth strategy.**

Jens Kalaene/picture-alliance/dpa/AP Images

Diversification
Company growth through starting up or acquiring businesses outside the company's current products and markets.

single-serve beverage market, Starbucks developed Via instant coffee, and it sells its coffees and Tazo teas in K-Cup packs that fit Keurig at-home brewers. And Starbucks continues to expand it lines of ready-to-drink beverages sold in grocery stores, such as Starbucks Doubleshot, Iced Expresso Classics, and Starbucks Refreshers caffeinated pick-me-up drinks.

Finally, Starbucks might consider **diversification**—starting up or buying businesses beyond its current products and markets. For example, the company recently created the ultra-premium Starbucks Reserve brand, with Starbucks Reserve Roasteries and Starbucks Reserve Bars featuring high-end immersive experiences. And within its Starbucks Reserve locations, the company is opening Princi Bakery and Café shops, offering artisan Italian food—from fresh-baked bread and pastries to flaky cornetti to focaccia sandwiches—based on the recipes of famed Italian baker Rocco Princi. Starbucks is also experimenting with standalone boutique Princi bakery stores, taking the company beyond coffee and snack shops. Such diversification into premium food and beverages fits well with the brand's "Starbucks Experience" positioning.

Companies must develop not only strategies for growing their business portfolios but also strategies for *downsizing* them. There are many reasons that a firm might want to abandon products or markets. A firm may have grown too fast or entered areas where it lacks experience. The market environment might change, making some products or markets less profitable. For example, in difficult economic times, many firms prune out weaker, less-profitable products and markets to focus their more limited resources on the strongest ones. Finally, some products or business units simply age and die.

When a firm finds brands or businesses that are unprofitable or that no longer fit its overall strategy, it must carefully prune, harvest, or divest them. For example, in past years, P&G has sold off dozens of major brands—from Crisco, Folgers, Jif, and Pringles to Duracell batteries, Right Guard deodorant, Aleve pain reliever, CoverGirl and Max Factor cosmetics, Wella and Clairol hair care products, and its Iams and other pet food brands—allowing the company to focus on household care and beauty and grooming products.

Author | Comment | Marketing can't go it alone in creating customer value. Under the company-wide strategic plan, marketing must work closely with other departments to form an effective internal company value chain and with other companies in the marketing system to create an external value delivery network that jointly serves customers.

Planning Marketing: Partnering to Build Customer Relationships

OBJECTIVE 2-3 Explain marketing's role in strategic planning and how marketing works with its partners to create and deliver customer value.

The company's strategic plan establishes what kinds of businesses the company will operate and its objectives for each. Then, within each business unit, more detailed planning takes place. The major functional departments in each unit—marketing, finance, accounting, purchasing, operations, information systems, human resources, and others—must work together to accomplish strategic objectives.

Marketing plays a key role in the company's strategic planning in several ways. First, marketing provides a guiding *philosophy*—the marketing concept—that suggests the company strategy should revolve around creating customer value and building profitable relationships with important consumer groups. Second, marketing provides *inputs* to strategic planners by helping to identify attractive market opportunities and assessing the firm's potential to take advantage of them. Finally, within individual business units, marketing designs *strategies* for reaching the unit's objectives. Once the unit's objectives are set, marketing's task is to help carry them out profitably.

Customer engagement and value are the key ingredients in the marketer's formula for success. However, as noted in Chapter 1, although marketing plays a leading role, it cannot act alone. It can be only a partner in attracting, engaging, and growing customers. In addition to *customer relationship management*, marketers must also practice *partner relationship management*. They must work closely with partners in other company departments to form an effective internal *value chain* that serves customers. Moreover, they must partner effectively with other companies in the marketing system to form a competitively superior external *value delivery network*. We now take a closer look at the concepts of a company value chain and a value delivery network.

Partnering with Other Company Departments

Value chain

The series of internal departments that carry out value-creating activities to design, produce, market, deliver, and support a firm's products.

Each company department can be thought of as a link in the company's internal **value chain**.[10] That is, each department carries out value-creating activities to design, produce, market, deliver, and support the firm's products. The firm's success depends not only on how well each department performs its work but also on how well the various departments coordinate their activities.

For example, Walmart's goal is to create customer value and satisfaction by providing shoppers with the products they want at the lowest possible prices. Marketers at Walmart play an important role. They learn what customers need and stock the stores' shelves, website, and mobile app with the desired products at unbeatable low prices. They prepare advertising and merchandising programs and assist shoppers with customer service. Through these and other activities, Walmart's marketers help to engage and deliver value to customers.

● **The value chain: Walmart's ability to help you "Save Money. Live Better." by offering the right products at lower prices depends on the contributions of people in all of the company's departments.**

Ann Parry/Alamy Stock Photo

However, the marketing department needs help from the company's other departments. ● Walmart's ability to help you "Save Money. Live Better." depends on the purchasing department's skill in developing the needed suppliers and buying from them at low cost. Walmart's information technology department must provide fast and accurate information about which products are selling in each store. The megaretailer's digital research and development group must apply the latest technologies to its web and mobile sites. And its operations people must provide effective, low-cost merchandise handling and develop effective delivery options.

A company's value chain is only as strong as its weakest link. Success depends on how well each group performs its work of adding customer value and on how the company coordinates the activities of various functions. At Walmart, if purchasing can't obtain the lowest prices from suppliers or if operations can't distribute merchandise at the lowest costs, then marketing can't deliver on its promise of unbeatable low prices.

Ideally, then, a company's different functions should work in harmony to produce value for consumers. But, in practice, interdepartmental relations are full of conflicts and misunderstandings. The marketing department takes the consumer's point of view. But when marketing tries to improve customer value and satisfaction, it can cause other departments to do a poorer job *in their terms*. Marketing department actions can increase purchasing costs, disrupt production schedules, increase inventories, and create budget headaches. Thus, other departments may resist the marketing department's efforts.

Yet marketers must find ways to get all departments to "think consumer" and develop a smoothly functioning value chain. Engaging customers today requires a whole-company commitment. Thus, whether you're an accountant, an operations manager, a financial analyst, an IT specialist, or a human resources manager, you need to understand marketing and your role in creating customer value. "From finance to customer service to manufacturing, every employee should see how their role plays a part in the customer experience," says one marketer. "Customer experience doesn't depend solely on the … marketing team, but [marketing] sets the tone and leads the way for all other departments."[11]

Partnering with Others in the Marketing System

In its quest to engage customers and create customer value, the firm needs to look beyond its own internal value chain and into the value chains of its suppliers, its distributors, and, ultimately, its customers. Consider fast-food chain Subway. People do not eat at Subway only because they love the chain's sandwiches. Consumers flock to the Subway *system*. Throughout the nation, Subway's finely tuned value delivery system consistently delivers fresh, fast, and tasty made-to-order sandwiches at affordable prices. Subway is effective only to the extent that it successfully partners with its franchisees, suppliers, and others to jointly carry out its "Make It What You Want" positioning promise.

More companies today are partnering with other members of the supply chain—suppliers, distributors, and, ultimately, customers—to improve the performance of the customer **value delivery network**. Competition no longer takes place only between individual competitors. Rather, it takes place between the entire value delivery network created by these competitors. Thus, Ford's performance against Toyota depends on the quality of Ford's overall value delivery network versus Toyota's. Even if Ford makes the best cars, it might lose in the marketplace if Toyota's dealer network provides a more customer-satisfying sales and service experience.

Value delivery network
A network composed of the company, suppliers, distributors, and, ultimately, customers who partner with each other to improve the performance of the entire system in delivering customer value.

Marketing Strategy and the Marketing Mix

OBJECTIVE 2-4 Describe the elements of a customer value–driven marketing strategy and mix and the forces that influence them.

The strategic plan defines the company's overall mission and objectives. Marketing's role is shown in ● **Figure 2.4**, which summarizes the major activities involved in managing a customer-driven marketing strategy and the marketing mix.

Consumers are at the center. The goal is to create value for customers and build profitable customer relationships. Next comes **marketing strategy**—the marketing logic by which the company hopes to create this customer value and achieve these profitable relationships. The company decides which customers it will serve (segmentation and targeting) and how (differentiation and positioning). It identifies the total market and then divides it into smaller segments, selects the most promising segments, and focuses on serving and satisfying the customers in these segments.

> Author Comment | Now that we've set the context in terms of company-wide strategy, it's time to discuss customer value–driven marketing strategies and programs.

Marketing strategy
The marketing logic by which the company hopes to create customer value and achieve profitable customer relationships.

● **FIGURE 2.4**
Managing Marketing Strategies and the Marketing Mix

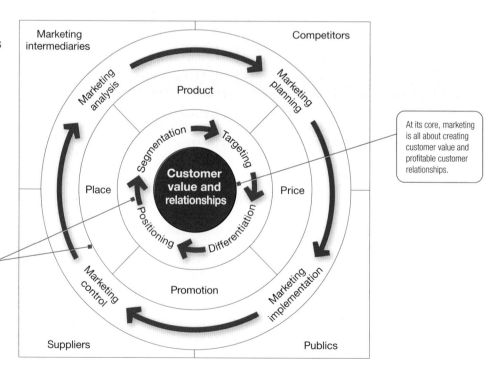

Marketing strategy involves two key questions: Which customers will we serve (segmentation and targeting)? and How will we create value for them (differentiation and positioning)? Then the company designs a marketing program—the four Ps—that delivers the intended value to targeted consumers.

At its core, marketing is all about creating customer value and profitable customer relationships.

Guided by marketing strategy, the company designs an integrated *marketing mix* made up of factors under its control—product, price, place, and promotion (the four Ps). To find the best marketing strategy and mix, the company engages in marketing analysis, planning, implementation, and control. Through these activities, the company watches and adapts to the actors and forces in the marketing environment. We will now look briefly at each activity. In later chapters, we will discuss each one in more depth.

Customer Value–Driven Marketing Strategy

To succeed in today's competitive marketplace, companies must be customer centered. They must win customers from competitors and then engage and grow them by delivering greater value. But before it can satisfy customers, a company must first understand customer needs and wants. Thus, sound marketing requires careful customer analysis.

Companies know that they cannot profitably serve all consumers in a given market—at least not all consumers in the same way. There are too many different kinds of consumers with too many different kinds of needs. Most companies are in a position to serve some segments better than others. Thus, each company must divide up the total market, choose the best segments, and design strategies for profitably serving chosen segments. This process involves *market segmentation, market targeting, differentiation*, and *positioning*.

Market Segmentation

Market segmentation

Dividing a market into distinct groups of buyers who have different needs, characteristics, or behaviors and who might require separate marketing strategies or mixes.

The market consists of many types of consumers, products, and needs. The marketer must determine which segments offer the best opportunities. Consumers can be grouped and served in various ways based on geographic, demographic, psychographic, and behavioral factors. The process of dividing a market into distinct groups of buyers who have different needs, characteristics, or behaviors and who might require separate marketing strategies or mixes is called **market segmentation**.

Every market has segments, but not all ways of segmenting a market are equally useful. For example, Tylenol would gain little by distinguishing between low-income and high-income pain-relief users if both respond the same way to marketing efforts. A **market segment** consists of consumers who respond in a similar way to a given set of marketing efforts. In the car market, for example, consumers who want the biggest, most comfortable car regardless of price make up one market segment. Consumers who care mainly about price and operating economy make up another segment. It would be difficult to make one car model that was the first choice of consumers in both segments. Companies are wise to focus their efforts on meeting the distinct needs of individual market segments.

Market segment

A group of consumers who respond in a similar way to a given set of marketing efforts.

Market Targeting

Market targeting

Evaluating each market segment's attractiveness and selecting one or more segments to serve.

After a company has defined its market segments, it can enter one or many of these segments. **Market targeting** involves evaluating each market segment's attractiveness and selecting one or more segments to enter. A company should target segments in which it can profitably generate the greatest customer value and sustain it over time.

A company with limited resources might decide to serve only one or a few special segments or market niches. Such nichers specialize in serving customer segments that major competitors overlook or ignore. For example, McLaren sold only 3,340 of its very-high-performance cars last year but at very high prices—such as its 570S model at $188,000 or a made-to-order FI model starting at an eye-popping $837,000. Most nichers aren't quite so exotic. Profitable low-cost airline Allegiant Air avoids direct competition with larger major airline rivals by targeting smaller, neglected markets and new fliers. Nicher Allegiant "goes where they ain't."

Alternatively, a large company (for example, car companies such as Honda and Ford) might decide to offer a complete range of products to serve all market segments. Or a company might choose to serve several related segments—perhaps those with different kinds of customers but with the same basic wants. The L'Oréal group serves major segments of the beauty market, and within each segment it caters to many sub-segments. L'Oréal targets the larger segments through its major divisions: L'Oréal Luxe, Consumer Products, Professional Products, Active Cosmetics, and the Body Shop. Within these major divisions, L'Oréal markets various brands that cater to customers of different ages, incomes, and lifestyles. For example, its Consumer Product division sells brands like Garnier, L'Oréal Paris,

Maybelline New York, Essie, and NYX Professional Make Up. Similarly, the L'Oréal Luxe division offers more than 15 brands, including Lancôme, Giorgio Armani, Urban Decay, Diesel, and Ralph Lauren.

Most companies enter a new market by serving a single segment; if this proves successful, they add more segments. For example, Southwest Airlines entered the crowded airline market almost 50 years ago as an upstart, no-frills commuter airline serving selected second-tier airports in Texas and other Southwestern states. Based on its early success in niche markets, Southwest has grown to become the nation's second-largest airline, serving 100 major destinations in the United States and 10 additional countries. The successful $22 billion airline has pulled in 46 straight years of profits.[12] Plant-based milk marketers have started targeting the small segment within the dairy milk market of people who have allergies, intolerances, or special nutritional requirements. The segment has grown bigger and bigger, attracting more customers with specific health, fitness, and lifestyle choices (see Real Marketing 2.2).

Market Differentiation and Positioning

Positioning

Arranging for a product to occupy a clear, distinctive, and desirable place relative to competing products in the minds of target consumers.

As the company decides which market segments to enter, it must also determine how to differentiate its market offering for each targeted segment and what positions it wants to occupy in those segments. **Positioning** is arranging for a product to occupy a clear, distinctive, and desirable place relative to competing products in the minds of target consumers. Marketers plan positions that distinguish their products from competing brands and give them the greatest advantage in their target markets.

For example, Volkswagen gives you "Think small," L'Oréal says "Because I'm worth it," British Airways claims to be "The world's favorite airline," Huawei tells you to "Make it Possible," and Siemens positions itself as "Ingenuity for life." Moreover, BMW promises "Sheer driving pleasure" and adidas tells people that "Nothing is impossible."

Such deceptively simple statements form the backbone of a product's marketing strategy. ● For example, adidas' slogan "Nothing is impossible" inspires people to push boundaries, set new goals, and achieve greatness. The company tries to position itself as the most inspirational sports apparel and athletic footwear brand. Using the stories that unfold in the campaign, adidas reminds athletes and non-athletes from every walk of life that they can make their own "impossible" come true. It emphasizes further on the act of attempting the seemingly impossible even if the effort does not result in riches or fame.[13]

In positioning its brand, a company first identifies possible customer value differences that provide competitive advantages on which to build the position. A company can offer greater customer value by either charging lower prices than competitors or offering more benefits to justify higher prices. But if the company *promises* greater value, it must then *deliver* that greater value.

● **Positioning: Adidas positions itself with "Nothing is impossible." This simple statement provides the backbone for its marketing strategy.**

PCN Photography/Alamy Stock Photo

Differentiation

Actually differentiating the market offering to create superior customer value.

Thus, effective positioning begins with **differentiation**—actually *differentiating* the company's market offering to create superior customer value. Once the company has chosen a desired position, it must take strong steps to deliver and communicate that position to target consumers. The company's entire marketing program should support the chosen positioning strategy.

Developing an Integrated Marketing Mix

Marketing mix

The set of tactical marketing tools—product, price, place, and promotion—that the firm blends to produce the response it wants in the target market.

After determining its overall marketing strategy, the company is ready to begin planning the details of the **marketing mix**, one of the major concepts in modern marketing. The marketing mix is the set of tactical marketing tools that the firm blends to produce the response it wants in the target market. The marketing mix consists of everything the firm can do to engage consumers and deliver customer value. The many possibilities can be

Real Marketing 2.2 | How Milk Is Becoming Dairy-Free

The dairy-free market has come into its own, and the consumers around the world are spoilt for choice of milk alternatives in the market. The non-dairy segment started off as an offshoot of the milk industry, but it has since become a huge industry itself with various segments of its own. For example, a quick search on the Waitrose website will give you over 30 different variants of milk alternatives. Driving the growth of the non-dairy milk industry are rising health concerns among consumers related to the use of dairy milk, the spread of vegan lifestyles, and new health and fitness trends. The needs and wants of the traditional milk consuming market have evolved, and the typical consumer now seeks different values from the milk they purchase. The milk market has seen new segments emerge that offer different value propositions to the differentiated needs of consumer with different preferences.

The global consumption of animal milk has been on the decline, a contrast to the sales of plant-based milk alternatives. There are several reasons for this: Lactose intolerance, the inability to digest a sugar in dairy products, is one of the better-known health conditions that force people to look for alternatives, but many also suffer from milk allergies that can cause rashes, diarrhea, vomiting, etc. Consumers are now also more aware of the environmental impact of animal husbandry, prompting many to adopt vegan diets, and of potential health risks associated with potential contaminants, including antibiotics, pesticides, and hormones.

Plant-based non-dairy drinks come from various sources and are marketed accordingly. These include almond milk, cashew milk, coconut milk, hemp milk, oat milk, pea protein milk, rice milk, quinoa milk, and soy milk. There are variants within each of these milk types too, such as sweetened, unsweetened, low-calorie, vanilla, chocolate, and banana flavored. The most popular plant-based milks are soy, almond, rice, and coconut. Soy milk has been the most popular daily milk substitute for over four decades, though many consumers do not care for the taste. Almond milk is believed to help in weight management and is a popular complement for smoothies or mixed with cereals and cookies. Coconut milk is particularly popular in Asia and South America but offers less protein and lower calories. All types of plant-based milks offer the advantage of longer shelf life compared to common dairy milk.

In 2018, the global market for plant-based milk was estimated at $16.3 billion, up from $7.4 billion in 2010, and it is forecasted that by 2024

the global plant milk market size will be valued at 10 billion liters, growing at a rate of about 10 percent annually between 2018 and 2023. North America has been leading the global sales of the plant-based milk, with 25 percent of the global market share. Europe's non-dairy milk market is forecasted to have a compound annual growth rate (CAGR) of 14.5 percent between 2018 and 2023. Asia-Pacific—including China, Japan, India, and South Korea—is also anticipated to record a high CAGR of 13 percent between 2017 and 2024.

The growth of the alternative milk segment has prompted many established players in the food and drinks industry to introduce brand extensions in the category. For instance, the Quaker Oats Company has announced that it will launch its own oats milk brand. For the dairy milk industry, however, the rapid growth, popularity, and easy availability of plant-based milk poses a major threat. Faced with a continuous decline in the consumption of cow's milk in many markets around the world, dairy milk producers have developed campaigns to position cow's milk as a complete natural food for healthy bones and teeth that cannot be substituted with plant-based alternatives. They have also argued that the plant-based alternatives cannot be labeled and marketed as milk. For example, in the European Union, a landmark ruling by the European Court of Justice stated that any vegan, dairy-alternative brand cannot be sold if it has used the words "milk," "butter," or "cheese"; however,

there are exemptions to this rule, such as almond milk, coconut milk, and peanut butter. For their part, plant-based milk producers contend that they have not fooled customers, for most of these products are positioned based on their sources or ingredients, and they offer different values and benefits to customers based on their preferences.

An interesting example of the ongoing dispute between dairy and non-dairy producers comes from Sweden, where non-dairy milk brand Oatly was taken to court by the country's dairy lobby. The latter argued that Oatly's campaign disparaged cow's milk as unhealthy through taglines in its ads such as "Like milk, but made for humans" and "Oh wow, no cow" and "No milk, no soy." The combined sales of the group that the lobby represented were 200 times greater than Oatly's sales, but the lawsuit actually increased the sales of the brand significantly.

Many companies have based their vision and mission on offering customers plant-based products, like Alpro, a Belgium-based company that started out by selling soy milk in 1980 and has since developed various other organic and non-organic plant-based products. Alpro aims to be the leading contributor in expanding plant-based food and drinks options. The company says that its vision is to see a world where more people's food items come directly from plants, and the company wants to change what people eat by offering tasty, natural, and healthy plant-based nutritious food.

The non-dairy segment started off as an offshoot of the milk industry but has now become a huge industry containing various segments within itself.

TY Lim/Shutterstock

For plant-based milk producers, Gen Z and Millennial families look to be the most profitable demographic segment as they generally have higher awareness of and concern for animal welfare as well as the nutritional contents and health benefits and risks of milk. They are also more willing to spend more on such products.

Both the dairy industry and the non-dairy industry are sure to witness more shifts as consumer preferences evolve. Product development will be a key factor in determining success. The non-dairy market can continue to look for alternative sources, new flavors, textures, formulations, and adaptations. The non-dairy industry will have to demonstrate that these products provide long-term health and sustainability benefits; at the same time, it must encourage more changes in product development and consumer behavior. Other areas of growth for non-dairy alternatives is their use in products like yogurt, frozen desserts and ice cream, creamers, and cheese.

Meanwhile, the old values of price, taste, and convenience that worked for the traditional dairy milk industry are being replaced by new values like wellness, health, safely, and social impact. The dairy industry needs to be more innovative and do more to connect better with consumers. For example, Arla, one of the biggest UK milk producers, is planning to launch a carbonated, fizzy milk product in the United Kingdom, Singapore, and the United Arab Emirates. Some predict that such products could successfully leverage the sparkling-water and flavored-milk trends among Millennials and the more experimental beverage users. Flavored milks generally have a longer shelf life too, so this could help in competing with plant-based milks on that basis.[14]

---

collected into four groups of variables—the four Ps. ● **Figure 2.5** shows the marketing tools under each P.

- *Product* means the goods-and-services combination the company offers to the target market. Thus, a Ford Escape consists of nuts and bolts, spark plugs, pistons, headlights, and thousands of other parts. Ford offers several Escape models and dozens of optional features. The car comes fully serviced and with a comprehensive warranty that is as much a part of the product as the tailpipe.
- *Price* is the amount of money customers must pay to obtain the product. For example, Ford calculates suggested retail prices that its dealers might charge for each Escape. But Ford dealers rarely charge the full sticker price. Instead, they negotiate the price with each customer, offering discounts, trade-in allowances, and credit terms. These actions adjust prices for the current competitive and economic situations and bring them into line with the buyer's perception of the car's value.
- *Place* includes company activities that make the product available to target consumers. Ford partners with a large body of independently owned dealerships that sell the company's many different models. Ford selects its dealers carefully and strongly supports them. The dealers keep an inventory of Ford automobiles, demonstrate them to potential buyers, negotiate prices, close sales, and service the cars after the sale.
- *Promotion* refers to activities that communicate the merits of the product and persuade target customers to buy it. Ford spent nearly $2.5 billion last year on U.S. advertising to tell consumers about the company and its many products.[15] Dealership salespeople assist potential buyers and persuade them that Ford is the best car for them. Ford and its dealers offer special promotions—sales, cash rebates, and low financing rates—as added purchase incentives. And Ford's websites and Facebook, Twitter, YouTube, Instagram, and other social media platforms engage consumers with the brand and each other.

An effective marketing program blends the marketing mix elements into an integrated marketing program designed to achieve the company's marketing objectives by engaging consumers and delivering value to them. The marketing mix constitutes the company's tactical tool kit for establishing strong positioning in target markets.

Some critics think that the four Ps may omit or underemphasize certain important activities. For example, they ask, "Where are services? Just because they don't start with a P doesn't justify omitting them." The answer is that services, such as banking, airline, and retailing services, are products too. We might call them *service products*. "Where is packaging?" the critics might ask. Marketers would answer that they include packaging as one of many product decisions. All said, as Figure 2.5 suggests, many marketing activities that might appear to be left out of the marketing mix are included under one of the four Ps. The issue is not whether there should be four, six, or ten Ps so much as what framework is most helpful in designing integrated marketing programs.

There is another concern, however, that is valid. It holds that the four Ps concept takes the seller's view of the market, not the buyer's view. From the buyer's viewpoint, in this age of customer value and relationships, the four Ps might be better described as the four As:[16]

Four Ps	Four As
Product	Acceptability
Price	Affordability
Place	Accessibility
Promotion	Awareness

Under this more customer-centered framework, *acceptability* is the extent to which the product exceeds customer expectations; *affordability* the extent to which customers are willing and able to pay the product's price; *accessibility* the extent to which customers can readily acquire the product; and *awareness* the extent to which customers are informed about the product's features, persuaded to try it, and reminded to repurchase. The four As relate closely to the traditional four Ps. Product design influences acceptability, price affects affordability, place affects accessibility, and promotion influences awareness. Marketers would do well to think through the four As first and then build the four Ps on that platform.

Managing the Marketing Effort and Marketing Return on Investment

OBJECTIVE 2-5 List the marketing management functions, including the elements of a marketing plan, and discuss the importance of measuring and managing marketing return on investment.

Managing the Marketing Effort

In addition to being good at the *marketing* in marketing management, companies also need to pay attention to the *management*. Managing the marketing process requires the five marketing management functions shown in ● **Figure 2.6**—*analysis, planning, implementation, organization,* and *control.* The company first develops company-wide strategic plans and then translates them into marketing and other plans for each division, product, and brand. Through implementation and organization, the company turns the plans into actions. Control consists of measuring and evaluating the results of marketing activities and taking

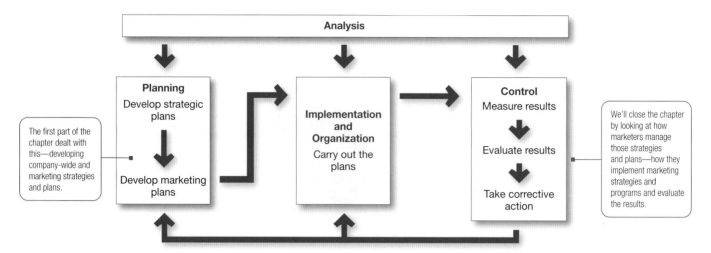

● FIGURE 2.6
Managing Marketing: Analysis, Planning, Implementation, and Control

corrective action where needed. Finally, marketing analysis provides the information and evaluations needed for all the other marketing activities.

Marketing Analysis

SWOT analysis
An overall evaluation of the company's strengths (S), weaknesses (W), opportunities (O), and threats (T).

Managing the marketing function begins with a complete analysis of the company's situation. The marketer should conduct a **SWOT analysis** (pronounced "swat analysis"), by which it evaluates the company's overall strengths (S), weaknesses (W), opportunities (O), and threats (T) (see **● Figure 2.7**). Strengths include internal capabilities, resources, and positive situational factors that may help the company serve its customers and achieve its objectives. Weaknesses include internal limitations and negative situational factors that may interfere with the company's performance. Opportunities are favorable factors or trends in the external environment that the company may be able to exploit to its advantage. And threats are unfavorable external factors or trends that may present challenges to performance.

The company should analyze its markets and marketing environment to find attractive opportunities and identify threats. It should analyze company strengths and weaknesses as well as current and possible marketing actions to determine which opportunities it can best pursue. The goal is to match the company's strengths to attractive opportunities in the environment while simultaneously eliminating or overcoming the weaknesses and minimizing the threats. Marketing analysis provides inputs to each of the other marketing management functions. We discuss marketing analysis more fully in Chapter 3.

Marketing Planning

Through strategic planning, the company decides what it wants to do with each business unit. Marketing planning involves choosing marketing strategies that will help the company attain its overall strategic objectives. A detailed marketing plan is needed for each business, product, or brand. What does a marketing plan look like? Our discussion focuses on product or brand marketing plans.

● FIGURE 2.7
SWOT Analysis: Strengths (S), Weaknesses (W), Opportunities (O), and Threats (T)

Internal

Strengths
Internal capabilities that may help a company reach its objectives

Weaknesses
Internal limitations that may interfere with a company's ability to achieve its objectives

External

Opportunities
External factors that the company may be able to exploit to its advantage

Threats
Current and emerging external factors that may challenge the company's performance

Positive   **Negative**

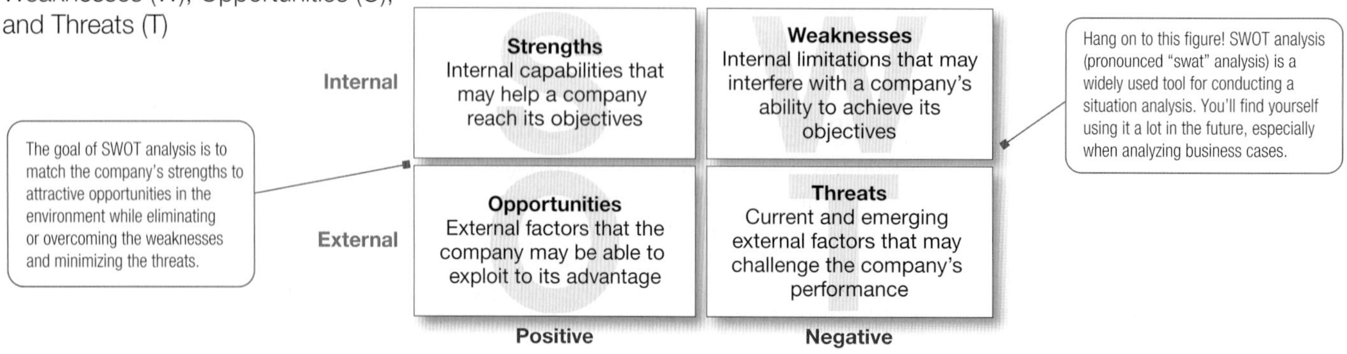

● **Table 2.2** outlines the major sections of a typical product or brand marketing plan. (See Appendix 1 for a sample marketing plan.) The plan begins with an executive summary that quickly reviews major assessments, goals, and recommendations. The main section of the plan presents a detailed SWOT analysis of the current marketing situation as well as potential threats and opportunities. The plan next states major objectives for the brand and outlines the specifics of a marketing strategy for achieving them.

A *marketing strategy* consists of specific strategies for target markets, positioning, the marketing mix, and marketing expenditure levels. It outlines how the company intends to engage target customers and create value in order to capture value in return. In this section, the planner explains how each strategy responds to the threats, opportunities, and critical issues spelled out earlier in the plan. Additional sections of the marketing plan lay out an *action program* for implementing the marketing strategy along with the details of a supporting *marketing budget*. The last section outlines the *controls* that will be used to monitor progress, measure return on marketing investment, and take corrective action.

Marketing Implementation

Marketing implementation

Turning marketing strategies and plans into marketing actions to accomplish strategic marketing objectives.

Planning good strategies is only a start toward successful marketing. A brilliant marketing strategy counts for little if the company fails to implement it properly. **Marketing implementation** is the process that turns marketing *plans* into marketing *actions* to accomplish strategic marketing objectives. Whereas marketing planning addresses the *what* and *why* of marketing activities, implementation addresses the *who, where, when,* and *how*.

Many managers think that "doing things right" (implementation) is as important as, or even more important than, "doing the right things" (strategy). The fact is that both are critical to success, and companies can gain competitive advantages through effective implementation. One firm can have essentially the same strategy as another yet win in the marketplace through faster or better execution. Still, implementation is difficult—it is often easier to think up good marketing strategies than it is to carry them out.

In an increasingly connected world, people at all levels of the marketing system must work together to implement marketing strategies and plans. At John Deere, for example, marketing implementation for the company's residential, commercial, agricultural, and industrial equipment requires day-to-day decisions and actions by thousands of people both inside and outside the organization. Marketing managers make decisions about target segments, branding, product development, pricing, promotion, and distribution. They talk with engineering about product design, with manufacturing about production and inventory levels, and with finance about funding and cash flows. They also connect with outside people, such as advertising agencies to plan ad campaigns and the news media to obtain publicity support. The sales force urges and supports independent John Deere dealers and large retailers like Lowe's in their efforts to convince residential, agricultural, and industrial customers that "Nothing Runs Like a Deere."

● **Marketers must continually plan their analysis, implementation, and control activities.**

Dmitriy Shironosov/123RF

Marketing Department Organization

The company must design a marketing organization that can carry out marketing strategies and plans. If the company is very small, one person might do all the research, selling, advertising, customer service, and other marketing work. ● As the company expands, however, a marketing department emerges to plan and carry out marketing activities. In large companies, this department contains many specialists—product and market managers, sales managers and salespeople, market researchers, and advertising and digital media experts, among others.

To head up such large marketing organizations, many companies have now created a *chief marketing officer* (or CMO) position. This person heads up the company's entire marketing operation and represents marketing on the company's top management team. The CMO position puts marketing on equal footing with other "C-level" executives, such as the chief operating officer (COO) and the chief financial officer (CFO).

● **Table 2.2** | **Contents of a Marketing Plan**

Section	Purpose
Executive summary	Presents a brief summary of the main goals and recommendations of the plan for management review, helping top management find the plan's major points quickly.
Current marketing situation	Describes the target market and the company's position in it, including information about the market, product performance, competition, and distribution. This section includes the following: • A *market description* that defines the market and major segments and then reviews customer needs and factors in the marketing environment that may affect customer purchasing. • A *product review* that shows sales, prices, and gross margins of the major products in the product line. • A review of *competition* that identifies major competitors and assesses their market positions and strategies for product quality, pricing, distribution, and promotion. • A review of *distribution* that evaluates recent sales trends and other developments in major distribution channels.
Threats and opportunities analysis	Assesses major threats and opportunities that the product might face, helping management to anticipate important positive or negative developments that might have an impact on the firm and its strategies.
Objectives and issues	States the marketing objectives that the company would like to attain during the plan's term and discusses key issues that will affect their attainment.
Marketing strategy	Outlines the broad marketing logic by which the business unit hopes to engage customers, create customer value, and build customer relationships, plus the specifics of target markets, positioning, and marketing expenditure levels. How will the company create value for customers in order to capture value from customers in return? This section also outlines specific strategies for each marketing mix element and explains how each responds to the threats, opportunities, and critical issues spelled out earlier in the plan.
Action programs	Spells out how marketing strategies will be turned into specific action programs that answer the following questions: *What* will be done? *When* will it be done? *Who* will do it? *How* much will it cost?
Budgets	Details a supporting marketing budget that is essentially a projected profit-and-loss statement. It shows expected revenues and expected costs of production, distribution, and marketing. The difference is the projected profit. The budget becomes the basis for materials buying, production scheduling, personnel planning, and marketing operations.
Controls	Outlines the controls that will be used to monitor progress, allow management to review implementation results, and spot products that are not meeting their goals. It includes measures of return on marketing investment.

As a member of top management, the CMO's role is to champion the customer's cause. To that end, many companies call their top marketer the "Chief Customer Experience Officer" or the "Chief Customer Value Officer." "Today's customer experiences must align with business strategy—and the CMO is the best candidate to drive these programs across the company," says one marketing analyst. "Instead of [just] creating big-picture marketing campaigns, CMOs are now responsible for the entire customer experience."[17]

Modern marketing departments can be arranged in several ways. The most common form of marketing organization is the *functional organization*, under which different marketing activities are headed by a functional specialist—a sales manager, an advertising manager, a marketing information manager, a customer service manager, or a new product manager. A company that sells across the country or internationally often uses a *geographic organization*, assigning sales and marketing people to specific countries, regions, and districts. Companies with many very different products or brands often create a *product management organization*. For companies that sell one product line to many different types of markets and customers who have different needs and preferences, a *market* or *customer management organization* might be best. Large companies that produce many different products flowing into many different geographic and customer markets usually employ some *combination* of the functional, geographic, product, and market organization forms.

Marketing organization has become an increasingly important issue in recent years. More and more, companies are shifting their brand management focus toward *customer management*—moving away from managing only product or brand profitability and toward managing customer profitability and customer equity. They think of themselves not as managing portfolios of brands but as managing portfolios of customers. And rather than managing the fortunes of a brand, they see themselves as managing customer–brand engagement, experiences, and relationships.

Marketing Control

Marketing control

Measuring and evaluating the results of marketing strategies and plans and taking corrective action to ensure that the objectives are achieved.

Because many surprises occur during the implementation of marketing strategies and plans, marketers must practice constant **marketing control**—evaluating results and taking corrective action to ensure that the objectives are attained. Marketing control involves four steps. Management first sets specific marketing goals. It then measures its performance in the marketplace and evaluates the causes of any differences between expected and actual performance. Finally, management takes corrective action to close the gaps between goals and performance. This may require changing the action programs or even changing the goals.

Operating control involves checking ongoing performance against the annual plan and taking corrective action when necessary. Its purpose is to ensure that the company achieves the sales, profits, and other goals set out in its annual plan. It also involves determining the profitability of different products, territories, markets, and channels. *Strategic control* involves looking at whether the company's basic strategies are well matched to its opportunities. Marketing strategies and programs can quickly become outdated, and each company should periodically reassess its overall approach to the marketplace.

Measuring and Managing Marketing Return on Investment

Marketing managers must ensure that their marketing dollars are being well spent. In the past, many marketers spent freely on big, expensive marketing programs and flashy advertising campaigns, often without thinking carefully about the financial returns on their spending. Their goal was often a general one—to "build brands and consumer preference." They believed that marketing produces intangible creative outcomes, which do not lend themselves readily to measures of productivity or return.

Marketing return on investment (marketing ROI)

The net return from a marketing investment divided by the costs of the marketing investment.

However, those free-spending days have been replaced by a new era of marketing measurement and accountability. More than ever, today's marketers are being held accountable for linking their strategies and tactics to measurable marketing performance outcomes. One important marketing performance measure is **marketing return on investment** (or **marketing ROI**). *Marketing ROI* is the net return from a marketing investment divided by the costs of the marketing investment. It measures the profits generated by investments in marketing activities.

Marketing ROI can be difficult to measure. In measuring financial ROI, both the *R* and the *I* are uniformly measured in dollars. For example, when buying a piece of equipment, the productivity gains resulting from the purchase are fairly straightforward. As of yet, however, there is no consistent definition of marketing ROI. For instance, returns such as engagement, advertising, and brand-building impact aren't easily put into dollar returns.

A company can assess marketing ROI in terms of standard marketing performance measures, such as brand awareness, social media responses, sales, or market share. Many companies are assembling such measures into *marketing dashboards*—meaningful sets of marketing performance measures in a single display used to monitor strategic marketing performance. Just as automobile dashboards present drivers with details on how their cars are performing, the marketing dashboard gives marketers the detailed measures they need to assess and adjust their marketing strategies. For example, VF Corporation

● FIGURE 2.8

Marketing Return on Investment

Source: Adapted from Roland T. Rust, Katherine N. Lemon, and Valerie A. Zeithaml, "Return on Marketing: Using Consumer Equity to Focus Marketing Strategy," *Journal of Marketing*, January 2004, p. 112. Used with permission.

Beyond measuring marketing return on investment in terms of standard performance measures such as sales or market share, many companies are using customer relationship measures, such as customer satisfaction, engagement, retention, and equity. These are more difficult to measure but capture both current and future performance.

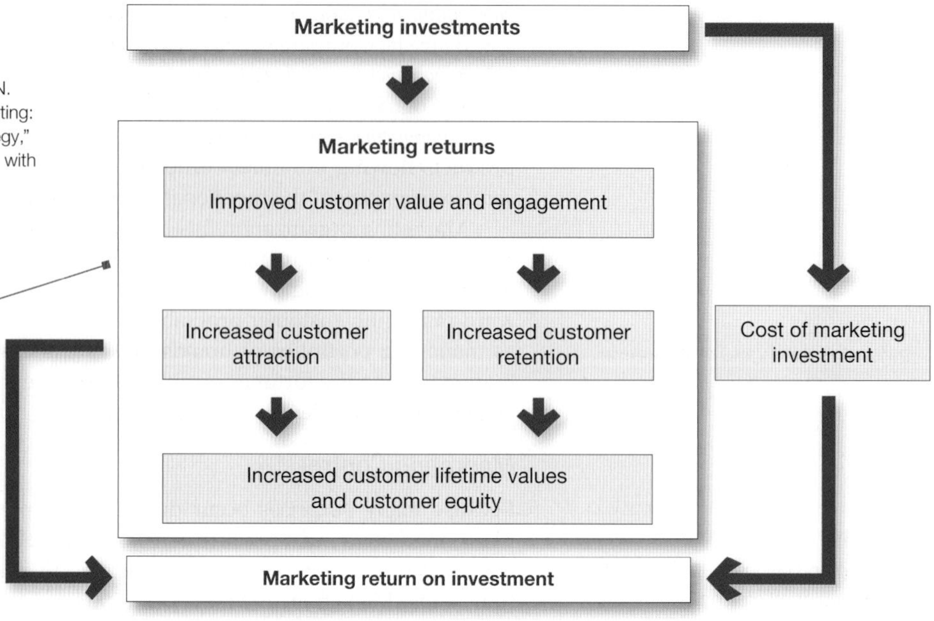

Marketing investments

Marketing returns

Improved customer value and engagement

Increased customer attraction

Increased customer retention

Increased customer lifetime values and customer equity

Cost of marketing investment

Marketing return on investment

uses a marketing dashboard to track the performance of its more than 30 lifestyle apparel brands—including Wrangler, Lee, The North Face, Vans, Nautica, 7 For All Mankind, Timberland, and others. VF's marketing dashboard tracks brand equity and trends, share of voice, market share, online sentiment, and marketing ROI in key markets worldwide, not only for VF brands but also for competing brands.[18]

Increasingly, however, beyond standard performance measures, marketers are using customer-centered measures of marketing impact, such as customer acquisition, customer engagement, customer experience, customer retention, customer lifetime value, and customer equity. These measures capture not only current marketing performance but also future performance resulting from stronger customer relationships.

● **Figure 2.8** views marketing expenditures as investments that produce returns in the form of more profitable customer engagement and relationships.[19] Marketing investments result in improved customer value, engagement, and satisfaction, which in turn increase customer attraction and retention. This increases individual customer lifetime values and the firm's overall customer equity. Increased customer equity, in relation to the cost of the marketing investments, determines return on marketing investment.

As one chief marketing officer says, "You have to be able to move on to those deeper engagement metrics, which show that for the money that I'm spending, here are the various programs that are working in terms of driving engagement with customers and ultimately driving purchase behavior and revenue."[20]

Reviewing and Extending the Concepts

Objectives Review

In Chapter 1, we defined marketing and outlined the steps in the marketing process. In this chapter, we examined company-wide strategic planning and marketing's role in the organization. Then we looked more deeply into marketing strategy and the marketing mix and reviewed the major marketing management functions. So you've now had a pretty good overview of the fundamentals of modern marketing.

OBJECTIVE 2-1 Explain company-wide strategic planning and its four steps. *(pp 58–62)*

Strategic planning sets the stage for the rest of the company's planning. Marketing contributes to strategic planning, and the overall plan defines marketing's role in the company.

Strategic planning involves developing a strategy for long-run survival and growth. It consists of four steps: (1) defining the company's mission, (2) setting objectives and goals, (3) designing a business portfolio, and (4) developing functional plans. The company's mission should be market oriented, realistic, specific, motivating, and consistent with the market environment. The mission is then transformed into detailed supporting goals and objectives, which in turn guide decisions about the business portfolio. Then each business and product unit must develop detailed marketing plans in line with the company-wide plan.

OBJECTIVE 2-2 Discuss how to design business portfolios and develop growth strategies. *(pp 62–66)*

Guided by the company's mission statement and objectives, management plans its business portfolio, or the collection of businesses and products that make up the company. The firm wants to produce a business portfolio that best fits its strengths and weaknesses to opportunities in the environment. To do this, it must analyze and adjust its current business portfolio and develop growth and downsizing strategies for adjusting the future portfolio. The company might use a formal portfolio-planning method. But many companies are now designing more-customized portfolio-planning approaches that better suit their unique situations.

OBJECTIVE 2-3 Explain marketing's role in strategic planning and how marketing works with its partners to create and deliver customer value. *(pp 66–68)*

Under the strategic plan, the major functional departments—marketing, finance, accounting, purchasing, operations, information technology, human resources, and others—must work together to accomplish strategic objectives. Marketing plays a key role in the company's strategic planning by providing a marketing concept philosophy and inputs regarding attractive market opportunities. Within individual business units, marketing designs strategies for reaching the unit's objectives and helps to carry them out profitably.

Marketers alone cannot produce superior value for customers. Marketers must practice partner relationship management, working closely with partners in other departments to form an effective *value chain* that serves the customer. And they must also partner effectively with other companies in the marketing system to form a competitively superior value delivery network.

OBJECTIVE 2-4 Describe the elements of a customer value–driven marketing strategy and mix and the forces that influence them. *(pp 68–73)*

Customer engagement, value, and relationships are at the center of marketing strategy and programs. Through market segmentation, targeting, differentiation, and positioning, the company divides the total market into smaller segments, selects segments it can best serve, and decides how it wants to bring value to target consumers in the selected segments. It then designs an integrated marketing mix to produce the response it wants in the target market. The marketing mix consists of product, price, place, and promotion decisions (the four Ps).

OBJECTIVE 2-5 List the marketing management functions, including the elements of a marketing plan, and discuss the importance of measuring and managing marketing return on investment. *(pp 73–78)*

To find the best strategy and mix and to put them into action, the company engages in marketing analysis, planning, implementation, and control. The main components of a marketing plan are the executive summary, the current marketing situation, threats and opportunities, objectives and issues, marketing strategies, action programs, budgets, and controls. Planning good strategies is often easier than carrying them out. To be successful, companies must also be effective at implementation—turning marketing strategies into marketing actions.

Marketing departments can be organized in one way or a combination of ways: functional marketing organization, geographic organization, product management organization, or market management organization. In this age of customer relationships, more and more companies are now changing their organizational focus from product or territory management to customer relationship management. Marketing organizations carry out marketing control, both operating control and strategic control.

More than ever, marketing accountability is the top marketing concern. Marketing managers must ensure that their marketing dollars are being well spent. In a tighter economy, today's marketers face growing pressures to show that they are adding value in line with their costs. In response, marketers are developing better measures of marketing return on investment. Increasingly, they are using customer-centered measures of marketing impact as a key input into their strategic decision making.

Key Terms

OBJECTIVE 2-1

Strategic planning (p 58)
Mission statement (p 59)

OBJECTIVE 2-2

Business portfolio (p 62)
Portfolio analysis (p 63)
Growth-share matrix (p 63)
Product/market expansion grid (p 65)
Market penetration (p 65)
Market development (p 65)

Product development (p 65)
Diversification (p 66)

OBJECTIVE 2-3

Value chain (p 67)
Value delivery network (p 68)

OBJECTIVE 2-4

Marketing strategy (p 68)
Market segmentation (p 69)
Market segment (p 69)

Market targeting (p 69)
Positioning (p 70)
Differentiation (p 70)
Marketing mix (p 70)

OBJECTIVE 2-5

SWOT analysis (p 74)
Marketing implementation (p 75)
Marketing control (p 77)
Marketing return on investment
  (marketing ROI) (p 77)

Discussion Questions

2-1 Discuss the role marketing plays in the company-wide strategic planning process. (AASCB: Written and Oral Communication)

2-2 Describe how a company's mission statement and objectives affect the way management plans its business portfolio. (AACSB: Communication; Reflective Thinking)

2-3 Explain the roles of market segmentation, market targeting, differentiation, and positioning in implementing an effective marketing strategy. (AACSB: Written and Oral Communication)

2-4 Discuss how a new brand manufacturer would go about defining their market segments and then begin to target them. (AACSB: Communication; Reflective Thinking)

2-5 Why do marketers need to practice constant marketing control? What steps are involved? (AACSB: Written and Oral Communication; Reflective Thinking)

2-6 What is marketing return on investment (ROI)? Why does it matter? (AACSB: Written and Oral Communication)

Critical Thinking Exercises

2-7 Examine the integrated marketing mix of the Japanese clothing brand UNIQLO. What are their key marketing mix ingredients? What about their brand, service, and IMC? (AASCB: Communication)

2-8 Locate the mission statements for the following organizations: (a) USAA, (b) United Airlines, (c) South Carolina State University (SC State), and (d) IKEA. Evaluate each statement using the criteria for creating a sound mission statement. What could be done to improve each

organization's mission statement? (AACSB: Written and Oral Communication; Reflective Thinking)

2-9 Create a mission statement for a nonprofit organization you would be interested in starting. Have another student evaluate your mission statement while you evaluate the other student's statement, suggesting areas for improvement. (AACSB: Written and Oral Communication; Reflective Thinking)

APPLICATIONS AND CASES

Online, Mobile, and Social Media Marketing Lush UK Abandons Social Media

Lush Fresh Handmade Cosmetics UK sells handmade premium beauty products such as body washes, bath bombs, and face masks through 900 cosmetics shops around the globe. Until recently, it engaged customers with captivating Instagram posts, which contributed to its massive following of more than 570,000 people. Therefore, people were surprised when the company announced it was abandoning social media because it inhibited the firm's ability to engage with fans. The announcement mentioned difficulties associated with talking directly to customers and challenges with changing algorithms the firm had to fight to appear in customers' newsfeeds. "We want social to be more about passions and less about likes," says Lush. Social media

platforms order posts by relevancy rather than chronology, which makes it harder for many brands to appear in consumers' social media feeds without paying to be there.

2-10 How will the market likely respond to Lush's abandoning its social media channels? (AACSB: Written and Oral Communication; Reflective Thinking)

2-11 As Lush UK implements the change, how can it measure the effects of leaving social media on the achievement of its marketing goals? (AACSB: Written and Oral Communication; Reflective Thinking)

Marketing Ethics Creating Value or Distracting Consumers?

In early 2014, Chipotle Mexican Grill announced that it would stop using genetically modified ingredients (GMOs) in its restaurants. Many observers applauded this move. However, critics of the fast-food chain cited a lack of evidence to support its anti-GMO stance. They suspected that Chipotle's anti-GMO claim was simply a ploy to distract consumers from a larger issue: the company's risky sanitation practices. Chipotle's anti-GMO policies may have won the burrito chain some health-conscious customers, but at the same time customers were becoming sick after eating at some Chipotle locations, calling into question the firm's food handling and safety practices.

Steve Ells, founder and co-CEO of Chipotle, said the GMO decision was "another step toward the visions we have of changing the way people think about and eat fast food. Just because food is served fast doesn't mean it has to be made with cheap raw ingredients, highly processed with preservatives and fillers and stabilizers and artificial colors and flavors." However, ridding Chipotle's supply chain of genetically altered components proved difficult. The chain discovered GMOs in basic ingredients such as baking powder, cornstarch, canola and soy oils,

cornmeal, and sugar. And many non-GMO ingredients were in short supply. For example, at one point, Chipotle found that it could not supply all its locations with enough non-GMO pork to make carnitas. Given the supply chain challenges, Chipotle decided to use non-GMO products in its food preparation but to continue to serve some soft drinks with sweeteners derived from genetically engineered corn.

2-12 Has Chipotle's focus on eliminating GMOs created value for its customers? Defend this market strategy. (AACSB: Written and Oral Communication; Ethical Understanding and Reasoning)

2-13 From an ethics standpoint, discuss Chipotle's focus on sourcing non-GMO food products rather than attention to food safety. In recent years, the company's oversights in food safety have resulted in numerous customers becoming ill (E. coli, norovirus, and salmonella). Discuss the challenges Chipotle still faces in overcoming the negative image that resulted. (AACSB: Written and Oral Communication; Reflective Thinking; Ethical Understanding and Reasoning)

Marketing by the Numbers Facebook versus Google

Facebook and Google are both giants in the tech industry. However, if you compare sales and profits, you would think that Google is a far better marketer than Facebook: Google's sales last year were more than double Facebook's sales, and its profits were 40 percent higher. Sales and profits provide information to compare the profitability of companies, but between these numbers is information regarding the efficiency of marketing efforts in creating those sales and profits. Appendix 2: Marketing by the Numbers, Marketing Performance Measures, discusses other marketing profitability measures beyond the return on marketing investment (marketing ROI) measure described in this chapter. Review the appendix to answer the questions using the following information from the two companies' incomes statements (all numbers are in thousands):

	Facebook	Google
Sales	$55,838,000	$136,819,000
Gross Profit	$46,483,000	$77,270,000
Marketing Expenses	$8,472,750	$18,344,250
Net Income (Profit)	$22,112,000	$30,736,000

2-14 Calculate profit margin, net marketing contribution, marketing return on sales (or marketing ROS), and marketing return on investment (or marketing ROI) for each company. Which company is performing better? (AACSB: Communication; Use of IT; Analytic Thinking)

2-15 Go to Yahoo! Finance (http://finance.yahoo.com/) and find the income statements for two other competing companies. Perform the same analyses for these companies that you performed for the previous question. Which company is doing better overall and with respect to marketing? For marketing expenses, use 75 percent of the company's reported "Selling General and Administrative" expenses, as not all of the expenses in that category are marketing expenses. (AACSB: Communication; Analytic Reasoning; Reflective Thinking)

Company Case Dyson: Solving Customer Problems in Ways They Never Imagined

The impact of Dyson Ltd. on various industries belies its relatively brief history. In just 25 years, Dyson has succeeded in causing revolution after revolution as it has reinvented the vacuum cleaner, the household fan, the hairdryer, and the commercial hand dryer. It did this across a variety of mature product categories thought to be anything but innovative, a tribute to the company's simple founding principles. First, every Dyson product must provide real consumer benefits that make life easier. Second, each product must take a totally unique approach to

accomplishing common, everyday tasks. Finally, each Dyson product must infuse excitement into products that are so mundane that most people never think much about them.

The Man behind the Name

James Dyson was born and raised in the United Kingdom. In 1979, he purchased what its maker claimed was the most powerful vacuum cleaner on the market. He found it to be anything but that. Instead, the vacuum did little more than move dirt around the room. This left Dyson wondering why no one had yet invented a decent vacuum cleaner. He remembered something he'd seen in an industrial sawmill—a cyclonic separator that removed dust from the air. Why wouldn't that approach work well in vacuum cleaners? "I thought no one was bothering to use technology in vacuum cleaners," said Dyson. Indeed, the core technology of vacuum motors at the time was more than 150 years old. "I saw a great opportunity to improve."

Dyson then did something that very few people would have the patience or the vision to do. Through trial and error, he spent 15 years and made 5,127 vacuum prototypes—all based on a bagless cyclonic separator—before he had the one that went to market. In his own words, "There were 5,126 failures. But I learned from each one. That's how I came up with a solution."

Dyson's all-new vacuum was far more than techno-gadgetry. Dyson had developed a completely new motor that ran at 110,000 revolutions per minute—three times faster than any other vacuum on the market. It provided tremendous suction that other brands simply couldn't match. The bagless design was very effective at removing dirt and particles from the air, and the machine was much easier to clean out than vacuums requiring the messy process of changing bags. The vacuum also was easier to maneuver and could reach places other vacuums could not. Dyson's vacuum really worked.

The major appliance companies and retailers of the time had no interest in Dyson's design. But Dyson gained distribution through a small mail-order catalog with an unusual sales pitch: "Your catalog is boring." Shortly thereafter, Dyson vacuums were picked up by other mail-order catalogs, then by small appliance chains, and then by large department stores. By the late 1990s, Dyson's full line of vacuums was being distributed in multiple global markets. Today, Dyson is the global leader in vacuum cleaners, with a line now dominated by lightweight, rechargeable units.

The Dyson Method

Throughout the development of Dyson's vacuums, a model for new products began to take shape: Take everyday products, focus on their shortcomings, and improve them to the point of reinvention. Dyson is known for saying, "I like going for unglamorous products and making them a pleasure to use." While taking this route, beyond finding solutions to the problems it is trying to solve, the company sometimes finds solutions for other problems.

For example, the vacuum motor Dyson developed sucked air with unprecedented strength. But the flipside of vacuum suction is exhaust. Why couldn't such a motor blow air at wet hands so fast that the water would be pressed off in a squeegee-like manner rather than the slow, evaporative approach employed by commercial hand dryers?

With that realization, Dyson created and launched the Airblade, a hand dryer that blows air through a .2-millimeter slot at 420 miles per hour. It dries hands in 12 seconds compared with the more typical 40 seconds required by other hand dryers. It also uses cold air—a huge departure from the standard warm air approach of existing commercial dryers. This not only reduces energy consumption by 75 percent—a major bonus for commercial enterprises that pay the electric bills—but customers are much more likely to use a product that works fast and does the job right.

With highly observable benefits, the Airblade was rapidly adopted by commercial customers. Meanwhile, guided by Dyson's customer-centric approach to developing products, the Airblade evolved. With the first Airblade, it was apparent that all that high-powered air is noisy. So Dyson spent seven years and a staggering $42 million to develop the V4 motor, one of the smallest and quietest commercial motors available. As a result, the Airblade grew quieter and lighter—almost six pounds lighter than the original. Dyson's innovation process led to variants of the Airblade, including the Blade V, 60 percent thinner and much sleeker than the Airblade, and the Airblade Tap, a faucet that washes *and* dries hands with completely touch-free operation.

Despite the fact that the lion's share of Dyson's business comes from vacuum cleaners, Dyson Ltd. does not define itself as a vacuum cleaner company. In fact, Dyson sees itself as a technology-driven company that develops products with the end user in mind. But rather than using traditional market research methods, Dyson takes a different approach. "Dyson avoids the kind of focus group techniques that are, frankly, completely averaging," says Adam Rostrom, group marketing director for Dyson. "Most companies start with the consumer and say, 'Hey Mr. or Mrs. X, what do you want from your toothbrush tomorrow or what do you want from your shampoo tomorrow?' The depressing reality is that you often won't get many inspiring answers."

Instead, Dyson's uses an approach it calls "interrogating products" to develop new technologies that produce real solutions to customer problems. After identifying the most obvious shortcomings for everyday products, it finds ways to improve them. Founder Dyson's philosophy is so focused on solving customer problems that he even developed the James Dyson Award—the top prize at an annual contest that challenges college students to design something that solves a problem. Once a problem-centered design is in place, the company then tests prototypes with real consumers under heavy nondisclosure agreements. In this manner, Dyson can observe consumer reactions in the context of real people using products in their real lives.

This approach enables Dyson to develop revolutionary products, such as those in its air treatment line of fans, air purifiers, humidifiers, and portable heating and cooling devices. It all started with the Air Multiplier, a fan that moves large volumes of air around a room with no blades. In fact, the Air Multiplier looks nothing like a fan. By using technology similar to that found in turbochargers and jet engines, driven by the power of its small digital motors, the Air Multiplier draws air in, amplifies it 18 times, and blows it back out in an uninterrupted stream that eliminates the buffeting and direct air pressure of conventional fans. The development of the Air Multiplier came about because of Dyson's approach to developing new products. "If you … asked people what they wanted from their fan tomorrow, they wouldn't say 'get rid of the blades,'" explains Rostrom. "Our approach is about product breakthroughs rather than the approach of just running a focus group and testing a concept."

The Next Big Thing

About three years ago, Dyson Ltd. shocked the world when it announced plans to enter the automotive business. Specifically, it planned to design and produce zero-emission, all-electric vehicles (EVs) with the ultimate goal of developing fully self-driving vehicles. Reactions to this announcement varied, but most experts and observers were skeptical and critical. After all, this venture was unlike any that Dyson had previously pursued. For starters, automobiles are hardly products that are "so mundane, most people never think much about them." In fact, the announcement came at a time characterized by more innovation in automotive design, propulsion systems, control systems, and even ownership models than perhaps ever before. Add the fact that no new automobile company had been successful in starting from scratch, penetrating the mass market, and sustaining business long term in well over 50 years. The barriers to entry in the automotive business far exceed those in the industries where Dyson currently competes.

Observers also scratched their heads as there were no readily apparent applications of Dyson technologies to the automobile industry. None of that has deterred Dyson. The company has committed more than $3 billion to get the business rolling and has begun construction of a manufacturing plant in Singapore with the express purpose of producing its EVs. In fact, Dyson is moving its main headquarters from the United Kingdom to Singapore, signaling the importance of this new venture. Dyson is also invested in the development and production of its own batteries to power the vehicles based on a new solid-state technology that promises batteries that are smaller, safer, lighter, longer-lasting between charges, and quicker-charging. And recently, as it applied for patents, the company revealed preliminary designs for both an EV and battery. It now asserts with confidence that Dyson will begin selling EVs in 2021.

What the outside world seems to overlook are the similarities between Dyson's self-driving EV project and its previous product development projects. It all started with another James Dyson observation on the status quo of an industry. "All I could see and smell were these huge clouds of diesel exhaust coming out," says Dyson. That led to the exploration of developing Dyson air filtering technologies for application in vehicle emissions. While emissions filtration showed promise, that project eventually led to the company's first and only acquisition of an outside company—Sakti3, a small startup that was developing solid-state batteries. Most experts agree that the entire future of EVs and rechargeable devices rests on better, more efficient batteries. Dyson simply acquired a technology it did not already have.

Beyond batteries, many core Dyson technologies could play significant roles in the development of self-driving EVs. Dyson

Ltd. has done more to advance electric motor technology than perhaps any other company today. True, Dyson's current consumer products motors are far too small to power a vehicle. But proprietary elements of Dyson motor designs are likely relevant to developing better, more efficient motors for cars. For example, Dyson's technologies could do for wet windshields what the Airblade does for wet hands. And then there's the Dyson robot vacuum, one of the most advanced on the market. Seventeen years in the making, Dyson's robot uses artificial intelligence, sophisticated sensors, and panoramic cameras to operate autonomously and learn its environments so that it can do its job without sucking up any stray socks or getting stuck behind furniture—capabilities on par with self-driving capabilities of today's most advanced vehicles.

With each step toward developing its new EVs, Dyson makes it more clear that it means business. When pressed for details about its electric car, James Dyson indicates that it won't be a sports car, it will likely be pricey, and it will have at least level 2 autonomy (hands-off). He also ads that Dyson's first EV may not look much like any car the world has ever seen. But its previous entries into new product categories didn't look much like vacuum cleaners, fans, hand dryers, and hair dryers either.

At Dyson Ltd., innovation never ends. The company not only continues to demonstrate that it can come up with winning products again and again, it is expanding throughout the world at a rapid pace. Dyson sells products in more than 50 global markets, emerging economies as well as developed nations. Dyson does well in both economic good times and recessionary periods. From a single vacuum cleaner to EVs in just over 20 years—that's quite an accomplishment.[21]

Questions for Discussion

2-16 Write a market-oriented mission statement for Dyson.

2-17 What are Dyson's goals and objectives?

2-18 Does Dyson have a business portfolio? Explain.

2-19 Is Dyson a customer-centered company? Explain.

2-20 Based on Dyson's past, predict the outcome of Dyson's future in the automotive business.

3

Analyzing the Marketing Environment

OBJECTIVES OUTLINE

OBJECTIVE 3-1 Describe the environmental forces that affect the company's ability to serve its customers. **See: The Microenvironment and Macroenvironment** *(pp 86–90)*

OBJECTIVE 3-2 Explain how changes in the demographic and economic environments affect marketing decisions. **See: The Demographic and Economic Environments** *(pp 90–98)*

OBJECTIVE 3-3 Identify the major trends in the firm's natural and technological environments. **See: The Natural and Technological Environments** *(pp 98–101)*

OBJECTIVE 3-4 Explain the key changes in the political and cultural environments. **See: The Political–Social and Cultural Environments** *(pp 101–109)*

OBJECTIVE 3-5 Discuss how companies can react to the marketing environment. **See: Responding to the Marketing Environment** *(pp 109–111)*

CHAPTER PREVIEW So far, you've learned about the basic concepts of marketing and the steps in the marketing process for engaging and building profitable relationships with targeted consumers. In this chapter, we'll begin digging deeper into the first step of the marketing process—understanding the marketplace and customer needs and wants. In this chapter, you'll see that marketing operates in a complex and changing environment. Other actors in this environment—suppliers, intermediaries, customers, competitors, publics, and others—may work with or against the company. Major environmental forces—demographic, economic, natural, technological, political, and cultural—shape marketing opportunities, pose threats, and affect the company's ability to engage customers and build customer relationships. To develop effective marketing strategies, a company must first understand the environment in which marketing operates.

To start, let's look at Microsoft, the technology giant that dominated the computer software world throughout the 1990s and much of the 2000s. Its Windows and Office products have long been must-haves in the PC market. But with the decline in standalone personal computers and the surge in digitally connected devices—everything from smartphones and tablets to internet-connected TVs—mighty Microsoft found itself struggling to find its place in a fast-changing environment. However, the tech giant has now reinvented itself as a relevant brand that consumers can't live without in the post-PC era.

MICROSOFT: Adapting to the Fast-Changing Marketing Environment

Twenty years ago, talking high-tech meant talking about the almighty personal computer. Intel provided the PC microprocessors while manufacturers such as Dell and HP built and marketed the machines. But it was Microsoft that really ruled the PC industry—it made the operating systems that kept most PCs humming. As the dominant software developer, Microsoft put its Windows operating system and Office productivity suite on almost every computer sold.

The huge success of Windows drove Microsoft's revenues, profits, and stock price to dizzying heights. By the start of the 2000s, Microsoft's was the most valuable company in corporate history. In those heady days, no company was more relevant than Microsoft. And from a competitive standpoint, no company was more powerful.

But times change. Moving through the first decade of the new millennium, PC sales growth flattened as the world fell in love with a rush of alluring new digital devices and technologies. The computing industry shifted rapidly from stationary standalones like the PC to connected mobile devices that linked users to an ever-on, ever-changing world of information, entertainment, and socialization options. But unlike PCs, those mobile devices didn't need Microsoft Windows.

In the new digitally connected world, Microsoft found itself lagging more-glamorous competitors such as Google, Apple, Samsung, and even Amazon and Facebook, which provided a complete slate of all things digital—not just the software but also the smart devices, connecting technologies, and even digital destinations. Although still financially strong and still the world's dominant PC software maker, Microsoft lost some of its luster. In turn, the company's growth stalled and profits languished at early 2000s' levels for a dozen years or more. Microsoft needed to change with the times, and fast.

So Microsoft began a sweeping transformation to align itself better with the new digital world order. More than just a PC software developer, Microsoft set out to become a full-line digital competitor. In tune with the times, the company pursued a new "mobile first, cloud first" strategy. It developed a mobile version of its Windows operating system—the long-time company cash cow. And it created Office 365—a cloud-based subscription version of its market-dominating suite of productivity apps.

At the same time, Microsoft unleashed a flurry of new, improved, or acquired digital products and services. These included an upgraded version of Skype, a OneDrive cloud storage solution, and even an innovative new digital hardware line—Microsoft Surface tablets and Microsoft Surface Book laptops—that it hoped would lead the way to even more innovative Windows devices. Microsoft also dabbled seriously with mobile phones, first buying then selling phone maker Nokia and then rumored to be soon introducing its own Windows-based Surface phone. Microsoft hoped that the Surface line, along with its Xbox console, would give it better access to three important digital screens beyond the PC—tablets, TVs, and phones.

But even with these new initiatives, Microsoft found itself still chasing rather than leading the pack of new digital competitors. The Microsoft Windows operating system still dominates the declining PC market, but its mobile versions capture only a sliver of the mobile operating system market dominated by Apple iOS and Google Android. Although its Surface tablets and laptops have done well, they still lag far behind those of Apple and Samsung. And Microsoft has yet to introduce a successful Surface phone.

Thus, to continue its massive makeover, Microsoft has made yet another significant shift. It started with a new mission. Microsoft's early mission was to "put a computer on every desk in every home." Not until 2013 did that changed to a grander but still-product-centered mission "to create a family of devices and services for individuals and businesses that empower people around the globe at home, at work, and on the go." Then in 2015, Microsoft announced a simpler mission "to empower every person and every organization on the planet to achieve more."

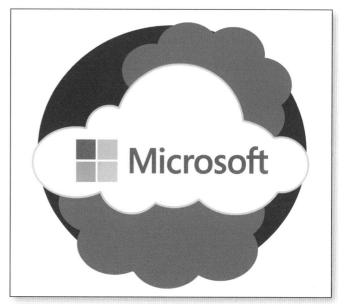

In the fast-changing digital marketing environment, Microsoft has transformed itself into a brand that consumers can't live without in the post-PC world.

imageBROKER/Alamy Stock Photo

The new mission focuses not on devices and services but on outcomes. Rather than chasing competitors in mobile devices and operating systems, Microsoft now intends to lead them in productivity tools. And instead of clinging to Windows as the linchpin in its future, Microsoft is taking its productivity apps and services headlong into the cloud. The old Microsoft didn't care what apps you ran as long as you ran them on Windows. In a dramatic shift, the new Microsoft doesn't care what operating system you run as long as you're using Microsoft apps and services.

At the center of Microsoft's cloud offerings is good old Microsoft Office, with its Word, Excel, Powerpoint, and other productivity apps. Although competitors Google and Apple have word processing, spreadsheet, and presentation apps, Office is still far and away the gold standard for getting things done, whether for large corporations, small businesses, students, or home users. In the old days, Office came bundled with Windows. But the plan now is to make Office accessible to anyone and everyone. Office 365 subscription services can be accessed from the cloud and run on any device or operating system—iOS, Android, or Windows.

Accessibility is only the start. Microsoft's goal is to make Office 365 the center for a whole new family of cloud-based online services that work seamlessly together. To that end, in addition to mobile versions of Word, Excel, and PowerPoint, Microsoft has been adding an ever-expanding set of mobile productivity apps to the Office 365 portfolio, such as Outlook Mobile (email) and To-Do (task management). Moreover, the

> Microsoft has undergone a dramatic transformation to better align itself with the new digital world. More than just making the software that makes PCs run, Microsoft now wants to empower every person and every organization on the planet to achieve more, regardless of what device or operating system they use.

cloud-based Office 365 increases the likelihood that subscribers will sign up for other Microsoft services, such as Skype, OneDrive cloud services, or Power BI data analytics and insights tools.

Another key part of Microsoft's new direction is artificial intelligence (AI)—the latest battleground for digital giants Amazon, Google, Samsung, and IBM. For example, Microsoft's Windows 10 AI voice assistant Cortana—already installed on hundreds of millions of Windows devices worldwide—is no match for Amazon's Alexa, Apple's Siri, or Google's "OK, Google." But rather than compete, Microsoft is taking a different path. Microsoft recently partnered with Amazon to let their formerly competing voice assistants work with and through each other; Alexa users can summon Cortana and vice versa. The partnership gives Amazon Echo users access to Microsoft's productivity apps. In turn, it gives Cortana users access to Alexa's smarthome capabilities, such as streaming music and controlling smarthome devices. Now,

Microsoft wants to create the same type of Cortana integration with Google Assistant.

So this is not your grandfather's Microsoft. With its sweeping transformation well under way, Microsoft now seems to be making the right moves to stay ahead of the times. As a result, sales and profit growth have rebounded. Although the Windows operating system remains a key component of Microsoft's current success, the company's future now lies in the cloud. And with nearly $27 billion in total commercial cloud revenues last year, a stunning 24 percent of its total revenues, Microsoft is now winning the cloud wars, ahead of Amazon, IBM, and a host of others.

Still, continued success will depend on Microsoft's ability to effectively adapt to—or even lead—the lightning-quick changes occurring in the marketing environment. "The opportunity ahead for Microsoft is vast," says Microsoft's CEO, "but to seize it, we must focus clearly, move faster, and continue to transform."[1]

Marketing environment
The actors and forces outside marketing that affect marketing management's ability to build and maintain successful relationships with target customers.

A COMPANY'S marketing environment consists of the actors and forces outside marketing that affect marketing management's ability to build and maintain successful relationships with target customers. Like Microsoft, companies must constantly watch and adapt to the changing environment—or, in many cases, lead those changes.

More than any other group in the company, marketers must be environmental trend trackers and opportunity seekers. Although every manager in an organization should watch the outside environment, marketers have two special aptitudes. They have disciplined methods—marketing research, marketing intelligence, and marketing analytics—for collecting information and developing insights about the marketing environment. They also spend more time in customer and competitor environments. By carefully studying the environment, marketers can adapt their strategies to meet new marketplace challenges and opportunities.

Author Comment | The microenvironment includes all the actors close to the company that affect, positively or negatively, its ability to engage with and create value for customers.

The Microenvironment and Macroenvironment

OBJECTIVE 3-1 Describe the environmental forces that affect the company's ability to serve its customers.

The marketing environment consists of a *microenvironment* and a *macroenvironment*. The **microenvironment** consists of the actors close to the company that affect its ability to engage and serve its customers—the company, suppliers, marketing intermediaries, customer markets, competitors, and publics. The **macroenvironment** consists of the larger societal forces that affect the microenvironment—demographic, economic, natural, technological, political, and cultural forces. We look first at the company's microenvironment.

Microenvironment
The actors close to the company that affect its ability to serve its customers—the company, suppliers, marketing intermediaries, customer markets, competitors, and publics.

The Microenvironment

Marketing management's job is to build relationships with customers by creating customer value and satisfaction. However, marketing managers cannot do this alone. ● Figure 3.1 shows the major actors in the marketer's microenvironment. Marketing success requires building relationships with other company departments, suppliers, marketing intermediaries, competitors, various publics, and customers, which combine to make up the company's value delivery network.

Macroenvironment
The larger societal forces that affect the microenvironment—demographic, economic, natural, technological, political, and cultural forces.

The Company

In designing marketing plans, marketing management takes other company groups into account—groups such as top management, finance, research and development (R&D), information technology, purchasing, operations, human resources, and accounting. All of these interrelated groups form the internal environment. Top management sets the company's

● FIGURE 3.1
Actors in the Microenvironment

In creating value for customers, marketers must partner with other firms in the company's value delivery network.

Marketers must work in harmony with other company departments to create customer value and relationships.

Customers are the most important actors in the company's microenvironment. The aim of the entire value delivery system is to serve target customers and create strong relationships with them.

mission, objectives, broad strategies, and policies. Marketing managers make decisions within these broader strategies and plans. Then, as we discussed in Chapter 2, marketing managers must work closely with other company departments. With marketing taking the lead, all departments—from manufacturing and finance to legal and human resources—share the responsibility for understanding customer needs and creating customer value.

Suppliers

Suppliers form an important link in the company's overall customer value delivery network. They provide the resources needed by the company to produce its goods and services. Supplier problems can seriously affect marketing. Marketing managers must watch supply availability and costs. Supply shortages or delays, natural disasters, and other events can cost sales in the short run and damage customer satisfaction in the long run. Rising supply costs may force price increases that can harm the company's sales volume.

Most marketers today treat their suppliers as partners in creating and delivering customer value. ● For example, home furnishings retailer IKEA knows the importance of building close relationships with its extensive network of suppliers:[2]

> IKEA, the world's largest furniture retailer, is the quintessential global cult brand. Last year, the Scandinavian retailer attracted more than 957 million visits to its 422 huge stores in 50 world markets plus an additional 2.5 *billion* website visits, generating more than $44 billion in sales. And despite the trouble worldwide retail environment in recent years, IKEA is growing at a healthy clip. But the biggest obstacle to growth isn't opening new stores and attracting customers. Rather, it's finding enough of the right kinds of *suppliers* to help design and produce the billions of dollars of goods that those customers will carry out of its stores. IKEA currently relies on about 1,000 suppliers in 51 countries to stock its shelves. At its current rate of growth, that number might have to double over the next decade.
>
> IKEA's mission is to create a better everyday life for customers by offering trendy but simple and practical home furnishings at prices so low that as many people as possible can afford them. But before it can sell the billions of dollars' worth of products its customers covet, IKEA must first develop a robust and reliable network of supplier–partners who can help it design and make all those products. IKEA does more than just buy from suppliers. The design process for a new IKEA product can take up to three years. IKEA's designers start with a basic customer value proposition and then work closely with key suppliers throughout the process to bring that proposition to life—refining the design, improving function, and reducing costs. "What makes the IKEA design process unique is that our suppliers play a very important role," says the company. It's a mutually beneficial partnership from start to finish, what IKEA refers to as "growing together as partners with passion for [creating] a better life at home. We strive to be the good link between suppliers and customers."

● **Suppliers: Giant furniture retailer IKEA doesn't just buy from its suppliers. It involves them deeply in the process of delivering the trendy but simple and affordable home furnishings to create a better everyday life for its customers.**

Used with permission of Inter IKEA Systems B.V.

Marketing Intermediaries

Marketing intermediaries
Firms that help the company to promote, sell, and distribute its goods to final buyers.

Marketing intermediaries help the company promote, sell, and distribute its products to final buyers. They include resellers, physical distribution firms, marketing services agencies, and financial intermediaries. *Resellers* are distribution channel firms that help the company find customers or make sales to them. These include wholesalers and retailers that buy and resell merchandise. *Physical distribution firms* help the company stock and move goods from their points of origin to their destinations. *Marketing services agencies* are the marketing research firms, advertising agencies, media firms, and marketing consulting firms that help the company target and promote its products to the right markets. *Financial intermediaries* include banks, credit companies, insurance companies, and other businesses that help finance transactions or insure against the risks associated with the buying and selling of goods.

Like suppliers, marketing intermediaries form an important component of the company's overall value delivery network. Thus, today's marketers recognize the importance of working with their intermediaries as partners rather than simply as channels through which they sell their products. ● For example, although Apple has hundreds of its own retail locations throughout the world, it also uses the services of authorized resellers who help the firm sell its products. In this arrangement, Apple's products are sold at identical prices both in its stores and in those of authorized resellers.[3]

Apple considers these authorized resellers as partners and has recently overhauled its premium resellers' partners program. The organization is co-funding the renovation of resellers' stores to follow Apple's own retail formula and make demo units display consistent with Apple's specifications. Apart from those who sell its products, Apple also has another set of intermediaries called authorized service providers. These are companies or individuals who represent organizations in providing repair and maintenance services to its customers. These intermediaries could belong to either of two categories, depending on the scale of the services that could be handled: authorized service providers or limited service providers. Apple gives its partners reimbursements for labor, travel, and parts, where applicable. It also gives them comprehensive access to products, upgrade information, service, troubleshooting, on-the-spot technical support for certified technicians, etc. In addition, the partners benefit from inclusion in the Apple resource locator system, whereby they are displayed on Apple's website for customers looking for nearby service providers.

● **Partnering with intermediaries: Apple provides its retail partners with much more than phones and smartwatches. It also pledges technical support.**
picturesbyrob/Alamy Stock Photo

Competitors

The marketing concept states that, to be successful, a company must provide greater customer value and satisfaction than its competitors do. Thus, marketers must do more than simply adapt to the needs of target consumers. They also must gain strategic advantage by positioning their offerings strongly against competitors' offerings in the minds of consumers.

No single competitive marketing strategy is best for all companies. Each firm should consider its own size and industry position compared with those of its competitors. Large firms with dominant positions in an industry can use certain strategies that smaller firms cannot afford. But being large is not enough. There are winning strategies for large firms, but there are also losing ones. And small firms can develop strategies that give them better rates of return than large firms enjoy.

Publics

The company's marketing environment also includes various publics. A **public** is any group that has an actual or potential interest in or impact on an organization's ability to achieve its objectives. We can identify seven types of publics:

Public
Any group that has an actual or potential interest in or impact on an organization's ability to achieve its objectives.

- *Financial publics.* This group influences the company's ability to obtain funds. Banks, investment analysts, and stockholders are the major financial publics.
- *Media publics.* This group carries news, features, editorial opinions, and other content. It includes television stations, newspapers, magazines, and blogs and other social media.
- *Government publics.* Management must take government developments into account. Marketers must often consult the company's lawyers on issues of product safety, truth in advertising, and other matters.
- *Citizen-action publics.* A company's marketing decisions may be questioned by consumer organizations, environmental groups, minority groups, and others. Its public relations department can help it stay in touch with consumer and citizen groups.
- *Internal publics.* This group includes workers, managers, volunteers, and the board of directors. Large companies use newsletters and other means to inform and motivate their internal publics. When employees feel good about the companies they work for, this positive attitude spills over to the external publics.
- *General public.* A company needs to be concerned about the general public's attitude toward its products and activities. The public's image of the company affects its buying behavior.
- *Local publics.* This group includes local community residents and organizations. Large companies usually work to become responsible members of the local communities in which they operate.

A company can prepare marketing plans and programs for major publics as well as for customer markets. ● NatWest, one of the leading UK banks, maintains a strong link with its local community through various cause-related activities:[4]

In 2016, across the group, NatWest gave a whooping £2.5 million to local charities, community groups, and social enterprises both in the United Kingdom and in Ireland. Many not-for-profit organizations have supported several people in deprived communities through the annual £2.5 million Skills and Opportunities Fund. Further, in 2015, the staff donated a total of £2.7 million to charity through the Pay-as-You-Earn Scheme and contributed 45,437 hours of volunteering for various communities and charity projects. The same year, it became an official sponsor of Sports Relief, a national event using sports personalities to raise money for charity. Over the years, it has been celebrated for supporting many other local charities to improve life, including Porchlight for the homeless, Discovery Park for tenants, and UKSA, a Youth charity. Its link to the Prince's Trust spans over 16 years. In 2014 alone, it ran an employability and mentoring program for 2,521 disadvantaged people through hours devoted to the Trust.

● Publics: NatWest shows its commitment to its local community by giving generously to local charities, community groups, and social enterprises.

Jeff Gilbert/Alamy Stock Photo

Customers

Customers are the most important actors in the company's microenvironment. The aim of the entire value delivery network is to engage target customers and create strong relationships with them. The company might target any or all of five types of customer markets. *Consumer markets* consist of individuals and households that buy goods and services for personal consumption. *Business markets* buy goods and services for further processing or use in their production processes, whereas *reseller markets* buy goods and services to resell at a profit. *Government markets* consist of government agencies that buy goods and services to produce public services or transfer the goods and services to others who need them. Finally, *international markets* consist of these buyers in other countries, including consumers, producers, resellers, and governments. Each market type has special characteristics that call for careful study by the seller.

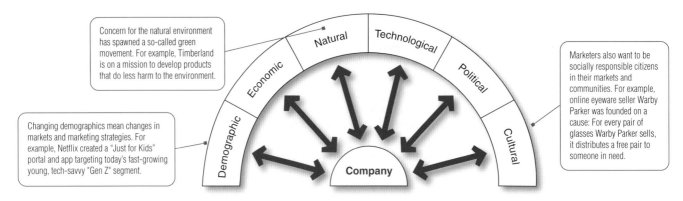

Concern for the natural environment has spawned a so-called green movement. For example, Timberland is on a mission to develop products that do less harm to the environment.

Marketers also want to be socially responsible citizens in their markets and communities. For example, online eyeware seller Warby Parker was founded on a cause: For every pair of glasses Warby Parker sells, it distributes a free pair to someone in need.

Changing demographics mean changes in markets and marketing strategies. For example, Netflix created a "Just for Kids" portal and app targeting today's fast-growing young, tech-savvy "Gen Z" segment.

● FIGURE 3.2
Major Forces in the Company's Macroenvironment

| Author Comment | The macroenvironment consists of broader forces that affect the actors in the microenvironment. |

The Macroenvironment

The company and all the other actors operate in a larger macroenvironment of forces that shape opportunities and pose threats to the company. ● **Figure 3.2** shows the six major forces in the company's macroenvironment. Even the most dominant companies can be vulnerable to the often turbulent and changing forces in the marketing environment. Some of these forces are unforeseeable and uncontrollable. Others can be predicted and handled through skillful management. Companies that understand and adapt well to their environments can thrive. Those that don't can face difficult times. One-time dominant market leaders such as Xerox, Sears, Sony, Blockbuster, and Kodak have learned this lesson the hard way. In the remaining sections of this chapter, we examine these forces and show how they affect marketing plans.

| Author Comment | Changes in demographics mean changes in markets, so they are very important to marketers. We first look at the biggest demographic trend—the changing age structure of the population. |

The Demographic and Economic Environments

OBJECTIVE 3-2 Explain how changes in the demographic and economic environments affect marketing decisions.

The Demographic Environment

Demography is the study of human populations in terms of size, density, location, age, gender, race, occupation, and other statistics. The demographic environment is of major interest to marketers because it involves people, and people make up markets. The world population is growing at an explosive rate. It now exceeds 7.5 billion people and is expected to grow to more than 8.6 billion by the year 2030.[5] The world's large and highly diverse population poses both opportunities and challenges.

Changes in the world demographic environment have major implications for business. Thus, marketers keep a close eye on demographic trends and developments in their markets. They analyze changing age and family structures, geographic population shifts, educational characteristics, and population diversity. Here, we discuss the most important demographic trends in the United States.

Demography
The study of human populations in terms of size, density, location, age, gender, race, occupation, and other statistics.

The Changing Age Structure of the Population

The U.S. population currently stands at more than 328 million and may reach almost 360 million by 2030.[6] The single most important demographic trend in the United States is the changing age structure of the population. Primarily because of falling birthrates and longer life expectancies, the U.S. population is rapidly getting older. In 1970, the median age was 28; it is now about 38.[7] This aging of the population will have a significant impact on markets and those who service them.

The U.S. population contains several generational groups. Here, we discuss the five major groups—the baby boomers, Generation X, the millennials, Generation Z, and Generation Alpha—and their impact on today's marketing strategies.

Baby boomers

The 72 million people born during the years following World War II and lasting until 1964.

The Baby Boomers. There are currently 72 million U.S. **baby boomers**, people born during the post–World War II baby boom from 1946 to 1964. Over the years, the baby boomers have been one of the most powerful forces shaping the marketing environment. The youngest boomers are now in their mid-50s; the oldest are in their 70s and well into retirement.

The baby boomers are the wealthiest generation in U.S. history. Today's baby boomers account for about 22 percent of the U.S. population but control 42 percent of the spending power.[8] The boomers constitute a lucrative market for financial services, new housing and home remodeling, new cars, travel and entertainment, eating out, health and fitness products, and just about everything else.

It's fashionable for some marketers these days to look past the boomers, instead targeting the highly coveted millennial generation. Some may stereotype the older boomers as stuck in the past, out of touch, and not interested in new products. However, it would be a mistake to think of older boomers as phasing out or slowing down. Rather than viewing themselves that way, many of today's boomers see themselves as entering new life phases.

More active boomers have no intention of abandoning their youthful lifestyles as they age. For example, adults over 50 now account for 80 percent of luxury travel spending in America. Contrary to the popular belief that they are staid in their ways, one recent survey found that 82 percent of boomers are open to new brands. Anything but tech-phobic, boomers are also digitally active and increasingly social media savvy. Some 70 percent of baby boomers now use mobile internet. And they are the fastest-growing shopper demographic online, outspending younger generations two to one.[9]

Thus, although boomers may buy lots of products that help them deal with issues of aging—from vitamins to blood pressure monitors to Good Grips kitchen tools—they tend to appreciate marketers who appeal to their youthful thinking rather than their advancing age. For example, after its research showed that older consumers were "perplexed, annoyed, and amused" by how little brands seemed to understand them, British insurance company Sun Life ran a "Welcome to life after 50" campaign challenging the stereotypes. In one ad, a distinguished older gentleman exits a boring cruise via a zip line into a cocktail bar, while a sunbathing beauty turns heads before removing her floppy hat to reveal that she is a "woman of 62." Sun Life's "Welcome to life after 50" website and blog are filled with stories about "amazing over-50s putting old on hold and making the world a better place."[10]

Companies across a wide range of industries have renewed their efforts to capture boomer consumers. For example, GEICO courts boomers with ads in both traditional and digital media. One well-timed "Peter Pan Reunion" ad, part of GEICO's long-running "It's what you do" campaign, targeted boomers about to turn 70. In the ad, Peter Pan showed up at a 50-year reunion and took humorous jabs at his aging former classmates. "If you're Peter Pan, you stay young forever. It's what you do," said the ad. "If you want to save 15 percent of more on car insurance, visit GEICO.com. It's what we do." Thanks to such targeting, during the past five years GEICO has gained more new boomer customers than any other insurance company.[11]

Generation X. The baby boom was followed by a "birth dearth," creating another generation of 55 million people born between 1965 and 1980.[12] Author Douglas Coupland calls them **Generation X** because they lie in the shadow of the boomers.

Generation X

The 55 million people born between 1965 and 1980 in the "birth dearth" following the baby boom.

Considerably smaller than the boomer generation that precedes them and the millennials who follow, the Generation Xers are a sometimes-overlooked "in-between" consumer group. Although they seek success, they are less materialistic than the other groups; they prize experience, not acquisition. For many of the Gen Xers who are parents and homeowners, family comes first—both children and their aging parents—and career second.

From a marketing standpoint, the Gen Xers are a more skeptical bunch. They are sensible shoppers who research products heavily before they consider a purchase, prefer quality to quantity, and tend to be less receptive to overt marketing pitches. But once they find a brand, they tend to be more loyal than other generational groups. They are more receptive to irreverent ad pitches that make fun of convention and tradition. Many Gen Xers grew up before the internet and adapted to digital technology during young adulthood. Most are now fully connected and embrace the benefits of new technology. For instance, one study found that more Gen Xers shop online than boomers or millennials. At the same time, however, Gen X viewers watch more network-produced TV shows than millennials.[13]

● **Targeting Gen Xers: Lowe's markets heavily to Gen X homeowners with ideas and advice on home-improvement projects and problems, urging them to "Never Stop Improving."**

Bryan Bedder/Getty Images for HGTV Home by Sherwin-Williams & Lowe's

The Gen Xers, now mostly in their 40s and early 50s, have grown up and are taking over. They have increasingly displaced the lifestyles, culture, and values of the baby boomers. They are firmly into their careers, and many are proud homeowners with growing families. They are the most educated generation to date, and they possess hefty annual purchasing power. Although Gen Xers make up less than a quarter of all U.S. adults, they pull in 29 percent of the nation's total income.[14]

With so much potential, many brands and organizations focus on Gen Xers as a prime target segment. For example, a full 82 percent of Gen Xers own their own homes, making them an important segment for home-and-hearth marketers. ● Home-improvement retailer Lowe's markets heavily to Gen X homeowners, urging them to "Never Stop Improving." Through ads, online videos, and a substantial social media presence, Lowe's provides ideas and advice on a wide range of indoor and outdoor home-improvement projects and problems, providing solutions that make life simpler for busy Gen X homeowners and their families. Its myLowe's app is like a 24/7 home-improvement concierge that lets customers build room-by-room profiles of their homes, archive their Lowe's purchases, build product lists with photos, receive reminders for things like changing furnace filters, and even consult with store employees online as they plan out home-improvement projects.[15]

Millennials (or Generation Y)
The 75 million children of the baby boomers born between 1981 and 1996.

Millennials. Both the baby boomers and Gen Xers will one day be passing the reins to the **millennials** (also called **Generation Y** or the echo boomers). Born between 1981 and 1996, these children of the baby boomers number 75 million or more, dwarfing the Gen Xers and now larger than the baby boomer segment. The 20- to 30-something millennials, by their sheer numbers, wield substantial buying power and make up a huge and attractive market, both now and in the future.

One thing that all millennials have in common is their comfort with digital technology. They don't just embrace technology; it's a way of life. The millennials were the first generation to grow up in a world filled with computers, mobile phones, satellite TV, iPods and iPads, and online social media. As a result, they engage with brands in an entirely new way, such as with mobile or social media. In one recent survey of millennials, when asked where they do most of their shopping, 75 percent said online mobile or online laptop. Ninety-two percent preferred to do their banking over a web or mobile device.[16]

More than sales pitches from marketers, millennials seek authenticity, value, and opportunities to shape their own brand experiences and share them with others. Compared with other generational groups, they tend to be frugal, practical, connected, mobile, and impatient. "The millennials are open to connecting with brands, drawn to bite-size content (paid or not), and intrigued by new information, product-wise," notes one analyst. "However, the main [caution] is that it all needs to get done in an [efficient], digestible, and fluid manner."[17]

Many brands have fielded specific products and marketing campaigns aimed at millennial needs and lifestyles. For example, in financial services, several app-based payment and banking brands have arisen that appeal to mobile-first millennial consumers. ● Consider Chime, the fast-growing mobile banking app and debit card:[18]

Chime simplifies and streamlines "traditional" banking services for a millennial generation that doesn't much favor big banks. Founded five years ago as an online, app-only bank, Chime eliminates typical checking account features that millennials dislike, such as minimum balances, monthly account fees, and costly overdraft protection. Chime customers have only a savings account, spending account, and debit card. Chime's no-frills, technology-driven approach appeals to millennials' desires for simplicity and mobility. "Chime's mobile app makes branchless banking a breeze," says the company. "Manage your money and account on the go, wherever you

● **Targeting millennials: Chime's no-frills, technology-driven approach to online banking appeals to millennials' needs for simplicity and mobility. Chime offers "Banking Made Awesome."**

Chime

Generation Z

People born between 1997 and 2012 who make up the tweens to twenty-something markets.

go." In the past four years, Chime's customer base has grown from 75,000 to more than 3,000,000 accounts, and the online-only bank is adding another 250,000 accounts per month. In all, says Chime, it's "Banking Made Awesome."[19]

Generation Z. Hard on the heels of the millennials is **Generation Z**, young people born between 1997 and 2012. This tweens to young twenty-somethings group is now the largest generation alive in the United States—80 million strong, making up 26 percent of the population. They are also the most ethnically and culturally diverse generation. Gen Zers spend an estimated $43 billion to $143 billion annually of their own money and influence up to $333 billion of family spending.[20] These young consumers also represent tomorrow's markets—they are now forming brand relationships that will affect their buying well into the future.

Even more than the millennials, the defining characteristic of Gen Zers is their utter fluency and comfort with digital technologies. Generation Z takes Wi-Fi, smartphones, tablets, internet-connected game consoles, and digital and social media for granted—they've always had them—making this group highly mobile, connected, and social. "If they're awake, they're online," quips one analyst. They have "digital in their DNA," says another.[21]

Gen Zers blend the online and offline worlds seamlessly as they socialize and shop. According to recent studies, despite their youth, more than half of all Generation Z tweens and teens do product research before buying a product or having their parents buy it for them. Some 39 percent of Gen Zer girls find shopping inspiration from social media, 35 percent read newsletters from brands, and 33 percent don't mind when brands work with influencers they like. Of Gen Zers who shop online, more than half *prefer* shopping online in categories ranging from electronics, books, music, sports equipment, and beauty products to clothes, shoes, and fashion accessories.[22]

Companies in almost all industries market products and services aimed at Generation Z. However, marketing to Gen Zers and their parents presents special challenges. Traditional media and brick and mortar stores are still important to this group. But marketers know they must meet Gen Zers where they hang out and shop. Increasingly, that's in the online and mobile worlds.

Today's youth are notoriously fickle and hard to pin down. The key is to engage these young consumers and let them help to define their brand experiences. For example, to engage young consumers more deeply, lifestyle apparel retail American Eagle (AE) even invited Gen Zers to create its latest marketing campaign. Selected through social media, 10 Gen Z "cast members" used their phones and disposable cameras to create self-portraits of themselves in their own environments. The campaign ran across AE's own and other social media, where cast members also shared their individual stories and American Eagle experiences. "Social media is a valuable platform for self-expression for digital-native Gen Z consumers," says one retail analyst. "Turning the creative over to the [GenZ] cast members [let AE] showcase the individuality of its style and promote diversity, empowerment, and inclusion," helping AE to "make authentic, emotional connections with its Gen Z consumer base."[23]

Generation Alpha

Kids born after 2012, largely the children of the millennials.

Generation Alpha. The latest generational group is **Generation Alpha**, kids born after 2012. Although still a relatively small market, by 2025 this group will grow larger even than the millennials. The Alphas hold great promise for marketers. "Generation Alpha will be the most formally educated generation ever, the most technology-supplied generation ever, and globally the wealthiest generation ever," claims the social researcher who gave the group its name.[24]

The emerging Generation Alpha group already exerts substantial influence on the household buying decisions of its mostly millennial parents. Born about the same time that the Apple iPad first appeared, today's kids take technology for granted. "Forget pleas for a puppy. Today's kids demand gadgets," says an analyst, who quotes a pint-sized participant in a recent video as saying, "I'd rather have an iPad—better than a dog."

Gen Alphas are an important gateway to their parents. In one recent survey, 81 percent of U.S. Gen Alpha parents said their latest technology purchase—including smartphones, tablets, and TVs—was influenced by the activities and needs of their children. But Gen Alpha influence reaches well beyond technology. Research has shown that kids influence family decisions ranging from entertainment options and eating out to car purchases and family vacations.

More than just influencers, Gen Alphas are important future consumers who are just beginning to establish brand preferences. By winning them over early, marketers hope to build loyalty that will carry into their later lives. For example, Fitbit now markets Fitbit Ace, a simple-to-use activity-monitoring device for children that was a popular gift during the recent holiday season. According to Fitbit's CEO, the Ace is expanding the brand's user base by helping to "create long-term relationships within the family."

As the children of cord-cutting millennials, Gen Alphas tend to watch less TV than previous generations. But they are perfectly comfortably with digital media and IoT technologies. As a result, marketers are testing innovative new ways to reach them. For example, P&G's Crest Kids brand has sponsored a "Chompers" Alexa skill for the Amazon Echo smart speaker that helps and encourages kids to brush their teeth properly. As kids brush for the recommended two minutes, Alexa tells them jokes, sings songs, and shares fun facts.

An important Generation Alpha marketing concern involves children's privacy and their vulnerability to marketing pitches. Companies marketing to this group must do so responsibly or risk the wrath of parents and public policy makers.

Generational Marketing. Do brands need to create separate products and marketing programs for each generation? Some experts warn that marketers need to be careful about turning off one generation each time they craft a product or message that appeals effectively to another. Others caution that each generation spans decades of time and many socioeconomic levels. For example, Generation Z spans tweens and teens to early 20s, each group with its own beliefs and behaviors.

Thus, marketers need to form more precise age-specific segments within each group. More important, defining people by their birth date may be less effective than segmenting them by lifestyle, life stage, or the common values they seek in the products they buy. We will discuss many other ways to segment markets in Chapters 5 and 7.

● **Generational marketing: Baby boomers and millennials are now moving over to make room for younger Generation Alpha.**

Syda Productions/Shutterstock

The Changing American Family

The traditional household consists of a husband, wife, and children (and sometimes grandparents). Yet the historic American ideal of the two-child, two-car suburban family has lately been losing some of its luster.

In the United States, fewer than half of today's households contain married couples, down from 76 percent in 1940. Married couples with children under 18 represent only about 19 percent of the nation's 128 million households. Married couples without children represent 30 percent, and single parents are another 8 percent. A full 35 percent are nonfamily households—singles living alone or unrelated adults of one or both sexes living together.[25]

More people are divorcing or separating, choosing not to marry, marrying later, remarrying, or marrying without intending to have children. Currently, 17 percent of all new marriages are interracial or interethnic, and 17 percent of married, same-sex couple households are raising children.[26] The changing composition of today's modern American families is increasingly reflected in popular movies and television shows, such as

Modern Family and Amazon's *Transparent*. Marketers must consider the special needs of nontraditional households because they are now growing more rapidly than traditional households. Each group has distinctive needs and buying habits.

The number of working women has also increased greatly, growing from 38 percent of the U.S. workforce in 1970 to about 57 percent of the workforce today. American women now make up 40 percent of primary family breadwinners in households with children under 18. Among households made up of married couples with children, 62 percent are dual-income households; only the husband works in 28 percent. Meanwhile, more men also stay home with their children and manage the household while their wives go to work.[27]

Companies are now adapting their marketing to reflect the changing dynamics of American families. For example, whereas fathers were once ignored or portrayed as dolts in family-oriented ads, today's advertisers are showing more caring and capable dads. For example, nobody puts much thought into a commodity like toilet paper, but Georgia-Pacific created emotional involvement for its Angel Soft brand and its "Be soft. Be strong." positioning with a heartwarming commercial featuring a single father raising a daughter, from infant to young adulthood. The ad shows the sensitive and caring dad alone helping his daughter though the full range of childhood and teenage hurdles, closing with this advice: "When you're raising a child, be soft. When you're doing it alone, be strong. Life takes softness and strength." Another ad in the series showed a caring dad advising and consoling his teenage son after the break-up of his first true love.[28]

Other ads reflect the evolving diversity in modern American households. For example, Campbell Soup's "Your Father" commercial—part of the brand's "Made for Real. Real Life" campaign—featured a real-life same-sex couple feeding their son Campbell's Star Wars soup as they mimicked Darth Vader's famous Star Wars line "I am your father." The commercial, like others in the campaign, aligned the brand with the company's purpose: "Real food that matters for real life moments." Similarly, General Mills ran a series of commercials for Cheerios featuring an interracial couple and their daughter portraying typical young family scenarios—from the daughter pouring Cheerios on her sleeping dad's chest after learning that Cheerios are good for your heart to her negotiating for a new puppy after learning that she is going to have a baby brother. Said a General Mills marketer, "At Cheerios, we know there are many kinds of families and we celebrate them all."[29]

Geographic Shifts in Population

Americans are a mobile people, with about 10 percent of all U.S. residents moving each year. Over the past few decades, the U.S. population has shifted from the Snowbelt states to the Sunbelt states. The West and South have grown, whereas the Midwest and Northeast states have lost population.[30] Such population shifts interest marketers because people in different regions buy differently.

Also, for more than a century, Americans have been moving from rural to metropolitan areas. In the 1950s, they made a massive exit from the cities to the suburbs. Today, the migration to the suburbs continues. And more and more Americans are moving to "micropolitan areas," small cities located beyond congested metropolitan areas, such as Minot, North Dakota; Boone, North Carolina; Traverse City, Michigan; and Concord, New Hampshire. These smaller micros offer many of the advantages of metro areas—jobs, restaurants, diversions, community organizations—but without the population crush, traffic jams, high crime rates, and high property taxes often associated with heavily urbanized areas.[31]

The shift in where people live has also caused a shift in where they work. For example, the migration to micropolitan and suburban areas has resulted in a rapid increase in the number of people who "telecommute"—working remotely at home or in a remote office with the help of PCs, tablets, smartphones, and broadband internet access. One recent study found that 43 percent of employed Americans spend at least some time working remotely.[32]

Many marketers are actively courting the lucrative telecommuting market. For example, online applications such as Citrix's GoToMeeting and Cisco's WebEx help people who telecommute or work remotely connect. And companies ranging from Salesforce.com to Google, IBM, and Slack offer cloud computing applications that let people collaborate

Slack takes the hardest part of all our jobs — communication — and makes it simpler, more pleasant, and more productive. Whether you're collaborating, brainstorming, striking deals, approving expenses, standing up with your team or sitting down with a new client, you can do that all in Slack. And then everyone is in the loop, no one's in the dark, and it's all time-stamped and searchable.

Research, sell, forecast, design, negotiate, deliberate, merge, deploy, resolve, secure, facilitate, build and create in one place. Slack. It's where work happens.

Try it with your team at
slack.com

⬤ Working remotely: Apps like Slack let people working remotely collaborate anywhere and everywhere through the internet and mobile devices.

Slack Technologies, Inc.

from anywhere and everywhere through the internet and mobile devices. ⬤ For example, Slack has been described as "a messaging app on steroids." It provides a shared digital workspace that connects people across remote offices and remote teams through real-time individual and group messaging, chat rooms, file sharing, video calls, and integrations with other cloud-based apps and services. Slack (an acronym for Searchable Log of All Conversations and Knowledge) is "where work happens, for millions of people around the world, every day."[33]

Additionally, for telecommuters who can't work fully at home, companies such as ShareDesk, DaVinci, and Regus rent out fully equipped shared office space. For a daily, monthly, or yearly fee, telecommuters who work away from a main office can rent shared space that includes the same amenities of a regular office, from networked computers, printers, and copiers to conference rooms and lounge spaces.

A Better-Educated, More White-Collar, More Professional Population

The U.S. population is becoming better educated. For example, in 2017, 90 percent of the U.S. population over age 25 had completed high school and 34 percent had a bachelor's degree or better, compared with 66 percent and 16 percent, respectively, in 1980.[34] The workforce also is becoming more white-collar. Job growth is now strongest for professional workers and weakest for manufacturing workers. Between 2016 and 2026, of 30 occupations projected to have the fastest employment growth, most require some type of postsecondary education.[35] The rising number of educated professionals affects not just what people buy but also how they buy.

Increasing Diversity

Countries vary in their ethnic and racial makeup. The United States has often been called a melting pot, where diverse groups from many nations and cultures have melted into a single, more homogenous whole. Instead, the United States seems to have become more of a "salad bowl" in which various groups have mixed together but have maintained their diversity by retaining and valuing important ethnic and cultural differences.

Marketers now face increasingly diverse markets, both at home and abroad, as their operations become more international in scope. The U.S. population is about 60 percent non-Hispanic white, with Hispanics at almost 19 percent, African Americans at over 13 percent, and Asian Americans at about 6 percent, with the remaining groups being Native Hawaiian, Pacific Islander, American Indian, Eskimo, or Aleut. The nation's ethnic populations are expected to explode in coming decades. By 2060, Hispanics will be about 28 percent of the population, African Americans will be about 15 percent, and Asian Americans will increase to 9 percent.[36]

Most large companies, from P&G, Walmart, and McDonald's to Toyota and Marriott, now target specially designed products, ads, and promotions to one or all of these diverse groups. For example, consider Marriott:[37]

> As part of its #LoveTravels campaign, Marriott launched a social media effort targeted specifically at Hispanic consumers. In a YouTube video series, Hispanic stars shared inspiring stories about their pride of heritage and related what travel means to them. In addition to YouTube videos, Marriott rolled out web and mobile ads on Pandora, Facebook, Twitter, and Instagram, hoping to inspire genuine and real conversations regarding culture and travel in the Hispanic community.
>
> More broadly, the long-running, award-winning Marriott #Love Travels campaign features inclusive efforts targeting a wide range of diverse groups, ranging from Hispanics, whites, Blacks, and Asians to same-sex couples with kids and the transgender community. The #LoveTravels website links visitors to more than a dozen inspiring video portraits of diverse Americans and their love of travel. "Marriott welcomes all," says the website. "Love is a universal language understood by all, and when it travels, it has the power to bridge cultures and inspire discovery around the world—connecting people, place, and purpose."

Diversity goes beyond ethnic heritage. For example, many major companies explicitly target gay and lesbian consumers. According to one estimate, the 4.5 percent of U.S. adults who identify themselves as lesbian, gay, bisexual, transgender, or questioning (or queer) (LGBTQ) have buying power of nearly $1 trillion.[38] As a result of TV shows such as *Modern Family, Transparent,* and *Gotham;* movies like *Boy Erased* and *Bohemian Rhapsody;*

and openly gay celebrities and public figures such as Neil Patrick Harris, Ellen DeGeneres, Jason Collins of the Washington Wizards, and Apple CEO Tim Cook, the LGBTQ community has increasingly emerged in the public eye.

Brands in a wide range of industries are now targeting the LGBTQ community with specific ads and marketing efforts. For example, Macy's and Best Buy run regular ads for their wedding registries featuring same-sex couples. Starbucks recently ran a holiday ad showing a same-sex couple leaning in for a kiss while holding a Starbucks cup together. Frito-Lay launched limited-edition Doritos Rainbows, multicolored chips demonstrating the brand's "expression of inclusion and support for individuality." And Wells Fargo became one of the first banks to feature an LGBTQ couple in a national TV ad campaign. The heartwarming commercial, featuring a lesbian couple adopting a deaf child, is part of a nine-commercial series that also spotlights other diverse customer groups. Says a Wells Fargo representative, "We. . . embrace diversity in every aspect, internally and externally. This [campaign] is a very important and natural progression of [that value] in how we serve our customers."[39]

Another attractive diversity segment is individuals with disabilities. One in four U.S. adults has a disability, representing a market of anywhere from $200 to $550 billion in annual spending power. Most individuals with disabilities are active consumers. For example, one study found that the segment spends $17.3 billion on 73 million business or leisure trips every year.[40]

● **Targeting consumers with disabilities: Toyota's "Start Your Impossible" campaign included ads highlighting inspirational real-life stories of athletes who overcame mobility challenges, such Paralympic gold medalist alpine skier Lauren Woolstencroft.**

Bonny Makarewicz/EPA/Shutterstock; Editorial/Alamy Stock Photo

How are companies trying to reach consumers with disabilities? Many marketers adapt their products and services to meet the needs of this market. For example, Microsoft's "accessibility team" adapts the company's products, services, and technologies to people with a wide range of disabilities, including vision, hearing, learning, mobility, or cognitive differences. As just one example, the company recently introduced the Xbox Adaptive Controller, a customizable device that lets gamers with disabilities play using whatever abilities they possess through their hands, feet, mouth, head, or otherwise. A recent ad features nine-year-old Owen, whose physical challenges make it difficult to use a typical controller, surrounded by friends urging him on as he wins a video game with the special Xbox controller. "What I like about the adaptive controller is no matter how your body is or how fast you are, you can play," says Owen. "When everybody plays, we all win," concludes the ad.[41]

Other marketers recognize that the worlds of people with disabilities and those without disabilities are often one in the same. Marketers such as McDonald's, Verizon Wireless, Nike, Samsung, Nordstrom, Toyota, and Apple have featured people with disabilities in their mainstream marketing. ● For instance, Toyota's "Start Your Impossible" campaign, which ran during the recent Olympic and Paralympic Winter Games, included ads highlighting inspirational real-life stories of athletes who overcame mobility challenges. One ad featured Canadian Para alpine skier Lauren Woolstencroft, born missing her left arm below the elbow as well as both legs below the knees, overcoming tremendous odds to become a legendary Paralympic gold medalist. "Toyota believes that mobility goes beyond cars," says the company. "It is about enabling everyone the freedom of movement."[42]

As the population in the United States grows more diverse, successful marketers will continue to diversify their marketing programs to take advantage of opportunities in fast-growing segments.

> **Author Comment** | The economic environment can offer both opportunities and threats. For example, in the post–Great Recession era of more sensible consumer spending, "value" has become the marketing watchword.

The Economic Environment

Markets require buying power as well as people. The **economic environment** consists of economic factors that affect consumer purchasing power and spending patterns. Economic factors can have a dramatic effect on consumer spending and buying behavior. For example, the Great Recession of 2008 to 2009 and its aftermath hit American consumers hard. After two decades of overspending, new economic realities forced consumers to bring their consumption back in line with their incomes and rethink their buying priorities.

Economic environment

Economic factors that affect consumer purchasing power and spending patterns.

In today's post-recession era, consumer spending is again on the rise. However, even as the economy has strengthened, rather than reverting to their old free-spending ways, Americans are retaining an enthusiasm for frugality. Each generational group faces financial challenges. For example, many boomers are watching their retirement accounts; many Gen Xers are facing the financial responsibilities of raising families, sending kids to college, and supporting aging parents; and many millennials are saddled with the expenses of paying back student loans and buying new homes.

As a result, consumers have now adopted a back-to-basics sensibility in their lifestyles and spending patterns that will likely persist for years to come. The new, more frugal spending values don't mean that people have resigned themselves to lives of deprivation. As the economy has improved, consumers are again indulging in luxuries and bigger-ticket purchases, just more sensibly. They are looking for greater value in the things they do buy. In turn, companies in all industries—from discounters such as Target to luxury brands such as Lexus and Tiffany—are focusing on value for the money, practicality, and durability in their product offerings and marketing pitches.

● **Economic environment: Consumers adopted a new back-to-basics sensibility in their lifestyles and spending patterns. To serve the tastes of these more financially frugal buyers, companies like Target are emphasizing the "pay less" side of their value propositions.**

M Spencer Green/AP/Shutterstock

● For example, for years discount retailer Target focused increasingly on the "Expect More" side of its "Expect More. Pay Less." value proposition. Its carefully cultivated "upscale-discounter" image successfully differentiated it from Walmart's more hard-nosed "lowest-price" position. But when the economy soured and as buyers increasingly shifted toward low-priced and convenient online retailers such as Amazon, many consumers worried that Target's trendier assortments and hip marketing also meant higher prices. So Target has shifted its balance more toward the "Pay Less" half of the slogan, making certain that its prices are in line with Walmart's and that customers know it. Although still chic and trendy, Target's marketing now emphasizes practical price and savings appeals. Offering "more for your money" holds a prominent place in the Target mission. "We think a lot about your budget and how to give you the best value every time you shop with us," says the company.[43]

In adjusting to the economy, companies may be tempted to cut their marketing budgets and slash prices to coax customers into opening their wallets. However, although cutting costs and offering selected discounts can be important marketing tactics, smart marketers understand that making cuts in the wrong places can damage long-term brand images and customer relationships. The challenge is to balance the brand's value proposition with the current times while also enhancing its long-term equity. Thus, rather than slashing prices in uncertain economic times, many marketers hold the line on prices and instead explain why their brands are worth it.

Marketers should pay attention to changes in major economic variables that have a large impact on the marketplace, such as income, cost of living, and savings and borrowing patterns. Companies watch and predict these variables using economic forecasting. Businesses do not have to be wiped out by an economic downturn or caught short in a boom. With adequate warning, they can take advantage of changes in the economic environment.

Author | Today's enlightened
Comment | companies are developing environmentally sustainable strategies in an effort to create a world economy that the planet can support indefinitely.

The Natural and Technological Environments

OBJECTIVE 3-3 Identify the major trends in the firm's natural and technological environments.

The Natural Environment

Natural environment
The physical environment and the natural resources that are needed as inputs by marketers or that are affected by marketing activities.

The **natural environment** involves the physical environment and the natural resources that are needed as inputs by marketers or that are affected by marketing activities. At the most basic level, unexpected happenings in the physical environment—anything from weather to natural disasters—can affect companies and their marketing strategies. For example, during a recent cold winter—in which the term *polar vortex* gusted into the American vocabulary—sales suffered across a wide range of businesses, from florists and auto dealers to restaurants, airlines, and tourist destinations. In contrast, the severe weather boosted demand for products such as salt, snowblowers, winter clothing, and auto repair centers.

Although companies can't prevent such natural occurrences, they should prepare for dealing with them. For example, shipping companies such as FedEx and UPS maintain corps of meteorologists on their staffs to anticipate weather conditions that might inhibit on-time deliveries around the world. "Someone awaiting a package in Bangkok doesn't care if it snowed in Louisville, Kentucky," says a UPS meteorologist. "They want their stuff."[44]

At a broader level, environmental sustainability concerns have grown steadily over the past several decades. In many cities around the world, air and water pollution have reached dangerous levels. World concern continues to mount about the possibilities of global warming, and many environmentalists fear that we soon will be buried in our own trash.

Marketers should be aware of trends in the natural environment. One major trend involves growing *shortages of raw materials*. Renewable resources, such as forests and food, must be used wisely. Nonrenewable resources, such as oil, coal, and various minerals, pose a serious problem. Firms making products that require these scarce resources face large cost increases even if the materials remain available. Another environmental trend is *increased pollution*. Industry will almost always damage the quality of the natural environment, and companies are now stepping up to reduce their environmental footprints in production, distribution, packaging, and many other areas.

A third trend is *increased government intervention* in natural resource management. The governments in many countries now vigorously pursue environmental quality policies that affect marketing actions. In the United States, the Environmental Protection Agency (EPA) was created in 1970 to create and enforce pollution standards and conduct pollution research. In the future, companies doing business in the United States can expect continued strong controls from government and pressure groups. Instead of opposing regulation, many marketers are now helping to develop solutions to the materials and energy problems facing the world.

Environmental sustainability

Developing strategies and practices that create a world economy that the planet can support indefinitely.

Concern for the natural environment has now spawned a movement toward **environmental sustainability**. Today, enlightened companies go beyond what government regulations dictate. They are developing strategies and practices that create a world economy that the planet can support indefinitely. Environmental sustainability means meeting present needs without compromising the ability of future generations to meet their needs.

Many companies are responding to consumer demands with more environmentally responsible products. Others are developing recyclable or biodegradable packaging, recycled materials and components, better pollution controls, and more energy-efficient operations. ● Consider Walmart, for example. Through its own environmental sustainability actions and its impact on the actions of suppliers, Walmart has emerged in recent years as the world's super "eco-nanny":[45]

When it comes to sustainability, perhaps no company in the world is doing more good these days than Walmart. That's right—big, bad Walmart. The giant retailer is now one of the world's biggest crusaders for the cause of saving the world for future generations. For starters, Walmart is rolling out new high-efficiency stores, each one saving more energy than the last. These stores use wind turbines to generate energy, high-output linear fluorescent lighting to reduce what energy stores do use, and native landscaping to cut down on watering and fertilizer. Store heating systems burn recovered cooking oil from the deli fryers

● The natural environment: Walmart has emerged in recent years as the world's super "eco-nanny" through its own sustainability practices and its impact on the actions of its huge network of suppliers.

grzegorz knec/Alamy Stock Photo; beboy/Shutterstock

and motor oil from the Tire and Lube Express centers. All organic waste, including produce, meats, and paper, is hauled off to a company that turns it into mulch for the garden. Walmart is committed to eventually using 100 percent renewable energy in all of its stores and distribution centers (it's currently at 28 percent) and sending zero waste to landfills (currently down to just 19 percent).

Walmart not only is greening up its own operations but also has laid down the eco-law to its vast network of suppliers to get them to do the same, asking them to examine the carbon life cycles of their products and rethink how they source, manufacture, package, and transport these goods. It has developed the Walmart Sustainability Index program, which helps suppliers understand, monitor, and enhance the sustainability of their products and the supply chain. Through its Project Gigaton, Walmart is working with suppliers to reduce value chain emissions by one gigaton between 2015 and 2030—equivalent to the emissions from 100 million homes or 211 million cars for a year. As a result, Walmart suppliers have cut energy, water, materials, toxic ingredients, and other inputs while creating less waste and fewer emissions—for themselves as well as for Walmart stores and consumers. With its immense buying power, Walmart can humble even the mightiest supplier. When imposing its environmental demands on suppliers, Walmart has even more clout than government regulators. Whereas the EPA can only level nominal fines, Walmart can threaten a substantial chunk of a supplier's business.

Companies are learning that what's good for customer well-being and the planet can also be good business. For example, Walmart's eco-charge is about more than just doing the right thing. It also makes good business sense. More efficient operations and less wasteful products are not only good for the environment but also save Walmart money. "From a brass tack standpoint," says Walmart's Director of Sustainability, "the efficiency gains that you get through programs like energy efficiency and operating a smarter, better system result in some real financial savings." Lower costs, in turn, let Walmart do more of what it has always done best—save customers money.

Many companies today are looking to do more than just good deeds. More and more, companies are making environmental sustainability a part of their core missions. For example, outdoor apparel and equipment maker Patagonia donates 1 percent of its revenue annually to environmental causes and adheres fiercely to a "cause no unnecessary harm" to the environment mantra. More than just implementing sustainability practices, Patagonia wants to "reimagine a world where we take only what nature can replace."

| Author | Technological advances
Comment | are perhaps the most
dramatic forces affecting today's
marketing strategies. Just think about
the tremendous impact on marketing
of digital technologies—which
have exploded in years. You'll see
examples of the fast-growing world
of online, mobile, and social media
marketing throughout every chapter,
and we'll discuss them in detail in
Chapter 14.

The Technological Environment

The **technological environment** is perhaps the most dramatic force now shaping our world. Technology has released such wonders as antibiotics, air travel, the internet, smartphones, artificial intelligence, and driverless cars. It also has released such horrors as nuclear missiles and assault rifles. Our attitude toward technology depends on whether we are more impressed with its wonders or its blunders.

Technological environment
Forces that create new technologies, creating new product and market opportunities.

Digital technologies and the dawn of the Internet of Things (IoT) have created a brave new world of marketing. The seemingly unending barrage of digital advances is affecting every aspect of how consumers learn about, shop for, buy, and experience brands. In turn, the digital age gives marketers exciting opportunities for understanding consumers, creating new products, and engaging customers in more direct and meaningful ways. Two decades ago, even wide-eyed futurists would have had difficulty envisioning today's digital world:

Digital has become an inseparable part of everything we do as consumers. You see it in the products we buy—from wearable technology like Fitbits and Apple watches; to connected IoT smarthome devices such as Nest monitors, Sonos wireless speakers, and Google smarthome gadgets; to digital-centric cars like the Tesla that can even self-drive for short periods. You see it in the ways we buy—from the massive shift from in-store to web and mobile shopping, to our reliance on apps and chatbots, to the way we relish brand experiences enhanced by augmented reality and other digital wizardry. It's evident in the ways we engage with brands, through digital brand communities, web and mobile apps, and our constant companions, the social media. Need more shopping information or assistance? Just ask Amazon's Alexa or Apple's Siri, or even let them do the buying for you. Today, our consumer lives—our lives in general—are inexorably linked to all things digital. It has become a part of us, almost like in a Dan Brown novel in which a futurist predicts that humans will eventually evolve into beings that are half human and half artificial intelligence–fueled machines. Fiction? Far-fetched? Who knows.

Disney takes full advantage of digital technology in creating magical customer experiences at its Walt Disney World Resort. Five years ago, it introduced My Disney Experience, a web and mobile app that helps guests plan their trips and then manage their visits in real time while at the resort. ● At the heart of the experience is an RFID-embedded wristband called the "MagicBand":[46]

● **Marketing technology: Disney takes full advantage of digital technology in creating magical customer experiences at its Walt Disney World Resort.**

GREGG MATTHEWS/The New York Times/Redux

Wearing a MagicBand at the Walt Disney World Resort opens up a whole new level of Disney's famed magic. After registering for cloud-based MyMagic+ services, with the flick of your wrist you can enter a park or attraction, buy dinner or souvenirs, skip lines at certain attractions, or even unlock your hotel room. But Disney has only begun to tap the MagicBand's potential for personalizing guest experiences. Future applications could be truly magical. Imagine, for example, the wonder of a child who receives a warm hug from Mickey Mouse or a bow from Prince Charming, who then greets the child by name and wishes her a happy birthday. Imagine animatronics that interact with nearby guests based on personal information supplied in advance. You get separated from family or friends? No problem. A quick scan of your MagicBand at a nearby directory could pinpoint the locations of your entire party. Linked to your Disney phone app, the MagicBand could trigger in-depth information about park features, ride wait times, FastPass check-in alerts, and your reservations schedule. Of course, the MagicBand also offers Disney a potential mother lode of digital data on guest activities and movements in minute detail, helping to improve guest logistics, services, and sales. If all this seems too Big Brother-ish, there will be privacy options—for example, letting parents opt out of things like characters knowing children's names. In all, such digital technologies promise to enrich the Disney experience for both guests and the company.

The technological environment changes rapidly, creating new markets and opportunities. However, every new technology replaces an older technology. Transistors hurt the vacuum-tube industry, digital photography hurt the film business, and digital downloads and streaming have hurt the DVD and book businesses. When old industries fight or ignore new technologies, their businesses decline. Marketers should watch the technological environment closely. Companies that do not keep up will soon find their products outdated. If that happens, they will miss new product and market opportunities.

As products and technologies become more complex, the public needs to know that these items are safe. Thus, government agencies investigate and ban potentially unsafe products. In the United States, the Food and Drug Administration (FDA) has created complex regulations for testing new drugs. The Consumer Product Safety Commission (CPSC) establishes safety standards for consumer products and penalizes companies that fail to meet them. Such regulations have resulted in much higher research costs and longer times between new product ideas and their introduction. Marketers should be aware of these regulations when applying new technologies and developing new products.

> Author | Even the strongest free-
> Comment | market advocates agree
> that the system works best with at
> least some regulation. But beyond
> regulation, most companies want
> to be socially responsible. We'll dig
> deeper into marketing and social
> responsibility in Chapter 20.

The Political–Social and Cultural Environments

OBJECTIVE 3-4 Explain the key changes in the political and cultural environments.

The Political and Social Environment

Political environment
Laws, government agencies, and pressure groups that influence and limit various organizations and individuals in a given society.

Marketing decisions are strongly affected by developments in the political environment. The **political environment** consists of laws, government agencies, and pressure groups that influence or limit various organizations and individuals in a given society.

Legislation Regulating Business

Even the strongest advocates of free-market economies agree that the system works best with at least some regulation. Well-conceived regulation can encourage competition and ensure fair markets for goods and services. Thus, governments develop *public policy* to guide commerce—sets of laws and regulations that limit business for the good of society as a whole. Almost every marketing activity is subject to a wide range of laws and regulations.

Legislation affecting business around the world has increased steadily over the years. The United States and many other countries have many laws covering issues such as competition, fair-trade practices, environmental protection, product safety, truth in advertising, consumer privacy, packaging and labeling, pricing, and other important areas (see ● **Table 3.1**).

Understanding the public policy implications of a particular marketing activity is not a simple matter. In the United States, there are many laws created at the national, state, and local levels, and these regulations often overlap. For example, aspirin products sold in Dallas are governed by both federal labeling laws and Texas state advertising laws. Moreover, regulations are constantly changing; what was allowed last year may now be prohibited, and what was prohibited may now be allowed. Marketers must work hard to keep up with changes in regulations and their interpretations.

Business legislation has been enacted for a number of reasons. The first is to *protect companies* from each other. Although business executives may praise competition, they sometimes try to neutralize it when it threatens them. Therefore, laws are passed to define and prevent unfair competition. In the United States, such laws are enforced by the Federal Trade Commission (FTC) and the Antitrust Division of the Attorney General's office.

The second purpose of government regulation is to *protect consumers* from unfair business practices. Some firms, if left alone, would make shoddy products, invade consumer privacy, mislead consumers in their advertising, and deceive consumers through their packaging and pricing. Rules defining and regulating unfair business practices are enforced by various agencies.

The third purpose of government regulation is to *protect the interests of society* against unrestrained business behavior. Profitable business activity does not always create a better quality of life. Regulation arises to ensure that firms take responsibility for the social costs of their production or products.

International marketers will encounter dozens, or even hundreds, of agencies set up to enforce trade policies and regulations. In the United States, Congress has established federal regulatory agencies, such as the FTC, the FDA, the Federal Communications Commission, the Federal Energy Regulatory Commission, the Federal Aviation Administration, the Consumer Product Safety Commission, the Environmental Protection Agency, and hundreds of others. Because such government agencies have some discretion in enforcing the laws, they can have a major impact on a company's marketing performance.

New laws and their enforcement will continue to increase. Business executives must watch these developments when planning their products and marketing programs. Marketers need to know about the major laws protecting competition, consumers, and society. They need to understand these laws at the local, state, national, and international levels.

Increased Emphasis on Ethics and Socially Responsible Actions

Written regulations cannot possibly cover all potential marketing abuses, and existing laws are often difficult to enforce. However, beyond written laws and regulations, business is also governed by social codes and rules of professional ethics.

Socially Responsible Behavior. Enlightened companies encourage their managers to look beyond what the regulatory system allows and simply "do the right thing." These socially responsible firms actively seek out ways to protect the long-run interests of their consumers and the environment.

● **Table 3.1** | **Major U.S. Legislation Affecting Marketing**

Legislation	Purpose
Sherman Antitrust Act (1890)	Prohibits monopolies and activities (price-fixing, predatory pricing) that restrain trade or competition in interstate commerce.
Federal Food and Drug Act (1906)	Created the Food and Drug Administration (FDA). It forbids the manufacture or sale of adulterated or fraudulently labeled foods and drugs.
Clayton Act (1914)	Supplements the Sherman Act by prohibiting certain types of price discrimination, exclusive dealing, and tying clauses (which require a dealer to take additional products in a seller's line).
Federal Trade Commission Act (1914)	Established the Federal Trade Commission (FTC), which monitors and remedies unfair trade methods.
Robinson-Patman Act (1936)	Amends the Clayton Act to define price discrimination as unlawful. Empowers the FTC to establish limits on quantity discounts, forbid some brokerage allowances, and prohibit promotional allowances except when made available on proportionately equal terms.
Wheeler-Lea Act (1938)	Makes deceptive, misleading, and unfair practices illegal regardless of injury to competition. Places advertising of food and drugs under FTC jurisdiction.
Lanham Trademark Act (1946)	Protects and regulates distinctive brand names and trademarks.
National Traffic and Safety Act (1958)	Provides for the creation of compulsory safety standards for automobiles and tires.
Fair Packaging and Labeling Act (1966)	Provides for the regulation of the packaging and labeling of consumer goods. Requires that manufacturers state what the package contains, who made it, and how much it contains.
Child Protection Act (1966)	Bans the sale of hazardous toys and articles. Sets standards for child-resistant packaging.
Federal Cigarette Labeling and Advertising Act (1967)	Requires that cigarette packages contain the following statement: "Warning: The Surgeon General Has Determined That Cigarette Smoking Is Dangerous to Your Health."
National Environmental Policy Act (1969)	Establishes a national policy on the environment. The 1970 Reorganization Plan established the Environmental Protection Agency (EPA).
Consumer Product Safety Act (1972)	Establishes the Consumer Product Safety Commission (CPSC) and authorizes it to set safety standards for consumer products as well as exact penalties for failing to uphold those standards.
Magnuson-Moss Warranty Act (1975)	Authorizes the FTC to determine rules and regulations for consumer warranties and provides consumer access to redress, such as the class action suit.
Children's Television Act (1990)	Limits the number of commercials aired during children's programs.
Nutrition Labeling and Education Act (1990)	Requires that food product labels provide detailed nutritional information.
Telephone Consumer Protection Act (1991)	Establishes procedures to avoid unwanted telephone solicitations. Limits marketers' use of automatic telephone dialing systems and artificial or prerecorded voices.
Americans with Disabilities Act (1991)	Makes discrimination against people with disabilities illegal in public accommodations, transportation, and telecommunications.

(Continued)

● **Table 3.1** | **Major U.S. Legislation Affecting Marketing (*Continued*)**

Legislation	Purpose
Children's Online Privacy Protection Act (2000)	Prohibits websites or online services operators from collecting personal information from children without obtaining consent from a parent and allowing parents to review information collected from their children.
Do-Not-Call Implementation Act (2003)	Authorizes the FTC to collect fees from sellers and telemarketers for the implementation and enforcement of a national Do-Not-Call Registry.
CAN-SPAM Act (2003)	Regulates the distribution and content of unsolicited commercial email.
Financial Reform Law (2010)	Created the Bureau of Consumer Financial Protection, which writes and enforces rules for the marketing of financial products to consumers. It is also responsible for enforcement of the Truth-in-Lending Act, the Home Mortgage Disclosure Act, and other laws designed to protect consumers.

Almost every aspect of marketing involves ethics and social responsibility issues. Unfortunately, because these issues usually involve conflicting interests, well-meaning people can honestly disagree about the right course of action in a given situation. Thus, many industrial and professional trade associations have suggested codes of ethics. And more companies are now developing policies, guidelines, and other responses to complex social responsibility issues.

The boom in online, mobile, and social media marketing has created a new set of social and ethical issues. Critics worry most about online privacy issues. There has been an explosion in the amount of personal digital data available. Users themselves supply some of it. They voluntarily place highly private information on social media sites, such as Facebook or LinkedIn, or on genealogy sites that are easily searched by anyone with a computer or a smartphone.

However, much of the information is systematically developed by businesses seeking to learn more about their customers, often without consumers realizing that they are under the microscope. Legitimate businesses track consumers' online browsing and buying behavior and collect, analyze, and share digital data from every move consumers with their connected devices. Critics worry that these companies may now know *too* much and might use digital data to take unfair advantage of consumers.

Although most companies fully disclose their internet privacy policies and most try to use data to benefit their customers, abuses do occur. In recent years, consumer data breaches of major companies such as Facebook, Yahoo!, credit agency Equifax, Target, Uber, Sony, Marriott, and many others have threatened the privacy of hundreds of millions or even billions of individuals.[47] As a result, companies are tightening their data security and public policy makers are acting to protect consumer privacy. In Chapters 4 and 20, we discuss these and other societal marketing issues in greater depth.

Cause-Related Marketing To exercise their social responsibility and build more positive images, companies often link themselves to worthwhile causes. These days, every product seems to be tied to some cause. For example, State Farm reinforces its "Good Neighbor" positioning with a "Neighborhood of Good" program that encourages policyholders to volunteer at charitable organizations in their communities. P&G's Pampers brand partners with UNICEF to provide vaccines to knock out neonatal tetanus in 58 countries while its Gillette brand runs ads rallying against "toxic masculinity"—bullying and sexual harassment. And Whirlpool's Care Counts program places washing machines and dryers in schools so that at-risk kids can have clean clothes, increasing both their confidence and their attendance. The program boosted the attendance of 91 percent of participating children.[48]

Some companies are founded on cause-related missions. Under the concept of "values-led business" or "caring capitalism," their mission is to use business to make the world a better place. ● For example, Ben & Jerry's, a division of Unilever, has long prided itself on being a "values-led business," one that creates "linked prosperity" for everyone connected to the brand—from suppliers to employees to customers and communities:[49]

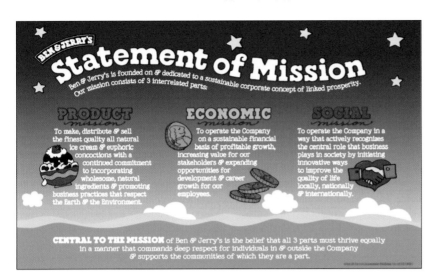

● **Cause-related marketing:** Ben & Jerry's three-part "linked prosperity" mission drives it to make fantastic ice cream (product mission), manage the company for sustainable financial growth (economic mission), and use the company "in innovative ways to make the world a better place" (social mission). Both Ben & Jerry's and its products are "Made of Something Better."

Ben & Jerry's Homemade Inc.

Under its three-part mission, Ben & Jerry's wants to make fantastic ice cream (product mission), manage the company for sustainable financial growth (economic mission), and use the company "in innovative ways to make the world a better place" (social mission). Ben & Jerry's backs its mission with actions. For example, the company is committed to using wholesome, natural, non-GMO, fair-trade-certified ingredients and buys from local farms. It employs business practices "that respect the earth and the environment," investing in wind energy, solar usage, travel offsets, and carbon neutrality. Its Caring Dairy program helps farmers develop more sustainable practices on the farm ("Caring Dairy means happy cows, happy farmers, and a happy planet"). The Ben & Jerry's Foundation awards nearly $2 million annually in grassroots grants to community service organizations and projects in communities across the nation. Ben & Jerry's also operates 14 PartnerShops, scoop shops that are independently owned and operated by community-based not-for-profit organizations. The company waives standard franchise fees for these shops.

Cause-related marketing has become a primary form of corporate giving. It lets companies "do well by doing good" by linking purchases of the company's products or services with benefiting worthwhile causes or charitable organizations (see Real Marketing 3.1). Brands with a higher purpose often produce better business results. According to one recent study, 64 percent of global consumers are now "belief-driven" buyers who will choose or avoid a brand based on its stand on societal issues.[50] Thus, beyond being socially admirable, cause-related marketing can make good economic sense for the company. For example, despite its values-led mission, or more probably because of it, Ben & Jerry's is the nation's second-largest ice cream brand behind only Breyers, with close to half a billion dollars in annual sales. And in addition to boosting school attendance, Whirlpool's Care Counts program also boosted the company's image, earning 350 million media impressions, more than 12 million video views across Facebook and YouTube, and a significant lift in purchase intent for the brand.[51]

Cause-related marketing has also stirred some controversy. Critics worry that cause-related marketing is more a strategy for selling than a strategy for giving—that "cause-related" marketing is really "cause-exploitative" marketing. Thus, companies using cause-related marketing might find themselves walking a fine line between an improved image and perceptions of exploitation or inauthenticity. However, if handled well, cause-related marketing can greatly benefit both the company and the cause. The company gains an effective marketing tool while building a more positive public image. The charitable organization or cause gains greater visibility and important new sources of funding and support. Spending on cause-related marketing in the United States skyrocketed from only $120 million in 1990 to $2.2 billion in 2019.[52]

Cultural environment

Institutions and other forces that affect society's basic values, perceptions, preferences, and behaviors.

> **Author | Comment |** Cultural factors strongly affect how people think and how they consume, so marketers are keenly interested in the cultural environment.

The Cultural Environment

The **cultural environment** consists of institutions and other forces that affect a society's basic values, perceptions, preferences, and behaviors. People grow up in a particular society that shapes their basic beliefs and values. They absorb a worldview that defines their relationships with others. The following cultural characteristics can affect marketing decision making.

Real Marketing 3.1

Cause-Related Marketing: Linking Brands, Consumers, and Causes

To see cause-related marketing in action, you need go no further than the checkout counter at your local retail store. Pay a dollar for a miracle balloon icon when checking out at Walmart or Sam's Club and you can support Children's Miracle Network Hospitals across the country. Throw in an extra dollar or two at Petco to help fund animal welfare and adoption programs. Point-of-sale donations at Best Buy benefit St Jude Children's Research Hospital. And the eBay for Charity program makes it easy for eBay's 171 million community members to donate to their favorite charities when buying or selling at the online market site. Such "checkout charity" programs raise hundreds of millions of dollars for worthy causes each year. At the same time, they add "purpose beyond profits" for retailers and their employees.

But cause-related marketing goes far beyond retailers. It seems that almost every brand supports some cause. And cause-related efforts go much deeper than simply collecting donations for charities. Instead, good cause-related marketing programs strategically link brands, causes, and consumers in authentic and meaningful ways that benefit all.

For example, for the past several years, Anheuser-Busch-owned Belgian brewer Stella Artois has teamed up with nonprofit Water.org to support the cause of providing clean water to people in developing countries. The partnership began with a Stella campaign titled "Buy a Lady a Drink," a series of videos that highlighted the plight of women around the world in their search for clean water. Research showed that women in developing areas spend a collective 200,000 hours each day collecting water; walking for miles, missing school, facing fights at public pumps, and going without when they fail.

The videos highlighted not only the woes of life without water but also the joys of life with it. Access to clean water allows women to care for their families, which allows families to earn incomes and pursue their dreams. Each video ended by urging viewers to "Help more women start new journeys" by buying limited-edition Stella beer glasses (chalices). Each artist-designed chalice was inspired by the cultural heritage of a specific country, including India, Ethiopia, Mexico, and Peru. For each chalice purchased, Stella gave $3.13 to Water.org, enough to give one person clean water for five years.

Stella Artois is still selling chalices, but the brand has extended the ways that consumers can support Water.org. For example, it recently launched a #PourItForward campaign. The campaign kicked off with a Super Bowl ad that resurrected two iconic characters—Jeff Bridges as "The Dude" from *The Big Lebowski* and Sara Jessica Parker as Carrie Bradshaw from *Sex and the City*. The two characters meet in a swanky restaurant, enjoy a Stella Artois, and "change up the usual." Beyond buying chalices, notes the ad, for every purchase of Stella Artois and every social media use of the hashtag #PourItForward, the company will make a donation to Water.org. "Together, we can change more lives," concludes Stella. "Together, let's #PourItForward." So far, with Stella's help. Water.org has positively transformed more than 17 million lives around the world with access to safe water and sanitation.

Some cause-related marketing efforts go beyond raising money and awareness for a specific cause—they become an integral part of a brand's positioning and identity. For example, five years ago, American Eagle Outfitter's Aerie intimate apparel and swimwear brand took a stand against the negative effects of the photoshopped images of female forms perpetuated by the media, marketers, and the modeling industry. It launched #AerieREAL, a campaign that pledged to use only unretouched images and videos of real women in its ads, stores, online, and social marketing content. The brand also committed to featuring women of all body types and ethnicities. Since then, #AerieREAL has grown into a full-blown body positivity and inclusivity movement.

As part of the far-reaching #AerieREAL campaign, Aerie has formed a partnership with the National Eating Disorder Association (NEDA). Aerie is the official corporate sponsor for NEDA Walks—community events filled with body-positive activities culminating in a walk symbolizing a unified fight against eating disorders. With thousands of supporters in more than 95 cities, NEDA Walks also raises money to fund eating disorder advocacy, research, and education.

Aerie supports the body positivity cause and NEDA with its ongoing #AerieREAL "Strong. Beautiful. Me." multimedia campaign. This year, the campaign features a new team of #AerieREAL role models, including plus-size model Iskra Lawrence, openly gay actress Samira Wiley, and Paralympian snowboarder Brenna Huckaby, each displaying their individuality in unretouched photos of themselves in Aerie apparel. To generate funds for NEDA, Aerie sells limited-edition "Strong. Beautiful. Me." tees and undies, donating 100 percent of sales to NEDA. Aerie is also matching customer donations as well as donating one dollar to NEDA for every unretouched swim photo shared in social media tagged @Aerie and #AerieREAL.

Whether it's something like checkout charity, supporting the work of a cause-related nonprofit, or making a cause an integral a part of the brand's identity, it's difficult to calculate the extent to which cause-related marketing contributes to a brand's prosperity. But research shows that today's consumers tend to favor brands with a purpose.

Aerie's #AerieREAL campaign pledges that it will use only unretouched images and videos of real women in its ads and other marketing content. The cause of body positivity and inclusivity is an integral part of the brand's identity.

MediaPunch Inc/Alamy Stock Photo

As for Aerie, the #AerieREAL campaign and positioning seems to be doing good things for both the cause and consumers. "By championing body diversity, Aerie is encouraging women and girls to live authentically," says NEDA's CEO. "We thank Aerie for helping to create a culture where all kinds of bodies are celebrated." And what's good for the cause and consumers is also good for the brand. American Eagle and Aerie consistently outperform competitors Abercrombie, Urban Outfitters, and Gap. Aerie is thriving at the same time that traditional mall apparel chains are declining. In fact, once-hot market leader Victoria's Secret, which still features oversexualized images of scantily clad models often aimed more at men than women—has faced steadily declining sales and market share in recent years, earning from one analyst the inglorious nickname "the Sears of Brassieres."[53]

The Persistence of Cultural Values

People in a given society hold many beliefs and values. Their core beliefs and values have a high degree of persistence. For example, most Americans believe in individual freedom, hard work, getting married, and achievement and success. These beliefs shape more specific attitudes and behaviors found in everyday life. *Core* beliefs and values are passed on from parents to children and are reinforced by schools, businesses, religious institutions, and government.

Secondary beliefs and values are more open to change. Believing in marriage is a core belief; believing that people should get married early in life is a secondary belief. Marketers have some chance of changing secondary values but little chance of changing core values. For example, family-planning marketers could argue more effectively that people should get married later than not get married at all.

Shifts in Secondary Cultural Values

Although core values are fairly persistent, cultural swings do take place. Consider the impact of popular music groups, movie personalities, and social media influencers on young people's style and clothing norms. Marketers want to predict cultural shifts to spot new opportunities or threats. The major cultural values of a society are expressed in people's views of themselves and others as well as in their views of organizations, society, nature, and the universe.

People's Views of Themselves. People vary in their emphasis on serving themselves versus serving others. Some people seek personal pleasure, wanting fun, change, and escape. Others seek self-realization through religion, recreation, or the avid pursuit of careers or other life goals. Some people see themselves as sharers and joiners; others see themselves as individualists. People use products, brands, and services as a means of self-expression, and they buy products and services that match their views of themselves.

Marketers can position their brands to appeal to specific self-view segments. For example, energy drink Red Bull targets 18- to 34-year-old athletes, busy professionals, college students, and travelers who view themselves as risk-taking fun-seekers—as active, adventuresome, youthful, and daring. The brand's energy-packed products, events, and marketing content fulfill its long-standing promise that "Red Bull gives you wings."

People's Views of Others. People's attitudes toward and interactions with others shift over time. In recent years, some analysts have voiced concerns that the digital age would result in diminished human interaction, as people buried themselves in social media pages or emailed and texted rather than interacting personally. Instead, today's digital technologies seem to be allowing allow people to connect more than ever. Basically, the more people meet, network, text, and socialize online, the more likely they are to eventually meet up with friends and followers in the real world.

However, these days, even when people are together, they are often "alone together." ● Groups of people may sit or walk in their own little bubbles, intensely connected to tiny screens and keyboards. One expert describes the latest communication skill as "maintaining eye contact with someone while you text someone else; it's hard but it can be done," she says. "Technology-enabled, we are

● People's views of others: These days, even when people are together, they are often "alone together."

Dmitriy Shironosov/123RF

able to be with one another, and also 'elsewhere,' connected to wherever we want to be."[54] Thus, whether technology-driven communication is a blessing or a curse is a matter of much debate.

This new way of interacting strongly affects how companies market their brands and communicate with customers. Consumers increasingly tap digitally into networks of friends and online brand communities to learn about and buy products and to shape and share brand experiences. As a result, it is important for brands to participate in these networks too.

People's Views of Organizations. People vary in their attitudes toward corporations, government agencies, trade unions, universities, and other organizations. By and large, people are willing to work for major organizations and expect them, in turn, to carry out society's work.

The past two decades have seen a sharp decrease in confidence in and loyalty toward America's business and political organizations and institutions. In the workplace, there has been an overall decline in organizational loyalty. Waves of company downsizings bred cynicism and distrust. In just the past decade, major corporate scandals, consumer data breaches, stories of Wall Street bankers' greed and incompetence, and other unsettling activities have resulted in a further loss of confidence in big business. Many people today see work not as a source of satisfaction but as a required chore to earn money to enjoy their nonwork hours. This trend suggests that organizations need to find new ways to win consumer and employee confidence.

People's Views of Society. People vary in their attitudes toward their society—patriots defend it, reformers want to change it, and malcontents want to leave it. People's orientation to their society influences their consumption patterns and attitudes toward the marketplace.

American patriotism has been increasing gradually for the past two decades. One annual consumer survey shows that some brands are highly associated with patriotism, such as Jeep, Levi Strauss, Disney, Coca-Cola, and Ford. Marketers respond with renewed "Made in America" pitches and ads with patriotic themes. For example, Coca-Cola launched a limited-edition red, white, and blue flag can surrounding the July 4 holiday with the patriotic song lyric "I'm proud to be an American" on the label.

Companies ranging from Jeep, The Home Depot, and Buffalo Wild Wings to National Geographic have run patriotic ads and promotions on Veteran's Day, Super Bowl Sunday, and other occasions. For example, Jeep's patriotic "More Than Just Words" ad, shown during the run-up to last year's Super Bowl and on digital and social platforms, struck a strong and sentimental chord with viewers. As the band OneRepublic plays "The Star Spangled Banner," the ad shows a succession of modern and historic images keyed to the words in the anthem—from kids playing baseball and farmers arising early to first responders at the scene, astronauts hurtling into space, and an aging veteran saluting. The two-minute video ad grabbed more than 52 million views on YouTube within just two months. "For all those who love this country, it's worth every second of viewing time," says one reporter.[55]

Although most such marketing efforts are tasteful and well received, waving the red, white, and blue can sometimes prove tricky. Flag-waving promotions can be viewed as corny or as token attempts to cash in on the nation's emotions.

People's Views of Nature. People vary in their attitudes toward the natural world—some feel ruled by it, others feel in harmony with it, and still others seek to master it. A long-term trend has been people's growing mastery over nature through technology and the belief that nature is bountiful. More recently, however, people have recognized that nature is finite and fragile; it can be destroyed or spoiled by human activities.

This renewed love of things natural has created a sizable market of consumers who seek out everything from natural, organic, and nutritional products to fuel-efficient cars and alternative medicines. For example, the U.S. organic food market now generates $44 billion in annual retail sales and is expected to reach $70 billion by 2025. And the market for organic, natural, and ethical beauty and personal care products is booming, with nearly 10 percent annual growth compared with only 2 percent grow for the market overall.[56]

As a result, almost every beauty and personal care products company offers organic and natural brands: Sephora's Future Naturals; Henkel's Nature Box; Garnier's Bio; and L'Oréal's Seed Phytonutrients, La Provençale Bio, and a host of others. P&G recently introduced Pure by Gillette shave gel and cream, a shaving line free from dyes, parabens, alcohol, and sulfates but rich in soothing ingredients such as aloe leaf juice, peppermint oil,

● Catering to the natural, organic, and ethical products trend: Unilever's Love Beauty and Planet brand has one goal: "To make you more beautiful and give a little love to our planet."

The Advertising Archives/Alamy Stock Photo

and menthol along with a fresh natural fragrance. ● And Unilever now markets Love Beauty and Planet, a complete line of hair, skin, and personal care products. Love Beauty and Planet products contain high-quality natural ingredients, sourced responsibly, and sold in packages made from post-consumer recycled plastics. They are free of silicones, parabens, and dyes; made with vegan formulas; and never tested on animals. "Love Beauty and Planet started with one goal," says the brand. "To make you more beautiful and give a little love to our planet."[57]

People's Views of the Universe. Finally, people vary in their beliefs about the origins of the universe and their place in it. Although most Americans practice religion, religious conviction and practice have been dropping off gradually through the years. According to a recent study, almost one in four (24 percent) Americans now say they are not affiliated with any particular faith, up from about 16 percent just one decade earlier. Among Americans under age 30, more than one-third say they are not currently affiliated with any particular religion.[58]

However, the fact that people are dropping out of organized religion doesn't mean that they are abandoning their faith. Some futurists have noted a renewed interest in spirituality, perhaps as a part of a broader search for a new inner purpose. People have been moving away from materialism and dog-eat-dog ambition to seek more permanent values—family, community, earth, faith—and a more certain grasp of right and wrong. Rather than calling it "religion," they call it "spirituality." One recent survey found that whereas Americans have become less religious in recent years, the share of people who feel a deep sense of "spiritual peace and well-being" as well as a deep sense of "wonder about the universe" has risen.[59] This changing spiritualism affects consumers in everything from the television shows they watch and the books they read to the products and services they buy.

Author Comment | Rather than simply watching and reacting to the marketing environment, companies should take proactive steps.

Responding to the Marketing Environment

OBJECTIVE 3-5 Discuss how companies can react to the marketing environment.

Someone once observed, "There are three kinds of companies: those who make things happen, those who watch things happen, and those who wonder what's happened." Many companies view the marketing environment as an uncontrollable element to which they must react and adapt. They passively accept the marketing environment and do not try to change it. They analyze environmental forces and design strategies that will help the company avoid the threats and take advantage of the opportunities the environment provides.

Other companies take a *proactive* stance toward the marketing environment. Rather than assuming that strategic options are bounded by the current environment, these firms develop strategies to change the environment. Companies and their products often create and shape new industries and their structures, products such as Ford's Model T car, Apple's iPod and iPhone, Google's search engine, and Amazon's online marketplace.

Even more, rather than simply watching and reacting to environmental events, proactive firms take aggressive actions to affect the publics and forces in their marketing environment. Such companies hire lobbyists to influence legislation affecting their industries and stage media events to gain favorable press coverage. They take to the social media and run blogs to shape public opinion. They press lawsuits and file complaints with regulators to keep competitors in line, and they form contractual agreements to better control their distribution channels.

By taking action, companies can often overcome seemingly uncontrollable environmental events. For example, whereas some companies try to hush up negative talk about their products, others proactively counter false information. Newell Rubbermaid's Crock-Pot slow cooker brand did this when an episode of a hit TV show wrongly portrayed the product as a potential home fire hazard:[60]

It happened in an episode of NBC's hit show *This Is Us.* The show's beloved patriarch died when the family's Pittsburgh home burned down in a fire caused by a faulty slow cooker much like your grandmother's 1970s' Crock-Pot. The incident went viral, creating a crisis for the Crock-Pot brand. Thousands of viewers took to Twitter to express both their grief and their intentions to toss out their Crock-Pots. As one fan tweeted: "Gee thanks #thisisus for ruining #CROCKPOT cooking. Now every time I use mine I'll be sad AND afraid."

Rather than sitting back, Crock-Pot reacted quickly with both humor and facts. It created its first-ever Twitter account—CrockPotCares—and posted a humorous "spoiler alert" to Facebook and other social media channels, complete with broken heart emojis and a Pittsburgh Steeler–branded Crock-Pot. "America's favorite dad and husband deserved a better exit and Crock-Pot shares in your devastation," read the message. "Don't further add to this tragedy by throwing your Crock-Pot Slow Cooker away. . . (grandma won't be too happy)." In the week that followed, Crock-Pot continued listening and responding online, expressing concern but with a bit of levity (#CrockPotIsInnocent). The brand also followed up with the facts. Media releases and social media posts noted, "For nearly 50 years, with over 100 million Crock-Pots sold, we have never received any consumer complaints similar to the fictional event portrayed in last night's episode." Thanks to its rapid "We miss him, too. But here are the facts" response, the Crock-Pot brand escaped with little or no long-term damage.

Marketing management cannot always control environmental forces. In many cases, it must settle for simply watching and reacting to the environment. For example, a company would have little success trying to influence geographic population shifts, the economic environment, or major cultural values. But whenever possible, smart marketing managers take a *proactive* rather than *reactive* approach to the marketing environment (see Real Marketing 3.2).

Real Marketing 3.2 | In the Social Media Age: When the Dialogue Gets Nasty

Marketers have hailed the internet and social media as the great way to engage customers and nurture customer relationships. In turn, today's more-empowered consumers use the digital media to share their brand experiences with companies and with each other. All of this back and forth helps both the company and its customers. But sometimes, the dialogue can get nasty. Consider the following examples:

• KFC has one of its worse weeks in history. It runs out of chicken. The blunder forces the company to close most of its 900 restaurants in England. Customers are not happy, igniting a social media firestorm. News crews interview angry customers, post the clips online, and then sit back and watch them go viral. In one, a woman rants that she was forced to eat at Burger King! In another, a young girl points to the closed KFC behind her and says, "Look at them. They're just chillin'. They're happy. Sorry, but I'm mad at them."

• Whole Foods Market is no stranger to folks taking online aim at its expensive gourmet products. But one experiment in the produce section causes quite a viral stir. Responding to high demand for convenience, the grocery chain puts single pre-peeled oranges in individual plastic containers at the eye-popping price of $5.99 a pound. But a single tweet puts the company on notice. Seeing a picture of the enshrined citrus at online image sharing community Imgur, customer Nathalie Gordon reposts the photo on Twitter with the quote "If only nature would find a way to cover these oranges so we didn't need to waste so much plastic on them." The hashtag #OrangeGate quickly takes flight, populated with negative Whole Foods Market potshots and memes.

• The airline industry thrives by overbooking flights. But one overbooked flight turns into a nightmare for United Airlines. With the boarding process complete, every seat is occupied by ticketed passengers. But United wants four seats for employees needing to make a connection to service another flight. After United's pleas for volunteers to give up their seats fail, the flight crew informs four passengers that they must vacate the plane. One man, a 67-year-old physician who claims he has to get home to work the next morning, refuses. The crew calls in the airport police, who forcibly remove the man, injuring him in the process, and drag him kicking and screaming from the plane. Within hours, video clips posted by troubled fellow passengers go viral, creating a well-earned image nightmare for United.

Extreme events? Not anymore. The internet and social media have turned the traditional power relationship between businesses and consumers upside down. In the good old days, disgruntled consumers could do little more than bellow at a company service rep or shout out their complaints from a street corner. Now, armed with only a smartphone

Today's empowered consumers: Whole Foods Market's decision to put single pre-peeled oranges in individual plastic containers caused a viral storm of #OrangeGate tweets. However, the retailer averted the potential PR disaster by responding within hours with its own humorous, self-critical social media posts admitting its mistake.

Kateryna Bibro/123RF

or tablet, they can take it public, airing their gripes to millions on social media sites, blogs, or even hate sites devoted exclusively to their least favorite corporations. "A consumer's megaphone is now [sometimes] more powerful than a brand's," says one ad agency executive. "Individuals can bring a huge company to its knees . . . simply by sharing their experiences and opinions on Facebook, Instagram, Twitter, Yelp, or other social forums."

Some online attacks air legitimate complaints that should be addressed. Others, however, are little more than anonymous, vindictive slurs that unfairly ransack brands and corporate reputations. Some of the attacks are only a passing nuisance; others can draw serious attention and create real headaches.

How should companies react to online attacks? The real quandary for targeted companies is figuring out how far they can go to protect their images without fueling the already-raging fire. One point on which all experts seem to agree: Don't try to retaliate in kind. "It's rarely a good idea to lob bombs at the fire starters," says one analyst. "Preemption, engagement, and diplomacy are saner tools." Such criticisms are often based on real consumer concerns and unresolved anger. Hence, the best strategy might be to proactively monitor and respond sincerely to the concerns they express.

For example, after its initial attempts to cool down angry British KFC customers with light-hearted Twitter posts only made them madder, KFC got serious and joined customers by talking a surprising shot at itself. It took out a full-page ad featuring an empty KFC bucket on which the letters in its brand were scrambled to form "FCK." The ad followed with a humble and sincere apology: "We're sorry. A chicken restaurant without chicken. It's not ideal. A huge apology to our customers. . . . Thank you for bearing with us." Although the ad might have been highly controversial in many countries, it was a perfect match for the British sense of humor. The artful response drew high praise in the social media, and when KFC restaurants reopened within the following week, they were once again serving chicken to throngs of cheerful customers.

Similarly, Whole Foods responded to #OrangeGate within hours with a response to the customer's viral tweet. "Definitely our mistake. These have been pulled. We hear you, and we will leave them in their natural packaging: the peel." The next day, Whole Foods even posted a humorous self-critical meme of its own. Over an image of four oranges in glass jars, the caption read, "IS THIS MORE A PEELING?" Whole Foods's prompt response derailed the negative #OrangeGate momentum and earned the company praise.

United Airlines's response to viral outrage over its forcible removal of a passenger was neither artful nor well-received. United's CEO fueled additional viral fury by taking 24 hours to issue a half-hearted apology only for "having to re-accommodate passengers," a response considered by both consumers and experts as "cold," "callous," and "a painfully-bad, jargony response." To make matters worse, the CEO circulated an internal memo to employees in which he referred to the removed passenger as "disruptive" and "belligerent." Within 48 hours, United's social sentiment had dropped 160 percent and its stock price had plummeted.

Many companies have now created teams of specialists who monitor online conversations and engage unhappy consumers. For example, Southwest Airlines has a state-of-the art social media listening center, staffed by 40 customer service experts who listen and respond 24/7 to customers online. They track Twitter comments, monitor Facebook groups, interact with bloggers, and check the company's presence on sites such as YouTube, Instagram, Flickr, and LinkedIn. So if someone posts an online comment, the company can respond promptly in a personal way.

Not long ago, Southwest's team helped avert what could have been a PR catastrophe when an engine exploded on a New York-to-Dallas flight, sending shrapnel through a window and leading to the airline's first-ever passenger fatality. Renowned for its emergency response strategy, only minutes after the incident, even as videos, images, and tweets of the incident were being posted by passengers on the flight, the Southwest listening center staff reacted. They crafted sincere, heartfelt responses and channeled the social media posts to people in various departments to assist in the response effort. The posting passengers were soon praising the company. "Southwest is a great company and they took really good care of us," said a firefighter who was onboard the flight. "There's no question in my mind as to who I'll be flying with again."

Thus, by monitoring and proactively responding to seemingly uncontrollable events in the environment, companies can prevent the negatives from spiraling out of control or even turn them into positives.[61]

Reviewing and Extending the Concepts

Objectives Review

In this and the next two chapters, you'll examine the environments of marketing and how companies analyze these environments to better understand the marketplace and consumers. Companies must constantly watch and manage the *marketing environment* to seek opportunities and ward off threats. The marketing environment consists of all the actors and forces influencing the company's ability to transact business effectively with its target market.

OBJECTIVE 3-1 Describe the environmental forces that affect the company's ability to serve its customers.

(pp 86–90)

The company's *microenvironment* consists of actors close to the company that combine to form its value delivery network or that affect its ability to serve customers. It includes the company's *internal environment*—its several departments and management levels—as it influences marketing decision making. *Marketing channel firms*—suppliers, marketing intermediaries, physical distribution firms, marketing services agencies, and financial intermediaries—cooperate to create customer value. *Competitors* vie with the company in an effort to serve customers better. Various *publics* have an actual or potential interest in or impact on the company's ability to meet its objectives. Finally, five types of customer *markets* exist: consumer, business, reseller, government, and international markets.

The *macroenvironment* consists of larger societal forces that affect the entire microenvironment. The six forces making up the company's macroenvironment are demographic, economic, natural, technological, political/social, and cultural forces. These forces shape opportunities and pose threats to the company.

OBJECTIVE 3-2 Explain how changes in the demographic and economic environments affect marketing decisions. *(pp 90–98)*

Demography is the study of the characteristics of human populations. Today's *demographic environment* shows a changing age structure, shifting family profiles, geographic population shifts, a better-educated and more white-collar population, and increasing diversity. The *economic environment* consists of factors that affect buying power and patterns. The economic environment is characterized by more frugal consumers who are seeking greater value—the right combination of good quality and service at a fair price. In turn, many companies are focusing on value for the money, practicality, and durability in their product offerings and marketing pitches.

OBJECTIVE 3-3 Identify the major trends in the firm's natural and technological environments. *(pp 98–101)*

The *natural environment* shows three major trends: shortages of certain raw materials, higher pollution levels, and more government intervention in natural resource management. Environmental concerns create marketing opportunities for alert companies. The *technological environment* creates both opportunities and challenges. The barrage of digital advances is affecting every aspect of how consumers learn about, shop for, buy, and experience brands. In turn, the digital age gives marketers exciting opportunities for understanding consumers, creating new products,

and engaging customers in more direct and meaningful ways. Companies that fail to keep up with technological change will miss out on new product and marketing opportunities.

OBJECTIVE 3-4 Explain the key changes in the political and cultural environments. *(pp 101–109)*

The *political environment* consists of laws, agencies, and groups that influence or limit marketing actions. The political environment has undergone changes that affect marketing worldwide: increasing legislation regulating business, strong government agency enforcement, and greater emphasis on ethics and socially responsible actions. The *cultural environment* consists of institutions and forces that affect a society's values, perceptions, preferences, and behaviors. The environment shows trends toward new technology-enabled communication, a lessening trust of institutions, increasing patriotism, greater appreciation for nature, a changing spiritualism, and the search for more meaningful and enduring values.

OBJECTIVE 3-5 Discuss how companies can react to the marketing environment. *(pp 109–111)*

Companies can passively accept the marketing environment as an uncontrollable element to which they must adapt, avoiding threats and taking advantage of opportunities as they arise. Or they can take a *proactive* stance, working to change the environment rather than simply reacting to it. Whenever possible, companies should try to be proactive rather than reactive.

Key Terms

Marketing environment (p 86)

OBJECTIVE 3-1

Microenvironment (p 86)
Macroenvironment (p 86)
Marketing intermediaries (p 88)
Public (p 88)

OBJECTIVE 3-2

Demography (p 90)
Baby boomers (p 91)
Generation X (p 91)
Millennials (Generation Y) (p 92)
Generation Z (p 93)
Generation Alpha (p 93)
Economic environment (p 97)

OBJECTIVE 3-3

Natural environment (p 98)
Environmental sustainability (p 99)
Technological environment (p 100)

OBJECTIVE 3-4

Political environment (p 101)
Cultural environment (p 105)

Discussion Questions

3-1 What are marketing intermediaries, and are they important for marketers? (AACSB: Written and Oral Communication; Reflective Thinking)

3-2 What are publics in the marketing context? Why are they important to marketers? Suggest the publics for a specific business. (AACSB: Communication; Reflective Thinking)

3-3 Why should marketers pay attention to geographic shifts in the U.S. population? (AACSB: Written and Oral Communication; Reflective Thinking)

3-4 Discuss the natural environment and the three trends that will impact future marketing plans. (AACSB: Written and Oral Communication)

3-5 Why should marketers play close attention to the political environment? (AASCB: Communication)

3-6 Provide an example of how people's views of nature might affect their food choices. (AACSB: Written and Oral Communication; Reflective Thinking)

Critical Thinking Exercises

3-7 Vice Media's Broadly site, which tells stories that focus on the experiences of women, gender-nonconforming people, and LGBTQ individuals, recently offered to the public The Gender Spectrum Collection, a stock photo library of more than 180 images of 15 transgender and nonbinary models (whose gender identities are not exclusively masculine or feminine). The goal was to avoid stereotypes that

result from misleading images of gender fluid and transgender people. Also, recent search results suggested that there is an unmet need for transgender and nonbinary models. How does the availability of the new stock photo library relate to diversity trends? (AACSB: Written and Oral Communication; Information Technology; Reflective Thinking)

3-8 Form a small group and discuss cultural trends in the United States. Research one of them in depth and create a presentation on the trend's impact on marketing. (AACSB: Written and Oral Communication; Reflective Thinking)

3-9 Visit engageforgood.com/halo-awards/ to learn about companies that have won Halo Awards for outstanding cause-related marketing programs. Present an award-winning case study to your class. (AACSB: Written and Oral Communication; Information Technology)

APPLICATIONS AND CASES

Online, Mobile, and Social Media Marketing #MeToo

Recent times have seen the rise of the #MeToo movement, focused on creating awareness and change relating to sexual harassment, assault, and violence in the workplace. At first, the movement centered on female Hollywood celebrities, such as Rose McGowan and Alyssa Milano, who alleged misconduct by producer Harvey Weinstein. However, once the silence was broken in Hollywood, many women around the world began using the #MeToo hashtag on Twitter and Facebook, pointing to their own experiences with workplace harassment or misconduct. The #MeToo wave rocked the world, ending the careers of several high-profile men, ranging from former news anchor Matt Lauer and celebrity chef Mario Batali to hip-hop mogul Russell Simmons and U.S. Senator Al Franken.

The #MeToo movement emboldened many women to step forward and speak out about toxic workplace environments and company cultures in high-profile companies. For example, after supermodel Kate Upton came forward alleging sexual harassment by Guess designer and co-founder Paul Marciano, Guess shares dropped 18 percent—more than $250 million in market value in one day. Many companies are reacting or taking proactive steps in response to the #MeToo movement. For example, after allegations surfaced regarding a toxic "bro culture" at ride-sharing service Uber, founder Travis Kalanick stepped down as CEO and the company fired many top-level executives. Newly hired CEO Dara Khosrowshahi took to LinkedIn to post Uber's new cultural norms.

3-10 Many businesses have now crafted responses to the #MeToo movement. Research the issue and discuss how companies are communicating their positions to customers. What online or social media platforms are they using? Are they communicating the message clearly and effectively? (AACSB: Written and Oral Communication; Information Technology; Reflective Thinking)

3-11 Is the #MeToo movement a marketing issue? How are customers likely to react to allegations of workplace harassment? How should companies deal with the issue, whether reactively or proactively? (AACSB: Written and Oral Communication; Reflective Thinking)

Marketing Ethics Automatic Auto Renewals

Consumers in the United Kingdom seem to be at the mercy of their own insurers. Hidden within the close print of the renewal notices is the true cost of renewing the insurance, often as much as a 100 percent increase. This is despite the fact that there have been no claims on the insurance and the value of the automobile may in fact have fallen since the previous year. Unwittingly, consumers have signed up to continuous payment authorities. In effect this means that the consumer has agreed to continue to buy the insurance year on year, regardless of any price increases, unless they contact the insurer and cancel it. If only cancelling were that simple. If the consumer fails to read the small print properly, they may be hit by a cancellation fee. With higher percentages of consumers checking insurance quotes on comparisons sites, insurers still take a chance on inertia when the customer receives their renewal notices. Insurers seem to rely on the fact that a certain percentage of consumers do not bother to read the documents, and if they do, they do not notice that the price is far higher than the previous year. The United Kingdom's Financial Conduct Authority, responsible for dealing with disputes arising out of financial services, receives around 500 complaints a year. However, this is just the tip of the iceberg. In response to the bad publicity the practice has had in the media, the Association of British Insurers (ABI) has proposed that renewal letters should state the amount that the consumer paid last year alongside the renewal price for the coming year. The suggestion has yet to be adopted.[62]

3-12 Discuss what it is about the competitive environment of the insurance industry that might allow this type of practice. (AACSB: Communication; Use of IT; Reflective Thinking)

3-13 Debate whether technology and access to comparison websites means that this type of practice is doomed. (AACSB: Communication; Use of IT; Reflective Thinking)

Marketing by the Numbers An Aging America

As marketers focus on millennials embarking on major first-time consumption decisions related to careers, homes, and families, another generation should not be forgotten: the aging baby boomers. The U.S. 65-and-older population will increase to almost 100 million people by 2060. One reason for this trend is the sheer size of the cohort to begin with—72 million people born between 1946 and 1964. Another major factor is that Americans are living longer. In 1950, the average life span was 68 years but is now 78.7 years. And the life-span gap between men and women is decreasing because of reduced smoking rates among men. In addition to longer life spans, families are spreading out—as children embark on careers and start their own families, they are no longer staying close to their hometowns. These factors contribute to a greater need for caregiver support for the elderly. There is already a proliferation of services such as "Visiting Angels" and "A Place for Mom." The number of boomers needing nursing home care could increase 75 percent by 2030, and the number of people with Alzheimer's disease could triple by 2050. The chart below shows the population estimates for the 65-and-over population for 2011 and 2016, the latest years for which data are available:

	2011	2016
Both sexes	41,364,093	49,244,195
Males	17,932,803	21,792,826
Females	23,431,290	27,451,369

3-14 Calculate the percentage change in the 65-and-over population between 2011 and 2016 for both sexes, males, and females. (AACSB: Analytic Reasoning)

3-15 How many more females than males age 65 and over were there in 2011 and 2016? What percentage of the population did females make up in each year? Draw some conclusions regarding these data. (AACSB: Written and Oral Communication; Analytic Reasoning)

Company Case Square: In Relentless Pursuit of a More Elegant Payment Experience

It happened one day at an art fair. Jim McKelvey, an artisan who worked in handblown glass, had an admirer of his work ready to buy a piece priced at $2,000. There was just one problem. The customer did not have that much cash, and Jim wasn't equipped to take credit cards. McKelvey couldn't close the deal and lost a valuable sale.

But there's a happy ending to this story. McKelvey quickly recognized that the problem he faced that day was common to small and medium-size businesses (SMBs) everywhere. Realizing how much money he was losing by not accepting credit cards got him going on solving the problem. McKelvey and partner Jack Dorsey came up with Square, the payment processing innovator that set fire to an industry. Today, Square is valued at $27 billion. So you might say that McKelvey's glass art piece is the most valuable piece of glass never sold.

Square's origins are not unlike the origins of most startup companies: The founders recognize a problem for which there is no current product or service solution and set out to solve it. The question is this: What created the problem that Jim McKelvey recognized that fateful day? The short answer: The consumer and marketing environment had changed, but businesses had yet to catch up.

The World before Square

When consumers used cash as the primary means of paying for goods and services, SMB owners had little problem selling their wares. But as the 1900s came to a close and more and more businesses accepted credit cards for payment, people carried less and less cash. This put SMBs at a disadvantage; many factors made the processing of credit cards difficult to impossible for them.

For starters, before Square and its many imitators, it was illegal for non-registered merchants to accept credit card payments. Registering with an approved credit card–processing terminal provider was expensive, with a substantial flat fee at the start and transaction fees higher than most SMBs could afford. Credit card processing was available to merchants only on a contract basis—when merchants signed, they were locked in. Adding to this complexity, the terms of the contracts were difficult to understand, often leading to unexpected fees.

If all this wasn't enough to keep most SMBs out of the credit card loop, when it came to accepting credit and debit cards, they still had to be approved. Like getting a bank loan, being approved for credit processing services was contingent on indications of financial strength and stability. Then, "even if you do get accepted by a traditional terminal provider to accept payments, you typically sign up for a contract that is at best opaque and probably not so fair," says Square's head of hardware. "There's a teaser rate, there are monthly fees, there's a variety of other fees, different cards cost different amounts."

Things started to change in the mid-1990s with the advent of e-commerce. As unlikely as it seems today, in the early days of eBay, buyers had to mail cash or a check to sellers before goods were shipped. Online payment processors like PayPal took care of that problem. But in the offline world, SMBs were still being excluded.

The Dongle That Changed Everything

Square launched in 2009. The idea was simple. Square would play the role of a big business, putting up the capital and assuming the risks of processing credit and debit card transactions. The promise of volume let Square form partnerships with credit card companies such as Visa and Mastercard, bypassing the credit card–processing companies altogether and negotiating lower fees. With low fees and minimal overhead, Square could make its services available to anyone—merchant or everyday individual—with no contract and no approval process. Merchants gained piece of mind from a simple structure of affordable transactions fees that were the same for all.

With the back-office part of payment processing sorted out, Square needed only to figure out the interface between the merchant and the customer. It developed the now-familiar Square dongle—a small yet elegant white plastic magstripe reader that plugged into the headphone port of Android or Apple iOs smartphones and tablets. The reader cost only $10 (free today), and the app that powered it was free. The combination of Square's hardware and software processed unencrypted, analog card information by digitizing it and sending it to Square's servers.

Thus, with nothing more than a smartphone, any small business owner could accept credit and debit card payments, whether selling from a traditional brick-and-mortar store, a street cart, a booth at an event, or even the trunk of a car. Highlighting the real benefits of Square, Dorsey notes that payment processing is "not even in the category of things [merchants] want to think about. They want to think about things like hiring people and introducing new ingredients."

Once Square launched, its founders quickly realized that it offered only one solution to a very narrow problem. Credit card payment processing was now available to all. But a one-size-fits-all solution is rarely perfect for anyone. For most SMBs, running a card through a reader connected to a smartphone did not give customers an impression of stability and security. There also remained the challenge of appealing to the segment of SMBs that already had contracts with terminal providers. "The biggest thing [we were] competing with, honestly, was that sellers tend to develop systems of doing things and it's the adage of 'If it's not broke, don't fix it,'" says Dorsey.

From its earliest days, Square's founders realized that they were far from solving the problems associated with payments. And given how rapidly the forces of the marketing environment were changing, their task would never be done. To meet the challenges, Dorsey and McKelvey developed a philosophy of never-ending innovation with the goal of making payments less painful and more elegant. By their nature, payments represented a transaction barrier to both buyer and seller. To remove the payment transaction barriers entirely, payments had to become perfectly seamless. And to fully accomplish that goal, Square would likely have to venture beyond the payment business.

Continuous Innovation

Following the original dongle, Square unleashed a string of products and services that rival the best of Silicon Valley for frequency and quality. Not only has Square partnered with Apple for various projects, references are often made to the "Apple-esque" design qualities of Square's hardware and software developments. Although the basic Square dongle is still available today, the device is the entry level and least sophisticated of Square's products. Consider the following:

Square Stand (2013). The Square Stand turned the Apple iPad into a more complete point-of-sale system. The integrated all-white stand sits on a merchant's countertop and serves as a customizable "register," letting employees ring up orders. Once the bill is finalized, Square Stand rotates to face customers, allowing them to swipe or insert their own card and sign on the touchscreen. Today, Square Stand has evolved to interface with commonly used peripherals such as printers, cash drawers, bar code scanners, and even Square's own Bluetooth Reader.

Square Bluetooth Reader (2015). Connecting to other Square devices via Bluetooth, the screenless Square Reader is a versatile device that reads chip-embedded cards as well as contactless forms of payment such as Apple Pay and Google Pay. The device can sit in an angled stand on a counter or can be handed to a customer to accept payment in almost any situation.

Square Register (2017). Despite the versatility of Square's many products, there were still customer transaction situations that were not yet "seamless." Enter Square Register—a stand-alone point-of-sale system designed and produced by Square. A stand holds the 13-inch anodized aluminum tablet that faces the employee. A second, smaller touchscreen faces the customer, either attached to the back of the stand or separate for situations where the customer is a bit removed from the register. Square Register interfaces with cards via magstripe or chip and also accepts contactless forms of payment. Like Stand, Register interfaces with a variety of peripherals.

Register saves money and time by not requiring an Apple iPad. But more important, Square developed Register to meet the needs of larger businesses that found Square's other products to be problematic. For example, iPads have to be updated frequently. For chains with multiple checkout lanes in multiple stores, updating each iPad in the company became a full-time job. Register solves this and other problems with a tablet that is stripped down in both hardware (for example, no battery) and software (only Square software). The result is a system that is faster, more powerful, and more reliable.

Square Terminal (2018). This is Square's all-in-one payment terminal. Like Register, the device is designed and produced by Square so that it doesn't rely on any additional hardware or software. It can stand alone or interface with other Square products. With a screen the size of a modern smartphone, Terminal accepts all forms of payment accepted by other Square products. Its touchscreen lets customers see and sign for their bill. And Terminal can also print receipts.

Square Terminal is Square's way of filling a niche that existed between its other products. More important, it seeks to fix "all the stuff" that's wrong with traditional credit card terminals. Square executives quickly point out the antiquity of standard terminals that still dominate the retail landscape, put in place by traditional payment processing companies such as Ingenico and First Data.

These devices have many issues that businesses and customers have just come to accept. For example, the keypad is small and clunky, resembling a handheld calculator of 40 years ago. The screens are tiny and do not let customers examine their complete bill. The older devices are also difficult to update with new capabilities, often requiring an entirely new hardware interface.

Beyond Exciting Hardware

Square designed each of its products with certain applications in mind. But the company's approach to innovation rests on the expectation that customers will apply its products in ways the company never imagined. "What's exciting to me about it is that it kind of resonates back to when we first started the company and we built the reader," explains Dorsey, referring to Terminal. "We had some idea of who would use it, but really no idea how it would end up being used. This has very similar properties where we'll probably be surprised at how people use it."

Once merchants get their hands on a Square device, they instinctively figure out how to make it work for them. While Square expected Terminal to be employed by everyone from "dentists to bowling alleys," it couldn't have imagined all the ways the product would be used. For example, field tests revealed that waitstaff in restaurants tote Terminal to diners' tables for on-the-spot payment. Salon operators hand Terminal to customers while they are still in the chair. In perhaps one of the most unexpected uses, a plastic surgeon began taking Terminal to the treatment room so that the bill could be reviewed with the patient and payment could be made in private, avoiding potential uncomfortable situations.

The Square universe also extends far beyond in-person payment processing. Square is invading PayPal's territory with online payment capabilities. It's Venmo-like Square Cash lets individuals send money to each other with the ease of an app. More important to SMBs, Square provides a full portfolio of business services, including creating and hosting online store platforms, omni-channel integration, payroll processing, loans, appointment scheduling, and much more. Thus, Terminal, Register, and Stand aren't just exciting pieces of hardware. They are gateways to an entire ecosystem of small-business essentials.

There's no question that Square has deeply disrupted the credit card payment establishment. Square's revenues have nearly tripled in the past three years to $3.3 billion. It also handled $84.66 billion in transaction payments—impressive but still a drop in the bucket when you consider that Square's potential market is "all transactions, online and off." More important is the potential of Square's portfolio. "Our approach has been to not just stop at the device, but the connection to the broader ecosystem of tools," says Dorsey. "We can handle your payroll, we can give you a loan, we can handle your appointments if you're a salon, in addition to walk-ins who come in to buy product and use [Terminal] to swipe a card. If we can tell a story that is bigger than one piece of hardware that is visible, then we tend to shift minds." In other words, Square's potential for growth is practically unlimited.[63]

Questions for Discussion

3-16 Describe how Square has evolved based on actors in the microenvironment.

3-17 Describe how Square has evolved based on the forces of the macroenvironment.

3-18 Are factors in the marketing environment not mentioned in this case affecting Square? Discuss.

3-19 Speculate on Square's future. What current and future trends may further shape the company?

4 Managing Marketing Information to Gain Customer Insights

OBJECTIVES OUTLINE

OBJECTIVE 4-1 Explain the importance of information in gaining insights about the marketplace and customers. See: **Marketing Information and Customer Insights** *(pp 118–120)*

OBJECTIVE 4-2 Define the marketing information system and discuss its parts. See: **Assessing Information Needs and Developing Data** *(pp 120–123)*

OBJECTIVE 4-3 Outline the role of marketing research and the steps in the marketing research process. See: **Marketing Research** *(pp 123–136)*

OBJECTIVE 4-4 Explain how companies analyze and use marketing information. See: **Analyzing and Using Marketing Information** *(pp 136–140)*

OBJECTIVE 4-5 Discuss the special issues some marketing researchers face, including public policy and ethics issues. See: **Other Marketing Information Considerations** *(pp 140–144)*

CHAPTER PREVIEW

In this chapter, we continue our exploration of how marketers gain insights into consumers and the marketplace. We look at how companies develop and manage information about important marketplace elements: customers, competitors, products, and marketing programs. To succeed in today's marketplace, companies must know how to turn mountains of marketing information from a slew of new sources into fresh customer insights that will help them engage customers and deliver greater value to them. As you'll see as the chapter unfolds, the marketing information and research industry is undergoing a major transformation. Traditional marketing research is giving way to an onslaught of new digital, online, mobile, and analytical technologies that enhance the marketer's ability to gather, analyze, communicate, and gain insights from data about consumers and markets.

Let's start with a story about marketing research and customer insights in action. In order to tailor its products to the market it operates in, Italian chocolate and confectionery manufacturer Ferrero derives fresh insights on customers and the marketplace from marketing information. The company's ability to use this information and capitalize on it by improving decision making and tailoring their offerings to the local market has been a key success factor in major and growing markets such as India.

FERRERO: Managing Marketing Information and Customer Insights

Ferrero SpA is an Italian manufacturer of branded chocolate and confectionery products and the third biggest chocolate producer and confectionery company in the world. Founded in 1946 in Alba, Italy, by Pietro Ferrero and still privately owned by the Ferrero family, it is among the reputable companies in the food-and-beverages sector: in the updated listings of Reputation Institute's Global RepTrak 100 for the year 2017, Ferrero was ranked highest for its innovation, governance, and citizenship. Its revenue in the fiscal year of 2017 was $13 billion, a 1.5 percent rise from the previous year. The company employs over 34,500 people worldwide. Because of its consistent commitment to innovation and customer focus, the company has outperformed its competitors in many markets.

The firm concentrates on meeting high standards; thus, it manufactures only in places where it is sure it can deliver consistently and establish a secure retail supply chain. The company strives to understand market preferences and has a proven track record of successfully managing marketing information and gaining customer insights. A prime example of this is when it created a new market for premium chocolate in India with the help of sophisticated marketing analysis.

When Ferrero entered India in 2004, the country did not really have a ready market for premium chocolates. India is a very price-sensitive country, and most brands offer products at low prices in small packs. Ferrero's sophisticated and ongoing analysis of the local market and its customers has paved the way for a new prod-

Ferrero is credited with developing the premium segment in India, a price-sensitive market where chocolates are sold at low prices in small packs.

Ekaterina Minaeva/Alamy Stock Photo

uct segment in that region. Premium chocolates now make up about 27 percent of the market in India. Besides Ferrero, several companies compete in this segment, including Cadbury, Nestlé, Mars, Hershey, and Lindt. Cadbury, with its Celebrations, Bourneville, and Silk brands, is the market leader, with more than 60 percent share in the premium segment and 70 percent overall. Within just a decade, Ferrero has garnered a 7.8 percent share of the Indian chocolate market. More notably, it is credited with developing the premium segment. When Ferrero launched its Rocher chocolates, the only competing brand was Cadbury Celebrations, which was priced between $1.50 and $2.65 per box. However, Ferrero has managed to successfully launch their product at $4.55 (per box of 12 chocolates). How did the Italian confectionery giant do it?

Ferrero launched Rocher in the country in 2007, and in 2009, it introduced the brands Tic Tac and Kinder Joy. The company continues to import Rocher, but in October 2011 it opened a factory in Baramati, in the state of Maharashtra, to produce a million Kinder Joy chocolates and 20 million pellets of Tic Tac daily, half of which is exported. India is now Ferrero's center for Asia, and the company has set up a branch office in Chennai, Tamil Nadu, to address this region's needs and expectations.

As early as 2004, Ferrero was convinced that there was a set of

consumers in India willing to pay a premium price for a box of chocolates. To gain and manage the appropriate marketing information and customer insights, Ferrero did not hire any market research firm when it was test-marketing Rocher but decided to approach the market on its own to better understand the Indian customer. The company set up a specific customer insights team as a center of excellence in market research. This team provided deep insight into the local market across all relevant aspects, such as new-product launches, packaging, recipes, and finding the ideal communication channels. In order to better understand the customer and their potential needs and wants as well as their habits, the Ferrero customer insights team as well as the management traveled to the metro cities as well as out of them, to Nagpur and other smaller markets in the interior. They also visited consumer homes to understand consumer habits and aspirations. As a result, Ferrero not only realized that there was a market for an expensive box of chocolates, even if it was sold in the local *kirana* store (a small neighborhood retail store in the Indian subcontinent), but they also discovered that consumers would buy expensive chocolates mostly during festivals, when they traditionally gift sweets.

Ferrero thus supplies Rocher all year round to modern retail stores, but *kirana* stores get these chocolates typically during the festival season (from October to

> Ferrero successfully analyzes and uses marketing information and customer insights to better tailor its offerings to the local market. Its ability to gain fresh understandings of customers and the marketplace from marketing information has become the basis for the company's success.

March). During the summer months, Ferrero distributors do not usually allow kirana stores to stock more than three to four boxes so that quality is not compromised because of a common lack of refrigeration facilities. Despite this limited availability during the summer, Ferrero Rocher had captured 14 percent share in the box chocolate category by 2014. In India, where the sheer variety of sweets is vast, where recipes vary from state to state, Ferrero has managed to lodge itself in the minds of the people as a luxury and exclusive product, and people are consuming and gifting these chocolates during local festivals in addition to other occasions when local sweets are consumed. It is worth emphasizing that Ferrero's growth comes despite a 30 percent import duty on chocolate.

Although both Cadbury and Nestlé sell premium brands, they derive the major share of their revenue from mass-market products. Ferrero, on the other hand, has successfully pursued a premium strategy instead of creating cheap variants. Tic Tac is priced at $0.15 while most mouth-freshener candies cost $0.01. Kinder Joy is an egg-shaped chocolate that comes with a toy for children, and to appeal to mothers it was positioned as a healthier alternative that contains more milk than cocoa.

The success behind Ferrero's product launches lies in its ability to manage marketing information and gain customer insights. New flavors of products are introduced only after conducting thorough research on Indian requirements and preferences. After further in-depth marketing research, the company successfully introduced an Indian flavor, "Elaichi Mint," to its Tic Tac brand in late 2014 to suit the local palate. This was the first time that the brand had introduced a local flavor in the market specifically to cater to the Indian audience. The new flavored Tic Tac mint had the strong flavor of cardamom and has the tag line "The Desi Mint." This condiment is widely used in India for its health benefits and as a mouth freshener after meals.

The Indian chocolate market has been growing at a rate of more than 19 percent between 2010 and 2020 and is projected to grow at an even higher rate in the future. In 2018 Ferrero's objective was to double its distribution network to one million retail outlets within a period of just 18-24 months. Although Nestlé and Cadbury together account for the majority of the chocolate market, Ferrero is expected to overtake Nestlé in the next few years thanks to the increasing popularity of Ferrero Rocher and Kinder Joy. The company's ability to capitalize on its management of marketing information by gaining customer insights and using them to improve decision-making may prove to be a valuable asset in this endeavor.[1]

AS THE FERRERO ROCHER STORY highlights, good products and marketing programs begin with good customer information and insights. Companies also need an abundance of information on competitors, resellers, and other actors and marketplace forces. But more than just gathering information, marketers must *use* the information to gain powerful *customer and market insights*.

Author Comment | Marketing information by itself has little value. The value is in the *customer insights* gained from the information and how marketers use these insights to make better decisions.

Marketing Information and Customer Insights

OBJECTIVE 4-1 Explain the importance of information in gaining insights about the marketplace and customers.

To create value for customers and build meaningful relationships with them, marketers must first gain fresh, deep insights into what customers need and want. Such customer insights come from good marketing information. Companies use these customer insights to develop a competitive advantage.

Although customer and market insights are important for building customer value and engagement, these insights can be very difficult to obtain. Customer needs and buying motives are often anything but obvious—consumers themselves usually can't tell you exactly what they need and why they buy. To gain good customer insights, marketers must effectively manage marketing information from a wide range of sources.

Marketing Information and Today's "Big Data"

With the recent explosion of information technologies, companies can now generate and find marketing information in great quantities. The marketing world is filled to the brim with information from innumerable sources—not just data collected from the company's marketing research and internal customer transaction data but real-time data flowing in from social media monitoring, connected devices, and other digital sources.

Consumers themselves are now generating tons of marketing information. Through their smartphones, PCs, and tablets—via online browsing and blogging, apps and social media interactions, texting and video, and geolocation data—consumers now volunteer a tidal wave of bottom-up information to companies and to each other.

Big data

The huge and complex data sets generated by today's sophisticated information generation, collection, storage, and analysis technologies.

Far from lacking information, most marketing managers are overloaded with data and often overwhelmed by it. This problem is summed up in the concept of **big data**. The term *big data* refers to the huge and complex data sets generated by today's sophisticated information generation, collection, storage, and analysis technologies. Every day, the people and systems of the world generate nearly 2.5 quintillion new bytes of data. Roughly 90 percent of the data in the world today has been created in only the past two years.[2]

Big data presents marketers with both big opportunities and big challenges. Companies that effectively tap this glut of data can gain rich, timely customer insights. However, accessing and sifting through so much data is a daunting task. For example, when a large consumer brand such as Coca-Cola or Apple monitors online discussions about its brand in tweets, blogs, social media posts, and other sources, it might take in a stunning 6 million public conversations a day, more than 2 billion a year. That's far more information than any manager can digest.

Thus, marketers don't need *more* information; they need *better* information. And they need to make better *use* of the information they already have. "When it rains, you can't just drink the water. It must be collected, purified, bottled, and delivered for consumption," observes a data expert. "Big data works the same way. It's a raw resource that is a few important steps away from being useful."[3]

Managing Marketing Information

Customer insights

Fresh marketing information-based understandings of customers and the marketplace that become the basis for creating customer value, engagement, and relationships.

The real value of marketing information lies in how it is used—in the **customer insights** that it provides. Based on such thinking, companies ranging from Unilever, PepsiCo, Starbucks, and McDonald's to Google and GEICO have restructured their marketing information and research functions. They have created *customer insights teams*, whose job it is to develop actionable insights from marketing information and work strategically with marketing decision makers to apply those insights. Consider Unilever:[4]

> Unilever's widespread marketing information activities are managed under its high-level Consumer & Market Insights (CMI) group. More than just doing marketing research, CMI is an "insights engine." Its job is to deeply understand consumer and market behaviors, to "inspire and provoke" actionable insights, and to feed those insights into decisions for its more than 400 brands. CMI works closely with managers to gather, consolidate, manage, and analyze data and insights from a rich variety of sources—ranging from focus groups, surveys, and subconscious measures to mingling with and observing customers in person and monitoring their digital and social media behaviors.
>
> CMI also helps Unilever marketers access insights from data already contained in the company's vast databases. For example, using artificial intelligence, one CMI program called PeopleWorld lets marketers use natural-language questions to mine information and insights from the company's huge global database of tens of thousands of research reports, troves of social media data, thousands of previous projects, and more. "A brand manager might ask, 'What hair-care problems concern middle-aged men in India?'" says one analyst. "PeopleWorld computers would intuit what's needed, search the vast repository of information on hair loss, dandruff, and similar topics, and instantly deliver a high-level overview." Through additional questions, the manager could drill down into the specifics of different consumer segments in various markets to form insights on how to serve them better.

Marketing information system (MIS)

People and procedures dedicated to assessing information needs, developing the needed information, and helping decision makers to use the information to generate and validate actionable customer and market insights.

Thus, companies must design effective marketing information systems that give managers the right information, in the right form, at the right time and help them to use this information to create customer value, engagement, and stronger customer relationships. A **marketing information system (MIS)** consists of people and procedures dedicated to assessing information needs, developing the needed information, and helping

● **FIGURE 4.1**
The Marketing
Information System

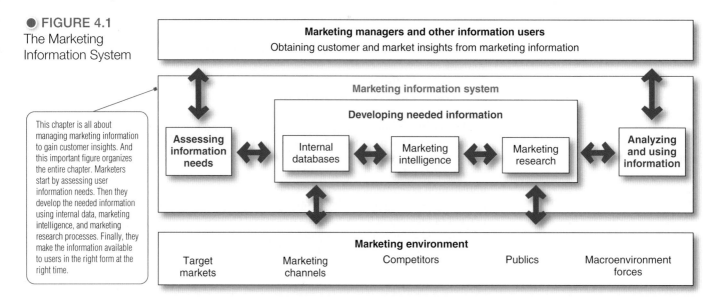

This chapter is all about managing marketing information to gain customer insights. And this important figure organizes the entire chapter. Marketers start by assessing user information needs. Then they develop the needed information using internal data, marketing intelligence, and marketing research processes. Finally, they make the information available to users in the right form at the right time.

decision makers use the information to generate and validate actionable customer and market insights.

● Figure 4.1 shows that the MIS begins and ends with information users—marketing managers, internal and external partners, and others who need marketing information and insights. First, it interacts with these information users to assess information needs. Next, it interacts with the marketing environment to develop needed information through internal company databases, marketing intelligence activities, and marketing research. Finally, the MIS helps users to analyze and use the information to develop customer insights, make marketing decisions, and manage customer engagement and relationships.

Author | The marketing information
Comment | system begins and
ends with users—assessing their
information needs and then delivering
information and insights that meet
those needs.

Assessing Information Needs and Developing Data

OBJECTIVE 4-2 Define the marketing information system and discuss its parts.

Assessing Marketing Information Needs

The marketing information system primarily serves the company's marketing and other managers. However, it may also provide information to external partners, such as suppliers, resellers, or marketing services agencies. For example, Walmart's Retail Link system gives key suppliers access to information on everything from customers' buying patterns and store inventory levels to how many items they've sold in which stores in the past 24 hours.[5]

A good marketing information system balances the information users would like to have against what they really need and what is feasible to offer. Some managers will ask for whatever information they can get without thinking carefully about what they really need. And in this age of big data, some managers will want to collect and store vast amounts of digital data simply because technology lets them. But too much information can be as harmful as too little. In contrast, other managers may omit things they ought to know, or they may not know to ask for some types of information they should have. The MIS must monitor the marketing environment to provide decision makers with information and insights they should have to make key marketing decisions.

Finally, the costs of obtaining, analyzing, storing, and delivering information can mount quickly. The company must decide whether the value of insights gained from additional information is worth the costs of providing it, and both value and cost are often hard to assess.

Developing Marketing Information

Author | The problem isn't *finding*
Comment | information; in this "big data" age, the world is bursting with information from a glut of sources. The real challenge is to find the *right* information—from inside and outside sources—and turn it into customer insights.

Marketers can obtain the needed information from *internal data, marketing intelligence*, and *marketing research*.

Internal Data

Internal databases

Collections of consumer and market information obtained from data sources within the company network.

Many companies build extensive **internal databases**, collections of consumer and market information obtained from data sources within the company's network. The marketing department furnishes information on customer characteristics and preferences, in-store and online sales transactions and interactions, and web and social media site visits. The customer service department keeps records of customer satisfaction or service problems. The accounting department provides detailed records of sales, costs, and cash flows. Operations reports on production, shipments, and inventories. The sales force reports on reseller reactions and competitor activities, and marketing channel partners provide data on sales transactions. Developing and harnessing such information can provide powerful customer insights and competitive advantage.

● For example, through skillful use of its richly developed internal customer database, online fashion retailer Stitch Fix has created a fast-growing core of satisfied and loyal customers:[6]

● **Internal data: Through skillful customer database development and use, Stitch Fix has built high levels of customer satisfaction and loyalty.**

Stitch Fix

Stitch Fix offers affordable personal styling services online to busy people on the go. It positions itself as "Your partner in personal style." Although "personal service" and "online" might seem a contradiction, Stitch Fix pulls it off with a team of more than 2,000 personal stylists and 80 data scientists who build and mine a deep customer database to determine each customer's unique sense of style. A customer begins by filling out a detailed style quiz that probes personal preferences with questions such as "What do you like to flaunt?" and "How adventurous do you want your Fix selections to be?" (One answer choice: "Frequently: Adventure is my middle name, bring it on!") The customer also rates photo montages of different fashions and can even submit links to her or his own social media pages.

Based on this rich customer database, combining sophisticated algorithms with large doses of human judgment (the stylist may completely override the algorithms), Stitch Fix assembles and ships the customer's fashion "Fix"—a box containing five clothing or accessory items carefully pegged to the customer's special tastes. The customer keeps what she or he likes and returns the rest, along with detailed feedback. The first Fix is the hardest because the stylist and algorithms are still learning. But after that, the Stitch Fix experience becomes downright addictive for many shoppers. Thanks to skillful use of its customer database, fast-growing Stitch Fix now sells more than $1.2 billion worth of clothing and accessories annually to more than 2.7 million clients.

Internal databases usually can be accessed more quickly and cheaply than other information sources, but they also present some problems. Because much internal information is often collected for other purposes, it may be incomplete or in the wrong form for making marketing decisions. Data also age quickly; keeping the database current requires a major effort. Finally, managing and mining the mountains of information that a large company produces require highly sophisticated equipment and techniques.

Competitive Marketing Intelligence

Competitive marketing intelligence

The systematic monitoring, collection, and analysis of publicly available information about consumers, competitors, and developments in the marketing environment.

Competitive marketing intelligence is the systematic monitoring, collection, and analysis of publicly available information about consumers, competitors, and developments in the marketplace. The goal of competitive marketing intelligence is to improve strategic decision making by understanding the consumer environment, assessing and tracking competitors' actions, and providing early warnings of opportunities and threats. Marketing intelligence techniques range from observing consumers firsthand to quizzing the company's own employees, benchmarking competitors' products, conducting online research, and monitoring social and mobile media in real-time.

Good marketing intelligence can help marketers gain insights into how consumers talk about and engage with their brands. Many companies send out teams of trained observers to mix and mingle personally with customers as they use and talk about the company's products. Other companies have set up state-of-the-art social media command centers that routinely monitor real-time brand-related online consumer and marketplace social and mobile media activity. Such centers can scour the digital environment, analyze brand-related conversations in real time to gain marketing insights, and respond quickly and appropriately.

● For example, Mastercard's digital intelligence command center—called the Conversation Suite—monitors, analyzes, and responds in real time to millions of online conversations around the world:[7]

The Conversation Suite monitors online brand-related conversations across 56 markets and 27 languages. It tracks social networks, blogs, on-line and mobile video, and traditional media—any and every digital place that might contain relevant content or commentary on Mastercard. At Mastercard's Purchase, New York, head-quarters, Conversation Suite staff huddle with managers from various Mastercard departments and business units in front of a giant 40-foot LED screen that displays summaries of ongoing global brand conversations, refreshed every four minutes. A rotating group of market-ing and customer service people spends two or three hours a day in the command center. "It's a real-time focus group," says a Mastercard marketing executive. "We track all mentions of Mastercard and any of our products, plus the competition."

Mastercard uses what it sees, hears, and learns in the Conversation Suite to improve its products and marketing, track brand performance, and spark meaningful customer conversations and engagement. Mastercard even trains "social am-bassadors," who can join online conversations and engage customers and brand influencers directly. "Today, almost everything we do [across the company] is rooted in insights we're gathering from the Conversation Suite," says another manager. "[It's] transforming the way we do business."

● **Competitive marketing intelligence: Mastercard's digital intelligence command center—called the Conversation Suite—monitors, analyzes, and responds in real time to millions of brand-related conversations across 43 markets and 26 languages around the world.**

Mastercard

Companies also need to actively monitor competitors' activities. They can monitor competitors' web and social media sites. For example, Amazon's Competitive Intelligence arm routinely purchases merchandise from competing sites to analyze and compare their assortment, speed, and service quality. Companies can use the internet to search specific competitor names, events, or trends and see what turns up. And tracking consumer con-versations about competing brands is often as revealing as tracking conversations about the company's own brands.

Firms use competitive marketing intelligence to gain early insights into competitor moves and strategies and to prepare quick responses. For example, Samsung routinely monitors real-time social media activity surrounding the introductions of Apple's latest iPhones, iPads, and other devices to quickly shape marketing responses for its own smart-phones and tablets. At the same time that Apple is unveiling the latest much-anticipated new models, Samsung marketing strategists are huddled around screens in a war room, monitoring not only each new device feature as it is presented but also the gush of online consumer commentary flooding blogs and social media channels. Even as the real-time consumer and competitive data surge in, the Samsung team is posting responses. Within only a few days, just as Apple's new models are hitting store shelves, Samsung is already airing TV, print, and social media responses that rechannel the excitement toward its own phone lines.[8]

Much competitor intelligence can be collected from people inside the company—executives, engineers and scientists, purchasing agents, and the sales force. The company can also obtain important intelligence information from suppliers, resellers, and key customers. Intelligence seekers can also pour through any of thousands of online databases. Some are free. For example, the U.S. Securities and Exchange Commission's database provides a huge stockpile of financial information on public competitors, and the U.S. Patent Office and Trademark database reveals patents that competitors have filed. For a fee, companies can also subscribe to any of the more than 3,000 online databases and information search services, such as D&B Hoover's, LexisNexis, and Dun & Bradstreet. Today's marketers have an almost overwhelming amount of competitor information only a few keystrokes away.

The intelligence and monitoring game goes both ways. Facing determined competitive marketing intelligence efforts by competitors, most companies take steps to protect their own information. Companies should try conducting marketing intelligence investigations of themselves, looking for potentially damaging information leaks. They should start by "vacuuming up" everything they can find in the public record, including job postings, court records, company advertisements and blogs, web pages, press releases, online business reports, social media site postings by customers and employees, and other information available to inquisitive competitors.

The growing use of marketing intelligence also raises ethical issues. Some intelligence-gathering techniques may involve questionable ethics. Clearly, companies should take advantage of publicly available information. However, they should not stoop to snoop. With all the legitimate intelligence sources now available, a company does not need to break the law or accepted codes of ethics to get good intelligence.

Marketing Research

Author Comment | Whereas marketing intelligence involves actively scanning the general marketing environment, marketing research involves more focused studies to gain customer insights related to specific marketing decisions.

OBJECTIVE 4-3 Outline the role of marketing research and the steps in the marketing research process.

In addition to marketing intelligence information about general consumer, competitor, and marketplace happenings, marketers often need formal studies that provide customer and market insights for specific marketing situations and decisions. For example, Starbucks wants to know how customers would react to a new breakfast menu item. Google wants to know how online and mobile searchers will react to a proposed redesign of its site. Or Samsung wants to know how many and what kinds of people will buy its next-generation, ultrathin televisions. In such situations, managers will need marketing research.

Marketing research
The systematic design, collection, analysis, and reporting of data relevant to a specific marketing situation facing an organization.

Marketing research is the systematic design, collection, analysis, and reporting of data relevant to a specific marketing situation facing an organization. Companies use marketing research in a wide variety of situations. For example, marketing research gives marketers insights into customer motivations, purchase behavior, and satisfaction. It can help them to assess market potential and market share or measure the effectiveness of pricing, product, distribution, and promotion activities.

Some large companies have their own research departments that work with marketing managers on marketing research projects. In addition, these companies—like their smaller counterparts—frequently hire outside research companies to consult with management on specific marketing problems and to conduct marketing research studies. Sometimes firms simply purchase data collected by outside firms to aid in their decision making.

Traditional Marketing Research in Transition

In recent years, as a host of new digital data-gathering technologies have burst onto the scene, traditional marketing research has undergone a major transformation. ● Traditional mainstays such as research surveys and focus groups, although still prevalent and powerful, are now giving way to newer, more agile, more immediate, and less costly digital data gathering methods. These new approaches—ranging from real-time social media, website, and online feedback monitoring to mobile device tracking—pose a threat to traditional marketing research. "The market research industry, as we have known it for decades, is disappearing," proclaims one industry observer. "It is being absorbed into a rapidly transforming collection of market intelligence subdisciplines."[9]

● **Marketing research in transition:** Traditional mainstays such as research surveys, although still prevalent and powerful, are now giving way to newer, more agile, more immediate, and less costly digital data gathering methods.

Andriy Popov/123RF

Today's fast and agile decision making often calls for fast and agile marketing information and research—call it *just-in-time research*. In such situations, speed often matters more than research rigor and precision. "If marketing managers can, at the tap of a button, see the views, clicks, likes, and shares of a new ad campaign, as well as listen to the roar—or silence, depending upon its success—of social media comments; then why would they be willing to wait four weeks for a [market research study's] bar chart to tell them that their spontaneous awareness has gone up?" asks an analyst. "Traditional research is in danger of being not only slower but also less insightful than other sources of information."[10] Marketing researchers must adjust to the new pace of information.

Although its role is changing, however, traditional marketing research is still widely used and very important. For many marketing decisions, information quality and rigor are more important than speed, convenience, and lower cost. The traditional research approaches, although often more time-consuming and expensive, can allow for deeper, more focused probing, especially into the whys and wherefores of consumer attitudes and behavior.

Thus, along with the threats, the rise of new digital research platforms also presents the marketing research industry with tremendous opportunities. When combined, the traditional and new digital approaches can greatly enhance the marketer's ability to gather, analyze, communicate, and gain insights from data about consumers and markets.

The key for marketers is to blend the traditional and new approaches into a unified marketing information system that yields agile but deep and complete marketing information and insights. New digital approaches can provide immediate and affordable access to real-time data on the wants, whens, wheres, and hows of consumer buying activities and responses. That frees traditional marketing research approaches to dig more deeply and rigorously into the whys. "In spite of all the benefits digital approaches can deliver," says one analyst, they "should be viewed not solely as a substitute for existing methods but as a new approach that can complement and enhance what has come before." "There has never been a better time to be an expert in market research," concludes another analyst. "But to meet the opportunity at hand, researchers need to get a handle on the biggest trends, tools, and technology shaping the industry."[11]

The marketing research process has four steps (see ● **Figure 4.2**): defining the problem and research objectives, developing the research plan, implementing the research plan, and interpreting and reporting the findings.

Defining the Problem and Research Objectives

Marketing managers and researchers must work together closely to define the problem and agree on research objectives. The manager best understands the decisions for which information is needed, whereas the researcher best understands marketing research and how to obtain the information. Defining the problem and research objectives is often the hardest step in the research process. The manager may know that something is wrong without knowing the specific causes.

In this age of big data, marketers might be tempted to simply turn their data scientists loose on mountains of big data in the search for problems and insights. But effective research calls for a blend of both well-directed and open-minded analysis. On the one hand, data analytics can be more effective when directed toward well-considered problems. The market researcher "must first ask smart questions," says one data expert, and

This first step is probably the most difficult but also the most important one. It guides the entire research process. It's frustrating and costly to reach the end of an expensive research project only to learn that you've addressed the wrong problem!

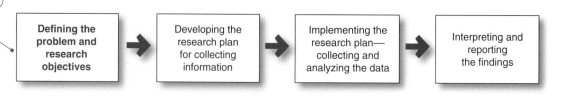

● FIGURE 4.2
The Marketing
Research Process

| Defining the problem and research objectives | Developing the research plan for collecting information | Implementing the research plan—collecting and analyzing the data | Interpreting and reporting the findings |

then "wrangle the relevant data and uncover insights." On the other hand, says another expert, "you must approach it with an open mind and be willing to embrace new insights. A lot of this is about turning over rocks and looking for little moments of surprise. That's where you find the magic."[12]

After the problem has been defined carefully, the manager and the researcher must set the research objectives. A marketing research project might have one of three types of objectives. The objective of **exploratory research** is to gather preliminary information that will help define the problem and suggest hypotheses. The objective of **descriptive research** is to describe things, such as the market potential for a product or the demographics and attitudes of consumers who buy the product. The objective of **causal research** is to test hypotheses about cause-and-effect relationships. For example, would a 10 percent decrease in tuition at a private college result in an enrollment increase sufficient to offset the reduced tuition? Managers often start with exploratory research and later follow with descriptive or causal research.

The statement of the problem and research objectives guides the entire research process. The manager and the researcher should put the statement in writing to be certain that they agree on the purpose and expected results of the research.

Developing the Research Plan

Once researchers have defined the research problem and objectives, they must determine the exact information needed, develop a plan for gathering it efficiently, and present the plan to management. The research plan outlines sources of existing data and spells out the specific research approaches, contact methods, sampling plans, and instruments that researchers will use to gather new data.

Research objectives must be translated into specific information needs. ● For example, suppose that Nordsee, the German-based seafood chain with more than 400 franchises throughout Europe, wants to know how consumers would react to the addition of "vegan fish" to its menu. In Germany, around 8 million people are vegetarian and 1.3 million are vegan. According to estimates, about 2,000 vegetarians and 200 vegans are added daily. However, vegan offerings at fast-food chains are usually limited to sides, such as fries or salads with no cheese. Adding vegan meals could help attract new customers and help Nordsee become a dominant player for vegan offerings. The proposed research might call for the following specific information:[13]

- The demographic, economic and lifestyle characteristics of current Nordsee customers: Do current customers have family members who do not eat fish? Would Nordsee need to target a new segment of customers?

- The characteristics and usage patterns of the broader population of fast-food and fast-casual diners: What do they need and expect from such restaurants? Where, when, and how do they use them, and what existing quality, price, and service levels do they value? The new Nordsee offering would require strong, relevant, and distinctive positioning in the crowded fast-food market.

- Impact on the Nordsee customer experience: Would vegan fish offerings be consistent in quality with its famous fish burgers?

- Nordsee employee reactions to vegan fish: Would restaurant employees buy into such a non-traditional product? Would they be able to prepare and present it properly?

- Forecast of vegan fish sales and profits: Would vegan fish create enough new sales to make it a lasting and profitable menu item?

Exploratory research

Marketing research to gather preliminary information that will help define problems and suggest hypotheses.

Descriptive research

Marketing research to better describe marketing problems, situations, or markets, such as the market potential for a product or the demographics and attitudes of consumers.

Causal research

Marketing research to test hypotheses about cause-and-effect relationships.

● A decision by Nordsee to add "vegan fish" would call for marketing research that provides specific information.

Toni Genes/Shutterstock

Nordsee's marketers would need these and many other types of information to decide whether to introduce vegan fish and, if so, the best way to do it.

Secondary data
Information that already exists somewhere, having been collected for another purpose.

Primary data
Information collected for the specific purpose at hand.

The research plan should be presented in a *written proposal*. A written proposal is especially important when the research project is large and complex or when an outside firm carries it out. The proposal should cover the management problems addressed, the research objectives, the information to be obtained, and how the results will help management's decision making. The proposal also should include estimated research costs.

To meet the manager's information needs, the research plan can call for gathering secondary data, primary data, or both. **Secondary data** consist of information that already exists somewhere, having been collected for another purpose. **Primary data** consist of information collected for the specific purpose at hand.

Gathering Secondary Data

Researchers usually start by gathering secondary data. The company's internal database provides a good starting point. However, the company can also tap into a wide assortment of external information sources.

Companies can buy secondary data from outside suppliers. For example, Nielsen sells shopper insight information from more than 900,000 participating stores around the world. Experian Simmons carries out a full spectrum of consumer studies that provide a comprehensive view of the American consumer. The U.S. MONITOR service by Kantar Futures sells information on important social and lifestyle trends. Kantar's Cultural Streetscapers can give marketers "an on-the-ground view of anything that's shaping the marketplace of tomorrow (and today): from broad societal shifts to breakthrough trends and unique consumer segments." These and other firms supply high-quality data to suit a wide variety of marketing information needs.[14]

Using *commercial online databases*, marketing researchers can conduct their own searches of secondary data sources. General database services such as ProQuest and LexisNexis put an incredible wealth of information at the fingertips of marketing decision makers. Beyond commercial services offering information for a fee, almost every industry association, government agency, business publication, and news medium offers free information to those tenacious enough to find their websites or apps.

Internet search engines can also be a big help in locating relevant secondary information sources. However, they can also be very frustrating and inefficient. For example, a Chick-fil-A marketer Googling "fast-food vegan chicken" would come up with more than 42 million hits. Still, well-structured, well-designed online searches can be a good starting point to any marketing research project.

Secondary data can usually be obtained more quickly and at a lower cost than primary data. Also, secondary sources can sometimes provide data an individual company cannot collect on its own—information that either is not directly available or would be too expensive to collect. For example, it would be too expensive for a consumer products brand such as Coca-Cola or Tide to conduct a continuing retail store audit to find out about the market shares, prices, and displays of its own and competitors' brands. But those marketers can buy store sales and audit data from IRI, which provides data from more than 100,000 retail stores in markets around the nation.[15]

Secondary data can also present problems. Researchers can rarely obtain all the data they need from secondary sources. For example, Chick-fil-A will not find existing information regarding consumer reactions about vegan chicken tenders in the fast-food setting. Even when data can be found, the information might not be very usable. The researcher must evaluate secondary information carefully to make certain it is *relevant* (fits the research project's needs), *accurate* (reliably collected and reported), *current* (up-to-date enough for current decisions), and *impartial* (objectively collected and reported).

Primary Data Collection

Secondary data provide a good starting point for research and often help to define research problems and objectives. In most cases, however, the company must also collect primary data. ● **Table 4.1** shows that designing a plan for primary data collection calls for decisions on *research approaches*, *contact methods*, the *sampling plan*, and *research instruments*.

● Table 4.1 | Planning Primary Data Collection

Research Approaches	Contact Methods	Sampling Plan	Research Instruments
Observation	Mail	Sampling unit	Questionnaire
Survey	Telephone	Sample size	Mechanical instruments
Experiment	Personal	Sampling procedure	
	Online		

Research Approaches

Research approaches for gathering primary data include observation, surveys, and experiments. We discuss each one in turn.

Observational research
Gathering primary data by observing relevant people, actions, and situations.

Observational Research. **Observational research** involves gathering primary data by observing relevant people, actions, and situations.

Researchers often observe consumer behavior to glean customer insights they can't obtain by simply asking customers questions. For instance, many new menu items at pizza giant Domino's come from its stores, where franchisees observe special requests from customers and fiddle accordingly to adapt existing offerings. The new menu ideas then come to corporate test kitchens, where they are tested using the company's 12 "sensory booths." Each booth is outfitted with a slot for sliding pizza slices to subjects and devices for getting feedback about product appearance, taste, and preferences. Beyond testing new products, Domino's also uses the observation booths to test improvements in existing products and reactions to ingredients from new suppliers.[16]

Ethnographic research
A form of observational research that involves sending trained observers to watch and interact with consumers in their "natural environments."

Marketers not only observe what consumers do but also observe what consumers are saying. As discussed earlier, marketers now routinely listen in on consumer conversations on social media, blogs, and websites. Observing such naturally occurring feedback can provide inputs that simply can't be gained through more structured and formal research approaches.

A wide range of companies also use **ethnographic research**. Ethnographic research involves sending observers to watch and interact with consumers in their "natural environments." The observers might be trained anthropologists and psychologists or company researchers and managers. Consider Intuit, maker of Turbo Tax and QuickBooks financial software:[17]

● Ethnographic research: Under Intuit's "follow me home" program, teams of Intuit employees visit customers in their homes or offices to watch them use the company's products in real life.

Pixel-Shot/Shutterstock

Most companies want to get close to their customers, but Intuit carries it to extremes. ● Under the company's "follow-me-home" program, small, well-trained teams of employees visit customers' homes and offices to watch them experience the company's products in real life—everything from removing the shrink-wrap to applying the software. The teams don't interview the customers; they simply observe. After each visit, the teams debrief immediately "so you get a complete picture faster," says Intuit CEO Brad Smith. Intuit conducts some 10,000 hours of follow-me-home visits a year; Smith himself devotes 60 to 100 hours a year to such visits. "The underlying reality is that you can't [always] believe what customers tell you," notes one observer. "Customer behavior is the truth." CEO Smith agrees: "What you get from a follow-me-home you can't get from a data stream. You've gotta look somebody in the eye and feel the emotion."

Observational and ethnographic research often yield the kinds of details that just don't emerge from traditional research questionnaires or focus groups. Whereas traditional quantitative research approaches seek to test known hypotheses and obtain answers to well-defined product or strategy questions, observational research can generate fresh customer and market insights that people are unwilling or unable to provide. It provides a window into customers' unconscious actions and unexpressed needs and feelings.

However, some things simply cannot be observed, such as attitudes, motives, or private behavior. Long-term or infrequent behavior is also difficult to observe. Finally, observations can be very difficult to interpret. Because of these limitations, researchers often use observation along with other data collection methods.

Survey research

Gathering primary data by asking people questions about their knowledge, attitudes, preferences, and buying behavior.

Survey Research. Long the backbone traditional marketing research, **survey research** is the most widely used method for primary data collection. Survey research is best suited for gathering descriptive information. A company that wants to know about people's knowledge, attitudes, preferences, or buying behavior can often find out by asking them directly.

The major advantage of survey research is its flexibility; it can be used to obtain many kinds of information in many different situations. Surveys addressing almost any marketing question or decision can be conducted by phone or mail, online, or in person.

However, survey research also presents some problems. Sometimes people are unable to answer survey questions because they cannot remember or have never thought about what they do and why they do it. People may be unwilling to respond to unknown interviewers or about things they consider private. Respondents may answer survey questions even when they do not know the answer just to appear smarter or more informed. Or they may try to help the interviewer by giving pleasing answers. Finally, busy people may not take the time, or they might resent the intrusion into their privacy.

Experimental research

Gathering primary data by selecting matched groups of subjects, giving them different treatments, controlling related factors, and checking for differences in group responses.

Experimental Research. Whereas observation is best suited for exploratory research and surveys for descriptive research, **experimental research** is best suited for gathering causal information. Experiments involve selecting matched groups of subjects, giving them different treatments, controlling unrelated factors, and checking for differences in group responses. Thus, experimental research tries to explain cause-and-effect relationships.

For example, before adding a new sandwich to its menu, McDonald's might use experiments to test the effects on sales of two different prices it might charge. It could introduce the new sandwich at one price in one city and at another price in another city. If the cities are similar and if all other marketing efforts for the sandwich are the same, then differences in sales in the two cities could be related to the price charged.

Online controlled experiments can be simple and inexpensive to run with immediate and revealing results. ● For example, to test a possible change in the way its Bing search engine displays ad headlines, Microsoft conducted an online "A/B test" or "split-run test" in which one group of users saw the old headline format (version A) while another group saw the new format (version B). Within only hours, the new headline variation was producing an astonishing 12 percent ad revenue increase without harming the user experience. Needless to say, Microsoft adopted the new format. Today, Microsoft and other digital companies such as Amazon, Google, and Facebook each conduct thousands of controlled experiments involving millions of users annually.[18]

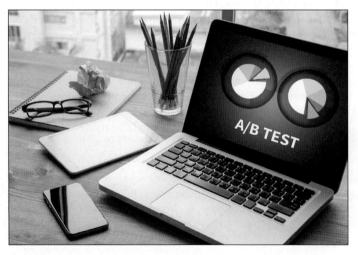

● **Experimental research: Online experiments can be simple and inexpensive. For example, an online "A/B test" for Microsoft's Bing search engine formatting yielded performance-enhancing results in only hours.**

One photo/Shutterstock

Contact Methods

Information can be collected by mail, by telephone, by personal interview, or online. Each contact method has its own particular strengths and weaknesses.

Mail, Telephone, and Personal Interviewing. *Mail questionnaires* can be used to collect large amounts of information at a low cost per respondent. Respondents may give more honest answers on a mail questionnaire than to an unknown interviewer in person or over the phone. Also, no interviewer is involved to bias respondents' answers. However, mail questionnaires are not very flexible; all respondents answer the same questions in a fixed order. And mail surveys usually take longer to complete and response rates are often low. As a result, more and more marketers are now shifting to faster, more flexible, and lower-cost email, online, and mobile phone surveys.

Telephone interviewing can be used by gather information quickly, and it provides greater flexibility than mail questionnaires. Interviewers can explain difficult questions and, depending on the answers they receive, skip some questions or probe on others. And interviewers can ask to speak to respondents with the desired characteristics or even by name.

However, with telephone interviewing, the cost per respondent is higher than with mail, online, or mobile questionnaires. Also, people may not want to discuss personal questions with an interviewer. The method introduces interviewer bias—the way interviewers talk, how they ask questions, and other differences that may affect respondents' answers. Finally, in this age of do-not-call lists, promotion-harassed consumers, caller ID, and mobile phones, potential survey respondents are increasingly not answering or are hanging up on telephone interviewers rather than talking with them. As a result, although telephone interviewing remains a valuable marketing research methodology, its use has declined in recent years.

Personal interviewing takes two forms: individual interviewing and group interviewing. *Individual interviewing* involves talking with people in their homes or offices, on the street, or in shopping malls. Such interviewing is flexible. Trained interviewers can guide interviews, explain difficult questions, and explore issues as the situation requires. They can show subjects actual products, packages, advertisements, or videos and observe reactions and behavior. However, individual personal interviews may cost three to four times as much as telephone interviews.

Focus Group Interviewing. *Group interviewing* consists of inviting small groups of people to meet with a trained moderator to talk about a product, service, or organization. Participants normally are paid a small sum for attending. A moderator encourages free and easy discussion, hoping that group interactions will bring out deeper feelings and thoughts. At the same time, the moderator "focuses" the discussion—hence the name **focus group interviewing**.

Focus group interviewing
Personal interviewing that involves inviting small groups of people to gather for a few hours with a trained interviewer to talk about a product, service, or organization. The interviewer "focuses" the group discussion on important issues.

In traditional focus groups, researchers and marketers watch the focus group discussions from behind a one-way mirror and video-record sessions for later study. Through videoconferencing and internet technology, marketers in far-off locations can look in and listen, even participate, as a focus group progresses.

Focus group interviewing remains one of the major qualitative marketing research tools for gaining fresh insights into consumer thoughts and feelings. In focus group settings, researchers not only hear consumer ideas and opinions, they also can observe facial expressions, body movements, group interplay, and conversational flows. However, focus group studies present some challenges. They usually employ small samples to keep time and costs down, and it may be hard to generalize from the results. Moreover, consumers in focus groups are not always open and honest about their real feelings, behaviors, and intentions in front of other people.

To overcome these problems, many researchers are tinkering with the focus group design. Some companies are changing the environments in which they conduct focus groups to help consumers relax and elicit more authentic responses. For example, Lexus hosts "An Evening with Lexus" dinners in customers' homes with groups of luxury car buyers to learn up close and personal why they did or did not buy a Lexus. Other companies use *immersion groups*—small groups of consumers who interact directly and informally with product designers without a focus group moderator present.

● Research and innovation consultancy The Mom Complex uses such immersion groups to help brand marketers from companies such as Unilever, Johnson & Johnson, Kimberly-Clark, Kellogg, Playskool, and Walmart understand and connect with their "mom customers":[19]

● **New focus group designs: The Mom Complex uses "Mom Immersion Sessions" to help brand marketers understand and connect directly with their "mom customers" on important brand issues.**

caia image/Alamy Stock Photo

According to The Mom Complex, America's 80 million moms control 85 percent of the nation's $2.4 trillion in household purchases, yet three out of four moms say marketers have no idea what it's like to be a mother. To change that, The Mom Complex arranges "Mom Immersion Sessions," in which brand marketers interact directly with groups of mothers, who receive $100 in compensation for a two-hour session. Rather than the usual focus group practice of putting the marketers behind a one-way mirror to observe groups of moms discussing their brands, the participants and marketers sit in the same room. Guided by a discussion facilitator, the moms begin by educating the marketers about the realities of motherhood—"the raw, real ugly truth about being a mom." Then the moms and marketers work together to address specific brand issues—whether it's new product ideas, current product problems, or positioning and communications strategy. The goal is to "turn the challenges of motherhood into growth opportunities for brands."

Individual and focus group interviews can add a personal touch as opposed to more numbers-oriented, big data–driven research. They can provide rich insights into the motivations and feelings behind the numbers and analytics. Things really come to life when you hear people say them. For that reason, focus groups are still the most widely used qualitative research tool.

Online marketing research

Collecting primary data through internet and mobile surveys, online focus groups, consumer tracking, experiments, and online panels and brand communities.

Online Marketing Research. Increasingly, researchers are collecting primary data through **online marketing research**: internet and mobile surveys, online focus groups, consumer tracking, experiments, and online panels and brand communities.

Online research can take many forms. A company can use the internet or mobile technology as a survey medium: It can include a questionnaire on its web or social media sites or use email or mobile devices to invite people to answer questions. It can create online panels that provide regular feedback or conduct live discussions or online focus groups. Researchers can also conduct online experiments. They can experiment with different prices, headlines, or product features on different web or mobile sites or at different times to learn the relative effectiveness of their offers. They can set up virtual shopping environments and use them to test new products and marketing programs. Or a company can learn about the behavior of online customers by following their movements they visit the online site and move to other sites.

Online and mobile channels are especially well suited to *quantitative* research—for example, conducting marketing surveys and collecting data. Almost 90 percent of all Americans now use the internet and some 77 percent own a smartphone, making online a fertile channel for reaching a broad cross-section of consumers.[20] As response rates for traditional survey approaches decline and costs increase, the internet is quickly replacing mail and the telephone as the dominant data collection methodology.

Internet-based survey research offers many advantages over traditional phone, mail, and personal interviewing approaches. The most obvious advantages are speed and low costs. By going online, researchers can quickly and easily distribute surveys to thousands of respondents simultaneously via email or by posting them on selected online, social media, and mobile sites. Responses can be almost instantaneous, and because respondents themselves enter the information, researchers can tabulate, review, and share research data as the information arrives.

Online research also usually costs much less than research conducted through mail, phone, or personal interviews. Using the internet eliminates most of the postage, phone, interviewer, and data-handling costs associated with the other approaches. Moreover, sample size and location have little impact on costs. Once the questionnaire is set up, there's little difference in cost between 10 respondents and 10,000 respondents on the internet or between local or globally distant respondents.

Its low cost puts online research well within the reach of almost any business, large or small. In fact, with internet and mobile channels, what was once the domain of research experts is now available to almost any would-be researcher. ● Even

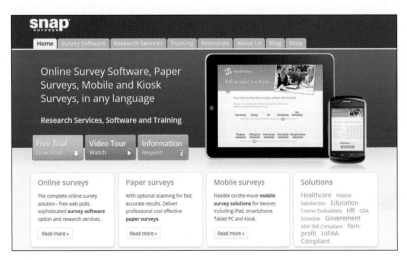

● Online research: Thanks to services such as Snap Surveys, almost any business, large or small, can create, publish, and distribute its own custom online or mobile survey in minutes.

smaller, less sophisticated researchers can use online survey services such as Snap Surveys, Qualtrics, SurveyMonkey, and SurveyGizmo to create, publish, and distribute their own custom online or mobile surveys in minutes.

Online and mobile surveys also tend to be more interactive and engaging, easier to complete, and less intrusive than traditional phone or mail surveys. As a result, they usually garner higher response rates. The internet is an excellent medium for reaching the hard-to-reach consumer—for example, the often-elusive teen, single, affluent, and well-educated audiences. It's also good for reaching people who lead busy lives, from working mothers to on-the-go executives. Such people are well represented online, and they can respond in their own space and at their own convenience.

Just as marketing researchers have rushed to use the internet for quantitative surveys and data collection, they are now also adopting *qualitative* online research approaches, such as online focus groups, blogs, and social networks. The internet can provide a fast, low-cost way to gain qualitative customer insights.

Online focus groups

Gathering a small group of people online with a trained moderator to chat about a product, service, or organization and gain qualitative insights about consumer attitudes and behavior.

A primary qualitative online research approach is **online focus groups**. ● For example, online research firm FocusVision offers its InterVu service, which lets companies connect with customers through interactive video and online focus groups. Groups can include participants at remote locations, anywhere in the world, at any time. InterVu participants can log on to focus sessions from their homes or offices and see, hear, and react to each other in real-time, face-to-face discussions.[21] Such focus groups can be conducted in any language and viewed with simultaneous translation. They work well for bringing together people from different parts of the country or world at low cost. Researchers can view the sessions in real time from just about anywhere, eliminating travel, lodging, and facility costs. Finally, although online focus groups require some advance scheduling, results are almost immediate.

● **Online focus groups: FocusVision's InterVu service lets focus group participants at remote locations see, hear, and react to each other in real-time, face-to-face discussions.**

Image provided courtesy of FocusVision, the leading research technology software provider for simple to sophisticated qualitative and quantitative projects.

Although growing rapidly, both quantitative and qualitative internet-based research have some drawbacks. One major problem is controlling who's in the online sample. Without seeing respondents, it's difficult to know who they really are. To overcome such sample and context problems, many online research firms use opt-in communities and respondent panels.

Alternatively, many companies have now developed their own "insight communities" from which they obtain customer feedback and insights. For example, ESPN has a long-standing digital insights community called FANography:[22]

> ESPN FANography consists of 12,000 dedicated ESPN fans who provide ongoing feedback across a wide range of topics—everything from marketing and advertising campaigns to program content. ESPN works to make FANography members feel like real insiders. It sends them custom-designed quarterly FANewsletters showing how others in the community responded to questions and how their feedback is being used. ESPN also hosts a private Facebook group for FANography members, with round-the-clock sports conversations and sneak peeks into breaking company news. "Our insight community provides quick yet deep customer insight to numerous ESPN divisions," says a brand marketing executive.

Online Behavioral and Social Tracking and Targeting. Thus, the internet has become an important tool for conducting research and developing customer insights. But today's marketing researchers are going even further—well beyond online surveys, focus groups, and insights communities. Increasingly, they are listening to and watching consumers by actively mining the rich veins of unsolicited, unstructured, "bottom-up" customer information already coursing around the internet. Whereas traditional marketing research provides more logical consumer responses to structured and intrusive research questions, online listening provides the passion and spontaneity of unsolicited, real-time consumer opinions.

Tracking consumers online might be as simple as scanning customer reviews and comments on the company's brand site or on shopping sites such as Amazon.com or BestBuy.com. Or it might mean using sophisticated online-analysis tools to deeply analyze the mountains of consumer brand-related comments and messages found in blogs or on social media sites. Listening to and engaging customers online can provide valuable insights into what consumers are saying or feeling about a brand. It can also provide opportunities for building positive brand experiences and relationships. Many companies now excel at listening online and responding quickly and appropriately.

Information about what consumers do while trolling the vast digital expanse—what searches they make, the online and mobile sites they visit, how they shop, and what they buy—is pure gold to marketers. And today's marketers are busy mining that gold. Then, in a practice called **behavioral targeting**, marketers use the online data to target ads and offers to specific consumers. Even further, they use *social targeting*, mining individual online social networking activity for the purpose of target ads and marketing efforts.

Online listening, behavioral targeting, and social targeting can help marketers to harness the massive amounts of consumer information swirling around the internet. However, as marketers get more adept at trolling social media, shopping sites, and other internet and mobile domains, many critics worry about consumer privacy. At what point does sophisticated online research cross the line into consumer stalking? Although behavioral and social targeting can benefit consumers with more relevant ads and products, if overdone or done badly, it can also strike customers as more than just a little creepy (see Real Marketing 4.1).

Regulators and others are stepping in. The Federal Trade Commission (FTC) has recommended the creation of a "Do Not Track" system (the online equivalent to the "Do Not Call" registry), which would let people opt out of having their actions monitored online. Such legislation has been slow to develop in the United States. However, the European Union recently a General Data Protection Regulation (GDPR), which sets strict standards for how companies around the world collect, process, and protect personal data on citizens of the European Union. GDPR affects any organization that holds and uses data on people inside the EU, regardless of where it is based. Companies that fail to comply with GDPR face substantial fines, up to €20 million or 4 percent of their global sales, whichever is larger.[23]

Sampling Plan

Marketing researchers usually draw conclusions about large groups of consumers by studying a small sample of the total consumer population. A **sample** is a segment of the population selected for marketing research to represent the population as a whole. Ideally, the sample should be representative so that the researcher can make accurate estimates of the thoughts and behaviors of the larger population.

Designing the sample requires three decisions. First, *who* is to be studied (what *sampling unit*)? The answer to this question is not always obvious. For example, to learn about the decision-making process for a family automobile purchase, should the subject be the husband, the wife, other family members, dealership salespeople, or all of these? Second, *how many* people should be included (what *sample size*)? Large samples give more reliable results than small samples. However, larger samples usually cost more, and it is not necessary to sample the entire target market or even a large portion to get reliable results.

Finally, *how* should the people in the sample be *chosen* (what *sampling procedure*)? ● **Table 4.2** describes different kinds of samples. Using *probability samples*, each population member has a known chance of being included in the sample, and researchers can calculate confidence limits for sampling error. But when probability sampling costs too much or takes too much time, marketing researchers often take *nonprobability samples* even though their sampling error cannot be measured. These varied ways of drawing samples have different costs and time limitations as well as different accuracy and statistical properties. Which method is best depends on the needs of the research project.

Research Instruments

In collecting primary data, marketing researchers have a choice of two main research instruments: *questionnaires* and *mechanical devices*.

Questionnaires. The questionnaire is by far the most common instrument, whether administered in person, by phone, by email, or online. Questionnaires are very flexible—there

Behavioral targeting
Using online consumer tracking data and analytics to target advertisements and marketing offers to specific consumers.

Sample
A segment of the population selected for marketing research to represent the population as a whole.

Real Marketing 4.1 | Behavioral and Social Targeting: Sophisticated Marketing or Just a Little Creepy?

Thanks to the burgeoning world of web browsing, social media, mobile apps, online shopping, and other internet activities, marketers now have real-time access to a flood of online consumer information. It's all there for the digging—what sites consumers visit, what searches they make, what apps they use, how they shop, what they buy, with whom they interact—digitally revealed as they navigate the internet.

Marketers routinely employ sophisticated big data tools to analyze the churning mass of online and mobile data in precise detail, using the resulting insights to target and personalize marketing ads and offers. On today's internet, everyone knows who you are. By combining online and offline data, marketers know your age, your gender, where you live, that you love dogs, what you bought recently at Amazon.com, and that you spent one hour and 21 minutes last Sunday morning browsing college basketball news and scores at ESPN.com.

Marketers use all that data to deliver ads and offers aimed squarely at individual consumers, wherever they travel on the internet, or even in stores. It's called *behavioral targeting*—tracking consumers' online behavior and using it to target ads and offers to them. So, for example, if you do a Google search for a Samsung TV you're thinking about buying, you'll probably see an ad for that very type of TV on your next visit to Facebook or your favorite buying site. Or as you're shopping in one section of your local Walgreen's, you might receive a real-time notification on your phone of a deal in another section of the store.

All this is amazing enough, but web analytics and targeting take online eavesdropping even further—from *behavioral* targeting to *social* targeting. Whereas behavioral targeting tracks consumer movements across online sites, social targeting also mines individual online social media connections and conversations. Research shows that consumers shop a lot like their friends and are five times more likely to respond to ads from brands friends use. Social targeting links customer data to social interaction data from social networking sites.

So, instead of just having a Zappos.com ad for running shoes pop up because you've recently searched for running shoes (behavioral targeting), an ad for a specific pair of running shoes pops up because a friend that you're connected to via Instagram or Twitter just bought those shoes from Zappos.com last week (social targeting).

Social targeting can even capture the dynamics of real-time conversations. For example, beyond just targeting 24- to 26-year-old males who are both sports fans and car enthusiasts, Chevrolet made its ad message even more relevant by targeting those consumers while they are talking about football on a mobile Twitter app during the Super Bowl. When they checked the app, targeted consumers saw an ad that prompted them to check out Chevy's Super Bowl video on YouTube.

Behavioral and social targeting require sophisticated analytics, so many marketers enlist the services of specialized ad networks with exotic names like Taboola, PulsePoint, and Adknowledge. These digital advertising networks obtain user browsing data by partnering with hundreds or even thousands of websites. The partners supply gobs of data on user browsing histories, web and mobile site usage, electronic shopping cart contents, and other details of what users do, where, and when.

The ad networks then apply high-powered big data analytics to identify consumers with similar interests, needs, behavior, and internet habits. This lets them merge audience data from one group of sites with ad placements on another. Armed with that information, the networks then work with advertisers to purchase ads that target the right customers. So if you're browsing lawn and garden sites, don't be surprised to see ads for Scotts lawn products the next time you visit Weather.com. Or if you seek car-buying advice at sites such as Edmunds.com or nadaguides.com, you might well see ads for the cars you researched the next time you visit Google News to catch up on what's happening around the nation and world.

The major social media have also gotten into behavioral targeting in a big way. Facebook, Google, Instagram, Twitter, Snapchat, and other social media dig deeply into user data to help their advertisers target more sharply. For example, some 2 billion people use Facebook every month. However, based on sophisticated analytics, Facebook offers powerful audience selection tools that help its advertisers target the right customer groups or even individuals on Facebook.

Advertisers can target Facebook users based on demographics (age, gender, education, relationship status, or even job titles), location (where they live or maybe within a radius around a store), interests (say, hobbies or favorite entertainment), or behaviors (what they buy, device usage, or other activities). Or Facebook can help advertisers create "custom audiences" by finding and reaching existing customers and contacts who also use Facebook. Advertisers can even build what Facebook calls "lookalike audiences," people on Facebook whose behaviors mirror those

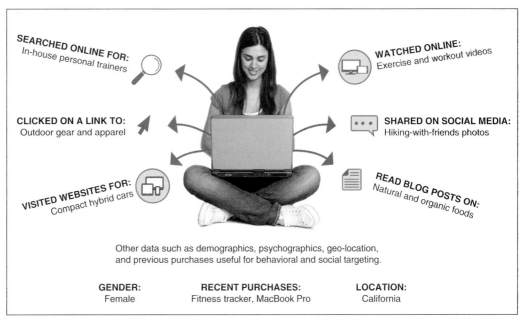

SEARCHED ONLINE FOR: In-house personal trainers

WATCHED ONLINE: Exercise and workout videos

CLICKED ON A LINK TO: Outdoor gear and apparel

SHARED ON SOCIAL MEDIA: Hiking-with-friends photos

VISITED WEBSITES FOR: Compact hybrid cars

READ BLOG POSTS ON: Natural and organic foods

Other data such as demographics, psychographics, geo-location, and previous purchases useful for behavioral and social targeting.

GENDER:	RECENT PURCHASES:	LOCATION:
Female	Fitness tracker, MacBook Pro	California

On today's internet, with today's advanced analytics, everyone knows who you are. Marketers use such insights to personalize online shopping experiences. But is it sophisticated marketing or "just a little creepy"?

Rido/Shutterstock

of their target customers. Thanks to such sophisticated targeting capabilities, Facebook now captures more that 15 percent of all online advertising dollars, second only to Google's more than 40 percent.

Online analytics. Behavioral targeting. Social targeting. All of these are great for marketers as they work to mine customer insights from the massive amounts of consumer information swirling around the internet. The biggest question? You've probably already guessed it. As marketers get more adept at trolling web and mobile sites, social media, and other digital domains, what happens to consumer privacy and personal data security?

Yup, that's the downside. At what point does sophisticated online research cross the line into unwelcome invasions of privacy?

Proponents claim that behavioral and social targeting benefit more than abuse consumers by feeding back ads and products that are more relevant to their interests. But to many consumers and public advocates, following consumers online and stalking them with ads feels more than just a little creepy. "Marketers must find a sweet spot between personalization and surveillance," says one analyst. "Customers can be creeped out when brands cross the thin line between knowing them like a friend and knowing them like a stalker."

Despite such concerns, behavior and social targeting continue to grow and to get smarter. And, with appropriate safeguards, they promise benefits for both companies and customers. Marketers who can plumb the depths of customer data and respond in meaningful, valuable ways without crossing the line will thrive. But it can be a delicate balance. As Snapchat's Privacy Center states, "We want you to feel understood. We want to understand what's relevant to you and your life, and we want to show you things that you'll care about. At the same time, we don't want to serve ads that are so custom-tailored that they feel invasive or uncomfortable."[24]

---

are many ways to ask questions. Closed-ended questions include all the possible answers, and subjects make choices among them. Examples include multiple-choice questions and scale questions. Open-ended questions allow respondents to answer in their own words. In a survey of airline users, Southwest Airlines might simply ask, "What is your opinion of Southwest Airlines?" Or it might ask people to complete a sentence: "When I choose an airline, the most important consideration is..." These and other kinds of open-ended questions often reveal more than closed-ended questions because they do not limit respondents' answers.

Open-ended questions are especially useful in exploratory research, when the researcher is trying to find out *what* people think but is not measuring *how many* people think in a certain way. Closed-ended questions, on the other hand, provide answers that are easier to interpret and tabulate.

Researchers should also use care in the *wording* and *ordering* of questions. They should use simple, direct, and unbiased wording. Questions should be arranged in a logical order. The first question should create interest if possible, and difficult or personal questions should be asked last so that respondents do not become defensive.

Mechanical Instruments. Although questionnaires are the most common research instrument, researchers also use mechanical instruments to monitor consumer behavior.

● Table 4.2 | **Types of Samples**

Probability Sample

Simple random sample	Every member of the population has a known and equal chance of selection.
Stratified random sample	The population is divided into mutually exclusive groups (such as age groups), and random samples are drawn from each group.
Cluster (area) sample	The population is divided into mutually exclusive groups (such as blocks), and the researcher draws a sample of the groups to interview.

Nonprobability Sample

Convenience sample	The researcher selects the easiest population members from which to obtain information.
Judgment sample	The researcher uses his or her judgment to select population members who are good prospects for accurate information.
Quota sample	The researcher finds and interviews a prescribed number of people in each of several categories.

For example, Nielsen Media Research attaches people meters to television sets in selected homes to record who watches which programs. Retailers use checkout scanners to record shoppers' purchases. Other marketers use mobile phone GPS technologies to track consumer movements in and near their stores.

Researchers also use a variety of physiological and neurological measures to gauge consumers' emotions and reactions. They apply *neuromarketing*, using EEG and MRI technologies to track brain electrical activity to learn how consumers feel and respond. Neuromarketing measures, often combined with *biometric* measures (such as heart rates, respiration rates, sweat levels, and facial and eye movements), can provide companies with insights into what turns consumers on and off regarding their brands and marketing.

● Online travel giant Expedia uses such devices in its "Usability Labs" to learn about the deep-down tensions and delights customers experience during their trip-planning journeys:[25]

One fall morning, a young woman named Megan in suburban Seattle goes online to make travel plans for an upcoming family vacation in Belize. She pulls up online travel agency Expedia, checking for available flights. Her anxiety grows as she navigates the maze of alternatives and learns that the cheapest seats on the best flights are already booked. After eight minutes, without having decided on a flight, Megan explores hotels. She smiles as she finds what looks like a good place but the smile turns to a frown as she finds it's not available on her planned travel dates. "That's so sad," she mutters. Through sweat and persistence, Megan finally finds a suitable flight and a pretty good place to stay. At that moment, a voice comes over a speaker to tell Megan that she's done.

Megan is planning an actual trip, but she's doing it in Expedia's Usability Lab at company headquarters. The voice belongs to an Expedia user-experience researcher, who's been sitting in the next room with members of Expedia's hotel-shopping and activities-booking teams, observing Megan through a two-way mirror and monitoring her biometric responses. Megan is wired with sensors that record the smallest changes in her facial muscles, and an eye tracker follows Megan's gaze as she navigates the Expedia screen. On a similar screen in the next room, the researchers can follow along: A yellow line shows where Megan is looking; a green line tracks her smiles and delight; a red line tracks furrowed brows that suggest tension and frustration.

Such lab results give Expedia's marketers deeper insights into the emotions of customers using web and mobile sites across its wide-ranging portfolio of travel-planning brands, from Expedia and Hotels.com to Hotwire, Trivago, and TripAdvisor. The insights drive everything from site design improvements to new and improved products that help reduce trip-planning tensions while increasing the pleasures. "The goal of Expedia's usability researchers is not only to make Expedia's various sites and mobile apps more efficient," says one analyst, "but also to make them an extension of the vacation fantasies that are always running in the back of our heads."

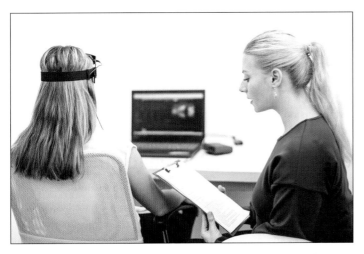

● **Biological and neurological measures: Online travel giant Expedia's "Usability Lab" uses biometics and observation to learn about the deep-down tensions and delights customers experience during their trip-planning journeys.**

ABO Photography/Shutterstock

Although neuromarketing techniques can measure consumer involvement and emotional responses second by second, such brain responses can be difficult to interpret. Thus, neuromarketing is usually used in combination with other research approaches to gain a more complete picture of what goes on inside consumers' heads.

Today's big data, Internet of Things (IoT) world has produced a flood of information from internet-connected devices. There are now more than 26 billion IoT-connected devices worldwide, not counting computers and phones.[26] They include everything from smart TVs and smart home devices to digital cameras, in-car navigation systems, and even robotic vacuum cleaners. Internet-connected devices offer huge potential for gathering data on consumer movements, actions, and activities. In the future, new technologies such as Amazon's Alexa, smart TVs, interactive store kiosks, or live interactive tools will offer startling opportunities to "read" users' emotions though audio and visual cues and react in real time. In fact, that's already happening.[27]

Implementing the Research Plan

The researcher next puts the marketing research plan into action. This involves collecting, processing, and analyzing the information. Data collection can be carried out by the company's marketing research staff, marketing managers, or outside firms. Researchers should watch closely to make sure that the plan is implemented correctly. They must guard against problems with data collection techniques and technologies, data quality, and timeliness.

Researchers must also process and analyze the collected data to isolate important information and insights. They need to check data for accuracy and completeness, tabulate the results, and compute statistical measures.

Interpreting and Reporting the Findings

The market researcher must now interpret the findings, draw conclusions, and report them to management. The researcher should not try to overwhelm managers with numbers and fancy statistical techniques. Rather, the researcher should present important findings and insights that are useful in the major decisions faced by management.

However, interpretation should not be left only to researchers. Although they are often experts in research design, statistics, and data science, the marketing manager knows more about the problem and the decisions that must be made. The best research means little if the manager blindly accepts faulty interpretations from the researcher. Similarly, managers may be biased. They might tend to accept research results that show what they expected and reject those that they did not expect or hope for. In many cases, findings can be interpreted in different ways, and discussions between researchers and managers will help point to the best interpretations. Thus, managers and researchers must work together closely when interpreting research results, and both must share responsibility for the research process and resulting decisions.

Author Comment | We've talked generally about managing customer relationships throughout the book. But here, *customer relationship management* (CRM) has a much narrower data-management meaning. It refers to capturing and using customer data from all sources to manage customer interactions, engage customers, and build customer relationships.

Analyzing and Using Marketing Information

OBJECTIVE 4-4 Explain how companies analyze and use marketing information.

Information gathered from internal databases, competitive marketing intelligence, and marketing research usually requires additional analysis. Managers may need help applying the information to gain customer and market insights that will improve their marketing decisions. This help may include advanced analytics to learn more about the relationships within sets of data. Information analysis might also involve the application of analytical models that will help marketers make better decisions.

Once the information has been processed and analyzed, it must be made available to the right decision makers at the right time. In the following sections, we look deeper into analyzing and using marketing information.

Customer Relationship Management (CRM)

The question of how best to analyze and use individual customer data presents special problems. In the current *big data* era, most companies are awash in information about their customers and the marketplace. Still, smart companies capture information at every possible customer *touch point*. These touch points include customer purchases, sales force contacts, service and support calls, web and social media site visits, satisfaction surveys, credit and payment interactions, market research studies—every contact between a customer and a company.

Unfortunately, this information is usually scattered widely across the organization or buried deep in separate company databases. To overcome such problems, many companies are now turning to **customer relationship management (CRM)** to manage detailed information about individual customers and carefully manage customer touch points to maximize customer loyalty.

CRM consists of sophisticated software and analysis tools from companies such as Salesforce.com, Oracle, Microsoft, and SAS that integrate customer and marketplace information from all sources, analyze it, and apply the results to build stronger customer

Customer relationship management (CRM)
Managing detailed information about individual customers and carefully managing customer touch points to maximize customer loyalty.

relationships. CRM integrates everything that a company's sales, service, and marketing teams know about individual customers, providing a 360-degree view of the customer relationship. For example, MetLife employs a CRM system that it calls "The MetLife Wall":[28]

> One of the biggest customer service challenges for MetLife's sales and service reps used to be quickly finding and getting to customer information—different records, transactions, and interactions stored in dozens of different company data locations and formats. The MetLife Wall solves that problem. The Wall uses a Facebook-like interface to serve up a consolidated view of each MetLife customer's service experience. The innovative CRM system draws customer data from 70 different MetLife systems containing 45 million customer agreements and 140 million transactions. It puts all of a given customer's information and related links into a single record on a single screen, updated in near real time. Now, thanks to The MetLife Wall—with only a single click instead of the 40 clicks it used to take—sales and service reps can see a complete view of a given customer's various policies, transactions, and claims filed and paid along with a history of all the interactions the customer has had with MetLife across the company's many touch points, all on a simple timeline. The Wall has given a big boost to MetLife's customer service and cross-selling efforts. According to a MetLife marketing executive, it's also had "a huge impact on customer satisfaction."

By using CRM to understand customers better, companies can provide higher levels of customer service and develop deeper customer relationships. They can use CRM to pinpoint high-value customers, target them more effectively, cross-sell the company's products, and create offers tailored to specific customer requirements.

Big Data, Marketing Analytics, and Artificial Intelligence

As noted at the start of the chapter, today's big data can yield big results. But simply collecting and storing huge amounts of data has little value. Marketers must sift through the mountains of data to mine the gems—the bits that yield customer insights. As one marketing executive puts it, "It's actually [about getting] *big insights* from big data. It's throwing away 99.999 percent of that data to find things that are actionable." Says another data expert, "*right* data trumps *big* data."[29] That's the job of *marketing analytics*.

Marketing analytics

The analysis tools, technologies, and processes by which marketers dig out meaningful patterns in big data to gain customer insights and gauge marketing performance.

Marketing analytics consists of the analysis tools, technologies, and processes by which marketers dig out meaningful patterns in big data to gain customer insights and gauge marketing performance. Marketers apply marketing analytics to the large and complex sets of data they collect from web, mobile, and social media tracking; customer transactions and engagements; and other big data sources.

● For example, Netflix uses sophisticated big data analytics to gain consumer insights, which it then uses to give customers exactly what they want:[30]

Netflix streams more movie and program content by far than any other video service. Worldwide, Netflix's 130 million paid subscribers watch more than 1 billion hours of movies, TV programs, and original Netflix content a week. But while avid Netflixers are busy watching Netflix videos, Netflix is also busy watching *them*—watching them very, very closely. Every day, Netflix tracks and parses member data on tens of millions of searches, ratings, and "plays." The company's bulging database contains every viewing detail for each individual subscriber—real-time data on what shows they watch, at what times, on what devices, at what locations, even when they hit the pause, rewind, or fast-forward buttons during programs. Netflix also employs experts to classify each video on hundreds of characteristics, such as talent, action, tone, genre, color, volume, scenery, and many, many others. Netflix supplements this already-massive database with consumer information purchased from Nielsen, Facebook, Twitter, and other sources.

Using this rich base of big data, Netflix builds detailed individual subscriber profiles and then uses these profiles to tailor each customer's viewing experience and make personalized recommendations based on what they've watched. According to Netflix, there

● **Netflix, big data, and CRM: While members are busy watching Netflix videos, Netflix is busy watching them—watching them very, very closely. Then it uses the big data insights to give customers exactly what they want.**

OJO Images Ltd/Alamy Stock Photo (photo); dennizn/Shutterstock (logo)

are 130 million different versions of Netflix, one for each individual subscriber worldwide. Netflix also uses the data to assess what additional content it should obtain or produce itself. "We always use our in-depth knowledge about what our members love to watch to decide what's available on Netflix," says a Netflix marketer. "If you keep watching, we'll keep adding more of what you love."

Artificial intelligence (AI)
Technology by which machines think and learn in a way that looks and feels human but with a lot more analytical capacity.

Such analytics employ **artificial intelligence (AI)**, technology by which machines think and learn in a way that looks and feels human but with a lot more analytical capacity. Artificial intelligence has taken the marketing—and about everything else in the world—by storm. Marketers are now using AI for everything from big data analytics to engaging customers to crafting personalized advertising and selling efforts. Although still in its infancy, AI offers vast potential for marketing. As Google's CEO suggests, AI "is more profound than fire or electricity." That's saying a great deal (see Real Marketing 4.2).[31]

The benefits of customer relationship management, big data analytics, and artificial intelligence don't come without costs or risks. The most common mistake is to view CRM, marketing analytics, and AI as technology processes only. Managers get buried in the big data details and miss the big picture. Or they can let machines make decisions rather than putting on their own thinking caps.

Yet technology alone cannot build profitable customer relationships. Companies can't improve customer relationships by simply installing some new software or analytics. Instead, marketers should start with the fundamentals of managing customer relationships and *then* employ high-tech data and analytics solutions. They should focus first on the R— it's the *relationship* that CRM is all about.

Distributing and Using Marketing Information

Marketing information has no value until it is used to make better marketing decisions. Thus, the marketing information system must make information readily available to managers and others who need it, when they need it. In some cases, this means providing managers with regular performance reports, intelligence updates, and reports on the results of research studies.

But marketing managers may also need access to nonroutine information for special situations and on-the-spot decisions. For example, a sales manager having trouble with a large customer may want a summary of the account's sales and profitability over the past year. Or a brand manager may want to get a sense of the amount of the social media buzz surrounding the recent launch of a new product. These days, therefore, information distribution involves making information accessible in a timely, user-friendly way. Many firms use company *intranets* and internal CRM systems to facilitate this process. These systems provide ready access to internal data, intelligence, and marketing research information; customer transaction and experience information; shared reports and documents; and more.

In addition, companies are increasingly allowing key customers and value-network members to access account, product, and other data on demand through *extranets*. Suppliers, customers, resellers, and select other network members may access a company's extranet to update their accounts, arrange purchases, and check orders against inventories to improve customer service.

For example, online shoes and accessories retailer Zappos considers suppliers to be "part of the Zappos family" and a key component in its quest to deliver "WOW" through great customer service. So it treats suppliers as valued partners, including sharing information with them. Through its ZUUL extranet (Zappos Unified User Login), thousands of suppliers are given full access to brand-related Zappos's inventory levels, sales figures, and even profitability. Suppliers can also use ZUUL to interact with the Zappos creative team and to enter suggested orders for Zappos buyers to approve.[32]

● **Extranets: Zappos shares marketing information and insights with suppliers through its ZUUL extranet. It considers suppliers to be "part of the Zappos family."**

Zappos

Thanks to modern technology, today's marketing managers can gain direct access to a company's information system at any time and from virtually anywhere. They can tap into the system from a home office, customer location, airport, or the local Starbucks—anyplace they can connect on a laptop, tablet,

Real Marketing 4.2

Artificial Intelligence in Marketing: "A Bigger Deal Than Fire or Electricity"

It's early morning, you're headed out to start your day, and you feel the urge for that first jolt of caffeine. As you get in your car, you tap the Starbucks app on your phone and ask for "the usual." Your Starbucks virtual barista replies in her familiar, cheerful voice: "One tall caramel latte!" She then politely suggests a breakfast snack—a Vermont maple nut muffin—not your usual, but it sure sounds good. You agree. "Thanks! Your order will be ready for pickup in five to seven minutes at University and 28th," she confirms. "Would you like to pay for that with your credit card on file?" You step inside the store, bypass the long lines, and grab your order—no fuss, no muss. Welcome to the world of artificial intelligence (AI).

This is just one example of how AI has exploded onto the marketing scene. Starbucks has long been into cutting-edge technology—a full 25 percent of its transactions are already placed through its smartphone apps. But My Starbucks Barista is more than just an ordering app. It uses artificial intelligence to create personalized customer experiences and manage real-time customer interactions, based on everything from customers' past transactions and preferences to demographics, store trends and inventories, and local traffic and weather conditions.

Artificial intelligence is sweeping the world. It involves machines that think and learn in a way that looks and feels human but with a lot more analytical capacity. The engine behind the AI's explosive growth is big data. Raw data is flowing in from everywhere: customer transaction and interaction data, web and social media data, news and environmental data, and data from more than 50 billion connected devices—everything from consumer wearables and GPS technology to household thermostats, washing machines, and cars. Companies need to make sense of all that data for their brands and consumers.

The human mind simply can't grapple with today's glut of big data. But machines can. However, more than just collecting and tabulating mountains of data, AI analyzes it at lightning speed to gain deep insights and apply them to accomplish designated tasks. AI learns as it goes along—the more data it ingests, the smarter and more accurate it gets. "AI is the planet we're headed to," says one AI expert. "Machine learning is the rocket that's going to get us there. And big data is the fuel."

Marketers use AI to assess, address, service, and sell to customers. In turn, AI can help customers manage their lives and their buying. It might be requesting a ride from Lyft via chat (Facebook Messenger or Slack) or voice (Amazon Echo's Alexa virtual assistant). Lyft's chatbot lets you know the current location of your driver along with a picture of the license plate and car model. Or it might be IBM's Watson supercomputer combing through vast amounts of data to unearth customer and market insights that help marketers sharpen their targeting, personalize customer engagements, design new products, and even craft better ads in real time.

Today's machines are smart and eerily human. IBM's Watson "is loquacious; it can tell jokes, answer questions, and write songs," notes one observer. "Google's AI can now read lips better than a professional and can master video games within hours. MIT's AI can predict action on video two seconds before it begins. Tesla's AI powers [its] innovative self-driving car."

Companies like Amazon have mastered AI, harnessing insights and interactions that let it understand and serve customers. Amazon's Echo brings Alexa's AI magic to nearly 50 million U.S. homes. Beyond serving as a valet for duties such as adjusting household appliances, controlling music, keeping shopping lists, sending text messages, and answering questions on about any subject, Echo and other similar AI devices, such as Google Home, have become voice-activated personal shopping assistants. Companies ranging from P&G and Clorox to 1-800-Flowers are hard at work perfecting ways to tap into Echo users who voice-shop from the comfort of their own kitchens.

At Amazon's shopping and video sites, AI powers recommendations that help consumers decide what to buy and what to watch. "Increasingly, Amazon will be selling you things you didn't even know you needed because it has learned what you like and are most inclined to buy," says an analyst. Amazon is so good at this that it's even considering what it calls "predictive delivery," sending consumers stuff they haven't even ordered yet. If customers don't want it, they would just keep it for free. Although such deliveries may still be a while off, Amazon uses such AI predictions to keep the right stock in warehouses or even on trucks to support its ever-more-popular one-day or even one-hour delivery promise.

Hosts of retailers are employing AI to improve how they service and sell to their customers. For example, home improvement retailer Lowe's is experimenting with LoweBots—five-foot something, fully mobile, AI-powered robots that roam stores helping customers. The LoweBots detect customers who might need assistance and engage them through voice and touchscreens. The AI robots tap store and external data to answers customer questions, offer solutions,

Artificial intelligence: The My Starbucks Barista uses artificial intelligence to create personalized customer experiences and manage real-time customer interactions, based on everything from customers' past transactions and preferences to local traffic and weather conditions.

Elias Stein Illustration

lead customers to merchandise in the store (or order online merchandise that's not in stock). They even offer text and video tutorials. Meanwhile, the LoweBots keep tabs on store-level data and analyze customer shopping patterns. They're "learning things that we never knew before," says a Lowe's Innovation Labs manager, like "what is happening at 3 o'clock on a Tuesday" in any given store.

AI does more than just serve customers. It also helps marketing managers shape marketing strategies and tactics. For example, IBM has formed a new division called Watson Advertising, built around its AI supercomputer Watson, which first gained public recognition when it bested human contestants and won $1 million on *Jeopardy!* Watson can ingest hundreds of millions of pages of data each second. IBM has now turned Watson's talents toward marketing. For example, factoring in emotion, tone, language, sentiment, purchase history, and social media interactions, Watson "can generate a psycholinguistic

profile of an individual in literally milliseconds," explains an IBM executive.

Using such analytics, Watson can give marketers precise, real-time views of customers and put the insights it learns into action, using its AI powers for everything from data analysis and media planning to audience targeting and actual content creation. According to one account:

> As part of a Toyota campaign, for example, Watson became a copywriter, crafting messaging for the carmaker's Mirai model based on [big data analysis of] tech and science fans' interests. Earlier this year, it transformed into a doctor, promoting Theraflu while answering questions about various flu symptoms. For Campbell's, Watson put on its chef's hat, personalizing recipes within display ads using data about consumers' locations and what ingredients they had on hand. For a major partnership with H&R Block, Watson turned into a tax expert, deploying an AI smart assistant to help clients find tax deductions."

IBM recently bought The Weather Company, which produces forecasts for 2.2

billion locations every 15 minutes, letting Watson munch on troves of data to gauge how weather affects consumers' moods, health, and buying. It recently used a combination of this weather data, consumer Google searches, and pollen counts to advise a medicine maker on which media to use in various markets and when.

Despite all these remarkable applications, AI is still in its early stages. "We're still in the dawn of AI adoption," says a technology expert. "It's a new frontier and one that will redefine the relationship between consumers and brands." As an industry, AI will skyrocket from current annual revenues of $8.1 billion to more $105 billion worldwide by 2025. And that doesn't include the trillions of dollars' worth of retail sales that AI will facilitate. "AI is going to be like electricity or the internet," says the Lowe's technology manager. "It becomes so interwoven…it takes all of this other stuff that we've been doing for so long and it makes it better than the sum of its parts." Google's CEO puts it more simply: "It's more profound than fire or electricity."[33]

or smartphone. Such systems allow managers to get the information they need directly and quickly and tailor it to their own needs.

> Author Comment | We finish this chapter by examining three special marketing information topics.

▶ Other Marketing Information Considerations

OBJECTIVE 4-5 Discuss the special issues some marketing researchers face, including public policy and ethics issues.

This section discusses marketing information in two special contexts: marketing research in small businesses and nonprofit organizations and international marketing research. Then we look at public policy and ethics issues in marketing research.

Marketing Research in Small Businesses and Nonprofit Organizations

Just like larger firms, small businesses and not-for-profit organizations need market information and the customer insights that it can provide. However, large-scale research studies are beyond the budgets of most small organizations. Still, many of the marketing research techniques discussed in this chapter can be used by smaller organizations in a less formal manner and at little or no expense.

Small businesses can obtain much useful market and customer insight without spending a lot of money. ● Consider Innocent Drinks:[34]

> As friends and students at Cambridge University in the early 1990s, Adam Balon, Richard Reed, and Jon Wright wanted to set up a business together. They believed that natural fruit smoothies would be a great healthy pursuit and would make it easy for people to do themselves some good. The lads began with very informal marketing research: instead of using a long questionnaire, they simply had people at festivals test their first batch of smoothies and just asked them whether they should quit their jobs to continue making these drinks. They had a simple bin that said "yes" and a bin that said "no," and at the end of the day, the "yes" bin was full of empty bottles.
>
> All of them returned to work the next day and quit their jobs. They took their first delivery of smoothies to 50 shops in London and offered them to the retailers for free; they only asked

them to call and order more if all had been sold—and about 45 retailers did. This market pull led the company to go to wholesalers and grow the business. Today, Innocent Drinks is one of Europe's most successful smoothie brands.

Thus, small businesses and not-for-profit organizations can obtain good marketing insights through observation, secondary data searches, or informal surveys using small convenience samples. Also, many associations, local media, and government agencies provide special help to small organizations. For example, the U.S. Small Business Administration offers dozens of free publications and a website (**www.sba.gov**) that give advice on topics ranging from starting, financing, and expanding a small business to ordering business cards. Other excellent research resources for small businesses include the U.S. Census Bureau (**www.census.gov**) and the Bureau of Economic Analysis (**www. bea.gov**).

Finally, small businesses can collect a considerable amount of information at very little cost online. They can check out online product and service review sites, use internet search engines to research specific companies and issues, and scour competitor and customer web, mobile, and social media sites.

In summary, secondary data collection, observation, surveys, and experiments can all be used effectively by small organizations with small budgets. However, although these informal research methods are less complex and less costly, they still must be conducted with care. Managers must think carefully about the objectives of the research, formulate questions in advance, recognize the biases introduced by smaller samples and less skilled researchers, and conduct the research systematically.[35]

● Innocent Drinks founders Adam Balon, Richard Reed, and Jon Wright started out with informal, affordable marketing research.

Martin Lee/Alamy Stock Photo

International Marketing Research

International researchers follow the same steps as domestic researchers, from defining the research problem and developing a research plan to interpreting and reporting the results. However, these researchers often face more and different problems. Whereas domestic researchers deal with fairly homogeneous markets within a single country, international researchers deal with diverse markets in many different countries. These markets often vary greatly in their levels of economic development, cultures and customs, and buying patterns.

In many foreign markets, the international researcher may have a tough time finding good secondary data. Whereas U.S. marketing researchers can obtain reliable secondary data from dozens of domestic research services, many countries have almost no research services at all. Some of the largest international research services operate in many countries. ● For example, the Nielsen Company (the world's largest marketing research company) has offices in more than 100 countries, from Schaumburg, Illinois, to Hong Kong to Nicosia, Cyprus.[36] However, most research firms operate in only a relative handful of countries. Thus, even when secondary information is available, it usually must be obtained from many varied sources on a country-by-country basis, making the information difficult to combine or compare.

Because of the scarcity of good secondary data, international researchers often must collect their own primary data. However, obtaining primary data may be no easy task. For example, it can be difficult simply to develop good samples. U.S. researchers can use current telephone directories, email lists, census tract data, and any of several sources of socioeconomic data to construct samples. However, such information is largely lacking in many countries.

Once the sample is drawn, the U.S. researcher usually can reach most respondents easily via any of multiple platforms—by phone, by mail, in person, or through online, social, or mobile media. However, reaching respondents by mail or phone is often not so easy in other parts of the world. As a result, surveys have now become the major means for conducting international research. However, the adoption of online and mobile technologies varies greatly worldwide. For example, most consumers in emerging markets, such as India or Africa, are accessing the internet for the first time largely from mobile devices. Survey research in such markets must be designed specifically for mobile, with all its inherent limitations.[37]

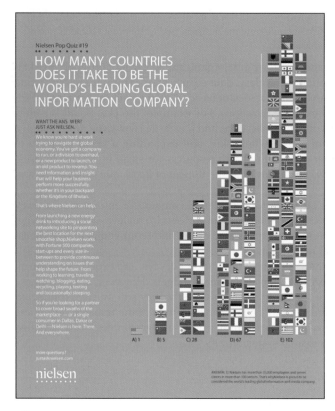

● **Some of the largest research services firms have large international organizations. Nielsen has offices in more than 100 countries.**

Cultural differences from country to country cause additional problems for international researchers. Language is the most obvious obstacle. For example, questionnaires must be prepared in one language and then translated into the languages of each country researched. Responses then must be translated back into the original language for analysis and interpretation. This adds to research costs and increases the risks of error. Even within a given country, language can be a problem. For example, in India, English is the language of business, but consumers may use any of 14 "first languages," with many additional dialects.

Translating a questionnaire from one language to another is anything but easy. Many idioms, phrases, and statements mean different things in different cultures. For example, a Danish executive noted, "Check this out by having a different translator put back into English what you've translated from English. You'll get the shock of your life. I remember [an example in which] 'out of sight, out of mind' had become 'invisible things are insane.'"[38]

Consumers in different countries also vary in their attitudes toward marketing research. People in one country may be very willing to respond; in other countries, nonresponse can be a major problem. Customs in some countries may prohibit people from talking with strangers. In certain cultures, research questions often are considered too personal. For example, in many Muslim countries, mixed-gender focus groups are taboo, as is videotaping female-only focus groups. In some countries, even when respondents are *willing* to respond, they may not be *able* to because of high functional illiteracy rates.

Despite these problems, as global marketing grows, global companies have little choice but to conduct these types of international marketing research. Although the costs and problems associated with international research may be high, the costs of not doing it—in terms of missed opportunities and mistakes—might be even higher. Once recognized, many of the problems associated with international marketing research can be overcome or avoided.[39]

Public Policy and Ethics in Marketing Research

Most marketing research benefits both the sponsoring company and its consumers. Through marketing research, companies gain insights into consumers' needs, resulting in more satisfying products and services and stronger customer relationships. However, the misuse of marketing research can also harm or annoy consumers. Three major public policy and ethics issues in marketing research are intrusions on consumer privacy, consumer data security and protection, and the misuse of research findings.

Intrusions on Consumer Privacy

Many consumers feel positive about marketing research and believe that it serves a useful purpose. Some actually enjoy being surveyed and giving their opinions. However, others strongly resent or even mistrust marketing research. They don't like being interrupted by researchers. They worry that marketers are building huge databases full of personal information about customers. Or they fear that researchers might use sophisticated techniques to probe our deepest feelings, track our internet and mobile device usage, or peek over our shoulders as we shop and then use this knowledge to manipulate our buying.

As a classic example, Target made some of its customers very uneasy recently when it used their buying histories to figure out that they had a baby on the way, including eerily accurate estimates of child gender and due date:[40]

> Target gives every customer a Guest ID number, tied to his or her name, credit card, or email address. It then tracks the customer's purchases in detail, along with demographic information from other sources. By studying the buying histories of women who'd previously signed up for its baby registries, Target found that it could develop a "pregnancy prediction" score for each customer based on her purchasing patterns across 25 product categories. It used this score to start sending personalized books of coupons for baby-related items to expectant parents, keyed to their pregnancy stages.

The strategy seemed to make good marketing sense—by hooking parents-to-be, Target could turn them into loyal buyers as their families developed. However, the strategy hit a snag when an angry man showed up at his local Target store, complaining that his high school–aged daughter was receiving Target coupons for cribs, strollers, and maternity clothes. "Are you trying to encourage her to get pregnant?" he demanded. The Target store manager apologized. But when he called to apologize again a few days later, he learned that Target's marketers had, in fact, known about the young woman's pregnancy before her father did. It turns out that many other customers were creeped out that Target knew about their pregnancies before they'd told even family and close friends. And they wondered what else Target might be tracking and profiling. As one reporter concluded: "The store's bull's-eye logo may now send a shiver…down the closely-watched spines of some [Target shoppers]."

When mining customer information, marketers must be careful not to cross over the privacy line. But there are no easy answers when it comes to marketing research and privacy. For example, is it a good or bad thing that some retailers use mannequins with cameras hidden in one eye to record customer demographics and shopping behavior in order to serve them better? Should we applaud or resent companies that monitor consumer posts on Facebook, Twitter, Instagram, YouTube, or other social media in an effort to be more responsive? Should we worry when marketers track consumers' mobile phone usage to issue location-based information, ads, and offers? Consider this example:[41]

SAP's Consumer Insight 365 service helps mobile service providers to "extract data about subscribers [and their] mobile-centric lifestyles." It ingests as many as 300 mobile web surfing, text messaging, phone call, and other mobile events per day for each of 20 to 25 million mobile subscribers across multiple carriers. The data tell marketers in detail where customers are coming from and where they go. According to one analyst, by combining the mobile data with other information, the service can tell businesses "whether shoppers are checking out competitor prices on their phones or just emailing friends. It can tell them the age ranges and genders of people who visited a store location between 10 a.m. and noon, and link location and demographic data with shoppers' web browsing histories. Retailers might use the information to arrange store displays to appeal to certain customer segments at different times of the day, or to help determine where to open new locations." Although such information can help marketers target customers with more useful offers, it might be "a little too close for comfort" from a consumer privacy viewpoint.

Increasing consumer privacy concerns have become a major problem for the marketing research industry. Companies face the challenge of unearthing valuable but potentially sensitive consumer data while also maintaining consumer trust. At the same time, consumers wrestle with the trade-offs between personalization and privacy. They want to receive relevant, personalized offers that meet their needs, but they worry or resent that companies may track them too closely. The key question: When does a company cross the line in gathering and using customer data?

Failure to address privacy issues could result in angry, less cooperative consumers and increased government intervention. As a result, the marketing research industry is considering several options for responding to intrusion and privacy issues. One example is the Marketing Research Association's "Your Opinion Counts" and "Respondent Bill of Rights" initiatives to educate consumers about the benefits of marketing research and distinguish it from telephone selling and database building.[42]

Most major companies—including Facebook, Apple, Microsoft, IBM, American Express, and even the U.S. government—have now appointed a chief privacy officer (CPO), whose job is to safeguard the privacy of customers. In the end, however, if researchers provide value in exchange for information, customers will gladly provide it. For example, Amazon's customers don't mind if the firm builds a database of previous purchases as a way to provide future product recommendations. This saves time and provides value. The best approach is for researchers to ask only for the information they need, use it responsibly to provide customer value, and avoid sharing information without the customer's permission.

Consumer Data Security and Protection

Today's large consumer data bases can pose serious data security challenges for companies. Most consumers trust that companies will take adequate steps to protect the personal data they collect. However, too often, that is not the case. In just the past few years, dozens of well-respected companies and brands have experienced major consumer data breaches, some affecting huge numbers of consumers.

For example, Facebook has recently reported two separate major breaches that exposed the personal information of 87 million and 50 million users, respectively, including information about people's personalities, social networks, and engagement on the platform. Major retailers such as Macy's, Saks Fifth Avenue, and Target have reported data security gaffs compromising payment card information for millions of their customers. Credit reporting agency Equifax revealed a massive breach that exposed sensitive data on more than 146 million consumers, including passport numbers, Social Security numbers, and driver's license information. And a few years back, Yahoo! announced the granddaddy of all data breaches, one affecting the personal information contained in more than 3 *billion* Yahoo! accounts.[43]

More recently, Marriott International revealed that hackers had breached its Starwood reservation system and stolen personal information on up to 500 million customers:[44]

Marriott-owned Starwood hotels (Sheraton, Westin, W Hotels, St. Regis, Aloft, and others) collect a treasure trove of information about guests: usually some combination of name, mailing address, phone number, email address, credit card numbers, Starwood Preferred Guest ("SPG") account information, date of birth, gender, arrival and departure information, reservation date, and communication preferences. For many, the information also includes travel history and passport numbers. The recent breach involved customers who made reservations for Starwood hotel brands from early 2014 to September 2018. When the breach was discovered, Marriott took immediate steps to notified both authorities and customers. However, the damage had already been done to Marriott's reputation. "They can say all they want that they take security seriously, but they don't if you can be hacked over a four-year period without noticing," said one data privacy advocate.

Such data security failures can harm consumers. But they can also do deep damage to companies and brands. First, they can be costly. For example, Equifax reported recovery costs of $400 million from its data breach incident; Marriott faced recovery costs and a host of immediate lawsuits. And given the size and duration of its massive data breach, Marriott may face hefty fines in Europe under the EU's General Data Projection Regulation (GDPR). Such incidents will invite even more government intervention. ● But most important, the massive data security lapses erode consumer trust harm hard-won customer–brand relationships. Thus, companies must take consumer data security very seriously.

● **Consumer data protection: Consumer data breaches can erode consumer trust damage hard-won customer–brand relationships. Companies must take consumer data security very seriously.**

Eyal Dayan Photography

Misuse of Research Findings

Research studies can be powerful persuasion tools; companies often use study results as claims in their advertising and promotion. Today, however, many research studies appear to be little more than vehicles for pitching the sponsor's products. In fact, in some cases, research surveys appear to have been designed just to produce the intended effect. For example, a Black Flag survey once asked: "A roach disk . . . poisons a roach slowly. The dying roach returns to the nest and after it dies is eaten by other roaches. In turn these roaches become poisoned and die. How effective do you think this type of product would be in killing roaches?" Not surprisingly, 79 percent said effective.

Few advertisers openly rig their research designs or blatantly misrepresent the findings—most abuses tend to be more subtle "stretches." Or disputes arise over the validity, interpretation, and use of research findings. Almost any research results can be variously interpreted depending on the researchers' bias and viewpoints.

Recognizing that marketing research can be abused, several associations—including the American Marketing Association, the Marketing Research Association, and the Council of American Survey Research Organizations (CASRO)—have developed codes of research ethics and standards of conduct. For example, the CASRO Code of Standards and Ethics for Survey Research outlines researcher responsibilities to respondents, including confidentiality, privacy, and avoidance of harassment. It also outlines major responsibilities in reporting results to clients and the public.[45]

In the end, however, unethical or inappropriate actions cannot simply be regulated away. Each company must accept responsibility for policing the conduct and reporting of its own marketing research to protect consumers' best interests as well as its own.

Reviewing and Extending the Concepts

Objectives Review

To create value for customers and build meaningful relationships with them, marketers must first gain fresh, deep insights into what customers need and want. Such insights come from good marketing information. Because of the recent explosion of "big data" and digital technologies, companies can now obtain great quantities of information, often even too much. Consumers themselves are now generating a tidal wave of bottom-up information through their smartphones, PCs, and tablets via online browsing, apps and social media interactions, texting and video, and geolocation data. The challenge is to transform today's vast volume of consumer information into actionable customer and market insights.

OBJECTIVE 4-1 Explain the importance of information in gaining insights about the marketplace and customers. (pp 118–120)

The marketing process starts with a complete understanding of the marketplace and consumer needs and wants. Thus, the company needs to turn sound consumer information into meaningful *customer insights* by which it can produce superior value for its customers. The company also requires information on competitors, resellers, and other actors and forces in the marketplace. Increasingly, marketers are viewing information not only as an input for making better decisions but also as an important strategic asset and marketing tool.

OBJECTIVE 4-2 Define the marketing information system and discuss its parts. (pp 120–123)

The *marketing information system* (MIS) consists of people and procedures for assessing information needs, developing the needed information, and helping decision makers use the information to generate and validate actionable customer and market insights. A well-designed information system begins and ends with users.

The MIS first *assesses information needs.* The MIS primarily serves the company's marketing and other managers, but it may also provide information to external partners. Then the MIS *develops information* from internal databases, marketing intelligence activities, and marketing research. *Internal databases* provide information on the company's own operations and departments. Such data can be obtained quickly and cheaply but often need to be adapted for marketing decisions. *Marketing intelligence* activities supply everyday information about developments in the external marketing environment, including listening and responding to the vast and complex digital environment. *Market research* consists of collecting information relevant to a specific marketing problem faced by the company. Last, the marketing information system helps users analyze and use the information to develop customer insights, make marketing decisions, and manage customer relationships.

OBJECTIVE 4-3 Outline the role of marketing research and the steps in the marketing research process.

(pp 123–136)

In recent years, as a host of new digital data gathering technologies have burst onto the scene, traditional marketing research has undergone a major transformation. Traditional mainstays such as research surveys and focus groups, although still prevalent and powerful approaches, are now giving way to newer, more agile, more immediate, and less costly digital data gathering methods. Although its role is changing, however, traditional marketing research is still widely used and important.

The first step in the marketing research process involves *defining the problem and setting the research objectives*, which may be exploratory, descriptive, or causal research. The second step consists of *developing a research plan* for collecting data from primary and secondary sources. The third step calls for *implementing the marketing research plan* by gathering, processing, and analyzing the information. The fourth step consists of *interpreting and reporting the findings.* Additional information analysis helps marketing managers apply the information and provides them with sophisticated statistical procedures and models from which to develop more rigorous findings.

Both *internal* and *external* secondary data sources often provide information more quickly and at a lower cost than primary data sources, and they can sometimes yield information that a company cannot collect by itself. However, needed information might not exist in secondary sources. Researchers must also evaluate secondary information to ensure that it is *relevant, accurate, current*, and *impartial.*

Primary research must also be evaluated for these features. Each primary data collection method—*observational, survey*, and *experimental*—has its own advantages and disadvantages. Similarly, each of the various research contact methods—mail, telephone, personal interview, and online—has its own advantages and drawbacks.

OBJECTIVE 4-4 Explain how companies analyze and use marketing information. (pp 136–140)

Information gathered in internal databases and through marketing intelligence and marketing research usually requires more analysis. To analyze individual customer data, many companies have now acquired or developed special software and analysis techniques—called *customer relationship management* (CRM)—that integrate, analyze, and apply the mountains of individual customer data to gain a 360-degree view of customers and build stronger the customer relationships. They apply *marketing analytics* and *artificial intelligence* to dig out meaningful patterns in big data and gain customer insights and gauge marketing performance.

Marketing information has no value until it is used to make better marketing decisions. Thus, the MIS must make the information available to managers and others who make marketing decisions or deal with customers. In some cases, this means providing regular reports and updates; in other cases, it means making nonroutine information available for special situations and on-the-spot decisions. Many firms use company intranets and extranets to facilitate this process. Thanks to modern technology, today's marketing managers can gain direct access to marketing information at any time and from virtually any location.

OBJECTIVE 4-5 Discuss the special issues some marketing researchers face, including public policy and ethics issues. *(pp 140–144)*

Some marketers face special marketing research situations, such as those conducting research in small business, not-for-profit, or international situations. Marketing research can be conducted effectively by small businesses and nonprofit organizations with limited budgets. International marketing researchers follow the same steps as domestic researchers but often face more and different problems. All organizations need to act responsibly concerning major public policy and ethical issues surrounding marketing research, including issues of intrusions on consumer privacy. Consumer data security and protection, and misuse of research findings.

Key Terms

OBJECTIVE 4-1

Big data (p 119)
Customer insights (p 119)
Marketing information system (MIS) (p 119)

OBJECTIVE 4-2

Internal databases (p 121)
Competitive marketing intelligence (p 121)

OBJECTIVE 4-3

Marketing research (p 123)
Exploratory research (p 125)
Descriptive research (p 125)
Causal research (p 125)
Secondary data (p 126)
Primary data (p 126)
Observational research (p 127)
Ethnographic research (p 127)
Survey research (p 128)
Experimental research (p 128)

Focus group interviewing (p 129)
Online marketing research (p 130)
Online focus groups (p 131)
Behavioral targeting (p 132)
Sample (p 132)

OBJECTIVE 4-4

Customer relationship management (CRM) (p 136)
Marketing analytics (p 137)
Artificial intelligence (AI) (p 138)

Discussion Questions

4-1 Explain how marketing intelligence differs from marketing research. Which is more valuable to a company? Why? (AACSB: Written and Oral Communication; Reflective Thinking)

4-2 Differentiate between exploratory research, descriptive research, and causal research. (AACSB: Communication; Reflective Thinking)

4-3 What three questions need to be answered when a researcher designs the sample? When would a marketing researcher use a nonprobability sample? What is the weakness of nonprobability samples relative to probability samples? (AACSB: Communication; Reflective Thinking)

4-4 What is behavioral targeting? Provide an example of behavioral targeting. How are firms responding to consumers and public advocates' contention that it is a means of stalking consumers? (AACSB: Communication; Reflective Thinking)

4-5 The marketing research process has several very distinct and important stages that need to be followed. In your opinion, which is the most important? Justify your view on this. (AACSB: Communication; Reflective Thinking)

4-6 What are the similarities and differences when conducting research in another country versus the domestic market? What research strategies might a company use to address the differences in various markets? (AACSB: Communication; Reflective Thinking)

Critical Thinking Exercises

4-7 Visit www.nielsen.com/us/en/insights/reports.html and select an example of a recent research report. Include the URL in a response that describes the study or studies that informed the report. Where did Nielsen get the data that informed the insights in the report? (The report may include more than one source of data.) What are the strengths and weaknesses of the types of data used? How is the information presented? How will people who see the results of the study likely respond based on the presentation? Provide one example of how the insight might be used by a marketer. (AACSB: Communication; Reflective Thinking)

4-8 In a small group, identify the steps a business organization might need to take to carry out market research in an overseas market. Discuss whether the business would be best advised to have someone do the research for them or do it themselves. (Objective 2) (AACSB: Communication; Reflective Thinking)

4-9 Go to Google Trends (trends.google.com). Assume you are a consumer goods marketer that oversees a sparkling water product. How could the Google Trends information help your company improve its understanding of its market? Conduct a search that could provide information that might increase profits. Explain what you searched and what insights you gained that could inform decision making. (AACSB: Communication; Use of IT; Reflective Thinking)

APPLICATIONS AND CASES

Online, Mobile, and Social Media Marketing Creepy Data

In each second of every day, personal information is being indexed and processed. Every device we use has a unique address that is being broadcast as long as you have wireless networking switched on. Many of us do not even realize that programs exist to find every picture you may have ever posted online. They can also pinpoint exactly where you were when you uploaded them. If you haven't set the right privacy settings, it will be fairly easy to work out exactly where you live, your habits, and when you are at home and when you are out. Some services are specifically designed to scare people about the information they are unintentionally leaking to the world, such as PleaseRobMe. com. This shows you whether you are sharing your location to prompt us to change our privacy settings.[46]

4-10 Make a careful list of all the websites, forums, social networks, and other places you have visited this week. What data have you left that could have value to a business? (AACSB: Communication; Use of IT)

4-11 Monetizing this data is the key to revealing its true value. Should marketers have access to such information? Discuss how you would use data trails left by individuals on the Internet if you ran a business. (AACSB: Communication; Ethical Reasoning)

Marketing Ethics WeChat

WeChat, an app in China, offers its users a "one-stop shop" for features. Users can chat, shop, form new social connections, order and pay for food, make payments, identify crowded locations, make investments, and make doctor's appointments—among other things—all without leaving the app. As a result, WeChat collects large amounts of valuable data about its consumers and their habits that it monetizes by selling advertising. Companies in China are required to share this information with the government, which has a history of human rights violations. Technology companies in the United States aim to develop similar capabilities in order to keep people engaged and gather volumes of valuable data, which may be one reason Facebook moved to allow users of Facebook Messenger, Instagram, and WhatsApp messengers to communicate across platforms. While consumers value the convenience

and personalized offers they gain by letting WeChat gather data, there are concerns about privacy intrusions and other entities that can access the data.

4-12 If you used an app like WeChat, what information would you be comfortable having tied to your identity? What information would you prefer not be tracked? What is the trade-off between convenience and privacy? (AACSB Communication; Reflective Thinking)

4-13 Is it ethical for marketers to gather massive amounts of data about everything a consumer does and sell advertising using the information. What types of protections do you value as a consumer? (AACSB: Communication; Ethical Reasoning)

Marketing by the Numbers What's Your Sample?

Decisions are often made by businesses on the basis of fairly small samples in relation to the actual size of the population or number of customers. Thus, the future of products and services is often determined by relatively small numbers of people. But just how reliable are small-scale samples? Larger samples cost more money; they take more time and ultimately may not be any more accurate than a smaller sample. Are businesses and organizations right to rely so heavily on these small samples? Statistically speaking, a small sample is probably just as accurate.

4-14 Go to http://www.surveysystem.com/sscalc.htm to determine the appropriate sample size for a population

in your country. Briefly explain what is meant by confidence interval and confidence level. Assuming a confidence interval of 5, how large should the sample of households be when desiring a 95 percent confidence level? How large for a 99 percent confidence level? (AACSB: Communication; Information Technology; Analytical Thinking)

4-15 What sample sizes are necessary to cover the population of the whole region in which you live with a confidence interval of 5 percent and a 95-percent confidence level? Explain the effect population size has on a required sample size. (AACSB: Written Communication; Information Technology; Analytical Thinking)

Company Case Bayer: Big Data for Customer Insights

Bayer Aktiengesellschaft, or Bayer AG, is a life sciences company and a global leader in healthcare and nutrition. Headquartered in Leverkusen, Germany, Bayer has a strong presence in Europe and more than 150 years of experience. To expand its operations, Bayer carefully examines the size of the market, determines its profitability, and analyzes the entry and exit barriers. Marketing information is vital for decisions on entering new markets and about adapting to existing ones, but Bayer must balance its information gathering against its policy on customers' data privacy as well as alignment with future operational objectives. When it comes to entering new markets, Bayer's analyses are based heavily on customer satisfaction and performance measures.

Reading the Customer's Mind

Bayer bases its various strategies on marketing information. Some of its markets are difficult to operate in; for example, pharmaceuticals involves multiple customers, distribution channels, purchasing arrangements and pricing methodologies, marketing techniques, and cost-control tools or prescription drug reimbursement systems. Gaining useful customer or marketplace insights from these various sources is challenging. Additionally, Bayer conducts research to discover new drugs and tests and validates their effectiveness and safety before introducing them to the market. As such, the company accumulates, analyzes, and stores vast amounts of clinical data from patients as well as healthy volunteers. Marketing information is also collected from laboratories and electronic devices but is automatically anonymized at the point of collection, following the guidelines and regulations created by local drugs administrations. Recently, Bayer deployed a microservices-based architecture for its data platform to enable easier and faster analysis of drug development data for company's researchers.

Bayer operates mainly as a business-to-business (B2B) company, but in the pharmaceuticals market, its focus is on researching, developing, and marketing specialty-focused medicines to businesses as well as individual consumers. Its products are distributed to hospitals and general practitioners, who also deliver useful marketplace insights. But Bayer carefully examines all information gathered even before it distributes to these intermediaries. For example, for distribution of the allergy drug Claritin, Bayer uses third-party analytics to analyze global warming data so that it can model the supply based on weather trends and allergy trends.

Bayer's customer insights and marketplace data are processed based mainly on how specialized products are received within the pharmaceutical market. Healthcare division insights are communicated between Bayer and the brands to which its products are distributed. Coupled with a large geographical footprint, this results in an enormous store of insights and techniques that can be used in marketing mix decision-making, formulation of marketing strategy, as well as daily business operations.

Bayer has market- and customer-specific distribution channels for each segment in which it operates. Through a number of programs, such as its Patient-Focused Transformation of Customer Engagement, the company draws on the experiences and challenges of participants to support business transformation initiatives at the company with the objective of shifting mindsets, implementing new processes, building new skills, or changing target behaviors. This customer engagement model has transformed information gathering into a single customer-centric and patient-focused model.

The consumer health and pharmaceuticals segments are connected to a global pharmaceutical monitoring system that includes safety management teams and experts across various disciplines. To detect potential safety concerns early on and identify changes in the risk–benefit profile, such teams must evaluate internal benefits, safety data, marketing studies, clinical trials, external databases, and scientific publications. These are all entered into Bayer's pharmacovigilance database, which is used in market research to test the viability of new products and services based on the responses of potential customers. The company is constantly investing in R&D—which generates information—but each product must also comply with the relevant regulatory environment.

Diving Deeper for Insights

At Bayer, internal data is information about customers—current and potential—collected primarily from four major sources: sales, finance, human resources, and marketing. However, gaining trade insights from each segment can be challenging due to legal requirements, especially from sources such as patients. For example, to collect customer satisfaction data, the company must follow different standards for prescription medicines and for non-prescription medicines.

Bayer's marketing activities focus on the local needs of its customers, but these needs can vary significantly. The company's customer-focused marketing activities take this into account. For instance, working together with Kansas City-based Consumer Orbit, Bayer combines the data it generates with the firm's databases, resulting in a total of 63 trillion pieces of data that enable Bayer to build a model of its customer base and deliver tailored messages to its customers through their preferred communications platform.

However, customer needs may differ merely because each country or state has its own set of rules and laws. The company must adhere to laws and regulations dealing with marketing practices; global, regional, and local industry codes; customer privacy and protection of consumer information and data; and recommendation and promotion only of lawful uses (for instance, there should be no off-label promotion for medicinal products). Ongoing dialogues with customers enable the company to take such local and country-specific regulatory frameworks into account and deploy optimization measures.

Bayer analyzes customer satisfaction reports and customer complaints to compare the company's performance in the individual segments, optimize its measures, and safeguard its long-term business strategy. Various marketing research techniques ensure accurate directions for shaping and redefining its marketing strategy. For instance, by using AI-driven diagnostic and treatment support for individual customers in the pharmaceuticals segment, the company accelerates the discovery of new drugs while combining processing power with the large data sets and advanced analytics available for marketing information. This allows Bayer to offer a personalized testing and treatment as well as personalized online medical consulting that examines customers' lifestyles, health, and diet directly through a website.

On June 7, 2018 Bayer acquired 100 percent of the outstanding shares of Monsanto Company. Bayer's strong position within the market is often contested by, for example, the fusion of Dow Chemical and Dupont, the two largest U.S. chemical groups. In crop science, Monsanto's position is more secure, so Bayer benefits from already present marketplace information and can outperform competitors. The acquisition strengthens Bayer's position as market leader in crop science, with the leading digital agriculture platform—Bayer now has better access to farmers than anybody else. The growing importance of data analysis and digital farming tools not only facilitates agronomic advice but also sales of seeds and pesticides.

Before taking any crucial decision, Bayer must determine in advance how the product works and what the market's regulatory environment is. For this purpose, the company collects external data to find out which market to enter and when is the best time to make an investment. This is where the big data from the Monsanto merger comes into play. Big data often opens new windows of opportunities; for instance, Bayer can now process terabytes of data into relevant information that helps farmers unleash their crops' full potential and achieve efficient yields that improve their financial results.

Big data is transforming agriculture to an almost overwhelming degree. Tractors and other farming devices equipped with sensors, mobile connectivity, and GPS; drones with infrared cameras and GPS patrolling the air and reporting on field conditions; satellites and phone apps monitoring soil and climate conditions—these are just a few sources of information. Recognizing the growing market for digital-based agricultural services, Bayer is increasingly employing data science methods in all R&D activities, bolstering its scientists' expertise with targeted data science learning programs. Bayer maintains a global network of R&D locations and employs about 17,300 researchers. In 2018, R&D investments increased by a nominal 16.5 percent to €5.2 billion. In addition, the company recently adopted data aggregation and direct partnerships with key vendors to further improve efficiencies.

Safeguarding Privacy

Bayer encapsulates its corporate values in what it calls the LIFE standard: Leadership, Integrity, Flexibility and Efficiency. It is followed in the marketing of their products and services as well. For instance, its standards of Integrity are reflected in the care with which the company handles privacy when it comes to customer data. Bayer ensures that specialized service contractors who handle customers' personal data work closely with the company to process the data strictly within its regulations and directives and follow respective data processor agreements; the company also monitors these contractors regularly.

The company's corporate compliance policy on responsible marketing and sales details multiple measures that are taken to prevent any ethical issues. Bayer's lobbyists are required to act according to certain standards, such as national laws and the respective jurisdiction in which the country carries out all lobbying activities.

Bayer recognizes that it is part of a global community and has stated that only a joint effort will provide the technologies and services required to feed the global population in 2050. Making the most of available farmland, increasing production on a long-term basis, and making breakthroughs in healthcare requires vast amounts of data. Through its use of big data, gathered from its collaborations with research institutes, leading scientists, international organizations, and government bodies across all the segments it operates in, Bayer is well poised to fulfill that need.[47]

Questions for Discussion

4-16 What opportunities are created for Bayer from the big data coming from the four segments it operates in and from the Monsanto merger?

4-17 How does Bayer gather relevant marketing information to keep up with customer demands in the four segments?

4-18 How does Bayer manage the information gathered from the various stakeholders mentioned in this case?

4-19 How are the steps of the marketing research process followed at Bayer?

4-20 How does Bayer safeguard customer privacy in its marketing research?

5 Consumer Markets and Buyer Behavior

OBJECTIVES OUTLINE

OBJECTIVE 5-1 Define the consumer market and construct a simple model of consumer buyer behavior. See: **Model of Consumer Behavior** *(pp 152–153)*

OBJECTIVE 5-2 Name the four major factors that influence consumer buyer behavior. See: **Characteristics Affecting Consumer Behavior** *(pp 153–167)*

OBJECTIVE 5-3 List and define the major types of buying decision behavior and the stages in the buyer decision process. See: **Buying Decision Behavior and the Buyer Decision Process** *(pp 167–172)*

OBJECTIVE 5-4 Describe the adoption and diffusion process for new products. See: **The Buyer Decision Process for New Products** *(pp 172–174)*

CHAPTER PREVIEW You've studied how marketers obtain, analyze, and use information to develop customer insights and assess marketing programs. In this chapter, we take a closer look at the most important element of the marketplace—customers. The aim of marketing is to engage customers and affect how they think and act. To affect the *whats, whens*, and *hows* of buyer behavior, marketers must first understand the *whys*. In this chapter, we look at *final consumer* buying influences and processes. In the next chapter, we'll study the buyer behavior of *business customers*.

You'll see that understanding buyer behavior is an essential but very difficult task.

To get a better sense of the importance of understanding consumer behavior, we begin by looking at Lenovo, the world's largest personal computer vendor by unit sales. Before it acquired IBM's computer business, you might never have heard of Lenovo. Yet few brands can match the avid enthusiasm and intense loyalty that Lenovo has generated in its customers. Its business model is thus built on customer satisfaction, innovation, and operational efficiency.

LENOVO: Understanding Customers and Building Profitable Relationships

Lenovo was established in Beijing, China, in 1984 by 11 members of the Computer Technology Research Institute. Originally founded as Legend by Liu Chunzhi with a group of 10 engineers, the company decided to abandon the brand name in 2002 to expand internationally, and so its name was changed to Lenovo. In 2005, the company acquired IBM's personal computer business, including the ThinkPad laptop and tablet lines. This acquisition accelerated access to foreign markets and made Lenovo the third-largest computer maker worldwide by volume. In 2018, Lenovo was the world's largest personal computer vendor in terms of units shipped and beat out HP and Dell for the year overall. The Chinese company, which is also the world's third largest smartphone company, has operations in more than 60 countries, with products sold in around 160 countries.

The global success of Lenovo is rooted in its deep and sound understanding of customers and its ability to build profitable relationships. The business model is thus built on customer satisfaction, innovation, and operational efficiency, so Lenovo's marketers focus on customers and their buying behavior: Who are they? What do they think? How do they feel about the products? What makes them tick? To find comprehensive answers to these questions, Lenovo's product design and engineering teams listen to their customers through their social media channels, forums, blogs, and fan clubs around the world. The company highly values the input of its customers and tracks it accordingly. For example, after Lenovo had introduced new variants of its Lenovo ThinkPad series in 2012 and 2013, customers complained on internet forums that the two physical TrackPoint buttons had been removed

Lenovo listens and communicates constantly with their customers and takes their input into consideration.
Lou-Foto/Alamy Stock Photo

from the touch-pad at the bottom of the keyboard. These buttons correspond to the left and right mouse buttons on a conventional mouse and work as a substitute to an external mouse or touch-pad. Always with an ear to the ground, Lenovo soon realized this issue and publicly admitted that they had made a big mistake. Soon afterwards, they brought back the TrackPoint buttons.

Lenovo's product development is always driven by deep customer understanding from around the globe. The company emphasizes on its websites that every time customers provide feedback in some form, they are actually and personally helping to influence the next wave of technology that it puts into the market. By listening and communicating constantly with their customers and taking into consideration their input when it comes to product development and improvement, Lenovo has been successful in building emotional relationships with their customers. They engage more directly with customers when they display traits such as honesty in admitting mistakes, as in case of the ThinkPad re-design. Through the years, Lenovo's emphasis on building emotional relationships with their customers has given them a more personal cast than a mere computer manufacturer.

In addition to listening to their customers, Lenovo also filters and analyzes the online behavior of visitors to its sites, focusing on purchasers and non-purchasers and their online buying behavior on the homepage and product

pages in particular. Studying them both enables Lenovo to develop and deliver the right message to the right users, turning non-purchasing users into purchasers. In order to achieve this objective, Lenovo permanently visualizes the in-page behavior of each customer segment via so-called heat maps, which provide deep insights into users' digital psychology.

Lenovo is continuously conducting consumer studies to identify areas for development in terms of customer experience. For example, when the company found out that purchasers were drawn to the main homepage banner and deals (whereas non-purchasers avoided the banner and were favoring product images and videos over text) the company used greater ratios of images and videos to text in order to guide those potential customers and engage with them to a greater extent.

Lenovo has also focused on integrating data and create a 360-degree view of customers. In order to achieve this, Lenovo uses Google Surveys 360, which allows them to get real-team, actionable insights that can be incorporated into the development process. For example, the design team had different versions of icons that would represent a specific functionality that it wanted to test. The team did not know which one would be most intuitive. They used Google Surveys 360 that gave them answers that helped them focus on and that too much faster than regular research studies.

> The global success of Lenovo is rooted in its deep and sound understanding of customers and its ability to build profitable relationships. The business model is thus built on customer satisfaction, innovation, and operational efficiency.

Understanding what's most important to the customer is paramount for Lenovo because the company continuously focuses on exceeding customer expectations and creating customer delight. For example, when the company noticed that many of the discussions about PCs, tablets, and other electronic devices were happening on blogs and third-party discussion forums, they spent a lot of time trying to understand the existing conversations and participating in discussions. Lenovo then decided that it wanted more ownership, even better customer understanding, and stronger leadership in the discussions about its products. Accordingly, Lenovo set up its own discussion forums and actively asked customers to share their ideas, user experience, and tips with Lenovo's product, design, and development teams. By doing so, Lenovo was able to better connect with its customers and provide even better customer service.

In all, Lenovo possesses a unique ability to achieve customer satisfaction and engagement. The company has positively shaped and influenced customers' perceptions of Lenovo's brand personality by trying to listen to and understand them. Consumers today—conditioned by mobile and powered by the Internet—need brands that can interact with them in real time. Lenovo engages in a consistent, respectful, two-way dialogue with their target audience. As a result, various satisfaction studies consistently place the company well ahead of its competitors in various satisfaction studies. For example, in its Corporate IT Buying Behavior and Customer Satisfaction studies, consultancy firm Technology Business Research named Lenovo the best computer brand for offering customer satisfaction and innovation that is second to none.[1]

Consumer buyer behavior

The buying behavior of final consumers—individuals and households that buy goods and services for personal consumption.

Consumer market

All the individuals and households that buy or acquire goods and services for personal consumption.

THE LENOVO EXAMPLE shows that factors at many levels affect consumer buying behavior. Buying behavior is never simple, yet understanding it is an essential task of marketing management. **Consumer buyer behavior** refers to the buying behavior of final consumers—individuals and households that buy goods and services for personal consumption. All of these final consumers combine to make up the **consumer market**. The American consumer market consists of more than 328 million people who consume more than $13 trillion worth of goods and services each year, making it one of the most attractive consumer markets in the world.[2]

Consumers around the world vary tremendously in age, income, education level, and tastes. They also buy an incredible variety of goods and services. How these diverse consumers relate with each other and with other elements of the world around them affects their choices among various products, services, and companies. Here we examine the fascinating array of factors that affect consumer behavior.

Author Comment | Despite the simple-looking model in Figure 5.1, understanding the whys of buying behavior is very difficult. Says one expert, "The mind is a whirling, swirling, jumbled mass of neurons bouncing around..."

Model of Consumer Behavior

OBJECTIVE 5-1 Define the consumer market and construct a simple model of consumer buyer behavior.

Consumers make many buying decisions every day, and the buying decision is the focal point of the marketer's effort. Most large companies research consumer buying decisions in great detail to answer questions about what consumers buy, where they buy, how and how much they buy, when they buy, and why they buy. Marketers mine mountains of big data on consumers to learn about their paths to purchase. But learning about the *whys* behind consumer buying behavior is not so easy—the answers are often locked deep within the consumer's mind. Often, consumers themselves don't know exactly what influences their purchases.

The central question for marketers is this: How do consumers respond to various marketing efforts the company might use? The starting point is the stimulus-response model of buyer behavior shown in ● **Figure 5.1**. This figure shows that marketing and other stimuli enter the consumer's "black box" and produce certain responses.

● FIGURE 5.1
The Model of Buyer Behavior

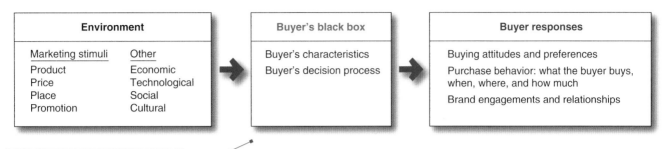

We can measure the whats, wheres, and whens of consumer buying behavior. But it's very diffcult to "see" inside the consumer's head and figure out the whys of buying behavior (that's why it's called the black box). Marketers spend a lot of energy and dollars trying to figure out what makes customers tick.

Marketers want to understand how the stimuli are changed into responses inside the consumer's black box, which has two parts. First, the buyer's characteristics influence how he or she perceives and reacts to the stimuli. These characteristics include a variety of cultural, social, personal, and psychological factors. Second, the buyer's decision process itself affects his or her behavior. This decision process—from need recognition, information search, and alternative evaluation to the purchase decision and postpurchase behavior—begins long before the actual purchase decision and continues long after. We look first at buyer characteristics as they affect buyer behavior and then discuss the buyer decision process.

Author | Many levels of factors
Comment | affect our buying
behavior—from broad cultural and social influences to motivations, beliefs, and attitudes lying deep within us.

Characteristics Affecting Consumer Behavior

OBJECTIVE 5-2 Name the four major factors that influence consumer buyer behavior.

Consumer purchases are influenced strongly by cultural, social, personal, and psychological characteristics, as shown in ● **Figure 5.2**. For the most part, marketers cannot control such factors, but they must take them into account.

Cultural Factors

Cultural factors exert a broad and deep influence on consumer behavior. Marketers need to understand the role played by the buyer's *culture, subculture*, and *social class*.

● FIGURE 5.2
Factors Influencing
Consumer Behavior

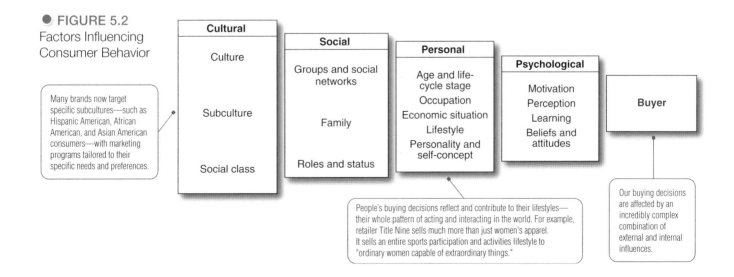

Many brands now target specific subcultures—such as Hispanic American, African American, and Asian American consumers—with marketing programs tailored to their specific needs and preferences.

People's buying decisions reflect and contribute to their lifestyles— their whole pattern of acting and interacting in the world. For example, retailer Title Nine sells much more than just women's apparel. It sells an entire sports participation and activities lifestyle to "ordinary women capable of extraordinary things."

Our buying decisions are affected by an incredibly complex combination of external and internal influences.

Culture

Culture
The set of basic values, perceptions, wants, and behaviors learned by a member of society from family and other important institutions.

Culture is the most basic cause of a person's wants and behavior. Human behavior is largely learned. Growing up in a society, a child learns basic values, perceptions, wants, and behaviors from his or her family and other important institutions. A child in the United States normally is exposed to the following values: equality, individualism, directness, informality, achievement and success, activity and involvement, time and its importance, material comfort, and health and fitness. Every group or society has a culture, and cultural influences on buying behavior may vary greatly from both county to county and country to country.

Marketers are always trying to spot *cultural shifts* to discover new products that might be wanted. For example, the cultural shift toward greater concern about health and fitness has created a huge industry for health-and-fitness services, exercise equipment and clothing, organic foods, and a variety of diets.

Subculture

Subculture
A group of people with shared value systems based on common life experiences and situations.

Each culture contains smaller **subcultures**, or groups of people with shared value systems based on common life experiences and situations. Subcultures include nationalities, religions, racial groups, and geographic regions. Many subcultures make up important market segments, and marketers often design products and marketing programs tailored to their needs. Examples of three such important subculture groups are Hispanic American, African American, and Asian American consumers.

Hispanic American Consumers. *Hispanics* represent a large, fast-growing market. The nation's more than 59 million Hispanic consumers have total annual buying power of $1.7 trillion. The U.S. Hispanic population will surge in coming decades, growing to represent nearly 29 percent of the total U.S. population by 2060. Hispanics are a youthful segment, with more than half under the age of 29.[3] Within the Hispanic market, there exist many distinct subsegments based on nationality, age, income, and other factors. A company's product or message may be more relevant to one nationality over another, such as Mexicans, Costa Ricans, Argentineans, or Cubans.

Although Hispanic consumers share many characteristics and behaviors with the mainstream buying public, there are also distinct differences. They tend to be deeply family oriented and make shopping a family affair—children have a big say in what brands they buy. And befitting their youthfulness, Hispanics are more active on mobile and social networks than other segments, making digital media ideal for reaching this segment.

For example, about 24 million of Twitter's 68 million active monthly U.S. users are Hispanics—they represent 35 percent of active Twitter users versus 18 percent of the U.S. population. Accordingly, Twitter recently created an internal U.S. Hispanic team to help advertisers reach its large and fast-growing Hispanic audience. Xfinity Comcast, for instance, used Twitter's bilingual targeting option during Hispanic Heritage Month to reach Hispanics who might be interested in its new bilingual remote control. ● And Nestlé's DiGiorno brand worked with Twitter's U.S. Hispanics team and the NFL on a football campaign with Spanish tweets.[4]

Companies ranging from Toyota, P&G, McDonald's, AT&T, Walmart, and State Farm to Google, Amazon, and L'Oréal have developed special targeting efforts for this fast-growing consumer segment. For example, working with its longtime Hispanic advertising agency Conill, Toyota has developed numerous Hispanic marketing campaigns that have helped make it the favorite automobile brand among Hispanic buyers. Consider its Toyota Tundra campaign during the 2018 FIFA World Cup soccer tournament.[5]

● Targeting Hispanic consumers: Nestle's DiGiorno brand worked with Twitter's U.S. Hispanics team and the NFL to create a football campaign with Spanish tweets.

Nestlé USA

During the FIFA World Cup soccer tournament in Russia in 2018, many American brands based their ad campaigns on the fact that the games were on U.S. TV very early. Toyota ran just such a campaign for its Tundra pickup truck aimed at Hispanic viewers, built around an actual super-strong coffee—Tundra Power Café Fuerte—sourced in Mexico. A tongue-in-cheek video run during the games showed groggy-eyed Hispanic consumers falling asleep at work after getting up early to view soccer matches. "Games are going to be really, really early," proclaimed the video in Spanish. "Someone has to do something."

The solution: The video shows a Tundra truck going deep into remote regions of Mexico during the murky morning hours collecting coffee beans. "That's why Toyota Tundra went to Mexico to bring you a coffee as strong as the truck that knows about getting up early and working hard all day long," says the announcer. Toyota also promoted the coffee on its Hispanic social media channels, handed out samples of the coffee at Tundra Power Mobile Coffee Shops near special viewing areas, and let fans order it to their homes using #TundraPower and #Ad.

African American Consumers. The U.S. *African American* population is growing in affluence and sophistication. The nation's 47 million black consumers wield $1.5 trillion in annual buying power. Although more price conscious than other segments, blacks are also strongly motivated by quality and selection. Brands are important. African American consumers are heavy users of digital and social media, providing access through a rich variety of marketing channels. Also, relative to the total population, black consumers tend more to pressure business to do and be better. For example, 38 percent of African Americans ages of 18 to 34 say they expect the brands they buy to support social causes, compared with only 4 percent of the broader population.[6]

Many companies develop special products, appeals, and marketing programs for African American consumers—from carmakers like Ford, Toyota, and Hyundai to consumer products companies like P&G and Unilever. ● For example, P&G has long been the leader in African American advertising. In addition to traditional product marketing efforts, however, P&G also supports a broader "My Black Is Beautiful" movement:[7]

Created more than a decade ago by a group of African American women at P&G, the movement aims "to ignite and support a sustained national conversation by, for, and about black women" and to "serve as the catalyst for a movement that effects positive change." The latest My Black Is Beautiful campaign focuses attention on issues of discrimination. It features an Emmy-winning video ad called "The Talk," which shows moving situations in which black parents convey to their children the prejudices they will face in life. Other "The Talk" videos, posted on the My Black Is Beautiful website, show how real people have dealt with negative bias in their everyday lives. Each video concludes by urging viewers to "talk about 'the talk' so we can end the need to have it," followed by, "It's time for everyone to #TalkAboutBias." Although the My Black Is Beautiful campaigns don't directly promote P&G products, they help to build positive relationships between P&G brands and black consumers.

● **Targeting African American consumers: P&G's "My Black Is Beautiful" campaign aims to spark conversation by, for, and about black women to effect positive change. The campaign helps to build positive relationships between P&G brands and black consumers.**

Tasia Wells/Stringer/Getty Images

Asian American Consumers. *Asian Americans* are the most affluent U.S. demographic segment. A relatively well-educated segment, they now number more than 20 million, with annual buying power of $1 trillion. Asian Americans are the nation's fastest-growing subsegment. And like the other subsegments, they are a diverse group. Chinese Americans constitute the largest group, followed by Filipinos, Asian Indians, Vietnamese, Korean Americans, and Japanese Americans. Yet, unlike Hispanics who all speak various dialects of Spanish, Asians speak many different languages from Japanese and Cantonese to Khmer and Taglish.[8]

As a group, Asian American consumers shop frequently and are the most brand conscious of all the ethnic groups. They can be fiercely brand loyal, especially to brands that work to build relationships with them. As a result, many firms now target the Asian American market. For example, insurer State Farm recently release two new spots across Asian digital platforms targeting different segments of the growing Asian American market:[9]

The first ad, a Mandarin-language spot called "Smart Living," provides a humorous take on cultural insights into the tech savviness of Asian Americans, who are leading adopters of smart home technologies. The ad shows a young Asian American couple being terrorized by their Alexa-like home system called SAL gone awry. SAL closes the garage door on their car, turns on their in-home sprinkler system, and blasts them out with loud music. However, State Farm agent Amy Loh assures them that while State Farm can't fix SAL, it can certainly cover the home and auto damages. A second spot—"Intuition"— plays off Asian Indian cultural insights. When a young couple's Asian Indian parents visit and offer unwanted advice with comedic results, State Farm agent Anu Sethi gives them in-language advice and is there to help life go right. "This creative work strikes a balance of providing information while recognizing and respecting cultural nuances," says State Farm's advertising director. "We really want humor to drive these stories in a way our audiences could completely see themselves."

Total Marketing Strategy

Total market strategy
Integrating ethnic themes and cross-cultural perspectives within a brand's mainstream marketing, appealing to consumer similarities across subcultural segments rather than differences.

Beyond targeting segments such as Hispanics, African Americans, and Asian Americans with specially tailored efforts, many marketers now embrace a **total market strategy**— the practice of integrating ethnic themes and cross-cultural perspectives within their main-stream marketing. An example is general-market commercials for brands such as Cheerios and IKEA that feature interracial and blended families and couples. A total market approach appeals to consumer similarities across subcultural segments rather than differences.[10]

Toyota uses a total market strategy that includes both ads targeting specific subcultural segments and cross-cultural ads aimed at the general market:[11]

A portion of the recent Toyota Camry "Sensations" marketing campaign features ads target-ing Hispanic, African American, and Asian American subsegments, prepared by specialized, ethnic-focused ad agencies. For example, a commercial titled "Captivating" captures the bond between a Chinese American father and daughter as they share the thrilling technology features of their new Camry, emphasizing the importance of family and technology to Asian American consumers. Another ad titled "Rebellious"—aired in both English and Spanish—shows a young Hispanic man in a red Camry hesitating before declining a call on his phone from his mother. It's an edgy move based on Hispanic generational insights. Still another ad, "Strut," features an African American man transforming a routine run to pick up pizza into "a cool slice of style." "We found that with African-Americans style really comes to the forefront in how we look at cars," says an executive at the agency that created the ad.

At the same time, the "Sensations" campaign also features overarching mainstream ads prepared by Toyota's general-market ad agency. These ads appeal to what Toyota's national manager of brand, multicultural, and crossline marketing strategy calls "the total transcultural market." They employ a diverse mix of actors and environments under a single, overall theme that focuses on shared, cross-cultural consumer values rather than cultural differences.

So, Toyota appears to cover all its bases under a comprehensive total marketing strategy. In the mainstream ads, "people like to see people of all ethnicities in what they're seeing because that's the life they're living in most of the U.S. today," says a Toyota brand executive. At the same time, in the ethnic-focused ads, "if a person of any group is looking for communication that is like them, that looks like them specifically, the good news is because of the breadth of something like a Camry campaign, they can find it."

Social Class

Social class
Relatively permanent and ordered divisions in a society whose members share similar values, interests, and behaviors.

Almost every society has some form of social class structure. **Social classes** are society's relatively permanent and ordered divisions whose members share similar values, interests, and behaviors. Social scientists have identified seven American social classes: upper-upper class, lower-upper class, upper-middle class, middle class, working class, upper-lower class, and lower-lower class.

Social class is not determined by a single factor, such as income, but is measured as a combination of occupation, income, education, wealth, and other variables. In some social systems, members of different classes are reared for certain roles and cannot change their social positions. In the United States, however, the lines between social classes are not fixed and rigid; people can move to a higher social class or drop into a lower one.

Marketers are interested in social class because people within a given social class tend to exhibit similar buying behavior. Social classes show distinct product and brand pref-erences in areas such as clothing, home furnishings, travel and leisure activity, financial services, and automobiles.

Social Factors

A consumer's behavior also is influenced by social factors, such as the consumer's *groups and social networks, family*, and *social roles and status*.

Groups, Social Networks, and Influencer Marketing

Reference group
A group that serves as direct or indirect point of comparison or reference in forming a person's attitudes or behavior.

Opinion leader
A person within a reference group who, because of special skills, knowledge, personality, or other characteristics, exerts social influence on others.

Word-of-mouth influence
The impact of the personal words and recommendations of trusted friends, family, associates, and other consumers on buying behavior.

Influencer marketing
Enlisting established influencers or creating new influencers to spread the word about a company's brands.

Online social networks
Online social communities—blogs, online social media, brand communities, and other online forums—where people socialize or exchange information and opinions.

Many groups influence a person's behavior. Groups that have a direct influence and to which a person belongs are called *membership groups*. In contrast, **reference groups** serve as direct (face-to-face interactions) or indirect points of comparison or reference in forming a person's attitudes or behavior. Marketers try to identify the reference groups of their target markets. Reference groups expose a person to new behaviors and lifestyles, influence the person's attitudes and self-concept, and create pressures to conform that may affect the person's product and brand choices.

The importance of group influence varies across products and brands. It tends to be strongest when the product is visible to others whom the buyer respects. Marketers of brands subjected to strong group influence must figure out how to reach **opinion leaders**—people within a reference group who, because of special skills, knowledge, personality, or other characteristics, exert social influence on others. Many marketers identify opinion leaders for their brands and direct marketing efforts toward them

Word-of-mouth influence can have a powerful impact on consumer buying behavior. The personal words and recommendations of trusted friends, family, associates, and other consumers tend to be more credible than those coming from commercial sources, such as advertisements or salespeople. Most word-of-mouth influence happens naturally: Consumers start chatting about a brand they use or feel strongly about one way or the other. Often, however, rather than leaving it to chance, marketers can help to create positive conversations about their brands.

Influencer marketing involves enlisting established influencers or creating new influencers to spread the word about a company's brands. ● For example, giant cosmetics maker CoverGirl has built its "I Am What I Make Up" ad campaign around a new, diverse team of well-known "badass" brand influencers—barrier-breaking women who bring the brand slogan to life. The influencer team includes, among others, Katy Perry; Issa Rae, star of the HBO series *Insecure*; Food Network host Ayesha Curry; fitness guru Massy Arias; 71-year-old model Maye Musk; and professional motorcycle racer Shelina Moreda. In the campaign, the influential CoverGirl ambassadors explain in their own words, in a personal and authentic way, what "I Am What I Make Up" means to them.[12]

Other marketers shape influence by tapping into **online social networks**, online communities where people socialize or exchange information and opinions. Social networking communities range from blogs (Mashable, Engadget, Gizmodo) and message boards (Craigslist) to social media sites (Facebook, Twitter, YouTube, Instagram, LinkedIn) and even communal shopping sites (Amazon.com and Etsy). Marketers are working to harness the power of these social networks to promote their products and build closer customer relationships. They hope to use digital, mobile, and social media to become an interactive part of consumers' conversations and lives.

Many influencer marketing campaigns involve building relationships with the army of self-made influencers already plying the internet, from social media personalities to independent bloggers. Along with internet mega-personalities stumping for big brands, you'll no doubt cross paths with the likes of climbers and skiers blogging for Patagonia, bikers blogging for Harley-Davidson, and foodies blogging for Whole Foods Market or Trader Joe's. The key is to find online influencers who have strong networks of relevant followers, a credible voice, and a good fit with the brand (see Real Marketing 5.1).

● **Influencer marketing: CoverGirl's "I Am What I Make Up" campaign uses a diverse team of influential brand ambassadors who explain authentically in their own words what the slogan means to them.**

Craig Barritt/Getty Images for Fast Company

Real Marketing 5.1

Influencer Marketing: Leveraging Relationships between Influencers and Their Followers

Influencer marketing is hot these days—companies are spending nearly $100 billion annually on influencer campaigns. Brands love influencer marketing because it builds on existing relationships between influencers and their followers. In a digital media world crammed with clutter, influencer marketing seems less intrusive than many other forms of marketing content at the same time that it's less likely to be ignored.

Influencer marketing campaigns are flexible. They range from small, quiet campaigns to big and booming ones. And because today's social media have democratized fame, a brand is as likely to hire a teen posting about her favorite cosmetics as it is to pay Kim Kardashian West a million dollars for a post about its fashion brand. Whatever form it takes, to be effective, influencer marketing must follow some simple strategic guidelines.

For starters, marketers must partner with influencers who fit naturally with their brands. And rather than just chasing large numbers of followers with one-time posts by big-name influencers, brands must build long-term relationships with influencers who resonate authentically with customers. Ideally, a brand can find influencers that have all three attributes—a fit with the brand, big numbers, and authentic brand-related connections with followers.

For example, adidas partners with supermodel, socialite, and reality TV personality Kylie Jenner, the youngest of the Jenner–Kardashian clan. At just 21 years old, Jenner has amassed more than 250 million highly engaged social media followers—132 million on Instagram alone. Jenner is Instagram's most lucrative influencer, commanding a cool $1 million per post. She keeps fans hooked with daily personal posts as well as posts for her own Kylie Cosmetics.

But when it comes to promoting other companies' brands, Jenner is very choosy. A few months ago, the former Puma girl began posting images of herself wearing adidas sneakers. Shortly thereafter, adidas announced that Jenner's posts were no coincidence. She was the brand's latest ambassador and the face of two new adidas lines: Falcon sneakers and the Coeeze collection of cropped hoodies, sweat suits, tees, and tights. Whether in the park with her daughter Stormi or on the go in her Rolls Royce Ghost, Jenner's looks and style in adidas apparel have inspired her fans and matched the brand's positioning beautifully.

The Kylie Jenner–adidas partnership illustrates another influencer marketing guideline:

Influencers should actually use the products they're being paid to represent. That might seem obvious. But overlooking this guideline has caused some high-profile influencer marketing gaffs. Take the time that, as part of a major campaign for Microsoft's Surface computers, Oprah Winfrey tweeted, "Gotta say love that SURFACE! Have bought 12 already for Christmas gifts. #FavoriteThings," The only problem: Oprah sent the post from the Twitter app on her Apple iPad. Such people-chasing efforts make both the brand and the influencer look inauthentic.

Not all influencer campaigns involve Kylie Jenner- or Oprah Winfrey-style celebrity mega-influencers. Far from it. Many campaigns employ less-known everyday voices. For example, companies ranging from Walmart and McDonald's to Disney tap into an army of social media moms as brand ambassadors. America's moms constitute a huge market; they are also heavy social media sharers and shoppers. Some 55 percent of moms on social media regularly base their buying decisions on personal stories, recommendations, and product reviews that they find in blogs and other social media. There are as many as 14.2 million U.S. mothers who blog, and some 4.4 million mom bloggers influence a million or more followers. Go-to social media platforms for mom influencers include Instagram ("Instamoms"), Facebook, and Twitter, but Pinterest and YouTube are also popular.

Disney has long recognized the power of moms in social media and the importance they play in planning family vacations. Eight years ago, the company assembled a group called Disney Social Media Moms, roughly 1,300 carefully selected mom bloggers (and some dads), travel bloggers, and active Disney-focused social media posters. Disney looks for influential moms who fit the brand's family-friendly focus, use social media heavily, and are active in their communities offline as well as online. An example is Wendy Wright, a homeschooling mother of two and a prolific blogger. Wendy describes herself as a "Disney nut" (she named her cats Mickey and Minnie), and she fills her blog with advice for planning Disney park visits, tips for holding Disney-themed parties, and reviews of Disney movies.

Disney Social Media Moms aren't paid; they participate because of their passion and enthusiasm for all things Disney. However, they do receive special educational attention from Disney, inside information, and occasional perks. For example, every year, Disney invites 175 to 200 of the moms and their families for a deeply discounted, four-day trip to attend its annual Disney Social Media Moms Celebration in Florida. The celebration is a mix of public relations event, educational conference, and family vacation with plenty of Disney magic for these important mom influencers.

The Disney Social Media Moms are under no obligation to post anything about Disney, and the company doesn't tell them what to say when they do post. However, the most recent celebration generated 28,500 tweets, 4,900 Instagram photos, and 88 blog posts

Harnessing the power of mom-to-mom influence: Each year, Disney invites 175 to 200 moms and their families to its Disney Social Media Moms Celebration in Florida, an affair that's a mix of public relations event, educational conference, and family vacation with plenty of Disney magic for these important mom influencers.

Mindy Marzec

full of ride reviews, videos of families meeting Disney characters, and a host of overwhelmingly positive comments. The Disney Social Media Moms effort costs the company very little but effectively harnesses the power of mom-to-mom influence to help sprinkle Disney's magical pixie dust on an important group of buyers.

Still other marketers have put together influencer campaigns using opinion leaders with very few followers but very authentic voices. For example, a recent campaign by Johnson & Johnson featured teens with only 500 to 1,500 Instagram followers as stars in videos for its Clean & Clear skincare products. The campaign began with six teens, selected from a larger group of 300 identified through searches of the social media and local press. An example is 18-year-old Dillon Eisman, who runs a nonprofit in Southern California that restores damaged apparel for homeless teens. *People* magazine named Eisman a "Hometown Hero" last year, but Eisman had never considered himself an "influencer." His Instagram following stands at a modest 1,471. But his Clean & Clear video grabbed 3.2 million YouTube views in only nine months. In addition to the J&J videos, the teens post their own self-created content.

In the Clean & Clear campaign, instead of using mega-celebrities as influencers, J&J opted for "influencers who weren't famous per se but [are] doing things that other kids responded to authentically, letting them tell their story and building the products and brands from there," says a J&J marketer. "The point where we knew we were doing the right thing was when we were…interrupting someone's feed with a paid post. That's normally where you see a lot of comments, usually 'I want to stop seeing this ad.' But this time most of our responses were 'Who is this person? How do I learn more about them?'"

In the nine months following launch, the influencer campaign helped boost Clean & Clear's sales by 19 percent. One product in particular—Clean & Clear oil-absorbing sheets—saw a 50-percent sales lift after years of stagnant growth. "When we gave the teens this product, it was one they really loved, and they created great content," says the J&J marketer. "They were using it all the time. Then we put it into paid media…and it really took off."[13]

We will dig deeper into online and social media as marketing tools in Chapter 17. However, although much current influencer marketing discussion focuses on digital, mobile, and social media, most brand conversations still take place the old-fashioned way—face-to-face. So effective influencer marketing programs usually begin with generating person-to-person brand conversations and integrating both offline and online social influence strategies. The goal is to get customers involved with brands, turn them into brand advocates, and help them share their brand passions and experiences with others in both their real and digital worlds.

Family

Family members can strongly influence buyer behavior. The family is the most important membership reference group and consumer buying organization in society. It has been researched extensively. Marketers are interested in the roles and influence of the husband, wife, and children on the purchase of different products and services.

Husband–wife involvement varies widely by product category and by stage in the buying process. Buying roles change with evolving consumer lifestyles. For example, in the United States, the wife traditionally has been considered the main purchasing agent for the family in the areas of food, household products, and clothing. But with more than 70 percent of all mothers now working outside the home and the willingness of husbands to do more of the family's purchasing, all this has changed in recent years. Recent surveys show that one-third of men do the majority of the house cleaning and 43 percent of men preform food preparation and cleanup activities. At the same time, women today purchase more than 50 percent of traditionally male products, including cars, electronics, and home improvement products.[14]

Such shifting roles signal a new marketing reality. Marketers in industries that have traditionally sold their products to only women or only men—from groceries and personal care products to cars, consumer electronics, and toys—are now carefully targeting the opposite sex. For example, a recent Tide ad shows a dad with kids in a busy household doing laundry and lauding the benefits of Tide with Ultra Oxi for Stains. And a 90-second ad for Barbie, shown during an NFL playoff game, shows heartwarming scenes of dads and daughters playing together with Barbies. The ad concludes, "Time spent in her imaginary world is an investment in her real world."[15]

Children may also have a strong influence on family buying decisions. A global survey in 30 countries with around 4,000 kids and parents showed that three-quarters of children wield influence on their parents' household purchase decisions, with boys and girls being equally successful in exerting their power. Furthermore, researchers found that their influence increases from the age of 10 and is biggest when it comes to decisions around entertainment, food, restaurants, electronics, and vacations.[16]

Marketers across a wide range of industries recognize such family influences in their marketing programs. For example, one ad for Honda's Odyssey minivan, titled "Keep the Peace," touts innovative features that satisfy the entire family. "When kids are happy, parents are happy, so the goal of this new campaign is to communicate that the all-new Honda Odyssey has the connectivity, functionality, flexibility, and fun-to-drive handling to keep everyone in the family happy," says a Honda marketer.[17]

Roles and Status

A person belongs to many groups—family, clubs, organizations, online communities. The person's position in each group can be defined in terms of both role and status. A role consists of the activities people are expected to perform according to the people around them. Each role carries a status reflecting the general esteem given to it by society.

People usually choose products appropriate to their roles and status. Consider the various roles a working mother plays. In her company, she may play the role of a brand manager; in her family, she plays the role of wife and mother; at her favorite sporting events, she plays the role of avid fan. As a brand manager, she will buy the kind of clothing that reflects her role and status in her company. At the game, she may wear clothing supporting her favorite team.

Personal Factors

A buyer's decisions also are influenced by personal characteristics such as the buyer's *occupation, age and stage, economic situation, lifestyle*, and *personality and self-concept*.

Occupation

A person's occupation affects the goods and services bought. Blue-collar workers tend to buy more rugged work clothes, whereas executives buy more business suits. Marketers try to identify the occupational groups that have an above-average interest in their products and services. A company can even specialize in making products needed by a given occupational group. ● A company can even specialize in making products needed by a given occupational group. For example, Caterpillar/CAT, the world's leading manufacturer of construction machinery, offers rugged mobile phones made for tough and challenging work environments. In demanding surroundings like the construction and heavy industry, normal smartphones are not durable, robust, or reliable enough. According to the device maker, consequential damage of handsets is a common problem for tradesmen in these professions, leaving them unnecessarily burdened with out-of-pocket expenses. The CAT S61, for example, withstands extreme drops, is dust- and waterproof, can be controlled with dry or wet gloves, and offers additional features for the trade, like thermal imaging or an indoor air quality monitor.[18]

● **Appealing to occupation segments: CAT makes rugged, durable phones for the construction and heavy industries.**

B Christopher/Alamy Stock Photo

Age and Life Stage

People change the goods and services they buy over their lifetimes. Tastes in food, clothes, furniture, and recreation are often age related. Buying is also shaped by the stage of the family life cycle—the stages through which families might pass as they mature over time. Life-stage changes usually result from demographics and life-changing events—marriage, having children, purchasing a home, divorce, children going to college, changes in personal income, moving out of the house, and retirement. Marketers often define their target markets in terms of life-cycle stage and develop appropriate products and marketing plans for each stage.

One of the leading life-stage segmentation systems is the Claritas PRIZM Lifestage Groups system. PRIZM classifies every American household into one of 68 distinct life-stage segments, which are organized into 11 major life-stage groups based on affluence, age, and family characteristics. The classifications consider a host of demographic factors such as age, education, income, occupation, family composition, ethnicity, and housing; and behavioral and lifestyle factors such as purchases, free-time activities, and media preferences.

The major PRIZM Lifestage groups carry names such as "**Striving Singles,**" "**Midlife Success,**" "**Young Achievers,**" "**Sustaining Families,**" "**Affluent Empty Nests,**" and "**Conservative Classics,**" which in turn contain subgroups such as "**Bright Lights, Li'l City,**" "**Kids & Cul-de-Sacs,**" "**Gray Power,**" and "**Big City Blues.**" The "**Young Achievers**" group consists of hip, single 20-somethings who rent apartments in or close to metropolitan neighborhoods. Their incomes range from working class to well-to-do, but the entire group tends to be politically liberal, listen to alternative music, and enjoy lively nightlife.[19]

Life-stage segmentation provides a powerful marketing tool for marketers in all industries to better find, understand, and engage consumers. Armed with data about the makeup of consumer life stages, marketers can create targeted, actionable, personalized campaigns based on how people consume and interact with brands and the world around them.

Economic Situation

A person's economic situation will affect his or her store and product choices. Marketers watch trends in spending, personal income, savings, and interest rates. In today's value-conscious times, most companies have taken steps to create more customer value by re-designing, repositioning, and repricing their products and services. For example, over the past decade, upscale discounter Target has put more emphasis on the "Pay Less" side of its "Expect More. Pay Less." positioning promise. And soon after Amazon purchased Whole Foods, the online giant took a knife to the upscale grocery chain's high prices. To help blunt the chain's "Whole Foods. Whole Paycheck." image, Amazon promised that the chain would offer "high-quality natural and organic food affordable for everyone."[20]

Lifestyle

Lifestyle
A person's pattern of living as expressed in his or her activities, interests, and opinions.

Personality
The unique psychological characteristics that distinguish a person or group.

People coming from the same subculture, social class, and occupation may have quite different lifestyles. **Lifestyle** is a person's pattern of living as expressed in his or her psychographics. It involves measuring consumers' major AIO dimensions—*activities* (work, hobbies, shopping, sports, social events), *interests* (food, fashion, family, recreation), and *opinions* (about themselves, social issues, business, products). Lifestyle captures something more than the person's social class or personality. It profiles a person's whole pattern of acting and interacting in the world.

When used carefully, the lifestyle concept can help marketers understand changing consumer values and how they affect buyer behavior. Consumers don't just buy products; they buy the values and lifestyles those products represent. ● The Body Shop's founder, Anita Roddick, had always been a strong advocate of ethical consumerism, human and animal rights issues, and environmental protection. Although The Body Shop was bought by Brazilian cosmetics group Natura in 2017, its social and environmental commitment remains in its marketing DNA today. For example, under its "Community Trade recycled plastic" scheme, the company will buy 250 tons of recycled plastic from India in 2019 to use in its production of bottles. In addition to counteracting plastic pollution, this initiative will also support Indian waste pickers.[21]

Marketers look for lifestyle segments with needs that can be served through special products or marketing approaches. Such segments might be defined by anything from family characteristics or outdoor interests to the foods people eat.

● Lifestyles: The Body Shop markets much more than just beauty products; its cosmetics seek to embody the ethical consumerism lifestyle.

UK retail Alan King/Alamy Stock Photo

Personality and Self-Concept

Each person's distinct personality influences his or her buying behavior. **Personality** refers to the unique psychological characteristics that distinguish a person or group. Personality is usually described in terms of traits such as self-confidence, dominance, sociability, autonomy, defensiveness, adaptability, and

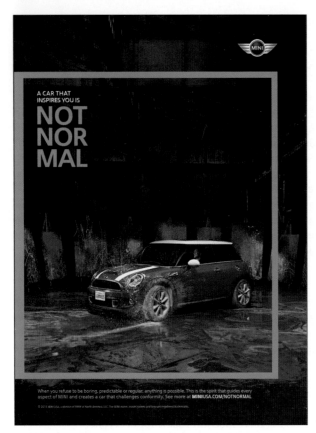

● **Brand personality: MINI markets to personality segments of people who are "adventurous, individualistic, open-minded, creative, tech-savvy, and young at heart"— anything but normal—just like the car.**

Used with permission of MINI Division of BMW of North America, LLC

aggressiveness. Personality can be useful in analyzing consumer behavior for certain product or brand choices.

The idea is that brands also have personalities, and consumers are likely to choose brands with personalities that match their own. A *brand personality* is the specific mix of human traits that may be attributed to a particular brand. One researcher identified five brand personality traits: *sincerity* (down-to-earth, honest, wholesome, and cheerful), *excitement* (daring, spirited, imaginative, and up-to-date), *competence* (reliable, intelligent, and successful), *sophistication* (glamorous, upper class, charming), and *ruggedness* (outdoorsy and tough).[22]

Most well-known brands are strongly associated with a particular trait: the Ford F150 with "ruggedness," Apple with "excitement," the *Washington Post* with "competence," Method with "sincerity," and Gucci with "class and sophistication." Many brands build their positioning and brand stories around such traits. For example, fast-growing lifestyle brand Shinola has crafted an "authentic, Detroit" persona that has made it one of America's hottest brands.

Many marketers use a concept related to personality—a person's *self-concept* (also called *self-image*). The idea is that people's possessions contribute to and reflect their identities—that is, "we are what we consume." Thus, to understand consumer behavior, marketers must first understand the relationship between consumer self-concept and possessions.

Hence, brands will attract people who are high on the same personality traits. ● For example, the MINI automobile has an instantly recognizable personality as a clever and sassy but powerful little car. MINI owners—who sometimes call themselves "MINIacs"—have a strong and emotional connection with their cars. More than targeting specific demographic segments, MINI appeals to personality segments—to people who are "adventurous, individualistic, open-minded, creative, tech-savvy, and young at heart"—anything but normal—just like the car.[23]

Psychological Factors

A person's buying choices are further influenced by four major psychological factors: *motivation, perception, learning,* and *beliefs and attitudes*.

Motivation

Motive (drive)
A need that is sufficiently pressing to direct the person to seek satisfaction of the need.

A person has many needs at any given time. Some are biological, arising from states of tension such as hunger, thirst, or discomfort. Others are psychological, arising from the need for recognition, esteem, or belonging. A need becomes a motive when it is aroused to a sufficient level of intensity. A **motive (or drive)** is a need that is sufficiently pressing to direct the person to seek satisfaction. Psychologists have developed theories of human motivation. Two of the most popular—the theories of Sigmund Freud and Abraham Maslow—carry quite different meanings for consumer analysis and marketing.

Sigmund Freud assumed that people are largely unconscious about the real psychological forces shaping their behavior. His theory suggests that a person's buying decisions are affected by subconscious motives that even the buyer may not fully understand. Thus, an aging baby boomer who buys a sporty BMW convertible might explain that he simply likes the feel of the wind in his thinning hair. At a deeper level, he may be trying to impress others with his success. At a still deeper level, he may be buying the car to feel young and independent again.

Consumers often don't know or can't describe why they act as they do. Thus, many companies employ teams of psychologists, anthropologists, and other social scientists to carry out *motivation research* that probes the subconscious motivations underlying consumers' emotions and behaviors toward brands. One ad agency routinely conducts one-on-one, therapy-like interviews to delve the inner workings of consumers. Another company asks consumers to describe their favorite brands as animals or cars (say, a Mercedes versus a Chevy) to assess the prestige associated with various brands. Still others rely on hypnosis, dream therapy, or soft lights and mood music to plumb the murky depths of consumer psyches.

Such projective techniques might seem pretty goofy, and some marketers dismiss such motivation research as mumbo jumbo. But many marketers use such touchy-feely approaches, now sometimes called *interpretive consumer research*, to dig deeper into consumer psyches and develop better marketing strategies.

Abraham Maslow sought to explain why people are driven by particular needs at particular times. Why does one person spend a lot of time and energy on personal safety and another on gaining the esteem of others? Maslow's answer is that human needs are arranged in a hierarchy, as shown in ● **Figure 5.3**, from the most pressing at the bottom to the least pressing at the top.[24] They include *physiological* needs, *safety* needs, *social* needs, *esteem* needs, and *self-actualization* needs.

A person tries to satisfy the most important need first. When that need is satisfied, it will stop being a motivator, and the person will then try to satisfy the next most important need. For example, starving people (physiological need) will not take an interest in the latest happenings in the art world (self-actualization needs) or in how they are seen or esteemed by others (social or esteem needs) or even in whether they are breathing clean air (safety needs). But as each important need is satisfied, the next most important need will come into play.

Perception

A motivated person is ready to act. How the person acts is influenced by his or her own perception of the situation. All of us learn by the flow of information through our five senses: sight, hearing, smell, touch, and taste. However, each of us receives, organizes, and interprets this sensory information in an individual way. **Perception** is the process by which people select, organize, and interpret information to form a meaningful picture of the world.

People can form different perceptions of the same stimulus because of three perceptual processes: selective attention, selective distortion, and selective retention. People are exposed to a huge number of stimuli every day. For example, individuals are exposed to an estimated 3,000 to 10,000 ad messages daily—from TV and magazine ads to billboards to social media ads and smartphones posts.[25] People can't possibly pay attention to all the competing stimuli surrounding them. *Selective attention*—the tendency for people to screen out most of the information to which they are exposed—means that marketers must work especially hard to attract the consumer's attention.

Even noticed stimuli do not always come across in the intended way. Each person fits incoming information into an existing mindset. *Selective distortion* describes the tendency of people to interpret information in a way that supports what they already believe. People

Perception

The process by which people select, organize, and interpret information to form a meaningful picture of the world.

● FIGURE 5.3
Maslow's Hierarchy of Needs

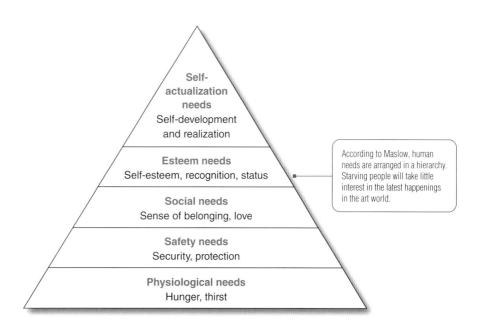

Self-actualization needs
Self-development and realization

Esteem needs
Self-esteem, recognition, status

Social needs
Sense of belonging, love

Safety needs
Security, protection

Physiological needs
Hunger, thirst

According to Maslow, human needs are arranged in a hierarchy. Starving people will take little interest in the latest happenings in the art world.

also will forget much of what they learn. They tend to retain information that supports their attitudes and beliefs. *Selective retention* means that consumers are likely to remember good points made about a brand they favor and forget good points made about competing brands. Because of selective attention, distortion, and retention, marketers must work hard just to get their messages through.

Interestingly, although most marketers worry about whether their offers will be perceived at all, some consumers worry that they will be affected by marketing messages without even knowing it—through *subliminal advertising*. More than 50 years ago, a researcher announced that he had flashed the phrases "Eat popcorn" and "Drink Coca-Cola" on a screen in a New Jersey movie theater every five seconds for 1/300th of a second. He reported that although viewers did not consciously recognize these messages, they absorbed them subconsciously and bought 58 percent more popcorn and 18 percent more Coke. Suddenly advertisers and consumer-protection groups became intensely interested in subliminal perception. Although the researcher later admitted to making up the data, the issue has not died. Some consumers still fear that they are being manipulated by subliminal messages.

Numerous studies by psychologists and consumer researchers have found little or no link between subliminal messages and consumer behavior. Although recent brain-wave studies have found that, in certain circumstances, our brains may register subliminal messages, it appears that subliminal advertising simply doesn't have the power attributed to it by its critics.[26] ● One classic ad from the American Association of Advertising Agencies pokes fun at subliminal advertising. "So-called 'subliminal advertising' simply doesn't exist," says the ad. "Overactive imaginations, however, most certainly do."

Interestingly, although subliminal messages might not influence human consumer behavior, they might be able to affect the behavior of smart devices without consumers knowing it. Researchers have recently shown that they can send hidden commands, buried in music or other background noise and undetectable to the human ear, to Apple's Siri, Amazon's Alexa, and Google's Assistant. In experimental settings, the researchers have been able to secretly activate the artificial intelligence systems on smart speakers and smartphones, getting them to dial phone numbers or open websites. "In the wrong hands, the technology could be used to unlock doors, wire money, or buy stuff online—simply with music playing over the radio," says an analyst. So far, it seems, such intrusions have happened only in research labs. But Amazon, Google, and other smart device makers are taking steps to protect users against such digital age subliminal commands.[27]

PEOPLE HAVE BEEN TRYING TO FIND THE BREASTS IN THESE ICE CUBES SINCE 1957.

The advertising industry is sometimes charged with sneaking seductive little pictures into ads.

Supposedly, these pictures can get you to buy a product without your even seeing them.

Consider the photograph above. According to some people, there's a pair of female breasts

hidden in the patterns of light refracted by the ice cubes.

Well, if you really searched you probably *could* see the breasts. For that matter, you could also see Millard Fillmore, a stuffed pork chop and a 1946 Dodge.

The point is that so-called "subliminal advertising" simply

doesn't exist. Overactive imaginations, however, most certainly do.

So if anyone claims to see breasts in that drink up there, they aren't in the ice cubes.

They're in the eye of the beholder.

ADVERTISING
ANOTHER WORD FOR FREEDOM OF CHOICE.
American Association of Advertising Agencies

● This classic ad from the American Association of Advertising Agencies pokes fun at subliminal advertising. "So-called 'subliminal advertising' simply doesn't exist," says the ad. "Overactive imaginations, however, most certainly do."

American Association of Advertising Agencies

Learning
Changes in an individual's behavior arising from experience.

Learning

When people act, they learn. **Learning** describes changes in an individual's behavior arising from experience. Learning theorists say that most human behavior is learned. Learning occurs through the interplay of drives, stimuli, cues, responses, and reinforcement.

A *drive* is a strong internal stimulus that calls for action. A drive becomes a motive when it is directed toward a particular *stimulus object*. For example, a person's drive for self-actualization might motivate him or her to look into buying a camera. The consumer's response to the idea of buying a camera is conditioned by the surrounding cues. *Cues* are minor stimuli that determine when, where, and how the person responds. The camera buyer might spot several camera brands in a shop window, hear of a special sale price, see buyer reviews on Amazon.com, or discuss cameras with a friend. These are all cues that might influence a consumer's *response* to his or her interest in buying the product.

Suppose the consumer buys a Nikon camera. If the experience is rewarding, the consumer will probably use the camera more and more, and his or her response will be *reinforced*. Then the next time he or she shops for a camera, or for binoculars or some similar product, the probability is greater that he or she will buy a Nikon product. The practical significance of learning theory for marketers is that they can build up demand for a product by associating it with strong drives, using motivating cues, and providing positive reinforcement.

Beliefs and Attitudes

Belief

A descriptive thought that a person holds about something.

Through doing and learning, people acquire beliefs and attitudes. These, in turn, influence their buying behavior. A **belief** is a descriptive thought that a person holds about something. Beliefs may be based on real knowledge, opinion, or faith and may or may not carry an emotional charge. Marketers are interested in the beliefs that people formulate about specific products and services because these beliefs make up product and brand images that affect buying behavior. If some of the beliefs are wrong and prevent purchase, the marketer will want to launch a campaign to correct them.

Attitude

A person's consistently favorable or unfavorable evaluations, feelings, and tendencies toward an object or idea.

People have attitudes regarding religion, politics, clothes, music, food, and almost everything else. **Attitude** describes a person's relatively consistent evaluations, feelings, and tendencies toward an object or idea. Attitudes put people into a frame of mind of liking or disliking things, of moving toward or away from them. Our camera buyer may hold attitudes such as "Buy the best," "The Japanese make the best camera products in the world," and "Creativity and self-expression are among the most important things in life." If so, the Nikon camera would fit well into the consumer's existing attitudes.

Attitudes are difficult to change. A person's attitudes fit into a pattern; changing one attitude may require difficult adjustments in many others. Thus, a company should usually try to fit its products into existing attitude patterns rather than attempt to change attitudes. Of course, there are exceptions. Repositioning or extending a brand calls for changing attitudes. So does introducing an innovative new brand that counters conventional thinking. For example, innovative women's shapewear brand SPANX succeeded by changing women's and retailers' long-held attitudes toward body-shaping foundation garments (see Real Marketing 5.2). And consider Beyond Meat, a startup company that is trying to disrupt the huge meat industry by creating healthier, eco-friendlier, plant-based alternatives to beef and chicken:[28]

Changing consumer attitudes and beliefs can be difficult. But Beyond Meat is off to a good start with its plant-based meat products. The Beyond Burger "cooks like a beef patty. It sizzles, it oozes. And sizzle, we know, is what sells."

Beyond Meat

Beyond Meat claims that it has invented a vegetarian burger—The Beyond Burger—that tastes like beef. The brand has a worthy mission: It seeks "a better way to feed the planet" by replacing animal protein with plant protein. That sounds great on a broad, societal level. However, changing firmly ingrained individual consumer attitudes toward meat will present real challenges. Americans love their meat—they are among the highest per capita meat eaters in the world.

But if the taste is right, products such as The Beyond Burger offer huge market potential. And for many consumers, the product's taste *is* a real attitude changer. "If the idea of building a juicy, tasty, 'I-can't-believe-it's a' veggie burger in a lab sounds totally sci-fi, then the future is here," says one food critic. Says another, "It 'cooks' like a beef patty. It sizzles, it oozes. And sizzle, we know, is what sells." As a result, Beyond Meat is off to a good start. After only one year, the meatless meat was available in more than 5,000 grocery stores—including Whole Foods and Safeway—as well as restaurants such as BurgerFi's, Carl's Jr, Subway, Disney World, and TGI Friday.

We can now appreciate the many forces acting on consumer behavior. The consumer's choice results from the complex interplay of cultural, social, personal, and psychological factors.

Real Marketing 5.2 | SPANX: Changing the Way Women Think about "Shapewear"

You probably know about SPANX—the market-leading company in women's shapewear—bodysuits, camis, slips, hosiery—SPANX even makes arm tights. With sub-brands such as Bra-llelujuh! and Slim Cognito, SPANX has grown quickly become a full-line brand of women's apparel, from underwear and hosiery to swimwear, shorts, skirts, and jeans. Its mission is "to help women feel great about themselves and their potential." But what you might not know is that SPANX is widely considered to be the company that saved an industry in decline. How? By changing women's attitudes toward undergarments.

It all started more than 20 years ago when SPANX founder Sara Blakely tried on a pair of designer slacks. She'd paid a premium price for an elegant pair of unlined cream-colored dress pants—a real stretch on her modest income as a fax machine sales rep. But although they were her favorite pants, she rarely wore them. "Every time I would go to wear them, you could see the undergarment," Blakely recalls. "Regular underwear left a panty line. The thong wasn't a great solution—it also left marks that you could see. And back then, the shapewear—the girdles—were so thick and overdone!" Thick waistbands caused ripples; ungainly leg bands left rumples.

Blakely was not alone in her garment–body woes. Women of all shapes and sizes often felt the same way. And it was nothing new: For centuries, women had wrestled with how to get their bodies to fit into fashionable clothing. From corsets in the sixteenth century to girdles in the 1900s, undergarments designed to deliver smooth and shapely figures were bulky, uncomfortable, and inconvenient. Even as clothing fashion trends changed rapidly throughout the twentieth century, the foundationwear industry saw surprisingly little innovation.

But there had to be something that could smooth Blakely's shape to the point where she felt comfortable wearing the pants she loved so much. That's when Blakely had an epiphany. As a working professional, she wore control top panty hose daily. Although she detested panty hose, they did smooth out her mid-section to where even her cream-colored pants looked good on her. But what to do about the ugly foot seams and reinforcements that showed through her open-toed shoes? Sara simply cut out the feet. That wouldn't work for skirts, but for pants, no one would be the wiser. So why couldn't someone design an undergarment that would take the "control top" concept to a higher level, perfecting the midsection and eliminating the feet and lower legs?

With no such innovations in sight from an apparel industry that seemed oblivious to the women's undergarment plight, Blakely took matters into her own hands. She scraped together funds, bought a sewing machine, created a prototype for her own miracle garment, designed the packaging, and came up with the name "SPANX"—kind of funny, kind of naughty, all about the rear end, and a fit with her outgoing personality. Then she beat the streets until she convinced a garment manufacturer to take a chance for a small piece of the action.

But the real challenge involved changing widespread attitudes toward foundation garments. Blakely's first hurdle was finding retail outlets. Her first stop was the corporate headquarters for premium retailer Neiman Marcus. But during the initial sales meeting, Blakely could tell that she wasn't getting through to the skeptical woman in charge of purchasing hosiery. So she took a big chance and invited the buyer join her in the restroom. The woman was taken aback, but Blakely clarified, "I want to show you my own product before and after." Once in the restroom, Blakely modeled the very cream-colored pants that started the whole project, first without SPANX and then with them. The Neiman Marcus buyer placed an order on the spot to begin a trial of SPANX in seven of the chain's stores.

With a quality product, a catchy brand name, and a premium retailer lined up, it seemed that SPANX would fly off the shelves. After all, women everywhere were begging for such a solution. But Blakely found that changing consumer attitudes was even more challenging than getting through to manufacturers and retailers. Part of the problem was that SPANX didn't fit into any existing garment category. Neiman Marcus placed SPANX in the hosiery department, allotting a single slot near the bottom of one rack. With a price tag many times higher than even the most expensive pantyhose, SPANX sat on the rack just as Blakely's cream-colored pants had stayed in her closet.

If SPANX was going to succeed, Blakely's innovative product had to change basic retailer and consumer attitudes toward foundation garments. And for that change to happen, women had to think about undergarments at the moments they were trying on clothes. That wouldn't happen in the hosiery department. So without asking permission, Blakely went into each of the seven Neiman Marcus stores and moved the SPANX from the hosiery department to racks near cash registers in the women's ready-to-wear clothing department, complete with "before and after" pictures. Putting SPANX in a new context caused customers to pause and break free of established mental boundaries. SPANX's sales surged.

Encouraged, Blakely forged ahead in her crusade to change attitudes. With no money

By changing long-held attitudes toward women's foundationwear, **SPANX began a shapewear revolution that has made founder Sara Blakely the world's youngest self-made female billionaire.**
Brian To/Variety/Shutterstock

to advertise, she sent samples to every imaginable celebrity, hoping that some would start wearing SPANX, talk about the brand, and model the results. She sent several gift baskets to Oprah Winfrey. When Oprah's hairdresser finally draped a pair of SPANX over the chair in Oprah's dressing room, Oprah tried them on and became an instant believer. Having battled with weight gain and loss for years, Oprah felt comfortable and confident in SPANX. She sang the product's praises on her show and even selected SPANX as her favorite product of the year. "Oprah made it okay to talk about whether your bra fits, and that shapewear is the fastest 10-minute fix you'll ever find," said one online retailing executive.

With Oprah's endorsement, SPANX took off. Other A-list celebrities such as Kate Winslet, Brooke Shields, and Julia Roberts started strutting their SPANX-clad bodies across the media, singing the shapewear's praises for slimming panty lines under unforgiving couture gowns. In one red-carpet interview, Gwyneth Paltrow even claimed that SPANX helped her post-baby body look better.

So began the SPANX revolution. Once something that nobody talked much about, foundationwear—now "shapewear"—became the new fashion trend and topic. With the changing attitudes, SPANX has given new life to an industry once in decline. Competitors ranging from traditional undergarment brands to Nike and Under Armour now feature shapewear. SPANX and the others have even started making shapewear for men. Experts predict that by 2022, the global shapewear market will reach $5.5 billion a year.

Thus, SPANX has changed the way women—and even men—think about both clothing and their body shapes. In the process, the innovative brand has modernized the foundationwear industry by giving new life to garments that long sat dormant in the backs of women's closets. And according to *Forbes*, the SPANX revolution has also made founder Sara Blakely the world's youngest self-made female billionaire. "Shapewear is the canvas and the clothes are the art," Blakely declares. "I know things are right on me by the way I feel."[29]

Buying Decision Behavior and the Buyer Decision Process

OBJECTIVE 5-3 List and define the major types of buying decision behavior and the stages in the buyer decision process.

Types of Buying Decision Behavior

Buying behavior differs greatly for a tube of toothpaste, a smartphone, financial services, and a new car. More complex decisions usually involve more buying participants and more buyer deliberation. ● **Figure 5.4** shows the types of consumer buying behavior based on the degree of buyer involvement and the degree of differences among brands.

Complex Buying Behavior

Complex buying behavior
Consumer buying behavior in situations characterized by high consumer involvement in a purchase and significant perceived differences among brands.

Consumers undertake **complex buying behavior** when they are highly involved in a purchase and perceive significant differences among brands. Consumers may be highly involved when the product is expensive, risky, purchased infrequently, and highly self-expressive. Typically, the consumer has much to learn about the product category. For example, someone buying a new car might not know what models, attributes, and accessories to consider or what prices to expect.

This buyer will pass through a learning process, first developing beliefs about the product, then attitudes, and then make a thoughtful purchase choice. Marketers of high-involvement products must understand the information-gathering and evaluation behavior of high-involvement consumers. They need to help buyers learn about product-class attributes and their relative importance. They need to differentiate their brand's features, perhaps by describing and illustrating the brand's benefits through printed promotional materials or in-depth online information and videos.

● **FIGURE 5.4**
Four Types of Buying Behavior
Source: Adapted from Henry Assael, *Consumer Behavior and Marketing Action* (Boston: Kent Publishing Company, 1987), p. 107. Used with permission of the author.

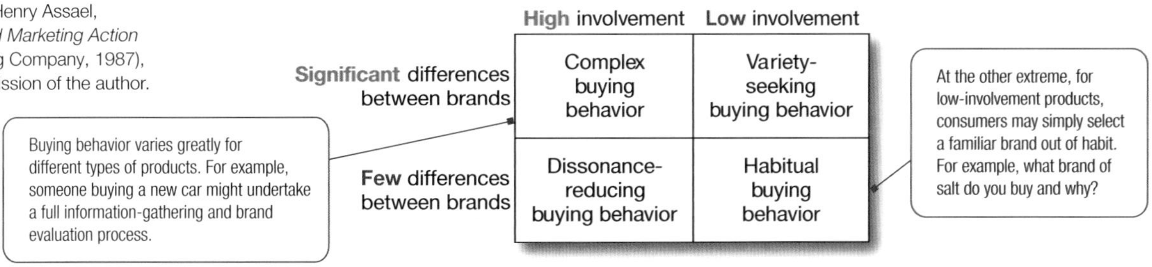

Buying behavior varies greatly for different types of products. For example, someone buying a new car might undertake a full information-gathering and brand evaluation process.

	High involvement	Low involvement
Significant differences between brands	Complex buying behavior	Variety-seeking buying behavior
Few differences between brands	Dissonance-reducing buying behavior	Habitual buying behavior

At the other extreme, for low-involvement products, consumers may simply select a familiar brand out of habit. For example, what brand of salt do you buy and why?

They must motivate store salespeople and the buyer's acquaintances to influence the final brand choice.

Dissonance-Reducing Buying Behavior

Dissonance-reducing buying behavior

Consumer buying behavior in situations characterized by high involvement but few perceived differences among brands.

Dissonance-reducing buying behavior occurs when consumers are highly involved with an expensive, infrequent, or risky purchase but see little difference among brands. For example, consumers buying carpeting may face a high-involvement decision because carpeting is expensive and self-expressive. Yet buyers may consider most carpet brands in a given price range to be the same. In this case, because perceived brand differences are not large, buyers may shop around to learn what is available but buy relatively quickly. They may respond primarily to a good price or purchase convenience.

After the purchase, consumers might experience *postpurchase dissonance* (after-sale discomfort) when they notice certain disadvantages of the purchased carpet brand or hear favorable things about brands not purchased. To counter such dissonance, the marketer's after-sale communications should provide evidence and support to help consumers feel good about their brand choices.

Habitual Buying Behavior

Habitual buying behavior

Consumer buying behavior in situations characterized by low consumer involvement and few significant perceived brand differences.

Habitual buying behavior occurs under conditions of low-consumer involvement and little significant brand difference. For example, take table salt. Consumers have little involvement in this product category—they simply go to the store and reach for a brand. If they keep reaching for the same brand, it is out of habit rather than strong brand loyalty. Consumers appear to have low involvement with most low-cost, frequently purchased products.

In such cases, consumer behavior does not pass through the usual belief-attitude-behavior sequence. Consumers do not search extensively for information about the brands, evaluate brand characteristics, and make weighty decisions about which brands to buy. Because they are not highly involved with the product, consumers may not evaluate the choice, even after purchase. Thus, the buying process involves brand beliefs formed by passive learning, followed by purchase behavior, which may or may not be followed by evaluation.

Because buyers are not highly committed to any brands, marketers of low-involvement products with few brand differences often use price and sales promotions to promote buying. Alternatively, they can add product features, varieties, enhancements, or marketing content to differentiate their brands from the rest of the pack and raise involvement.

For example, Morton Salt's Next Door Chef campaign creates brand involvement by showing consumers that there's more to salt than first meets the eye. In a series of 30-second TV spots and longer-form videos posted on the brand's web, Twitter, and Facebook pages, the Morton Salt campaign pairs home chefs with famous local chefs who coach them through meal preparation. Notes one observer, the pros "use each of several different types of Morton salt to neatly summarize the purpose of each: kosher for seasoning and prep; fine sea salt for precision and flavor; and course, sea salt for texture and finish." The home cooks are then urged to hold their own "home restaurant" events and post photos and recipes that include Morton kosher or sea salts using the hashtag "#NextDoorChef." The campaign raises involvement for an otherwise low-involvement product by demonstrating that which Morton salt you use for what purpose can make a big difference.[30]

Variety-Seeking Buying Behavior

Variety-seeking buying behavior

Consumer buying behavior in situations characterized by low consumer involvement but significant perceived brand differences.

Consumers undertake **variety-seeking buying behavior** in situations characterized by low consumer involvement but significant perceived brand differences. In such cases, consumers often do a lot of brand switching. For example, when buying cookies, a consumer may hold some beliefs, choose a cookie brand without much evaluation, and then evaluate that brand during consumption. But the next time, the consumer might pick another brand out of boredom or simply to try something different. Brand switching occurs for the sake of variety rather than because of dissatisfaction.

In such product categories, the marketing strategy may differ for the market leader and minor brands. The market leader will try to encourage habitual buying behavior by dominating shelf space, keeping shelves fully stocked, and running frequent reminder advertising. Challenger firms will encourage variety seeking by offering lower prices, special deals, coupons, free samples, and advertising that presents reasons for trying something new.

The Buyer Decision Process

> Author Comment | The actual purchase decision is part of a much larger buying process—from recognizing a need through postpurchase behavior. Marketers want to be involved throughout the entire buyer decision process.

Now that we have looked at the influences that affect buyers, we are ready to look at how consumers make buying decisions. ● **Figure 5.5** shows that the buyer decision process consists of five stages: *need recognition, information search, evaluation of alternatives*, the *purchase decision*, and *postpurchase behavior*. Clearly, the buying process starts long before the actual purchase and continues long after. Marketers need to focus on the entire buying process rather than on the purchase decision only.

Figure 5.5 suggests that consumers pass through all five stages with every purchase in a considered way. But buyers may pass quickly or slowly through the buying decision process. And in more routine purchases, consumers often skip or reverse some of the stages. Much depends on the nature of the buyer, the product, and the buying situation. A person buying a regular brand of toothpaste would recognize the need and go right to the purchase decision, skipping information search and evaluation. However, we use the model in Figure 5.5 because it shows all the considerations that arise when a consumer faces a new and complex purchase situation.

Need Recognition

Need recognition
The first stage of the buyer decision process, in which the consumer recognizes a problem or need.

The buying process starts with **need recognition**—the buyer recognizes a problem or need. The need can be triggered by *internal stimuli* when one of the person's normal needs—for example, hunger or thirst—rises to a level high enough to become a drive. A need can also be triggered by *external stimuli*. For example, an advertisement or a chat with a friend might get you thinking about buying a new car. At this stage, the marketer should research consumers to find out what kinds of needs or problems arise, what brought them about, and how they led the consumer to this particular product.

Information Search

Information search
The stage of the buyer decision process in which the consumer is motivated to search for more information.

An interested consumer may or may not search for more information. If the consumer's drive is strong and a satisfying product is near at hand, he or she is likely to buy it then. If not, the consumer may store the need in memory or undertake an **information search** related to the need. For example, once you've decided you need a new car, at the least, you will probably pay more attention to car ads, cars owned by friends, and car conversations. And you may actively search car brands and buying sites online, talk with friends, and gather information in other ways.

Consumers can obtain information from any of several sources. These include *personal sources* (family, friends, neighbors, acquaintances), *commercial sources* (advertising, salespeople, dealer and manufacturer web and mobile sites, packaging, displays), *public sources* (mass media, consumer rating organizations, social media, online searches and peer reviews), and *experiential sources* (examining and using the product). The relative influence of these information sources varies with the product and the buyer.

Traditionally, consumers have received the most information about a product from commercial sources—those controlled by the marketer. The most effective sources, however, tend to be personal. Commercial sources normally *inform* the buyer, but personal sources *legitimize* or *evaluate* products for the buyer. Few advertising campaigns can be

> The buying process starts long before the actual purchase and continues long after. In fact, it might result in a decision not to buy. Therefore, marketers must focus on the entire buying process, not just the purchase decision.

● FIGURE 5.5
Buyer Decision Process

Alternative evaluation
The stage of the buyer decision process in which the consumer uses information to evaluate alternative brands in the choice set.

Purchase decision
The buyer's decision about which brand to purchase.

as effective as a next-door neighbor leaning over the fence and raving about a wonderful experience with a product you are considering.

Increasingly, that "neighbor's fence" is a digital one. Today, consumers share product opinions, images, and experiences freely across social media. And buyers can find an abundance of user-generated reviews alongside the products they are considering at sites ranging from Amazon.com or BestBuy.com to Yelp, TripAdvisor, and Epicurious. ● For example, Yelp's goal is "to connect people with great local businesses" by maintaining a huge, searchable collection of candid reviews from people who've used those businesses. Over the past decade, Yelpers have written more than 171 million reviews of local restaurants and stores, service business, arts and entertainment activities, and other services in cities across the nation. Its mobile website receives some 75 million unique visitors per month seeking reviews and ratings.[31] Although individual user reviews at Yelp and other sites vary widely in quality, an entire body of reviews often provides a reliable product assessment—straight from the fingertips of people like you who've actually purchased and experienced the product. "Reviews for anything you could need," says Yelp. "We know just the place."

As more information is obtained, the consumer's awareness and knowledge of the available brands and features increase. In your car information search, you may learn about several brands that are available. The information might also help you to drop certain brands from consideration. A company must design its marketing mix to make prospects aware of and knowledgeable about its brand. It should carefully identify consumers' sources of information and the importance of each source.

Evaluation of Alternatives

We have seen how consumers use information to arrive at a set of final brand choices. Next, marketers need to know about **alternative evaluation**, that is, how consumers process information to choose among alternative brands. Unfortunately, consumers do not use a simple and single evaluation process in all buying situations. Instead, several evaluation processes are at work.

How consumers go about evaluating purchase alternatives depends on the individual consumer and the specific buying situation. In some cases, consumers use careful calculations and logical thinking. At other times, the same consumers do little or no evaluating. Instead, they buy on impulse and rely on intuition. Sometimes consumers make buying decisions on their own; sometimes they turn to friends, online reviews, or salespeople for buying advice.

Suppose you've narrowed your car choices to three brands. And suppose that you are primarily interested in four attributes—price, style, operating economy, and performance. By this time, you've probably formed beliefs about how each brand rates on each attribute. Clearly, if one car rated best on all the attributes, the marketer could predict that you would choose it. However, the brands will no doubt vary in appeal across the attributes. By knowing the importance that you assigned to each attribute, the marketer could predict and affect your car choice more reliably.

Marketers should study buyers to find out how they evaluate brand alternatives. If marketers know what evaluative processes go on, they can take steps to influence the buyer's decision.

Purchase Decision

In the evaluation stage, the consumer ranks brands and forms purchase intentions. Generally, the consumer's **purchase decision** will be to buy the most preferred brand, but two factors can come between the purchase *intention* and the purchase *decision*. The first factor is the *attitudes of others*. If someone important to you thinks that you should buy the lowest-priced car, then the chances of you buying a more expensive car are reduced.

The second factor is *unexpected situational factors*. The consumer may form a purchase intention based on factors such as expected income, expected price, and expected

Postpurchase cognitive dissonance: Postpurchase customer satisfaction is a key to building profitable customer relationships. Most marketers go beyond merely meeting the customer expectations—they aim to delight customers.

Dusit/Shutterstock

Postpurchase behavior
The stage of the buyer decision process in which consumers take further action after purchase, based on their satisfaction or dissatisfaction.

Cognitive dissonance
Buyer discomfort caused by postpurchase conflict.

Customer journey
The sum of the ongoing experiences consumers have with a brand that affect their buying behavior, engagement, and brand advocacy over time.

product benefits. However, unexpected events may change the purchase intention. For example, the economy might take a turn for the worse, a close competitor might drop its price, or a friend might report being disappointed in your preferred car. Thus, preferences and even purchase intentions do not always result in an actual purchase choice.

Postpurchase Behavior

The marketer's job does not end when the product is bought. After purchasing the product, the consumer will either be satisfied or dissatisfied and will engage in **postpurchase behavior** of interest to the marketer. What determines whether the buyer is satisfied or dissatisfied with a purchase? The answer lies in the relationship between the *consumer's expectations* and the product's *perceived performance*. If the product falls short of expectations, the consumer is disappointed; if it meets expectations, the consumer is satisfied; if it exceeds expectations, the consumer is delighted. The larger the negative gap between expectations and performance, the greater the consumer's dissatisfaction. This suggests that sellers should promise only what their brands can deliver so that buyers are satisfied.

Almost all major purchases, however, result in **cognitive dissonance**, or discomfort caused by postpurchase conflict. After the purchase, consumers are satisfied with the benefits of the chosen brand and are glad to avoid the drawbacks of the brands not bought. However, every purchase involves compromise. So consumers feel uneasy about acquiring the drawbacks of the chosen brand and about losing the benefits of the brands not purchased. Thus, consumers feel at least some postpurchase dissonance for every purchase.

Why is it so important to satisfy the customer? Customer satisfaction is a key to building profitable relationships with consumers—to keeping and growing consumers and reaping their customer lifetime value. Satisfied customers buy a product again, talk favorably to others about the product, pay less attention to competing brands and advertising, and buy other products from the company. ● Many marketers go beyond merely *meeting* the expectations of customers—they aim to *delight* customers.

A dissatisfied consumer responds differently. Bad word of mouth often travels farther and faster than good word of mouth. It can quickly damage consumer attitudes about a company and its products. But companies cannot simply wait for dissatisfied customers to volunteer their complaints. Most unhappy customers never tell the company about their problems. Therefore, a company should measure customer satisfaction regularly. It should set up systems that *encourage* customers to complain. In this way, the company can learn how well it is doing and how it can improve.

By studying the overall buyer decision process, marketers may be able to find ways to help consumers move through it. For example, if consumers are not buying a new product because they do not perceive a need for it, marketing might launch advertising messages that trigger the need and show how the product solves customers' problems. If customers know about the product but are not buying because they hold unfavorable attitudes toward it, marketers must find ways to change either the product or consumer perceptions.

The Customer Journey

Rather than viewing the buying process only as a specific set of stages, many marketers view it as a broader **customer journey**—as the sum of the ongoing experiences consumers have with a brand. Almost all discussions of the customer journey begin with customer brand awareness and end with the customer advocating the brand to others. However, customers rarely move consistently through any or all of these stages. Rather, in their brand relationship-building journey, customers collect a portfolio of brand experiences.

● **The customer journey: By understanding the customer journey, marketers can work to create brand experiences that will result in positive purchase behavior, engagement, and brand advocacy over time.**

Rodrigo Reyes Marin/AFLO/Alamy Live News

They move from touch point to touch point, sometimes circling back or moving off the path altogether. Under the customer journey concept, marketers focus not just on what customers do across the stages and touch points in the buying process but also on understanding and shaping the evolving customer experience.

The customer journey is unique to each customer. ● For example, while shopping at Amazon.com, customers might be exposed to a display ad for Amazon Echo smart speakers featuring the "Alexa" personal digital assistant. Ideally, a customer would become immediately interested, buy an Echo on the spot, install it at home, have positive experiences, and then later advocate it to others in a review at the Amazon site. However, some consumers might not even notice the Echo ad and end their customer journey there. Others might see the ad, be motivated to search and compare a range of smart speaker brands, and end up buying a Google Home smart speaker instead. Still others might miss the ad but see an Echo in use at a friend's home and want one for themselves. For consumers who buy an Echo, their use, loyalty, and advocacy will differ with their experiences.

The sum of a customer's experiences throughout the customer journey will shape his or her continuing behavior and attitudes toward the brand. Beyond learning what paths customers are taking, marketers must dig deeper to learn the whys. To that end, most marketers mine masses of consumer data to gain insights into the customer journey. For example, for customers who buy an Echo but never blossom into advocates, Amazon might learn that they've simply never learned about everything that Alexa can do for them and how to make things happen. To improve the Echo experience for such customers, Amazon sends them weekly "What's new with Alexa" emails announcing new features and suggesting new things to try.

"In an ideal world," concludes one analyst, "the journey people take to become loyal customers would be a straight shot down a highway: See your product. Buy your product. Use your product. Repeat. In reality, this journey is often more like a sightseeing tour with stops, exploration, and discussion along the way—all moments when you need to convince people to pick your brand and stick with it instead of switching to a competitor."[32] Thus, the marketer's goal is to deeply understand the ongoing customer journey, mapping customer touch points and experiences in detail. By understanding the customer journey, marketers can work to create brand experiences that will result in positive purchase behavior, engagement, and brand advocacy over time.

Author | Here we look at some
Comment | special considerations in
new product buying decisions.

New product
A good, service, or idea that is perceived by some potential customers as new.

Adoption process
The mental process through which an individual passes from first hearing about an innovation to final adoption.

The Buyer Decision Process for New Products

OBJECTIVE 5-4 Describe the adoption and diffusion process for new products.

We now look at how buyers approach the purchase of new products. A **new product** is a good, service, or idea that is perceived by some potential customers as new. It may have been around for a while, but our interest is in how consumers learn about products for the first time and make decisions on whether to adopt them. We define the **adoption process** as the mental process through which an individual passes from first learning about an innovation to final adoption. *Adoption* is the decision by an individual to become a regular user of the product.[33]

Stages in the Adoption Process

Consumers go through five stages in the process of adopting a new product:

- *Awareness.* The consumer becomes aware of the new product but lacks information about it.
- *Interest.* The consumer seeks information about the new product.

- *Evaluation.* The consumer considers whether trying the new product makes sense.
- *Trial.* The consumer tries the new product on a small scale to improve his or her estimate of its value.
- *Adoption.* The consumer decides to make full and regular use of the new product.

This model suggests that marketers should think about how to help consumers move through these stages. For example, if a company finds that many consumers are considering its products but are still tentative about buying one, it might offer sales prices or special promotions that help get consumers over the decision hump. ● For instance, when Beyond Meat first entered the supermarket aisles, the company offered "Try Some Free" coupons for free packages of its Beyond Beef and Beyond Chicken products at local supermarkets. The promotion helped get interested consumers to take the next step and try the product.

● The adoption process: To help get tentative consumers over the buying decision hump, Beyond Meat invited consumers to "try some free—zip, zero, zilch" at their local grocery store.

Beyond Meat

Individual Differences in Innovativeness

People differ greatly in their readiness to try new products in a category. In each product area, there are "consumption pioneers" and early adopters. Other individuals adopt new products much later. People can be classified into the adopter categories shown in ● **Figure 5.6**.[34] As shown by the curve, after a slow start, an increasing number of people adopt the new product. As successive groups of consumers adopt the innovation, it eventually reaches its cumulative saturation level. Innovators are defined as the first 2.5 percent of buyers to adopt a new idea (those beyond two standard deviations from mean adoption time); the early adopters are the next 13.5 percent (between one and two standard deviations); and then come early mainstream, late mainstream, and lagging adopters.

The five adopter groups have differing values. *Innovators* are venturesome—they try new ideas at some risk. *Early adopters* are guided by respect—they are opinion leaders in their communities and adopt new ideas early but carefully. *Early mainstream* adopters are deliberate—although they rarely are leaders, they adopt new ideas before the average person. *Late mainstream* adopters are skeptical—they adopt an innovation only after a majority of people have tried it. Finally, *lagging adopters* are tradition bound—they are suspicious of changes and adopt the innovation only when it has become something of a tradition itself.

This adopter classification suggests that an innovating firm should research the characteristics of innovators and early adopters in their product categories and direct initial marketing efforts toward them.

● FIGURE 5.6
Adopter Categories Based on Relative Time of Adoption of Innovations

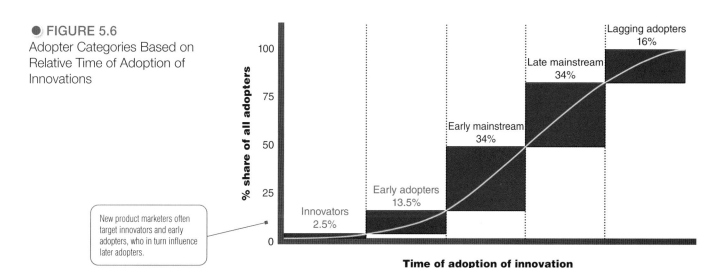

New product marketers often target innovators and early adopters, who in turn influence later adopters.

Influence of Product Characteristics on Rate of Adoption

The characteristics of the new product affect its rate of adoption. Some products catch on almost overnight. For example, Apple's iPod, iPhone, and iPad flew off retailers' shelves at an astounding rate from the day they were first introduced. Others take a longer time to gain acceptance. For example, all-electric cars were first introduced in the United States in 2010, led by models such as the Nissan Leaf and the Tesla Model S. However, although sales are picking up lately, electric vehicles still account for less than 2 percent of total U.S. automobile sales. It will likely be years or even decades before they replace gasoline-powered cars.[35]

Five characteristics are especially important in influencing an innovation's rate of adoption. For example, consider the characteristics of all-electric vehicles in relation to their rate of adoption:

Relative advantage. The degree to which the innovation appears superior to existing products. All-electric cars require no gas and use clean, less costly energy. This will accelerate their rate of adoption. However, they have limited driving range before recharging and cost more initially, which will slow the adoption rate.

Compatibility. The degree to which the innovation fits the values and experiences of potential consumers. Electric cars are driven the same way as gas-powered cars. However, they are not compatible with the nation's current refueling network. Plug-in electric charging stations are few and far between. Increased adoption will depend on the development of a national network of recharging stations, which may take considerable time.

Complexity. The degree to which the innovation is difficult to understand or use. Electric cars are not different or complex to drive, which will help to speed up adoption. However, the "conceptual complexity" of the new technologies and concerns about how well they will likely work slow the adoption rate.

Divisibility. The degree to which the innovation may be tried on a limited basis. Consumers can test-drive electric cars, a positive for the adoption rate. However, current high prices to own and fully experience these new technologies will likely slow adoption.

Communicability. The degree to which the results of using the innovation can be observed or described to others. To the extent that electric cars lend themselves to demonstration and description, their use will spread faster among consumers.

Other characteristics influence the rate of adoption, such as initial and ongoing costs, risk and uncertainty, and social approval. The new product marketer must research all these factors when developing the new product and its marketing program.

Reviewing and Extending the Concepts

Objectives Review

The American consumer market consists of more than 328 million people who consume more than $13 trillion worth of goods and services each year, making it one of the most attractive consumer markets in the world. Consumers vary greatly in terms of cultural, social, personal, and psychological makeup. Understanding how these differences affect consumer buying behavior is one of the biggest challenges marketers face.

OBJECTIVE 5-1 Define the consumer market and construct a simple model of consumer buyer behavior. *(pp 152–153)*

The *consumer market* consists of all the individuals and households that buy or acquire goods and services for personal consumption. The simplest model of consumer buyer behavior is the stimulus-response model. According to this model, marketing stimuli (the four Ps) and other major forces (economic, technological, political, cultural) enter the consumer's "black box" and produce certain responses. Once in the black box, these inputs produce observable buyer responses, such as brand choice, purchase location and timing, and brand engagement and relationship behavior.

OBJECTIVE 5-2 Name the four major factors that influence consumer buyer behavior. *(pp 153–167)*

Consumer buyer behavior is influenced by four key sets of buyer characteristics: cultural, social, personal, and psychological. Although many of these factors cannot be influenced by the marketer, they can be useful in identifying interested buyers and shaping products and appeals to serve consumer needs better. *Culture* is the most basic determinant of a person's wants and behavior. *Subcultures* are "cultures within cultures" that have distinct values and lifestyles and can be based on anything from age to ethnicity. Many companies focus their marketing programs on the special needs of certain cultural and subcultural segments, such as Hispanic American, African American, and Asian American consumers.

Social factors also influence a buyer's behavior. A person's *reference groups*—family, friends, social networks, an other influencers—strongly affect product and brand choices. The buyer's age, life-cycle stage, occupation, economic circumstances, personality, and other *personal characteristics* influence his or her buying decisions. Consumer *lifestyles*—the whole pattern of acting and interacting in the world—are also an important influence on purchase decisions. Finally, consumer buying behavior is influenced by four major *psychological factors*: motivation, perception, learning, and beliefs and attitudes. Each of these factors provides a different perspective for understanding the workings of the buyer's black box.

OBJECTIVE 5-3 List and define the major types of buying decision behavior and the stages in the buyer decision process. *(pp 167–172)*

Buying behavior may vary greatly across different types of products and buying decisions. Consumers undertake *complex buying behavior* when they are highly involved in a purchase and perceive significant differences among brands. *Dissonance-reducing behavior* occurs when consumers are highly involved but see little difference among brands. *Habitual buying behavior* occurs under conditions of low involvement and little significant brand difference. In situations characterized by low involvement but significant perceived brand differences, consumers engage in *variety-seeking buying behavior*.

When making a purchase, the buyer goes through a decision process consisting of need recognition, information search, evaluation of alternatives, purchase decision, and postpurchase behavior. The marketer's job is to understand the buyer's behavior at each stage and the influences that are operating. During *need recognition*, the consumer recognizes a problem or need that could be satisfied by a product or service in the market. Once the need is recognized, the consumer is aroused to seek more information and moves into the *information search* stage. With information in hand, the consumer proceeds to *alternative evaluation*, during which the information is used to evaluate brands in the choice set. From there, the consumer makes a *purchase decision* and actually buys the product. In the final stage of the buyer decision process, *postpurchase behavior*, the consumer takes action based on satisfaction or dissatisfaction.

More broadly, marketers must understand the *customer journey*—the sum of ongoing experiences consumers have with a brand. By understanding the customer journey, marketers can work to create brand experiences that will result in positive purchase behavior, engagement, and brand advocacy over time.

OBJECTIVE 5-4 Describe the adoption and diffusion process for new products. *(pp 172–174)*

The product *adoption process* is made up of five stages: awareness, interest, evaluation, trial, and adoption. New-product marketers must think about how to help consumers move through these stages. With regard to the *diffusion process* for new products, consumers respond at different rates, depending on consumer and product characteristics. Consumers may be innovators, early adopters, early mainstream, late mainstream, or lagging adopters. Each group may require different marketing approaches. Marketers often try to bring their new products to the attention of potential early adopters, especially those who are opinion leaders. Finally, several characteristics influence the rate of adoption: relative advantage, compatibility, complexity, divisibility, and communicability.

Key Terms

OBJECTIVE 5-1

Consumer buyer behavior (p 152)
Consumer market (p 152)

OBJECTIVE 5-2

Culture (p 154)
Subculture (p 154)
Total market strategy (p 156)
Social class (p 156)
Reference group (p 157)
Opinion leader (p 157)
Word-of-mouth influence (p 157)
Influencer marketing (p 157)

Online social networks (p 157)
Lifestyle (p 161)
Personality (p 161)
Motive (drive) (p 162)
Perception (p 163)
Learning (p 164)
Belief (p 165)
Attitude (p 165)

OBJECTIVE 5-3

Complex buying behavior (p 167)
Dissonance-reducing buying behavior
  (p 168)

Habitual buying behavior (p 168)
Variety-seeking buying behavior (p 168)
Need recognition (p 169)
Information search (p 169)
Alternative evaluation (p 170)
Purchase decision (p 170)
Postpurchase behavior (p 171)
Cognitive dissonance (p 171)
Customer journey (p 171)

OBJECTIVE 5-4

New product (p 172)
Adoption process (p 172)

Discussion Questions

5-1 What characteristics affect consumers' purchase decisions? (AACSB: Written and Oral Communication; Reflective Thinking)

5-2 What is a *total market strategy,* and why do marketers use this approach? Provide a recent example of a product or service that uses the total market strategy approach and discuss the components that make it effective or ineffective. (AACSB: Written and Oral Communication, Diverse and Multicultural Work Environments, Reflective Thinking)

5-3 Name and briefly describe each of the four psychological factors that affect consumer behavior. (AACSB: Written and Oral communication, Reflective Thinking)

5-4 What is the significance of complex consumer buying behavior and the level of consumer involvement to marketers? (AACSB: Communication; Reflective Thinking)

5-5 How is need recognition triggered in the buyer decision making process? Provide examples of the two different types of triggers. (AACSB: Communication; Reflective Thinking)

5-6 How might the marketing strategy for a market leader in a product category that is high in variety-seeking buying behavior (low consumer involvement, high perceived brand differences) differ from the marketing strategy for a minor brand? (AACSB: Written and Oral Communication; Reflective Thinking)

Critical Thinking Exercises

5-7 Late adopters are those who tend to be suspicious of new technology and new products. Generally, they fail to see the value of the new capabilities or they don't feel they can engage with it. These are not necessarily all older consumers. How would you target them? (AACSB: Communication; Reflective Thinking)

5-8 Your manager suggests you do everything in your power to limit customer complaining. Make an argument about why your firm should encourage consumers to complain. (AACSB: Written and Oral Communication; Reflective Thinking)

5-9 The grocery store shopping experience often falls short of customer expectations or desires due in part to limited assortments in trending product categories and the absence of pleasant interactions with other people. How should the in-store grocery shopping experience affect the customer journey for a brand? Support your answer with examples. (AACSB: Written and Oral Communication; Reflective Thinking)

APPLICATIONS AND CASES

Online, Mobile, and Social Media Marketing Blogvertorials

Bloggers can be highly influential. On the one hand, we read their pieces because we value their opinions and ideas, but on the other, do we really know their motivations? There is a growing trend for social media and public relations agencies to approach bloggers to get them to "blogvertize" on their behalf.

The agencies also insist that such bloggers make no mention of the fact that they are being paid to make positive statements about certain products and services. In the United Kingdom, the Advertising Standards Authority (ASA) states that it is acceptable for a blogger to receive payment for a positive review, but the blogger has to be clear that they are advertising. The ASA suggests signposting paid-for posts. The ASA argues that just like in any other media, consumers need to be able to judge whether or not they are seeing an advertisement. The clear rules are that advertisements must be obviously identifiable as such and not likely to mislead.

5-10 Have you encountered this type of blog posting before? Was it clear that the post was an advertisement? How does the fact that the blogger was paid for an opinion change your view? Write a brief report of your observations. (AACSB: Use of IT; Communication; Reflective Thinking)

5-11 Are there clear rules in your country concerning blogvertorials, such as the U.S. Federal Trade Commission's disclosure rules on using social media for the promotion of products and services? If yes, can the rules help in controlling blogvertorials written in other countries? What sanctions should be imposed on those who promote blogvertorials without calling them so? (AACSB: Communication; Reflective Thinking)

Marketing Ethics Make Yourself Feel Good

The Ethical Superstore (http://www.ethicalsuperstore.com) states its mission as enabling customers to make choices that let them feel good about their purchases. To this end, they offer a broad range of products from ethical sources around the world. The Ethical Superstore takes all the angst out of ethically conscious buying and relies on customers' passions rather than price sensitivity. The website is a one-stop-shop to protect the planet, find eco-friendly alternatives, support farmers and small businesses in developing countries, buy fair-trade items, use local resources, and cut carbon emissions. With scarcely a thought, the

environmentally concerned consumer has had all the hard work taken out of purchasing decisions. Customers can even make an extra charitable donation at checkout!

5-12 What are the likely buying factors for customers making purchases from a business like this? (AACSB: Communication; Reflective Thinking)

5-13 Is it ethical to charge a premium price for ethically sourced products? (AACSB: Communication; Ethical Reasoning)

Marketing by the Numbers Evaluating Alternatives

One way consumers can evaluate alternatives is to identify important attributes and assess how alternative choices perform on those attributes. Consider a consumer deciding among various fitness centers. Each attribute considered, such as price, class offerings, and so on, is given a score to reflect its level of importance to that consumer. In this example, the consumer gives each attribute a score of 1 to 10 to reflect how important that attribute is to her or him. Then the consumer evaluates each alternative on each attribute (that is, her or his belief about how an alternative performs on each attribute). For example, in the table below, location (with an importance score of 9) is the most important attribute for this consumer. This consumer believes that Peak Fitness performs best on this attribute because it is closest to home, rating it 8 (higher ratings indicate better perceived performance), but also believes this alternative to be the most expensive (belief rating of 3). The consumer believes Revolution Fitness offers the best price, but it is located relatively far away. Class offerings is the least important attribute for this consumer.

A score can be calculated for each alternative by multiplying the importance rating for each attribute by the alternative's perceived rating on that attribute. These scores are then summed to determine the score for that brand. For example, $Score_{Revolution} = (5 \times 10) + (9 \times 4) + (6 \times 5) + (2 \times 6) = 50 + 36 + 30 + 12 = 128$. This consumer will calculate the scores for each brand in a similar way and select the brand with the highest score.

5-14 Calculate the scores for 24/7 Fitness and Peak Fitness. Which fitness center would this consumer likely choose? (AACSB: Communication; Analytic Reasoning)

5-15 Which brand is this consumer least likely to select? Discuss two ways the marketer of this alternative can enhance consumer likelihood of joining its fitness club. (AACSB: Communication; Reflective Thinking; Analytic Reasoning)

Attributes Considered	Importance of Each Attribute	Alternatives Considered		
		Revolution Fitness Beliefs	24/7 Fitness Beliefs	Peak Fitness Beliefs
Price	5	10	7	2
Location	9	4	6	7
Hours of operation	6	5	10	4
Class offerings	2	6	1	8

Company Case Kraft Heinz: Once a Taste Maker Now Struggles as Consumer Tastes Change

In the era of high-tech Silicon Valley startups, the Googles, Amazons, and Facebooks of the world seem to get all the attention. But plenty of companies today have been leading their industries for decades, some since the start of the Industrial Revolution. Kraft Heinz is one such company. Tracing its roots back to the late 1800s, Kraft Heinz has played a big role in shaping the packaged food industry with innovative processing, production, and distribution methods. Today, you'd be hard pressed to find a household in the United States and many other parts of the world that doesn't have Kraft Macaroni and Cheese, Heinz Ketchup, Oscar Mayer deli products, Jell-O, Miracle Whip, or one of Kraft Heinz's numerous other blockbuster brands on hand.

But in recent years, the company that's put so many beloved brands on American tables has encountered some head-scratching market conditions. All of a sudden, Kraft Heinz's once-golden brands have lost some of their sauce. In an age of rapidly increasing health awareness and the expansion of store brands, consumer tastes and preferences have shifted fast. Brand managers and product developers at Kraft Heinz have tweaked and extended the company's brands as always. But in the past few years, little has worked. After years of steady growth, Kraft Heinz's revenues have been flat for three years running. Even worse, last year Kraft Heinz posted a net loss of more than $10 billion—an amount nearly identical to the net profit posted the year before. At the same time, the company was forced to write down the value of some of its best-known brands by $15.4 billion. With its stock price in a free fall, Kraft Heinz is now desperately trying to figure out how to once again please the pallets and tickle the taste buds of consumers worldwide.

The Men behind the Brands

Henry John Heinz was born near Pittsburgh in 1844. By the age of 15, he was bottling and selling condiments—horseradish and pickles at first. A few decades later, Heinz Tomato Ketchup made its debut. Right about that time, James Lewis Kraft was born. Getting his start in the cheese business, Kraft founded the company bearing his family name and opened its first cheese manufacturing plant in Chicago in 1914.

In the early 1900s, fewer people were farming and more people were working in mines and factories. Thus, fewer people were growing and raising their own food. As a result, many were getting sick from foodborne illnesses. At that time, "healthy" mostly meant "stable." With demand for food products with long shelf lives skyrocketing, both the H.J. Heinz Company and J.L. Kraft and Brothers were quick to oblige.

Canning was already a known method for making food shelf-stable for months. Heinz took it further, applying science and technology to solve problems like bacterial contamination as well. Similarly, Kraft got crafty with cheese, bringing it in to the industrial age with pasteurization techniques. Kraft also developed canning and dehydration methods that led to the development of brands such as Miracle Whip and Kraft Macaroni and Cheese. Both companies played key roles in stabilizing foods, making them safer as well as easier to ship and store. These characteristics played well not just with U.S. consumers but also with institutional customers. The United States and foreign governments became the biggest food-buying customers throughout two world wars and the reconstruction efforts

that followed. Both Kraft and Heinz became some of the largest food producers in the world while also establishing standards for processed foods and consumer packaged goods in general.

As the twentieth century came to a close and a new millennium dawned, both Heinz and Kraft experienced various mergers and acquisitions. In 2015, the two companies combined to form the Kraft Heinz Company—the world's fifth-largest food corporation.

Like other large and established packaged food companies, Kraft Heinz is no stranger to shifting consumer preferences and trends. Kraft Heinz brands have evolved considerably over the years based on such trends. Take Kraft Macaroni and Cheese, a brand launched as a direct response to specific consumer needs. Introduced in 1937 during the depths of the Great Depression, the box of dried pasta with the familiar packet of processed cheese powder was launched in the United States and Canada as *Kraft Dinner*—a meal for four at the low price of just 18 cents. Kraft sold eight million boxes the first year and 50 million boxes throughout World War II.

Today, the original-format boxed and dried Kraft Macaroni & Cheese Dinner is still the most popular version of the world-renowned brand. But you can also get your mac-and-cheese fix in microwaveable single-serve containers as well as in a creamy Deluxe form in varieties ranging from White Cheddar and Bacon to Cheddar Broccoli Cheese. And Macaroni & Cheese Shapes not only puts letters and numbers in kids' bowls but entertains them with Star Wars, Sponge Bob, Finding Dory, Trolls, and Teenage Mutant Ninja Turtles shapes as well.

A New Kind of Food Consumer

While Kraft Heinz has successfully adapted to consumer trends and has even set some trends of its own, recent shifts have stymied the company. One of the biggest shifts has been toward healthier fare. Consumers today are far more aware of the link between food and health, including the role that foods can play in the development of major diseases. This trend has been unfolding for some time, and Kraft Heinz has not sat idly by. In attempting to appeal to consumer demand for healthier products, the company initially took a "no problem, we'll fix it" approach by doing what it has always done. Customers wanted healthier food, so the company eliminated artificial flavors, colors, and preservatives from many of its brands. Still not enough? Kraft offered whole grain and organic versions of consumer favorites.

But such new products have largely missed the mark. Although such products were "health*ier*," discerning parents and individuals still did not view them as "healthy enough." For example, Kraft Heinz launched CapriSun Organic, made from organic juice concentrates without added sugars or artificial ingredients. But critics and activists quickly pointed out that healthier in some areas doesn't compensate for unhealthy in others. CapriSun Organic may have left out all the unnatural ingredients, but it still packs nearly as many calories and carbohydrates per ounce as good old-fashioned soda pop.

Health trends are nothing new to the food industry. But today's time-starved and health-aware consumers are looking for more than just buzz words on labels of the same old products. Customers today want ready-to-eat foods that emphasize the "prepared" but eliminate the "processed." As a result, food-buying customers are spending more time in the produce sections as well as the refrigerated and frozen food aisles of grocery stores. These aisles are exploding with options that have the look, taste, and nutrition of something you might have just made yourself from scratch. Individual food items and complete meal kits are proliferating. And at price points close to the cost of buying all the individual ingredients and making the dish, consumers are gobbling up these options about as fast as they hit the shelves.

More than just the foods inside the packages, it's the packaging itself. Customers are favoring labels that are simple and clean with nutritional information that is easy to find and interpret. Moreover, the very image of established food brands often seems to be incompatible with current consumer perceptions of "healthy."

Beyond health issues, another trend in consumer food purchases hits at the very core of big food companies like Kraft Heinz. Consumers are turning away from tried-and-true national brands and toward private label and niche brands. More and more, customers are finding greater value in store brands such as Archer Farms (Target), Kirkland Signature (Costco), and Wickedly Prime (Amazon), which offer lower prices with exceptional variety and quality. Some of the fastest-growing grocery chains—such as Trader Joe's, ALDI, and Lidl—sell mostly store brands. With so many good grocery options, many consumers are questioning the logic of paying $1.59 for a plain old box of Kraft Macaroni & Cheese when they can get the Whole Foods 365 brand through Amazon Prime for 99 cents and the organic version for $1.69.

Turning the Tables

With control over customer purchase and traffic data—not to mention shelf and display space—retailers have been quick to identify and respond to consumer trends. As a result, many of the hot new food items in stores now bear store-brand labels. In-store real estate itself is changing as the center aisles dominated by processed foods are shrinking while the fresher food sections around the perimeter of the store are growing. In other words, the grocery space where Kraft Heinz has thrived the most in the past is getting smaller. In the sections that are growing, the company has little that fits current consumer needs.

Many of Kraft Heinz's current woes are due in part to the major cost-cutting efforts it launched immediately following the merger four years ago. In cutting costs, it forgot that the most important thing for a food company is to make tasty products that people want to buy. At the same time, Kraft Heinz is not alone in its struggles. Other food giants such as General Mills, Smucker, and Kellogg are having similar problems. On average, year-over-year revenues for large food conglomerates are flat, whereas those of small, niche-oriented food companies are growing by double digits. Private label food brands are posting similar fast growth. One study shows that 90 of the top 100 consumer-packaged goods brands have lost market share over the past four years. Meanwhile, private-label brands now account for 17 percent of all groceries, a market share figure that has been rising for years.

Kraft Heinz and its peers won't likely disappear. But the degree to which they continue to lead the industry they created will depend on their ability to adapt. Each is making efforts. In some cases, those efforts are in R&D, such as Nestlé working to develop a "hollow" sugar molecule that will let it make the same candies with 40 percent less sugar. In other cases, established companies are acquiring successful niche brands—General Mills now owns Annie's, ConAgra owns Smart Balance and Udi's, Mondelēz owns Tate's Bake Shop, and Kellogg owns RXBAR. But the price of acquiring hot, niche food brands is on the rise, even as Kraft Heinz's cash-on-hand declines. The bottom line: Unless Kraft Heinz can adapt to changing consumer tastes and preferences, it will continue to see both its treasured brands and its fortunes shrink.[36]

Questions for Discussion

5-16   Of the factors that influence consumer behavior, which category or categories (cultural, social, personal, or psychological) best explain Kraft Heinz's current situation?

5-17   Choose the specific consumer behavior factor (for example, culture, family, occupation, attitudes) that most accounts for Kraft Heinz's current situation.

5-18   With respect for buying groceries, discuss the buyer decision process and how it has changed in recent years.

5-19   Make recommendations for Kraft Heinz that you think will turn its situation around.

6 | Business Markets and Business Buyer Behavior

OBJECTIVES OUTLINE

OBJECTIVE 6-1 Define the business market and explain how business markets differ from consumer markets. **See: Business Markets** *(pp 182–184)*

OBJECTIVE 6-2 Identify the major factors that influence business buyer behavior. **See: Business Buyer Behavior** *(pp 184–189)*

OBJECTIVE 6-3 List and define the steps in the business buying decision process. **See: The Business Buyer Decision Process** *(pp 189–191)*

OBJECTIVE 6-4 Discuss how online, mobile, and social media have changed business-to-business marketing. **See: Engaging Business Buyers with Digital and Social Marketing** *(pp 192–193)*

OBJECTIVE 6-5 Compare the institutional and government markets and explain how institutional and government buyers make their buying decisions. **See: Institutional and Government Markets** *(pp 193–197)*

CHAPTER PREVIEW In the previous chapter, you studied *final consumer* buying behavior and factors that influence it. In this chapter, we'll do the same for *business customers*—those that buy goods and services for use in producing their own products and services or for resale to others. As when selling to final buyers, firms marketing to businesses must engage business customers and build profitable relationships with them by creating superior customer value.

To start, let's look at LinkedIn. You probably know LinkedIn as the place to go for professional networking. What you may not realize, however, is that LinkedIn is also a powerful marketing platform for business-to-business marketers. With its hundreds of millions of professional networking members, Microsoft-owned LinkedIn has become an ideal site for marketers looking to engage business customers in a meaningful way. But LinkedIn's services don't sell themselves. LinkedIn's success rests on its skill in convincing businesses to use the platform. Thus, beyond being a great B-to-B marketing platform, LinkedIn must itself also be a great B-to-B marketer.

LINKEDIN: The Place to Be for B-to-B

Over the past decade, social selling has become the hottest trend in business-to-business (B-to-B) marketing. Today's B-to-B marketers can choose from any of dozens of digital and social media to engage business buyers and market their wares to other companies. But one social media platform stands out as *the* go-to B-to-B social selling leader. It's LinkedIn, the social network specifically designed to connect business professionals and to help them cultivate their businesses and careers.

LinkedIn boasts a fast-growing membership of 590 million business professionals in more than 200 countries. According to LinkedIn, four out of five of its members drive business decisions. Some 44 percent of LinkedIn members log on every day, seeking content that can change the way they do business. LinkedIn's content feed nabs an eye-popping 9 billion views each week—more than 468 billion content impressions a year.

LinkedIn lets B-to-B marketers target business decision makers with a precision other social networks just can't match. Along with basic demographic factors such as gender, age, income, and location, LinkedIn allows targeting by company industry, company size, company connections, job titles, job functions, job seniority, years of experience, skills, and various educational background factors.

All that makes LinkedIn a prime platform for marketing to B-to-B audiences. "Marketing on LinkedIn helps you engage a community of professionals to drive actions that are relevant to your business," says LinkedIn. B-to-B marketers seem to agree. Among B-to-B companies using social media, 94 percent use LinkedIn.

But LinkedIn's advantages don't sell themselves. LinkedIn's success rests on its convincing businesses to use the platform and helping them do that effectively. So at the same time that LinkedIn is a great B-to-B marketing platform, LinkedIn itself is a great B-to-B marketer. The giant professional social network skillfully markets itself to its own business customers as an ideal platform for engaging their customers. Then, LinkedIn's marketers do everything they can to make social selling on LinkedIn easy and effective.

LinkedIn's Business Solutions group works arm in arm with business customers to help them create, execute, and monitor powerful business-to-business marketing campaigns using LinkedIn. It shows customers how they can tap into LinkedIn's huge professional audience to generate sales leads, drive website traffic, increase brand awareness, launch new products, strengthen customer relationships, recruit new employees, or any combination of the above.

LinkedIn promises its business customers "Success. Powered by relationships." Different sections of LinkedIn's Business Solutions website provide step-by-step advice to customers on how to use LinkedIn to *Market* ("Market to the world's largest professional audience."), *Sell* ("Power your social selling efforts with real-time sales intelligence."), *Hire* ("Attract talent and recruit candidates from the world's largest talent pool."), and *Train* ("Develop talent and keep skills current with personalized eLearning.").

Marketing on LinkedIn starts with setting up a free LinkedIn company page. The main company page serves as a brand-building tool within the LinkedIn community and a landing page for the company's LinkedIn ads and other content. Business marketers can then expand their page presence

With a fast-growing membership of more than 590 million business professionals, LinkedIn stands out as the go-to B-to-B social selling platform. It lets B-to-B marketers "market to who matters."

AlexandraPopova/Shutterstock

with LinkedIn Showcase Pages, linked subpages that focus on more specific company brands or target specific audience segments with content relevant to them.

For example, IBM's main LinkedIn page provides basic information about and links to IBM, along with job postings and interesting and informational posts about IBM products, programs, and developments. The main page also links to a dozen Showcase Pages focusing on various IBM divisions and initiatives, ranging from IBM Analytics, IBM Mobile, and IBM Security to IBM Research and IBM Watson Internet of Things. In all, worldwide, companies large and small offer some 26 million LinkedIn company pages.

Beyond LinkedIn pages, LinkedIn offers B-to-B marketers a broad portfolio of advertising options, including sponsored content, display ads, text ads, and personalized messages sent through its Sponsored InMail messaging system. The company also gives customers all the tools and assistance they need to create LinkedIn ads and content on their own with the help of LinkedIn experts. LinkedIn's Business Solutions page is crammed with testimonials and success stories of LinkedIn ad campaigns by companies of all sizes, from giants like parent company Microsoft, SAP, Verizon, and American Express to smaller clients such as Utah State University.

For example, American Express in Australia used LinkedIn to target small to medium-sized business owners as customers for its small business funding products and services. With the help of LinkedIn, American Express created a campaign using sponsored content, sponsored InMail, and personalized dynamic LinkedIn

> When it comes to online social selling, LinkedIn stands out as the go-to business-to-business social media platform. But at the same time that it's a great B-to-B marketing platform, LinkedIn is itself a great B-to-B marketer.

display ads. "The targeting capabilities of the LinkedIn platform helped us to identify the right people and engage them with the right content at the right time," says an American Express digital marketer, enabling "us to not only sustain but grow the volume of quality leads." The LinkedIn campaign accounted for 55 percent of American Express's media-driven leads, and an amazing 22 percent of LinkedIn leads converted to customers.

In another example, Utah State University took advantage of LinkedIn's demographic targeting capabilities with a campaign designed to recruit high-caliber students to its graduate programs. The campaign consisted of LinkedIn display ads and Sponsored InMail carefully targeted to LinkedIn members by region, job title, and undergraduate degrees. The campaign converted an impressive 71 percent of clicks into requests for information and resulted in a 20-to-1 return on investment. "The ability to target our marketing efforts on LinkedIn by region, expertise, and career level made it possible to reach and engage with the precise audience we needed," says a Utah State marketer. The university also maintains and ongoing LinkedIn page with an active content feed and several Showcase Pages.

LinkedIn markets another powerful tool to its business customers. Called Campaign Manager, it helps business customers manage their LinkedIn accounts, select target audiences, create content, and—importantly—track the performance of their LinkedIn campaigns. Using Campaign Manager, LinkedIn customers can see campaign performance metrics—such as impressions, ad demographics, click-through rates, and average cost per click—as they view their campaigns or downloaded as performance reports. LinkedIn's marketers know that nothing breeds customer loyalty like success. And Campaign Manager's metrics give most customers ample incentive keep using the LinkedIn platform.

Thus, LinkedIn masters B-to-B marketing on two important levels. First, LinkedIn is a great B-to-B marketing platform for reaching business decision makers. Second, LinkedIn is itself a great B-to-B marketer. As a result, LinkedIn's fortunes are soaring within parent company Microsoft's digital empire. Over the past two years, LinkedIn's membership has grown 26 percent. In the past year alone, its revenues have doubled and membership sessions have grown by 41 percent. Clearly, for business marketers, LinkedIn is the place to be for B-to-B.[1]

· ·

ONE WAY OR ANOTHER, most large companies sell to other organizations. Companies such as IBM, Boeing, DuPont, Caterpillar, GE, and countless other firms sell *most* of their products to other businesses. Even large consumer products companies, which make products used by final consumers, must first sell their products to other businesses. For example, General Mills makes many familiar consumer brands—Big G cereals (Cheerios, Wheaties, Trix, Chex, Total, Fiber One), baking products (Pillsbury, Betty Crocker, Bisquick, Gold Medal flour), snacks (Nature Valley, Bugles, Chex Mix), Yoplait yogurt, Häagen-Dazs ice cream, and many others. But to sell these products to consumers, General Mills must first sell them to its wholesaler and retailer customers, who in turn serve the consumer market.

Business buyer behavior

The buying behavior of organizations that buy goods and services for use in the production of other products and services that are sold, rented, or supplied to others.

Business buyer behavior refers to the buying behavior of organizations that buy goods and services for use in the production of other products and services that are sold, rented, or supplied to others. It also includes the behavior of retailing and wholesaling firms that acquire goods to resell or rent to others at a profit. In the **business buying process**, business buyers determine which products and services their organizations need to purchase and then find, evaluate, and choose among alternative suppliers and brands. *Business-to-business (B-to-B) marketers* must do their best to understand business markets and business buyer behavior. Then, like businesses that sell to final buyers, they must engage business customers and build profitable relationships with them by creating superior customer value.

Business buying process

The decision process by which business buyers determine which products and services their organizations need to purchase and then find, evaluate, and choose among alternative suppliers and brands.

Author Comment | Business markets operate "behind the scenes" to most consumers. Most of the things you buy involve many sets of business purchases before you ever see them.

Business Markets

OBJECTIVE 6-1 Define the business market and identify the major factors that influence business buyer behavior.

The business market is *huge*. In fact, business markets involve far more dollars and items than do consumer markets. For example, think about the large number of business transactions involved in the production and sale of a single set of Goodyear tires. Various suppliers sell Goodyear the rubber, steel, equipment, and other goods that it needs to produce tires. Goodyear then sells the finished tires to retailers, which in turn sell them to consumers. Thus, many sets of *business* purchases were made for only one set of *consumer* purchases. In addition, Goodyear sells tires as original equipment to manufacturers that install them on new vehicles and as replacement tires to companies that maintain their own fleets of company cars, trucks, or other vehicles.

In some ways, business markets are similar to consumer markets. Both involve people who assume buying roles and make purchase decisions to satisfy needs. However, business markets differ in many ways from consumer markets. The main differences are in *market structure and demand*, the *nature of the buying unit*, and the *types of decisions and the decision process* involved.

Market Structure and Demand

The business marketer normally deals with *far fewer but far larger buyers* than the consumer marketer does. Even in large business markets, a few buyers often account for most of the purchasing. For example, when Goodyear sells replacement tires to final consumers, its potential market includes millions of car owners around the world. But its fate in business markets depends on getting orders from only a handful of large automakers.

Further, many business markets have *inelastic and more fluctuating demand*. The total demand for many business products is not much affected by price changes, especially in the short run. A drop in the price of leather will not cause shoe manufacturers to buy much more leather unless it results in lower shoe prices that, in turn, increase consumer demand for shoes. And the demand for many business goods and services tends to change more— and more quickly—than does the demand for consumer goods and services. A small percentage increase in consumer demand can cause large increases in business demand.

Derived demand

Business demand that ultimately comes from (derives from) the demand for consumer goods.

Finally, business demand is **derived demand**—it ultimately derives from the demand for consumer goods. ● For example, demand for Gore-Tex fabrics derives from consumer purchases of outdoor apparel brands made from Gore-Tex. If consumer demand for these products increases, so does the demand for the Gore-Tex fabrics they contain. So to boost demand for Gore-Tex, Gore advertises to final consumers to educate them on the benefits of Gore-Tex fabrics in the brands they buy. It also directly markets brands containing Gore-Tex—from Rukka, Marmot, The North Face, Burton and L.L. Bean to Adidas, Under Armour, and New Balance— on its own web and mobile sites. As a result, consumers around the world have learned to look for the familiar Gore-Tex brand label, and both Gore and its partner brands win.[2]

Nature of the Buying Unit

Compared with consumer purchases, a business purchase usually involves *more decision participants* and a *more professional purchasing effort*. Often, business buying is done by trained purchasing agents who spend their working lives learning how to buy better. The more complex the purchase, the more likely it is that several people will participate in the decision-making process. Buying committees composed of technical experts and top management are common in the buying of major goods. Beyond this, B-to-B marketers now face a new breed of higher-level, better-trained supply managers. And these supply managers are well-versed in today's digital, mobile, and social media technologies for finding and evaluating purchase

● **Derived demand: To increase demand for Gore-Tex fabrics, Gore markets directly to buyers of the outdoor and athletic apparel brands made using its products and technologies. This ad encourages runners to "take on the muck, …take on the sludge, …take off and run," thanks to Gore-Tex technology in their running shoes. Both Gore and its partner brands win.**

Courtesy: Gore-Tex, Shine United, Eric Cook (art director), James Breen (copywriter), John Krull (creative director), Michael Kriefski (executive creative director), Mike Tittle (photographer), and Scott Lanza (photographer).

● The business buyer decision process: More than just supplying networking equipment and systems to its business customers, "Cisco is firmly focused on being the most strategic partner for our customers and helping them succeed in today's world."

Kristoffer Tripplaar/Alamy Stock Photo

alternatives. Therefore, companies must have well-trained marketers, salespeople, and digital support personnel to deal with these well-trained, technology-oriented buyers.

Types of Decisions and the Decision Process

Business buyers usually face *more complex* buying decisions than do consumer buyers. Business purchases often involve large sums of money, complex technical and economic considerations, and interactions among people at many levels of the buyer's organization. The business buying process also tends to be *longer* and *more formalized*. Large business purchases usually call for detailed product specifications, written purchase orders, careful supplier searches, and formal approval.

Finally, in the business buying process, the buyer and seller are often much more *dependent* on each other. B-to-B marketers may roll up their sleeves and work closely with customers during all stages of the buying process—from helping customers define problems to finding solutions to supporting after-sale operation. In the short run, sales go to suppliers who meet buyers' immediate product and service needs. In the long run, however, business-to-business marketers keep customers by meeting current needs *and* by partnering with them to help solve their problems. ● For example, digital networking giant Cisco Systems doesn't just sell networking hardware, software, and systems to its business customers. It partners with them to create long-term customer success:[3]

> Cisco provides its business customers with equipment and technologies that connect people, data, computers systems, and digital networks, within the company and with their customers and others in the broader world. But more than simply selling connecting technologies *to* customers, Cisco sees itself as a strategic partner that helps its clients *use* those technologies serve their own customers better and more profitably. Cisco's CEO likes to the story about the financial services customer that defined itself as an outstanding technology company that was secondarily good at banking. It was limited only by the extent to which its internal and external digital networks could deliver exceptional customer experiences. It didn't want just networking hardware and software; it wanted successful connections with its customers. And it wanted Cisco to be its long-term partner in this digital transformation.
>
> To serve such business customers, says the company, "Cisco is firmly focused on being the most strategic partner for our customers and helping them succeed in today's world." Cisco works closely with customers to help them build what it calls "the bridge to possible." "Amazing things can happen when you connect the unconnected," says Cisco. "An integral part of our DNA is creating long-lasting customer partnerships, working together to identify our customers' needs and provide solutions that fuel their success."

In recent years, relationships between most customers and suppliers have been changing from downright adversarial to close and chummy. In fact, many customer companies are now practicing **supplier development**, systematically developing networks of supplier-partners to ensure a dependable supply of the products and materials that they use in making their own products or reselling to others. For example, Walmart doesn't have a "Purchasing Department"; it has a "Supplier Development Department." The giant retailer knows that it can't just rely on spot suppliers who might be available when needed. Instead, Walmart manages a huge network of supplier-partners that help provide the hundreds of billions of dollars of goods that it sells to its customers each year.

Supplier development
Systematic development of networks of supplier-partners to ensure an appropriate and dependable supply of products and materials for use in making products or reselling them to others.

Author | Business buying decisions
Comment | can range from routine to incredibly complex, involving only a few or very many decision makers and buying influences.

Business Buyer Behavior

OBJECTIVE 6-2 Identify the major factors that influence business buyer behavior.

At the most basic level, marketers want to know how business buyers will respond to various marketing stimuli. ● **Figure 6.1** shows a model of business buyer behavior. In this model, marketing and other stimuli affect the buying organization and produce certain buyer responses. To design good marketing strategies, marketers must understand what happens within the organization to turn stimuli into purchase responses.

A Model of Business Buyer
Behavior

In some ways, business markets are similar to consumer markets—this model looks a lot like the model of consumer buyer behavior presented in Figure 5.1. But there are some major differences, especially in the nature of the buying unit, the types of decisions made, and the decision process.

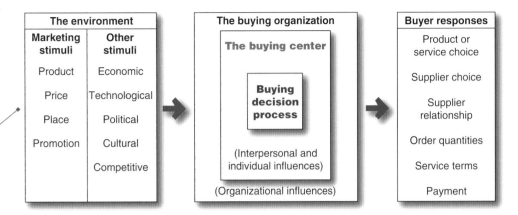

The environment		The buying organization	Buyer responses
Marketing stimuli	**Other stimuli**	**The buying center**	Product or service choice
Product	Economic		Supplier choice
Price	Technological	**Buying decision process**	Supplier relationship
Place	Political		Order quantities
Promotion	Cultural	(Interpersonal and individual influences)	Service terms
	Competitive	(Organizational influences)	Payment

Straight rebuy

A business buying situation in which the buyer routinely reorders something without modifications.

Modified rebuy

A business buying situation in which the buyer wants to modify product specifications, prices, terms, or suppliers.

New task

A business buying situation in which the buyer purchases a product or service for the first time.

Systems selling (or solutions selling)

Buying a packaged solution to a problem from a single seller, thus avoiding all the separate decisions involved in a complex buying situation.

Within the organization, buying activity consists of two major parts: the *buying center*, composed of all the people involved in the buying decision; and the *buying decision process*. The model shows that the buying center and the buying decision process are influenced by internal organizational, interpersonal, and individual factors as well as external environmental factors.

The model in Figure 6.1 suggests four questions about business buyer behavior: What buying decisions do business buyers make? Who participates in the business buying process? What are the major influences on buyers? How do business buyers make their buying decisions?

Major Types of Buying Situations

There are three major types of buying situations.[4] In a **straight rebuy**, the buyer reorders something without any modifications. It is usually handled on a routine basis by the purchasing department. To keep the business, "in" suppliers try to maintain customer engagement and product and service quality. "Out" suppliers try to find new ways to add value or exploit dissatisfaction so that the buyer will consider them.

In a **modified rebuy**, the buyer wants to modify product specifications, prices, terms, or suppliers. The "in" suppliers may become nervous and feel pressured to put their best foot forward to protect an account. "Out" suppliers may see the modified rebuy situation as an opportunity to make a better offer and gain new business.

A company buying a product or service for the first time faces a **new task** situation. In such cases, the greater the cost or risk, the larger the number of decision participants and the greater the company's efforts to collect information. The new task situation is the marketer's greatest opportunity and challenge. The marketer not only tries to reach as many key buying influences as possible but also provides help and information. The buyer makes the fewest decisions in the straight rebuy and the most in the new task decision.

Many business buyers prefer to buy a complete solution to a problem from a single seller rather than buying separate products and services from several suppliers and putting them together. The sale often goes to the firm that engages business customers deeply and provides the most complete *system* for meeting a customer's needs and solving its problems. Such **systems selling (or solutions selling)** is often a key business marketing strategy for winning and holding accounts. ● Consider UPS and its customer Overstock.com:[5]

● **Solutions selling: UPS not only delivers packages for online retailer Overstock.com, it also manages much of Overstock's complex order and returns process in an efficient, customer-pleasing way.**

Ken James/Bloomberg via Getty Images

Online retailer Overstock.com sells more than $1.7 billion worth of furniture, home décor, bedding and bath, kitchen, and home improvement items annually to tens of millions of customers. It offers an inventory of more than 2.8 million different products. But with all those sales come big delivery headaches and hundreds of thousands of hard-to-handle returns. Until recently, Overstock.com handled all its sales and returns out of its own warehouse space in Salt Lake City, Utah. But as sales increased, outbound shipping and inbound returns became increasingly complex and costly, especially for customers on the east coast.

So Overstock.com turned to UPS, which had handled Overstock.com's package delivery for years. But more than just shipping, UPS helped come up with a total systems solution. It took over a big chunk of Overstock.com's east coast inventory and returns operations; lock, stock, and barrel. UPS now manages transportation, staffing, and warehousing for much of Overstock.com's sales and returns—at its own Hebron, Kentucky, transportation and logistics hub, efficiently processing tens of thousands of returns each month. The UPS hub now serves 78 percent of the east coast and 66 percent of the nation with customer-pleasing two-day delivery. "We have developed a world-class process for returns," says an Overstock.com executive. "UPS as a partner has been integral to this success."

Participants in the Business Buying Process

Who does the buying of the trillions of dollars' worth of goods and services needed by business organizations? The decision-making unit of a buying organization is called its **buying center**. It consists of all the individuals and units that play a role in the business purchase decision-making process. This group includes the actual users of the product or service, those who make the buying decision, those who influence the buying decision, those who do the actual buying, and those who control buying information.

The buying center includes all members of the organization who play any of five roles in the purchase decision process.[6]

Buying center

All the individuals and units that play a role in the purchase decision-making process.

- **Users** are members of the organization who will use the product or service. In many cases, users initiate the buying proposal and help define product specifications.
- **Influencers** often help define specifications and also provide information for evaluating alternatives. Technical personnel are particularly important influencers.
- **Buyers** have formal authority to select the supplier and arrange terms of purchase. Buyers may help shape product specifications, but their major role is in selecting vendors and negotiating. In more complex purchases, buyers might include high-level officers participating in the negotiations.
- **Deciders** have formal or informal power to select or approve the final suppliers. In routine buying, the buyers are often the deciders or at least the approvers.
- **Gatekeepers** control the flow of information to others. For example, purchasing agents often have authority to prevent salespersons from seeing users or deciders. Other gatekeepers include technical personnel and even personal secretaries.

Users

Members of the buying organization who will actually use the purchased product or service.

Influencers

People in an organization's buying center who affect the buying decision; they often help define specifications and also provide information for evaluating alternatives.

Buyers

People in an organization's buying center who make an actual purchase.

Deciders

People in an organization's buying center who have formal or informal power to select or approve the final suppliers.

Gatekeepers

People in an organization's buying center who control the flow of information to others.

The buying center is not a fixed and formally identified unit within the buying organization. It is a set of buying roles assumed by different people for different purchases. Within the organization, the size and makeup of the buying center will vary for different products and for different buying situations. For some routine purchases, one person—say, a purchasing agent—may assume all the buying center roles and serve as the only person involved in the buying decision. For more complex purchases in large companies, the buying center may include 20, 30, or even more people from different levels and departments in the organization.

The buying center concept presents a major marketing challenge. The business marketer must learn who participates in the decision, each participant's relative influence, and what evaluation criteria each decision participant uses. This can be difficult.

The buying center usually includes some obvious participants who are involved formally in the buying decision. For example, the decision to buy a corporate jet will probably involve the company's CEO, the chief pilot, a purchasing agent, some legal staff, a member of top management, and others formally charged with the buying decision. It may also involve less obvious, informal participants, some of whom may actually make or strongly affect the buying decision. Sometimes, even the people in the buying center are not aware of all the buying participants. For example, the decision about which corporate jet to buy may actually be made by a corporate board member who has an interest in flying and who knows a lot about airplanes. This board member may work behind the scenes to sway the decision. Many business buying decisions result from the complex interactions of ever-changing buying center participants.

Major Influences on Business Buyers

Business buyers are subject to many influences when they make their buying decisions. Some marketers assume that the major influences are economic. They think buyers will favor the supplier who offers the lowest price or the best product or the most service. They concentrate on offering strong economic benefits to buyers. Such economic factors are very important to most buyers, especially in a tough economy. However, business buyers actually respond to both economic and personal factors. Far from being cold, calculating, and impersonal, business buyers are human and social as well. They react to both reason and emotion.

Today, most B-to-B marketers recognize that emotion plays an important role in business buying decisions. Consider this example:[7]

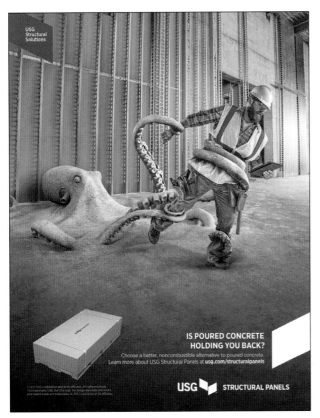

● Ads like this one for USG concrete structural panels suggest that emotions play a role even in heavily performance-based business-to-business decision making.

USG

● USG Corporation is a leading manufacturer of building materials for the construction and remodeling industries. Given its construction contractor, architect, and builder audience, you might expect USG's B-to-B ads to focus heavily on detailing performance features and benefits, such as strength, impact resistance, ease of installation, and costs. USG does promote these benefits. However, the imagery in its B-to-B ads packs a decided emotional wallop. For example, overall sales and marketing for USG's concrete structural panels stresses durability, light weight, and ease of installation versus traditional poured concrete, which is comparatively heavy, slow, and expensive. But rather than state these benefits directly, a USG ad for its structural panels features a dramatic image of a structural engineer caught hand and foot in the grasp of the tentacles of a concrete octopus emerging from a poured concrete floor. The ad asks, "Is poured concrete holding you back?" and then refers customers to USG's website for detailed performance features and comparisons. This and other USG ad recognize that emotions can play a role even in heavily performance-based decisions.

● **Figure 6.2** lists various groups of influences on business buyers: environmental, organizational, interpersonal, and individual. Business buyers are heavily influenced by factors in the current and expected *economic environment*, such as the level of primary demand, the economic outlook, and the cost of money. Another environmental factor is the *supply* of key materials. Business buyers also are affected by *technological, political*, and *competitive* developments in the environment. Finally, *culture and customs* can strongly influence business buyer reactions to the marketer's behavior and strategies, especially in the international marketing environment (see Real Marketing 6.1). The business buyer

● FIGURE 6.2
Major Influences on Business Buyer Behavior

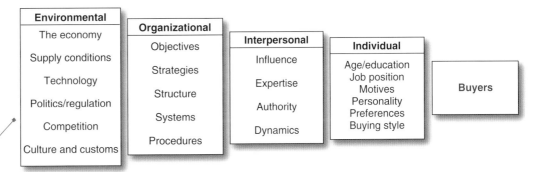

Like consumer buying decisions in Figure 5.2, business buying decisions are affected by an incredibly complex combination of environmental, interpersonal, and individual influences, but with an extra layer of organizational factors thrown into the mix.

Environmental	Organizational	Interpersonal	Individual	
The economy	Objectives	Influence	Age/education	Buyers
Supply conditions	Strategies	Expertise	Job position	
Technology	Structure	Authority	Motives	
Politics/regulation	Systems	Dynamics	Personality	
Competition	Procedures		Preferences	
Culture and customs			Buying style	

Real Marketing 6.1 | International Marketing Manners

Picture this: Consolidated Amalgamation Inc. thinks it's time that the rest of the world enjoyed the same fine products it has offered American consumers for two generations. It dispatches Vice President Harry E. Slicksmile to Europe, Asia, and Africa to explore the territory. Mr. Slicksmile stops first in London, where he makes short work of some bankers—he rings them up on the phone. He handles Parisians with similar ease: After securing a table at La Tour d'Argent, he greets his luncheon guest, the director of an industrial engineering firm, with the words "Just call me Harry, Jacques." In Germany, Mr. Slicksmile is a powerhouse. He licks the meeting off with a good joke. Then, whisking through a flashy multimedia presentation on his iPad and an ultra-compact projector, he shows 'em that this Georgia boy knows how to make a buck.

Mr. Slicksmile next swings through Saudi Arabia, where he coolly presents a potential client with a multimillion-dollar proposal in a classy pigskin binder. Heading on to Moscow, Harry strikes up a conversation with the Japanese businessman sitting next to him on the plane. Harry compliments the man's cuff links several times, recognizing him as a man of importance. As the two say goodbye, the man gifts his cuff links to Harry, presents his business card with both hands, and bows at the waist. Harry places his hand firmly on the man's back to express sincere thanks and then slips his own business card into the man's shirt pocket.

Harry takes Russia by storm as he meets with the CEO of a startup tech firm. Feeling very at ease with the Russia executive, Harry sheds his suit coat, leans back, crosses one foot over the other knee, and slips his hands into his pockets. At his next stop in Beijing, China, Harry talks business over lunch with a group of Chinese executives. After completing the meal, he drops his chopsticks into his bowl of rice and presents each guest with a gift as a gesture of his desire to do business with them—an elegant Tiffany clock.

A great tour, sure to generate a pile of orders, right? Wrong. Six months later, Consolidated Amalgamation has nothing to show for the extended trip but a stack of bills. Abroad, they weren't wild about Harry.

This hypothetical case has been exaggerated for emphasis. Americans are seldom such dolts. But experts say success in international business has a lot to do with knowing the territory and its people. By learning English and extending themselves in other ways, the world's business leaders have met Americans more than halfway. In contrast, Americans too

often do little except assume that others will march to their music. "We want things to be 'American' when we travel. Fast. Convenient. Easy. So we become 'ugly Americans' by demanding that others change," says one American world trade expert. "I think more business would be done if we tried harder."

Poor Harry tried, all right, but in all the wrong ways. The British do not, as a rule, make deals over the phone as much as Americans do. It's not so much a "cultural" difference as a difference in approach. A proper Frenchman neither likes instant familiarity nor refers to strangers by their first names. "That poor fellow, Jacques, probably wouldn't show anything, but he'd not be pleased," explains an expert on French business practices.

Harry's flashy presentation would likely have been a flop with the Germans, who dislike overstatement and showiness and to whom jokes are not appreciated in a business context. And to the Saudi Arabians, the pigskin binder would have been considered vile. An American salesperson who actually presented such a binder was unceremoniously tossed out of the country and his company was blacklisted from working with Saudi businesses.

Harry also committed numerous faux pas with his new Japanese acquaintance. Because the Japanese strive to please others, especially when someone admires their possessions, the executive likely felt obligated rather than pleased to give up his cuff links. Harry's "hand on the back" probably labeled him as disrespectful and presumptuous. Japan, like many Asian countries, is a "no-contact culture" in which even shaking hands is a strange experience. Harry made matters worse with his casual treatment of the business cards. Japanese people revere the business card as an extension of self and as an indicator of rank. They do not hand it to people; they present it—with both hands.

Things didn't go well in Russia, either. Russian businesspeople maintain a conservative, professional appearance, with dark suits and dress shoes. Taking one's coat off during negotiations of any kind is taken as a sign of weakness. Placing hands in one's pockets is considered rude, and showing the bottoms of one's shoes is a disgusting gesture. Similarly, in China, Harry casually dropping his chopsticks could have been misinterpreted as an act of aggression. Stabbing chopsticks into a bowl of rice and leaving them signifies death to the Chinese. The clocks Harry offered as gifts might have confirmed such dark intentions. To "give a clock" in Chinese sounds the same as "seeing someone off to his end."

Thus, to compete successfully in global markets or even to deal effectively with international firms in their home markets, companies must help their managers to understand the needs, customs, and cultures of international business buyers. Several companies now offer smartphone apps that provide tips to international travelers and help prevent them from making embarrassing mistakes while abroad. Cultures around the world differ greatly, and marketers must dig deeply to make certain they adapt to these differences. "When doing business in a foreign country and a foreign culture ... take nothing for granted," advises an international business specialist. "Turn every stone. Ask every question. Dig into every detail."[8]

International marketing manners: To compete successfully in global markets, companies must help their managers to understand the needs, customs, and cultures of international business buyers.
Rawpixel.com/Shutterstock

must watch these factors, determine how they will affect the buyer, and try to turn these challenges into opportunities.

Organizational factors are also important. Each buying organization has its own objectives, strategies, structure, systems, and procedures, and the business marketer must understand these factors well. Questions such as these arise: How many people are involved in the buying decision? Who are they? What are their evaluative criteria? What are the company's policies and limits on its buyers?

The buying center usually includes many participants who influence each other, so *interpersonal factors* also influence the business buying process. However, it is often difficult to assess such interpersonal factors and group dynamics. Buying center participants do not wear tags that label them as "key decision maker" or "not influential." Nor do buying center participants with the highest rank always have the most influence. Participants may influence the buying decision because they control rewards and punishments, are well liked, have special expertise, or have a special relationship with other important participants. Interpersonal factors are often very subtle. Whenever possible, business marketers must try to understand these factors and design strategies that take them into account.

Each participant in the business buying decision process brings in personal motives, perceptions, and preferences. These *individual factors* are affected by personal characteristics such as age, income, education, professional identification, personality, and attitudes toward risk. Also, buyers have different buying styles. Some may be technical types who make in-depth analyses of competitive proposals before choosing a supplier. Other buyers may be intuitive negotiators who are adept at pitting the sellers against one another for the best deal.

The Business Buyer Decision Process

OBJECTIVE 6-3 List and define the steps in the business buying decision process.

● **Figure 6.3** lists the eight stages of the business buyer decision process.[9] Buyers who face a new task buying situation usually go through all stages of the buying process. Buyers making modified or straight rebuys, in contrast, may skip some of the stages. We will examine these steps for the typical new task buying situation.

Problem Recognition

Problem recognition
The first stage of the business buying process in which someone in the company recognizes a problem or need that can be met by acquiring a good or a service.

The buying process begins when someone in the company recognizes a problem or need that can be met by acquiring a specific product or service. **Problem recognition** can result from internal or external stimuli. Internally, the company may decide to launch a new product that requires new production equipment and materials. Or a machine may break down and need new parts. Perhaps a purchasing manager is unhappy with a current supplier's product quality, service, or prices. Externally, the buyer may get some new ideas at a trade show, see an ad or website, or receive a call from a salesperson who offers a better product or a lower price.

● FIGURE 6.3
Stages of the Business Buyer Decision Process

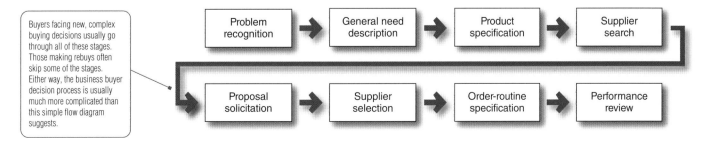

Buyers facing new, complex buying decisions usually go through all of these stages. Those making rebuys often skip some of the stages. Either way, the business buyer decision process is usually much more complicated than this simple flow diagram suggests.

Problem recognition → General need description → Product specification → Supplier search → Proposal solicitation → Supplier selection → Order-routine specification → Performance review

● **Problem recognition:** Salesforce's "Blaze your trail" ads show how it solves problems for some of its high-profile customers, such as Intuit, suggesting that it can do the same for new customers.
Salesforce.com, inc.

General need description
The stage in the business buying process in which a buyer describes the general characteristics and quantity of a needed item.

Product specification
The stage of the business buying process in which the buying organization decides on and specifies the best technical product characteristics for a needed item.

Supplier search
The stage of the business buying process in which the buyer tries to find the best vendors.

In fact, business marketers often alert customers to potential problems and then show how their products and services provide solutions. ● For example, CRM solutions firm Salesforce's "Blaze your trail" ads show how Salesforce solves problems for some of its high-profile customers, suggesting that it can do the same for new customers.[10] "How Intuit Gets a Better View of Their Customers," says one Salesforce ad headline. "Running a business with millions of customers can be like manning air traffic control," the ad continues. "How do you keep everyone on the right flight path? Intuit does it with Salesforce. The Customer Success Platform, powered by Einstein artificial intelligence, gives employees the insights they need to work smarter. And apps connect customers to real-time help, right when they need it. What if you had a way to track every one of your customers, no matter where they were headed?"

General Need Description

Having recognized a need, the buyer next prepares a **general need description** that describes the characteristics and quantity of the needed item. For standard items, this process presents few problems. For complex items, however, the buyer may need to work with others—engineers, users, consultants—to define the item. The team may want to rank the importance of reliability, durability, price, and other attributes desired in the item. In this phase, the alert business marketer can help the buyers define their needs and provide information about the value of different product characteristics.

Product Specification

The buying organization next develops the item's technical **product specifications**, often with the help of a value analysis engineering team. *Product value analysis* is an approach to cost reduction in which components are studied carefully to determine if they can be redesigned, standardized, or made by less costly methods of production. The team decides on the best product characteristics and specifies them accordingly. Sellers, too, can use value analysis as a tool to help secure a new account. By showing buyers a better way to make an object, outside sellers can turn straight rebuy situations into new task situations that give them a chance to obtain new business.

Supplier Search

The buyer now conducts a **supplier search** to find the best vendors. The buyer can compile a small list of qualified suppliers by reviewing trade directories, doing online searches, or phoning other companies for recommendations. Today, more and more companies are turning to the internet to find suppliers. For marketers, this has leveled the playing field—the internet gives smaller suppliers many of the same advantages as larger competitors. The newer the buying task and the more complex and costly the item, the greater the amount of time the buyer will spend searching for suppliers. The supplier's task is to get listed in major directories, create a robust online presence, and build a good reputation in the marketplace. Salespeople should watch for companies in the process of searching for suppliers and make certain that their firm is considered.

Proposal Solicitation

In the **proposal solicitation** stage of the business buying process, the buyer invites qualified suppliers to submit proposals. In response, some suppliers will refer the buyer to their website or promotional materials or send a salesperson to call on the prospect. However,

Proposal solicitation
The stage of the business buying process in which the buyer invites qualified suppliers to submit proposals.

when the item is complex or expensive, the buyer will usually require a detailed written proposal or formal presentation from each potential supplier.

Business marketers must be skilled in researching, writing, and presenting proposals in response to buyer proposal solicitations. They should be skilled at connecting digitally with buyers to understand their needs and requirements. Proposals should be marketing documents, not just technical documents. Presentations should inspire confidence and should make the marketer's company stand out from the competition.

Supplier Selection

Supplier selection
The stage of the business buying process in which the buyer reviews proposals and selects a supplier or suppliers.

The members of the buying center now review the proposals and select a supplier or suppliers. During **supplier selection**, the buying center often will draw up a list of the desired supplier attributes and their relative importance. Such attributes include product and service quality, reputation, on-time delivery, ethical corporate behavior, honest communication, and competitive prices. The members of the buying center will rate suppliers against these attributes and identify the best suppliers.

Buyers may attempt to negotiate with preferred suppliers for better prices and terms before making the final selections. In the end, they may select a single supplier or a few suppliers. Many buyers prefer multiple sources of supplies to avoid being totally dependent on one supplier and to allow comparisons of prices and performance of several suppliers over time. Today's supplier development managers want to develop a full network of supplier-partners that can help the company bring more value to its customers.

Order-Routine Specification

Order-routine specification
The stage of the business buying process in which the buyer writes the final order with the chosen supplier(s), listing the technical specifications, quantity needed, expected time of delivery, return policies, and warranties.

The buyer now prepares an **order-routine specification**. It includes the final order with the chosen supplier or suppliers and lists items such as technical specifications, quantity needed, expected delivery time, return policies, and warranties. In the case of maintenance, repair, and operating items, buyers may use blanket contracts rather than periodic purchase orders. A blanket contract creates a long-term relationship in which the supplier promises to resupply the buyer as needed at agreed prices for a set time period.

Many large buyers now practice *vendor-managed inventory*, in which they turn over ordering and inventory responsibilities to their suppliers. Under such systems, buyers share sales and inventory information directly with key suppliers. The suppliers then monitor inventories and replenish stock automatically as needed. For example, most major suppliers to large retailers such as Walmart, Target, Home Depot, and Lowe's assume vendor-managed inventory responsibilities.

Performance Review

Performance review
The stage of the business buying process in which the buyer assesses the performance of the supplier and decides to continue, modify, or drop the arrangement.

In this stage, the buyer reviews supplier performance. The buyer may contact users and ask them to rate their satisfaction. The **performance review** may lead the buyer to continue, modify, or drop the arrangement. The seller's job is to monitor the same factors used by the buyer to make sure that the seller is giving the expected satisfaction.

In all, the eight-stage buying-process model shown in Figure 6.3 provides a simple view of the business buying as it might occur in a new task buying situation. However, the actual process is usually much more complex. In the modified rebuy or straight rebuy situation, some of these stages would be compressed or bypassed. Each organization buys in its own way, and each buying situation has unique requirements.

Different buying center participants may be involved at various stages of the process. Although certain buying-process steps usually do occur, buyers do not always follow them in the same order, and they may add other steps. Often, buyers will repeat certain stages of the process. Finally, a customer relationship might involve many different types of purchases ongoing at a given time, all in different stages of the buying process. And for most business customers, individual purchases are made within the framework of an ongoing, long-term customer relationship. The seller must manage the total *customer relationship*, not just individual purchases.

Engaging Business Buyers with Digital and Social Marketing

OBJECTIVE 6-4 Discuss how online, mobile, and social media have changed business-to-business marketing.

As in every other area of marketing, the explosion of information technologies and online, mobile, and social media has changed the face of the B-to-B buying and marketing process. In the following sections, we discuss two important technology advancements: *e-procurement and online purchasing* and *B-to-B digital and social media marketing*.

E-procurement and Online Purchasing

E-procurement

Purchasing through electronic connections between buyers and sellers—usually online.

Advances in information technology have dramatically affected the face of the B-to-B buying process. ● Online purchasing, often called **e-procurement**, has grown rapidly in recent years. Virtually unknown two decades ago, online purchasing is standard procedure for most companies today. In turn, business marketers can connect with customers online to share marketing information, sell products and services, provide customer support services, and maintain ongoing customer relationships.

Companies can do e-procurement in any of several ways. They can conduct *reverse auctions*, in which they put their purchasing requests online and invite suppliers to bid for the business. Or they can engage in online *trading exchanges*, through which companies work collectively to facilitate the trading process. Companies also can conduct e-procurement by setting up their own *company buying sites*. For example, GE operates a company trading site on which it posts its buying needs and invites bids, negotiates terms, and places orders. Or companies can create *extranet links* with key suppliers. For instance, they can create direct procurement accounts with suppliers such as Dell or Staples through which company buyers can purchase equipment, materials, and supplies directly. Staples operates a business-to-business procurement division called Staples Business Advantage, which serves the office supplies and services buying needs of businesses of any size, from 10 employees to the *Fortune* 1000.

● **Online procurement is standard procedure for most companies today, letting business marketers connect with customers online to sell products and services, provide customer support services, and maintain ongoing customer relationships.**

icetray/123RF

Business-to-business e-procurement yields many benefits. First, it shaves transaction costs and results in more efficient purchasing for both buyers and suppliers. E-procurement reduces the time between order and delivery. And an online-powered purchasing program eliminates the paperwork associated with traditional requisition and ordering procedures and helps an organization keep better track of all purchases. Finally, beyond the cost and time savings, e-procurement frees purchasing people from a lot of drudgery and paperwork. Instead, they can focus on more-strategic issues, such as finding better supply sources and working with suppliers to reduce costs and develop new products.

The rapidly expanding use of e-procurement, however, also presents some problems. For example, although the internet makes it possible for suppliers and customers to share business data and even collaborate on product design, it can also erode decades-old customer–supplier relationships. Many buyers now use the power of the internet to pit suppliers against one another and search out better deals, products, and turnaround times on a purchase-by-purchase basis.

Business-to-Business Digital and Social Media Marketing

B-to-B digital and social media marketing

Using digital and social media marketing approaches to engage business customers and manage customer relationships anywhere, any time.

In response to business customers' rapid shift toward online buying, today's B-to-B marketers are now using a wide range of digital and social media marketing approaches—from websites, blogs, mobile apps, e-newsletters, and proprietary online networks to mainstream social media such as Facebook, LinkedIn, Instagram, YouTube, and Twitter—to engage business customers and manage customer relationships anywhere, anytime.

B-to-B digital and social media marketing isn't just growing, it's exploding. Digital and social media marketing have rapidly become the new space for engaging business

" *Social media is about communication, not marketing. It's about engaging, not pushing. And social media is definitely not just about the media side.*

● Container shipping giant Maersk Line engages business customers through a boatload of digital and social media. "The goal is...to get closer to our customers."

A.P. Møller-Mærsk A/S

customers. ● Consider Maersk Line, the world's leading container shipping and transport company, serving business customers through 374 offices in 160 countries:[11]

> You might not expect much by way of new-age marketing from an old-line container shipping company, but think again. Maersk Line is one of the most forward-looking and accomplished B-to-B digital and social media marketers in any industry. Maersk Line has sailed full steam ahead into the social media waters with eight global accounts on primary social media networks including Facebook, LinkedIn, Twitter, and YouTube. Maersk Line has more than 2.4 million Facebook followers, making Facebook a platform for engaging a broad audience of customers and other stakeholders interested in the brand. On Instagram, the company shares customer and employee images and stories to help visualize the brand. On YouTube it posts informational and educational videos detailing Maersk Line's activities, services, and people. Maersk Line's Twitter feed presents the latest news and events, creating conversation and buzz with and among its more than 73,000 Twitter followers. The company's LinkedIn account, with more than 466,000 followers, lets Maersk Line engage customers, opinion leaders, and industry influencers, who share information and discuss industry challenges and opportunities with shipping and logistics experts. Why all this social media? "The goal is to use social media to get closer to our customers," says Maersk Line. "Social media is about engaging, not pushing."

Compared with traditional media and sales approaches, digital and social media can create greater customer engagement and interaction. B-to-B marketers know that they aren't really targeting *businesses,* they are targeting *individuals* in those businesses who affect buying decisions. And today's business buyers are always connected via their digital devices—whether it's computers, tablets, or smartphones.

Digital and social media play an important role in engaging these always-connected business buyers in a way that personal selling alone cannot. Instead of the old model of sales reps calling on business customers at work or maybe meeting up with them at trade shows, the new digital approaches facilitate anytime, anywhere connections between a wide range of people in the selling and customer organizations. It gives both sellers and buyers more control of and access to important information. B-to-B marketing has always been social network marketing, but today's digital environment offers an exciting array of new networking tools and applications.

Some B-to-B companies mistakenly assume that today's digital and social media are useful primarily to consumer products and services companies. But no matter what the industry, digital platforms can be powerful tools for engaging customers and other important publics. For example, B-to-B technology giant IBM uses a wide array of digital and social media not just to engage and support its business customers directly but also to tell the compelling IBM brand story and to keep the company relevant, contemporary, and accessible (see Real Marketing 6.2).

Author | These two nonbusiness
Comment | organizational markets provide attractive opportunities for many companies. Because of their unique nature, we give them special attention here.

Institutional and Government Markets

OBJECTIVE 6-5 Compare the institutional and government markets and explain how institutional and government buyers make their buying decisions.

Institutional Markets

Institutional market
Schools, hospitals, nursing homes, prisons, and other institutions that provide goods and services to people in their care.

The **institutional market** consists of schools, hospitals, nursing homes, prisons, and other institutions that provide goods and services to people in their care. Institutions differ from one another in their sponsors and their objectives. For example, Community Health Systems runs 115 for-profit hospitals in 20 states, generating $15 billion in annual revenues. By contrast, the Shriners Hospitals for Children is a nonprofit organization

Real Marketing 6.2 | IBM: Staying Nimble and Relevant with B-to-B Digital and Social Media Marketing

IBM is a household word to most of us. However, throughout the years, IBM's fortunes have come not from final consumers but from large business and institutional customers. "Big Blue"—as it's often called—is the quintessential B-to-B brand. It sells complex, big-ticket solutions to big-customer problems. The $79 billion technology giant has survived and thrived for more than 100 years, something no other *Fortune* top-25 company has managed.

Its long-term success in a turbulent industry means that IBM has mastered the art of innovation and transformation. "We're 104 years old," says IBM's CEO. "The reason we're the only tech company still here at 104 is how many times we've transformed." Twenty years ago, IBM focused heavily on its state-of-the art mainframe computers and software. But today's customers don't need just computers and software. Instead, they need total solutions to ever-more-bewildering data, information, and analytics problems.

To meet customers' vastly changing needs, IBM has shifted deeply into consulting with customers on data analytics, cloud computing, cybersecurity, social networking, mobile technology, and other digital-age problems. The transformed IBM now works arm in arm with B-to-B customers on everything from assessing, planning, designing, and implementing their data and analytics systems to actually running those systems for customers and helping them apply the results.

The IBM brand is largely shaped by the interactions that IBMers have with customers. Through the decades, IBM has nurtured customer relationships primarily through its legendary sales forces. But just as IBM has transformed its product and services portfolio to meet the needs of the digital revolution, it has also transformed how it engages with customers. Although one of the oldest companies around, when it comes to grasping digital and social media, good-old Big Blue is young, nimble, and relevant.

IBM's leap to social media prominence didn't happen overnight. At first, the company simply encouraged employees to talk publicly in the social media—to each other and to customers—and let them go about it with no intervention or oversight. And go about it they did. Tens of thousands of IBMers became important brand advocates for the company, through internal blogs, IBM's own internal Facebook-like network, and individual involvement on Twitter, Instagram, LinkedIn, Facebook, YouTube, and other public social media.

Such IBMer-led social networking drove an incredible amount of interaction among IBM employees, customers, and suppliers. However, at times, it was also chaotic and unfocused. So as the digital environment matured, IBM centralized its social media strategy to give it more customer focus and impact.

At a core level, IBM now covers the digital basics well through a wide variety of platforms that inform and engage business customers directly, connect them with IBM salespeople, and promote customer purchasing and relationships. For example, IBM's various divisions offer dozens of market- and industry-specific websites, containing thousands of individual site areas and tens of thousands of pages that provide B-to-B customers with purchasing solutions, product overviews, detailed technical information, and real-time customer support. IBM also helps its sales force engage business customers more deeply through a comprehensive presence in major social media.

But IBM knows that digital and social media marketing is about more than just driving sales. It's about building a brand. It's about creating brand personality and ongoing relationships. It's about telling great IBM stories of innovation, big data, artificial intelligence, cloud computing, and technology consulting. The goal is to make the IBM brand relevant, contemporary, and accessible, a task ideally suited to digital and social media.

To that end, over the past several years, IBM has unleashed a remarkable array of digital content that connects the brand with customers across a full array of digital platforms and positions the iconic company as a contemporary technology leader. As part of a broad-based, carefully crafted marketing content program, each social media platform plays a unique role in telling the IBM story.

For example, IBM's Instagram posts provide eye-catching bursts of colorful, stimulating content consistent with that platform's penchant for visual creativity. Posts tell interesting stories about IBM product developments, creative uses of IBM technology, and snippets of IBM's storied history. In what one analyst calls a "hyper-glossy, high-end B-to-B brochure," IBM's Instagram pages turn innovations into art and make complex technologies digestible. One post tells how IBM applied artificial intelligence to on-court and off-court data at the U.S. Open tennis championships to improve the fan experience and help players and coaches improve their approaches to the game. Another post tells how IBM Watson directs tourists through an iconic coastal drive. Still another post shows how in 1981, the iconic IBM 5150 PC "set a worldwide computing standard and helped to establish a multibillion-dollar industry."

The Instagram posts are designed not to sell but to showcase IBM's products, prowess, and impact. For example, posts feature

Although IBM is one of the oldest companies around, when it comes to grasping digital and social media, good-old Big Blue is young, nimble, and relevant.

Courtesy of International Business Machines Corporation, © (2019) International Business Machines Corporation.

visually engaging images of products such as IBM Z mainframe servers with little text and no clear sales pitch. Posts don't spell out the product's selling points—IBM knows that people commenting on the posts will take care of that. IBM reps can participate in the dialogues and direct interested parties to the right places to learn more.

IBM's numerous Twitter feeds (IBM Watson, IBM Cloud, IBM Analytics, IBM Research, IBM News Room, and others) play a different role. Although Twitter posts include striking images and video content, their emphasis is less on visual artistry and more on current news, information, and education. Each post includes newsworthy links to articles or blogs on IBM's website, where customers can dig deeper on topics of interest, such as blockchain innovations, IBM

Watson's newest AI venture, or even the company's most recent quarterly earnings. Daily Twitter posts supply a constant flow of rich content that keeps followers engaged and IBM relevant.

IBM uses Facebook to build brand community. Although it features much of the same content as its Instagram and Twitter feeds, IBM also uses Facebook to post longer videos that would not work well on platforms like Twitter where viewers have shorter attention spans. IBM's Facebook pages also include some more motivational and inspirational content. For example, one recently posted video shows a 13-year-old developer who built a pizza delivery bot with IBM Watson. IBM also excels on LinkedIn, perhaps the most popular forum for B-to-B social media marketing. Its more than a dozen LinkedIn feeds focus

on business-related content. With 5.3 million LinkedIn followers, IBM ranks among LinkedIn's most popular companies.

In all, through its skillful use of digital and social media marketing, IBM achieves one of the largest social marketing followings of any B-to-B company. In this digital age, by constantly transforming not only its products and services but also its digital approaches to engaging customers, the century-old IBM remains as nimble and relevant as its much younger competitors. And more than just producing views, comments, likes, and click-throughs, IBM's digital transformation has helped the company turn customer engagement and relationships into revenues and profits. Despite its advanced age, IBM now ranks as the second-most-valuable B-to-B brand behind only Microsoft[12].

---

with 22 facilities that provide free specialized health care for children, whereas the government-run Veterans Affairs Medical Centers located across the country provide special services to veterans.[13] Each institution has different buying needs and resources.

Institutional markets can be huge. Consider the massive and expanding U.S. prisons economy. U.S. prisons spend about $80 billion annually to keep their facilities running, an amount greater than the GDP of 144 nations.[14] This market presents a unique opportunity for marketers of food, medical, maintenance, education, technology, security, and other products and services.

Many institutional markets are characterized by low budgets and captive patrons. For example, in the United States alone has almost 100,000 public schools. It costs more than $668 billion each year—$13,000 on average per student—to run those schools.[15] Unless students and teachers brown bag it, they have little choice but to eat whatever food the school provides. The school district purchasing agent who buys the food must adhere to strict nutritional guidelines to follow and is often constrained by a tight budget. Thus, food vendors can play an important role in helping such buyers to meet or exceed the guidelines and affordable prices.

Many marketers set up separate divisions to meet the special characteristics and needs of institutional buyers. ● For example, Nestlé Professional helps institutional food service customers in any of several industries find creative meal solutions using Nestlé's broad assortment of food and beverage brands. And P&G's Professional Division markets professional cleaning and laundry formulations and systems to educational, healthcare, and other institutional and commercial customers.[16]

Government Markets

Government market

Governmental units—federal, state, and local—that purchase or rent goods and services for carrying out the main functions of government.

The **government market** offers large opportunities for many companies, both big and small. In most countries, government organizations are major buyers of goods and services. In the United States alone, federal, state, and local governments contain tens of thousands of buying units that purchase more than $2.3 trillion in goods and services each year.[17] Government buying and business buying are similar in many ways. But there are also differences that must be understood by companies that wish to sell products and services to governments. To succeed in the government market, sellers must locate key decision makers, identify the factors that affect buyer behavior, and understand the buying decision process.

Government organizations typically require suppliers to submit bids, and normally they award the contract to the lowest bidder. In some cases, a governmental unit will make allowances for the supplier's superior quality or reputation for completing contracts on time.

Creative Food and Beverage Solutions

FAST CASUAL

CONVENIENCE STORE

FOODSERVICE AT RETAIL

COLLEGE & UNIVERSITY

HEALTHCARE

BUSINESS & INDUSTRY

● **Institutional markets: Nestlé Professional helps foodservice customers in any of several industries find creative meal solutions using Nestlé's broad assortment of food and beverage brands.**
Nestlé Brands®

Governments will also buy on a negotiated contract basis, primarily in the case of complex projects involving major R&D costs and risks and in cases where there is little competition.

Government organizations tend to favor domestic suppliers over foreign suppliers. A major complaint of multinationals operating in Europe is that each country shows favoritism toward its nationals in spite of superior offers that are made by foreign firms. The European Economic Commission is gradually removing this bias.

Like consumer and business buyers, government buyers are affected by environmental, organizational, interpersonal, and individual factors. One unique thing about government buying is that it is carefully watched by outside publics, ranging from Congress to a variety of private groups interested in how the government spends taxpayers' money. Because their spending decisions are subject to public review, government organizations require considerable documentation from suppliers, who often complain about excessive paperwork, bureaucracy, regulations, decision-making delays, and frequent shifts in procurement personnel.

Given all the red tape, why would any firm want to do business with the U.S. government? The reasons are quite simple: The U.S. government is the world's largest buyer of products and services—about $450 billion last year—and its checks don't bounce. The government buys everything from socks to stealth bombers.

Most governments provide would-be suppliers with detailed guides describing how to sell to the government. For example, the U.S. Small Business Administration provides on its website detailed advice for small businesses seeking government contracting opportunities (www.sba.gov/federal-contracting/contracting-guide/how-win-contracts). And the U.S. Commerce Department's website is loaded with information and advice on international trade opportunities (www.commerce.gov/work-with-us/grants-and-contract-opportunities).

In several major cities, the General Services Administration operates *Business Service Centers* with staffs to provide a complete education on the way government agencies buy, the steps that suppliers should follow, and the procurement opportunities available. Various trade magazines and associations provide information on how to reach schools, hospitals, highway departments, and other government agencies. And almost all of these government organizations and associations maintain internet sites offering up-to-date information and advice. Still, suppliers have to master the system and find ways to cut through the red tape, especially for large government purchases.

Noneconomic criteria are playing a growing role in government buying. Government buyers are asked to favor depressed business firms and areas; small business firms; minority-owned firms; and business firms that avoid race, gender, or age discrimination. Sellers need to keep these factors in mind when seeking government business.

Many companies that sell to the government have not been very marketing oriented for a number of reasons. Total government spending is determined by elected officials rather than by any marketing effort to develop this market. Government buying has emphasized price, making suppliers invest their effort in technology to bring costs down. When the product's characteristics are specified carefully, product differentiation is not a marketing factor. Nor do advertising or personal selling matter much in winning bids on an open-bid basis.

Several companies, however, have established separate government marketing departments, including Boeing, Goodyear, and Raytheon. Other companies, such as global security and aerospace company Lockheed Martin, sell primarily to government buyers. Lockheed Martin receives more than 69 percent of its sales from the U.S. government, either as a prime contractor or a subcontractor. Another 30 percent of its sales are primarily foreign military sales contracted though the U.S. government.[18] Such companies anticipate government needs and projects, participate in the product specification phase, gather competitive intelligence, prepare bids carefully, and build long-term, value-adding relationships with government buying centers.

Other companies have established customized marketing programs for government buyers. For example, Dell has specific business units tailored to meet the needs of federal as well as state and local government buyers. Dell offers its customers tailor-made Premier web pages that include special pricing, online purchasing, and service and support for each city, state, and federal government entity.

During the past decade, a great deal of the government's buying has gone online. The Federal Business Opportunities website (www.fbo.gov) provides a single point of entry through which commercial vendors and government buyers can post, search, monitor, and retrieve opportunities solicited by the entire federal contracting community. The three federal agencies that act as purchasing agents for the rest of government have also launched websites supporting online government purchasing activity. The General Services Administration, which influences more than one-quarter of the federal government's total procurement dollars, has set up a GSA Advantage! website (www.gsaadvantage.gov). The Defense Logistics Agency offers an Internet Bid Board System (www.dibbs.bsm.dla.mil) for purchases by America's military services. And the Department of Veterans Affairs facilitates e-procurement through its VA Advantage! website (https://VAadvantage.gsa.gov).

Such sites allow authorized defense and civilian agencies to buy everything from office supplies, food, and information technology equipment to construction services through online purchasing. The General Services Administration, the Defense Logistics Agency, and the Department of Veterans Affairs not only sell stocked merchandise through their websites but also create direct links between government buyers and contract suppliers. For example, the branch of the Defense Logistics Agency that sells 160,000 types of medical supplies to military forces transmits orders directly to vendors such as Bristol-Myers Squibb. Such online systems promise to eliminate much of the hassle sometimes found in dealing with government purchasing.[19]

Reviewing and Extending the Concepts

Objectives Review

Business markets and consumer markets are alike in some key ways. For example, both include people in buying roles who make purchase decisions to satisfy needs. But business markets also differ in many ways from consumer markets. For one thing, the business market is *huge*, far larger than the consumer market. Within the United States alone, the business market includes organizations that annually purchase trillions of dollars' worth of goods and services.

OBJECTIVE 6-1 Define the business market and explain how business markets differ from consumer markets. *(pp 182–184)*

The *business market* comprises all organizations that buy goods and services for use in the production of other products and services or for the purpose of reselling or renting them to others at a profit. As compared to consumer markets, business markets usually have fewer but larger buyers. Business demand is derived demand, which tends to be more inelastic and fluctuating than consumer demand. The business buying decision usually involves more, and more professional, buyers. Business buyers usually face more complex buying decisions, and the buying process tends to be more formalized. Finally, business buyers and sellers are often more dependent on each other.

OBJECTIVE 6-2 Identify the major factors that influence business buyer behavior. *(pp 184–189)*

Business buyers make decisions that vary with the three *types of buying* situations: straight rebuys, modified rebuys, and new tasks. The decision-making unit of a buying organization—*the buying center*—can consist of many different persons playing many different roles. The business marketer needs to know the following: Who are the major buying center participants? In what decisions do they exercise influence and to what degree? What evaluation criteria does each decision participant use? The business marketer also needs to understand the major environmental, organizational, interpersonal, and individual influences on the buying process.

OBJECTIVE 6-3 List and define the steps in the business buying decision process. *(pp 189–191)*

The business buying decision process itself can be quite involved, with eight basic stages: problem recognition, general need description, product specification, supplier search,

proposal solicitation, supplier selection, order-routine specification, and performance review. Buyers who face a new task buying situation usually go through all stages of the buying process. Buyers making modified or straight rebuys may skip some of the stages. However, most B-to-B purchases are made within the framework of the broader, longer-term customer relationship. Companies must manage the overall customer relationship, which often includes many different buying decisions in various stages of the buying decision process.

OBJECTIVE 6-4 Discuss how online, mobile, and social media have changed business-to-business marketing. *(pp 192–193)*

Rapid advances in information and digital technology have given birth to "e-procurement," by which business buyers are purchasing all kinds of products and services online. The internet gives business buyers access to new suppliers, lowers purchasing costs, and hastens order processing and delivery. Today's business marketers also connect extensively with customers online and through digital, mobile, and social media to engage customers, share marketing information, sell products and services, provide customer support services, and maintain ongoing customer relationships.

OBJECTIVE 6-5 Compare the institutional and government markets and explain how institutional and government buyers make their buying decisions. *(pp 193–197)*

The *institutional market* consists of schools, hospitals, prisons, and other institutions that provide goods and services to people in their care. These markets are characterized by low budgets and captive patrons. The *government market*, which is vast, consists of government units—federal, state, and local—that purchase or rent goods and services for carrying out the main functions of government.

Government buyers purchase products and services for defense, education, public welfare, and other public needs. Government buying practices are highly specialized and specified, with open bidding or negotiated contracts characterizing most of the buying. Government buyers operate under the watchful eye of the U.S. Congress and many private watchdog groups. Hence, they tend to require more forms and signatures and respond more slowly and deliberately when placing orders.

Key Terms

Business buyer behavior (p 182)
Business buying process (p 182)

OBJECTIVE 6-1

Derived demand (p 183)
Supplier development (p 184)

OBJECTIVE 6-2

Straight rebuy (p 185)

Modified rebuy (p 185)
New task (p 185)
Systems selling (solutions selling) (p 185)
Buying center (p 186)
Users (p 186)
Influencers (p 186)
Buyers (p 186)

Deciders (p 186)
Gatekeepers (p 186)

OBJECTIVE 6-3

Problem recognition (p 189)
General need description (p 190)
Product specification (p 190)
Supplier search (p 190)

Proposal solicitation (p 190)
Supplier selection (p 191)
Order-routine specification (p 191)
Performance review (p 191)

OBJECTIVE 6-4
E-procurement (p 192)
B-to-B digital and social media
marketing (p 192)

OBJECTIVE 6-5
Institutional market (p 193)
Government market (p 195)

Discussion Questions

6-1 How are business markets similar to consumer markets? How are they different?

6-2 Briefly discuss a business buyer's straight rebuy and modified rebuy strategies. What are the similarities and differences? When might it be beneficial to use one approach over the other? (AACSB: Written and Oral Communication, Reflective Thinking)

6-3 What are systems or solutions selling? How can an organization be successful in this area of sales? What are customers looking for from suppliers? (AACSB: Communication; Reflective Thinking)

6-4 List the participants in the business buying process. What factors influence the buying decision? Discuss the major influences on business buyers. (AACSB: Written and Oral Communication; Reflective Thinking)

6-5 Discuss the major influences on business buyers. (AACSB: Written and Oral Communication; Reflective Thinking)

6-6 What are the benefits of business-to-business e-procurement? (AACSB: Written and Oral Communication; Reflective Thinking)

Critical Thinking Exercises

6-7 Business buying can be a very involved process. Many companies employ procurement or purchasing experts dedicated to managing the firm's buying process. Visit www.glassdoor.com/Salaries and www.indeed.com/salary to conduct a search of the salary ranges for "procurement specialists," "procurement manager," or similar positions in purchasing. Present your findings. Can e-procurement help to streamline the buying process? Might it eventually replace employees in these careers? Discuss if it is possible for all buying functions to be performed through e-procurement? (AACSB: Written and Oral Communication; Reflective Thinking; Information Technology)

6-8 At various times, many governments have favored a procurement process that requires government buyers to choose domestic rather than foreign suppliers. This

approach has also been used by some retailers as integral parts of their advertising, encouraging consumers to buy domestic rather than overseas brands. Investigate the government procurement policy in your own country and try to find a retailer that has run an advertising campaign like this. How were these policies and campaigns received? What was their longevity? (AACSB: Communication; Reflective Thinking)

6-9 Following a sales pitch, an individual at a company recognizes the need for one of the hybrid-electric airships like those you were selling in Exercise 6-8. What happens next in the buying process? (AACSB: Written and Oral Communication; Reflective Thinking)

APPLICATIONS AND CASES

Online, Mobile, and Social Media Marketing E-procurement and Mobile Procurement

Gone are the days of tedious, paper-laden, labor-intensive B-to-B procurement duties. E-procurement is changing the way buyers and sellers do business, specifically via mobile procurement that offers cloud-based platforms that reduce the search, order, and approval cycle. Most large companies have adopted some form of e-procurement. A recent study found that almost 70 percent of companies utilize some form of e-procurement, mobile procurement, or supply chain management applications. A leading industry platform, Coupa, provides a suite of cloud-based applications for finance, including accounts payable, sourcing, procurement, and expense management that allows customers full functionality from their mobile devices. Employees now enjoy the flexibility and time savings of viewing, approving, or denying requisitions, purchase orders, and invoices. One of Coupa's large

retail clients claimed a reduction from 10 days to only 5 hours in its requisition-approval-process cycle by implementing Coupa's mobile procurement platform. Talk about savings! Visit www.coupa.com/software/procurement/ to learn more about how this company is revolutionizing the e-procurement and mobile procurement environments.

6-10 Discuss the advantages of e-procurement to both buyers and sellers. What are the disadvantages? (AACSB: Written and Oral Communication; Reflective Thinking)

6-11 Research mobile procurement and discuss the roles in the buying center that are affected most by this technology. (AACSB: Written and Oral Communication; Reflective Thinking)

Marketing Ethics Big Tech for Military Activities

The U.S. government has appealed to tech giants, including Amazon, Google, and Microsoft, indicating it is the patriotic duty of American tech firms to help the military use advanced technology such as artificial intelligence. However, some tech firm employees have protested the use of the tools they develop by the government—in particular, if the tools are used for military activities they consider immoral. Thus, the technology firms have concerns about how technology might be used in the future, about how the government contracts may affect recruiting efforts, and about how the contracts might affect consumer attitudes toward the brand.

6-12   Take a position: If you were Microsoft, would you pursue a government contract to adapt HoloLens, an augmented reality headset, for use by soldiers in the battlefield? Why or why not? (AACSB: Written and Oral Communication; Reflective Thinking)

6-13   What other factors more generally associated with government contracts might Microsoft's marketers want to keep in mind when bidding for a government contract? (AACSB: Written and Oral Communication; Reflective Thinking)

Marketing by the Numbers From Gaming to Public Safety

Edgybees, formerly a drone gaming company, is applying augmented reality (AR) technology from gaming uses to public safety uses, with applications for the military and emergency first responders. New fifth-generation (or 5G) cellular technology has opened doors for companies like Edgybees to overlay real-time drone video feeds with geo-information layers such as maps, building layouts, and other data. For example, the company recently provided intelligence to firefighters battling one of Northern California's worst wildfires, giving them real-time footage of their surroundings and ultimately saving lives. Edgybees is a small company but has recently raised $6 million in venture capital funding to expand. One market it wants to target is first responders. These business customers need more than just to be sold a product—they need a relationship with Edgybees to ensure that the latest technology is meeting their needs. Thus, Edgybees would need to visit customers at least twice per year, often for hours at a time. If Edgybees decides to go with its own sales force, each salesperson will earn $50,000 plus 5 percent commission on all sales. Refer to the Increase Distribution Coverage heading in Appendix 2: Marketing by the Numbers to answer the questions below.

6-14   How many salespeople does Edgybees need if it wants to obtain 500 first-responder customer accounts, such as fire departments and police stations, which need to be called on twice per year? Each sales call lasts approximately 2.5 hours, and each sales rep has approximately 1,250 hours per year to devote to customers. (AACSB: Communication; Analytical Reasoning)

6-15   If Edgybees realizes an overall contribution margin of 40 percent, as the company expands, by how much will sales have to increase to break even on each additional sales representative? (AACSB: Communication; Analytical Reasoning)

Company Case Shopify: An E-commerce Giant That Doesn't Sell to End Users

What do Budweiser, Tesla, *The New York Times,* Bombas Socks, and Kylie Cosmetics have in common? Each company sells direct-to-consumer (DTC) merchandise primarily online. But more, each has an online store created, managed, and powered by Shopify—the biggest e-commerce company that most people have never heard of. In the age of DTC companies, Shopify is behind-the-scenes business that takes care of everything for anyone wanting to sell something online—a genuine end-to-end commerce platform for everyone from the young entrepreneur who has never started a company to large, well-known corporations needing an online store.

The concept is simple. For a monthly fee, Shopify helps individuals or corporations sell their merchandise online. It supplies everything merchants need to go online, including customizable store templates, inventory management systems, analytics, payment processing, and shipping. Shopify also provides consultative services and a network of partners to handle manufacturing, promotion, and order fulfillment. Shopify's platform not only sells merchandise directly from the merchant's online store or mobile app, it plugs into a growing number of broader platforms, including online marketplaces like Amazon, social media channels like Instagram Stories, and even brick-and-mortar locations. The system is completely cloud-based, which means zero investment in hardware and software. It also means that business owners can manage things from anywhere on any device with an internet connection. In short, Shopify's mission is to make e-commerce easier and better for everyone.

Although that mission seems a bit lofty, Shopify is well on its way. In 2015, the nearly 10-year-old company went public at a value of $1.3 billion. The preceding year, Shopify's 140,000 stores had sold more than $3.7 billion worth of merchandise. And Shopify has been lauded by experts and organizations the world over for its growth and impact, including being named as one of the world's most innovative companies by *Fast Company* this year. How has Shopify come so far so fast yet remain relatively unknown to the average consumer?

From Snowboards to Startups

It all started in the early 2000s in Ottawa, Quebec, when Tobi Lütke and Scott Lake met and bonded over their love of technology and snowboarding. The pair joined forces to open Snowdevil, an online store selling high-end snowboards. Building the site proved to be an exercise in frustration. Working with popular software options of the day, such as Microsoft Commerce and Yahoo! Stores, was difficult and expensive. So Lütke—who had dropped out of high school at the age of 17 to work as a programming apprentice at Siemens—decided to build his own e-commerce platform from scratch. He came up with something much simpler, faster, and more visually pleasing than anything from existing web design vendors.

Snowdevil.com's sales were meager at best. But Lütke and Lake quickly realized that the most valuable entity they possessed was the platform beneath Snowdevil. So in 2006 they launched Shopify as a platform for creating online stores. The going was slow at first, but as they continued to improve the platform with innovative tools, the client base grew steadily. Shopify also developed a corporate culture based on authenticity, free thinking, and what the company calls the "trust battery"—a perceptual gauge of an individual's potential based less on what they've already done and more on what they might do in the future.

The Anti-Amazon

Building the Shopify e-commerce platform required carefully defining what that platform is. But key to Shopify's strategy is also to define what the platform is not. In short, Shopify is not a marketplace. Although Shopify sets up and runs e-commerce operations for DTC companies, it operates in the shadows, silently and invisibly. So when customers visit Leesa.com to buy a mattress, every interaction take place with Leesa, the company and brand. Customers browsing for temporary tattoos at Tattly.com know only that they are experiencing a selection of creative, high-quality temporary tattoos exclusive to Tattly. When DTC brands sell on Amazon—whether fulfilled by Amazon or by the third-party vendors—customers are buying from Amazon, and the brands themselves gain little by way of brand equity. But visitors to the e-commerce stores powered by Shopify typically have no idea that Shopify even exists, let alone that it's the company behind the engine that drives their interactions. The DTC brand itself stands out, not the platform.

Shopify thinks of itself as the anti-Amazon, not because it is against the e-commerce giant but because it offers DTC companies a path to selling their goods that is so different in concept and outcome. Although Amazon takes care of everything down to operations and fulfillment, vendors don't so much build their own brands as they do Amazon's. As Amazon has grown, more sellers have complained openly that they have little control over their sales, customer relations, and the data generated from shopping. In many cases, controlling those assets has allowed Amazon to develop private-label brands that compete directly against its sellers' brands. With Shopify, the merchant, not the marketplace, owns access to the end user.

Being a non-marketplace e-commerce platform gives Shopify a unique competitive advantage: Shopify is neutral. It interfaces with and even plugs into numerous existing marketplaces but doesn't favor any. And short of monitoring to prevent illegal activity on the part of vendors, Shopify does not interfere in their businesses. This neutrality has allowed Shopify to easily interface with the likes of Pinterest, Instagram, Facebook, Amazon, and numerous other companies that feature their own marketplaces. Thus, Shopify clients have access to any and all partner marketplaces.

A Big Boost from Lipstick

Since going public, Shopify's growth has accelerated. The company got its biggest publicity lift in August 2018, when the cover of *Forbes* featured Kylie Jenner in a black business suit with the headline "America's Women Billionaires." The cover story described how Jenner would become the youngest-ever self-made billionaire at age 21 by leveraging her fame into a cosmetics empire. More important, the article noted that Jenner's online store, kyliecosmetics.com, was powered by Shopify. Less than one year after joining Shopify, Kylie Cosmetics had gone from selling its signature lip kits to selling a full line of more than 50 different cosmetics products generating more than $300 million in annual sales. Paying tribute to the power of Jenner's fame as a factor in the young brand's success, *Forbes* also pointed out that Shopify was the e-commerce platform behind online stores for Drake, Justin Bieber, and Jenner's own half-sister Kim Kardashian West.

More recently, Shopify has taken things to an entirely new level, releasing a range of new tools that let small and medium-sized businesses better compete with e-commerce giants. These include Shopify Ping—a powerful customer service tool that lets merchants interact with customers over Facebook Messenger—and Dynamic Checkout—a checkout system that eliminates roadblocks that lead customers to abandon their carts. Although small businesses and startups are still the backbone of Shopify, the company now offers Shopify Plus—an e-commerce platform and services for companies with revenues of $1 million or more each year.

Today, just four years after the company went public, Shopify hosts more than 800,000 active client stores that have sold more than $100 billion worth of merchandise. During that same period, its stock price has increased by 600 percent, giving the company a value of more than $22 billion. For its efforts, Shopify's cut of client store sales came to more than $1 billion last year, making it the youngest software-as-a-service company ever to reach the billion-dollar revenue mark. "The 21st-century brand is the direct-to-consumer brand," says Shopify's chief marketing officer. "We run the gamut of a retail operating system," he says, indicating that the company intends to be a major force in powering DTC companies for a long time to come.

Despite its momentum, Shopify faces plenty of challenges ahead. For starters, Amazon recently launched its own Shopify fighter, Amazon Storefronts. Billed as "a new way for small and medium-sized businesses to sell products directly through Amazon," Storefronts highlights small businesses and their collections of unique products in a separate section. And although Shopify has a clear lead in the end-to-end e-commerce platform business, some analysts speculate that its model would be easy to replicate. In fact, many of the companies that Shopify partners with to provide process pieces for its e-commerce platform—such as PayPal and MailChimp—already possess data that could allow them to expand the e-commerce services they provide to their own DTC clients. Forgoing short-term profits, Shopify continues to invest heavily in Shopify Plus, international expansion, and innovations it believes will continue to make it the leading e-commerce platform provider.[20]

Questions for Discussion:

6-16 Compare and contrast the nature of the business market structure and demand relative to consumer market structure and demand for Shopify's services.

6-17 Discuss how a potential client for Shopify might go through the business buyer decision.

6-18 How does the concept of the buying center apply to Shopify?

6-19 How much of a threat does competition pose in Shopify's future?

7 | Customer Value–Driven Marketing Strategy:
Creating Value for Target Customers

OBJECTIVES OUTLINE

OBJECTIVE 7-1 Define the major steps in designing a customer value–driven marketing strategy: market segmentation, targeting, differentiation, and positioning. **See: Marketing Strategy** *(pp 204–205)*

OBJECTIVE 7-2 List and discuss the major bases for segmenting consumer and business markets. **See: Market Segmentation** *(pp 205–213)*

OBJECTIVE 7-3 Explain how companies identify attractive market segments and choose a market-targeting strategy. **See: Market Targeting** *(pp 213–220)*

OBJECTIVE 7-4 Discuss how companies differentiate and position their products for maximum competitive advantage. **See: Differentiation and Positioning** *(pp 221–227)*

CHAPTER PREVIEW So far, you've learned what marketing is and about the importance of understanding consumers and the marketplace. We now delve deeper into marketing strategy and tactics. This chapter looks further into key customer value–driven marketing strategy decisions—dividing markets into meaningful customer groups (*segmentation*), choosing which customer groups to serve (*targeting*), creating market offerings that best serve targeted customers (*differentiation*), and positioning the offerings in the minds of consumers (*positioning*). The chapters that follow explore the tactical marketing tools—the four Ps—by which marketers bring these strategies to life.

To open our discussion of segmentation, targeting, differentiation, and positioning, let's look at Henkel. For nearly 140 years, Henkel has wielded a leader's influence with its varied offering of products that address the specialized needs of global customers. Henkel's brand Persil has revolutionized the Middle Eastern market through sophisticated segmentation and targeting, with each product line offering a unique value proposition to a distinct segment of customers.

Henkel's Persil in the Gulf States

Henkel AG & Company, KGaA, a well-known German multinational company active both in the consumer and industrial sector, was founded in September 1876 by Fritz Henkel in Aachen, Germany. The first product it launched was a silicate-based universal detergent; ever since, the company has been successful through continuous innovation in new products that satisfy a range of diverse customers and their different needs and preferences across the globe. Today, Henkel—which is headquartered in Düsseldorf, Germany—is globally ranked among the Fortune Global 2000 companies. In the fiscal year 2017, Henkel reported sales of $22.79 billion and an operating profit of $3.48 billion. In 2016, Henkel was the only German company in the Top 50 of the world's biggest consumer-goods manufacturers worldwide according to consulting firm OC&C's study "Trends and Strategies on the Consumer-goods Market." Henkel solidified its status as one of the most reputable companies in its industry category in *Fortune's* 2018 "World's Most Admired Companies" ranking, where it finished in fourth place.

Henkel's force of around 53,000 employees worldwide is working hard to gain the trust of a customer base in more than 120 countries with several successful brands, particularly Persil. Since its invention in 1907, Persil has been regarded as the expert in sparkling clean laundry. Its name has stood for quality and trust, making it, for example, the most trusted laundry detergent in Germany. The Persil product line has included many successful products since it was first introduced in the market back in 1907 and revolutionized the laundry process. The product combined sodium silicate with sodium perborate, which releases fine pearling oxygen when the laundry is boiled. The result is an especially textile-friendly and odorless bleach, in contrast to the chlorine used till then. It also reduces the strenuous and time-consuming rubbing, swinging, and scrubbing of laundry that had hitherto been the norm. The first self-acting detergent was born: Persil.

Over its history, Henkel has wielded a leader's influence through different brands and technology, enabling people to live easier and better lives. The company has managed to successfully capitalize on its customer-driven "glocal" marketing strategy, blending global understanding with local implementation, as in Saudi Arabia, which is one of the Gulf Cooperation Council (GCC) countries. The other member states are Bahrain, Kuwait, Oman, Qatar, and the United Arab Emirates. Each of these countries has very different needs based on its culture. Saudi Arabia offers an excellent example that illustrates Henkel's marketing strategy in more depth.

Since its foundation, Henkel Saudi Arabia has enjoyed tremendous growth, and its workforce is currently comprised of more than 1,600 people, with Persil cornering 75 percent of the market. As Amitabh Bose, the former Marketing Head of Henkel Saudi Arabia, notes, Henkel's brand presence is epitomized by the success of its premium laundry detergent Persil, which has revolutionized the Middle Eastern market with its focus on developing strong brand equity, generating consumer insights, and evolving outstanding marketing campaigns. The Saudi Arabia region was targeted by Henkel a couple of years ago across two main segments—men and women—with three exceptionally innovative and, later, extremely successful products: Persil Abaya Shampoo for women, and Persil White liquid detergent and Persil Starch Spray for men.

Persil's success in the Middle East is predominantly due to a deep understanding of the regional consumers' needs and preferences.
Newscast Online Limited/Alamy Stock Photo

The introduction of both lines of products was based on extensive market research on regional consumer insights and preferences. Research by Henkel proved that nearly 75 percent of GCC consumers wash thobes (long white dresses traditionally worn by men in the region) with a mix of detergent and bleach, which, in time, negatively affects the brightness of the garments' white color. Research also revealed the lack of a suitable starch spray in the detergent market that would give thobes the right level of firmness preferred by local consumers. Persil White and Persil Starch Spray, the first range of laundry products aimed at GCC men, achieved an enormous market share and sales 90 percent above forecasts within only four months after its launch. This success as a new laundry product was predominantly based on a deep understanding of the regional consumers' needs and preferences.

In addition, women traditionally wear abayas, loose robe-like garments that are typically black. As local men take pride in the brightness of their thobes' white color and the fabric's firmness, women exercise great care in maintaining the depth of their abayas' black color and the richness of the fabric. Amal Murad, a well-known fashion designer, emphasizes that it is paramount that women take care of their abayas in order to maintain its look, feel, and color.

> By focusing on generating insights to understand market trends and customers' special needs in different regions, Henkel found huge success with its brands in the Middle East.

As a result, Persil Abaya Shampoo (also known as Persil Black) was developed to offer the perfect retention of the black color by using the new Henkel technology "black color lock." Abaya Shampoo also safeguards the fabric and gives the abaya an enduring floral scent. Research on local consumers revealed that almost 50 percent of them adopt inappropriate and damaging practices in cleaning their abayas, such as using powdered detergents, fabric softeners, or even hair and body shampoo. That's why Persil Abaya Shampoo was viewed as revolutionary in the regional world of laundry.

The marketing strategy applied by Henkel serves as an excellent example of how the mix of common global technology and scale (economies of scale or low-cost production) can be combined with a local and regional marketing strategy. The Persil brands have common product formulations but region-specific packaging and marketing communication. Persil Abaya launched in the Gulf States with a mix of TV commercials and a very successful online viral campaign. An interactive website was set up and Henkel also sponsored a reality TV designer competition in cooperation with Swarovski Elements in order to show that the abaya is not only a traditional garment but can also be an individual fashion and personality statement. By focusing on generating insights to understand market trends and customers' special needs in different regions, Henkel found huge success with its brands. Its marketing strategy has been considered a successful example of a totally customer-driven strategy.[1]

COMPANIES TODAY RECOGNIZE that they cannot appeal to all buyers in the marketplace—or at least not to all buyers in the same way. Buyers are too numerous, widely scattered, and varied in their needs and buying practices. And companies themselves vary widely in their abilities to serve different market segments. Instead, companies must identify the parts of the market they can serve best and most profitably. They must design customer-driven marketing strategies that build the right relationships with the right customers.

Moreover, today's new technologies—from big data analytics to digital and social media platforms—have greatly expanded marketers' capacity to understand and reach consumers on an individualized basis. Thus, most companies have moved away from mass marketing and toward *target marketing:* identifying market segments, selecting one or more of them, and developing products and marketing programs tailored to each.

Author Comment | Market segmentation addresses the first simple-sounding marketing question: What customers will we serve?

Marketing Strategy

OBJECTIVE 7-1 Define the major steps in designing a customer value–driven marketing strategy: market segmentation, targeting, differentiation, and positioning.

● **Figure 7.1** shows the four major steps in designing a customer value–driven marketing strategy. In the first two steps, the company selects the customers that it will serve. **Market segmentation** involves dividing a market into distinct groups of buyers who have different needs, characteristics, or behaviors and who might require separate marketing strategies or mixes. The company identifies different ways to segment the market and develops profiles of the resulting market segments. **Market targeting (or targeting)** consists of evaluating each market segment's attractiveness and selecting one or more market segments to enter.

In the final two steps, the company decides on a value proposition—how it will create value for target customers. **Differentiation** involves actually differentiating the firm's market offering to create superior customer value. **Positioning** consists of arranging for

Market segmentation
Dividing a market into distinct groups of buyers who have different needs, characteristics, or behaviors and who might require separate marketing strategies or mixes.

● FIGURE 7.1
Designing a Customer Value–
Driven Marketing Strategy

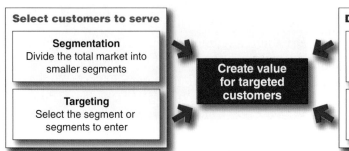

In concept, marketing boils down to two questions: (1) Which customers will we serve? and (2) How will we serve them? Of course, the tough part is coming up with good answers to these simple-sounding yet difficult questions. The goal is to create more value for the customers we serve than competitors do.

Market targeting (targeting)
Evaluating each market segment's attractiveness and selecting one or more segments to serve.

Differentiation
Actually differentiating the market offering to create superior customer value.

Positioning
Arranging for a market offering to occupy a clear, distinctive, and desirable place relative to competing products in the minds of target consumers.

a market offering to occupy a clear, distinctive, and desirable place relative to competing products in the minds of target consumers. We discuss each of these steps in turn.

Market Segmentation

OBJECTIVE 7-2 List and discuss the major bases for segmenting consumer and business markets.

Buyers in any market differ in their wants, resources, locations, buying attitudes, and buying practices. Through market segmentation, companies divide large, diverse markets into smaller segments that can be reached more efficiently and effectively with products and services that match their unique needs. In this section, we discuss four important segmentation topics: segmenting consumer markets, segmenting business markets, segmenting international markets, and the requirements for effective segmentation.

Segmenting Consumer Markets

There is no single way to segment a market. A marketer has to try different segmentation variables, alone and in combination, to find the best way to view market structure. ● Table 7.1 outlines variables that might be used in segmenting consumer markets. Here we look at the major *geographic, demographic, psychographic*, and *behavioral* variables.

Geographic Segmentation

Geographic segmentation
Dividing a market into different geographical units, such as nations, states, regions, counties, cities, or even neighborhoods.

Geographic segmentation calls for dividing the market into different geographical units, such as nations, regions, states, counties, cities, or even neighborhoods. A company may decide to operate in one or a few geographical areas or operate in all areas but pay attention to geographical differences in needs and wants. Moreover, many companies today are localizing their products, services, advertising, promotion, and sales efforts to fit the needs of individual regions, cities, and other localities.

For example, many large retailers—from Target and Walmart to Kohl's and Staples—are now opening smaller-format stores designed to fit the needs of smaller markets or densely packed urban neighborhoods in larger cities not suited to their typical large suburban superstores. For example, Target is opening more than 100 small-format stores over the next three years in college towns and crowded urban areas:[2]

> The smaller Target stores are about one-third the size of a regular Target. They carry a limited assortment of products carefully tailored toward local patrons to create personalized shopper experiences. For example, its campus stores are designed to fit the on-the-go, budget-conscious lifestyles of college students. Each small-format store analyzes its customers' characteristics, purchases, and feedback to shape assortments. A Target campus store at Florida State would be very different from one near the Northwestern University campus. Target's Chicago Belmont store features Chicago Cubs gear and gay pride banners in the front window to match fit its location near Wrigley Field and a local gay community.

Hyperlocal social marketing
Location-based targeting to consumers in local communities or neighborhoods using digital and social media.

The surge in digital and mobile technology has caused a corresponding surge in **hyperlocal social marketing**—location-based targeting to consumers in local communities or neighborhoods using digital and social media. ● For example, Mazda, the Japanese

● **Table 7.1** | **Major Segmentation Variables for Consumer Markets**

Segmentation Variable	Examples
Geographic	Nations, regions, states, counties, cities, neighborhoods, population density (urban, suburban, rural), climate
Demographic	Age, life-cycle stage, gender, income, occupation, education, religion, ethnicity, generation
Psychographic	Lifestyle, personality
Behavioral	Occasions, benefits, user status, usage rate, loyalty status

● **Hyperlocal social marketing: Mazda uses personalized ads for customers within a certain radius of a dealer.**

Car Collection/Alamy Stock Photo

multinational automaker, realized that car buyers do not travel beyond a certain maximum radius. Thus, the company used geographic data to maximize revenues and set up dynamically personalized mobile ads that would be triggered every time the user entered the radius of a local Mazda dealership. As a result, 20 percent of all targeted consumers interacted with the ad and were 53 percent more likely to make an inquiry at their local Mazda dealership.[3]

Alternatively, many of the major social media, such as Facebook and Instagram, let advertisers select audiences by geographic location. Companies can sign up with Google Maps to show their locations and ads in response to "near me" or "nearby" Google searches. For instance, a search of "auto repairs near me" brings up several ads for anything from your local Sears service center to local auto repair shops. If you search "hotels in Poughkeepsie, NY," the search results are topped by ads for Expedia.com, Booking.com. Tripadvisor.com, and KAYAK.com, followed by several specific hotel listings with site links and a map showing each location. Such hyperlocal targeting lets advertisers refine tailor their marketing content to local consumer locations and search intent.

Demographic Segmentation

Demographic segmentation divides the market into segments based on variables such as age, life-cycle stage, gender, income, occupation, education, religion, ethnicity, and generation. Demographic factors are the most popular bases for segmenting customer groups. One reason is that consumer needs, wants, and usage rates often vary closely with demographic variables. Another is that demographic variables are easier to measure than many other types of variables. Even when marketers first define segments using other bases, such as benefits sought or behavior, they must know a segment's demographic characteristics to assess the size of the target market and reach it efficiently.

● **Gender segmentation: In line with the "athleisure" trend that has more women wearing workout gear as everyday fashion, Dick's Sporting Goods recently launched its first-ever ads aimed directly at fitness-minded women.**

DICK'S Sporting Goods

Age and Life-Cycle Stage. Consumer needs and wants change with age. Some companies use **age and life-cycle segmentation**, offering different products or using different marketing approaches for different age and life-cycle groups. For example, P&G's Crest White Brilliance toothpaste targets seniors and older adults—it helps "seniors turn their tooth stains into a brighter, whiter smile." In contrast, Crest Pro-Health Jr. toothpaste targets young children by featuring packages adorned with *Frozen* and *Star Wars* characters and offering a Magic Timer App "to help even the most reluctant child to brush longer."[4]

Marketers must be careful to guard against stereotypes when using age and life-cycle segmentation. For example, although some 80-year-olds fit the stereotypes of doddering shut-ins with fixed incomes, others ski and play tennis. Similarly, whereas some 40-year-old couples are sending their children off to college, others are just beginning new families. Thus, age is often a poor predictor of a person's life cycle, health, work or family status, needs, and buying power.

Gender. **Gender segmentation** has long been used in marketing clothing, cosmetics, toiletries, toys, and magazines. For example, P&G was among the first to use gender segmentation with Secret, a deodorant brand specially formulated for a woman's chemistry, packaged and advertised to reinforce the female image.

More recently, the men's personal care industry has exploded, and many cosmetics brands that previously catered mostly to women—from L'Oréal, Nivea, and Sephora to Unilever's Dove brand—now successfully market men's lines. For example, Dove's Men+Care believes that "Care makes a stronger man." The brand provides a full line of body washes, body bars, deodorants, face care, and hair care.[5]

Going in the other direction, brands that have traditionally targeted men are now targeting women. ● For example, in line with the "athleisure" trend in which more women are wearing workout gear as

Demographic segmentation
Dividing the market into segments based on variables such as age, life-cycle stage, gender, income, occupation, education, religion, ethnicity, and generation.

Age and life-cycle segmentation
Dividing a market into different age and life-cycle groups.

Gender segmentation
Dividing a market into different segments based on gender.

Income segmentation
Dividing a market into different income segments.

everyday fashion, sports apparel makers and retailers—from Nike, Adidas, and Under Armour to Dick's Sporting Goods—are boosting their marketing efforts aimed at women buyers. Women now make up half of all sporting good shoppers:[6]

> Dick's Sporting Goods launched its first-ever ads aimed directly at fitness-minded women, as part of its broader "Who Will You Be?" campaign. The ads feature women who must juggle their busy lives to meet their fitness goals. The first ad in the series showed one mom jogging rather than driving to pick up her sons at school. Another mom jogs on a treadmill while listening to her baby monitor. "Who will you be?" asks the ad. "Every run. Every workout. Every day. Every choice. Every season begins with Dick's Sporting Goods." Dick's wants women buyers to know that "we understand the choices that they have to make every single day…to fit in fitness," says the retailer's chief marketer.

Income. The marketers of products and services such as automobiles, clothing, cosmetics, financial services, and travel have long used **income segmentation**. Many companies target affluent consumers with luxury goods and convenience services. For example, credit card companies target affluent customers with premium cards that offer luxury and more perks but at hefty annual fees. For example, consider American Express:[7]

> The American Express Platinum card costs members $550 per year. It comes with perks such as special airport lounge access, airline fee credits, Uber credits, elite status at hotel and car rental chains, and extra bonus airline travel points. But for the really well heeled, American Express offers the Centurion Black Card, perhaps the world's most exclusive credit card. The Amex Centurion Black Card targets high-net-worth individuals who earn at least $1 million annually and charge at least $100,000 to $450,000 a year. Application is by invitation only, and cardholders pay an initiation fee of $7,500 plus a $2,500 annually. Black Card members receive exclusive experiences—many kept secret—not available to Platinum Card holders. For example, it includes the Centurion Concierge, a kind of personal assistant who tends to every need, such as priority seating in hot restaurants, first dibs on show tickets, and research for that exotic vacation. And, of course, the Amex Black Card comes with status and bragging rights that you just can't get with other cards.

Psychographic segmentation
Dividing a market into different segments based on lifestyle or personality characteristics.

Not all companies that use income segmentation target the affluent. For example, many retailers—such as the Dollar General, Family Dollar, and Dollar Tree store chains—successfully target low- and middle-income groups. The core market for such stores is represented by families with annual incomes under $50,000. When Family Dollar real estate experts scout locations for new stores, they look for lower-middle-class neighborhoods where people wear less-expensive shoes and drive old cars that drip a lot of oil. With their low-income strategies, dollar stores are now the fastest-growing retailers in the nation.

Psychographic Segmentation

Psychographic segmentation divides buyers into different segments based on lifestyle or personality characteristics. People in the same demographic group can have very different psychographic characteristics.

In Chapter 5, we discussed how the products people buy reflect their *lifestyles*. As a result, marketers often segment their markets by consumer lifestyles and base their marketing strategies on lifestyle appeals. For example, fast-casual restaurant Panera caters to a lifestyle segment of people who want more than just good-tasting food—they want food that's good for them, too. To better meet the needs of this healthy-living lifestyle segment, Panera recently announced that it would soon banish more than 150 artificial preservatives, sweeteners, colors, and flavors from its food. It then launched a marketing campaign tagged "Food as it should be," showing happy customers eating better at Panera. "100% of our food is 100% clean," says one ad. According to Panera, food should do more than just fill your stomach. "Food should taste good. It should feel good. It should do good things for you and the world around you. That's food as it should be." If that kind of thinking fits your lifestyle, suggests Panera's head of marketing, "then yeah, come on in…that's why we're here."[8]

Marketers also use *personality* variables to segment markets. For example, Loews, a luxury-boutique hotel chain that offers high-level personal service, targets "personas" segments, such as "weekend explorer couples," "confident business travelers," "serious planners," "luxury jet-setters," "vacationing families" and "Loews loyalists." The chain creates

● Lifestyle segmentation: Panera caters to a healthy-eating lifestyle segment of people who want more than just good-tasting food—they want food that's good for them, too.

Panera LLC

personalized offers, messages, and media plans for each segment, keyed to stages of planning and staying at a Loews hotel—what Loews calls a "SmartJourney." For example, communications aimed at luxury jetsetters might start with an email offering opportunities to enhance their experiences with special room upgrades. Next come Loews mobile app notifications offering additional pre-stay options, such as reservations for fine dining. Once on site, the travelers in this persona group receive high-touch, personal attention tailored to their preferences, say, app notifications of a special "chef's tasting" or spa treatments. In the year following the start of the SmartJourney approach, Loews customer email engagement rates improved 40 percent and rebookings were up 20 percent.[9]

Behavioral Segmentation

Behavioral segmentation

Dividing a market into segments based on consumer knowledge, attitudes, uses of a product, or responses to a product.

Behavioral segmentation divides buyers into segments based on their knowledge, attitudes, uses, or responses to a product. Many marketers believe that behavior variables are the best starting point for building market segments.

Occasion segmentation

Dividing the market into segments according to occasions when buyers get the idea to buy, actually make their purchase, or use the purchased item.

Occasions. Buyers can be grouped according to occasions when they get the idea to buy, actually make their purchases, or use the purchased items. **Occasion segmentation** can help firms build up product usage. Campbell's advertises its soups more heavily in the cold winter months; and P&G boosts its marketing for it Vicks Nyquil, DayQuil, VapoRub, and VapoDrops remedies during the cold and flu season. And for more than 15 years, Starbucks has welcomed the autumn season with its pumpkin spice latte (PSL). Sold only in the fall and now available in more than 50 countries, PSL is Starbucks's top-selling seasonal beverage of all time.[10]

Still other brands try to boost consumption by promoting usage during nontraditional occasions. For example, consider the American Egg Board (AEB), an association of U.S. egg producers that works to increase demand for eggs through research, education, and promotion. Many consumers think of eggs primarily as a breakfast food. But the AEB's "How Do You Like Your Eggs?" campaign is aimed at getting people to think about "The Incredible Egg" beyond breakfast. The campaign takes a humorous, pairing colorful characters with a variety of egg dishes, such as a nun who loves deviled eggs or Santa, who of course prefers his eggs "nogged." "There's no wrong answer to the question How Do You Like Your Eggs?" says an AEB marketing executive. The AEB hopes "to help consumers unleash new ways to enjoy the incredible egg from breakfast to dinner and everything in between." Beyond ads and other digital content, the AEB supplies a host of innovative egg recipes. "The possibilities are truly endless."[11]

Benefit segmentation

Dividing the market into segments according to the different benefits that consumers seek from the product.

Benefits Sought. A powerful form of segmentation is grouping buyers according to the different *benefits* that they seek from a product. **Benefit segmentation** requires finding the major benefits people look for in a product class, the kinds of people who look for each benefit, and the major brands that deliver each benefit. For example, people buying bicycles are looking for any of numerous benefits, from competitive racing and sports performance to recreation, fitness, touring, transportation, and just plain fun. ● To meet varying benefit preferences, Schwinn makes affordable, quality bikes in seven major benefit groups: cruisers, hybrid, bike path, mountain, road, electric, and kids. Schwinn's *bike path* bikes are "Perfect for riders who want a comfortable and easy-riding bike with convenient features for casual riding."[12] *Mountain* bikes are "for riders who want a solid, rugged, and durable bike to ride over all surfaces." Schwinn *electric* bikes are "for riders who want an extra boost to help make the morning commute or ride around town a little bit easier."

● Benefit segmentation: Schwinn makes bikes for every benefit segment. For example, its e-bikes "help make the morning commute or ride around town a little bit easier."

In all, Schwinn makes dozens of lines of bikes, each designed for a specific benefit segment or subsegment. For example, Schwinn's S-series cruisers (priced at an affordable $250 to $340) are steel-frame classic cruiser bikes with coaster brakes that sell at mass retailers. Riding "has never been easier and at such a great value." In contrast, Schwinn's high-end Sycamore models are "stylish sport hybrid e-bikes" (priced at $2099). They sport a hub-drive electric motor and offer five different levels of e-assistance up to 20 miles per hour, providing "a new adventure in biking or commuting." "No matter what you're looking for," says Schwinn, "we've got a line of bikes for you."

User Status. Markets can be segmented into nonusers, ex-users, potential users, first-time users, and regular users of a product. Marketers want to reinforce and retain regular users, attract targeted nonusers, and reinvigorate relationships with ex-users. Included in the potential users group are consumers facing life-stage changes—such as new parents and newlyweds—who can be turned into heavy users. For example, to get new parents off to the right start, P&G makes certain that its Pampers Swaddlers are the diaper most U.S. hospitals provide for newborns and then promotes them as "the #1 choice of hospitals."[13]

Usage Rate. Markets can also be segmented into light, medium, and heavy product users. Heavy users are often a small percentage of the market but account for a high percentage of total consumption. ● For instance, fast-growing Southeastern fast-food chain Bojangles' Famous Chicken 'n Biscuits targets everything it does toward the tastes and tendencies of its core of regulars.[14]

● Targeting heavy users: Fast-growing Southeastern fast-food chain Bojangles' Famous Chicken 'n Biscuits targets everything it does toward the tastes and tendencies of hungry regulars.

Milesbeforeisleep/Shutterstock

The company calls them Bo Fanatics or Bo'lievers, people who crave lots and lots of Bojangles' signature fried chicken, made-from-scratch biscuits, and "Legendary Sweet Tea." North Carolinian Brandon Sanders, a 36-year-old basketball trainer, is a typical Bo'liever. Brandon has eaten in more than 100 of Bojangles' 759 stores. "He picks up on the subtle differences between locations like a fried chicken sommelier," notes a reporter. Brandon's Bojangles' obsession began with childhood family meals. His father's side of the family eats regular Bojangles' takeout; his mother's side ate often in the restaurant. So Brandon got Bojangles' on both sides. As an adult, he's cut back—he's now down to only two or three Bo visits per week. He could eat at KFC or some other fried chicken place, but "they don't have the soul for it." The brand has even created Bomojis, including one featuring a Bo'liever kneeling and holding a Bo Box of chicken toward the heavens as thanks to the gods. For hungry Bo'lievers, the company's long-time brand slogan says it all. No matter where or when; rain or shine; morning, noon, or night; "It's Bo Time!"

Loyalty Status. A market can also be segmented by consumer loyalty. Consumers can be loyal to brands (Tide), stores (Target), and companies (Apple). Buyers can be divided into groups according to their degree of loyalty. Some consumers are completely loyal—they buy one brand all the time and can't wait to tell others about it. Other consumers are somewhat loyal—they are loyal to two or three brands of a given product or favor one brand while sometimes buying others. Still other buyers show no loyalty to any brand—they either want something different each time they buy, or they buy whatever's on sale.

A company can learn a lot by analyzing loyalty patterns in its market. It should start by studying its own loyal customers. Highly loyal customers can be a real asset. They often promote the brand through personal word of mouth and social media. Instead of just marketing *to* loyal customers, companies should engage them fully and make them partners in building the brand and telling the brand story. For example, in the United Arab Emirates, its leading telecommunications company launched a youth-targeted brand that allows its customers to choose data plans based on their usage (see Real Marketing 7.1).

Some companies actually put loyalists to work for the brand. For example, Patagonia relies on its most tried-and-true customers—what it calls Patagonia ambassadors—to field-test products in harsh environments, provide input for "ambassador-driven" lines of apparel and gear, and share their product experiences with others.[15] In contrast, by studying its less-loyal buyers, a company can detect which brands are most competitive with its own. By looking at customers who are shifting away from its brand, the company can learn about its marketing weaknesses and take actions to correct them.

Real Marketing 7.1 │ Swyp: Are You Young Enough for It?

For the longest time, the telecommunications sector in the United Arab Emirates was a duopoly with only two players, Etisalat and Du, both of which are majority-owned by the government. In 2017, there were over 19 million mobile phone subscribers in the United Arab Emirates. Etisalat was the market leader, with 54.6 percent market share, and Du followed with 45.4 percent. Etisalat launched its mobile operations in the country back in 1982, and Du entered the market much later in 2006; both have led the country into an era of fast digital connectivity. The mobile penetration rate of the United Arab Emirates is now reported as among the highest over the last few years; according to one study, in 2017, mobile penetration in the country was the highest in world at 173 percent.

The main reason for this is the country's wealthy consumers and the demographics of its large expat population, which is young and employed and wants to be more digitally connected. The estimated population of the country in 2018 was 9.54 million, with a median age of 30.3 years. Nearly 90 percent of the population are expatriates and nearly 94 percent of the population over the age of 15 is literate. The average monthly household income of UAE residents is more than $4,500.

Although the United Arab Emirates boasts one of the highest mobile penetration rates in the world, the sector has been highly regulated, with little or no liberalization or foreign investment until recently with the entry of two new mobile providers. In September 2017, Virgin Mobile made big news by launching its services in the United Arab Emirates, becoming its third mobile phone company. Virgin Mobile UAE is owned by Emirates Integrated Telecommunications Company (EITC), the same company that owns Du. EITC wanted to treat Virgin Mobile a separate brand so that they could target a different segment. The expectation was that a multiple-brand strategy would lead to a better coverage strategy and help to increase its consumer offering in the saturated UAE market, a problem that Du and Etisalat had in common.

Virgin Mobile UAE aimed to serve younger, more digitally savvy consumers by offering differentiated services. Virgin mobile services offered a different subscription-based model in which all its services were offered through the Virgin Mobile UAE app. This meant that consumers would not have to visit the store; they could simply use the app, choose their mobile number, develop a customized mobile plan, scan their ID, and get a sim delivered to their doorstep (within the United Arab Emirates) in an hour.

To make the service more appealing for the target segment, Virgin Mobile did not require its customers to make any long-term contractual commitment; they could fix their own monthly spend limits. The app also enabled users to track their data in real time. Virgin Mobile catered to both light and heavy users by offering a range of plans, from basic ones comprising 1GB (+1GB free) data and 50 minutes/SMS to higher level ones that included 7GB (+7GB free) and 300 minutes/SMS. Although Virgin Mobile was targeting the youth, its products were open to all ages and could therefore appeal to a much wider segment. Virgin Mobile's launch included a promotion offering users a month's free trial of its services.

Within days of Virgin mobile's entry in the United Arab Emirates came the news that another mobile phone brand would be launching soon in the market. Not to be left behind, Etisalat soon launched its own youth-centric mobile phone brand, Swyp.

The country's fourth mobile-phone brand also specifically targeted the youth, but Swyp was strictly a youngsters' brand, with an age limit of between 15 and 29 years as a prerequisite to sign up for the SIM. The users were even asked to show their ID when they collected their SIMs. However, a registered user who crossed the 29-year-old limit could continue with the mobile service provider.

Swyp augmented its offering to the youth segment with many promotional features and discounts across various product categories as part of its subscription package. At the start of every month, consumers receive multiple vouchers and discounts for restaurants, shops, theme parks, cinemas, and more, irrespective of the mobile plan. Swyp's most basic plan is $14, with 5 GB of social media data. Consumers can then choose add-ons like voice minutes, texting, and general data. Registering for Swyp services is easy; customers just have to visit any of Etisalat's stores across the United Arab Emirates, and they can also be bought, registered, and managed through its app. Like Virgin Mobile, Swyp also offered customers the option of having the SIM card delivered directly to them or picking up the SIM from any one of ten selected Etisalat stores after the order is placed through the Swyp app. Swyp

Swyp has specifically targeted the youth, focusing on users between the ages of 15 and 29.
Rawpixel.com/Shutterstock

subscribers also get access to Swyp's network of Wi-Fi hotspots throughout the city, most of which are connected to Etisalat's network.

Swyp's advertising clearly targeted Millennials and focused on data and app-based features. Swyp's brand name—an acronym for "So, What's Your Plan?"—was also used as a tagline in many of its advertisements. To make its product offering even more appealing to the youth, Swyp also developed packages specifically for Instagram and Snapchat.

Over a year since its launch, Virgin mobile UAE claims that it remains unmatched in its ability to deliver the SIM within one hour and in terms of the flexibility its app offers, creating a totally different customer experience. In terms of pricing, Swyp is also more restrictive, as its users are required to make additional payments to purchase general data, whereas Virgin Mobile offers general data as part of its base offering. For example, a consumer would have to pay at least $4 for 1 GB

of general data for web browsing or streaming, which increases their overall bill. However, both Virgin Mobile UAE and Swyp have significantly cheaper data rates (per 1 GB) than Etisalat and Du. As the new providers vie for command of the Millennial market, what's certain is that Virgin Mobile UAE and Swyp have changed the mobile market in the United Arab Emirates, creating further potential for more sub-brands to launch in the future and more flexible packages that appeal to their young segment's needs.[16]

Using Multiple Segmentation Bases

Marketers rarely limit their segmentation analysis to only one or a few variables. Rather, they often use multiple segmentation bases in an effort to identify smaller, better-defined target groups. Several business information services—such as Acxiom, Nielsen, Esri, and Experian—provide multivariable segmentation systems that merge geographic, demographic, lifestyle, and behavioral data to help companies segment their markets down to zip codes, neighborhoods, and even households.

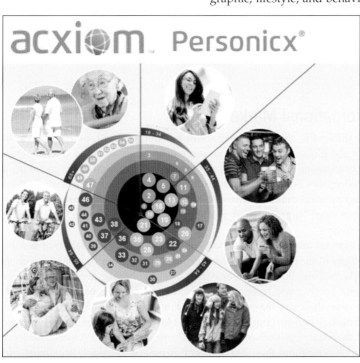

● Using Acxiom's Personicx segmentation system, marketers and paint a surprisingly precise picture of who you are and what you buy. Personicx clusters carry such colorful names as "Skyboxes and Suburbans," "Shooting Stars," "Hard Chargers," "Soccer and SUVs," "Raisin' Grandkids," "Truckin' and Stylin'," "Pennywise Mortgagees," and "Cartoons and Carpools."

Acxiom Corporation

● For example, Acxiom's Personicx Lifestage system classifies U.S. households into one of 70 distinct clusters within 21 life stage groups.[17] Personicx segments carry colorful descriptive names such as "Summit Estates," "Skyboxes and Suburbans," "Hard Chargers," "Toys and Tots," "Country Single," "Raisin' Grandkids," "Truckin' and Stylin'," "Farmland Families," "Downtown Dwellers," "Pennywise Mortgagees," and "Cartoons and Carpools."

Each segment has its own pattern of demographics, lifestyles, likes and dislikes, and purchase behaviors. Using the Personicx system, marketers can paint a surprisingly precise picture of who consumers are and what they might buy. For instance, the Personicx "Cartoons and Carpools" cluster consists of solidly middle-income, married, mid-30s couples with children of all ages. They lay dead center in terms of income, education, and home values and provide comfortably for their families. The cluster has a high concentration of Hispanics and blue-collar occupations. "Cartoons and Carpools" consumers drive minivans and pickups, buy lots of clothes and shoes for their kids, and enjoy family activities such as visiting zoos, going to theme parks, and camping.[18]

Personicx and other such systems can help marketers to segment people and locations into marketable groups of like-minded consumers. Such rich segmentation provides a powerful tool for marketers of all kinds. It can help companies identify and better understand key customer segments, reach them more efficiently, and tailor market offerings and messages to their specific needs.

Segmenting Business Markets

Consumer and business marketers use many of the same variables to segment their markets. Business buyers can be segmented geographically, demographically (industry, company size), or by benefits sought, user status, usage rate, and loyalty status. Yet business marketers also use some additional variables, such as customer *operating characteristics, purchasing approaches, situational factors,* and *personal characteristics.*

Almost every company serves at least some business markets. For example, Starbucks has developed distinct marketing programs for various commercial segments, such as colleges and universities, government and military, and office coffee. In the office coffee segment, Starbucks Branded Solutions markets a variety of workplace coffee services to businesses of any size, helping them to make Starbucks coffee and related products available to their employees in their workplaces. Starbucks helps these business customers design the best office solutions involving its coffees (the Starbucks, Seattle's Best, and Torrefazione Italia brands), syrups, and branded paper products and methods of serving them—brewed, premium self-service, or ready to drink. The college and university segment offers various platforms of providing Starbucks products, such as premium-self-service, ready to drink, and licensed stores. Starbucks provides not only the coffee, tea, and paper products to its business customers but also equipment, training, and marketing and merchandising support.[19]

Many companies establish separate systems for dealing with larger or multiple-location customers. For example, Steelcase, a major producer of office furniture systems, first divides customers into several segments: health-care, education, hospitality, legal, U.S. and Canadian governments, state and local governments, and architects and designers. Next, company salespeople work with independent Steelcase dealers to handle smaller, local, or regional Steelcase customers in each segment. But many national, multiple-location customers, such as ExxonMobil or IBM, have special needs that may reach beyond the scope of individual dealers. Therefore, Steelcase uses national account managers to help its dealer networks handle national accounts and global account managers who deal with accounts that operate across both national and international regions.[20]

Segmenting International Markets

Few companies have either the resources or the will to operate in all, or even most, of the countries that dot the globe. Although some large companies, such as Coca-Cola or Unilever, sell products in more than 200 countries, most international firms focus on a smaller set. Different countries, even those that are close together, can vary greatly in their economic, cultural, and political makeup. Thus, just as they do within their domestic markets, international firms need to group their world markets into segments with distinct buying needs and behaviors.

Companies can segment international markets using one or a combination of several variables. They can segment by *geographic location*, grouping countries by regions such as Western Europe, the Pacific Rim, South Asia, or Africa. Geographic segmentation assumes that nations close to one another will have many common traits and behaviors. Although this is sometimes the case, there are many exceptions. For example, some U.S. marketers lump all Central and South American countries together. However, the Dominican Republic is no more like Brazil than Italy is like Sweden. Many Central and South Americans don't even speak Spanish, including more than 200 million Portuguese-speaking Brazilians and the millions in other countries who speak a variety of indigenous languages.

World markets can also be segmented based on *economic factors*. Countries might be grouped by population income levels or by their overall level of economic development. A country's economic structure shapes its population's product and service needs and therefore the marketing opportunities it offers. For example, many companies are now targeting the BRICS countries—Brazil, Russia, India, China, and South Africa—which are fast-growing developing economies with rapidly increasing buying power.

Countries can be segmented by *political and legal factors* such as the type and stability of government, receptivity to foreign firms, monetary regulations, and amount of bureaucracy. *Cultural factors* can also be used, grouping markets according to common languages, religions, values and attitudes, customs, and behavioral patterns.

Segmenting international markets based on geographic, economic, political, cultural, and other factors presumes that segments should consist of clusters of countries. However, thanks to technologies such as social media, mobile phones, and satellite TV, today's marketers can define and reach segments of like-minded consumers no matter where in the

● **Intermarket segmentation: Today's technologies let fast-fashion retailer Zara target like-minded style-conscious but value-seeking consumers anywhere in the world they live.**

Eyal Dayan Photography

Intermarket (cross-market) segmentation

Forming segments of consumers who have similar needs and buying behaviors even though they are located in different countries.

world. Using **intermarket segmentation** (also called **cross-market segmentation)**, marketers form segments of consumers who have similar needs and buying behaviors even though they are located in different countries.

● For example, Zara—the world's largest fast-fashion retailer—targets fashion-conscious but value-seeking shoppers spread across cultures in over 96 countries. All of Zara's more than 2,250 stores and nearly 40 online marketplaces globally feature similar appeals, a kind of "reverse sticker shock" based on stylish, good quality, and constantly refreshed fashions offered at a fraction of the price of high-end brands. Beyond its stores, Zara leverages today's digital technologies to engage like-minded target consumers directly no matter where they live. For example, the brand has more than 30 million Instagram followers, 27 million Facebook followers, 636,000 Pinterest followers, and 70,000 YouTube subscribers. Connect with Zara from anywhere on the planet and you'll see the same with appeals targeting the same kinds of customers.[21]

Requirements for Effective Segmentation

Clearly, there are many ways to segment a market, but not all segmentations are effective. For example, buyers of table salt could be divided into blonde and brunette customers. But hair color obviously does not affect the purchase of salt. Furthermore, if all salt buyers bought the same amount of salt each month, believed that all salt is the same, and wanted to pay the same price, the company would not benefit from segmenting this market.

To be useful, market segments must be

- *Measurable.* The size, purchasing power, and profiles of the segments can be measured.
- *Accessible.* The market segments can be effectively reached and served.
- *Substantial.* The market segments are large or profitable enough to serve. A segment should be the largest possible homogeneous group worth pursuing with a tailored marketing program. It would not pay, for example, for an automobile manufacturer to develop cars especially for people whose height is greater than seven feet.
- *Differentiable.* The segments are conceptually distinguishable and respond differently to different marketing mix elements and programs. If men and women respond similarly to marketing efforts for soft drinks, they do not constitute separate segments.
- *Actionable.* Effective programs can be designed for attracting and serving the segments. For example, although one small airline identified seven market segments, its staff was too small to develop separate marketing programs for each segment.

Author Comment | After dividing the market into segments, it's time to answer that first seemingly simple marketing strategy question we raised in Figure 7.1: Which customers will the company serve?

Market Targeting

OBJECTIVE 7-3 Explain how companies identify attractive market segments and choose a market-targeting strategy.

Market segmentation reveals the firm's market segment opportunities. The firm then has to evaluate the various segments and decide how many and which segments it can serve best. We now look at how companies evaluate and select target segments.

Evaluating Market Segments

In evaluating different market segments, a firm must look at three factors: segment size and growth, segment structural attractiveness, and company objectives and resources. First, a company wants to select segments that have the right size and growth characteristics. But "right size and growth" is a relative matter. The largest, fastest-growing segments are not always the most attractive ones for every company. Smaller companies may lack the skills and resources needed to serve larger segments. Or they may find these segments too competitive. Such companies may target segments that are smaller and less attractive, in an absolute sense, but that are potentially more profitable for them.

The company also needs to examine major structural factors that affect long-run segment attractiveness.[22] For example, a segment is less attractive if it already contains many strong and aggressive *competitors* or if it is easy for *new entrants* to come into the segment. The existence of many actual or potential *substitute products* may limit prices and the profits that can be earned in a segment. The relative *power of buyers* also affects segment attractiveness. Buyers with strong bargaining power relative to sellers will try to force prices down, demand more services, and set competitors against one another—all at the expense of seller profitability. Finally, a segment may be less attractive if it contains *powerful suppliers* that can control prices or reduce the quality or quantity of ordered goods and services.

Even if a segment has the right size and growth and is structurally attractive, the company must consider its own objectives and resources. Some attractive segments can be dismissed quickly because they do not mesh with the company's long-run objectives. Or the company may lack the skills and resources needed to succeed in an attractive segment. For example, the economy segment of the automobile market is large and growing. But given its objectives and resources, it would make little sense for luxury-performance carmaker Mercedes-Benz to enter this segment. A company should only enter segments in which it can create superior customer value and gain advantages over its competitors.

Selecting Target Market Segments

Target market

A set of buyers who share common needs or characteristics that a company decides to serve.

After evaluating different segments, the company must decide which and how many segments it will target. A **target market** consists of a set of buyers who share common needs or characteristics that a company decides to serve. Market targeting can be carried out at several different levels. ● **Figure 7.2** shows that companies can target very broadly (*undifferentiated marketing*), very narrowly (*micromarketing*), or somewhere in between (*differentiated or concentrated marketing*).

Undifferentiated Marketing

Undifferentiated (mass) marketing

A market-coverage strategy in which a firm decides to ignore market segment differences and go after the whole market with one offer.

Using an **undifferentiated marketing** (or **mass marketing**) strategy, a firm might decide to ignore market segment differences and target the whole market with one offer. Such a strategy focuses on what is *common* in the needs of consumers rather than on what is *different*. The company designs a product and a marketing program that will appeal to the largest number of buyers.

As noted earlier in the chapter, most modern marketers have strong doubts about this strategy. Difficulties arise in developing a product or brand that will satisfy all consumers. Moreover, mass marketers often have trouble competing with more-focused firms that do a better job of satisfying the needs of specific segments and niches. Finally, new digital technologies let marketers "have their cake and eat it too," targeting large numbers of consumers with more individually tailored marketing offers and messages.

Differentiated Marketing

Differentiated (segmented) marketing

A market-coverage strategy in which a firm targets several market segments and designs separate offers for each.

Using a **differentiated marketing** (or **segmented marketing**) strategy, a firm targets several market segments and designs separate offers for each. ● For example, Marriott International maintains a portfolio of 30 differentiated hotel brands, ranging from Ritz-Carlton and St. Regis to Westin Hotels, Sheraton, and Marriott to Courtyard, Residence Inn, and Aloft. Each hotel brand caters to one of a dozen or more travel and hospitality segments.

This figure covers a broad range of targeting strategies, from mass marketing (virtually no targeting) to individual marketing (customizing products and programs to individual customers). An example of individual marketing: At mymms.com you can order a batch of M&M's with your face and personal message printed on each little candy.

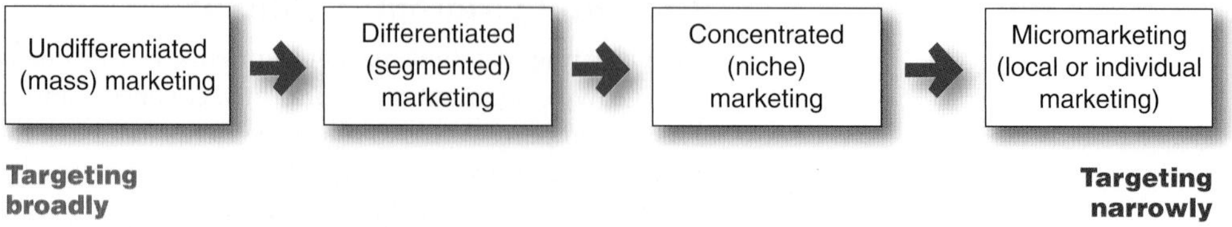

Undifferentiated (mass) marketing	→	Differentiated (segmented) marketing	→	Concentrated (niche) marketing	→	Micromarketing (local or individual marketing)

Targeting broadly   **Targeting narrowly**

● **FIGURE 7.2**
Market-Targeting Strategies

● **Differentiated marketing: With more than 30 differentiated hotel brands, Marriott International dominates the hotel industry, capturing a much larger share of the travel and hospitality market than it could with any single brand alone.**

Associated Press

For instance, Ritz-Carlton, St. Regis, and W Hotels serve the luxury segment. The Marriott, Sheraton, and Westin brands serve more mainstream but still upscale travelers. Courtyard by Marriott focuses on more affordable rooms for business travelers, and Residence Inn by Marriott targets extended-stay business and leisure travelers. Aloft offers "an affordable alternative for the tech-savvy and confidently social—travelers who love open spaces, open thinking, and open expression." The Marriott Vacation Club gives travelers a timeshare option. In all, the Marriott portfolio of brands offers something for every travel segment.[23]

By offering product and marketing variations to segments, companies hope for higher sales and a stronger position within each market segment. Developing a stronger position within several segments creates more total sales than undifferentiated marketing across all segments. Thanks to its differentiated approach, Marriott International dominates the hotel industry, capturing a much larger share of the travel and hospitality market than it could with any single brand alone.[24]

But differentiated marketing also increases the costs of doing business. A firm usually finds it more expensive to develop and produce, say, 10 units of 10 different products than 100 units of a single product. Developing separate marketing plans for separate segments requires extra marketing research, forecasting, sales analysis, promotion planning, and channel management. Trying to reach different market segments with different advertising campaigns increases promotion costs. And having too many overlapping brands can confuse customers, and different brands might cannibalize each other's customers. For example, does Marriott really need 30 different bands, many of which compete with each other in a given segment? Thus, a company must weigh the advantages against the disadvantages when deciding on how many brands it will offer and how differentiated they will be.

Concentrated Marketing

Concentrated (niche) marketing
A market-coverage strategy in which a firm goes after a large share of one or a few segments or niches.

When using a **concentrated marketing** (or **niche marketing**) strategy, instead of going after a small share of a large market, a firm goes after a larger share of one or a few smaller segments or niches. For example, consider apparel company nicher American Giant:[25]

Nicher American Giant makes and sells a limited line of American-made, back-to-basics apparel, sold only at its own web and mobile sites. It began in 2012 as an online startup selling high-quality sweatshirts at reasonable prices online (what *Slate Magazine* called "the best hoodie known to man"). From the start, American Giant's back-to-basics approach focused on a few, high-quality, classic American style products—such as the hoodie, with new technology like a double lining and ribbed panels at the shoulders and waist for improve functionality and durability. The company formed lasting relationships with American growers and mills to produce high-quality, American-made fabrics and apparel.

Although American Giant has expanded its lines to include basic styles of tees, work shirts, crew sweaters, polos, vests, jackets, and denim, it has stuck with the basics of simplicity, quality, durability, and value. For example, its first denim offering is a classic five-pocket, straight-leg, relaxed design jean—the 218 Straight—in one color, one fit, and one price. It's manufactured by a 173-year-old American textile company, Mount Vernon Mills, in Trion, Georgia. Beyond its product lines, American Giant's entire approach is pretty much a back-to-basics one. "American Giant does little or no marketing, has no retail outlets, does not chase trends, and pays premium wages to American labor to produce top-shelf quality products at a middle shelf price," says one analyst. Although still tiny compared with major competitors such as Gap and Levi-Strauss, American Giant has grown explosively in its niche.

Through concentrated marketing, the firm achieves a strong market position because of its greater knowledge of consumer needs in the niches it serves and the special reputation it acquires. It can market more *effectively* by fine-tuning its products, prices, and programs to the needs of carefully defined segments. It can also market more *efficiently*, targeting its products or services, channels, and communications programs toward only consumers that it can serve best and most profitably.

Real Marketing 7.2 | Fila Sneaks Back into Fashion

In many cities across the world, it is not uncommon now to see people out on the streets dressed up in sports clothing as if they are headed to a yoga class, Pilates studio, or the gym—even if they aren't. Sports-based fashion like gym gear, yoga pants, workout clothes, and sneakers have entered the mainstream in the fashion and apparel industry worldwide. This trend has given opportunities to many non-traditional sportswear brands, and people have started to take more fashion risks and experiment with brands they might not have purchased before.

Recent sports fashion trends have created newer segments with different value propositions for those who are enjoying the new styles, designs, and innovation, especially in athletic footwear. The sports shoe market can be divided into five segments with different value propositions for each target group:

- The **sports segment** is the traditional one, consisting of consumers who are actively and regularly involved in fitness or sports on a regular basis. They prefer well-known, higher-quality, higher-priced brands.
- The **elite sports segment** includes consumers who are committed to a particular sport like running, cycling, basketball, etc. They actively train for it, so they look for specialty shoes for their specific sports. The purchase is a high-involvement one for them, and they tend to be loyal to their brand.
- The **everyday sneaker wearers segment** includes common sports shoe users. Sports shoes are part of their day-to-day lifestyle, but they are not particular about any specific sport. The main criteria they look for in sports shoes are comfort and good value for money. They prefer well-known brands, regarding them as safer, low-risk purchases.
- The **fashion sports market segment** is a developing segment that comprises young working adults and teenagers. They buy shoes for style, design, and brand image as a reflection of their social and self-identity. They want fashionable sports shoe brands, but not necessarily the brands their parents wore.
- The **budget-conscious segment** consists of consumers who buy cheaper shoes. They look for low-priced—which usually means lower-quality—shoes that have a sporty look. This segment mostly includes families,

retirees, and consumers looking for an extra pair of shoes for casual, everyday wear.

The fashion sports market is a fast-growing segment widely referred to "athleisure." Various social and demographic factors, like greater health consciousness, are driving the pursuit of more active lifestyle habits and, in turn, the popularity of athletic wear. The athleisure segment is particularly popular now as it involves easy assimilation of sports-related attire in people's wardrobes for casual and versatile use, a same-for-less value proposition. Established and new brands alike, including Under Armour, Lulu Lemon, New Balance, Converse, Vans, Fila, and Champions, have widened their product offerings to cater to the needs of the various segments in the sports fashion market. One of the brands that have benefited from the athleisure trend is the Italian sportswear brand Fila, which has reemerged as a popular fashion brand, particularly in the sneakers segment.

Fila was a popular sportswear brand in the 1990s but lost much of its market share to the growing dominance of the mainstream sports brands. However, in 2017–2018, the brand made a comeback by cutting its prices and reinventing itself as an on-trend fashion brand through effective brand positioning

and targeting strategies. In a manner similar to Adidas's turnaround, Fila positioned its brand at the crossroads of fashion and sports. This gave Fila a lot of visibility as its value proposition clicked well with younger consumers who wanted a trendy, athletic look.

There has been a retro revival wave for everything related to the 1990s: movies, TV shows, even cereal. Fila used to be a very popular and important brand during this decade, and the era's resurgence became a great opportunity for it to leverage the trend. Fila's Disruptor 2 line, especially popular among the younger segment, is part of the "ugly shoe movement" pioneered by the brand but adopted by high-fashion brands like Balenciaga and Fendi and celebrities like Kim Kardashian. It has become a point of pride for the company that the bulky shoe look, which it claims as part of its "DNA," has quickly become one of the most sought-after styles and made the brand an on-trend fashion essential. However, the company has stated that its future is not just about looking at past strategies and current trends; it aims to be a sports fashion brand that can balance past, present, and future.

Fila's repositioning and comeback efforts were successful because they were able to get the attention of target

Fila owes its resurgence not only to the retro wave but the brand's ability to create a narrative about its products.

sozon/Shutterstock

consumers. Referring to the story of the chunky shoe, from its popularity in the 1990s, to its disappearance, to its re-emergence in the market, the company said that its brand conversations have reinforced stories about the past to inspire the younger customer. Fila wants to offer a unique value to its customers by telling a fashion story—a sneaker from the past coming back in vogue again—and believes that footwear trends are evolving to suit brands' positioning as well as the value proposition of stylish, in-vogue trendy sports shoes at a lower price.

Fila's sales and popularity continue to grow: the company reported a growth of 28 percent in its revenue to reach approximately $640 million in the last quarter of 2018. Fila knows that its target customers are looking for more value and authenticity but also want to be more on-trend in their fashion statements. The company positions itself as a mid-market brand that is closer to its customers and therefore more focused on their target market selection—with smaller operational scales—and more flexible and responsive to trends. This is where the Fila thinks it has an advantage over bigger companies, which take more time to catch on to trends. Millennials and the Gen Z have shown a clear preference for casual clothing, which could drive the sportswear market in the coming years. Although established brands have key advantages, more experimental brands that have clear visions and disruptive concepts—like Fila—are better placed to be embraced by the younger market.[26]

Niching lets smaller companies focus their limited resources on serving niches that may be overlooked by larger competitors. Choosing the right value proposition is important and helps to connect with consumers by offering them unique brand differences. For example, Fila, an Italian sports brand, has reached out to Generation Z by offering affordable but stylish fashion sports footwear. (See Real Marketing 7.2.)

Many companies start as nichers to get a foothold against larger, more resourceful competitors and then grow into broader competitors. For example, Southwest Airlines began by serving intrastate, no-frills commuters in Texas but is now one of the nation's largest airlines. Enterprise Rent-A-Car began by building a network of neighborhood offices rather than competing with Hertz and Avis in airport locations but is now the nation's largest car rental company. And Amazon began by selling books online but now sells anything and everything as the nation's largest online emporium.

Concentrated marketing can be highly profitable, giving nichers an advantage in their corners of the market. At the same time, it involves higher-than-normal risks. Companies that rely on one or a few segments for all of their business will suffer greatly if the segment turns sour. Or larger competitors, threatened by successful nichers, may decide to enter the same segment with greater resources. Or they may attack or even acquire nichers to safeguard their own markets. Harry's and Dollar Shave Club experienced both of these competitor responses in the direct-to-consumer razor market.

In fact, many large companies develop or acquire niche brands of their own. For example, Coca-Cola's Venturing & Emerging Brands unit markets a cooler full of niche beverages. Its brands include Honest (the nation's number one organic bottled teas, lemonades, and sparkling sodas), Hubert's Lemonade, FUZE (a fusion of tea, fruit, and other flavors), Suja (the nation's leading organic and cold-pressured juice brand), Fairlife (ultra-filtered milk), and many others. Such brands let Coca-Cola compete effectively in smaller, specialized markets, and some will grow into future powerhouse brands. In fact, the Coca-Cola Venturing & Emerging Brands unit's mission is "to identify and nurture brands with billion-dollar potential."[27]

Micromarketing

Micromarketing

Tailoring products and marketing programs to the needs and wants of specific individuals and local customer segments; it includes local marketing and individual marketing.

Differentiated and concentrated marketers tailor their offers and marketing programs to meet the needs of various market segments and niches. At the same time, however, they do not customize their offers to each individual customer. **Micromarketing** is the practice of tailoring products and marketing programs to suit the tastes of specific individuals and local customer segments. Rather than seeing a customer in every individual, micromarketers see the individual in every customer. Micromarketing includes *local marketing* and *individual marketing*.

Local marketing

Tailoring brands and marketing to the needs and wants of local customer segments—cities, neighborhoods, and even specific stores.

Local Marketing. **Local marketing** involves tailoring brands and promotions to the needs and wants of local customers. For example, Marriott's Renaissance Hotels has a

● **Geographic segmentation:** Marriott's Renaissance Hotels' Navigator program helps guests experience "the hidden gems throughout the neighborhood of each hotel through the eyes of those who know it best." Navigator Jennifer Portuhondo at the Renaissance New York Times Square Hotel "lives and breathes New York."

Marriott International, Inc.

Navigator program, which hyper-localizes guest experiences at each of its more than 160 lifestyle hotels around the world:[28]

> Renaissance Hotels' Navigator program puts a personal and local face on each location by "microlocalizing" recommendations for guests' food, shopping, entertainment, and cultural experiences at each destination. The program is anchored by on-site Renaissance Hotels "Navigators" at each location. Navigators are extensively trained locals who are deeply passionate about the destination and often have a personal connection to the locale.
> ● An example is Jennifer Portuhondo, a restaurant-loving Manhattanite at the Renaissance New York Times Square Hotel who "lives and breathes New York." Based on hours of intense training plus their own personal experiences and ongoing research, navigators work with guests personally to help them experience the hidden gems in the neighborhood of each hotel through their own experienced eyes.
> In addition, Renaissance Hotels engages locals in each city to participate by inviting them to follow their local Navigator via social media as well as adding their own favorites to the system, creating each hotel's own version of Yelp. Navigators then cull through submitted tips and feature the best recommendations alongside their own for sharing on its web, mobile, and social media channels or in the hotel lobby on a tablet or in a printed Local Navigator Guide. The hotels also offer an R Navigator phone app that lets guests "uncover the most authentic hidden gems the city you're visiting has to offer. Eat, drink, shop and more—at locations handpicked and continually updated by our local Navigators themselves."

Advances in communications technology have given rise to new high-tech versions of location-based marketing. Thanks to the explosion in smartphones and tablets that integrate geolocation technology, companies can now track consumers' whereabouts closely and engage them on the go with localized deals and information fast, wherever they may be. Retailers ranging from Home Depot and Starbucks to Walgreens and Sephora have jumped onto the hyperlocal bandwagon. For example, Home Depot's app localizes trend information and product suggestions—customers in Oregon receive different recommendations from those living in Florida. And when customers visit a store, the Home Depot app shifts into "store mode" to show product locations. Some stores even offer Waze-like navigation of store aisles.

Local marketing has some drawbacks, however. It can drive up manufacturing and marketing costs by reducing the economies of scale. It can also create logistics problems as companies try to meet the varied requirements of different local markets. Still, as companies face increasingly fragmented markets and as new supporting digital technologies develop, the advantages of local marketing often outweigh the drawbacks.

Individual marketing

Tailoring products and marketing programs to the needs and preferences of individual customers.

Individual Marketing. In the extreme, micromarketing becomes **individual marketing**—tailoring products and marketing to the needs and preferences of individual customers. Individual marketing has also been labeled one-to-one marketing, mass customization, and markets-of-one marketing.

The widespread use of mass marketing has obscured the fact that for centuries consumers were served as individuals: The tailor custom-made a suit, the cobbler designed shoes for an individual, and the cabinetmaker made furniture to order. Today, new technologies are permitting many companies to return to customized marketing. Detailed databases, robotic production and flexible manufacturing, and interactive technologies such as smartphones and online and social media have combined let brands address and serve customers individually.

Companies these days are hyper-customizing everything from food, artwork, earphones, and sneakers to high-end luxury products. At one end of the spectrum, candy lovers can go to mymms.com and buy M&Ms with personalized messages or pictures embossed on each little candy. Visit Nike ID online to design and order your very own personalized sneakers. Jerry Harvey Audio makes customized earphones based on molds of customers' ears to provide optimized fit and better and safer sound. The company even laser-prints designs on

● **Individual marketing: The Rolls-Royce Bespoke design team works closely with individual customers to help them create their own unique Rolls-Royces.**

WENN Ltd/Alamy Stock Photo

the tiny ear buds—some people request a kid for each ear; others prefer a dog.

At the other extreme are "bespoke" luxury goods (a fancy word for "custom-made" or "made to order"). For the right price, well-heeled customers can buy custom-designed goods ranging from bespoke fashions and accessories by Hermès and Gucci to bespoke cars from Aston Martin or Rolls-Royce. ● Ninety-five percent of Rolls-Royce buyers customize their cars in some way. Customers can sit down with a Rolls-Royce Bespoke design team—color experts, leather-smiths, master woodworkers—in a lounge filled with images, materials, and other inspirational elements to design their own unique Rolls-Royces. One customer even wanted his car's interior trim to be made from a favorite tree that had recently fallen on his estate. After analyzing a sample, a Rolls-Royce craftsman deemed the wood acceptable, and the customer's tree will now live forever in the dash and door panels of his custom Rolls-Royce.[29]

Beyond customizing products, marketers also personalize advertising messages, marketing offers, and service encounters on a one-to-one basis. Given today's data and analytics technologies, almost any customer engagement can be fine-tuned to individual customer characteristics, preferences, and behaviors.

Choosing a Targeting Strategy

Companies need to consider many factors when choosing a market-targeting strategy. Which strategy is best depends on the company's resources. When the firm's resources are limited, concentrated marketing makes the most sense. The best strategy also depends on the degree of product variability. Undifferentiated marketing is more suited for uniform products, such as grapefruit or steel. Products that can vary in design, such as cars or fashions, are more suited to differentiation or concentration. The product's life-cycle stage also must be considered. When a firm introduces a new product, it may be practical to launch one version only, and undifferentiated marketing or concentrated marketing may make the most sense. In the mature stage of the product life cycle, however, differentiated marketing often works better.

Another factor is *market variability*. If most buyers have the same tastes, buy the same amounts, and react the same way to marketing efforts, undifferentiated marketing is appropriate. Finally, *competitors' marketing strategies* should be considered. When competitors use differentiated or concentrated marketing, undifferentiated marketing can be suicidal. Conversely, when competitors use undifferentiated marketing, a firm can gain an advantage by using differentiated or concentrated marketing, focusing on the needs of buyers in specific segments.

Socially Responsible Target Marketing

Smart targeting helps companies become more efficient and effective by focusing on the segments that they can satisfy best and most profitably. Targeting also benefits consumers—companies serve specific groups of consumers with offers carefully tailored to their needs. However, target marketing sometimes generates controversy and concern. The biggest issues usually involve the targeting of vulnerable or disadvantaged consumers with controversial or potentially harmful products.

For example, fast-food chains have generated controversy over the years by their attempts to target inner-city minority consumers. They've been accused of pitching their high-fat, salt-laden fare to low-income, urban residents who are much more likely than suburbanites to be heavy consumers. Similarly, big banks and mortgage lenders have been criticized for targeting consumers in poor urban areas with attractive home mortgages that they can't really afford.

Children are seen as an especially vulnerable audience. Marketers in a wide range of industries—from cereal, soft drinks, and fast food to toys, fashion, and social media—have been criticized for their marketing efforts directed toward children. Critics worry that enticing premium offers and high-powered advertising appeals will overwhelm children's defenses. For instance, YouTube has been accused by some consumer groups of profiting by enticing children into what one advocate calls an "ad-filled digital playground" where toy, theme park, and sneaker ads can surface alongside kid-oriented videos. YouTube's terms of use discourage children under 13 years of age from using the site, but most kids don't know about or ignore these conditions. "Google profits handsomely from selling advertising to kid-directed programs that it packages," says the advocate.[30]

Such digital technologies may make children even more vulnerable to targeted marketing messages. Traditional child-directed TV and print ads usually contain fairly obvious pitches that are easily detected and controlled by parents. However, marketing in digital media may be subtly embedded within the content and viewed by children on personal, small-screen devices that are beyond even the most watchful parent's eye. In digital platforms, the lines between educational, entertainment, and commercial content are often blurred. Thus, as children consume increasing amounts of online and digital content, experts advise close parental supervision of children using digital devices.

● **Socially responsible targeting: Digital technologies may make children even more vulnerable to targeted marketing messages.**

subbotina/123RF

More broadly, the growth of the internet, smartphones, and other carefully targeted direct media has raised fresh concerns about potential targeting abuses. The internet and mobile marketing allow more precise targeting, letting the makers of questionable products or deceptive advertisers zero in on the most vulnerable audiences. Unscrupulous marketers can now send tailor-made, deceptive messages by email directly to millions of unsuspecting consumers. For example, the Federal Bureau of Investigation's Internet Crime Complaint Center website alone received almost 300,000 complaints last year.[31]

Today's marketers are also using sophisticated analytical techniques to track consumers' digital movements and to build amazingly detailed customer profiles containing highly personal information. Such profiles can then be used to hypertarget individual consumers with personalized brand messages and offers. However, with such targeting, marketers often walk a fine line between serving customers better and stalking them:

How well does your smartphone know you? What stories could your laptop tell? Whatever you do—at work, at play, socializing, shopping—your phone, tablet, laptop, or desktop is almost always a part of the action. These devices go where you go, entertain you, connect you with friends, take you browsing and shopping, feed you news and information, and listen in on even your most intimate voice, text, and email conversations. And more and more, these devices are sharing all that personal information with marketers. Companies have now developed sophisticated analytics that border on wizardry to extract intimate insights about consumers.

Marketers argue that using all of this up-close-and-personal information better serves both customers and a company. Customers receive tailored, relevant information and offers from brands that really understand and interest them. However, many consumers and privacy advocates are concerned that such intimate information in the hands of unscrupulous marketers can result in more harm than benefit. They often view big data and hypertargeting less as "serving consumers better" and more as "stalking" and "profiling" consumers. Although most consumers are willing to share some personal information if it means getting better service or deals, many consumers worry that marketers might go too far.

Thus, in target marketing, the issue is not really *who* is targeted but rather *how* and for *what*. Controversies arise when marketers attempt to profit at the expense of targeted segments—when they unfairly target vulnerable segments or target them with questionable products or tactics. Socially responsible marketing calls for segmentation and targeting that serve not just the interests of the company but also the interests of those targeted.

Author Comment | At the same time that a company is answering the first simple-sounding question (Which customers will we serve?), it must also be asking the second question (How will we serve them?).

Product position
The way a product is defined by consumers on important attributes—the place it occupies in consumers' minds relative to competing products.

Differentiation and Positioning

OBJECTIVE 7-4 Discuss how companies differentiate and position their products for maximum competitive advantage.

Beyond deciding which segments of the market it will target, the company must decide on a *value proposition*—how it will create differentiated value for targeted segments and what positions it wants to occupy in those segments. A **product position** is the way a product is *defined by consumers* on important attributes—the place the product occupies in consumers' minds relative to competing products. Products are made in factories, but brands happen in the minds of consumers.

In the automobile market, the Honda Fit and Nissan Versa are positioned on economy, Mercedes and Cadillac on luxury, and Porsche and BMW on performance. Your Visa card is "Everywhere you want to be"; with American Express, "Don't live life without it." Gillette is "The best a man can get," but with Dollar Shave Club you "Shave time. Shave money." ● And whereas Bose gives you "Better sound through research," Sonos unleashes "All the music on earth, in every room of your house, wirelessly." Such simple sounding statements form the backbone of a brand's value proposition.

● Positioning: Sonos does more than just sell speakers; it unleashes "All the music on earth, in every room of your house, wirelessly."

The Advertising Archives/Alamy Stock Photo

Consumers are overloaded with information about products and services. They cannot reevaluate products every time they make a buying decision. To simplify the buying process, consumers organize products, brands, and companies into categories and "position" them in their minds. A product's position is the complex set of perceptions, impressions, and feelings that consumers have for the product compared with competing products.

Consumers position products with or without the help of marketers. But marketers do not want to leave their products' positions to chance. They must *plan* positions that will give their products the greatest advantage in selected target markets, and they must design marketing mixes to create these planned positions.

Positioning Maps

In planning their differentiation and positioning strategies, marketers often prepare *perceptual positioning maps* that show consumer perceptions of their brands versus those of competing products on important buying dimensions. ● Figure 7.3 shows a positioning map for the U.S. large luxury SUV market.[32] The position of each circle on the map indicates the brand's perceived positioning on two dimensions: price and orientation (luxury versus performance). The size of each circle indicates the brand's relative market share.

● FIGURE 7.3
Positioning Map: Large Luxury SUVs

The location of each circle shows where consumers position a brand on two dimensions: price and luxury-performance orientation. The size of each circle indicates the brand's relative market share in the segment. Thus, Toyota's Land Cruiser is a niche brand that is perceived to be relatively expensive and more performance oriented.

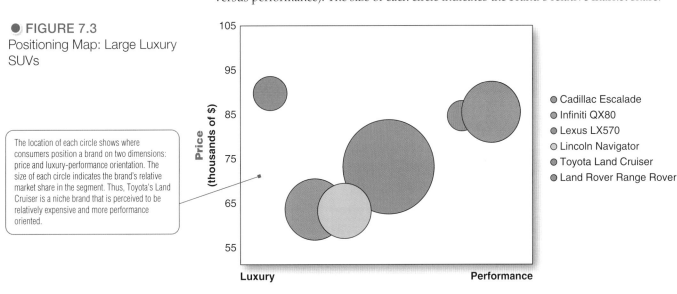

Thus, relative to other luxury SUVs, customers view the market-leading Cadillac Escalade as a moderately priced, large, luxury SUV with a balance of luxury and performance. The Escalade is positioned on urban luxury, and in its case, "performance" probably means power and safety performance. You'll find no mention of off-road adventuring in an Escalade ad.

Choosing a Differentiation and Positioning Strategy

Some firms find it easy to choose a differentiation and positioning strategy. For example, a firm well known for quality in certain segments will go after this position in a new segment if there are enough buyers seeking quality. But in many cases, two or more firms will go after the same position. Then each will have to find other ways to set itself apart. Each firm must differentiate its offer by building a unique bundle of benefits that appeal to a substantial group within the segment.

Above all else, a brand's positioning must serve the needs and preferences of well-defined target markets. For example, although both Dunkin' and Starbucks are coffee and snack shops, they target very different customers who want very different things from their favorite coffee seller. Starbucks targets more upscale professionals with more high-brow, "third place" positioning. In contrast, Dunkin' targets the "average Joe" with a decidedly more low-brow, "everyman" kind of "America runs on Dunkin'" positioning. Yet each brand succeeds because it creates just the right value proposition for its unique mix of customers.

The differentiation and positioning task consists of three steps: identifying a set of differentiating competitive advantages on which to build a position, choosing the right competitive advantages, and selecting an overall positioning strategy. The company must then effectively communicate and deliver the chosen position to the market.

Identifying Possible Value Differences and Competitive Advantages

To build profitable relationships with target customers, marketers must understand customer needs and deliver more customer value better than competitors do. To the extent that a company can differentiate and position itself as providing superior customer value, it gains **competitive advantage**.

But solid positions cannot be built on empty promises. If a company positions its product as *offering* the best quality and service, it must actually differentiate the product so that it *delivers* the promised quality and service. Companies must do much more than simply shout out their positions with slogans and taglines. They must first *live* the slogan. For example, Clorox positions its Glad trash bag as "Glad: The Toughest Trash Bag." But this positioning would ring hollow if its products didn't live up to the promise. So to prove its positioning claim, Glad ran a "Torture Test" campaign in which a homemaker packed a Glad Force Flex Plus kitchen trash bag full of garments and other items and checked it as normal baggage on a trip through seven major U.S. airports. A 90-second ad video showed footage from hidden cameras as they followed the bag's tortuous ordeals at the hands of unforgiving baggage handlers throughout the journey. The bag emerged unscathed. "The bag made it," the ad concluded. "If it can handle this, it can handle your trash! Be happy, it's Glad."[33]

To find points of differentiation, marketers must think through the customer's entire experience with the company's product or service. An alert company can find ways to differentiate itself at every customer contact point in the customer journey. In what specific ways can a company differentiate itself or its market offer? It can differentiate along the lines of *product, services, channels, people,* or *image.*

Through *product differentiation*, brands can be differentiated on features, performance, or style and design. Thus, premium audio brand Bose positions its audio products on the innovative, high-quality listening experiences it gives users. Bose

Competitive advantage
An advantage over competitors gained by offering greater customer value either by having lower prices or providing more benefits that justify higher prices.

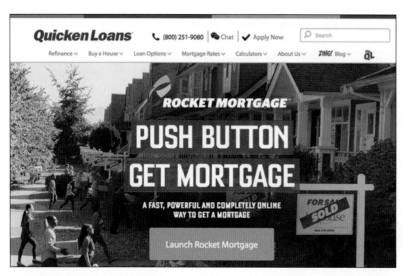

● **Services differentiation: QuickenLoans' Rocket Mortgage doesn't just offer mortgage loans; its online-only interface lets users get a loan decision in only minutes.**

Quicken Loans

promises "better sound through research." And BMW positions itself as "The Ultimate Driving Machine" that's "designed for driving pleasure."

Beyond differentiating its physical product, a firm can also differentiate the services that accompany the product. Some companies gain *services differentiation* through speedy, convenient service. ● QuickenLoans' Rocket Mortgage unit doesn't just offer mortgage loans; its online-only website or mobile app interface lets users easily upload financial details and get a loan decision in only minutes. Other firms promise high-quality customer service. For example, in an age where customer satisfaction with airline service is in constant decline, Singapore Airlines sets itself apart through extraordinary customer care and the grace of its flight attendants.

Firms that practice *channel differentiation* gain competitive advantage through the way they design their channel's coverage, expertise, and performance. Amazon and GEICO, for example, set themselves apart with their smooth-functioning direct channels. Companies can also gain a strong competitive advantage through *people differentiation*—hiring and training better people than their competitors do. People differentiation requires that a company select its customer-contact people carefully and train them well. For example, East Coast supermarket chain Wegmans has long been recognized as a customer service champ with a cult-like loyalty among its shoppers. The secret to its extraordinary customer service lies in its carefully selected, superbly trained, happy employees, who personify Wegmans's commitment to customers: "Everyday You Get Our Best." For example, the chain's cashiers aren't allowed to interact with customers until they've had at least 40 hours of training. "We're committed to hiring good people who are passionate about food and ready to learn and grow with us," says a Wegmans store manager.[34]

Even when competing offers look the same, buyers may perceive a difference based on company or brand *image differentiation*. A company or brand image should convey a product's distinctive benefits and positioning. Developing a strong and distinctive image calls for creativity and hard work. A company cannot develop an image in the public's mind overnight by using only a few ads. If Ritz-Carlton means quality, this image must be supported by everything the company is, says, and does.

Symbols, such as the McDonald's golden arches, the colorful Google logo, the Twitter bird, the Nike swoosh, or Apple's "bite mark" logo, can provide strong company or brand recognition and image differentiation. The company might build a brand around a famous person, as Nike did with its Michael Jordan and LeBron James basketball shoe and apparel collections. Some companies even become associated with colors, such as Coca-Cola (red), IBM (blue), or UPS (brown). The chosen symbols, characters, and other image elements must be communicated through advertising that conveys the company's or brand's personality.

Choosing the Right Competitive Advantages

Suppose a company is fortunate enough to discover several potential differentiations that provide competitive advantages. It now must choose the ones on which it will build its positioning strategy. It must decide how many differences to promote and which ones.

How Many Differences to Promote. Many marketers think that companies should aggressively promote only one benefit to the target market. Former advertising executive Rosser Reeves, for example, said a company should develop a *unique selling proposition (USP)* for each brand and stick to it. Each brand should pick an attribute and tout itself as "number one" on that attribute. Buyers tend to remember number one better, especially in this overcommunicated society. Thus, Walmart promotes its unbeatable low prices and Burger King promotes personal choice—"have it your way."

Other marketers think that companies should position themselves on more than one differentiator. This may be necessary if two or more firms are claiming to be best on the same attribute. ● For example, Toyota positions its Land Cruiser on both luxury and off-road performance. The Land Cruiser began in 1951 as a four-wheel-drive, jeep-like vehicle designed to conquer the world's most grueling terrains and

● Positioning on multiple competitive advantages: Toyota positions its Land Cruiser as "a sophisticated blend of off-road prowess, on-road comfort, and unparalleled refinement."

David Hare/Alamy Stock Photo

climates. In recent years, the vehicle has retained this adventure and performance positioning but with luxury added. Its website brags of a "timeless icon" with "a sophisticated blend of off-road prowess, on-road comfort, and unparalleled refinement."[35] Toyota's challenge is to convince buyers that one brand can provide both luxury and off-road performance.

Today, in a time when the mass market is fragmenting into many small segments, companies and brands are trying to broaden their positioning strategies to appeal to more segments.

Which Differences to Promote. Not all brand differences are meaningful or worthwhile, and each difference has the potential to create company costs as well as customer benefits. A difference is worth establishing to the extent that it satisfies the following criteria:

- *Important.* The difference delivers a highly valued benefit to target buyers.
- *Distinctive.* Competitors do not offer the difference, or the company can offer it in a more distinctive way.
- *Superior.* The difference is superior to other ways that customers might obtain the same benefit.
- *Communicable.* The difference is communicable and visible to buyers.
- *Preemptive.* Competitors cannot easily copy the difference.
- *Affordable.* Buyers can afford to pay for the difference.
- *Profitable.* The company can introduce the difference profitably.

Many companies have introduced differentiations that failed one or more of these tests. When the Westin Stamford Hotel in Singapore once advertised itself as the world's tallest hotel, it was a distinction that was not important to most tourists; in fact, it turned many off. Similarly, Coca-Cola's classic product failure—New Coke—failed the superiority and importance tests among core Coca-Cola drinkers:

> Extensive blind taste tests showed that 60 percent of all soft drink consumers chose a new, sweeter Coca-Cola formulation over the original Coke, and 52 percent chose it over Pepsi. So the brand dropped its original-formula Coke and, with much fanfare, replaced it with New Coke, a sweeter, smoother version. However, in its research, Coca-Cola overlooked the many intangibles that have made Coca-Cola so popular for 130 years. To loyal Coke drinkers, the original beverage stands alongside baseball, apple pie, and the Statue of Liberty as an American institution. As it turns out, Coca-Cola differentiates its brand not just by taste but by tradition. By dropping the original formula, Coca-Cola trampled on the sensitivities of the huge core of loyal Coke drinkers who loved Coke just the way it was. After only three months, the company brought the classic Coke back.

Thus, choosing competitive advantages on which to position a product or service can be difficult, yet such choices are crucial to success. Choosing the right differentiators can help a brand stand out from the pack of competitors.

Selecting an Overall Positioning Strategy

Value proposition
The full positioning of a brand—the full mix of benefits on which it is positioned.

The full positioning of a brand is called the brand's **value proposition**—the full mix of benefits on which a brand is differentiated and positioned. It is the answer to the customer's question "Why should I buy your brand?" BMW's "ultimate driving machine/designed for driving pleasure" value proposition hinges on performance but also includes luxury and styling, all for a price that is higher than average but seems fair for this mix of benefits.

● **Figure 7.4** shows possible value propositions on which a company might position its products. In the figure, the five green cells on the top and right represent winning value propositions—differentiation and positioning that give the company a competitive advantage. The red cells at the lower left, however, represent losing value propositions. The center cell represents at best a marginal proposition. In the following sections, we discuss the five winning value propositions: more for more, more for the same, the same for less, less for much less, and more for less.

More for More. *More-for-more* positioning involves providing the most upscale product or service and charging a higher price to cover the higher costs. A more-for-more market offering not only offers higher quality, it also gives prestige to the buyer. It symbolizes status and a loftier lifestyle. Four Seasons hotels, Patek Philippe watches, Starbucks coffee, Louis

● **FIGURE 7.4**
Possible Value Propositions

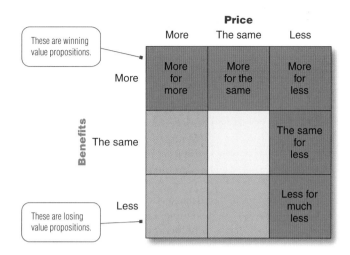

Vuitton handbags, Mercedes automobiles, SubZero appliances—each claims superior quality, craftsmanship, durability, performance, or style and therefore charges a higher price.

Similarly, the marketers of Hearts On Fire diamonds have created a more-for-more niche as "The World's Most Perfectly Cut Diamond." ● Hearts On Fire diamonds have a unique "hearts and arrow" design. When viewed under magnification from the bottom, a perfect ring of eight hearts appears; from the top comes a perfectly formed Fireburst of light. Hearts On Fire diamonds aren't for everyone, says the company. "Hearts On Fire is for those who expect more and give more in return." The brand commands a 15 to 20 percent price premium over comparable competing diamonds.[36]

Although more-for-more can be profitable, this strategy can also be vulnerable. It often invites imitators who claim the same quality but at a lower price. For example, more-for-more brand Starbucks now faces "gourmet" coffee competitors ranging from Dunkin' to McDonald's to the local corner coffee roaster. Also, luxury goods that sell well during good times may be at risk during economic downturns when buyers become more cautious in their spending.

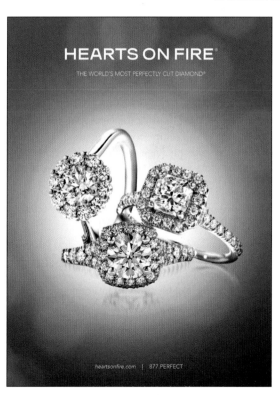

● **More-for-more positioning: Hearts On Fire diamonds have created a more-for-more niche as "The World's Most Perfectly Cut Diamond—for those who expect more and give more in return."**

Hearts On Fire

More for the Same. A company can attack a competitor's value proposition by positioning its brand as offering more for the same price. For example, Target positions itself as the "upscale discounter." It claims to offer more in terms of store atmosphere, service, stylish merchandise, and classy brand image but at prices comparable to those of Walmart, Kohl's, and other discounters.

The Same for Less. Offering *the same for less* can be a powerful value proposition—everyone likes a good deal. Discount stores such as Walmart and "category killers" such as Costco, PetSmart, and DSW Shoes use this positioning. They don't claim to offer different or better products. Instead, they offer many of the same brands as department stores and specialty stores but at deep discounts based on superior purchasing power and lower-cost operations. Other companies develop imitative but lower-priced brands in an effort to lure customers away from the market leader. For example, Amazon's Kindle Fire tablets sell for less than 40 percent of the price of the Apple iPad or Samsung Galaxy tablet. Amazon claims that it offers "Premium products at non-premium prices."

Less for Much Less. A market almost always exists for products that offer less and therefore cost less. Few people need, want, or can afford "the very best" in everything they buy. In many cases, consumers will gladly settle for less-than-optimal performance or give up some of the bells and whistles in exchange for a lower price. Less-for-much-less positioning involves meeting consumers' lower performance or quality requirements at a much lower price.

For example, at ALDI grocery stores, customers pay super-low prices but must settle for less in terms of selection and services. ALDI offers a narrower selection with fewer national brands and does no promotional pricing or price matching—it just sticks with its efficient everyday very low prices. Customers bring their own bags (or purchase them from ALDI for a small charge), bag their own groceries (ALDI provides no baggers), and return shopping carts on their own (to get back a 25-cent deposit). "You can't eat frills," says ALDI, "so why pay for them?"

More for Less. Of course, the winning value proposition would be to offer *more for less*. Many companies claim to do this. And, in the short run, some companies can actually achieve such lofty positions. For example, when it first opened for business, Home Depot had arguably the best product selection, the best service, *and* the lowest prices compared with local hardware stores and other home-improvement chains.

Yet in the long run, companies find it very difficult to sustain such best-of-both positioning. Offering more usually costs more, making it difficult to deliver on the "for-less" promise. Companies that try to deliver both may lose out to more focused competitors. For example, facing determined competition from Lowe's stores, Home Depot must decide whether it wants to compete primarily on superior service or on lower prices.

All said, each brand must adopt a positioning strategy designed to serve the needs and wants of its target markets. *More for more* will draw one target market, *less for much less* will draw another, and so on. In any market, there is usually room for many different companies, each successfully occupying different positions. The important thing is that each company must develop its own winning positioning strategy, one that makes the company special to its target consumers.

Developing a Positioning Statement

Positioning statement

A statement that summarizes company or brand positioning using this form: To (target segment and need) our (brand) is (concept) that (point of difference).

Company and brand positioning should be summed up in a **positioning statement**. The statement should follow the form: To (target segment and need) our (brand) is (concept) that (point of difference).[37] Here is an example using online retailer Brandless: "For value- and convenience-seeking buyers, Brandless is an online food and household goods retailer that makes better stuff accessible and affordable to more people in a responsible way."

Note that the positioning statement first states the brand's membership in a category (online food and household goods retailer) and then shows its point of difference from other members of the category (makes better stuff accessible and affordable to more people in a responsible way). In what one analyst likens to "an online Trader Joe's," Brandless offers some 350 own-brand product items online—including organic and specialty goods—all at a magical price of $3. "Better stuff, fewer dollars. It's that simple," says Brandless. The online retailer also believes in giving back to its communities. Through its "Tangible Acts of Kindness" initiative, in partnership with Feeding America, every time anyone checks out at Brandless, the company donates a meal to someone facing hunger.[38]

Placing a brand in a specific category suggests similarities that it might share with other products in the category. But the case for the brand's superiority is made on its points of difference. For example, the U.S. Postal Service ships packages just like UPS and FedEx, but it differentiates its Priority Mail from competitors with convenient, low-price, flat-rate shipping boxes and envelopes. "If it fits, it ships," promises USPS.

Communicating and Delivering the Chosen Position

Once it has chosen a position, the company must take strong steps to deliver and communicate the desired position to its target consumers. All the company's marketing mix efforts must support the positioning strategy.

Positioning the company calls for concrete action, not just talk. If the company decides to build a position on better quality and service, it must first *deliver* that position. Designing the marketing mix—product, price, place, and promotion—involves working out the tactical details of the positioning strategy. Thus, a firm that seizes on a more-for-more position knows that it must produce high-quality products, charge a high price, distribute through high-quality dealers, and advertise in high-quality media. It must hire and train more service people, find retailers that have a good reputation for service, and develop sales and advertising content that supports its superior offer. This is the only way to build a consistent and believable more-for-more position.

Companies often find it easier to come up with a good positioning strategy than to implement it. Establishing a position or changing one usually takes a long time. In contrast, positions that have taken years to build can quickly be lost. Once a company has built the desired position, it must take care to maintain the position through consistent performance and communication. It must closely monitor and adapt the position over time to match changes in consumer needs and competitors' strategies. However, the company should avoid abrupt changes that might confuse consumers. Instead, a product's position should evolve gradually as it adapts to the ever-changing marketing environment.

Reviewing and Extending the Concepts

Objectives Review

In this chapter, you learned about the major elements of a customer value–driven marketing strategy: segmentation, targeting, differentiation, and positioning. Marketers know that they cannot appeal to all buyers in their markets—or at least not to all buyers in the same way. Therefore, most companies today practice *target marketing*—identifying market segments, selecting one or more of them, and developing products and marketing mixes tailored to each.

OBJECTIVE 7-1 Define the major steps in designing a customer value–driven marketing strategy: market segmentation, targeting, differentiation, and positioning. *(pp 204–205)*

A customer value–driven marketing strategy begins with selecting which customers to serve and determining a value proposition that best serves the targeted customers. It consists of four steps. *Market segmentation* is the act of dividing a market into distinct groups of buyers who have different needs, characteristics, or behaviors and who might require separate marketing strategies or mixes. Once the groups have been identified, *market targeting* evaluates each market segment's attractiveness and selects one or more segments to serve. *Differentiation* involves actually differentiating the market offering to create superior customer value. *Positioning* consists of positioning the market offering in the minds of target customers. A customer value–driven marketing strategy seeks to build the *right relationships* with the *right customers*.

OBJECTIVE 7-2 List and discuss the major bases for segmenting consumer and business markets. *(pp 205–213)*

There is no single way to segment a market. Therefore, the marketer tries different variables to see which give the best segmentation opportunities. For consumer marketing, the major segmentation variables are geographic, demographic, psychographic, and behavioral. In *geographic segmentation*, the market is divided into different geographical units, such as nations, regions, states, counties, cities, or even neighborhoods. In *demographic segmentation*, the market is divided into groups based on demographic variables, including age, life-cycle stage, gender, income, occupation, education, religion, ethnicity, and generation. In *psychographic segmentation*, the market is divided into different groups based on social class, lifestyle, or personality characteristics. In *behavioral segmentation*, the market is divided into groups based on consumers' knowledge, attitudes, uses, or responses concerning a product.

Business marketers use many of the same variables to segment their markets. But business markets also can be segmented by business *demographics* (industry, company size), *operating*

characteristics, purchasing approaches, situational factors, and *personal characteristics*. The effectiveness of the segmentation analysis depends on finding segments that are *measurable, accessible, substantial, differentiable*, and *actionable*.

OBJECTIVE 7-3 Explain how companies identify attractive market segments and choose a market-targeting strategy. *(pp 213–220)*

To target the best market segments, the company first evaluates each segment's size and growth characteristics, structural attractiveness, and compatibility with company objectives and resources. It then chooses one of four market-targeting strategies—ranging from very broad to very narrow targeting. The seller can ignore segment differences and target broadly using *undifferentiated* (or *mass*) *marketing*. This involves mass producing, mass distributing, and mass promoting the same product in about the same way to all consumers. Or the seller can adopt *differentiated marketing*—developing different market offers for several segments. *Concentrated marketing* (or *niche marketing*) involves focusing on one or a few market segments only. Finally, *micromarketing* is the practice of tailoring products and marketing programs to suit the tastes of specific individuals and locations. Micromarketing includes *local marketing* and *individual marketing*. Which targeting strategy is best depends on company resources, product variability, product life-cycle stage, market variability, and competitive marketing strategies.

OBJECTIVE 7-4 Discuss how companies differentiate and position their products for maximum competitive advantage. *(pp 221–227)*

As the company is deciding which segments to enter, it must also decide on its *differentiation and positioning strategy*. The differentiation and positioning task consists of three steps: identifying a set of possible differentiations that create competitive advantage, choosing advantages on which to build a position, and selecting an overall positioning strategy.

The brand's full positioning is called its *value proposition*—the full mix of benefits on which the brand is positioned. In general, companies can choose from one of five winning value propositions on which to position their products: more for more, more for the same, the same for less, less for much less, or more for less. Company and brand positioning are summarized in positioning statements that state the target segment and need, the positioning concept, and specific points of difference. The company must then effectively communicate and deliver the chosen position to the market.

Key Terms

OBJECTIVE 7-1

Market segmentation (p 204)
Market targeting (targeting) (p 205)
Differentiation (p 205)
Positioning (p 205)

OBJECTIVE 7-2

Geographic segmentation (p 205)
Hyperlocal social marketing (p 205)
Demographic segmentation (p 207)
Age and life-cycle segmentation (p 207)
Gender segmentation (p 207)

Income segmentation (p 207)
Psychographic segmentation (p 207)
Behavioral segmentation (p 208)
Occasion segmentation (p 208)
Benefit segmentation (p 208)
Intermarket (cross-market)
  segmentation (p 213)

OBJECTIVE 7-3

Target market (p 214)
Undifferentiated (mass) marketing
  (p 214)

Differentiated (segmented) marketing
  (p 214)
Concentrated (niche) marketing (p 215)
Micromarketing (p 217)
Local marketing (p 217)
Individual marketing (p 218)

OBJECTIVE 7-4

Product position (p 221)
Competitive advantage (p 222)
Value proposition (p 224)
Positioning statement (p 226)

Discussion Questions

7-1 How would you describe the key differences between differentiation and positioning? Do businesses use both techniques? (AACSB: Communication)

7-2 How is demographic segmentation used in consumer markets? Provide an example where marketers have used demographic segmentation. (AACSB: Written and Oral Communication; Reflective Thinking)

7-3 What is the value of intermarket segmentation for global businesses? (AACSB: Communication)

7-4 Discuss the challenges marketers face with international market segmentation. (AACSB: Communication)

7-5 Explain the differences between differentiated and undifferentiated marketing. Can a business effectively use both strategies? (AACSB: Communication; Reflective Thinking)

7-6 What is a value proposition? Discuss the five winning value propositions on which a company might position its products and give an example of each. (AACSB: Written and Oral Communication)

Critical Thinking Exercises

7-7 Identify a product or service that you are familiar with but consider a niche product. You have been asked to come up with a strategy that aims to transform the product from niche to a more mass-market position. (AACSB: Communication; Reflective Thinking)

7-8 The breakfast cereal market is highly competitive and marketers for the many varieties of cereal attempt to differentiate their brands to appeal to specific segments. Choose five different breakfast cereal brands and match them with the segmentation variables that marketers

might be using to target a specific market. Explain why you matched each cereal with the specific segmentation variables. (AACSB: Written and Oral Communication; Reflective Thinking)

7-9 In a small group, look at InsomniaCookies.com. Using the steps described in the chapter, describe the company's customer value-driven marketing strategy. Write as a positioning statement for this business. (AACSB: Written and Oral Communication; Reflective Thinking)

APPLICATIONS AND CASES

Online, Mobile, and Social Media Marketing Influence Not Accepted as Payment

Recently, Mr. Gianluca Casaccia, manager and co-owner of the White Banana Beach Club on an island in the Philippines, posted the following message on Facebook:

> "We are receiving many messages regarding collaborations with influencers, Instagram influencers. We kindly would like to announce that White Banana is not interested to "collaborate" with self-proclaimed "influencers." And we would like to suggest to try another way to eat, drink, or sleep for free. Or try to actually work."

Despite prior efforts to work with "real influencers," which Mr. Casaccia classified as travelers with 500,000 or more Instagram followers, he was bothered by "wannabe freeloaders." The message went viral, with mixed responses. Some suggested that the travelers were entrepreneurial and that it did not hurt to ask. Others suggested that the number of requests had become a challenge to manage and equated influencers to beggars. Further, if a

U.S.-based Instagram influencer is compensated for a post, she or he must note that the content is sponsored (see www.ftc.gov/news-events/press-releases/2017/04/ftc-staff-reminds-influencers-brands-clearly-disclose/).

7-10 Should the White Banana Beach Club sponsor Instagram influencers that have less than 500,000 followers to help position its offering? Should it sponsor Instagram influencers that have more than 500,000 followers? In each case, explain why or why not? (AACSB: Written and Oral Communication; Information Technology; Reflective Thinking)

7-11 How does using an Instagram influencer with more than 500,000 followers compare to a micro-marketing strategy? Which would you recommend to the White Banana Beach Club? Why? (AACSB: Written and Oral Communication; Reflective Thinking)

Marketing Ethics Allegiant Airlines: Value Creation or Flying Public at Risk?

With millions of American passengers selecting air travel to reach their intended destinations, Allegiant Airlines has cornered the market by providing exceptionally low fares, consistent customer service, and excellent returns for investors. While Allegiant is known for its bargain fares, it is also now known for its in-flight breakdowns and mechanical failures. According to a *60 Minutes* investigation in 2018, Allegiant Airlines, which has the oldest fleet of airplanes in the industry, experienced more than 100 serious mechanical incidents between January 2016 and October 2017, ranging from engine failures and fires, aborted takeoffs, and smoke and fumes in the passenger cabin to rapid descents and flight control malfunctions. Experts believe that Allegiant's problems stem from its aggressive cost-reduction business practices, which have produced sixty consecutive quarters of profitability, with profit margins near 30 percent. To achieve these results,

Allegiant has maintained or decreased costs as much as possible and kept its fleet flying as often as possible. To view the full video and clips, visit: www.cbsnews.com/news/allegiant-air-the-budget-airline-flying-under-the-radar/.

7-12 Companies have long struggled to balance the need for profit with consumer value. How has Allegiant differentiated and positioned itself in the airline industry? How has this differentiation and positioning strategy impacted its corporate decision making? (AACSB: Written and Oral communication; Ethical Understanding and Reasoning)

7-13 Give an example of another airline that positions itself in a way that differentiates it from Allegiant? Which airline would you rather fly? (AACSB: Written and Oral Communication; Reflective Thinking)

Marketing by the Numbers See the Clot, Bust the Clot, Save a Life

Stroke is the fifth-leading cause of death among Americans, claiming more than 130,000 lives each year. Almost 800,000 people suffer a stroke each year in the United States, one every 40 seconds. These grim statics are actually not as grim as they used to be. New technologies and treatments are increasing the survival rate among sufferers of the most common type of stroke caused by a clot blocking a blood vessel supplying blood to the brain. A procedure known as thrombectomy busts or removes clots and increases survival rates if patients are treated within 6 to 24 hours of symptom presentation. However, less than 5 percent of patients present symptoms within this short time window. Neural Analytics, Inc. has a solution: its Lucid Robotic System. The system is a combination of two products: transcranial ultrasound and a robotic system. The ultrasound, taken from a natural "window into the brain" near a patient's ear, lets medical professionals see if a clot is blocking blood flow. The robotic system, using artificial intelligence (AI), then compares the image to thousands of stored images of severe strokes to identify candidates for the life-saving thrombectomy procedure. This device will help hospital emergency departments to better identify the 10 to 15 percent of stroke patients who qualify for a thrombectomy and send them to one of the country's 100

certified stroke centers. Neural Analytics plans to market its Lucid Robotic System to hospitals first, with the ultimate goal of getting a lower-priced portable system into every emergency response vehicle in the United States.

7-14 There are 5,534 certified hospitals in the United States, and 95 percent have emergency departments. Assuming the price of the Lucid Robotic System is $50,000 and that hospitals with emergency departments purchase one system, use the chain ratio method described in Market Potential and Sales Estimates in Appendix 2: Marketing by the Numbers to calculate the market potential for this product. (AACSB: Analytic Reasoning)

7-15 There are approximately 50,000 emergency response vehicles operated by private ambulance companies, municipal fire departments, and hospitals. Assuming the price of the portable Lucid Robotic System is $5,000 and that each emergency response vehicle would be equipped with one system, calculate the market potential of this target market. (AACSB: Analytic Reasoning)

Company Case 5-Hour Energy: Hours of Energy without the Beverage

You've no doubt heard of 5-Hour Energy—the small red bottles filled with an energy-infused elixir, located alongside the candy and gum near the checkout at most grocery and convenience stores. Chances are good that you've tried one. You may even be among the more than 4 million people in the United States who have collectively consumed 9 million bottles of 5-Hour Energy in just the past seven days. This upstart brand has had a huge impact on the beverage industry. How did 5-Hour Energy become so big so fast? By targeting the right kinds of customers with a product that gives them exactly what they want at precisely the right moment.

Discovering an Unmet Need

It all started in the early 2000s. India-born Manoj Bhargava had sold his company—an outdoor furniture components maker—and retired to Michigan with his wife and son. But after only a couple of months, he grew tired of doing nothing and began looking for a product he could license and turn into the "next big thing." With that in mind, he attended a natural products trade show in Anaheim, California.

Amid meetings with numerous companies, he happened upon the booth for an energy drink developed by a group of PhDs. The 16-ounce concoction claimed to boost energy for hours. Knowing he faced meetings until 10 p.m. that evening, Bhargava was concerned that he not would be able to stay awake, let alone pay attention. So, he tried a can of the energy drink. The results were almost instantaneous. "For the next six or seven hours, I was in great shape," Bhargava recalls. Not only was he wide awake, but his levels of focus and awareness were enhanced. "I thought, 'Wow, this is amazing. I can sell this.'"

But when he talked with the drink's owners to discuss potential partnerships, Bhargava learned that they were not interested in selling or even licensing the rights for the product. He looked over the label and made a mental note of its ingredients and thought, "How hard can it be?" Most people without a science or nutrition background would never dream of trying to come up with their own recipe for a product intended for human consumption. But Bhargava was not deterred. He got to work setting up his own lab and forming a company he called Living Essentials.

Bhargava quickly realized that a 16-ounce beverage would not succeed in a market saturated with long-standing brands peddled by deep-pocketed companies. As an energy-giving beverage, the new product would have to compete for refrigerator and shelf space with an ever-increasing batch of brands, the biggest of which was Red Bull. It would also face off against some of the most established brands in the world put out by the likes of the Coca-Cola and PepsiCo.

But Bhargava's new concoction didn't have to be a 16-ounce beverage or, for that matter, a beverage at all. "If I'm tired, am I also thirsty? Is that like having a headache and a stomachache?" mused Bhargava. After all, Tylenol didn't sell a 16-ounce single serving version of its pain-killing product. As he developed the formula through trial and error—he always tried the experimental versions out on himself—he contemplated the customer he was trying to reach and how the product could be positioned to appeal to them.

Profile of an Unfulfilled Customer

In defining that customer, Bhargava thought about himself at the trade show. He needed energy to stay awake. But he also needed to be able to pay attention—to focus on what was happening as he met with people from various companies. He needed energy and focus quickly, preferably in a form that wouldn't weigh him down or produce unwanted side effects. Once he thought in those terms, he considered other types of people who also need those benefits—people working two jobs to make ends meet, truck drivers who spend hours at a time behind the wheel, the Wall Street trader grinding out 16-hour days, or the person who works on a Hollywood movie set. All those people have two things in common—they work long hours and they need to be able to focus on their work.

From his own experience and observation, Bhargava knew that energy drinks, caffeinated soft drinks, and even coffee all focused on providing energy and the ability to stay awake. But consuming enough of any of those beverages to get the right amount of energy put a lot of liquid in people's bellies, tending to weigh them down and make them feel sluggish. Additionally, product's containing sugar might produce an initial jolt of energy, but that spike is short-lived, followed by a carbohydrate-induced crash into grogginess.

With the target customer in mind, Bhargava set the form—a sugar-free two-ounce shot that contained enough caffeine (200 milligrams by some estimates) to produce a substantial boost in energy along with a blend of vitamins and amino acids known to increase the human brain's ability to focus. The small dose of liquid wasn't so much a beverage as it was a delivery system.

Positioning through the Marketing Mix

With the product's form established, Bhargava created the name: 5-Hour Energy—simple and functional, precisely communicating the product's benefit. The product's form was important for ease of consumption and for differentiating it from other beverage options. But it was necessary for another key component of Bhargava's marketing mix strategy—to get the product into stores in its own spot, away from the refrigerated beverages and right next to the cash registers.

The first retail chain that 5-Hour Energy's marketing team targeted for distribution was GNC—the largest chain of vitamin and nutrition stores in the country. 5-Hour Energy was a perfect fit for GNC's customers—fitness and health-oriented people who spent hours working out each day on top of their jobs and other life pursuits. GNC's buyers agreed, placing 5-Hour Energy in a small display next to the cash register.

After the first week, however, 5-Hour Energy sold only 200 bottles across GNC's 1,200 stores. The premium price of more than $3 for the little shot was a hurdle. But Bhargava wasn't worried. He knew that the product was sound, the location was perfect, and the price was right to establish an image as a quality product. His hunches were right. After six months, 5-Hour Energy was selling 10,000 bottles a week.

That success gained 5-Hour Energy entry into Walgreen's, CVS, and various convenience store chains throughout the country. With increased distribution, the company ran ads on TV and the internet. The ads were simple—even low-budget in appearance. But the message was right on. "You know what 2:30 in the afternoon feels like, right? Sleepy? Groggy? Dying for a nap?" said a young, hip, white-collar worker, navigating his way around a typical corporate office. "What do you do? Run for the coffee? Grab a soda? But how long does that last, before you're back for more?" After detailing the benefits provided by 5-Hour Energy, the ad ended with the tagline, "Hours of energy now, no 2:30 feeling later."

Adding multiple flavors in regular, extra strength, and even decaf forms, 5-Hour Energy rose to new heights with distribution in Walmart and every other major U.S. grocery chain. By that time, many other companies were taking notice of the upstart brand and opportunities in the new energy shot category. If 5-Hour Energy had been created by a guy with no background in the business, certainly, they could do it better.

Soon, Coca-Cola, Pepsi, Red Bull, Monster, and a host of other established beverage makers began distributing their own versions of the two-ounce shot, pressing for their share of limited counter space next to cash registers. And they weren't the only new entrants. At one point, there were literally hundreds of brands of two-ounce shots on the market, most from small, opportunistic companies looking to score a quick buck. Almost all came in at price-points cheaper than 5-Hour Energy. And the deep-pocketed veteran brands threw their muscle into distribution channels and promoting their newest offerings.

Initially, the new competition made a dent in 5-Hour Energy's fortunes. Within months, the brand's market share dropped from 93 percent to 67 percent. "Everybody tried their products," reports Bhargava. "However, the one thing they all forgot was, you have to have a great product." Bhargava remains a big believer in product quality. "It's not the little bottle. It's not the placement. It's the product. You can con people one time, but nobody pays $3 twice."

As the energy shot market has evolved, Bhargava has been proven right. Even as the market has continued to grow in overall volume, competitors have dropped by the wayside. With little repeat purchase and not enough incentive to stay in the game, even the big brands have decided the battle isn't worth it.

Today, 5-Hour Energy again commands more than 95 percent of the category it created. The number two brand? NVE Pharmaceutical's "Stacker," at just over three percent of the market. When asked what other brand 5-Hour Energy most resembles, Bhargava replies, "WD-40." He considers the two brands to be similar in that they are both brands without categories. "Usually, to be a category, there have to be at least two major players. This shot area...it's really not so much a category as a brand."

With the competition neutralized, Living Essentials continues to keep 5-Hour Energy at the forefront of consumers' minds with new ads that feature simple, functional slogans like "Back to 100 Percent", and "Energy on the Go." The brand also continues to develop new varieties, including 5-Hour Tea—a two-ounce shot in a white bottle boasting caffeine derived from green tea leaves.

As a private company, Living Essentials doesn't disclose its performance. But industry estimates put 5-Hour Energy's annual retail sales at more than $1 billion. About 25 percent of that retail figure filters down to Living Essentials' net profit. That's enough for Bhargava to have amassed an estimated net worth somewhere between $1.5 billion and $4 billion. Yet, with 5-Hour Energy's rapid growth and market domination, Bhargava sees much more potential before the market becomes saturated. "If we sold 5-Hour Energy to everyone who needs it, we'd be selling twenty times more."[39]

Questions for Discussion

7-16 Consider the variables commonly used to segment markets. Which of these best represents how the makers of 5-Hour Energy segmented the market?

7-17 Which market targeting strategy is 5-Hour Energy following? Justify your answer.

7-18 Write a positioning statement for 5-Hour Energy.

7-19 What potential challenges does 5-Hour Energy faces in the future?

8 Products, Services, and Brands
Building Customer Value

OBJECTIVES OUTLINE

OBJECTIVE 8-1 Define *product* and describe the major classifications of products and services. **See: What Is a Product?** *(pp 234–239)*

OBJECTIVE 8-2 Describe the decisions companies make regarding their individual products and services, product lines, and product mixes. **See: Product and Service Decisions** *(pp 239–247)*

OBJECTIVE 8-3 Identify the four characteristics that affect the marketing of services and the additional marketing considerations that services require. **See: Services Marketing** *(pp 247–252)*

OBJECTIVE 8-4 Discuss branding strategy—the decisions companies make in building and managing their brands. **See: Branding Strategy: Building Strong Brands** *(pp 252–261)*

CHAPTER PREVIEW After examining customer value–driven marketing strategy, we now take a deeper look at the marketing mix: the tactical tools that marketers use to implement their strategies, engage customers, and deliver superior customer value. In this and the next chapter, we study how companies develop and manage products, services, and brands. Then, in the chapters that follow, we look at pricing, distribution, and marketing communication tools. The product and brand are usually the first and most basic marketing consideration. We start with a seemingly simple question: What *is* a product? As it turns out, the answer is not so simple.

Before getting into the chapter, let's look at a remarkable brand story. Marketing is all about building brands that connect deeply with customers. When you think about top brands, which ones pop up first? Maybe it's traditional megabrands such as Coca-Cola, Nike, or McDonald's, or maybe a trendy tech brand such as Google, Facebook, or Apple. If we asked you to focus on home furnishing, though, you'd probably name IKEA. When it comes to your life and home furnishing, IKEA has it covered.

IKEA: Building a Cult Brand

IKEA has a remarkably devoted following. In 2018, IKEA had over 957 million visits to their stores, and opened 19 new stores including their first in India. When IKEA opened their first store in Croatia, 68,000 customers visited it in its first four days. The company received 100,000 job applications for their new story in Valencia, Spain, temporarily shutting down their servers.

IKEA achieved this level of success by offering a unique value proposition to consumers: leading-edge Scandinavian design at extremely low prices. Part of the reason why IKEA can afford such prices is because most items come boxed and require assembly when the customer brings them home. This allows savings in transport and better use of shelf space. In addition, IKEA sources its products from multiple companies all over the world rather than a handful of suppliers as many competitors do, ensuring the lowest price possible. Other products may be sold at higher prices, but IKEA ensures that they are still quite affordable. The company aims to drive prices down across its whole product range by an average of 2–3 percent per year.

While the modern consumer is presented with a dizzying array of choices for everything they buy, IKEA provides a single venue for everything "cool," a safe space for like-minded people who have good taste and know value for money. That vision extends to the names of its products: customers can live in a BoKlok home and sleep in a Leksvik bed under a Brunskära quilt. Founder Ingvar Kamprad, who was dyslexic, believed that it was easier to remember product names rather than codes or numbers, so the beds are named after Norwegian cities and the bedding after flowers and plants. The strategy has obviously paid off, for the Swedish retailer accounts for 5 to 15 percent of the furniture market in each country in which it operates.

IKEA has succeeded in building a global cult brand. In 2018, after 12 years of planning and six years after they announced their intentions, IKEA opened the first of its new stores in Hyderabad in India. The vast 13 acre complex in Hitec City has a display area with over 7,500 product lines. In the run up to the opening, teams from IKEA visited over 1,000 typical homes in India from range of income levels and lifestyles in order to understand their new customers. The Hyderabad store is the first of 25 projected sites across India to be opened by 2025. In 2019, IKEA launched their e-commerce site for India based in Mumbai; it will now roll out e-commerce operations in cities where it can support sales with fulfilment, delivery and assembly services locally. IKEA looks set to be an enormous hit in India with upwards of 40,000 customers visiting the store on the opening day alone. IKEA maintains this performance even while it steadily cuts prices, achieving an operating margin of approximately 10 percent, which ranks among the best in the global market for home furnishing.

To maintain its growth, IKEA has continued opening new stores around the world, with up to 20 per year at a cost of $80–100 million per store on average. IKEA has boosted its profile in three of its fastest-growing markets: the United States, Russia, and China. In the United States, the number of stores has grown from 25 in 2005 to 48 in 2018. IKEA is also investing in emerging markets such as Croatia, Slovenia, and the Ukraine.

The key success factor for these roll-outs is in preserving the strong enthusiasm IKEA evokes. What unites and enchants shoppers all over the world is the store visit, a customer experience that is common to every country IKEA operates in. IKEA provides a unique shopping experience with its blue-and-yellow buildings averaging 300,000 square feet (27,871 square meters). The sheer number of items is a major advantage. IKEA's stores are located, on average, about 25 miles from most city centers, which helps keep land costs down and taxes low. In order to bring IKEA closer to its customers, the company announced that they will further extend its network of stores; for example, in Germany, one of the most important countries for IKEA, the company aims to build 20 new stores by 2025. In addition, the company also has started an online initiative that encompasses

IKEA stores are designed for the customer to experience the whole store and be drawn by a wide variety of items along the way.
Chih-Chung Johnny Chang/Alamy Stock Photo

the installation of so-called pick-up points, where customers can collect items they had previously ordered online.

For customers, a visit to an IKEA store is more of an exciting and engaging excursion than a simple shopping trip, and this is testament to the strength of the brand and the loyalty of its customers. Many stores resemble a large box with few windows, and doors and are painted bright yellow and blue—Sweden's national colors. Shopping at IKEA is a different experience from other retailers. To begin, customers can drop off their children at the playroom near the entrance, which encourages a more relaxed shopping experience. The floor plan is designed to follow a one-way path, so the customer experiences the entire store by proceeding along a marked path through the different showrooms. The furniture is arranged in fully accessorized displays to inspire customers and increase spending. Along the way, the customer's attention is continuously drawn by strategically placed items, from pencils to picture frames. The shopping experience constantly surprises, as IKEA replaces a third of its product line every year. There is usually a restaurant at the center of the store to give shoppers a rest before they move on to the warehouse, where nearly all the big items are flat-packed.

IKEA has created a clear positioning of what the brand stands for: it is more than just value-priced, assemble-it-yourself furniture and home furnishings; IKEA offers a comprehensive lifestyle solution for its consumers. IKEA does things differently from its competitors: it determines what the price for a product should be and then challenges its designers to create a beautifully designed product that can be sold for that specified price. By doing so, IKEA fuses cost focus with a strong design culture. Due to excellent design and materials as well as good value for money, more wealthy people are also choosing to shop at IKEA.

> IKEA'S success comes from a deep understanding that it's selling much more than just home furnishing at low prices—it offers customers a lifestyle both affordable and comprehensive.

Moreover, IKEA knows their customers and customizes its offerings by selling products people want to buy. For example, the company produced a quarter of a million plastic placemats for the Chinese market to honor the year of the rooster. In just three weeks, they were sold out.

For every fan who shops at IKEA, there seems to be one working for the company. The "IKEA Spirit" calls for workers to take care of each other and inspire each other. Employees at IKEA enjoy autonomy, very little hierarchy, and a familial culture. In return, they absorb IKEA's values of frugality and design. This is supported heavily by the use of social media platforms by the company, predominantly Facebook, Twitter, Instagram, and Pinterest. The company continuously posts promotions, discounts, unique giveaways, events, and news; and they also use it as a platform to share their content. In addition, IKEA is always responsive to their followers, and they're quick to address any customer complaints. The results display the cult like image of the brand, with 27 million Facebook fans, 2 million followers just on their U.S. Instagram account, and more than 10 million monthly visitors to their German Pinterest account alone. The IKEA Group has not only successfully built a global cult brand but continues to capitalize on it, to grow, and to enable more fans to live an affordable life at home.[1]

AS THE IKEA STORY shows, in their quest to create customer relationships, marketers must build and manage products and brands that connect with customers. This chapter begins with a deceptively simple question: *What is a product?* After addressing this question, we look at ways to classify products in consumer and business markets. Then we discuss the important decisions that marketers make regarding individual products, product lines, and product mixes. Next, we examine the characteristics and marketing requirements of a special form of product—services. Finally, we look into the critically important issue of how marketers build and manage product and service brands.

> Author Comment | As you'll see, this deceptively simple question has a very complex answer. For example, think back to the opening IKEA story. What is the IKEA "product"?

What Is a Product?

OBJECTIVE 8-1 Define *product* and describe the major classifications of products and services.

We define a **product** as anything that can be offered to a market for attention, acquisition, use, or consumption that might satisfy a want or need. Products include more than just tangible objects, such as cars, clothing, or smartphones. Broadly defined, products also include services, events, persons, places, organizations, and ideas or a mixture of these. Throughout this text, we use the term *product* broadly to include any or all these entities. Thus, an Apple iPhone, a Toyota Camry, and a Caffé Mocha at Starbucks are products. But so are a trip to Las Vegas, Schwab online investment services, your Instagram account, and advice from your family doctor.

Because of their importance in the world economy, we give special attention to services. **Services** are a form of product that consists of activities, benefits, or satisfactions offered for sale that are essentially intangible and do not result in the ownership of anything. Examples include banking, hotel, airline travel, retail, wireless communication, and home-repair services. We will look at services more closely later in this chapter.

Product
Anything that can be offered to a market for attention, acquisition, use, or consumption that might satisfy a want or need.

Service
An activity, benefit, or satisfaction offered for sale that is essentially intangible and does not result in the ownership of anything.

Products, Services, and Experiences

Products are a key element in the overall *market offering*. Marketing mix planning begins with building an offering that brings value to target customers. This offering becomes the basis on which the company builds profitable customer relationships.

A company's market offering often includes both tangible goods and services. At one extreme, the market offer may consist of a *pure tangible good*, such as soap, toothpaste, or salt; no services accompany the product. At the other extreme are *pure services*, for which the market offer consists primarily of a service. Examples include a doctor's exam and financial services. Between these two extremes, however, many goods-and-services combinations are possible.

Today, as products and services become more commoditized, many companies are moving to a new level in creating value for their customers. To differentiate their offers, beyond simply making products and delivering services, they are creating and managing customer *experiences* with their brands or companies.

Experiences have always been an important part of marketing for some companies. Disney has long manufactured dreams and memories through its movies and theme parks—it wants theme park cast members to deliver a thousand "small wows" to every customer. And Nike has long declared, "It's not so much the shoes but where they take you." Today, however, all kinds of firms are recasting their traditional goods and services to create experiences. ● For example, your local Buffalo Wild Wings restaurant doesn't just serve up wings and beer; it gives customers the ultimate "Wings. Beer. Sports." fan experience:[2]

"Wings. Beer. Sports." That's the long-standing motto for the Buffalo Wild Wings restaurant chain. "B-Dubs"—as it's known to avid regulars—focuses on food and sports and "everything in between." There's no doubt about it. Buffalo Wild Wings more than lives up to the "wings" and "beer" parts of the equation. It serves up wings in an abundant variety and each B-Dubs restaurant pours as many as 30 different draft beers. You won't go hungry or thirsty at B-Dubs.

But the Buffalo Wild Wings recipe for success goes much deeper than just selling wings and beer for profit. What really packs 'em in and keeps 'em coming back is the B-Dubs experience. Customers come to B-Dubs to watch sports, trash talk, cheer on their sports teams, and meet old friends and make new ones—that is, a total eating and social experience. "We realize that we're not just in the business of selling wings," says the company. "We're something much bigger. We're in the business of fueling the sports fan experience." Catering to the customer experience has paid big dividends for Buffalo Wild Wings. B-Dubs is now the nation's number-one seller of chicken wings and largest pourer of draft beer.

● **Creating customer experiences: Your local Buffalo Wild Wings restaurant doesn't just serve up wings and beer; it gives customers the ultimate "Wings. Beer. Sports." fan experience.**
Buffalo Wild Wings, Inc.

Levels of Product and Services

Product planners need to think about products and services on three levels (see ● **Figure 8.1**). Each level adds more customer value. The most basic level is the *core customer value*, which addresses the question: *What is the buyer really buying?* When designing products, marketers must first define the core, problem-solving benefits, services, or experiences that consumers seek. A woman buying lipstick buys more than lip color. Charles Revson of Revlon saw this early: "In the factory, we make cosmetics; in the store, we sell hope."

● FIGURE 8.1
Three Levels of Product

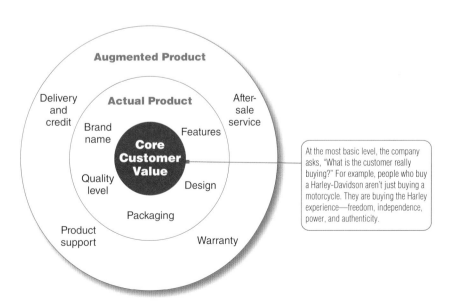

At the most basic level, the company asks, "What is the customer really buying?" For example, people who buy a Harley-Davidson aren't just buying a motorcycle. They are buying the Harley experience—freedom, independence, power, and authenticity.

● **Core product:** People who buy a Harley-Davidson are buying more than just a motorcycle. They are buying self-expression, lifestyles, aspirations, and dreams.

John Powell Photographer/Alamy Stock Photo

● And people who buy a Harley-Davidson motorcycle are buying much more than a machine that gets them from point A to point B:[3]

> Remove the helmets and the leathers of a hard-core Harley enthusiast, and there's no telling whom you'll find. It might be a guy with tattoos and unruly hair, but it's just as likely to be a CEO, investment banker, or gourmet chef. More than 12 percent of Harley purchasers today are women. "Harley brings together all walks of life," says Harley's chief marketing officer. "You'll find a neurosurgeon talking and riding with a janitor. It's a family."
>
> But no matter who they are, Harley-Davidson disciples share a common, deeply held attraction to the brand. The core Harley appeals are these: freedom, independence, power, and authenticity. A Harley renews your spirits and announces your freedom and independence. "It's all about the *experience*," says an analyst, "one forged in heavy metal thunder, living free, and peeling wheel down Route 66. It's an experience that allows middle-aged accountants to don black, studded leather and forget about debits and credits for a little while."

At the second level, product planners must turn the core benefit into an *actual product*. They need to develop product and service features, a design, a quality level, a brand name, and packaging. For example, a Harley-Davidson motorcycle is an actual product. Its name, styling, features, sounds, parts, and other attributes have all been carefully combined to deliver the core customer values of freedom and independence.

Finally, product planners must build an *augmented product* around the core benefit and actual product by offering additional consumer services and benefits. Thus, when consumers buy a Harley, Harley-Davidson and its dealers also give buyers a warranty on parts and workmanship, quick repair services when needed, a showroom full of accessories, and web and mobile sites to use if they have problems or questions. The Harley Owners Group (H.O.G.) provides additional benefits such as roadside assistance, H.O.G. rallies and other events, and regular issues of *HOG* magazine, packed with H.O.G. news, product information, riding stories, and more.

Consumers see products as complex bundles of benefits that satisfy their needs. When developing products, marketers first must identify the *core customer value* that consumers seek from the product. They must then design the *actual* product and find ways to *augment* it to create customer value and a full and satisfying brand experience.

Product and Service Classifications

Products and services fall into two broad classes based on the types of consumers who use them: *consumer products* and *industrial products*. Broadly defined, products also include other marketable entities such as experiences, organizations, persons, places, and ideas.

Consumer Products

Consumer product

A product bought by final consumers for personal consumption.

Convenience product

A consumer product that customers usually buy frequently, immediately, and with minimal comparison and buying effort.

Consumer products are products and services bought by final consumers for personal consumption. Marketers usually classify these products and services further based on how consumers go about buying them. Consumer products include *convenience products, shopping products, specialty products*, and *unsought products*. These products differ in the ways consumers buy them and, therefore, in how they are marketed (see ● **Table 8.1**).

Convenience products are consumer products and services that customers usually buy frequently, immediately, and with minimal comparison and buying effort. Examples include laundry detergent, candy, magazines, and fast food. Convenience products are usually low priced, and marketers place them in many locations to make them readily available when customers need or want them.

● **Table 8.1 | Marketing Considerations for Consumer Products**

Marketing Considerations	Type of Consumer Product			
	Convenience	**Shopping**	**Specialty**	**Unsought**
Customer buying behavior	Frequent purchase; little planning, little comparison or shopping effort; low customer involvement	Less frequent purchase; much planning and shopping effort; comparison of brands on price, quality, and style	Strong brand preference and loyalty; special purchase effort; little comparison of brands; low price sensitivity	Little product awareness or knowledge (or, if aware, little or even negative interest)
Price	Low price	Higher price	Highest price	Varies
Distribution	Widespread distribution; convenient locations	Selective distribution in fewer outlets	Exclusive distribution in only one or a few outlets per market area	Varies
Promotion	Mass promotion by the producer	Advertising and personal selling by both the producer and resellers	More carefully targeted promotion by both the producer and resellers	Aggressive advertising and personal selling by the producer and resellers
Examples	Toothpaste, magazines, and laundry detergent	Major appliances, televisions, furniture, and clothing	Luxury goods, such as Rolex watches or fine crystal	Life insurance and Red Cross blood donations

Shopping product
A consumer product that the customer, in the process of selecting and purchasing, usually compares on such attributes as suitability, quality, price, and style.

Specialty product
A consumer product with unique characteristics or brand identification for which a significant group of buyers is willing to make a special purchase effort.

Unsought product
A consumer product that the consumer either does not know about or knows about but does not normally consider buying.

Industrial product
A product bought by individuals and organizations for further processing or for use in conducting a business.

Shopping products are less frequently purchased consumer products and services that customers compare carefully on suitability, quality, price, and style. When buying shopping products and services, consumers spend much time and effort in gathering information and making comparisons. Examples include furniture, clothing, major appliances, and hotel services. Shopping product marketers usually distribute their products through fewer outlets but provide deeper sales support to help customers in their comparison efforts.

Specialty products are consumer products and services with unique characteristics or brand identifications for which a significant group of buyers is willing to make a special purchase effort. Examples include specific brands of cars, high-priced photography equipment, designer clothes, gourmet foods, and the services of medical or legal specialists. A Lamborghini automobile, for example, is a specialty product because buyers are usually willing to travel great distances to buy one. Buyers normally do not compare specialty products. They invest only the time needed to reach dealers carrying the wanted brands.

Unsought products are consumer products that a consumer either does not know about or knows about but does not normally consider buying. Most major new innovations are unsought until consumers become aware of them through marketing. Classic examples of known but unsought products and services are life insurance, preplanned funeral services, and blood donations to the Red Cross. By their very nature, unsought products require a lot of promoting, personal selling, and other marketing efforts.

Industrial Products

Industrial products are those products purchased for further processing or for use in conducting a business. Thus, the distinction between a consumer product and an industrial product is based on the *purpose* for which the product is purchased. If a consumer buys a lawn mower for use around home, the lawn mower is a consumer product. If the same consumer buys the same lawn mower for use in a landscaping business, the lawn mower is an industrial product.

The three groups of industrial products and services are materials and parts, capital items, and supplies and services. *Materials and parts* include raw materials as well as manufactured materials and parts. *Capital items* are industrial products that aid in the buyer's production or operations, including installations and accessory equipment. The final group of industrial products is *supplies and services*. Supplies include operating supplies and repair and maintenance items. Business services include maintenance and repair services and business advisory services.

Organizations, Persons, Places, and Ideas

In addition to tangible products and services, marketers have broadened the concept of a product to include other market offerings: organizations, persons, places, and ideas.

Organizations often carry out activities to "sell" the organization itself. *Organization marketing* consists of activities undertaken to create, maintain, or change the attitudes and behavior of target consumers toward an organization. Both profit and not-for-profit organizations practice organization marketing. Business firms sponsor corporate marketing campaigns to market themselves, their images, and their ideals.

For example, outdoor apparel and gear marketer Patagonia does little or no advertising for specific products. Instead, its marketing promotes the company's environmental purpose and values, whether its print ads promoting responsible consumption or an activist social media campaign to save the world's public lands. According to Patagonia's European marketing director, when someone buys something from Patagonia, "we want to make sure… they understand why we exist as a company, how we have chosen to bring that product into existence, what they need to use that product for and how they will—with our support— care for that garment." Patagonia's marketing is about more than just selling products. It's about "building a movement" based on the values it shares with its communities.[4]

People can also be thought of as products. *Person marketing* consists of activities undertaken to create, maintain, or change attitudes or behavior toward particular people. People ranging from presidents, entertainers, and sports figures to professionals such as doctors, lawyers, and architects use person marketing to build their reputations. And businesses, charities, and other organizations use well-known personalities to help sell their products or causes. For example, tennis superstar and entrepreneur Serena Williams earns nearly $20 million a year from endorsements for brands ranging from Nike, Gatorade, and Beats to JPMorgan Chase. Williams herself has become a marketable brand. She recently launched a fashion line—Serena—inspired by her own personal model of femininity, strength, and authenticity.[5]

Place marketing involves activities undertaken to create, maintain, or change attitudes or behavior toward particular places. Cities, states, regions, and even entire nations compete to attract tourists, new residents, conventions, and company offices and factories. For example, Detroit's city website celebrates Detroit as "American's Great Comeback City" and promotes the best places to eat, things to do, and events to attend. Tourism Ireland tells travelers to "Fill your heart with Ireland—discover heart-warming moments and spectacular sight." It tells businesses, "Ireland, right place right time—our people and your business, a winning combination."[6]

Ideas can also be marketed. In one sense, all marketing is the marketing of an idea, whether it is the general idea of brushing your teeth or the specific idea that Crest toothpastes "improve the health of your smile." Here, however, we narrow our focus to the marketing of *social ideas*. This area has been called **social marketing** and consists of using traditional business marketing concepts and tools to encourage behaviors that will create individual and societal well-being.

Social marketing
The use of traditional business marketing concepts and tools to encourage behaviors that will create individual and societal well-being.

Many companies engage in social marketing to support ideas they believe in. ● Microsoft's "Make What's Next" campaign encourages girls to enter tech and science fields. The company promotes the program with inspirational ads, social media videos and events, and a dedicated website. The website also offers an experiential tool called Career Explorer, powered by professional LinkedIn, that shows girls how to pursue their passions and skills in

● Marketing ideas: Microsoft's "Make What's Next" campaign markets the company's support for the idea of encouraging girls to enter tech and science fields.
Microsoft Corporation

specific areas. "When we encourage girls to pursue science, technology, engineering, and math (STEM)," says Microsoft, "we double the potential to solve problems. If she stays in STEM, she could be the one to change the world."[7]

Social marketing programs cover a wide range of issues. The Ad Council of America (www.adcouncil.org), for example, has developed dozens of social advertising campaigns involving issues ranging from health care, education, and environmental sustainability to preventing teen bullying and confronting sexual harassment. But social marketing involves much more than just advertising. It involves a broad range of marketing strategies and marketing mix tools designed to bring about beneficial social change.[8]

Author Comment | Now that we've answered the "What is a product?" question, we dig into the specific decisions that companies must make when designing and marketing products and services.

Product and Service Decisions

OBJECTIVE 8-2 Describe the decisions companies make regarding their individual products and services, product lines, and product mixes.

Marketers make product and service decisions at three levels: individual product decisions, product line decisions, and product mix decisions. We discuss each in turn.

Individual Product and Service Decisions

Figure 8.2 shows the important decisions in the development and marketing of individual products and services. We will focus on decisions about *product attributes, branding, packaging, labeling and logos,* and *product support services.*

Product and Service Attributes

Developing a product or service involves defining the benefits that it will offer. These benefits are communicated and delivered by product attributes such as *quality, features,* and *style and design.*

Product quality
The characteristics of a product or service that bear on its ability to satisfy stated or implied customer needs.

Product Quality. **Product quality** is one of the marketer's major positioning tools. Quality affects product or service performance; thus, it is closely linked to customer value and satisfaction. In the narrowest sense, quality can be defined as "no defects." But most marketers go beyond this narrow definition. Instead, they define quality in terms of creating customer value and satisfaction. The American Society for Quality defines quality as the characteristics of a product or service that bear on its ability to satisfy stated or implied customer needs. Similarly, Siemens defines quality this way: "Quality is when our customers come back and our products don't."[9]

Companies can take any of several approaches to product quality. *Total quality management (TQM)* is an approach in which all the company's people are involved in constantly improving the quality of products, services, and business processes. For most top companies, customer-driven quality has become a way of doing business.[10] Today, companies are taking a *return-on-quality (ROQ)* approach, viewing quality as an investment and holding quality efforts accountable for bottom-line results.

Product quality has two dimensions: level and consistency. In developing a product, the marketer must first decide on a *quality level* that will support the product's positioning. Here, product quality means *performance quality*—the product's ability to perform its functions. For example, a Rolls-Royce provides higher performance quality than a Chevrolet: It has a smoother ride, lasts longer, and provides more handcraftsmanship, custom design, luxury, and "creature comforts." Companies rarely try to offer the highest possible performance quality level; few customers want or can afford the high levels of quality offered in products such as a Rolls-Royce automobile, a Viking range, or a Rolex watch. Instead, companies choose a quality level that matches target market needs and the quality levels of competing products.

● FIGURE 8.2
Individual Product Decisions

Don't forget Figure 8.1. The focus of all of these decisions is to create core customer value.

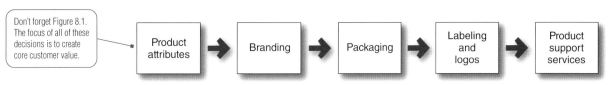

Beyond quality level, high quality also can mean high levels of quality consistency. Here, product quality means *conformance quality*—freedom from defects and consistency in delivering a targeted level of performance. All companies should strive for high levels of conformance quality. In this sense, a Chevrolet can have just as much quality as a Rolls-Royce. Although a Chevy doesn't perform at the same level as a Rolls-Royce, it can just as consistently deliver the quality that customers pay for and expect.

Similarly, the Chick-fil-A fast-food chain doesn't aspire to provide gourmet dining experiences. But it excels at delighting customers by exceeding their quality expectations day in and day out. And Americas Best Value Inn—the fast-growing economy hotel chain—doesn't offer a luxury Ritz-Carlton experience. However, it consistently delivers on its promise to gives customers "The Best Bang for Your Buck." Its locally owned and operated hotels consistently "provide an honest stay and reliable service." By consistently meeting and exceeding customer quality expectations, Americas Best Value Inn recently earned the J.D. Power Award for highest customer satisfaction among the nation's economy hotels. "A good stay doesn't require any complicated formula," says the hotel. "We focus on a comfortable bed to sleep in, complimentary breakfast each morning, and the promise of a great day ahead. It is that simple."[11]

Product Features. A product can be offered with varying features. A stripped-down model, one without any extras, is the starting point. The company can then create higher-level models by adding more features. Features are a competitive tool for differentiating the company's product from competitors' products. Being the first producer to introduce a valued new feature is one of the most effective ways to compete.

How can a company identify new features and decide which ones to add? It should periodically survey buyers who have used the product and ask these questions: How do you like the product? Which specific features of the product do you like most? Which features could we add to improve the product? The answers to these questions provide the company with a rich list of feature ideas. The company can then assess each feature's *value* to customers versus its *cost* to the company. Features that customers value highly in relation to costs should be added.

Product Style and Design. Another way to add customer value is through distinctive *product style and design*. Design is a larger concept than style. *Style* simply describes the appearance of a product. Styles can be eye catching or yawn producing. A sensational style may grab attention and produce pleasing aesthetics, but it does not necessarily make the product *perform* better. Unlike style, *design* is more than skin deep—it goes to the very heart of a product. Good design contributes to a product's usefulness as well as to its looks.

Good design doesn't start with brainstorming new ideas and making prototypes. Design begins with observing customers, understanding their needs, and shaping their product-use experience. Product designers should think less about technical product specifications and more about how customers will use and benefit from the product. For example, consider PopSockets:[12]

PopSockets, those back-of-the-phone buttons you see everywhere, didn't start in a big-company design lab. They began when a philosophy professor's iPhone earbuds kept getting tangled up in his pocket and he needed something to wrap his cord around. He observed that many others experienced this same problem, along with a boatload of other frustrations in handling and using their smartphones. So he invested his life savings, taught himself how to use 3-D design software, and set out to create a solution. After 100 tries, he came up with PopSockets. The collapsible, silver-dollar-size buttons in colorful, trendy designs are useful for a lot more than just cord storage. They're also handy for gripping the device, propping it up on an angle for hands-free use, and preventing drops and breaks by selfie-takers. Thanks to user-centered design, PopSocket sales have soared to tens of millions of units per year.

Branding

Brand
A name, term, sign, symbol, or design or a combination of these that identifies the products or services of one seller or group of sellers and differentiates them from those of competitors.

Perhaps the most distinctive skill of professional marketers is their ability to build and manage brands. A **brand** is a name, term, sign, symbol, or design or a combination of these that identifies the maker or seller of a product or service. Consumers view a brand as an important part of a product, and branding can add value to a consumer's purchase. Customers attach meanings to brands and develop brand relationships. As a result, brands have meaning well beyond a product's physical attributes.

Real Marketing 8.1

Nike Pro Hijab: Combining Branding and an Innovative Design

A world-class brand offering a well-designed, innovative product to an underserved market segment is already a success. In many ways, Nike's Pro Hijab, a sports hijab launched in 2017, was more than that. "Hijab" is an Arabic word that means "barrier" or "partition"; in clothing, it usually refers to a head covering, like a head scarf, worn by Muslim women. The Nike Pro Hijab was named one the winners of the Designs of the Year by the Design Museum in London. Hailing its potential for revolutionizing the face of sports for Muslim women, the judges were taken by the single-layer, stretchy, high-performance Hijab. Commenting on its design functionality, one of the judges said she was hugely impressed with the product as soon as she saw it; it seemed to tackle an important issue in a simple and elegant way.

Nike's decision to launch the Pro Hijab goes back to 2012, when track-and-field athlete Sarah Attar represented Saudi Arabia at the 2012 Olympics, motivating more Muslim women to take up competitive sports. In the 2016 Rio Olympics, 14 Muslim women won medals, and a record number of Muslim women athletes are expected to participate in the 2020 Olympics. For years, Muslim sportswomen who needed to participate while covered had no choice but to wear hijabs in traditional fabrics to compete. These traditional fabrics are not an ideal option for a workout; for example, cotton absorbs and retains water, which would keep perspiration on the head.

Nike put special focus on the design and style of the sports hijab, which took more than 13 months to perfect. By working with female athletes from the United Arab Emirates, Nike learned that the main requirements of Arab sportswomen were a hijab that is lightweight and more breathable. Therefore, providing more customer value meant using a lighter and softer garment, something that would be similar to Nike Pro's other products—inconspicuous and like a second skin. Additionally, Nike also recognized that different Muslim countries had their own hijab styles, so it wanted to create a design that would accommodate these different cultural preferences. Nike therefore asked local communities and advocates to make sure its protype design met the cultural requirements of their markets.

The final product included an easy pull-on design made of durable single-layer fabric. The fabric used is Nike's most breathable, a lightweight polyester mesh with small holes that are strategically placed to allow greater breathability while maintaining the opaqueness of the fabric. The back of the hijab is styled to be longer so that it cannot become untucked. Another feature of the hijab is the use of fluff threads at the neck to minimize rubbing and irritation caused as a result of sweat. The product is available in XS/S and M/L sizes, to allow for a better fit, and in the neutral colors black, white, gray, and navy blue.

Product attributes such as design, quality, brand, and logo also contributed toward a successful launch in the sportswear industry through their focus on a specific segment. Based on feedback from the athletes, the hijab's designers placed the signature Nike Swoosh just above the left ear to highlight the hijab's peak performance standard and Nike's brand values. The brand message and image was fully integrated into the advertising campaign too. The product's launch was accompanied by the "What Will They Say About You?" campaign, with an advertisement featuring five prominent female athletes from the Arab world pursuing different sports and questioning the limitations the society puts on women. Nike said that its Pro Hijab is very much in line with its "just do it" spirit of pushing oneself and is part of an ongoing cultural shift that has seen more women embracing sports than ever before. The advertisement communicated—and reinforced—its brand values by using the direct, simple, and commanding language that has been associated with the brand for a long time.

The launch of the Pro Hijab clearly fits the company's mission and vision and became the natural next step for Nike. The word "Pro" in the product's name sets it firmly within the family of similar Nike products such the Nike Pro Shorts and the Nike Pro Leggings. The Pro line uses a durable, stretchy DRI FIT fabric that is preferred by many professional athletes as it absorbs sweat and moisture well and enables them to focus more on their performance. Initially developed for golfers, this trademark fabric, first introduced in 1991, is also used by runners, football players and other athletes to feel comfortable and look stylish.

The product's packaging is simple, a black box that features the face of a woman athlete wearing the hijab. The front of the box highlights key product features and the brand message. At the top right corner of the box is the word "performance" in bold letters. The lower right side of the box has the Nike Swoosh, the brand name, and the main product quality attribute, the Dri Fit technology used for other Nike products. As a brand element, the logo helps connect with the consumers and builds the brand's association; Nike's logo is visible at two spots on the front of the package. The back of the package lists three main features of the product that matter most to users: sweat wicking

Nike collaborated with Arab athletes on the design and style of its first sports hijab.

Independent Photo Agency Srl/Alamy Stock Photo

material, breathable fabric, and full coverage of the head and neck.

As the Islamic world rapidly modernizes in the twenty-first century, Nike is reaching out to Muslims across the world and winning their loyalty. Referring to the Nike Pro Hijab, the company has stated that its decision to introduce a product designed specifically for Muslim women was meant to serve and inspire more women and girls across the Muslim world. The product is the first of its kind, and its popularity has continued to increase; in 2019, it was one of the world's most popular clothing items according to Lyst, the largest global fashion search platform. Indeed, in May 2019, Lyst reported that the demand for product rose by 125 percent over the quarter.[13]

● A classic stunt by former bargain footwear retailer Payless dramatically illustrated the power of brands in shaping consumer perceptions:[14]

As part of a viral advertising campaign to shift consumer perceptions of its brand, Payless and its marketing agency DCX Growth Accelerator created a fake luxury brand—Palessi. They put the fake name on a former Armani store in an upscale shopping mall, stocked the store with

footwear that usually sold at Payless for $19.99 to $39.99, and invited 60 VIP fashion influencers to the made-up brand's launch party. With no idea that they were looking at discount wares, the fashionistas praised the design and fabrication of the Palessi shoes and paid as much as $645 for the footwear. "It's just stunning. Elegant, sophisticated," said one shopper of a normally low-budget stiletto heel. Payless rang up the sales but later gave the influencers their money back along with free shoes. The influencers' reactions, along with the priceless "gotcha moments" when they learned they'd been pranked, were captured in campaign ad videos. According to Payless's then-chief marketer, "the campaign aimed to remind shoppers that Payless strikes the right balance of stylistic relevance and affordability." Said an analyst, "the stunt indicates how powerful branding is in today's society."

● **A classic stunt by former bargain footwear retailer Payless dramatically illustrated the power of brands in shaping perceptions. Fashion influencers paid as much as $645 for "Palessi" shoes for that normally sell for less than $40.**

Collective Brands Inc.

Branding has become so strong that today hardly anything goes unbranded. Salt is packaged in branded containers, common nuts and bolts are packaged with a distributor's label, and automobile parts—spark plugs, tires, filters—bear brand names that differ from those of the automakers. Even fruits, vegetables, dairy products, and poultry are branded—Cuties mandarin oranges, Dole Classic salads, Wonderful Pistachios, Perdue chickens, Eggland's Best eggs, and Avocados From Mexico.

Branding helps buyers in many ways. Brand names help consumers identify products that might benefit them. Brands also say something about product quality and consistency—buyers who always buy the same brand know that they will get the same features, benefits, and quality each time they buy. Branding also gives the seller several advantages. The seller's brand name and trademark provide legal protection for unique product features that otherwise might be copied by competitors. Branding helps the seller to segment markets. For example, rather than offering just one general product to all consumers, Toyota can offer the different Lexus, Toyota, and Scion brands, each with numerous sub-brands—such as Avalon, Camry, Corolla, Prius, Yaris, Tundra, and Land Cruiser.

Finally, a brand name becomes the basis on which a whole story can be built about a product's special qualities. For example, the goal of Avocados From Mexico—a not-for-profit organization that represents both Mexican avocado growers and U.S. importers and packers—is to convince U.S. consumers that avocados are a must-have snack ("No Guac. No Game!"). It wants consumers to know that the Avocados From Mexico brand stands for great avocados that make for good times, good food, and good health. To promote the brand, the organization spends $20 million a year on advertising, including big-budget ads in four consecutive Super Bowls. During last year's Super Bowl, Avocados From Mexico was the most mentioned advertiser across Instagram and Twitter and #Guacworld was the most used hashtag. As a result of such brand building, U.S. avocado sales have seen double-digit growth during the past few years, and the Avocados From Mexico brand now accounts for nearly 80 percent of all U.S. avocado sales.[15] We will discuss branding strategy in more detail later in the chapter.

Packaging

Packaging

The activities of designing and producing the container or wrapper for a product.

Packaging involves designing and producing the container or wrapper for a product. Traditionally, the primary function of the package was to hold and protect the product. In recent times, however, packaging has become an important marketing tool as well. Increased competition and clutter on retail store shelves means that packages must now perform many sales tasks—from attracting buyers to communicating brand positioning to closing the sale. Not every customer will see a brand's advertising, social media pages, or other marketing content. However, all consumers who buy and use a product will interact regularly with its packaging. Thus, the humble package represents prime marketing space.

Companies realize the power of good packaging to create immediate consumer recognition of a brand. For example, an average supermarket stocks about 30,000 items; the average Walmart supercenter carries 142,000 items. And according to recent studies, 55 percent of shoppers decide what brand to buy while shopping, and 81 percent say they have tried something new because of the packaging. In this highly competitive environment, the package may be the seller's best and last chance to influence buyers. So the package itself becomes an important promotional medium.[16]

Innovative packaging can give a company an advantage over competitors and boost sales. Distinctive packaging may even become an important part of a brand's identity. For example, an otherwise plain brown carton imprinted with the familiar curved arrow from the Amazon.com logo—variously interpreted as "a to z" or even a smiley face—leaves no doubt as to who shipped the package sitting at your doorstep. And Tiffany's distinctive blue boxes have come to embody the exclusive jewelry retailer's premium legacy and positioning. As the company puts it, "Glimpsed on a busy street or resting in the palm of a hand, Tiffany Blue Boxes make hearts beat faster and epitomize Tiffany's great heritage of elegance, exclusivity, and flawless craftsmanship."[17]

Poorly designed packages can cause headaches for consumers and lost sales for the company. Think about all those hard-to-open packages, such as packaging with finger-splitting wire twist-ties or sealed plastic clamshell containers that cause "wrap rage" and send thousands of people to the hospital each year with lacerations and puncture wounds. Another packaging issue is overpackaging—as when a tiny USB flash drive in an oversized cardboard and plastic display package is delivered in a giant corrugated shipping carton. Overpackaging creates an incredible amount of waste, frustrating those who care about the environment.

In making packaging decisions, the company also must heed growing environmental concerns. Fortunately, many companies have gone "green" by reducing their packaging and using environmentally responsible packaging materials. Product safety has also become a major packaging concern in recent years. ● For example, consider P&G's Tide PODS unit-dose laundry detergent packets. To prevent children from accidentally eating the colorful, candy-looking but toxic packets, P&G spent three years perfecting a Child-Guard Pack and Child Guard Tub. These packaging innovations likely saved P&G's Tide PODS and other unit-dose brands.[18]

Labeling and Logos

Labels and logos range from simple tags attached to products to complex graphics that are part of the packaging. They perform several functions. At the very least, the label *identifies* the product or brand.

● **Innovative Child Guard safety packaging likely saved P&G's fast-growing Tide PODS and other unit-dose laundry detergent brands.**

Gary Armstrong

The label might also *describe* several things about the product—who made it, where it was made, when it was made, its contents, how it is to be used, and how to use it safely. Finally, the label and logo help to *promote* the brand and engage customers. For many companies, labels and logos have become important elements in broader marketing campaigns.

Labels and logos must be redesigned from time to time. Companies have always taken great care to craft simple, easily recognized logos that quickly identify their brands and trigger positive consumer associations. However, in today's digital world, brand logos are being asked to do much more. A logo is no longer just a static symbol placed on a printed page, package, TV ad, billboard, or store display. Instead, todays logos must also meet the demands of an ever-more-diverse set of media. ● Thus, many brands are adapting their logos to meet the needs of new digital devices and interactive platforms such as mobile apps and social media. From Google and Uber to Southwest Airlines, Pizza Hut, and Audi, it's out with the old and in with the new:

Most logo changes focus on creating simpler, brighter, more modern designs that present better on digital screens and platforms. Pizza Hut's new logo consists of a simple pizza-shaped medallion with the brand name and familiar roof symbol reversed out in white. Southwest went from black all-capital letters beneath a jumbo jet image to bright blue letters in title format accompanied by its signature heart icon in rainbow colors. The old IHOP logo had white letters on a blue field with a downward-curving red banner containing the word "restaurant." Now, IHOP's letters are blue on a white field, a design that stands out better against the white backgrounds on most web, mobile, and social media sites. The new logo also replaces the old frown-like "restaurant" banner with an upward curving red line under the "o" and the "p," creating a smiley face that adds a burst of happiness to the brand.

Many logos today are wordless, using only a brand symbol with no mention of the brand name at all. Think Apple, Twitter, Nike, and Airbnb. Carmaker Audi recently redesigned its logo, dropping the red Audi wordmark altogether. It turned its signature four 3D interlocking chrome rings to flat black and let the rings themselves become the logo. The new logo seems plainer but is also less restrictive and more interactive across today's digital formats, from screens inside the car to Audi's website, mobile apps, and even wearables.

● **Brand logo makeovers:** Many companies are redesigning their logos to keep them in sync with the rapidly evolving digital times.

Pizza Hut, Inc.; Southwest Airlines; International House of Pancakes, LLC, and Audi of America.

Companies need to move carefully when changing their brand logos. Customers often form strong connections to the visual representations of their brands—consider the feelings evoked by the logos of companies such as Google, Coca-Cola, Twitter, Apple, and Nike. Consumers may react strongly to changes in their favorite brand symbols. Moreover, such changes often require a huge investment. For example, Southwest's seemingly simple logo redesign requires sweeping changes that touch almost every aspect of the company's operations. Just think of all the places you see Southwest's logo—from its advertising, web, and social media activities to the graphics on its airplanes and the design of its airport gates to its corporate letterhead. Everything must be redone to reflect the new logo look, a process that requires resources and must be carried out with strategic precision.

Along with the positives, there has been a long history of legal concerns about labels and packaging. The Federal Trade Commission Act of 1914 held that false, misleading, or deceptive labels or packages constitute unfair competition. Labels can mislead customers, fail to describe important ingredients, or fail to include needed safety warnings. As a result, several federal and state laws regulate labeling. The most prominent is the Fair Packaging and Labeling Act of 1966, which set mandatory labeling requirements, encouraged voluntary industry packaging standards, and allowed federal agencies to set packaging regulations in specific industries. The Nutritional Labeling and Educational Act of 1990 requires sellers to provide detailed nutritional information on food products, and recent sweeping actions by the Food and Drug Administration (FDA) regulate the use of health-related terms such as *low fat, light, high fiber,* and *organic.* Sellers must ensure that their labels contain all the required information.

Product Support Services

Customer service is another element of product strategy. A company's offer usually includes some support services, which can be a minor part or a major part of the total offering. Later in this chapter, we will discuss services as products in themselves. Here, we discuss services that augment actual products.

Support services are an important part of the customer's overall brand experience. Lexus knows that good marketing doesn't end with making a sale. Keeping customers happy *after* the sale is the key to building lasting relationships. Lexus believes that if you delight the customer, and continue to delight the customer, you will have a customer for life. So Lexus dealers across the country will go to almost any lengths to take care of customers and keep them coming back:[19]

Lexus Covenant

Lexus will enter the most competitive, prestigious automobile race in the world. Over 50 years of Toyota automobile experience has culminated in the creation of Lexus cars. They will be the finest cars ever built.

Lexus will win the race because Lexus will do it right from the start. Lexus will have the finest dealer network in the industry. Lexus will treat each customer as we would a guest in our home.

If you think you can't you won't... If you think you can, you will! We can, we will.

● **Customer service: From the start, under the Lexus Covenant, Lexus's high-quality support services create an unmatched car ownership experience and some of the world's most satisfied car owners.**
Toyota Motor Sales, USA, Inc.

From the very start, Lexus set out to revolutionize the auto ownership experience. ● In its "Lexus Covenant," the company vows that it will make "the finest cars ever built"—high-quality cars that need little servicing. However, the covenant also vows to value customers as important individuals and "treat each customer as we would a guest in our own home." So, when a car does need servicing, Lexus goes out of its way to make it easy and painless. Many dealers will even pick up a car and then return it when the maintenance is finished. You might even be surprised to find that they've touched up a door ding to help restore the car to its fresh-from-the-factory luster. By all accounts, Lexus has lived up to its ambitious customer-satisfaction promise. It has created what appear to be the world's most satisfied car owners. Lexus regularly tops industry customer-satisfaction ratings in both the United States and globally.

The first step in designing support services is to survey customers periodically to assess the value of current services and obtain ideas for new ones. Next, the company can take steps to fix problems and add new services that will both delight customers and yield profits to the company.

Many companies use a sophisticated mix of phone, email, online, social media, mobile, and interactive voice and data technologies to provide support services that were not possible before. For example, home-improvement store Lowe's offers a vigorous dose of customer service at both its store and online locations that makes shopping easier, answers customer questions, and handles problems. Customers can access Lowe's extensive support by phone, email (CareTW@lowes.com), website, mobile app, and Twitter via @LowesCares. The Lowe's website and mobile app link to a buying guide and how-to library. In its stores, Lowe's has equipped employees with phones filled with custom apps and add-on hardware, letting them perform service tasks such as checking inventory at nearby stores, looking up specific customer purchase histories, sharing how-to videos, and checking competitor prices—all without leaving the customer's side.

Product Line Decisions

Beyond decisions about individual products and services, product strategy also calls for building a product line. A **product line** is a group of products that are closely related because they function in a similar manner, are sold to the same customer groups, are marketed through the same types of outlets, or fall within given price ranges. For example, Nike produces several lines of athletic shoes and apparel. And Google-owned Nest offers a full line of smart-home products, from smart thermostats and smoke alarms to home security cams, video boor bells, and key-free locks.

The major product line decision involves *product line length*—the number of items in the product line. The line is too short if the manager can increase profits by adding items; the line is too long if the manager can increase profits by dropping items. Managers need to analyze their product lines periodically to assess each item's sales and profits and understand how each item contributes to the line's overall performance.

A company can expand its product line in two ways: by *line filling* or *line stretching*. *Product line filling* involves adding more items within the present range of the line.

Product line
A group of products that are closely related because they function in a similar manner, are sold to the same customer groups, are marketed through the same types of outlets, or fall within given price ranges.

There are several reasons for product line filling: reaching for extra profits, satisfying dealers, using excess capacity, being the leading full-line company, and plugging holes to keep out competitors. However, line filling is overdone if it results in cannibalization (eating up sales of the company's own existing products) and customer confusion. The company should ensure that new items are noticeably different from existing ones.

Product line stretching occurs when a company lengthens its product line beyond its current range. The company can stretch its line downward, upward, or both ways. Companies located at the upper end of the market can stretch their lines *downward*. A company may stretch downward to plug a market hole or to respond to a competitor's attack on the upper end. Or it may add lower-end products to attract new entry-level buyer segments. For example, Nest stretched downward with its Nest Thermostat E to draw in more budget-conscious and first-time buyers. The Thermostat E has many of the same features as the original Nest Learning Thermostat but with a simpler design and lower resolution display at a 30 percent lower price. Companies can also stretch their product lines *upward*. Sometimes, companies stretch upward to add prestige to their current products or to reap higher margins. Ridesharing service Uber traded up with UberBLACK ("high-end rides with professional drivers"). And competitor Lyft added Lyft Lux ("add a little luxury to your ride and arrive in style").

As they grow and expand, many companies both stretch and fill their product lines. Consider BMW:[20]

● **Product line stretching and filling:** Through skillful line stretching and filling, BMW now has brands and lines that successfully appeal to the rich, the super-rich, and the hope-to-be-rich.

dpa picture alliance archive/Alamy Stock Photo

Over the years, BMW Group has transformed itself from a single-brand, five-model automaker into a powerhouse with three brands, 14 "Series," and dozens of distinct models. The company has expanded downward with its MINI Cooper line and upward with Rolls-Royce. Its BMW line brims with models from the low end to the high end to everything in between. The brand's seven "Series" lines range from the entry-level 1-Series subcompact to the luxury-compact 3-Series to the midsize 5-Series sedan to the luxurious full-size 7-Series. In between, BMW has filled the gaps with X1, X3, X4, X5, and X6 SUVs; M-Series performance models; and the i3 and i8 hybrids. ● Thus, through skillful line stretching and filling, while staying within its premium positioning, BMW now has brands and lines that successfully appeal to the rich, the super-rich, and the hope-to-be-rich.

Product Mix Decisions

Product mix (or product portfolio)
The set of all product lines and items that a particular seller offers for sale.

An organization with several product lines has a product mix. A **product mix** (or **product portfolio**) consists of all the product lines and items that a particular seller offers for sale. For example, Colgate-Palmolive is perhaps best known for its toothpaste and other oral care products. But, in fact, Colgate is a $15.5 billion consumer products company that makes and markets a full product mix consisting of many familiar lines and brands. Colgate divides its overall product mix into four major lines: oral care, personal care, home care, and pet nutrition. Each product line consists of many brands and items.[21]

A company's product mix has four important dimensions: width, length, depth, and consistency. Product mix *width* refers to the number of different product lines the company carries. ● For example, Colgate markets a fairly wide product mix, consisting of many brands that constitute the "Colgate World of Care"—products that "every day, people like you trust to care for themselves and the ones they love."

Product mix *length* refers to the total number of items a company carries within its product lines. Colgate carries several brands within each line. For example, its personal care line includes Softsoap liquid soaps and body washes, Tom's of Maine, Irish Spring bar soaps, Speed Stick deodorants, Afta, and Colgate toiletries and shaving products, among others. The Colgate home care line includes Palmolive and AJAX dishwashing products, Suavitel fabric conditioners, and Murphy Oil Soap cleaners. The pet nutrition line houses the Hill's Science Diet pet food brand.

● **The product mix: Colgate-Palmolive's nicely consistent product mix contains many brands that constitute the "Colgate World of Care"—products that "every day, people like you trust to care for themselves and the ones they love."**

Used with permission of Colgate-Palmolive Company

Product line *depth* refers to the number of versions offered of each product in the line. Colgate toothpastes come in numerous varieties, ranging from Colgate Total, Colgate Optic White, and Colgate Tartar Protection to Colgate Sensitive, Colgate Enamel Health, Colgate PreviDent, and Colgate Kids. Then each variety comes in its own special forms and formulations. For example, you can buy Colgate Total in regular, clean mint, advanced whitening, deep clean, total daily repair, 2in1 liquid gel, or any of several other versions.

Finally, the *consistency* of the product mix refers to how closely related the various product lines are in end use, production requirements, distribution channels, or some other way. Colgate's product lines are consistent insofar as they are consumer products that go through the same distribution channels. The lines are less consistent insofar as they perform different functions for buyers.

These product mix dimensions provide the handles for defining the company's product strategy. A company can increase its business in four ways. It can add new product lines, widening its product mix. In this way, its new lines build on the company's reputation in its other lines. A company can lengthen its existing product lines to become a more full-line company. It can add more versions of each product and thus deepen its product mix. Finally, a company can pursue more product line consistency—or less—depending on whether it wants to have a strong reputation in a single field or in several fields.

From time to time, a company may also have to streamline its product mix to pare out marginally performing lines and to better align with its markets. For example, in response to shifts in car-buyer preferences toward SUVs, crossovers, hatchbacks, and trucks, GM recently dropped several long-established sedan models: the Buick LaCrosse, Cadillac CT6, Cadillac XTS, Chevrolet Cruze, and Chevrolet Impala. And as the market has shifted toward electric vehicles, GM dropped its plug-in electric hybrid sedan Chevy Volt to focus more on the Chevy Bolt and other all-electric models.

Author Comment | As noted at the start of this chapter, services are "products," too—intangible ones. So all the product topics we've discussed so far apply to services as well as to physical products. However, in this section, we focus on the special characteristics and marketing needs that set services apart.

Services Marketing

OBJECTIVE 8-3 Identify the four characteristics that affect the marketing of services and the additional marketing considerations that services require.

Services have grown dramatically in recent years. They now account for more than 80 percent of the U.S. gross domestic product (GDP). Services are growing even faster in the world economy, making up 63 percent of the gross world product.[22]

Service industries vary greatly. *Governments* offer services through courts, employment services, hospitals, military services, police and fire departments, the postal service, and schools. *Private not-for-profit organizations* offer services through museums, charities, churches, colleges, foundations, and hospitals. In addition, a large number of *business organizations* offer services—airlines, banks, hotels, insurance companies, consulting firms, real estate firms, retailers, medical and legal practices, entertainment and telecommunications companies, digital and social media platforms, and others.

The Nature and Characteristics of a Service

A company must consider four special service characteristics when designing marketing programs: intangibility, inseparability, variability, and perishability (see ● **Figure 8.3**).

Service intangibility means that services cannot be seen, tasted, felt, heard, or smelled before they are bought. For example, people undergoing cosmetic surgery cannot see the result before the purchase. Airline passengers have nothing but a ticket and a promise that they and their luggage will arrive safely at the intended destination, hopefully at

Service intangibility
Services cannot be seen, tasted, felt, heard, or smelled before they are bought.

● **FIGURE 8.3**
Four Service Characteristics

Although services are "products" in a general sense, they have special characteristics and marketing needs. The biggest differences come from the fact that services are essentially intangible and that they are created through direct interactions with customers. Think about your experiences with an airline or Google versus Nike or Apple.

Intangibility

Services cannot be seen, tasted, felt, heard, or smelled before purchase

Inseparability

Services cannot be separated from their providers

Services

Variability

Quality of services depends on who provides them and when, where, and how

Perishability

Services cannot be stored for later sale or use

the same time. To reduce uncertainty, buyers look for *signals* of service quality. They draw conclusions about quality from the place, people, price, equipment, and communications that they can see. Therefore, the service provider's task is to make the service tangible in one or more ways and send the right signals about quality. Oscar Insurance Corporation does this well:[23]

● **Oscar Health personalizes and tangibilizes heath care in an industry that is notoriously complex and difficult to navigate. The young company's business is booming.**

Oscar Health Insurance

To most people, traditional health insurance companies are little more than faceless corporate entities. And for individuals who don't get their health insurance through an employer, buying insurance in the open marketplace can be a complex and uncertain process. ● Fast-growing startup Oscar Insurance Corporation is changing all that. "Insurance is confusing. Oscar makes it simple," says the company. Oscar gives you "health insurance that won't make your head explode, …and if it does, you're covered."

Predominantly web-based Oscar targets young, digitally savvy consumers with simple, affordable health insurance plans. It offers a slew of high-tech features that make the user experience more personal and tangible. For example, every member is assigned a dedicated Oscar concierge team: "You talk to the same people each time, so you get personalized help when you need it." Oscar's innovative web and mobile apps make it easier for members to manage their health care. They can use the apps for everything from accessing their health histories and account information to finding a doctor, having a free virtual visit, and getting prescriptions. Oscar also offers free 24/7 doctor consultation and telemedicine services. It's "stupidly easy," says the company. Just open the Oscar app, request a call from a doctor, and get a call back in about 10 minutes. You can even attach a picture of your symptoms.

Personalizing and tangibilizing the user experience has paid off for Oscar. At a time when larger health insurance companies are scaling back on individual health care, Oscar is surging. During the past three years, its business has soared from 40,000 members and $200 million in yearly revenues to an estimated 250,000 members and well over $1 billion in revenues.

Physical goods are produced, then stored, then later sold, and then still later consumed. In contrast, services are first sold and then produced and consumed at the same time. **Service inseparability** means that services cannot be separated from their providers, whether the providers are people or machines. If a service employee provides the service, then the employee becomes a part of the service. And customers don't just buy and use a service; they play an active role in its delivery. Customer coproduction makes *provider–customer interaction* a special feature of services marketing. Both the provider and the customer affect the service outcome.

Service variability means that the quality of services depends on who provides them as well as when, where, and how they are provided. For example, some hotels—say, Marriott—have reputations for providing better service than others. Still, within a given Marriott hotel, one registration-counter employee may be cheerful and efficient, whereas another standing just a few feet away may be grumpy and slow. Even the quality of a

Service inseparability
Services are produced and consumed at the same time and cannot be separated from their providers.

Service variability
The quality of services may vary greatly depending on who provides them and when, where, and how they are provided.

single Marriott employee's service varies according to his or her energy and frame of mind at the time of each customer encounter.

Service perishability

Services cannot be stored for later sale or use.

Service perishability means that services cannot be stored for later sale or use. Some doctors charge patients for missed appointments because the service value existed only at that point and disappeared when the patient did not show up. The perishability of services is not a problem when demand is steady. However, when demand fluctuates, service firms often have difficult problems. For example, when demand mushrooms during the end-of-year holiday season, Amazon must ramp up its delivery capacity, as must parcel delivery firms such as UPS, FedEx, and the USPS. To meet such demand surges, Amazon hires thousands of its own seasonal drivers and supplies them with vans to help deliver parcels. Other service firms often design strategies for producing a better match between demand and supply. Hotels and resorts charge lower prices in the off-season to attract more guests. And restaurants hire part-time employees to serve during peak periods.

Marketing Strategies for Service Firms

Just like manufacturing businesses, good service firms use marketing to position themselves strongly in chosen target markets. Enterprise Rent-A-Car says, "You drive. We'll take care of the rest"; Zipcar offers "An alternative to car rental." At CVS Pharmacy, "Health is everything"; Walgreens meets you "at the corner of happy & healthy." And St. Jude Children's Hospital is "Finding cures. Saving children." These and other service firms establish their positions through traditional marketing mix activities. However, because services differ from tangible products, they often require additional marketing approaches.

The Service Profit Chain

In a service business, the customer and the front-line service employee *interact* to co-create the service. Effective interaction, in turn, depends on the skills of front-line service employees and on the support processes backing these employees. Thus, successful service companies focus their attention on both their customers and their employees. They understand the **service profit chain**, which links service firm profits with employee and customer satisfaction. This chain consists of five links:[24]

Service profit chain

The chain that links service firm profits with employee and customer satisfaction.

- *Internal service quality.* Superior employee selection and training, a quality work environment, and strong support for those dealing with customers, which results in ...
- *Satisfied and productive service employees.* More satisfied, loyal, and hardworking employees, which results in ...
- *Greater service value.* More effective and efficient customer value creation, engagement, and service delivery, which results in ...
  - *Satisfied and loyal customers.* Satisfied customers who remain loyal, make repeat purchases, and refer other customers, which results in ...
  - *Healthy service profits and growth.* Superior service firm performance.

● For example, supermarket chain Wegmans—a perennial customer service champion—has developed a cult-like customer following by putting its employees first:[25]

Wegmans customers absolutely love the place. One recent survey put Wegmans at #2 in consumers perceptions among the 100 best known brands, behind only Amazon. Another survey placed Wegmans at #2 on its list of Most Loved Brands, behind only Disney. "Every time I shop at Wegmans," says one customer, "the stores are filled with people happy to be shopping there." Says another customer, "I'd never move anywhere there isn't a Wegmans."

What's the secret behind Wegmans's avid and loyal customer following? "In order to be a great place to shop, we must first be a great place to work," declares a Wegmans marketing executive. A superior customer experience begins with superbly trained, happy employees. To that end, Wegmans

● The service-profit chain: Perennial customer service champion Wegmans knows that "In order to be a great place to shop, we must first be a great place to work."

Wegmans Food Markets Inc.

● **FIGURE 8.4**
Three Types of Services
Marketing

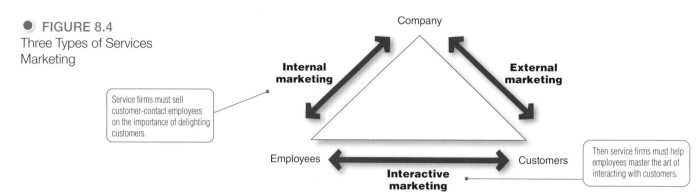

Service firms must sell customer-contact employees on the importance of delighting customers.

Then service firms must help employees master the art of interacting with customers.

invests $50 million each year on employee development and another $5 million for scholarships. It provides a flexible work environment and plenty of career advancement opportunities. Wegman's listens to employees and acts on their feedback—through "Open Door Days, Huddles, Focus Groups, and a two-way Q&A blog." "Building a culture where employees can thrive and develop in is not a one-time thing," says Wegmans, "it's something we work hard at every day." Not surprisingly, then, along with all its lofty customer satisfaction ratings, Wegmans has spent 21 straight years on the *Fortune* 100 Best Companies to Work For list, this year at #2.

Services marketing requires more than just traditional external marketing using the four Ps. ● **Figure 8.4** shows that services marketing also requires *internal marketing* and *interactive marketing*. **Internal marketing** means that the service firm must orient and motivate its customer-contact employees and supporting service people to work as a team to provide customer satisfaction. Marketers must get everyone in the organization to be customer centered. In fact, internal marketing must *precede* external marketing. For example, Wegmans starts by hiring the right people and carefully orienting and inspiring them to give unparalleled customer service. The idea is to make certain that employees themselves believe in the brand so that they can authentically deliver Wegmans's promise to customers that "Every day we give our best."

Interactive marketing means that service quality depends heavily on the quality of the buyer–seller interaction during the service encounter. In product marketing, product quality often depends little on how the product is obtained. But in services marketing, service quality depends on both the service deliverer and the quality of delivery. Service marketers, therefore, have to master interactive marketing skills. Thus, Wegmans hires only the people who fit the company's culture and instructs them carefully in the fine art of interacting with customers to satisfy their every need.

Today, as competition and costs increase and as productivity and quality decrease, more services marketing sophistication is needed. Service companies face three major marketing tasks: They want to increase their *service differentiation*, *service quality*, and *service productivity*.

Managing Service Differentiation

In these days of intense price competition, service marketers often complain about the difficulty of differentiating their services from those of competitors. To the extent that customers view the services of different providers as similar, they care less about the provider than the price. The solution to price competition is to develop a differentiated offer, delivery, and image.

The differentiated offer can include innovative features that set one company's offer apart from competitors' offers. ● For example, Emirates recently added first-class suites to its Boeing 777 airplanes featuring door-to-ceiling sliding doors, closets for hanging clothes, wireless tablets with 2,500 channels, 32-inch TV screens, personal minibars, and "inspiration kits" containing moisturizing pajamas and skin care kits. Some retailers differentiate themselves with offerings

Internal marketing
Orienting and motivating customer-contact employees and supporting service employees to work as a team to provide customer satisfaction.

Interactive marketing
Training service employees in the fine art of interacting with customers to satisfy their needs.

● **Service differentiation: Emirates offers first-class suites in its Boeing 777 airplanes featuring door-to-ceiling sliding doors, closets for hanging clothes, wireless tablets with 2,500 channels, 32-inch TV screens, personal minibars, and "inspiration kits" containing moisturizing pajamas and skin care kits.**

Christian Charisius/picture-alliance/dpa/AP Images

that take you well beyond the products they stock. At any of several large REI stores, consumers can get hands-on experience with merchandise before buying it via the store's mountain bike test trail, gear-testing stations, a huge rock climbing wall, or an in-store simulated rain shower.

Service companies can differentiate their service *delivery* by having more able and reliable customer-contact people, developing a superior physical environment in which the service product is delivered, or designing a superior delivery process. For example, many grocery chains now offer online ordering with curbside pick-up or home delivery as a better way to shop than having to drive, park, wait in line, and tote groceries home. CVS Health offers fast and convenient walk-in medical services through Minute Clinics in its own and Target stores, saving you a trip and long wait at the doctor's office for immunizations, treatment of minor illnesses, and other health-care needs. Minute Clinic gives you "The care you need on your schedule."

Finally, service companies also can work on differentiating their *images* through symbols and branding. Well-known service characters and symbols include the GEICO gecko, Progressive Insurance's Flo, McDonald's golden arches, Allstate's "good hands," the Twitter bird, and the freckled, red-haired, pig-tailed Wendy's girl. The KFC Colonel has become a popular pop culture figure, portrayed in a series of delightfully awful ads over the past few years by a dozen or more celebrities, from Rob Lowe, George Hamilton, and Norm McDonald to country singer Reba McEntire.

Managing Service Quality

A service firm can differentiate itself by delivering consistently higher quality than its competitors provide. Like manufacturers before them, most service industries have now joined the customer-driven quality movement. And like product marketers, service providers need to identify what target customers expect in regard to service quality.

Unfortunately, service quality is harder to define and judge than product quality. For instance, it is harder to agree on the quality of a haircut than on the quality of a hair dryer. Customer retention is perhaps the best measure of quality; a service firm's ability to hang onto its customers depends on how consistently it delivers value to them.

Top service companies set high service-quality standards. They watch service performance closely, both their own and that of competitors. They do not settle for merely good service—they strive for 100 percent defect-free service. A 98 percent performance standard may sound good, but using this standard, the U.S. Postal Service would lose or misdirect 412,000 pieces of mail each hour, and U.S. pharmacies would misfill more than 2.2 million prescriptions each week.[26]

Unlike product manufacturers who can adjust their machinery and inputs until everything is perfect, service quality will always vary, depending on the interactions between employees and customers. As hard as they may try, even the best companies will have an occasional late delivery, burned steak, or grumpy employee. However, good *service recovery* can turn angry customers into loyal ones. In fact, good recovery can win more customer purchasing and loyalty than if things had gone well in the first place. For example, a Marriott study of guest repeat business grouped customers stays into three groups: nothing bad happened, something bad happened but Marriott fixed the problem, and something bad happened but Marriott did not fix it. The percentages of these three groups that intended to return were 89 percent, 94 percent, and 69 percent, respectively. Thus, the best outcomes were those where Marriott turned a negative into a positive.[27]

Many companies train their frontline employees in the art of service recovery.  For example, Starbucks Baristas learn the LATTE method for recognizing disgruntled customers and addressing their concerns in positive ways. LATTE stands for *Listen* to the customer, *Acknowledge* their complaint, *Take action* by solving the problem, *Thank* them, and then *Explain* why the problem occurred. By listening and taking positive action, Starbucks employees can often turn upset customers into delighted ones.[28]

● Service quality: Good service recovery can turn angry customer into loyal ones. Starbucks trains its employees to "LATTE" upset customers: Listen, Acknowledge, Take action, Thank them, and Explain what happened.

B.O'Kane/Alamy Stock Photo

These days, social media such as Facebook, Instagram, and Twitter can help companies root out and remedy customer dissatisfaction with service. As discussed in Chapter 4, companies now monitor the digital space to spot customer issues quickly and respond in real time. For example, Southwest Airlines has a dedicated team of 29 people who respond to roughly 80,000 Facebook and Twitter posts monthly. Southwest and other airlines have become adept at responding quickly to social media inquiries and comments. A recent study shows that Southwest's response time to customers on Twitter averages just 6 minutes and 36 seconds. A quick and thoughtful response can turn a dissatisfied customer into a brand advocate.[29]

Managing Service Productivity

With their costs rising rapidly, service firms are under great pressure to increase service productivity. They can do so in several ways. They can train current employees better or hire new ones who will work harder or more skillfully. Or they can increase the quantity of their service by giving up some quality. Finally, a service provider can harness the power of technology. Although we often think of technology's power to save time and costs in manufacturing companies, it also has great—and often untapped—potential to make service industries more efficient and productive. For example, the Vdara Hotel and Spa in Las Vegas uses robots for room service. Two delivery robots—named Fetch and Jett, designed to look like dogs—can remotely call an elevator, bring food items from the hotel's café directly to guests' rooms, and alert guests via automated phone messages before they arrive.[30]

However, companies must avoid pushing productivity so hard that doing so reduces quality. Attempts to streamline a service or cut costs can make a service company more efficient in the short run. But that can also reduce its longer-run ability to innovate, maintain service quality, or respond to consumer needs and desires. For example, the Vdara in Las Vegas envisions using technology to eliminate fronts desks altogether, letting customers check in by phone. But automating such customer services might be risky if it reduces the hotel's human touch. That won't happen, says a marketing executive at MGM Resorts International, which manages the Vdara. More efficient check-in allows more personal service elsewhere. "The people that were at those front desks are still there," he says. "They're there to customize your journey, there to greet you at the car, and they're there to escort you to your room to make sure you have everything you need. You can't replace that engagement."[31]

Thus, in attempting to improve service productivity, companies must be mindful of how they create and deliver customer value. They should be careful not to take *service* out of the service. In fact, a company may purposely lower service productivity to improve service quality, in turn allowing it to maintain higher prices and profit margins.

> **Author Comment** | A brand represents everything that a product or service means to consumers. As such, brands are valuable assets to a company. For example, when you hear someone say "Coca-Cola," what do you think, feel, or remember? What about "Target"? Or "Instagram"?

Branding Strategy: Building Strong Brands

OBJECTIVE 8-4 Discuss branding strategy—the decisions companies make in building and managing their brands.

Some analysts see brands as *the* major enduring asset of a company, outlasting the company's specific products and facilities. John Stewart, former CEO of Quaker Oats, once said, "If this business were split up, I would give you the land and bricks and mortar, and I would keep the brands and trademarks, and I would fare better than you." A former CEO of McDonald's declared, "If every asset we own, every building, and every piece of equipment were destroyed in a terrible natural disaster, we would be able to borrow all the money to replace it very quickly because of the value of our brand.... The brand is more valuable than the totality of all these assets."[32]

Thus, brands are powerful assets that must be carefully developed and managed. In this section, we examine the key strategies for building and managing product and service brands.

Brand Equity and Brand Value

Brands are more than just names and symbols. They are a key element in the company's relationships with consumers. Brands represent consumers' perceptions and feelings about a product and its performance—everything that the product or the service *means* to consumers. In the final analysis, brands exist in the heads of consumers. As one well-respected marketer once said, "Products are created in the factory, but brands are created in the mind."[33]

Brand equity

The differential effect that knowing the brand name has on customer response to the product or its marketing.

A powerful brand has high *brand equity*. **Brand equity** is the differential effect that knowing the brand name has on customer response to the product and its marketing. It's a measure of the brand's ability to capture consumer preference and loyalty. A brand has positive brand equity when consumers react more favorably to it than to a generic or unbranded version of the same product. It has negative brand equity if consumers react less favorably than to an unbranded version.

Brands vary in the amount of power and value they hold in the marketplace. Some brands—such as Coca-Cola, Nike, Disney, Apple, McDonald's, Harley-Davidson, and others—become larger-than-life icons that maintain their power in the market for years, even generations. Other brands—such as Amazon, Google, Instagram, Airbnb, Uber, and Waze—create fresh consumer excitement and loyalty. These brands win in the marketplace not simply because they deliver unique benefits or reliable service. Rather, they succeed because they forge deep connections with customers.

People really do have relationships with brands. ● For example, to the world's more than 800 million Instagram users, the Instagram brand stands for something much more than just a photo and video sharing service. Instagram stands for sharing important moments with friends through pictures as they happen. It means growing closer to friends and family through shared experiences in the moment, whether it's a new puppy, someone getting married, your kid's first steps, or seeing a beautiful double rainbow in Hawaii.[34]

Ad agency Young & Rubicam's BrandAsset Valuator measures brand strength along four consumer perception dimensions: *differentiation* (what makes the brand stand out), *relevance* (how consumers feel it meets their needs), *knowledge* (how much consumers know about the brand), and *esteem* (how highly consumers regard and respect the brand). Brands with strong brand equity rate high on all four dimensions. The brand must be distinct, or consumers will have no reason to choose it over other brands. However, the fact that a brand is highly differentiated doesn't necessarily mean that consumers will buy it. The brand must stand out in

● Consumers' relationships with brands: To devoted Instagram users, the brand stands for much more than just a photo sharing service. It means growing closer to friends and family through shared experiences in the moment.

Eyal Dayan Photography

ways that are relevant to consumers' needs. Even a differentiated, relevant brand is far from a shoo-in. Before consumers will respond to the brand, they must first know about and understand it. And that familiarity must lead to a strong, positive consumer-brand connection.[35]

Thus, positive brand equity derives from consumer feelings about and connections with a brand. A brand with high brand equity is a very valuable asset. **Brand value** is the total financial value of a brand. Measuring such value is difficult. However, according to one estimate, the brand value of Apple is a whopping $316 billion, with Google at $313 billion, Amazon at $279 billion, Microsoft at $215 billion, Facebook at $161 billion, and AT&T at $106 billion. Other brands rating among the nation's most valuable include Visa, IBM, and McDonald's.[36]

Brand value

The total financial value of a brand.

High brand equity provides a company with many competitive advantages. A powerful brand enjoys a high level of consumer brand awareness and loyalty. Because consumers expect stores to carry the particular brand, the company has more leverage in bargaining with resellers. Because a brand name carries high credibility, the company can more easily launch line and brand extensions. A powerful brand also offers the company some defense against fierce price competition and other competitor marketing actions.

Above all, however, a powerful brand forms the basis for building strong and profitable customer engagement and relationships. The fundamental asset underlying brand equity is *customer equity*—the value of customer relationships that the brand creates. A powerful brand is important, but what it really represents is a profitable set of loyal customers. The proper focus of marketing is building customer equity, with brand management serving as a major marketing tool. Companies need to think of themselves not as portfolios of brands but as portfolios of customers.

Building Strong Brands

Branding poses challenging decisions to the marketer. ● **Figure 8.5** shows that the major brand strategy decisions involve *brand positioning, brand name selection, brand sponsorship,* and *brand development.*

Brand Positioning

Marketers need to position their brands clearly in target customers' minds. They can position brands at any of three levels.[37] At the lowest level, they can position the brand on *product or service attributes*. For example, FedEx can position itself on attributes such as speed, reliability, quality, and convenience of package delivery. In general, however, attributes are the least desirable level for brand positioning. Competitors can easily copy attributes. More important, customers are not interested in attributes as such—they are interested in what the attributes will do for them.

A brand can be better positioned by associating its name with a desirable *benefit*. Thus, FedEx can go beyond product attributes and talk about benefits such as the peace of mind in knowing that packages will be delivered where and when they must be. For example, for years, FedEx built its positioning around the slogan "When it absolutely, positively has to be there on time." Some successful brands positioned on benefits are Walmart (save money) and Instagram (capturing and sharing moments).

The strongest brands go beyond attribute or benefit positioning. They are positioned on strong *beliefs, values, and feelings,* engaging customers on a deep, emotional level. For example, FedEx's more recent "What we deliver by delivering" campaign goes beyond pragmatic attributes and benefits. It shows that the brand is about more than efficient package deliveries; it's about what those package deliveries mean to the people shipping and receiving them. For instance, one soft and sentimental ad—titled "The Tortoise & The Hare"—tells the story of a young girl's joy when her beloved stuffed tortoise is returned to her by FedEx after being left behind in a motel on a family vacation. Another ad—titled "Memories"—shows a young man receiving a FedEx package containing an old family photo album and being transported back to a quaint 1920s-era European wedding ceremony, presumably that of his immigrant grandparents. "To us, it's not just about packages and pallets," says the company, "it's about what we do for people and communities."[38]

Brands that connect with consumers on an emotional level can inspire substantial loyalty. Brands like Disney, Apple, Nike, Coca-Cola, and Starbucks have achieved this status with many of their customers. Customers don't just like these brands; they have strong emotional connections with them and love them unconditionally. ● For example, consider Disney. As one Walt Disney World Resort regular affirms: "I have a deep love and bond to all things Disney. Walking down Main Street and seeing Cinderella's castle for the first time always makes my heart jump. It's a moment I can guarantee and rely

> Brands are powerful assets that must be carefully developed and managed. As this figure suggests, building strong brands involves many challenging decisions.

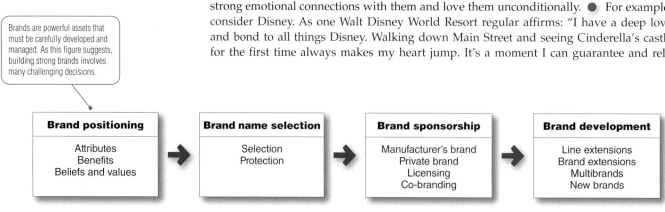

Brand positioning	**Brand name selection**	**Brand sponsorship**	**Brand development**
Attributes Benefits Beliefs and values	Selection Protection	Manufacturer's brand Private brand Licensing Co-branding	Line extensions Brand extensions Multibrands New brands

● **FIGURE 8.5** Major Brand Strategy Decisions

● **Brand positioning: Brands like Disney form strong emotional connections with customers. Says one Disney World Resort regular: """I have a deep love and bond to all things Disney."**

Art of Drawing/Alamy Stock Photo

on. A constant in my life. No matter what I'm going through...suddenly the world is filled with magic and wonder and possibilities all over again and I feel a wave of happiness flow over me and a smile creep back onto my face easily, not forced or painted on. A real, true smile."[39]

When positioning a brand, the marketer should establish a mission for the brand and a vision of what the brand must be and do. A brand is the company's promise to deliver a specific set of features, benefits, services, and experiences consistently to buyers. The brand promise must be clear, simple, and honest. Motel 6, for example, offers clean rooms, low prices, and good service but does not promise expensive furnishings or large bathrooms. In contrast, the Ritz-Carlton offers luxurious rooms and a truly memorable experience but does not promise low prices.

Brand Name Selection

A good name can add greatly to a product's success. However, finding the best brand name is a difficult task. It begins with a careful review of the product and its benefits, the target market, and proposed marketing strategies. After that, naming a brand becomes part science, part art, and a measure of instinct.

Desirable qualities for a brand name include the following: (1) It should suggest something about the product's benefits and qualities: Beautyrest, Slimfast, Facebook, Airbnb. (2) It should be easy to pronounce, recognize, and remember: iPad, Beats, Jelly Belly, Twitter, JetBlue. (3) The brand name should be distinctive: Panera, Swiffer, Zappos, Nest. (4) It should be extendable—Amazon.com began as an online bookseller but chose a name that would allow expansion into other categories. (5) The name should translate easily into foreign languages: Coca-Cola translates in Chinese to "Ke Kou Ke Le," which means "tasty fun." (6) It should be capable of registration and legal protection. A brand name cannot be registered if it infringes on existing brand names.

Choosing a new brand name is hard work. After a decade of choosing quirky names (Yahoo!, Google) or trademark-proof made-up names (Novartis, Aventis, Accenture), today's style is to build brands around names that have real meaning. For example, names like Silk (soy milk), Method (home products), Smartwater (beverages), and Snapchat (photo messaging) are simple and make intuitive sense. But with trademark applications soaring, *available* new names can be hard to find. Try it yourself. Pick a product and see if you can come up with a better name for it. How about Moonshot? Tickle? Treehugger? Avocado? Simplicity? Mindbender? Bearhug? Google them and you'll find that they are already taken.

Once chosen, the brand name must be protected. Many firms try to build a brand name that will eventually become identified with the product category. Brand names such as Kleenex, JELL-O, BAND-AID, Scotch Tape, Velcro, Formica, Magic Marker, Post-it Notes, and Ziploc have succeeded in this way. However, their very success may threaten the company's rights to the name. Many originally protected brand names—such as cellophane, aspirin, nylon, kerosene, linoleum, yo-yo, trampoline, escalator, thermos, and shredded wheat—are now generic names that any seller can use.

To protect their brands, marketers present them carefully using the word brand and the registered trademark symbol. ● For example, a recent Kleenex ad advises advertisers and others that the name Kleenex should always be followed by the registered trademark symbol and the words "Brand Tissue." "You may not realize it, but by using the name Kleenex® as a generic term for tissue," says the ad, "you risk erasing our coveted brand name that we've worked so hard for all these years."

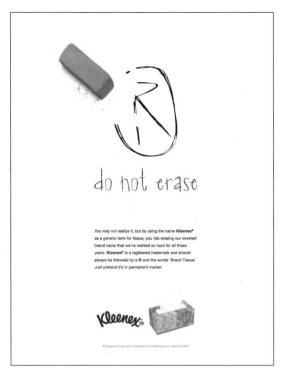

● **Protecting the brand name:** This ad asks advertisers and others to always add the registered trademark symbol and the words "Brand Tissue" to the Kleenex name, helping to keep from "erasing our coveted brand name that we've worked so hard for all these years."

©Kimberly-Clark Worldwide, Inc. Reprinted with permission.

Store brand (or private brand)
A brand created and owned by a reseller of a product or service.

Companies often go to great lengths to protect their names and brand symbols. For example, insurance company Travelers zealously pursues companies that infringe in even the slightest way on its familiar trademarked red umbrella symbol. It once threatened a tiny consulting firm in Anchorage, Alaska—Human Resource Umbrella—with legal action for hanging an umbrella above the two *l*'s in its name. Such actions might seem unneeded, but they are serious business to Travelers. "Mary Poppins might want to consider lawyering up," quips one industry lawyer.[40]

Brand Sponsorship

A manufacturer has four sponsorship options. The product may be launched as a *national brand* (or *manufacturer's brand*), as when Samsung and Kellogg sell their output under their own brand names (the Samsung Galaxy tablet or Kellogg's Frosted Flakes). Or the manufacturer may sell to resellers who give the product a *private brand* (also called a *store brand*). Although most manufacturers create their own brand names, others market licensed brands. Finally, two companies can join forces and *co-brand* a product. We discuss each of these options in turn.

National Brands versus Store Brands. National brands (or manufacturers' brands) have long dominated the retail scene. In recent times, however, increasing numbers of retailers and wholesalers have created their own **store brands** (or **private brands**). Store brands have been gaining strength for decades, but recent years have seen a store-brand boom.

Many large retailers skillfully market a deep assortment of store-brand merchandise. For example, Kroger's private brands—the Kroger house brand, Private Selection, Heritage Farm, Simple Truth (natural and organic), Psst, Check This Out (savings), and others—add up to a whopping 25 percent of the giant grocery retailer's sales, nearly $23 billion worth annually. At thrifty grocery chain ALDI, more than 90 percent of sales come from private brands such as Baker's Choice, Friendly Farms, Simply Nature, and Mama Cozzi's Pizza Kitchen. Even online retailer Amazon has developed a stable of private brands, including AmazonBasics (mostly electronics), Amazon Elements (nutritional supplements), Strathwood (outdoor furniture), GoodThreads (menswear), and Denali (tools).[41]

Store brands were once known as "generic" or "no-name" brands. Online grocery retailer Brandless still positions them that way, claiming that its customers avoid the "brand tax" that name-brand products levy to cover the costs of building and promoting their brands.[42] However, most of today's store brands have shed their image as less expensive knockoffs of national brands. Store brands now offer much greater selection, and they are rapidly achieving name-brand quality. In fact, retailers such as Target and Trader Joe's are out-innovating many of their national-brand competitors. ● Kroger even offers a Kroger brand guarantee— "Try it, like it, or get the national brand free." As a result, consumers are becoming loyal to store brands for reasons besides price. In some cases, consumers are even willing to pay more for store brands that have been positioned as gourmet or premium items. Beyond just price and value, the customer experience has become an important motive behind store brand success (see Real Marketing 8.2).

In the so-called *battle of the brands* between national and private brands, retailers have many advantages. They control what products they stock, where they go on the shelf, what prices they charge, and which ones they will feature in local promotions. Retailers often price their store brands lower than comparable national brands and feature the price differences in side-by-side comparisons on store shelves. Although store brands can be hard to establish and costly to stock and promote, they also yield higher profit margins for

● **Store brands:** Kroger's store brands—from Private Selection to Simple Truth—account for 25 percent of the grocery retailer's sales. Kroger even offers a "Try it, like it, or get the national brand free" guarantee.

Al Behrman/AP Images

Real Marketing 8.2 | Store Brands: Price Is Important, but It's More about the Customer Experience

Store brands are surging, grabbing market share from national brands in categories ranging from groceries and apparel to household goods, consumer electronics, and tools. Saving money is part of the reason. But gone are the days when store brands were little more than cheap, no-name knockoffs. Today's store brands often equal national brands in quality, and they are backed by retailers with reputations that match or exceed those of national brand manufacturers. For example, who do you have a closer relationship with, Kraft or Trader Joe's? Wrangler or Target?

Beyond offering good value, large retailers offer something else that brand-name manufacturers can't—shopping convenience and selection across a wide range of products. Store brands help take the work out of buying. Today's shoppers are often overwhelmed with options. Store brands can reduce the time and mental effort needed to make brand choices. For example, Costco affixes its highly successful Kirkland Signature brand to products in a dozen or more categories, from food and clothing to health and beauty items, household and cleaning goods, and even pet supplies. So whether you're buying laundry detergent, baby wipes, organic chicken stock, or a no-iron dress shirt, brand choice at Costco is easier.

Similarly, a single trip to Target brings customers face-to-face with a broad selection of store brands that includes Archer Farms and Market Pantry (food and grocery), A New Day (women's apparel), Simply Balanced (organic and healthy foods), Threshold (premium home goods), Room Essentials (budget-friendly home goods), Goodfellow & Co, (menswear), JoyLab (women's fashion performance), Cat & Jack (children's apparel), and Up & Up (low-priced essentials in various categories). If you like Target, chances are good that you will like its store brands too. Whereas Target has struggled in recent years in the murky retail market, its store brands have been a beacon. Target now boasts more than 30 store brands, many of them billion-dollar-a-year brands. For example, just one year after its launch, A New Day became a billion-dollar brand. Cat & Jack children's apparel has spurted to a mammoth $2 billion a year.

Unlike the early days, consumers have learned to trust major store brands, just as they trust the stores that sell them. For example, customers flock to Trader Joe's *because* of its store brands, which are about all that the trendy retailer sells. Trader Joe's sells novel brands that you just can't get anywhere else, at great value for the price and backed by a no-questions-asked refund policy.

Are Trader Joe's brands really as good as national brands? In many cases, they are produced by the same manufacturers. Trader Joe's makes very few if any of the products it sells. Instead, it partners with third-party producers, many of them national brand manufacturers who agree to sell some of their products under Trader Joe's labels. Although the retailer is notoriously tight-lipped about the identity of its suppliers, analysts have sleuthed out likely makers of many Trader Joe's products. These include Wonderful Pistachios, Naked Juice, Tate's Bake Shop, Tribe Mediterranean Foods, Snack Factory, Stauffer's, and big conglomerates like ConAgra (maker of Hunt's brand foods). But Trader Joe's fans don't think of the retailer's wares as "generics" sourced elsewhere. "[They think] 'it's Trader Joe's—that's the brand,'" says an analyst, "and it's a special brand you can only get here."

When it comes to marketing their brands, retailers have another big advantage over name-brand marketers—direct customer access and control over the customer experience. Perhaps no retailer knows this better than Amazon. Amazon launched its first store brand—Pinzon bedding and bath products—just over a decade ago. Since then, Amazon has launched a blitz of private brands in almost every imaginable category. Today, Amazon sells more than 4,600 unique products across more than 100 of its own brands. That makes good sense. Once on Amazon.com, customers have access to a broad selection of Amazon store brands that reduce buying uncertainty and make filling their shopping carts a lot easier. Why spend time evaluating a long list of brands when you can just buy an AmazonBasics cable or battery or bath towel and trust that you'll be getting good quality and value (confirmed by customer reviews)?

AmazonBasics is Amazon's bread-and-butter store brand. It covers a wide range of everyday electronics and household items, from electronics accessories and batteries to bedsheets, bath towels, knife sets, and yoga mats. The Amazon Essentials brand covers basic clothing items, and Amazon Elements includes vitamins, supplements, and other health-related items, pitched as "Premium Product. Transparent Origins. Exclusive to Amazon."

But Amazon is now moving rapidly beyond Basics, Essentials, and Elements toward store brands with more fashion and flair. Its more-recently launched store brands include the likes of Lark & Ro (sleek women's wear), Mae (intimate apparel), Franklin Tailored (men's dress wear), Buttoned Down (men's dress shirts), Goodthreads (men's casual wear), Scout + Ro (children's clothing), Presto! (bio-based household cleaners), Wag (pet products), Mama Bear (baby products), and Happy Belly (gourmet snack foods).

Despite their newness, Amazon's store brands are soaring. Last year alone, sales of Amazon-owned brands reached $7.5 billion, triple the sales of two years earlier. AmazonBasics brand batteries now account for more than 30 percent of all batteries sold, beating out name-brand Duracell. And Amazon Elements Baby Wipes are poised to soon overtake Pampers and Huggies. Amazon's store brands are helping the online

Store brands: Amazon has launched a blitz of private brands in almost every imaginable category. Why spend time evaluating a long list of brands when you can just buy an AmazonBasics product and trust that you'll be getting good quality and value (confirmed by customer reviews)?

Gary Armstrong

retailer dominate in other unexpected categories as well. For example, including sales of its own and national brands, experts predict that Amazon will soon pass Walmart as the nation's largest apparel and footwear retailer, with apparel sales reaching $85 billion by 2020. An increasing share of those apparel sales will come from Amazon's own brands.

It's easy to understand the dramatic growth of store brands that have Amazon in the name— AmazonBasics, Amazon Essentials, and Amazon Elements. When shoppers see the trusted Amazon name on an everyday product, they believe that they'll get good quality at a fair price. Amazon Prime will deliver it to their doorsteps within a few hours or a few days, and if they have issues with the product, Amazon will fix things without question.

But for store brands that don't include its name, Amazon must build customer trust, satisfaction, and advocacy. In its usual fashion, with its store brands, Amazon is putting the customer experience before short-term profits. As just one example, Amazon representatives recently met with fashion designer Jackie Wilson to discuss making a women's knit top that would be sold under an Amazon private label. Wilson later reported that Amazon's quality specifications are on par with those of name-brand apparel sellers. "They are not concerned at all about how many units they sell, and they're not focused on margins," says Wilson, whose company makes clothing for Kohl's, American Eagle Outfitters, and JCPenney. "They're concerned about customer satisfaction. They want five-star reviews."[43]

---

the reseller. And they give resellers exclusive products that cannot be bought from competitors, resulting in greater store traffic and loyalty. Retailer Trader Joe's, which carries approximately 90 percent store brands, largely controls its own brand destiny rather than relying on producers to make and manage the brands it needs to serve its customers best.

To compete with store brands, national brands must sharpen their value propositions, especially when appealing to today's more frugal consumers. Many national brands are fighting back by rolling out more discounts and coupons to defend their market shares. In the long run, however, leading brand marketers must compete by investing in new brands, new features, and quality improvements that set them apart. They must design strong advertising programs to maintain high awareness and preference. And they must find ways to partner with major distributors to find distribution economies and improve joint performance.

Licensing. Most manufacturers take years and spend millions to create their own brand names. However, some companies license names or symbols previously created by other manufacturers, names of well-known celebrities, or characters from popular movies and books. For a fee, any of these can provide an instant and proven brand name.

Apparel and accessories sellers pay large royalties to adorn their products—from blouses to ties and linens to luggage—with the names or initials of well-known fashion innovators such as Calvin Klein, Tommy Hilfiger, Gucci, or Armani. Sellers of children's products attach an almost endless list of character names to clothing, toys, school supplies, linens, dolls, lunch boxes, cereals, and other items. Licensed character names range from classics such as Sesame Street, Disney, Star Wars, Scooby Doo, Hello Kitty, SpongeBob SquarePants, and Dr. Seuss characters to the more recent Doc McStuffins, Monster High, Frozen, and Minions. And currently, numerous top-selling retail toys are products based on television shows and movies.

Name and character licensing has grown rapidly in recent years. Annual retail sales of licensed products worldwide have grown from only $4 billion in 1977 to $55 billion in 1987 and almost $300 billion today. ● The Smurfs is a Belgian TV brand based on the lives of small blue creatures that live in mushrooms. Created in 1958 as a series of comic characters, The Smurfs today are a multi-million-dollar licensing company selling products under the Smurfs brand name like video games, toys, magazines, and school items. In 2011, *The Smurfs* feature film was released, which gave a boost to the popularity of the Smurfs and the sales of its licensed products.[44]

Co-branding

The practice of using the established brand names of two different companies on the same product.

● After release of the movie *The Smurfs*, the popularity of its characters and branded offerings, including shows, games, toys, school items, and clothing, rose considerably.

Moviestore collection Ltd./Alamy Stock Photo

Co-branding. **Co-branding** occurs when two established brand names of different companies are used on the same product. Co-branding offers many advantages. Because each brand operates in a different category, the combined brands create broader consumer appeal and greater brand equity. For example, Uber partnered with Spotify to allow you to control the music during your Uber ride. Sherwin-Williams and Pottery Barn joined forces to create a special collection of Sherwin-Williams paint colors designed to perfectly coordinate with Pottery Barn's furnishings and accents. And Taco Bell and Doritos teamed up to create the Doritos Locos Taco. Taco Bell sold more than 100 million of the tacos in just the first 10 weeks. It quickly added Cool Ranch and Fiery versions and has since sold more than a billion. More than just co-branding, these companies are "co-making" these products.

Co-branding can take advantage of the complementary strengths of two brands. It also allows a company to expand its existing brand into a category it might otherwise have difficulty entering alone. For example, Yale and Nest co-branded the Nest × Yale lock, a key-free deadbolt lock that connects to the Nest app and lets people lock and unlock their doors from anywhere. The Nest × Yale arrangement gives Yale a presence in the smart home market. At the same time, it adds another device to Nest's product portfolio, complete with Yale's long-established lock expertise and the trusted Yale name.

Co-branding can also have limitations. Such relationships usually involve complex legal contracts and licenses. Co-branding partners must carefully coordinate their advertising, sales promotion, and other marketing efforts. Finally, when co-branding, each partner must trust that the other will take good care of its brand. If something damages the reputation of one brand, it can tarnish the co-brand as well.

Brand Development

A company has four choices when it comes to developing brands (see ● **Figure 8.6**). It can introduce *line extensions, brand extensions, multibrands*, or *new brands*.

Line extension

Extending an existing brand name to new forms, colors, sizes, ingredients, or flavors of an existing product category.

Line Extensions. **Line extensions** occur when a company extends existing brand names to new forms, colors, sizes, ingredients, or flavors of an existing product category. For example, over the years, KFC has extended its "finger lickin' good" chicken lineup well beyond original recipe, bone-in Kentucky fried chicken. It now offers grilled chicken, boneless fried chicken, chicken tenders, hot wings, chicken bites, chicken popcorn nuggets, chicken sandwiches, and KFC Go Cups—chicken and potato wedges in a handy car-cup holder that lets customers snack on the go.

A company might introduce line extensions as a low-cost, low-risk way to introduce new products. Or it might want to meet consumer desires for variety, use excess capacity, or simply command more shelf space from resellers. However, line extensions involve some risks. An overextended brand name might cause consumer confusion or lose some of its specific meaning.

At some point, additional extensions might add little value to a line. For instance, the original Doritos Tortilla Chips have morphed into a U.S. roster of more than 20 different types of chips and flavors, plus dozens more in foreign markets. Flavors include everything from Nacho Cheese and Taco flavor to Tapatío, Spicy Sweet Chili, and Salsa Verde. Or how about spicy chicken flavored Late Night or garlic shrimp flavored Royal, served up in Japan? Although the line is doing great—Doritos is the number-two chip brand in the United States (Lay's is number one)—the original Doritos chips now seem like just another flavor.[45] And how much would adding yet another flavor steal from Doritos' own sales versus those of competitors? A line extension works best when it takes sales away from competing brands, not when it "cannibalizes" the company's other items.

● **FIGURE 8.6**
Brand Development Strategies

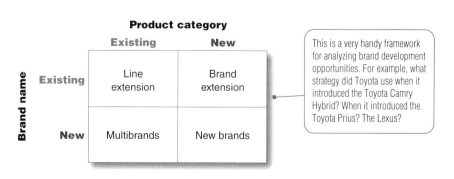

Brand extension

Extending an existing brand name to new product categories.

Brand Extensions. A **brand extension** extends a current brand name to new or modified products in a new category. For example, most consumers know the Birkenstock brand for its classic premium sandals and other footwear. And it's no surprise that Birkenstock has added other apparel and accessories items to its lines, such as legwear, belts, and bags. But in recent years, Birkenstock has extended its brand to interesting new categories, including Birkenstock natural skin care products and even Birkenstock sleep systems. ● Although some might see the concept of Birkenstock beds as a stretch, the company sees it as a natural extension of its footwear positioning. The brand has long positioned its sandals and shoes as "footbeds" with functional and orthopedic benefits. So with sleep systems, says the company, it's just "taking a great idea one step further, from anatomically shaped footbeds into anatomically shaped beds. Just like the original Birkenstock footbed, our anatomically designed sleep systems also adapt to the shape of your body. This enables our mattresses, slatted frames, and beds to support and ease the strain on the human body in an ideal manner when lying—helping you sleep as comfortably as possible."[46]

● Brand extensions: Classic footwear maker Birkenstock has extended its brand to sleep systems. It's just "taking a great idea one step further, from anatomically shaped foot beds into anatomically shaped beds."

dpa picture alliance/Alamy Stock Photo

These days, a large majority of new products are extensions of already-successful brands. Compared with building new brands, extensions can create immediate new-product familiarity and acceptance at lower development costs. For example, it's not just any new wireless charging mat for your mobile devices, it's a Duracell Powermat. And it's not just a new, no-name over-the-counter sleep aid, it's Vicks ZzzQuil. Extensions such as the Duracell Powermat and Vicks ZzzQuil make good sense—they connect well with the core brand's values and build on its strengths.

At the same time, a brand extension strategy involves some risk. The extension may confuse the image of the main brand—for example, how about Zippo perfume or Fruit of the Loom laundry detergent? Brand extensions such as Cheetos lip balm, Heinz pet food, Colgate ready meals, and Life Savers gum met early deaths.[47] Furthermore, a brand name may not be appropriate to a particular new product, even if it is well made and satisfying—would you consider flying on Hooters Air or wearing an Evian water-filled padded bra (both failed)? And if a brand extension fails, it may harm consumer attitudes toward other products carrying the same brand name. Thus, a company can't just take a familiar brand name and slap it on a product in another category. Instead, a good brand extension should fit the parent brand, and the parent brand should give the extension competitive advantage in its new category.

Multibrands. Companies often market many different brands in a given product category. For example, in the United States, PepsiCo markets at least 10 brands of carbonated soft drinks (Pepsi, Sierra Mist, Mountain Dew, Manzanita Sol, Mirinda, Tropicana Twister, Mug root beer, Paso de los Toros, Stubborn Soda, and Caleb's Cola), two brands of energy drinks (Mountain Dew AMP and AMP Energy Organic,), six brands of ready to drink teas and coffees (Lipton, Brisk, Pure Leaf, SoBe, Tazo, Starbucks), seven brands of bottled waters (Aquafina, H2OH!, PACt, Propel, SoBe, Bubly, Ocean Spray), and nine brands of juices and juice drinks (Brisk, Dole, IZZE, Looza, Ocean Spray, Tropicana, and others). Each brand includes a long list of sub-brands. For instance, PepsiCo's ready-to-drink coffees in partnership with Starbucks include regular, Cold Brew, Refreshers, Frappuccino, Iced Coffee, Double Shot, Iced Latte, and Iced Espresso Classics.

Multibranding offers a way to establish different features that appeal to different customer segments, lock up more reseller shelf space, and capture a larger market share. For example, although PepsiCo's many brands of beverages compete with one another on supermarket shelves, the combined brands reap a much greater overall market share than any single brand ever could. Similarly, by positioning multiple brands in multiple segments, Pepsi's 10 soft drink brands combine to capture much more market share than any single brand could capture by itself.

A major drawback of multibranding is that each brand might obtain only a small market share, and none may be very profitable. The company may end up spreading its resources over many brands instead of building a few brands to a highly profitable level. These companies should reduce the number of brands they sell in a given category and set up tighter screening procedures for new brands.

New Brands. A company might believe that the power of its existing brand name is waning so a new brand name is needed. Or it may create a new brand name when it enters a new product category for which none of its current brand names is appropriate. For example, Toyota created the separate Lexus brand aimed at luxury car consumers.

As with multibranding, offering too many new brands can result in a company spreading its resources too thin. And in some industries, such as consumer packaged goods, consumers and retailers have become concerned that there are already too many brands with too few differences between them. Thus, P&G, PepsiCo, Kraft, GA, and other large marketers of consumer products are now pursuing megabrand strategies—weeding out weaker or slower-growing brands and focusing their marketing dollars on brands that can achieve the number-one or number-two market share positions with good growth prospects in their categories.

For example, over the past decade or more, P&G has sold off dozens of major brands ranging from Jif peanut butter, Crisco shortening, Folgers coffee, Pringles snack chips, and Sunny Delight drinks to Noxzema skin care products, Right Guard deodorant, Aleve pain reliever, Duracell batteries, CoverGirl and Max Factor cosmetics, Wella and Clairol hair care products, and Iams and other pet food brands. These divestments allow P&G to focus investment and energy on the 65 core brands—including 23 billion-dollar-plus brands—that yield most of its sales and profits. "Less [can] be much more," says P&G's CEO.

Managing Brands

Companies must manage their brands carefully. First, the brand's positioning must be continuously communicated to consumers. Major brand marketers often spend huge amounts on advertising to create brand awareness and build preference and loyalty. For example, worldwide, Coca-Cola spends $4 billion annually to advertise its many brands, Google spends $5.1 billion, Unilever spends $8.5 billion, and P&G spends an astounding $10.5 billion.[48]

Such advertising campaigns can help create name recognition, brand knowledge, and perhaps even some brand preference. However, the fact is that brands are not maintained by advertising but by customers' *engagement* with brands and customers' *brand experiences*. Today, customers come to know a brand through a wide range of contacts and touch points along the customer journey. These include advertising but also personal experiences with the brand, word of mouth and social media, company websites and mobile apps, and many others. The company must put as much care into managing these touch points as it does into producing its ads. As one former Disney top executive put it: "A brand is a living entity, and it is enriched or undermined cumulatively over time, the product of a thousand small gestures."[49]

The brand's positioning will not take hold fully unless everyone in the company lives the brand. Therefore, the company needs to train its people to be customer centered. Even better, the company should carry on internal brand building to help employees understand and be enthusiastic about the brand promise. Many companies go even further by training and encouraging their distributors and dealers to serve their customers well.

Finally, companies need to periodically audit their brands' strengths and weaknesses. They should ask: Does our brand excel at delivering benefits that consumers truly value? Is the brand properly positioned? Do all our consumer touch points support the brand's positioning? Do the brand's managers understand what the brand means to consumers? Does the brand receive proper, sustained support? The brand audit may turn up brands that need more support, brands that need to be dropped, or brands that must be rebranded or repositioned because of changing customer preferences or new competitors.

Reviewing and Extending the Concepts

Objectives Review

A product is more than a simple set of tangible features. Each product or service offered to customers can be viewed on three levels. The *core customer value* consists of the core problem-solving benefits that consumers seek when they buy a product. The *actual product* exists around the core and includes the quality level, features, design, brand name, and packaging. The *augmented product* is the actual product plus the various services and benefits offered with it, such as a warranty, free delivery, installation, and maintenance.

OBJECTIVE 8-1 Define *product* and describe the major classifications of products and services.
(pp 234–239)

Broadly defined, a *product* is anything that can be offered to a market for attention, acquisition, use, or consumption that might satisfy a want or need. Products include physical objects but also services, events, persons, places, organizations, ideas, or mixtures of these entities. *Services* are products that consist of activities, benefits, or satisfactions offered for sale that are essentially intangible, such as banking, hotel, tax preparation, and home-repair services.

Products and services fall into two broad classes based on the types of consumers who use them. *Consumer products*—those bought by final consumers—are usually classified according to consumer shopping habits (convenience products, shopping products, specialty products, and unsought products). *Industrial products*—those purchased for further processing or for use in conducting a business—include materials and parts, capital items, and supplies and services. Other marketable entities—such as organizations, persons, places, and ideas—can also be thought of as products.

OBJECTIVE 8-2 Describe the decisions companies make regarding their individual products and services, product lines, and product mixes. *(pp 239–247)*

Individual product decisions involve product attributes, branding, packaging, labeling, and product support services. *Product attribute* decisions involve product quality, features, and style and design. *Branding* decisions include selecting a brand name and developing a brand strategy. *Packaging* provides many key benefits, such as protection, economy, convenience, and promotion. Package decisions often include designing *labels and logos*, which identify, describe, and possibly promote the product. Companies also develop *product support services* that enhance customer service and satisfaction and safeguard against competitors.

Most companies produce a product line rather than a single product. A *product line* is a group of products that are related in function, customer-purchase needs, or distribution channels. All product lines and items offered to customers by a particular seller make up the *product mix*. The mix can be described by four dimensions: width, length, depth, and consistency. These dimensions are the tools for developing the company's product strategy.

OBJECTIVE 8-3 Identify the four characteristics that affect the marketing of services and the additional marketing considerations that services require.
(pp 247–252)

Services are characterized by four key aspects: they are *intangible, inseparable, variable*, and *perishable*. Each characteristic poses problems and marketing requirements. Marketers work to find ways to make the service more tangible, increase the productivity of providers who are inseparable from their products, standardize quality in the face of variability, and improve demand movements and supply capacities in the face of service perishability.

Good service companies focus attention on *both* customers and employees. They understand the *service profit chain*, which links service firm profits with employee and customer satisfaction. Services marketing strategy calls not only for external marketing but also for *internal marketing* to motivate employees and *interactive marketing* to create service delivery skills among service providers. To succeed, service marketers must create *competitive differentiation*, offer high *service quality*, and find ways to increase *service productivity*.

OBJECTIVE 8-4 Discuss branding strategy—the decisions companies make in building and managing their brands. *(pp 252–261)*

Some analysts see brands as *the* major enduring asset of a company. Brands are more than just names and symbols; they embody everything that the product or the service *means* to consumers. *Brand equity* is the positive differential effect that knowing the brand name has on customer response to the product or the service. A brand with strong brand equity is a very valuable asset.

In building brands, companies need to make decisions about brand positioning, brand name selection, brand sponsorship, and brand development. The most powerful *brand positioning* builds around strong consumer beliefs and values. *Brand name selection* involves finding the best brand name based on a careful review of product benefits, the target market, and proposed marketing strategies. A manufacturer has four *brand sponsorship* options: It can launch a *national brand* (or manufacturer's brand), sell to resellers that use a *private brand* (or store brand), market *licensed brands*, or join forces with another company to *co-brand* a product. A company also has four choices when it comes to developing brands. It can introduce *line extensions, brand extensions, multibrands*, or *new brands*.

Companies must build and manage their brands carefully. The brand's positioning must be continuously communicated to consumers. Advertising can help. However, brands are not maintained by advertising but by customers' *brand experiences*. Customers come to know a brand through a wide range of contacts and interactions. The company must put as much care into managing these touch points as it does into producing its ads. Companies must periodically audit their brands' strengths and weaknesses.

Key Terms

OBJECTIVE 8-1

Product (p 234)
Service (p 234)
Consumer product (p 236)
Convenience product (p 236)
Shopping product (p 237)
Specialty product (p 237)
Unsought product (p 237)
Industrial product (p 237)
Social marketing (p 238)

OBJECTIVE 8-2

Product quality (p 239)
Brand (p 240)
Packaging (p 243)
Product line (p 245)
Product mix (or product portfolio) (p 246)

OBJECTIVE 8-3

Service intangibility (p 247)
Service inseparability (p 248)
Service variability (p 248)

Service perishability (p 249)
Service profit chain (p 249)
Internal marketing (p 250)
Interactive marketing (p 250)

OBJECTIVE 8-4

Brand equity (p 253)
Brand value (p 253)
Store brand (or private brand) (p 256)
Co-branding (p 258)
Line extension (p 259)
Brand extension (p 260)

Discussion Questions

8-1 Define *consumer products*. Describe the characteristics of each type of consumer product and give examples of each. (AACSB: Oral and Written Communication; Reflective Thinking)

8-2 Name and explain the five important decisions that marketers must make in developing and marketing individual products and services. (AACSB: Written and Oral Communication)

8-3 What is a product mix? How is the product mix organized? What decisions are made in the creation of this mix? (AACSB: Communication; Reflective Thinking)

8-4 Describe the service profit chain. Provide an example. (AACSB: Written and Oral Communication; Reflective Thinking)

8-5 Explain the four key brand strategy options for a business. Provide an example of each. (AACSB: Communication; Reflective Thinking)

8-6 Explain the four choices a company has when developing brands and illustrate each with an example. (AACSB: Written and Oral Communication; Reflective Thinking)

Critical Thinking Exercises

8-7 A vehicle hire company wants to introduce a service-profit chain process linking their profits with employee and customer satisfaction. How would they go about doing this? What would you recommend to them? (AACSB: Communication; Reflective Thinking)

8-8 Coca-Cola recently introduced Coca-Cola Orange No Sugar as a limited edition flavor. Why would Coca-Cola market this product using the Coca-Cola brand name instead of creating a new brand? What are the trade-offs associated with adding the line extension? (AACSB: Written and Oral Communication; Reflective Thinking)

8-9 Musical performer Rihanna recently launched her own makeup line called Fenty. If Fenty makeup does not succeed, how could it affect Rihanna as a person brand? (AACSB: Written and Oral Communication; Reflective Thinking)

APPLICATIONS AND CASES

Online, Mobile, and Social Media Marketing Engaging Rival Brand Fans

Brands often focus their marketing efforts on encouraging fans to engage with them on their web and social media sites. But what happens when fans of competing brands engage with the brand and its fans on its social media pages— sometimes called "trolling"? Brand managers may have heard not to "feed the trolls." However, recent research suggests that when rival brand fans engage, it provides an opportunity for marketing managers to influence the rival brand's customers and to strengthen their own brand's message. The research also suggests that posts from rival brand fans can motivate central brand fans to react in a positive way that increases engagement and positive brand messages about the central brand.

8-10   Consider ad agency Young & Rubicam's BrandAsset Valuator. How might the central brand fans speaking up in support of a brand affect the four consumer perception dimensions? (AACSB: Written and Oral Communication; Reflective Thinking)

8-11   What are the potential drawbacks of leveraging or encouraging dialogue from brand rivals? (AACSB: Written and Oral Communication; Reflective Thinking)

Marketing Ethics   Cutthroat Prices

Multinational corporations such as Gillette were widely criticized in 2017 for perpetuating the price differential between men's and women's razors. A survey by *The Times* in 2016 revealed that clothes, beauty products, toys, and other products were routinely more expensive for women than men. According to the newspaper, the prices were 37 percent higher across several product categories. This price discrimination is not new; neither is it restricted to women's clothes, pink razors, and dolls. A report by the New York City Department of Consumer Affairs ("From Cradle to Cane: The Cost of Being a Female Consumer," 2015) found that across 800 identical products, on average the female version was 7 percent more expensive. Perhaps part of the explanation is price sensitivity. In other situations, a business will attempt to increase the price out of balance to the increase in cost to them if they can manage it. Sellers do rely on making a greater profit by sneaking "add-ons"

or personalizing products. In these cases, the buyer effectively self-selects the higher price. It may be a simple extra topping on a dessert, a super-sized version of the standard product, or even a vanilla syrup shot in a coffee. All attract a nice mark-up for the seller.

8-12   Is price discrimination reasonable and a viable approaching in the marketing of products and services? Explain why the approach might be contrary to customer value–driven strategies. (AACSB: Communication; Ethical Reasoning)

8-13   There are other forms of price discrimination that are routinely used by businesses. Identify the different types and comment on their impact on customer value–driven approaches. (AACSB: Communication; Reflective Thinking)

Marketing by the Numbers   Diet Coke with Fiber

Coca-Cola launched Coca-Cola Plus in a limited market in Japan last year and now plans to launch it nationwide in that country. Coca-Cola Plus is a zero-calorie soda (essentially Diet Coke) with 5 grams of an indigestible dietary fiber called dextrin. Although some might just call it Diet Coke with a laxative, Coca-Cola Plus is touted in Japan as a health food that suppresses the absorption of fat and keeps blood triglycerides at moderate levels. In fact, the product has earned the Japanese government's "gold label," designating it as a government-approved Food of Specific Health Use (FOSHU). Although the new Coca-Cola Plus reaps a higher wholesale price for the company ($1.20 per 470-milliliter bottle versus $1.15 per bottle for the original Diet Coke), it also comes with higher variable costs ($0.65 per bottle versus $0.55 per bottle for the original product). Although some Diet Coke drinkers will switch to Coca-Cola Plus, the company believes the new product will attract new customers because of its health benefits. Coca-Cola is no stranger to introducing new products in Japan. The company released Coca-Cola Coffee

Plus last year and recently introduced its first alcoholic beverage called Lemon Do.

8-14   What brand development strategy is Coca-Cola undertaking? (AACSB: Communication; Reflective Thinking)

8-15   Assume the company expects to sell 5 million bottles of Coca-Cola Plus in the first year after introduction but that 60 percent of those sales will come from buyers who would normally purchase Diet Coke (that is, cannibalized sales). Assuming the sales of Diet Coke are normally 300 million bottles per year and that the company will incur an increase in fixed costs of $500,000 during the first year to launch Coca-Cola Plus, will the new product be profitable for the company? Refer to the Financial Analysis of Marketing Tactics: Extend the Product Line section in Appendix 2: Marketing by the Numbers for an explanation regarding how to conduct this analysis. (AACSB: Communication; Analytical Reasoning)

Company Case   MINI: Focus on the Essential—Maximize the Experience

Long-term brands face a balancing act. On the one hand, they must remain true to the characteristics that endear them to their throngs of loyal customers. On the other hand, the longer a brand remains, the more it must develop new attributes that appeal to new generations of customers. Maintaining this balance between consistency and relevancy is difficult. Brands

that can do this for decades are truly special. Take BMW's MINI—the modern representation of the iconic British people's car. MINIs continue to roll off the assembly line after more than 60 years. Not only has MINI remained true to the original brand while keeping up with changing customer dynamics, it has done so despite having been owned by six different companies.

A Classic Is Born

In 1956, the Suez Crisis brought on a major worldwide fuel shortage. As a result, the demand for small, fuel-efficient vehicles spiked. The British Motor Corporation (BMC) gave Sir Alec Issigonis the job of designing a vehicle with a unique challenge—minimize dimensions and amenities while maximizing efficiency and utility. That challenge became the heart and soul of the MINI brand.

Measuring only ten feet long, four-and-a-half feet wide, and four-and-a-half feet high, the original MINI rode on tiny ten-inch wheels. But with its wheels pushed out to the extreme corners and its 40-horsepower engine mounted sideways, the tiny car could seat four people comfortably with room in the back for cargo. It was fuel efficient and boasted a sturdy frame and suspension. The innovative design of the original MINI gave it nimble reflexes and go kart-like handing. Available in a variety of basic colors, the car offered optional niceties such as adjustable seats, opening rear side windows, rubber mats, and a heater.

Customers were thrilled with the MINI and its small-on-size-big-on-function design. Those initial characteristics of the brand were soon enhanced even further through a partnership between BMC and John Cooper, the legendary Formula One driver and race car designer. Recognizing the MINI's potential as a race car based on its small size, low weight, and stiff chassis, Cooper designed performance modifications for the drivetrain, suspension, and brakes. Cooper's hunches were right. MINI won the Monte Carlo Rally three times between 1958 and 1962 against veteran racing brands such as Ferrari, Maserati, and Lotus. With Cooper performance modifications added to the options list, the MINI was poised to deliver more value than ever.

Based on its design and options, key characteristics of the brand began to emerge. Round headlights and a "smiley face" bumper contributed to a friendly and fun brand personality. As the options offered by BMC and by aftermarket companies evolved, MINI soon became one of the most customizable car brands, giving it a strong appeal to those who wanted a car that would express their individuality. It's not surprising that MINI quickly became the perfect blend of practical and cool that was irresistible to everyone, regardless of class and culture. MINI's popularity really took off as iconic celebrities became fans. At one point, all four Beatles were counted among the growing body of MINI owners.

Under BMC during its first decade, the MINI was sold in coupe, wagon, and van versions as a sub-brand of various marks (Morris MINI-Minor and the Austin Seven MINI, among others). In 1969, MINI became a standalone brand. But as BMC experienced financial difficulties in the late 1960s, MINI bounced from one company to another for the better part of 25 years before finding a home with BMW in 1994 where it has remained ever since.

Although the MINI's pedigree is confusing, the car changed very little during its first 41 years, staying true to the original design. But safety and emissions regulations as well as changing consumer needs brought MINI production to a halt in October of 2000. It was then that MINI number 5,387,862—a red Cooper Sport—was driven off the line and immediately parked in the Heritage Motor Centre in Gaydon, England, right alongside the first MINI ever made—a tribute to the most popular British car of all time. Just one year before, a jury of 126 automotive experts from 32 countries had voted the MINI the runner up to Ford's Model T as the Car of the Century.

Redesigning an Iconic Brand

Although the writing was on the wall signaling the end of the original MINI design, BMW was hard at work designing its replacement. The brand had far too much equity and heritage to let it die. However, BMW faced a challenge in recreating one of the most iconic automobiles ever made. Modern customers called for more of everything—more power, larger size, safer design, and more features and options. But the heritage of the brand demanded an automobile for the new millennium that was unmistakably a MINI.

In 2001, the first of the new two-door MINI hatchbacks rolled off the assembly line in England and hit showroom floors. Although the length and width of the new MINI was substantially greater than the original (22 inches longer and 11 inches wider), the new MINI was very small relative to average vehicles of the time. Various engine options delivered between 75 and 245 horsepower. BMW's modern version delivered on fuel efficiency, practicality, and driving performance. With nimble reflexes and rally car handling, it was easy to drive and park. Yet taller-than-average occupants found plenty of headroom and legroom, not to mention superb visibility in any direction. Round headlights and a happy-face grill gave the new design a look that was unmistakably MINI.

Sticking with the original MINI's appeal to individuality, BMW provided a lengthy list of options with various wheel packages, paint schemes, and latex appliques that could be fitted to give the roof, mirrors, hood, and hatch seemingly endless appearance options. Within a few years, the two-door hatch spawned convertible and wagon variants.

The goal of the new MINI's branding was to sell "lifestyles defined by freedom, good cheer, and camaraderie." To that end, MINI unleashed the "Let's Motor" campaign, employing a rich mix of unconventional media, carefully integrated to create personality for the car and excited buzz among consumers. The company put MINIs in all kinds of imaginative places. It mounted them atop Ford SUVs and drove them around 22 major cities, highlighting the car's sensible size. It set up "MINI Ride" displays outside department stores, featuring an actual MINI that looked like a children's ride. Displays in airport terminals featured oversize newspaper vending machines showing the undersized MINI and proclaiming, "Makes everything else seem too big." Equally creative were integrated print, online, and direct mail ads.

The "Let's Motor" campaign not only won awards, it was a smashing success in achieving BMW's goals. Together with company-sponsored owner events, MINI developed a cult-like following of devoted owners. Although the new MINI didn't please all purists, many were impressed. Like the original, the new MINI drew drivers of all demographics despite the fact that BMW targeted drivers between the ages of 20 and 30 who enjoyed the pleasure of driving. Sales were initially strong and steadily increased to more than 300,000 units sold in 2012—a figure that rivaled the best sales years ever of the classic MINI.

The Soul of the Brand Lives On

With the MINI's popularity stronger than ever, in the summer of 2015 BMW announced that it would again reinvent the brand, complete with new designs, a new logo, and a new positioning for its cars. Many observers asked the obvious question, "With things are going so well for MINI, why was it reinventing itself?" The simple answer is, BMW was proactively staying ahead of shifts in market conditions. Keeping tabs, BMW noticed that its target customer—affluent urban dwellers in their 20s and 30s who enjoy fun, freedom, and individuality—had changed considerably. When the brand first launched in 2001, consumers were brimming with confidence from a booming world economy. But rapid technological change, geo-political uncertainty, and the financial crash of 2008 combined to fundamentally alter consumer values. MINI's core customer had become more practical—focused on the essentials. For a brand built on a lifestyle defined by fun, adventure, and sharing good times, BMW managers none-the-less believed that MINI was better positioned than perhaps any other brand to meet this new focus on practicality.

The new MINI logo was toned down from the 3D version to a more simple 2D black and white rendition. MINI also simplified its approach to advertising. Gone were the tongue-in-cheek creatives that broke with convention. Instead, new, simpler MINI ads focused on the features and functions of the cars. MINI also updated its website with videos and visuals that helped customers better understand the benefits of the car. These branding changes suggested that MINI was authentic, practical, and ready to play a bigger role in society.

As part of the new branding philosophy, BMW planned to rollout complete revisions of each of its five models—now referring to them as the "Five Superheroes"—the Hardtop 2 Door, the Hardtop 4 Door, the Convertible, the wagon-esque Clubman, and the all-wheel drive Countryman crossover. All models would receive substantial technological updates. In a departure from the past, branding efforts for each new model would emphasize a unique identity, including color schemes and aesthetics tailored to each car. With this approach, MINI created a brand with five product lines that appealed to a broader range of customers. For example, the Clubman was aimed at attracting more families to the brand. Advertising focused on the car's functionality and elegant design. And at over 14 feet in length and six feet in width, it was MINI's largest and roomiest car ever.

With this redesign, did MINI abandon its original brand values? Not according to MINI's head of brand management.

"With our five 'superheroes' we want to make it very clear that each of those cars has its own character. The Clubman is the most extreme example in terms of moving in a direction away from the past, but you should still expect a lot of fun from the different models as each character emerges." Those at the company emphasize that MINI's brand values are still in line with the minimizing, practical instincts of Issigonis on the one hand contrasted with the maximizing, performance-driven approach of Cooper on the other.

"MINI has always been about new ideas, inspiration, and a lot of passion, and these things are not going to change," said another MINI representative. Since the unveiling of the new generation of MINIs, the company continues to innovate with state-of-the-art features like MINI Connected Concierge services, wireless smartphone charging, and anti-dazzle adaptive headlights with a matrix high beam—a rarity on small city cars. In an even bolder move, buyers of new MINIs can custom design interior appointments like dashboard inserts, side scuttles, and door sills that are produced on 3D printers and installed in the car before the buyer takes ownership. In addition, MINI's high-performance models will soon see higher performance than ever. And in the coming year, the MINI Copper SE will make its debut, the first in a new line of fully electric MINIs.

Based on MINI's recent sales numbers, it seems that the new direction is right on the money. For each of the past four years, MINI has sold substantially more vehicles than any year prior to the 2015 rebranding, moving more than 360,000 vehicles into garages around the world last year. As MINI moves boldly into the future with efforts to stay relevant in a changing world, it must also stay true to the qualities that have made it iconic for so long. The folks at MINI seem to get that. "Mini crosses cultures, class, gender, and age," says MINI's head of design. "Anyone who buys a MINI feels immediately younger while driving it. It just puts a smile on your face."[50]

Questions for Discussion

8-16 Discuss how MINI has endured for 60 years as a brand, despite being owned by various companies.

8-17 Does MINI have high brand equity? Explain.

8-18 Over the years, has MINI been positioned based on attributes, benefits, or values? Explain.

8-19 Is BMW taking MINI in the right direction with its current branding strategy? Why or why not?

9

Developing New Products
and Managing the Product Life Cycle

OBJECTIVES OUTLINE

OBJECTIVE 9-1 Explain how companies find and develop new product ideas. **See: New Product Development Strategy** *(pp 270–271)*

OBJECTIVE 9-2 List and define the steps in the new product development process and the major considerations in managing this process. **See: The New Product Development Process** *(pp 271–281)*

OBJECTIVE 9-3 Describe the stages of the product life cycle and how marketing strategies change during a product's life cycle. **See: Product Life-Cycle Strategies** *(pp 281–287)*

OBJECTIVE 9-4 Discuss two additional product issues: socially responsible product decisions and international product and services marketing. **See: Additional Product and Service Considerations** *(pp 288–289)*

CHAPTER PREVIEW In the previous chapter, you learned how marketers manage and develop products and brands. In this chapter, we examine two additional product topics: developing new products and managing products through their life cycles. New products are the lifeblood of an organization. However, new product development is risky, and many new products fail. So, the first part of this chapter lays out a process for finding and growing successful new products. Once introduced, marketers then want their products to enjoy long and happy lives. In the second part of the chapter, you'll see that every product passes through several life-cycle stages, and each stage poses new challenges requiring different marketing strategies and tactics. Finally, we wrap up our product discussion by looking at two additional considerations: social responsibility in product decisions and international product and services marketing.

For openers, consider Google, one of the world's most innovative companies. Google seems to come up with an almost unending flow of knock-your-eye-out new technologies, products, and services. The company's entire culture encourages, supports, and rewards innovation. At Google and its parent company Alphabet, innovation isn't just a process. It's in the very spirit of the place.

GOOGLE (...er, Alphabet): The New Product Moonshot Factory

Google is wildly innovative. Over the past decade and a half, it has become a top-five fixture in every list of most-innovative companies. Google simply refuses to get comfortable with the way things are. Instead, it innovates constantly, plunging into new markets and taking on new competitors.

Google began as an online search company with a mission "to organize the world's information and make it universally accessible and useful." In that mission, Google has been spectacularly successful. Despite formidable competition from giants Microsoft, Yahoo!, and China's Baidu, Google's share of worldwide online search stands at a breathtaking 90 percent—a virtual Google-opoly. Its grasp on mobile search is even stronger at 94 percent. Google also dominates in paid search-related advertising revenue, which accounted for a large majority of the company's $136 billion in revenues last year. And Google is growing at a blistering rate, with revenues more than doubling in just the past four years.

But Google is now much more than just an online search and advertising company. In Google's view, information is a kind of natural resource—one to be mined, refined, and universally distributed. That broad perspective gives Google's engineers and developers a blank canvas, a broad brush, and plenty of incentive to innovate. At many companies, new product development is a cautious, step-by-step affair that might take years to unfold. In contrast, Google's freewheeling new product development process moves at the speed of light. In the time that it takes most competitors to refine and approve an initial idea for a major new product or serviced, Google has already implemented it.

Google's famously chaotic innovation process has unleashed a seemingly unending flurry of diverse products, many of which are market leaders in their categories. Although diverse, many of these innovations are tied in one way or another to Google's Internet-related information mission. Google's megahits include an email service (Gmail), projects for mapping and exploring the world (Google Maps and Google Earth), a digital media store (Google Play), an online payment service (Google Pay), a photo sharing service (Google Photos), a mobile operating system (Google Android), a suite of cloud computing services (Google Cloud), and a cloud-friendly Internet browser (Chrome).

Although Google has traditionally focused on software-based innovations, it now has a strong presence in hardware with smartphones, tablets, and laptops (Pixel); an AI virtual assistant (Google Home); connected smarthome devices (Nest), a state-of-the-art virtual reality headset (Daydream VR); and a small, wireless smart camera (Google Clips). Google connects its hardware and information worlds by infusing the hardware with sophisticated algorithms and artificial intelligence. For example, Google's Pixel phone can turn standard snapshots into beautiful portraits by blurring everything but the foreground subject. Pixel Buds are more than just wireless headphones—they interface with Google Assistant and put Google Translate front and center, letting people talk to others in multiple languages. And the Google Clips hands-free camera uses AI to automatically recognize great expressions, lighting, and framing to capture spontaneous images.

Google acquired Nest Labs as its entry into the Internet of Things (IoT). The subsequent development of Google Home and Google Assistant has added voice control and AI technology to Nest's fast-growing smarthome presence. Nest now includes its own expanding portfolio of smart

Google and parent company Alphabet are wildly innovative. The company's innovation machine is renowned for producing new product "moonshots," futuristic long shots that, if successful, will profoundly change how people live.

VovanIvanovich/Shutterstock

and stylish home control and monitoring devices, along with "Works with Nest" smart products from other companies. Nest will soon be helping consumers run their entire homes, an enormous potential market.

Google's wild-eyed innovation process has also taken the company down paths far afield from its main information mission—everything from self-driving cars to earth-imaging satellites and even a crusade to increase human life spans. With so many ventures and innovations becoming more and more diverse, Google created a parent holding company called Alphabet to contain them all.

Google is the largest Alphabet company—it continues to house information and Internet-related software and hardware products. But along with Google, Alphabet provides an independent home for the company's more far-reaching projects and businesses. These include what Alphabet calls "moonshots"—futuristic, breathtakingly idealistic longshots that, if successful, will profoundly change how people live. To foster moonshots, the company created X—a secretive innovation lab and kind of nerd heaven charged with developing things that seem audacious, even for Alphabet.

The X innovation lab is Alphabet's incubator for earth-shaking projects that may or may not pay for themselves in the long run. To get the green light at X, a project must address a huge problem that affects millions or even billions of people, propose a radical solution, and require a breakthrough technology to bring about that solution. The goal is to hatch new Googles. Those stringent requirements "cause us to throw out more than 99 percent of

> Google's famously chaotic innovation process has unleashed a seemingly unending flurry of diverse new products. But at Google, innovation is more than a process. It's part of the company's DNA. "Where does innovation happen at Google? It happens everywhere."

our ideas," says X's director, whose official title is Captain of Moonshots. Secreted behind X's curtain are numerous exotic projects, such as Malta (a molten salt thermal energy storage system), Free Space Optical Communications (high-speed data transmission via beams of light), and Makani (kite-like wind-energy production).

Many X projects have already become full-fledged Alphabet companies. There's Waymo, the self-driving car project that's on a mission to make it safe and easy to for people and things to move around. Medical technology project Verily creates health-care devices, such as glucose-monitoring contact lenses that could help identify cancer cells. In just the past year, three big X hatchlings have emerged: Chronicle employs sophisticated analytics tools that can predict and fight cybercrimes before they happen. Project Loon (a Wi-Fi-distributing high-altitude balloon network) carries Wi-Fi to underserved areas of the world. And Project Wing (a drone delivery system) will soon be delivering packages in Finland.

Lesser-known Alphabet companies include investment arms GV (funding for bold new startups) and CapitalG (funding for long-term tech projects), Calico (research into fighting age-related disease and increasing life spans), and DeepMind (AI research and applications). According to Google co-founder Larry Page, Alphabet's goal is "to keep tremendous focus on the extraordinary opportunities" that exist and will exist within Google and the other companies.

In the end, at Google and parent company Alphabet, in-novation is more than a process—it's part of the company's DNA. "Where does innovation happen at Google? It happens everywhere," says a Google research scientist.

Talk to Googlers at various levels and departments, one pow-erful theme emerges: These people feel that their work can change the world. The marvel of Google is its ability to con-tinue to instill a sense of creative fearlessness and ambition in its employees. Prospective hires are often asked, "If you could change the world using Google's resources, what would you build?" But here, this isn't a goofy or even theoretical ques-tion: Google wants to know because thinking—and building—on that scale is what Google does. When it comes to innovation, Google is different. But the difference isn't tangible. It's in the air—in the spirit of the place.[1]

AS THE GOOGLE STORY SUGGESTS, companies that excel at developing and managing new products reap big rewards. Every product seems to have a life cycle: It is born, goes through several phases, and eventually dies as newer products come along that create new or greater value for customers.

This product life cycle presents two major challenges: First, because all products even-tually decline, a firm must be good at developing new products to replace aging ones (the challenge of *new product development*). Second, a firm must be good at adapting its market-ing strategies in the face of changing tastes, technologies, and competition as products pass through stages (the challenge of *product life-cycle strategies*). We first look at the problem of finding and developing new products and then at the problem of managing them success-fully over their life cycles.

<table>
<tr><td>Author
Comment</td><td>New products are the lifeblood of a company. As old products mature and fade away, companies must develop new ones to take their place. For example, the iPhone and iPad have been around for only a little over a decade but are now Apple's two top-selling products.</td></tr>
</table>

New Product Development Strategy

OBJECTIVE 9-1 Explain how companies find and develop new product ideas.

A firm can obtain new products in two ways. One is through *acquisition*—by buying a whole company, a patent, or a license to produce someone else's product. For example, Google got into the smarthome market by acquiring Nest and into mobile navigation by acquiring Waze. The other is through the firm's own **new product development** efforts. By *new products* we mean original products, product improvements, product modifica-tions, and new brands that the firm develops through its own product development. Most of Google's products and services were developed this way. In this chapter, we concentrate on new product development.

New products are important to both customers and the marketers who serve them: They bring new solutions and variety to customers' lives, and they are a key source of growth for companies. In today's fast-changing environment, many companies rely on new products for the majority of their growth. For example, new products have almost completely transformed Apple in recent years. The iPhone and iPad—introduced little more than a decade ago—are now the company's two biggest-selling products, with the iPhone alone bringing in 63 percent of Apple's total global revenues. And to remain competitive, Apple releases a steady stream of new products and new versions of existing ones.[2]

New product development
The development of original products, product improvements, product modifications, and new brands through the firm's own product development efforts.

Yet innovation can be very expensive and very risky. New products face tough odds. For example, by one estimate, of the more than 30,000 new products introduced every year, 95 percent fail.[3] Why do so many new products fail? There are several reasons. Although an idea may be good, the company may overestimate market size. The actual product may be poorly designed. Or it might be incorrectly positioned, launched at the wrong time, priced too high, or poorly advertised. A high-level executive might push a favorite idea despite poor marketing research findings. Sometimes the costs of product development are higher than expected, and sometimes competitors fight back harder than expected.

So, companies face a problem: They must develop new products, but the odds weigh heavily against success. To create successful new products, a company must understand its consumers, markets, and competitors and develop products that deliver superior value to customers.

> Author | Companies can't just
> Comment | hope that they'll stumble
> across good new products. Instead,
> they must develop a systematic new
> product development process.

The New Product Development Process

OBJECTIVE 9-2 List and define the steps in the new product development process and the major considerations in managing this process.

Rather than leaving new products to chance, a company must carry out strong new product planning and set up a systematic, customer-driven *new product development process* for finding and growing new products. ● **Figure 9.1** shows the eight major steps in this process.

Idea Generation

Idea generation
The systematic search for new product ideas.

New product development starts with **idea generation**—the systematic search for new product ideas. A company typically generates hundreds—even thousands—of ideas to find a few good ones. Major sources of new product ideas include internal sources and external sources such as customers, competitors, distributors and suppliers, and others.

Internal Idea Sources

Using *internal sources*, the company can find new ideas through formal R&D. For example, Ford operates an innovation and mobility center in Silicon Valley staffed by engineers, app developers, and scientists working on everything from driverless cars to Works with Nest apps that let consumers control home heating, lighting, and appliances from their vehicles. Chick-fil-A has set up three large innovation centers. The first, called Hatch, is an idea hatchery where Chick-fil-A staff and partners explore new ideas in food, design, and service. "It's a place to explore and imagine the future in order to hatch new food and restaurant ideas and bring them to life."[4]

Beyond its internal R&D process, a company can pick the brains of its own people—from executives to salespeople to scientists, engineers, and manufacturing staff. Many companies have developed successful internal social networks and intrapreneurial programs that encourage employees to develop new product ideas. An example is Google's "Area 120":[5]

New product development starts with good new product ideas—lots of them. For example, during the past decade, AT&T's The Innovation Pipeline (TIP) employee crowdsourcing program has attracted more than 40,000 innovation ideas from members in all 50 states and 54 countries.

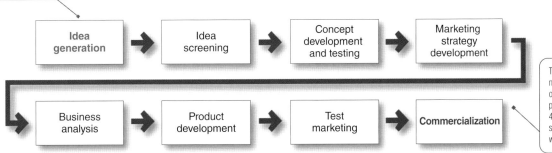

The remaining steps reduce the number of ideas and develop only the best ones into profitable products. Of the 40,000 AT&T TIP ideas submitted, only 80 TIP projects were funded.

● FIGURE 9.1
Major Stages in New Product Development

● **Internal new product ideas: Many companies—such as Facebook—use hackathons to pick the brains of their own employees for innovative ideas.**

Hero Images Inc./Alamy Stock Photo

Google has long offered employees "20% time," letting them spend up to a fifth of their work time on projects that might later benefit the company. The program has birthed many highly successful innovations, including Gmail, Google News, and the Cardboard VR headset. But as employees' day jobs became more demanding, many found that the time spent on personal projects became more of an add-on to their normal work hours than a part of them. That is, Google's famed "20% time" became "120% time." So two years ago, to encourage continued internal innovation, Google set up Area 120, an in-house innovation incubator that lets selected employees devote full time to their dream projects. Google employees pitch their project ideas to Area 120 leaders. If selected, the employees leave their previous jobs and receive full financial and Google-wide technological expertise to turn their brainchildren into real businesses. It's still too early to tell how successful Area 120 will be. But so far, it has received more than 1,000 project pitches, of which 50 have been accepted and 25 are still in the works.

Many companies sponsor periodic internal "hackathons," in which employees take a day or a week away from their day-to-day work to develop new ideas. ● Such hackathons are legendary at Facebook. During a Facebook hackathon, "a few hundred of our engineers unleash their talents in epic, all-night coding sessions and often end up with products that hit the internal and external versions of the site within weeks," says one Facebook employee. The social media giant's hackathons have produced major innovations such as the "Like" button and friend tagging. Such events not only produce fresh new ideas, they can also boost employee morale and engagement. As the employee explains, "the camaraderie, productivity, and occasional insanity of hackathons have helped make Facebook what it is."[6]

External Idea Sources

Companies can also obtain good new product ideas from any of a number of external sources. For example, *distributors and suppliers* can contribute ideas. Distributors are close to the market and can pass along information about consumer problems and new product possibilities. Suppliers can tell the company about new concepts, techniques, and materials that can be used to develop new products.

● **New product ideas from customers: Salesforce's IdeaExchange invites customers to suggest, discuss, and vote on new software features and product enhancements. Over the past 10 years, customers have submitted more than 60,000 ideas and cast millions of votes.**

Salesforce Inc.

Competitors are another important source. Companies watch competitors' ads to get clues about their new products. They buy competing new products, take them apart to see how they work, analyze their sales, and decide whether they should bring out a new product of their own. Other idea sources include trade magazines, shows, websites, and seminars; government agencies; advertising agencies; marketing research firms; university and commercial laboratories; and inventors.

Perhaps the most important sources of new product ideas are *customers* themselves. The company can analyze customer questions and complaints to find new products that better solve consumer problems. Or it can invite customers to share suggestions and ideas. ● For example, Salesforce—the leading customer relationship management (CRM) solutions company—hosts an online IdeaExchange, where it invites customers to suggest, discuss, and vote on new software features and product enhancements. Over the past 10 years, customers have submitted more than 60,000 ideas and cast millions of votes.

Often, the best results come more from the ensuing collaboration and brainstorming than from the initial idea. A Salesforce executive estimates that one-third of a product management team's thinking is influenced by IdeaExchange. The system also greatly improves the customer experience. It builds two-way relationships where customers feel listened to and valued.[7]

Crowdsourcing

Crowdsourcing

Inviting broad communities of people—customers, employees, independent scientists and researchers, and even the public at large—into the new product innovation process.

More broadly, many companies are now developing crowdsourcing or open-innovation new product idea programs. Through **crowdsourcing**, a company invites broad communities of people—customers, employees, independent scientists and researchers, and even the public at large—into the innovation process. Tapping into a breadth of sources—both inside and outside the company—can produce unexpected and powerful new ideas.

Companies large and small, across all industries, are crowdsourcing product innovation ideas rather than relying only on their own R&D labs. For example, Ben & Jerry's ran a "Do the World a Flavor" campaign, an online video game on the company's website and social media by which fans could create and name new flavors. ● Food container giant Tupperware recently sponsored the Clever Container Challenge, a crowdsourcing contest seeking ideas for integrating Internet-of-Things technologies into food containers for future smart kitchens. It asked for "easy to use but technologically advanced" designs for affordable, reusable containers that provide real value in storage and preventing waste, whether in the kitchen or on the go. And Under Armour sponsors an annual crowdsourcing competition called the Future Show Innovation Challenge, in which it invites entrepreneurs and inventors from around the nation to submit new product ideas, with finalists pitching their products in a splashy, *Shark Tank*–like reality TV setting. "We need to be humble enough to know that the next great thing might come from some kid playing college football who happens to have a better idea," says the Under Armour innovation chief.[8]

Thus, truly innovative companies don't rely only on one source or another for new product ideas. Instead, they develop extensive innovation networks that capture ideas and inspiration from every possible source, from employees and customers to outside innovators and multiple points beyond.

● **Crowdsourcing: Food container giant Tupperware sponsored the Clever Container Challenge contest seeking ideas for integrating Internet-of-Things technologies into food containers for future smart kitchens.**

Giddy Io. Inc

Idea Screening

Idea screening

Screening new product ideas to spot good ones and drop poor ones as soon as possible.

The purpose of idea generation is to create a large number of ideas. The purpose of the succeeding stages is to *reduce* that number. The first idea-reducing stage is **idea screening**, which helps spot good ideas and drop poor ones as soon as possible. Product development costs rise greatly in later stages, so the company wants to go ahead only with those product ideas that will turn into profitable products.

Many companies require their executives to write up new product ideas in a standard format that can be reviewed by a new product committee. The write-up describes the product or the service, the proposed customer value proposition, the target market, and the competition. It makes rough estimates of market size, product price, development time and costs, manufacturing costs, and rate of return. The committee then evaluates the idea against a set of general criteria.

One marketing expert describes an R-W-W ("real, win, worth doing") new product screening framework that asks three questions.[9] First, *Is it real?* Is there a real need and desire for the product, and will customers buy it? Is there a clear product concept, and will such a product satisfy the market? Second, *Can we win?* Does the product offer a sustainable competitive advantage? Does the company have the resources to make such a product a success? Finally, *Is it worth doing?* Does the product fit the company's overall growth strategy? Does it offer sufficient profit potential? The company should be able to answer yes to all three R-W-W questions before developing the new product idea further.

Concept Development and Testing

Product concept

A detailed version of the new product idea stated in meaningful consumer terms.

An attractive idea must then be developed into a **product concept**. It is important to distinguish between a product idea, a product concept, and a product image. A *product idea* is an idea for a possible product that the company can see itself offering to the market. A *product concept* is a detailed version of the idea stated in meaningful consumer terms. A *product image* is the way consumers perceive an actual or potential product.

● **All-electric cars: This is Tesla's initial all-electric full-sized sedan. Its more recent Model 3 compact travels up to 310 miles on a single charge and costs pennies per mile to operate.**

Salwan Georges/The Washington Post via Getty Images

Concept Development

Suppose a car manufacturer has developed a practical battery-powered, all-electric car. Its initial models were a sleek, sporty roadster convertible selling for more than $100,000 followed by a full-size sports sedan priced at $78,000.[10] ● However, it now plans to introduce a more-affordable, mass-market compact version that will compete with hybrid-electric or all-electric cars such as the Nissan Leaf, Chevy Bolt EV, and KIA Soul EV. This 100 percent plug-in electric car will accelerate from 0 to 60 miles per hour in five seconds, travel up to 310 miles on a single charge, recharge in two hours from a normal 120-volt electrical outlet, and cost about one penny per mile to power.

Looking ahead, the marketer's task is to develop this new product into alternative product concepts, find out how attractive each concept is to customers, and choose the best one. It might create the following product concepts for this all-electric car:

- *Concept 1.* An affordably priced compact car designed as a second family car to be used around town for running errands and visiting friends.
- *Concept 2.* A mid-priced sporty compact appealing to young singles and couples.
- *Concept 3.* A "green" everyday car appealing to environmentally conscious people who want practical, no-polluting transportation.
- *Concept 4.* A compact crossover SUV appealing to those who love the space SUVs provide but lament the poor gas mileage.

Concept Testing

Concept testing

Testing new product concepts with a group of target consumers to find out if the concepts have strong consumer appeal.

Concept testing calls for testing new product concepts with groups of target consumers. The concepts may be presented to consumers symbolically or physically. Here, in more detail, is concept 3:

> An efficient, fun-to-drive, battery-powered compact car that seats five. This 100 percent electric wonder provides practical and reliable transportation with no pollution. It goes 310 miles on a single charge and costs pennies per mile to operate. It's a sensible, responsible alternative to today's pollution-producing gas guzzlers. Its fully equipped base price is $35,000.

Many firms routinely test new product concepts with consumers before attempting to turn them into actual new products. For some concept tests, a word or picture description might be sufficient. However, a more concrete and physical presentation of the concept will increase the reliability of the concept test. After being exposed to the concept, consumers then may be asked to react to it by answering questions similar to those in ● **Table 9.1**.

The answers to such questions will help the company decide which concept has the strongest appeal. For example, the last question asks about the consumer's intention to buy. Suppose 2 percent of consumers say they "definitely" would buy and another 5 percent say "probably." The company could project these figures to the full population in this target group to estimate sales volume. Even then, however, the estimate is uncertain because people do not always carry out their stated intentions.

● Table 9.1 | Questions for the All-Electric Car Concept Test

1. Do you understand the concept of a battery-powered electric car?
2. Do you believe the claims about the car's performance?
3. What are the major benefits of an all-electric car compared with a conventional car?
4. What are its advantages compared with a hybrid gas-electric car?
5. What improvements in the car's features would you suggest?
6. For what uses would you prefer an all-electric car to a conventional car?
7. What would be a reasonable price to charge for the car?
8. Who would be involved in your decision to buy such a car? Who would drive it?
9. Would you buy such a car (definitely, probably, probably not, definitely not)?

Marketing Strategy Development

Marketing strategy development

Designing an initial marketing strategy for a new product based on the product concept.

Suppose the carmaker finds that concept 3 for the new electric car model tests best. The next step is **marketing strategy development**, designing an initial marketing strategy for introducing this car to the market.

The *marketing strategy statement* consists of three parts. The first part describes the target market; the planned value proposition; and the sales, market-share, and profit goals for the first few years. Thus:

> The target market is younger, well-educated, moderate- to high-income individuals, couples, or small families seeking stylish but practical and environmentally responsible transportation. The car will be positioned as more fun to drive, less polluting, and higher in technology than today's internal combustion engine or hybrid cars. The company will aim to sell 50,000 cars in the first year at a loss of not more than $15 million. In the second year, the company will aim for sales of 90,000 cars and a profit of $25 million.

The second part of the marketing strategy statement outlines the product's planned price, distribution, and marketing budget for the first year:

> The battery-powered all-electric car will be offered in three colors—red, white, and blue—and will have a full set of accessories as standard features. It will sell at a base retail price of $35,000 with 15 percent off the list price to dealers. Dealers who sell more than 10 cars per month will get an additional discount of 5 percent on each car sold that month. A marketing budget of $50 million will be split 30-40-30 among a national media campaign, online and social media marketing, and local event marketing. Advertising, the web and mobile sites, and various social media content will emphasize the car's fun spirit, advanced technology, high status, and low emissions. During the first year, $200,000 will be spent on marketing research to find out who is buying the car and what their satisfaction levels are.

The third part of the marketing strategy statement describes the planned long-run sales, profit goals, and marketing mix strategy:

> We intend to capture a 3 percent long-run share of the total auto market and realize an after-tax return on investment of 15 percent. To achieve this, product quality will start high and be improved over time. Price will be raised in the second and third years if competition and the economy permit. The total marketing budget will be raised each year by about 10 percent. Marketing research will be reduced to $60,000 per year after the first year.

Business Analysis

Business analysis

A review of the sales, costs, and profit projections for a new product to find out whether these factors satisfy the company's objectives.

Once management has decided on its product concept and marketing strategy, it can evaluate the business attractiveness of the proposal. **Business analysis** involves a review of the sales, costs, and profit projections for a new product to find out whether they satisfy the company's objectives. If they do, the product can move to the product development stage.

To estimate sales, the company might look at the sales history of similar products and conduct market surveys. It can then estimate minimum and maximum sales to assess the range of risk. After preparing the sales forecast, management can estimate the expected costs and profits for the product, including marketing, R&D, operations, accounting, and finance costs. The company then uses the sales and cost figures to analyze the new product's financial attractiveness.

Product Development

Product development

Developing the product concept into a physical product to ensure that the product idea can be turned into a workable market offering.

For many new product concepts, a product may exist only as a word description, a drawing, or perhaps a crude mock-up. If the product concept passes the business test, it moves into **product development**. Here, R&D or engineering develops the product concept into a physical product. The product development step, however, now calls for a huge jump in investment. It will show whether the product idea can be turned into a workable product.

The R&D department will develop and test one or more physical versions of the product concept. R&D hopes to design a prototype that will satisfy and excite consumers and that can be produced quickly and at budgeted costs. Developing a successful prototype can take days, weeks, months, or even years depending on the product and prototype methods.

Often, products undergo rigorous tests to make sure that they perform safely and effectively or that consumers will find value in them. Companies can do their own product testing or outsource testing to other firms that specialize in testing.

Marketers often involve actual customers in product development and testing. ● For example, Brooks, maker of high-performance running gear and apparel, has enlisted an army of users it calls Lab Rats and Wear Testers to test its products. It studies the Lab Rats in its Biomechanics Lab at headquarters, where it places them on treadmills wearing Brooks gear and watches how they run, making sure that Brooks products enhance rather than impede performance. The Wear Testers use Brooks running shoes and gear in the field and report back regarding fit, design, style, and function. "It's pretty simple," says Brooks. "We send you gear, you use it. You use it on morning jogs, on race days, in the sun and in the snow. Any time and any place you run and then let us know how it worked (or didn't work) for you. Your feedback is what helps determine fit, function, and design of all our future products."[11]

A new product must have the required functional features and also convey the intended psychological characteristics. The all-electric car, for example, should strike consumers as being well built, comfortable, and safe. Management must learn what makes consumers decide that a car is well built. To some consumers, this means that the car has "solid-sounding" doors. To others, it means that the car can withstand a heavy impact in crash tests. Consumer tests are conducted in which consumers test-drive the car and rate its attributes.

● Product testing: Brooks has enlisted an army of users it calls Lab Rats and Wear Testers to test its products. "Your feedback is what helps determine fit, function, and design of all our future products."

Brooks Sports Inc.

Test Marketing

Test marketing

The stage of new product development in which the product and its proposed marketing program are tested in realistic market settings.

If the product passes both the concept test and the product test, the next step is **test marketing**, the stage at which the product and its proposed marketing program are tested in realistic market settings. Test marketing gives the marketer experience with marketing a product before going to the great expense of full introduction. It lets the company test the product and its entire marketing program—targeting and positioning strategy, advertising, distribution, pricing, branding and packaging, and budget levels.

The amount of test marketing needed varies with each new product. When introducing a new product requires a big investment, when the risks are high, or when management is not sure of the product or its marketing program, a company may do a lot of test marketing. For instance, Taco Bell took three years and 45 prototypes before introducing Doritos Locos Tacos, now the most successful product launch in the company's history. And Starbucks spent 20 years developing Starbucks VIA instant coffee—one of its most risky product rollouts ever—and several months testing the product in Starbucks shops in Chicago and Seattle before releasing it nationally. Starbucks VIA is now a best-selling coffee brand.[12]

However, test marketing costs can be high, and testing takes time that may allow market opportunities to slip by or competitors to gain advantages. A company may do little or no test marketing when the costs of developing and introducing a new product are low or when management is already confident about the new product. For example, companies often do not test-market simple line extensions or copies of competitors' successful products.

Companies may also shorten or skip testing in the face of fast-changing market developments. ● For example, to take advantage of digital and mobile trends, Starbucks quickly introduced a less-than-perfect mobile payments app and then worked out the flaws during the six months after launch. The Starbucks mobile order and pay app now accounts for more than 20 percent of all Starbucks U.S. revenues. "We don't think it is okay if things aren't perfect," says Starbucks' chief digital officer, "but we're willing to innovate and have speed to market trump a 100 percent guarantee that it'll be perfect."[13]

As an alternative to extensive and costly standard test markets, companies can use controlled test markets or simulated test markets. In *controlled test markets*, new products and tactics are tested among controlled panels of shoppers and stores. By combining information on each test consumer's purchases with consumer demographic and media viewing information, the company can assess the impact of in-store and in-home marketing efforts. Using *simulated test markets*, researchers measure consumer responses to new products and marketing tactics in laboratory stores or simulated online shopping environments. Both controlled test markets and simulated test markets reduce the costs of test marketing and speed up the process.

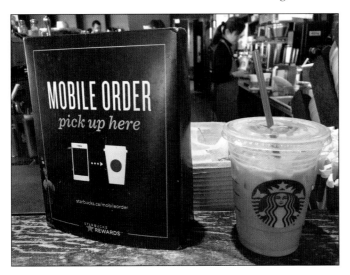

● Companies sometimes shorten or skip test marketing to take advantage of fast-changing market developments, as Starbucks did with its hugely successful mobile payments app.

SamaraHeisz5/Shutterstock

Commercialization

Commercialization
Introducing a new product into the market.

Test marketing gives management the information needed to make a final decision about whether to launch the new product. If the company goes ahead with **commercialization**—introducing the new product into the market—it will face high costs. For example, the company may need to build or rent a manufacturing facility. And, in the case of a major new consumer product, it may spend hundreds of millions of dollars for advertising, sales promotion, and other marketing efforts in the first year. For instance, Nintendo spent an estimated $18 million in a single month on TV advertising to introduce its Nintendo Switch console/hand-held hybrid game system. Tide spent $150 million on a campaign to launch Tide Pods in the highly competitive U.S. laundry detergent market. And to introduce the original Surface tablet, Microsoft spent close to $400 million on an advertising blitz that spanned TV, print, radio, outdoor, the internet, events, public relations, and sampling.[14]

A company launching a new product must first decide on introduction *timing*. If the new product will eat into the sales of other company products, the introduction may be delayed. If the product can be improved further or if the economy is down, the company may wait until the following year to launch it. However, if competitors are ready to introduce their own competing products, the company may push to introduce its new product sooner.

Next, the company must decide *where* to launch the new product—in a single location, a region, the national market, or the international market. Some companies may quickly introduce new models into the full national market. Companies with international distribution systems may introduce new products through swift global rollouts. For example, in its fastest-ever global rollout, Apple launched the iPhone X in 55 countries on the same day.[15]

> **Author** | Above all else, new **Comment** | product development must focus on creating customer value. Says a senior Samsung executive, "We get our ideas from the market. The market is the driver."

Managing New Product Development

The new product development process shown in Figure 9.1 highlights the important activities needed to find, develop, and introduce new products. However, new product development involves more than just going through a set of steps. Companies must take a holistic approach to managing this process. Successful new product development requires a customer-centered, team-based, and systematic effort.

Customer-Centered New Product Development

Above all else, new product development must be customer centered. When looking for and developing new products, companies often rely too heavily on technical research in their R&D laboratories. But like everything else in marketing, successful new product development begins with a thorough understanding of what consumers need and value. **Customer-centered new product development** focuses on finding new ways to solve customer problems and create more customer-satisfying experiences.

Customer-centered new product development

New product development that focuses on finding new ways to solve customer problems and create more customer-satisfying experiences.

One study found that the most successful new products are ones that are differentiated, solve major customer problems, and offer a compelling customer value proposition. Another study showed that companies that directly engage their customers in the new product innovation process had twice the return on assets and triple the growth in operating income of firms that did not. Thus, customer involvement has a positive effect on the new product development process and product success.

● Leading toymaker The LEGO Group is a strong proponent of customer-centered new product development:[16]

> Fifteen years ago, The LEGO Group (TLG) was near bankruptcy as the age of the internet, video games, mobile devices, and high-tech playthings pushed traditional toys such as LEGO bricks to the back of the closet. So TLG set out to rebuild its aging product lines. The LEGO makeover, however, didn't start with engineers working in design labs. It started with listening to and engaging customers.
>
> TLG embedded researchers with families, observed children at play, interviewed parents, and shopped with customers. The research produced a lot of "Aha! Moments." For example, TLG had long offered only basic, unstructured building sets that it thought would foster creativity. But in today's tech-rich world, children get bored easily and welcome more-structured play experiences. So TLG now offers a seemingly endless selection of themed, specialized kits with detailed instructions by which kids can construct anything from fire trucks and helicopters to crave-worthy ninja castles. Research also showed that, for children today, the digital and physical worlds blend as one. This insight led to TLG's "One Reality" products, which combine digital and real-world play experiences that involve building with LEGO bricks alongside software running on a phone or tablet app.
>
> TLG also actively taps its avid user community for new customer insights and ideas. For example, the LEGO Ideas website, a kind of branded version of Kickstarter, invites customers to submit ideas and to evaluate and vote on the ideas of others. Such customer co-creation resulted in TLG's most popular product ever, LEGO MINDSTORMS, a series of building sets complete with hardware and software for making customizable robots that are programmable from a smartphone app. Thanks to customer-centered new product development, LEGO now runs neck and neck with Mattel as the world's largest toymaker.

● **Customer-centered new product development: Toymaker LEGO listens to its customers and actively taps its user community for new product ideas, making it what one observer calls "the Apple of Toys."**

Photo by S. Clyde/U.S. Department of Transportation, Federal Highway Administration

Thus, today's innovative companies get out of the research lab and connect with customers in search of fresh ways to meet customer needs. Customer-centered new product development begins and ends with understanding customers and involving them in the process.

Team-Based New Product Development

Good new product development also requires a total-company, cross-functional effort. Some companies organize their new product development process into the orderly sequence of steps shown in Figure 9.1, starting with idea generation and ending with commercialization. Under this *sequential product development* approach, one company department works individually to complete its stage of the process before passing the new product along to the next department and stage. This orderly, step-by-step process can help bring control to complex and risky projects. But it can also be dangerously slow. In fast-changing, highly competitive markets, such slow-but-sure product development can result in product failures, lost sales and profits, and crumbling market positions.

Team-based new product development

New product development in which various company departments work closely together, overlapping the steps in the product development process to save time and increase effectiveness.

To get their new products to market more quickly, many companies use a **team-based new product development** approach. Under this approach, company departments work closely together in cross-functional teams, overlapping the steps in the product development process to save time and increase effectiveness. Instead of passing the new product from department to department, the company assembles a team of people from various departments that stays with the new product from start to finish. Such teams usually include people from the marketing, finance, design, manufacturing, and legal departments and even supplier and customer companies. In the sequential process, a bottleneck at one phase can seriously slow an entire project. In the team-based approach, however, if one area hits snags, it works to resolve them while the team moves on.

The team-based approach does have some limitations, however. For example, it sometimes creates more organizational tension and confusion than the more orderly sequential approach. However, in rapidly changing industries facing increasingly shorter product life cycles, the rewards of fast and flexible product development far exceed the risks. Companies that combine a customer-centered approach with team-based new product development gain a big competitive edge by getting the right new products to market faster.

Systematic New Product Development

Finally, the new product development process should be holistic and systematic rather than compartmentalized and haphazard. Otherwise, few new ideas will surface, and many good ideas will sputter and die. To avoid these problems, a company can install an *innovation management system* to collect, review, evaluate, and manage new product ideas.

The company can appoint a respected senior person to be its innovation manager. It can set up web-based idea management software and encourage all company stakeholders—employees, suppliers, distributors, dealers—to become involved in finding and developing new products. It can assign a cross-functional innovation management committee to evaluate proposed new product ideas and help bring good ideas to market. It can also create recognition programs to reward those who contribute the best ideas.

The innovation management system approach yields two favorable outcomes. First, it helps create an innovation-oriented company culture. It shows that top management supports, encourages, and rewards innovation. Second, it will yield a larger number of new product ideas, among which will be found some especially good ones. The good new ideas will be more systematically developed, producing more new product successes. No longer will good ideas wither for the lack of a sounding board or a senior product advocate.

Thus, new product success requires more than simply thinking up a few good ideas, turning them into products, and finding customers for them. It requires a holistic approach for finding new ways to create valued customer experiences, from generating and screening new product ideas to creating and rolling out want-satisfying products to customers.

More than this, successful new product development requires a whole-company commitment. At companies known for their new product prowess, such as Google, Samsung, Apple, 3M, and P&G, the entire culture encourages, supports, and rewards innovation. For example, at Nestlé, a world-leading food and beverage giant and one of the world's most innovative companies, innovation is at the heart of everything it does (see Real Marketing 9.1).

Real Marketing 9.1 | Nestlé: How the Food Industry Leader Utilizes New Product Development and Innovation

Nestlé S.A. is a Swiss global food and beverage company formed in 1905 through the merger of the Anglo-Swiss Milk Company and Farine Lactée Henri Nestlé. Since its founding by Henri Nestlé, the company has become the largest food company in the world by revenue and was ranked 34th in the Top 100 companies on the Fortune Global 500 list in 2017.

Innovation and new product development have always been at the heart of Nestlé since its beginning, for it has had to keep up with an ever-changing environment as well as to define and to drive new markets. This would not be possible without Nestlé's extensive R&D capability. In 2018, the company announced that the Nestlé Research Center and Nestlé Institute of Health Sciences (NIHS) would be combined into one organization called Nestlé Research based in Switzerland and employing 800 people. The move was designed to speed up the process from invention to market. Each of Nestlé's products has a team of scientists, engineers, nutritionists, designers, regulatory specialists, and consumer care representatives behind it. In recent years it has focused on becoming a nutrition, health, and wellness company; as such, part of the company's vision is to make its products tastier as well as offer healthier choices.

Let us look at an example from the United Kingdom: Maggi—A Natural Choice, a new brand that was developed solely to target customers in the United Kingdom as a result of extensive market and customer analysis. In the United Kingdom, Maggi consists of a range of culinary aid products such as bouillons, soups, seasonings, and sauces to aid cooking and add flavor. Nestlé found that the UK foodservice market is not only highly competitive but companies must also apply high standards to products and their nutritional content to meet strict food safety and labeling laws. Furthermore, as a result of food scares and greater incidences of food allergies, customers worldwide are becoming increasingly knowledgeable and demanding about what they eat, leading to even more stringent specifications.

The Maggi brand came to be seen as uninteresting and old-fashioned in the United Kingdom due to its dehydrated format and flavor, resulting in declining sales. Nestlé decided to act to meet customers' increasing requirements for fresh-tasting culinary aids and regain market share. A central element of the innovation and new product development process at Nestlé is to put the customers at the core of its innovation movement. Maggi first commissioned face-to-face qualitative research to gauge the views and attitudes of chefs and consumers. The results showed that customers believed that fresh was best.

However, the views and attitudes of chefs were different. They generally stated that their customers preferred that everything be made from scratch (that is, made from basic raw ingredients), but they do not have the time and the money to do this. Consequently, the research showed that there was a sizeable market potential for chefs who aim to please their customers with time- and money-saving culinary aid products with natural qualities that make their cooking as fresh tasting as possible. Following these market research results, Nestlé launched the brand Maggi—A Natural Choice with the brand proposition to combine real and fresh ingredients with the time- and cost-saving effects of culinary aid products.

Using chefs and their customers as external idea sources and drivers for innovation and new product development, Nestlé decided that in addition to needing a more natural taste, the new products needed to offer value for money at the same time. Following its internal and generic new product development process, the first step involved a clearly written product brief for Maggi's factories based on the new brand proposition. The brief gives comprehensive product specifications, specific dietary requirements (such as "gluten-free"), as well as the final price range. In the second step, Maggi's food technologists develop a variety of kitchen samples that are then presented before a panel of specialist taste testers, including chefs and their customers. The third step involves reporting the results of the product testing in the framework of an interactive and revolving process in which any changes needed are incorporated into further samples. The final step of the product development process is the sign-off stage, in which an agreement on the samples is confirmed along with the pricing. The Maggi factories then commence production. In parallel, front labels are designed, product photography commissioned, recipe sheets produced, and sales presenters briefed to ensure a successful product launch.

The final products developed and launched under the Maggi—A Natural Choice range were lower in salt and made using sunflower oil. Nutritional information and allergy warnings on the packaging inform chefs about the products so they in turn can advise their customers as necessary. For the product launch itself, select trade media such as *Catering Update* and *Caterer and Hotelkeeper* carried advertising and promotional material.

In addition, eight-page supplements were produced to communicate the new brand proposition, supported by direct mailing of

The brand proposition of Maggi—A Natural Choice was to combine the goodness and taste of real and fresh ingredients with the time- and cost-saving effects of culinary aid products.

Shebeko/Shutterstock

informative literature to chefs and other users. Maggi also sponsors events for chefs that involve using Maggi—A Natural Choice products, such as the Nestlé Toque d'Or competition, in which teams have to battle against each other and the clock in a live cooking arena. This event has become the top event for the top talents in the United Kingdom. Maggi works closely with the main food services wholesalers and cash-and-carry operators and supports them with promotional material about new products to coincide with the launch.

Against the background of its customer centered new product development, Nestlé continues to improve its range further and extend its approach to providing healthier food. In Thailand, the Nestlé brand Milo has launched a low-sugar, ready-to-drink beverage. Alongside this is a sports program that aims to encourage a balanced diet and active lifestyle for children aged 6–12 years. As of 2018, the program has grown to reach over a million children across 1,000 schools. Nestlé are also very active in the area of bio-fortification. This is a GM approach to

boosting the nutritional value of crops as a means of helping to improve the nutrition of millions of people in a sustainable manner. This is a long-term project, and in 2017, Nestlé began working with the International Food Policy Research Institute (IFPRI) to accelerate progress.

Nestlé's work has yielded dividends. In April 2016, Nestlé ranked second in Oxfam's Behind the Brands scorecard, which ranks the world's Top 10 consumer food-and-beverage companies on their policies and commitments to improve food security and sustainability.[17]

Author Comment | A company's products are born, grow, mature, and then decline, just as living things do. To remain vital, the firm must continually develop new products and manage them effectively throughout their life cycles.

Product life cycle (PLC)
The course of a product's sales and profits over its lifetime.

Product Life-Cycle Strategies

OBJECTIVE 9-3 Describe the stages of the product life cycle and how marketing strategies change during a product's life cycle.

After launching the new product, management wants that product to enjoy a long and happy life. Although it does not expect the product to sell forever, the company wants to earn a decent profit to cover all the effort and risk that went into launching it. Management is aware that each product will have a life cycle, although its exact shape and length are not known in advance.

● **Figure 9.2** shows a typical **product life cycle (PLC)**, the course that a product's sales and profits take over its lifetime. The PLC has five distinct stages:

1. *Product development:* The company finds and develops a new product idea. During product development, sales are zero, and the company's investment costs mount.
2. *Introduction:* A period of slow sales growth as the product is introduced in the market. Profits are nonexistent in this stage because of the heavy expenses of product introduction.
3. *Growth:* A period of rapid market acceptance and increasing profits.
4. *Maturity:* A period of slowdown in sales growth because the product has achieved acceptance by most potential buyers. Profits level off or decline because of increased marketing outlays to defend the product against competition.
5. *Decline:* The period when sales fall off and profits drop.

Not all products follow all five stages of the PLC. Some products are introduced and die quickly; others stay in the mature stage for a long, long time. Some enter the decline stage and are then cycled back into the growth stage through strong promotion or repositioning. It seems that a well-managed brand could live forever. Venerable brands like Coca-Cola, Gillette, IBM, American Express, Wells Fargo, Levi-Strauss, Crayola, and Quaker, for

● FIGURE 9.2
Sales and Profits over the Product's Life from Inception to Decline

Some products die quickly; others stay in the mature stage for a long, long time. For example, Crayola Crayons have been around for more than 115 years. However, to keep the brand young, the company has added a continuous stream of contemporary new products, such as Color Alive, which lets kids color cartoons, scan them, and then watch as an app animates them.

● FIGURE 9.3
Styles, Fashions, and Fads

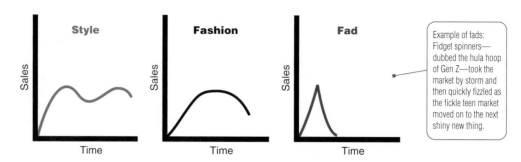

Example of fads: Fidget spinners—dubbed the hula hoop of Gen Z—took the market by storm and then quickly fizzled as the fickle teen market moved on to the next shiny new thing.

instance, are still going strong after more than 100 years. The 150-year-old TABASCO sauce brand brags that it's "over 150 years old and still able to totally whup your butt!"

The PLC concept can describe a *product class* (gasoline-powered automobiles), a *product form* (SUVs), or a *brand* (the Ford Escape). The PLC concept applies differently in each case. Product classes have the longest life cycles; the sales of many product classes stay in the mature stage for a long time. Product forms, in contrast, tend to have the standard PLC shape. Product forms such as dial telephones, VHS tapes, and film cameras passed through a regular history of introduction, rapid growth, maturity, and decline.

A specific brand's life cycle can change quickly because of changing competitive attacks and responses. For example, although laundry soaps (product class) have enjoyed a long life cycle, the life cycles of laundry product forms and specific brands have tended to be shorter. Powdered detergents (product form) have increasingly given way to liquids and pods. And today's leading U.S. brands of laundry detergent are Tide and Gain; the leading brands 100 years ago were Fels-Naptha and Octagon.

The PLC concept also can be applied to what are known as styles, fashions, and fads. Their special life cycles are shown in ● Figure 9.3. A **style** is a basic and distinctive mode of expression. For example, styles appear in homes (colonial, ranch, transitional), clothing (formal, casual), and art (realist, surrealist, abstract). Once a style is invented, it may last for generations, passing in and out of vogue. A style has a cycle showing several periods of renewed interest.

A **fashion** is a currently accepted or popular style in a given field. For example, the more formal "business attire" look of corporate dress of the 1980s and 1990s gave way to the "business casual" look of the 2000s and 2010s. Fashions tend to grow slowly, remain popular for a while, and then decline slowly.

Fads are temporary periods of intense sales driven by short-term consumer enthusiasm. A fad may be part of an otherwise normal life cycle, as in the case of recent surges in the sales of poker chips and accessories. Or the fad may comprise a brand's or product's entire life cycle.

Style
A basic and distinctive mode of expression.

Fashion
A currently accepted or popular style in a given field.

Fad
A temporary period of unusually high sales driven by consumer enthusiasm and immediate product or brand popularity.

● An example is the fidget spinner—the small, three-pronged ball-bearing device that you flick and spin to relieve stress or just because it's fun to do. Dubbed the "hula hoop of Gen Z," the spinners took the preteen and teen market by storm in early 2017. By early May of that year, the gizmos accounted for an amazing 17 percent of daily online toy sales. However, like most fads, sales quickly started to fizzle. By June, then widely sold by mass merchants like Walmart and Target, the gadgets were becoming too common to be cool. It didn't help that schools began banning the toys as distractions. Notoriously fickle teens lost interest and moved on to the next shiny new thing. Other examples of fads include selfie sticks, Silly Bandz, and Pokemon Go.[18]

Marketers can apply the product life-cycle concept as a useful framework for describing how products and markets work. And when used carefully, the PLC concept can help in developing good marketing strategies for the different life-cycle stages. However, using the PLC concept for forecasting product performance or developing marketing strategies presents some practical problems. For example, in practice, it is difficult to forecast the sales level at each PLC stage, the length of each stage, and the shape of the PLC curve. Using the PLC concept to develop marketing strategy also can be difficult because strategy is both

● **Fads:** Dubbed the "hula hoop of Gen Z," fidget spinners took the preteen and teen market by storm. However, like most fads, sales quickly fizzled as fickle teens moved on to the next shiny new thing.

3Baboons/Shutterstock

a cause and a result of the PLC. The product's current PLC position suggests the best marketing strategies, and the resulting marketing strategies affect product performance in later stages.

Moreover, marketers should not blindly push products through the traditional product life-cycle stages. Instead, marketers often defy the "rules" of the life cycle and position or reposition their products in unexpected ways. By doing this, they can rescue mature or declining products and return them to the growth phase of the life cycle. Or they can leapfrog obstacles that slow consumer acceptance and propel new products forward into the growth phase.

The moral of the product life cycle is that companies must continually innovate; otherwise, they risk extinction. To grow, the company must develop a steady stream of new products that bring new value to customers. And no matter how successful its current product lineup, a company must skillfully manage the life cycles of existing products for future success. Financial-software maker Intuit does this well. Rather than sitting on its successful products, it systematically reinvents them before competitors can. So Intuit's products stay in a perpetual PLC growth stage and never reach maturity or go into decline.

We looked at the product development stage of the PLC in the first part of this chapter. We now look at strategies for each of the other life-cycle stages.

Introduction Stage

Introduction stage
The PLC stage in which a new product is first distributed and made available for purchase.

The **introduction stage** starts when a new product is first launched. Introduction takes time, and sales growth is apt to be slow. Well-known products such as frozen foods, HDTVs, and all-electric cars lingered for many years before they entered a stage of more rapid growth.

In this stage, as compared to other stages, profits are negative or low because of the low sales and high distribution and promotion expenses. Much money is needed to attract distributors and build their inventories. Promotion spending is relatively high to inform consumers of the new product and get them to try it. Because the market is not generally ready for product refinements at this stage, the company and its few competitors produce basic versions of the product. These firms focus their selling on those buyers who are the most ready to buy.

A company, especially the *market pioneer*, must choose a launch strategy that is consistent with the intended product positioning. It should realize that the initial strategy is just the first step in a grander marketing plan for the product's entire life cycle. If the pioneer chooses its launch strategy to make a "quick killing," it may be sacrificing long-run revenue for the sake of short-run gain. The pioneer has the best chance of building and retaining market leadership if it plays its cards correctly from the start.

Growth Stage

Growth stage
The PLC stage in which a product's sales start climbing quickly.

If the new product satisfies the market, it will enter a **growth stage** in which sales will start climbing quickly. The early adopters will continue to buy, and later buyers will start following their lead, especially if they hear favorable word of mouth. Attracted by the opportunities for profit, new competitors will enter the market. They will introduce new product features and the market will expand. The increase in competitors leads to an increase in the number of distribution outlets, and sales jump just to build reseller inventories. Prices remain where they are or decrease only slightly. Companies keep their promotion spending at the same or a slightly higher level. Educating the market remains a goal, but now the company must also meet the competition.

Profits increase during the growth stage as promotion costs are spread over a large volume and as unit manufacturing costs decrease. The firm uses several strategies to sustain rapid market growth for as long as possible. It improves product quality and adds new product features and models. It enters new market segments and new distribution channels. It shifts some advertising from building product awareness to building product conviction and purchase, and it lowers prices at the right time to attract more buyers.

In the growth stage, the firm faces a trade-off between high market share and high current profit. By spending a lot of money on product improvement, promotion, and distribution, the company can capture a dominant position. In doing so, however, it gives up maximum current profit, which it hopes to make up in the next stage.

Real Marketing 9.2

Managing L'Oréal's Product Life Cycle: More Than Just Makeup

Founded in 1909, L'Oréal has devoted itself to one business over the century: beauty. Headquartered in Clichy near Paris, the company has become the largest cosmetics company worldwide, operating in 130 countries with 44 international brands. Its mother brand, L'Oréal Paris, is the no. 1 beauty brand in the world.

In the increasingly dynamic environment of the cosmetics industry, L'Oréal has to ensure a continuous and sophisticated management of the life cycle of its products and services to bring new value and appeal to its customers. By tradition, the makeup market has long been driven by classic mass marketing brands such as Maybelline New York and Max Factor. In addition, competition is intensified by brands selling directly to customers, such as Avon, and, in particular, low-cost brands such as Essence and Kiko. While competition is fierce and challenging, the makeup market is growing fast. To a large extent this growth is driven by so-called makeup artist brands, which are product lines initially used by professionals or named after famous makeup artists such as MAC, Benefit, and Bobby Brown. There are also many makeup brands that bear the names of perfume or luxury ready-to-wear brands, such as Shiseido, Chanel, or Yves Saint Laurent.

L'Oréal's makeup brand L'Oréal Paris has a long tradition of 30 years in the market, and it currently ranks no. 2 in the global market after Estee Lauder. The global makeup market has seen steady growth from $55 billion in 2012, and by 2024 it is estimated that it will be worth $85 billion. Even though L'Oréal's makeup brand performed better than the market with a significant market share increase, it was outperformed by the makeup artist brands. With respect to the product life cycle, the L'Oréal makeup brand was close to the maturity phase, as the competition was fierce, profits were slowing down, and the brand's customers were aging. An initial analysis of the market and its competitors indicated that the two fastest growing types of brands—makeup artist brands and low-cost brands—had something in common: a very large variety of colors that appealed to customers. Although L'Oréal's makeup brand was still performing, the company realized that this might not be sustainable enough in the future to compete with its rivals. By tradition, the brand was particularly strong when it comes to foundation and mascara products but had been increasingly challenged by the fashionable segment of color variety and selection.

Yann Joffredo, Senior Vice President, Global Product Development, has emphasized that the traditional market has shifted and that today's women shop "looks" rather than products. As a result, conventional channels are no longer the only key in this new era of internet sales, cross-channel purchasers and connected beauty. Instead of pursuing an exit strategy and dropping out of the makeup market like Nivea did in 2011, L'Oréal wanted to continue building its makeup brand and avoid the decline stage.

In order to achieve this target, the company looked at various market research reports and conducted a battery of tests. One study carried out in Europe showed that L'Oréal Paris was seen as a trustworthy brand whose products were highly effective and innovative, enhancing beauty in an elegant manner while bringing self-esteem to women. However, the study also discovered that the brand was not seen as the most dynamic and trendy in the industry, particularly when it came to the younger generation, who said that L'Oréal did not offer the right shades. All findings were analyzed in detail in order to determine the right strategy with respect to competition and the marketing environment while still hewing close to the company's culture and values.

L'Oréal decided to choose a different positioning from the low-cost brands. Without the cost structure that L'Oréal has, with a team of over 3,800 researchers, the low-cost brands would always win the battle of costs.

Consequently, the decision was made to learn from the makeup artist brands' success by repositioning the brand and developing an innovative color statement that appealed to young consumers. L'Oréal Paris established a new strategy platform, moving from a generalist brand to a multi-specialist one. In 2014, the name of the brand was changed to L'Oréal Makeup Designer Paris.

The value proposition is that the products are developed and endorsed by the greatest makeup artists and spokespeople. The brand is positioned on three pillars: L'Art du Regard (The Art of Looks), L'Architecture du Teint (The Architecture of Complexion), and L'Obsession de la Couleur (Color Obsession). In order to evolve from proposing products to offering an experience, the brand needed to create an interactive relationship with its audience at all customer touchpoints, offline and particularly online. Therefore, the new positioning and strategy was primarily driven by the creation of the revolutionary Makeup Genius App, an easy-to-use smartphone iOS application that gives customers the ability to "shop" their look instantly.

Thanks to head and expression tracking features as well as face texture 3D analysis, this application enabled users to be the designers of their own looks through a real-time interactive mirror. In addition, L'Oréal Paris developed a fully integrated digital approach in order to bring valuable services to consumers, inspiring conversations and building relationships through social

L'Oréal had to contend with the perception that it was not trendy enough for the younger generation.

ITAR-TASS News Agency/Alamy Stock Photo

media platforms. The campaign kicked off on three continents, starting in France, the United States, and China in May 2014. Cyril Chapuy, L'Oréal Paris International General Manager, stated that the strategy successfully positioned the company at the vanguard of creativity and fashion. As a result, L'Oréal has grown its Facebook followers to 35 million at the global level in the past 5–6 years. Makeup Genius has become the first beauty app in the world and has been downloaded over 20 million times since May 2014. Since then, the company has seen a strong acceleration of its sales.

In all, L'Oréal has successfully repositioned and relaunched its makeup brand by managing the product life cycle in a sophisticated way. By entering a new era of digital beauty through its Makeup Genius App, L'Oréal has successfully lived up to its ambition of creating tomorrow's beauty services.[19]

Maturity Stage

Maturity stage
The PLC stage in which a product's sales growth slows or levels off.

At some point, a product's sales growth will slow down, and it will enter the **maturity stage**. This maturity stage normally lasts longer than the previous stages, and it poses strong challenges to marketing management. Most products are in the maturity stage of the life cycle, and therefore most of marketing management deals with the mature product.

The slowdown in sales growth results in many producers with many products to sell. In turn, this overcapacity leads to greater competition. Competitors begin marking down prices, increasing their advertising and sales promotions, and upping their product development budgets to find better versions of the product. These steps lead to a drop in profit. Some of the weaker competitors start dropping out, and the industry eventually contains only well-established competitors.

Although many products in the mature stage appear to remain unchanged for long periods, most successful ones are actually evolving to meet changing consumer needs. Product managers should do more than simply ride along with or defend their mature products—a good offense is the best defense. They should consider modifying the market, product offering, and marketing mix.

In *modifying the market*, the company tries to increase consumption by finding new users and new market segments for its brands. For example, L'Oréal, a longtime leader in women's beauty care, has created new products aimed at men. It offers full lines of L'Oréal Men Expert grooming products, from deodorants and shower gels to skin care, hair care, and beard care products. Scientifically tailored to the special characteristics of men's skin, the lines include items such as Hydra Energetic Recharging Tissue Mask, Hydra Energetic Wake Up Boost Wash, Hydra Sensitive Soothing Birch Sap Moisturizer, and Vita Lift Anti-Wrinkle & Firming Moisturizer. L'Oréal's Men Expert products are "Built with men in mind."[20]

The company may also look for ways to increase usage among present customers. For example, Campbell encourages people to use more of its soups and other product by offering meal ideas and recipes. Using the Campbell's Kitchen website or phone app (www.campbells.com/kitchen/), meal planners can search for or exchange recipes, create their own personal recipe box, learn ways to eat healthier, calculate meal costs, and sign up for a daily or weekly Meal Mail program. At the Campbell's Facebook, Pinterest, and Twitter sites, consumers can join in and share on Campbell's Kitchen Community conversations.

The company might also try *modifying the product*—changing characteristics such as quality, features, style, packaging, or technology platforms to retain current users or attract new ones. Thus, most home appliance manufacturers are rapidly adapting their products for today's smart homes, with everything from Bluetooth and camera-laden kitchen appliances to voice-activated faucets. For example, Samsung's Chef Collection built-in appliances are all Wi-Fi or Bluetooth enabled, letting users monitor and control them while at home or away with a smartphone app. View-inside cameras let consumers see what's inside their refrigerators from anywhere, including remotely from the grocery store. The refrigerators have FlexZone compartments that transition from a fridge to a freezer with the touch of an app button. The dishwasher automatically opens the door when the cycle is done, to speed up drying times, and notifies users when the load is complete. The Chef Collection app lets users remotely preheat their ovens and set precise cooking temperatures. Or better

yet, the oven's smart-cooking algorithm can automatically sense what's in the oven and set its own temperatures and cooking times.[21]

Finally, the company can try *modifying the marketing mix*—improving sales by changing one or more marketing mix elements. The company can offer new or improved services to buyers. It can cut prices to attract new users and competitors' customers. It can launch a better advertising campaign or use aggressive sales promotions. In addition to pricing and promotion, the company can also move into new marketing channels to help serve new users.

PepsiCo has use all these market, product, and marketing mix modification approaches to continually reinvigorate its venerable Quaker Oats brand:[22]

● The 140-year-old Quaker brand is acting anything but its age. In recent years, far beyond its legacy oatmeal products, Quaker has added a kitchen cabinet full of contemporary new products and a full slate of modern marketing approaches. Quaker calls its new product developments "oatsperiments." According to a recent Malaysian ad, "We played with our oats. We spiced it up. For 140 years, we've experimented with our oats to create filling breakfast products that help you power through the day, and that's never going to stop." To that end, Quaker offers a full and ever-evolving line of energy-packed hot and cold cereals, snack bars, cookies, and other products that give contemporary families healthy lifestyle choices.

More than just new product additions, Quaker modernizes every other element of the brand to keep it fresh. For example, it recently slimmed down the iconic Befitting the more mobile and connected lifestyles of the young families it targets, Quaker's marketing campaigns incorporate healthy doses of digital media, including mobile ads, extensive social media content, and an information-packed community website.

● **Managing the product life cycle:** The 140-year-old Quaker brand is acting anything but its age. Through what it calls "oatsperiments," the brand has added a kitchen cabinet full of contemporary new products and a full slate of modern marketing approaches.

Provided courtesy of The Quaker Oat Company.

Decline Stage

The sales of most product forms and brands eventually dip. The decline may be slow, as in the cases of postage stamps and mainframe computers, or rapid, as in the case of VHS tapes. Sales may plunge to zero, or they may drop to a low level where they continue for many years. This is the **decline stage**.

Decline stage
The PLC stage in which a product's sales fade away.

Sales decline for many reasons, including technological advances, shifts in consumer tastes, and increased competition. As sales and profits decline, some firms withdraw from the market. Those remaining may prune their product offerings. In addition, they may drop smaller market segments and marginal trade channels, or they may cut the promotion budget and reduce their prices further.

Carrying a weak product can be very costly to a firm, and not just in profit terms. There are many hidden costs. A weak product may take up too much of management's time. It often requires frequent price and inventory adjustments. It requires advertising and sales-force attention that might be better used to make "healthy" products more profitable. A product's failing reputation can cause customer concerns about the company and its other products. The biggest cost may well lie in the future. Keeping weak products delays the search for replacements, creates a lopsided product mix, hurts current profits, and weakens the company's foothold on the future.

For these reasons, companies must identify products in the decline stage and decide whether to maintain, harvest, or drop them. Management may decide to *maintain* its brand, repositioning or reinvigorating it in hopes of moving it back into the growth stage of the product life cycle. ● Radio Flyer—the 100-year-old iconic red wagon maker—did this:[23]

Less than 20 years ago, Radio Flyer was declining and unprofitable. But rather giving in to the product life cycle, the brand engineered a turnaround. It sent designers out to visit homes, playgrounds, and side-street sidewalks around the country to watch firsthand how today's kids

● **Reinvigorating an iconic brand:** Thanks to customer-centered new product development, the 100-year-old Radio Flyer is once again growing and profitable.

Courtesy of Radio Flyer, Inc.

were using wagons, tricycles, and other items that Radio Flyer makes. At headquarters, it built a Play Lab with a test-track sidewalk, where it videotaped how kids ride. It also studied parents. "We'll say to Mom, 'OK, take this wagon and put it into your trunk,' and then we watch: Is it clumsy? Is it awkward?" says Radio Flyer's CEO.

Such customer-focused new product development paid off. For example, after watching small children ride the toys, the Radio Flyer team came up with a scooter that had a wider deck, two front wheels, and a less-wobbly ride. "We went from not having a product in this category to becoming the number one brand…in scooters for little kids," says the CEO. Thanks to this and other products successes, Radio Flyer is now once again rolling and profitable, recently earning it a spot on the *Forbes* list of America's Best Small Companies.

Management may decide to *harvest* the product, which means reducing various costs (plant and equipment, maintenance, R&D, advertising, sales force), hoping that sales hold up. If successful, harvesting will increase the company's profits in the short run. Finally, management may decide to *drop* the product from its line. The company can sell the product to another firm or simply liquidate it at salvage value. In recent years, Ford has sold off or discontinued several major brands such as Mercury and Volvo. And to meet market shifts, Ford recently shed most of its Ford brand sedan models, including the Ford Focus, the Ford Fiesta, and the once best-selling Ford Taurus. Dropping these slumping models let Ford focus on its more popular SUVs, crossovers, and pickups, which now account for a sizable majority all U.S. new vehicle sales.

● **Table 9.2** summarizes the key characteristics of each stage of the PLC. The table also lists the marketing objectives and strategies for each stage.[24]

● **Table 9.2** | **Summary of Product Life-Cycle Characteristics, Objectives, and Strategies**

	Introduction	Growth	Maturity	Decline
Characteristics				
Sales	Low sales	Rapidly rising sales	Peak sales	Declining sales
Costs	High cost per customer	Average cost per customer	Low cost per customer	Low cost per customer
Profits	Negative	Rising profits	High profits	Declining profits
Customers	Innovators	Early adopters	Mainstream adopters	Lagging adopters
Competitors	Few	Growing number	Stable number beginning to decline	Declining number
Marketing objectives				
	Create product engagement and trial	Maximize market share	Maximize profit while defending market share	Reduce expenditure and milk the brand
Strategies				
Product	Offer a basic product	Offer product extensions, service, and warranty	Diversify brand and models	Phase out weak items
Price	Use cost-plus	Price to penetrate market	Price to match or beat competitors	Cut price
Distribution	Build selective distribution	Build intensive distribution	Build more intensive distribution	Go selective: phase out unprofitable outlets
Advertising	Build product awareness among early adopters and dealers	Build engagement and interest in the mass market	Stress brand differences and benefits	Reduce to level needed to retain hardcore loyals
Sales promotion	Use heavy sales promotion to entice trial	Reduce to take advantage of heavy consumer demand	Increase to encourage brand switching	Reduce to minimal level

Source: Based on Philip Kotler and Kevin Lane Keller, *Marketing Management*, 15th ed. (Hoboken, NJ: Pearson Education, 2016), p. 358. © 2016. Printed and electronically reproduced by permission of Pearson Education, Inc., Hoboken, New Jersey.

Author | Let's look at just a few
Comment | more product topics,
including regulatory and social
responsibility issues and the special
challenges of marketing products
internationally.

Additional Product and Service Considerations

OBJECTIVE 9-4 Discuss two additional product issues: socially responsible product decisions and international product and services marketing.

We wrap up our discussion of products and services with two additional considerations: social responsibility in product decisions and issues of international product and services marketing.

Product Decisions and Social Responsibility

Marketers should carefully consider public policy issues and regulations regarding acquiring or dropping products, patent protection, product quality and safety, and product warranties.

Regarding new products, the government may prevent companies from adding products through acquisitions if the effect threatens to lessen competition. Companies dropping products must be aware that they have legal obligations, written or implied, to their suppliers, dealers, and customers who have a stake in the dropped product. Companies must also obey U.S. patent laws when developing new products. A company cannot make its product illegally similar to another company's established product.

Manufacturers must comply with specific laws regarding product quality and safety. The Federal Food, Drug, and Cosmetic Act protects consumers from unsafe and adulterated food, drugs, and cosmetics. Various acts provide for the inspection of sanitary conditions in the meat- and poultry-processing industries. Safety legislation has been passed to regulate fabrics, chemical substances, automobiles, toys, and drugs and poisons. The Consumer Product Safety Act of 1972 established the Consumer Product Safety Commission, which has the authority to ban or seize potentially harmful products and set severe penalties for violation of the law.

If consumers have been injured by a product with a defective design, they can sue manufacturers or dealers. A recent survey of manufacturing companies found that product liability was the second-largest litigation concern, behind only labor and employment matters. Tens of thousands of product liability suits are now tried in U.S. district courts each year. Although manufacturers are found to be at fault in only a small percentage of all product liability cases, when they are found guilty, awards can run into the tens or even hundreds of millions of dollars. Class action suits can run into the billions. For example, after admitting that it had rigged its diesel engine cars to cheat on emissions tests, Volkswagen agreed to pay fines of more than $4 billion in the United States alone, settled one class action suit from another $25 billion, and agreed to buy back 600,000 diesel vehicles from American consumers. Other fines and lawsuits were expected.[25]

This litigation phenomenon has resulted in huge increases in product liability insurance premiums, causing big problems in some industries. Some companies pass these higher rates along to consumers by raising prices. Others are forced to discontinue high-risk product lines. Some companies are now appointing *product stewards*, whose job is to protect consumers from harm and the company from liability by proactively ferreting out potential product problems.

International Product and Services Marketing

International product and services marketers face special challenges. First, they must figure out what products and services to introduce and in which countries. Then they must decide how much to standardize or adapt their products and services for world markets.

On the one hand, companies would like to standardize their offerings. Standardization helps a company develop a consistent worldwide image. It also lowers the product design, manufacturing, and marketing costs of offering a large variety of products. On the other hand, markets and consumers around the world differ widely. Companies must usually respond to these differences by adapting their product offerings.

For example, McDonald's operates in more than 100 countries, with sometimes widely varying local food preferences. So although you'll find its signature burgers and fries in most locations around the world, the chain has added menu items that meet the unique taste buds of customers in local markets. McDonald's serves salmon burgers in Norway, mashed-potato burgers in China, shrimp burgers in Japan, a Samurai Pork Burger in Thailand,

● **Global product adaptation: By adapting its menu and operations to the needs and preferences of French consumers and their culture, McDonald's has turned France into its second-most-profitable world market.**

PRM/SIPA/Newscom

chicken porridge in Malaysia, and Spam and eggs in Hawaii. In a German McDonald's, you'll find the Nürnburger (three large bratwurst on a soft roll with lots of mustard, of course); in Israel, there's the McFalafel (chickpea fritters, tomatoes, cucumber, and cheese topped with tahini and wrapped in lafa). Menus in Turkey feature a chocolate orange fried pie (Brazil adds banana, Egypt taro, and Hawaii pineapple). And French consumers love baguettes, so McDonald's bakes them fresh in its restaurants and sells them in oh-so-French McBaguette sandwiches.[26]

In many major global markets, McDonald's adapts more than just its menu. It also adjusts its restaurant design and operations. ● Although a McDonald's in Paris might at first seem a lot like one in Chicago, McDonald's has carefully adapted its French operations to suit French lifestyles. For example, French meal times tend to be longer, with more food consumed per sitting. So McDonald's has refined its restaurant interiors to create a comfortable, welcoming environment where customers want to linger and perhaps order an additional coffee or dessert. McDonald's even provides tableside service. Thanks to such menu and operations adaptations, the fast-food giant has turned France into its second-largest world market.[27]

Service marketers also face special challenges when going global. Some service industries have a long history of international operations. For example, the commercial banking industry was one of the first to grow internationally. Banks had to provide global services to meet the foreign exchange and credit needs of their home-country clients who wanted to sell overseas. In recent years, many banks have become truly global. Germany's Deutsche Bank, for example, serves more than 20 million customers through 2,400 branches in more than 70 countries. For its clients around the world who wish to grow globally, Deutsche Bank can raise money not only in Frankfurt but also in Zurich, London, Paris, Tokyo, and Moscow.[28]

Retailers are among the latest service businesses to go global. As their home markets become saturated, American retailers such as Walmart, Office Depot, and Saks Fifth Avenue are expanding into faster-growing markets abroad. For example, Walmart now has more than 11,700 stores in 27 countries; its international division's sales account for 24 percent of total sales. Foreign retailers are making similar moves. Asian shoppers can now buy American products in French-owned Carrefour stores. Carrefour—the world's ninth-largest retailer—now operates more than 12,000 stores in more than 30 countries. It is the leading retailer in Europe, Brazil, and Argentina and the largest foreign retailer in China.[29]

The trend toward growth of global service companies will continue, especially in banking, airlines, telecommunications, and professional services. Today, service firms are no longer simply following their manufacturing customers. Instead, they are taking the lead in international expansion.

Reviewing and Extending the Concepts

Objectives Review

A company's products face limited life spans and must be replaced by newer products. But new products can fail—the risks of innovation are as great as the rewards. The key to successful innovation lies in a customer-focused, holistic, total-company effort; strong planning; and a systematic new product development process.

OBJECTIVE 9-1 Explain how companies find and develop new product ideas. (pp 270–271)

Companies find and develop new product ideas from a variety of sources. Many new product ideas stem from *internal sources*. Companies conduct formal R&D, or they pick the brains of their employees, urging them to think up and develop new product

ideas. Other ideas come from *external sources*. Companies track *competitors'* offerings and obtain ideas from *distributors and suppliers* who are close to the market and can pass along information about consumer problems and new product possibilities.

Perhaps the most important sources of new product ideas are *customers* themselves. Companies observe customers, invite them to submit their ideas and suggestions, or even involve customers in the new product development process. Many companies are now developing *crowdsourcing* or *open-innovation* new product idea programs, which invite broad communities of people—customers, employees, independent scientists and researchers, and even the general public—into the new product innovation process. Truly innovative companies do not rely only on one source for new product ideas.

OBJECTIVE 9-2 List and define the steps in the new product development process and the major considerations in managing this process. *(pp 271–281)*

The new product development process consists of eight sequential stages. The process starts with *idea generation*. Next comes *idea screening,* which reduces the number of ideas based on the company's own criteria. Ideas that pass the screening stage continue through *product concept development,* in which a detailed version of the new product idea is stated in meaningful consumer terms. This stage includes *concept testing,* in which new product concepts are tested with a group of target consumers to determine whether the concepts have strong consumer appeal. Strong concepts proceed to *marketing strategy development,* in which an initial marketing strategy for the new product is developed from the product concept. In the *business-analysis* stage, a review of the sales, costs, and profit projections for a new product is conducted to determine whether the new product is likely to satisfy the company's objectives. With positive results here, the ideas become more concrete through *product development* and *test marketing* and finally are launched during *commercialization*.

New product development involves more than just going through a set of steps. Companies must take a systematic, holistic approach to managing this process. Successful new product development requires a customer-centered, team-based, systematic effort.

OBJECTIVE 9-3 Describe the stages of the product life cycle and how marketing strategies change during a product's life cycle. *(pp 281–287)*

Each product has a *life cycle* marked by a changing set of problems and opportunities. The sales of the typical product follow an S-shaped curve made up of five stages. The cycle begins with the *product development* stage in which the company finds and develops a new product idea. *The introduction stage* is marked by slow growth and low profits as the product is distributed to the market. If successful, the product enters a *growth stage,* which offers rapid sales growth and increasing profits. Next comes a *maturity stage* in which the product's sales growth slows down and profits stabilize. Finally, the product enters a *decline stage* in which sales and profits dwindle. The company's task during this stage is to recognize the decline and decide whether it should maintain, harvest, or drop the product. The different stages of the PLC require different marketing strategies and tactics.

OBJECTIVE 9-4 Discuss two additional product issues: socially responsible product decisions and international product and services marketing. *(pp 288–289)*

Marketers must consider two additional product issues. The first is *social responsibility*. This includes public policy issues and regulations involving acquiring or dropping products, patent protection, product quality and safety, and product warranties. The second involves the special challenges facing international product and services marketers. International marketers must decide how much to standardize or adapt their offerings for world markets.

Key Terms

OBJECTIVE 9-1

New product development (p 270)

OBJECTIVE 9-2

Idea generation (p 271)
Crowdsourcing (p 273)
Idea screening (p 273)
Product concept (p 274)
Concept testing (p 274)

Marketing strategy development (p 275)
Business analysis (p 275)
Product development (p 276)
Test marketing (p 276)
Commercialization (p 277)
Customer-centered new product development (p 278)
Team-based new product development (p 279)

OBJECTIVE 9-3

Product life cycle (PLC) (p 281)
Style (p 282)
Fashion (p 282)
Fad (p 282)
Introduction stage (p 283)
Growth stage (p 283)
Maturity stage (p 285)
Decline stage (p 286)

Discussion Questions

9-1 Explain how firms obtain new products and why it is an important process for companies and customers. (AACSB: Written and Oral Communication; Reflective Thinking)

9-2 Why do so many new products fail? (AACSB: Written and Oral Communication)

9-3 What actions are performed in the test marketing step of the new product development process? How does a business carry out this step? (AACSB: Communication)

9-4 Why might a business adopt a customer-centered approach to new product development? (AACSB: Communication)

9-5 Distinguish between a market modifying strategy and a marketing mix modifying strategy in the product life cycle process. (AACSB: Communication)

9-6 What special challenges do international product and services marketers face? (AACSB: Written and Oral Communication)

Critical Thinking Exercises

9-7 After it admitted that it had rigged its diesel engine cars to cheat on emissions tests, Volkswagen agreed to pay $4 billion in fines, buy back 600,000 diesel vehicles from American consumers, and settle a class action suit for $25 billion. How does the past scandal affect Volkswagen's ability to market its present-generation diesel engines based on its pollutant emissions? What strategy should it use? (AACSB: Written and Oral Communication; Information Technology; Reflective Thinking)

9-8 In small groups, research the Owlet Smart Sock. Where is this product in the new product life cycle? After examining the company website, assess what the company does well. What challenges will it face? (AACSB: Written and Oral Communication; Information Technology; Reflective Thinking)

9-9 Goat yoga is yoga practiced in the presence of live goats. Goatyoga.net describes it as "animal-assisted therapy in a natural setting with an unexpectedly smart, social, and profoundly cuddly animal. It's not a cancer cure, but it *is* an unbelievable distraction from politics, work, stress, sickness or depression." Is goat yoga (see goatyoga.net) a fad? What is its likely product life cycle? Please respond in a way that reflects your understanding of fads. (AACSB: Written and Oral Communication; Reflective Thinking)

APPLICATIONS AND CASES

Online, Mobile, and Social Media Marketing Share the Robot Vacuum Love

Although robot vacuums have been around for more than a decade, recent updates made them smarthome gadgets, allowing consumers to provide cleaning instructions from a smartphone. The upgrade increased the adoption of the innovation and the number of competitors in the market. iRobot (www.irobot.com), which offers a number of different robot cleaning machines, invites consumers to share the #iRobotLove on social media. The #iRobotLove campaign is iRobot's initiative to move the conversation about owning an iRobot vacuum—positioned based on the benefit of a cleaner home every day—onto social media. The customers are focused on the benefit of freedom from the mundane work, and they share their passion for the product that enables the freedom.

9-10 Visit a social media channel (Twitter, Instagram, or Facebook) and search for the hashtag #iRobotLove.

What do the user posts suggest about iRobot's ability to solve major customer problems? How could the user-generated content inform the new product development process? (AACSB: Written and Oral Communications; Reflective Thinking)

9-11 Visit www.pcmag.com/roundup/341251/the-best-robot-vacuums. How do the reviews of iRobot vacuums compare to competitive robot vacuums? Does the information from the review match the value proposition that is communicated using the user-generated content? What are the implications of your observations for consumer evaluations of the iRobot robot vacuums? (AACSB: Written and Oral Communication; Reflective Thinking)

Marketing Ethics Autonomous Autos

The road to autonomous cars could be right around the corner, but automakers will likely face twists and turns getting there as these vehicles make their way to the marketplace. Companies like Waymo, General Motors, Tesla, and even Uber and Lyft are piloting various autonomous vehicle technologies that will likely be seen on streets within the next three years. In one futuristic forecast, Goldman Sachs predicts that "robo-taxis will help the ride-hailing and ride-sharing business grow from $5 billion in revenue today to $285 billion by 2030…Without drivers, operating margins could be in the 20 percent range, more than twice what carmakers generate right now. If that kind of growth and profit come to pass—very big ifs—it would be almost three times what GM makes in a year." As this potentially lucrative technology looms on the horizon, consumers and industry groups, such as the Insurance Institute for Highway Safety, are concerned about safety measures and developing realistic consumer expectations. Test programs of self-driving vehicles on public roads have produced some high-profile accidents, some resulting in fatalities.

9-12 Discuss the ethical issues surrounding the testing and introduction of self-driving vehicles. Is there sufficient research to support the claims and safety of these new products? (AACSB: Written and Oral Communication; Ethical Understanding and Reasoning)

9-13 Would you use such a product? Why or why not? Support your answer. (AACSB: Written and Oral Communication; Reflective Thinking)

Marketing by the Numbers Taking It on the Road

According to the American Massage Therapy Association, the therapeutic massage industry grew more than 7 percent between 2013 and 2018, reaching $18 billion in revenue. The industry will continue to grow an estimated 4 percent or more through 2022. Although the majority of massages are performed in spas, massage therapy offices, or franchises such as Massage Envy, almost 30 percent occur in clients' homes. That has gotten the attention of many licensed massage therapists who see it as an opportunity to expand their businesses beyond their offices or spas. Some in-home patients are wealthy and prefer the personal service, whereas others are disabled or elderly homebounds who cannot get out to receive needed therapy. In-home massages require additional equipment, such as a portable massage table, and supplies such as flannel sheets, pillows, towels, lotions, massage stones, and relaxing music in addition to a vehicle. Additionally, because the production and consumption of services such as massages occur simultaneously, to really expand business, more massage therapists must be hired to cater to more clients.

9-14   Refer to Increase Distribution Coverage in Appendix 2: Marketing by the Numbers to answer the following question. Assume that adding this mobile service will increase fixed costs by $32,500 and that a contribution margin of 65 percent is desired. Determine the increase in sales necessary to break even on adding the service. (AACSB: Communication; Analytical Thinking)

9-15   What other factors must a therapist consider before adding this in-home service to his or her in-office service? (AACSB: Communication; Reflective Thinking)

Company Case Toyota: Developing a Million New Product Ideas Every Year

Toyota is one of the car industry's biggest success stories. Founded in 1918 as Toyota Spinning and Weaving company, it only started to produce automobiles in 1937, but since then the company has continued to grow to become one of the most important car manufacturers in the world. In this regard the company has been a global trailblazer in several areas related to product and product design, with some of its strategies, like the Toyota Product Development System (TPDS), becoming industry standards.

From Concept to Decision Hall

The new product development strategy at Toyota is realized mainly in five distinct steps:

1. *Creation of Concept.* This step is defined by the collection of ideas, mainly from employees but also from the general public through programs such as Ideas for Good. Major points taken into consideration are customer profile and future car trends. Designers then create an initial sketch.
2. *Development of the Idea.* After the initial sketches have been penciled out, a team of experienced designers create a complete 3D computer model with full details. Emphasis is on the realism of the project (how close it is to the final product) as well as creativity and visual appeal.
3. *Color Choice.* Toyota takes great care with minor details, even color. Every color is analyzed based on its fit with the general product idea and concept. For example, red might fit a sports car like the Toyota GTR but not a Toyota Offroader. Moreover, special attention is given to how the colors of different car parts fit with each other.
4. *Mock-Up.* A realistic mockup is created using clay, which the designers and engineers analyze to find errors.
5. *Decision Hall.* A few models are built and taken to a hall where they are analyzed in realistic environmental conditions. Light and rain are generated to see how the car looks in these settings.

Toyota believes in co-creation value in which all stakeholders are involved, potential customers included. The company uses three main sources of product ideas: employees in the engineering and design departments, other employees across the whole company, and people from outside the company. Toyota also gathers new product ideas from dealerships worldwide, as this is where customers bring their cars in for repairs. Ideas from engineers and designers are generated through the TPDS.

Toyota Creative Idea and Suggestion System

In 1951, the company developed the Toyota Creative Idea and Suggestion System (TCISS) to allow every employee to offer feedback on any topic they could bring an improvement to.

The TCISS was put in place to empower every employee to make informed suggestions regarding the production process, especially employees at the sharp end of production, arguably the ones most likely to highlight potential issues. The company offers an individual annual award for ideas submitted through the TCISS, for which employees can earn gold, silver, or bronze medals.

Since the TCISS was set up, the company has expanded its ideas creation process to include people from outside. It organized multiple idea contests and has received a growing number of creative submissions: in 1974, it exceeded a million; by 1984, 10 million; by 1988, 20 million; and by 2011, 40 million ideas—and the number continues to rise. In 2007, as an extension to the TCISS, the company launched an Innovation Fair where teams from the sales, financial, and IT departments compete in an idea-based tournament. It was at the 2007 Fair that hydrogen-powered vehicles were presented, and at the 2014 Fair, Bluetooth low-energy beacons to help dealers get better inventory management information were debuted and won funding.

Supporting and Rewarding Creativity

Fundamental to the TPDS is the human value of Toyota's employees. The company seeks to create an environment of creativity where ideas flow freely and contributions from every team member are encouraged and rewarded. To separate good ideas from bad ones, those who submit ideas must always explain how they contribute to the overall project. Additionally, each topic or problem receives multiple ideas, and each idea is verified based on a performance-based approach. Finally, to avoid "reinventing the wheel," all ideas are centralized in an easy-to-access ideas management system. This system, especially in the engineering department, involves the most exceptional and experienced engineers, who also serve in the role of teacher.

At Toyota, the boss can perform their subordinate's tasks at a higher level, so the creation process is not hindered by employees' differences with bureaucratically selected management. At higher echelons, managers are expected not only to possess advanced technical skills but also to see the bigger picture by carefully coordinating the work of multiple distinct departments working on the same project. As such, this facilitates the top management support that is so crucial for the new product development process.

In 2010, Toyota extended its search for new ideas to the general public through the "Ideas for Good" campaign, encouraging people to imagine new ways in which its technologies could be used for the betterment of their lives beyond the automotive world. The best ideas are selected by a panel of Toyota employees, and the winners are invited to participate in the Toyota design process for a future product related to their idea.

The Toyota Prius

Toyota's product life cycle is shaped by the launch of numerous generations of the same model. This strategy can extend the growth and maturity phases of the cycle by decades and involve multiple product generations. Consider the Toyota Prius, arguably its most successful model. Here, each phase of the product life cycle corresponds to a generation of the Prius.

1. *Introduction Phase*: The first generation of Toyota Prius was launched in 1997, after five years of design. As one of the world's first commercial hybrid vehicles, it was revolutionary; in fact, the design proved so successful that it has been maintained in all Toyota models since. The car was an immediate success in Japan, selling 40,000 units by the year 2000. Although it initially had slow external sales, by the end of 2003, when the first-generation production ended, the model had sold more than 123,000 units in all markets.

2. *Growth Phase*: This phase is represented by the second-generation Toyota Prius, which had more electrical features and a new hybrid motor that could achieve peak performance based only on the electrical part of the engine. The car was larger and fuel performance was improved by 15 percent. It was an immediate commercial success: by 2004, it had already sold more than the previous model over its entire lifespan. By 2012, when production stopped, worldwide sales had reached over 1,190,000 units.

3. *Maturity Phase*: This phase is represented by the third-generation Prius, which had incremental improvements: CO_2 emissions decreased by 14 percent, engine power increased by 22 percent, and fuel efficiency increased by 10 percent. This model also broke internal sales records, with a total of 3,360,000 units sold by 2014.

4. *Decline Phase*: This is what we can consider the current phase of the Prius. In 2016, the number of Priuses sold in the U.S. was half the number in 2012. The reasons range from lower gasoline prices to the emergence of full electric vehicles like Tesla.

Acting Responsibly for the World

Social responsibility at Toyota is incorporated in innovative ideas toward the environmental goal of reducing CO_2 emissions by more than 22 percent between 2010 and 2020. The company plans to produce only electric vehicles and hybrids by 2050 and to drop total CO_2 emissions by 90 percent until then. Toyota's website currently presents six electric vehicles, the latest being the Toyota Concept-I Ride, launched at the Tokyo Motor Show in 2017. These vehicles are small urban compacts designed to travel short distances in a busy city environment. The show also unveiled the Concept-i WALK, an electric personal transporter that operates like a Segway.

Technologies are being developed to ensure that Toyota's vehicles maintain the highest performance as well as environmental friendliness. Continuous improvement is cultivated. For example, the company recently discovered a method to create magnets for electric vehicles that uses 50 percent less critically rare materials than regular magnets. This means lower production costs for the same performance and a lower reliance on raw minerals. Partnerships with two Chinese battery companies, CATL and BYD, ensure a smooth entry into the full electric vehicle market.

Social responsibility at Toyota is also reflected in its testing of electric technologies in urban environments. Between 2014 and 2017, Toyota partnered with the French city of Grenoble, French energy provider EDF, and carpooling company City Lib to conduct an experiment on the integration of electric vehicles in public transportation. Toyota provided a fleet of electric vehicles using its proprietary technology and powering stations to complement the city's public transport—the result was 90 percent satisfaction among the people who used these services.

Toyota introduced multiple safety systems in all vehicles to reduce traffic accidents, such as emergency driver assistance and the Intelligent Clearance Sonar system, and has organized information campaigns on traffic safety, environmentalism, and society and culture. Toyota has also held cell vehicle classes at elementary schools in Iwaki City, and along with the China Soong Ching Ling Foundation, the company has provided scholarships to over 2,000 Chinese students to attend university.

At Toyota, workplace culture includes basing responsible product decisions on employees' volunteer activities. For instance, the company signed its employees up for the Tokyo Paralympic Games in 2019 to get a better understanding of different types of disabilities. In Belgium, Toyota donated the money collected through different employee activities to an NGO that deals with refugees and disadvantaged people. The Toyota Foundation has supported several public programs, including the Traffic Congestion Mitigation Project in Bangkok, the Station Access & Mobility Programme for the Bengaluru metro system, and the Ueyama Mobility Project to make traffic easier in mountainous regions in Okayama Prefecture, Japan. Toyota also sets itself apart with its policy toward Conflict Minerals, which are mined in war-torn zones, usually by warlords, gangsters, and local dictators. Toyota refuses to purchase minerals acquired through human rights violations, and it is a member of international organizations that monitor the routes of conflict minerals.[30]

Questions for Discussion

9-16 Provide a short explanation for each of the five steps of the product development strategy that Toyota follows.

9-17 Explain how ideas at Toyota are gathered and managed.

9-18 Describe the Toyota Creative Idea and Suggestion System and give examples of benefits that such a system can bring.

9-19 Explain the strategies during each stage of the product life cycle for the Toyota Prius.

9-20 Give examples of publicly responsible decisions that Toyota has recently been involved in. What is their impact on the society?

10

Pricing
Understanding and Capturing Customer Value

OBJECTIVES OUTLINE

OBJECTIVE 10-1 Answer the question "What is price?" and discuss the importance of pricing in today's fast-changing environment. **See: What Is Price?** *(pp 296–297)*

OBJECTIVE 10-2 Define price, identify the three major pricing strategies, and discuss the importance of understanding customer-value perceptions, company costs, and competitor strategies when setting prices. **See: Major Pricing Strategies** *(pp 297–306)*

OBJECTIVE 10-3 Identify and define the other important external and internal factors affecting a firm's pricing decisions. **See: Other Internal and External Considerations Affecting Price Decisions** *(pp 306–310)*

CHAPTER PREVIEW In this chapter, we look at the second major marketing mix tool—pricing. If effective product development, promotion, and distribution sow the seeds of business success, effective pricing is the harvest. Firms successful at creating customer value with the other marketing mix activities must still capture some of this value in the prices they earn. In this chapter, we discuss the importance of pricing, dig into three major pricing strategies, and look at internal and external considerations that affect pricing decisions. In the next chapter, we examine some additional pricing considerations and approaches.

For openers, let's examine Apple's pricing strategy. Apple has always set its prices substantially above those of even its highest-priced competitors. The company's vision has been to provide innovative designs and superior user experiences that make its premium prices secondary in the minds of customers who covet Apple products. Recently, however, as Apple faces stiffer global competition from lower-priced brands, some customers may now be questioning just how much more they are willing to pay for the iconic brand.

APPLE: Premium Priced and Worth It?

Apple is the prototypical premium pricer. Whether it's an iPhone, iPad, MacBook laptop, or Apple Watch, customers pay more for an Apple than for competing devices—a lot more. For example, the Apple iPhone's average selling price last year was well over $800, three times higher than the overall industry average. Similarly, a standard MacBook Pro costs hundreds of dollars more than a comparable Dell or HP laptop.

Yet despite such sky-high prices, Apple's products have flown off shelves for decades, as eager customers lined up to grab the latest models before they would inevitably sell out.

This has put Apple in an envious position: It has charged the highest prices and still captured market-leading revenue shares in most of its product categories. How has Apple pulled that off?

For Apple, success has never been about prices. Instead, it's been about the Apple user experience. Many tech companies make products that just occupy space and complete the tasks at hand. By contrast, Apple creates "life-feels-good" experiences. Ask Apple users and they'll tell you that their Apple devices simply work better and are easier to use. And they love Apple's clean, simple designs that ooze style.

From the beginning, Apple was an innovative leader, churning out one cutting-edge product after another, each working seamlessly with other products in Apple's portfolio. Making products customers wanted—usually before consumers themselves even knew what they wanted—resulted in one Apple-led revolution after another. Apple has always demonstrated a genius for wrapping technology beautifully around human needs in a way that puts its customers at the front of the crowd. In turn, Apple has built a huge corps of avid Apple enthusiasts. For more than four decades, its customers have anointed Apple as the undisputed keeper of all things cool. Such enthusiasm and support create demand for Apple products beyond the limits of price. Not only are Apple fans willing to pay more, they believe deep down that the value they receive is well worth the higher price.

One of the best illustrations of Apple's premium pricing power is the Apple Watch. Apple was hardly a pioneer in introducing a smartwatch. Dozens of companies were already selling wearables across a broad range of price points. In the year prior to the launch of the Apple Watch, competitors sold 6.8 million smartwatches at an average price of $189. Apple unveiled its own smartwatch in three versions. The least expensive version, the basic Apple Watch Sport, sold for $349, nearly twice the average industry price. At the other extreme was the ultra-premium Apple Watch Edition, made of solid 18-karat gold with sapphire crystal glass. Fully loaded, it sold for as much as $17,000. Even as the price of the Apple Watch has escalated with each new series, the company sold over 30 million Apple Watches last year, grabbing more than 50 percent of the rapidly expanding smartwatch market.

Apple's ability to command higher prices has produced stunning revenue and profit results. In smartphones, for example, Apple captures a 15 percent global unit market share, second to Samsung's 21 percent unit share. However, thanks to its much higher prices and margins, in the fourth quarter of last year, Apple grabbed an impressive 51 percent share of global smartphone revenues, compared to Samsung's 15.7 percent. And it reaped a stunning 87 percent of global smartphone profits, almost nine times Samsung's 10 percent. Apple enjoys similar revenue and profit dynamics for its laptops and other products.

Overall, Apple has become one of the largest and most valuable companies in the world. In just the past four years, Apple's sales have risen 45 percent to $266 billion, placing the company at number three among *Fortune*

Avid fans have long anointed Apple as the keeper of all things cool, believing deep down that the value they receive is worth the premium price.

Mark Lennihan/AP/Shutterstock

500 companies. Even more notable, Apple's record profits of $59 billion were higher than any other company's. And brand tracker Interbrand has rated Apple as the world's most valuable brand for six straight years.

Even with all this success, however, many analysts see signs that the superheated demand for all things Apple at any price may be cooling down. Although Apple posted record revenues and profits last year, the company's stock price experienced a year-end tailspin that erased some 35 percent of the company's value. The decline resulted from slowing sales growth for Apple products, primarily the iPhone, which accounts for a massive 60 percent of Apple's annual revenues.

Sales growth for smartphones in general has slowed as global economies struggle and phone ownership reaches saturation in many markets. Moreover, Apple appears to be losing some of its innovation edge—even its low-price competitors are closing the technology gap. Apple's premium prices make it particularly vulnerable to such market dynamics, especially in the world's rapidly growing emerging markets. But even at home, iPhone loyalists appear to be keeping their old Apple phones longer. Prices keep rising with each new model, and the new Apple phones don't seem different enough to justify the upgrade.

Apple's pricing dilemma is most apparent in emerging global markets. Consider China, the world's largest smartphone market and Apple's second-largest market behind the United States. Once China's top-selling phone, the iPhone now places

> Apple has always set its prices way above those of competitors, reaping the rewards of higher revenues and profits. But as Apple faces stiffer global competition from lower-priced brands, some customers may be questioning just how much more they are willing to pay for the iconic brand.

fifth behind fast-growing, low-priced local competitors such as Huawei and Xiaomi. Chinese market leader Huawei has spurted globally in recent years and now runs dead even with Apple as the world's second-largest smartphone producer behind Samsung. Huawei sells a wide range of phones, many with features similar to those of the iPhone but at much lower prices.

Similarly, Xiaomi has come from nowhere in the past several years by producing low-cost smartphones, laptops, and other devices modeled closely after Apple products. Xiaomi packs potent technology and stunning design into dirt-cheap phones that sell at a fraction of Apple's prices. For instance, an entry-level iPhone sells in China for about $900, compared with an entry-level Xiaomi smartphone at only $150. With its smart designs and lower prices, Xiaomi is targeting the "technically inclined, geeky, typically younger sort of customer who can't afford a top-of-the-line Apple or Samsung phone," says one tech blogger. Such consumers make up the fastest-rising tech segment not just in China but also in other emerging markets like India, where Apple captures only 2 percent of the smartphone market.

So far, Apple neither has nor intends to have an affordable answer for the types of consumers that provide strong growth for Xiaomi, Huawei, and other cheaper brands. Low-end products simply don't fit Apple's operating style or premium positioning. And Apple, perhaps appropriately for now, is reluctant to give up the high profit margins that go with its high prices.

Still, feeling competitive pressures and the recent stumble in sales growth, Apple has now relaxed its prices, at least a little. In the United States, it promoted its latest entry-level phone with a trade-in allowance of up to $300. And in a rare move, Apple recently cut prices on some of its flagship phones in non-U.S. markets—only the second time in the iPhone's 12-year history that Apple has made an across-the-board price cut.

Some tech analysts are calling for Apple to make permanent price cuts to the entire iPhone line, both at home and abroad. Some are even urging Apple to create lower-range phones, as Samsung has done, to compete with cheaper brands in global markets. That's a difficult decision for Apple, whose premium pricing has long been a winner. But whatever it decides about prices, Apple must regain and retain its innovative edge, ensuring that customers are getting full value for whatever price they pay. Only truly premium products can earn premium prices.[1]

● Pricing: No matter what the state of the economy, companies should sell value, not price.

magicoven/Shutterstock.com

COMPANIES TODAY FACE a fierce and fast-changing pricing environment. Value-seeking. smartphone-wielding customers have put increased pricing pressure on many companies. Thanks to tight economic times in recent years, the pricing power of the internet, and value-driven retailers such as Walmart and Amazon, today's consumers are pursuing more frugal spending strategies. In response, it seems that almost every company has been looking for ways to cut prices.

● Yet cutting prices is often not the best answer. Reducing prices unnecessarily can lead to lost profits and damaging price wars. It can cheapen a brand by signaling to customers that price is more important than the customer value a brand delivers. Instead, in both good economic times and bad, companies should sell value, not price. In some cases, that means selling lesser products at rock-bottom prices. But in most cases, it means persuading customers that paying a higher price for the company's brand is justified by the greater value they gain.

What Is Price?

OBJECTIVE 10-1 Answer the question "What is price?" and discuss the importance of pricing in today's fast-changing environment.

In the narrowest sense, **price** is the amount of money charged for a product or a service. More broadly, price is the sum of all the values that customers give up to gain the benefits of having or using a product or service. Historically, price has been the major factor affecting buyer choice. In recent decades, however, nonprice factors have gained increasing importance. Even so, price remains one of the most important elements that determine a firm's market share and profitability.

Price is the only element in the marketing mix that produces revenue; all other elements represent costs. Price is also one of the most flexible marketing mix elements. Unlike product features and channel commitments, prices can be changed

Price
The amount of money charged for a product or service, or the sum of the values that customers exchange for the benefits of having or using the product or service.

quickly. At the same time, pricing is the number-one problem facing many marketing executives, and many companies do not handle pricing well. Some managers view pricing as a big headache, preferring instead to focus on other marketing mix elements.

However, smart managers treat pricing as a key strategic tool for creating and capturing customer value. Prices have a direct impact on a firm's bottom line. A small percentage improvement in price can generate a large percentage increase in profitability. More important, as part of a company's overall value proposition, price plays a key role in creating customer value and building customer relationships. So, instead of shying away from pricing, smart marketers embrace it as an important competitive asset.[2]

> Author Comment | Setting the right price is one of the marketer's most difficult tasks. A host of factors come into play. But as the opening story about Apple illustrates, finding and implementing the right pricing strategy is critical to success.

Major Pricing Strategies

OBJECTIVE 10-2 Define price, identify the three major pricing strategies, and discuss the importance of understanding customer-value perceptions, company costs, and competitor strategies when setting prices.

The price the company charges will fall somewhere between one that is too low to produce a profit and one that is too high to produce any demand. ● **Figure 10.1** summarizes the major considerations in setting prices. Customer perceptions of the product's value set the ceiling for its price. If customers perceive that the product's price is greater than its value, they will not buy the product. Likewise, product costs set the floor for a product's price. If the company prices the product below its costs, the company's profits will suffer. In setting its price between these two extremes, the company must consider several external and internal factors, including competitors' strategies and prices, the overall marketing strategy and mix, and the nature of the market and demand.

Figure 10.1 suggests three major pricing strategies: customer value–based pricing, cost-based pricing, and competition-based pricing. We discuss each strategic pricing approach in turn.

> Author Comment | Like everything else in marketing, good pricing starts with customers and their perceptions of value.

Customer Value–Based Pricing

In the end, the customer will decide whether a product's price is right. Pricing decisions, like other marketing mix decisions, must start with customer value. When customers buy a product, they exchange something of value (the price) to get something of value (the benefits of having or using the product). Effective customer-oriented pricing involves understanding how much value consumers place on the benefits they receive from the product and setting a price that captures that value.

Customer value–based pricing
Setting price based on buyers' perceptions of value rather than on the seller's cost.

Customer value–based pricing uses buyers' perceptions of value as the key to pricing. Value-based pricing means that marketers cannot design a product and marketing program and then set the price. They must consider price along with all other marketing mix variables *before* they set a marketing program.

● **Figure 10.2** compares value-based pricing with cost-based pricing. Although costs are an important consideration in setting prices, cost-based pricing is often product

● FIGURE 10.1
Considerations in Setting Price

If customers perceive that a product's price is greater than its value, they won't buy it. If the company prices the product below its costs, profits will suffer. Between the two extremes, the "right" pricing strategy is one that delivers both value to the customer and profits to the company.

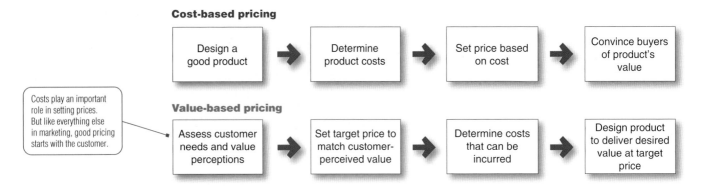

Cost-based pricing

| Design a good product | → | Determine product costs | → | Set price based on cost | → | Convince buyers of product's value |

Costs play an important role in setting prices. But like everything else in marketing, good pricing starts with the customer.

Value-based pricing

| Assess customer needs and value perceptions | → | Set target price to match customer-perceived value | → | Determine costs that can be incurred | → | Design product to deliver desired value at target price |

● **FIGURE 10.2**
Value-Based Pricing versus Cost-Based Pricing

driven. The company designs what it considers to be a good product, adds up the costs of making the product, and sets a price that covers costs plus a target profit. Marketing must then convince buyers that the product's value at that price justifies its purchase. If the price turns out to be too high, the company must settle for lower markups or lower sales, both resulting in disappointing profits.

Value-based pricing reverses this process. The company first assesses customer needs and value perceptions. It then sets its target price based on customer perceptions of value. The targeted value and price drive decisions about what costs can be incurred and the resulting product design. As a result, pricing begins with analyzing consumer needs and value perceptions, and the price is set to match perceived value.

It's important to remember that "good value" is not the same as "low price." ● For example, some consumers consider premium YETI coolers to be a real bargain, even at their eye-popping prices:[3]

● **Customer value–based price: Most customers consider a premium YETI cooler to be a real value, even at eye-popping prices ranging from $299 to $1,299.**

Ty Sprague

What's a cooler worth—one of those insulated containers you take camping or haul to a picnic or tailgate party? If it's a YETI cooler, you can expect to pay from $299 to as much as $1,299 for the top-of-the-line Tundra model. However, despite their high prices and spare, boxy designs, YETI coolers have achieved an almost cult-like status among outdoor enthusiasts and on constructions sites, ranches, football stadium parking lots, or even military bases. The company's founding slogan "YETI Coolers—Wildly Stronger. Keep Ice Longer!" suggests the reasons why. Devoted users will tell you that a YETI does keep things cooler—with a FatWall design (with twice the insulation of competitors) and an interlocking lid system with a gasket that keeps the cold in. And rugged YETI coolers are made to last—no more busted hinges, failed latches, or caved-in lids. They're even certified as grizzly bear–proof by the Interagency Grizzly Bear Committee. One ad describes a YETI as "The cooler you've always wanted. And the last cooler you'll ever need." So, is a YETI cooler worth the premium price compared to less expensive coolers made by Igloo or Rubbermaid? To many consumers, a YETI would be a real value at twice the price.[4]

A company will often find it hard to measure the value customers attach to its product. For example, calculating the cost of ingredients in a meal at a fancy restaurant is relatively easy. But assigning value to other measures of satisfaction such as taste, environment, relaxation, conversation, and status is very hard. Such value is subjective; it varies for both different consumers and different situations.

Still, consumers will use these perceived values to evaluate a product's price, so the company must work to measure them. Sometimes, companies ask consumers how much they would pay for a basic product and for each benefit added to the offer. Or a company might conduct experiments to test the perceived value of different product offers. According to an old Russian proverb, there are two fools in every market—one who asks too much and one who asks too little. If the seller charges more than the buyers' perceived value, the company's sales will suffer. If the seller charges less, its products will sell very well, but they will produce less revenue than they would if they were priced at the level of perceived value.

We now examine two types of value-based pricing: *good-value pricing* and *value-added pricing*.

Good-Value Pricing

Recent years have seen a shift in consumer attitudes toward price and quality. Increasingly, consumers want to know that they are getting good value for their money. In response, many companies have changed their pricing approaches to bring them in line with changing price and value perceptions. More and more, marketers have adopted the strategy of **good-value pricing**—offering the right combination of quality and good service at a fair price.

In many cases, this has involved introducing less-expensive versions of established brand name products or new lower-price lines. For example, Kroger carries three low-priced product lines—Heritage Farm, Check This Out, and Psst, which offers thrift-conscious customers rock-bottom prices on grocery staples such as chicken, toilet paper, and sugar. Good-value prices are a relative thing—even premium brands can launch value versions. ● Mercedes-Benz released its CLA Class, entry-level models starting at $31,500. From its wing-like dash and diamond-block grille to its 208-hp turbo inline-4 engine, the CLA Class gives customers "The Art of Seduction. At a price reduction."[5]

In other cases, good-value pricing involves redesigning existing brands to offer more quality for a given price or the same quality for less. Some companies even succeed by offering less value but at very low prices. For example, the ALDI supermarket chain has established an impressive good-value pricing position by which it gives customers a basic assortment of quality items at super-low everyday prices (see Real Marketing 10.1).

ALDI practices an important type of good-value pricing at the retail level called *everyday low pricing* (EDLP). EDLP involves charging a constant, everyday low price with few or no temporary price discounts. Perhaps the king of EDLP is Walmart, which practically defined the concept. Except for a few sale items every month, Walmart promises everyday low prices on everything it sells. In contrast, *high-low pricing* involves charging higher prices on an everyday basis but running frequent promotions to lower prices temporarily on selected items. Department stores such as Kohl's and JCPenney practice high-low pricing by having frequent sale days, early-bird savings, and bonus earnings for store credit-card holders.

The art of seduction. At a price reduction.

The Concept Style Coupe set the auto show circuit abuzz with its dramatic design and athletic presence. Snowgoers had only one request: Build it. The CLA brings an international sensation to life with nothing lost in translation, from its diamond-block grille to its frameless door glass to its sweeping taillamps, all at a down-to-earth price.

● **Good-value pricing: Even premium brands can launch good-value versions. The Mercedes CLA Class gives customers "The Art of Seduction. At a price reduction."**
© Courtesy of Daimler AG

Good-value pricing
Offering just the right combination of quality and good service at a fair price.

Value-added pricing
Attaching value-added features and services to differentiate a company's offers and charging higher prices.

Value-Added Pricing

Value-based pricing doesn't mean simply charging what customers want to pay or setting low prices to meet competition. Instead, many companies adopt **value-added pricing** strategies. Rather than cutting prices to match competitors, they add quality, services, and value-added features to differentiate their offers and thus support their higher prices.

● For example, Philips has relied on its investments in meticulous research and innovation based on customer insights to offer greater value. Philips's lighting division, for instance, works on creating energy-efficient solutions for home and office users. More than 20 percent of

● **Value-added pricing: Philips uses R&D and innovation rather than low prices to differentiate its lighting solutions.**
Sergiy Palamarchuk/Alamy Stock Photo

Real Marketing 10.1 | ALDI: Doing Things "Differentli" to Bring Customers Amazingly Low Prices

When asked to name the world's largest grocery chains, you'd probably come up with Walmart, the world's largest retailer; and maybe Kroger, the largest U.S. grocery-only merchant. One name that probably wouldn't come to mind is Germany-based discount grocer ALDI. Yet, surprisingly, with more than $85 billion in annual revenues and more than 11,000 stores in 20 countries, ALDI is the world's eighth-largest retailer overall and the second-largest grocery-only retailer behind Kroger. What's more, ALDI is taking the United States and other country markets by storm, growing faster than any of its larger rivals.

How does ALDI do it? Its simple formula for success is no secret: Give customers a basic assortment of good-quality items at everyday extra-low prices. These days, many grocers brag about low prices. But at ALDI, they are an absolute fact. The rapidly expanding chain invites customers to "Shop differentli"—ALDI's way of promising customers a unique shopping experience that delivers quality products while saving both money and time. ALDI has redesigned the food shopping experience to reduce costs and give customers prices that it claims are up to 50 percent lower than those of rival supermarkets. "ALDI does things differentli to bring you amazing low prices," says the company.

To get those super-low prices, however, ALDI customers must settle for a little less in terms of many of the extras they've come to expect from competitors. For example, they get a smaller selection. To keep costs and prices down, ALDI operates smaller, energy-saving stores (about one-fourth the size of traditional supermarkets) that stock only about 1,400 of the fastest-moving grocery items (the typical supermarket carries about 40,000 items). ALDI also carries fewer national brands; more than 90 percent of its items are ALDI's own store brands. (ALDI claims customers are paying for the product itself, not national brand advertising and marketing.) And ALDI does no promotional pricing or price matching—it just sticks with its efficient everyday very low prices. "We don't match other stores' prices because that would mean raising ours," say ALDI.

In trimming costs and passing savings along to customers, ALDI leaves no stone unturned. Even customers themselves help to keep costs low: They bring their own bags (or purchase them from ALDI for a small fee), bag their own groceries (ALDI provides no bagger), and return shopping carts on their own (to get back a 25-cent deposit). But to ALDI fans, the savings

make it all worthwhile. ALDI tells customers "You can't eat frills, so why pay for them?"

Whereas ALDI cuts operating costs to the bone, it doesn't scrimp on quality. With its preponderance of store brands, ALDI exercises complete control over the quality of the products on its shelves, and the chain promises that it checks and rechecks everything it sells to "meet or exceed the quality of national name brands." The company operates its own test kitchens, taste testing more than 30,000 products each year to ensure that customers get more than just low prices. ALDI is so confident that its products stand up to national brands that it backs every grocery item with its "Twice as Nice" guarantee: "If for any reason you are not 100-percent satisfied with any product, we will gladly replace the product *and* refund your money."

To improve the quality of its assortment, ALDI has progressively added items that aren't usually associated with "discount" grocers. Beyond the typical canned, boxed, and frozen food basics, ALDI carries fresh meats and fish, baked goods, and fresh produce. It also features ALDI Finds—limited-time specialty goods that are "Here today, gone tomorrow"—such as Castello Aged Havarti, Fusia Fresh Spicy Surimi roll, Season's Choice Steamable Edamame, and Fresh USDA tenderloin filet mignon. ALDI even offers an extensive selection of organic, gluten-free, and vegan foods. Beyond that, every ALDI branded product is completely free of certified synthetic color, added MSG, and partially hydrogenated oils. Many customers rave about their favorite ALDI products, items they can't live without and

can't get anywhere else. With items like these and clean, bright stores, ADLI targets not just low-income customers but frugal middle-class and upper-middle-class customers as well.

None of this is news to German shoppers, who have loved ALDI for decades. In Germany, the chain operates 4,200 stores, accounting for about 12 percent of the market. Together with discount grocery competitors Lidl and Netto, the German market has more than its share of discount grocers. That might explain why Walmart gave up in Germany just nine years after entering the market. Against competitors like ALDI, Walmart's normally low prices were just too expensive for frugal German consumers.

ALDI's no-frills basic approach isn't for everyone. Whereas some shoppers love the low prices, basic assortments, exclusive store brands, and simple store atmosphere, others can't imagine life without at least some of the luxuries and amenities offered by traditional grocery chains. But most people who shop at ALDI quickly become true believers. Testimonials from converts litter the internet. "My favorite grocery store! Mind blowingly cheaper than anywhere else," proclaims one customer. Another fervent fan, a mother shopping on a tight budget for her family, used to scour the papers for coupons and shop at two or three different stores on a typical grocery trip. Now, she gets everything on her list in a single stop at ALDI, with money left over for extra items not on the list. "I cannot believe how much I saved!" she says. "ALDI is now my immediate go-to grocery store! I'm totally team ALDI."[6]

Fast-growing grocery chain ALDI has redesigned the food shopping experience to reduce costs and create customer value.

AKP Photos/Alamy Stock Photo

the world's total electricity is used by lighting these days, and 75 percent of current urban lighting is energy inefficient. As the public sector in many countries invests heavily in more energy-efficient technologies, Philips is surging ahead with its innovative lighting solutions. One of its latest offerings is connected LED lighting systems and services, which it claims will save energy as well as enable their customers to work more efficiently and productively. The company intends to win the consumer market in professional lighting systems and is gearing up to do this by driving more innovation and by becoming more customer centric.[7]

Cost-Based Pricing

Author Comment | Costs set the floor for price, but the goal isn't always to minimize costs. In fact, many firms invest in higher costs so that they can claim higher prices and margins (think back about YETI coolers or Bose audio products). The key is to manage the spread between costs and prices—how much the company makes for the customer value it delivers.

Whereas customer value perceptions set the price ceiling, costs set the floor for the price that the company can charge. **Cost-based pricing** involves setting prices based on the costs of producing, distributing, and selling the product plus a fair rate of return for the company's effort and risk. A company's costs may be an important element in its pricing strategy.

Some companies, such as Walmart or ALDI, work to become the *low-cost producers* in their industries. Companies with lower costs can set lower prices that result in smaller margins but greater sales and profits. However, other companies—such as Apple, BMW, and Steinway—intentionally pay higher costs so that they can add value and claim higher prices and margins. For example, it costs more to make a "handcrafted" Steinway piano than a Yamaha production model. But the higher costs result in higher quality, justifying an average $87,000 price. To those who buy a Steinway, price is nothing; the Steinway experience is everything. The key is to manage the spread between costs and prices—how much the company makes for the customer value it delivers.

Types of Costs

Cost-based pricing

Setting prices based on the costs of producing, distributing, and selling the product plus a fair rate of return for effort and risk.

A company's costs take two forms: fixed and variable. **Fixed costs** (also known as **overhead**) are costs that do not vary with production or sales level. For example, a company must pay each month's bills for rent, heat, interest, and executive salaries regardless of the company's level of output. **Variable costs** vary directly with the level of production. Each smartphone or tablet produced by Samsung involves a cost of computer chips, wires, plastic, packaging, and other inputs. Although these costs tend to be the same for each unit produced, they are called variable costs because the total varies with the number of units produced. **Total costs** are the sum of the fixed and variable costs for any given level of production. Management wants to charge a price that will at least cover the total production costs at a given level of production.

Fixed costs (overhead)

Costs that do not vary with production or sales level.

Variable costs

Costs that vary directly with the level of production.

Total costs

The sum of the fixed and variable costs for any given level of production.

The company must watch its costs carefully. If it costs the company more than its competitors to produce and sell a similar product, the company will need to charge a higher price or make less profit, putting it at a competitive disadvantage.

Costs at Different Levels of Production

To price wisely, management needs to know how its costs vary with different levels of production. For example, suppose Lenovo built a plant to produce 1,000 tablet computers per day. ● **Figure 10.3A** shows the typical short-run average cost curve (SRAC). It shows that the cost per tablet is high if Lenovo's factory produces only a few per day. But

● **FIGURE 10.3**
Cost per Unit at Different Levels of Production per Period

What's the point of all the cost curves in this and the next few figures? Costs are an important factor in setting price, and companies must understand them well!

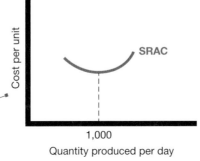

A. Cost behavior in a fixed-size plant

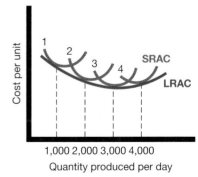

B. Cost behavior over different-size plants

as production moves up to 1,000 tablets per day, the average cost per unit decreases. This is because fixed costs are spread over more units, with each one bearing a smaller share of the fixed cost. Lenovo can try to produce more than 1,000 tablets per day, but average costs will increase because the plant becomes inefficient. Workers have to wait for machines, the machines break down more often, and workers get in each other's way.

If Lenovo believed it could sell 2,000 tablets a day, it should consider building a larger plant. The plant would use more efficient machinery and work arrangements. Also, the unit cost of producing 2,000 tablets per day would be lower than the unit cost of producing 1,000 units per day, as shown in the long-run average cost (LRAC) curve (● Figure 10.3B). In fact, a 3,000-capacity plant would be even more efficient, according to Figure 10.3B. But a 4,000-daily production plant would be less efficient because of increasing diseconomies of scale—too many workers to manage, paperwork slowing things down, and so on. Figure 10.3B shows that a 3,000-daily production plant is the best size to build if demand is strong enough to support this level of production.

Costs as a Function of Production Experience

Suppose Lenovo runs a plant that produces 3,000 tablets per day. As Lenovo gains experience in producing tablets, it learns how to do it better. Workers learn shortcuts and become more familiar with their equipment. With practice, the work becomes better organized, and Lenovo finds better equipment and production processes. With higher volume, Lenovo becomes more efficient and gains economies of scale. As a result, the average cost tends to decrease with accumulated production experience. This is shown in ● Figure 10.4.[8] Thus, the average cost of producing the first 100,000 tablets is $10 per tablet. When the company has produced the first 200,000 tablets, the average cost has fallen to $8.50. After its accumulated production experience doubles again to 400,000, the average cost is $7. This drop in the average cost with accumulated production experience is called the **experience curve** (or the **learning curve**).

A downward-sloping experience curve exists is highly significant for a company. Not only will the company's unit production cost fall, but it will fall faster if the company makes and sells more during a given time period. But the market has to stand ready to buy the higher output. And to take advantage of the experience curve, Lenovo must get a large market share early in the product's life cycle. This suggests the following pricing strategy: Lenovo should price its tablets lower; its sales will then increase, its costs will decrease through gaining more experience, and then it can lower its prices further.

Some companies have built successful strategies around the experience curve. However, a single-minded focus on reducing costs and exploiting the experience curve will not always work. Experience-curve pricing carries some major risks. The aggressive pricing might give the product a cheap image. The strategy also assumes that competitors are weak and not willing to fight it out by meeting the company's price cuts. Finally, while the company is building volume under one technology, a competitor may find a lower-cost technology that lets it start at prices lower than those of the market leader, which still operates on the old experience curve.

Cost-Plus Pricing

The simplest pricing method is **cost-plus pricing** (or **markup pricing**)—adding a standard markup to the cost of the product. Construction companies, for example, submit job bids by estimating the total project cost and adding a standard markup for profit. Lawyers, accountants, and other professionals typically price by adding a standard markup to their costs. Some sellers tell their customers they will charge cost plus a specified markup; for example, aerospace companies often price this way to the government.

To illustrate markup pricing, suppose a toaster manufacturer had the following costs and expected sales:

Variable cost	$10
Fixed costs	$300,000
Expected unit sales	50,000

Then the manufacturer's cost per toaster is given by the following:

$$\text{unit cost} = \text{variable cost} + \frac{\text{fixed cost}}{\text{unit sales}} = \$10 + \frac{\$300,000}{50,000} = \$16$$

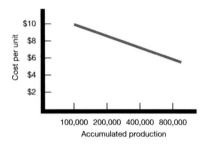

● FIGURE 10.4
Cost per Unit as a Function of Accumulated Production: The Experience Curve

Experience curve (learning curve)
The drop in the average per-unit production cost that comes with accumulated production experience.

Cost-plus pricing (markup pricing)
Adding a standard markup to the cost of the product.

Now suppose the manufacturer wants to earn a 20 percent markup on sales. The manufacturer's markup price is given by the following:[9]

$$\text{markup price} = \frac{\text{unit cost}}{(1 - \text{desired return on sales})} = \frac{\$16}{1 - 0.2} = \$20$$

The manufacturer would charge dealers $20 per toaster and make a profit of $4 per unit. The dealers, in turn, will mark up the toaster. If dealers want to earn 50 percent on the sales price, they will mark up the toaster to $40 ($20 + 50% of $40). This number is equivalent to a *markup on cost* of 100 percent ($20/$20).

Does using standard markups to set prices make sense? Generally, no. Any pricing method that ignores demand and competitor prices is not likely to lead to the best price. Still, markup pricing remains popular for many reasons. First, sellers are more certain about costs than about demand. By tying the price to cost, sellers simplify pricing; they do not need to make frequent adjustments as demand changes. Second, when all firms in the industry use this pricing method, prices tend to be similar, so price competition is minimized. Third, many people feel that cost-plus pricing is fairer to both buyers and sellers. Sellers earn a fair return on their investment but do not take advantage of buyers when buyers' demand becomes great.

Break-Even Analysis and Target Profit Pricing

Break-even pricing (target return pricing)

Setting price to break even on the costs of making and marketing a product, or setting price to make a target return.

Another cost-oriented pricing approach is **break-even pricing** (or a variation called **target return pricing**). The firm sets a price at which it will break even or make the target return on the costs of making and marketing a product.

Target return pricing uses the concept of a *break-even chart*, which shows the total cost and total revenue expected at different sales volume levels. ● **Figure 10.5** shows a break-even chart for the toaster manufacturer discussed here. Fixed costs are $300,000 regardless of sales volume. Variable costs are added to fixed costs to form total costs, which rise with volume. The total revenue curve starts at zero and rises with each unit sold. The slope of the total revenue curve reflects the price of $20 per unit.

The total revenue and total cost curves cross at 30,000 units. This is the *break-even volume*. At $20, the company must sell at least 30,000 units to break even, that is, for total revenue to cover total cost. Break-even volume can be calculated using the following formula:

$$\text{break-even volume} = \frac{\text{fixed cost}}{\text{price} - \text{variable cost}} = \frac{\$300,000}{\$20 - 10} = 30,000$$

If the company wants to make a profit, it must sell more than 30,000 units at $20 each. Suppose the toaster manufacturer has invested $1,000,000 in the business and wants to set a price to earn a 20 percent return, or $200,000. In that case, it must sell at least 50,000 units at $20 each. If the company charges a higher price, it will not need to sell as many toasters to achieve its target return. But the market may not buy even this lower volume at the higher price. Much depends on price elasticity and competitors' prices.

● **FIGURE 10.5**
Break-Even Chart for Determining Target Return Price and Break-Even Volume

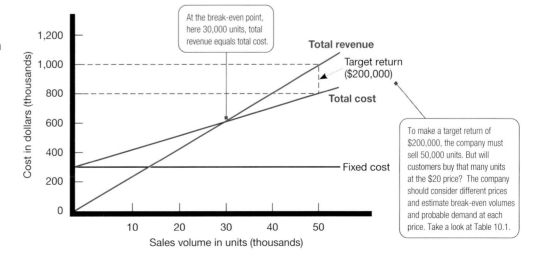

At the break-even point, here 30,000 units, total revenue equals total cost.

Total revenue

Target return ($200,000)

Total cost

Fixed cost

To make a target return of $200,000, the company must sell 50,000 units. But will customers buy that many units at the $20 price? The company should consider different prices and estimate break-even volumes and probable demand at each price. Take a look at Table 10.1.

Cost in dollars (thousands)

Sales volume in units (thousands)

The manufacturer should consider different prices and estimate break-even volumes, probable demand, and profits for each. This is done in ● **Table 10.1**. The table shows that as price increases, the break-even volume drops (column 2). But as price increases, the demand for toasters also decreases (column 3). At the $14 price, because the manufacturer clears only $4 per toaster ($14 less $10 in variable costs), it must sell a very high volume to break even. Even though the low price attracts many buyers, demand still falls below the high break-even point, and the manufacturer loses money. At the other extreme, with a $22 price, the manufacturer clears $12 per toaster and must sell only 25,000 units to break even. But at this high price, consumers buy too few toasters, and profits are negative. The table shows that a price of $18 yields the highest profits. Note that none of the prices produce the manufacturer's target return of $200,000. To achieve this return, the manufacturer will have to search for ways to lower the fixed or variable costs, thus lowering the break-even volume.

> **Author Comment** | In setting prices, the company must also consider competitors' prices. No matter what price it charges—high, low, or in between—the company must be certain to give customers superior value for that price.

Competition-Based Pricing

Competition-based pricing involves setting prices based on competitors' strategies, costs, prices, and market offerings. Consumers will base their judgments of a product's value on the prices that competitors charge for similar products.

Competition-based pricing

Setting prices based on competitors' strategies, prices, costs, and market offerings.

In assessing competitors' pricing strategies, a company should ask several questions. First, how does the company's market offering compare with competitors' offerings in terms of customer value? If consumers perceive that the company's product or service provides greater value, the company can charge a higher price. If consumers perceive less value relative to competing products, the company must either charge a lower price or change customer perceptions to justify a higher price.

Next, how strong are current competitors, and what are their current pricing strategies? If the company faces a host of smaller competitors charging high prices relative to the value they deliver, it might charge lower prices to drive weaker competitors from the market. If the market is dominated by larger, lower-price competitors, a company may decide to target unserved market niches by offering value-added products and services at higher prices.

Importantly, the goal is not to match or beat competitors' prices. Rather, the goal is to set prices according to relative value. If a company creates greater value for customers, higher prices are justified. For example, Caterpillar makes high-quality, heavy-duty construction and mining equipment. It dominates its industry despite charging higher prices than competitors such as Komatsu. Loyal Caterpillar customers have learned that, even though they pay more up front for a Cat, thanks to Caterpillar's high quality and extraordinary dealer support, it will cost them less in the long run (see Real Marketing 10.2).

What principle should guide decisions about prices to charge relative to those of competitors? The answer is simple in concept but often difficult in practice: No matter what price you charge—high, low, or in between—be certain to give customers superior value for that price.

● **Table 10.1** | **Break-Even Volume and Profits at Different Prices**

Price	Unit Demand Needed to Break Even	Expected Unit Demand at Given Price	Total Revenue (1) × (3)	Total Costs*	Profit (4) − (5)
$14	75,000	71,000	$994,000	$1,010,000	–$16,000
16	50,000	67,000	1,072,000	970,000	102,000
18	37,500	60,000	1,080,000	900,000	180,000
20	30,000	42,000	840,000	720,000	120,000
22	25,000	23,000	506,000	530,000	–24,000

*Assumes fixed costs of $300,000 and constant unit variable costs of $10.

Real Marketing 10.2 | Caterpillar: Adding Value for the Price Keeps the Big Cat Purring

For more than nine decades, Caterpillar has dominated the heavy construction and mining equipment industry. Its familiar yellow tractors, crawlers, loaders, bulldozers, and trucks are a common sight at any construction area around the world. And after all those years, the big Cat is still purring. It sells hundreds of different products in nearly 200 countries, with annual sales reaching $55 billion. During the past two years, as the struggling global construction industry has stabilized, Caterpillar's sales have shot up 45 percent and profits have soared. Caterpillar captures a 16.4 percent share of the worldwide heavy-equipment business, well ahead of number-two Komatsu at 12 percent.

Heavy construction and mining equipment represents a huge purchase for industrial customers. And the industry is highly competitive, served by quality competitors the likes of Caterpillar, Komatsu, John Deere, Hitachi, and Volvo. As a result, when buying high-priced construction equipment, customers thoroughly analyze and compare competitive products on quality, service, and price. Surprisingly, in this cutthroat environment, Caterpillar maintains its dominance despite charging higher prices than competitors.

But Caterpillar knows that customers consider much more than just initial purchase prices. They also look at how much the equipment will cost to operate over the long haul in terms of fuel, routine maintenance, repairs, and downtime. Caterpillar has long stressed that its products yield the lowest total cost of ownership over the lifetime of the equipment. That's a powerful claim. By one estimate, the total cost of ownership on a medium-size piece of equipment is two to three times the initial purchase price. The ratio gets much higher with larger, more expensive pieces of equipment that have very long life spans. Loyal Caterpillar customers have learned that even though they pay more up front for a Cat, it will cost them less in the long run.

It all starts with the reliability of Caterpillar equipment. Over the years, Cat has produced a steady stream of innovative, high-quality products. The company thoroughly engineers low cost of ownership into every piece of Cat equipment, from design through manufacturing. But perhaps even more important, Caterpillar has developed a vast global network of 172 outstanding independent dealers, employing 157,000 people at 2,163 branches, who help customers maintain that equipment and keep it working.

According to a former Caterpillar CEO: "After the product leaves our door, the dealers take over. They're the ones who live with the product for its lifetime. They're the ones customers see. ...They service a product frequently throughout its life, carefully monitoring a machine's health and scheduling repairs to prevent costly downtime. [They] create the image of a company that doesn't just stand *behind* its products but *with* its products, anywhere in the world. Our dealers are the reason that our motto—Buy the Iron, Get the Company—is not an empty slogan."

"Buy the Iron, Get the Company"—that's a powerful value proposition. It means that when customers buy Cat equipment, they become members of the Caterpillar family. Caterpillar and its dealers work in close harmony with customers to help them get the most out of their Cat equipment. The company's large dealer network gives customers rapid access to parts and service, minimizing downtime and maximizing productivity.

In the heavy-equipment industry, downtime can mean big losses. Caterpillar's exceptional service gives it a huge advantage in winning and keeping customers. Consider BHP Billiton, a Caterpillar customer that operates the huge Antamina copper and zinc mine in Peru. More than a mile in length, the mine sits 14,100 oxygen-deprived feet above sea level in the Peruvian Andes. Every hour of every day, Cat machines—giant trucks, mechanical shovels, scrapers, and other brutes—carve out massive amounts of minerals from the earth. All told, BHP uses more than $200 million worth of Caterpillar machinery at Antamina—and it will spend another $200 million servicing them over their working life. When equipment breaks down, BHP loses money fast. It gladly pays a premium price for machines and service it can count on. And it knows it can count on Caterpillar and its dealer network for superb support and long machine life.

For example, the BHP equipment at Antamina includes a fleet of 49 mammoth 250-ton Caterpillar series 793 trucks—43-foot-high machines costing millions of dollars each and powered by a diesel engine with more oomph than a tank. Thanks to initial quality and Caterpillars unrelenting support, the 793s have an unmatched reputation for durability and longevity. "Our very first 793 truck, placed in service 27 years ago, is still in service delivering best-in-class cost-per-ton," says Caterpillar's global production manager. One of the longest-running 793s has amassed 173,000 operating hours—the equivalent of nearly 20 years nonstop.

Caterpillar's extraordinary dealer support extends to the company's parts delivery system, the fastest and most reliable in the industry. Through a vast network of distribution centers and service facilities around the world, Caterpillar and its dealers guarantee parts delivery within 48 hours anywhere in the world, from the Alaskan tundra to the deserts of Timbuktu. In contrast, it's not unusual for competitors' customers to wait four or five costly days for a part.

Pricing versus competitors: Caterpillar dominates the heavy equipment industry despite charging premium prices. Customers believe that Caterpillar gives them a lot more value for the price over the lifetime of its machines.

Kristoffer Tripplaar/Alamy Stock Photo

Thus, Caterpillar doesn't try to meet or beat competitors' prices. Instead, it offers greater value that justifies its higher prices. When a commercial customer once asked a Caterpillar dealer why it should pay $500,000 for a big Caterpillar bulldozer when it could get an "equivalent" Komatsu dozer for $420,000, the Caterpillar dealer famously provided an analysis like the following:

$420,000	the Caterpillar's price if equivalent to the competitor's bulldozer

+$50,000	the value added by Caterpillar's superior reliability and durability
+$40,000	the value added by Caterpillar's superior service
+$40,000	the value added by Caterpillar's lower lifetime operating costs
+$20,000	the value added by Caterpillar's longer parts warranty

= $570,000	the total value-added price for Caterpillar's bulldozer
−$70,000	discount
= $500,000	final price

So while the customer paid an $80,000 price premium for the Caterpillar bulldozer, it was actually getting $150,000 in added value over the product's lifetime. The customer chose the Caterpillar bulldozer.[10]

Other Internal and External Considerations Affecting Price Decisions

OBJECTIVE 10-3 Identify and define the other important external and internal factors affecting a firm's pricing decisions.

Beyond customer value perceptions, costs, and competitor strategies, the company must consider several additional internal and external factors. Internal factors affecting pricing include the company's overall marketing strategy, objectives, and marketing mix as well as other organizational considerations. External factors include the nature of the market and demand and other environmental factors.

Overall Marketing Strategy, Objectives, and Mix

Price is only one element of the company's broader marketing strategy. So, before setting price, the company must decide on its overall marketing strategy for the product or service. If a company has selected its target market and positioning carefully, then its marketing mix strategy, including price, will be fairly straightforward. For example, Tesla targets high-end, technology-driven buyers with sophisticated all-electric cars that "accelerate the advent of sustainable transportation." Such elevated targeting and positioning dictate charging premium prices.

Sometimes companies build their strategies around a price and value story. For example, in recent years, dozens of direct-to-consumer startups have positioned themselves as offering good quality at great value. Online mattress and bedding seller Casper offers "a better night's sleep for an amazing value." Shaving products marketer Harry's declares "You deserve a great shave at a fair price." And online grocery and home goods retailer Brandless promises "Better stuff, fewer dollars. It's that simple."

● No-frills Spirit Airlines positions itself entirely on what it calls "Bare Fare" pricing. It promises "Less Money. More Go.":[11]

● No-frills Spirit Airlines builds its entire marketing strategy around "Bare Fare" pricing. You don't get much when you fly Spirit. Then again, you don't pay for what you don't get.
Larry MacDougal/AP Photo

Spirit is an unrivaled "ultra-low-cost carrier," with prices much lower than those of competitors—up to 90 percent lower in some cases. But to cash in on such rock-bottom fares, customers must accept less in return. Buying a ticket on a Spirit flight gets you one thing and one thing only—a seat on a plane to your destination. If you want more, you pay for it. For example, whereas most airlines provide free beverages, Spirit charges $3 for a bottle of water or can of soda. Want a pillow or a blanket? Glad to oblige—that'll be $7, please. Getting a seat assignment costs $15, and it will cost you $10 extra to have a check-in agent print out your boarding pass. A full-size carry-on bag runs another $37. Adding insult to injury, seats on Spirit flights are crammed much closer together (what Spirit calls "a little cozier seating"), and the seats don't recline. If you do want a little more breathing room—you guessed it—for a fee you can get an exit row or first-class-sized front-row seat. Although some customers view this a cheap nickel-and-diming or, worse, complain that it's unfair and deceitful, Spirit is thriving with its Bare Fare approach. The airline claims that it gives customers more control over what they pay for and what they don't. True, you don't get much when you fly Spirit. Then again, you don't pay for what you don't get. If paying for the extras bothers you, declares Spirit, don't buy them. Or just fly another airline and pay the full up-front fare.

Pricing may play an important role in helping to accomplish company objectives at many levels. A firm can set prices to attract new customers or profitably retain existing ones. It can set prices low to prevent competition from entering the market or set prices at competitors' levels to stabilize the market. It can price to keep the loyalty and support of resellers or avoid government intervention. Prices can be reduced temporarily to create excitement for a brand. Or one product may be priced to help the sales of other products in the company's line.

Price decisions must be coordinated with product design, distribution, and promotion decisions to form a consistent and effective integrated marketing mix program. Decisions made for other marketing mix variables may affect pricing decisions. For example, a decision to position the product on high-performance quality will mean that the seller must charge a higher price to cover higher costs. And producers whose resellers are expected to support and promote their products may have to build larger reseller margins into their prices.

Target costing

Pricing that starts with an ideal selling price and then targets costs that will ensure that the price is met.

Companies often position their products on price and then tailor other marketing mix decisions to the prices they want to charge. Here, price is a crucial product-positioning factor that defines the product's market, competition, and design. Many firms support such price-positioning strategies with a technique called **target costing**. Target costing reverses the usual process of first designing a new product, determining its cost, and then asking, "Can we sell it for that?" Instead, it starts with an ideal selling price based on customer value considerations and then targets costs that will ensure that the price is met. For example, when Honda initially designed the Honda Fit, it began with a $13,950 starting price point and highway mileage of 33 miles per gallon firmly in mind. It then designed a stylish, peppy little car with costs that allowed it to give target customers those values.

Other companies deemphasize price and use other marketing mix tools to create *nonprice* positions. Often, the best strategy is not to charge the lowest price but rather to differentiate the marketing offer to make it worth a higher price. ● For example, Sleep Number puts high value into its mattresses and charges a higher price to match that value.

At the most basic level, a Sleep Number mattress lets you adjust each side to your ideal level of firmness and support. Add SleepIQ technology and you can track and optimize for the best possible night's sleep. Sleep Number lets you "Know. Adjust. Sleep." SleepIQ technology inside the bed monitors restful sleep time, heart rate, breathing rate, movements, and other factors. Then the SleepIQ app reports on your night's SleepIQ score and how you slept. The app recommends adjustments that will change your sleep for the better. The Sleep Number children's mattress line helps parents track how their kids sleep. It even lets parents know when their kids get out of bed at night and includes a head tilt for stuffy heads, star-based rewards for sleep habits, and a clever "monster detector." Sleep Number beds cost more than a traditional mattresses—models run from $900 to more than $7,000 compared with

● **Nonprice positioning: Sleep Number beds cost more than traditional mattresses, but the brand's highly satisfied customers are willing to pay more to get more. After all, it's hard to put a price on a good night's sleep.**

Select Comfort Corporation

good-quality traditional mattresses at $1,000 or less. But Sleep Number's satisfied customers are willing to pay more to get more. After all, it's hard to put a price on a good night's sleep.[12]

Thus, marketers must consider the total marketing strategy and mix when setting prices. But again, even when featuring price, marketers need to remember that customers rarely buy on price alone. Instead, they seek products that give them the best value in terms of benefits received for the prices paid.

Organizational Considerations

Management must decide who within the organization should set prices. Companies handle pricing in a variety of ways. In small companies, prices are often set by top management rather than by the marketing or sales departments. In large companies, pricing is typically handled by divisional or product managers. In industrial markets, salespeople may be allowed to negotiate with customers within certain price ranges. Even so, top management sets the pricing objectives and policies, and it often approves the prices proposed by lower-level management or salespeople.

In industries in which pricing is a key factor (airlines, aerospace, steel, railroads, oil companies), companies often have pricing departments to set the best prices or help others set them. These departments report to the marketing department or top management. Others who have an influence on pricing include sales managers, production managers, finance managers, and accountants.

The Market and Demand

As noted earlier, good pricing starts with understanding how customers' perceptions of value affect the prices they are willing to pay. Both consumer and industrial buyers balance the price of a product or service against the benefits of owning it. Thus, before setting prices, the marketer must understand the relationship between price and demand for the company's product. In this section, we take a deeper look at the price–demand relationship and how it varies for different types of markets. We then discuss methods for analyzing the price–demand relationship.

Pricing in Different Types of Markets

The seller's pricing freedom varies with different types of markets. Economists recognize four types of markets, each presenting a different pricing challenge.

Under *pure competition*, the market consists of many buyers and sellers trading in a uniform commodity, such as wheat, copper, or financial securities. No single buyer or seller has much effect on the going market price. In a purely competitive market, marketing research, product development, pricing, advertising, and sales promotion play little or no role. Thus, sellers in these markets do not spend much time on marketing strategy.

Under *monopolistic competition*, the market consists of many buyers and sellers trading over a range of prices rather than a single market price. A range of prices occurs because sellers can differentiate their offers to buyers. Because there are many competitors, each firm is less affected by competitors' pricing strategies than in oligopolistic markets. Sellers try to develop differentiated offers for different customer segments and, in addition to price, freely use branding, advertising, and personal selling to set their offers apart.

● Thus, Google attempts to set its Pixel smartphones apart from the profusion of other

Introducing Pixel 2 XL
Phone by Google
Ask more of your phone.

● **Pricing in monopolistic competition markets: Google attempts to set its Pixel smartphones apart not by price but by the power of its brand and the host of differentiating features. Pixel ads tell consumers to "Ask more of your phone."**

Google

phones not by price but by the power of its brand and the host of differentiating features. Pixel ads tell consumers to "Ask more of your phone." Its Pixel phones promise a more ultra-vivid display, more beautiful portraits, the best smartphone camera, faster battery charging, water resistance, free cloud storage, Google Lens, more help from Google Assistant, more fun, more memories, and more, more, more, more... Google spent close to $40 million in one month on TV advertising alone to introduce the Pixel 2 and drive home these differentiating features.[13]

Under *oligopolistic competition*, the market consists of only a few large sellers. For example, only a handful of providers—Comcast, Spectrum, AT&T, and Dish Network— control a lion's share of the cable/satellite television market. Because there are few sellers, each seller is alert and responsive to competitors' pricing strategies and marketing moves. In the battle for subscribers, price becomes a major competitive tool. For example, to woo customers away from competitors, they offers special discounts, free equipment upgrades, and lock-in prices.

In a *pure monopoly*, the market is dominated by one seller. The seller may be a government monopoly (the U.S. Postal Service), a private regulated monopoly (a power company), or a private unregulated monopoly (De Beers and diamonds). Pricing is handled differently in each case.

Analyzing the Price–Demand Relationship

Each price the company might charge will lead to a different level of demand. The relationship between the price charged and the resulting demand level is shown in the **demand curve** in ● Figure 10.6 The demand curve shows the number of units the market will buy in a given time period at different prices that might be charged. In the normal case, demand and price are inversely related—that is, the higher the price, the lower the demand. Thus, the company would sell less if it raised its price from P_1 to P_2. In short, consumers with limited budgets probably will buy less of something if its price is too high.

Understanding a brand's price-demand curve is crucial to good pricing decisions. ConAgra Foods has learned this lesson when pricing its Banquet frozen dinners:[14]

> Banquet has charged about $1 per dinner since its start way back in 1953. And that's what many customers still expect. The $1 price is a key component in the brands appeal. Nine years ago, when ConAgra tried to cover higher commodity costs by raising the list price of Banquet dinners from $1 to $1.25, consumers turned up their noses to the higher price. Sales dropped sharply, forcing ConAgra to drop its prices back to a buck a dinner. To make money at that price, ConAgra tried to do a better job of managing costs by shrinking portions and substituting less expensive ingredients for costlier ones. But as commodity prices continue to rise, Banquet just can't make a decent dinner for a dollar anymore. So it's cautiously raising prices again. Some smaller meals are still priced at $1. For example, the chicken finger meal still comes with macaroni and cheese but no longer includes a brownie. But classic meals such as Salisbury steak are now back up to $1.29. ConAgra has also introduced Banquet Select Recipes meals at a startling $1.50 and larger-portion Mega meals and bowls at more than $2. Despite the price increases, ConAgra's frozen food sales are growing modestly. Banquet is an entry-point brand, notes ConAgra's CEO, but "that doesn't mean it's married to a dollar. It [just] needs to be the best value for our core customer." And times are changing. "When we think about millennials shopping in frozen [foods], the notion of them wanting to buy a meal at 88 cents doesn't compute because their latte costs $4.37," says the CEO.

Most companies try to measure their demand curves by estimating demand at different prices. The type of market makes a difference. In a monopoly, the demand curve shows the total market demand resulting from different prices. If the company faces competition, its demand at different prices will depend on whether competitors' prices stay constant or change with the company's own prices.

Price Elasticity of Demand

Marketers also need to know **price elasticity**—how responsive demand will be to a change in price. If demand hardly changes with a small change in price, we say demand is *inelastic*. If demand changes greatly, we say the demand is *elastic*.

● FIGURE 10.6
Demand Curve

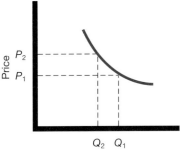

Quantity demanded per period

Demand curve
A curve that shows the number of units the market will buy in a given time period at different prices that might be charged.

Price elasticity
A measure of the sensitivity of demand to changes in price.

If demand is elastic rather than inelastic, sellers will consider lowering their prices. A lower price will produce more total revenue. This practice makes sense as long as the extra costs of producing and selling more do not exceed the extra revenue. At the same time, most firms want to avoid pricing that turns their products into commodities. In recent years, forces such as deregulation and the instant price comparisons afforded by the internet and mobile and other technologies have increased consumer price sensitivity, turning products ranging from phones and computers to new automobiles into commodities in some consumers' eyes.

The Economy

Economic conditions can have a strong impact on the firm's pricing strategies. Economic factors such as a boom or recession, inflation, and interest rates affect pricing decisions because they affect consumer spending, consumer perceptions of the product's price and value, and the company's costs of producing and selling a product.

In the aftermath of the Great Recession of 2008–2009, many consumers rethought the price-value equation. They tightened their belts and become more value conscious. Consumers have continued their thriftier ways well beyond the economic recovery. As a result, many marketers have increased their emphasis on value-for-the-money pricing strategies.

The most obvious response to the new economic realities is to cut prices and offer discounts. Thousands of companies have done just that. Lower prices make products more affordable and help spur short-term sales. However, such price cuts can have undesirable long-term consequences. Lower prices mean lower margins. Deep discounts may cheapen a brand in consumers' eyes. And once a company cuts prices, it's difficult to raise them again when the economy recovers.

Rather than cutting prices on their main-market brands, many companies are holding their price positions but redefining the "value" in their value propositions. Other companies have developed "price tiers," adding both more affordable lines or premium lines that span the varied means and preferences of different customer segments. For example, to boost the "pay less" side of its "Expect More. Pay Less." mantra and to meet the needs of cost-conscious customers with tighter budgets, Target introduced lower-priced store brands such as Room Essentials (budget-friendly home goods) and Up & Up (low-priced essentials in various categories). ● One ad for Up & Up states, "Quality and value can be friends forever. And, like wildflowers, laughter, or an extra hour of sleep, beautiful things don't have to be spendy."

Remember that even in tough economic times, consumers do not buy based on prices alone. They balance the price they pay against the value they receive. For example, despite selling its shoes for as much as $200 a pair, Nike commands the highest consumer loyalty of any brand in the footwear segment. Customers perceive the value of Nike's products and the Nike ownership experience to be well worth the price. Thus, no matter what price they charge—low or high—companies need to offer great *value for the money*.

Other External Factors

Beyond the market and the economy, the company must consider several other factors in its external environment when setting prices. It must know what impact its prices will have on other parties in its environment. How will *resellers* react to various prices? The company should set prices that give resellers a fair profit, encourage their support, and help them to sell the product effectively. The *government* is another important external influence on pricing decisions. Finally, *social concerns* may need to be taken into account. In setting prices, a company's short-term sales, market share, and profit goals may need to be tempered by broader societal considerations. We will examine public policy issues later in Chapter 11.

● Pricing and the economy: To meet the needs of cost-conscious customers with tighter budgets, Target introduced lower-priced store brands such as Up & Up. "Beautiful things don't have to be spendy."
Gary Armstrong

Reviewing and Extending the Concepts

Objectives Review

Companies today face a fierce and fast-changing pricing environment. Firms successful at creating customer value with the other marketing mix activities must still capture some of this value in the prices they earn. This chapter examines the importance of pricing, general pricing strategies, and the internal and external considerations that affect pricing decisions.

OBJECTIVE 10-1 Answer the question "What is a price?" and discuss the importance of pricing in today's fast-changing environment. *(pp 296–297)*

Price can be defined narrowly as the amount of money charged for a product or service. Or it can be defined more broadly as the sum of the values that consumers exchange for the benefits of having and using the product or service. The pricing challenge is to find the price that will let the company make a fair profit by getting paid for the customer value it creates.

Despite the increased role of nonprice factors in the modern marketing process, price remains an important element in the marketing mix. It is the only marketing mix element that produces revenue; all other elements represent costs. More important, as a part of a company's overall value proposition, price plays a key role in creating customer value and building customer relationships. Smart managers treat pricing as a key strategic tool for creating and capturing customer value.

OBJECTIVE 10-2 Define *price,* identify the three major pricing strategies, and discuss the importance of understanding customer-value perceptions, company costs, and competitor strategies when setting prices. *(pp 297–306)*

Companies can choose from three major pricing strategies: customer value–based pricing, cost-based pricing, and competition-based pricing. *Customer value–based pricing* uses buyers' perceptions of value as the basis for setting price. Good pricing begins with a complete understanding of the value that a product or service creates for customers and setting a price that captures that value. Customer perceptions of the product's value set the ceiling for prices. If customers perceive that a product's price is greater than its value, they will not buy the product.

Companies can pursue either of two types of value-based pricing. *Good-value pricing* involves offering just the right combination of quality and good service at a fair price. EDLP is an example of this strategy. *Value-added pricing* involves attaching value-added features and services to differentiate the company's offers and support charging higher prices.

Cost-based pricing involves setting prices based on the costs for producing, distributing, and selling products plus a fair rate of return for effort and risk. Company and product costs are an important consideration in setting prices. Whereas customer value perceptions set the price ceiling, costs set the floor for pricing. However, cost-based pricing is product driven rather than customer driven. The company designs what it considers to be a good product and sets a price that covers costs plus a target profit. If the price turns out to be too high, the company must settle for lower markups or lower sales, both resulting in disappointing profits. If the company prices the product below its costs, its profits will also suffer. Cost-based pricing approaches include *cost-plus pricing* and *break-even pricing* (or target profit pricing).

Competition-based pricing involves setting prices based on competitors' strategies, costs, prices, and market offerings. Consumers base their judgments of a product's value on the prices that competitors charge for similar products. If consumers perceive that the company's product or service provides greater value, the company can charge a higher price. If consumers perceive less value relative to competing products, the company must either charge a lower price or change customer perceptions to justify a higher price.

OBJECTIVE 10-3 Identify and define the other important external and internal factors affecting a firm's pricing decisions. *(pp 306–310)*

Other *internal* factors that influence pricing decisions include the company's overall marketing strategy, objectives, and marketing mix, as well as organizational considerations. Price is only one element of the company's broader marketing strategy. If the company has selected its target market and positioning carefully, then its marketing mix strategy, including price, will be fairly straightforward. Common pricing objectives might include customer retention and building profitable customer relationships, preventing competition, supporting resellers and gaining their support, or avoiding government intervention. Price decisions must be coordinated with product design, distribution, and promotion decisions to form a consistent and effective marketing program. Finally, in order to coordinate pricing goals and decisions, management must decide who within the organization is responsible for setting price.

Other *external* pricing considerations include the nature of the market and demand and environmental factors such as the economy, reseller needs, and government actions. Ultimately, the customer decides whether the company has set the right price. The customer weighs the price against the perceived values of using the product—if the price exceeds the sum of the values, consumers will not buy. So the company must understand such concepts as demand curves (the price–demand relationship) and price elasticity (consumer sensitivity to prices).

Economic conditions can have a major impact on pricing decisions. The Great Recession caused consumers to rethink the price–value equation, and consumers have continued their thriftier ways well beyond the economic recovery. Marketers have responded by increasing their emphasis on value-for-the-money pricing strategies. No matter what the economic times, however, consumers do not buy based on prices alone. Thus, no matter what price they charge—low or high—companies need to offer superior value for the money.

Key Terms

OBJECTIVE 10-1

Price (p 297)

OBJECTIVE 10-2

Customer value–based pricing (p 297)
Good-value pricing (p 299)
Value-added pricing (p 299)

Cost-based pricing (p 301)
Fixed costs (overhead) (p 301)
Variable costs (p 301)
Total costs (p 301)
Experience curve (learning curve) (p 302)
Cost-plus pricing (markup pricing) (p 302)

Break-even pricing (target return pricing) (p 303)
Competition-based pricing (p 304)

OBJECTIVE 10-3

Target costing (p 307)
Demand curve (p 309)
Price elasticity (p 309)

Discussion Questions

10-1 Why is finding and implementing the right pricing strategy critical to a company's success? (AACSB: Written and Oral Communication)

10-2 What is cost-based pricing? How do companies use fixed and variable costs in cost-based pricing models? (AACSB: Written and Oral Communication)

10-3 Two different types of costs form the total cost in setting a product price in cost-based pricing. Explain what these two costs are and which one is the most important in determining price.

10-4 Briefly explain the four types of markets companies must consider for pricing decisions. Are these markets relevant for all types of products?

10-5 List and briefly explain what internal factors companies must consider for pricing decisions. How important are these, in your opinion?

10-6 How is target costing different from other pricing strategies?

Critical Thinking Exercises

10-7 Congratulations! You just won your state lottery and will be receiving a check for $1 million. You have always wanted to own your own business and have noticed the increase in the number of food trucks in your local area. A new food truck with a kitchen and related equipment costs about $100,000. Other fixed costs include salaries, gas for the truck, and license fees and are estimated to be about $50,000 per year. You decide to offer traditional Mediterranean cuisine. Variable costs include food and beverages estimated at $6 per platter (meat, rice, vegetable, and pita bread). Meals will be priced at $10. Calculate the break-even for your food truck business. After reviewing your break-even, what changes would you consider? Is this how you want to spend your lottery winnings? (AACSB: Written and Oral Communication; Reflective Thinking)

10-8 Economic conditions can have a strong impact on a firm's pricing strategies. In the aftermath of the recent Great Recession, many companies adjusted prices by cutting prices or offering discounts. Nike's approach was somewhat different considering their value of products and customer loyalty. Identify key factors and reflect on Nike's approach to pricing after the recent recession.

10-9 Your company has developed a new weight-loss breakfast shake that has proven to be successful in the test market phase. Users have experienced an average weight loss of two pounds per week. You hold a patent on the product. The cost to produce the shake is relatively low, with total manufacturing costs running about $0.05 per ounce. Each shake is eight ounces. What pricing strategy do you recommend for this product? (AACSB: Communication; Use of IT; Reflective Thinking)

APPLICATIONS AND CASES

Online, Mobile, and Social Media Marketing Sold Out

Even before tickets went on general sale for the Rugby World Cup 2015, tickets were being offered on the secondary market for up to $14,000 for a $200 ticket—around 44 times the face value of the ticket. The 1 million general sale tickets were later offered for sale by ballot. The over-priced tickets were thought to have been legitimately secured hospitality packages bought by an individual or company in the hope that they could turn a big profit on them. At the same time, tickets for the final match of the sports competition were being offered at around $7,000 each. Although there is no suggestion that StubHub or Viagogo, the two resale sites in this case, had done anything illegal in hosting a third-party sale, it does illustrate the fact that within minutes of an event's tickets being available online, they are sold out. In many cases, tickets are being offered even before the tickets are officially on sale, and at inflated prices. The ticket resellers need to be fairly confident that they can secure the tickets. This is usually done with the help of specially programmed software that they use to ensure their ticket orders get to the front of the queue, making a huge profit for them.

10-10 Is there a ticket resale market active in your own country? How does ticketing work? Are tickets bought directly or via agents and brokers? Write a report on the ticketing industry in your country. (AACSB: Written and Oral Communication; Information Technology)

10-11 Inflated ticket prices can reflect very badly on the sport, event, or celebrity, even though the activities of resellers have nothing to do with them. Discuss how resellers could be cut out of the market. (AACSB: Written and Oral Communication; Information Technology)

Marketing Ethics Hidden Cities

Some travelers use cheap travel websites and book at off-peak times to save money. Other travelers have tried to increase their savings by booking a one-way ticket through a connecting city where they intend to stay in the layover city. For example, a traveler flying from Los Angeles to New York City may find it is less expensive to book a one-stop flight to Providence that connects through New York City and then not take the last leg to Providence. This practice, known as using a hidden city fare or skiplagging, can save the consumer money on the trip. However, it prevents the airline from selling the empty seat.

10-12 Why would an airline charge less for a longer flight that passes through the destination city than for a shorter flight to the destination city? (AACSB: Communication; Ethical Reasoning)

10-13 In your opinion, is it ethical for consumers to skiplag/use hidden cities to save money? Why or why not? (AACSB: Communication; Ethical Reasoning)

Marketing by the Numbers Rock Bottom Promotional Pricing

Rock Bottom Golf is an online golf equipment retailer that sells clubs, shoes, balls, and all the other gadgets golfers could ever need. Rock Bottom's prices are lower than those of most brick-and-mortar golf and sporting goods retailers, but they often go even lower with limited-time promotional pricing, especially around major holidays. For example, the Father's Day promotion offers $50 off Rock Bottom's already low price on select clubs and range finders that normally cost hundreds of dollars. One current offer is $50 off the Tour Edge EX10 Driver that Rock Bottom normally sells for $249.99. To get the word out about the offer, Rock Bottom spent $10,000 on banner ads on golf-related websites like golfchannel.com and pga.com. Rock Bottom understands that promotional pricing cuts into its profits for each sale but also knows that such pricing generates excitement and a sense of urgency among buyers because of the limited time the promotional price is available. In fact, Rock Bottom's research of past Father's Day promotions shows that it's mostly men buying the clubs and gadgets for themselves!

10-14 Assuming Rock Bottom's cost of goods sold (COGS) is 60 percent, calculate Rock Bottom's margin per driver before the $50 off promotional price and after the promotional price. What effect does the promotional pricing have on the margin Rock Bottom earns for every driver sold? Refer to Break-Even and Margin Analysis in Appendix 2: Marketing by the Numbers to learn how to perform this analysis. (AACSB: Communication; Analytic Reasoning; Reflective Thinking)

10-15 How many additional drivers must Rock Bottom sell at the lower margin to break even on the increase in advertising promotion? Assume the $10,000 spent on banner ads is the only fixed cost associated with this promotion. Refer to Financial Analysis of Marketing Tactics: Increase Advertising Expenditure in Appendix 2: Marketing by the Numbers to learn how to perform this analysis. (AACSB: Analytic Reasoning)

Company Case Gillette: Searching for the Right Price in a Volatile Market

Few brands dominate their industry with a more than 50 percent global market share. Gillette has done that for decades. Under its slogan "The Best a Man Can Get," Gillette has long been the razor-market leader, with veteran brands Schick and Bic running a distant second and third. Gillette achieved its market dominance by selling the highest-quality razors at a premium price.

For more than 100 years, by launching more razor innovations than any other company, Gillette has stood out as the brand in relentless pursuit of the closest, most-irritation-free shave.

With all that history and success, you might think that Gillette's marketers have few worries. But even as the storied brand continues to dominate the razor market, managers at

Gillette and parent company P&G are not resting well these days. Instead, the bigger story is that Gillette's market share has plummeted. Capturing a 50 percent market share is fantastic for most brands. But it's not so great for Gillette, which held a whopping 70 percent market share only 10 years ago. And there is no end in sight to Gillette's current decline.

Why this dramatic change? While there are many factors at play, they all point to one thing—more and more consumers are discovering high-quality blades elsewhere for a fraction of the price. And the fact that many of today's competing products are also more conveniently available presents even more difficult challenges for Gillette.

More Is Better

Gillette's quest for the ultimate shave began when the company started selling safety razors in 1900. For more than 70 years, it was all about creating a single thinner, stronger, and sharper disposable blade for its reusable handles. But the big leap forward came in 1972 when Gillette introduced the TRAC II—the first twin-blade shaving system. That innovation launched Gillette on a 40-year journey of convincing consumers that more blades make for a better shave. Gillette upped that proposition in 1998 with its MACH3—the first three-blade cartridge—and again in 2006 with its FUSION5—the first razor system with five blades. Beyond its "more is better" product developments, in pursuit of the perfect shave, Gillette modified each new razor generation with innovations such as pivoting heads, lubrication strips, and even vibrating mechanisms.

With each new innovation, Gillette established a pattern: Introduce the new product at a high price point while lowering the price of the existing Gillette razors. This pattern relied on one thing—convincing the public that the new product provided a big enough improvement to be worth the higher price. If that happened, the new, more expensive version became Gillette's best seller as the older technology faded away. Once customers were hooked on the new razor, they would buy expensive refill cartridges for years. This high-margin approach worked to perfection with the TRAC II and the MACH3. It worked so well, in fact, that billionaire Warren Buffett became one of Gillette's largest investors, adding to his fortunes when P&G acquired the number-one razor company for a whopping $57 billion in 2005.

The Law of Diminishing Returns

But a decade ago, Gillette's go-to-market model began to show signs of fatigue. For one, as razor performance increased with each new generation, the incremental improvement became less noticeable. When the MACH3 hit the market in the late 1990s, shavers everywhere embraced it as giving the closest, smoothest shave ever. With such a noticeable difference over twin-blade razors, customers happily paid nearly $2 per cartridge, a 35 percent premium over Gillette's previous flagship razor. But when the five-bladed FUSION debuted at $3 per cartridge nearly a decade later, customers were less enthusiastic. In fact, while Gillette intended to rapidly phase down the MACH3 as sales for the FUSION increased, demand for the MACH3 remained strong

and the two razor brands sold side by side on store shelves. Then, five years ago when Gillette announced that it had "rebuilt" shaving with its Fusion ProGlide FlexBall razor at $5 per cartridge, the writing was already on the wall.

Another factor in Gillette's fall from market dominance came in the form of a new generation of direct-to-consumer (DTC) competitors. Startup companies such as Dollar Shave Club and Harry's targeted a customer niche with a refreshing proposition—comparable-quality razors for a fraction of the price with the convenience of online purchase and home delivery. The DTC razor brands grew quickly and soon drew the attention of big-name retailers and consumer packaged goods companies. Unilever recently purchased Dollar Shave Club for approximately $1 billion, and Edgewell Personal Care Company (which owns Schick) followed suit by paying even more for Harry's. Today, both brands not only sell online but are carried by Target, Walmart, and other major retailers.

In addition to the fierce competition from DTC brands, Gillette is also facing stiff competition from the very retailers that have sold its products for decades. Not long ago, Walmart and Costco began selling their own store brand cartridges that fit Gillette handles. Many consumers can't tell the difference between a shave with a MACH3 cartridge and one with a comparable 3-blade cartridge sold under Walmart's Equate or Costco's Kirkland Signature brands. And with the store brands priced as low as $1 per cartridge, many customers find little reason to pay Gillette's higher prices.

Gillette Fights Back

In response to the challenges from the DTC and store brands, Gillette has stepped up efforts to defend its place at the top of the market. For starters, it launched its own online service—now dubbed Gillette On Demand—selling its same products at the same prices via the more convenient DTC channel. Gillette faithful responded but mostly at the expense of cannibalizing Gillette's in-store sales.

But Gillette has also had plenty of new product ideas up its sleeve. First, it introduced customized products with Razor Maker—a site where individuals can create their own customer razor handle via 3D printing. It also continued with new versions of its FUSION5. Then, in what seemed like a startling reversal, it unveiled the SkinGuard Sensitive—a state-of-the-art twin-blade system targeting shavers with sensitive skin. And in a dramatic upmarket move, Gillette recently launched the super-premium Heated Razor—a high-tech rechargeable that heats to 122 degrees. Available only through the Gillette On Demand site and company-owned Art of Shaving retail stores, the high-tech marvel sells at a whopping $200 plus $25 for a four-pack of replacement cartridges. With each new model, however, critics question whether Gillette's innovations provide substantive improvements.

In perhaps its biggest move yet to combat low-priced competition, two years ago, Gillette announced a 12 percent across-the-board price cut. "You told us our blades can be too expensive and we listened," Gillette declared on its website. However, although the price cut brings Gillette products closer to the competition, it also risks lowering perceptions of Gillette's quality. Perhaps worse, the price cut angered some consumers who demanded to know why Gillette had charged such a premium for so many years if it could now afford to sell its products for less. Whatever the case, Gillette's price cut signaled the brand's desperation and competitive vulnerability, a position the veteran razor brand has rarely if ever experienced.

However, things are far from over for Gillette. The brand is still far and away the market leader in total sales. Even in online sales, Gillette's late entry has earned it the number-two position behind Dollar Shave Club but ahead of Harry's. And with online sales representing the fastest-growing segment in the shaving market, Gillette could make great strides in that area. Gillette's vast experience in product development and marketing gives it an acute edge in the razor wars. Even as some observers have suggested that P&G sell Gillette, currently one of the company's poorest-performing businesses, insiders reaffirm P&G's intention

to stay the course with the brand. "This is a business that we not only want to keep but that we like and feel can win," says P&G's chief financial officer. But future success hinges on whether Gillette can find the right pricing strategy in a rapidly changing market.[15]

Questions for Discussion

10-16 Based on the concept of customer value–based pricing, explain Gillette's rise to market dominance.

10-17 Historically, did Gillette employ good-value pricing or value-added pricing? Explain.

10-18 Based on those same concepts of value-based pricing, explain how Gillette's pricing strategy stopped working.

10-19 What can Gillette do to improve its position in the market?

11

Pricing Strategies
Additional Considerations

OBJECTIVES OUTLINE

OBJECTIVE 11-1 Describe the major strategies for pricing new products. **See: New Product Pricing Strategies** *(pp 318–319)*

OBJECTIVE 11-2 Explain how companies find a set of prices that maximizes the profits from the total product mix. **See: Product Mix Pricing Strategies** *(pp 319–321)*

OBJECTIVE 11-3 Discuss how companies adjust their prices to take into account different types of customers and situations. **See: Price Adjustment Strategies** *(pp 321–330)*

OBJECTIVE 11-4 Discuss the key issues related to initiating and responding to price changes. **See: Price Changes** *(pp 330–333)*

OBJECTIVE 11-5 Discuss the major public policy concerns and key pieces of legislation that affect pricing decisions. **See: Public Policy and Pricing** *(pp 333–336)*

CHAPTER PREVIEW In the previous chapter, you learned that price is an important marketing mix tool for both creating and capturing customer value. You explored the three main pricing strategies—customer value–based, cost-based, and competition-based pricing—and the many internal and external factors that affect a firm's pricing decisions. In this chapter, we'll look at some additional pricing considerations: new product pricing, product mix pricing, price adjustments, and initiating and reacting to price changes. We close the chapter with a discussion of public policy and pricing.

To start, we'll look at Peloton, the fitness startup that's turning its industry upside down. Peloton sells its in-home, internet-connected stationary bikes at a substantial price premium over the competition. Yet it has quickly attracted a large and growing cult following of users who like what they get for the price they pay. For the Peloton faithful, it isn't just about the price of a Peloton bike. It's about inspiration, streaming content, and membership in a dynamic, closely connected Peloton community of like-minded exercise enthusiasts.

PELOTON: Premium Priced. But's It's Not about the Price

Peloton in-home exercise bikes sell at a steep price of $1,995, compared with the typical bikes you'd find at your local sporting goods store for as little as $200 or $300. What's more, buying a Peloton requires an additional $250 delivery and setup charge plus a $39 monthly membership fee. But even at those prices, Peloton sales are really rolling. The company has sold more than 500,000 bikes, and its annual sales have doubled each of the past two years

to nearly $800 million, an amazing feat for a six-year-old startup.

Although the price might seem steep, when consumers buy a Peloton, they're getting much more for their money than just a premium home fitness bike. They're buying into an absorbing lifestyle and a closely connected community of like-minded exercise enthusiasts, who ride together through classes on-demand or live-streamed from Peloton's studios to an internet-connected tablet on the bike. As one writer says, it's "the allure of sweating buckets and feverishly cycling en masse to the beat of Beyoncé as an all-too enthusiastic instructor shouts encouragement about 'feeling the burn, baby!,'" all from the comfort and convenience of your own home.

In recent years, a fast-growing number of fitness boutiques have popularized "spinning"—high-intensity, indoor cycling workout classes led by popular instructors in upscale exercise studios. With names like SoulCycle, Flywheel, Revolve, and Swerve, these studios evoke a vibe that is more swanky private club than sweaty fitness gym. For example, cyclists in one of SoulCycle's candle-lit "soul studios" pay $34 for an instructor-led 45-minute class. But more than a workout, SoulCycle promises "A powerful mind-body experience. Change your body. Find your SOUL."

Peloton founder John Foley—a triathlete and then new father—enjoyed spinning. But as the SoulCycle spinning craze grew in popularity, he found it increasingly difficult to book the classes and popular instructors that he wanted. Like others, his time-challenged lifestyle often made it tough to get to an exercise studio, and sometimes he just wanted more privacy when working out. So Foley found a better way. Instead of making customers go to spinning classes, he would take the spinning classes to customers. Working with a team of engineers, instructors, and sales reps, Foley designed Peloton around the tech-forward, time-starved, on-demand lifestyles of today's consumers.

Every premium Peloton cycle comes mounted with a large touch-screen tablet by which riders can track their performance, stream content from Peloton, or interact with others in the Peloton online community. Peloton streams 24 hours of live content daily and offers more than 8,000 on-demand cycling classes and other "Beyond the Ride" classes such as yoga, arms, legs, stretching, and core strengthening. Riders can select their favorite instructors, class length, class type, and even music genre. They can follow and compete with other riders in real time. And they can do all that from the comfort and convenience of home.

Peloton's early adopters were affluent riders who weren't deterred by the high price of admission. The brand quickly earned a cult following of well-off users, including celebrities ranging from Mark Zuckerberg, Richard Branson, David Beckham, and Sean "Diddy" Combs to Ellen DeGeneres and Michelle Obama. Peloton's initial promotional campaign conveyed a mix of function and inspiration in upscale settings. In one ad, a fit woman on a Peloton bike takes a high-intensity virtual class in her home, with the camera zooming

For the Peloton faithful, it isn't just about the price of a Peloton bike. It's about the values received from membership in the dynamic, closely connected Peloton community.

Peloton Interactive

in on the bike's user interface. After her workout, she walks down the stairs of her luxurious home to join her family for breakfast.

But based on customer data gathered through the Peloton network, the company soon discovered opportunities among less affluent riders. "We realized, through conversations with our community, that there was a huge opportunity with people who thought $2,000 was a huge investment but were [buying] it over and over again because the product was so important to them," says Peloton's head of brand marketing. So Peloton began offering a financing option that bundled the bike with a monthly subscription for $97 a month for 39 months. By comparison, two in-studio spinning classes a week at any Peloton competitor costs from $200 to $300 a month. Three spins a week in a New York City studio runs a hefty $500 a month. That makes Peloton a real bargain in the eyes of its fans.

But again, for the Peloton faithful, it isn't just about the price of a bike. Joining Peloton provides benefits that customers can't get from either stand-alone bikes or in-person spinning studios: owning a premium bike, workout and scheduling convenience, access to quality content, and membership in a dynamic, thriving community. Because an unlimited number of people can participate in a given Peloton class, the company can spend generously to produce a wide selection of top-quality classes taught by the best instructors. And Peloton collects tons of user data that helps shape future content offerings, making it what some analysts have called the "Netflix of fitness."

> Peloton sells its in-home stationary bikes at a substantial price premium over the competition. Yet it has attracted a large and growing cult following of users who like the value they get for the price they pay.

More than a fitness brand, Peloton is a "microcultural" phenomenon. Members self-select into "tribes" on Facebook based on age, height, profession, location, instructor preferences, and other characteristics. And Peloton tribes don't just get together for virtual rides; they interact between rides. They communicate online, offering advice and encouragement and congratulating each other on reaching new milestones. They meet up at local showrooms and travel cross-country to attend Peloton's annual Homecoming—a three-day gathering of classes, meetups, cocktails, and meet-and-greets with Peloton's celebrity-like instructors. When one Peloton member posted on the Official Peloton Page that he needed to sell his recently purchased bike to cover his wife's medical expenses, fellow riders set up a GoFundMe page that raised $25,000 in just 48 hours.

Peloton now sells bikes and subscriptions all over the world through its online store and 70 showrooms throughout the United State, Canada, and the United Kingdom. In turn, competitors like SoulCycle and Flywheel are feeling the burn of Peloton's success. Peloton recently overtook SoulCycle as the most popular stationary cycling brand, doubling its subscribers last year while the number of active SoulCycle patrons

dropped by 10 percent. And executive-level shakeups at both rival companies suggest that they are redesigning their businesses to include their own bike-selling, ride-at-home offerings. Flywheel has even offered "limited time" discounts of half-off for classes—an industry first.

All of this makes Peloton an interesting study in pricing strategy. Although at first blush, the price might seem unreasonably high, most customers see it as a bargain for what they are getting. In fact, Peloton initially set lower prices to attract more customers. But raising prices actually increased demand. "It was interesting psychology that we teased out," says Foley. "In the very, very early days, we charged $1,200 for the Peloton bike for the first couple of months. And what turned out happening is we heard from customers that the bike must be poorly built if you're charging $1,200 for it. We charged $2,000 for it, and sales increased, because people said, 'Oh, it must be a quality bike.'"

Whatever the psychology, with its cult-like following and the largest membership base in the industry, even at its high price, Peloton appears to be giving riders more than their money's worth.[1]

AS THE PELOTON STORY SUGGESTS, and as we learned in the previous chapter, pricing decisions are subject to a complex array of company, environmental, and competitive forces. To make things even more complex, a company does not set a single price but rather a *pricing structure* that covers different items in its line. This pricing structure changes over time as products move through their life cycles. The company adjusts its prices to reflect changes in costs and demand and to account for variations in buyers and situations. As the competitive environment changes, the company considers when to initiate price changes and when to respond to them.

This chapter examines additional pricing approaches used in special pricing situations or to adjust prices to meet changing situations. We look in turn at *new product pricing* for products in the introductory stage of the product life cycle, *product mix pricing* for related products in the product mix, *price adjustment tactics* that account for customer differences and changing situations, and strategies for initiating and responding to *price changes*.

New Product Pricing Strategies

OBJECTIVE 11-1 Describe the major strategies for pricing new products.

Pricing strategies usually change as the product passes through its life cycle. The introductory stage is especially challenging. Companies bringing out a new product face the challenge of setting prices for the first time. They can choose between two broad strategies: *market-skimming pricing* and *market-penetration pricing*.

Market-Skimming Pricing

Market-skimming pricing (price skimming)

Setting a high price for a new product to skim maximum revenues layer by layer from the segments willing to pay the high price; the company makes fewer but more profitable sales.

Many companies that invent new products set high initial prices to *skim* revenues layer by layer from the market. Apple frequently uses this strategy, called **market-skimming pricing** (or **price skimming**). With each new generation of Apple iPhone, iPad, or MacBook laptop, new models start at a high price then work their way down as newer models are introduced. In this way, Apple skims the maximum amount of revenue and margins from the various segments of the market. For example, as noted in the previous chapter's opening story, through smart premium pricing, Apple vacuums up as much as 60 to 87 percent of all global smartphone profits.[2]

Market skimming makes sense only under certain conditions. First, the product's quality and image must support its higher price, and enough buyers must want the product at that price. Second, the costs of producing a smaller volume cannot be so high that they cancel the advantage of charging more. Finally, competitors should not be able to enter the market easily and undercut the high price.

Market-Penetration Pricing

Market-penetration pricing

Setting a low price for a new product in order to attract a large number of buyers and a large market share.

Rather than setting a high initial price to skim off small but profitable market segments, some companies use **market-penetration pricing**. Companies set a low initial price to *penetrate* the market quickly and deeply—to attract a large number of buyers quickly and win a large market share. Or a firm might use penetration pricing to win customers initially and then turn them into loyal long-term customers.

Amazon does this for some of its digital products and services. For example, to attract first-time customers and tie them into its Internet-of-Things (IoT) platform, Amazon sells its introductory-level Echo Dot smart speakers with the Alexa digital assistant at a penetration price of less than $50. Once on board with an Echo device, customers are more likely to buy additional Amazon IoT devices and services rather than those of competitors such as Google, Samsung, or Apple. Moreover, people who own Amazon smart speakers spend 66 percent more at Amazon.com than other consumers. ● Similarly, Amazon used penetration pricing to make headway against Netflix and build a customer base for its Prime Video service in more than 240 countries where Prime Video isn't already bundled with Amazon Prime subscriptions. Amazon offered Prime Video for only $2.99 per month for a six-month introductory period and only $5.99 thereafter, compared with Netflix's more than $10 monthly rate.[3]

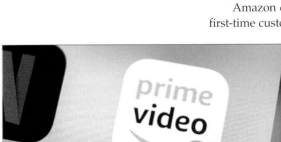

● **Penetration pricing: Amazon used penetration pricing for Amazon Prime Video in more than 240 international markets to build a customer base and make headway against higher priced Netflix.**

BigTunaOnline/Shutterstock

Several conditions must be met for penetration pricing to work. First, the market must be highly price sensitive so that a low price produces more market growth. Second, production and distribution costs must decrease as sales volume increases. Finally, the low price must help keep out the competition, and the penetration pricer must maintain its low-price position. Otherwise, the price advantage may be only temporary.

> **Author Comment** | Most individual products are part of a broader product mix and must be priced accordingly. For example, Gillette prices its Fusion razors low. But once you buy the razor, you're a captive customer for its higher-margin replacement cartridges.

Product Mix Pricing Strategies

OBJECTIVE 11-2 Explain how companies find a set of prices that maximizes the profits from the total product mix.

The strategy for setting a product's price often has to be changed when the product is part of a product mix. In this case, the firm looks for a set of prices that maximizes its profits on the total product mix. Pricing is difficult because the various products have related demand and costs and face different degrees of competition. We now take a closer look at the five product mix pricing situations summarized in ● **Table 11.1**: *product line pricing, optional-product pricing, captive-product pricing, by-product pricing,* and *product bundle pricing.*

Product Line Pricing

Product line pricing

Setting the price steps between various products in a product line based on cost differences between the products, customer evaluations of different features, and competitors' prices.

Companies usually develop product lines rather than single products. In **product line pricing**, management must determine the price steps to set between the various products in a line. The price steps should take into account cost differences between products in the line. More important, they should account for differences in customer perceptions of the value of different features.

● Table 11.1 | **Product Mix Pricing**

Pricing Situation	Description
Product line pricing	Setting prices across an entire product line
Optional-product pricing	Pricing optional or accessory products sold with the main product
Captive-product pricing	Pricing products that must be used with the main product
By-product pricing	Pricing low-value by-products to get rid of or make money on them
Product bundle pricing	Pricing bundles of products sold together

For example, Microsoft offers full lines of Surface tablets, laptops, and PCs, from the ultra-portable Surface Go tablet starting at $399, to Surface Pro tablet/laptops starting at $899, to Surface Book combination laptops starting at $1,149, to the Surface Studio all-in-one PC starting at $2,999. Then each of these lines features a range of prices depending on the chosen configuration. For example, an upgraded Surface Go can cost as much as $679, and a fully featured Microsoft Surface Studio 2 runs as much as $4,799. Microsoft's task is to establish perceived value differences that support price differences for different buyers and uses.

Optional-Product Pricing

Optional-product pricing
The pricing of optional or accessory products along with a main product.

Captive-product pricing
Setting a price for products that must be used along with a main product, such as blades for a razor and games for a video-game console.

Many companies use **optional-product pricing**—pricing optional or accessory products along with the main product. For example, a car buyer may choose to order a remote engine start system and premium sound system. Refrigerators come with optional ice makers. And when you order a new laptop, you can select from a bewildering array of processors, drives, docking systems, software options, and service plans. Pricing these options is a sticky problem. Companies must decide which items to include in the base price and which to offer as options.

Captive-Product Pricing

Companies that make products that must be used along with a main product are using **captive-product pricing**. Examples of captive products are razor blade cartridges, printer cartridges, single-serve coffee pods, e-books, and video games. Producers of the main products (razors, e-readers, printers, single-cup coffee brewing systems, and video-game consoles) often price them low and set high markups on supplies and supplemental products. ● For example, Nintendo makes little or no profit on its Switch video game consoles. The company spends an estimated $257 on parts alone to make each Switch, which then sells at retail for only $299.99. That means that Nintendo might probably loses money on the consoles themselves. However, it hopes to more than make up for thin console margins through sales of Switch video games, which yield much higher unit sales and margins. For example, whereas Nintendo sold about 32 million Switch consoles last year, it sold more than 163 million higher-margin game units.[4]

Captive products can account for a substantial portion of a brand's sales and profits. For example, Gillette has long sold razor handles at low prices and made its money on higher-price replacement blade cartridges. "The razor

● Captive-product pricing: Nintendo makes little or no profit on its Switch video game console but makes up for it through sales of higher-margin video games.

Wachirawit Iemlerkchai/Alamy Stock Photo

business is all about the blades," says an analyst. "Get consumers hooked on your razor, and they buy the highly profitable refill blades forever." Last year, Gillette sold well over half a billion dollars' worth of refill blades at prices ranging up to a hefty $5 per cartridge.

However, companies that use captive-product pricing must be careful. Finding the right balance between the main-product and captive-product prices can be tricky. Even more, consumers trapped into buying expensive captive products may come to resent the brand that ensnared them. For example, Gillette has lost market share in recent years as price-fatigued customers have shifted to lower-priced private-label upstarts such as Dollar Shave Club and Harry's. To compete, it was recently forced to slash cartridge prices across the board by 15 to 20 percent.[5]

In the case of services, captive-product pricing is called *two-part pricing*. The price of the service is broken into a *fixed fee* plus a *variable usage rate*. Thus, at Six Flags and other amusement parks, you pay a daily ticket or season pass charge plus additional fees for food and other in-park features.

By-Product Pricing

By-product pricing

Setting a price for by-products to help offset the costs of disposing of them and help make the main product's price more competitive.

Producing products and services often generates by-products. If the by-products have no value and if getting rid of them is costly, this will affect the pricing of the main product. Using **by-product pricing**, the company seeks a market for these by-products to help offset the costs of disposing of them and help make the price of the main product more competitive.

The by-products themselves can even turn out to be profitable—turning trash into cash. For example, Americans eat some nine billion chickens a year but not the feet. Chinese, on the other hand, consider chicken feet (or what the industry calls "chicken paws") to be a real delicacy. That solves a lot of problems for poultry processors such as Perdue Farms, which once couldn't give the feet away and even had to pay to dispose of them. But thanks to the huge demand in China, chicken feet are now a huge profit center. Perdue sells some $40 million of the otherwise value-less by-product to China annually. Interestingly, the opposite is true for pork ribs. European meatpackers sell most of their pork products to China. But the Chinese only want full-flesh cuts such as loins and pork bellies; they're not interested in the bones. So the European packers sell the ribs as by-products to U.S. foodservice chains at a bargain. "They like feet, we like bones," says an industry insider. "And round and round we go.[6]

Product Bundle Pricing

Product bundle pricing

Combining several products and offering the bundle at a reduced price.

Using **product bundle pricing**, sellers often combine several products and offer the bundle at a reduced price. For example, fast-food restaurants bundle a burger, fries, and a soft drink at a "combo" price. Microsoft Office 365 subscriptions are sold as a bundle of software products, including Word, Excel, PowerPoint, and Outlook. And Comcast, AT&T, Spectrum, Verizon, and other telecommunications companies bundle TV, phone, and high-speed internet services at a low combined price. Price bundling can promote the sales of products consumers might not otherwise buy, but the combined price must be low enough to get them to buy the bundle.

> Author | Setting the base price for
> Comment | a product is only the start.
> The company must then adjust the price to account for customer and situational differences. When was the last time you paid the full suggested retail price for something?

Price Adjustment Strategies

OBJECTIVE 11-3 Discuss how companies adjust their prices to take into account different types of customers and situations.

Companies usually adjust their basic prices to account for various customer differences and changing situations. Here we examine the seven price adjustment strategies summarized in ● **Table 11.2**: *discount and allowance pricing, segmented pricing, psychological pricing, promotional pricing, geographical pricing, dynamic and personalized pricing,* and *international pricing*.

Discount and Allowance Pricing

Most companies adjust their basic price to reward customers for certain responses, such as paying bills early, volume purchases, and off-season buying. These price adjustments—called *discounts* and *allowances*—can take many forms.

● Table 11.2 | Price Adjustments

Strategy	Description
Discount and allowance pricing	Reducing prices to reward customer responses such as volume purchases, paying early, or promoting the product
Segmented pricing	Adjusting prices to allow for differences in customers, products, or locations
Psychological pricing	Adjusting prices for psychological effect
Promotional pricing	Temporarily reducing prices to spur short-run sales
Geographical pricing	Adjusting prices to account for the geographic location of customers
Dynamic and personalized pricing	Adjusting prices continually to meet the characteristics and needs of individual customers and situations
International pricing	Adjusting prices for international markets

Discount

A straight reduction in price on purchases during a stated period of time or of larger quantities.

One form of **discount** is a *cash discount*, a price reduction to buyers who pay their bills promptly. A typical business example is "2/10, net 30," which means that although payment is due within 30 days, the buyer can deduct 2 percent if the bill is paid within 10 days. A *quantity discount* is a price reduction to buyers who buy large volumes. A seller offers a *functional discount* (also called a *trade discount*) to trade-channel members who perform certain functions, such as selling, storing, and record keeping. A *seasonal discount* is a price reduction to buyers who buy merchandise or services out of season.

Allowance

Promotional money paid by manufacturers to retailers in return for an agreement to feature the manufacturer's products in some way.

Allowances are another type of reduction from the list price. For example, *trade-in allowances* are price reductions given for turning in an old item when buying a new one. Trade-in allowances are most common in the automobile industry, but they are also given for other durable goods. *Promotional allowances* are payments or price reductions that reward dealers for participating in advertising and sales-support programs.

Segmented Pricing

Segmented pricing

Selling a product or service at two or more prices, where the difference in prices is not based on differences in costs.

Companies will often adjust their basic prices to allow for differences in customers, products, and locations. In **segmented pricing**, the company sells a product or service at two or more prices, even though the difference in prices is not based on differences in costs.

Segmented pricing takes several forms. Under *customer-segment pricing*, different customers pay different prices for the same product or service. For example, museums, movie theaters, and retail stores may charge lower prices for students, people in the military, and senior citizens. ● Microsoft, Apple Samsung, and other electronics brands have launched dedicated online stores for military members, veterans, and their families, with discounts of 10 percent or more on the wide range of products offered there. And Walgreens holds periodic Senior Discount Day events, offering 20 percent price reductions to AARP members and to its Balance Rewards members age 55 and over. "Grab Granny and go shopping!" advises one Walgreens ad.

Under *product form pricing*, different versions of the product are priced differently but not according to differences in their costs. For instance, a round-trip economy seat on a flight from New York to London might cost $500, whereas a business-class seat on the same flight might cost $6,000 or more. Although business-class customers receive roomier, more comfortable seats and higher-quality food and service, the differences in costs to the airlines are much less than the additional prices to passengers. However, to passengers who can afford it, the additional comfort and services are worth the extra charge.

● **Customer-segment pricing: Microsoft and other electronics brands have launched dedicated online stores for military members, veterans, and their families, with discounts of 10 percent or more on the wide range of products offered there.**

Microsoft Corporation

Using *location-based pricing*, a company charges different prices for different locations, even though the cost of offering each location is the same. For instance, state universities charge higher tuition for out-of-state students, and theaters vary their seat prices because of audience preferences for certain locations. Finally, using *time-based pricing*, a firm varies its price by the season, the month, the day, and even the hour. For example, movie theaters charge matinee pricing during the daytime, and resorts give weekend and seasonal discounts.

For segmented pricing to be an effective strategy, certain conditions must exist. The market must be segmentable, and segments must show different degrees of demand. The costs of segmenting and reaching the market cannot exceed the extra revenue obtained from the price difference. Of course, the segmented pricing must also be legal.

Most important, segmented prices should reflect real differences in customers' perceived value. Consumers in higher price tiers must feel that they're getting their extra money's worth for the higher prices paid. Otherwise, segmented pricing practices can cause consumer resentment. For example, buyers reacted negatively when a New York City Department of Consumer Affairs (DCA) investigation found that women consumers often pay a "pink tax," paying more for female versions of products that are virtually identical to male versions except for gender-specific packaging.[7] The DCA compared the prices of male and female versions for nearly 800 products—including adult apparel, personal care products, home goods and children's toys and clothing. It found that items marketed to girls and women cost an average of 7 percent more than similar items aimed at boys and men, and as much as 13 percent more in some categories. Although no laws prohibit gender-based pricing differences, such glaring disparities can damage a brand's credibility and reputation.

Companies must also be careful not to treat customers in lower price tiers as second-class citizens. Otherwise, in the long run, the practice will lead to customer resentment and ill will. For example, in recent years, the airlines have incurred the wrath of frustrated customers at both ends of the airplane. Passengers paying full fare for business- or first-class seats often feel that they are being gouged. At the same time, passengers in lower-priced coach seats feel that they're being ignored or treated poorly.

Psychological Pricing

Price says something about the product. For example, many consumers use price to judge quality. A $100 bottle of perfume may contain only $3 worth of scent, but some people are willing to pay the $100 because this price indicates something special.

Psychological pricing

Pricing that considers the psychology of prices and not simply the economics; the price is used to say something about the product.

In using **psychological pricing**, sellers consider the psychology of prices, not simply the economics. For example, consumers usually perceive higher-priced products as having higher quality. When they can judge the quality of a product by examining it or by calling on past experience with it, they use price less to judge quality. But when they cannot judge quality because they lack the information or skill, price becomes an important quality signal. For instance, who's the better lawyer, one who charges $50 per hour or one who charges $500 per hour? You'd have to do a lot of digging into the respective lawyers' credentials to answer this question objectively; even then, you might not be able to judge accurately. Most of us would simply assume that the higher-priced lawyer is better.

● **Psychological pricing: Dunkin's S!p coffee experiment showed that price and context can affected brand perceptions.**
Dunkin' Brands

Reference prices
Prices that buyers carry in their minds and refer to when they look at a given product.

Promotional pricing
Temporarily pricing products below the list price, and sometimes even below cost, to increase short-run sales.

● Dunkin' proved this psychological pricing point when it opened a hip-looking, high-end pop-up espresso cafe in Portland, Maine, named it S!p, and served its Dunkin' espresso products disguised in S!p packaging. A Dunkin' video shows local foodies waxing ecstatic about the quality of the coffee before learning to their surprise and delight that the supposedly high-end S!p was really good old Dunkin's new handcrafted espresso drinks. The event shows how price and context can shape brand perceptions.[8]

Another aspect of psychological pricing is **reference prices**— prices that buyers carry in their minds and refer to when looking at a given product. The reference price might be formed by noting current prices, remembering past prices, or assessing the buying situation. Sellers can influence or use these consumers' reference prices when setting price. For example, a grocery retailer might place its store brand of bran flakes and raisins cereal priced at $2.49 next to Kellogg's Raisin Bran priced at $3.79. Or a company might offer more expensive models that don't sell very well to make its less expensive but still-high-priced models look more affordable by comparison. For example, Williams-Sonoma once offered a fancy bread maker at the steep price of $279. However, it then added a $429 model. The expensive model flopped, but sales of the cheaper model doubled.[9]

For most purchases, consumers don't have all the skill or information they need to figure out whether they are paying a good price. They don't have the time, ability, or inclination to research different brands or stores, compare prices, and get the best deals on every item they buy. Instead, they may rely on certain cues that signal whether a price is high or low. Interestingly, such pricing cues are often provided by sellers, in the form of sales signs, price-matching guarantees, loss-leader pricing, and other helpful hints.

Even small differences in price can signal product differences. A 9 or 0.99 at the end of a price often signals a bargain. You see such prices everywhere. For example, browse the online sites of top discounters such as Target, Best Buy, or Overstock.com, where almost every price ends in 9. In contrast, high-end retailers might favor prices ending in a whole number (for example, $6, $25, or $200). Others use 00-cent endings on regularly priced items and 99-cent endings on discount merchandise.

Premium phone maker Apple uses 9-endings to take a little of the psychological sting out of its highest-in-market phone prices. For instance, when it introduced the iPhone X, it assigned a starting price of $999, keeping it just under the then-key market threshold of $1,000. The $1 difference is surprisingly bigger in psychological terms. Interestingly, Apple set the initial starting price of the iPhone X at £999 in the United Kingdom (almost $1,400).[10]

Although actual price differences might be small, the impact of such psychological tactics can be big. For example, in one study, people were asked how likely they were to choose among LASIK eye surgery providers based only on the prices they charged: $299 or $300. The actual price difference was only $1, but the study found that the psychological difference was much greater. Preference ratings for the providers charging $300 were much higher. Subjects perceived the $299 price as significantly less, but the lower price also raised stronger concerns about quality and risk. Some psychologists even argue that each digit has symbolic and visual qualities that should be considered in pricing. Thus, eight (8) is round and even and creates a soothing effect, whereas seven (7) is angular and creates a jarring effect.[11]

Promotional Pricing

With **promotional pricing**, companies will temporarily price their products below list price—and sometimes even below cost—to create buying excitement and urgency. Promotional pricing takes several forms. A seller may simply offer *discounts* from normal prices to increase sales and reduce inventories. Sellers also use *special-event pricing* in certain seasons to draw more customers. Thus, TVs and other consumer electronics are promotionally priced in November and December to attract holiday shoppers into the stores. *Limited-time offers*, such as online *flash sales*, can create buying urgency and make buyers feel lucky to have gotten in on the deal.

Manufacturers sometimes offer *cash rebates* to consumers who buy the product from dealers within a specified time; the manufacturer sends the rebate directly to the customer. Rebates have been popular with automakers and producers of phones and small appliances, but they are also used with consumer packaged goods. Some manufacturers offer *low-interest financing, longer warranties,* or *free maintenance* to reduce the consumer's "price." This practice has become another favorite of the auto industry.

Promotional pricing can help move customers over humps in the buying decision process. For example, to encourage consumers to convert to its Windows 10 operating system, Microsoft ran an Easy Trade-Up promotion offering buyers $200 trade-ins on their old devices when purchasing new Windows 10 PCs costing $599 or more at the Microsoft Store. It sweetened the deal to $300 for trade-ins of Apple MacBooks or iMacs. In the past, Microsoft has offered customers up to $650 toward the purchase of a Surface Pro when they trade in a MacBook Air. Such aggressive price promotions can provide powerful buying and switching incentives.

Promotional pricing, however, can have adverse effects. During most holiday seasons, for example, it's an all-out bargain war. Marketers bombard consumers with deals, causing buyer wear-out and pricing confusion. Constantly reduced prices can erode a brand's value in the eyes of customers. And used too frequently, price promotions can create "deal-prone" customers who wait until brands go on sale before buying them. ● For example, ask most regular shoppers at home goods retailer Bed Bath & Beyond, and they'll likely tell you that they never shop there without a stack of 20-percent-off or 5-dollar-off coupons in hand. As one reporter put it: "Shopping with a coupon at Bed Bath & Beyond has begun to feel like a given instead of like a special treat, and that's bad news for the chain's bottom line." In fact, greater coupon redemption rates have increasingly eaten into the retailer's profit margins.[12]

● **Promotional pricing: Some marketers bombard consumers with endless price promotions, eroding the brand's value. "Shopping with a coupon at Bed Bath & Beyond has begun to feel like a given instead of like a special treat."**

Keri Miksza

Geographical Pricing

Geographical pricing

Setting prices for customers located in different parts of the country or world.

A company also must decide how to price its products for customers located in different parts of the United States or the world. Should the company risk losing the business of more-distant customers by charging them higher prices to cover the higher shipping costs? Or should the company charge all customers the same prices regardless of location? We will look at five **geographical pricing** strategies for the following hypothetical situation:

> The Peerless Paper Company is located in Atlanta, Georgia, and sells paper products to customers all over the United States. The cost of freight is high and affects the companies from which customers buy their paper. Peerless wants to establish a geographical pricing policy. It is trying to determine how to price a $10,000 order to three specific customers: Customer A (Atlanta), Customer B (Bloomington, Indiana), and Customer C (Compton, California).

FOB-origin pricing

Pricing in which goods are placed free on board a carrier; the customer pays the freight from the factory to the destination.

One option is for Peerless to ask each customer to pay the shipping cost from the Atlanta factory to the customer's location. All three customers would pay the same factory price of $10,000, with Customer A paying, say, $100 for shipping; Customer B, $150; and Customer C, $250. Called **FOB-origin pricing**, this practice means that the goods are placed *free on board* (hence, *FOB*) a carrier. At that point, the title and responsibility pass to the customer, who pays the freight from the factory to the destination. Because each customer picks up its own cost, supporters of FOB pricing feel that this is the fairest way to assess freight charges. The disadvantage, however, is that Peerless will be a high-cost firm to distant customers.

Uniform-delivered pricing

Pricing in which the company charges the same price plus freight to all customers, regardless of their location.

Uniform-delivered pricing is the opposite of FOB pricing. Here, the company charges the same price plus freight to all customers, regardless of their location. The freight charge is set at the average freight cost. Suppose this is $150. Uniform-delivered pricing therefore results in a higher charge to the Atlanta customer (who pays $150 freight instead of $100) and a lower charge to the Compton customer (who pays $150 instead of $250). Although the Atlanta customer would prefer to buy paper from another local paper company that uses FOB-origin pricing, Peerless has a better chance of capturing the California customer.

Zone pricing

Pricing in which the company sets up two or more zones. All customers within a zone pay the same total price; the more distant the zone, the higher the price.

Zone pricing falls between FOB-origin pricing and uniform-delivered pricing. The company sets up two or more zones. All customers within a given zone pay a single total price; the more distant the zone, the higher the price. For example, Peerless might set up an East Zone and charge $100 freight to all customers in this zone, a Midwest Zone in which it charges $150, and a West Zone in which it charges $250. In this way, the customers within a given price zone receive no price advantage from the company. For example, customers in Atlanta and Boston pay the same total price to Peerless. The complaint, however, is that the Atlanta customer is paying part of the Boston customer's freight cost.

Basing-point pricing

Pricing in which the seller designates some city as a basing point and charges all customers the freight cost from that city to the customer.

Using **basing-point pricing**, the seller selects a given city as a "basing point" and charges all customers the freight cost from that city to the customer location, regardless of the city from which the goods are actually shipped. For example, Peerless might set Chicago as the basing point and charge all customers $10,000 plus the freight from Chicago to their locations. This means that an Atlanta customer pays the freight cost from Chicago to Atlanta, even though the goods may be shipped from Atlanta. If all sellers used the same basing-point city, delivered prices would be the same for all customers, and price competition would be eliminated.

Freight-absorption pricing

Pricing in which the seller absorbs all or part of the freight charges in order to get the desired business.

Finally, the seller who is anxious to do business with a certain customer or geographical area might use **freight-absorption pricing**. Using this strategy, the seller absorbs all or part of the actual freight charges to get the desired business. The seller might reason that if it can get more business, its average costs will decrease and more than compensate for its extra freight cost. Freight-absorption pricing is used for market penetration and to hold on to increasingly competitive markets.

Dynamic and Personalized Pricing

Throughout most of history, prices were set by negotiation between buyers and sellers. A *fixed-price* policy—setting one price for all buyers—is a relatively modern idea that arose with the development of large-scale retailing at the end of the nineteenth century. Today, most prices are set this way. However, with advances in digital technologies, many companies are now reversing the fixed-pricing trend. They are using **dynamic pricing**—adjusting prices continually to meet changing conditions and situations in the marketplace.

Dynamic pricing

Adjusting prices continually to meet changing conditions and situations in the marketplace.

Dynamic pricing offers many advantages for marketers. Services ranging from retailers, airlines, and hotels to sports teams change prices on the fly to optimize sales according to changes in demand, costs, or competitor pricing, adjusting what they charge for specific items on a daily, hourly, or even continuous basis.

Personalized pricing

Adjusting prices in real time to fit individual customer needs, situations, locations, and buying behaviors.

Today's digital environment also lets marketers practice **personalized pricing**, adjusting prices in real time to fit individual customer situations, locations, and buying behaviors. It seems that every seller knows what prices competitors are charging and customers are paying—for anything and everything it sells, minute by minute, and down to the penny. For example, in this digital age of big data, online sellers such as Amazon, L.L.Bean, or Apple can mine their databases to gauge a specific shopper's desires, measure his or her means, check out competitors' prices, and instantaneously personalize prices and offers to fit individual shopper's situations.

These days, online offers and prices might well be based on what specific customers search for and buy, how much they pay for other purchases, what neighborhood they live in, and whether they might be willing and able to spend more. For example, a consumer from a snooty zip code area who recently went online to purchase a first-class ticket to Paris or customize a new Mercedes coupe might later get a higher quote on a new Bose Wave Radio. By comparison, a friend from a less affluent area with a more modest online search and purchase history might receive an offer of 5 percent off and free shipping on the same radio.

Dynamic pricing doesn't happen only online. For example, many store retailers and other organizations now adjust prices by the day, hour, or even minute. For example, Kohl's uses electronic price tags in its stores to adjust prices instantly based on supply, demand, and store traffic factors. It can now stage sales that last only hours instead of days, much as its online competitors do.

Ride-sharing services such as Uber and Lyft adjust their fares dynamically during slow or peak times, a practice called "surge pricing." Similarly, supply and demand dictates minute-to-minute price adjustments these days for everything from theater tickets to parking spots and golf course greens fees. Tollways in Texas even shift toll prices every five minutes depending on traffic—the fare for one 11-mile stretch, for example, ranges between 94 cents and $8.38 depending on the speed of the traffic. Some unhappy consumers think of this as "highway robbery."[13]

Dynamic and personalized pricing make sense in many contexts—they adjust prices according to market forces and consumer situations. However, done poorly, they can trigger margin-eroding price wars and damage customer relationships and trust. Customers may resent what they see as unfair pricing practices or price gouging. For example, when the fatal derailment of Amtrak Train 188 shut down rail service on the heavily traveled Washington, D.C.-to-New York City line for nearly a week, demand for airline tickets between the two cities jumped dramatically. As demand surged, the airlines' dynamic pricing bots kicked in to coldly raise fares by as much as five times, infuriating travelers and leading to a Department of Transportation investigation.

Such extreme dynamic pricing transgressions are rare. However, even lesser lapses caused by poorly executed dynamic and personalized pricing can also cause shopper confusion, disgruntlement, or brand distrust (see Real Marketing 11.1). Companies must be careful not to cross the fine line between smart dynamic pricing strategies and damaging ones.

Just as dynamic and personalized pricing can benefit sellers, however, consumers can use it to their own benefit. ● Thanks to the internet, consumers with smartphones can now routinely compare prices online while at home, in stores, or anywhere in between. They can get instant product and price comparisons and price alerts from mobile apps such as ShopSavvy, Amazon's Price Check, or Price.com. In fact, retailers are finding that ready online access to comparison prices is giving consumers *too* much of an edge. Such information lets smart shoppers take advantage of the constant price skirmishes among sellers, snap up good deals, leverage retailer price-matching policies, or simply buy items online at lower prices.

Store retailers are now implementing strategies to combat such cross-channel price comparisons and shopping or, better, to turn it into an advantage. For example, Best Buy has a "Price Match Guarantee" where it will match the prices of major online merchants or store competitors. Once it has neutralized price as a buying factor, Best Buy reasons, it can convert shoppers into in-store buyers with its nonprice advantages, such as immediacy, convenient locations, personal assistance by well-trained associates, and the ability to order goods online and pick up or return them in the store. Best Buy has also sharpened its own online and mobile marketing.

● **Dynamic online pricing benefits both sellers and buyers. Consumers armed with instant access to product and price comparisons can often negotiate better in-store prices.**

Yakobchuk Viacheslav/Shutterstock

International Pricing

Companies that market their products internationally must decide what prices to charge in different countries. In some cases, a company can set a uniform worldwide price. For example, Boeing sells its jetliners at about the same price everywhere, whether the buyer is in the United States, Europe, or a third-world country. However, most companies adjust their prices to reflect local market conditions and cost considerations.

The price that a company should charge in a specific country depends on many factors, including economic conditions, competitive situations, laws and regulations, and the nature of the wholesaling and retailing system. Consumer perceptions and preferences also may vary from country to country, calling for different prices. Or the company may have different marketing objectives in various world markets, which require changes in pricing strategy.

Real Marketing 11.1 | Dynamic and Personalized Pricing: Walking a Fine Line

Dynamic pricing has become a competitive necessity in today's marketplace. Consumers armed with digital devices—whether shopping online at home or on the go—routinely cross-check the latest prices offered by different sellers. The sale often goes to the best pricer. In this age of big data, most sellers adjust prices automatically and continuously based on supply, demand, competitor prices, and even individual shopper characteristics and buying situations.

Online giant Amazon has mastered the science of dynamic pricing. According to one source, Amazon's automated, AI-driven dynamic pricing system changes the price on as many as 80 million items throughout a given day on its mammoth site, based on a host of marketplace factors. As a result, Amazon competes very effectively pricewise. Over the most recent Black Friday holiday weekend, Amazon's prices averaged nearly 14 percent lower than same-product prices at competing retailers, including Walmart and Target.

But dynamic pricing is a complex process, and it doesn't always sit well with customers. Done poorly, it can cause customer confusion, frustration, or even resentment, damaging hard-won customer relationships. Consider this Amazon shopper's experience:

Nancy Plumlee had just taken up mahjong, a Chinese game of tiles similar to rummy. She browsed Amazon.com and, after sifting through several pages of options, settled on a set for $54.99. She placed it in her [shopping cart] and continued shopping for some scorecards and game accessories. A few minutes later, she scanned the cart and noticed the $54.99 had jumped to $70.99. Plumlee thought she was going crazy. She checked her computer's viewing history and, indeed, the game's original price was listed at $54.99. Determined, she cleared out the cart and tried again. [This time,] the game's price jumped from $54.99 to $59.99. "That just doesn't feel like straight-up business honesty. Shame on Amazon," said Plumlee, who called [Amazon] and persuaded the online retailer to refund her $5.

Despite the hiccups, Amazon defends its dynamic pricing practices and its shopping cart pricing. Amazon lets customers hold items in their carts indefinitely, and that requires regular updates of purchase terms such as price, availability, and shipping dates to match current conditions. "Items in your shopping cart will always reflect the most recent price displayed on the item's product detail page," says Amazon on its pricing policies webpage. "Placing an item in your cart

doesn't reserve the price shown at that time." However, Amazon does notify customers upon purchase confirmation if a product's price has changed while in the cart. And, Amazon points out, this policy works both ways—if the price of an item drops after it is placed in the shopping cart, the customer gets the lower price.

For multichannel retailers—those selling both online and in physical stores—dynamic pricing poses additional challenges. To compete effectively with Amazon and other sellers, omni-channel retailers must continuously monitor competitor prices and match them dynamically at their web and mobile stores as well. But whereas it's relatively easy to change online prices, trying to constantly adjust in-store prices would create havoc, if it's possible at all. "The problem with dynamic pricing offline is cost," says one expert. "You would have to go to all those little shelf facings and change them."

Thus, discrepancies between store and online prices are common, often causing consumer confusion and displeasure. One avid Target shopper learned this the hard way:

After evaluating an Epilator on her Target app inside the store, Miranda Artz bought it for the $99.99 price listed on both the app and the store shelf. But when she reached the parking lot, she noticed something strange. "My app was still open and it was still on that product and when I got to my car I noticed it said $69.99. I was a little confused. I thought maybe I had misread it in the store or something." Returning to the store, Artz confirmed

that both the app and shelf prices were $99.99. "I went back out to my car and again it was $69.99. So, I took a screen shot this time and brought it back in and got a price match."

Artz's Target story repeated itself a few weeks later. She was shopping for a tent on the Target app and found one she liked at a reduced price of $83.99. This time, she took a screen shot before going into the Target store. Her intuition paid off. As soon as she stepped inside the store, the Target app adjusted the price of the tent to its regular price of $119.99—a difference of $37. Artz is a little disappointed in Target. It's still her favorite store, but she's now a wiser shopper.

Based on reports of similar customer experiences, various news agencies have conducted their own experiments on Target's "parking lot price switch." These studies compared the app prices outside and inside the store on lists of 10 to 20 items. The results showed that the Target app posted a higher in-store price for 40 to 50 percent of the items. For some, the price difference was small—20 cents more for a 24-pack of Scott toilet paper or 10 cents more for a one-liter bottle of Listerine mouthwash. On other items, however, the price difference was startling—$72 higher for a Graco child car seat or a whopping $148 higher for a Dyson Cyclone V10 Motorhead vacuum cleaner.

What's behind Target's parking lot versus in-store price differences? The Target app uses phone location data to determine where customer is then "geo-fencing" to set app prices for that customer. "When in the

Dynamic pricing is a competitive necessity. But as Target shoppers learned, it can be difficult to implement, especially for omni-channel retailers.

Eyal Dayan Photography

store, all prices listed in the app resemble the prices listed in the store," says a retail analyst. "Outside of the store is a different story. That is where Target must compete with other online stores and the rest of the world, and the prices there mimic those of Target.com."

In response to inquiries, Target stated that it is "committed to providing value to our guests and that includes being priced competitively online and in our stores, and as a result, pricing and promotions may vary." However, the retailer has made some changes to its app that make its pricing policies clearer. Target also stresses its price-matching policy: "If a guest finds any item for a lower price across any of the ways they can shop Target, we'll price match it." And it notes that customers can avoid the problem by opting out of the Target app's geolocation capabilities. But that means also giving up some of the app's attractive features, such as in-store product location and store aisle navigation mapping.

Most consumers have experienced first-hand the joys and frustrations of dynamic and personalized pricing. And many consumers have learned how to navigate the pricing maze to their own benefit. From the seller's side, done well, dynamic pricing can create competitive advantage. But it must be practiced with care. Like everything else in marketing, it should be used to create value for customers and to enhance brand–customer relationships. If a company gets that right, it will gain value in return.[14]

● **International prices: Companies often must change their pricing strategies from country to country. For example, Apple sells its latest phones at premium prices to affluent Chinese customers but is under pressure to target China's mid-range customers with lower-priced phones.**

FRED DUFOUR/AFP/Getty Images

● For example, Apple uses its premium pricing strategy to introduce sophisticated, feature-rich, premium smartphones in carefully segmented mature markets in developed countries and to affluent consumers in emerging markets. By contrast, it's now under pressure to discount older models and develop cheaper, more basic phone models for sizable but less affluent markets in developing countries, where even discounted older Apple phones sell at prices three to five times those of those of competing low-price models. For example, in China, Apple's latest premium phones sell well and profitably to affluent consumers. However, as Samsung and large Chinese competitors like Huawei and Xiaomi bring sophisticated but lower-priced phones to the highly competitive Chinese market, Apple is struggling to maintain market share there. Says one analyst, "If Apple wants to grow iPhone volume higher in China in the future, it will have to push down, not up, the pricing curve, to target more mid-range consumers who can no longer afford a full-featured iPhone."[15]

Costs play an important role in setting international prices. Travelers abroad are often surprised to find that goods that are relatively inexpensive at home may carry outrageously higher price tags in other countries. A pair of Levi's 501 selling for $54 in Los Angeles might go for $118 in Paris. A McDonald's Big Mac selling for $5 in New York might cost nearly $7 in Zurich, and an Oral-B toothbrush selling for $2.49 at home may cost $10 in China. Conversely, a Gucci handbag going for only $1,470 in Milan, Italy, might fetch $1,790 in the United States.

In some cases, such *price escalation* may result from differences in selling strategies or market conditions. In most instances, however, it is simply a result of the higher costs of selling in another country—the additional costs of operations, product modifications, shipping and insurance, exchange-rate fluctuations, and physical distribution. Import tariffs and taxes can also add to costs. For example, the Indian government imposes a 150 percent tariff on U.S. wine imports, driving up the prices of American wines in India relative to domestic wines.[16]

Price has become a key element in the international marketing strategies of companies attempting to enter less affluent emerging markets. Typically, entering such markets has meant targeting the exploding middle classes in developing countries such as China, India, Russia, Brazil, and South Africa, whose economies have been growing rapidly. More recently, however, many companies are shifting their sights to include a new target—the so-called "bottom of the pyramid," the vast untapped market consisting of the world's poorest consumers.

Not long ago, the preferred way for many brands to market their products in developing markets—whether consumer products or cars, computers, and smartphones—was to paste new labels on existing models and sell them at higher prices to the privileged few who could afford them. However, such a pricing approach put many products out of the reach of the tens of millions of poor consumers in emerging markets. As a result, many companies developed smaller, more basic and affordable product versions for these markets. For example, whereas Apple has focused on ever-more sophisticated and more expensive phones in global markets, Samsung leads all competitors worldwide in unit smartphone sales by also marketing mid- and lower-priced phones in fast-growing emerging markets such as India and China.

Most companies are learning that selling profitably to the bottom of the pyramid requires more than just repackaging or stripping down existing products and selling them at low prices. Just like more well-to-do consumers, low-income buyers want products that are both functional *and* aspirational. Thus, companies today are innovating to create products that not only sell at low prices but also give bottom-of-the-pyramid consumers more for their money, not less. For instance, to strengthen its position further in such markets, Samsung is now putting more cutting-edge technology into mid-range phones that still sell at affordable prices.[17]

International pricing presents many special problems and complexities. We discuss international pricing issues in more detail in Chapter 19.

Author | When and how should
Comment | a company change its
price? What if costs rise, putting
the squeeze on profits? What if
the economy sags and customers
become more price sensitive? Or
what if a major competitor raises
or drops its prices? As Figure 11.1
suggests, companies face many
price-changing options.

Price Changes

OBJECTIVE 11-4 Discuss the key issues related to initiating and responding to price changes.

After developing their pricing structures and strategies, companies often face situations in which they must initiate price changes or respond to price changes by competitors.

Initiating Price Changes

In some cases, the company may find it desirable to initiate either a price cut or a price increase. In both cases, it must anticipate possible buyer and competitor reactions.

Initiating Price Cuts

Several situations may lead a firm to consider cutting its price. One such circumstance is excess capacity. Another is falling demand in the face of strong price competition or a weakened economy. In such cases, the firm may aggressively cut prices to boost sales and market share. But as the airline, fast-food, automobile, retailing, and other industries have learned in recent years, cutting prices in an industry loaded with excess capacity may lead to price wars as competitors try to hold on to market share.

A company may also cut prices in a drive to dominate the market through lower costs. Either the company starts with lower costs and prices than its competitors, or it cuts prices in the hope of gaining market share that will further cut costs through larger volume. For example, AGIT Global used low prices to quickly build demand for its Wavestorm surfboards. Before Wavestorm, surfers and would-be surfers typically bought custom-made or high-end surfboards at local surf shops, where entry-level boards typically run $800 to $1,000. But to make surfing more accessible, AGIT began mass-producing good-quality soft-foam surfboards and selling them through big-box stores at very low prices. For example, it initially sold an entry-level, eight-foot, blue-and-white Wavestorm board at Costco for only $99.99. A dozen years later, the boards still sell at Costco for only $149.99. Thanks to heavy price cuts relative to established brands, Wavestorm is now the market leader, selling an estimated five times more boards than the other largest surfboard brands.[18]

Initiating Price Increases

A successful price increase can greatly improve profits. For example, if the company's profit margin is 3 percent of sales, a 1 percent price increase will boost profits by 33 percent if sales volume is unaffected. A major factor in price increases is cost inflation. Rising costs squeeze profit margins and lead companies to pass cost increases along to customers.

Another factor leading to price increases is over-demand: When a company cannot supply all that its customers need, it may raise its prices, ration products to customers, or both.

When raising prices, the company must avoid being perceived as a *price gouger*. For example, when gasoline prices rise rapidly, angry customers often accuse the major oil companies of enriching themselves at the expense of consumers. Customers have long memories, and they will eventually turn away from companies or even whole industries that they perceive as charging excessive prices. In the extreme, claims of price gouging may even bring about increased government regulation.

There are some techniques for avoiding these problems. One is to maintain a sense of fairness surrounding any price increase. Price increases should be supported by company communications telling customers why prices are being raised.

● Brands must be careful when raising prices. When Mondelēz reduced the amount of chocolate in its Toblerone bar (effectively raising the price), British consumers found the change in Toblerone's iconic shape hard to stomach, sparking online outrage.

DARREN STAPLES/REUTERS/Newscom

Wherever possible, the company should consider ways to meet higher costs or demand without raising prices. For example, it might be more cost-effective in how it produces or distributes its products. It can "unbundle" its market offering, removing features, packaging, or services and separately pricing elements that were formerly part of the offer. Or it can shrink the product or substitute less-expensive ingredients instead of raising the price, a process sometimes called "shrinkflation." Kimberly-Clark raised Kleenex prices by "desheeting"—reducing the number of sheets of toilet paper or facial tissues in each same-priced package. ● And Mondelēz recently cut the size of its popular Toblerone chocolate bar by about 12 percent in the UK, not by shortening the bar but by increasing the spacing between its signature triangles. "Shrinkflation is actually quite a successful tactic because a lot of shoppers are more sensitive to a price change than to a weight change," says a pricing expert. However, British consumers found the too-obvious change to Toblerone's iconic shape hard to stomach, sparking online outrage.[19]

Buyer Reactions to Price Changes

Customers do not always interpret price changes in a straightforward way. A price *increase*, which would normally lower sales, may have some positive meanings for buyers. For example, what would you think if Rolex *raised* the price of its latest watch model? On the one hand, you might think that the watch is even more exclusive or better made. On the other hand, you might think that Rolex is simply being greedy by charging what the traffic will bear.

Similarly, consumers may view a price *cut* in several ways. For example, what would you think if Rolex were to suddenly cut its prices? You might think that you are getting a better deal on an exclusive product. More likely, however, you'd think that quality had been reduced, and the brand's luxury image might be tarnished. A brand's price and image are often closely linked. A price change, especially a drop in price, can adversely affect how consumers view the brand.

Competitor Reactions to Price Changes

A firm considering a price change must worry about the reactions of its competitors as well as those of its customers. Competitors are most likely to react when the number of firms involved is small, when the product is uniform, and when the buyers are well informed about products and prices.

How can the firm anticipate the likely reactions of its competitors? The problem is complex because, like the customer, the competitor can interpret a company price cut in many ways. It might think the company is trying to grab a larger market share or that it's doing poorly and trying to boost its sales. Or it might think that the company wants the whole industry to cut prices to increase total demand.

The company must assess each competitor's likely reaction. If all competitors behave alike, this amounts to analyzing only a typical competitor. In contrast, if the competitors do not behave alike—perhaps because of differences in size, market shares, or policies—then separate analyses are necessary. However, if some competitors will match the price change, there is good reason to expect that the rest will also match it.

Responding to Price Changes

Here we reverse the question and ask how a firm should respond to a price change by a competitor. The firm needs to consider several issues: Why did the competitor change the price? Is the price change temporary or permanent? What will happen to the company's market share and profits if it does not respond? Are other competitors going to respond? Besides these issues, the company must also consider its own situation and strategy and possible customer reactions to price changes.

● **Figure 11.1** shows the ways a company might assess and respond to a competitor's price cut. Suppose a company learns that a competitor has cut its price and decides that this price cut is likely to harm its sales and profits. It might simply decide to hold its current price and profit margin. The company might believe that it will not lose too much market share or that it would lose too much profit if it reduced its own price. Or it might decide that it should wait and respond when it has more information on the effects of the competitor's price change. However, waiting too long to act might let the competitor get stronger and more confident as its sales increase.

If the company decides that effective action can and should be taken, it might make any of four responses. First, it could *reduce its price* to match the competitor's price. It may decide that the market is price sensitive and that it would lose too much market share to the lower-priced competitor. However, cutting the price will reduce the company's profits in the short run. Some companies might also reduce their product quality, services, and marketing communications to retain profit margins, but this will ultimately hurt long-run market share. The company should try to maintain its quality as it cuts prices.

Alternatively, the company might maintain its price but *raise the perceived value* of its offer. It could improve its communications, stressing the relative value of its product over that of the lower-price competitor. The firm may find it cheaper to maintain price and spend money to improve its perceived value than to cut price and operate at a lower margin. Or the company might *improve quality* and *increase price*, moving its brand into a higher price–value position. The higher quality creates greater customer value, which justifies the higher price. In turn, the higher price preserves the company's higher margins.

Finally, the company might launch a *low-price "fighter brand"*—adding a lower-price item to the line or creating a separate lower-price brand. This is necessary if the

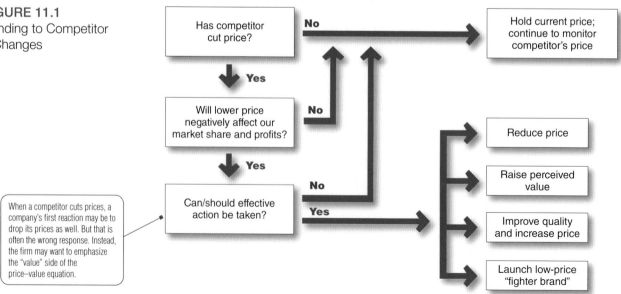

● FIGURE 11.1
Responding to Competitor
Price Changes

When a competitor cuts prices, a company's first reaction may be to drop its prices as well. But that is often the wrong response. Instead, the firm may want to emphasize the "value" side of the price–value equation.

● Fighter brands: To counter store brands and other low-price entrants, P&G turned a number of its brands into fighter brands. Charmin Essentials Soft is "soft on your butt and budget."

Kelly Tippett/Shutterstock

particular market segment being lost is price sensitive and will not respond to arguments of higher quality. For example, to counter store brands and other low-price entrants, P&G turned a number of its brands into fighter brands. Luvs disposable diapers give parents "premium stretch and ultra leakage protection for less than the pricey brands." And P&G offers popular budget-priced essentials versions of several of its major brands. ● For instance, Charmin Essentials Soft is "soft on your butt and budget," and Bounty Essentials is the "affordable picker upper." Tide Simply Clean & Fresh is about 35 percent cheaper than regular Tide detergent—it's "tough on odors and easy on your wallet." However, companies must use caution when introducing fighter brands, as such brands can tarnish the image of the main brand. In addition, although they may attract budget buyers away from lower-priced rivals, they can also take business away from the firm's higher-margin brands.

<table>
<tr><td>Author Comment</td><td>Pricing decisions are often constrained by social and legal issues. For example, think about the pharmaceuticals industry. Are rapidly rising prescription drug prices justified? Or are the drug companies unfairly lining their pockets by gouging consumers who have few alternatives? Should the government step in?</td></tr>
</table>

Public Policy and Pricing

OBJECTIVE 11-5 Discuss the major public policy concerns and key pieces of legislation that affect pricing decisions.

Price competition is a core element of our free-market economy. In setting prices, companies usually are not free to charge whatever prices they wish. Many federal, state, and even local laws govern the rules of fair play in pricing. In addition, companies must consider broader societal pricing concerns. In setting their prices, for example, pharmaceutical firms must balance their development costs and profit objectives against the sometimes life-and-death needs of prescription drug consumers (see Real Marketing 11.2).

The most important pieces of legislation affecting pricing are the Sherman Act, the Clayton Act, and the Robinson-Patman Act, initially adopted to curb the formation of monopolies and regulate business practices that might unfairly restrain trade. Because these federal statutes can be applied only to interstate commerce, some states have adopted similar provisions for companies that operate locally.

● **Figure 11.2** shows the major public policy issues in pricing. These include potentially damaging pricing practices within a given level of the channel (price-fixing and predatory pricing) and across levels of the channel (retail price maintenance, discriminatory pricing, and deceptive pricing).[21]

● **FIGURE 11.2**
Public Policy Issues in Pricing

Source: Adapted from Dhruv Grewal and Larry D. Compeau, "Pricing and Public Policy: A Research Agenda and Overview of the Special Issue," *Journal of Public Policy and Marketing*, Spring 1999, pp. 3–10.

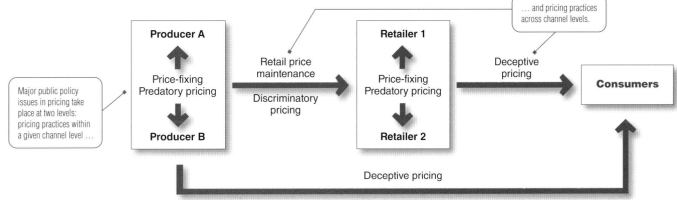

Real Marketing 11.2 | Pharmaceutical Pricing: No Easy Answers

The U.S. pharmaceutical industry has historically been one of the nation's most profitable industries. In most situations, we'd applaud such high-performing companies and industries. However, when it comes to pharmaceutical firms, critics claim, healthy sales and profits may not be so healthy for consumers.

Somehow, learning that major pharmaceutical companies such as Johnson & Johnson, Roche, Pfizer, Novartis, Merck, and GlaxoSmithKline are reaping big profits leaves a bad taste in the mouths of many consumers. It's like learning that the oil companies are profiting when gas prices rocket upward. Although most consumers appreciate the steady stream of beneficial drugs produced by pharmaceutical companies, they worry that the industry's huge success may be coming at their own expense—literally.

Americans spent about $360 billion last year on prescription medications, up 6.5 percent from the prior year. Prescription prices have risen rapidly over the years, and healthcare costs continue to jump. For example, the prices of popular brand name drugs jumped 190 percent during the past decade.

The critics claim that competitive forces don't operate well in the pharmaceuticals market, allowing the pharmaceutical companies to charge excessive prices. Unlike purchases of other consumer products, drug purchases cannot be postponed. And consumers don't usually shop for the best deals on medicines—they simply take what the doctor orders. Because physicians who write the prescriptions don't pay for the medicines they recommend, they have little incentive to be price conscious. Moreover, third-party payers—insurance companies, health plans, and government programs—often pay all or part of the bill. Finally, because of patent protection and the huge investment and time needed to develop and test new drugs, there are fewer competing brands to force lower prices.

The critics claim that these market factors leave pharmaceutical companies free to practice monopoly pricing, sometimes resulting in unfair practices or even seemingly outlandish cases of price gouging. One classic case made headlines when entrepreneur Martin Shkreli and his company Turing Pharmaceuticals acquired Daraprim, a 62-year-old, lifesaving medication used by AIDS patients. Turing immediately jacked up the price of Daraprim from $13.50 per pill to an astounding $750 per pill, a more than 5,000 percent increase. The pill itself costs only about a dollar to produce.

Major drug companies would never commit such atrocities. "He is not us," said Merck's CEO of Turing's Shkreli. Nevertheless, mainstream pharmaceutical makers routinely boost the prices of their cancer, diabetes, MS, and cholesterol-reducing drugs by 10 percent or more per year, much faster than inflation. As just one example, take Gleevec, a drug sold by Novartis to treat blood-based cancer. Gleevec seemed pretty expensive when it first came to market in 2001 at about $26,000 for a year's supply. Yet, for reasons unknown, Novartis has since quadrupled Gleevec's price, leading one industry economist to remark that she could find no economic theory to explain how pharmaceutical companies set or raise their drug prices.

The prices of some new lifesaving drugs seem more than exorbitant. For example, Bavencio, a recently approved cancer drug, costs patients about $156,000 a year. And a new muscular dystrophy drug recently debuted at an eye-popping $300,000 annually. But even older drugs that have been on the market for a long time have seen major price increases. Take the price of 40-year-old EpiPen, a lifesaving allergy medication. Its price increased 400 percent in just five years, sparking public outrage. Similarly, a congressional investigation revealed that the price of insulin tripled between 2002 and 2013 despite few changes in the drug.

To add insult to injury, the critics say, drug companies pour more than $10 billion a year into direct-to-consumer advertising and spend another $20 billion on marketing to doctors. Proponents claim that such promotions inform and empower patients to participate in their own health care. But critics charge that these marketing efforts dictate higher prices at the same time that they build demand for more expensive remedies. Thus, the severest critics say, the big drug companies may be profiting unfairly—or even at the expense of human life—by promoting and pricing products beyond the reach of many people who need them.

But there's another side to the drug-pricing issue—the industry's side. Industry proponents point out that, over the years, the drug companies have developed a steady stream of medicines that transform people's lives. Developing such new drugs is risky and expensive, involving legions of scientists, expensive technology, and years of effort with no certainty of success. Last year, the pharmaceutical industry spent more than $172 billion on R&D. On average, it takes 12 to 15 years and costs between $660 million and $2.7 billion to bring a new drug to market. Thus, the proponents say, although the prices of new prescription drugs seem high, they're needed to fund the development of important future drugs. As one recent Pfizer ad states: "It takes an average of 1,600 scientists 12 years to bring one Pfizer medicine to life. That's a lot of collective brain power dedicated to finding medicines that improve lives." GlaxoSmithKline (GSK) puts it this way: "Inventing new medicines isn't easy, but it's worth it. . . . Today's medicines finance tomorrow's miracles."

And so the controversy continues. As drug prices climb, the pharmaceutical companies face pressure from the federal government,

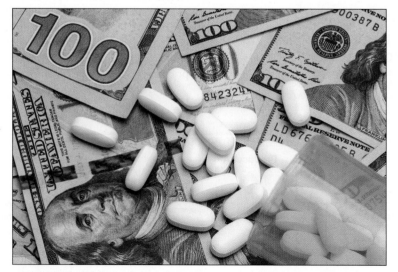

Responsible pharmaceutical pricing: Most consumers understand that they'll have to pay the price for beneficial drugs. They just want to be treated fairly in the process.

pixelrobot/123RF

insurance companies, managed-care providers, and consumer advocacy groups to exercise restraint in setting prices. However, rather than waiting for tougher legislation on prices—or simply because it's the right thing to do—many of the drug companies are taking action on their own. For example, some companies have committed to keeping their average price hikes at or below inflation. Others employ tiered pricing—selling their medicines in different countries at varying prices based on ability to pay in each country. Most pharmaceutical companies now sponsor patient assistance programs that provide prescription medicines free or at low cost to people who cannot afford them, and they regularly donate free medicines in response to disaster relief efforts around the globe.

In all, pharmaceutical pricing is no easy issue. For the pharmaceutical companies, it's more than a matter of sales and profits. In setting prices, short-term financial goals must be tempered by broader societal considerations. For example, GSK's heartfelt mission is "to help people do more, feel better, live longer." Accomplishing this mission won't come cheap. Most consumers understand that. One way or another, they know, they'll have to pay the price. All they really ask is that they be treated fairly in the process.[20]

Pricing within Channel Levels

Federal legislation on *price-fixing* states that sellers must set prices without talking to competitors. Otherwise, price collusion is suspected. Price-fixing is illegal per se—that is, the government does not accept any excuses for price-fixing. Recently, governments at the state and national levels have been aggressively enforcing price-fixing regulations in industries ranging from gasoline, insurance, and concrete to credit cards, computer chips, and e-books. Companies found guilty of price-fixing practices can pay heavy penalties. For example, Apple paid $450 million in fines for conspiring with publishers to fix prices on e-books. Four major U.S. airlines—United, Delta, Southwest, and American—agreed to pay $60 million to settle a class action suit and still face a U.S. Department of Justice investigation for conspiring to artificially inflate air fares to "reap huge profits." And Visa and Mastercard recently agreed to pay $6.2 billion to settle a price-fixing case brought by retailers over allegedly inflated card fees.[22]

Sellers are also prohibited from using *predatory pricing*—selling below cost with the intention of punishing a competitor or gaining higher long-run profits by putting competitors out of business. This protects small sellers from larger ones that might sell items below cost temporarily or in a specific locale to drive them out of business. The biggest problem is determining just what constitutes predatory pricing behavior. Selling below cost to unload excess inventory is not considered predatory; selling below cost to drive out competitors is. Thus, a given action may or may not be predatory depending on intent, and intent can be very difficult to determine or prove.

● **Predatory pricing: Some industry critics have accused Amazon.com of pricing books at fire-sale prices that harm competing booksellers. But is it predatory pricing or just plain good competitive marketing?**

imageBROKER/Alamy Stock Photo

In recent years, several large and powerful companies have been accused of predatory pricing. However, turning an accusation into a lawsuit can be difficult. ● For example, many publishers and booksellers have expressed concerns about Amazon.com's predatory practices, especially its book pricing:[23]

> Many booksellers and publishers complain that Amazon's book pricing policies are destroying their industry. Amazon routinely sells best-selling hardback books as loss leaders at cut-rate prices. And it peddles e-books at fire-sale prices in order to win customers for its Kindle e-reader and tablets. Such very low book prices have caused considerable damage to competing booksellers, many of whom view Amazon's pricing actions as predatory. According to some industry groups, such practices "harm the interests of America's readers, impoverish the book industry as a whole, and impede the free flow of ideas in our society." Still, no predatory pricing charges have ever been filed against Amazon. It would be extremely difficult to prove that such loss-leader pricing is purposefully predatory as opposed to just plain good competitive marketing. "But wait a minute," states one analyst. "Isn't that what business is supposed to do—compete to lower prices?"

Pricing across Channel Levels

The Robinson-Patman Act seeks to prevent unfair *price discrimination* by ensuring that sellers offer the same price terms to customers at a given level of trade. For example, every retailer is entitled to the same price terms from a given manufacturer, whether the retailer is REI or a local bicycle shop. However, price discrimination is allowed if the seller can prove that its costs are different when selling to different retailers—for example, that it costs less per unit to sell a large volume of bicycles to REI than to sell a few bicycles to the local dealer.

The seller can also discriminate in its pricing if the seller manufactures different qualities of the same product for different retailers. The seller has to prove that these differences are proportional. Price differentials may also be used to "match competition" in "good faith," provided the price discrimination is temporary, localized, and defensive rather than offensive.

Laws also prohibit *retail (or resale) price maintenance*—a manufacturer cannot require dealers to charge a specified retail price for its product. Although the seller can propose a manufacturer's *suggested* retail price to dealers, it cannot refuse to sell to a dealer that takes independent pricing action, nor can it punish the dealer by shipping late or denying advertising allowances. For example, the Florida attorney general's office investigated Nike for allegedly fixing the retail price of its shoes and clothing. It was concerned that Nike might be withholding items from retailers who were not selling its most expensive shoes at prices the company considered suitable.

Deceptive pricing occurs when a seller states prices or price savings that mislead consumers or are not actually available to consumers. This might involve bogus reference or comparison prices, as when a retailer sets artificially high "regular" prices and then announces "sale" prices close to its previous everyday prices. For example, luxury apparel and accessories retailer Michael Kors recently settled a class action lawsuit alleging that it used deceptive pricing at its outlet stores. The retailer was charged with tagging products with false "manufacturer's suggested retail prices" to make its supposed discounted prices more appealing when, in fact, the products were sold only in the outlet stores. Such artificial comparison pricing is widespread in retailing. Retailers ranging from TJMaxx, Kohl's, and JCPenney to Zara, Neiman Marcus, and Michael Kors have drawn complaints and lawsuits over this issue.[24]

Although comparison pricing claims are legal if they are truthful, the Federal Trade Commission's "Guides against Deceptive Pricing" warn sellers not to advertise (1) a price reduction unless it is a savings from the usual retail price, (2) "factory" or "wholesale" prices unless such prices are what they are claimed to be, and (3) comparable value prices on imperfect goods.[25]

Other deceptive pricing issues include *scanner fraud* and price confusion. The widespread use of scanner-based computer checkouts has led to increasing complaints of retailers overcharging their customers. Most of these overcharges result from poor management, such as a failure to enter current or sale prices into the system. Other cases, however, involve intentional overcharges.

Many federal and state statutes regulate against deceptive pricing practices. For example, the Automobile Information Disclosure Act requires automakers to attach a statement on new vehicle windows stating the manufacturer's suggested retail price, the prices of optional equipment, and the dealer's transportation charges. However, reputable sellers go beyond what is required by law. Treating customers fairly and making certain that they fully understand prices and pricing terms are an important part of building strong and lasting customer relationships.

Reviewing and Extending the Concepts

Objectives Review

In this chapter, we examined some additional pricing considerations—new product pricing, product mix pricing, price adjustments, initiating and reacting to prices changes, and pricing and public policy. A company sets not a single price but rather a *pricing structure* that covers its entire mix of products. This pricing structure changes over time as products move through their life cycles. The company adjusts product prices to reflect changes in costs and demand and account for variations in buyers and situations. As the competitive environment changes, the company considers when to initiate price changes and when to respond to them.

OBJECTIVE 11-1 Describe the major strategies for pricing new products. *(pp 318–319)*

Pricing is a dynamic process. Companies design a *pricing structure* that covers all their products. They change this structure over time and adjust it to account for different customers and situations. Pricing strategies usually change as a product passes through its life cycle. In pricing innovative new products, a company can use *market-skimming pricing* by initially setting high prices to "skim" the maximum amount of revenue from various segments of the market. Or it can use *market-penetrating pricing* by setting a low initial price to penetrate the market deeply and win a large market share.

OBJECTIVE 11-2 Explain how companies find a set of prices that maximizes the profits from the total product mix. *(pp 319–321)*

When the product is part of a product mix, the firm searches for a set of prices that will maximize the profits from the total mix. In *product line pricing*, the company decides on price steps for the entire set of products it offers. In addition, the company must set prices for *optional products* (optional or accessory products included with the main product), *captive products* (products that are required for use of the main product), *by-products* (waste or residual products produced when making the main product), and *product bundles* (combinations of products at a reduced price).

OBJECTIVE 11-3 Discuss how companies adjust their prices to take into account different types of customers and situations. *(pp 321–330)*

Companies apply a variety of *price adjustment strategies* to account for differences in consumer segments and situations. One is *discount and allowance pricing*, whereby the company establishes cash, quantity, functional, or seasonal discounts, or varying types of allowances. A second strategy is *segmented pricing*, where the company sells a product at two or more prices

to accommodate different customers, product forms, locations, or times. Sometimes companies consider more than economics in their pricing decisions, using *psychological pricing* to better communicate a product's intended position. In *promotional pricing*, a company offers discounts or temporarily sells a product below list price as a special event, sometimes even selling below cost as a loss leader. Another approach is *geographical pricing*, whereby the company decides how to price to near or distant customers. In *dynamic and personalized pricing*, companies adjust prices continually to meet the characteristics and needs of individual customers and situations. Finally, *international pricing* means that the company adjusts its price to meet different conditions and expectations in different world markets.

OBJECTIVE 11-4 Discuss the key issues related to initiating and responding to price changes. *(pp 330–333)*

When a firm considers initiating a *price change*, it must consider customers' and competitors' reactions. There are different implications to *initiating price cuts* and *initiating price increases*. Buyer reactions to price changes are influenced by the meaning customers see in the price change. Competitors' reactions flow from a set reaction policy or a fresh analysis of each situation.

There are also many factors to consider in responding to a competitor's price changes. The company that faces a price change initiated by a competitor must try to understand the competitor's intent as well as the likely duration and impact of the change. If a swift reaction is desirable, the firm should preplan its reactions to different possible price actions by competitors. When facing a competitor's price change, the company might sit tight, reduce its own price, raise perceived quality, improve quality and raise price, or launch a fighting brand.

OBJECTIVE 11-5 Discuss the major public policy concerns and key pieces of legislation that affect pricing decisions. *(pp 333–336)*

Price competition is a core element of our free-market economy. In setting prices, companies usually are not free to charge whatever prices they wish. Marketers must heed federal, state, and local laws govern pricing. In addition, companies must consider broader societal pricing concerns. The major public policy issues in pricing include potentially damaging pricing practices within a given level of the channel (price-fixing and predatory pricing) and across levels of the channel (retail price maintenance, discriminatory pricing, and deceptive pricing). Reputable marketers go beyond what is required by law. Treating customers fairly and making certain that they fully understand prices and pricing terms are an important part of building strong and lasting customer relationships.

Key Terms

OBJECTIVE 11-1

Market-skimming pricing (price skimming) (p 318)
Market-penetration pricing (p 319)

OBJECTIVE 11-2

Product line pricing (p 319)
Optional-product pricing (p 320)
Captive-product pricing (p 320)

By-product pricing (p 321)
Product bundle pricing (p 321)

OBJECTIVE 11-3

Discount (p 322)
Allowance (p 322)
Segmented pricing (p 322)
Psychological pricing (p 323)
Reference prices (p 324)
Promotional pricing (p 324)

Geographical pricing (p 325)
FOB-origin pricing (p 325)
Uniform-delivered pricing (p 325)
Zone pricing (p 326)
Basing-point pricing (p 326)
Freight-absorption pricing (p 326)
Dynamic pricing (p 326)
Personalized pricing (p 326)

Discussion Questions

11-1 Discuss the two new product pricing strategies and the conditions that must be met for companies to successfully launch new products under each of these strategies. (AACSB: Written and Oral Communication)

11-2 Why might the strategy for setting a product's price need to be changed when a product is part of a product mix? What are the five product mix pricing strategies? Provide an example for each. (AACSB: Written and Oral Communication; Reflective Thinking)

11-3 What is promotional pricing, and how is it used by sellers? Give an example. (AACSB: Communication)

11-4 Discuss some situations that may prompt companies to initiate price cuts. (AACSB: Communication)

11-5 Why would a company choose to introduce a low-price, fighter brand? Provide an example. What should the company be wary of when it launches a low-price fighter brand? (AACSB: Written and Oral Communication)

11-6 Discuss the major public policy issues in pricing practices within a given channel level and across channel levels. (AACSB: Communication)

Critical Thinking Exercises

11-7 Alesya sells her high-end laptop bags and coordinating wallets online through her own website and in high-end retailers in Charleston, South Carolina. She encourages her mailing list customers to purchase products from her retail partners. She does this to maintain her presence in their physical locations, which helps increase awareness of her products among other customers and establishes the high-end, prestigious image she desires. She currently encourages customers to shop at the retailers to bypass shipping fees and avoid the wait. She is considering using a geofence to send a personalized, discount price to mailing list subscribers who come within five miles of a retail location that they can redeem in the store. Should she use this type of promotion? Why or why not? (AACSB: Written and Oral Communication; Reflective Thinking)

11-8 A company that delivers subscription boxes of children's clothes to customers all over the United States is considering different geographical pricing strategies. If the company wants to penetrate the market and hold its market share in a competitive market, which geographical pricing policy should it use? Why is your chosen strategy better than the other geographical pricing policies you considered? (AACSB: Written and Oral Communication; Reflective Thinking)

11-9 Josue's firm is deciding if it should sell a stripped-down version of its stylized, solar-powered battery charger to consumers at the bottom of the pyramid in India. What factors should Josue consider as he makes a recommendation to his manager? (AACSB: Written and Oral Communication; Reflective Thinking)

APPLICATIONS AND CASES

Online, Mobile, and Social Media Marketing Krazy Coupon Lady

Price-conscious consumers are all about finding the best deal. Some even make a sport out of it! Krazy couponers Heather and Joanie have been showcased on many national television shows and in web and print articles. The two friends run a highly successful company that works tirelessly to uncover the best deals so enabling families to save money. Posted on their website, www.krazycouponlady.com, is the company mantra "You'd be krazy not to be one of us!" The website features promotions and alerts to special pricing on products as well as coupons and discounts to help consumers stretch their dollars. Also featured are retailers with sale priced merchandise, coupons, and promotions. Community members post their best deals in the brag section.

11-10 Visit www.krazycouponlady.com and browse a deal you would consider purchasing. After identifying the deal, conduct an online price comparison at various retailers to determine the range of prices you would typically pay for the product. Present your conclusions. (AACSB: Written and Oral Communication; Information Technology; Reflective Thinking)

11-11 Using www.krazycouponlady.com, click on Stores, Coupons, and Deals on the navigation bar and make a list of the featured products. Identify the pricing strategy used by the retailer. (AACSB: Written and Oral Communication; Information Technology; Reflective Thinking)

Marketing Ethics Pink Tax

Your firm did market research and realized it can maintain demand and charge $20 more for a pink version of a bicycle helmet than the blue version. Both helmets cost the same amount to produce. Your manager asks you whether the firm should charge a higher price for the pink helmet. As you research your response, you come across a recent report by the Government Accountability Office. The report found that about half of the items it evaluated—which included deodorant, shaving gel/cream, razors, perfumes and body sprays, and financial products—cost more when they were marketed to women, which is sometimes referred to as a "pink tax." Gender-based pricing differences are legal, and the GAO could not conclude that bias was to blame for the price differences. However, you also find information that suggests consumers have requested laws that punish retailers and manufacturers that charge higher prices for women's versions of products when there is no cost-based justification. Further, you

learn that consumer activists are publicly shaming brands that charge higher prices for certain population segments.

11-12 Should the firm charge $20 more for the pink helmet? Why or why not? (AACSB: Written and Oral Communication; Ethical Understanding and Reasoning; Reflective Thinking)

11-13 One of your coworkers makes the argument that the higher price on the pink helmet makes sense because it is an example of value-based pricing. Her argument is that a consumer who does not want to pay the higher price for the pink helmet can buy the blue version. Respond to her argument. (AACSB: Written and Oral Communication; Reflective Thinking)

Marketing by the Numbers Lose Some Customers, Be Better Off?

For the past several years, large food manufacturers followed Kraft-Heinz's lead by aggressively slashing costs to improve profitability. That hasn't work out well for Kraft-Heinz or for other manufacturers such as General Mills, marketer of Yoplait yogurt, Cheerios and other breakfast cereals, Häagen-Dazs ice cream, and dozens of other popular brands. Such cost cutting has hurt the quality of well-known brands. In response, General Mills took a different tack, raising prices 20 percent. Some may argue that this has not worked out well for General Mills either, noting that sales volume slipped in the first quarter following the price hikes. Although General Mills' sales decreased, however, the company's margins improved, making it more profitable. Companies realize that sales volumes will decrease after price hikes, but they also know that they can maintain or even enhance profitability even though sales drop.

11-14 Assuming a contribution margin of 25 percent and sales of $4 billion, with a 20 percent price increase, by how much can sales decrease before profitability (total contribution) drops below its current level? Refer to Financial Analysis of Marketing Tactics: Price Decrease in Appendix 2: Marketing by the Numbers to learn how to perform this analysis, but determine the maximum *drop* in sales before total contribution is negatively affected. (AACSB: Communication; Analytic Reasoning)

11-15 What absolute change and percentage change in sales does this represent? (AACSB: Communication; Analytic Reasoning)

Company Case Casper: A Pricing Strategy That Flipped the Mattress Industry

The mood was whimsical at Casper's New York headquarters—the online mattress startup had flipped its industry upside down. Celebrating Casper's fifth anniversary, the celebration seemed more like a birthday party for a five-year-old, complete with face painting, piñatas, and a balloon artist who crafted everything from an intricate jet pack to a knockoff Chanel bag. "But the

magician canceled at the last minute," said Casper's chief technology officer, "which kind of sucked." About the only indication that this was gathering of adults was the free-flowing open bar.

Although the party was unusual for a successful New York firm, young Casper's five founders had plenty to celebrate. Against all odds, the startup had finished the prior year selling

$400 million worth of mattresses and other sleep-related goods. And it accomplished that feat using an innovative direct-to-consumer (DTC) "bed-in-a-box" model. Although not exactly reaping market-leading revenue numbers, Casper had taken a notable slice of the $14 billion U.S. mattress market—a market dominated by a handful of mattress companies and specialty retailers. Perhaps more amazing, Casper had just raised an additional $100 million in funding, bringing its total to $340 million in venture capital. That huge influx of cash combined with the young company's rapid growth gave Casper a valuation of $1.1 billion, nearly one-third the value of 140-year-old mattress stalwart Tempur Sealy International.

Casper has succeeded for numerous reasons. But at the core of its trampoline-like launch is an idea as old as beds themselves—break into a mature market with a quality product at a fraction of the price charged by the ruling brands. For good measure, Casper made shopping and buying simple. Consumer response to this approach demonstrates the extent of unmet consumer need lurking beneath the sheets—unmet need that has led to a revolution in the mattress industry.

An Industry Begging for DTC

Casper's five founders had crossed paths through various other business ventures and unsuccessful startups. Each was looking to start something new. As their discussions evolved, one thing became clear. The modern marketing environment was fueling a direct-to-consumer (DTC) model in countless industries that were dominated by veteran companies charging high prices despite little innovation. What Warby Parker did with eyewear was being repeated over and over again in other industries by companies such as Dollar Shave Club (razors), Bonobos (men's clothing), and The Honest Company (cleaning and baby products). The entire sharing economy, which propelled the likes of Airbnb and Uber to upend their industries, was rooted in the same characteristics—customers were sick of paying high prices for warmed-over options that gave them little satisfaction.

Casper's founders set their sights on the mattress industry—one that was ripe for change. The industry was dominated by two firms—Tempur Sealy and Serta Simmons—that captured a combined 60 percent of the global mattress market and 75 percent of the U.S. market. The two firms sold mattresses under the Sealy, Tempur-Pedic, Serta, Simmons, Stearns & Foster, Beautyrest, and other brands. Mattress retail sales were also dominated by a small circle of specialty retailer chains like Mattress Firm and Sleepy's. Nearly all mattresses were sold through one of these stores as well as through furniture stores or department stores where salespeople earning high commissions used old-school tactics to persuade customers to part with their money.

From the customer viewpoint, there wasn't much difference between shopping for a mattress and shopping for a new car. Conventional wisdom held that customers simply would not buy a mattress without lying down on several to find the perfect fit for their slumbers. But the mattress-shopping process required hours of effort filled with sales presentations, mattress testing, and transactions riddled with paperwork. The bed companies further complicated matters by manufacturing different mattress models for each retailer, making price comparisons impossible. Moreover, most customers had no idea that retailers marked up mattress prices by as much as 100 percent over wholesale price. Mattress prices for the big brands ranged from hundreds of dollars for a basic twin to more than $5,000 for a top-of-the-line

king. Not surprisingly, many mattress purchases required long-term financing.

Casper's idea of "cutting out the middleman" and selling mattresses at low prices directly to consumers wasn't exactly new. Nor was the memory foam bed-in-a-box concept. In fact, BedInABox.com began selling mattresses online in 2006, and a handful of other companies had more recently followed suit. But the concept was largely unknown to most consumers and had yet to take off. Most beds sold at the time were of coil spring construction, requiring a bulky box spring base. But various companies—including IKEA with its own mattress brands—were selling viscoelastic memory foam mattresses of the type perfected by Tempur-Pedic. These mattresses could be compressed, rolled, and boxed to make shipping a reasonable option.

An Unexpected Reaction

Casper flipped the switch on its e-commerce platform in April 2014 with just one foam mattress model in twin, full, queen, and king sizes. Each mattress was tightly packed in a blue-and-white heavy-duty box. Watching the mattress unroll and expand when unboxed was magical. Each mattress came with a 100-day money-back-guarantee and was delivered for free via UPS. And the price—just $850 for a queen—was less than the retail markup on many comparable name-brand mattresses. Targeting millennials, Casper was confident that a nimble, low-overhead online brand with a cool vibe and an irresistibly low price could capture a small but profitable slice of the market while avoiding the attention of the deep-pocket market leaders. It set a modest 18-month revenue goal of just $1.8 million, a goal that seemed reachable based on a low-cost promotion plan using social media and influencers.

By the end of the first day, Casper was already rethinking its sales goal. Orders flooded in so fast that Casper's initial inventory was quickly depleted. The fledgling company surpassed its original 18-month sales goal in only eight weeks. During its first full fiscal year, Casper delivered $100 million worth of mattresses to customer's doorsteps. Originally planning only to nibble at the edges of the mattress market, Casper had taken a big bite right out of the center.

Early success led Casper's founders down a path that other DTC mattress brands had not yet tried—raising venture capital. "At the beginning, we met with dozens of investors who all said, 'No one is ever going to buy a mattress online. This is a dumb idea,'" said Neil Parikh, one of the original Casper founders. But when Casper mattresses started flying out of the warehouse, there was no shortage of interested funders. Through venture capital firms, early investors included actors Leonardo DiCaprio and Ashton Kutcher and rappers Nas and 50 Cent, lending celebrity clout as well as funds. And then there were the influencers. About a year after Casper launched, Kylie Jenner posted a picture of herself standing next to a Casper box in her new mansion. "So much work to still be done. IM SO EXCITED. The first thing I'm gonna open are my new Casper mattresses." Jenner's post racked up an immediate 870,000 likes. "When Kylie Jenner posted about Casper I think it broke our website," Parikh said.

Success Draws Competition

Perhaps more amazing than its immediate popularity is that Casper's sales exploded even as numerous companies with the same idea began selling mattresses. In fact, some of today's leading DTC mattress companies launched the same year that Casper did, including Leesa, Yogabed, Purple, and Bear

Mattress. With a low cost of entry, the early startups gave way to an explosion of new mattress companies, each with its own spin on boxable mattresses and nearly all priced much lower than traditional brands. With all this activity, established mattress companies took notice. Serta Simmons bought Tuft & Needle, Sealy launched Cocoon, and Tempur-Pedic launched Tempur-Cloud, a familiar option for DTC customers given that Tempur-Pedic was already far and away the number-one memory foam mattress peddler.

Today, there are well over 100 DTC mattress brands. Is that too many? Experts don't think so. Not all will survive. But at the rate the DTC mattress market is growing, there's plenty of room for numerous successful DTC bed sellers. And e-commerce mattress purchases still capture only 5 to 10 percent of all mattress sales, which means it will be awhile before the dust settles. Making matters even more promising for DTC mattress sales, the conventional mattress market seems to be going the wrong direction. After retailer Mattress Firm acquired Sleepy's, it promptly rebranded all 1,000 Sleepy's stores, resulting in 3,500 Mattress Firm outlets. The move didn't end well. Mattress Firm filed for bankruptcy, only to be rescued by South African retail giant Steinhoff in a deal valued at $3.8 billion.

Although Casper began as a one-product company looking to fill a hole in the market, the company is now embracing the future by shaping a brand platform that looks at sleep as a consumer category not unlike travel or cooking. "If I wake up in the morning and say, 'I want to sleep a little bit better,' I have to go and get a mattress from a furniture store, sheets from Bed Bath & Beyond—you end up having to get things from all these different places," says Parikh. "But if you wake up in the morning and say…'I want to eat healthier,' great, go to Whole Foods. There's nothing like that for sleep." Casper aims to change that. With its "cheaper-than-the-leading-brands" image secure, the company now sells three mattress lines, sheets, duvets, pillows, and a high-tech sleep light. It even has a line of dog beds. And with its products now being sold in the real world through Target stores and in its own growing chain of Casper Sleep Shops, Casper looks unstoppable.[26]

Questions for Discussion

11-16 Explain Casper's product offering in terms of customer value.

11-17 Which new product pricing strategy does Casper employ? Why does it work?

11-18 Could Casper have achieved the same level of success with a different pricing strategy? Explain.

11-19 Based on principles of price changes, make some predictions for the mattress industry.

12

Marketing Channels
Delivering Customer Value

OBJECTIVES OUTLINE

OBJECTIVE 12-1 Explain why companies use marketing channels and discuss the functions these channels perform. **See: Supply Chains and the Value Delivery Network** *(pp 344–348)*

OBJECTIVE 12-2 Discuss how channel members interact and how they organize to perform the work of the channel. **See: Channel Behavior and Organization** *(pp 348–355)*

OBJECTIVE 12-3 Identify the major channel alternatives open to a company. **See: Channel Design Decisions** *(pp 355–359)*

OBJECTIVE 12-4 Explain how companies select, motivate, and evaluate channel members. **See: Channel Management Decisions** *(pp 359–362)*

OBJECTIVE 12-5 Discuss the nature and importance of marketing logistics and integrated supply chain management. **See: Marketing Logistics and Supply Chain Management** *(pp 362–369)*

CHAPTER PREVIEW We now look at the third marketing mix tool—distribution. Companies rarely work alone in engaging customers, creating customer value, and building profitable customer relationships. Instead, most are only a single link in a larger supply chain and marketing channel. As such, a firm's success depends not only on how well *it* performs but also on how well its *entire marketing channel* competes with competitors' channels. The first part of this chapter explores the nature of marketing channels and the marketer's channel design and management decisions. We then examine physical distribution—or logistics—an area that has grown dramatically in importance and sophistication. In the next chapter, we'll look more closely at two major channel intermediaries: retailers and wholesalers.

We start by looking at Netflix. Through innovative distribution, Netflix has become the world's largest video subscription service. But as baseball great Yogi Berra, known more for his mangled phrasing than for his baseball prowess, once said, "The future ain't what it used to be." To stay atop the churning video distribution industry, Netflix must continue to innovate at a break-neck pace or risk being pushed aside.

NETFLIX: Finding the Future by Abandoning the Past

Time and again, Netflix has innovated its way to the top in video entertainment distribution. In the early 2000s, Netflix's revolutionary DVD-by-mail service put all but the most powerful movie-rental stores out of business. In 2007, Netflix's then-groundbreaking move into digital streaming once again revolutionized how people accessed movies and other video content. Since then, Netflix has continued to break new ground by making its services available through any and all digital and mobile devices and by creating its own original content. With Netflix leading the pack, video distribution has now become a roiling pot of emerging technologies and high-tech competitors, one that offers both mind-bending opportunities and stomach-churning risks.

Just ask Blockbuster, the former brick-and-mortar movie-rental chain that once flat-out owned the industry. Then along came Netflix, the fledgling DVD-by-mail service. First thousands, then millions, of subscribers were drawn to Netflix's innovative distribution model, catching market-leading Blockbuster off guard and eventually pulling the rug out from under it. Once-mighty Blockbuster fell into bankruptcy and shuttered its doors as Netflix surged.

The Blockbuster riches-to-rags story underscores the turmoil that typifies the video distribution business today. In the decade since Blockbuster's demise, a glut of video access options has materialized. At the same time that Netflix ascended and Blockbuster plunged, Coinstar's Redbox came out of nowhere to build a novel national network of $1-a-day DVD-rental kiosks. Then high-tech venues such as Hulu and Crackle began pushing on-demand digital streaming through a model of ad-supported free viewing.

All along the way, Netflix has acted boldly to stay ahead of the competition. For example, by 2007, Netflix had mailed out its one-billionth DVD. But rather than rest on success, Netflix and its CEO, Reed Hastings, set their sights on a then-revolutionary new video distribution model: Deliver Netflix to any and every Internet-connected screen—from laptops to Internet-ready TVs to smartphones and other Wi-Fi-enabled devices. Netflix launched its Watch Instantly service, which let members stream movies to their Internet-connected devices as part of their monthly fee, even if it came at the expense of the company's still-hot DVD-by-mail business.

Although Netflix didn't pioneer digital streaming, it poured resources into improving the technology and building the largest streaming content library. It built a huge subscriber base and sales and profits soared. With its massive physical DVD library and a growing streaming library accessible on just about anything with a screen, it seemed that nothing could stop Netflix.

But Netflix's stunning success drew a slew of resourceful competitors. Video giants such as Google's YouTube and Apple's iTunes began renting movie downloads, and Hulu and Amazon expanded their libraries and added subscription-based streaming services with Hulu Plus and Amazon

Netflix's innovative distribution strategy: From DVDs by mail to Watch Instantly to streaming on almost any device and creating original content, Netflix has led the howling pack by doing what it does best—revolutionize distribution. What's next?
sitthiphong/Shutterstock

Prime Video. To stay ahead—even to survive—Netflix needed to keep the innovation pedal to the metal. So in the summer of 2011, in an ambitious but risky move, CEO Hastings made an all-in bet on digital streaming. He split off Netflix's still-thriving DVD-by-mail service into a separate business with a separate subscription fee.

Although subscribership dipped temporarily as some customers jumped ship, Hastings had made a visionary move. While Netflix still provides its classic DVDs-by-mail service, only a few million customers still check their mailboxes for videos. In contrast, 98 percent of the company's 139 million paid subscribers are now streaming-only customers. Netflix subscribers stream an astounding 1 billion hours of movies and TV programs every week. On an average weeknight, Netflix commands one-third of all internet traffic in North American homes. And the company has expanded globally into more than 190 countries.

Despite its sustained success, Netflix knows that it can't rest its distribution innovation machine. Competition continues to move at a blurring rate. For example, Amazon's Prime Instant Video offers streaming access to its ever-expanding library of movies and TV shows to Prime members at no extra cost. YouTube's Premium subscription service, backed by parent Google's deep pockets, offers ad-free access to videos and to members-only original shows and movies. And even as Netflix has been the prime force behind the cord-cutting trend—in which consumers abandon traditional cable or satellite TV services in favor of over-the-top video

> Time and again, Netflix has innovated its way to the top in the distribution of video entertainment. But to stay atop its boiling, roiling industry, Netflix must keep the distribution innovation pedal to the metal.

streaming—the traditional networks and services are fighting back with their own subscription streaming options, such as Comcast's Xfinity Streampix, HBO GO, CBS All Access, and DirecTV Now, to name only a few. And whereas access to live TV has been the biggest deterrent to cord cutting, numerous services today provide paid access to live TV streaming, including AT&T, DirecTV, YouTube, Hulu, and many newcomers.

For years, as the industry has settled into streaming as the main delivery model, Netflix has known that content—not just delivery—is key to staying ahead in video distribution. Given its head start, Netflix remains ahead in the content race. But with more competitors working feverishly to sign contracts with big movie and television content providers, content-licensing deals are harder and more expensive to get and keep.

So, in yet another innovative twist, to decrease its reliance on content from outside sources, Netflix has been producing and distributing its own original content at a torrid pace. Eight years ago, it shocked the industry when it paid $100 million to out-bid HBO and AMC for exclusive rights to air the first two seasons of *House of Cards*. The show was a huge success, and Netflix moved rapidly to develop other original series and movies, including *Orange Is the New Black, Stranger Things, Black Mirror, GLOW*, and *Bird Box*.

Although Netflix's streaming competitors have once again followed the leader by creating their own original content, Netflix still has the upper hand. Last year, it spent an astounding $13 billion to produce an estimated 700 original series and 80 movies, more than any single network, cable channel, or

Hollywood studio. To watch all that new original Netflix content, a person would have to spend more than four hours every day for an entire year. The company's original content has been well received. For example, the Netflix horror movie *Bird Box* was watched by more than 80 million people within the first 10 days of its release. And Netflix tallied more Emmy award nominations last year than any other network—112 in all—breaking HBO's 17-year winning streak.

Such efforts have left the rest of the industry scrambling to keep up. And Netflix is just getting started. For the coming year, Netflix has announced that it will spend more on developing original content than in any past year. In the ever more tumultuous video environment, Netflix intends to control its own destiny by locking down ownership of its content. Netflix's original content now comprises more than half of its vast video library.

Thus, from DVDs by mail, to Watch Instantly, to video streaming on almost any device, to dominating with original content, Netflix has stayed ahead of the howling pack by doing what it does best—innovate and revolutionize distribution. In *Fast Company*'s most recent list of the 50 most innovative companies, Netflix is number two, trailing only Apple. In just the past two years, Netflix's subscriber base has grown nearly 58 percent, and revenues have surged more than 80 percent.

What's next? No one really knows. But one thing seems certain: Whatever's coming, if Netflix doesn't lead the change, it risks being left behind—and quickly. In this fast-changing business, new tricks grow old in a hurry. To stay ahead, as one headline suggests, Netflix must "find its future by abandoning its past."[1]

AS THE NETFLIX STORY SHOWS, good distribution strategies can contribute strongly to customer value and create competitive advantage for a firm. But firms cannot bring value to customers by themselves. Instead, they must work closely with other firms in a larger value delivery network.

> Author Comment | These are pretty hefty terms for a really simple concept: A company can't go it alone in creating customer value. It must work within a broader network of partners to accomplish this task. Individual companies and brands don't compete; their entire value delivery networks do.

Supply Chains and the Value Delivery Network

OBJECTIVE 12-1 Explain why companies use marketing channels and discuss the functions these channels perform.

Producing a product or service and making it available to buyers requires building relationships not only with customers but also with key suppliers and resellers in the company's *supply chain*. This supply chain consists of upstream and downstream partners. Upstream from the company is the set of firms that supply the raw materials, components, parts, information, finances, and expertise needed to create a product or service. Marketers, however, have traditionally focused on the downstream side of the supply chain—the *marketing channels* (or *distribution channels*) that look toward the customer. Downstream marketing channel partners, such as wholesalers and retailers, form a vital link between the firm and its customers.

The term *supply chain* may be too limited, as it takes a *make-and-sell* view of the business. It suggests that raw materials, productive inputs, and factory capacity should

● **Value delivery network: In making and marketing its lines of cars, Toyota manages a huge network of people within the company plus thousands of outside suppliers, dealers, and marketing service firms that work together to deliver the brand's "Let's Go Places" and "Let's Go Beyond" promises.**

Pras Nazri/Shutterstock

Value delivery network

A network composed of the company, suppliers, distributors, and, ultimately, customers who partner with each other to improve the performance of the entire system in delivering customer value.

serve as the starting point for market planning. A better term would be *demand chain* because it suggests a *sense-and-respond* view of the market. Under this view, planning starts by identifying the needs of target customers, to which the company responds by organizing a chain of resources and activities with the goal of creating customer value.

Yet even a demand chain view of a business may be too limited because it takes a step-by-step, linear view of purchase-production-consumption activities. Instead, most large companies today are engaged in building and managing a complex, continuously evolving value delivery network. As defined in Chapter 2, a **value delivery network** is made up of the company, suppliers, distributors, and, ultimately, customers who "partner" with each other to improve the performance of the entire system. ● For example, Toyota makes great cars. But to make and market just one of its many lines—say, its best-selling Camry model—Toyota manages a huge network of people within the company, from marketing and sales people to folks in finance and operations. It also coordinates the efforts of thousands of suppliers, dealers, and advertising agencies and other marketing service firms. The entire network must function together to create customer value and establish the brand's "Let's Go Places" and "Let's Go Beyond" positioning.

This chapter focuses on marketing channels—on the downstream side of the value delivery network. We examine four major questions concerning marketing channels: What is the nature of marketing channels and why are they important? How do channel firms interact and organize to do the work of the channel? What problems do companies face in designing and managing their channels? What role do physical distribution and supply chain management play in attracting and satisfying customers? In the next chapter, we will look at marketing channel issues from the viewpoints of retailers and wholesalers.

Author | In this section, we look
Comment | at the downstream side
of the value delivery network—the marketing channel organizations that connect the company and its customers. To understand their value, imagine life without retailers—say, without grocery stores or department stores.

The Nature and Importance of Marketing Channels

Few producers sell their goods directly to final users. Instead, most use intermediaries to bring their products to market. They try to forge a **marketing channel** (or **distribution channel**)—a set of interdependent organizations that help make a product or service available for use or consumption by the consumer or business user.

A company's channel decisions directly affect every other marketing decision. Pricing depends on whether the company works with national discount chains, uses high-quality specialty stores, or sells directly to consumers online. The firm's sales force and communications decisions depend on how much persuasion, training, motivation, and support its channel partners need. Whether a company develops or acquires certain new products may depend on how well those products fit the capabilities of its channel members.

Companies often pay too little attention to their distribution channels—sometimes with damaging results. In contrast, many companies have used imaginative distribution systems to gain a competitive advantage. Enterprise Rent-A-Car revolutionized the car-rental business by setting up off-airport rental offices. Apple turned the retail music business on its head by selling music via the internet on iTunes. FedEx's creative and imposing distribution system made it a leader in express package delivery. Uber and Airbnb, with their sharing models, have disrupted the taxi and hospitality businesses. And Amazon.com forever changed the face of retailing by selling anything and everything online without using physical stores.

Marketing channel (distribution channel)

A set of interdependent organizations that help make a product or service available for use or consumption by the consumer or business user.

Distribution channel decisions often involve long-term commitments to other firms. For example, companies such as Ford, McDonald's, or Nike can easily change their advertising, pricing, or promotion programs. They can scrap old products and introduce new ones as market tastes demand. But when they set up distribution channels through contracts with franchisees, independent dealers, or large retailers, they cannot readily replace these channels with company-owned stores or online sites if the conditions change. Therefore, management must design its channels carefully, with an eye on both today's likely selling environment and tomorrow's as well.

How Channel Members Add Value

Why do producers give some of the selling job to channel partners? After all, doing so means giving up some control over how and to whom they sell their products. Producers use intermediaries because they create greater efficiency in making goods available to target markets. Through their contacts, experience, specialization, and scale of operation, intermediaries usually offer the firm more than it can achieve on its own.

● **Figure 12.1** shows how using intermediaries can provide economies. Figure 12.1A shows three manufacturers, each using direct marketing to reach three customers. This system requires nine different contacts. Figure 12.1B shows the three manufacturers working through one distributor, which contacts the three customers. This system requires only six contacts. In this way, intermediaries reduce the amount of work that must be done by both producers and consumers.

From the economic system's point of view, the role of marketing intermediaries is to transform the assortments of products made by producers into the assortments wanted by consumers. Producers make narrow assortments of products in large quantities, but consumers want broad assortments of products in small quantities. Marketing channel members buy large quantities from many producers and break them down into the smaller quantities and broader assortments desired by consumers.

For example, Unilever makes millions of bars of Dove Beauty Bar soap each week. However, you most likely want to buy only a few bars at a time. Therefore, big food, drug, and discount retailers, such as Safeway, Walgreens, and Target, buy Dove by the truckload and stock it on their stores' shelves. In turn, you can buy a single bar of Dove along with a shopping cart full of small quantities of toothpaste, shampoo, and other related products as you need them. Thus, intermediaries play an important role in matching supply and demand.

In making products and services available to consumers, channel members add value by bridging the major time, place, and possession gaps that separate goods and services from those who use them. Members of the marketing channel perform many key functions. Some help to complete transactions:

- *Information.* Gathering and distributing information about consumers, producers, and other actors and forces in the marketing environment needed for planning and aiding exchange.
- *Promotion.* Developing and spreading persuasive communications about an offer.
- *Contact.* Finding and engaging customers and prospective buyers.

● **FIGURE 12.1**
How a Distributor Reduces the Number of Channel Transactions

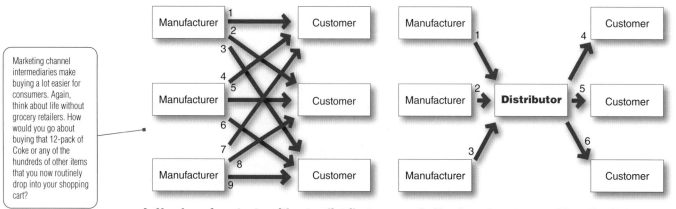

Marketing channel intermediaries make buying a lot easier for consumers. Again, think about life without grocery retailers. How would you go about buying that 12-pack of Coke or any of the hundreds of other items that you now routinely drop into your shopping cart?

A. Number of contacts without a distributor

B. Number of contacts with a distributor

- *Matching*. Shaping offers to meet the buyer's needs, including activities such as manufacturing, grading, assembling, and packaging.
- *Negotiation*. Reaching an agreement on price and other terms so that ownership or possession can be transferred.

Others help to fulfill the completed transactions:

- *Physical distribution*. Transporting and storing goods.
- *Financing*. Acquiring and using funds to cover the costs of the channel work.
- *Risk taking*. Assuming the risks of carrying out the channel work.

The question is not *whether* these functions need to be performed—they must be—but rather *who* will perform them. To the extent that the manufacturer performs these functions, its costs go up; therefore, its prices must be higher. When some of these functions are shifted to intermediaries, the producer's costs and prices may be lower, but the intermediaries must charge more to cover the costs of their work. In dividing the work of the channel, the various functions should be assigned to the channel members that can add the most value for the cost.

Number of Channel Levels

Companies can design their distribution channels to make products and services available to customers in different ways. Each layer of marketing intermediaries that performs some work in bringing the product and its ownership closer to the final buyer is a **channel level**. Because both the producer and the final consumer perform some work, they are part of every channel.

The *number of intermediary levels* indicates the *length* of a channel. ● **Figure 12.2** shows both consumer and business channels of different lengths. Figure 12.2A shows several common consumer distribution channels. Channel 1, a **direct marketing channel**, has no intermediary levels—the company sells directly to consumers. For example, Pampered Chef, Mary Kay Cosmetics, and Amway sell their products through home and office sales parties and online websites and social media; companies ranging from GEICO insurance to Quicken Loans to Casper Mattress sell directly to customers via internet, mobile, and telephone channels. The remaining channels in Figure 12.2A are **indirect marketing channels**, containing one or more intermediaries.

Channel level

A layer of intermediaries that performs some work in bringing the product and its ownership closer to the final buyer.

Direct marketing channel

A marketing channel that has no intermediary levels.

Indirect marketing channel

A marketing channel containing one or more intermediary levels.

● FIGURE 12.2
Consumer and Business
Marketing Channels

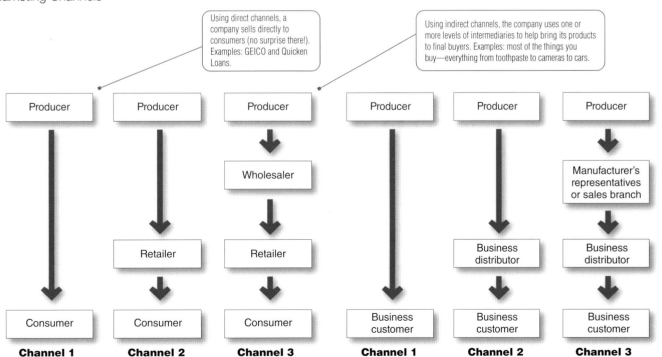

Using direct channels, a company sells directly to consumers (no surprise there!). Examples: GEICO and Quicken Loans.

Using indirect channels, the company uses one or more levels of intermediaries to help bring its products to final buyers. Examples: most of the things you buy—everything from toothpaste to cameras to cars.

A. Consumer marketing channels

B. Business marketing channels

Figure 12.2B shows some common business distribution channels. The business marketer can use its own sales force or the internet to sell directly to business customers. Or it can sell to various types of intermediaries, which in turn sell to these customers. Although consumer and business marketing channels with even more levels can sometimes be found, these are less common. From the producer's point of view, a greater number of levels means less control and greater channel complexity. Moreover, all the institutions in the channel are connected by several types of *flows*. These include the *physical flow* of products, the *flow of ownership*, the *payment flow*, the *information flow*, and the *promotion flow*. These flows can make even channels with only one or a few levels very complex.

> **Author Comment** | Channels are made up of more than just boxes and arrows on paper. They are behavioral systems consisting of real companies and people who interact to accomplish their individual and collective goals. Like groups of people, sometimes they work well together and sometimes they don't.

Channel Behavior and Organization

OBJECTIVE 12-2 Discuss how channel members interact and how they organize to perform the work of the channel.

Distribution channels are more than simple collections of firms tied together by various flows. They are complex behavioral systems in which people and companies interact to accomplish individual, company, and channel goals. Some channel systems consist of only informal interactions among loosely organized firms. Others consist of formal interactions guided by strong organizational structures. Moreover, channel systems do not stand still—new types of intermediaries emerge and whole new channel systems evolve. Here we look at channel behavior and how members organize to do the work of the channel.

Channel Behavior

A marketing channel consists of firms that have partnered for their common good. Each channel member depends on the others. For example, a Ford dealer depends on Ford to design cars that meet customer needs. In turn, Ford depends on the dealer to engage customers, persuade them to buy Ford cars, and service the cars after the sale. Each Ford dealer also depends on other dealers to provide good sales and service that will uphold the brand's reputation. In fact, the success of individual Ford dealers depends on how well the entire Ford marketing channel competes with the channels of Toyota, GM, Honda, and other auto manufacturers.

Each channel member plays a specialized role in the channel. For example, Samsung's role is to produce electronics products that consumers will covet and create demand through national advertising. Best Buy's role is to display these Samsung products in convenient locations, answer buyers' questions, and complete sales. The channel will be most effective when each member assumes the tasks it can do best.

Ideally, because the success of individual channel members depends on the overall channel's success, all channel firms should work together smoothly. They should understand and accept their roles, coordinate their activities, and cooperate to attain overall channel goals. However, individual channel members rarely take such a broad view. Cooperating to achieve overall channel goals sometimes means giving up individual company goals. Although channel members depend on one another, they often act alone in their own short-run best interests. They often disagree on who should do what and for what rewards. Such disagreements over goals, roles, and rewards generate **channel conflict**.

Horizontal conflict occurs among firms at the same level of the channel. For instance, some Ford dealers in Chicago might complain that other dealers in the city steal sales from them by pricing too low or advertising outside their assigned territories. Or Hampton Inn franchisees might complain about other Hampton Inn operators overcharging guests or giving poor service, hurting the overall Hampton Inn image.

Vertical conflict, conflict between different levels of the same channel, is even more common. ● For example, McDonald's has recently faced growing conflict with its corps of 3,100 independent franchisees:[2]

Channel conflict

Disagreements among marketing channel members on goals, roles, and rewards—who should do what and for what rewards.

● **Channel conflict:** A high level of franchisee discontent is worrisome to McDonald's. There's a huge connection between franchisee satisfaction and customer service.

Ratana21/Shutterstock

Recent surveys of McDonald's franchise owners have reflected substantial franchisee discontent with the corporation. The most basic conflicts are financial. McDonald's makes its money from franchisee royalties based on total system sales. In contrast, franchisees make money on margins—what's left over after their costs. To turn around steadily declining sales in recent years, McDonald's has emphasized aggressive discounting—in the form of value menus—a strategy that increases corporate sales but squeezes franchisee profits. Franchisees also grumble about adding popular but more complex menu items—such as customizable burgers, fresh beef, McCafé beverages, and all-day breakfasts—that increase the top-line growth for McDonald's but add preparation, equipment, and staffing costs for franchisees while slowing down service. McDonald's has also asked franchisees to make costly restaurant upgrades and overhauls that owners claim don't add value to the customer. As a result, many franchisees are highly disgruntled. The most recent survey rates McDonald's current franchisee relations at an all-time low 1.81 out of a possible 5, in the "fair" to "poor" range. That's worrisome for McDonald's, whose franchise owners operate 93 percent of its locations. Studies show that there's a huge connection between franchisee satisfaction and customer service.

Some conflict in the channel takes the form of healthy competition. Such competition can be good for the channel; without it, the channel could become passive and noninnovative. For example, the McDonald's conflict with its franchisees might represent normal give-and-take over the respective rights of the channel partners. However, severe or prolonged conflict can disrupt channel effectiveness and cause lasting harm to channel relationships. McDonald's should manage the long-running channel conflict carefully to keep it from getting out of hand.

Vertical Marketing Systems

For the channel as a whole to perform well, each channel member's role must be specified, and channel conflict must be managed. The channel will perform better if it includes a firm, agency, or mechanism that provides leadership and has the power to assign roles and manage conflict.

Historically, *conventional distribution channels* have lacked such leadership and power, often resulting in damaging conflict and poor performance. One of the biggest channel developments over the years has been the emergence of *vertical marketing systems* that provide channel leadership. ● **Figure 12.3** contrasts the two types of channel arrangements.

A **conventional distribution channel** consists of one or more independent producers, wholesalers, and retailers. Each is a separate business seeking to maximize its own profits, perhaps even at the expense of the system as a whole. No channel member has

Conventional distribution channel
A channel consisting of one or more independent producers, wholesalers, and retailers, each a separate business seeking to maximize its own profits, perhaps even at the expense of profits for the system as a whole.

● FIGURE 12.3
Comparison of Conventional Distribution Channel with Vertical Marketing System

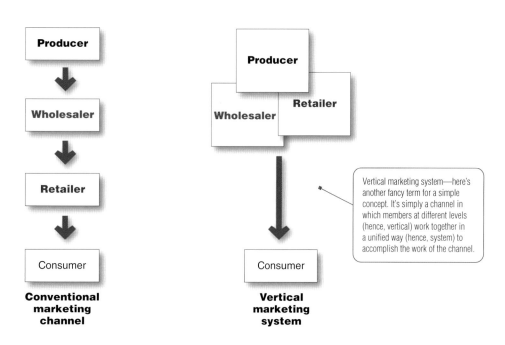

much control over the other members, and no formal means exists for assigning roles and resolving channel conflict.

In contrast, a **vertical marketing system (VMS)** consists of producers, wholesalers, and retailers acting as a unified system. One channel member owns the others, has contracts with them, or wields so much power that they must all cooperate. The VMS can be dominated by the producer, the wholesaler, or the retailer.

We look now at three major types of VMSs: *corporate, contractual,* and *administered.* Each uses a different means for setting up leadership and power in the channel.

Corporate VMS

A **corporate VMS** integrates successive stages of production and distribution under single ownership. Coordination and conflict management are attained through regular organizational channels. For example, European eyewear maker EssilorLuxottica has a firm grip on the global eyewear channel from producer to consumer. It produces many famous eyewear brands—including its own Ray-Ban, Oakley, Persol, and Vogue Eyewear brands and licensed brands such as Burberry, Chanel, Polo Ralph Lauren, Dolce & Gabbana, DKNY, Prada, Versace, and Michael Kors. It also produces and sells more than 40 percent of the world's prescription lenses. It then controls the distribution of these brands through some of the world's largest optical chains—LensCrafters, Pearle Vision, Sunglass Hut, Target Optical, and others—which it also owns. In all, through vertical integration, EssilorLuxottica makes and sells close to 1 billion pairs of lenses and frames a year.[3]

A corporate VMS can give a company more channel control and flexibility. ● Consider Amazon. Rather than depending only on FedEx, UPS, the USPS, and other package shippers, Amazon is now developing its own package delivery capabilities. For instance, it owns a fleet of cargo planes called Prime Air, and its Uber-like Amazon Flex operation pays people by the hour to deliver packages with their own cars. Amazon has also launched a program to develop a fleet of independent Amazon Prime courier partners who will deliver its packages locally in Amazon branded vans and uniforms. By developing its own delivery network, Amazon hopes to rein in delivery expenses and gain more control over how its packages are delivered. Integrating vertically can also help Amazon expand its same-day delivery capabilities and compete more effectively with store retailers that have order-online-and-pick-up-in-store services, something FedEx and UPS can't do. For the longer run, Amazon is looking into bolstering its own delivery services through futuristic technologies such as delivery drones, driverless vehicles, and package-handling robots.[4]

● **Corporate VMS: To rein in delivery expenses and gain more control over how its packages are delivered, Amazon is now developing its own package delivery capabilities.**

KYLE JOHNSON/The New York Times/Redux

Contractual VMS

A **contractual VMS** consists of independent firms at different levels of production and distribution that join together through contracts to obtain more economies or sales impact than each could achieve alone. Channel members coordinate their activities and manage conflict through contractual agreements.

The **franchise organization** is the most common type of contractual relationship. In this system, a channel member called a *franchisor* links several stages in the production-distribution process. In the United States alone, almost 760,000 franchise outlets account for more than $450 billion of economic output.[5] Almost every kind of business has been franchised—from motels and fast-food restaurants to dental centers and dating services; from wedding consultants and handyman services to funeral homes, fitness centers, moving services, and hair salons. Franchising allows entrepreneurs with good business concepts to grow their businesses quickly and profitably.

● For example, consider Sport Clips Haircuts, the sports-themed hair salon that caters to men and boys, a place where you can "Get your hair in the game." Through

---

Vertical marketing system (VMS)
A channel structure in which producers, wholesalers, and retailers act as a unified system. One channel member owns the others, has contracts with them, or has so much power that they all cooperate.

Corporate VMS
A vertical marketing system that combines successive stages of production and distribution under single ownership—channel leadership is established through common ownership.

Contractual VMS
A vertical marketing system in which independent firms at different levels of production and distribution join together through contracts.

Franchise organization
A contractual vertical marketing system in which a channel member, called a franchisor, links several stages in the production-distribution process.

● Franchising systems: Through franchising, Sport Clips—where you can "Get your hair in the game"—has grown rapidly to more than 1,700 locations.

Sport Clips, Inc.

franchising, since the mid-1990s, Sport Clips has grown rapidly and now has more than 1,700 locations across the United States and Canada pulling in more than $600 million in annual system-wide sales. Last year, Sport Clips ranked among the top 20 on the *Entrepreneur* Franchise 500 list of top franchise opportunities, just below franchising heavyweights such as Pizza Hut, Ace Hardware, and 7-Eleven.[6]

There are three types of franchises. The first type is the *manufacturer-sponsored retailer franchise system*—for example, Ford and its network of independent franchised dealers. The second type is the *manufacturer-sponsored wholesaler franchise system*—Coca-Cola licenses bottlers (wholesalers) in various world markets that buy Coca-Cola syrup concentrate and then bottle and sell the finished product to retailers locally. The third type is the *service-firm-sponsored retailer franchise system*—for example, Sonic Drive-In has more than 3,600 franchisee-operated restaurants in the United States. Other examples can be found in everything from auto rentals (Hertz, Avis), apparel retailers (The Athlete's Foot, Plato's Closet), and motels (Holiday Inn Express, Hampton Inn) to supplemental education (Huntington Learning Center, Kumon Math & Reading Centers) and personal services (Two Men and a Truck, Mr. Handyman, Great Clips, Planet Fitness).

The fact that most consumers cannot tell the difference between contractual and corporate VMSs shows how successfully the contractual organizations compete with corporate chains. The next chapter on retailing presents a fuller discussion of the various contractual VMSs.

Administered VMS

Administered VMS
A vertical marketing system that coordinates successive stages of production and distribution through the size and power of one of the parties.

In an **administered VMS**, leadership is assumed not through common ownership or contractual ties but through the size and power of one or a few dominant channel members. Manufacturers of a top brand can obtain strong trade cooperation and support from resellers. For example, P&G and Samsung can command unusual cooperation from many resellers regarding displays, shelf space, promotions, and price policies. In turn, large retailers such as Walmart, Home Depot, Kroger, Best Buy, and Walgreens can exert strong influence on the many manufacturers that supply the products they sell.

For example, in the normal push and pull between Home Depot and its suppliers, giant Home Depot—the nation's fifth-biggest retailer and largest home improvement merchant—usually gets its way. Take specialty coatings and sealants supplier RPM International, for instance. You may never have heard of RPM International, but you've probably used one or more of its many familiar do-it-yourself brands—such as Rust-Oleum paints, Plastic Wood and Dap fillers, Mohawk and Watco finishes, and Testors hobby cements and paints—all of which you can buy at your local Home Depot store. Home Depot is a very important customer to RPM, accounting for a significant share of its consumer sales. However, Home Depot's sales of more than $100 billion are almost 20 times RPM's sales of $5.3 billion. As a result, the giant retailer can, and often does, use this power to gain channel cooperation and support from RPM and thousands of other smaller suppliers.[7]

Horizontal Marketing Systems

Horizontal marketing system
A channel arrangement in which two or more companies at one level join together to follow a new marketing opportunity.

Another channel development is the **horizontal marketing system**, in which two or more companies at one level join together to follow a new marketing opportunity. By working together, companies can combine their financial, production, or marketing resources to accomplish more than any one company could alone.

Companies might join forces with competitors or noncompetitors. They might work with each other on a temporary or permanent basis, or they may create a separate company. For example, Target partners with noncompetitor Starbucks to place coffee stands in its stores. Starbucks benefits from Target's heavy store traffic, and Target keeps its shoppers caffeinated and ready to shop. ● Target also partners with CVS Health, which operates CVS pharmacies and Minute Clinics in Target stores through a store-within-a-store

● Horizontal marketing systems: Target partners with CVS Health, who operates stores-within-stores to the benefit of all—Target, CVS, and their mutual customers.

CVS Caremark

format. The partnership gives CVS Health more than 1,700 pharmacies and 80 clinics at prime locations inside Target stores. At the same time, it frees up Target focus on its core product design, merchandising, and marketing strengths while still offering customers the expert pharmacy and healthcare services they want.[8]

Horizontal channel arrangements also work well globally. For example, most of the world's major airlines have joined to together in one of three major global alliances: Star Alliance, Skyteam, or Oneworld. Star Alliance consists of 28 airlines "working in harmony," including United, Air Canada, Lufthansa, Air China, Turkish Airlines, and almost two dozen others. It offers more than 18,800 combined daily departures to more than 1,300 airports around the world. Such alliances tie the individual carriers into massive worldwide air travel networks with joint branding and marketing, co-locations at airports, interline scheduling and smoother global flight connections, and shared rewards and membership privileges.[9]

Multichannel Distribution Systems

In the past, many companies used a single channel to sell to a single market or market segment. Today, with the proliferation of customer segments and channel possibilities, more and more companies have adopted **multichannel distribution systems**. Such multichannel marketing occurs when a single firm sets up two or more marketing channels to reach one or more customer segments.

● **Figure 12.4** shows a multichannel marketing system. In the figure, the producer sells directly to consumer segment 1 using catalogs and online and mobile channels and reaches consumer segment 2 through retailers. It sells indirectly to business segment 1 through distributors and dealers and to business segment 2 through its own sales force.

These days, almost every large company and many small ones distribute through multiple channels. For example, John Deere sells its familiar green-and-yellow lawn and garden tractors, mowers, and outdoor power products to consumers and commercial users through several channels, including John Deere retailers, Lowe's home improvement stores, and online. It sells and services its tractors, combines, planters, and other agricultural equipment through its premium John Deere dealer network. And it sells large construction and forestry equipment through selected large, full-service John Deere dealers and their sales forces.

Multichannel distribution systems offer many advantages to companies facing large and complex markets. With each new channel, the company expands its sales and market

Multichannel distribution system

A distribution system in which a single firm sets up two or more marketing channels to reach one or more customer segments.

● FIGURE 12.4
Multichannel Distribution System

Most large companies distribute through multiple channels. For example, you could buy a familiar green-and-yellow John Deere lawn tractor from a neighborhood John Deere dealer or from Lowe's. A large farm or forestry business would buy larger John Deere equipment from a premium full-service John Deere dealer and its sales force.

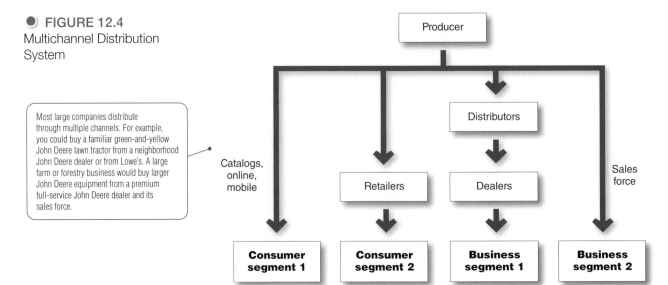

coverage and gains opportunities to tailor its products and services to the specific needs of diverse customer segments. But such multichannel systems are harder to control, and they can generate conflict as more channels compete for customers and sales. For example, when John Deere first began selling selected consumer products through Lowe's home improvement stores, many of its independent dealers complained loudly. To avoid such conflicts in its online marketing channels, the company routes all of its online sales to John Deere dealers.

Changing Channel Organization

Disintermediation

The cutting out of marketing channel intermediaries by product or service producers or the displacement of traditional resellers by radical new types of intermediaries.

Changes in technology and the explosive growth of direct and online marketing are having a profound impact on the nature and design of marketing channels. One major trend is toward **disintermediation**—a big term with a clear message and important consequences. Disintermediation occurs when product or service producers cut out intermediaries and go directly to final buyers or when radically new types of channel intermediaries displace traditional ones.

Thus, in many industries, traditional intermediaries are dropping by the wayside, as is the case with online marketers taking business from traditional brick-and-mortar retailers. For example, online music download services such as iTunes and Amazon pretty much put traditional music-store retailers out of business. In turn, however, streaming music services such as Spotify, Amazon Prime Music, and Apple Music are now disintermediating digital download services. Music downloads fell 24 percent last year while on-demand audio streaming rose 42 percent.[10]

Disintermediation presents both opportunities and problems for producers and resellers. Channel innovators who find new ways to add value in the channel can displace traditional resellers and reap the rewards. For example, app-based ride-hailing services Lyft and Uber have recently stormed onto the scene, rapidly disintermediating traditional taxi and car-for-hire services by offering better customer experiences at lower fares.

In turn, traditional intermediaries must continue to innovate to avoid being swept aside. ● For example, Toys"R"Us pioneered the superstore format that once made it the go-to place for buying toys and baby products, driving most small independent toy stores out of business. But in recent years, Toys"R"Us failed to adapt to major shifts in toy market sales, first toward big discounters such as Walmart and Target and then toward online merchants like Amazon. An estimated 28 percent of toy and baby product purchases are now made online, where Toys"R"Us lagged badly. Amazon leads in online toys sales, with Walmart hot on its digital heels. As a result, Toy "R" Us ended up declaring declared bankruptcy and shuttering its U.S. and UK stores.[11]

● Disintermediation: Toys"R"Us pioneered the superstore format that once made it the go-to place for buying toys. But after falling victim to shifts in toy market sales to big discounters like Walmart and online merchants like Amazon, the retail giant was forced to close down operations and shutter its stores.

Sundry Photography/Shutterstock

Like resellers, to remain competitive, product and service producers must develop new channel opportunities, such as the internet, mobile, and other direct channels. However, developing these new channels often brings them into direct competition with their established channels, resulting in conflict. To ease this problem, companies often look for ways to make going direct a plus for the entire channel. For example, Stanley Black & Decker knows that many customers would prefer to buy its power tools, outdoor power equipment, and small appliances directly from the company online. But selling directly through its web and mobile sites would create conflicts with important and powerful retail partners, such as Home Depot, Wal-Mart, and Amazon.com. So, although Stanley Black & Decker's online sites provide detailed information about the company's products, you can't buy a Black & Decker cordless drill, laser level, leaf blower, power garden shears, stick vac, or anything else there. Instead, the Black & Decker site refers you to resellers' sites and stores. Thus, Stanley Black & Decker's direct marketing helps both the company and its channel partners.

Real Marketing 12.1 | Zara: Though Disintermediation to the Top of World Fashion

Unlike their competitors Gap, Beneton, and H&M, Spanish clothing and accessories retailer Zara controls most of the steps in the supply chain as well as the designing, manufacturing, and distributing of its products. While some competitors outsource all production to developing countries, particularly in Asia, Zara makes its most fashionable items, accounting for about 50 percent of its merchandise, at a dozen company-owned factories in Spain and Portugal. Zara, which was founded in 1975 and is the flagship brand of the Inditex group, has over 7,400 stores strategically located in leading cities, such as New York, Paris, Tokyo, and Buenos Aires, and operates in 96 countries in Europe, South America, Oceania, and Africa. In the fiscal year 2017, Inditex had sales of $28.8 billion, a 9 percent increase, and far stronger than many of its competitors, making Zara the world's largest apparel retailer—not despite but because of its production and manufacturing strategy.

The secret of its success stems from Zara's vertically integrated marketing system (VMS), which combines successive stages of production and distribution under single ownership. Controlling the entire distribution chain from design and production to its own worldwide distribution network has turned Zara into the world's fastest growing retailer. Zara resisted the temptation of locating its production in Asian countries like China, where labor cost is low. By going against the trend, Zara was able to hold control over its supply chain. As a vertically integrated retailer, Zara pursues a disintermediation strategy, which as the name suggests involves the removal of intermediaries in a supply chain. Instead of going through traditional distribution channels, Zara deals with every customer directly—the company designs, produces, and distributes the products by itself.

Disintermediation means that Zara has to monitor all its processes clearly in order to be efficient and fast. Effective disintermediation and vertical integration make Zara faster, more flexible, and more efficient than its competitors. Zara's key competitive advantage lies in its ability to match fashion trends that change quickly. A new line can be created in less than 15 days, and the latest trending look can be found in Zara stores less than a month later, far below the industry average of six months. Speeding up the process is the fact that 51 to 55 percent of its clothing is manufactured in relatively close locations like Spain, Portugal, Turkey, and Morocco instead of Asia. It is no wonder that versions of latest designs by fashion designers in Paris, London, New York, and Tokyo are in Zara stores within a very short time of appearing on the runway. One of the most fascinating things about Zara is that it became popular not in spite of but because of its lack of originality, as shoppers around the world are thrilled to buy Zara's catwalk copycat designs at affordable prices.

Zara stores are located in city center streets and are owned by the company, so it has total control of its image and sales data. The stores collect data about preferences, styles, colors, etc. and send them back to Zara's headquarters in Spain through a sophisticated marketing information system. At the end of each day, Zara sales assistants report inventory levels to the respective store manager, who immediately informs Zara's central design and distribution departments about what consumers are purchasing, demanding, and avoiding, all of which have to be recorded accordingly. Top-selling items are requested by the store managers and reach the store within one to two days. At the same time, the commercial team liaises with the designers to identify sales trends based on store data as well as the catwalk and then develop new products. These are made in relatively small batches so that failures can be disregarded after their first appearance and new batches of popular items can be produced quickly. By producing smaller batches of clothing, Zara adds an air of exclusivity that encourages customers to shop more often. Indeed, whereas shoppers visit most high-street stores in Spain three times a year on average, Zara can expect its customers to visit up to 17 times.

As fresh inventory is key to Zara's sales strategy, its stores are stocked with new designs twice a week, faster than most of its competitors. This means that the product range in Zara stores changes quickly; rather than focusing on one product range per season, Zara promotes four or five. In the stores, around 60 percent of Zara's products are lasting, and the remaining 40 percent vary continually. Thus, the retailer can offer considerably more products than its rivals. Zara launches 10,000 new styles a year, compared to 2,000 to 4,000 by its key competitors. Consequently, the chain does not have to slash prices, as rivals often do, to move mass quantities of out-of-season stock.

Zara has grown with little or no advertising, and it has been observed that it hardly even has a marketing department. Where other brands spend money on TV spots or print ads, the company invests instead in the design, appeal, and location of its shops, which

● **Zara's key competitive advantage lies in its ability to match fashion trends that change quickly.**
Mira/Alamy Stock Photo

are really the best display and advertisement for Zara and its brand image. Zara's flexibility and speed have resulted in steady expansion and growth. Over the past few years, like-for-like sales have grown by 17 percent, and Zara wants to expand its shop space by 8 to 10 percent every year for the next three to five years.

Zara continues to enhance its impressive channel management system and disintermediation strategy. Establishing the prototype of the "fast-fashion" retailer, the strategy has left thousands of fashion retailers worldwide pop-eyed. Daniel Piette, the chairman of LVMH Investment Funds and the former fashion director for the luxury house that owns brands like Louis Vuitton, Givenchy, Marc Jacobs, and Hublot, has hailed Zara as possibly the most innovative and devastating retailer.

Stacey Cartwright, former CFO of Burberry Group plc, stated that Zara is a fantastic case study of how to get products to the stores at amazing speeds; indeed, Burberry itself has an eye on their techniques. The so-called Spanish success story has transformed shoppers' expectations of a high-street clothing store and promises to continue to thrive as one of the world's biggest fashion retailers.[12]

<table>
<tr><td>

Author | Like everything else
Comment | in marketing, good
channel design begins with analyzing customer needs. Remember, marketing channels are really customer value delivery networks.

</td></tr>
</table>

Channel Design Decisions

OBJECTIVE 12-3 Identify the major channel alternatives open to a company.

We now look at several channel design decisions manufacturers face. In designing marketing channels, manufacturers struggle between what is ideal and what is practical. A new firm with limited capital usually starts by selling in a limited market area. In this case, deciding on the best channels might not be a problem: The problem might simply be how to convince one or a few good intermediaries to handle the line.

If successful, the new firm can branch out to new markets through existing intermediaries. In smaller markets, the firm might sell directly to retailers; in larger markets, it might sell through distributors. In one part of the country, it might grant exclusive franchises; in another, it might sell through all available outlets. Then it might add an online store that sells directly to customers. In this way, channel systems often evolve to meet market opportunities and conditions.

For maximum effectiveness, however, channel analysis and decision making should be more purposeful. **Marketing channel design** calls for analyzing consumer needs, setting channel objectives, identifying major channel alternatives, and evaluating the alternatives.

Marketing channel design

Designing effective marketing channels by analyzing customer needs, setting channel objectives, identifying major channel alternatives, and evaluating those alternatives.

Analyzing Consumer Needs

As noted previously, marketing channels are part of the overall *customer value delivery network*. Each channel member and level add value for the customer. Thus, designing the marketing channel starts with finding out what target consumers want from the channel. Do consumers want to buy nearby, or are they willing to travel to more centralized locations? Would customers rather buy in person, by phone, or online? Do they value breadth of assortment, or do they prefer specialization? Do consumers want many add-on services (delivery, installation, repairs), or will they obtain these services elsewhere? The faster the delivery, the greater the assortment provided, and the more add-on services supplied, the greater the channel's service level.

Providing the fastest delivery, the greatest assortment, and the most services, however, may not be possible, practical, or desired. The company and its channel members may not have the resources or skills needed to provide all the desired services. Also, higher levels of service result in higher costs for the channel and higher prices for consumers. The success of modern discount retailing shows that consumers often accept lower service levels in exchange for lower prices. For example, Walmart typically rates near the bottom in rankings of grocery retailers on customer shopping experience and satisfaction compared to the likes of Wegmans, Publix, Kroger, Trader Joe's, Whole Foods, or about any other grocery retailer. Yet it captures a 26 percent share of the U.S. grocery market.[13]

Many companies, however, position themselves on higher service levels, and customers willingly pay the higher prices. ● For example, Four Seasons Hotels and Resorts invests heavily in top-flight service that creates customer delight:[14]

● **Meeting customers' channel service needs: Four Seasons Hotels and Resorts has perfected the art of high-touch, carefully crafted service. "If there's a heaven, I hope it's run by Four Seasons."**

Four Seasons Hotel Prague

Four Seasons has perfected the art of high-touch, carefully crafted service. Whether it's at the tropical island paradise at the Four Seasons Resort Mauritius or the luxurious sub-Saharan "camp" at the Four Seasons Safari Lodge Serengeti, guests paying $1,000 or more a night expect to have their minds read. For these guests, Four Seasons doesn't disappoint. It spares no expense in the quality of the Four Seasons staff and the high level of service they provide. Four Seasons hires the best people, pays them well, orients them carefully, instills in them a sense of pride, and rewards them for outstanding service deeds. According to one travel rating service, each Four Seasons property strives "to go above and beyond every day for their guests." As one Four Seasons Maui guest once told a manager, "If there's a heaven, I hope it's run by Four Seasons."

Thus, companies must balance consumer needs not only against the feasibility and costs of meeting these needs but also against customer price preferences.

Setting Channel Objectives

Companies should state their marketing channel objectives in terms of targeted levels of customer service. Usually, a company can identify several segments wanting different levels of service. The company should decide which segments to serve and the best channels to use in each case. In each segment, the company wants to minimize the total channel cost of meeting customer service requirements.

The company's channel objectives are also influenced by the nature of the company, its products, its marketing intermediaries, its competitors, and the environment. For example, the company's size and financial situation determine which marketing functions it can handle itself and which it must give to intermediaries. Companies selling perishable products, for example, may require more direct marketing to avoid delays and too much handling.

In some cases, a company may want to compete in or near the same outlets that carry competitors' products. For example, Maytag and other appliance makers want their products displayed alongside competing brands to facilitate comparison shopping. In other cases, companies may avoid the channels used by competitors. The Pampered Chef, for instance, sells high-quality kitchen tools directly to consumers through its corps of more than 60,000 consultants worldwide rather than going head-to-head with other kitchen tool makers for scarce positions in retail stores. GEICO and USAA primarily market insurance and banking products to consumers via phone and internet channels rather than through agents. ● And unlike competing carmakers that use franchise dealerships, Tesla sells its cars online, supported by a network of company-owned Tesla stores or "galleries," where customers can see sample vehicles and get more information.

Finally, environmental factors such as economic conditions and legal constraints may affect channel objectives and design. For example, in a depressed economy, producers will want to distribute their goods in the most economical way, using shorter channels and dropping unneeded services that add to the final price of the goods.

Identifying Major Alternatives

When the company has defined its channel objectives, it should next identify its major channel alternatives in terms of the *types* of intermediaries, the *number* of intermediaries, and the *responsibilities* of each channel member.

Types of Intermediaries

A firm should identify the types of channel members available to carry out its channel work. Most companies face many channel member choices. For example, Dell initially sold directly to final

● **Channel objectives: Unlike competing carmakers, Tesla sells its cars online, supported by a network of only a few company-owned Tesla stores in major cities, where customers can see sample vehicles and get more information.**

Chon Kit Leong/Alamy Stock Photo

consumers and business buyers only through its sophisticated phone and online marketing channel. It also sold directly to large corporate, institutional, and government buyers using its direct sales force. However, to reach more consumers and match competitors such as Samsung, Apple, and HP, Dell now sells indirectly through retailers such as Best Buy, Staples, and Walmart. It also sells indirectly through *value-added resellers*, independent distributors and dealers that develop computer systems and applications tailored to the special needs of small and medium-sized business customers.

Using many types of resellers in a channel provides both benefits and drawbacks. For example, by selling through retailers and value-added resellers in addition to its own direct channels, Dell can reach more and different kinds of buyers. However, these are more difficult to manage and control. In addition, the direct and indirect channels compete with each other for many of the same customers, causing potential conflict. In fact, Dell often finds itself "stuck in the middle," with its direct sales reps complaining about competition from retail stores, whereas its value-added resellers complain that the direct sales reps are undercutting their business.

Number of Marketing Intermediaries

Intensive distribution

Stocking the product in as many outlets as possible.

Exclusive distribution

Giving a limited number of dealers the exclusive right to distribute the company's products in their territories.

Selective distribution

The use of more than one but fewer than all of the intermediaries that are willing to carry the company's products.

Companies must also determine the number of channel members to use at each level. Three strategies are available: intensive distribution, exclusive distribution, and selective distribution. Producers of convenience products and common raw materials typically seek **intensive distribution**—a strategy in which they stock their products in as many outlets as possible. These products must be available where and when consumers want them. For example, toothpaste, candy, and other similar items are sold in millions of outlets to provide maximum brand exposure and consumer convenience. P&G, Coca-Cola, Kimberly-Clark, and other consumer goods companies distribute their products in this way.

By contrast, some producers purposely limit the number of intermediaries handling their products. The extreme form of this practice is **exclusive distribution**, in which the producer gives only a limited number of dealers the exclusive right to distribute its products in their territories. Exclusive distribution is often found in the distribution of luxury brands. Breitling watches—positioned as "Instruments for Professionals" and selling at prices from $5,000 to more than $100,000—are sold by only a few authorized dealers in any given market area. For example, the brand sells through only one jeweler in Chicago and only six jewelers in the entire state of Illinois. Exclusive distribution enhances Breitling's distinctive positioning and earns greater dealer support and customer service.

Between intensive and exclusive distribution lies **selective distribution**—the use of more than one but fewer than all of the intermediaries who are willing to carry a company's products. Most consumer electronics, furniture, and home appliance brands are distributed in this manner. ● For example, outdoor power equipment maker STIHL doesn't sell its chain saws, blowers, hedge trimmers, and other products through mass merchandisers such as Lowe's and Home Depot. Instead, it sells through a select corps of independent hardware and lawn and garden dealers. By using selective distribution, STIHL can develop good working relationships with dealers and expect a better-than-average selling effort. Selective distribution also enhances the STIHL brand's image and allows for higher markups resulting from greater value-added dealer service. "We count on our select dealers every day and so can you," says one STIHL ad.

● **Selective distribution: STIHL sells its chain saws, blowers, hedge trimmers, and other products through a select corps of independent hardware and lawn and garden retailers. "We count on them every day and so can you."**

STIHL Incorporated

Responsibilities of Channel Members

The producer and intermediaries need to agree on the terms and responsibilities of each channel member. They should agree on price policies, conditions of sale, territory rights, and the specific services to be performed by each party. The producer should establish a list price and a fair set of discounts for the intermediaries. It must define each channel member's territory, and it should be careful about where it places new resellers.

Mutual services and duties need to be spelled out carefully, especially in franchise and exclusive distribution channels. For example, Subway provides franchisees with access to proprietary formulas and operational systems, promotional and advertising support, intensive training, site selection assistance, and general management guidance. In turn, franchisees must meet company standards for physical facilities and food quality, provide requested information, buy specified food products, cooperate with new promotion programs and pay and advertising fund fee, and pay an 8 percent royalty to Subway.[15]

Evaluating the Major Alternatives

Suppose a company has identified several channel alternatives and wants to select the one that will best satisfy its long-run objectives. Each alternative should be evaluated against economic, control, and adaptability criteria.

Using *economic criteria*, a company compares the likely sales, costs, and profitability of different channel alternatives. What will be the investment required by each channel alternative, and what returns will result? The company must also consider *control issues*. Using intermediaries usually means giving them some control over the marketing of the product, and some intermediaries take more control than others. Other things being equal, the company prefers to keep as much control as possible. Finally, the company must apply *adaptability criteria*. Channels often involve long-term commitments, yet the company wants to keep the channel flexible so that it can adapt to environmental changes. Thus, to be considered, a channel involving long-term commitments should be greatly superior on economic and control grounds.

Designing International Distribution Channels

International marketers face many additional complexities in designing their channels. Each country has its own unique distribution system that has evolved over time and changes very slowly. These channel systems can vary widely from country to country. Thus, global marketers must usually adapt their channel strategies to the existing structures within each country.

There are large differences in the numbers and types of intermediaries serving each country market and in the transportation infrastructure serving these intermediaries. For example, whereas large-scale retail chains dominate the U.S. scene, most of the retailing in other countries is done by small, independent retailers. In India or Indonesia, millions of retailers operate tiny shops or sell in open markets.

Even in world markets containing similar types of sellers, retailing practices can vary widely. For example, you'll find plenty of Walmarts, Carrefours, Tescos, and other retail superstores in major Chinese cities. But whereas consumer brands sold in such stores in Western markets rely largely on self-service, brands in China hire armies of uniformed in-store promoters—called "promoter girls" or "push girls"—to dispense samples and pitch their products person to person. In a Beijing Walmart, on any given weekend, you might find 100 or more such promoters acquainting customers with products from Kraft, Unilever, P&G, Johnson & Johnson, and a slew of local competitors. "Chinese consumers know the brand name through media," says the director of a Chinese retail marketing service, "but they want to feel the product and get a detailed understanding before they make a purchase."[16]

When selling in emerging markets, companies must often overcome distribution infrastructure and supply challenges. For example, in Nigeria, Domino's Pizza has had to dig wells and install water-treatment plants behind many of its restaurants to obtain clean water. Similarly, after having difficulty sourcing quality beef in South Africa, rather than buying scarce beef from scrawny cattle raised by local herdsmen, Burger King finally invested $5 million in its own local cattle ranch.[17]

And to serve northeast Brazil's Amazon River

● **International distribution: To overcome distribution infrastructure problems in Brazil's Amazon River basin, Nestlé even launched a floating supermarket to take goods directly to customers.**

Marcia Zoet/Bloomberg via Getty Images

basin, which lacks a solid network of good roads, Nestlé even launched a floating super-market to take goods directly to customers. The boat served 800,000 consumers in 18 river-side towns with 300 different Nestlé products, spending one day at each stop.[18]

<table>
<tr><td>Author | Now it's time to
Comment | implement the chosen
channel design and work with
selected channel members to manage
and motivate them.</td></tr>
</table>

Channel Management Decisions

OBJECTIVE 12-4 Explain how companies select, motivate, and evaluate channel members.

Once the company has reviewed its channel alternatives and determined the best channel design, it must implement and manage the chosen channel. **Marketing channel management** calls for selecting, managing, and motivating individual channel members and evaluating their performance over time.

Marketing channel management
Selecting, managing, and motivating individual channel members and evaluating their performance over time.

Selecting Channel Members

Producers vary in their ability to attract qualified marketing intermediaries. Some producers have no trouble signing up channel members. For example, when Toyota first introduced its Lexus line in the United States, it had no trouble attracting new dealers. In fact, it had to turn down many would-be resellers.

At the other extreme are producers that have to work hard to line up enough qualified intermediaries. For example, when Timex first tried to sell its inexpensive watches through regular jewelry stores, most jewelry stores refused to carry them. The company then managed to get its watches into mass-merchandise outlets. This turned out to be a wise decision because of the rapid growth of mass merchandising.

Even established brands may have difficulty gaining and keeping their desired distribution, especially when dealing with powerful resellers. ● For example, Amazon.com refuses to sell some of Google's line of Nest smart home products or its Google Home voice assistant speakers, saying that they compete with its own Amazon Echo, Ring, and other products. In turn, Google has removed its YouTube from Amazon's FireTV and Echo show/Spot streaming products. The feud between the two digital giants deprives both companies of significant distribution opportunities while also inconveniencing their mutual customers.[19]

● **Selecting channels: Even established brands may have difficulty getting desired channels. For example, Amazon refuses to sell many Google- and Nest-branded products.**

BigTunaOnline/Shutterstock

When selecting intermediaries, the company should determine what characteristics distinguish the better ones. It will want to evaluate each channel member's years in business, other lines carried, location, growth and profit record, cooperativeness, and reputation.

Managing and Motivating Channel Members

Once selected, channel members must be continuously managed and motivated to do their best. The company must sell not only *through* the intermediaries but also *to* and *with* them. Most companies see their intermediaries as first-line customers and partners. They practice strong *partner relationship management* to forge long-term partnerships with channel members. This creates a value delivery system that meets the needs of both the company and its marketing partners.

In managing its channels, a company must convince suppliers and distributors that they can succeed better by working together as a part of a cohesive value delivery system. Companies must work in close harmony with others in the channel to find better ways to bring value to customers. For example, the growing success Microsoft's Azure cloud computing services unit derives from its unique partnership-building capabilities. Microsoft is "the best partner there is," says one customer (see Real Marketing 12.2). And automaker Toyota forges beneficial relationships with its large network of suppliers to gain mutual competitive advantage:[20]

Real Marketing 12.2 │ Microsoft Azure: Partnering with Customers in the Cloud

Just as it does in online retailing, Amazon dominates the public cloud computing services industry. Based on Amazon's own amazing online success, its Amazon Web Services (AWS) unit supplies its business customers with the platforms, services, applications, and expertise that help them operate successfully on the internet (the "cloud"). As a public cloud provider, AWS provides all-things-cloud to its clients, relieving them of the expenses, burdens, and risks of building and managing their own data centers. AWS pioneered these kinds of cloud computing services, and it captures a bigger market share than its next four public cloud competitors combined, including tech heavyweights Microsoft, Google, and IBM. As one analyst puts it, "In the [public] cloud business, there's Amazon Web Services, and there's everybody else."

Still, Amazon Web Services has some vulnerabilities that leave the door ajar for competitors. And second-place Microsoft is shouldering its way through that door with Microsoft Azure, which lets companies build, deploy, and manage applications and services via the internet through Microsoft's own data centers. For one thing, some of the largest cloud services customers are themselves bitter rivals to Amazon. In the public cloud computing business, "'Not Amazon' is a strong position when pitching to retailers, grocers, and other cloud customers that would prefer to avoid lining [Amazon's] pockets while [it is] competing directly against them," notes the analyst. As a result, a growing number of major retailers have turned to Microsoft Azure for cloud solutions, including the likes of Walmart, Kroger, Walgreen's, Albertsons, and Gap.

But Microsoft Azure's growing success in public cloud services runs much deeper than simply being an alternative to Amazon. Instead, Azure's biggest advantage derives from its partnership-building capabilities. AWS is known for providing off-the-shelf cloud services that are largely modified versions of Amazon's own cloud products. Whereas this easy-to-use, "self-serve" approach works well for some companies, it is a turn-off for others. Cloud customers are increasingly looking for supplier-partners that can help them customize and manage their cloud solutions. And when it comes to partnering with clients, nobody beats Microsoft.

Microsoft has spent more than four decades fine-tuning the art of forging customer relationships. It has a sales team of more than 3,000 software engineers already in place. So

whereas AWS takes a kind of arm's-length, self-service approach to selling cloud services, Azure takes a decidedly more human-partnering one. Microsoft has turned its sales force into a roving cloud development and management consultancy. When clients sign on with Azure, they gain immediate access to a sales team that pitches in and partners with them to help them get the most out of cloud services.

For example, large grocery and drug retailer Albertsons recently invited Microsoft to help it develop cloud services that would "digitally transform the customer journey." "We are reimagining the future to serve customers in a way they want to interact with us across all channels," says Albertsons chief information officer. Partnering with Microsoft's Azure, Azure AI, and Azure Cognitive Science units, Albertsons is developing cloud solutions that improve the customer experience both in store and digitally.

The Azure–Albertsons partnership is already bearing fruit at Albertsons fuel stops in the form of a new One Touch Fuel app. The app uses Microsoft Azure and geofencing to let customers complete almost all gas-buying tasks—from paying for gas and collecting rewards to activating the pump—with a single tap on the phone. By eliminating the hassle of prompts at the pump, the app saves customers an average of 90 seconds per fuel-up.

Microsoft Azure has another partnering advantage. It already has many long-standing relationships with companies using its signature Windows and Office software products. Customers already using Office cloud applications are more likely to stay with Microsoft when they move their own servers and data centers to the cloud. That's why candy maker and pet food company Mars recently picked Microsoft Azure over AWS. "Our philosophy is to drive deeper relationships with partners we already have," says Mars's chief technology officer. "We didn't have that same sort of relationship with AWS."

Similarly, good partnering is the reason that cloud file sharing company and Dropbox rival Egnyte shifted most of its services to the Microsoft Azure cloud. The two companies are now working together to develop joint cloud products. Egnyte had previously relied on Google Cloud for most of its cloud computing needs. In fact, Egnyte was funded early on by Google Ventures. But it now sees Microsoft as the best fit, given that most of its clients already use Microsoft cloud products. "We both win by providing one integrated solution," says Egnyte's CEO. "We're not seeing that level of integration or go-to-market programs put together by Amazon [or Google]." Microsoft is "the best partner there is."

Amazon's AWS is still far and away the public cloud computing market leader. Despite its recent successes, Microsoft Azure

Cloud services customers want supplier-partners that can help them customize and manage their cloud solutions. And when it comes to partnering, nobody beats Microsoft's Azure.

Piotr Swat/Shutterstock

still captures only about one-third of AWS's cloud services revenues. But Azure now has a firm and growing lock on second place, with twice the market share of runners-up Google and IBM. And thanks to its supplier–customer partnership building prowess, Azure is growing leaps and bounds to close the gap with AWS.

In response, Azure's competitors have been bolstering their own relationship-building capabilities. For example, feeling the pressure, AWS is now "spending more time cultivating relationships with top executives and CIOs," says a tech reporter. "It's hosting dinners with prospective clients to address their concerns in more intimate settings and bringing more of a human touch to these relationships." And Google is now building its own cloud sales force from scratch. Says the reporter, "Even Google, a company that has been generally allergic to using people for anything a machine can do, has seen the value of having a human sales force."[21]

Achieving satisfying supplier relationships has long been a cornerstone of Toyota's stunning success. Historically, Toyota's U.S. competitors often alienate their suppliers through self-serving, heavy-handed dealings. By contrast, rather than bullying suppliers, Toyota partners with them and helps them to meet its very high expectations. It learns about their businesses, conducts joint improvement activities, helps train supplier employees, gives daily performance feedback, and actively seeks out supplier concerns. It even recognizes top suppliers with annual performance awards.

As a result, for 16 of the past 18 years, Toyota has received the top supplier relations score in the respected North American Automotive Supplier Working Relations Index Study. The study rates companies on financial dealings with suppliers, valuing suppliers and treating them fairly, open and honest communication, and providing opportunities to make profits. The study suggests that Toyota suppliers consider themselves true partners with the automotive giant. Creating satisfied suppliers helps Toyota produce lower-cost, higher-quality cars, which in turn results in more satisfied customers. As Toyota puts it on its supplier website, "not everything our diverse suppliers do is easily seen...but everything they do shows in every Toyota."

Many companies are now installing integrated high-tech partnership relationship management (PRM) systems to coordinate their whole-channel marketing efforts. Just as they use customer relationship management (CRM) software systems to help manage relationships with important customers, companies can now use PRM and supply chain management (SCM) software to help recruit, train, organize, manage, motivate, and evaluate relationships with channel partners.

Evaluating Channel Members

The company must regularly check channel member performance against standards such as sales quotas, average inventory levels, customer delivery time, treatment of damaged and lost goods, cooperation in company promotion and training programs, and services to the customer. The company should recognize and reward intermediaries that are performing well and adding good value for consumers. Those that are performing poorly should be assisted or, as a last resort, replaced. Finally, companies need to be sensitive to the needs of their channel partners. Those that treat their partners poorly risk not only losing their support but also causing some legal problems. The next section describes various rights and duties pertaining to companies and other channel members.

Public Policy and Distribution Decisions

For the most part, companies are legally free to develop whatever channel arrangements suit them. In fact, the laws affecting channels seek to prevent the exclusionary tactics of some companies that might keep another company from using a desired channel. Most channel law deals with the mutual rights and duties of channel members once they have formed a relationship.

Many producers and wholesalers like to develop exclusive channels for their products. When the seller allows only certain outlets to carry its products, this strategy is called *exclusive distribution*. When the seller requires that these dealers not handle competitors' products, its strategy is called *exclusive dealing*. Both parties can benefit from exclusive arrangements: The seller obtains more loyal and dependable outlets, and the dealers obtain a steady source of supply and stronger seller support. But exclusive arrangements also exclude other producers from selling to these dealers. This situation brings exclusive dealing contracts under the scope of the Clayton Act of 1914. They are legal as long as they do not substantially lessen competition or tend to create a monopoly and as long as both parties enter into the agreement voluntarily.

Exclusive dealing often includes *exclusive territorial agreements*. The producer may agree not to sell to other dealers in a given area, or the buyer may agree to sell only in its own territory. The first practice is normal under franchise systems as a way to increase dealer enthusiasm and commitment. It is also perfectly legal—a seller has no legal obligation to sell through more outlets than it wishes. The second practice, whereby the producer tries to keep a dealer from selling outside its territory, has become a major legal issue.

Producers of a strong brand sometimes sell it to dealers only if the dealers will take some or all of the rest of its line. This is called *full-line forcing*. Such *tying agreements* are not necessarily illegal, but they violate the Clayton Act if they tend to lessen competition substantially. The practice may prevent consumers from freely choosing among competing suppliers of these other brands.

Finally, producers are free to select their dealers, but their right to terminate dealers is somewhat restricted. In general, sellers can drop dealers "for cause." However, they cannot drop dealers if, for example, the dealers refuse to cooperate in a doubtful legal arrangement, such as exclusive dealing or tying agreements.

Marketing Logistics and Supply Chain Management

> Author Comment | Marketers used to call this plain-old "physical distribution." But as these titles suggest, the topic has grown in importance, complexity, and sophistication.

OBJECTIVE 12-5 Discuss the nature and importance of marketing logistics and integrated supply chain management.

In today's global marketplace, selling a product is sometimes easier than getting it to customers. Companies must decide on the best way to store, handle, and move their products and services so that they are available to customers in the right assortments, at the right time, and in the right place. Logistics effectiveness has a major impact on both customer satisfaction and company costs. Here we consider the nature and importance of logistics management in the supply chain, the goals of the logistics system, major logistics functions, and the need for integrated supply chain management.

Nature and Importance of Marketing Logistics

Marketing logistics (physical distribution)

Planning, implementing, and controlling the physical flow of materials, final goods, and related information from points of origin to points of consumption to meet customer requirements at a profit.

To some managers, marketing logistics means only trucks and warehouses. But modern logistics is much more than this. **Marketing logistics**—also called **physical distribution**—involves planning, implementing, and controlling the physical flow of goods, services, and related information from points of origin to points of consumption to meet customer requirements at a profit. In short, it involves getting the right product to the right customer in the right place at the right time profitably.

In the past, physical distribution planners typically started with products at the plant and then tried to find low-cost solutions to get them to customers. However, today's *customer-centered* logistics starts with the marketplace and works backward to the factory or even to sources of supply. Marketing logistics involves not only *outbound logistics* (moving products from the factory to resellers and ultimately to customers) but also *inbound logistics* (moving products and materials from suppliers to the factory) and *reverse logistics* (reusing, recycling, refurbishing, or disposing of broken, unwanted, or excess products returned by consumers or resellers). That is, it involves the entirety of **supply chain management**—managing upstream and downstream value-added flows of materials, final goods, and related information among suppliers, the company, resellers, and final consumers, as shown in ● **Figure 12.5**.

Supply chain management

Managing upstream and downstream value-added flows of materials, final goods, and related information among suppliers, the company, resellers, and final consumers.

The logistics manager's task is to coordinate the activities of suppliers, purchasing agents, marketers, channel members, and customers. These activities include forecasting, information systems, purchasing, production planning, order processing, inventory, warehousing, and transportation planning.

Companies today are placing greater emphasis on logistics for several reasons. First, companies can gain a powerful competitive advantage by using improved logistics to give

● FIGURE 12.5
Supply Chain Management

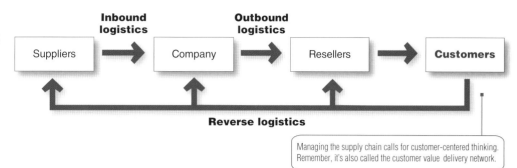

Managing the supply chain calls for customer-centered thinking. Remember, it's also called the customer value delivery network.

customers better service or lower prices. Second, improved logistics can yield tremendous cost savings to both a company and its customers. As much as 20 percent of an average product's price is accounted for by shipping and transport alone.

American companies spend $1.5 trillion each year—about 7.7 percent of GDP—to wrap, bundle, load, unload, sort, reload, and transport goods. That's more than the total national GDPs of all but nine countries worldwide. ● By itself, General Motors has hundreds of millions of tons of finished vehicles, production parts, and aftermarket parts in transit at any given time, running up an annual logistics bill of about $8 billion. Shaving off even a small fraction of logistics costs can mean substantial savings. For example, GM recently announced a logistical overhaul that would save nearly $2 billion over two years in North America alone.[22]

● The importance of logistics: At any given time, GM has hundreds of millions of tons of finished vehicles and parts in transit, running up an annual logistics bill of about $8 billion. Even small savings can be substantial.

A.J. Mast

Third, the explosion in product variety has created a need for improved logistics management. For example, in 1916 the typical Piggly Wiggly grocery store carried only 605 items. Today, a Piggly Wiggly carries a stock of between 20,000 and 35,000 items, depending on store size. A Walmart Supercenter store carries 142,000 products, 30,000 of which are grocery products. Amazon.com carries a bewildering 12 million products, or nearly 353 million products if Amazon Marketplace sellers are included.[23] Ordering, shipping, stocking, and controlling such a variety of products presents a sizable logistics challenge.

Improvements in information technology have also created opportunities for major gains in distribution efficiency. Today's companies are using sophisticated supply chain management software, internet-based logistics systems, point-of-sale scanners, RFID tags, satellite tracking, and electronic transfer of order and payment data. Such technology lets them quickly and efficiently manage the flow of goods, information, and finances through the supply chain.

Finally, more than almost any other marketing function, logistics affects the environment and a firm's environmental sustainability efforts. Transportation, warehousing, packaging, and other logistics functions are typically the biggest supply chain contributors to the company's environmental footprint. Therefore, many companies are now developing *green supply chains*.

Sustainable Supply Chains

Companies have many reasons for reducing the environmental impact of their supply chains. For one thing, if they don't green up voluntarily, a host of sustainability regulations enacted around the world will soon require them to. For another, many large customers—from Walmart and Nike to the federal government—are demanding it. Even consumers are demanding it: According to one survey, 73 percent of millennials are willing to pay more for sustainable products.[24] Thus, environmental sustainability has become an important factor in supplier selection and performance evaluation. But perhaps even more important than *having* to do it, designing sustainable supply chains is simply the *right* thing to do. It's one more way that companies can contribute to saving our world for future generations.

But that's all pretty heady stuff. As it turns out, companies have a more immediate and practical reason for turning their supply chains green. Not only are sustainable channels good for the world, they're also good for a company's bottom line. The very logistics activities that create the biggest environmental footprint— such as transportation, warehousing, and packaging—also account for a lion's share of logistics costs. Companies green up their supply chains through greater efficiency, and greater efficiency means lower costs and higher profits. In other words, developing a sustainable supply chain is not only environmentally responsible, it can also be profitable. ● Consider Levi Strauss & Co.:[25]

Water is essential to every step in Levi Strauss's jeans-making process. Making just one pair of Levi's jeans consumes 3,781 liters of water—about three days' worth of water for one U.S. household.

To conserve water, Levi's launched a series of innovative techniques called Water<Less, which saves up to 96 percent of the water in the denim finishing process alone. So far, Water<Less innovations have saved more than 2 billion liters of water. But more than being good for the planet, Water<Less has also been good for Levi Strauss's bottom line, saving the company more than $1.6 million. Says Levi's vice president of Sustainability, "Sustainability should actually cost less, because, by definition, if you're more sustainable, you're consuming fewer resources, which means you have fewer input costs."

Beyond manufacturing, however, the greatest environmental impact from a pair of jeans occurs in after-purchase care. So to save even more water, Levi Strauss launched a Water<Less line of jeans made specifically to require no machine washing. The company tells consumers that washing their jeans less, washing them in cold water, and line drying them can reduce the full life-cycle climate change impact of a pair of jeans by as much as 50 percent. Once again, what's good for consumers is also good for Levi Strauss. "Being known as a progressive brand also has helped carry Levi's through difficult business times," says the executive. "After all, consumers love a sustainable company."

● **Green supply chains: Levi Strauss's Water<Less innovations are good for the planet, consumers, and the company's bottom line. "Sustainability should actually cost less..."**

Levi Strauss & Co.

Goals of the Logistics System

Some companies state their logistics objective as providing maximum customer service at the least cost. Unfortunately, as nice as this sounds, no logistics system can *both* maximize customer service *and* minimize distribution costs. Maximum customer service implies rapid delivery, large inventories, flexible assortments, liberal returns policies, and other services—all of which raise distribution costs. In contrast, minimum distribution costs imply slower delivery, smaller inventories, and larger shipping lots—which represent a lower level of overall customer service.

The goal of marketing logistics should be to provide a *targeted* level of customer service at the least cost. A company must first research the importance of various distribution services to customers and then set desired service levels for each segment. The objective is to maximize *profits*, not sales. Therefore, the company must weigh the benefits of providing higher levels of service against the costs. Some companies offer less service than their competitors and charge a lower price. Other companies offer more service and charge higher prices to cover higher costs.

Major Logistics Functions

Given a set of logistics objectives, the company designs a logistics system that will minimize the cost of attaining these objectives. The major logistics functions are *warehousing, inventory management, transportation*, and *logistics information management*.

Warehousing

Production and consumption cycles rarely match, so most companies must store their goods while they wait to be sold. For example, Snapper, Toro, and other lawn mower manufacturers run their factories all year long and store up products for the heavy spring and summer buying seasons. The storage function overcomes differences in needed quantities and timing, ensuring that products are available when customers are ready to buy them.

A company must decide on *how many* and *what types* of warehouses it needs and *where* they will be located. The company might use either *storage warehouses* or *distribution centers.* Storage warehouses store goods for moderate to long periods. In contrast, **distribution centers** are designed to move goods rather than just store them. They are large and highly automated warehouses designed to receive goods from various plants and suppliers, take orders, fill them efficiently, and deliver goods to customers as quickly as possible.

For example, Amazon operates more than 150 giant distribution centers in the United States, called fulfillment centers, which fill online orders and handle returns. These centers are huge and highly automated. For example, the Amazon fulfillment center in Tracy, California, covers 1.2 million square feet (equivalent to 27 football fields). At the center, 3,000 employees control an inventory of 21 million items and ship out up to 700,000 packages a day to Amazon customers in Northern California and parts of the Pacific Northwest. During last year's Thanksgiving weekend, customers ordered more than 180 million items from Amazon. Amazon's fulfillment center network filled customer orders at a rate of more than 961 items per second globally.[26]

Like almost everything else these days, warehousing has seen dramatic changes in technology in recent years. Outdated materials-handling methods are steadily being replaced by newer, automated systems requiring fewer employees. Computers and scanners read orders and direct lift trucks, electric hoists, or robots to gather goods, move them to loading docks, and issue invoices. ● For example, Amazon uses an army of robots to make its fulfillment centers more efficient:[27]

When you buy from Amazon, the chances are good that your order will still be plucked and packed by human hands. However, the humans in Amazon's fulfillment centers are now assisted by an army of more than 100,000 squat, ottoman-size, Day-Glo-orange robots, developed by the digital giant's own Amazon Robotics division. The robots bring racks of merchandise to workers, who in turn fill boxes with orders. The robots make warehouse work less tedious and physically taxing for employees while also creating efficiencies let that a customer order something as small as dental floss and receive it within two days. Dubbed the "magic shelf," racks of items simply materialize in front of workers, with red lasers pointing to items to be picked. The robots then drive off and new shelves appear. The super-efficient robots work tirelessly 16 hours a day, seven days a week. They never complain about the workload or ask for pay raises, and they are pretty much maintenance free. "The robot will work the same all day long," says an Amazon warehouse supervisor. And "their stomachs don't grumble."

● **High-tech distribution centers: Amazon employs teams of super-retrievers—Day-Glo-orange Kiva robots—to keep its fulfillment centers humming.**
David Paul Morris/Bloomberg via Getty Images

Inventory Management

Inventory management also affects customer satisfaction. Here, managers must maintain the delicate balance between carrying too little inventory and carrying too much. With too little stock, the firm risks not having products when customers want to buy. To remedy this, the firm may need costly emergency shipments or production. Carrying too much inventory results in higher-than-necessary inventory-carrying costs and stock obsolescence. Thus, in managing inventory, firms must balance the costs of carrying larger inventories against resulting sales and profits.

Many companies have greatly reduced their inventories and related costs through *just-in-time* logistics systems. With such systems, producers and retailers carry only small inventories of parts or merchandise, often enough for only a few days of operations. New stock arrives exactly when needed rather than being stored in inventory until being used. Just-in-time systems require accurate forecasting along with fast, frequent, and flexible delivery so that new supplies will be available when needed. However, these systems result in substantial savings in inventory-carrying and inventory-handling costs.

When it comes to managing inventories, Walmart doesn't mess around with its suppliers. With the goal of having just enough but not too much inventory on its shelves, Walmart demands "On-Time, In-Full" deliveries to its stores. Suppliers who miss the designated delivery window pay the price. "Two days late? That'll earn you a fine," says an analyst. "One day early? That's a fine, too. Right on time but goods aren't packed properly? You guessed it—fine." While this delivery policy seems severe, Walmart pays a huge price for having too little inventory (lost sales) or too much (inventory carrying costs). Inventory "variability is the No. 1 killer in the supply chain," says a Walmart operations manager.[28]

Marketers are always looking for new ways to make inventory management more efficient. For example, many companies now use some form of RFID or "smart tag" technology, by which small transmitter chips are embedded in or placed on products, packaging, and shipping pallets for everything from flowers, fashions, and razors to tires. Such smart tags can make the entire supply chain—which accounts for up to 75 percent of a product's cost—intelligent and automated. Many large and resourceful marketing companies, such as Walmart, Macy's, P&G, and IBM, are investing heavily to make the full use of RFID technology a reality.

Transportation

The choice of transportation carriers affects the pricing of products, delivery performance, and the condition of goods when they arrive—all of which will affect customer satisfaction. In shipping goods to its warehouses, dealers, and customers, the company can choose among five main transportation modes: truck, rail, water, pipeline, and air along with an alternative mode for digital products—the internet.

Trucks have increased their share of transportation steadily and now account for 65 percent of total tons transported in the United States. Trucks are highly flexible in their routing and time schedules, and they can usually offer faster service than railroads. They are efficient for short hauls of high-value merchandise. Trucking firms have evolved in recent years to become full-service providers of global transportation services. For example, large trucking firms now offer everything from satellite tracking, internet-based shipment management, and logistics planning software to cross-border shipping operations.[29]

Railroads account for 10 percent of the total tons shipped. They are one of the most cost-effective modes for shipping large amounts of bulk products—coal, sand, minerals, and farm and forest products—over long distances. In recent years, railroads have increased their customer services by designing new equipment to handle special categories of goods, providing flatcars for carrying truck trailers by rail (piggyback), and providing in-transit services such as the diversion of shipped goods to other destinations en route and the processing of goods en route.

Water carriers, which account for 4 percent of goods transported, transport large amounts of goods by ships and barges on U.S. coastal and inland waterways. Although the cost of water transportation is very low for shipping bulky, low-value, nonperishable products such as sand, coal, grain, oil, and metallic ores, water transportation is the slowest mode and may be affected by the weather. *Pipelines*, which account for 16 percent of the tonnage transported, are a specialized means of shipping petroleum, natural gas, and chemicals from sources to markets. Most pipelines are used by their owners to ship their own products.

Although *air* carriers transport less than 1 percent of the of the nation's goods, they are an important transportation mode. Airfreight rates are much higher than rail or truck rates, but airfreight is ideal when speed is needed or distant markets have to be reached. Among the most frequently airfreighted products are perishables (such as fresh fish, cut flowers) and high-value,

Transportation: In shipping goods to their warehouses, dealers, and customers, companies can choose among many transportation modes, including truck, rail, water, pipeline, and air. Much of today's shipping requires multiple modes.

DigitalPen/Shutterstock

low-bulk items (technical instruments, jewelry). Companies find that airfreight also re-duces inventory levels, packaging costs, and the number of warehouses needed.

The *internet* carries digital products from producer to customer via satellite, cable, phone wire, or wireless signal. Software firms, the media, music and video companies, and education all make use of the internet to deliver digital content. The internet holds the potential for lower product distribution costs. Whereas planes, trucks, and trains move freight and packages, digital technology moves information bits.

Shippers also use **multimodal transportation**—combining two or more modes of transportation. *Piggyback* describes the use of rail and trucks; *fishyback*, water and trucks; *trainship*, water and rail; and *airtruck*, air and trucks. Combining modes provides advan-tages that no single mode can deliver. Each combination offers advantages to the shipper. For example, not only is piggyback cheaper than trucking alone, but it also provides flex-ibility and convenience. Numerous logistics companies provide single-source multimodal transportation solutions.

Multimodal transportation
Combining two or more modes of transportation.

Logistics Information Management

Companies manage their supply chains through information. Channel partners often link up to share information and make better joint logistics decisions. From a logistics perspec-tive, flows of information, such as customer transactions, billing, shipment and inventory levels, and even customer data, are closely linked to channel performance. Companies need simple, accessible, fast, and accurate processes for capturing, processing, and sharing channel information.

Information can be shared and managed in many ways, but most sharing takes place through *electronic data interchange* (*EDI*), the digital exchange of data between organiza-tions, which primarily is transmitted via the internet. Walmart, for example, requires EDI links with its more than 100,000 suppliers through its Retail Link sales data system. If new suppliers don't have the required EDI capability, Walmart will work with them to find and implement the needed tools.[30]

In some cases, suppliers might actually be asked to generate orders and arrange de-liveries for their customers. Many large retailers—such as Walmart and Home Depot—work closely with major suppliers such as P&G or Moen to set up *vendor-managed inven-tory (VMI)* systems or *continuous inventory replenishment* systems. Using VMI, the customer shares real-time data on sales and current inventory levels with the supplier. The supplier then takes full responsibility for managing inventories and deliveries. Some retailers even go so far as to shift inventory and delivery costs to the supplier. Such systems require close cooperation between the buyer and seller.

Integrated Logistics Management

Integrated logistics management
The logistics concept that emphasizes teamwork—both inside the company and among all the marketing channel organizations—to maximize the performance of the entire distribution system.

Today, more and more companies are adopting the concept of **integrated logistics man-agement**. This concept recognizes that providing better customer service and trimming distribution costs require *teamwork*, both inside the company and among all the marketing channel organizations. Inside, the company's various departments must work closely to-gether to maximize its own logistics performance. Outside, the company must integrate its logistics system with those of its suppliers and customers to maximize the performance of the entire distribution network.

Cross-Functional Teamwork Inside the Company

Most companies assign responsibility for various logistics activities to many different departments—marketing, sales, finance, operations, IT, and purchasing. Too often, each function tries to optimize its own logistics performance without regard for the activities of the other functions. However, transportation, inventory, warehousing, and information management activities interact, often in an inverse way. Lower inventory levels reduce inventory-carrying costs. But they may also reduce customer service and increase costs from stockouts, backorders, special production runs, and costly fast-freight shipments. Because distribution activities involve strong trade-offs, decisions by various functions must be coordinated to achieve better overall logistics performance.

The goal of integrated supply chain management is to harmonize all of the company's logistics decisions. Close working relationships among departments can be achieved in

Integrated logistics management: Oracle's supply chain management software solutions help companies to "gain sustainable advantage and drive innovation by transforming their traditional supply chains into integrated value chains."

Oracle Corporation

several ways. Some companies have created permanent logistics committees composed of managers responsible for different physical distribution activities. Companies can also create supply chain manager positions that link the logistics activities of functional areas. For example, P&G has created product supply managers who manage all the supply chain activities for each product category. Many companies have a vice president of logistics or a supply chain VP with cross-functional authority.

Finally, companies can employ sophisticated, system-wide supply chain management software, now available from a wide range of software enterprises large and small, from Oracle and SAP to Logility. ● For example, Oracle's supply chain management software solutions help companies to "gain sustainable advantage and drive innovation by transforming their traditional supply chains into integrated value chains."[31] It coordinates every aspect of the supply chain, from value chain collaboration to inventory optimization to transportation and logistics management. The important thing is that the company must coordinate its logistics, inventory investments, demand forecasting, and marketing activities to create high market satisfaction at a reasonable cost.

Building Logistics Partnerships

Companies must do more than improve their own logistics. They must also work with other channel partners to improve whole-channel distribution. The members of a marketing channel are linked closely in creating customer value and building customer relationships. One company's distribution system is another company's supply system. The success of each channel member depends on the performance of the entire supply chain. For example, furniture retailer IKEA can create its stylish but affordable furniture and deliver the "IKEA lifestyle" only if its entire supply chain—consisting of thousands of merchandise designers and suppliers, transport companies, warehouses, and service providers—operates at maximum efficiency and with customer-focused effectiveness.

Smart companies coordinate their logistics strategies and forge strong partnerships with suppliers and customers to improve customer service and reduce channel costs. Many companies have created *cross-functional, cross-company teams*. For example, Nestlé's Purina pet food unit has a team of dozens of people working in Bentonville, Arkansas, the home base of Walmart. The Purina Walmart team members work jointly with their counterparts at Walmart to find ways to squeeze costs out of their distribution system. Working together benefits not only Purina and Walmart but also their shared, final consumers.

Other companies partner through *shared projects*. For example, many large retailers conduct joint in-store programs with suppliers. Home Depot allows key suppliers to use its stores as a testing ground for new merchandising programs. The suppliers spend time at Home Depot stores watching how their product sells and how customers relate to it. They then create programs specially tailored to Home Depot and its customers. Clearly, both the supplier and the customer benefit from such partnerships. The point is that all supply chain members must work together in the cause of bringing value to final consumers.

Third-Party Logistics

Third-party logistics (3PL) provider

An independent logistics provider that performs any or all of the functions required to get a client's product to market.

Although most big companies love to make and sell their products, many loathe the associated logistics "grunt work." They detest the bundling, loading, unloading, sorting, storing, reloading, transporting, customs clearing, and tracking required to supply their factories and get products to their customers. They hate it so much that many firms outsource some or all of their logistics to **third-party logistics (3PL) providers** such as Ryder, Penske Logistics, BAX Global, DHL Logistics, FedEx Logistics, and UPS Business Solutions.

For example, UPS knows that, for many companies, logistics can be a real nightmare. But logistics is exactly what UPS does best. To UPS, logistics is today's most powerful force for creating competitive advantage. To its supply chain customers, UPS stands for "United Problem Solvers." At one level, UPS can simply handle a company's package shipments. But on a deeper level, UPS can help businesses sharpen their own logistics systems to cut costs and serve customers better. At a still deeper level, companies can let UPS take over and manage part or all of their logistics operations.

For example, UPS not only delivers packages for online retailer Overstock.com, it also manages Overstock's complex order returns process in an efficient, customer-pleasing way. Consumer electronics maker Toshiba lets UPS handle its entire laptop PC repair process— lock, stock, and barrel. Individuals simply drop their computers off at a nearby UPS store, which forwards them to a special UPS facility next to its Worldport central hub for repair. The UPS–Toshiba computer repair process is so efficient that laptops brought in one day can often be sent back to the owner the next day. "Customers are expecting the world from you," says UPS. "We can help you deliver."[32]

3PL providers like UPS can help clients tighten up sluggish, overstuffed supply chains; slash inventories; and get products to customers more quickly and reliably. According to one report, 90 percent of *Fortune* 500 companies now use 3PL (also called *outsourced logistics* or *contract logistics*) services, compared to only 46 percent in 2001. General Motors, P&G, and Walmart each use 50 or more 3PLs. And the 3PL market is expected to grow to about $1.5 trillion by 2025.[33]

Companies use third-party logistics providers for several reasons. First, because getting the product to market is their main focus these providers can often do it more efficiently and at lower cost. Second, outsourcing logistics frees a company to focus more intensely on its core business. Finally, integrated logistics companies understand increasingly complex logistics environments.

Reviewing and Extending the Concepts

Objectives Review

Some companies pay too little attention to their distribution channels; others, however, have used imaginative distribution systems to gain a competitive advantage. A company's channel decisions directly affect every other marketing decision. Management must make channel decisions carefully, incorporating today's needs with tomorrow's likely selling environment.

OBJECTIVE 12-1 Explain why companies use marketing channels and discuss the functions these channels perform. (pp 344–348)

In creating customer engagement and value, a company can't go it alone. It must work within an entire network of partners—a value delivery network—to accomplish this task. Individual companies and brands don't compete; their entire value delivery networks do.

Most producers use intermediaries to bring their products to market. They forge a *marketing channel* (or *distribution channel*)—a set of interdependent organizations involved in the process of making a product or service available for use or consumption by the consumer or business user. Through their contacts, experience, specialization, and scale of operation, intermediaries usually offer the firm more than it can achieve on its own.

Marketing channels perform many key functions. Some help complete transactions by gathering and distributing *information* needed for planning and aiding exchange, developing and spreading persuasive *communications* about an offer, performing *contact* work (finding and communicating with prospective buyers), *matching* (shaping and fitting the offer to the buyer's needs), and entering into *negotiation* to reach an agreement on price and other terms of the offer so that ownership can be transferred. Other functions help to *fulfill* the completed transactions by offering *physical distribution* (transporting and storing

goods), *financing* (acquiring and using funds to cover the costs of the channel work), and *risk taking* (assuming the risks of carrying out the channel work.

OBJECTIVE 12-2 Discuss how channel members interact and how they organize to perform the work of the channel. (pp 348–355)

The channel will be most effective when each member assumes the tasks it can do best. Ideally, because the success of individual channel members depends on overall channel success, all channel firms should work together smoothly. They should understand and accept their roles, coordinate their goals and activities, and cooperate to attain overall channel goals. By cooperating, they can more effectively sense, serve, and satisfy the target market.

In a large company, the formal organization structure assigns roles and provides needed leadership. But in a distribution channel composed of independent firms, leadership and power are not formally set. Traditionally, distribution channels have lacked the leadership needed to assign roles and manage conflict. In recent years, however, new types of channel organizations have appeared that provide stronger leadership and improved performance.

OBJECTIVE 12-3 Identify the major channel alternatives open to a company. (pp 355–359)

Channel alternatives vary from direct selling to using one, two, three, or more intermediary *channel levels*. Marketing channels face continuous and sometimes dramatic change. Three of the most important trends are the growth of *vertical*, *horizontal*, and *multichannel marketing systems*. These trends affect channel cooperation, conflict, and competition.

Channel design begins with assessing customer channel service needs and company channel objectives and constraints. The company then identifies the major channel alternatives in terms of the *types* of intermediaries, the *number* of intermediaries, and the *channel responsibilities* of each. Each channel alternative must be evaluated according to economic, control, and adaptive criteria. *Channel management* calls for selecting qualified intermediaries and motivating them. Individual channel members must be evaluated regularly.

OBJECTIVE 12-4 Explain how companies select, motivate, and evaluate channel members.
(pp 359–362)

Producers vary in their ability to attract qualified marketing intermediaries. Some producers have no trouble signing up channel members, whereas others have to work hard to line up enough qualified intermediaries. When selecting intermediaries, the company should evaluate each channel member's qualifications and select those that best fit its channel objectives.

Once selected, channel members must be continuously motivated to do their best. The company must sell not only *through* the intermediaries but also *with* them. It should forge strong partnerships with channel members to create a marketing system that meets the needs of both the manufacturer *and* the partners.

OBJECTIVE 12-5 Discuss the nature and importance of marketing logistics and integrated supply chain management. *(pp 362–369)*

Marketing logistics (or *physical distribution*) is an area of potentially high cost savings and improved customer satisfaction. Marketing logistics addresses not only *outbound logistics* but also *inbound logistics* and *reverse logistics*. That is, it involves the entire *supply chain management*—managing value-added flows between suppliers, the company, resellers, and final users. No logistics system can both maximize customer service and minimize distribution costs. Instead, the goal of logistics management is to provide a *targeted* level of service at the least cost. The major logistics functions are *warehousing, inventory management, transportation*, and *logistics information management*.

The *integrated supply chain management concept* recognizes that improved logistics requires teamwork in the form of close working relationships across functional areas inside the company and across various organizations in the supply chain. Companies can achieve logistics harmony among functions by creating cross-functional logistics teams, integrative supply manager positions, and senior-level logistics executive positions with cross-functional authority. Channel partnerships can take the form of cross-company teams, shared projects, and information-sharing systems. Today, some companies are outsourcing their logistics functions to third-party logistics (3PL) providers to save costs, increase efficiency, and gain faster and more effective access to global markets.

Key Terms

OBJECTIVE 12-1

Value delivery network (p 345)
Marketing channel (distribution channel) (p 345)
Channel level (p 347)
Direct marketing channel (p 347)
Indirect marketing channel (p 347)

OBJECTIVE 12-2

Channel conflict (p 348)
Conventional distribution channel (p 349)
Vertical marketing system (VMS) (p 350)

Corporate VMS (p 350)
Contractual VMS (p 350)
Franchise organization (p 350)
Administered VMS (p 351)
Horizontal marketing system (p 351)
Multichannel distribution system (p 352)
Disintermediation (p 353)

OBJECTIVE 12-3

Marketing channel design (p 355)
Intensive distribution (p 357)
Exclusive distribution (p 357)
Selective distribution (p 357)

OBJECTIVE 12-4

Marketing channel management (p 359)

OBJECTIVE 12-5

Marketing logistics (physical distribution) (p 362)
Supply chain management (p 362)
Distribution center (p 365)
Multimodal transportation (p 367)
Integrated logistics management (p 367)
Third-party logistics (3PL) provider (p 368)

Discussion Questions

12-1 Describe a value delivery network. How does it differ from a supply chain? Explain. (AACSB: Written and Oral Communication; Reflective Thinking)

12-2 Why is it often necessary and advantageous to have intermediaries in a marketing or distribution channel? (AACSB: Communication; Reflective Thinking)

12-3 How would you distinguish between exclusive and selective distribution? (AACSB: Communication; Reflective Thinking)

12-4 Define *disintermediation* and describe how it affects the nature and design of marketing channels. (AACSB: Written and Oral Communication; Reflective Thinking)

12-5 Define *integrated logistics management* and discuss its importance in a firm achieving its corporate goals. (AACSB: Written and Oral Communication; Reflective Thinking)

12-6 Identify three reasons why companies use third-party logistics (3PL) providers. (AACSB: Written and Oral Communication; Reflective Thinking)

Critical Thinking Exercises

12-7 Explain how channel members help candy maker Mars, Inc. deliver value to consumers. Could Mars take on any of these distribution functions itself? (AACSB: Written and Oral Communication; Information Technology; Reflective Thinking)

12-8 It has been estimated that the top 100 third-party logistics companies worldwide control around a third of the estimated $270 billion outsourced logistics. Market growth is between 6 and 8 percent. Do some research to find out why this logistics model is so successful. (AACSB: Communication; Use of IT; Reflective Thinking)

12-9 Research how vendor-managed inventory (VMI) compares to a traditional inventory management system. Given their benefits, why wouldn't all suppliers and retailers establish VMI systems? (AACSB: Written and Oral Communication; Information Technology; Reflective Thinking)

APPLICATIONS AND CASES

Online, Mobile, and Social Media Marketing Petco's Partnership with Shipt

Petco recently formed a partnership with Target-owned Shipt to expand its same-day delivery options, which it already offers in some markets through Instacart's PetcoNow service. Shipt now delivers goods from Petco stores to nearly 70 million households in as little as one hour. Many analysts were positive about Petco's move to maximize same-day delivery coverage for its customers. Same-day delivery is now an expectation for online consumers in almost every category. However, critics of the partnership questioned why Target would offer its Shipt service to competitors like Petco instead of using Shipt exclusively to deliver its own pet products, including its private-label Boots & Barkley brand. Critics also noted Petco's frequent in-store stockouts, which would affect its ability to deliver desired products.

12-10 Is it wise for Petco to expand its same-day delivery offerings to additional customers through Shipt? Why or why not? (AACSB: Written and Oral Communication; Reflective Thinking; Information Technology)

12-11 Transportation, inventory, warehousing, and information management activities can interact in inverse ways. What trade-offs will Petco have to make in offering its customers same-day delivery? (AACSB: Written and Oral Communication; Reflective Thinking; Information Technology)

Marketing Ethics Ethical Sourcing

Lush, the fresh handmade cosmetics company, was launched in 1995, and included the same creative team who designed many amazing products for The Body Shop. In less than 20 years of its establishment, Lush grew to a network of over 850 stores in more than 50 countries worldwide and over 6,000 employees. From the outset, the company was keen on ensuring that they sourced their product ingredients ethically. This has become their key USP, and together with the anti-animal-testing stance and the ethos of making fresh cosmetics, the business stands apart from most of its competitors. It does mean that the prices of their products are marginally higher, but this is offset by the unique, minimalist packaging and general vibe of the brand. When Lush looks for suppliers, they consider the whole picture; they take into account the conditions under which the workers may operate and also consider how the production of the ingredients affects the environment. For Lush, it is important that the ingredients

used for the cosmetics should be vegetarian, not tested on animals, and have minimal impact as far as transportation is concerned. Today, the company indirectly supports 400 women in Ghana who supply fair-trade shea butter and has stopped using palm oil from Indonesia in order to protect the natural habitat of the orangutan. They also buy directly from small farmers in Tunisia, Costa Rica, the Dominican Republic, and Laos.

12-12 Write a brief report on a business of your choice that supports ethical sourcing. What criteria are being used to establish the ethical standards under which they operate? (AACSB: Written and Oral Communication; Reflective Thinking)

12-13 Should ethical sourcing be the default standard for all businesses? (AACSB: Written and Oral Communication; Reflective Thinking; Ethical Understanding and Reasoning)

Marketing by the Numbers Drinking from the Source

The post-Prohibition "three-tier system" requires the separation of the production, distribution, and retailing of alcohol in most states. That wasn't much of an issue for craft brewers during the explosive growth years between 2011 and 2015, when craft beers doubled their percentage of the beer market and could hardly keep up with demand. However, craft beer volume through the three-tier system is now slowing down, growing less than 2 percent per year, causing craft brewers to turn to direct distribution for growth. Adding direct distribution, mainly through operating

taprooms and brewpubs, resulted in 24 percent volume growth. Taprooms are located in working breweries where consumers can buy beer, and brewpubs are restaurants with a brewery. Such establishments now account for almost 10 percent of all U.S. bar traffic and for as much as 35 percent of traffic in Denver and San Diego. Some independent craft beer bar chains are closing locations in states like Texas because of lost sales following a 2013 law that relaxed the three-tier system and allowed breweries to sell 5,000 barrels a year for onsite consumption. Small craft brewers are excited about this trend—they make higher margins selling direct compared to using an indirect channel of distributors and bars. A brewer's average cost per keg of craft beer is $60, and a keg sells to distributors for $90. The distributor then resells the keg to a bar for $120. Each keg serves more than one hundred 14.5-ounce glasses, the amount typically poured into a 16-ounce glass at a bar to accommodate a foam head. A bar's cost per glass of craft beer poured is $0.88 per glass. The standard in the bar industry is to have 20 percent liquor cost, meaning 20 percent of the price to consumers represents the bar's cost of goods sold, leaving 80 percent for the bar's margin.

12-14 Calculate the price at which a bar will sell one 14.5-ounce glass of craft beer if the desired 80 percent margin is based on selling price. What is the bar's dollar markup on a glass of craft beer? Refer to Setting Price Based on External Factors in Appendix 2: Marketing by the Numbers to learn how to do this analysis. (AACSB: Analytic Reasoning)

12-15 Determine the brewer's cost per 14.5-ounce serving (one glass). What price would a brewer sell that glass of beer for to achieve an 80 percent margin based on its selling price at its own taproom or brewpub? What dollar and percentage margin would a brewer realize if the glass of beer was sold for the same price as it is sold in bars? Is the brewer better off using the direct channel compared to the "three-tiered system" indirect channel? (AACSB: Communication; Analytic Reasoning; Reflective Thinking)

Company Case Target: A Serious Contender in the Same-Day Delivery Business

Once upon a time, there were two major forces dominating the discount retail market: Walmart and Target. The two retailers offered similar merchandise assortments, and their stores were close to one another—often facing off from opposite sides of major boulevards. The two were constantly compared—the press rarely covered one without mentioning the other.

Walmart was far and away the market leader. And although Target was a distant runner-up, its stylish "cheap chic" positioning and "Expect More. Pay Less." mantra made it a formidable challenger to Walmart's always-lowest-price positioning. In fact, for years Target grew at a faster rate than Walmart, nibbling away at the giant's market share and posing a genuine threat.

But what a difference a decade makes. Since the Great Recession of 2008, Walmart's annual revenues have increased by more than $140 billion while Target's have barely moved. Not only has Walmart improved its game, but increased competition from Amazon, Costco, Kohl's, and dollar stores have flattened Target's growth. Still, Target hasn't given up. It has doubled down on improving its customer experience while at the same time cutting corporate costs. So far, however, its efforts haven't seemed to make much difference.

All that may soon change. Target has made a major investment that it hopes will help it to regain its edge in the retail world and restore its growth. For a cool $550 million in cash, Target recently acquired Shipt, the exploding startup with a thriving same-day delivery network across the United States. With online grocery sales exploding, the future of retail favors companies that can deliver goods fast and cheap. With the Shipt acquisition, Target is sending a message—it's serious about establishing a competitive advantage in home delivery. Target plans not only to increase sales of its current inventory but also to become a major player in an area of retail where it has languished—groceries.

A New Way to Deliver Groceries

Founded in 2014 by a 32-year-old high school dropout, Shipt quickly established itself as a force in the home delivery business. After a few failed models, Shipt focused on groceries. Members get unlimited same-day grocery delivery on orders of $35 or more for just $99 a year. The Shipt app and website offer users a seamless experience for ordering and receiving groceries and general merchandise.

But Shipt is not a grocer. It's a home delivery service. Rather than invest in its own inventory, Shipt built its business by partnering with grocery chains such as Kroger, Publix, and, of course, Target. When a customer places an order, employees at partner stores don't have to do anything. Instead, one of Shipt's personal shoppers goes to the store, plucks the products from shelves, and delivers them to the customer's home. Shipt shoppers wear green T-shirts with the company logo. But similar to Uber and Lyft, they are independent contractors. They drive their own vehicles and work when they want to. A Shipt personal shopper makes between $16 and $22 an hour. Shipt finished its most recent fiscal year with approximately 100,000 shoppers delivering approximately $1 billion worth of groceries and other merchandise.

Experts have predicted a reliable model for home grocery delivery to the masses for the past 20 years. Until now, however, efforts have moved slowly, leaving behind many casualties. Today, same-day grocery delivery is a rapidly growing sector with many large retail competitors entering the fray. Fueled by the explosion in mobile devices and consumer expectations for instant everything, same-day grocery delivery is more in demand than ever. "One-stop shopping was convenient in the 1990s," says one retail analyst. "But for today's families you have to be able to do instant food delivery as well." According to a recent report, online grocery shopping in the United States could expand fivefold, eclipsing $100 billion in annual sales by 2025.

Why Partner When You Can Buy?

Although the Shipt acquisition may seem sudden for Target, it was actually a long time coming. Target has always striven to stand out from the rest of the discount retail world by offering a more high-end customer experience. With Amazon and Walmart fast establishing their same-day grocery delivery capabilities, Target knew it had to make a move or risk falling further behind. But why buy Shipt instead of simply partnering with it? For starters, the acquisition sends a strong signal to competitors and customers that Target is serious about the grocery business and about delivering its goods better and faster than larger competitors.

Purchasing rather than partnering with Shipt also gives Target more control. The acquisition lets the company take full advantage of the Shipt technology platform across its entire network of stores, letting it to provide faster and more convenient same-day delivery on a wide variety of goods. Now, just over a year after the acquisition, Target customers can take delivery via Shipt of groceries, home goods, and electronics, among other things. "By the end of 2019, we'll offer same-day delivery on all major product categories at Target," claims John Mulligan, Target's chief operating officer.

Prior to the acquisition, Target was already partnering with Shipt rival Instacart. But the strong compatibility between Target and Shipt was apparent to both companies. "What sets us apart, and really one of the big reasons we were drawn to Target, is the value we place on delivering quality, personalized experiences to our customers," notes Shipt's founder. "Our localized network of...shoppers goes above and beyond to make sure our customers are well served."

In the Race or Out in Front?

The Shipt purchase was primarily prompted by developments at Target's main competitors. At the time of the Shipt purchase, Walmart offered same-day grocery delivery in only six U.S. markets but had announced partnerships with delivery services Point Pickup, Skipcart, AxleHire, and Roadie that would expand capabilities rapidly. Well on its way, Walmart will provide same-day delivery from 1,600 of its stores in 300 U.S. markets by the end of the current fiscal year. For same-day delivery, Walmart customers pay a flat fee of $9.95 on minimum orders of $30. Similar to Shipt, Walmart also uses personal shoppers to assemble orders from shelves. But these shoppers are actual Walmart employees who also pick orders for its curbside pickup, a service that will be offered at 3,100 Walmart Supercenters and Neighborhood Market stores by the end of this year. All orders are taken to a designated holding area at the front of the store. But whereas Shipt uses the same delivery mechanism systemwide, Walmart's store-to-household delivery is fragmented across a mix of service providers, including its own subsidiary Jet.com.

Amazon is also establishing itself as a leader in same-day grocery delivery. As the owner of Whole Foods Market, the dominant e-commerce retailer now has a bigger stake in the grocery business. And with its AmazonFresh service, Prime members who pay an additional $14.99 per month can get same-day grocery delivery on minimum orders of $50. Customers can even have orders auto-delivered every two weeks. Available in numerous markets throughout the United States, AmazonFresh warehouses groceries in its own facilities. In some markets, delivery is carried out by Amazon drivers and a fleet of big green Amazon Fresh box trucks. In other markets, AmazonFresh is delivered by the U.S. Postal Service.

So far, the quality of AmazonFresh delivery has been spotty, prompting complaints by loyal Amazon customers about late orders, missed orders, and missing items. "I feel like Amazon now has two very distinct divisions," said one Los Angeles customer. "While I love Amazon Prime and even Prime Now, I don't know what's going on with AmazonFresh. It really leaves a bad taste in my mouth, because there are other companies that do grocery so much better." The disruptions have led Amazon to pull back temporarily, halting AmazonFresh service in nine states where it relied on the USPS. But Amazon assures the public that it is regrouping, promising more cooperation over time between Whole Foods, AmazonFresh, and Prime Now.

Although Target now owns Shipt, it's business as usual at the Birmingham-based startup. Target is allowing Shipt to continue operating independently, and Shipt will continue to service its other clients and Target competitors. For now, that's just fine by Target. The retailer gains an immediate strength in the same-day delivery business through one of the strongest players in the market. For Shipt, the acquisition provides a big boost to its already growing network, one that reaches 260 U.S. cities and counting.

So how does Target stack up against its larger competitors? Target may now be in the best position of all grocers to establish reliable nationwide same-day delivery. Although Amazon is in the lead when it comes to all online grocery sales, it's AmazonFresh same-day service lags behind Shipt and Instacart. According to one Moody's analyst, "The fact that Target will have this service in place ... will significantly improve its online competitive position." Based on calculations for the average home, Shipt's service is the cheapest compared to Walmart and Amazon. More important, the consistency and reliability of the Shipt delivery system give Target the highest-quality customer experience.

With the capability to extend its services in a more modern and flexible way, Target is making one thing clear—it won't simply fade away. It will continue to do whatever it takes to serve its customer base. The competition in the same-day grocery sector gives even more options to shoppers looking for time savings and convenience. For customers, that's good news. For the retailers, only time will tell.[34]

Questions for Discussion

12-16 As completely as possible, diagram the value delivery network for Target's grocery business, from raw materials to finished consumer goods.

12-17 Is Target a producer, a customer, or an intermediary? How about Shipt? Explain.

12-18 Discuss Target's channel management procedures.

12-19 Regarding the same-day delivery venture, why are Target's partnerships important?

12-20 Will Target's acquisition of Shipt result in growing revenues in the coming years? Explain.

13 Retailing and Wholesaling

OBJECTIVES OUTLINE

CHAPTER PREVIEW We now look more deeply into the two major intermediary marketing channel functions: retailing and wholesaling. You already know something about retailing—retailers of all shapes and sizes serve you every day, both in stores and online. However, you probably know much less about the hoard of wholesalers working behind the scenes. In this chapter, we examine the characteristics of different kinds of retailers and wholesalers, the marketing decisions they make, and trends for the future.

Fast Retailing, Asia's top apparel retailer and the world's fourth largest, has revolutionized the retail clothing industry by creating and fostering innovative retail experiences. The company has turned Uniqlo, its key brand, into a global one by living up to its "Made for All" credo. The company has built long-term relationships with material manufacturers and cooperates with them to offer high-quality products at affordable prices. Uniqlo's specific attention to customer service has further contributed to its global success.

Uniqlo: The Innovative Route in Fashion Retailing

Uniqlo Co., Ltd. is a Japanese casual wear designer, manufacturer, and retailer. Since 2005, the company has been a wholly owned subsidiary of Fast Retailing Co., Ltd. Uniqlo Japan is the nation's largest apparel retail chain, with a 6.5 percent market share of the Japanese apparel market and a network of 1,241 stores at the end of November 2018, generating annual net sales in the year (ending August 31) of over $7.66 billion. The company contributes more than 51 percent of the group's net sales. From there, Uniqlo International has been driving group growth by opening new stores each year in various countries outside Japan. The company has more than 3,445 stores as of August 2018 worldwide, including Australia, Bangladesh, Canada, China, France, Germany, Russia, and the United Kingdom. Uniqlo

International's revenue overtook Uniqlo Japan for the first time in 2018. This makes Fast Retailing the latest global company from Japan and Asia's top—as well as the world's third-largest—apparel retailer, following Inditex (Zara) and Hennes & Mauritz (H&M).

Founded by President and CEO Tadashi Yanai, Uniqlo's first store opened as a "unique clothing warehouse" selling unisex casual clothing in Hiroshima in 1984. It was later renamed Fast Retailing Co. in 1991. At this time, the company was simply reselling garments that it bought from other manufacturers, but a key turning point for the brand came about when it decided in 1997 to take on more elements of the value chain and begin producing its own clothes. This transformed Uniqlo from a suburban casual clothing store into a Japanese household name, and the company became Japan's first specialty store retailer of private label apparel (known as an SPA). Ever since, the company has refined this business model, allowing sophisticated control of the entire business process, from planning and design to material procurement and sales. As a consequence, Uniqlo won the fiscal 2014 Retailer of the Year Award from the World Retail Congress for exceptional, world-class performance and has successfully developed into a global brand. Tadashi Yanai believes that this global development and growth reflects Uniqlo's positioning as the world's only "lifewear" brand, which means everyday high-quality clothes that are fashionable, affordable, and comfortable.

How did Fast Retailing manage to turn Uniqlo into a global fashion retail brand? Steered by the philosophy "Made for All," Uniqlo offers high-quality products at affordable prices; for example, a pair of jeans may be priced as low as $9. Direct relationships with material manufacturers globally and bulk purchases enable the Uniqlo Material Development Team to procure high-quality materials at low costs. In addition, the company's highly experienced technical specialists, the Takumi Team, are sent directly to Uniqlo's partner factories in China to give technical instruction and share their experience. Supervisors from the production department at the Shanghai office also make weekly visits to partner factories to check the quality and progress of production.

Uniqlo positions itself as the world's only "lifewear" brand, which means everyday clothes that are high quality, fashionable, affordable, and comfortable.
Pawan Kumar/Alamy Stock Photo

Moreover, Uniqlo has continuously innovated in functional materials through collaborations with manufacturers and suppliers as well as customers. For example, it developed a heat-generating material known as HEATTECH with Toray Industries, Inc. Launched in 2003, HEATTECH is a unique, highly functional line of innerwear that preserves body warmth and has won over a multitude of customers. As Uniqlo believes that it must be highly reactive to customer opinions and needs, HEATTECH products are continuously refined each year based on customer feedback—approximately 100,000 comments from customers annually—to ensure the highest quality.

In addition to the affordable prices of Uniqlo products, their trendy designs also attract customers. Uniqlo partners with renowned artists and designers from across the globe, such as German designer Jil Sander. Following a five-year absence from designing, she created a collection for Uniqlo named +J, which was launched globally and sold out in most countries in the first week. In order to position Uniqlo as a socially functional brand and not just another fashion brand, the company appoints influential brand ambassadors like chef David Chang, technology entrepreneur David Karp of Tumblr, jazz musician Esperanza Spalding, professional tennis player Novak Djokovic, and Australian golfer Adam Scott.

> In a growing global environment in which cheap can also mean chic and feeling good, Uniqlo has found the best cut in fabric.

Another positive characteristic that Uniqlo has integrated is the world-renowned Japanese characteristic of attentiveness in customer service. At Uniqlo stores, there are "advisors" who help customers find what they need and keep the store neat and tidy at all times. Advisors are trained to project the Uniqlo way of interacting with customers.

Fast Retailing continues to revolutionize the retail clothing industry by creating innovative retail experiences. In 2013, Uniqlo's joint project with New York's Museum of Modern Art successfully enhanced the company's visibility worldwide by enabling Uniqlo to offer a range of sweatshirts and T-shirts with cutting-edge design from both contemporary artists and established luminaries like Andy Warhol.

In 2016 Uniqlo partnered with Paris designer Christophe Lemaire. Together they developed a range of flexible everyday wear. The range was so successful that in July 2018, the partners announced a five-year extension to the relationship. Uniqlo acquired a minority stake in Lemaire's business in order to access the design expertise and talent in the French business.

Fast Retailing aims to achieve consolidated Group sales of $61.2 billion by 2020 with a continuous growth rate of 20 percent per year in order to become the world's biggest specialty retailer of private label apparel. In a growing global environment in which cheap and chic also means looking and feeling good, Uniqlo has definitely found the best cut in fabric.[1]

THE UNIQLO STORY sets the stage for examining the fast-changing world of today's resellers. This chapter looks at *retailing* and *wholesaling*. In the first section, we look at the nature and importance of retailing, the major types of retailers, the decisions retailers make, and the future of retailing. In the second section, we discuss these same topics as they apply to wholesalers.

> Author Comment | You already know a lot about retailers. You deal with them every day—store retailers, service retailers, online and mobile retailers, and others.

Retailing

OBJECTIVE 13-1 Explain the role of retailers in the distribution channel and describe the major types of retailers.

Retailing
All the activities involved in selling goods or services directly to final consumers for their personal, nonbusiness use.

Retailer
A business whose sales come *primarily* from retailing.

What is retailing? We all know that Costco, Home Depot, Best Buy, and Trader Joe's are retailers, but so are Amazon.com, the local Hampton Inn, and a doctor seeing patients. **Retailing** includes all the activities involved in selling products or services directly to final consumers for their personal, nonbusiness use. Many institutions—manufacturers, wholesalers, and retailers—do retailing. But most retailing is done by **retailers**, businesses whose sales come *primarily* from retailing. Retailing plays a very important role in most marketing channels. Last year, retailers accounted for more than $6 trillion of sales to final consumers.[2]

Retailing: Connecting Brands with Consumers

Shopper marketing
Focusing the entire marketing process on turning shoppers into buyers as they move along toward the point of sale, whether during in-store, online, or mobile shopping.

Retailers connect brands with consumers throughout the buying process and at the point of purchase. In fact, many marketers are now embracing the concept of **shopper marketing**, focusing the entire marketing process—from product and brand development to logistics, promotion, and merchandising—toward turning shoppers into buyers as they move along toward the point of sale. Of course, every well-designed marketing effort focuses on customer buying behavior. What differentiates the concept of shopper marketing is the suggestion that these efforts should be coordinated around the customer's buying journey itself.

Shopper marketing builds around what P&G has long called the "First Moment of Truth"—the critical three to seven seconds that a shopper considers a product on a store shelf. However, with the dramatic growth of online and mobile shopping, the retailing "moment of truth" no longer takes place only in stores. Instead, Google defines a "zero moment of truth" and "micro-moments," brief seconds of decision making when consumers turn to their online or mobile devices to search for, learn about, or buy something. According to Google, consumers have no brand in mind during 90 percent of their micro-moments. And 73 percent of consumers make a purchase decision based on which brand is most useful during micro-moments of retail research.[3] Thus, these days, shopper marketing and the "point of purchase" go well beyond in-store buying.

The Shifting Retailing Model

Online and mobile technologies have caused a massive shift in how and where people buy. Today's consumers are increasingly *omni-channel buyers,* who make little distinction between in-store and online shopping and for whom the path to a retail purchase runs across multiple channels.

More than ever, consumers are "mobile-first" shoppers who begin—and sometimes end—their buying processes on mobile devices. Purchases often consist of researching a product online and buying it from an online retailer without ever setting foot in a retail store. Or they might involve using a smartphone to research a purchase on the fly or while in retail store aisles. Although 90 percent of all purchases are still made in stores, one recent study found that mobile devices drive more than half of all retail sales. And during this past holiday season, 46 percent of online purchases were made on mobile devices. "The retail customer journey is now almost unrecognizable from just a few years ago," says a retail analyst.[4]

Such dramatic shifts in buying have caused a massive upheaval in the retailing industry. Increased online buying means less need for physical stores and shopping malls. As Amazon and other online merchants have boomed, traditional store retailers have struggled. Amazon has grown by more than three Macy's in just the past three years. In what some analysts have called a "retail apocalypse," retail bankruptcies and store closings have soared to record levels recent years. Even as overall retail spending grows, retail icons ranging from JCPenney, Sears, and Macy's to Kohl's and The Limited have shuttered stores as their sales have stagnated and profits have shrunk. Even retail stars like Walmart, Target, and Best Buy have made major adjustments to adapt to the new retailing challenges posed by today's connected customers.[5]

Omni-channel retailing
Creating a seamless cross-channel buying experience that integrates in-store, online, and mobile shopping.

● **The new retailing model: Digital technologies have caused a massive shift in how and where people buy. Today's retailers must adopt omni-channel retailing that integrates in-store, online, and mobile shopping.**

Stanisic Vladimir/123RF

Given these incredible shifts in consumer buying, some experts are predicting an end to retailing as we know it today and perhaps even the eventual death of physical stores altogether. That won't happen. The Amazons of the world aren't likely to swallow up the brick-and-mortar retailing world. But it's no longer a matter of online sellers *versus* brick-and-mortar stores. ● Instead, successful retailers of the future must adopt **omni-channel retailing**, creating a seamless cross-channel buying experience that integrates in-store, online, and mobile shopping. Thus, to meet the needs of customers who work across multiple channels as they shop, traditional store retailers are rapidly integrating digital, online, and mobile shopping into their operations. And many once-online-only retailers—such as Amazon, Warby Parker, and Glossier—are setting up physical stores.

We discuss online and omni-channel retailing in detail later in this chapter and in Chapter 17. But first, because a large majority of retailing still happens in stores, we examine the various types of store retailers.

Types of Store Retailers

Retailer stores come in all shapes and sizes—from your local hairstyling salon or family-owned restaurant to national specialty chain retailers such as REI or Williams-Sonoma to megadiscounters such as Costco or Walmart. The most important types of retail stores are described in ● Table 13.1 and discussed in the following sections. They can be classified in terms of several characteristics, including the *amount of service* they offer, the breadth and depth of their *product lines*, the *relative prices* they charge, and how they are *organized*.

Amount of Service

Different types of customers and products require different amounts of service. To meet these varying service needs, retailers may offer one of three service levels: self-service, limited service, and full service.

Self-service retailers serve customers who are willing to perform their own *locate-compare-select* process to save time or money. Self-service is the basis of all discount operations and is typically used by retailers selling convenience goods (such as supermarkets) and nationally branded, fast-moving shopping goods (such as Target or Kohl's). *Limited-service retailers*, such as Macy's or JCPenney, provide more sales assistance because they carry more shopping goods about which customers need information. Their increased operating costs result in higher prices.

Full-service retailers, such as high-end specialty stores (for example, Tiffany or Williams-Sonoma) and first-class department stores (such as Nordstrom or Neiman Marcus), assist customers in every phase of the shopping process. Full-service stores usually carry more specialty goods for which customers need or want assistance or advice. They provide more services, which results in much higher operating costs. These higher costs are passed along to customers as higher prices.

● **Table 13.1** | **Major Store Retailer Types**

Type	Description	Examples
Specialty store	A store that carries a narrow product line with a deep assortment, such as apparel stores, sporting-goods stores, furniture stores, florists, and bookstores.	REI, Sunglass Hut, Sephora, Williams-Sonoma
Department store	A store that carries several product lines—typically clothing, home furnishings, and household goods—with each line operated as a separate department managed by specialist buyers or merchandisers.	Macy's, Neiman Marcus
Supermarket	A relatively large, low-cost, low-margin, high-volume, self-service operation designed to serve the consumer's total needs for grocery and household products.	Kroger, Publix, Safeway, SuperValu
Convenience store	A relatively small store located near residential areas, open 24/7, and carrying a limited line of high-turnover convenience products at slightly higher prices.	7-Eleven, Circle K, Speedway, Sheetz
Superstore	A very large store that meets consumers' total needs for routinely purchased food and nonfood items. This includes *supercenters*, combined supermarket and discount stores, and *category killers*, which carry a deep assortment in a particular category.	Walmart Supercenter, SuperTarget, Meijer (discount stores); Best Buy, Petco, Staples, Bed Bath & Beyond (category killers)
Discount store	A store that carries standard merchandise sold at lower prices with lower margins and higher volumes.	Walmart, Target, Kohl's
Off-price retailer	A store that sells merchandise bought at less-than-regular wholesale prices and sold at less than retail. These include *factory outlets* owned and operated by manufacturers; *independent off-price retailers* owned and run by entrepreneurs or by divisions of larger retail corporations; and *warehouse (or wholesale) clubs* selling a limited selection of goods at deep discounts to consumers who pay membership fees.	Mikasa (factory outlet); TJ Maxx (independent off-price retailer); Costco, Sam's Club, BJ's (warehouse clubs)

Product Line

Specialty store
A retail store that carries a narrow product line with a deep assortment within that line.

Retailers can also be classified by the length and breadth of their product assortments. Some retailers, such as **specialty stores**, carry narrow product lines with deep assortments within those lines. Williams-Sonoma stores focus deeply on kitchenware's; REI offers a deep selection of outdoor clothing and gear. Today, specialty stores are flourishing. The increasing use of market segmentation, market targeting, and product specialization has resulted in a greater need for stores that focus on specific products and segments.

Department store
A retail store that carries a wide variety of product lines, each operated as a separate department managed by specialist buyers or merchandisers.

By contrast, **department stores** carry a wide variety of product lines. In recent years, mainstream department stores have been squeezed between more focused and flexible specialty stores on the one hand and more efficient, lower-priced discounters on the other. In response, many have added promotional pricing to meet the discount threat. Others have stepped up the use of store brands and single-brand *shop-in-shop* concepts to compete with specialty stores. High-end department stores such as Nordstrom, Saks, and Neiman Marcus are emphasizing exclusive merchandise and high-quality service.

The shift toward online and mobile buying has also hit department stores hard, causing many major chains—from Sears and JCPenney to Macy's and Dillard's—to close stores and adapt their strategies. Most major chains have added direct and online selling but still have a long way to go to catch up with the Amazons of the retailing world. "The world is moving faster than department stores are adapting," says a store retailing executive.[6]

Supermarket
A large, low-cost, low-margin, high-volume, self-service store that carries a wide variety of grocery and household products.

Supermarkets are the most frequently visited type of retail store. Today, however, they are facing slow sales growth because of slower population growth and an increase in competition from discounters (Walmart, Costco, and Dollar General) on the one hand and specialty food stores (Whole Foods Market, Trader Joe's, ALDI, Sprouts, Lidl) on the other.

Like department stores, supermarkets are also facing challenges from Amazon and other online shopping options, such as food and recipe delivery services like Blue Apron and HelloFresh. Online grocery shopping captured more than 5 percent of annual sales last year and will reach an estimated 20 percent of total grocery retail sales by 2025. And more than half of all grocery purchases are now impacted by what consumers have seen or researched online.[7]

In the battle for "share of stomachs," some supermarkets are competing head-on with large discounters such as Costco and Walmart by cutting costs, establishing more-efficient operations, and lowering prices. Other supermarkets have moved upscale, providing improved store environments and higher-quality food offerings, such as from-scratch bakeries, gourmet deli counters, natural and organic foods, and fresh seafood departments. Still others are adding online buying options, such as online ordering for home delivery, in-store pick-up, or curbside pick-up. They are beefing up their websites and mobile apps shopping list creators, recipes and meal ideas, and other features.

● For example, to stay ahead of the digital and delivery trends sweeping the food retailing industry, Texas supermarket chain H-E-B recently set up a "world-class" technology innovation lab tasked with developing "the ultimate digital experience for our customers." In the lab, the chain's digital team develops technologies and strategies to expand H-E-B's online ordering, personal shopper, on-demand delivery, curbside pick-up, and other omni-channel services. To accelerate its digital and delivery offerings, H-E-B also recently acquired innovative on-demand delivery service Favor Delivery. Through these and other strategic investments, 114-year-old H-E-B is building on the success of its traditional "brick-and-mortar operations by growing its online presence to meet

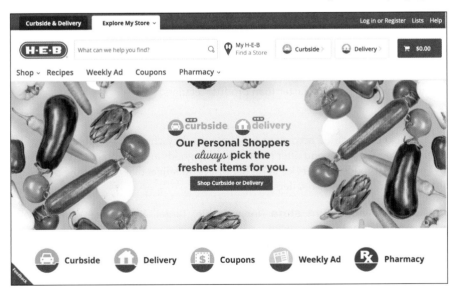

● To stay ahead of the digital and delivery trends sweeping the supermarket industry, 114-year-old H-E-B is expanding its online ordering, personal shopper, on-demand delivery, curbside pick-up, and other omni-channel services. It wants to deliver "the ultimate digital experience for our customers."

H-E-B

customers' evolving needs and expectations, …enabling customers to choose how they shop, pay for, and receive products."[8]

Convenience stores are small stores that carry a limited line of high-turnover convenience goods. After several years of stagnant sales due to fewer cigarette sales and rising gas prices, these stores are now experiencing growth. Many convenience store chains have expanded beyond their primary market of young, blue-collar men by redesigning their stores to attract female shoppers. They are shedding the image of a "truck stop" where men go to buy gas, beer, cigarettes, or shriveled hot dogs on a roller grill and are instead offering freshly prepared foods and cleaner, safer, more-upscale environments.

Many convenience stores are expanding their offerings to attract "fill-in" shoppers—people looking to pick up a few items between major grocery store trips. For example, Midwestern convenience chain Kwik Trip has expanded its offerings to become the one quick stop customers need to help get dinner on the table when they're rushing home from work:[9]

> Walk into a Kwik Trip and you can buy everything from buns, bread, and milk to fresh produce, salads, and fresh meat. Yes, fresh meat like ground beef, brats, chicken, and steaks—whatever's in demand. It's not always easy to persuade customers to buy fresh groceries in stores better known for selling cigarettes, beer, and lottery tickets. Kwik Trip strategically places a cold case of meat, fresh vegetables, and fruits near the front of its stores to help convince shoppers that a Kwik Trip is their "neighborhood market"—a valid place to stop and buy what they need for dinner. It offers the basics in fresh groceries but also seasonal produce such as fresh cherries, preaches, and strawberries, "just to keep it interesting for our guests," says one of Kwik Trips registered dieticians. The "fill-in" approach has been successful for Kwik Trip, especially in rural areas where the chain helps fill the gap left by the decline of rural grocery stores.

Superstores are much larger than regular supermarkets and offer a large assortment of routinely purchased food products, nonfood items, and services. Walmart, Target, Meijer, and other discount retailers offer *supercenters*, very large combination food and discount stores. The average Walmart supercenter brings in about three times the sales of a traditional supermarket.[10]

Some superstores that are actually giant specialty stores, the so-called **category killers** (for example, Best Buy, Home Depot, Petco, and Bed Bath & Beyond). They feature stores the size of airplane hangars that carry a very deep assortment of a particular line. Category killers are found in a wide range of categories, including electronics, home-improvement products, books, home goods, sporting goods, and even pet supplies. Category killers grew rapidly during the 1980s and 1990s, and many are still doing well. However, others have faced hard times at the hands of mass-market retailers such as Walmart, Target, and Amazon. Once-thriving category killers such as Borders, Toys"R"Us, Circuit City, Sports Authority, Blockbuster, and others have shuttered their stores in recent years.

Finally, for many retailers, the product line is actually a service. **Service retailers** include hotels and motels, banks, airlines, restaurants, colleges, hospitals, movie theaters, tennis clubs, bowling alleys, repair services, hair salons, and dry cleaners. Service retailers in the United States are growing faster than product retailers.

Relative Prices

Retailers can also be classified according to the prices they charge (see Table 13.1). Most retailers charge regular prices and offer normal-quality goods and customer service. Others offer higher-quality goods and service at higher prices. Retailers that feature low prices are discount stores and "off-price" retailers.

Discount Stores. A **discount store** (for example, Target, Kohl's, or Walmart) sells standard merchandise at lower prices by accepting lower margins and selling higher volume. The early discount stores cut expenses by offering few services and operating in warehouse-like facilities in low-rent, heavily traveled districts. Today's discounters have improved their store environments and increased their services while at the same time keeping prices low through lean, efficient operations.

Leading "big-box" discounters, such as Walmart and Target, now dominate the retail scene. However, even "small-box" discounters are thriving in the current economic environment. ● One example is Leader Price, which has carved out a place as one of France's leading discount stores against hypermarket "big box" discounters such as Carrefour.

Convenience store

A small store, located near a residential area, that is open long hours seven days a week and carries a limited line of high-turnover convenience goods.

Superstore

A store much larger than a regular supermarket that offers a large assortment of routinely purchased food products, nonfood items, and services.

Category killer

A giant specialty store that carries a very deep assortment of a particular line.

Service retailer

A retailer whose product line is actually a service; examples include hotels, airlines, banks, colleges, and many others.

Discount store

A retail operation that sells standard merchandise at lower prices by accepting lower margins and selling at higher volume.

● **Leader Price, one of France's leading "small box" discounters, took on France's "big box" discounters by offering low price, high quality, and convenience.**

GAUTIER Stephane/SAGAPHOTO.COM/Alamy Stock Photo

Leader Price understands that French consumers seek value-oriented items, wish to spend responsibly, and expect their retailers to demonstrate their responsibility to the planet. Leader Price's core value proposition is to offer French families low prices while maintaining high quality. To do so, product ranges are carefully selected so consumers don't need to look elsewhere for better value for money. The company offers the regular array of fast-moving consumer goods but limits the number of products offered in each category. A typical Leader Price store stocks about 4,000 products, of which 3,000 are produced and branded by the company, allowing them control over quality and margins and ensuring that consumers get the best value for money. Recognizing that some consumers are loyal to certain brands, Leader Price stocks 300 of the largest (like Coke) and offers eco-friendly, organic, and fair-trade products. All the fruit, vegetables, and meat offered are seasonal to ensure the best prices, with daily delivery ensuring quality. Leader Price strives to offer a simple and pleasant shopping experience, so their store design is well-organized and inviting as well as located in urban areas, near parking or public transport for easy access.

Off-price retailer

A retailer that buys at less-than-regular wholesale prices and sells at less than retail.

Off-Price Retailers. As the major discount stores traded up, a new wave of **off-price retailers** moved in to fill the ultralow-price, high-volume gap. Ordinary discounters buy at regular wholesale prices and accept lower margins to keep prices down. By contrast, off-price retailers buy at less-than-regular wholesale prices and charge consumers less than retail. Off-price retailers can be found in all areas, from food, clothing, and electronics to no-frills banking and discount brokerages.

The three main types of off-price retailers are *independents, factory outlets,* and *warehouse clubs.* **Independent off-price retailers** either are independently owned and run or are divisions of larger retail corporations. An example is online furniture, home décor, bedding and bath, kitchen, and home improvement goods retailer Overstock.com, which began by buying excess inventory and closeout merchandise from manufacturers, distributors, and other retailers and reselling it online at steep discounts. Overstock.com still sells closeouts and overstocks but now also sells new branded merchandise at low prices. Although many off-price operations are run by smaller independents, most large off-price retailer operations are owned by bigger retail chains. Examples include store retailers such as TJ Maxx, Marshalls, and HomeGoods, all owned by TJX Companies. TJ Maxx promises brand-name and designer fashions for 20 to 60 percent off department store prices.

Independent off-price retailer

An off-price retailer that is independently owned and operated or a division of a larger retail corporation.

Factory outlets—manufacturer-owned and operated stores by firms such as J.Crew, Gap, Levi Strauss, and others—sometimes group together in *factory outlet malls* and *value-retail centers.* At these centers, dozens of outlet stores offer prices as much as 50 percent below retail on a wide range of mostly surplus, discounted, or irregular goods. Whereas outlet malls consist primarily of manufacturers' outlets, value-retail centers combine manufacturers' outlets with off-price retail stores and department store clearance outlets.

Factory outlet

An off-price retailing operation that is owned and operated by a manufacturer and normally carries the manufacturer's surplus, discontinued, or irregular goods.

These malls in general are now moving upscale—and even dropping *factory* from their descriptions. A growing number of outlet malls now feature luxury brands such as Coach, Polo Ralph Lauren, Dolce & Gabbana, Giorgio Armani, Burberry, and Versace. As consumers become more value-minded, even upper-end retailers are accelerating their factory outlet strategies, placing more emphasis on outlets such as Nordstrom Rack, Neiman Marcus Last Call, Bloomingdale's Outlets, and Saks Off 5th. Many companies now regard outlets not simply as a way of disposing of problem merchandise but as an additional way of gaining business for fresh merchandise. The combination of highbrow brands and lowbrow prices found at outlets provides powerful shopper appeal, especially in thriftier times.

Warehouse club

An off-price retailer that sells a limited selection of brand name grocery items, appliances, clothing, and other goods at deep discounts to members who pay annual membership fees.

Warehouse clubs (also known as *wholesale clubs* or *membership warehouses*), such as Costco, Sam's Club, and BJ's, operate in huge, warehouse-like facilities and offer few

● **Warehouse clubs: Costco is a retail treasure hunt, where both low-end and high-end products meet deep-discount prices.**

Oleksiy Maksymenko Photography/Alamy Stock Photo

frills. In exchange for the bare-bones environment, they offer ultralow prices and surprise deals on selected branded merchandise. Warehouse club retailers appeal not only to low-income consumers seeking bargains on bare-bones products but also to all kinds of customers shopping for a wide range of goods, from necessities to extravagances.

● Consider Costco, now the world's second-largest retailer behind only Walmart. Low price is an important part of Costco's equation, but what really sets Costco apart is the products it carries and the sense of urgency that it builds into the Costco shopper's store experience:

Costco is a retail treasure hunt, where both low-end and high-end products meet deep-discount prices. Alongside the gallon jars of peanut butter, four-packs of toothpaste, and 2,250-count packs of Q-Tips, Costco offers an ever-changing assortment of high-quality products—even luxuries—all at tantalizingly low margins. Last year, Costco sold more than 110 million hot dog and soda combinations (still only $1.50, as they have been for more than three decades). At the same time, it sold more than 100,000 carats of diamonds at up to $100,000 per item. It is the nation's biggest baster of poultry (nearly 70,000 rotisserie chickens a year at $4.99 and a million whole turkeys during a holiday season), but it's also the country's biggest seller of fine wines. Just for the fun of it, a Costco in Arizona once sold an extremely limited-edition bottle of Macallan Lalique single-malt scotch for $17,000 (actually a $6,000 discount). And Costco.com once offered a Pablo Picasso drawing at only $129,999.99!

Each Costco store is a theater of retail that creates buying urgency and excitement. Mixed in with its regular stock of staples, Costco features a glittering, constantly shifting array of one-time specials on brands such as Andrew Marc, Calvin Klein, Chanel, Prada, and Breitling—deals you just won't find anywhere else. In fact, 25 percent of the items that Costco carries are designated as "treasure items" (Costco's words). The deals come and go quickly, and the changing assortment and great prices keep people coming back, wallets in hand. There was a time when only the great, unwashed masses shopped at off-price retailers, but Costco has changed all that. Now, even people who don't have to pinch pennies shop there.

Organizational Approach

Although many retail stores are independently owned, others band together under some form of corporate or contractual organization. ● Table 13.2 describes four major types of retail organizations—*corporate chains, voluntary chains, retailer cooperatives*, and *franchise organizations*.

● **Table 13.2 | Major Types of Retail Organizations**

Type	Description	Examples
Corporate chain	Two or more outlets that are commonly owned and controlled. Corporate chains appear in all types of retailing but they are strongest in department stores, discount stores, food stores, drugstores, and restaurants.	Macy's (department stores), Target (discount stores), Kroger (grocery stores), CVS (drugstores)
Voluntary chain	Wholesaler-sponsored group of independent retailers engaged in group buying and merchandising.	Independent Grocers Alliance (IGA), Western Auto (auto supply), True Value (hardware)
Retailer cooperative	Group of independent retailers who jointly establish a central buying organization and conduct joint promotion efforts.	Associated Grocers (groceries), Ace Hardware (hardware)
Franchise organization	Contractual association between a franchisor (a manufacturer, wholesaler, or service organization) and franchisees (-independent businesspeople who buy the right to own and operate one or more units in the franchise system).	McDonald's, Subway, Pizza Hut, Jiffy Lube, Meineke Mufflers, 7-Eleven

Corporate chains

Two or more outlets that are commonly owned and controlled.

Franchise

A contractual association between a manufacturer, wholesaler, or service organization (a franchisor) and independent businesspeople (franchisees) who buy the right to own and operate one or more units in the franchise system.

Corporate chains are two or more outlets that are commonly owned and controlled. They have many advantages over independents. Their size allows them to buy in large quantities at lower prices and gain promotional economies. They can hire specialists to deal with areas such as pricing, promotion, merchandising, inventory control, and sales forecasting.

The great success of corporate chains caused many independents to band together in one of two forms of contractual associations. One is the *voluntary chain*—a wholesaler-sponsored group of independent retailers that engages in group buying and common merchandising. Examples include the Independent Grocers Alliance (IGA), Western Auto, and True Value hardware stores. The other type of contractual association is the *retailer cooperative*—a group of independent retailers that bands together to set up a jointly owned, central wholesale operation and conduct joint merchandising and promotion efforts. Examples are Associated Grocers and Ace Hardware. These organizations give independents the buying and promotion economies they need to meet the prices of corporate chains.

Another form of contractual retail organization is a **franchise**. The main difference between franchise organizations and other contractual systems (voluntary chains and retail cooperatives) is that franchise systems are normally based on some unique product or service; a method of doing business; or the trade name, goodwill, or patent that the franchisor has developed. Franchising has been prominent in fast-food restaurants, motels, health and fitness centers, auto sales and service dealerships, and real estate agencies.

However, franchising covers a lot more than just burger joints and fitness centers. Franchises have sprung up to meet just about any need. For example, Mad Science Group franchisees put on science programs for schools, scout troops, and birthday parties. Soccer Shots offers programs that give kids ages two to eight an introduction to basic soccer skills at daycare centers, schools, and parks. Mr. Handyman provides repair services for homeowners, while Merry Maids tidies up their houses and Mosquito Joe rids their yards of mosquitos. ● Century 21 franchises provide residential real estate sales services. A subsidiary of franchise giant Realogy, which also owns the Coldwell Banker real estate franchise, Century 21 consists of over 127,000 independent agents working in more than 9,400 franchise offices in 80 countries.[11]

Franchises now command about 50 percent of all retail sales in the United States. These days, it's nearly impossible to stroll down a city block or drive on a city street without seeing a McDonald's, Subway, Jiffy Lube, or Hampton Inn. One of the best-known and most successful franchisers, McDonald's, now has more than 37,000 stores in more than 100 countries. It serves 69 million customers a day and racks up more than $95 billion in annual systemwide sales. More than 90 percent of McDonald's restaurants worldwide are owned and operated by franchisees.[12]

● Franchising covers a lot more than just burger joints and fitness centers. Century 21 consists of over 127,000 independent agents working in more than 9,400 franchise offices in 80 countries.

Century 21 Real Estate LLC

Author Comment | To succeed in this age of retail upheaval, traditional retailers must adapt to the ways that today's digitally connected customers shop, providing seamless cross-channel buying experiences.

Omni-Channel Retailing: Blending In-Store, Online, Mobile, and Social Media Channels

OBJECTIVE 13-2 Discuss how retailers are using omni-channel retailing to meet the cross-channel shopping behavior of today's digitally connected consumers.

As discussed earlier in the chapter, the retail shopping process has changed radically in recent years. Not all that long ago, shopping consisted mostly of going store to store—or perhaps flipping through catalogs—to gather product information, make price comparisons, and purchase goods. That was then. Now—in this age of websites, smartphones, mobile apps, social media, and other things digital—shopping typically involves a dazzling array of channels and platforms.

Online retailing is thriving. Although it currently accounts for only about 10 percent of total U.S. retail sales, online buying is growing at a much brisker pace than retail buying as a whole. Last year's U.S. online retail sales grew 16.5 percent over the previous year versus a 5 percent increase in overall retail sales. Beyond direct online sales, retailer online sites, mobile apps, and social media also influence a large amount of in-store buying. It's estimated that more than half of total U.S. retail sales are either transacted directly or influenced by online research.[13]

Today's omni-channel consumers readily research products and prices online, shopping digitally from home, from work, in stores, or anywhere in between. They scour retailer websites and social media for buying ideas, inspiration, and advice. They might see products in stores and order them online, see products online then buy them in stores, or buy goods online for in-store pick-up or home delivery. According to a recent study, 60 percent of shoppers use their smartphones while shopping, and 54 percent chose to shop with retailers who send them special offers while in the store.[14]

This massive shift in how people shop calls for massive changes in how store retailers operate. Omni-channel *buying* calls for omni-channel *retailing*, integrating all available shopping channels and devices into a seamless customer shopping experience. The boundaries between in-store and online retailing are rapidly blurring. For most customers, it's no longer a matter of deciding whether to shop in a store *or* to shop online. Today's omni-channel buyers shift seamlessly across online and in-store channels throughout the buying process. They've gotten used to researching and buying anywhere, anytime—whether it's in the store, online, on the go, or even online while in the store.

An increasing share of the growth in online sales is being captured by omni-channel retailers who successfully merge the virtual and physical worlds. Physical store operators are expanding to the digital world via websites, mobiles apps, and the social media. Meanwhile, many online merchants—including Amazon—are moving into the physical world with showrooms, pop-up shops, their own stores, and other ways of meeting shoppers face-to-face.

Retailers have learned that shoppers with smartphones are doing far more than just checking online prices. More often, they are filling in the information gap. "The consumer has never been more informed, and that information comes from their phone," says a senior marketer at outdoor-gear retailer REI. "We love when someone enters the store holding their phone saying, 'I want this tent. I want this bike. Help me find this.'" This type of activity shows how digital and store retailing can come together to make a sale. By one estimate, mobile devices will influence more than 40 percent of in-store sales by 2022.[15]

But omni-channel retailing goes way beyond just helping in-store customers as they cross-shop on mobile devices. It requires carefully integrating the entire range of available shopping channels, both in store and out, from discovery to purchase in the buying process. To that end, most large retailers are now boosting their own online and digital selling options and linking them with stores.

For example, Walmart has upped its emphasis on in-store pick-ups and free two-day delivery. It tells customers that they can order from its Walmart.com site, pick up items on the same day, avoid shipping fees, and easily return items to the store if not satisfied. Customers now pick up half of all Walmart.com purchases in stores, often buying additional merchandise during the visit. Similarly, Target acquired same-day delivery service Shipt. As with Amazon's Prime, Target customers in major urban areas can pay an annual membership to have same-day delivery of online orders.

In addition to websites, omni-channel retailers are integrating other digital shopping channels. Walmart, Target, Macy's, and other major retailers offer handy mobile apps that pull customers to both their websites and stores, let them prepare shopping lists, help them locate merchandise inside stores, and send daily alerts and exclusive discounts to their phones. A recent study showed that 44 percent of shoppers regularly or occasionally purchase on their phones from within a retail store from that store's website. Ten percent of Walmart purchases via mobile devices are made from inside a Walmart store.[16]

Social media also play an important part in omni-channel retailing. In a recent survey, 58 percent of respondents indicated that social media influences their purchase decisions, up from 45 percent just two years earlier. Thirty percent of shoppers made purchases via social media last year, 44 percent discovered new products via social networks, and 49 percent made purchases based on referrals from social media. In turn, most large store retailers now use social media extensively to engage customers, build community, and link buyers to their websites and stores.[17]

But simply creating a digital-friendly store, high-powered website, and extensive social media presence doesn't constitute good omni-channel retailing. The key is to integrate these elements to create that critical seamless, anywhere, anytime, omni-channel shopping experience that today's customers seek. For example, rather than folding under the onslaught of Amazon and the digital retailing tidal wave, electronics superstore Best Buy now thrives by blending in-store and online shopping into an integrated omni-channel experience that provides the best overall customer value (see Real Marketing 13.1). ● And consider used-car giant CarMax:[18]

CarMax's marketing and digital people work closely together in cross-functional teams consisting of product managers, user experience designers, software developers, and data scientists. They even share the same office space. Their goal is to make the entire used-car buying experience simple and seamless across CarMax's digital and in-store shopping channels. On the CarMax website or mobile app, customers can research used-car models of interest, receive personalized vehicle recommendations, view 360-degree photos of the interiors of cars in stock, apply for preapproved financing, and get an appraisal offer for their trade-in. Then they can visit the nearest CarMax location, take the cars they're considering for a spin, sign the papers, and drive away. CarMax even offers home delivery and a "try and buy at home or work" option, with test drives delivered so that customers can try before buying without coming to a store. "Buy a car your way," says CarMax, "however you like to shop, whatever you want to buy. Online or in store, browse, reserve,

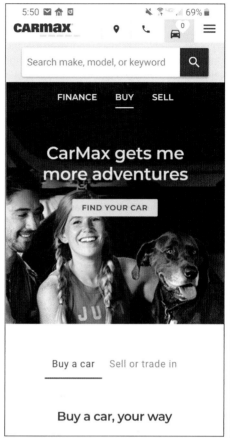 

● **Omni-channel retailing: Used-car giant CarMax makes the entire used-car buying experience simple and seamless across its digital and store shopping channels.**

CarMax; pictures are representative of customer facing materials and may vary by location or season.

and have cars brought to you from any CarMax." By seamlessly blending digital and in-store experiences across the omni-channel customer journey, CarMax remains the nation's top used-car merchant, selling more than 720,000 vehicles in its 188 locations last year and generating more the $17 billion in revenues.

Author Comment | Not surprisingly, retailers must make the same types of segmentation, positioning, and marketing mix of decisions as any other marketer.

Retailer Marketing Decisions

OBJECTIVE 13-3 Describe the major retailer marketing decisions.

Retailers are always searching for new marketing strategies to attract and hold customers. In the past, retailers attracted customers with unique product assortments and more or better services. Today, the assortments and services of various retailers are looking more and more alike. You can find most consumer brands not only in department stores but also in mass-merchandise discount stores, in off-price discount stores, and all over the internet. Thus, it's now more difficult for any one retailer to offer exclusive merchandise.

Service differentiation among retailers has also eroded. Many department stores have trimmed their services, whereas discounters have increased theirs. In addition, customers have become smarter and more price sensitive. They see no reason to pay more for identical brands, especially when service differences are shrinking. For all these reasons, many retailers today are rethinking their marketing strategies.

Real Marketing 13.1 | Best Buy: Thriving in the Age of Amazon

Consumer electronics superstore Best Buy burst onto the retailing scene in the late 1960s and grew quickly to dominate the category. Its prime locations offered a huge selection of consumer electronics, CDs, and videos at low prices. By the late 1990s, Best Buy was the nation's largest electronics chain with 3,900 superstores in 14 countries.

Then came Amazon. The burgeoning online retailer offered even more selection, more shopping convenience, and lower prices. Best Buy and other store retailers fell victim to *showrooming,* as consumers armed with smartphones routinely visited stores to see an item, compare prices online while in the store, and then request price matches or simply buy the item online at a lower price. Amazon usually had a bigger selection, lower prices, and good delivery, leaving Best Buy to shoulder store operating and inventory costs while Amazon got the sale.

By early 2012, under pressure from the digital takeover, Best Buy was floundering. "A lot of our businesses simultaneously got worse, fast," says a former Best Buy CEO. Adds an analyst, "Stores fell into disrepair, the staff became complacent, sales tanked, the stock price dropped, and to maintain some measure of profitability, the company gave up competing on price." Best Buy shut down its international operations and began shuttering U.S. stores. Competitors such as Circuit City and CompUSA went out of business entirely, and analysts predicted a slow death for once-mighty Best Buy. "Everyone thought we were going to die," says Best Buy's current CEO.

But Best Buy didn't die. In fact, it's now thriving in the age of Amazon. How is Best Buy succeeding where so many other store retailers are failing? Through true omni-channel retailing. Best Buy came to realize that the real challenge isn't in-store shopping versus online shopping. It's more a matter of using both to provide the best overall customer shopping experience and value. Although online-only sellers may have some cost, price, assortment, and convenience advantages, store retailers offer their own unique benefits, such as, well, stores. They also have multichannel advantages, combining in-store and online capabilities that online-only retailers can't match. So their best strategy isn't to *combat* showrooming and digital buying. Instead, Best Buy now *embraces* it.

In line with this new thinking, Best Buy launched a broad-based "Building the New Blue" omni-channel retailing strategy. The plan involves improving the customer in-store experience, building its own online marketing

capabilities, and integrating in-store and online to create the omni-channel shopping experience today's consumer seek.

In its stores, Best Buy now routinely matches the prices of Amazon and other major online merchants. Once it has neutralized price as a buying factor, Best Buy reasons, it can convert showroomers into in-store buyers with its nonprice advantages, such as immediacy, convenient locations, personal assistance by well-trained associates, and easy returns. Best Buy has refreshed and modernized its store layouts and merchandise assortments in line with emerging consumer electronics trends like home theaters, smartphones, and smarthome technologies.

One thing that Best Buy has a lot more of than Amazon is stores, and it's now using its showrooms to full advantage. *Showrooming* is no longer a bad word at Best Buy— although the retailer prefers to call it *showcasing.* Best Buy now works closely with several consumer technology giants to create store-within-store showcases for their brands. Inside most Best Buys, you'll find one or more exclusive display areas each for Apple, Samsung, Microsoft, Sony, and other big brands, staffed by their own salespeople or by specially trained Best Buy associates. These brands pay for the space, helping to offset showrooming costs.

Best Buy even gives mini-store space to Amazon and Google to showcase their

smarthome products. The two are bitter rivals: Amazon refuses to sell competing Google Home and many Google Nest products. Best Buy serves as a neutral ground where shoppers can examine the latest Amazon and Google devices alongside those of Apple and Samsung. That's good for the tech brands, and it makes Best Buy an attractive one-stop shop for shoppers.

Along with improvements in its stores, in line with the "Building the New Blue" omni-channel retailing blueprint, Best Buy has also sharpened its own online and mobile marketing, carefully integrating digital marketing with store operations. The chain has expanded its online offerings, streamlined the online buying process, and developed faster and more efficient delivery. Delivery was once a serious drawback, but Best Buy now offers more delivery options than Amazon. The chain offers free two-day delivery of online orders over $35 and same-day delivery for a nominal fee in many cities. And with 70 percent of the U.S population living within 15 minutes of a Best Buy store, most customers can order online for in-store pick-up. The company even has an "On My Way" function on its app that ensures that customers' orders will be ready and waiting when they arrive at the store. Improvements in Best Buy's online experience are paying dividends. Last year, the chain pulled in record online revenues of $6 billion, up 25 percent from the previous

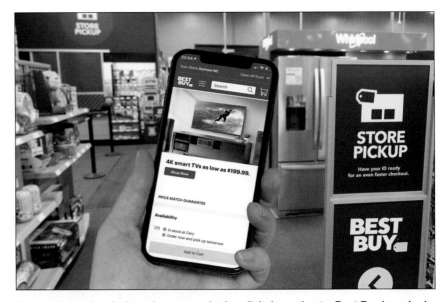

To meet the onslaught from Amazon and other digital merchants, Best Buy launched a broad-based "Building the New Blue" omni-retailing strategy that integrates in-store and online to create the onni-channel shopping experience today's customers seek.

Eyal Dayan Photography

year and accounting for 14 percent of total revenues.

Perhaps the most important piece of the "Building a New Blue" strategy is the recognition that, in today's ever-more-complex technology environment, customers need more than just products—they need advice and solutions. "It's really about building more aggressively toward serving customers and helping change lives with technology," says Best Buy's chief marketer. The company's recent "Let's talk about what's possible" marketing campaign positions Best Buy as an inspiring friend that can help consumers achieve their electronics goals.

With more than 100,000 blue-shirted employees engaging customers face-to-face daily in 1,000 stores, Best Buy is better positioned than any online competitor to provide personalized customer service. Sales associates don't work on commission, so their major focus is on helping customers, not selling products. Says Best Buy, "We are continuing to invest in the proficiency of our store associates and their ability to truly connect with customers, understand what they are trying to accomplish, and find solutions to satisfy their needs."

In addition to its sales associates, Best Buy's Geek Squad—now 20,000 agents strong—helps customers with repairs, installations, and tech support in their homes, in stores, by phone, or online. Best Buy is building a Total Tech Support platform that gives customers quick and easy access to Geek Squad tech experts, including a new app with video chat capabilities.

And taking personal service to a new level, Best Buy is now developing a core of in-home advisors—tech-oriented personal consultants who provide free, in-home consultations to help customers find solutions across a full range of products and services. These highly trained advisors are walking, talking experts on all things technical, from the latest TVs and sound systems to smarthome security cameras, doorbells, garage door openers, smoke alarms, shades, lighting, and thermostats. Like Best Buy associates, the in-home advisors are salaried not commissioned employees, placing emphasis on helping customers "talk about what's possible" rather than selling more products.

So rather than folding under the onslaught of Amazon and the digital retailing tidal wave, Best Buy is now thriving. Its sales grew 7 percent last year and 9 percent during the year-end holiday season, the biggest holiday gain in 15 years. And although Amazon's success almost spelled Best Buy's doom less than a decade ago, the relationship between the nation's largest consumer electronics store retailer and the largest online retailer seems almost congenial. "You won't get me to say a bad word about Amazon," says Best Buy's CEO. "There's a lot of room for both of us. It's not a zero-sum game." In turn, Best Buy has earned the respect of its online rival. According to Amazon founder and CEO Jeff Bezos, "The last five years [at Best Buy] have been remarkable."[19]

As shown in ● **Figure 13.1**, retailers face major marketing decisions about *segmentation and targeting, store differentiation and positioning*, and the *retail marketing mix*.

Segmentation, Targeting, Differentiation, and Positioning Decisions

Retailers must first segment and define their target markets and then decide how they will differentiate and position themselves in these markets. Should they focus on upscale, midscale, or downscale shoppers? Do target shoppers want variety, depth of assortment, convenience, or low prices? Until they define and profile their markets, retailers cannot make consistent decisions about product assortment, services, pricing, advertising, store décor, online and mobile site design, or any of the other decisions that must support their positions.

● FIGURE 13.1
Retailer Marketing Strategies

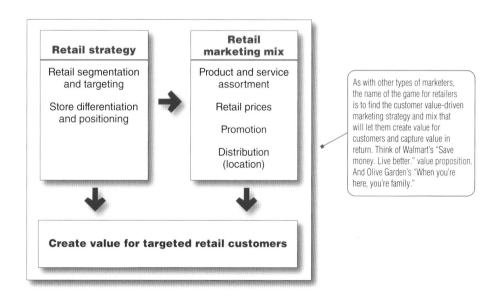

Successful retailers define their target markets well and position themselves strongly. For example, Trader Joe's has established its "cheap gourmet" value proposition. Walmart is powerfully positioned on low prices and what those always-low prices mean to its customers. And highly successful outdoor products retailer Bass Pro Shops positions itself strongly as being "as close to the Great Outdoors as you can get indoors!"

With solid targeting and positioning, a retailer can compete effectively against even larger and stronger competitors. ● For example, compare small Lush Fresh Handmade Cosmetics to larger rivals such as Sephora or L'Oréal. Lush has about 900 cosmetics shops dotting the globe, with annual sales of about $660 million. By contrast, much larger Sephora sells nearly $7 billion worth of cosmetics and personal care products annually through more than 2,300 stores globally. And cosmetics industry leader L'Oréal swamps both, selling more than $30 billion worth of cosmetics, skincare, body, fragrance, and other products annually through tens of thousands of retail outlets in 150 countries. How does Lush compete with the giants of the cosmetics world? It doesn't—at least not directly. Instead, Lush succeeds by carefully positioning itself *away* from its competitors:[20]

● **Retail targeting and positioning: Lush Fresh Handmade Cosmetics succeeds by carefully positioning itself away from its larger competitors. It makes premium beauty products made by hand from the freshest possible natural ingredients.**

Lush is known for "Fresh Handmade Cosmetics"—premium beauty products made by hand from the freshest possible natural ingredients. It sells products with evocative names such as Flying Fox shower gel, Angels on Bareskin cleanser, and Honey I Washed the Kids soap. But Lush does much more than just make and sell body care products for profit. It also positions itself on doing right by customers, employees, the environment, and society. Its do-good mission is spelled out in a seven-point positioning statement titled "A Lush Life: We Believe…." For example, the company believes in inventing and making its own products from fresh organic fruits and vegetables using little or no preservatives or packaging. Lush has a strict policy against animal testing and supports fair trade and community trade efforts. Each year, the company invests heavily in sustainable initiatives and support of grassroots charities. Lush takes care of its employees—"We believe in happy people making happy soap …" In fact, Lush seems to wish well to everyone, everywhere—"We believe in long candlelit baths, sharing showers, massage, filling the world with perfume, and the right to make mistakes, lose everything, and start again." Only in its final belief does Lush mention profits—"We believe our products are good value, that we should make a profit, and that the customer is always right." Thanks to its strong and unique positioning, Lush is thriving like fresh flowers in springtime. Whereas L'Oréal's sales are growing nicely at about 5 percent a year, Lush boasts four-year average annual sales growth of 36 percent.

Product Assortment and Services Decision

Retailers must decide on three major product variables: product assortment, services mix, and store atmosphere. These decisions, more than any other, can help store retailers differentiate themselves from online sellers. Of course, store retailers must blend effective web and mobile elements to into marketing mixes. But they must also leverage assets that the Amazons of retailing can't match, such as their own private brands, personal service, and store experiences.

"When Amazon zigs, retailers must zag," says a retailing expert. "The…bigger Amazon gets, the more opportunity it creates for fresh, local alternatives. The more Amazon pushes robot-powered efficiency, the more space there is for warm and individualized service. The more that people interact with Amazon through its AI-based assistant Alexa, the more they will crave the insight and personal connection of fellow humans."[21]

The retailer's *product assortment* should differentiate it while matching target shoppers' expectations. One strategy is to offer a highly targeted product assortment: Torrid carries plus-size clothing for teens and young adults; Five Below offers "hot stuff. cool prices."—all priced at $1 to $5; and Battery Depot offers about every imaginable kind of replacement battery. Alternatively, a retailer can differentiate itself by offering merchandise that no other competitor carries, such as store brands or national brands on which it holds exclusive rights. For example, Kohl's gets exclusive rights to carry well-known labels such as Simply Vera by Vera Wang and a Food Network–branded line of kitchen tools, utensils, and appliances. Kohl's also offers its own private-label lines, such as Sonoma, Croft & Barrow, Candies, EVRI, and Apt. 9, which bring in nearly half of Kohl's annual sales.

The *services mix* can also help set one retailer apart from another. For example, some retailers invite customers to ask questions or consult service representatives in person or via phone or tablet. Home Depot offers a diverse mix of services to do-it-yourselfers, from "how-to" classes and "do-it-herself" and kid workshops to a proprietary credit card. Nordstrom delivers top-notch service and promises to "take care of the customer, no matter what it takes."

The *store's atmosphere* is another important element in the reseller's product arsenal. Retailers want to create a unique store experience, one that suits the target market, enhances brand positioning, and moves customers to buy. Many retailers practice *experiential retailing*. ● For example, consider adidas' flagship store on Fifth Avenue in New York City, its largest store in the world:[22]

> The mammoth four-story adidas store carries pretty much every product that adidas offers, for men, women, and children in separate areas for soccer, basketball, tennis, and outdoor gear. But the store focuses as much on offering customer experiences as on selling products. "Customers today are not necessarily just looking for products," says an adidas retailing executive. "They're also buying experiences, so creating an emotional attachment is important."
>
> The Fifth Avenue emporium showcases an adidas design concept that mimics a sports arena. Customers enter through a tunnel-like entrance, climb cement stairs to reach different floors, sit on bleachers to watch games broadcast live on large screens, and pay for their purchases at stations designed to look like ticket booths. The store features a miniature running track where customers can take a test run or get their stride analyzed to ensure they're buying the right shoe. Another floor includes a turf field where customers can test soccer balls, kettle bells, and other workout equipment. There are four customization stations throughout the store where shoppers can create their own sneakers and a print shop where they can customize clothing. The store even offers fitness consultants, a concierge service, and same-day hotel delivery.
>
> In the future, this adidas store design will be applied to other adidas stores around the world, tailored to each specific location. Retail locations operated by the adidas account for almost 60 percent of revenues. "Retail is exceptionally important to the brand," says the adidas marketing executive. "It's important because we can provide the consumer with the experience we want them to have."

● **Experiential retailing: adidas's stadium-like flagship store on Fifth Avenue in New York City carries about every product that adidas offers. But the store focuses as much on offering customer experiences as on selling products.**

Eyal Dayan Photography

Successful retailers carefully orchestrate virtually every aspect of the consumer store experience. The next time you step into a retail store—whether it sells consumer electronics, hardware, food, or high fashion—stop and carefully consider your surroundings. Think about the store's layout and displays. Listen to the background music. Check out the colors. Smell the smells. Chances are good that everything in the store, from the layout and lighting to the music and even the colors and smells, has been carefully orchestrated to help shape the customers' shopping experiences—and open their wallets.

For example, many large retailers have developed signature scents that you smell only in their stores.[23] Anytime Fitness pipes in "Inspire," a eucalyptus-mint fragrance to create a uniform scent from store to store and mask that "gym" smell. Bloomingdale's uses different essences in different departments: the soft scent of baby powder in the baby store, coconut in the swimsuit area, lilacs in intimate apparel, and sugar cookies and evergreen scent during the holiday season. Scents can subtly reinforce a brand's imagery and positioning. For example, the Hard Rock Café Hotel in Orlando added a scent of the ocean in its lobby to help guests imagine checking into a seaside resort (even though the hotel is located an hour from the coast). To draw customers into the hotel's often-overlooked downstairs ice cream shop, the hotel put a sugar cookie aroma at the top of the stairs and a whiff of waffle cone at the bottom. Ice cream sales jumped 45 percent in the following six months. By contrast, negative scents can be a turnoff. For example, a decade ago, Starbucks stopped selling breakfast sandwiches because the egg sandwich smells were overpowering the coffee smells.

Such experiential retailing confirms that retail stores are much more than simply assortments of goods. They are environments to be experienced by the people who shop in them.

Price Decision

A retailer's price policy must fit its target market and positioning, product and service assortment, the competition, and economic factors. All retailers would like to charge high markups and achieve high volume, but the two seldom go together. Most retailers seek *either* high markups on lower volume (most specialty stores) *or* low markups on higher volume (mass merchandisers and discount stores).

Thus, 120-year-old Bergdorf Goodman caters to the upper crust by selling apparel, shoes, and jewelry created by designers such as Chanel, Prada, Hermès, and Jimmy Choo. The upmarket retailer pampers its customers with services such as a personal shopper and in-store showings of the upcoming season's trends with cocktails and hors d'oeuvres. ● By contrast, TJ Maxx sells brand-name clothing at everyday discount prices aimed at middle-class Americans. TJ Maxx buyers are constantly on the lookout for deals. "So when a designer overproduces and department stores overbuy," says the company, "we swoop in, negotiate the lowest possible price, and pass the savings on. No sales. No gimmicks. Just brand name and designer fashions for you…for up to 60 percent off department store prices."[24]

Retailers must also decide on the extent to which they will use sales and other price promotions. Some retailers use no price promotions at all, competing instead on product and service quality rather than on price. For example, it's difficult to imagine Bergdorf Goodman holding a two-for-the-price-of-one sale on Chanel handbags, even in a tight economy. Other retailers—such as Walmart, Costco, ALDI, and Family Dollar—practice *everyday low pricing (EDLP)*, charging constant, everyday low prices with few sales or discounts.

Still other retailers practice *high-low pricing*—charging higher prices on an everyday basis coupled with frequent sales and other price promotions to increase store traffic, create a low-price image, or attract customers who will buy other goods at full prices (Macy's, Kohl's, JCPenney, for example). Recent fierce retail competition, both online and offline, has caused a rash of high-low pricing, as retailers have poured on price cuts and promotions to coax bargain-hunting customers into their stores. Which pricing strategy is best depends on the retailer's overall marketing strategy, the pricing approaches of its competitors, and the economic environment.

● Retail price positioning: TJ Maxx sells brand-name clothing at everyday discount prices aimed at middle-class Americans.

Matthew Staver/Bloomberg/Getty Images

Promotion Decision

Retailers use various combinations of the five promotion tools—advertising, personal selling, sales promotion, public relations, and direct and social media marketing—to reach consumers. They advertise in newspapers and magazines and on radio and television. Advertising may be supported by newspaper inserts and catalogs. Store salespeople greet customers, meet their needs, and build relationships. Sales promotions may include in-store demonstrations, displays, sales, and loyalty programs. PR activities, such as new-store

● **Retailer promotion: Most retailers interact digitally with customers using websites and digital catalogs, mobile and social media, and other digital platforms. CVS's myWeekly Ad program distributes personalized versions of its weekly circulars to the chain's ExtraCare loyalty program members.**

CVS Health

openings, special events, newsletters and blogs, store magazines, and public service activities, are also available to retailers. Most retailers also interact digitally with customers using mobile ads and apps, websites and digital catalogs, social media, blogs, and email. Almost every retailer, large or small, maintains a full social media presence.

Digital promotions let retailers personalize offers to individual customers with carefully targeted messages. ● For example, CVS/pharmacy distributes personalized versions of its weekly circulars to the chain's 80 million ExtraCare loyalty program members. Called myWeekly Ad, customers can view their circulars by logging into their personal accounts on CVS.com or through the CVS app on their phones. Based on ExtraCare members' characteristics and previous purchases, the personalized promotions highlight sales items and special offers of special interest to each specific customer. For example, if a customer buys a certain shampoo, CVS will highlight that shampoo when it's on sale in the myWeekly Ad. Or customers with allergies might receive special ads and promotions on their apps when the pollen count is high in their areas. CVS ExtraCare members who access their personal digital promotions tend to save three times more than customers who don't.[25]

Place Decision

Store retailers often point to three critical factors in retailing success: location, location, and location! It's very important that retailers select locations that are accessible to the target market in areas that are consistent with the retailer's positioning. For example, Apple locates its stores in high-end malls and trendy shopping districts—such as the Magnificent Mile on Chicago's Michigan Avenue or Fifth Avenue in Manhattan—not low-rent strip malls on the edge of town. By contrast, to keep costs down and support its "cheap gourmet" positioning, Trader Joe's places its stores in lower-rent, out-of-the-way locations. Small retailers may have to settle for whatever locations they can find or afford. Large retailers, however, usually employ specialists who use advanced methods to select store locations.

Most stores cluster together to increase their customer pulling power and give consumers the convenience of one-stop shopping. Central business districts were the main form of retail cluster until the 1950s. Every large city and town had a central business district with department stores, specialty stores, banks, and movie theaters. When people began moving to the suburbs, however, many of these central business districts, with their traffic, parking, and crime problems, began to lose business. In recent years, many cities have joined with merchants to revive downtown shopping areas, generally with only mixed success.

Shopping center

A group of retail businesses built on a site that is planned, developed, owned, and managed as a unit.

A **shopping center** is a group of retail businesses built on a site that is planned, developed, owned, and managed as a unit. A *regional shopping center*, or *regional shopping mall*, the largest and most dramatic shopping center, has from 50 to more than 100 stores, including two or more full-line department stores. It is like a covered mini-downtown and attracts customers from a wide area. A *community shopping center* contains between 15 and 50 retail stores. It normally contains a branch of a department store or variety store, a supermarket, specialty stores, professional offices, and sometimes a bank. Most shopping centers are *neighborhood shopping centers* or *strip malls* that generally contain between 5 and 15 stores. These centers, which are close and convenient for consumers, usually contain a supermarket, perhaps a discount store, and several service stores—dry cleaner, drugstore, hardware store, local restaurant, or other stores.[26]

Power centers are huge unenclosed shopping centers consisting of a long strip of retail stores, including large, freestanding anchors such as Walmart, Home Depot, Costco, Best Buy, Michaels, PetSmart, and Office Depot. Each store has its own entrance with parking directly in front for shoppers who wish to visit only one store. By contrast, *lifestyle centers* are smaller, open-air malls with upscale stores, convenient locations, and nonretail activities, such as a playground, skating rink, hotel, dining establishments, and a movie theater complex.

The past few years have brought hard times for many shopping centers. The country has long been "overmalled"—between 1970 and 2015, U.S. malls grew at twice the rate of the population. More recently, online shopping has siphoned off shoppers and reduced the need for mall-going. And as embattled department store and specialty chains have announced record store closings, vacancy rates at the nation's enclosed malls have soared.

Although the largest and best regional malls are still prospering, many weaker and smaller regional malls are suffering. Power centers have also been hard hit hard as their big-box retailer tenants such as Kmart, Circuit City, Borders, Sports Authority, Mervyns, Toys"R"Us, and Linens N Things have gone out of business and others such as Sears, JCPenney, Macy's, Gap, Barnes & Noble, and Office Depot have reduced the number or size of their stores. In all, according to one prediction, one out of every three U.S. malls is at risk of dying off as a result of store closings.[27]

Despite these grim predictions, the future for the stronger malls is bright. Traditional malls are reinventing themselves to meet the changing needs of shoppers. They are adding lifestyle elements—such as fitness centers, restaurants, children's play areas, common areas, and multiplex theaters—to make themselves more social and welcoming. In all, today's centers are more like places to hang out rather than just places to shop.

Author | Retailers must constantly
Comment | adapt their marketing
strategies and mixes to today's
challenging, fast-changing retail
environment.

Retailing Trends and Developments

OBJECTIVE 13-4 Discuss the major trends and developments in retailing.

Retailers operate in a harsh and fast-changing environment, which offers threats as well as opportunities. Consumer demographics, lifestyles, and spending patterns are changing rapidly, as are retailing technologies. To be successful, retailers need to choose target segments carefully and position themselves strongly. They need to take the following retailing developments into account as they plan and execute their competitive strategies.

Tighter Consumer Spending

Following many years of good economic times, the Great Recession of 2008–2009 turned many relatively free-spending consumers into value-seeking ones. Even as the economy has recovered, retailers will feel the effects of changed consumer spending patterns well into the future.

Some retailers actually benefit from more frugal consumer spending. For example, as consumers cut back and looked for ways to spend less on what they bought, big discounters such as Costco scooped up new business from bargain-hungry shoppers. And price-oriented and off-price retailers such as ALDI, Dollar Tree, and Marshalls have attracted greater shares of more frugal buyers.

For other retailers, however, tighter consumer spending has required marketing strategy and tactics adjustments. As the economy has improved and as consumers have retained their thriftier ways, many retailers have added new value pitches to their positioning. For example, Home Depot replaced its older "You can do it. We can help." theme with a thriftier one: "More saving. More doing." Retailers ranging from Walmart and Kohl's to Macy's and Kroger have boosted their emphasis on more economical private-label brands. And to compete with the boom in fast-casual restaurants such as Panera Bread and Chipotle, traditional sit-down restaurants have added value offerings of their own. For example, Applebee's has a 2 for $20 menu—two meals and one appetizer, all for just $20. ● TGI Fridays offers Fridays 5, "a selection of delicious drinks and appetizers, all for $5 each, … all the options you could want, whenever you want, even late night."

● Value positioning: To attract today's more value-oriented consumers, TGI Friday offers Fridays 5, "a selection of delicious drinks and appetizers, all for $5 each...whenever you want.".

When reacting to economic shifts, retailers must be careful that their short-run actions don't damage their long-run images and positions. For example, cost-cutting and drastic price discounting can increase immediate sales but damage brand loyalty. One analyst calls this "death by discount" and suggests that "virtually every retailer—at both the high and the low end—has fallen so deeply into the trap that discounting has become an expectation of customers rather than a bonus."[28] A stroll through your local shopping mall confirms this assessment.

Iconic retailer Macy's has fallen into this trap. To prop up sales, it offers a never-ending stream of deep discounts, damaging its profit margins. To prop up its profits, it has centralized its merchandising and reduced its sales staff, resulting in less customer service. "Macy's has worked very hard to kill their points of difference—sales help," laments one consultant. "The sales professionals who knew their customers got trashed in the name of efficiency." Because of such actions, Macy's sales and profits have declined steadily over the past several years, forcing it to shutter many locations.[29] Instead of relying on cost-cutting and price reductions, Macy's and other retailers should focus on building greater customer value within their long-term store positioning strategies.

New Retail Forms, Shortening Retail Life Cycles, and Retail Convergence

New retail forms continue to emerge to meet new situations and consumer needs, but the life cycle of new retail forms is getting shorter. Department stores took about 100 years to reach the mature stage of the life cycle; more recent forms, such as warehouse stores, reached maturity in about 10 years. In such an environment, seemingly solid retail positions can crumble quickly. Of the top 10 discount retailers in 1962 (the year that the first Walmart, Kmart, Target, and Kohl's stores first opened), not one still exists today. Even the most successful retailers can't sit back with a winning formula. To remain successful, they must keep adapting.

New retail forms are always emerging. As discussed, one of the most recent block-buster retailing trends is the advent of online retailing, by both online-only and store retailers, via websites, mobile apps, and social media. But other innovations occur regularly. For example, many retailers now use limited-time *pop-up stores* that let them promote their brands to seasonal shoppers and create buzz in busy, high-rent areas.

Shopping malls are also jumping in with pop-up options to freshen their store mixes. Large mall operator Simon has set up a permanent section for pop-ups—called "The Edit @ Roosevelt Field"—in one of its New York area malls. Offering short-term leases (versus standard five- to ten-year leases), The Edit @ Roosevelt Field hosts numerous pop-ups, primarily online-only retailers that want to experiment with retail to reach consumers who may hesitate to buy online without seeing and touching the goods. The mix of retailers at The Edit @ Roosevelt Field is rotated periodically. Recent pop-ups at The Edit @ Roosevelt Field include Lively (bras), Beltology (belts), Raden (luggage), JARS (desserts), and Winky Lux (cosmetics).[30]

The online and mobile equivalent of pop-ups is online *flash sales.* ● Originally found on flash sale-only sites, such as Gilt and Zulily, flash sales can help move inventory or create buzz and excitement. For example, Target has one-day only flash sales on specific product lines, such as Halloween costumes on a day in October. And Amazon runs flash sales—called Lightning Deals—throughout the year and especially during the holiday season. The Lightning Deals are offered in limited quantities for a short period of time, one per customer, until available inventory runs out.[31]

● **New retail forms: Online and mobile flash sales, originated on flash-sale only sites such as Zulily, can help move inventory or create buzz and excitement.**

M4OS Photos/Alamy Stock Photo

Today's retail forms appear to be converging. Increasingly, different types of retailers now sell the same products at the same prices to the same consumers thanks in part to the pricing transparency the internet provides. For example, you can buy brand-name home appliances at department stores, discount stores, home-improvement stores, off-price retailers, electronics superstores, and a slew of online sites that all compete for the same customers. If you can't find the microwave oven you want at Home Depot or Lowe's, you can step across the street and find one for a better price at Target or Best Buy—or just order one online from Amazon.com or Build.com. This merging of consumers, products, prices, and retailers is called *retail convergence*. Such convergence means greater competition for retailers and greater difficulty in differentiating the product assortments of various types of retailers.

The Rise of Megaretailers

The rise of huge mass merchandisers and specialty superstores, the formation of vertical marketing systems, the rapid growth of online retailers like Amazon, and a rash of retail mergers and acquisitions have created a core of superpower megaretailers. With their size and buying power, these giant retailers can offer better merchandise selections, good service, and strong price savings to consumers. As a result, they grow even larger by squeezing out their smaller, weaker competitors.

The megaretailers have shifted the balance of power between retailers and producers. A small handful of retailers now controls access to enormous numbers of consumers, giving them the upper hand in their dealings with manufacturers. For example, in the normal push and pull between Walmart and its consumer goods suppliers, giant Walmart—the biggest grocer in the United States with a more than 26 percent share of all U.S. grocery sales—usually gets its way. Take supplier Clorox, for instance. Although The Clorox Company's strong consumer brand preference gives it significant negotiating power, Walmart simply holds more cards. Sales to Walmart make up 27 percent of Clorox's sales, whereas Clorox products account for only one-third of 1 percent of Walmart's purchases, making Walmart by far the dominant partner. Similarly, Cal-Maine Foods with its Eggland's Best brand relies on Walmart for almost 33 percent of its sales yet tallies only about one-tenth of 1 percent of Walmart's volume. And it's not just smaller brands that operate under Walmart's influence. P&G relies on Walmart for about $9 billion in annual sales and 13.5 percent of its yearly revenues but makes up only 1.75 percent of Walmart's total sales.[32]

Growing Importance of Retail Technology

As digital and omni-channel shopping become the norm, retail technologies have become critically important as competitive tools. Progressive retailers are using advanced information technology and software systems to produce better forecasts, control inventory costs, interact digitally with suppliers, send information between stores, and even sell to customers within stores. They have adopted sophisticated systems for checkout scanning, RFID inventory tracking, merchandise handling, information sharing, and customer interactions.

Perhaps the most startling advances in retail technology concern the ways in which retailers are assessing and connecting with consumers. In this age of big data, retailers large and small can apply advanced analytics to mountains of in-store and online data to gain insights into customer needs and behaviors. Using artificial intelligence, they can tailor merchandise, promotions, recommendations, and service to individual customer profiles.

As the surge in online and mobile shopping has changed retail customer shopping behavior and expectations, a wide range of retailers are merging the physical and digital worlds to create new-age experiential retailing environments. Amazon is doing this in its futuristic Amazon Go stores:[33]

● **Retail technology: "If you want to glimpse the future of retail, check out an Amazon Go store."**

Naum Chayer/Alamy Stock Photo

"Imagine a world where you never wait in line, or even open your wallet," posits one retailing analyst. "A world where stores know so much about you that they recommend products and lead you right to them." There's no need to imagine that world—it's already a reality at a fast-growing number of Amazon Go checkout-free convenience stores. Shoppers simply enter an Amazon Go store with an app, grab items off the shelves, and walk out without waiting in line. Cameras and sensors track what customers pick up and put down, make recommendations or even special offers based on individual shopper data, and automatically charge purchases to a credit card when they leave. Moments later, the phone app provides a receipt with details of what customers bought, what they paid, and even how long they spent in the store. Besides making shopping easier for customers, the Amazon Go "just walk out" system reduces operating costs, facilitates inventory management, and yields a gold mine of customer data. Amazon reportedly plans to open as many as 3,000 Amazon Go stores within the next few years. Says another analyst, "If you want to glimpse the future of retail, check out an Amazon Go store."

Many other advanced technologies are finding their way into retail showrooms. One is beacon technology, Bluetooth connections that greet and engage customers via their smartphones as they shop around in stores. For example, when opted-in customers enter a Target store, a beacon signal wakes up the Target app on their smartphones. The app then shows shoppers' locations on a map as they move through the store. It also shows the locations of items on their shopping lists and identifies nearby Cartwheel deals. The beacon-based Target technology may one day soon also offer a scan-and-go feature that simply tracks what items customers select and automatically charges them to a credit card without going through checkout, much like the Amazon Go stores described previously but on a bigger scale. "We want to save guests time and money by helping them find what they're looking for, discover new products, and receive offers and services that are relevant and timely," says a Target marketer.[34]

Other retailers are experimenting with *augmented (AR)* and *virtual reality (VR)* to enhance the shopping experience. For example, customers at North Face's Manhattan store can don virtual-reality headsets that transport them to remote hiking, climbing, or even base-jumping locations where they can experience gutsy jumps off a 420-foot cliff, all while using North Face gear. Marriott guests can put on virtual-reality goggles for up-close tours of destinations such as Hawaii or London. Intel has developed a "smart" dressing room, dubbed the MemoryMirror, in which shoppers, using augmented reality, can change outfits and colors with a wave of the hand. Although augmented and virtual reality technologies are difficult and expensive to implement now, they hold exciting promise for the future (see Real Marketing 13.2).[35]

Green Retailing

Today's retailers are increasingly adopting environmentally sustainable practices. They are greening up their stores and operations, promoting more environmentally responsible products, launching programs to help customers be more responsible, and working with channel partners to reduce their environmental impact.

At the most basic level, most large retailers are making their stores more environmentally friendly through sustainable building design, construction, and operations. ● For example, under its "People & Planet Positive" sustainability strategy, home furnishings retailer IKEA's long-term goal is to become 100 percent sustainable:[36]

The "People & Planet Positive" strategy begins with making IKEA's 355 giant stores in 29 countries more energy independent and efficient. To power its stores, IKEA has committed to owning and operating 416 wind turbines and has installed 750,000 solar panels—90 percent of its U.S. stores have solar panels. IKEA now generates as much energy as it uses from renewable sources. Inside its stores, IKEA uses only energy-efficient LED lighting. Most stores also sort food waste from in-store customer restaurants for composting or send it to treatment centers where it is turned into animal feed or biogas to fuel cars and buses. Some IKEAs offer customer recycling centers for products such as plastic, paper, CFL light bulbs, batteries, and even end-of-life appliances.

● **Green retailing: Under its "People & Planet Positive" sustainability strategy, home furnishings retailer IKEA's long-term goal is to become 100 percent sustainable, both in its operations and in the products it sells.**

Used with the permission of Inter IKEA Systems B.V.

Real Marketing 13.2 │ AR and VR in Retailing: Extending and Enhancing the Shopping Experience

Remodeling a dated kitchen or bathroom can be a Herculean task, and many customers simply throw up their hands and say, "Forget it!" To help solve this customer dilemma, home-improvement retailer Lowe's created a virtual reality program called Holoroom that let customers in some stores try out power tools or redo rooms to see how they would look without ever knocking down a wall.

Dubbed "Minecraft for Moms," Holoroom let customers use an in-store tablet app to design their dream room, selecting cabinets, countertops, faucets, appliances, tile, and paint colors in endless configurations (all with Lowe's products, of course). Customers then donned an HTC Vive headset and found themselves standing in the middle of the re-designed space in 3D virtual reality. Based on what they saw, they could fine-tune the design until it looked just right. Then they could export it to YouTube 360 for sharing and viewing at home with Google Cardboard.

Welcome to the fast-growing world of augmented and virtual reality in retailing. Retailers are increasingly using sophisticated digital technologies to extend and enhance the customer shopping experience, bring the outside world into their stores, and bring their stores to the outside world. They are using augmented reality (AR) and virtual reality (VR), fueled by artificial intelligence (AI), to create enhanced, personalized, and highly engaging retail experiences that transcend real-world limits.

Augmented reality merges digitally augmented objects with real-world images. AR can help consumers design, try out, and visualize products before buying them. For example, Sephora's Virtual Artist makeup app scans a customer's face and lets her experiment with different combinations of eye, lip, and cheek makeup until she finds one she likes. It also offers "virtual tutorials" that show customers how to apply makeup and digitally overlays the results on their faces. Similarly, Sherwin-Williams Color Visualizer app lets you "Color It Before You Paint It!" by uploading actual room images and painting them virtually. And IKEA's AR app, IKEA Place, lets customers place furniture items virtually in their homes to see what they look like before buying.

At the NIKEiD Direct Studio in London, augmented video mapping lets visitors design their own one-of-a-kind Nikes and watch the designs come to life before their very eyes. Customers start by placing an all-white version of the Nike Air Force 1 into the NIKEiD Direct configurator—a small booth that serves as the display area. Then, as customers select colors, materials, and patterns from the options on a tablet interface, their selections are projected onto the shoe in real time. Final designs go into production at the NIKEiD factory. Such AR applications can greatly enrich and personalize customer shopping experiences.

Whereas AR augments customers' existing environments, VR immerses them in whole new virtual environments. For example, automaker Audi has installed VR in 1,000 dealer showrooms. Customers use tablets to select any Audi model and customize each element. They then put on a headset and earphones to experience the sights and sounds of their customized car in virtual reality. They can move around the outside of the car, open the trunk and doors, check under the hood, and even sit in the driver's seat. Future versions may even add the cool feel of the leather upholstery and the rich new car smells.

Retailers can use VR to help customers experience products in simulated real-world environments. For example, Walmart is experimenting with VR applications that enhance "the contextual shopping experience." The retail giant's innovation arm—called Store No. 8 (named after an early Walmart store remembered by founder Sam Walton as an "experiment")—recently demonstrated a VR app that allows shoppers to try out camping gear in a virtual Yosemite National Park. "You can see the tent in the environment in which you'll use it," says the head of Store No. 8. "You can unzip the opening, get inside, lay on the ground and say, 'You know what? this is too tight,' then swipe your hand to try another tent." Whereas Walmart doesn't have room to set up even one or two tents in its physical stores, with virtual reality, it can let customers experience its entire inventory. "The ability to have a real-life experience, to see how the tent's fabric is woven and what type of zipper it's using, has the potential to be the next generation of merchandising," adds the Walmart developer.

Beyond using VR to draw shoppers into stores or to give them out-of-store experiences, retailers can use it to bring their stores to shoppers, wherever they might be. For example, you won't likely find a Nike store in a small town. But Nike could create a virtual Nike store and put it anywhere. Using artificial intelligence, such virtual stores could provide interactive experiences personalized to each shopper's demographics, preferences, purchase histories, and actions while navigating the store. Because some VR gear can track exactly what a user is viewing, virtual store apps could use AI to adapt an individual shopper's experience based on what he or she is most interested in. "Right now stores have zero customization, so they're trying to appeal to everyone," says the analyst. "VR solves that."

Wild-eyed VR futurists envision virtual stores—or even real stores—populated by AI-driven salespeople synched to individual shopper characteristics and preferences. Customers in some stores or situations

AR and VR in retailing: Carmaker Audi has installed virtual reality in many of its showrooms, letting customers put on a headset and earphones to experience the sights and sounds of their customized car in realistic virtual environments.
Audi of America

might prefer assistance from a man, others from a woman. Some might need salespeople with a specific look or knowledge set. A physical store can only hire so many salespeople. With virtual reality, stores can create whatever the customer wants. For instance, imagine walking into a Nike store and being approached by a holographic Serena Williams, tennis superstar and Nike spokesperson. You could ask virtual Serena Williams anything, and it would understand and respond personally as the real Williams might.

AR and VR are still in their infancy. The hardware remains expensive and awkward, and the impact of virtual apps on shoppers is still untested and uncertain. Thus, retailers are still only experimenting with these potentially powerful technologies for attracting and engaging customers. But most retailers view AR and VR, fueled by AI, as the wave of the future. Says a VR consultant, "When you take a three-dimensional world like VR or AR and combine that with a smart [AI] system that can replicate a human, suddenly the experience is leaps and bounds ahead of where we've been."[38]

Retailers are also greening up their product assortments. For example, IKEA now sells only LED lighting products in its stores, and a growing proportion of the home furnishing products it sells are made from sustainable and renewable cotton, wood, and other resources. IKEA suppliers must adhere to the retailer's IWAY supplier code of conduct sustainability standards. IKEA's goal is have all of its home furnishings made from renewable, recyclable, or recycled materials. "At IKEA, sustainability is central to our business," says the company, "to ensure that we have a positive impact on people and the planet."

Many retailers have also launched programs that help consumers make more environmentally responsible decisions. Staples's Easy Sustainability Program helps customers to identify green products sold in its stores and to recycle printer cartridges, mobile phones, computers, and other office technology products. Staples recycles some 30 million printer cartridges and 10 million pounds of old technology each year.[38]

Finally, many large retailers are joining forces with suppliers and distributors to create more sustainable products, packaging, and distribution systems. For example, Amazon.com works closely with the producers of many of the products it sells to reduce and simplify their packaging. And beyond its own substantial sustainability initiatives, Walmart wields its huge buying power to urge its army of suppliers to improve their environmental impact and practices. The retailer has even developed a worldwide Sustainable Product Index by which it rates suppliers. It plans to translate the index into a simple rating for consumers to help them make more sustainable buying choices.[39]

Green retailing yields both top- and bottom-line benefits. Sustainable practices lift a retailer's top line by attracting consumers looking to support environmentally friendly sellers and products. They also help the bottom line by reducing costs. For example, Amazon.com's reduced-packaging efforts increase customer convenience and eliminate "wrap rage" while at the same time saving packaging costs. And IKEA's more energy-efficient buildings not only appeal to customers and help save the planet but also cost less to operate.

Global Expansion of Major Retailers

Retailers with unique formats and strong brand positions are increasingly moving into other countries. Many are expanding internationally to escape saturated home markets. Over the years, some giant U.S. retailers, such as McDonald's and Walmart, have become globally prominent because of their marketing prowess.

However, some U.S. retailers are still significantly behind Europe and Asia when it comes to global expansion. Although 10 of the world's top 20 retailers are U.S. companies, only five of these retailers have set up operations outside North America (Walmart, Home Depot, Walgreens, Amazon, and Costco). Of the 10 non-U.S. retailers in the world's top 20, eight have stores in at least 10 countries. Foreign retailers that have gone global include France's Carrefour, Groupe Casino, and Groupe Auchan; Germany's Metro, Lidl, and ALDI chains; Britain's Tesco; and Japan's Seven & I.[40]

International retailing presents challenges as well as opportunities. Retailers can face dramatically different retail environments when crossing countries, continents, and cultures. Simply adapting the operations that work well in the home country is usually not enough to create success abroad. Instead, when going global, retailers must understand and meet the needs of local markets.

Author | Whereas retailers
Comment | primarily sell goods and
services directly to final consumers
for personal use, wholesalers sell
primarily to those buying for resale or
business use. Because wholesalers
operate behind the scenes, they are
largely unknown to final consumers.
But they are very important to their
business customers.

Wholesaling

All the activities involved in selling goods
and services to those buying for resale or
business use.

Wholesaler

A firm engaged *primarily* in wholesaling
activities.

Wholesaling

OBJECTIVE 13-5 Explain the major types of wholesalers and their marketing
decisions.

Wholesaling includes all the activities involved in selling goods and services to those
buying them for resale or business use. Firms engaged *primarily* in wholesaling activities
are called **wholesalers**.

Wholesalers buy mostly from producers and sell mostly to retailers, industrial consumers, and other wholesalers. As a result, many of the nation's largest and most important wholesalers are largely unknown to final consumers. For example, how much do you
know about McKesson, the huge $208 billion diversified health-care-services provider and
the nation's leading wholesaler of pharmaceutical, health and beauty care, home health-
care, and medical supply and equipment products? Or how about wholesaler Arrow
Electronics, which supplies $30 billion worth of computer chips, capacitors, and other
electronics and computer components annually to more than 125,000 original equipment
manufacturers and commercial customers through a global network of more than 465 locations serving over 90 countries? ● And you may never have heard of a company called
Grainger, even though it is very well known and much valued by its more than 3.2 million
business and institutional customers in more than 150 countries:[41]

● **Wholesaling: Many of the nation's largest and most important
wholesalers—like Grainger—are largely unknown to final
consumers. But they are very well known and much valued by the
business customers they serve.**

Kristoffer Tripplaar/Alamy Stock Photo

Grainger may be the biggest market leader you've never heard of.
It's a $10.4 billion business that offers more than 1.6 million main-
tenance, repair, and operating (MRO) products from 5,000 manufacturers to more than 3.2 million active customers. Through its
branch network, service centers, sales reps, catalog, and online and
social media sites, Grainger links customers with the supplies they
need to keep their facilities running smoothly—everything from
light bulbs, cleaners, and display cases to nuts and bolts, motors,
valves, power tools, test equipment, and safety supplies. Grainger's
nearly 600 branches, 33 strategically located distribution centers,
more than 25,000 employees, and innovative web and mobile sites
handle more than 100,000 transactions a day. Grainger's customers
include organizations ranging from factories, garages, and grocers
to schools and military bases.

Grainger operates on a simple value proposition: to make it
easier and less costly for customers to find and buy MRO supplies.
It starts by acting as a one-stop shop for products needed to maintain facilities. On a broader level, it builds lasting relationships with
customers by helping them find *solutions* to their overall MRO problems. Acting as consultants, Grainger sales reps help buyers with
everything from improving their supply chain management to reducing inventories and streamlining warehousing operations. We're
"here to help you build, fix, and move our world," says Grainger.

So, how come you've never heard of Grainger? Perhaps it's because the company operates in the not-so-glamorous world of MRO supplies, which are important to businesses
but not so important to consumers. More likely, it's because Grainger is a wholesaler. And
like most wholesalers, it operates behind the scenes, selling mostly to other businesses.

Why are wholesalers important to sellers? For example, why would a producer use
wholesalers rather than selling directly to retailers or consumers? Simply put, wholesalers
add value by performing one or more of the following channel functions:

- *Selling and promoting.* Wholesalers' sales forces help manufacturers reach many small
customers at a low cost. The wholesaler has more contacts and is often more trusted
by the buyer than the distant manufacturer.
- *Buying and assortment building.* Wholesalers can select items and build assortments
needed by their customers, thereby saving much work.
- *Bulk breaking.* Wholesalers save their customers money by buying in carload lots and
breaking bulk (breaking large lots into small quantities).
- *Warehousing.* Wholesalers hold inventories, thereby reducing the inventory costs and
risks of suppliers and customers.
- *Transportation.* Wholesalers can provide quicker delivery to buyers because they are
closer to buyers than are producers.

- *Financing.* Wholesalers finance their customers by giving credit, and they finance their suppliers by ordering early and paying bills on time.
- *Risk bearing.* Wholesalers absorb risk by taking title and bearing the cost of theft, damage, spoilage, and obsolescence.
- *Market information.* Wholesalers give information to suppliers and customers about competitors, new products, and price developments.
- *Management services and advice.* Wholesalers often help retailers train their salesclerks, improve store layouts and displays, and set up accounting and inventory control systems.

Types of Wholesalers

Merchant wholesaler
An independently owned wholesale business that takes title to the merchandise it handles.

Wholesalers fall into three major groups (see ● Table 13.3): *merchant wholesalers, brokers and agents*, and *manufacturers' and retailers' branches and offices*. **Merchant wholesalers** are the largest single group of wholesalers, accounting for roughly 50 percent of all wholesaling. Merchant wholesalers include two broad types: full-service wholesalers and

● **Table 13.3 | Major Types of Wholesalers**

Type	Description
Merchant wholesalers	Independently owned businesses that take title to all merchandise handled. There are full-service wholesalers and limited-service wholesalers.
Full-service wholesalers	Provide a full line of services: carrying stock, maintaining a sales force, offering credit, making deliveries, and providing management assistance. Full-service wholesalers include wholesale merchants and industrial distributors.
Wholesale merchants	Sell primarily to retailers and provide a full range of services. General merchandise wholesalers carry several merchandise lines, whereas general line wholesalers carry one or two lines in great depth. Specialty wholesalers specialize in carrying only part of a line.
Industrial distributors	Sell to manufacturers rather than to retailers. Provide several services, such as carrying stock, offering credit, and providing delivery. May carry a broad range of merchandise, a general line, or a specialty line.
Limited-service wholesalers	Offer fewer services than full-service wholesalers. Limited-service wholesalers are of several types:
Cash-and-carry wholesalers	Carry a limited line of fast-moving goods and sell to small retailers for cash. Normally do not deliver.
Truck wholesalers (or truck jobbers)	Perform primarily a selling and delivery function. Carry a limited line of semiperishable merchandise (such as milk, bread, snack foods), which is sold for cash as deliveries are made to supermarkets, small groceries, hospitals, restaurants, factory cafeterias, and hotels.
Drop shippers	Do not carry inventory or handle the product. On receiving an order, drop shippers select a manufacturer, who then ships the merchandise directly to the customer. Drop shippers operate in bulk industries, such as coal, lumber, and heavy equipment.
Rack jobbers	Serve grocery and drug retailers, mostly in nonfood items. Rack jobbers send delivery trucks to stores, where the delivery people set up toys, paperbacks, hardware items, health and beauty aids, or other items. Rack jobbers price the goods, keep them fresh, set up point-of-purchase displays, and keep inventory records.
Producers' cooperatives	Farmer-owned members that assemble farm produce for sale in local markets. Producers' cooperatives often attempt to improve product quality and promote a co-op brand name, such as Sun-Maid raisins, Sunkist oranges, or Diamond nuts.
Mail-order or web wholesalers	Send catalogs to or maintain websites for retail, industrial, and institutional customers featuring jewelry, cosmetics, specialty foods, and other small items. Its primary customers are businesses in small outlying areas.

(Continued)

● **Table 13.3 | Major Types of Wholesalers (*Continued*)**

Type	Description
Brokers and agents	Do not take title to goods. The main function is to facilitate buying and selling, for which they earn a commission on the selling price. Generally specialize by product line or customer type.
Brokers	Bring buyers and sellers together and assist in negotiation. Brokers are paid by the party who hired the broker and do not carry inventory, get involved in financing, or assume risk. Examples include food brokers, real estate brokers, insurance brokers, and security brokers.
Agents	Represent either buyers or sellers on a more permanent basis than brokers do. There are four types:
Manufacturers' agents	Represent two or more manufacturers of complementary lines. Often used in such lines as apparel, furniture, and electrical goods. A manufacturer's agent is hired by small manufacturers who cannot afford their own field sales forces and by large manufacturers who use agents to open new territories or cover territories that cannot support full-time salespeople.
Selling agents	Have contractual authority to sell a manufacturer's entire output. The selling agent serves as a sales department and has significant influence over prices, terms, and conditions of sale. Found in product areas such as textiles, industrial machinery and equipment, coal and coke, chemicals, and metals.
Purchasing agents	Generally have a long-term relationship with buyers and make purchases for them, often receiving, inspecting, warehousing, and shipping the merchandise to buyers. Purchasing agents help clients obtain the best goods and prices available.
Commission merchants	Take physical possession of products and negotiate sales. Used most often in agricultural marketing by farmers who do not want to sell their own output. Take a truckload of commodities to a central market, sell it for the best price, deduct a commission and expenses, and remit the balance to the producers.
Manufacturers' and retailers' branches and offices	Wholesaling operations conducted by sellers or buyers themselves rather than operating through independent wholesalers. Separate branches and offices can be dedicated to either sales or purchasing.
Sales branches and offices	Set up by manufacturers to improve inventory control, selling, and promotion. Sales branches carry inventory and are found in industries such as lumber and automotive equipment and parts. Sales offices do not carry inventory and are most prominent in the dry goods and notions industries.
Purchasing offices	Perform a role similar to that of brokers or agents but are part of the buyer's organization. Many retailers set up purchasing offices in major market centers, such as New York and Chicago.

Broker

A wholesaler who does not take title to goods and whose function is to bring buyers and sellers together and assist in negotiation.

Agent

A wholesaler who represents buyers or sellers on a relatively permanent basis, performs only a few functions, and does not take title to goods.

Manufacturers' and retailers' branches and offices

Wholesaling by sellers or buyers themselves rather than through independent wholesalers.

limited-service wholesalers. *Full-service wholesalers* provide a full set of services, whereas the various *limited-service wholesalers* offer fewer services to their suppliers and customers. The different types of limited-service wholesalers perform varied specialized functions in the distribution channel.

Brokers and *agents* differ from merchant wholesalers in two ways: They do not take title to goods, and they perform only a few functions. Like merchant wholesalers, they generally specialize by product line or customer type. A **broker** brings buyers and sellers together and assists in negotiation. **Agents** represent buyers or sellers on a more permanent basis. *Manufacturers' agents* (also called *manufacturers' representatives*) are the most common type of agent wholesaler. The third major type of wholesaling is that done in **manufacturers' and retailers' branches and offices** by sellers or buyers themselves rather than through independent wholesalers.

Wholesaler Marketing Decisions

Wholesalers now face growing competitive pressures, more-demanding customers, new technologies, and more direct-buying programs on the part of large industrial, institutional, and retail buyers. As a result, they have taken a fresh look at their marketing strategies. As with retailers, their marketing decisions include choices of segmentation and targeting, differentiation and positioning, and the marketing mix—product and service assortments, price, promotion, and distribution (see ● **Figure 13.2**).

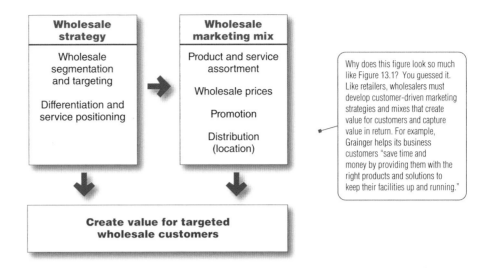

● FIGURE 13.2
Wholesaler Marketing Strategies

Segmentation, Targeting, Differentiation, and Positioning Decisions

Like retailers, wholesalers must segment and define their target markets and differentiate and position themselves effectively—they cannot serve everyone. They can choose a target group by size of customer (for example, large retailers only), type of customer (convenience stores only), the need for service (customers who need credit), or other factors. Within the target group, they can identify the more profitable customers, design stronger offers, and build better relationships with them. They can propose automatic reordering systems, establish management-training and advisory systems, or even sponsor a voluntary chain. They can discourage less-profitable customers by requiring larger orders or adding service charges to smaller ones.

Marketing Mix Decisions

Like retailers, wholesalers must decide on product and service assortments, prices, promotion, and place. Wholesalers add customer value though the *products and services* they offer. They are often under great pressure to carry a full line and stock enough for immediate delivery. But this practice can damage profits. Wholesalers today are cutting down on the number of lines they carry, choosing to carry only the more profitable ones. They are also rethinking which services count most in building strong customer relationships and which should be dropped or paid for by the customer. The key for companies is to find the mix of services most valued by their target customers.

Price is also an important wholesaler decision. Wholesalers usually mark up the cost of goods by a standard percentage and operate on small margins. As retail and industrial customers face increasing costs and margins pressures, they turn to wholesalers, looking for lower prices. Wholesalers may, in turn, cut their margins on some lines to keep important customers. They may also ask suppliers for special price breaks in cases when they can turn them into an increase in the supplier's sales.

Although *promotion* can be critical to wholesaler success, most wholesalers are not promotion minded. They have historically used largely scattered and unplanned trade advertising, sales promotion, personal selling, and public relations. Like other business-to-business marketers, wholesalers need to make a team effort to sell, build, and service major accounts. Wholesalers also need to adopt some of the nonpersonal promotion techniques used by retailers. They need to develop an overall promotion strategy and make greater use of supplier promotion materials and programs.

Digital and social media are playing an increasingly important role in wholesaler promotion. For example, Grainger maintains an active presence on Facebook, YouTube, Twitter, LinkedIn, and Instagram. It also provides a feature-rich mobile app. On its YouTube channel, Grainger lists more than 700 videos on topics ranging from the company and its products and services to keeping down inventory costs.

Finally, *distribution* (location) is important. Wholesalers must choose their locations, facilities, and other locations carefully. There was a time when wholesalers could locate in low-rent, low-tax areas and invest little money in their buildings, equipment, and systems. Today, however, as technology zooms forward, such behavior results in outdated systems for material handling, order processing, and delivery.

Instead, today's large and progressive wholesalers have reacted to rising costs by investing in automated warehouses and IT systems. Orders are fed from the retailer's information system directly into the wholesaler's, and the items are picked up by mechanical devices and automatically taken to a shipping platform where they are assembled. Most large wholesalers use technology to carry out accounting, billing, inventory control, and forecasting. Modern wholesalers are adapting their services to the needs of target customers and finding cost-reducing methods of doing business. They are also transacting more business online. For example, e-commerce is Grainger's fastest-growing sales channel. Online and mobile purchasing now account for more than half of the wholesaler's total sales.[42]

Trends in Wholesaling

Today's wholesalers face considerable challenges. The industry remains vulnerable to one of its most enduring trends—the need for ever-greater efficiency. Tight economic conditions and retailer woes have led to demands for even lower prices and the winnowing out of suppliers who are not adding value based on cost and quality. Progressive wholesalers constantly watch for better ways to meet the changing needs of their suppliers and target customers. They recognize that their only reason for existence comes from adding value, which occurs by increasing the efficiency and effectiveness of the entire marketing channel.

As with other types of marketers, the goal is to build value-adding customer relationships. ● For example, consider Sysco, the $55 billion wholesale food distribution company that operates behind the scenes to supply more than 425,000 restaurants, schools, hospitals, colleges, and other commercial customers that prepare meals away from home.[43]

● Giant food distribution wholesaler Sysco lives up to its "Good things come from Sysco" motto by procuring and delivering food and food service supplies more dependably, efficiently, and cheaply than customers could ever hope to do on their own.

Sysco Corporation

Whether it's a hot dog from Reliant Stadium in Houston, the original Italian sub from Jersey Mike's, crab cakes from a Hilton Hotel, or a ham and cheese sandwich at the local hospital cafeteria, the chances are good that the ingredients were supplied by Sysco, the nation's top food supplier. Sysco supplies anything and everything needed to run an eating establishment, from boxes of seafood, chicken, and beef to 25-pound bags of rice or pasta to gallon jars of ketchup or salsa to boxes of plastic gloves and jugs of dishwashing detergent. What makes Sysco so valuable to its customers is that it procures and delivers these supplies more dependably, efficiently, and cheaply than customers could ever hope to do on their own.

For example, Lowell's, the iconic restaurant in Seattle's Pike Place Market, procures almost all of its products conveniently through the Sysco Market online ordering system. Its orders are processed quickly and accurately at Sysco's automated distribution center. Then Lowell's—by itself or with the help of Sysco sales associates and dispatchers—can track the location of individual deliveries via the My Sysco Truck program. Sysco constantly seeks new ways to add more value and build trust, from product traceability for safety to sourcing products from local, small to mid-sized farms, ranches, and processors to serve the needs of customers whose businesses are positioned on sustainability and community. In short, Sysco more than lives up to its motto: "Good things come from Sysco."

The distinction between large retailers and large wholesalers continues to blur. Many retailers now operate formats such as wholesale clubs and supercenters that perform many wholesale functions. In return, some large wholesalers are setting up their own retailing operations. For example, SuperValu is one of the nation's largest food wholesalers, and it's also one of the country's largest food retailers. About one-third of the company's sales come from its Cub Foods, Farm Fresh, Hornbacher's, Shop 'n Save, and Shoppers stores.[44]

Wholesalers will continue to increase the services they provide to retailers—retail pricing, cooperative advertising, marketing and management information services, accounting services, online transactions, and others. However, both the more value-focused environment and the demand for increased services have put the squeeze on wholesaler profits. Wholesalers that do not find efficient ways to deliver value to their customers will soon drop by the wayside. Fortunately, the increased use of computerized, automated, and internet-based systems will help wholesalers contain the costs of ordering, shipping, and inventory holding, thus boosting their productivity.

Reviewing and Extending the Concepts

Objectives Review

Retailing and wholesaling consist of many organizations bringing goods and services from the point of production to the point of use. In this chapter, we examined the nature and importance of retailing, the major types of retailers, the decisions retailers make, and the future of retailing. We then examined these same topics for wholesalers.

OBJECTIVE 13-1 Explain the role of retailers in the distribution channel and describe the major types of retailers. *(pp 376–383)*

Retailing includes all the activities involved in selling goods or services directly to final consumers for their personal, non-business use. Retailers play an important role in connecting brands to consumers in the final phases of the buying process. *Shopper marketing* involves focusing the entire marketing process on turning shoppers into buyers as they move along toward the point of sale, whether during in-store, online, or mobile shopping.

Recent dramatic shifts in how today's connected consumers shop and buy have caused a massive upheaval in the retailing industry. Today's buyers are omni-channel consumers who work across multiple channels as they shop, changing the role of retail stores in the buying process. As Amazon and other online merchants have boomed, traditional store retailers have struggled. Successful retailers of the future must adopt *omni-channel retailing*, creating a seamless cross-channel buying experience that integrates in-store, online, and mobile shopping.

Retail stores come in all shapes and sizes, and new retail types keep emerging. Store retailers can be classified by the *amount of service* they provide (self-service, limited service, or full service), *product line sold* (specialty stores, department stores, supermarkets, convenience stores, superstores, and service businesses), and *relative prices* (discount stores and off-price retailers). Today, many retailers are banding together in corporate and contractual *retail organizations* (corporate chains, voluntary chains, retailer cooperatives, and franchise organizations).

OBJECTIVE 13-2 Discuss how retailers are using omni-channel retailing to meet the cross-channel shopping behavior of today's digitally connected consumers. *(pp 383–385)*

The retail shopping process has changed radically in this age of websites, smartphones, mobile apps, social media, and other things digital. Today's omni-channel buyers shift easily across online and in-store channels throughout the buying process. They readily research products and prices online, shopping digitally from home, from work, in stores, or anywhere in between. This massive shift in how people shop calls for massive changes in how store retailers operate. Omni-channel *buying* calls for omni-channel *retailing*, integrating all available shopping channels and devices into a seamless customer shopping experience.

Omni-channel retailing goes beyond just helping in-store customers as they cross-shop on mobile devices. It requires carefully integrating the entire range of available shopping channels, both in-store and out, from discovery to purchase in the buying process. To that end, most large retailers are now boosting their online and digital selling options and linking them with stores. The key is to integrate these elements to create the critical seamless, anywhere, anytime, omni-channel shopping experience that today's customers seek.

OBJECTIVE 13-3 Describe the major retailer marketing decisions. *(pp 385–392)*

Retailers are always searching for new marketing strategies to attract and hold customers. They face major marketing decisions about segmentation and targeting, store differentiation and positioning, and the retail marketing mix.

Retailers must first segment and define their target markets and then decide how they will differentiate and position themselves in these markets. Those that try to offer "something for everyone" end up satisfying no market well. By contrast, successful retailers define their target markets well and position themselves strongly.

Guided by strong targeting and positioning, retailers must decide on a retail marketing mix—product and services assortment, price, promotion, and place. Retail stores are much more than simply an assortment of goods. Beyond the products and services they offer, today's successful retailers carefully orchestrate virtually every aspect of the consumer store experience. A retailer's price policy must fit its target market and positioning, products and services assortment, and competition. Retailers use various combinations of the five promotion tools—advertising, personal selling, sales promotion, PR, and direct and digital marketing—to reach consumers. Online, mobile, and social media tools are playing an ever-increasing role in helping retailers to engage customers. Finally, it's very important that retailers select locations that are accessible to the target market in areas that are consistent with the retailer's positioning.

OBJECTIVE 13-4 Discuss the major trends and developments in retailing. *(pp 392–397)*

Retailers operate in a harsh and fast-changing environment, which offers threats as well as opportunities. Following years of good economic times, retailers have now adjusted to the new economic realities and more thrift-minded consumers. New retail forms continue to emerge. At the same time, however, different types of retailers are increasingly serving similar customers with the same products and prices (retail convergence), making differentiation more difficult. Other trends in retailing include the rise of megaretailers, the growing importance of retail technology, a surge in green retailing, and the global expansion of major retailers.

OBJECTIVE 13-5 Explain the major types of wholesalers and their marketing decisions. *(pp 398–403)*

Wholesaling includes all the activities involved in selling goods or services to those who are buying for resale or business use. Wholesalers fall into three groups. First, *merchant wholesalers* take possession of the goods. They include *full-service wholesalers* and *limited-service wholesalers*. Second, *brokers* and *agents* do not take possession of the goods but are paid a commission for aiding companies in buying and selling. Finally, *manufacturers' and retailers' branches and offices* are wholesaling operations conducted by non-wholesalers to bypass the wholesalers.

Like retailers, wholesalers must target carefully and position themselves strongly. And, like retailers, wholesalers must decide on product and service assortments, prices, promotion, and place. Progressive wholesalers constantly watch for better ways to meet the changing needs of their suppliers and target customers. They recognize that, in the long run, their only reason for existence comes from adding value, which occurs by increasing the efficiency and effectiveness of the entire marketing channel. As with other types of marketers, the goal is to build value-adding customer relationships.

Key Terms

OBJECTIVE 13-1

Retailing (p 376)
Retailer (p 376)
Shopper marketing (p 376)
Omni-channel retailing (p 377)
Specialty store (p 379)
Department store (p 379)
Supermarket (p 379)
Convenience store (p 380)
Superstore (p 380)
Category killer (p 380)

Service retailer (p 380)
Discount store (p 380)
Off-price retailer (p 381)
Independent off-price retailer (p 381)
Factory outlet (p 381)
Warehouse club (p 381)
Corporate chains (p 383)
Franchise (p 383)

OBJECTIVE 13-3

Shopping center (p 391)

OBJECTIVE 13-5

Wholesaling (p 398)
Wholesaler (p 398)
Merchant wholesaler (p 399)
Broker (p 400)
Agent (p 400)
Manufacturers' and retailers' branches and offices (p 400)

Discussion Questions

13-1 Define *omni-channel retailing* and explain its connection to *shopper marketing*. (AACSB: Written and Oral Communication)

13-2 How would you describe the process of devising a workable retail marketing mix? (AACSB: Communication)

13-3 Distinguish between a warehouse club and a factory outlet. What is distinctive about them?

13-4 Does a business need agents and brokers? (AACSB: Communication; Reflective Thinking)

13-5 List and describe the functions wholesalers perform that add value to both retailers and consumers. (AACSB: Written and Oral Communication)

13-6 Discuss the marketing mix decisions faced by wholesalers. What current challenges do wholesalers face? (AACSB: Written and Oral Communication)

Critical Thinking Exercises

13-7 You need a new pair of jeans, and you have many retail options. Using the information in your text, choose three different major store retailer types and select a specific store for each type chosen. Visit each store (in person or online) and describe each store's segmentation and positioning strategy and retail marketing mix—product, price, place, and promotion. How do the product assortments differ? What is each store's pricing approach? What promotional tools are used? Discuss store locations. (AACSB: Written and Oral Communication; Reflective Thinking; Information Technology)

13-8 In a small group, present a plan for a new retail store. Who is the store's target market? Describe the merchandise, atmospherics, price points, services provided, location, and how you would promote your retail store. Describe how you will differentiate your store from competitors. (AACSB: Written and Oral Communication; Reflective Thinking)

13-9 In a small group, present a plan for a new wholesaler. Identify and describe what type of wholesaler it will be, the target market it will serve, and which channel functions it will provide to add value to its target market. (AACSB: Written and Oral Communication; Reflective Thinking)

APPLICATIONS AND CASES

Online, Mobile, and Social Media Marketing Kohl's Courts Millennials with Merchandise Curated by Social Media Influencers

Kohl's developed shopper loyalty among middle-aged moms but had challenges appealing to millennials. Millennial fashion trends are often driven by social media influencers. Further, millennials are comfortable shopping online and do not want to waste time roaming around in big-box retailers looking for the right sizes and styles. Based on feedback from millennials, Kohl's launched an "Outfit Bar" that was inspired by Pinterest. Kohl's customers can shop online or in the store for outfits and find their favorite "look." The in-store experience features signage and merchandise that seem tailor-made for Instagram. The online site has a companion landing page that lets customers shop by outfit. Social media personalities will curate the Outfit Bar selections, which will be updated every 30 days with new looks.

13-10 What benefits and challenges will Kohl's have in introducing its Outfit Bar? (AACSB: Written and Oral Communication; Information Technology; Reflective Thinking)

13-11 If a Kohl's Outfit Bar was available at a location near you, would your friends use it? Why or why not? Based on your response, what advice would you give Kohl's management in advance of rolling out the Outfit Bar initiative nationwide? (AACSB: Written and Oral Communication; Reflective Thinking)

Marketing Ethics Footloose and Tax-Free

In the United Kingdom, in the summer of 2013, there were mass protests against several global brands operating in the country. Starbucks, Google, Amazon, and Vodafone immediately came under fire. Shortly afterward, the Arcadia Group, Boots, and Fortnum & Mason were singled out for attention. The reason: they were all avoiding paying UK taxes on UK sales. Everything they were doing was legal, however; it was tax avoidance, not tax evasion. Starbucks, despite sales of almost $500 million, had paid no corporation tax. It was instead paying royalties to a Dutch sister company, buying coffee beans in Switzerland, and paying extortionate interest on loans to other parts of the business. Meanwhile, Amazon, enjoying sales of $5.5 billion, had somehow contrived to pay less than $3 million in tax. Similarly, Google, with a turnover of $640 million, had paid under $10 million in tax. How is this legally achieved? The first tried-and-tested method is to locate facilities in low-tax jurisdictions, as when Starbucks located its coffee wholesaling business in Switzerland. Google's UK operation is actually based in the Republic of Ireland and Bermuda. The second method is known as transfer pricing. By locating factories, services, and distribution in low-tax countries, the business is able to bill the subsidiary in a high-tax country. In effect, the money is siphoned out of the high-tax country into a low-tax one.

13-12 Why do global businesses use such strategies? Are the financial benefits greater than the loss in customer confidence and trust? (AACSB: Communication; Reflective Thinking)

13-13 Consider the Marketplace Fairness Act of 2013, which would enable state governments in the United States to collect sales taxes from online retailers. How do you think such an act would impact small retailers? (AACSB: Communication; Ethical Reasoning; Reflective Thinking)

Marketing by the Numbers Grocery Stores Offering Meal Kits

Half of Americans' food dollars are spent eating out, and many meals eaten at home are not actually cooked there, trends that are eating into grocery store sales. More recently, firms such as HelloFresh, Blue Apron, Plated, and others have begun delivering meal kits that include premeasured ingredients to be cooked at home, further eroding grocery store sales. Although the meal kit industry has exploded to $2 billion in annual sales, it has had problems achieving scale and profitability. To combat this, Blue Apron and HelloFresh are distributing meals kits through supermarkets and wholesale clubs. Other meal kit firms are being acquired by grocery chains. For example, Kroger, the largest U.S. supermarket chain, purchased Home Chef, the largest privately owned meal kit company. In addition to increasing its online delivery, Kroger also intends to sell meal kits in its stores. However, the meal kit business could be difficult for Kroger. Online subscription meal kit operators have found that it's not good to offer too many recipe options. But how many different recipes are optimal? Kroger thinks that its no-subscription requirement and price ($14 to $18 for a two-person meal kit compared to $50 or more for regular home-delivery meal kits) will attract more sales. But finding the right balance of kit offerings and stocking

levels is challenging. Not stocking enough merchandise—in this case varied meal kits—results in lost sales. But carrying too much inventory increases costs and lowers margins, especially because of perishability. Both conditions reduce profits. One measure of a reseller's inventory management effectiveness is its *stockturn rate* (also called *inventory turnover rate* for manufacturers). Retailers want to realize a large volume of sales on as little inventory as possible while maintaining enough stock to meet customer demand. To determine this, Kroger ran several market tests in selected stores to determine the optimum inventory levels.

13-14 Using the data below, determine Kroger's weekly stockturn rate for meal kits during one of the market tests. Refer to Analytic Ratios in Appendix 2: Marketing by the Numbers to learn how to calculate stockturn rate. (AACSB: Analytical Reasoning)

13-15 Interpret your answers from the previous question. Is Kroger's weekly stockturn rate good or bad? What factors should be considered to determine this? (AACSB: Communication; Reflective Thinking)

Company Case Ulta Beauty: Where the Experience Is Beautiful

In today's retail environment, there is plenty of buzz about the "retail apocalypse"—the growing phenomenon that will likely result in more than 6,000 brick-and-mortar chain store closings this year. Numerous longtime specialty retailers such as Radio Shack, Sports Authority, Toys "R" Us, and Payless Shoe Source have gone out of business in recent years. Still others such as The Gap, J.Crew, and Victoria's Secret have been closing stores and showing signs of distress. And once massive general merchandise retailers such as Sears and JCPenney have been shrinking for years, leaving many to speculate that they will soon be out of business entirely.

But all the buzz about ailing retail chains overlooks the retail areas that are thriving. And it's more than e-commerce. Plenty of brick-and-mortar chains are booming. One such company is Ulta Beauty—the largest U.S. beauty retailer and the premier destination for cosmetics, fragrance, skin care products, hair care products, and salon services. Not only is Ulta the market leader, its revenues have doubled in the past four years as the chain grew from 874 to nearly 1,200 stores. What's the secret to Ulta's success? Customers of all kinds enthusiastically flock to Ulta because, more than any other retailer, the chain offers a complete beauty experience.

Ulta opened its first store more than 27 years ago. But until a handful of years ago, Ulta operated quietly in the shadow of former leading beauty retailer Sephora. Ulta's sales were good, but the company had a lackluster market presence and a tepid brand image. It had always operated as a beauty superstore where shoppers could find hundreds of beauty brands. But that wasn't enough set it apart from rivals—discount merchandise megachains such as Walmart and Target and the increasingly growing presence of online behemoth Amazon. It wasn't until Mary Dillon took over as Ulta's CEO that the brand really started to shine.

Strengthening Its Competitive Advantage

Dillon built a strategy that capitalizes on competitive advantages that store-based beauty retailers have over online competitors.

Shopping for beauty products is a deeply personal, uniquely emotional experience. Only in a real-world store can customers perfectly match a shade, see how a fragrance suits them, or feel the effects of a product's performance. Customers often need advice about options or instructions on using products, something the online world has yet to perfect. And when a person needs a product *immediately*, even same-day delivery will not suit.

Dillon's strategy amplifies the "personal" and "emotional" elements of the beauty shopping experience. For starters, Ulta invested heavily to hire, train, and reward the right employees, creating an army of frontline associates who not only welcome customers but make them feel at home. Ulta employees are pros at reading customers, understanding their needs and motives, and making recommendations that feel perfect to them. In turn, this builds trust, and trust increases the time and money customers spend in a store.

To make stores more fulfilling, Ulta also created an unparalleled product assortment. It boasts of "more than 25,000 products from approximately 500 brands." But that's only part of the product story. Ulta also focuses on introducing hot, new cosmetic brands such as Morphe, Revolution Beauty, and Jeffree Star, many with exclusive distribution rights. For example, until last year, the exploding Kylie Cosmetics brand was available only through its own online store. But Ulta scored a huge victory by becoming the only physical store chain to carry the brand's growing beauty portfolio. With one of the biggest and youngest social media followings, Kylie Cosmetics is a perfect example of brands that have increased Ulta's store traffic and sales. Such "gotta-have-it" new brands are bringing in younger consumers, giving Ulta a strong base across all age demographics.

Ulta has developed other enticements to enhance the shopping experience. Cosmetic shoppers love samples. Not only are they free, samples let customers try a product for a limited time to see how they like it. Although most beauty retailers provide instore "testers" as well as mini versions of products to take home, they do so only for higher-end brands. But Ulta offers samples across a wider range of products than other retailers, including so-called "drugstore" brands such as Maybelline and CoverGirl.

Beyond its amazing selection of goods, Ulta distinguishes itself by offering in-store services such as haircuts and facials. This not only drives store traffic and generates additional revenue, the sights, sounds, and smells of these services enhance the energy level in stores. Ulta's data shows that salon services guests spend almost three times as much as other customers. This prompted Dillon to move the Benefit Brow Bar—a station for eyebrow shaping—to the front of the store so that shoppers would see services being performed the moment they enter. It worked. Salon sales increased by 15 percent in just nine months following this move.

The Power of Rewards

One of Dillon's strongest strategy moves is the makeover of Ulta's previously stale loyalty program. Now with well over 30 million active members, the newly branded Ultamate Rewards program is far more simple and engaging. Like any good loyalty program, the new and improved Ultamate Rewards positively affects the customer experience in multiple ways. For starters, rather than simply tossing out gratuitous giveaways, it lets Ulta use pricing as a relationship-building tool. Rather than the former blunt-force approach that doled out freebies for reaching certain points milestones, Ultamate Rewards now lets customers use their accumulated points as store credit for items of their own choosing. This not only gives customers more autonomy, it lets them apply points to high-end brands such as Urban Decay—brands that never go on sale.

Ultamate Rewards also lets Ulta interact with each customer in a personal way. It can design messages, incentives, and rewards to suit individuals based on all the information in company databases, including shopping history. "There's a lot of information we have to work with to deliver that targeted offer to the right person," says Ulta's director of loyalty marketing. "The majority of our promotions and engagement with guests has transitioned to the loyalty program, so we're now creating even more value in the currency around points and the ability to accrue them toward other products." As icing on the cake, Ulta can pair Ultamate Rewards with a company credit card for an immediate customer benefit of double-points. The new rewards program is working well. Ultamate Rewards membership grew more than 14 percent last year, and rewards members account for a whopping 90 percent of company sales.

Ulta's chain of brick-and-mortar stores give it substantial competitive advantage. However, the chain also has a strong e-commerce presence, making it a true omni-channel retailer. When it comes to online beauty products sales, Amazon is far-and-away the leader. In fact, Beauty and Personal Care is Amazon's second-most-shopped category and one of its fastest-growing ones. But in addition to lacking face-to-face interaction with customers, Amazon makes a sizable portion of its cosmetics sales through third-party vendors, priced 35-to-40 percent higher than the same products at Ulta. Even with its massive scale, Amazon achieved less than two-thirds Ulta's revenue in beauty products last year. And of all beauty products Amazon sells, cosmetics is showing the lowest growth.

Although Dillon believes that building physical stores is critical to the company's growth, she is equally committed to boosting Ulta's online shopping experience. Recent investments in Ulta's distribution system have dramatically improved its e-commerce processing. But Ulta has also made major improvements in its online customer interface with an infusion of tutorials, tips, and social content. "People want to buy online, and they want to come into the store and try things," says Dillon. She notes that Ulta can more effectively guide customers through the shopping process and into new experiences online than in stores. Although Ulta has yet to break the billion-dollar mark in online revenues, its e-commerce business is growing far more rapidly than in-store sales. Thus, e-commerce is both a key part of the Ulta customer experience and a major contributor to the company's financial performance.

Under Dillon's guidance, Ulta has now put the customer experience at the forefront in all aspects of its retail business. This focus has played a key role in helping the company to escape the negative effects of the "retail apocalypse." More broadly, beauty and cosmetics remains a genuine growth industry. While Ulta is the market leader, Sephora continues to do well even as Amazon thrives. So long as Ulta focuses on continually improving the customer experience, its future looks as bright and vibrant as the palettes of colors throughout its stores.[45]

Questions for Discussion

13-16 Describe Ulta Beauty's targeting strategy. Does the chain provide a truly differentiated customer experience?

13-17 How did Ulta Beauty become the nation's leading beauty retailer based on the retail marketing mix.

13-18 In terms of the major types of retailers, how would you classify Ulta Beauty?

13-19 Can Ulta Beauty continue to maintain its edge against the competition in coming years? Explain.

14

Engaging Consumers and Communicating Customer Value
Integrated Marketing Communications Strategy

OBJECTIVES OUTLINE

OBJECTIVE 14-1 Define the five promotion mix tools for communicating customer value. **See: The Promotion Mix** *(pp 410–411)*

OBJECTIVE 14-2 Discuss the changing communications landscape and the need for integrated marketing communications. **See: Integrated Marketing Communications** *(pp 411–416)*

OBJECTIVE 14-3 Outline the communication process and the steps in developing effective marketing communications. **See: Developing Effective Marketing Communication** *(pp 416–422)*

OBJECTIVE 14-4 Explain the methods for setting the promotion budget and factors that affect the design of the promotion mix. **See: Setting the Total Promotion Budget and Mix** *(pp 422–429)*

CHAPTER PREVIEW In this and the next three chapters, we'll examine the last of the marketing mix tools—promotion. Companies must do more than just create customer value. They must also clearly and persuasively communicate that value. Promotion is not a single tool but rather a mix of several tools. Ideally, under the concept of *integrated marketing communications,* a company will carefully coordinate these promotion elements to engage customers and build clear, consistent, and compelling messages and content about an organization and its products.

We'll begin by introducing the various promotion mix tools. Next, we'll examine the rapidly changing communications environment—especially the addition of digital, mobile, and social media—and the need for integrated marketing communications.

Finally, we'll discuss the steps in developing marketing communications and the promotion budgeting process. In the next three chapters, we'll present the specific marketing communications tools: advertising and public relations (Chapter 15); personal selling and sales promotion (Chapter 16); and direct, online, mobile, and social media marketing (Chapter 17).

Let's start by looking at good integrated marketing communications in action at Burger King. The world's number-two burger chain has mastered the art and science of blending traditional media channels with the latest digital, mobile, and social media platforms to create bold and edgy campaigns that engage consumers, support its Home of the Whopper positioning, win industry awards, and feed steady growth in today's fiercely competitive quick-service food industry.

BURGER KING: Anything but Traditional Integrated Marketing Communications

Burger King is the world's second-largest fast-food hamburger chain behind industry leader McDonald's. But although Burger King trails in sales, it routinely dominates McDonald's when it comes to innovative, attention-getting, and effective marketing communications. Year after year, Burger King runs a seemingly unending series of award-winning campaigns, with bold, edgy promotions that pique the imagination, engage brand fans and the public, and keep the Burger King brand fresh and contemporary.

Although Burger King's often whacky campaigns might strike some observers as impetuous or even reckless, they unite around long-held positioning themes that set Burger King apart from competitors. Burger King is "Home of the Whopper," the iconic "flame-grilled, 100% beef" creation that keeps loyal customers coming back. It's a place where you can "have it your way"—every Whopper is prepared to order by hand. And then there's "The King"—Burger King's quirky, ceramic-headed robed mascot, who routinely pops up in unexpected places.

Burger King campaigns are anything but traditional; brand fans have learned to expect the unexpected. Many of the chain's campaigns are built around provocative stunts and pranks. But more than just naive one-off stunts, the campaigns use a rich, carefully integrated mix of traditional and digital media for maximum impact. One example is the classic Whopper Freakout campaign, now more than a decade old but still much remembered. To celebrate the 50th anniversary of the Whopper, Burger King set out to show what would happen if it suddenly removed the sandwich from its menu "forever." It dropped the Whopper in selected restaurants and used hidden cameras to capture the real-time reactions of stricken customers. It then shared the results in an integrated, multipronged promotional campaign.

The campaign began with coordinated TV, print, and radio spots announcing, "We stopped selling the Whopper for one day to see what would happen. …What happened was, people freaked!" The ads drove consumers to whopperfreakout.com, which featured a video documentary outlining the entire experiment. The documentary was also uploaded to YouTube and other social media. At the website, visitors could view hilarious Freakout ads showing the disbelieving, often angry, and sometimes profane reactions of a dozen or more customers. Customers themselves extended the campaign with spoofs and parodies posted on YouTube.

Whopper Freakout became the most recalled campaign in Burger King's history. It won a Grand Effie—the marketing industry's highest award for marketing effectiveness. The whopperfreakout.com website site received 4 million views in only the first three months, and the campaign drove store traffic and sales of the Whopper up a whopping 29 percent.

Burger King has created any number of imaginative sources for advertising content. For example, to drive home the flame-grilled qualities of its burgers, the chain recently launched a Twitter

Burger King's often wacky campaigns might strike some observers as impetuous or even reckless. But they unite around the long-held positioning that Burger King is "Home of the Whopper," the iconic "flame-grilled, 100% beef" creation that keeps loyal customers coming back.

dpa picture alliance/Alamy Stock Photo

campaign enticing customers with a free Whopper for "burning" its rivals' ads using augmented reality on the Burger King app. "After all," the promotion concluded, "flame-grilled is always better." In another effort, last year on Good Samaritan Day the chain posted a video showing a car on fire at the side of a desert highway—a vintage convertible, hood propped up, smoke pouring out, and a driver trying to wave down help. But when passers-by stopped to give aid, they didn't find an engine fire under the hood. Instead, it was the Burger King flipping patties on a flaming grill where the engine was supposed to be. The video went viral and generated a lot of media coverage.

Yet another flame-grilling campaign—"Burning Stores"—consisted of a series of print ads with striking pictures of actual Burger King stores on fire, firefighters and all, with the simple headline "Flame-grilled since 1954." Together, the images and headline created what one analyst called a perfect "a-ha" moment in readers. Industry experts agreed: The "Burning Stores" campaign won a prestigious Cannes Grand Prix advertising award.

Burger King has mastered the art and science of blending traditional and new-age digital platforms. For example, consider its brief but sophisticated "Google Home of the Whopper" campaign. The campaign began with a 15-second TV spot in which a Burger King employee explained that the ad's short length didn't give him time to say fully what makes the Whopper so great. Instead, he leans into the camera and says, "Okay Google, what is the Whopper burger?" That phrase,

> Year after year, Burger King runs a seemingly unending series of award-winning, bold, and edgy integrated marketing communications campaigns that engage brand fans and keep the Burger King brand fresh and contemporary.

blasted out on TVs, laptops, and mobile devices, triggered the Google Assistant on Google Home devices across the nation, prompting them to read aloud the Wikipedia entry for Burger King's Whopper.

Google responded quickly, shutting down the Whopper search. But Burger King was ready with additional spots on late-night talk shows using alternative key words targeting Google Home devices. The campaign was brief, but the effect was massive. With Burger King and the Whopper at center stage, media headlines, bloggers, and the social media engaged in heated debates about privacy, the vulnerability of technology, and the role of advertising in a rapidly evolving digital world. The campaign's genius earned Burger King $135 million worth of measured media coverage and more top creative honors at Cannes.

The "Google Home of the Whopper" campaign also supported the notion that some of the most effective promotions are those that people initially find annoying. In that regard, Burger King isn't afraid to take risks with its marketing content—in fact, it seems to relish controversy. For example, consider the brand's Super Bowl LIII ad, "Eat Like Andy," a 45-second spot consisting of vintage footage of pop artist Andy Warhol seated at a table quietly eating a Whopper. Following the big game, Burger King posted the TV ad along with a four-and-a-half-minute video version on its web and social media channels. In an ad showcase like the Super Bowl, alongside a host of best-of-the-best ads, Burger King's "Eat Like Andy" left most viewers scratching their heads. The *USA Today* ad meter ranked it number 58—dead last. Media tracker Ace Metrix revealed that the Warhol ad scored second in two categories—"Eerie" and "WTF."

"We're proud of that," said Burger King's chief marketer. "Ad meter was never our objective. The whole campaign was designed to create conversation." Mission accomplished. People in droves shared #EatLikeAndy images, memes, and videos; wondered if Andy Warhol was still alive and why he was eating a Whopper; and debated whether that was the real Warhol or just an actor. One artist posted framed prints from the spot priced at $7,292—the speculated price of the airtime for a single frame of the 45-second ad. Despite initial confusion and negative reactions, later surveys showed that, among those who viewed the ad, positive Burger King buzz soared 36 percent overall and 52 percent among the coveted 18-to-34 age group. The ad also earned more than 4 billion media impressions. "We've never seen such a strong shift in brand attributes like what we've seen with this campaign," says the Burger King marketer.

In just the past two years, Burger King's wacky but well-crafted integrated marketing communications campaigns have earned the chain a trophy cabinet full of some of the most prestigious awards in the advertising industry, including Cannes' Creative Marketer of the Year, *Advertising Age*'s Innovator of the Year, and *Ad Week*'s Grand Brand Genius. And thanks in large part to Burger King's award-winning promotional campaigns, even as McDonald's revenue growth has stagnated in recent years, Burger King's systemwide sales have grown at an average 9 percent annually. In a competitive environment bustling with healthier, fresher-fare fast-casual restaurants and premium cult-loved burger chains like Smashburger, Five Guys, and The Habit, that's a whopper of an accomplishment.[1]

• •

BUILDING GOOD CUSTOMER RELATIONSHIPS calls for more than just developing a good product, pricing it attractively, and making it available to target customers. Companies must also engage consumers and communicate their value propositions to customers, and what they communicate should not be left to chance. All communications must be planned and blended into carefully integrated programs. Just as good communication is important in building and maintaining any other kind of relationship, it is a crucial element in a company's efforts to engage customers and build profitable customer relationships.

> **Author** | The promotion mix is the
> **Comment** | marketer's bag of tools
> for engaging and communicating with
> customers and other stakeholders.
> To deliver a clear and compelling
> message, each tool must be carefully
> coordinated under the concept of
> integrated marketing communications
> (IMC).

The Promotion Mix

OBJECTIVE 14-1 Define the five promotion mix tools for communicating customer value.

Promotion mix (marketing communications mix)
The specific blend of promotion tools that the company uses to persuasively communicate customer value and build customer relationships.

A company's total **promotion mix**—also called its **marketing communications mix**—consists of the specific blend of advertising, public relations, personal selling, sales promotion, and direct and digital marketing tools that the company uses to engage consumers, persuasively communicate customer value, and build customer relationships. The five major promotion tools are defined as follows:[2]

Advertising

Any paid form of nonpersonal presentation and promotion of ideas, goods, or services by an identified sponsor.

Sales promotion

Short-term incentives to encourage the purchase or sale of a product or a service.

Personal selling

Personal presentation by the firm's sales force for the purpose of engaging customers, making sales, and building customer relationships.

Public relations (PR)

Building good relations with the company's various publics by obtaining favorable publicity, building a good corporate image, and creating favorable events, stories, and other marketing content.

Direct and digital marketing

Engaging directly with carefully targeted individual consumers and customer communities to both obtain an immediate response and build lasting customer relationships.

> **Author Comment** | Integrated marketing communications—IMC—is a really hot topic these days. No other area of marketing is changing more quickly and profoundly. A big part of the reason is the huge surge in customer engagement through digital media—online, mobile, and social media marketing.

- **Advertising**. Any paid form of nonpersonal presentation and promotion of ideas, goods, or services by an identified sponsor.
- **Sales promotion**. Short-term incentives to encourage the purchase or sale of a product or service.
- **Personal selling**. Personal customer interactions by the firm's sales force to engage customers, make sales, and build customer relationships.
- **Public relations (PR)**. Activities designed to engage the company's various publics and build good relations with them.
- **Direct and digital marketing**. Engaging directly with carefully targeted individual consumers and customer communities to both obtain an immediate response and build lasting customer relationships.

Each category involves specific promotional tools that are used to communicate with customers. For example, *advertising* includes broadcast, print, online, mobile, outdoor, and other forms. *Sales promotion* includes discounts, coupons, displays, demonstrations, and events. *Personal selling* includes sales presentations, trade shows, and incentive programs. *Public relations* includes stories, sponsorships, events, and webpages. And *direct and digital marketing* includes direct mail, email, catalogs, online and social media, mobile marketing, and more.

At the same time, marketing communication goes beyond these specific promotion tools. The product's design, its price, the shape and color of its package, and the stores that sell it—*all* communicate something to buyers. Thus, although the promotion mix is the company's primary engagement and communications activity, the entire marketing mix—promotion *and* product, price, and place—must be coordinated for greatest impact.

Integrated Marketing Communications

OBJECTIVE 14-2 Discuss the changing communications landscape and the need for integrated marketing communications.

In past decades, marketers perfected the art of mass marketing: selling highly standardized products to masses of customers. In the process, they developed effective mass-media communication techniques to support these strategies. Large companies now routinely invest millions or even billions of dollars in television, magazine, or other mass-media advertising, reaching tens of millions of customers with a single ad. Today, however, marketing managers face some new marketing communications realities. Perhaps no other area of marketing is changing so profoundly as marketing communications, creating both exciting and challenging times for marketing communicators.

The New Marketing Communications Model

Several major factors are changing the face of today's marketing communications. First, *consumers* are changing. In this digitally connected, mobile age, consumers are better informed and more communications empowered. Rather than relying on marketer-supplied information, they can use the internet, social media, and other technologies to find information on their own. They can connect easily with other consumers to exchange brand-related information or even create their own brand messages and experiences.

Second, *marketing strategies* are changing. As mass markets have fragmented, marketers are shifting away from mass marketing. More and more, they are developing focused marketing programs designed to engage customers and build customer relationships in more narrowly defined micromarkets.

Finally, sweeping advances in *digital technology* have caused remarkable changes in the ways companies and customers communicate with each other. The digital age has spawned a host of new information and communication tools—from smartphones and tablets to the many faces of the internet (brand websites, email, blogs, streamed content, social media and online communities, the mobile web, and so much more). Just as mass marketing once gave rise to a new generation of mass-media communications, digital and social media have given birth to a more targeted, social, and engaging marketing communications model.

Although network television, magazines, newspapers, and other traditional mass media remain very important, their dominance is declining. In their place, advertisers have added a broad selection of more-specialized and highly targeted media to engage smaller customer communities with more personalized, interactive content. The new media range from specialty cable television channels and made-for-the-web videos to online ads, email and texting, blogs, mobile catalogs and coupons, and a burgeoning list of social media. Such new media have taken marketing by storm.

Some advertising industry experts even predict that the old mass-media communications model will eventually become obsolete. Mass-media costs are rising, audiences are shrinking, ad clutter is increasing, and viewers are gaining control of message exposure through technologies such as streamed content or DVRs that let them skip disruptive television commercials. As a result, the skeptics suggest, marketers have shifted ever-larger portions of their marketing budgets away from old-media mainstays and to online, social, and mobile media.

In recent years, although TV remains a potent advertising medium, TV ad spending growth has declined. Ad spending in magazines, newspapers, and radio has also lost significant ground. Meanwhile, spending in digital media has surged. Total digital ad spending now captures more than 50 percent of all U.S. ad spending and will grow to an estimated 67 percent of total ad spending by 2023. Advertising on mobile devices now accounts for almost two-thirds of all digital ad spending and by itself exceeds the amount spent on TV advertising.[3]

● The new marketing communications model: Marketers are shifting ever-larger portions of their marketing budgets away from old-media mainstays to online, social, and mobile media. Adidas now uses only digital channels to engage its younger consumers.

Dan Freebairn

More and more, large advertisers—from Nike and P&G to Unilever—are moving toward a "digital-first" approach to building their brands. For example, Unilever, one of the world's largest advertisers, now spends as much as 40 percent of its more than $9 billion global marketing budget on digital media.[4] Some marketers now rely almost entirely on digital and social media. ● For example, adidas has now abandoned TV altogether and uses only digital channels to reach younger consumers. "It's clear that the younger consumer engages with us predominantly over the mobile device," says adidas's CEO.[5]

In the current marketing communications world, rather than using old approaches that interrupt customers and force-feed them mass messages, new media formats let marketers reach smaller communities of consumers in more engaging ways. For example, think about television viewing these days. Consumers can now watch their favorite programs on just about any screen—on televisions but also tablets, smartphones, or laptops. And they can choose to watch programs whenever and wherever they wish, often without commercials. Increasingly, programs, ads, and videos are being produced only for online viewing.

Despite the shift toward digital media, however, traditional mass media still capture a sizable share of the promotion budgets of most major marketing firms. Thus, rather than the old-media model collapsing completely, most marketers foresee a shifting mix of both traditional mass media and online, mobile, and social media that engage more-targeted consumer communities in a more personalized way. In the end, regardless of the communications channel, the key is to integrate all of these media in a way that best engages customers, communicates the brand message, and enhances the customer's brand experiences.

As the marketing communications environment shifts, so will the role of marketing communicators. Rather than just creating and placing "TV ads" or "print ads" or "Instagram stories," many marketers now view themselves more broadly as **content marketing** managers. As such, they create, inspire, and share brand messages and conversations with and among customers across a fluid mix of *paid, owned, earned,* and *shared* communication channels. These channels include media that are both traditional and new as well as controlled and not controlled. It's not just advertising anymore, notes one ad agency executive. "It's about [communications] context and channels now, rather than just the message itself. It's about mapping the customer journey to start a conversation with consumers, one that leads to engagement, purchase, loyalty, and advocacy at different touchpoints against this integrated journey" (see Real Marketing 14.1).[6]

Content marketing
Creating, inspiring, and sharing brand messages and conversations with and among consumers across a fluid mix of paid, owned, earned, and shared channels.

Real Marketing 14.1 | Just Don't Call It Advertising: It's Content Marketing

In the good old days, life seemed so simple for advertisers. When a brand needed an advertising campaign, everybody knew what that meant. The brand team and ad agency came up with a creative strategy, developed a media plan, produced and placed a set of TV commercials and magazine or newspaper ads, and maybe issued a press release to stir up some news. But in these digital times, the old practice of placing "advertisements" in well-defined "media" within the tidy framework of a carefully managed "advertising campaign" just doesn't work anymore.

Instead, the lines are rapidly blurring between traditional advertising and new digital content. To be relevant, today's brand messages must be social, mobile, interactively engaging, and multi-platformed. Says one industry insider: "Today's media landscape keeps getting more diverse—it's broadcast, cable, and streaming; it's online, tablet, and smartphone; it's video, rich media, social media, branded content, banners, apps, in-app advertising, and interactive technology products."

The new digital landscape has called into question the very definition of advertising. "What Is Advertising Anyway?" asks one provocative headline. Call it whatever you want, admonishes another, but "Just Don't Call It Advertising." Instead, according to many marketers these days, it's "content marketing," creating and distributing a broad mix of compelling content that engages customers, builds relationships with and among them, and moves them to act and advocate the brand to others. To feed today's digital and social media machinery and to sustain "always-on" consumer conversations, brands need a constant supply of fresh content across a breadth of traditional and digital platforms.

Many advertisers and marketers now view themselves more broadly as content marketing managers who create, inspire, share, and curate marketing content—both their own content and that created by consumers and others. Rather than using traditional media breakdowns, they subscribe to a new framework that builds on how and by whom marketing content is created, controlled, and distributed. The new classification identifies four major types of media: paid, owned, earned, and shared (POES):

Paid media—promotional channels paid for by the marketer, including traditional media (such as TV, radio, print, or outdoor) and online and digital media (paid search ads, web and social media display ads, mobile ads, or email marketing).

Owned media—promotional channels owned and controlled by the company, including company websites, corporate blogs, owned social media pages, proprietary brand communities, sales forces, and events.

Earned media—PR media channels, such as television, newspapers, blogs, online video sites, and other media not directly paid for or controlled by the marketer but that include the content because of viewer, reader, or user interest.

Shared media—media shared by consumers with other consumers, such as social media, blogs, mobile media, and viral channels as well as traditional word of mouth.

In the past, advertisers have focused on traditional paid (broadcast, print) or earned (public relations) media. Now, however, content marketers have rapidly added the new digital generation of owned (websites, blogs, brand communities) and shared (online social, mobile, email) media. Whereas a successful paid ad used to be an end in itself, marketers are now developing integrated marketing content that leverages the combined power of all the POES channels. Thus, many TV ads often aren't just TV ads anymore. They're "video content" you might see anywhere—on a TV screen but also on a tablet or phone. Other video content looks a lot like TV advertising but was never intended for TV, such as

made-for-online videos posted on websites or social media. Similarly, printed brand messages and pictures no longer appear only in carefully crafted magazine ads or catalogs. Instead, such content, created by a variety of sources, pops up in anything from formal ads and online brand pages to mobile and social media and independent blogs.

The new "content marketing" campaigns look a lot different from the old "advertising" campaigns. For example, consider Intuit. Until recently, Intuit was the biggest software company you'd never heard of. It's TurboTax, Mint, and QuickBooks brands were household names, but Intuit wanted to unite its products under a common and compelling corporate brand. To make that happen, Intuit developed a bold promotional campaign. But to engage consumers in today's complex media environment, Intuit went well beyond traditional TV advertising. Instead, it created a content-rich campaign spanning a full slate of traditional and digital platforms.

Although the initial campaign included a Super Bowl ad, it centered on a four-minute animated video shared on YouTube, Facebook, and Intuit's websites. The video, a Pixar-like animated short film titled "Giant Story," introduced a likeable giant robot, representing the power of Intuit's various products. The beautifully animated video tells the story of Pari, an engineer who watches

Content marketing: As the lines are rapidly blurring between traditional advertising and new digital content, many marketers now view themselves more broadly as content marketing managers who create, inspire, share, and curate marketing content—both their own and that created by consumers and others.

designer491/Shutterstock

her friend Pete struggle with the financial burdens of owning and operating his own flower shop in a futuristic world. Pari invents an enormous but gentle Intuit Giant that harnesses the power of TurboTax, QuickBooks, and Mint to help Pete spend less time managing his small business's finances and more time doing the things that will help his business prosper.

The Giant Story campaign largely targets self-employed entrepreneurs who are working hard and have big but vulnerable dreams. "There are 750 million people who work for themselves around the world who juggle managing their finances while pursuing their passions," says Intuit's chief marketer. "With today's economy and the pressures of managing time and money, sometimes it can seem like the odds are stacked against them. But Intuit exists to work for them." The Giant Story campaign positions QuickBooks, Mint, and TurboTax as an ecosystem—as a go-to suite of products that work on their behalf and deliver on Intuit's "powering prosperity" promise.

A deluge of other Giant Story content, including the Super Bowl and other TV ads plus shorter clips on Facebook, Instagram, and Twitter, presented more compact versions of the Intuit story and encouraged viewers to go to YouTube to watch the full video. "A Giant Story is here," announced one Instagram ad. "Watch it and see what an Intuit Giant can do for you."

Skillfully integrated across POES channels, Intuit's Giant Story campaign produced striking results. On the day the four-minute video was first posted, before any paid media kicked in, Intuit employees helped drive more than 1 million views. The video grabbed 22 million YouTube views in the first three months plus an additional 3 million on Facebook. More important, in the wake of the Giant Story campaign, Intuit's ad recall was up 26 percent, brand awareness increased 17 percent, and brand favorability jumped 27 percent.

Intuit followed with a second Giant campaign, featuring a 60-second spot— "A Prosperity Story"—in which the Intuit Giant helps another young entrepreneur named Luisa turn her penchant for design into a successful clothing shop. The giant shows Luisa positive cash flow through QuickBooks, financial health and tax cuts with TurboTax, and financial management with Mint. The campaign is supported by a full schedule of other television, online, and social media elements, including a social media campaign in which Intuit invites customers share with others what prosperity means to them.

So, we can't just call it "advertising" anymore. Today's shifting and sometimes chaotic marketing communications environment calls for more than just creating and placing ads in well-defined and controlled media spaces. Rather, today's marketing communicators must be marketing content strategists, creators, connectors, and catalysts who manage brand conversations with and among customers and help those conversations catch fire across a fluid mix of channels. That's a tall order, but with today's new thinking, anything is POES-ible![7]

The Need for *Integrated* Marketing Communications

The shift toward a richer mix of media and content approaches poses a problem for marketers. Consumers today are bombarded by brand messages from a broad range of sources. But all too often, companies fail to integrate their various communication channels. Mass-media ads say one thing, whereas company's website, social media pages and posts, videos, or emails say something altogether different.

One problem is that marketing content often comes from different parts of the company. Advertising messages are prepared by the advertising department or an ad agency. Other company departments or agencies prepare public relations messages, sales promotion events, and web, mobile, or social media content. However, consumers don't distinguish between content sources the way marketers do. In the consumer's mind, brand-related content from different sources—whether it's a Super Bowl ad, in-store display, mobile app, or friend's social media post—all merge into a single message about the brand or company. Conflicting content from these different sources can result in confused company images, brand positions, and customer relationships.

Thus, the explosion of online, mobile, and social media marketing presents tremendous opportunities but also big challenges. It gives marketers rich new tools for understanding and engaging customers. At the same time, it complicates and fragments overall marketing communications. The challenge is to bring it all together in an organized way. To that end, most companies practice the concept of **integrated marketing communications (IMC)**. Under this concept, as illustrated in ● **Figure 14.1**, the company carefully integrates its many communication channels to deliver a clear, consistent, and compelling message about the organization and its brands.

Often, different media play unique roles in engaging, informing, and persuading consumers. For example, a recent study showed that more than two-thirds of advertisers and their agencies are planning video ad campaigns that stretch across multiple viewing platforms, such as traditional TV and digital, mobile, and social media. Such *cross-platform* campaigns combine TV's core strength—vast reach—with digital's better targeting, interaction, and engagement. These varied media and roles must be carefully coordinated under the overall integrated marketing communications plan.

● One good example of a well-integrated marketing communications effort is automaker Land Rover's "Above and Beyond" marketing campaign, which integrates the clout and reach of traditional media with the power of digital media to create deep customer engagement:[8]

Integrated marketing communications (IMC)
Carefully integrating and coordinating the company's many communications channels to deliver a clear, consistent, and compelling message about the organization and its products.

● **FIGURE 14.1**
Integrated Marketing
Communications

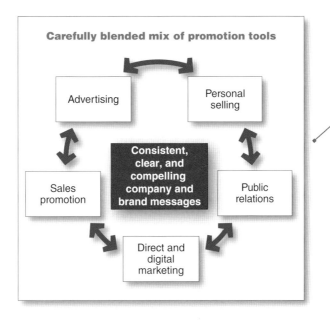

The 70-year-old Range Rover brand uses plenty of good old traditional media. It runs big-budget television ads—including Super Bowl spots—that drive home its luxury performance and outdoor adventure positioning. It supports those mass-market ads with more targeted broadcast ads on AMC, ESPN, Food Network, and NFL Network and print ads in *Architectural Digest, GQ, Wired, Vogue,* and *The Wall Street Journal.*

But the Range Rover campaign also includes a carefully integrated flow of web and social media content that enriches the customer experience in ways that traditional media can't. For example, the Land Rover Stories section of the brand's website features travelogues in which adventure photographers relate their personal experiences riding Land Rovers through rugged and picturesque landscapes, each story illustrated with stunning visuals. But that's just a start. The brand recently produced a video series capturing the adventures of a couple and their young child during a trip across Europe in a Land Rover Discovery, and it created a 360-degree video by which viewers could sail with the Land Rover team in Bermuda ahead of the 35th America's Cup.

Land Rover shares such video stories and other carefully crafted content with brand fans via social media. The brand boasts 16 million Facebook followers, 290,000 YouTube subscribers, 723,000 Twitter followers, and 4.9 million Instagram faithful who engage by the thousands with every post. The social media followings of competitors pale by comparison (for example, competitor Toyota Landcruiser has only 336,000 Facebook followers and 88,000 Instagram fans). No matter what the platform, all content—from television spots to web videos to Instagram posts—is carefully coordinated under Range Rover's "Above and Beyond" luxury adventure mantra. The integrated marketing campaign seems less about selling vehicles and more about reinforcing the Range Rover experience and keeping customers deeply engaged.

In the past, no one person or department was responsible for thinking through the communication roles of the

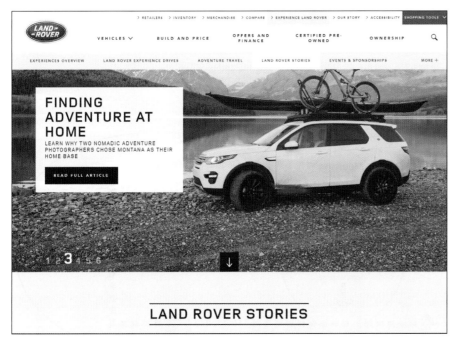

● **Integrated marketing communications: Land Rover's "Above and Beyond" marketing campaign integrates the clout and reach of traditional media with the power of digital and social media to create deep and personal customer engagement.**

Jaguar Land Rover North America, LLC

various promotion tools and coordinating the promotion mix. To help implement integrated marketing communications, many companies now appoint a marketing communications director who has overall responsibility for the company's communications efforts. This helps to produce better communications consistency and greater sales impact. It places the responsibility in someone's hands to unify the company's image as it is shaped across ever-expanding cross-platform communications activities.

Author Comment | To develop effective marketing communications, you must first understand the general communication process.

Developing Effective Marketing Communication

OBJECTIVE 14-3 Outline the communication process and the steps in developing effective marketing communications.

A View of the Communication Process

Integrated marketing communications involves identifying the target audience and shaping a well-coordinated promotional program to obtain the desired audience response. Too often, marketing communications focus on immediate awareness, image, or preference goals in the target market. But this approach to communication is too shortsighted. Today, marketers are moving toward viewing communications as managing ongoing customer engagement and relationships with the company and its brands.

Because customers differ, communications programs must be developed for specific segments, niches, and even individuals. And, given today's interactive communications technologies, companies must ask not only "How can we engage our customers?" but also "How can we let our customers engage us and each other?"

Thus, the communications process should start with an audit of all the potential touch points that target customers may have with the company and its brands. For example, someone purchasing a new wireless phone plan may talk to others, see television or magazine ads, visit various online sites for prices and reviews, and check out plans at Best Buy, Walmart, or a wireless provider's kiosk or store. Marketers need to assess what influence each communication experience will have at different stages of the buying process. This understanding helps marketers allocate their communication dollars more efficiently and effectively.

To communicate effectively, marketers need to understand how communication works. Communication involves the nine elements shown in ● **Figure 14.2**. Two of these elements are the major parties in a communication—the *sender* and the *receiver*.

● **FIGURE 14.2**
Elements in the Communication Process

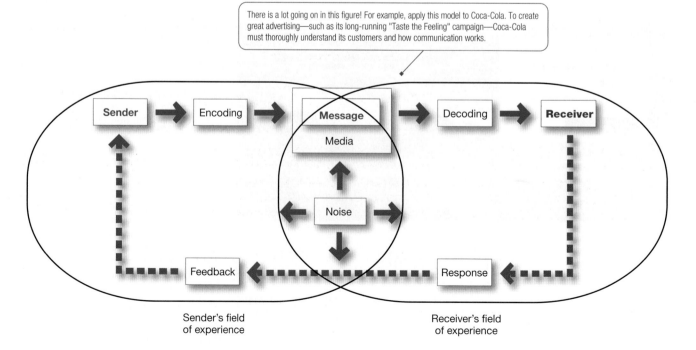

There is a lot going on in this figure! For example, apply this model to Coca-Cola. To create great advertising—such as its long-running "Taste the Feeling" campaign—Coca-Cola must thoroughly understand its customers and how communication works.

Sender's field of experience

Receiver's field of experience

Another two are the major communication tools—the *message* and the *media*. Four more are major communication functions—*encoding, decoding, response*, and *feedback*. The last element is *noise* in the system. Definitions of these elements follow and are applied to a Coca-Cola "Taste the Feeling" television commercial.

- *Sender.* The *party sending the message* to another party—here, Coca-Cola.
- *Encoding.* The process of *putting thought into symbolic form*—for example, Coca-Cola's ad agency assembles words, sounds, and illustrations into a TV ad that will convey the intended message.
- *Message.* The *set of symbols* that the sender transmits—the actual Coca-Cola ad.
- *Media.* The *communication channels* through which the message moves from the sender to the receiver—in this case, television and the specific television programs that Coca-Cola's selects.
- *Decoding.* The process by which the receiver *assigns meaning to the symbols* encoded by the sender—a consumer watches the Coca-Cola commercial and interprets the words and images it contains.
- *Receiver.* The *party receiving the message* sent by another party—the customer who watches the Coca-Cola ad.
- *Response.* The *reactions of the receiver* after being exposed to the message—any of hundreds of possible responses, such as the consumer likes Coca-Cola better, is more likely to drink Coca-Cola next time, advocates Coca-Cola to a friend, or does nothing.
- *Feedback.* The part of the *receiver's response communicated back to the sender*—Coca-Cola's research shows that consumers are either struck by and remember the ad or they email Coca-Cola or post messages on its social media sites praising or criticizing the ad or its products.
- *Noise.* The *unplanned static or distortion* during the communication process, which results in the receiver getting a different message than the one the sender sent—the consumer is distracted while watching the commercial and misses its key points.

For a message to be effective, the sender's encoding process must mesh with the receiver's decoding process. The best messages consist of words and other symbols that are familiar to the receiver. The more the sender's field of experience overlaps with that of the receiver, the more effective the message is likely to be. Marketing communicators may not always *share* the customer's field of experience. For example, an advertising copywriter from one socioeconomic level might create content for customers from another level—say, wealthy business owners. However, to communicate effectively, the marketing communicator must *understand* the customer's field of experience.

This model points out several key factors in good communication. Senders need to know what audiences they wish to reach and what responses they want. They must be good at encoding messages that take into account how the target audience decodes them. They must send messages through media that reach target audiences, and they must develop feedback channels so that they can assess an audience's response to the message. Also, in today's interactive media environment, companies must be prepared to "flip" the communications process—to become good receivers of and responders to messages sent by consumers.

> **Author Comment** | Now that we understand how communication works, it's time to turn all of those promotion mix elements into an actual marketing communications program.

Steps in Developing Effective Marketing Communication

We now examine the steps in developing an effective integrated communications and promotion program. Marketers must do the following: identify the target audience, determine the communication objectives, design a message, choose the media through which to send the message, select the message source, and collect feedback.

Identifying the Target Audience

A marketing communicator starts with a clear target audience in mind. The audience may be current users or potential buyers, those who make the buying decision or those who influence it. The audience may be individuals, groups, special publics, or the general public. The target audience will heavily affect the communicator's decisions on *what* will be said, *how* it will be said, *when* it will be said, *where* it will be said, and *who* will say it.

Determining the Communication Objectives

Once the target audience has been defined, marketers must determine the desired response. Of course, in many cases, they will seek a purchase response. But as discussed in Chapter 5, purchase decisions are only part of a broader customer journey, the sum of the ongoing experiences consumers have with a brand. More broadly, marketing communicators want to help build customer–brand relationships and guide customers through the **five As** of the customer journey: *awareness* (I know about the product), *appeal* (I like the product), *ask* (I want to know more about the product and be more engaged with the brand), *act* (I'm buying and relating to the product), and *advocacy* (I'm telling others about the product).[9] The goal is to create content experiences that will keep customers on the path from brand awareness and preference to purchasing the brand and advocating it to others.

Five As

The five customer journey stages on the path from awareness of a brand to advocating it to others: awareness, appeal, ask, act, and advocacy.

The marketing communicator's target market may be totally unaware of the brand. More likely, consumers may know about the brand but not actively consider or engage with it. Thus, marketers often must first build active awareness and engagement, then move consumers to purchase and advocacy. ● For example, most consumers know about the 103-year-old Planters nuts brand. However, in past years, Planters has sometimes found itself lost amid the clutter of competing brands in the shifting snack food market. So to reawaken awareness, involvement, preference, and purchase, Planters launched a major multi-platform promotional campaign tagged "Always There in Crunch Time."[10]

The campaign began with Planters's first-ever Super Bowl ad. In the dramatic spot, Planters mascot Mr. Peanut took a wild ride on the Planters Nutmobile to rescue Yankees legend Alex Rodriguez from eating bland kale chips. To increase engagement during the game, Planters ran a live online promotion giving surprise prizes—such as signed Rodriguez memorabilia or having Mr. Peanut as your personal driver in the Nutmobile for a week—to selected fans who engaged with the brand by following @MrPeanut on Twitter. In the days following the big game, Planters continued its live consumer engagement with innovative Twitter and other social media content.

● Moving customers through the customer journey: Planters's "Crunch Time" communications campaign boosted awareness, engagement, and purchase consideration for the iconic brand.

The Kraft Heinz Company

Based on the success of the Super Bowl campaign, Planters soon followed with a second "Crunch Time" effort, this one an interactive social media campaign for Valentine's Day. It partnered with famous analyst Dr. Ruth to help answer people's relationship questions. "With #ValentinesDay around the corner, it's officially #CrunchTime!" said Mr. Peanut in one tweet. "But don't worry, I've got your back. Together with @AskDrRuth, we are answering YOUR relationship questions." The "Crunch Time" campaigns and other brand content efforts have paid off for the nostalgic Planters brand. Consumer ad awareness and engagement are at all-time highs, leading to a significant boost in purchase consideration.

Of course, marketing communications alone cannot create positive engagement, preference, and purchases for Planters products. The product itself must provide superior value for customers. In fact, outstanding marketing communications can actually speed the demise of a poor product. The more quickly potential buyers learn about a poor product, the more quickly they become aware of its faults. Thus, good marketing communications call for "good deeds followed by good words."

Designing a Message

Having defined the desired audience response, the communicator then turns to developing an effective message. When putting a message together, the marketing communicator must decide what to say (message content) and how to say it (message structure and format).

Message Content. The marketer has to figure out an appeal or theme that will produce the desired responses. There are three types of appeals: rational, emotional, and moral. Rational appeals relate to the audience's self-interest. They show that the product will produce the desired benefits. Examples are messages showing a product's quality, economy, value, or performance. Thus, an ad for Aleve makes this matter-of-fact claim: "More pills doesn't mean more pain relief. Aleve has the strength to keep back, body, and arthritis pain away all day with fewer pills than Tylenol." And in a recent ad from Sprint's "Look Who Switched" campaign, a customer who switched from Verizon to Sprint states simply: "You get a highly reliable network and save 50% off most of the rates other wireless carriers charge."[11]

● Google's "100 Billion Words" ad uses warmly emotional appeals that position Google Translate, and language in general, as a great international unifier.

Emotional appeals attempt to stir up either positive or negative emotions that can motivate purchase. Communicators may use emotional appeals ranging from love, joy, and humor to fear and guilt. Advocates of emotional messages claim that they attract more attention and create more belief in the sponsor and the brand. The idea is that consumers often feel before they think, and persuasion is emotional in nature.

● For example, Google's most recent Super Bowl ad focuses not on the rational functions of its search engine, phones, or smarthome devices but on the emotions surrounding Google Translate, its 12-year-old multilingual translation app. The 60-second spot—titled "100 Billion Words," denoting the number of words that users process every day—uses emotional appeals that position Google Translate, and language in general, as an international unifier. Composed of a series of inspiring scenes in various languages, the ad shows how Translate brings people of all nationalities and persuasions together through shared experiences. "Every day," the ad concludes, "the most translated words in the world are 'how are you,' 'thank you,' and 'I love you.'"[12]

Moral appeals are directed to an audience's sense of what is "right" and "proper." They are often used to urge people to support social causes, such as a cleaner environment or aid to the disadvantaged. For example, a Colgate ad campaign urges people to "Close the tap while brushing" their teeth to conserve water. One ad shows a young boy in a developing economy with a water bucket atop his head, noting, "What you waste in two minutes is all his family needs for a day."

Message Structure. Marketers must also decide how to handle three message structure issues. The first is whether to draw a conclusion or leave it to the audience. Research suggests that, in many cases, rather than drawing a conclusion, the advertiser is better off asking questions and letting buyers come to their own conclusions. The second message structure issue is whether to present the strongest arguments first or last. Presenting them first gets strong attention but may lead to an anticlimactic ending.

The third message structure issue is whether to present a one-sided argument (mentioning only the product's strengths) or a two-sided argument (touting the product's strengths while also admitting its shortcomings). Usually, a one-sided argument is more effective in sales presentations—except when audiences are highly educated or likely to hear opposing claims or when the communicator has a negative association to overcome. In this spirit, Heinz once ran the message "Heinz Ketchup is slow good," and Listerine ran the message "Listerine tastes bad twice a day." In such cases, two-sided messages can enhance an advertiser's credibility and make buyers more resistant to competitor attacks.

Message Format. The marketing communicator also needs a strong *format* for the message. In a print ad, the communicator has to decide on the headline, copy, illustration, and colors. To attract attention, advertisers can use novelty and contrast; eye-catching pictures and headlines; distinctive formats; message size and position; and color, shape, and movement. ● For example, Reese's Peanut Butter Cup ads are bold and simple. They feature the brand's familiar orange, yellow, and brown colors with text overlaying images of the classic candy. They feature clever headlines that unite the candy's two distinctive ingredients, such as "Chocolate and peanut butter walked into a bar. The rest is history." and "Ever

CHOCOLATE AND PEANUT BUTTER WALK INTO A BAR. THE REST IS HISTORY.

Reese's perfect

● Message format: To attract attention, advertisers can use novelty and contrast, eye-catching images and headlines, and distinctive formats, as in this Reese's ad.

The Hershey Company

since peanut butter hooked up with chocolate, peanut butter still talks to jelly, but the relationship is very strained."

Presenters plan every detail carefully, from start to finish. If the message is to be communicated by television or video content, the communicator must incorporate motion, pace, and sound. If the message is carried on the product or its package, the communicator must watch texture, scent, color, size, and shape. For example, color alone can significantly enhance message recognition for a brand—think about Target (red), McDonald's (yellow and red), John Deere (green and yellow), Twitter (blue), or Home Depot (orange). Thus, in designing effective marketing communications, marketers must consider color and other seemingly unimportant details carefully.

Choosing Communication Channels and Media

The communicator must now select the *channels of communication*. There are two broad types of communication channels: *personal* and *nonpersonal*.

Personal communication channels

Channels through which two or more people communicate directly with each other, including face-to-face, on the phone, via mail or email, or even through an internet "chat."

Word-of-mouth influence

The impact of the personal words and recommendations of trusted friends, family, associates, and other consumers on buying behavior.

Buzz marketing

Cultivating opinion leaders and getting them to spread information about a product or a service to others in their communities.

Personal Communication Channels. In **personal communication channels**, two or more people communicate directly with each other. They might communicate face-to-face, on the phone, via mail or email, or through texting or chat. Personal communication channels are effective because they allow for personal addressing and feedback.

Some personal communication channels are controlled directly by the company. For example, company salespeople contact business buyers. But other personal communications about the product may reach buyers through channels not directly controlled by the company. These channels might include independent experts—consumer advocates, bloggers, and others—making statements to buyers. Or they might be neighbors, friends, family members, associates, or other consumers talking to target buyers, in person or via social media or other interactive channels. This last channel, **word-of-mouth influence**, has considerable effect in many product areas.

Personal influence carries great weight, especially for products that are expensive, risky, or highly visible. One survey found that recommendations from friends and family are far and away the most powerful influence on consumers worldwide: 83 percent of consumers said that a recommendation from a friend or family member makes them more likely to purchase a product or service. Fifty percent of Americans would choose online or offline word of mouth if they had to pick one source of information.[13]

Is it any wonder, then, that few consumers buy a big-ticket item before checking out what existing users have to say about the product at a site such as Amazon.com? Who hasn't made an Amazon purchase based on another customer's review or the "Customers who bought this also bought…" section or decided against purchase because of negative customer reviews?

Companies can take steps to put personal communication channels to work for them. For example, as discussed in Chapter 5, they can hire or create *opinion leaders* for their brands—people whose opinions are sought by others—by supplying influencers with the product on attractive terms or by educating them so that they can inform others. **Buzz marketing** involves cultivating opinion leaders and getting them to spread information about a product or a service to others in their communities.

For example, Red Bull has created "The Wings Team," a group of 2,800 brand ambassadors who connect with Red Bull fans at events and through stacks of user-generated digital content showing their extreme and active lifestyles. Wings are "the face of the brand." Red Bull describes them as "charming, fun-loving, entrepreneurial, and dynamic individuals…who drive product trial, support sales, and work at Red Bull Events, …winning the hearts and minds of our customers through highly personalized interactions.[14]

● Similarly, athleisure apparel retailer Lululemon has cultivated a network of more than 1,600 brand ambassadors. The group includes global yoga ambassadors (eight experienced instructors), elite ambassadors (more than 75 professional

● **Personal communications channels: Lululemon's brand ambassadors represent the brand to customers and nurture impact in their communities. "Let's do big things," Lululemon tells its ambassadors.**

fizkes/Shutterstock; Arne Beruldsen/Shutterstock

athletes from soccer, cycling, and more), and grassroots store ambassadors (more than 1,500 local influencers in personal training, yoga, running, and other active pursuits). Lululemon recruits people who are dedicated to what it calls "the sweatlife: sweat, grow, and connect." Lululemon supports the ambassadors with development experiences, products to try out, "a network of like-minded people, and a humungous cheer squad." The ambassadors represent the brand to customers and nurture impact in their communities but also give valuable feedback to Lululemon. "Let's do big things," Lululemon tells its ambassadors. "When you're an ambassador, …you're an extension of our brand and an inspiration to our guests."[15]

Nonpersonal Communication Channels

Nonpersonal communication
channels

Media that carry messages without personal contact or feedback, including major media, atmospheres, and events.

Nonpersonal communication channels are media that carry messages without personal contact or feedback. They include major media, atmospheres, and events. Major *media* include broadcast media (television, radio), print media (newspapers, magazines, direct mail), display media (billboards, signs, posters), and online and digital media (email, websites, and mobile and social media). *Atmospheres* are designed environments that create or reinforce the buyer's leanings toward buying a product. Thus, lawyers' offices and banks are designed to communicate confidence and other qualities that might be valued by clients. *Events* are staged occurrences that communicate messages to target audiences. For example, brands arrange shows and exhibits, public tours, and other events.

Nonpersonal communication affects buyers directly. In addition, using mass media often affects buyers indirectly by causing more personal communication. For example, communications might first flow from television, magazines, and other mass media to opinion leaders and then from these opinion leaders to others. Thus, influencers step between the mass media and their audiences and carry messages to people who are less exposed to media. Interestingly, marketers often use nonpersonal communication channels to replace or stimulate personal communications by embedding consumer endorsements or word-of-mouth testimonials in their ads and other promotions.

Selecting the Message Source

In either personal or nonpersonal communication, the message's impact also depends on how the target audience views the communicator. Messages delivered by highly credible or popular sources are more persuasive. Thus, many food companies promote to doctors, dentists, and other health-care providers to motivate these professionals to recommend specific food products to their patients. And marketers hire celebrity endorsers—well-known athletes, actors, musicians, and even cartoon characters—to deliver their messages. A host of NBA superstars lend their images to brands such as Nike, McDonald's, and Coca-Cola. Actress Sophia Vergara speaks for CoverGirl, State Farm, Comcast, Rooms to Go, and other brands and has her own Kmart clothing line. Actor George Clooney loves his Nestle Nespresso expresso machine, and tennis great Serena Williams endorses Gatorade, Nike, and Beats By Dre.

But companies must be careful when selecting celebrities to represent their brands. Picking the wrong spokesperson can result in embarrassment and a tarnished image. For example, a dozen or more big brands—including Nike, Anheuser-Busch, Oakley, Trek bikes, and Giro helmets—faced embarrassment when pro cyclist Lance Armstrong was stripped of his Tour de France titles and banned for life from competitive cycling for illegal use of performance-enhancing drugs. Previously considered a model brand spokesman, Armstrong once earned nearly $20 million in endorsement income in a single year. "Arranged marriages between brands and celebrities are inherently risky," notes one expert. "Ninety-nine percent of celebrities do a strong job for their brand partners," says another, "and 1 percent goes off the rails."[16] More than ever, it's important to pick the right celebrity for the brand.

Collecting Feedback

After sending the message or other brand content, the communicator must research its effect on the target audience. This involves asking target audience members whether they remember the content, how many times they saw it, what points they recall, how they felt about the content, and their past and present attitudes toward the brand and company.

The communicator would also like to measure behavior resulting from the content—how many people bought the product, advocated it to others, or visited the store.

Feedback on marketing communications may suggest changes in the promotion program or in the product offer itself. For example, Macy's uses television, newspaper, and mobile advertising to inform area consumers about its stores, services, and merchandising events. Suppose feedback research shows that 80 percent of all shoppers in an area recall seeing the store's ads and are aware of its merchandise and sales. Sixty percent of these aware shoppers have visited a Macy's store in the past month, but only 20 percent of those who visited were satisfied with the shopping experience.

These results suggest that although promotion is creating awareness, Macy's stores aren't giving consumers the satisfaction they expect. Therefore, Macy's needs to improve the shopping experience while staying with the successful communications program. In contrast, suppose research shows that only 40 percent of area consumers are aware of the store's merchandise and events, only 30 percent of those aware have shopped recently, but 80 percent of those who have shopped return soon to shop again. In this case, Macy's needs to strengthen its promotion program to take advantage of its power to create customer satisfaction in the store.

Author | In this section, we'll
Comment | look at the promotion budget–setting process and at how marketers blend the various marketing communication tools into a smoothly functioning integrated promotion mix.

Setting the Total Promotion Budget and Mix

OBJECTIVE 14-4 Explain the methods for setting the promotion budget and factors that affect the design of the promotion mix.

We have looked at the steps in planning and sending communications to a target audience. But how does the company determine its total *promotion budget* and the division among the major promotional tools to create the *promotion mix*? By what process does it blend the tools to create integrated marketing communications? We now look at these questions.

Setting the Total Promotion Budget

One of the hardest marketing decisions facing a company is how much to spend on promotion. John Wanamaker, the department store mogul, once said, "I know that half of my advertising is wasted, but I don't know which half. I spent $2 million for advertising, and I don't know if that is half enough or twice too much." ● For example, PepsiCo spends more than $1 billion annually on advertising for its many brands, but is that too little, just right, or too much? Thus, it is not surprising that industries and companies vary widely in how much they spend on promotion. Promotion spending may be 10 to 12 percent of sales for consumer packaged goods, 20 percent for cosmetics, and only 1.9 percent for household appliances. Within a given industry, both low and high spenders can be found.[17]

Affordable method

Setting the promotion budget at the level management thinks the company can afford.

How does a company determine its promotion budget? Here, we look at four common methods used to set the total budget for promotion: the *affordable method*, the *percentage-of-sales method*, the *competitive-parity method*, and the *objective-and-task method*.

Affordable Method

Some companies use the **affordable method**: They set the promotion budget at the level they think the company can afford. Small businesses often use this method, reasoning that the company cannot spend more on promotion than it has. They start with total revenues, deduct operating expenses and capital outlays, and then devote some portion of the remaining funds to promotion.

● Setting the promotion budget: PepsiCo spends more than $1 billion a year on promotion campaigns for its many brands, such as its current Pepsi "For the Love of It" campaign. But is that too little, just right, or too much?

PEPSI, the Pepsi Globe and FOR THE LOVE OF IT are the trademarks of PepsiCo, Inc. Used with permission.

Unfortunately, this method of setting budgets completely ignores the effects of promotion on sales. It tends to place promotion last among spending priorities, even in situations in which promotion is critical to the firm's success. It leads to an uncertain annual promotion budget, which makes long-range market planning difficult. Although the affordable method can result in overspending on promotion, it more often results in underspending.

Percentage-of-Sales Method

Percentage-of-sales method

Setting the promotion budget at a certain percentage of current or forecasted sales or as a percentage of the unit sales price.

Other companies use the **percentage-of-sales method**, setting their promotion budget at a certain percentage of current or forecasted sales. Or they budget a percentage of the unit sales price. The percentage-of-sales method is simple to use and helps management think about the relationships between promotion spending, selling price, and profit per unit.

Despite these claimed advantages, however, the percentage-of-sales method has little to justify it. It wrongly views sales as the *cause* of promotion rather than as the *result*. Although studies have found a positive correlation between promotional spending and brand strength, this relationship often turns out to be effect and cause, not cause and effect. Stronger brands with higher sales can afford the biggest ad budgets.

Thus, the percentage-of-sales budget is based on the availability of funds rather than on opportunities. It may prevent the increased spending sometimes needed to turn around falling sales. Because the budget varies with year-to-year sales, long-range planning is difficult. Finally, the method does not provide any basis for choosing a *specific* percentage, except what has been done in the past or what competitors are doing.

Competitive-Parity Method

Competitive-parity method

Setting the promotion budget to match competitors' outlays.

Still other companies use the **competitive-parity method**, setting their promotion budgets to match competitors' outlays. They monitor competitors' promotion activity or get industry promotion spending estimates from publications or trade associations and then set their budgets based on the industry average.

Two arguments support this method. First, competitors' budgets represent the collective wisdom of the industry. Second, spending what competitors spend helps prevent promotion wars. Unfortunately, neither argument is valid. There are no grounds for believing that the competition has a better idea of what a company should be spending on promotion than does the company itself. Companies differ greatly, and each has its own special promotion needs. Finally, there is no evidence that budgets based on competitive parity prevent promotion wars.

Objective-and-Task Method

Objective-and-task method

Developing the promotion budget by (1) defining specific promotion objectives, (2) determining the tasks needed to achieve these objectives, and (3) estimating the costs of performing these tasks. The sum of these costs is the proposed promotion budget.

The most logical budget-setting method is the **objective-and-task method**, whereby the company sets its promotion budget based on what it wants to accomplish with promotion. This budgeting method entails (1) defining specific promotion objectives, (2) determining the tasks needed to achieve these objectives, and (3) estimating the costs of performing these tasks. The sum of these costs is the proposed promotion budget.

The advantage of the objective-and-task method is that it forces management to spell out its assumptions about the relationship between dollars spent and promotion results. But it is also the most difficult method to use. Often, it is hard to figure out which specific tasks will achieve the stated objectives. For example, suppose Samsung wants a 95-percent-awareness level for its latest Galaxy smartphone model during the two-month introductory period. What specific advertising messages, brand content, and media schedules should Samsung use to attain this objective? How much would this content and media cost? Samsung management must consider such questions, even though they are hard to answer.

Author Comment | In this section, we'll look at how marketers blend the various marketing communication tools into a smooth-functioning, integrated, and engaging promotion mix.

Shaping the Overall Promotion Mix

The concept of integrated marketing communications suggests that the company must blend the promotion tools carefully into a coordinated *promotion mix*. But how does it determine what mix of promotion tools to use? Companies within the same industry differ greatly in the design of their promotion mixes. For example, direct-to-consumer mattress maker Casper promotes its products primarily through digital content on its website and social media pages. By contrast, Sleep Number promotes its mattresses and bed systems through a broad mix of promotional tools, from television ads and digital content to in-store personal selling and promotions. We now look at factors that influence the marketer's choice of promotion tools.

The Nature of Each Promotion Tool

Each promotion tool has unique characteristics and costs. Marketers must understand these characteristics in shaping the promotion mix.

Advertising. Advertising can reach masses of geographically dispersed buyers at a low cost per exposure, and it enables the seller to repeat a message many times. Television advertising can reach huge audiences. For example, more than 98 million Americans watched the most recent Super Bowl on TV; the recent Oscars telecast pulled in almost 30 million viewers.[18]

What's more, a popular TV ad's reach can be extended through online and social media. For instance, 42 percent of football fans watched Super Bowl 53 ads on YouTube before, during, and after the big game. One study that tracked 28 Super Bowl ads across 24 video and social media platforms (including YouTube, Facebook, Instagram, Twitter, and TikTok) found that the ads were viewed about 105 million times during the two days *before* the game even aired. Verizon's "Team That Wouldn't Be Here" commercial—highlighting the real stories of 12 NFL stars who'd faced life-threatening situations and honoring the first responders who'd saved them—captured the nearly 100 million TV viewers during the Super Bowl, then got more than 16 million views on YouTube alone during the two weeks following the game.[19] Thus, for companies that want to reach a mass audience, TV is the place to be.

Beyond its reach, large-scale advertising says something positive about the seller's size, popularity, and success. Because of advertising's public nature, consumers tend to view advertised products as more legitimate. Advertising is also very expressive; it allows the company to dramatize its products through the artful use of visuals, print, sound, and color. On the one hand, advertising can be used to build up a long-term image for a product (such as Coca-Cola ads). On the other hand, advertising can trigger quick sales (as when Kohl's advertises weekend specials).

Advertising also has some drawbacks. Although it reaches many people quickly, mass-media advertising is impersonal and lacks the direct persuasiveness of company salespeople. For the most part, advertising can carry on only one-way communication with an audience, and the audience does not feel that it has to pay attention or respond. In addition, advertising can be very costly. Although some advertising forms—such as newspaper, radio, or online advertising—can be done on smaller budgets, other forms, such as network TV advertising, require very large budgets. For example, the 90-second Amazon Echo "Not Everything Makes the Cut" Super Bowl 53 ad cost almost $16 million for media time alone—more than $175,000 per tick of the clock—not counting the costs of producing the ad, paying for talent (Forrest Whittaker and Harrison Ford), and licensing a Queen song ("Don't Stop Me Now").[20]

Personal Selling. Personal selling is the most effective tool at certain stages of the buying process, particularly in building up buyers' preferences, convictions, and actions. It involves personal interaction between two or more people, so each person can observe the other's needs and characteristics and make quick adjustments. Personal selling also allows all kinds of customer relationships to spring up, ranging from matter-of-fact selling relationships to personal friendships. An effective salesperson keeps the customer's interests at heart to build a long-term relationship by solving a customer's problems. Finally, with personal selling, the buyer usually feels a greater need to listen and respond, even if the response is a polite "No, thank you."

These unique qualities come at a cost, however. A sales force requires a longer-term commitment than does advertising—advertising can be turned up or down, but the size of a sales force is harder to change. Firms can spend up to three times as much on personal selling as they do on advertising.

Sales Promotion. Sales promotion includes a wide assortment of tools—coupons, contests, discounts, premiums, and others—all of which have many unique qualities. They attract consumer attention, engage consumers, offer strong incentives to engage, and can be used to dramatize product offers and boost sagging sales. Sales promotions invite and reward quick response. Whereas advertising says, "Buy our product," sales promotion says, "Buy it now." Sales promotion effects can be short lived, however, and often are not as effective as advertising or personal selling in building long-run brand preference and customer relationships.

Public Relations. Public relations (PR) is very believable—news stories, features, sponsorships, and events seem more real and believable to readers than ads do. PR can also reach many prospects who avoid salespeople and advertisements—the message gets to buyers as "news and events" rather than as a sales-directed communication. And, as with advertising, public relations can dramatize a company or product. Marketers tend to underuse public relations or use it as an afterthought. Yet a well-thought-out public relations campaign used with other promotion mix elements can be very effective and economical.

Direct and Digital Marketing. The many forms of direct and digital marketing— from traditional direct mail, catalogs, and telephone marketing to newer online, mobile, and social media—all share some distinctive characteristics. Direct marketing is more targeted: It's usually directed to a specific customer or customer community. Direct marketing is immediate and personalized: Content can be prepared quickly— even in real time—and tailored to appeal to individual consumers or brand groups. Finally, direct marketing is interactive: It allows a dialogue between the marketing team and the consumer, and messages can be altered depending on the consumer's response. Thus, direct and digital marketing are well suited to highly targeted marketing efforts, creating customer engagement, and building one-to-one customer relationships.

Promotion Mix Strategies

Marketers can choose from two basic promotion mix strategies: *push* promotion or *pull* promotion. ● **Figure 14.3** contrasts the two strategies. The relative emphasis given to the specific promotion tools differs for push and pull strategies. A **push strategy** involves "pushing" the product through marketing channels to final consumers. The producer directs its marketing activities (primarily personal selling and trade promotion) toward channel members to induce them to carry the product and promote it to final consumers. For example, John Deere does very little promoting of its lawn mowers, garden tractors, and other residential consumer products to final consumers. Instead, John Deere's sales force works with Lowe's, Home Depot, independent dealers, and other channel members, who in turn push John Deere products to final consumers.

Using a **pull strategy**, the producer directs its marketing activities (primarily advertising, consumer promotion, and direct and digital media content) toward final consumers to induce them to engage with and buy the product. For example, P&G promotes its Tide laundry products directly to consumers using TV and print ads, websites and social media,

Push strategy
A promotion strategy that calls for using the sales force and trade promotion to push the product through channels. The producer promotes the product to channel members who in turn promote it to final consumers.

Pull strategy
A promotion strategy that calls for spending a lot on consumer advertising, promotion, and other content to induce final consumers to engage with and buy the product, creating a demand vacuum that "pulls" the product through the channel.

● **FIGURE 14.3**
Push versus Pull Promotion Strategy

In a push strategy, the company "pushes" the product to resellers, which in turn "push" it to consumers.

In a pull strategy, the company promotes directly to final consumers, creating a demand vacuum that "pulls" the product through the channel. Most companies use some combination of push and pull.

Push strategy

Pull strategy

and other channels. If the pull strategy is effective, consumers will then demand the brand from retailers such as Walmart, Target, Kroger, Walgreens, or Amazon, which will in turn demand it from P&G. Thus, under a pull strategy, consumer demand "pulls" the product through the channels.

Some industrial-goods companies use only push strategies; likewise, some direct marketing companies use only pull strategies. However, most large companies use some combination of both. For example, P&G spends more than $4.3 billion each year on U.S. consumer advertising to create brand preference and pull customers into stores that carry its products.[21] At the same time, it uses its sales force and trade promotions to push its brands through the channels so that they will be available on store shelves when consumers come calling.

Companies consider many factors when designing their promotion mix strategies, including the type of product and market. For example, the importance of different promotion tools varies between consumer and business markets. Business-to-consumer companies usually pull more, putting more of their funds into advertising, followed by sales promotion, personal selling, and then public relations. In contrast, business-to-business marketers tend to push more, putting more of their funds into personal selling, followed by sales promotion, advertising, and public relations.

Integrating the Promotion Mix

Having set the promotion budget and mix, the company must now take steps to see that each promotion mix element is smoothly integrated. Guided by the company's overall communications strategy, the various promotion elements should work together to carry the firm's unique brand messages and selling points. Integrating the promotion mix starts with customers. Whether it's advertising, personal selling, sales promotion, public relations, or digital and direct marketing, communications at each customer touch point must deliver consistent marketing content and positioning. An integrated promotion mix ensures that communications efforts occur when, where, and how *customers* need them.

To achieve an integrated promotion mix, all of the firm's functions must cooperate to jointly plan communications efforts. Many companies even include customers, suppliers, and other stakeholders at various stages of communications planning. Scattered or disjointed promotional activities across the company can result in diluted marketing communications impact and confused positioning. By contrast, an integrated promotion mix maximizes the combined effects of all a firm's promotional efforts.

Socially Responsible Marketing Communication

In shaping its promotion mix, a company must be aware of the many legal and ethical issues surrounding marketing communications. Most marketers work hard to communicate openly and honestly with consumers and resellers. Still, abuses may occur, and public policy makers have developed a substantial body of laws and regulations to govern advertising, sales promotion, personal selling, and direct marketing. In this section, we discuss issues regarding advertising, sales promotion, and personal selling. We discuss digital and direct marketing issues in Chapter 17.

Advertising and Sales Promotion

By law, companies must avoid false or deceptive advertising. Advertisers must not make false claims, such as suggesting that a product cures something when it does not. They must avoid ads that have the capacity to deceive, even though no one actually may be deceived. An automobile cannot be advertised as getting 32 miles per gallon unless it does so under typical conditions, and diet bread cannot be advertised as having fewer calories simply because its slices are thinner.

Sellers must avoid bait-and-switch advertising that attracts buyers under false pretenses. For example, a large retailer advertised a sewing machine at $179. However, when consumers tried to buy the advertised machine, the seller downplayed its features, placed faulty machines on showroom floors, understated the machine's performance, and took other actions in an attempt to switch buyers to a more expensive machine. Such actions are both unethical and illegal.

Real Marketing 14.2 | Promoting Social Responsibility: It's the Right Thing to Do

Most companies today have made social responsibility part of their corporate strategy, and they use advertising and marketing to promote socially responsible programs, actions, and ideas. Rather than focusing only on profits, they recognize that company success is inexorably linked to the welfare of their customers and the world around them.

Companies in almost every industry now support and promote a wide range of social and environmental issues. In the past two seasons, for example, 20 percent of all Super Bowl ads have connected brands with a wide range of issues. Last season, Microsoft ran an inspirational ad featuring children with physical and cognitive disabilities rising to the top of their games with the help of its Xbox Adaptive Controller. "The story illustrates Microsoft's commitment to building accessible technology that levels the playing field and creates opportunity for all of us," says Microsoft. "When everyone plays, we all win." And an Anheuser-Busch Super Bowl ad featured the Budweiser Dalmatian, ears flapping in the breeze, sitting atop a wagon pulled by the Budweiser Clydesdales through a field of golden grain on a wind turbine farm, set to Bob Dylan's "Blowin' In the Wind." "Wind never felt better," the ad concluded, noting that Budweiser is "now brewed with 100% renewable energy. This Bud's for a better tomorrow."

Thus, more and more, companies are using advertising and marketing to take a stand on relevant social and environmental issues, not just to make a buck but because it's the right thing to do. Let's look more deeply into three successful campaigns promoting social responsibility.

Google: "Made with Code"

Five years ago, Google launched a $50 million "Made with Code" marketing and advertising campaign that encourages young girls to pursue science and technology careers. The company found that 74 percent of middle school girls express interest in science, technology, engineering, and math (STEM), but by high school, less than 1 percent of girls plan to major in computer science. Jobs in computer science will be among the highest paid jobs over the coming decade. Yet women are underrepresented in the roles that make technology happen.

Through ads, dedicated digital and social media sites, events, and partnerships with dozens of not-for-profit organizations, Google's campaign promotes the idea that

the things young girls love, from their smartphone apps to fashions to their favorite movies are "made with code." "Simply put, code is a tool that lets you write your story with technology," says Google.

The Made with Code website offers resources to help kids learn coding, communities for discussing and sharing coding projects and discoveries, and support from coding mentors. Made with Code Twitter, Instagram, and Tumblr pages are loaded with images, news, and stories that bring coding to life. "Girls start out with a love of science and technology but lose it somewhere along the way," says Google. "Let's help encourage that passion."

Walgreens: "Red Nose Day"

Walgreens did not invent Red Nose Day, a global fundraising effort to help end child poverty. But more than any other organization,

Walgreens has made Red Nose Day famous in the United States. To back its corporate commitment to child health, education, and well-being, Walgreens stepped forward five years ago to become the official and exclusive retailer for Red Nose Day in the United States. Every year, in the weeks leading up to Red Nose Day (the fourth Thursday in May), Walgreens promotes and sells the iconic red noses online and in each of its 9,000 U.S. stores. It sells the red noses for $1 each, individually or in boxes of 60 or 360, and donates all proceeds to the Red Nose Day Fund.

Beyond just selling red noses, Walgreens supports Red Nose Day with a fully integrated marketing content campaign. In addition to TV ads, online video, and website and social media support, Walgreens also promotes Red Nose Day with events and challenges. For example, its Red Nose Challenge invites everyone everywhere to

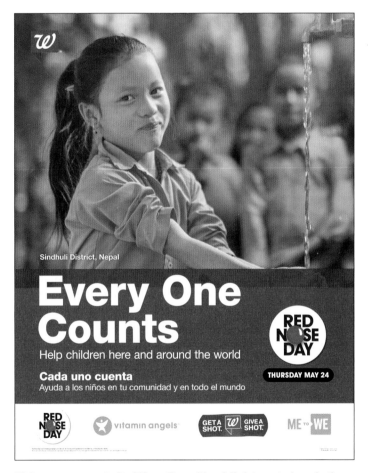

Walgreens supports Red Nose Day with a fully integrated marketing content campaign. It creates "a powerful opportunity for our customers and the communities we serve to come together to help make an impact on a worthwhile cause like child poverty."
Walgreen Co.

"get seriously silly" on social media or share their #NosesOn selfies.

Walgreens isn't alone in supporting Red Nose Day in the United States—dozens of brands take part. But as the only outlet where official Red Nose Day noses can be purchased, it plays an essential role in driving promotional content and in moving people to donate. Last year, Walgreens generated 180 million media impressions and 267,000 engagements for Red Nose Day. More important, Walgreens alone raised more than $28 million for Red Nose Day, bringing its five-year total to more than $100 million. "By focusing our efforts on initiatives like Red Nose Day," says a Walgreens executive, "we create a unique and powerful opportunity for our customers and the communities we serve to come together to help make an impact on a worthwhile cause like child poverty. By choosing Walgreens, our customers choose to make a difference in the life of a child in need."

Gillette: "The Best Men Can Be"

Gillette has been closely associated with images of men and masculinity for decades. Recently, the brand has attempted to use that association as an agent for social change. In response to the #metoo movement, Gillette

has taken a stand. "Turn on the news today and it's easy to believe that men are not at their best," says Gillette. "It's time we acknowledge that brands like ours play a role in influencing culture. And as a company that encourages men to be their best, we have a responsibility to make sure we are promoting positive, attainable, inclusive, and healthy versions of what it means to be a man."

To get things started, Gillette released a short video ad—"The Best Men Can Be"—that plays off of its 30-year slogan, "The Best a Man Can Get." The video lays out the case that men need to come together to address issues of "toxic masculinity," including sexual harassment, sexual discrimination, and bullying. It invites men to support positive change, "to strive to be better, to make us better, and to help each other be better."

Gillette simultaneously launched a new brand site, TheBestMenCanBe.org, which details the campaign's purpose and pledges that the brand will "actively challenge the stereotypes and expectations of what it means to be a man everywhere you see Gillette. In the ads we run, the images we publish to social media, the words we choose, and so much more." Gillette also pledged to donate $1 million annually to nonprofit organizations offering programs that help men of all ages "achieve their personal best and become role

models for the next generation." "We've got work to do," says the brand. "And it starts today."

Gillette's "The Best Men Can Be" campaign has received praise from many quarters. But not surprisingly, taking a stand on a hot issue often generates controversy. Within 48 hours, the video had received 20 million views and Gillette had racked up 1.5 million social media mentions, explosively more than the mere 10,000 mentions during the same period the prior week. On YouTube, the responses ran two-to-one "thumbs down." Most naysayers agreed that there is a need for change but accused Gillette of polarizing a sensitive issue, lumping all men into one category, and being preachy. One prominent broadcaster even accused Gillette of contributing to the so-called "global assault on masculinity."

Despite the controversy, Gillette has continued to support the campaign and the cause. The company expected the "Best Men Can Be" campaign to spark a difficult dialogue. "Successful brands today have to be relevant and engage consumers in topics that matter to them," said a Gillette marketer. "If we get people to pause, reflect, and to challenge themselves and others to ensure that their actions reflect who they really are, then this campaign will be a success."[22]

A company's trade promotion activities also are closely regulated. For example, under the Robinson-Patman Act, sellers cannot favor certain customers through their use of trade promotions. They must make promotional allowances and services available to all resellers on proportionately equal terms.

Beyond simply avoiding legal pitfalls, such as deceptive or bait-and-switch advertising, companies can use advertising and other forms of promotion to encourage and promote socially responsible programs, actions, and ideas. Companies in almost every industry now promote a wide range of social and environmental causes and issues related to their brands (see Real Marketing 14.2).

An all-time classic example is the long-running "Dove Campaign for Real Beauty," which set out to change stereotypical definitions of beauty with ads featuring candid and confident images of real women with all sorts of body types (not glamorous actresses or skinny models). "Our mission is to make more women feel beautiful every day by broadening the definition of beauty," says Dove. Over the years, the constantly evolving "Campaign for Real Beauty"—consisting of ads, heavily viewed digital videos, and other content—has done much to serve the cause of helping women to be comfortable in their own skin. And although the campaign has noble motives beyond sales and profits, it has also contributed to Dove's success. During the first decade of the campaign, the brand's annual revenues grew from $2.5 billion to more than $4 billion. Fifteen years later, the Dove Campaign for Real Beauty campaign is still going strong.[23]

Personal Selling

A company's salespeople must follow the rules of "fair competition." Most states have enacted deceptive sales acts that spell out what is not allowed. For example, salespeople may not lie to consumers or mislead them about the advantages of buying a particular product. To avoid bait-and-switch practices, salespeople's statements must match advertising claims.

Different rules apply to consumers who are called on at home or who buy at a location that is not the seller's permanent place of business versus those who go to a store in search of a product. Because people who are called on may be taken by surprise and may be especially vulnerable to high-pressure selling techniques, the Federal Trade Commission (FTC) has adopted a *three-day cooling-off rule* to give special protection to customers who are not seeking products. Under this rule, customers who agree in their own homes, workplace, dormitory, or facilities rented by the seller on a temporary basis—such as hotel rooms, convention centers, and restaurants—to buy something costing more than $25 have 72 hours in which to cancel a contract or return merchandise and get their money back—no questions asked.

Reviewing and Extending the Concepts

Objectives Review

In this chapter, you learned how companies use integrated marketing communications (IMC) to communicate customer value. Modern marketing calls for more than just creating customer value by developing a good product, pricing it attractively, and making it available to target customers. Companies also must clearly and persuasively engage current and prospective consumers and *communicate* that value to them. To do this, they must blend five promotion mix tools, guided by a well-designed and implemented IMC strategy.

OBJECTIVE 14-1 Define the five promotion mix tools for communicating customer value. (pp 410–411)

A company's total *promotion mix*—also called its *marketing communications mix*—consists of the specific blend of *advertising, personal selling, sales promotion, public relations,* and *direct and digital marketing* tools that the company uses to engage consumers, persuasively communicate customer value, and build customer relationships. *Advertising* includes any paid form of nonpersonal presentation and promotion of ideas, goods, or services by an identified sponsor. In contrast, *public relations* focuses on building good relations with the company's various publics. *Personal selling* is personal presentation by the firm's sales force for the purpose of making sales and building customer relationships. Firms use *sales promotion* to provide short-term incentives to encourage the purchase or sale of a product or service. Finally, firms seeking immediate response from targeted individual customers use *direct and digital marketing* tools to engage directly with customers and cultivate relationships with them.

OBJECTIVE 14-2 Discuss the changing communications landscape and the need for integrated marketing communications. (pp 411–416)

The explosive developments in communications technology and changes in marketer and customer communication strategies have had a dramatic impact on marketing communications. Advertisers have now added a broad selection of more-specialized and highly targeted media and content—including online, mobile, and social media—to reach smaller customer segments with more-personalized, interactive messages. As they adopt richer but more fragmented media and promotion mixes to reach their diverse markets, they risk creating a communications hodgepodge for consumers. To prevent this, companies have adopted the concept of *integrated marketing communications (IMC)*. Guided by an overall IMC strategy, the company works out the roles that the various promotional tools and marketing content will play and the extent to which each will be used. It carefully coordinates the promotional activities and the timing of when major campaigns take place.

OBJECTIVE 14-3 Outline the communication process and the steps in developing effective marketing communications. (pp 416–422)

The communication process involves nine elements: two major parties (sender, receiver), two communication tools (message, media), four communication functions (encoding, decoding, response, and feedback), and noise. To communicate effectively, marketers must understand how these elements combine to communicate value to target customers.

In preparing marketing communications, the communicator's first task is to *identify the target audience* and its characteristics. Next, the communicator has to determine the *communication objectives* and define the response sought. Beyond purchase, marketing communicators want to help build customer–brand relationships and guide customers through the five As of the customer journey: *awareness, appeal, ask, act,* and *advocacy.* Then a *message* should be constructed with an effective content and structure. *Media* must be selected, both for personal and nonpersonal communication. The communicator must find highly credible sources to deliver messages. Finally, the communicator must collect *feedback* by watching how much of the market becomes aware, tries the product, and is satisfied in the process.

OBJECTIVE 14-4 Explain the methods for setting the promotion budget and factors that affect the design of the promotion mix. (pp 422–429)

The company must determine how much to spend for promotion. The most popular approaches are to spend what the company can afford, use a percentage of sales, base promotion on competitors' spending, or base it on an analysis and costing of the communication objectives and tasks. The company has to divide the *promotion budget* among the major tools to create the *promotion mix.* Companies can pursue a *push* or a *pull* promotional strategy—or a combination of the two. People at all levels of the organization must be aware of the many legal and ethical issues surrounding marketing communications.

Companies must work hard and proactively at communicating openly, honestly, and agreeably with their customers and resellers.

Key Terms

OBJECTIVE 14-1

Promotion mix (or marketing communications mix) (p 410)
Advertising (p 411)
Sales promotion (p 411)
Personal selling (p 411)
Public relations (PR) (p 411)
Direct and digital marketing (p 411)

OBJECTIVE 14-2

Content marketing (p 412)

Integrated marketing communications (IMC) (p 414)

OBJECTIVE 14-3

Five As (p 418)
Personal communication channels (p 420)
Word-of-mouth influence (p 420)
Buzz marketing (p 420)
Nonpersonal communication channels (p 421)

OBJECTIVE 14-4

Affordable method (p 422)
Percentage-of-sales method (p 423)
Competitive-parity method (p 423)
Objective-and-task method (p 423)
Push strategy (p 425)
Pull strategy (p 425)

Discussion Questions

14-1 Name and describe the five major promotion tools used in a company's marketing communications mix. (AASCB: Written and Oral Communication)

14-2 How has the role of marketing communicators shifted in response to the increasingly fragmented and digital communications environment? (AACSB: Written and Oral Communication)

14-3 What is integrated marketing communications (IMC), and how does a company go about implementing it? (AACSB: Written and Oral Communication; Reflective Thinking)

14-4 Discuss the main marketing communication objectives and the ideal responses from audiences. (AACSB: Communication)

14-5 How does a company determine its promotional budget? (AACSB: Written and Oral Communication)

Critical Thinking Exercises

14-6 Integrated marketing communications are highly coordinated. Identify a new product or service and research the IMC across different platforms and media. Is the message consistent? (AACSB: Communication; Use of IT; Reflective Thinking)

14-7 In a small group, create a video advertisement for Ulta Beauty (www.ulta.com) that appropriately addresses each aspect of the communication process shown in Figure 14.2. Illustrate how each element is represented in the advertisement. Discuss how the advertisement, by itself, does or does not constitute effective marketing communication for Ulta Beauty. (AACSB: Written and Oral Communication; Reflective Thinking)

14-8 Recently, a former creative director from Netflix founded a canned water startup called Liquid Death Mountain Water. The brand positions itself as a sustainable alternative to energy drinks and soda and targets the straight-edge punk crowd that abstains from drugs and alcohol using the tagline: "Murder Your Thirst." The brand aims to make the world's healthiest beverage, water, as funny and entertaining as unhealthy brands in other categories (energy drinks, soda, beer). The brand sells water in tall-boy cans that resemble beer cans for $1.83, which includes delivery. It donates 5 cents from every can sold to clean up plastic garbage from the ocean. Should Liquid Death emphasize a push or pull strategy? Explain. (AACSB: Written and Oral Communication; Ethical Reasoning; Reflective Thinking)

APPLICATIONS AND CASES

Online, Mobile, and Social Media Marketing Spot the Difference

Online newspapers and magazines need most of the content they publish to be current, up-to-date, and in vogue. However, very few readers actually want to pay to access that content. The solution seems simple: use thinly disguised advertorial content instead. Interestingly, the more the content is read, the greater the advertising revenue. To many readers, it would now appear that few online content sites are prepared to take the trouble of paying a proper journalist or travel writer to create an article or a piece of high-quality copy. Instead, content is either advertorial material or fairly dull practical advice. This also means that opportunities of making a living for journalists are dwindling. The subscription systems put people off, and it is impossible to subscribe to a specific section of a newspaper or magazine to keep up with news and events from a specific perspective. A great deal of writing on news and media sites has become an integral part of public relations rather than conventional journalism. Some sites simply reprint press releases without comment or changes. Others will turn to business organizations that have customized-content providers to create a piece for them in different styles to match the look of different news websites. A major marketing trend has been to create content for brands. This has blurred the fine line between paid media coverage or advertisements and earned media coverage, which is more about convincing a journalist that a brand deserves to be written about. This has also created a conflict between different parts of the marketing industry. PR specialists would suggest they are better placed to write the customized content and they can find a newsworthy

story for a brand. Advertising specialists claim they are the ones with the greatest affinity with advertorials, and they would know better to make something stand out. As the distinction between opinionated news content and customized content presented with a clear opinion and purpose become ever more blurred, it is becoming increasingly difficult for the reader to tell the difference. As advertising revenue becomes more diluted with increased competition, should we blame the media for looking for a new income stream? Brands deserve their own story too, and it looks like the media are ready to write it for them.

14-9 Find examples of advertorials on various news websites. Create a presentation with screenshots showing the content and how it is identified. Has the content been shared with others via social media? (AACSB: Communication; Information Technology)

14-10 Should there be a clear warning on content that has been sponsored or customized? Should there be legislation or guidelines to identify and control this activity? (AACSB: Communication; Reflective Thinking)

Marketing Ethics Western Stereotypes

In January 2014, the Japanese airline All Nippon Airways (ANA) was forced to pull a TV advertisement after being accused of racist stereotyping by viewers. The TV commercial featured two Japanese men in ANA uniforms. They were discussing, in English with Japanese subtitles, how they could boost the image of ANA as an international airline. The punch line of the commercial saw one of them suggesting that they change the image of Japanese people. The camera then cut back to the other man, who was now wearing a blonde wig and a long rubber nose. These are stereotypical Japanese images of what Westerners look like. This is by no means the first and probably not the last time potentially racist stereotyping of Westerners has been employed in Japanese advertisements. In 2013, Toshiba featured a Japanese girl with a

blonde wig and a fake nose in an advertisement for a bread maker. In 2010, Nagasaki Prefecture promoted its foreign-designed buildings with Japanese tourists wearing blonde wigs and big noses. At other times, Westerners have been portrayed as hapless visitors, a stereotype that has not been met with widespread viewer approval.

14-11 Westerners are comparatively rare in countries such as Japan. Is it right to portray them in this way? Explain why or why not. (AACSB: Communication; Reflective Thinking; Ethical Understanding and Reasoning)

14-12 Find other examples of marketing strategies that have employed racial stereotypes which could be considered inappropriate by viewers outside a specific culture. (AACSB: Written and Oral Communication; Reflective Thinking)

Marketing by the Numbers Never-Ending Cola War

Although consumption of carbonated beverages has been decreasing, it is still an $81 billion industry in North America, which far exceeds alternatives such as water ($23 billion) and sports drinks ($9.4 billion). That's why Coca-Cola and Pepsi still battle it out. Coca-Cola's market share increased from 17.3 percent to 17.8 percent during the past decade. That might not seem like much, but one share point equals 1 percent of market sales, so half a share point represents $405 million. Pepsi's market share decreased from 10.3 percent to 8.4 percent during the same period—a loss of 1.9 share points or $1.5 billion. The war is not yet over, though. PepsiCo increased its advertising budget $500 million in 2018, resulting in a $1.13 billion increase in sales compared to Coca-Cola's almost $4 billion decrease in sales. Many marketers budget an upcoming year's advertising expenditures using a percentage-of-sales method based on past or projected sales. The industry average advertising-to-sales ratio for beverages is 4.1 percent of sales. Below are the worldwide advertising expenditures and sales revenues for the two combatants (all numbers are in billions of dollars):

Year	PepsiCo		Coca-Cola	
	Advertising	**Sales**	**Advertising**	**Sales**
2014	$2.30	$66.68	$3.50	$46.00
2015	$2.40	$63.06	$3.98	$44.29
2016	$2.50	$62.80	$4.00	$41.86
2017	$2.40	$63.53	$3.96	$35.41
2018	$2.90	$64.66	$4.00	$31.86

14-13 Calculate both companies' advertising-to-sales ratios for each year. What is each's average ratio over the five-year period? Refer to the percentage-of-sales method in the chapter to learn about this method. (AACSB: Analytical Reasoning)

14-14 If PepsiCo had decided to base its 2018 advertising budget on the industry average advertising-to-sales ratio for beverages, which is 4.1 percent, how much would PepsiCo have budgeted for advertising based on last year's sales? How much of a budget increase is that? Compare that to the actual 2018 $500 million increase in advertising expenditures. Was Pepsi's action effective? (AACSB: Analytic Reasoning; Reflective Thinking)

Company Case Nestlé: Integrating Marketing Communication into Daily Operations

With more than 2000 brands, from global icons to local favorites, and present in 190 countries, Nestlé is one of the world's largest food-and-beverage companies. It operates in four different strategic business units: beverages, milk and milk products, prepared dishes and cooking aides, and chocolates. To design a proper marketing mix for all four product groups, Nestlé employs country- and market-specific marketing teams to design an IMC strategy, regardless of the product group.

Have a Break from TV. Have a KitKat.

KitKat serves as a good representative of Nestlé's promotional strategies. Its "take a break" message enjoys high-level recognition in more than 80 countries globally. The official website follows that philosophy faithfully: it literally just asks the visitor to take a break and have a KitKat. The brand's promotion is concentrated mainly in TV commercials and posters, where the powerful colors of the pack and the product reinforce the marketing message.

Advertising plays an important role in the confectionery industry, which Nestlé is a part of, so it is not surprising that the company heavily invests in it. In 2016, for example, it spent £10 million on advertising for KitKat. The brand has a history of very successful campaigns, like one in 2012, in which customers who discovered one of the six GPS-enabled chocolate bars were delivered a prize of £10,000 by helicopter. The campaign drew a huge number of visitors to its website and Facebook and Twitter pages, all eager to see how many bars were yet to be found. Building on its success, an additional contest was organized to win £2,012, the year in which the campaign was launched, by entering the code on the inside of their KitKat wrapper into a custom-made Facebook application. Customers were only allowed to enter after they had liked the KitKat page.

Another creative ad was the KitKat's 2015 Christmas commercial, which showed a blank screen for 30 seconds—a break from the holiday noise of the season. More conventionally, for the 2019 winter season in the UK and Ireland, KitKat launched on-pack promotion where customers who found a golden ticket in their KitKat won a "holiday break" to one of ten sunny exotic locations. The winning chocolate bar featured the name of the destination written on it in white chocolate. Besides the ten holidays, the company offered other prizes to be won every day, like beach towels, luggage tags, sun visors, and KitKat-branded passport covers.

Besides advertising, Nestlé has used a wide range of IMC tools for KitKat, including sales promotion activities. Personal selling is costly, but large companies like Nestlé can afford it. One of its classic campaigns was a direct vendor selling activity in the summer months of June, July, and August in Lahore, Pakistan, during which a team of vendors clad in branded t-shirts, caps, and jackets, sold chilled 0.5-liter bottles to commuters on all major intersections. The brand got great mileage out of this innovative idea of personal selling in terms of brand awareness, paid trial, image, as well as real sales.

KitKat has become a particular obsession in Japan, where sales and profits are higher than in any other market. The introduction of KitKat Green Tea (Uji Matcha) in 2004 has not only expanded the over 350 KitKat varieties that have been available in Japan over the years but also drawn more attention to the brand and increased sales volume. After its massive success in Japan, in February 2019, the KitKat Matcha was introduced in Europe.

In direct marketing, Nestlé has even used physical mail creatively. For instance, it sent out a mailer made to look like the card left by postal workers when they are unable to deliver a parcel, saying that the package, the KitKat chunky, was "too chunky for your letterbox." The recipients could exchange their card at their local news agency for a free KitKat Chunky.

Direct and Digital Marketing

Apart from being the most used channel, digital marketing now has the highest audience reach. Nestlé is active in social media marketing and connects and interacts with more than 11 million Facebook fans, 250,000 followers on Twitter, and more than 180,000 followers on Instagram. The company makes sure that its products are positioned for the wider but also the most appropriate audience using brilliant ideas for creative advertising. A campaign launched in India in 2015 provided a fresh take on its signature tag line. This campaign was about "celebrating the breakers," and recognized that people take many different types of breaks. Animated videos and ad photos of people snoozing at their desk, listening to music, and partying all night were posted with the hashtag #mybreak on Instagram, which was the ideal platform to tell this story visually and engage followers. The campaign was a success, with a 42-point lift in ad recall and 6-point lift in message association.

Nestlé constantly responds to rapid technological changes in the marketing environment. In 2011, the company launched the Digital Acceleration Team (DAT) to design a better mix of traditional and digital IMC tools and enhance its product marketing and e-commerce. Inspired by hackathon culture, this involves an intensive and highly entrepreneurial eight-month training program where diverse high-potential leaders from across the globe gather at Nestlé's HQ in Switzerland to exchange marketing experiences. The DAT works on specific digital marketing topics, and the team returns with the expertise needed to lead the digital transformation in their home units. Beyond DAT, Nestlé has also endeavored to become more digitally connected by having an internal social network where more than 200 employees can engage with one another, and by enabling employees to blog and inspire or influence customers as daily practice.

Developing Effective Communications

At Nestlé, the process of developing an effective IMC strategy for promotions begins with identifying the target audience, such as current and potential customers and those who make the buying decision or those who influence it. For KitKat the target audience is *everyone*—the mass consumer market. Next, the communication objectives, such as building awareness and knowledge, and providing information value for the customers, are determined. As KitKat is already a well-known product globally, the company advertises not so much to boost sales as to remind the customers about their favorite chocolate bar. It then decides on the suitable media, including personal and non-personal channels, for the marketing message: should it choose personal address or a wide exposure? Nestlé uses all possible channels, including print media (newspapers, magazines, direct mail) for its cost effectiveness and non-intrusiveness, which is a struggle in the digital era.

KitKat uses broadcast (radio, television) and display (billboards, signs, posters) media to reach a broader target audience. It uses print media mostly in form of posters that celebrate an event in a funny way, focusing on the "Take a Break" slogan. In one example, when a "no Wi-Fi zone" was introduced in downtown Amsterdam in 2013, a street sign was installed with the "Take a Break" slogan. Nestlé also uses events: in 2013, Android launched its new operating system using the KitKat name. Another aspect of effective communications is message source selection—one of KitKat's brand ambassadors is musician Chance the Rapper, who has appeared in various ads since 2016, to appeal to his young Millennial following.

Feedback is vital for measuring the effectiveness of communication tools, so Nestlé analyzes big data from retailers and internal processes such as how many people bought a product, talked to others about it, or visited a store. Insights from these analyses are then used by Nestlé for suggesting changes in the IMC strategy or in the product offer itself.

Budget-Setting

Nestlé sets its promotion budget based on what it wants to accomplish, defining specific promotion objectives, determining the tasks needed to achieve them, and estimating the costs of performing these tasks. The sum of these costs is the proposed promotion budget, which is then divided among various IMC tools. For example, KitKat announced that it would double its media spend in 2015 with the launch of a £10 million multimedia campaign after losing sales in the sweet biscuits category the year before. Seeking to reclaim the 11 percent of sales lost, the campaign involved heavy promotion in-store as well as on social media. Budget-setting is also in line with pricing policy: the price is dependent on the market of each individual product, so market leaders Nescafé and Maggi are priced with higher margins for the company as compared to the competition. To deliver a clear, consistent, and compelling message about the products, Nestlé ensures close cooperation with market- and marketing-specific local-country teams to consider culture and market differences.

Nestlé has worked hard to make sure that its traditional marketing approaches blend well with newer, tech-savvy ones, like printing of QR codes on candy bars and boosting social media engagement. Sales promotion is also done through interactive and responsive websites. For example, in the UK, the company printed individual codes on KitKat packaging that could either be entered on a dynamic website or texted on a mobile phone to win a prize—proof that traditional promotion can co-exist with digital tools. The particular blend of channels—of traditional and digital media—is based on observation of customer behavior. For instance, when marketing analytics indicate that a product appeals to a younger generation, digital is clearly the way for the company to go. However, this doesn't mean that Nestlé should abandon more traditional approaches; it continues to find ways to use traditional marketing to raise brand awareness with creative ideas that reinforce the marketing message.

Through high-quality messages that increase ad recall, such as the "celebrate the breakers" campaign, Nestlé maximizes returns on brand-building investments as it leverages social media to drive marketing and capitalize on digital channels. By developing a highly engaging customer base and enhancing earned media benefits, the company keeps pace with an ever-changing communication landscape. Digital and social media marketing strategies, social network initiatives, and digital formats are implemented across global operations.

To continue building attractive and rewarding brand experiences for customers, Nestlé designs its IMC strategy collaboratively with other groups, such as sales and e-business, R&D, technical applications, and agency partners. Through these well-defined steps in IMC and budget-setting, Nestlé has executed multiple campaigns with great success and is all set to continue that trend in the future.[24]

Questions for Discussion

14-15 What steps did Nestlé undertake to design KitKat's IMC and promotion program?

14-16 Should all companies have a digital acceleration team? What benefits did Nestlé get from having one?

14-17 How is the budget for IMC set at Nestlé? What factors might possibly influence it?

14-18 What IMC tool has Nestlé mainly used to promote KitKat and increase sales?

14-19. Explain the benefits of IMC efforts based on examples given in this case.

15 | Advertising and Public Relations

CHAPTER PREVIEW

After analyzing overall integrated marketing communications (IMC) planning, we dig more deeply into the specific marketing communication tools. In this chapter, we explore advertising and public relations (PR). Advertising involves communicating the company's or brand's value proposition by using paid media to inform, persuade, and remind consumers. PR involves building good relations with various company publics—from consumers and the general public to the media, investor, donor, and government publics. As with all the promotion mix tools, advertising and PR must be blended into the overall IMC program. In Chapters 16 and 17, we will discuss the remaining promotion mix tools: personal selling, sales promotion, and direct and digital marketing.

Let's start by looking at a one of the most successful advertising campaigns in recent history. In the fiercely competitive snack and candy industry, where well-established brands are fighting for survival, the inspired-yet-durable Snickers "You're not you when you're hungry" content campaign has given the iconic brand new life. No matter where you see the message—on TV, on a mobile screen, in a friend's post, or even on a Snickers candy bar wrapper—the imaginative campaign clearly and consistently drives home the brand's "Snickers satisfies" and "You're not you when you're hungry" positioning in an engaging and memorable way. It has also made Snickers the world's leading sweet snack. The message: Good advertising really does matter.

SNICKERS: "You're Not You When You're Hungry"

It all started with a now-classic Snickers ad in the 2010 Super Bowl. In the ad, during a neighborhood pickup football game, then-octogenarian Golden Girl Betty White appeared as a football player who was "playing like Betty White"—that is, very poorly. But after biting into a Snickers bar, she morphed back into a young, athletic footballer who played more like his usual self. The ad ended with the now-familiar slogan "You're not you when you're hungry" followed by the tagline "Snickers satisfies."

The Betty White ad generated tremendous buzz, reinvigorating the then-stagnant Snickers candy bar brand. According to Nielsen, it was the "best-liked spot" of that year's Super Bowl, and it achieved the highest score on the *USA Today* Ad Meter rankings. The ad went viral, racking up tens of millions of views online and earning seemingly endless media attention. The "You're not you when you're hungry" slogan went on to become the cornerstone of a long-running, highly successful advertising communications campaign that has propelled Snickers to the top of the global confectionary market.

Every great advertising campaign starts with a unique brand message, something that sets the brand apart. For decades, Mars, Incorporated has positioned Snickers on one overriding brand attribute: Snickers is satisfying. Heartier than most candy bars, Snickers combines ingredients like chocolate, nougat, and caramel with the protein power of peanuts. The "Snickers satisfies" tagline emphasizes the bar's stomach-filling properties. Before the current campaign, Snickers pitched the bar to young athletic males as a meal alternative. One classic print ad, for example, showed an approving mother sending her son off to football practice with a Snickers bar.

But by the early 2000s, Snickers was in a rut. Its positioning had grown stale; its sales and market share had flattened. The brand needed a new creative concept—something that would rejuvenate Snickers and broaden its market appeal. Rather than abandoning its established positioning, however, Mars extended it with the fresh "You're not you when you're hungry" theme. So while "Snickers satisfies" remains the brand's baseline positioning, "You're not you" is the creative "big idea" that now brings the positioning to life in a clever and engaging way.

"You're not you when you're hungry" taps into a powerful and universal emotional appeal—hunger. It reaches a broad market. Almost everyone can relate to how being hungry changes who you are. The positioning is as powerful for women as for men; for older generations as for younger ones; for office workers, factory workers, or students. It works across global cultural lines. Finally, the "You're not you" theme lends itself to no end of imaginative and entertaining ads and executions across varied media platforms.

From that first Betty White Super Bowl ad, the "You're not you" campaign has spawned a host of creative ads in more than 80 countries. One memorable TV ad featured the late Robin Williams as a football coach instructing his team to "kill them—with kindness" by making balloon animals and tea cosies. Then there was the Snickers Brady Bunch ad for Super Bowl XLIX in which roughneck Danny Trejo portrayed a snarling Marcia and quirky Steve Buscemi played a disgruntled Jan. That ad ranked third-highest among that year's Super Bowl ads in terms of earned impressions and went on to win a first-ever Super Clio (the Academy Awards of advertising). During Super Bowl 50, another Snickers ad mimicked the iconic photo shoot featuring Marilyn Monroe in a white dress standing over a breezy subway grate—only this time, the updraft revealed grumpy-faced Willem Dafoe's bony legs and tighty-whiteys. That ad pulled in more than 11 million views on the Snickers YouTube channel alone.

The "You're not you" campaign also works well in print.

The Snickers "You're not you when you're hungry" mantra taps into a powerful and universal emotional appeal—hunger. Everyone can relate to how being hungry changes who you are.
Mars Incorporated

One print ad shows three sprinters in start position on a track, one of them facing the wrong direction. Another shows four soccer players in position to block a free kick, all with their cupped hands protecting important body parts save one who is unguarded, hands above his head with his jersey pulled over his face. Still another ad gets the point across without using humans at all. In a reversal of roles, it shows a zebra in hot pursuit of a lion. Each simple visual is accompanied by a cross-section of a Snickers bar and the phrase "You're not you when you're hungry. Snickers satisfies."

Beyond TV and print ads, the "You're not you" appeal works across a range of advertising media including digital and mobile. For example, a global Twitter campaign

> The enduring Snickers "You're not you when you're hungry" advertising content campaign clearly and consistently drives the brand's "Snickers satisfies" positioning in an engaging and memorable way, helping to make Snickers the world's leading sweet snack.

asking users what happens #WhenYouAreHungry drew nearly 5 million tweets in only one week. And a "Snap a Selfie with your Snickers Bar" contest invited the brand's more than 11 million Facebook followers to share photos of "who R U when U R hungry"—the winner received $100,000 and his own personalized Snickers bars.

The Snickers "You're not you when you're hungry" creative concept even transfers to the candy bar's packaging. Snickers's "Hunger Bar" candy wrappers directly reinforce the campaign message, with labels containing mood descriptors such as Cranky, Loopy, Spacey, Whiny, Snippy, Feisty, Grouchy, and Drama Mama. This clever execution urges customers to action by calling out contrarian-acting friends with an appropriately labeled Snickers bar.

The "You're not you" campaign has also extended well to new products lines. For example, Snickers recently put a twist on the long-running slogan to introduce its new line of Creamy Snickers—a bar filled with fresh, smooth ground nut butters rather than the brand's traditional nougat. During the NFL Countdown prior to Super Bowl LIII, a 30-second Creamy Snickers spot called "Heist" showed three men with stockings pulled over their faces blowing open the door of an armored truck stuck in traffic. At that critical moment, two of the thugs looked disbelievingly at the third—he was wearing a fishnet stocking mast, making his face completely visible. "What?" says the culprit. "We said pantyhose, right?" In the background, a women yells, "Pete Zagarine? That's Peter. I taught him social studies. Peter, what are you doing over there?" The add ends with the tagline "You're not smooth when you're hungry." Each

new "You're not smooth" ad, plus a plentiful supply of supporting #SmoothItOver digital and social media content, presents out-of-sorts behavior smoothed over by a Creamy Snickers bar.

Despite its diversity, no matter what the platform—whether print or packaging, TV or mobile screens, or something else—the Snickers campaign is much more than just a scattered collection of clever content. What makes the campaign so powerful is that all its pieces are carefully integrated under the brand's long-running "Snickers satisfies" and "You're not you when you're hungry" positioning. No matter where you are in the world or how you receive the message, the campaign delivers a clear and consistent brand message.

Thus, after nearly 10 years, the "You're not you" campaign still packs energy. Prior to the campaign, Snickers was losing market share. However, not long after Betty White made her Super Bowl debut, Snickers surpassed Mars's own M&Ms to become the planet's best-selling candy, a position it still holds today. With an expanded lineup that now includes Creamy Snickers, Snickers Almond, Snickers & Hazelnut, Snickers Crisper, Snickers Crunchy Peanut Butter, Snickers Bites, and Snickers Ice Cream bars, the multibillion-dollar Snickers brand contributes an estimate 10 percent or more of giant Mars, Inc.'s total annual revenues. Thanks in large part to the innovative "You're not you when you're hungry" content campaign, the brand's long-standing claim holds truer than ever, for both the company and its customers: "Snickers satisfies."[1]

· ·

COMPANIES MUST DO MORE than simply create customer value. They must also engage target customers and clearly and persuasively communicate that value to them. In this chapter, we take a closer look at two marketing communications tools: advertising and public relations.

Advertising

Any paid form of nonpersonal presentation and promotion of ideas, goods, or services by an identified sponsor.

Advertising

OBJECTIVE 15-1 Define the role of advertising in the promotion mix.

Advertising can be traced back to the very beginnings of recorded history. Archaeologists working in countries around the Mediterranean Sea have dug up signs announcing various events and offers. The Romans painted walls to announce gladiator fights, and the Phoenicians painted pictures on large rocks to promote their wares along parade routes. During the golden age in Greece, town criers announced the sale of cattle, crafted items, and even cosmetics. An early "singing commercial" went as follows: "For eyes that are shining, for cheeks like the dawn/For beauty that lasts after girlhood is gone/For prices in reason, the woman who knows/Will buy her cosmetics from Aesclyptos."

Modern advertising, however, is a far cry from these early efforts. U.S. advertisers now run up an estimated annual bill of more than $210 billion on measured advertising media; worldwide ad spending is an estimated $563 billion. P&G, the

● FIGURE 15.1
Major Advertising Decisions

Objectives setting	Budget decisions	Message decisions	Advertising evaluation
Communication objectives Sales objectives	Affordable approach Percent of sales Competitive parity Objective and task	Message strategy Message execution Media decisions Impact and engagement Major media types Specific media vehicles Media timing	Communication impact Sales and profit impact Return on advertising

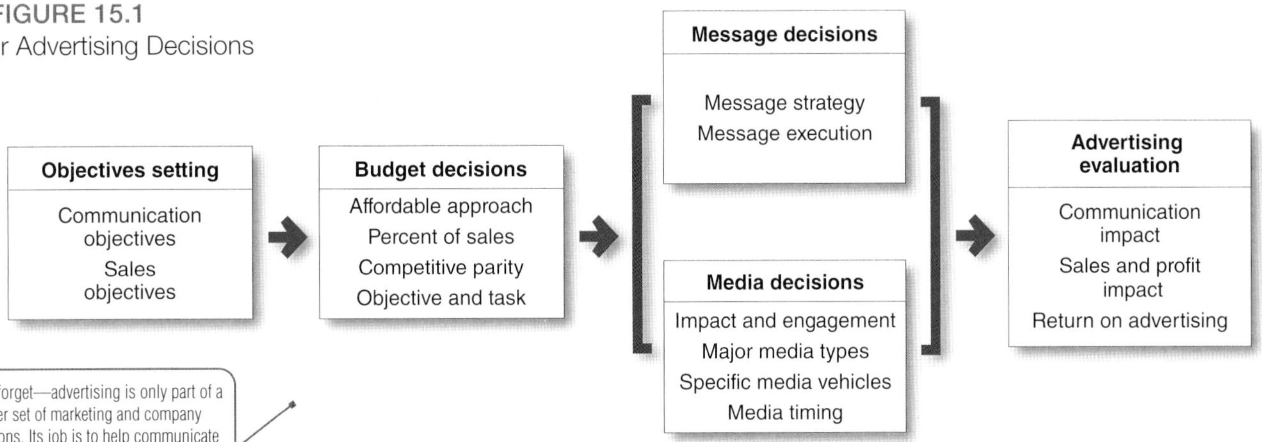

Don't forget—advertising is only part of a broader set of marketing and company decisions. Its job is to help communicate the brand's value proposition to target customers. Advertising must blend well with other promotion and marketing mix decisions.

world's largest advertiser, spends more than $4.3 billion on U.S. advertising and $10.5 billion worldwide.[2]

Although advertising is used mostly by business firms, a wide range of not-for-profit organizations, professionals, and social agencies also use advertising to promote their causes to various target publics. In fact, the 46th-largest U.S. advertising spender is a not-for-profit organization—the U.S. government, which advertises in many ways. For example, the U.S. Army alone spends some $400 million a year to attract new recruits.[3] Advertising is a good way to engage, inform, and persuade, whether the purpose is to sell Coca-Cola worldwide, attract recruits to the armed forces, or educate people in developing nations on how to lead healthier lives.

Marketing management must make four important decisions when developing an advertising program (see ● Figure 15.1): *setting advertising objectives, setting the advertising budget, developing advertising strategy (message decisions and media decisions)*, and *evaluating advertising effectiveness.*

Major Advertising Decisions

OBJECTIVE 15-2 Describe the major advertising decisions involved in developing an advertising plan.

Setting Advertising Objectives

The first step is to set *advertising objectives*. These objectives should be based on past decisions about the target market, positioning, and the marketing mix, which define the job that advertising must do in the total marketing program. The overall advertising objective is to help engage customers and build customer relationships by communicating customer value. Here, we discuss specific advertising objectives.

Advertising objective

A specific communication *task* to be accomplished with a specific *target* audience during a specific period of *time*.

An **advertising objective** is a specific communication *task* to be accomplished with a specific *target* audience during a specific period of *time*. Advertising objectives can be classified by their primary purpose—to *inform, persuade*, or *remind*. ● Table 15.1 lists examples of each of these specific objectives.

Informative advertising is used heavily when introducing a new product category. In this case, the objective is to build primary demand. Thus, early producers of all-electric vehicles (EVs) have first had to inform consumers of the economic and performance benefits of the new class of products. *Persuasive advertising* becomes more important as competition increases. Here, the company's objective is to build selective demand. For example, as EVs catch on, GM is now trying to persuade consumers that its Chevy Bolt offers more value for the price than the Tesla Model 3 or Nissan Leaf. Such advertising wants to engage customers and create brand preference.

Some persuasive advertising has become *comparative advertising* (or *attack advertising*), in which a company directly or indirectly compares its brand with one or more other brands. You see examples of comparative advertising in almost every product

● **Table 15.1 | Possible Advertising Objectives**

Informative Advertising

Communicating customer value	Suggesting new uses for a product
Building a brand and company image	Informing the market of a price change
Telling the market about a new product	Describing available services and support
Explaining how a product works	Correcting false impressions

Persuasive Advertising

Building brand preference	Persuading customers to purchase now
Encouraging switching to a brand	Creating customer engagement
Changing customer perceptions of product value	Building brand community

Reminder Advertising

Maintaining customer relationships	Reminding consumers where to buy the product
Reminding consumers that the product may be needed in the near future	Keeping the brand in a customer's mind during off-seasons

category, ranging from fast food and soft drinks to car rentals, credit cards, wireless plans, and smartphones. For example, Samsung Galaxy ads have long unabashedly bashed Apple's iPhone. Over the past decade, in one campaign after another, Samsung ads have featured direct comparisons of its phones to Apple's. The ads smugly depict iPhone owners as either disappointed in their phones by comparison or secretly envious of people using the latest Galaxy model. "When it comes to the way Samsung is marketing its new devices," say an analyst, "it appears to be fixated on just bashing Apple."[4]

● In another classic ad battle, Wendy's recent advertising has taken direct aim at McDonald's frozen-beef burgers:

Wendy's has long touted that it uses "fresh, never frozen" beef in its burgers. So when in mid-2017 McDonald's tweeted out that it would begin making all of its Quarter Pounders in most of its restaurants with fresh beef, Wendy's responded within only an hour or two: "@McDonalds So you'll still use frozen beef in MOST of your burgers in ALL of your restaurants?" That response turned out to be one of the brand's top tweets ever, logging as many as 600 million impressions in just over a day. Wendy's fresh-not-frozen onslaught escalated with a humorous Super Bowl LII ad supported by social media content. In the ad, Wendy's called out McDonald's boast that it uses flash-frozen beef that is "ground fresh and then quickly frozen to seal in fresh flavor." "The iceberg that sank the Titanic was frozen, too," quipped the Wendy's ad. "We only use fresh never frozen beef, on *every* hamburger *every* day. So skip the hamburgers at the Frozen Arches." The ad gained attention and produced results: "The impact of the Super Bowl stuff was terrific for us," says Wendy's chief marketer. Based on that success, Wendy's continued with new ads listing all the burgers made with frozen patties at McDonald's. In all, the comparative advertising campaign has given new voice to Wendy's heritage "fresh, never frozen" positioning.[5]

● **Comparative advertising:** Wendy's recent advertising has taken direct aim at McDonald's frozen-beef burgers, giving a fresh, new voice to its heritage "fresh, never frozen" positioning.

rafapress/Shutterstock

Comparative advertising campaigns often create controversy. Many times, that's the point of using them.

Whereas established market leaders want to exclude other brands from the consumer's choice set, challengers want to shake things up, inject their brands into the consumer conversation, and put themselves on equal footing with the leader. Still, advertisers should use comparative advertising with caution. All too often, such ads invite competitor responses, resulting in an advertising war that neither competitor can win. Upset competitors might also take more drastic action, such as filing complaints with the self-regulatory National Advertising Division of the Council of Better Business Bureaus or even filing false-advertising lawsuits. Consider the reactions of competitors to comparative ads by Chobani:[6]

> One Chobani Simply 100 yogurt ad showed a woman scrutinizing the label on a container of Yoplait Greek 100 yogurt and promptly discarding it as the ad voiceover says, "Potassium sorbate? Really? That stuff is used to kill bugs." The ad concluded by noting that Chobani Simply 100 Greek yogurt contains zero preservatives. Another ad portrayed a woman sitting poolside tossing a container of Dannon Light and Fit into the trash as a voiceover declared, "Sucralose, why? That stuff has chlorine added to it. Chobani Simply 100 is the only 100-calorie yogurt sweetened naturally." Competitors didn't take kindly to the jabs. Yoplait maker General Mills filed a lawsuit against Chobani for misleading advertising. And Dannon's lawyers sent Chobani a cease-and-desist letter asking it to discontinue the campaign. In turn, Chobani sued Dannon asking the courts to confirm that Chobani's advertising is not misleading. In both lawsuits, the courts concluded that the information about competitors was misleading and ruled that Chobani could not run the ads.

Reminder advertising is important for mature products; it helps to maintain customer relationships and keep consumers thinking about the product. For example, a recent ad campaign for Silk soy milk tells consumers to "Fall back in love with Soymilk," reminding them of the many reasons that "Silk helps you bloom." And expensive Coca-Cola television ads primarily build and maintain the Coca-Cola brand relationship rather than inform consumers or persuade them to buy it in the short run.

Advertising's goal is to help move consumers through the buying process. Some advertising is designed to move people to immediate action. For example, a direct-response television ad by Weight Watchers urges consumers to go online and sign up right away, and a Walgreens mobile ad promoting weekend specials encourages immediate store visits. However, many ads focus on building or strengthening long-term customer relationships. For example, a Nike video spot in which everyday athletes work through extreme challenges in their Nike gear never directly pitches products or asks for a sale. Instead, the goal is to engage customers and somehow change the way they think or feel about the brand.

Setting the Advertising Budget

Advertising budget

The dollars and other resources allocated to a product or a company advertising program.

After determining its advertising objectives, the company next sets its **advertising budget** for each product. Four commonly used methods for setting promotion budgets are discussed in Chapter 14. Here we discuss some specific factors that should be considered when setting the advertising budget.

A brand's advertising budget often depends on its stage in the product life cycle. For example, new products typically need relatively large advertising budgets to build awareness and to gain consumer trial. In contrast, mature brands usually require lower budgets as a ratio to sales. Also, brands in a market with many competitors and high advertising clutter must be advertised more heavily to be noticed above the marketplace noise. Undifferentiated brands—those that closely resemble other brands in their product class (soft drinks, laundry detergents)—may require heavy advertising to set them apart. When the product differs greatly from those of competitors, advertising can be used to point out the differences to consumers.

No matter what method is used, setting the advertising budget is no easy task. How does a company know if it is spending the right amount, or spending it or on the right advertising content and media? Even within the overall budget, specific media buys can be difficult to assess. For example, dozens of advertisers spend lavishly on high-profile Super Bowl ads each year. Although they sense that the returns are worth the sizable investment, few could fully measure or prove it (see Real Marketing 15.1).

As a result of such thinking, advertising is one of the easiest budget items to cut when economic times get tough. Cuts in brand-building advertising appear to do little

Real Marketing 15.1

The Super Bowl: The Mother of All Advertising Events—But Is It Worth It?

The Super Bowl is the mother of all advertising events. Each year, dozens of blue-chip advertisers showcase some of their best work to huge audiences around the world. But all this doesn't come cheap. Last year, major advertisers plunked down an average of $5.25 million per 30-second spot—that's $175,000 per second! Throw in ad production costs—which can run millions more per ad—and running even a single Super Bowl ad becomes a super-expensive proposition.

So each year, up pops the big debate: Is Super Bowl advertising worth all that money? Super Bowl stalwarts such as Anheuser-Busch and PepsiCo must think it's a good investment—they come back year after year. But for every big brand that invests in the Super Bowl, there are lots of others that just don't think the returns justify the costs.

The naysayers make some pretty good arguments. Super Bowl advertising is outrageously expensive. And beyond the costs, the competition for attention during the Super Bowl is fierce. Every single ad represents the best efforts of a major marketer trying to design a knock-your-socks-off spectacular. Many advertisers feel they can get more for their dollar in venues that aren't so crowded with bigger-than-life commercials.

Still, the Super Bowl has much to offer advertisers. It plays to a huge and receptive audience. Of the 20 most-watched television broadcasts ever, 19 are Super Bowl games. A typical game draws more than 100 million U.S. viewers. What's more, during a typical Super Bowl, the ads draw as much or more viewership than the game. As a result, according to one study, the return on investment for one Super Bowl ad can equal that of as many as 250 regular TV ads.

More important these days, a Super Bowl ad itself usually is only the centerpiece of something much, much bigger. Long before the game begins and long after it ends, consumers, ad critics, media pundits, and advertisers are previewing, reviewing, discussing, rating, and rehashing the commercials. "What used to be a one-day event, with some postgame water-cooler chat, is now an eight- to 13-week experience," says one Super Bowl marketer. In this digital, mobile, and social media age, rather than surprising viewers with their blockbuster ads during the game, most sponsors begin weeks in advance to build anticipation for their Super Bowl moments. They flood online and social media channels with related promotions, teasers, or even the entire ads themselves.

For example, by the time Super Bowl LIII kicked off, Doritos, Jeep, Hyundai, Microsoft, Amazon, and 37 other brands—comprising 64 percent of all brands that ended up advertising during the game—had already posted 135 related creative pieces on social media, grabbing more than 154 million online views. Consider Budweiser's "Wind Never Felt Better" spot—a heartwarming ad featuring the Budweiser Dalmatian happily embracing the breeze atop a wagon pulled by the iconic Budweiser Clydesdales through a field of golden grain on a wind turbine farm to the tune of Bob Dylan's "Blowin' in the Wind." Before the game ever began, that ad had already claimed more than 14 million views and 27,000 engagements.

Rather than stealing thunder from the super-spendy game day ads, the previews appear to make them even more effective. According to one study, 60 percent of the most-shared Super Bowl spots of all time were introduced before the game was aired. And on average, commercials uploaded to YouTube before the game generated 3.4 times more views than ads released on game day. Thanks to the viral power of the social media, building buzz around one great ad can have a much bigger impact than spending the same amount on a string of lesser ads.

Many companies go well beyond simply placing and previewing ads; they build promotional spectaculars around the entire Super Bowl event. For example, during Super Bowl LIII in Atlanta, PepsiCo—an NFL sponsor for more than 35 years—aired ads for its Pepsi, Doritos, and Bubly brands. And like many other advertisers, it posted the ads before the game to build hype. But more, PepsiCo served yet again as title sponsor of the much-watched Pepsi Halftime show. And still more, a week before the game, Pepsi painted rival Coca-Cola's hometown of Atlanta Pepsi blue, plastering more than 350 huge ads on everything from billboards and recycling bins to train station walls. "Pepsi in Atlanta. How refreshing," taunted one billboard near the World of Coca-Cola museum. "Hey Atlanta, thanks for hosting. We'll bring the drinks," jabbed another. PepsiCo's comprehensive Super Bowl campaign help make it the hands-down winner in the battle of the colas in Coke's own backyard.

Beyond the pregame antics, Super Bowl advertisers are also working harder these days to create ads that engage consumers interactively during the game itself. Ads increasingly incorporate hashtags, prompts, and incentives that spark online brand conversations and draw viewers to a brand's web, mobile, and social media sites. All those digital nods are paying off. For example, viewership of last year's Super Bowl ads on YouTube increased by 58 percent overall and 78 percent on mobile devices over the previous year's Big Game. According to one account, Super Bowl ads near and during game time generated 48 million total online views, 1.1 million social actions, and 2.9 billion social media impressions.

Finally, for most Super Bowl advertisers, the marketing content machine is still cranking long after the game ends. Next-day "water cooler" discussions about Super Bowl ads have been going on for decades. There is no end to the number of organizations and pundits posting their ranking of Super Bowl ads. But digital, mobile, and social media

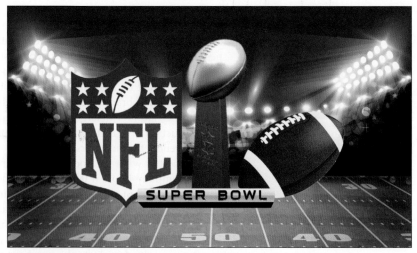

Advertising budgets: Each year, dozens of advertisers spend lavishly to showcase their ads during the Super Bowl. But do the returns justify the outrageous costs?

Photoraidz/Shutterstock; CharacterFamily/Shutterstock; grzegorz knec/Alamy Stock Photo; h_f_a/Shutterstock

have taken post-game buzz into the stratosphere. For days or even weeks following the game, online social channels hum with ad views and reviews, likes, shares, and comments. Becoming a part of all that online conversation and sharing can substantially extend return on the game-day investment.

Capturing viewer impressions, online buzz, and ad popularity can reflect meaningful brand engagements resulting from a Super Bowl ad. However, marketers must also look beyond those numbers and assess the *nature* of the buzz *behind* the numbers. Every advertiser wants to create ads that are both popular *and* effective, but the two don't necessarily go hand in hand. A popular ad that is much discussed for its own sake but is soon forgotten may contribute little to a brand's message and positioning. In contrast, an ad that is less popular and less discussed might

still be very effective if it gets the right people buzzing about the right message.

For example, in Super Bowl LIII, Budweiser's "Wind Never Felt Better" ad did both: It placed among the top 10 most-popular ads in the *USA Today* ad meter ratings. And even after the social media buzz dwindled, online conversation stayed strong for the brand's message that it is brewed with 100 percent renewable energy and the brand's willingness to take a stand. In contrast, dating app Bumble's Super Bowl LIII ad, in which tennis great Serena Williams told women to "make the first move," received only fair-to-middling ad meter reactions. Yet it generated strong online interest for Bumble throughout the following week, with nearly all conversations focusing on how the app works and how it compares to other dating apps. Thus, to be worth the cost, Super Bowl

ads must do more than just build buzz. They must create effective buzz.

So—back to the original question. Is Super Bowl advertising really worth the huge investment? The Super Bowl is certainly not for every brand. But for the right brands, and the brands that do it right, the answer is a resounding "yes." It's not just about running an ad or two during the Big Game. Instead, it's about consumers by the millions watching, streaming, sharing, commenting, debating, and buzzing about ads and brands before the game, in the moment, and after the main event. "The Super Bowl isn't an ad platform—it's a theater," says one advertising executive. "The Super Bowl is a one-of-a-kind moment with a massive, engaged audience and enormous value," says another. "The cost is not the issue that holds people back—it's nailing the content that matters the most."[7]

---

short-term harm to sales. In the long run, however, slashing ad spending may cause long-term damage to a brand's image and market share. In fact, companies that can maintain or even increase their advertising spending while competitors are decreasing theirs can gain competitive advantage.

For example, during the Great Recession, while competitors were cutting back, car maker Audi actually increased its marketing and advertising spending. Audi "kept its foot on the pedal while everyone else [was] pulling back," said an Audi ad executive. "Why would we go backwards now when the industry is generally locking the brakes and cutting spending?" As a result, Audi's brand awareness and buyer consideration reached record levels during the recession, outstripping those of BMW, Mercedes, and Lexus and positioning Audi strongly for the post-recession era. Audi is now one of the hottest auto brands on the market, neck and neck with BMW and Mercedes in global luxury car sales.[8]

Developing Advertising Strategy

Advertising strategy
The strategy by which the company accomplishes its advertising objectives. It consists of two major elements: creating advertising messages and selecting advertising media.

Advertising strategy consists of two major elements: creating advertising *messages* and selecting advertising *media*. In the past, companies often viewed media planning as secondary to the message-creation process. After the creative department created good advertisements, the media department then selected and purchased the best media for carrying those advertisements to the desired target audiences. This often caused friction between creatives and media planners.

Today, however, soaring media costs, more-focused target marketing strategies, and the blizzard of new online, mobile, and social media have promoted the importance of the media-planning function. The decision about which media to use for an ad campaign—television, newspapers, magazines, video, a website, social media, mobile devices, or email—is now sometimes more critical than the creative elements of the campaign. Also, brand content is now often co-created through interactions with and among consumers. As a result, most advertisers orchestrate a close harmony between their messages and the media that deliver them. As discussed in the previous chapter, the goal is to create and manage brand content across a full range of media, whether they are paid, owned, earned, or shared.

Creating the Advertising Message and Brand Content

No matter how big the budget, advertising can succeed only if it engages consumers and communicates well. Good advertising messages and content are especially important in today's costly and cluttered advertising environment.

Today, the average U.S. household receives more than 200 TV channels and consumers have nearly 7,200 magazines from which to choose.[9] Add in the countless radio stations and a continuous barrage of catalogs, direct mail, out-of-home media, email, and online, mobile, and social media exposures, and consumers are being bombarded with ads and brand content at home, work, and all points in between. For example, Americans are exposed to an estimated 5.3 trillion online ad impressions each year and a daily diet of 500 million tweets, 432,000 hours of YouTube videos, 95 million photos shared on Instagram, 5 million article pins on Pinterest, and 4.75 billion pieces of shared content on Facebook.[10]

Breaking through the Clutter. If all this clutter bothers some consumers, it also causes huge headaches for marketers. Take the situation facing network television advertisers. They pay an average of $350,000 to produce a single 30-second commercial. Then each time they show it, they pay an average of $123,000 for 30 seconds of advertising time during a popular primetime program. They pay even more if it's an especially popular program, such as *Sunday Night Football* ($666,000), *This Is Us* ($434,000), or a mega-event such as the Super Bowl (averaging $5.25 million per 30 seconds!). Then their ads are sandwiched in with a clutter of other commercials, network promotions, and other nonprogram material totaling as much as 20 minutes per primetime hour, with long commercial breaks coming every six minutes on average. Such clutter in television and other ad media has created an increasingly hostile advertising environment.[11]

It used to be that television viewers were pretty much a captive audience for advertisers. But today's viewers have a rich new set of information and entertainment options—the internet, video streaming, social and mobile media, tablets and smartphones, and others. More and more consumers are becoming "cord cutters"—skirting their cable and satellite subscriptions in favor of often ad-free internet-based or wireless streaming. ● Today's consumers can easily skip, mute, or block TV and digital content they don't want to watch. And, increasingly, they are choosing not to watch ads.

Thus, advertisers can no longer force-feed the same old cookie-cutter messages and content to captive consumers through traditional media. Simply interrupting or disrupting consumers no longer works. Unless ads provide content that is engaging, useful, or entertaining, many consumers will simply ignore or skip them.

● Advertising clutter: Today's consumers can easily skip, mute, or block TV and digital content they don't want to watch. And, increasingly, they are choosing not to watch ads.

cgstock/Shutterstock

Merging Advertising and Entertainment. To break through the clutter, most marketers are now merging of advertising and entertainment to create new avenues for reaching consumers with more engaging messages.

This merging of advertising and entertainment takes one of two forms: advertainment or brand integrations. The aim of *advertainment* is to make ads and brand content themselves so entertaining or so useful that people *want* to watch them. There's no chance that you'd watch ads on purpose, you say? Think again. For example, the Super Bowl has become an annual advertainment showcase. Tens of millions of people tune in to the Super Bowl each year, as much to watch the entertaining ads as to see the game. And ads and related content posted online before, during, and after the big game draw hundreds of millions of views. These days, it's common to see an entertaining ad on YouTube long before you see it on TV or to share it with friends after seeing it.

Advertisers are also creating content forms that look less like ads and more like short films or shows. A range of brand messaging platforms—from webisodes and blogs to long-form online videos and social media posts—now blur the line between ads and other consumer content. For example, Pizza Hut recently developed a two-part documentary-style "Hometown Heroes" video series aimed at creating an emotional connection between the brand and football fans.[12]

The "Hometown Heroes" video series, run on Yahoo! Sports, gave fans a behind-the-scenes glimpse of two top NFL athletes giving back to their local communities. In one episode, running back Alvin Kamara surprises a lucky group of youth football players in New Orleans's Ninth Ward with new gear and a Pizza Hut pizza party. In another, wide receiver Tyler Lockett stops by a Seattle area middle school, pizza in hand, to talk about the days of his youth and the power of books, reading, and imagination. The branded "Hometown Heroes" series generated more than 120 million impressions. And although the videos focused on the players and their stories, with almost no direct mention of Pizza Hut, they boosted the brand's association with football and the NFL by 86 percent.

Marketers have tested all kinds of novel ways to break through today's clutter and engage consumers. For example, JCPenney once posted incoherent tweets, grabbing widespread attention and leading to speculation that the retailer's social media person was either drunk or had been hacked. Instead, says JCPenney, the person was tweeting with mittens on to promote its winter merchandise. P&G's Charmin brand's #tweetfromtheseat Twitter campaign used irreverent humor to create engagement and drive buzz, with questions such as "Charmin asks: What are your thoughts on streaming while streaming?" and "There's no toilet paper left on the roll, do you yell for help, wiggle and air dry, text someone for help?"[13]

Brand integrations (or *branded entertainment*) involve making the brand an inseparable part of some other form of entertainment or content. The most common form of brand integration is product placements—embedding brands as props within other programming. It might be characters drinking from Starbucks cups in episodes of *Will & Grace*, Jimmy Dean sausage in a scene on *Young Sheldon,* or characters in *The Big Bang Theory* working at the Cheesecake Factory. It could be scenes from the latest *Avengers* movie in which Black Widow rides a Harley-Davidson Livewire.

Or the product placement might be scripted into a movie or episodes of TV shows. For example, a storyline in one episode of *Black-ish* was built around a Buick Encore, which characters Dre and Bow purchased for their daughter, Zoey. Another episode was scripted around a super-competitive game of Hasbro's Monopoly, which brings out the worst competitive instincts of each family member. In yet another show, Dre's ad agency discusses an ad campaign for P&G. Then there's the one in which Dre learns to deal with his newly discovered type 2 diabetes—ads between segments feature Tresiba Long-Lasting Insulin and diabetes management drug Victoza, both developed and marketed by pharmaceutical giant Novo Nordisk. Other *Black-ish* episodes feature storylines built around brands ranging State Farm Insurance to Disney.

Native advertising
Advertising or other brand-produced online content that looks in form and function like the other natural content surrounding it on a web or social media platform.

Originally created with TV in mind, brand integration spread quickly into other sectors of the entertainment industry. If you look carefully, you'll see product placements in movies, video games, comic books, Broadway musicals, and even pop music. For example, the highly acclaimed film *The LEGO Movie* was pretty much a 100-minute product placement for iconic LEGO construction bricks. According to one writer, "The audience happily sits through a cinematic sales pitch … that shows off the immense versatility of the product while placing it in a deeply personal context. …This film [is] product placement perfection." *The LEGO Movie* boosted The LEGO Group's sales by 13 percent the year after it opened. ● A follow-up movie, *The LEGO Movie 2: The Second Part*, offered product placement opportunities for other brands as well. For example, it featured a LEGO version of the recently redesigned Chevrolet Silverado. Chevrolet launched tie-in ads on Facebook, Twitter, and Instagram showing characters from the movie, Emmet and Lucy, riding in a LEGO-sized Silverado.[14]

A related form of brand integration is **native advertising** (also called *sponsored content*), advertising or other brand-produced content that appears to be "native to" the web or social media site in which it is placed. The brand content looks in form and function like the other natural content surrounding it. It might be an article on a website such as *The Huffington Post, BuzzFeed, Mashable,* or even *The New York Times* or *The Wall Street Journal* that is paid for, written by, and placed by an advertiser but uses the same format as articles written by the editorial staff.

● The highly acclaimed film *The LEGO Movie* was pretty much a 100-minute product placement for iconic LEGO construction bricks. The sequel offered product placement opportunities for other brands, such as a LEGO version of the Chevy Silverado.

WENN Rights Ltd/Alamy Stock Photo; Barry King/Alamy Stock Photo

Or it might be brand-prepared videos, pictures, posts, or pages integrated into social media such as Facebook, YouTube, Instagram, Pinterest, or Twitter that match the form and feel of native content on those media. Examples include Twitter's promoted tweets, Facebook Stories ads, *BuzzFeed*'s sponsored posts, or Instagram stories ads.

Native advertising is an increasingly popular form of brand content. It lets advertisers create relevant associations between brand and consumer content. It bypasses ad blockers but seems less intrusive than pop-up ads or banners. One recent study found that viewers pay 53 percent more attention to native advertising that to banner ads. As a result, native advertising grew more than 25 percent last year and now accounts for more about two-thirds of all digital display advertising spending.[15]

Thus, through the blending of advertising and entertainment, the goal for today's advertising and content marketers is to make brand messages a part of the broader flow of consumer content and conversation rather than an intrusion or interruption of it. As advertising agency JWT puts it, "We believe advertising needs to stop *interrupting* what people are interested in and *be* what people are interested in." However, advertisers must be careful that the new content forms themselves don't become too cluttered. With all the new brand content formats and integration, the merging of advertising and entertainment might create even more of the very clutter that it was designed to break through.

Creative concept
The compelling "big idea" that will bring an advertising message strategy to life in a distinctive and memorable way.

Message and Content Strategy. The first step in creating effective advertising content is to plan a message strategy—the general message that will be communicated to consumers. The purpose of advertising and other content is to get consumers to engage with or react to the product or company in a certain way. People will engage and react only if they believe they will benefit from doing so. Thus, developing an effective message strategy begins with identifying customer *benefits* that can be used as content appeals. Ideally, the message strategy will follow directly from the company's broader positioning and customer value-creation strategies.

Message strategy statements tend to be plain, straightforward outlines of benefits and positioning points that the advertiser wants to stress. The advertiser must next develop a compelling **creative concept**—or *big idea*—that will bring the message strategy to life in a distinctive and memorable way. At this stage, simple message ideas become great ad campaigns. The creative concept may emerge as a visualization, a phrase, or a combination of the two.

The creative concept will guide the choice of specific appeals to be used in an advertising campaign. *Advertising appeals* should have three characteristics. First, they should be *meaningful*, pointing out benefits that make the product more desirable or interesting to consumers. Second, appeals must be *believable*. Consumers must believe that the product or service will deliver the promised benefits.

However, the most meaningful and believable benefits may not be the best ones to feature. Appeals should also be *distinctive*. They should tell how the product is better than competing brands. For example, the most meaningful benefit of owning a wristwatch is that it keeps accurate time, yet few watch ads feature this benefit. For years, Timex has been the affordable watch that "takes a licking and keeps on ticking." In contrast, Rolex ads talk about the brand's "obsession with perfection" and the fact that "Rolex has been the preeminent symbol of performance and prestige for more than a century."

Similarly, the most meaningful benefits of high-quality work boots are ruggedness and durability. ● But Wolverine sets its Cat Earthmovers footwear apart through its association with the well-respected Caterpillar construction equipment brand. Cat Earthmovers boots are "born from bulldozers."[16] "Cat Footwear comes from a world of industry and action," says the brand. "A world where you can build anything. Where effort is everything. Where hard work pays off. Where others see obstacles, we see opportunity. We are Earthmovers."

● Distinctive advertising appeals: Wolverine sets its Cat Earthmovers footwear apart through its association with the well-respected Caterpillar brand. Cat Earthmovers boots are "born from bulldozers."

Courtesy Young & Laramore and Cat Footwear

Message Execution. The advertiser now must turn the big idea into an actual ad execution that will capture the target market's attention and interest. The creative team must find the best approach, style, tone, words, and format for executing the message. The message can be presented in various **execution styles**, such as the following:

Execution style
The approach, style, tone, words, and format used for executing an advertising message.

- *Slice of life.* This style shows one or more "typical" people using the product in a normal setting. For example, IKEA content—from microsites and Instagram posts to print ads, catalogs, and television commercials—features people living in rooms furnished with IKEA furniture and household goods.
- *Lifestyle.* This style shows how a product fits in with a particular lifestyle. For example, an ad for Athleta activewear shows a woman in a complex yoga pose and states: "If your body is your temple, build it one piece at a time."
- *Fantasy.* This style creates a fantasy around the product or its use. For example, an ad for Nestlé Pure Life water shows a young girl diving into a water-filled fantasy land where children blow soap bubbles high on a gondola lift and paddle a boat through the clouds, suggesting "a future full of possibilities starts by drinking pure bottled water now."
- *Mood or image.* This style builds a mood or image around the product or service, such as beauty, love, intrigue, serenity, or pride. Few claims are made about the product or service except through suggestion. For example, a warm, soul-stirring three-minute "Little Moments" ad for HP's phone-sized Sprocket printer captures through printed images the evolving relationship between a father and his moody 12-year-old daughter as she starts sixth grade. "Hold onto the ones you love," the ad urges. "Reinvent memories."
- *Musical.* This style employs music or dance to engage viewers with the brand. For example, Apple introduced its Siri-powered HomePod with a captivating four-minute musical short in which English singer-dancer FKA Twigs revives body and soul after arriving home at the end of a hard day's work by dancing to inspirational music selected for her by Siri.
- *Personality symbol.* This style creates a character that represents the product. The character might be animated (Mr. Clean, the GEICO Gecko, or the Travelocity Gnome) or real (perky Progressive Insurance spokeswoman Flo, KFC's Colonel Sanders, or Ronald McDonald).
- *Technical expertise.* This style shows the company's expertise in making the product. Thus, Jim Koch of the Boston Beer Company tells about his many years of experience in brewing Samuel Adams beer.
- *Scientific evidence.* This style presents survey or scientific evidence that the brand is better or better liked than one or more other brands. For years, Crest toothpaste has used scientific evidence to convince buyers that Crest is better than other brands at fighting cavities.
- *Testimonial evidence or endorsement.* This style features a highly believable or likable source endorsing the product. It could be ordinary people saying how much they like a given product. For example, in its "It's Free" marketing campaign, Angie's List features a variety of real customers endorsing the service. Or it might be a celebrity presenting the product, such as Dwayne "The Rock" Johnson for Under Armour or Steve Carrell and Cardi B in a Super Bowl ad for Pepsi.

The advertiser also must choose a *tone* for the ad. For example, P&G always uses a positive tone: Its ads say something very positive about its products. Other advertisers now use edgy humor to break through the commercial clutter. Doritos, Burger King, and Budwesier commercials are famous for this.

The advertiser must use memorable and attention-getting *words* in the ad. For example, rather than just saying that its prescription sunglass lenses protect your eyes and look good at the same time, a LensCrafters ad announces, "Sunblock Never Looked So Good." Rather than claiming that "a BMW is a well-engineered automobile," BMW uses more creative and higher-impact phrasing: "The ultimate driving machine." And instead of stating plainly that it delivers inexpensive shaving products direct to your door, Dollar Shave Club invites you to "Shave Time. Shave Money."

Finally, *format* elements make a difference in an ad's impact as well as in its cost. A small change in an ad's design can make a big difference in its effect. In a

● **Novel formats can make an advertisement stand out. This Quicken Loans Rocket Mortgage ad compels readers to flip the ad, where they get the brand's "Go Waitless" message.**

Quicken Loans

print or display ad, the *illustration* is the first thing the reader notices—it must be strong enough to draw attention. Next, the *headline* must effectively entice the right people to read the copy. Finally, the *copy*—the main block of text in the ad—must be simple but strong and convincing. Moreover, these three elements must effectively work *together* to engage customers and persuasively present customer value. However, novel formats can help an ad stand out from the clutter. ● For example, in a recent Quicken Loans Rocket Mortgage ad, the headline and subhead are upside down, suggesting that the person in the ad is floating weightlessly above the ground. Curious readers are compelled to flip the ad and the headline becomes clear: "Go Waitless—Don't get held down by an outdated mortgage process. Go completely online for a fast, convenient approval."

Consumer-Generated Content. Taking advantage of today's digital and social media technologies, many companies are now tapping consumers for marketing content, message ideas, or even actual ads and videos. Sometimes the results are outstanding; sometimes they are forgettable. If done well, however, user-generated content can incorporate the voice of the customer into brand messages and generate greater customer engagement.

Perhaps the best-known consumer-generated content effort is the former "Crash the Super Bowl Challenge" held annually by PepsiCo's Doritos brand. For more than a decade, Doritos invited consumers to create their own 30-second video ads, with winners receiving cash awards and having their ads run during the Super Bowl.

Consumer-generated content can make customers an everyday part of the brand. For example, as part of its #AerieREAL campaign (discussed in the previous chapter), swimwear and lingerie brand Aerie includes user-submitted content in its social media. Promoting Aerie's pledge to never use retouched images in its marketing, #AerieREAL invites users to submit their own untouched photos captioned with the hashtag. It then donates $1 to the National Eating Disorders Association for every photo submitted. Such content creates consumer interest and involvement in a way that naturally showcases the brand's #AerieREAL body positivity and inclusivity positioning.[17]

Similarly, trendy home furnishings maker West Elm runs a campaign called #MyWestElm. The campaign collects user-generated photos of West Elm products shared online and uses them in promotional posts on its web, Facebook, Instagram, and Pinterest sites along with links to similar products on the company's online store. It even includes user-generated photos on its product pages to show buyers how fellow customers use the products in the real world. The click-through rate for these user-generated photos is 2.6 times higher than for traditional, professionally produced photos.[18]

Not all consumer-generated content efforts, however, are successful. As many big companies have learned, ads and other content made by amateurs can be … well, pretty amateurish. If done well, however, consumer-generated content efforts can produce new creative ideas and fresh perspectives on the brand from consumers who actually experience it. Such campaigns can boost consumer engagement and get customers talking about a brand and its value to them.

Selecting Advertising Media

Advertising media
The vehicles through which advertising messages are delivered to their intended audiences.

The major steps in **advertising media** selection are (1) determining *reach, frequency, impact*, and *engagement*; (2) choosing among major *media types*; (3) selecting specific *media vehicles*; and (4) choosing *media timing*.

Determining Reach, Frequency, Impact, and Engagement. To select media, the advertiser must determine the reach and frequency needed to achieve the advertising objectives. *Reach* is a measure of the *percentage* of people in the target market who are exposed to an ad campaign during a given period of time. For example, the advertiser might try to reach 70 percent of the target market during the first three months of a campaign. *Frequency* is a measure of how many *times* the average person in the target market is exposed to a message. For example, the advertiser might want an average exposure frequency of three.

But advertisers want to do more than just reach a given number of consumers a specific number of times. The advertiser also must determine the desired *media impact*—the *qualitative value* of message exposure through a given medium. For example, the same message in one magazine (say, *Travel+Leisure*) may be more believable than in another (say, the *National Enquirer*). For products that need to be demonstrated, television ads or video content may have more impact than print or radio messages because they use sight, motion, *and* sound. Products for which consumers provide input on design or brand experiences might be better promoted at a website or social media page than in a direct mailing.

More generally, an advertiser wants to choose media that will *engage* consumers rather than simply reach them. Using any medium, the relevance of ad content for its audience is often much more important than how many people it reaches. ● For example, when adidas wanted to connect personally with avid runners and influencers, it launched a "Here to Create Legend" Boston Marathon campaign that created personalized highlight videos for each of 30,000 marathon participants:[19]

> Using data generated by RFID chips on bibs worn by runners and video footage captured by eight cameras along the 26.2-mile course, adidas blended personal highlights with general race day scenes and inspirational music, creating 30,000 unique videos for 30,000 runners. Participants could retrieve their videos at an adidas "Here to Create Legend" website within hours of the race and share them via Facebook, Twitter, Instagram, and other social media. Although the campaign didn't deliver the big audience numbers of a TV ad campaign, such ultrapersonalization and engagement could be achieved only with digital media. More than 57 percent of runners who completed the race viewed their videos, and more than one-quarter shared the video on Facebook. Across all social media, the content drew hundreds of thousands of views, resulting in a nearly 1,200 percent spike in online sales.

Although Nielsen is beginning to measure *media engagement* levels for some television, radio, and social media, such measures are still hard to find in most cases. Current media measures are things such as ratings, readership, listenership, and click-through rates. However, engagement happens inside the head of the consumer. It's hard enough to measure how many people are exposed to a given television ad, video, or social media post, let alone measure the depth of engagement with that content. Still, marketers need to know how customers connect with an ad and brand idea as a part of the broader brand relationship.

● Engaging the right consumers with the right media: The "Here to Create Legend" Boston Marathon campaign created ultrapersonalized highlight videos for each of 30,000 marathon participants. Such ultrapersonalization and engagement could be achieved only with digital and social media.

Marcio Jose Bastos Silva/Shutterstock

Engaged consumers are more likely to act upon brand messages and even share them with others. Thus, rather than simply tracking consumer *impressions* for a media placement—how many people see, hear, or read an ad—Coca-Cola also tracks the consumer *expressions* that result, such as a comment, a "Like," uploading a photo or video, or sharing brand content on social networks. Today's empowered consumers often generate more messages about a brand than a company can.

Choosing among Major Media Types. As summarized in ● **Table 15.2**, the major media types are television; digital, mobile, and social media; newspapers; direct mail; magazines; radio; and outdoor. Each medium has its advantages and its limitations. Media

● **Table 15.2 | Profiles of Major Media Types**

Medium	Advantages	Limitations
Television	Good mass-marketing coverage; low cost per exposure; combines sight, sound, and motion; appealing to the senses	High absolute costs; high clutter; fleeting exposure; less audience selectivity
Digital, mobile, and social media	High selectivity; low cost; immediacy; engagement capabilities	Potentially low impact; high audience control of content and exposure
Newspapers	Flexibility; timeliness; good local market coverage; high believability	Short life; poor reproduction quality; small pass-along audience
Direct mail	High audience selectivity; flexibility; no ad competition within the same medium; allows personalization	Relatively high cost per exposure; "junk mail" image
Magazines	High geographic and demographic selectivity; credibility and prestige; high-quality reproduction; long life and good pass-along readership	Long ad purchase lead time; high cost; no guarantee of position
Radio	Good local acceptance; high geographic and demographic selectivity; low cost	Audio only; fleeting exposure; low attention ("the half-heard" medium); fragmented audiences
Outdoor	Flexibility; high repeat exposure; low cost; good positional selectivity	Little audience selectivity; creative limitations

planners want to choose a mix of media that will effectively and efficiently present the advertising message to target customers. Thus, they must consider each medium's impact, message effectiveness, and cost.

As discussed earlier in the chapter, traditional mass media still make up a significant portion of today's media mixes. However, as mass-media costs rise and audiences shrink, companies have added larger portions of digital, mobile, and social media that cost less, target more effectively, and engage consumers more fully. Today's marketers are assembling a full mix of *paid, owned, earned, and shared media* that create and deliver engaging brand content to target consumers.

In addition to the explosion of online, mobile, and social media, cable and satellite television systems are still thriving. Such systems allow narrow programming formats, such as all sports, all news, nutrition, arts, home improvement and gardening, cooking, travel, history, finance, and others that target select groups. Comcast and other cable operators are even testing systems that will let them target specific types of ads to TVs in specific neighborhoods or individually to specific types of customers. For example, ads for a Spanish-language channel would run in only Hispanic neighborhoods, or only pet owners would see ads from pet food companies.

Finally, in their efforts to find less costly and more highly targeted ways to reach consumers, advertisers have discovered a dazzling collection of *alternative media*. These days, no matter where you go or what you do, you will probably run into some new form of advertising:

Tiny billboards attached to shopping carts urge you to buy Pampers, while ads roll by on the store's checkout conveyor touting your local Chevy dealer. Step outside, and there goes a city trash truck sporting an ad for Glad trash bags or a school bus displaying a Little Caesar's pizza ad. A nearby fire hydrant is emblazoned with advertising for KFC's "fiery" chicken wings. You escape to the ballpark, only to find billboard-size video screens running Budweiser ads while a blimp with an electronic message board circles lazily overhead. ● On a rainy day, as thunder booms and the rain begins, groundskeepers cover the infield with a colorful Skittles-branded "Taste the Rainbow" tarp.

These days, you're likely to find ads—well—anywhere. Taxicabs sport electronic messaging signs tied to GPS location sensors that can pitch local stores and restaurants wherever they

● **Marketers have discovered as dazzling array of alternative media, like this colorful Skittles-branded "Taste the Rainbow" infield groundcover tarp.**

Carolyn Kaster/AP Photo

roam. Ad space is being sold on parking-lot tickets, airline boarding passes, subway turnstiles, highway toll booth gates, ATMs, municipal garbage cans, and even police cars, doctors' examining tables, and church bulletins. One company even sells space on toilet paper furnished free to restaurants, stadiums, and malls—the paper carries advertiser logos, coupons, and codes you can scan with your smartphone to download digital coupons or link to advertisers' social media pages. Now that's a captive audience.

Such alternative media seem a bit far-fetched, and they sometimes irritate consumers who resent it all as "ad nauseam." But for many marketers, these media can save money and provide a way to hit selected consumers where they live, shop, work, and play.

Another important trend affecting media selection is the rapid growth in the number of *media multitaskers*, people who absorb more than one medium at a time. For example, it's not uncommon to find someone watching TV with a smartphone in hand, tweeting, Snapchatting with friends, and chasing down product information on Google. One recent survey found that 88 percent of consumers use another digital device while watching TV. Another study found that millennials and Gen X consumers engage in an average of three additional media activities while watching television, including online browsing, text messaging, and reading email. Although some of this multitasking is related to TV viewing—such as looking up related product and program information—most multitasking involves tasks unrelated to the shows or ads being watched. Marketers need to take such media interactions into account when selecting the types of media they will use.[20]

Selecting Specific Media Vehicles. Media planners must also choose the best media vehicles—specific media within each general media type. For example, television vehicles include *Modern Family* and *ABC World News Tonight*. Magazine vehicles include *People, Better Homes and Gardens,* and *ESPN The Magazine.* Online and mobile vehicles include Twitter, Facebook, Instagram, and YouTube.

Media planners must compute the cost per 1,000 persons reached by a vehicle. For example, if a full-page, four-color advertisement in the national edition of *People* magazine costs $402,900 and *People*'s readership is 3,400,000 people, the cost of reaching each group of 1,000 persons is about $119. The same advertisement in *Forbes* may cost $169,988 and but reach only 650,000 people—a cost per 1,000 of about $262.[21] The media planner ranks each magazine by cost per 1,000 and often favors those magazines with the lower cost per 1,000 for reaching target consumers. In the previous case, if a marketer is targeting business managers, *Forbes* would likely be the more cost-effective buy, even at lower overall readership and a higher cost per thousand.

Media planners must also consider the costs of producing ads for different media. Whereas newspaper ads may cost very little to produce, flashy television ads can be very costly. Many online and social media ads cost little to produce, but costs can climb when producing made-for-the-web or mobile video and ad series.

In selecting specific media vehicles, media planners must balance media costs against several media effectiveness factors. First, the planner should evaluate the media vehicle's audience quality. For a Huggies disposable diapers ad, for example, *Parents* magazine would have a high exposure value; men's lifestyle magazine *Maxim* would have a low exposure value. Second, the media planner should consider audience engagement. Readers of *Vogue*, for example, typically pay more attention to ads than do *People* readers. Third, the planner should assess the vehicle's editorial quality. *People* and *The Wall Street Journal* are more believable and prestigious than *Star* or the *National Enquirer*.

Deciding on Media Timing. An advertiser must also decide how to schedule the advertising over time. Suppose sales of a product peak in December and drop in March (for winter outdoor gear, for instance). The firm can vary its advertising to follow the seasonal pattern, oppose the seasonal pattern, or be the same all year. Most firms do some seasonal advertising. For example, weight-loss product and service marketers tend to heavy up after the first of the year, targeting consumers who let their appetites get the better of them over the holiday season. Weight Watchers, for instance, spends more than a quarter of its annual advertising budget in January. ● By contrast, Peeps, the perennial Easter favorite marshmallow chicks and bunnies candies, launched an "Every Day Is a Holiday" campaign to broaden demand beyond Easter, which accounts for an estimated 70 percent of the brand's business. The campaign now promotes Peeps at Valentine's Day, Halloween, Thanksgiving, Christmas, and other holiday seasons. Some marketers do *only* seasonal advertising: For instance, P&G advertises its Vicks NyQuil mostly during the cold and flu season.[22]

Today's online and social media let advertisers create content that responds to events in real time. In a classic example, Oreos reacted in a timely way to a power outage during Super Bowl XLVII with an outage-related "Power out? No problem. You can still dunk in the dark" tweet ad. The fast-reaction ad was retweeted and shared tens of thousands of times in only 15 minutes, attracting more attention for Oreo than the brand's big-budget first-quarter advertisement. In today's digital and social media environment, however, effective real-time marketing involves much more than only spontaneous, one-off tweets. Instead, it requires well-planned, equity-building campaigns and a steady flow of content that engages consumers in the moment (see Real Marketing 15.2).

● Peeps' "Every Day Is a Holiday" campaign promotes the favorite marshmallow chicks and bunnies candies at holiday seasons other the just Easter, here Christmas.

Keith Homan/Alamy Stock Photo

Brands large and small care take advantage of real-time marketing's immediacy and targeting qualities. For example, Red Roof Inn regularly links airline flight data from flight tracking service FlightAware with Google's online search ads to beam real-time ads to stranded travelers facing flight cancellations. For example, when Chicago's O'Hare Airport recently experienced a major bout of flight cancellations, Red Roof managed to secure the top ad spot in three-quarters of the Google search results for "hotels near O'Hare," resulting in a 60 percent jump in bookings from those searches.[23]

Evaluating Advertising Effectiveness and the Return on Advertising Investment

Return on advertising investment
The net return on advertising investment divided by the costs of the advertising investment.

Measuring advertising effectiveness and the **return on advertising investment** has become a hot issue for most companies. Top management at many companies is asking marketing managers, "How do we know that we're spending the right amount on advertising?" and "What return are we getting on our advertising investment?"

Advertisers should regularly evaluate two types of advertising results: the communication effects and the sales and profit effects. Measuring the *communication effects* of an ad or ad campaign tells whether the ads and media are communicating the ad message well. Individual ads can be tested before or after they are run. Before an ad is placed, the advertiser can show it to consumers, ask how they like it, and measure message recall or attitude changes resulting from it. After an ad is run, the advertiser can measure how the ad affected consumer recall or product awareness, engagement, knowledge, and preference. Pre- and post-evaluations of communication effects can be made for entire advertising and content campaigns as well.

Advertisers have gotten pretty good at measuring the communication effects of their ads and ad campaigns. However, *sales and profit* effects of advertising and other content are often much harder to measure. For example, what sales and profits are produced by an ad campaign that increases brand awareness by 20 percent and brand preference by 10 percent? Sales and profits are affected by many factors other than advertising—such as product features, price, and availability.

One way to measure the sales and profit effects of advertising is to compare past sales and profits with past advertising expenditures. Another way is through experiments. For

Real Marketing 15.2 | Real-Time Marketing: Engaging Consumers in the Moment

A funny thing happened during Super Bowl XLVII in New Orleans. Early in the third quarter, the lights in the Mercedes-Benz Superdome suddenly went out. As 71,000 attendees and 106 million viewers restlessly bided their time and scratched their heads, engineers worked feverishly for a full 34 minutes to repair the power outage and bring the lights back on. But whereas the blackout was a disaster for Superdome management and CBS Sports and an annoyance for players and fans, at least one marketer saw it as an opportunity. Shortly after the blackout began, Nabisco's Oreo brand tweeted out a simple message: "Power out? No problem. You can still dunk in the dark."

That now-famous single tweet, conceived and approved within just minutes, grabbed more attention for Oreo than the brand's extravagant first-quarter advertisement. Within an hour, the "dunk in the dark" message was retweeted nearly 16,000 times and racked up more than 20,000 Facebook likes, resulting in tens of millions of favorable exposures. In the following days, Oreo received tons of media coverage and was hailed as "The Brand That Won the Blackout Bowl." Those were pretty impressive results for a one-off joke by a cookie maker.

Oreo's successful Super Bowl one-liner triggered a surge in real-time marketing. Brands of all kinds began trying to create their own "Oreo moments" by aligning marketing content with real-world events and trending topics through timely tweets, videos, blog entries, and social media posts. But six years later, such spontaneous one-offs have become almost commonplace, and very few such quick hitters generate as much interest or response. In today's cluttered marketing content environment, even the famous Oreo "Dunk in the dark" moment might go largely unnoticed.

For sure, real-time marketing is now bigger than ever. But today, as brands master the mysteries of digital and social media, real-time consumer interaction has become a day-in, day-out, never-ending, unremitting process. Nowadays, real-time marketing success results from well-planned, equity-building campaigns and steady in-the-moment consumer engagements that make brands an authentic part of real-time consumer conversations. "It's more of a long game now than a lightning-in-a-bottle thing," says one digital marketing strategist.

For example, unlike Oreo's spontaneous tweet, P&G's Super Bowl LII real-time marketing campaign for Tide took months of careful planning. Instead of waiting for something to happen and reacting to it, the Tide brand team made their own moment, monitored consumers' social media reactions, and seamlessly integrated the brand into the conversation.

The campaign centered on four "It's a Tide Ad" ads featuring *Stranger Things* actor David Harbour asking viewers to question every ad they saw during the game. If they were seeing clean clothes, it was a Tide ad. A 45-second ad in the game's first quarter set things up. It featured various teaser scenarios of car, beer, shaving, and other ads before revealing, "No, it's a Tide ad." How do you know? "Look at those clean clothes." The opening ad left viewers wondering which of the ads they'd see later was actually a Tide ad.

Ads in each subsequent quarter kept the question alive and even cross-promoted other P&G brands. An ad with Isaiah Mustafa on a horse must certainly be an Old Spice ad, right? No, it's a Tide ad. An ad with Mr. Clean dancing with a woman cleaning her home? Also a Tide ad. P&G even worked with Anheuser-Busch, airing a fourth-quarter ad featuring a classic Budweiser Clydesdale in slow motion before giving way to Harbour in a cowboy hat announcing it to be yet another Tide ad.

Here's where the real-time campaign kicked in. As the big game began, Tide's Madison Avenue war room came alive. The Tide team—including brand marketers, social media specialists, ad agency representatives, and even Twitter sales reps—had preplanned six to 10 tweets for each quarter plus additional video clips to post on Facebook and YouTube. The team was also prepared to ad-lib as events unfolded. For example, when the TV feed suddenly went black during the game, the team cleverly tweeted, à

la Oreos, "Clean clothes are still clean in the dark. If it's clean, it's a #TideAd." To increase the drama, the team even poked fun at other brands. During a Mercedes ad, for instance, it posted "Rugged, sleek, dependable, #1 in initial customer satisfaction." And instead of posting a tweet showing Harbour in bed with a "Good Morning" message on the following day as intended, the team called a last-minute audible and posted it as the final piece of that night's Super Bowl content with the parting message, "Sweet dreams, you beautiful clean you."

The "It's a Tide Ad" real-time campaign was nothing short of a Super Bowl coup. Within seconds of the first-quarter ad, the social media lit up with tweets and retweets of comments such "Okay, this #TideAd is brilliant," "Every commercial is a #TideAd now,"

Real-time marketing: Oreo's now-famous "You can still dunk in the dark" tweet triggered a surge in real-time marketing. But today, real-time marketing success results from well-planned and steady in-the-moment consumer engagements that make brands an authentic part of real-time consumer conversations.

Sean Strong Photography/Shutterstock

and "Darn, Tide! You have people wondering now #TideAd." The campaign even reached beyond commercial breaks with tweets like "This whole *game* is a #TideAd," and "MY *LIFE* IS A #TideAd." In the days that followed, bloggers, journalists, morning show hosts, and sportscasters buzzed about the campaign. Other brands, from M&Ms to competitor Persil, jumped on the "It's a Tide Ad." hype with clever ads of their own clarifying, "This is not a @Tide commercial."

During the Super Bowl broadcast, Tide social media mentions spiked to 163,800 while social engagements soared 2,500 percent. When the dust had settled many days later, Tide had earned an eye-popping 3.6 billion media impressions and a 35 percent sales boost. *Time* magazine even proclaimed, "Tide Won the Super Bowl."

Although Tide's real-time marketing moment was a huge success, it was still only a moment, built around a specific mega-event. Such events are infrequent, and once over, the magic soon fades. Thus, to be consistently successful, real-time marketing must become part of a broader, carefully conceived strategy that makes the brand itself an ongoing part of consumers' social sharing. "The [real-time] war room has given way to a campsite," says the digital strategist. "Real-time marketing needs to be a built-in strategy all year round."

Take Wendy's, for example. The burger chain is well known for its edgy twitter roasts calling out competitors and other posters, much to the delight of its more than 3 million Twitter fans. "We like our tweets the same way we like to make hamburgers: better than anyone expects from a fast food joint," proclaims the chain. When one tweeter asked, "@Wendy's How much does a Big Mac cost?," Wendy's responded, "Your dignity." When a Burger King fan posted, "Yo @Wendys, y'all can use my mixtape to flame-grill your burgers if you want #JustSayin," Wendy's responded, "We'd prefer to keep our food fresh and hot." And when Planter's Mr. Peanut prompted Wendy's on National Roast Day with an "Alright, @Wendy's. Roast this nut!" tweet, Wendy's came back quickly with a tongue-in-cheek "Congratulations on being the worst part of trail mix." Such real-time commentary keeps the Wendy's faithful coming back for more. "While marketers wanted to be Oreo in 2013, now they want to be Wendy's," says an analyst. "People tweet at Wendy's and everyone waits and watches with bated breath for what the burger brand will say back."

Like Wendy's, most brands—whether its Nike, Starbucks, Moonpie, or Pop Tarts—are now working to harness real-time marketing's power to engage customers in the moment. Some do it well; others are still learning. But done right, real-time marketing can connect a brand with what's happening and important in consumers' lives and keep the conversation going. "Real-time marketing used to be just the content," says the strategist. "But now the content is the spark for conversation and helps brands build a relationship with followers."[24]

---

example, to test the effects of different advertising spending levels, Coca-Cola could vary the amount it spends on advertising in different market areas and measure the differences in the resulting sales and profit levels. More complex experiments could be designed to include other variables, such as differences in the ads or media used.

However, because so many factors affect advertising effectiveness, some controllable and others not, pretesting ads and measuring the results of advertising spending remains an inexact science. Managers often must rely on large doses of judgment along with quantitative analysis when assessing content and advertising performance. That's especially true in this content-hungry digital age, where large quantities of ads and other content are produced and run on a virtual real-time basis. Thus, whereas companies tend to carefully pretest traditional big-budget media ads before running them, digital marketing content often goes untested.

Other Advertising Considerations

In developing advertising strategies and programs, the company must address two additional questions. First, how will the company organize its advertising and content function—who will perform which advertising tasks? Second, how will the company adapt its advertising strategies and programs to the complexities of international markets?

Organizing for Advertising

Different companies organize in different ways to handle advertising. In small companies, advertising might be handled by someone in the sales department. Large companies have advertising departments whose job it is to set the advertising budget, work with ad agencies, and handle other advertising not done by an agency. However, most large companies use outside advertising agencies because they offer several advantages.

Advertising agency

A marketing services firm that assists companies in planning, preparing, implementing, and evaluating all or portions of their advertising programs.

How does an **advertising agency** work? Advertising agencies originated in the mid- to late 1800s from salespeople and brokers who worked for the media and received a commission for selling advertising space to companies. As time passed, the salespeople began to help customers prepare their ads. Eventually, they formed agencies and grew closer to the advertisers than to the media.

Today's agencies employ specialists who can often perform advertising and brand content tasks better than the company's own staff can. Agencies also bring an outside point of view to solving the company's problems along with lots of experience from working with different clients and situations. So, today, even companies with strong advertising departments of their own use advertising agencies.

Some ad agencies are huge; Y&R, one of the largest U.S. agency groups, has annual gross U.S. revenues of $4.1 billion. In recent years, many agencies have grown by gobbling up other agencies, thus creating huge agency holding companies. The largest of these megagroups, WPP, includes several large advertising, PR, digital, and promotion agencies with combined worldwide revenues of more than $19.7 billion.[25]

Most large advertising agencies have the staff and resources to handle all phases of an advertising campaign for their clients, from creating a marketing plan to developing ad and content campaigns and preparing, placing, and evaluating ads and content. Large brands commonly employ several agencies that handle everything from mass-media advertising campaigns to shopper marketing to social media content.

International Advertising Decisions

International advertisers face many complexities not encountered by domestic advertisers. The most basic issue concerns the degree to which global advertising should be adapted to the unique characteristics of various country markets.

Some advertisers have attempted to support their global brands with highly standardized worldwide advertising, with campaigns that work as well in Bangkok as they do in Baltimore. For example, Coca-Cola follows a "one brand" strategy under which it unifies its creative elements and brand presentation under a global "Taste the Feeling" theme. Oreo's "Open Up with Oreo" runs in 50 global markets with a simple universal message—

● **International advertising: Chevrolet unifies its global advertising under a "Find New Roads" theme that has meaning in all markets, here Russia.**

General Motors

"Open your heart to people who are different and you will discover similarities." ● And five years ago, Chevrolet swapped out its previous, American-focused "Chevy Runs Deep" positioning and advertising theme with a more global "Find New Roads" theme. The new theme "works in all markets," says a GM marketing executive. "The theme has meaning in mature markets like the U.S. as well as emerging markets like Russia and India, where the potential for continued growth is the greatest." The time was right for a more globally consistent Chevy brand message. Chevrolet sells cars in more than 140 countries, and nearly two-thirds of its sales are now outside the United States, compared with only about one-third a decade ago.[26]

In recent years, the increased popularity of online marketing and social media sharing has boosted the need for advertising standardization for global brands. Connected consumers can now zip easily across borders via the internet and social media, making it difficult for advertisers to roll out adapted campaigns in a controlled, orderly fashion. As a result, at the very least, most global consumer brands coordinate their digital sites internationally. For example, Coca-Cola web and social media sites around the world, from Australia and Argentina to France, Romania, and Russia, are surprisingly uniform. All feature splashes of familiar Coke red, iconic Coke bottle shapes, and Coca-Cola's music and "Taste the Feeling" themes.

Standardization produces many benefits—lower advertising costs, greater global advertising coordination, and a more consistent worldwide image. But it also has drawbacks. Most important, it ignores the fact that country markets differ greatly in their cultures, demographics, and economic conditions. Thus, most international advertisers "think globally but act locally." They develop global advertising *strategies* that make their worldwide efforts more efficient and consistent. Then they adapt their advertising *programs* to make them more responsive to consumer needs and expectations within local markets. For example, although Visa employs its "Everywhere you want to be" theme globally, ads in specific locales employ local language and inspiring local imagery that make the theme relevant to the local markets in which they appear.

Global advertisers face several special problems. For instance, advertising media costs and availability differ vastly from country to country. Countries also differ in the extent to

Author Comment | Not long ago, public relations was considered a marketing stepchild because of its limited marketing use. That situation has changed rapidly in recent years, however, as more marketers recognize PR's brand building, customer engagement, and social power.

which they regulate advertising practices. Many countries have extensive systems of laws restricting how much a company can spend on advertising, the media used, the nature of advertising claims, and other aspects of the advertising program. Such restrictions often require advertisers to adapt their campaigns from country to country.

Thus, although advertisers may develop global strategies to guide their overall advertising efforts, specific advertising programs must usually be adapted to meet local cultures and customs, media characteristics, and regulations.

Public Relations

OBJECTIVE 15-3 Define the role of public relations in the promotion mix.

Public relations (PR)

Activities designed to engage the company's various publics and build good relations with them.

Another major promotion tool, **public relations (PR)**, consists of activities designed to engage the company's various publics and build good relations with them. PR may include any or all of the following functions:[27]

- Press relations or press agency. Creating and placing newsworthy information in the media to attract attention to a person, product, or service.
- Product and brand publicity. Publicizing specific products and brands.
- Public affairs. Building and maintaining national or local community relationships.
- Lobbying. Building and maintaining relationships with legislators and government officials to influence legislation and regulation.
- Investor relations. Maintaining relationships with shareholders and others in the financial community.
- Development. Working with donors or members of nonprofit organizations to gain financial or volunteer support.

Public relations is used to promote products, people, places, ideas, activities, organizations, and even nations. Companies use PR to build good relations with consumers, investors, the media, and their communities. PR is often used to build support for newsworthy company events and actions. For example, a few years ago when CVS Health announced its bold decision to stop selling cigarettes and tobacco products in its stores, even though it meant sacrificing $2 billion in tobacco-related revenues, it knew that the decision would make headlines. But it left little to chance about how the full story would be told. Instead, CVS crafted a comprehensive "CVS Quits for Good" public relations campaign to tell consumers, Wall Street, and the health-care community that the decision would benefit both customers and the company:[28]

> The "CVS Quits" PR campaign kicked off with full-page ads in *The New York Times, The Wall Street Journal, The Boston Globe,* and other major newspapers along with multimedia news releases featuring video announcements from CVS's president and other company leaders. The ads and releases explained that dropping tobacco products "is simply the right thing to do for the good of our customers and our company," consistent "with our purpose— helping people on their path to better health." CVS also created an information-packed cvsquits.com website along with a #cvsquits hashtag and banners announcing the decision on the company's many web and social media sites. The "CVS Quits" story was snapped up by major print and broadcast media, creating some 2,557 broadcast mentions and more than 218 million total media impressions. The news also went viral online, becoming a top trending topic on both Facebook and Twitter and generating 200,000 social media mentions and 152,000 shares.
>
> On the day the decision was activated, CVS's CEO rang the New York Stock Exchange bell, and CVS Health executives snuffed out a 50-foot-high cigarette at an event in New York City's Bryant Park. Both events received substantial media coverage. Finally, at the same time that it nixed tobacco products, CVS launched a nationwide campaign to help smokers kick the habit, cementing the company's message of "helping people on their path to better health" and generating even more positive news.
>
> The "CVS Quits" PR campaign achieved impressive results. On Capitol Hill, eight U.S. senators, 12 House members, and other influential leaders released statements urging other retailers to follow in CVS's footsteps. CVS's stock price jumped 9.2 percent in the three weeks following the announcement. And a survey showed that one in four consumers not currently shopping at CVS pharmacies said they would switch their prescriptions there after it quit tobacco. "CVS Quits" was named *PR Week*'s campaign of the year. "This is a new standard in PR," said one judge. "Great business decision that led to amazing PR results [that had] a real business impact on stock value, consumer behavior, and brand reputation."

The Role and Impact of PR

Like other promotional forms, public relations has the power to engage consumers and make a brand part of their lives and conversations. However, public relations can have a strong impact at a much lower cost than advertising can. Interesting brand stories, events, videos, or other content can be picked up by different media or shared virally by consumers, giving it the same impact as or even greater impact than advertising that would cost millions of dollars. 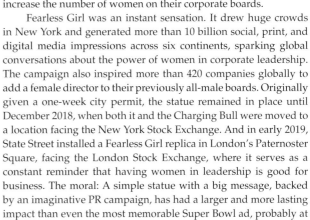 Consider a recent PR campaign by large Wall Street investment firm State Street Global Advisors:[29]

On the eve of International Women's Day 2017, State Street placed a small, 4-foot-high bronze statue in the heart of New York City's financial district, opposite Wall Street's much larger Charging Bull statue, the iconic symbol of strength in corporate America. Though small in stature, the statue—named "Fearless Girl"—sent a powerful message. It depicted a proudly defiant young girl with hands on hips and chin held high. It was intended to promote State Street's "Gender Diversity Index" fund, which invests in large companies that rank high in gender diversity across their senior leadership. More important, it kicked off a Fearless Girl campaign that highlighted State Street's support of gender diversity on corporate boards. The plaque below the statue read: "Know the power of women in leadership. SHE makes a difference." (SHE is also the fund's NASDAQ ticker symbol.) On the day that it unveiled the statue, State Street called on the more than 3,500 companies it invests in on behalf of clients to take steps to increase the number of women on their corporate boards.

Fearless Girl was an instant sensation. It drew huge crowds in New York and generated more than 10 billion social, print, and digital media impressions across six continents, sparking global conversations about the power of women in corporate leadership. The campaign also inspired more than 420 companies globally to add a female director to their previously all-male boards. Originally given a one-week city permit, the statue remained in place until December 2018, when both it and the Charging Bull were moved to a location facing the New York Stock Exchange. And in early 2019, State Street installed a Fearless Girl replica in London's Paternoster Square, facing the London Stock Exchange, where it serves as a constant reminder that having women in leadership is good for business. The moral: A simple statue with a big message, backed by an imaginative PR campaign, has had a larger and more lasting impact than even the most memorable Super Bowl ad, probably at a lower cost.

 The power of public relations: A simple statue with a big message, backed by an imaginative PR campaign, has had a larger and more lasting impact than even the most memorable Super Bowl ad, probably at a lower cost.

AP/Shutterstock

Despite its potential strengths, public relations is occasionally described as a marketing stepchild because of its sometimes limited and scattered use. The PR department is often located at corporate headquarters or handled by a third-party agency. Its staff is so busy dealing with various publics—stockholders, employees, legislators, and the press—that PR programs to support product marketing objectives may be ignored. Moreover, marketing managers and PR practitioners do not always speak the same language. Whereas many PR practitioners see their jobs as simply communicating, marketing managers tend to be much more interested in how advertising and PR affect brand building, sales and profits, and customer engagement and relationships.

This situation is changing, however. Although public relations still captures only a modest portion of the overall marketing budgets of many firms, PR can be a powerful brand-building tool. Especially in this digital age, the lines between advertising, PR, and other content are becoming more and more blurred. For example, are brand websites, blogs, video content, and social media activities advertising, PR, or something else? All are marketing content. And as the use of earned and shared digital content grows rapidly, PR is playing a bigger role in marketing content management.

More than any other department, PR has always been responsible for creating relevant marketing content that draws consumers to a brand rather than pushing messages out. "PR pros are an organization's master storytellers. In a word, they *do* content," says one expert. "The rise of social media [is] moving public relations professionals from the backroom, crafting press releases and organizing events, to the forefront of brand development and customer engagement," says another. PR professionals "have an edge because they have always had to earn attention, while [ad people] have bought attention."[30] The point is that PR should work hand in hand with advertising within an integrated marketing communications program to help build customer engagement and relationships.

Major Public Relations Tools

OBJECTIVE 15-4 Explain how companies use PR to communicate with their publics.

Public relations uses several tools. One of the major tools is *news*. PR professionals find or create favorable news about the company and its products or people. Sometimes news stories occur naturally; sometimes the PR person can suggest events or activities that would create news. Another common PR tool is *special events*, ranging from news conferences and speeches, brand tours, and sponsorships to multimedia presentations or educational programs designed to reach and interest target publics.

Public relations people also prepare *written materials* to reach and influence their target markets. These materials include annual reports, brochures, articles, and company newsletters and magazines. *Videos* are being used increasingly as communication tools. *Corporate identity materials* can also help create a corporate identity that the public immediately recognizes. Logos, stationery, brochures, signs, business forms, business cards, buildings, uniforms, and company cars and trucks all become marketing tools when they are attractive, distinctive, and memorable. Finally, companies can improve public goodwill by contributing money and time to *public service activities*.

As previously discussed, the web and social media are also important PR channels. Websites, blogs, and social media provide ways to reach and engage people. As noted, storytelling and engagement are core PR strengths, and that plays well into the use of online, mobile, and social media.

As with the other promotion tools, in considering when and how to use product public relations, management should set PR objectives, choose the PR messages and vehicles, implement the PR plan, and evaluate the results. The firm's PR should be blended smoothly with other promotion activities within the company's overall integrated marketing communications effort.

Reviewing and Extending the Concepts

Objectives Review

Companies must do more than make good products; they have to engage consumers, inform them persuasively about product benefits, and carefully position products in consumers' minds. To do this, they must master *advertising* and *public relations*.

OBJECTIVE 15-1 Define the role of advertising in the promotion mix. *(pp 436–437)*

Advertising—the use of paid media by a seller to inform, persuade, and remind buyers about its products or its organization—is an important promotion tool for engaging customers and communicating the value that marketers create for customers. American marketers spend more than $210 billion each year on advertising; worldwide spending exceeds $563 billion. Advertising takes many forms and has many uses. Although advertising is employed mostly by business firms, a wide range of not-for-profit organizations, professionals, and social agencies also employ advertising to promote their causes to various target publics. *Public relations*—engaging the company's various publics and building good relations with them—is the least used of the major promotion tools, although it has great potential for building consumer awareness and preference.

OBJECTIVE 15-2 Describe the major decisions involved in developing an advertising program. *(pp 437–454)*

Advertising decision making involves making decisions about the advertising objectives, budget, messages and media, and evaluation of the results. Advertisers should set clear target, task, and timing objectives, whether the aim is to inform, engage, persuade, or remind buyers. Advertising's goal is to move consumers through the customer journey stages discussed in Chapter 14. Some advertising is designed to move people to immediate action. However, many of the ads you see today focus on building or strengthening long-term customer engagement and relationships. The advertising budget depends on many factors. No matter what method is used, setting the advertising budget is no easy task.

Advertising strategy consists of two major elements: creating advertising messages and content and selecting advertising media. The message decision calls for planning a message strategy and executing it effectively. Good messages and other content are especially important in today's costly and cluttered advertising environment. Just to gain and hold attention, today's messages must be better planned, more imaginative, more entertaining, and more rewarding to consumers. In fact, many marketers are now merging advertising and entertainment to break through the clutter. The *media decision* involves defining reach, frequency, impact, and engagement goals; choosing major media types; selecting media vehicles; and choosing media timing. Message and media decisions must be closely coordinated for maximum campaign effectiveness.

Finally, *evaluation* calls for evaluating the communication and sales effects of advertising before, during, and after ads are placed. Advertising accountability has become a hot issue for most companies. Increasingly, top management is asking: "What return are we getting on our advertising investment?" and "How do we know that we're spending the right amount?" Other important advertising issues involve *organizing* for advertising and dealing with the complexities of *international* advertising.

OBJECTIVE 15-3 Define the role of public relations in the promotion mix. *(pp 454–456)*

Public relations, or *PR,* is used to promote products, people, places, ideas, activities, organizations, and even nations. Companies use PR to engage and build good relationships with consumers, investors, the media, and their communities. PR can have a strong impact on public awareness at a much lower cost than advertising can, and PR results can sometimes be spectacular. Although PR still captures only a modest portion of the overall marketing budgets of many firms, it is playing an increasingly important brand-building role. In the digital, mobile, and social media age, the lines between advertising and PR are becoming more and more blurred.

OBJECTIVE 15-4 Explain how companies use PR to communicate with their publics. *(p 456)*

Companies use PR to communicate with their publics by setting PR objectives, choosing PR messages and vehicles, implementing the PR plan, and evaluating PR results. To accomplish these goals, PR professionals use several tools, such as news and special events. They also prepare written, video, and corporate identity materials and contribute money and time to public service activities. The internet has also become an increasingly important PR channel, as websites, blogs, and social media are providing interesting new ways to reach more people.

Key Terms

OBJECTIVE 15-1

Advertising (p 436)

OBJECTIVE 15-2

Advertising objective (p 437)
Advertising budget (p 439)
Advertising strategy (p 441)

Native advertising (p 443)
Creative concept (p 444)
Execution style (p 445)
Advertising media (p 446)
Return on advertising investment (p 450)
Advertising agency (p 452)

OBJECTIVE 15-3

Public relations (PR) (p 454)

Discussion Questions

15-1 What major decisions should a marketing manager consider when developing an advertising program? (AACSB: Written and Oral Communication)

15-2 What is native advertising and why has its usage by marketers increased? (AACSB: Written and Oral Communication)

15-3 What is meant by the term "native advertising"? (AACSB: Communication)

15-4 What three characteristics should advertising appeals have? (AACSB: Written and Oral Communication)

15-5 Explain how the Internet has become a key area for public relations activities. (AACSB: Communication)

15-6 Discuss the major tools used by the public relations team to communicate relevant marketing content. (AACSB: Written and Oral Communication)

Critical Thinking Exercises

15-7 Search YouTube for three of your favorite television commercials, each using a different execution style. For each ad, identify the execution style used and the audience targeted. Is it a good ad? Be prepared to present the commercials and support your conclusions. (AACSB: Written and Oral Communication; Information Technology; Reflective Thinking)

15-8 Visit the website for the OBIE Awards, which celebrates creative excellence in advertising. Go to the section for current winners and select one of the winning campaigns (obieawards.org/Current-Winners). Evaluate the campaign. Describe how the advertiser used the media vehicle(s) to reach the target audience and get them to engage. (AACSB: Written and Oral Communication; Information Technology; Reflective Thinking)

15-9 Nike recently offered a Snapchat Lens that lets users wear the U.S. women's soccer kit virtually. Fans of the U.S. women's national soccer team could try on home and away jerseys through an augmented reality filter then swipe-up to purchase it at Nike.com. What factors may have influenced Nike's decision to advertise in this way? (AACSB: Written and Oral Communication; Information Technology; Reflective Thinking)

APPLICATIONS AND CASES

Online, Mobile, and Social Media Marketing Plum Organics: Patenting Unfiltered

Plum Organics, an organic baby food brand, recently created a video-led campaign called Parenting Unfiltered that celebrated the messiness and complications associated with parenting. The campaign did not feature a product; it was a lifestyle campaign designed to get parents talking to each other and engaging with the brand. It showed videos of real parents having real, unfiltered moments (for example, a goldfish funeral) and partnered with influential parents who engaged consumers on a variety of platforms using #ParentingUnfiltered. Plum launched a multi-platform social campaign to support the launch of the videos. It aimed to create a conversation that others could go back and reference over time and offered user-generated content, in the form of realistic holiday cards people could share, to increase engagement. The campaign resulted in more than four million video views and hundreds of thousands of engagements across platforms.

15-10 Plum Organics chose to focus its advertising on lifestyle dimensions associated with parenting rather than on its products. What are the positives and negatives of this approach? (AACSB: Written and Oral Communication; Reflective Thinking)

15-11 Create an outline for a marketing-focused public relations campaign to run alongside the Parenting Unfiltered advertising campaign. What would the public relations campaign encompass? How would it complement the advertising campaign? (AACSB: Written and Oral Communication; Reflective Thinking)

Marketing Ethics Burger King's Real Meals

Burger King recently launched "Real Meals" in select markets to deliver an important message about mental health. Real Meals come in five varieties, including a Pissed Meal (for when you're mad) and a Blue Meal (for when you're sad). The ads extend Burger King's concept of letting customers have it their way to the idea that they should also feel their way. The campaign leveraged Burger King's rivalry with competitor McDonald's, which launched the Happy Meal in 1979, by noting that no one is happy all the time. However, Burger King's objective was to increase visibility of issues related to mental well-being during Mental Health Awareness Month (May) and to donate a portion of sales to Mental Health America. It noted that social media may encourage people to appear happy and perfect; Burger King wants consumers to be themselves. Social media users reacted positively to the chain's decision to include mental health in the social issues that it addresses. Other issues included the pink tax and net neutrality.

15-12 What challenges might Burger King face if it chose to take this campaign global? (AACSB: Written and Oral Communication; Reflective Thinking)

15-13 Is it ethical for Burger King to use advertising that emphasizes negative emotions to sell its products? (AACSB: Written and Oral Communication; Ethical Reasoning; Reflective Thinking)

Marketing by the Numbers Advertising Costs

A common measure of advertising efficiency is cost per thousand (CPM), which is the ad cost per thousand potential audience contacts. Although all audience members are important for advertisers, those in the 18-to-49 demographic is the most coveted by many because they are the most difficult to reach with advertising messages. Because these viewers basically make or break a television show's success, television networks break out this demographic when giving audience numbers. The chart shown at right illustrates average costs and audience sizes for some of America's favorite primetime television shows during a five-week period in 2018.

Although cost-per-thousand calculations for television programs are normally done on a household basis rather than viewer basis, comparing CPM per overall audience members versus CPM per 18-to-49 demographic audience members can help advertisers select appropriate media vehicles (that is, appropriate television programs) when trying to reach this demographic.

Program	Average Cost per 30-Second Spot	Average Number of Viewers (in millions)	18-to-49 Demo Viewers (in millions)
This Is Us	$433,866	9.309	2.47
The Big Bang Theory	$285,934	12.483	2.27
Empire	$227,494	5.387	1.67
Young Sheldon	$213,536	10.731	1.74
The Voice (Mon.)	$212,618	9.816	1.99
Grey's Anatomy	$204,792	6.739	1.73
The Connors	$201,065	10.563	2.35
The Voice (Tues.)	$193,140	9.372	1.91

15-14 Calculate both the overall CPM and the CPM for the 18-to-49 demographic for each show. Refer to the "Selecting Specific Media Vehicles" section of "Selecting Advertising Media" in the chapter to learn how to do this calculation. Which programs are the most efficient media buys for advertisers? (AACSB: Analytical Reasoning; Reflective Thinking)

15-15 If an advertiser wants to reach the 18-to-49 demographic, which programs would you suggest? Explain. (AACSB: Communication; Analytical Reasoning; Reflective Thinking)

Company Case Allstate: Bringing Mayhem to the Auto Insurance Advertising Wars

In the spring of 1950, the teenage daughter of Allstate general sales manager Davis Ellis was stricken with hepatitis shortly before she was to graduate from high school. The worried executive arrived home from work one evening just as his wife returned from the hospital where their daughter was admitted. As he met her at the front door, his wife reported, "The hospital said not to worry . . . we're in good hands with the doctor."

Later that year, Ellis became part of a team charged with developing the first major national advertising campaign for the Allstate Insurance Company. As the team discussed the message they wanted the brand to convey, Ellis recalled his wife's "we're in good hands" remark and how good it made him feel. The phrase projected security, reassurance, and responsibility, exactly the traits the team wanted customers to associate with Allstate. Thus was born the slogan, "You're in Good Hands with Allstate."

By the early 2000s, a study by Northwestern University found that the long-standing Allstate catchphrase was the most recognized slogan in the United States. For years, Allstate held the position as the second-largest personal lines insurer, trailing only State Farm. Shortly thereafter, Allstate hired actor Dennis Haysbert as the brand's spokesperson. After starring in dozens of Allstate commercials—each culminating with the question "Are you in good hands?"—Haysbert's deep voice became a comforting familiarity to television viewers. Today, the "good hands" slogan is the oldest surviving slogan for a paid campaign.

An Advertising Shakeup

Although Allstate's advertising served it well for decades, the company eventually fell into the same routine as the rest of the insurance industry. Big auto insurance companies were spending modestly on sleepy ad campaigns featuring touchy-feely, reassuring messages such as Allstate's "You're in good hands" or State Farm's "Like a good neighbor." In an industry characterized by low budgets and even lower-key ads, no brand's marketing stood out.

However, the advertising serenity ended with the first appearance of the now-iconic GEICO Gecko, backed by a big budget, pitching direct sales and low prices. That single GEICO ad campaign sparked a frenzy of ad spending and creativity in the insurance industry that quickly escalated into a full-scale advertising war. Once-conservative car insurance ads became creative showstoppers, as edgy and creative as ads found in any industry. Here are a few highlights:

- **GEICO:** GEICO got the auto insurance advertising wars rolling when it was acquired by billionaire Warren Buffet's Berkshire Hathaway company and given a blank check to aggressively increase market share. That led to an onslaught of advertising the likes of which the auto insurance industry had never seen. A string of creative GEICO campaigns featured everything from

civilized cavemen to a stack of cash with googly eyes. But it was the GEICO Gecko that had the biggest impact. With his signature English accent, the Gecko made GEICO's simple message clear—"15 minutes can save you 15 percent or more on car insurance." More than any other industry spokesperson, the Gecko lent personality and pizzazz to the previously sleepy insurance industry and its staid brands. Since the first appearance of the Gecko, GEICO has continued to drive home its message and entertain the masses with ads featuring Maxwell the Pig, the GEICO squirrels, the Hump Day camel, and various parodies.

- **Progressive:** Following GEICO's lead, Progressive created its own perky and endearing personality—Flo. Progressive created the ever-upbeat, ruby-lipped sales clerk to help convince consumers who are already in the market that they can get an even better price deal from Progressive. Flo helped put Progressive hot on the heels of rising GEICO as the fourth-largest auto insurer. Flo assists people when they are ready to shop. The Flo campaign has carried on like a beloved TV series, revealing new characters and scenarios each year. And to avoid the risk of Flo burn-out, Progressive also introduced complementary campaigns featuring the Messenger—the mustachioed, leather-jacket-wearing stranger—and Brad—the easy-going, self-assured man with an absurdly funny sense of self-esteem who refers to himself only in the third person. Like the GEICO Gecko, Flo, the Messenger, and Brad have pitched price savings as their primary appeal.

- **State Farm:** As GEICO and Progressive shook up the industry with their direct, low-price, high-profile selling models, conventional agent-based auto insurers were forced to respond. 90-year-old State Farm, the long-time industry leader, was hardly a stranger to advertising. Like Allstate, State Farm had a long-standing, widely recognized slogan—"Like a good neighbor, State Farm is there"—a jingle written by pop music icon Barry Manilow way back in 1971. Sensing the threat from the rising newcomers, State Farm fought back vigorously with a new campaign centered on its enduring jingle. In its "magic jingle" campaign, State Farm agents magically appear when summoned with the jingle by young drivers in trouble—including the likes of LeBron James. The campaign's goal—to convince consumers that they still need the services of one of State Farm's 18,000 agents. To help make the point more forcefully, State Farm doubled its ad budget.

"Good Hands" Meets Mayhem

Amid this surge in competition and advertising creativity, Allstate struggled just to hold its own, let alone to grow. In the wake of the Gecko and Flo, Allstate had lost market share for two years running, even with Haysbert's presence as company pitchman. The brand needed its own over-the-top personality. So Allstate tapped ad agency Leo Burnett to bring mayhem to life—literally. With the creepy Mayhem character played by actor Dean

Winters, Allstate created a villainous counterpart to Haysbert's soothing hero. The campaign's goal: to convince consumers that there is more to buying car insurance than just price. "We knew we needed…a loud thunderclap to tell people that we cared about them," said Lisa Cochrane, senior VP of marketing at Allstate. "Mayhem is there to change the conversation, to disrupt the commoditization of insurance, and to provide you with something to think about to make sure that you have the right coverage." A Leo Burnett executive put it more bluntly— "We wanted to kick Flo's ass."

Mayhem portrays all of the unlikely events that can lead to a major auto insurance claim. He first appeared as a tree branch falling on a car, then as an emotionally compromised teenager ramming her pink SUV into an unsuspecting vehicle. According to Cochrane, after only these two early ads, "it made an impression." The possible situations for Mayhem are endless. As a deer, Mayhem jumps into the path of a moving car at night, "because that's what we deer do." As a torrential downpour, he loves leaky sunroofs. As a malfunctioning GPS, he sends a driver swerving into another car. As snow, he weighs down the roof of a garage until it collapses, smashing the car within. Each quirky ad ends with the statement and question "If you have cut-rate insurance, you could be paying for this yourself. Are you in good hands?"

Through such clever ads, Allstate's creative "Mayhem. It's Everywhere." campaign has put a contemporary, attention-grabbing twist on the company's long-standing "You're in good hands with Allstate" slogan, helping to position the brand as a superior alternative to price-oriented competitors. Even with its long-standing "Good Hands" campaign, Allstate needed something unconventional. In fact, mayhem didn't just describe the Allstate campaign—it characterized the entire world of auto insurance advertising.

The Mayhem campaign was not only well received by consumers, it earned critical acclaim, winning approximately 80 advertising awards in the first year. But perhaps a bigger indication of the campaign's impact is the extent to which the character has become ingrained in the pop culture. Although Mayhem only has a little more than a third of Flo's 4.5 million Facebook fans, he commands an engagement score roughly five times that of Progressive's perky spokeswoman. And when the character's creator recently saw a Mayhem-costumed trick-or-treater walking down her street, she called it "a career highlight that gave her chills."

More than just popular, Mayhem is right on message. At the end of each ad, he warns, "If you've got cut-rate insurance, you could be paying for this yourself." Then the reassuring voice of Haysbert provides the solution: "Are you in good hands?" he asks. "Get Allstate. You can save money and be better protected from Mayhem." This "worth-paying-a-little-more" message puts Allstate back at the top in terms of customer value.

Mayhem Redux

Allstate's ads were not only creative, they were effective. After a few years of Mayhem ads complementing Haysbert's Good Hands ads, Allstate's unaided brand awareness of 74 percent trailed State Farm's by only a slight margin despite State Farm's 60 percent greater ad spending. And for a time, the Mayhem campaign halted Allstate's market share slide. According to Allstate CEO Thomas Wilson, "It's working. If you look at our quotes and our new business, it's way up." All this prompted Allstate to extend the campaign, including the introduction of Mayhem's Hispanic cousin, Mala Suerte (bad luck), aimed at Hispanic consumers.

To extend the campaign, Allstate took Mayhem to the next level, giving the character his own Twitter account. Seemingly late to the Twitter party, Allstate executives indicated that the delay was intentional. "We've been very careful about not overdoing Mayhem and not overexposing [him]," said Jennifer Egeland, Allstate's director of advertising. "[We wanted] the right idea for launching him in the Twitter space."

The right idea was to conform to Mayhem's persona. At the beginning of an NFL season, Mayhem polled followers about what he should portray in the next ad—a charcoal grill or a cheap bungee cord. Consumers voted for the cord. Mayhem disobeyed, tweeting: "Too bad I'm a tailgate grill. Who's got a light?" He followed that up with online videos of a car set on fire from a grill mishap. Allstate then released two new Mayhem ads—"Tailgate Grill Fire" and "Cheap Bungee Cord"—making everyone happy. Also driving traffic to its social media sites was the "#MayhemSale" installment, a spot in which unsuspecting football fans Matt and Shannon had their house raided by a social-media savvy burglar. The spot drove significant web traffic and won an American Advertising Federation gold ADDY award.

With all this activity and positive public response, Allstate seems to have found a weapon for maintaining its market position. But the all-out auto insurance advertising war illustrates just how critical it is to stay one step ahead of the competition. Even as Allstate has increased its annual ad budget to roughly $1 billion, it is only keeping pace with market leader State Farm. However, both company's ad spending lags well behind GEICO's nearly $2 billion advertising budget. Today, no less than 12 car insurance brands are running national TV advertising campaigns, with Liberty Mutual as the latest to enter the mascot game with LiMu the emu. Combined, the auto insurers now spend more than $6 billion each year to get their messages out. That makes things confusing for consumers, who struggle under the deluge of clever ads, which also creates difficulties for the insurers.

Still, Allstate is holding its own when it comes to advertising effectiveness. Allstate's Mayhem has now been causing advertising industry mayhem for some nine years via more than 25 TV ads plus a slew of radio spots, billboard placements, and internet banner ads. And a recent study of nearly 500 consumer brands found that refreshed Mayhem and "Good Hands" campaigns have boosted Allstate to number one as the brand with the most talk-worthy marketing.

Still, intense competition, big budgets, and a focus on consumer advertising have kept industry market shares dynamic. In fact, during the past last year, number-two GEICO increased its market share substantially, narrowing the gap to within only a few percentage points of market-leading State Farm's 17 percent share. Progressive and Allstate both soldier on with 11 percent and 9 percent shares, respectively. Although Allstate has grown its auto insurance business in recent years, GEICO and Progressive have remained consistently stronger. That leaves Allstate to reconsider the value it's getting out of its advertising and how it might slow down its rivals and retake its former number-two market position.[31]

Questions for Discussion

15-16 Why has Allstate's "good hands" slogan withstood the test of time to become advertising's longest-running slogan?

15-17 Analyze Allstate's Mayhem ads based on the process of creating an advertising message as outlined in the text (for the latest Mayhem ads, check www.allstate .com/mayhem-is-everywhere.aspx).

15-18 Discuss issues of selecting advertising media for the Mayhem campaign. How might this process differ from that of campaigns for other companies?

15-19 Based on the information in this case, how might Allstate measure the effectiveness of the Mayhem campaign?

15-20 Has the Mayhem campaign been effective? Support your answer.

16

Personal Selling and Sales Promotion

OBJECTIVES OUTLINE

OBJECTIVE 16-1 Discuss the role of a company's salespeople in engaging customers, creating customer value, and building customer relationships. **See: Personal Selling** *(pp 464–466)*

OBJECTIVE 16-2 Identify and explain the six major sales force management steps. **See: Managing the Sales Force** *(pp 466–476)*

OBJECTIVE 16-3 Discuss the personal selling process, distinguishing between transaction-oriented marketing and relationship marketing. **See: The Personal Selling Process** *(pp 476–479)*

OBJECTIVE 16-4 Explain how sales promotion campaigns are developed and implemented. **See: Sales Promotion** *(pp 479–486)*

CHAPTER PREVIEW In the previous chapter, you learned about engaging customers and communicating customer value through integrated marketing communications (IMC) and two elements of the promotion mix: advertising and public relations. In this chapter, we examine two more IMC elements: personal selling and sales promotion. Personal selling is the interpersonal arm of marketing communications, in which the sales force engages customers and prospects to build relationships and make sales. Sales promotion consists of short-term incentives to encourage the purchase or sale of a product or service. Although this chapter presents personal selling and sales promotion as separate tools, they must be carefully integrated with the other elements of the promotion mix.

First, let's look at a real-life sales force. When you think of salespeople, perhaps you think of pushy retail sales clerks, "yell and sell" TV pitchmen, or the stereotypical glad-handing "used-car salesman." But such stereotypes don't fit the reality of most of today's salespeople—sales professionals who succeed not by taking advantage of customers but by listening to their needs and helping to forge solutions. Consider Salesforce—the industry leader in customer relationship management solutions. Salesforce not only produces market-leading sales management software services, it also excels at practicing what it preaches—effective personal selling.

SALESFORCE: You Need a Great Sales Force to Sell Salesforce

Salesforce is way out front in the $48 billion market for customer relationship management (CRM) solutions. The Salesforce logo, set inside the image of a cloud, underscores Salesforce's highly successful cloud-based computing model (no software to install or own). Cloud-based systems are common today, but they were state-of-the-art when Salesforce pioneered the concept more than 20 years ago. Since then, the company has established itself as a leading innovator, constantly finding new ways to help client companies connect with customers and achieve greater sales force effectiveness using the latest online, mobile, social, artificial intelligence (AI), and cloud technologies.

Salesforce helps businesses to "supercharge their sales." It supplies what it calls a "Customer Success Platform," a wide array of cloud-based customer relationship management tools across sales, marketing, ecommerce, and customer service. Salesforce's Einstein artificial intelligence system even lets clients predict customer outcomes based on sales data without their own data science teams. From its home in the cloud, Salesforce makes all these data and analyses readily available anytime, from anywhere, on any device with online access—desktops, laptops, tablets, or smartphones. Salesforce also provides real-time customer engagement and collaboration on its Salesforce Chatter platform, a kind of Facebook for enterprises.

Salesforce's innovative products have made it the world's number-one and fastest-growing CRM platform, ahead of blue-chip competitors such as Microsoft, Oracle, SAP, and IBM. The company's revenues hit $13.3 billion last year, up an impressive 27 percent over the previous year and more than triple what they were just five years ago. Salesforce has placed first or second on the *Forbes* World's Most Innovative Company list for seven straight years. With the ongoing digital transformation causing a surge in the CRM market, Salesforce has set a bold target of $23 billion in annual revenue by 2022.

Innovative products and platforms have played a major role in Salesforce's stunning success. But even the best products don't sell themselves. You need a great sales force to sell Salesforce, and the company excels at practicing what it preaches—effective personal selling. Like the companies that buy its services, Salesforce has its own army of experienced, well-trained, highly motivated sales reps who take the company's products to customers. In many respects, Salesforce's own sales force serves as a model for the products and services it sells—not just for using the Salesforce cloud but more generally for achieving the "supercharged" sales force results that the company promises its clients.

At Salesforce, developing an outstanding sale force starts with recruiting and hiring top-notch salespeople. Salesforce's aggressive but highly selective recruiting program skims the cream off the top of the global sales rep candidate pool. Experience counts. Salesforce expects a minimum of two years of prior sales experience for small-business sales reps and up to two decades of experience for sales execs assigned to major accounts. Salesforce counts on its high-energy culture and strong compensation package to attract experienced and successful candidates into the Salesforce fold.

Once hired, as you might expect, Salesforce salespeople have access to all the latest high-tech selling tools. In fact, the first major assignment of new hires is to study 20 hours of at-home video that teaches them the ins and outs of the Salesforce technologies that they won't be just selling but also using. But Salesforce would be the first to tell you that, although its cloud wizardry can help to optimize customer contact and the selling process, it doesn't take the place of good personal selling skills. So in

Salesforce's cloud-based "Customer Success Platform" provides a wide array of customer relationship management tools that help its customers "supercharge their sales."
Salesforce.com Inc.

training and fine-tuning its own sales force, the company starts by preaching tried-and-true selling fundamentals, tempered by its own modern twists.

The first fundamental of good selling at Salesforce is to *listen and learn*. As new recruits go through Salesforce's week-long selling boot camp, taught at the company's Salesforce U, they learn that they should begin building customer relationships by asking probing questions and getting customers to talk, seeking to understand everything they can about a customer's situation and needs. "Eighty-five percent of salespeople don't slow down enough to really understand their customer's business," says a senior Salesforce sales executive.

Understanding the customer leads to a second selling fundamental: *empathize*—let customers know that you understand their issues and feel their pain. Empathy builds rapport and trust, an important step toward closing sales and building long-term customer relationships. Listening, learning, and empathizing are important first steps, but more is needed. "If all you are is responsive and helpful, then all you are is an administrative assistant," says the Salesforce sales executive.

So the next important step is to *offer solutions*—to show how Salesforce's cloud-based solutions will help clients make their sales forces more effective and productive in connecting with and selling to customers. Salesforce believes that the best way to offer solutions is by telling good stories that highlight other customers' successes with its products. "Storytelling is very, very important," says Salesforce's sales productivity promoter. "It can be the foundation of things like

> Salesforce leads the market in sales force automation and customer relationship management solutions. But even Salesforce's innovative products won't sell themselves. The company knows that it needs a great sales force to sell Salesforce.

the corporate pitch and your interactions with your customers and prospects." When it comes to handling objections—such as "I don't trust putting our data in the cloud," "My current system is working fine," or "It costs too much"—Salesforce tells its salespeople that stories can be the most powerful tools they have. "When faced with objections, we always relate it back to a customer story," says a Salesforce marketing manager. "We're not the hero in our customer's stories," says another manager. "It's how the customer succeeded, not how we saved them."

When it comes to competitors, Salesforce's salespeople are ferocious. But Salesforce reps are trained to take the high road—to sell Salesforce's strengths, not competitors' weaknesses. And even though Salesforce boasts the best sales and customer connection tools in the business, backed by big data and combined with AI and plenty of other new-school techniques, its sales reps stay focused on old-school selling principles. At Salesforce—or anywhere else—good selling starts with the fundamentals of engaging and listening to customers, understanding and empathizing with their problems, and building relationships by offering meaningful solutions for mutual gain. That's how you build an incredibly successful sales force and Salesforce.[1]

IN THIS CHAPTER, we examine two more promotion mix tools: *personal selling* and *sales promotion*. Personal selling consists of interpersonal interactions with customers and prospects to make sales and maintain customer relationships. Sales promotion involves using short-term incentives to encourage customer purchasing, reseller support, and sales force efforts.

> Author Comment | Personal selling is the interpersonal arm of the promotion mix. A company's sales force creates and communicates customer value by personally engaging customers and building customer relationships.

Personal Selling

OBJECTIVE 16-1 Discuss the role of a company's salespeople in engaging customers, creating customer value, and building customer relationships.

Robert Louis Stevenson once noted, "Everyone lives by selling something." Companies around the world use sales forces to sell products and services to business customers and final consumers. But sales forces are also found in many other kinds of organizations. For example, colleges use recruiters to attract new students. Museums and fine arts organizations use fundraisers to contact donors and raise money. Even governments use sales forces. The U.S. Postal Service, for instance, uses a sales force to sell Express Mail and other shipping and mailing solutions to corporate customers. In the first part of this chapter, we examine personal selling's role in the organization, sales force management decisions, and the personal selling process.

The Nature of Personal Selling

Personal selling
Personal presentations by the firm's sales force for the purpose of engaging customers, making sales, and building customer relationships.

Personal selling is one of the oldest professions in the world. The people who do the selling go by many names, including salespeople, sales representatives, agents, district managers, account executives, sales consultants, and sales engineers.

People hold many stereotypes of salespeople—including some unfavorable ones. *Salesman* may bring to mind the image of Dwight Schrute, the opinionated Dunder Mifflin paper salesman from the old TV show *The Office*, who lacks both common sense and social skills. Or you may think of the real-life "yell and sell" TV pitchmen, who hawk everything from the Flex Seal to the INSANITY Workout and the Power Air Fryer in infomercials. However, the majority of salespeople are a far cry from these unfortunate stereotypes.

As the opening Salesforce story shows, most salespeople are well-educated and well-trained professionals who add value for customers and maintain long-term customer relationships. They listen to their customers, assess customer needs, and organize the company's efforts to solve customer problems. The best salespeople are the ones who work closely with customers for mutual gain. ● Consider Boeing, the aerospace giant

● **Professional selling: It takes more than fast talk and a warm smile to sell expensive airplanes. Boeing's real challenge is to win business by building partnerships—day in, day out, year in, year out—with its customers.**

Stephen Brashear/Getty Images

competing in the rough-and-tumble worldwide commercial aircraft market. It takes more than fast talk and a warm smile to sell expensive airplanes:

> Selling high-tech aircraft at $125 million or more a copy is complex and challenging. A single big sale to an airline, air-freight carrier, government, and military customer can easily run into billions of dollars. Boeing salespeople head up an extensive team of company specialists—sales and service technicians, financial analysts, planners, engineers—all dedicated to finding ways to satisfy a large customer's needs. On the customer side, buying a batch of jetliners involves dozens or even hundreds of decision makers from all levels of the buying organization and layer upon layer of subtle and not-so-subtle buying influences. The selling process is nerve-rackingly slow—it can take two or three years from the first sales presentation to the day the sale is announced. After getting the order, salespeople then must stay in almost constant touch to keep track of the account's equipment needs and to make certain the customer stays satisfied. The real challenge is to win buyers' business by building day-in, day-out, year-in, year-out partnerships with them based on superior products and close collaboration.

Salesperson
An individual who represents a company to customers by performing one or more of the following activities: prospecting, communicating, selling, servicing, information gathering, and relationship building.

The term **salesperson** covers a wide range of positions. At one extreme, a salesperson might be largely an *order taker*, such as the department store salesperson standing behind the counter. At the other extreme are *order getters*, whose positions demand *creative selling*, *social selling*, and *relationship building* for products and services ranging from appliances, industrial equipment, and airplanes to insurance and IT services. In this chapter, we focus on the more creative types of selling and the process of building and managing an effective sales force.

The Role of the Sales Force

Personal selling is the interpersonal arm of the promotion mix. It involves interpersonal interactions and engagement between salespeople and individual customers—whether face-to-face, by phone or text, via email or social media, through video or online conferences, or by other means. Personal selling can be very effective in complex selling situations. Salespeople can probe customers to learn more about their problems and then adjust the marketing offer and presentation to fit each customer's special needs.

The role of personal selling varies from company to company. Some firms have no salespeople at all—for example, companies that sell only online or companies that sell through manufacturers' reps, sales agents, or brokers. In most firms, however, the sales force plays a major role. In companies that sell business products and services, such as IBM, DuPont, Intel, or GE, salespeople work directly with customers. In consumer product companies such as P&G or Nike, the sales force plays an important behind-the-scenes role. It works with wholesalers and retailers to gain their support and help them be more effective in selling the company's products to final buyers.

Linking the Company with Its Customers

The sales force serves as a critical link between a company and its customers. In many cases, salespeople serve two masters—the seller and the buyer. First, they *represent the company to customers*. They find and develop new customers and communicate information about the company's products and services. They sell products by engaging customers and learning about their needs, presenting solutions, answering objections, negotiating prices and terms, closing sales, servicing accounts, and maintaining account relationships.

At the same time, salespeople *represent customers to the company*, acting inside the firm as "champions" of customers' interests and managing the buyer–seller relationship. Salespeople relay customer concerns about company products and actions back inside to those who can handle them. They learn about customer needs and work with other marketing and nonmarketing people in the company to develop greater customer value.

In fact, to many customers, the salesperson *is* the company—the only tangible manifestation of the company that they see. Hence, customers may become

● **Salespeople link the company with its customers. To many customers, the salesperson is the company.**

dotshock/Shutterstock

loyal to salespeople as well as to the companies and products they represent. This concept of *salesperson-owned loyalty* lends even more importance to the salesperson's customer-relationship-building abilities. Strong relationships with the salesperson will result in strong relationships with the company and its products. Conversely, poor salesperson relationships will probably result in poor company and product relationships.

Coordinating Marketing and Sales

Ideally, the sales force and other marketing functions (marketing planners, brand managers, marketing content managers, and researchers) should work together closely to jointly create value for customers. Unfortunately, however, some companies still treat sales and marketing as separate functions. When this happens, the separate sales and marketing groups may not get along well. When things go wrong, marketers blame the sales force for its poor execution of what they see as an otherwise splendid strategy. In turn, the sales team blames the marketers for being out of touch with what's really going on with customers. Neither group fully values the other's contributions. However, if not repaired, such disconnects between marketing and sales can damage customer relationships and company performance.

A company can take several actions to help bring its marketing and sales functions closer together. At the most basic level, it can increase communications between the two groups by arranging joint meetings and spelling out communication channels. It can create opportunities for salespeople and marketers to work together. Brand managers and researchers can tag along on sales calls or sit in on sales planning sessions. In turn, salespeople can sit in on marketing planning sessions and share their firsthand customer knowledge.

A company can also create joint objectives and reward systems for sales and marketing teams or appoint marketing-sales liaisons—people from marketing who "live with the sales force" and help coordinate marketing and sales force programs and efforts. Finally, it can appoint a high-level marketing executive to oversee both marketing and sales. Such a person can help infuse marketing and sales with the common goal of creating value for customers to capture value in return.

> **Author Comment** Here's another definition of sales force management: "planning, organizing, leading, and controlling personal contact programs designed to achieve profitable customer relationships." Once again, the goal of every marketing activity is to create customer value, engage customers, and build profitable customer relationships.

Managing the Sales Force

OBJECTIVE 16-2 Identify and explain the six major sales force management steps.

We define **sales force management** as analyzing, planning, implementing, and controlling sales force activities. It includes designing sales force strategy and structure as well as recruiting, selecting, training, compensating, supervising, and evaluating the firm's salespeople. These major sales force management decisions are shown in ● **Figure 16.1** and discussed in the following sections.

Sales force management
Analyzing, planning, implementing, and controlling sales force activities.

Designing the Sales Force Strategy and Structure

Marketing managers face several sales force strategy and design questions. How should salespeople and their tasks be structured? How big should the sales force be? Should salespeople sell alone or work in teams with other people in the company? Should they sell in the field, by phone, or using online and social media? We address these issues next.

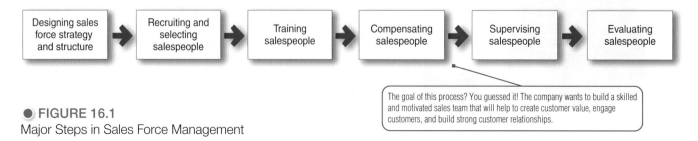

● **FIGURE 16.1**
Major Steps in Sales Force Management

The goal of this process? You guessed it! The company wants to build a skilled and motivated sales team that will help to create customer value, engage customers, and build strong customer relationships.

The Sales Force Structure

A company can divide sales responsibilities along any of several lines. The structure decision is simple if the company sells only one product line to one industry with customers in many locations. In that case the company would use a *territorial sales force structure*. However, if the company sells many products to many types of customers, it might need a *product sales force structure*, a *customer sales force structure*, or a combination of the two.

In the **territorial sales force structure**, each salesperson is assigned to an exclusive geographic area and sells the company's full line of products or services to all customers in that territory. This organization clearly defines each salesperson's job and fixes accountability. It also increases the salesperson's desire to build local customer relationships that, in turn, improve selling effectiveness. Finally, because each salesperson travels within a limited geographic area, travel expenses are relatively small. A territorial sales organization is often supported by many levels of sales management positions. For example, individual territory sales reps may report to area managers, who in turn report to regional managers, who report to a director of sales.

If a company has numerous and complex products, it can adopt a **product sales force structure**, in which the sales force specializes along product lines. For example, GE employs different sales forces for and within different product and service divisions of its major businesses. For instance, the company has separate sales forces for aviation, power, transportation, and healthcare products and technologies. Within GE Healthcare, the company employs different sales forces for diagnostic imaging, life sciences, and integrated IT products and services. No single salesperson can become expert in all of these product categories, so product specialization is required. In all, a company as large and complex as GE might have dozens of separate sales forces serving its diverse product and service portfolio.

Using a **customer (or market) sales force structure**, a company organizes its sales force along customer or industry lines. Separate sales forces may be set up for different industries, serving current customers versus finding new ones, and serving major accounts versus regular accounts. Organizing the sales force around customers can help a company build closer relationships with important customers. Many companies even have special sales forces to handle the needs of individual large customers. For example, P&G sales reps are integrated into Customer Business Development (CBD) teams. Each CBD team is assigned to a major P&G customer, such as Walmart, Safeway, or CVS Health.

● P&G's Walmart CBD team consists of more than 200 P&Gers who partner with Walmart buyers in Walmart's hometown of Bentonville, Arkansas. The CBD organization places the focus on serving the complete needs of each major customer. It lets P&G "grow our business by working as a 'strategic partner' (as opposed to just a supplier) with those who ultimately sell our products to consumers."[2]

When a company sells a wide variety of products to many types of customers over a broad geographic area, it often employs a *complex sales force structure*, which combines several types of organization. Salespeople can be specialized by customer and territory; product and territory; product and customer; or territory, product, and customer. For example, P&G specializes its sales force by customer (with different sales teams for Walmart, Safeway, CVS Health, or other large customers) *and* by territory for each key customer group (territory CBD representatives, territory managers, regional managers, and so on). No single structure is best for all companies and situations. Each company should select a sales force structure that best serves the needs of its customers and fits its overall marketing strategy.

Territorial sales force structure
A sales force organization that assigns each salesperson to an exclusive geographic territory in which that salesperson sells the company's full line.

Product sales force structure
A sales force organization in which salespeople specialize in selling only a portion of the company's products or lines.

Customer (or market) sales force structure
A sales force organization in which salespeople specialize in selling only to certain customers or industries.

● **Customer sales force structure: P&G's Walmart Customer Business Development sales team consists of hundreds of P&Gers who work closely with Walmart buyers in Walmart's hometown of Bentonville, Arkansas.**

grzegorz knec/Alamy Stock Photo

Sales Force Size

Once the company has set its structure, it is ready to consider *sales force size*. Sales forces may range in size from only a few salespeople to tens of thousands. Some sales forces are huge—for example, AT&T employs almost 40,000 salespeople around the world; PepsiCo, 24,300; Microsoft, 16,000; and IBM,14,000.[3] Salespeople constitute one of the company's most productive—and most expensive—assets. Therefore, increasing their numbers will increase both sales and costs.

A company might use some form of *workload approach* to set sales force size. Using this approach, a company first groups accounts into different classes according to size, account status, or other factors related to the amount of effort required to maintain the account. It then determines the number of salespeople needed to call on each class of accounts the desired number of times.

The company might think as follows: Suppose we have 1,000 A-level accounts and 2,000 B-level accounts. A-level accounts require 36 calls per year, and B-level accounts require 12 calls per year. In this case, the sales force's *workload*—the number of calls it must make per year—is 60,000 calls [(1,000 × 36) + (2,000 × 12) = 36,000 + 24,000 = 60,000]. Suppose our average salesperson can make 1,000 calls a year. Thus, we need 60 salespeople (60,000 ÷ 1,000).

Other Sales Force Strategy and Structure Issues

Sales management must also determine who will be involved in the selling effort and how various sales and sales-support people will work together.

Outside and Inside Sales Forces. A company may have an **outside sales force** (or **field sales force**), an **inside sales force**, or both. Outside salespeople travel to call on customers in the field. In contrast, inside salespeople conduct business from their offices via phone, online and social media interactions, or visits from buyers. The use of inside sales has grown in recent years as a result of increased outside selling costs and the surge in online, mobile, and social media technologies.

Some inside salespeople provide support for the outside sales force, freeing them to spend more time selling to major accounts and finding new prospects. For example, *technical sales-support people* provide technical information and answers to customers' questions. Sales assistants provide research and administrative backup for outside salespeople. They track down sales leads, call ahead and confirm appointments, follow up on deliveries, and answer customers' questions when outside salespeople cannot be reached. Using such combinations of inside and outside salespeople can help serve important customers better. The inside rep provides daily access and support, whereas the outside rep provides face-to-face collaboration and relationship building.

Other inside salespeople do more than just provide support. Telemarketers and online sellers use the phone, internet, and social media to find new leads, learn about customers and their business, or sell and service accounts directly. Telemarketing and online selling can be very effective, less costly ways to sell to smaller, harder-to-reach customers. Depending on the complexity of the product and customer, for example, a telemarketer can make from 20 to 33 decision-maker contacts a day compared with the average of four that an outside salesperson can make. In addition, whereas the cost of a business-to-business (B-to-B) field sales call can average close to $600, a routine industrial telemarketing or online contact might average only $25 to $75.[4]

Although the federal government's Do Not Call Registry put a dent in telephone sales to consumers, telemarketing remains a vital tool for most B-to-B marketers. For some smaller companies, telephone and online selling may be the primary sales approaches. However, most of the larger companies also use these tactics extensively, either to sell directly to small and midsize customers or to assist their sales forces in selling to larger ones.

● In addition to costs savings, in today's digital, mobile, and social media environments, many buyers are more receptive to—or even prefer—phone and online contact versus the high level of face-to-face contact once required. Today's customers are more inclined to gather their own information online—one study showed that a typical buyer reports contacting a sales rep only after independently completing about 60 percent of the buying process. Then

Outside sales force (or field sales force)
Salespeople who travel to call on customers in the field.

Inside sales force
Salespeople who conduct business from their offices via telephone, online and social media interactions, or visits from prospective buyers.

● **Outside and inside sales: In today's digital, mobile, and social media environment, inside selling is growing much faster than in-person selling. And a growing proportion of outside selling is now done over a phone or mobile device.**

LDProd/Shutterstock

buyers routinely use the phone, online meetings, and social media interactions to engage sellers and close deals.

As a result of these trends, telephone and virtual selling are growing much faster than in-person selling. Moreover, the lines are blurring between outside and inside selling, creating a new breed of "hybrid sales reps"—a modern cross between a field sales rep and an inside rep—who often work virtually when connecting with customers. One recent survey of 2,900 sales professionals concluded that "in an era of unprecedented connections, sales reps are increasingly likely to chat with a customer or prospect from behind a computer screen, rather than by slogging to their office."[5]

Team Selling. As products become more complex and as customers grow larger and more demanding, a single salesperson simply can't handle all of a large customer's needs. Instead, most companies now use **team selling** to service large, complex accounts. Sales teams can unearth problems, solutions, and sales opportunities that no individual salesperson could. Such teams might include experts from any area or level of the selling firm—sales, marketing, technical and support services, research and development, engineering, operations, finance, and others.

In many cases, the move to team selling mirrors similar changes in customer buying organizations. Many large customer companies have implemented team-based purchasing, requiring marketers to employ equivalent team-based selling. When dealing with large, complex accounts, one salesperson can't be an expert in everything the customer needs. Instead, selling is done by strategic account teams, quarterbacked by senior account managers or customer business managers.

For example, the 200-person P&G Walmart Customer Business Development team is a complete, multifunctional customer service unit. The team includes a CBD manager and several CBD account executives (each responsible for a specific P&G product category), supported by specialists in marketing strategy, product development, operations, information systems, logistics, finance, and human resources.

Team selling does have some pitfalls, however. For example, salespeople are by nature competitive and have often been trained and rewarded for outstanding individual performance. Salespeople who are used to having customers all to themselves may have trouble learning to work with and trust others on a team. In addition, selling teams can confuse or overwhelm customers who are used to working with only one salesperson. Finally, difficulties in evaluating individual contributions to the team-selling effort can create some sticky compensation issues.

Recruiting and Selecting Salespeople

At the heart of any successful sales force operation is the recruitment and selection of good salespeople. The performance difference between an average salesperson and a top salesperson can be substantial. In a typical sales force, the top 30 percent of the salespeople might bring in 60 percent of the sales. Thus, careful salesperson selection can greatly increase overall sales force performance.

Beyond the differences in sales performance, poor selection results in costly turnover. When a salesperson quits, the costs of finding and training a new salesperson—plus the costs of lost sales—can be very high. One sales consulting firm calculates the total 12-month cost of a bad sales hire at a whopping $382,000.[6] Also, a sales force with many new people is less productive, and turnover disrupts important customer relationships and sales team morale.

What sets great salespeople apart from all the rest? In an effort to profile top sales performers, Gallup Consulting, a division of the well-known Gallup polling organization, has interviewed hundreds of thousands of salespeople. Its research suggests that the best salespeople possess four key talents: intrinsic motivation, a disciplined work style, the ability to close a sale, and, perhaps most important, the ability to build relationships with customers.[7]

Super salespeople are motivated from within—they have an unrelenting drive to excel. Some salespeople are driven by money, a desire for recognition, or the satisfaction of competing and winning. Others are driven by the desire to provide service and build relationships. The best salespeople possess some of each of these motivations. However, another analysis found that the best salespeople are driven by a strong sense of

Team selling
Using teams of people from sales, marketing, engineering, finance, technical support, and even upper management to service large, complex accounts.

 **Great salespeople: The best salespeople possess intrinsic motivation, a disciplined work style, the ability to close a sale, and, perhaps most important, the ability to build relationships with customers.**

nd3000/Shutterstock

purpose: "The salespeople who sold with noble purpose, who truly want to make a difference to customers, consistently outsold the salespeople focused on sales goals and money." Selling with such a sense of customer-related purpose is not only more successful, it's also more profitable and more satisfying to salespeople.[8]

Super salespeople also have a disciplined work style. They lay out detailed, organized plans and then follow through in a timely way. But motivation and discipline mean little unless they result in closing more sales and building better customer relationships. Super salespeople build the skills and knowledge they need to get the job done. ● Perhaps most important, top salespeople are excellent customer problem solvers and relationship builders. They understand their customers' needs. Talk to sales executives and they'll describe top performers in these terms: good listeners, empathetic, patient, caring, and responsive. Top performers can put themselves on the buyer's side of the desk and see the world through their customers' eyes. They don't want just to be liked; they want to add value for their customers.

That said, there is no one right way to sell. Each successful salesperson uses a different approach, one that best applies his or her unique strengths and talents. For example, some salespeople enjoy the thrill of a harder sell in confronting challenges and winning people over. Others might apply "softer" talents to reach the same goal. "The truth is, no two great sales reps are alike," says one sales consultant. "You might thrive on fierce competition, while a colleague wins by being a super-analytical problem solver. Or maybe you have a tremendous talent for building relationships, while your fellow top performer is a brilliant strategist. What's most important is that you win business your way."[9]

When recruiting, a company should analyze the sales job itself and the characteristics of its most successful salespeople to identify the traits needed by a successful salesperson in its industry. Then it must recruit the right salespeople. The human resources department looks for applicants by getting names from current salespeople, using employment agencies, searching the internet and online social media, posting ads and notices on its website and industry media, and working through college placement services. Another source is to attract top salespeople from other companies. Proven salespeople need less training and can be productive immediately.

Recruiting will attract many applicants from which the company must select the best. The selection procedure can vary from a single informal interview to lengthy testing and interviewing. Many companies give formal tests to sales applicants. Tests typically measure sales aptitude, analytical and organizational skills, personality traits, and other characteristics. But test scores provide only one piece of information in a set that includes personal characteristics, references, past employment history, and interviewer reactions.

Training Salespeople

New salespeople may spend anywhere from a few weeks or months to a year or more in training. After the initial training ends, most companies provide continuing sales training via seminars, sales meetings, and online learning throughout the salesperson's career. According to one source, U.S. firms spend approximately $88 billion on sales training each year. Although training can be expensive, it can also yield important returns.[10]

Training programs have several goals. First, salespeople need to know about customers and how to build relationships with them. Therefore, the training program must teach them about different types of customers and their needs, buying motives, and buying habits. It must also teach them how to sell effectively and train them in the basics of the selling process. Salespeople also need to know and identify with the company, its products, and its competitors. Therefore, an effective training program teaches them about the company's objectives, organization, products, and the strategies of major competitors.

Today, many companies are adding digital components to their sales training programs. Online training may range from simple self-paced text- and video-based product training and internet-based sales exercises that build sales skills to sophisticated simulations that recreate the dynamics of real-life sales calls. Companies are also blending digital training with live classroom events and one-to-one coaching. Although much online training is web-based, companies now offer on-demand training from anywhere via almost any mobile device or other digital platform. Training online instead of on-site can cut travel and other training costs, and it takes up less of a salesperson's selling time. It also makes on-demand training available to salespeople, letting them train as little or as much as needed, whenever and wherever needed.

Compensating Salespeople

To attract good salespeople, a company must have an appealing compensation plan. Compensation consists of four elements: a fixed amount, a variable amount, expenses, and fringe benefits. The fixed amount, usually a salary, gives the salesperson some stable income. The variable amount, which might be commissions or bonuses based on sales performance, rewards the salesperson for greater effort and success.

● **Sales force compensation: A good compensation plan both motivates salespeople and directs their activities.**

Luca Bertolli/123RF

● A sales force compensation plan can both motivate salespeople and direct their activities. Compensation should direct salespeople toward activities that are consistent with the overall sales force and marketing objectives. For example, if the strategy is to acquire new business, grow rapidly, and gain market share, the compensation plan might include a larger commission component coupled with a new account bonus to encourage high sales performance and new account development. In contrast, if the goal is to maximize current account profitability, the compensation plan might contain a larger base-salary component with additional incentives for current account sales or customer satisfaction.

In fact, more and more companies are moving away from high-commission plans that may drive salespeople to make short-term grabs for business. They worry that a salesperson who is pushing too hard to close a deal may ruin the customer relationship. Instead, companies are designing compensation plans that reward salespeople for building customer relationships and growing the long-run value of each customer.

When times get tough economically, some companies are tempted to cut costs by reducing sales compensation. However, although some cost-cutting measures make sense when business is sluggish, cutting sales force compensation across the board is usually an action of last resort. Top salespeople are always in demand, and paying them less might mean losing them at a time when they are needed most. Thus, short-changing key salespeople can result in short-changing important customer relationships. If the company must reduce its compensation expenses, rather than making across-the-board cuts, companies should continue to pay top performers well while turning loose low performers.

Supervising and Motivating Salespeople

New salespeople need more than a territory, compensation, and training—they need supervision and motivation. The goal of *supervision* is to help salespeople "work smart" by doing the right things in the right ways. The goal of *motivation* is to encourage salespeople to "work hard" and energetically toward sales force goals. If salespeople work smart and work hard, they will realize their full potential—to their own and the company's benefit.

Supervising Salespeople

Companies vary in how closely they supervise their salespeople. Many help salespeople identify target customers and set call objectives. Some may also specify how much time the sales force should spend prospecting for new accounts and set other time management priorities. One tool is the weekly, monthly, or annual *call plan* that shows which customers and prospects to call on and which activities to carry out. Another tool is *time-and-duty analysis*.

In addition to time spent selling, the salesperson spends time planning, traveling, in meetings, processing orders, and doing administrative chores. Surprisingly, studies show that, on average, salespeople spend only 34 percent of their time on active selling.[11] Companies are always looking for ways to save time—simplifying administrative duties, developing better sales-call and routing plans, supplying more and better customer information, and using phone, email, online, or mobile conferencing instead of traveling.

Many firms have adopted *sales force automation systems*: computerized, digitized sales force operations that let salespeople work more effectively anytime, anywhere.

 Companies now routinely equip their salespeople with laptops or tablets, smartphones, videoconferencing technologies, and customer-contact and relationship management software. Armed with these technologies, salespeople can more effectively and efficiently profile customers and prospects, analyze and forecast sales, engage customers, make presentations, prepare sales and expense reports, and manage account relationships. The result is better time management, improved customer service, lower sales costs, and higher sales performance. In all, technology has reshaped the ways in which salespeople carry out their duties and engage customers.

Sales force automation: To help salespeople work more efficiently and effectively anytime, anywhere, companies routinely equip their salespeople with laptops or tablets, smartphones, wireless connections, videoconferencing technologies, and customer relationship management software.

kantver/123RF

Motivating Salespeople

Beyond directing salespeople, sales managers must also motivate them. Some salespeople will do their best without any special urging from management. To them, selling may be the most fascinating job in the world. But selling can also be frustrating. Salespeople often work alone, and they must sometimes travel away from home. They may also face aggressive competing salespeople and difficult customers. Therefore, salespeople often need special encouragement to do their best.

Management can boost sales force morale and performance through its organizational climate, sales quotas, and positive incentives. *Organizational climate* describes the feeling that salespeople have about their opportunities, value, and rewards for a good performance. Some companies treat salespeople as if they are not very important, so performance suffers accordingly. Other companies treat their salespeople as valued contributors and allow virtually unlimited opportunity for income and promotion. Not surprisingly, these companies enjoy higher sales force performance and less turnover.

Sales quota

A standard that states the amount a salesperson should sell and how sales should be divided among the company's products.

Many companies motivate their salespeople by setting **sales quotas**—standards stating the amount they should sell and how sales should be divided among the company's products. Compensation is often related to how well salespeople meet their quotas. Companies also use various *positive incentives* to increase the sales force effort. *Sales meetings* provide social occasions, breaks from the routine, chances to meet and talk with "company brass," and opportunities to air feelings and identify with a larger group. Companies also sponsor *sales contests* to spur the sales force to make a selling effort above and beyond what is normally expected. Other incentives include honors, merchandise and cash awards, trips, and profit-sharing plans.

Evaluating Salespeople and Sales Force Performance

We have thus far described how management communicates what salespeople should be doing and how it motivates them to do it. This process requires good feedback, which means getting regular information about salespeople to evaluate their performance.

Management gets information about its salespeople in several ways. The most important source is *sales reports*, including weekly or monthly work plans and longer-term territory marketing plans. Salespeople also write up their completed activities on *call reports* and turn in *expense reports* for which they are partly or wholly reimbursed. The company can also monitor the sales and profit performance data in the salesperson's territory. Additional information comes from personal observation, customer surveys, and talks with other salespeople.

Using various sales force reports and other information, sales management evaluates the members of the sales force. It evaluates salespeople on their ability to "plan their work and work their plan." Formal evaluation forces management to develop and communicate clear standards for judging performance. It also provides salespeople with constructive feedback and motivates them to perform well.

On a broader level, management should evaluate the performance of the sales force as a whole. Is the sales force accomplishing its customer relationship, sales, and profit objectives? Is it working well with other areas of the marketing and company organization? Are sales force costs in line with outcomes? As with other marketing activities, the company wants to measure its *return on sales investment*.

> **Author** | Like just about everything
> **Comment** | else these days, selling
> has been affected in a big way by
> digital technologies. Today's sales
> forces are mastering the use of online,
> mobile, and social media tools to
> engage business customers, build
> relationships, and make sales.

Social selling

Using online, mobile, and social media to engage customers, build stronger customer relationships, and augment sales performance.

Social Selling: Online, Mobile, and Social Media Tools

The fastest-growing sales trend is the explosion in **social selling**—the use of online, mobile, and social media to engage customers, build stronger customer relationships, and augment sales performance. Digital sales force technologies are creating exciting avenues for connecting with and engaging customers. Some analysts even predict that the internet will mean the death of person-to-person selling, as salespeople are ultimately replaced by websites, online social media, mobile apps, video and conferencing technologies, AI-driven sales assistants, and other tools that allow direct customer contact. Such predictions are much overstated. Online and social media technologies won't likely make salespeople obsolete (see Real Marketing 16.1). However, digital technologies are rapidly changing the role of face-to-face selling.

When used properly, digital technologies can make salespeople more productive and effective. They provide powerful tools for identifying and learning about prospects, engaging customers, creating customer value, closing sales, and nurturing customer relationships. Social selling technologies can produce big organizational benefits for sales forces. They help conserve salespeople's valuable time, save travel dollars, and give salespeople new vehicles for selling and servicing accounts.

Social selling hasn't really changed the fundamentals of selling. Sales forces have always taken the primary responsibility for reaching out to and engaging customers and managing customer relationships. Now, more of that is being done digitally. However, because online and social media are dramatically changing the customer buying process, they are also changing the selling process. In today's digital world, many customers no longer rely as much as they once did on information and assistance provided by salespeople. Instead, they carry out more of the buying process on their own—especially the early stages. Increasingly, they use online and social media resources to analyze their own problems, research solutions, get advice from colleagues, and rank buying options before ever speaking to a salesperson. One study of business buyers found that 68 percent of buyers prefer to research independently online and 62 percent develop a selection criteria before they reach out to a sales rep.[12]

Thus, today's customers have much more control over the sales process than they had in the days when brochures, pricing, and product advice were available only from sales reps. Customers can now browse corporate websites and social media sites to identify and qualify sellers. They can hobnob with other buyers on social media such as LinkedIn, Twitter, or Facebook to share experiences, identify solutions, and evaluate products they are considering.

As a result, if and when salespeople do enter the buying process, customers often know almost as much about a company's products as the salespeople do. And when customers do call in salespeople, they are more often doing it digitally, with the expectation of real-time engagement. These days, they want more than product and pricing information from salespeople—they want problem solving and solutions.

In response to this new digital buying environment, sellers are reorienting their selling processes around the new customer buying process. They are "going where customers are"—social media, web forums, online communities, blogs—in order to engage customers earlier. They are engaging customers not just where and when they are buying but also where and when they are learning about and evaluating what they will buy.

Salespeople now routinely use digital tools that monitor customer social media exchanges to spot trends, identify prospects, and learn what customers would like to buy, how they feel about a vendor, and what it would take to make a sale. They generate lists

Real Marketing 16.1 | B-to-B Salespeople: In This Digital and Social Media Age, Who Needs Them Anymore?

It's hard to imagine a world without salespeople. But based on declining numbers in recent years, some analysts predict that the nation's corps of B-to-B salespeople will continue to shrink in future years or even fade away. With the explosion of the internet, mobile devices, social media, and other technologies that link customers directly with companies, they reason, who needs face-to-face selling anymore?

The doubters point out that various sales jobs are rapidly being replaced by websites, email, mobile apps, blogs, video sharing, virtual trade shows, social media, artificial intelligence–driven sales assistants, and a host of other digital-age interaction tools. "The world no longer needs salespeople," one doomsayer proclaims. "Sales is a dying profession and soon will be as outmoded as oil lamps and the rotary phone."

So, is B-to-B selling really dying? Will the internet, mobile technologies, social media, and AI reps replace the age-old art of selling face-to-face? To most sales analysts, the answer is a resounding "no." "A lot of people who are experts in sales … would predict the fall of the sales rep," says one sales expert. "I hear people say that and I think, 'no way.'"

Most experts do agree on one thing: Technology is radically transforming the selling profession. Today's revolutionary changes in how people communicate are affecting every aspect of business, and selling is no exception. But digital technologies won't soon replace person-to-person buying and selling. Technology can greatly enhance the selling process, but it can't replace many of the functions that salespeople perform. "The internet can take orders and disseminate content, but what it can't do is discover customer needs," says another sales expert. "It can't build relationships and it can't prospect on its own." Adds another, "Someone must define the company's value proposition and unique message and communicate it to the market, and that person is the sales rep."

What is dying, however, is the account-maintenance role—the order taker who stops by the customer's office on Friday and says, "Hey, got anything for me?" Likewise, there's not much of a future for explainers, reps who simply convey product and service information that can be obtained more quickly and easily online. Such salespeople are not creating value and can easily be replaced by automation. However, salespeople who excel at new customer acquisition, relationship

management, problem solving, and account growth with existing customers will always be in high demand. And digital technologies will only make those salespeople better.

There's no doubt about it—technology is transforming the selling profession. Instead of relying on salespeople for basic information and education, customers can now do much of their own prepurchase research via websites, online searches, phone apps, social media contacts, and other venues. A recent study found that 91 percent of B-to-B buyers are active in social media and that the decisions of 75 percent of buyers are influenced by digital and social media activities. Many customers now start the sales process online and do their homework about problems, competing products, and suppliers before the first sales meeting ever takes place.

Another study found that business buyers are at least 60 percent of the way through the buying process by the time they reach out to a vendor. They don't need basic information or product education; they need solutions and new insights. So today's salespeople need to excel at solving customer problems and building relationships. In fact, even as lower-order sales jobs disappear in coming years, jobs for such consultant-type sales reps are expected to grow at a healthy clip.

Beyond the mechanics of the selling process, buying and selling involve emotional

exchanges as well as transactional ones. Even with new artificial intelligence applications that put an almost-human face on sales force automation, digital technologies still can't replace the human touch—the empathy, instinct, and understanding that are essential to good selling. Rather than replacing salespeople, technology is augmenting them. Today's top salespeople aren't really doing anything fundamentally new. They've always done customer research, problem solving, social networking, and relationship building. Today, however, they are doing it on steroids, using a new kit of high-tech digital tools and applications.

As discussed in Chapter 6, IBM provides a good example of how companies are using social selling to make an already strong sales force even better. For more than 100 years, IBM has relied on its legendary sales force to build customer relationships and sales. But in recent years, IBM has significantly transformed how its sales force engages with B-to-B customers to meet their needs in the digital age. IBM now employs a wide variety of platforms that inform and engage business customers directly, connect them with IBM salespeople, and promote customer purchasing and relationships.

For example, IBM's various divisions offer dozens of market- and industry-specific websites, containing thousands of individual

Digital and social selling technologies—from websites, social media, and mobile apps to AI-driven sales assistants—have rapidly changed the face of personal selling. But rather than replacing salespeople, such efforts extend their reach and effectiveness.

Gerd Altmann/Pixabay

site areas and tens of thousands of pages. Customers can access the websites to do their own digging into IBM product and service overviews, detailed technical information, and purchasing details with real-time customer support as needed. Customers can connect even more deeply and interactively with the IBM community through the company's comprehensive digital and social media network—mobile apps, Twitter channels, LinkedIn groups, Facebook and Instagram pages, YouTube channels, and more—where they can discover, discuss, evaluate, and even buy IBM solutions and services.

However, although IBM's digital and social media presence draws in new potential customers and takes them through many of the initial stages of product discovery and evaluation, it doesn't replace IBM's salespeople.

Instead, it extends their reach and effectiveness. Digital and social media not only give customers more effective access to IBM, they give IBM's salespeople more effective access to customers.

The real value of IBM's social selling is the flood of sales leads it creates and the customer connections it develops. Once prospective customers have discovered and evaluated IBM solutions online, they will likely initiate contact, request a proposal, or start the negotiation process. That's where the person-to-person selling begins. And once sales agreements are inked, digital and social media give IBM's salespeople a rich reservoir of connecting tools with which to maintain and build long-term customer relationships.

All this suggests that B-to-B selling isn't dying, it's just changing. In fact, according

to the Bureau of Labor Statistics, overall employment of B-to-B sales representatives is projected to grow 5 percent through 2026, equal to the average growth for all occupations. But now more than ever, salespeople must blend more traditional approaches with new digital experiences. The tools and techniques may be different as sales forces leverage and adapt to selling in the digital and social media age. But whatever the tools, B-to-B marketers still need strong sales teams composed of salespeople who can engage customers, discover customer needs, solve customer problems, and build relationships. Especially for big-ticket B-to-B sales, "all the new technology may make it easier to sell by building strong ties to customers even before the first sit-down, but when the signature hits the dotted line, there will be a sales rep there."[13]

of prospective customers from online databases and social networking sites, such as InsideView, Hoovers, and LinkedIn. They create dialogues when prospective customers visit their web and social media sites through live chats with the sales team. They use internet conferencing tools such as WebEx, Zoom, GoToMeeting, or TelePresence to talk live with customers about products and services. They provide videos and other information on their YouTube channels and Facebook pages.

Today's sales forces have also ramped up their own use of digital content and social media to engage customers throughout the buying process. A recent survey of business-to-business marketers found that although they have recently cut back on traditional media and event spending, they are investing more in digital content, ranging from proprietary online customer communities to webinars and social media and mobile apps. Consider Makino, a leading manufacturer of metal cutting and machining technology:[14]

● There's a hot new video on YouTube these days, featured at the Makino Machine Tools YouTube channel. It shows a Makino five-axis vertical machining center in action, with metal chips flying as the machinery mills a new industrial part. Sound exciting? Probably not to you. But to the right industrial customer, the video is downright spellbinding. YouTube is just one of a wide variety of social media content initiatives that Makino uses to complement its salespeople in their efforts to engage and inform customers and enhance customer relationships. For example, Makino hosts an ongoing series of industry-specific webinars that position the company as an industry thought leader. Makino produced and archived hundreds of webinars on topics ranging from how to get the most out of your machine tools to how metal-cutting processes are done. Webinar content is tailored to specific industries, such as aerospace or medical, and is promoted through carefully targeted online ads and email invitations. The webinars help to build Makino's customer database, generate sales leads, build customer relationships, and prepare the way for salespeople by serving up relevant information and educating customers online. Makino also uses Facebook, YouTube, and Twitter to inform customers and prospects about the latest Makino innovations and events and to demonstrate the company's machines in action. Such digital content and social media don't replace salespeople. Instead, they help salespeople build even more fruitful customer relationships. When it comes to B-to-B selling these days, Makino has learned, social marketing is *the* space to be.

● Social selling: Machine tool manufacturer Makino engages customers through extensive digital content and social media, which complement sales force efforts to engage customers and build product–customer relationships.

Courtesy of Makino

Ultimately, social selling technologies are helping to make sales forces more efficient, cost-effective, and productive. The technologies help salespeople do what good salespeople have always done—build customer relationships by solving customer problems—but do it better, faster, and cheaper.

However, social selling also has some drawbacks. For starters, it's not cheap. But even more, there are some things you just can't present or teach via the internet—things that require personal engagement, insight, and interaction. For these reasons, some technology experts recommend that sales executives use online and social media technologies to spot prospects and opportunities, provide information, maintain customer contact, and make preliminary client sales presentations but resort to old-fashioned, face-to-face meetings when the time draws near to close a big deal.

The Personal Selling Process

OBJECTIVE 16-3 Discuss the personal selling process, distinguishing between transaction-oriented marketing and relationship marketing.

Author Comment | So far, we've examined how sales management develops and implements overall sales force strategies and programs. In this section, we'll look at how individual salespeople and sales teams sell to customers and build relationships with them.

We now turn from designing and managing a sales force to the personal selling process. The **selling process** consists of several steps that salespeople must master. These steps focus on the goal of getting new customers and obtaining orders from them. However, most salespeople spend much of their time maintaining existing accounts and building long-term customer relationships. We will discuss the relationship aspect of the personal selling process in a later section.

Selling process
The steps that salespeople follow when selling, which include prospecting and qualifying, preapproach, approach, presentation and demonstration, handling objections, closing, and follow-up.

Steps in the Selling Process

As shown in ● **Figure 16.2**, the selling process consists of seven steps: prospecting and qualifying, preapproach, approach, presentation and demonstration, handling objections, closing, and follow-up.

Prospecting and Qualifying

Prospecting
The sales step in which a salesperson or company identifies qualified potential customers.

The first step in the selling process is **prospecting**—identifying qualified potential customers. Approaching the right customers is crucial to selling success. Salespeople don't want to call on just any potential customers. They want to call on those who are most likely to appreciate and respond to the company's value proposition—those the company can serve well and profitably.

A salesperson must often approach many prospects to get only a few sales. Although the company supplies some leads, salespeople need skill in finding their own. The best source is referrals. Salespeople can ask current customers for referrals and cultivate other referral sources, such as suppliers, dealers, noncompeting salespeople, and online or social media contacts. They can also search for prospects in directories or on the internet and

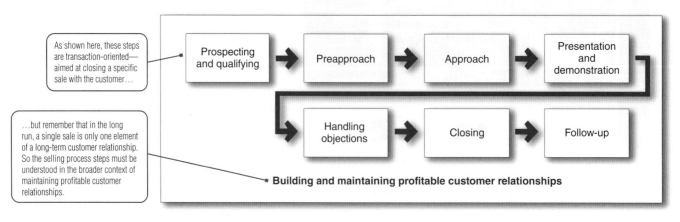

● **FIGURE 16.2**
Steps in the Selling Process

track down leads using the phone, email, and social media. Or, as a last resort, they can drop in unannounced on various offices (a practice known as *cold calling*).

Salespeople also need to know how to *qualify* leads—that is, how to identify the good ones and screen out the poor ones. Prospects can be qualified by looking at their financial ability, volume of business, special needs, location, and possibilities for growth.

Companies are increasingly using artificial intelligence and other advanced analytics to identify and evaluate sales prospects. They are using AI to amass and sift through the mountains of data regarding potential customers' characteristics, behaviors, and purchasing patterns to generate and rank good sales leads. AI can also be used to assess prospective client needs and suggest company solutions that might make salespeople more effective in landing new business. In recent years, says one analyst, AI "has gone from predictive to prescriptive, meaning it can suggest the prospect to call that is most likely to result in a sale, or the best combination of offers to construct a successful [sale]."[15]

Preapproach

> **Preapproach**
> The sales step in which a salesperson learns as much as possible about a prospective customer before making a sales call.

Before calling on a prospect, the salesperson should learn as much as possible about the organization (what it needs, who is involved in the buying) and its buyers (their characteristics and buying styles). This step is known as **preapproach**. A successful sale begins long before the salesperson makes initial contact with a prospect. Preapproach begins with good research and preparation. The salesperson can consult standard industry and online sources, acquaintances, and others to learn about the company. He or she can scour the prospect's web and social media sites for information about its products, buyers, and buying processes. The company's AI activities can supply data and analyses on the prospects characteristics and needs. Then the salesperson must apply the research gathered to develop a customer strategy.

The salesperson should set *call objectives*, which may be to qualify the prospect, gather information, or make an immediate sale. Another task is to determine the best approach, which might be a personal visit, a phone call, an email, or a text. The ideal timing should be considered carefully because many prospects are busiest at certain times of the day or week. Finally, the salesperson should give thought to an overall sales strategy for the account.

Approach

> **Approach**
> The sales step in which a salesperson meets the customer for the first time.

During the **approach** step, the salesperson should know how to meet and greet the buyer and get the relationship off to a good start. The approach might take place offline or online, in-person or via digital conferencing or social media. This step involves the salesperson's appearance, opening lines, and follow-up remarks. The opening lines should be positive to build goodwill from the outset. This opening might be followed by some key questions to learn more about the customer's needs or by showing a display or sample to attract the buyer's attention and curiosity. As in all stages of the selling process, listening to the customer is crucial.

Presentation and Demonstration

> **Presentation**
> The sales step in which a salesperson tells the "value story" to the buyer, showing how the company's offer solves the customer's problems.

During the **presentation** step of the selling process, the salesperson tells the "value story" to the buyer, showing how the company's offer solves the customer's problems. The *customer-solution approach* fits better with today's relationship marketing focus than does a hard sell or glad-handing approach.

The goal should be to show how the company's products and services fit the customer's needs. Buyers today want insights and solutions, not smiles; results, not razzle-dazzle. Moreover, buyers don't want just products; they want to know how those products will add value to their businesses. They want salespeople who listen to their concerns, understand their needs, and respond with the right products and services.

But before salespeople can *present* customer solutions, they must *develop* solutions to present. The solutions approach calls for good listening and problem-solving skills. The qualities that buyers *dislike most* in salespeople include being pushy, late, deceitful, unprepared, disorganized, or overly talkative. The qualities they *value most* include good listening, empathy, honesty, dependability, thoroughness, and follow-through. ● Great salespeople know how to sell, but more important, they know how to listen and build strong customer relationships. According to an old sales adage, "You have two ears and one mouth. Use them proportionally." A classic ad from office products maker Boise Cascade

● **Great salespeople know how to sell, but more important, they know how to listen and build strong customer relationships.**

Tony Garcia/The Image Bank/Getty Images

Handling objections
The sales step in which a salesperson seeks out, clarifies, and overcomes any customer objections to buying.

Closing
The sales step in which a salesperson asks the customer for an order.

Follow-up
The sales step in which a salesperson follows up after the sale to ensure customer satisfaction and repeat business.

makes the listening point. It shows a Boise salesperson with huge ears drawn on. "With Boise, you'll notice a difference right away, especially with our sales force," says the ad. "At Boise… our account representatives have the unique ability to listen to your needs."

Finally, salespeople must also plan their presentation methods. Good interpersonal communication skills count when it comes to engaging customers and making effective sales presentations. However, the current media-rich and cluttered communications environment presents many new challenges for sales presenters. Today's information-overloaded customers demand richer presentation experiences. For their part, presenters now face multiple distractions during presentations from mobile phones, text messages, and other digital competition. As a result, salespeople must deliver their messages in more engaging and compelling ways.

Thus, today's salespeople are employing advanced presentation technologies that allow for full multimedia presentations to only one or a few people. The venerable old sales presentation flip chart has been replaced with tablets, sophisticated presentation software, online presentation technologies, interactive whiteboards, and digital projectors.

Handling Objections

Customers almost always have objections during the presentation or when asked to place an order. The objections can be either logical or psychological, and they are often unspoken. In **handling objections**, the salesperson should use a positive approach, seek out hidden objections, ask the buyer to clarify any objections, take objections as opportunities to provide more information, and turn the objections into reasons for buying. Every salesperson needs training in the skills of handling objections.

Closing

After handling the prospect's objections, the salesperson next tries to close the sale. However, some salespeople do not get around to **closing** or don't handle it well. They may lack confidence, feel guilty about asking for the order, or fail to recognize the right moment to close the sale. Salespeople should know how to recognize closing signals from the buyer, including physical actions, comments, and questions. For example, the customer might sit forward and nod approvingly or ask about prices and credit terms.

Salespeople can use any of several closing techniques. They can ask for the order, review points of agreement, offer to help write up the order, ask whether the buyer wants this model or that one, or note that the buyer will lose out if the order is not placed now. The salesperson may offer the buyer special reasons to close, such as a lower price, an extra quantity at no charge, or additional services.

Follow-Up

The last step in the selling process—**follow-up**—is necessary if the salesperson wants to ensure customer satisfaction and repeat business. Right after closing, the salesperson should complete any details on delivery time, purchase terms, and other matters. The salesperson then should schedule a follow-up call after the buyer receives the initial order to make sure proper installation, instruction, and servicing occur. This visit would reveal any problems, assure the buyer of the salesperson's interest, and reduce any buyer concerns that might have arisen since the sale.

Personal Selling and Managing Customer Relationships

The steps in the just-described selling process are *transaction oriented*—their aim is to help salespeople close a specific sale with a customer. But in most cases, the company is not simply seeking a sale. Rather, it wants to engage the customer over the long haul in a mutually profitable *relationship*. The sales force usually plays an important role in customer relationship building.

Thus, as shown in Figure 16.2, the selling process must be understood in the context of building and maintaining profitable customer relationships. Moreover, as discussed in a previous section, today's buyers are increasingly moving through the early stages of the buying process themselves, before ever engaging sellers. Salespeople must adapt their selling process to match the new buying process. That means discovering and engaging customers on a relationship basis rather than a transaction basis.

Successful sales organizations recognize that winning and keeping accounts requires more than making good products and directing the sales force to close lots of sales. If the company wishes only to close sales and capture short-term business, it can do this by simply slashing its prices to meet or beat those of competitors. Instead, most companies want their salespeople to practice *value selling*—demonstrating and delivering superior customer value and capturing a return on that value that is fair for both the customer and the company.

● Value selling: Sales management's challenge is to transform salespeople from customer advocates for price cuts into company advocates for value.

almagami/123RF

Unfortunately, in the heat of closing sales, salespeople too often take the easy way out by cutting prices rather than selling value. ● Sales management's challenge is to transform salespeople from customer advocates for price cuts into company advocates for value. Here's how Rockwell Automation sells value and relationships rather than price:[16]

Under pressure from Walmart to lower its prices, a condiment producer asked several competing supplier representatives—including Rockwell Automation sales rep Jeff Policicchio—to help it find ways to reduce its operating costs. After spending a day in the customer's plant, Policicchio quickly put his finger on the major problem: Production was suffering because of downtime due to poorly performing pumps on the customer's 32 large condiment tanks. Quickly gathering cost and usage data, Policicchio used his Rockwell Automation laptop value-assessment tool to develop an effective solution for the customer's pump problem.

The next day, as he and competing reps presented their cost-reduction proposals to plant management, Policicchio offered the following value proposition: "With this Rockwell Automation pump solution, through less downtime, reduced administrative costs in procurement, and lower spending on repair parts, your company will save at least $16,268 per pump—on up to 32 pumps—relative to our best competitor's solution." Compared with competitors' proposals, Policicchio's solution carried a higher initial price. However, no competing rep offered more than fuzzy promises about possible cost savings. Most simply lowered their prices.

Impressed by Policicchio's value proposition—despite its higher initial price—the plant managers opted to buy and try one Rockwell Automation pump. When the pump performed even better than predicted, the customer ordered all of the remaining pumps. By demonstrating tangible value rather than simply selling on price, Policicchio not only landed the initial sale but also earned a loyal future customer.

Thus, value selling requires listening to customers, understanding their needs, and carefully coordinating the whole company's efforts to create lasting relationships based on customer value.

Author | Sales promotion is the
Comment | most short-term of the promotion mix tools. Whereas advertising or personal selling says "buy," sales promotions say "buy now."

Sales Promotion

OBJECTIVE 16-4 Explain how sales promotion campaigns are developed and implemented.

Personal selling and advertising often work closely with another promotion tool: sales promotion. **Sales promotion** consists of short-term incentives to encourage the purchase or sales of a product or service. Whereas advertising offers reasons to buy a product or service, sales promotion offers reasons to buy *now*.

Sales promotion
Short-term incentives to encourage the purchase or sale of a product or a service.

● **Sales promotions are found everywhere. For example, stores at your local mall are peppered with signs announcing special sales.**

Gary Armstrong

● Examples of sales promotions are found everywhere. A 20-page Best Buy freestanding insert in the Sunday paper offers hundreds of great Black Friday Doorbuster deals; a Rooms to Go insert offers special prices and 60 months free interest. At the mall, stores are peppered with signs announcing seasonal sales; one store promises to give you $20 in store cash for every $20 you spend plus an extra 60 percent off markdown prices. Buy a new Samsung tablet and get a free memory upgrade. A hardware store chain receives a 10 percent discount on selected Stihl power lawn and garden tools if it agrees to advertise them in local newspapers. Sales promotion includes a wide variety of promotion tools designed to stimulate earlier or stronger market response.

The Rapid Growth of Sales Promotion

Sales promotion tools are used by most organizations, including manufacturers, distributors, retailers, and not-for-profit institutions. They are targeted toward final buyers (*consumer promotions*), retailers and wholesalers (*trade promotions*), business customers (*business promotions*), and members of the sales force (*sales force promotions*). In all, by one estimate, sales promotion spending accounts for about 20 percent of all marketing spending in the United States.[17]

Several factors have contributed to these high sales promotion levels, particularly in consumer markets. First, inside the company, product managers face great pressures to increase current sales, and they view promotion as an effective short-run sales tool. Second, externally, the company faces stiff competition, and competing brands are increasingly less differentiated. Sales promotion can help to differentiate their offers. Third, advertising efficiency has declined because of rising costs, media clutter, and legal restraints. Finally, consumers have become very deal oriented. Consumers are demanding lower prices and better deals. Sales promotions can help attract today's more value-oriented consumers.

The heavy use of sales promotion has resulted in *promotion clutter*, which is similar to advertising clutter. With so many products being sold on deal these days, a given promotion runs the risk of being lost in a sea of other promotions, weakening its ability to trigger an immediate purchase. Manufacturers are now searching for ways to rise above the clutter, such as offering larger coupon values, creating more dramatic point-of-purchase displays, or delivering promotions through digital, mobile, and social media. Digital promotions can help drive both in-store and online sales.

In developing a sales promotion program, a company must first set sales promotion objectives and then select the best tools for accomplishing these objectives.

Sales Promotion Objectives

Sales promotion objectives vary widely. Sellers may use *consumer promotions* to urge short-term customer buying or boost customer-brand engagement. Objectives for *trade promotions* include getting retailers to carry new items and more inventory, buy ahead, or promote the company's products and give them more shelf space. *Business promotions* are used to generate business leads, stimulate purchases, reward customers, and motivate salespeople. For the sales force, objectives include getting more sales force support for current or new products and getting salespeople to sign up new accounts.

Sales promotions are usually used together with advertising, personal selling, direct and digital marketing, or other promotion mix tools. Consumer promotions must usually be advertised and can add excitement and pulling power to ads and other marketing content. Trade and business sales promotions support the firm's personal selling process.

When the economy tightens and sales lag, it's tempting to offer deep promotional discounts to spur consumer spending. In general, however, rather than creating only short-term sales or temporary brand switching, sales promotions should help to reinforce the product's position and build long-term customer relationships. If properly designed, every sales promotion tool has the potential to build both short-term excitement and long-term

● **Customer loyalty programs: Membership in the IKEA Family loyalty club gives customers special benefits, rewards, and discounts. More important, it lets IKEA create special experiences designed just for them.**

Hadrian/Shutterstock

consumer engagement and relationships. Marketers should avoid "quick fix," price-only promotions in favor of promotions that are designed to build brand equity. Examples include the various *frequency marketing programs* and loyalty cards. Most hotels, supermarkets, and airlines offer frequent-guest/buyer/flier programs that give rewards to regular customers to keep them coming back. Such promotional programs can build loyalty through added value rather than discounted prices.

● For example, IKEA invites customers to join its IKEA Family loyalty club. In addition to special discounts on purchases, IKEA Family members receive sneak preview access to IKEA events, 90-day price protection, financing options, a record of purchases, and a subscription to IKEA Family Magazine, loaded with decorating tips and tricks. Members can opt in for emails that offer "rewards and inspiration." Swiping the membership card at a local IKEA store gives members a chance to win a $100 IKEA gift card every month. And members who complete an IKEA Family Profile receive special treatment, such as tailored offers and "Happy Birthday treats" in their email boxes. "We want to get to know your tastes, ideas, and plans to create the perfect IKEA experience just for you," says IKEA. "Together, we bring ideas to life."[18]

Major Sales Promotion Tools

Many tools can be used to accomplish sales promotion objectives. Descriptions of the main consumer, trade, and business promotion tools follow.

Consumer Promotions

Consumer promotions

Sales promotion tools used to boost short-term customer buying and engagement or enhance long-term customer relationships.

Consumer promotions include a wide range of tools—from samples, coupons, refunds, premiums, and point-of-purchase displays to contests, sweepstakes, and event sponsorships.

Samples are offers of a trial amount of a product. Sampling is the most effective—but most expensive—way to introduce a new product or create new excitement for an existing one. Some samples are free; for others, the company charges a small amount to offset its cost. The sample might be sent by mail, handed out in a store or at a kiosk, attached to another product, or featured in an ad, email, or mobile offer. Samples are sometimes combined into sample packs, which can then be used to promote other products and services. Sampling can be a powerful promotional tool. ● For example, every year 7-Eleven celebrates its self-proclaimed 7-Eleven Day on July 11 (7/11) by handing out free Slurpees. Last year it gave out about 9 million of the frozen treats. Free Slurpee Day is followed by a "seven deals in seven days" promotion that gives 7Rewards loyalty club members and 7-Eleven app users a week of sample deals on other 7-Eleven products—such as a free Big Gulp soft drink with the purchase of a Snickers bar. Thus, the popular sampling program pulls new customers into the stores but also rewards loyal customers and encourages them to "maybe try something they haven't." It also generates plenty of buzz about the brand.[19]

Coupons are certificates that save buyers money when they purchase specified products. Most consumers love coupons. U.S. consumer packaged-goods companies distributed 267 billion coupons last year. Consumers redeemed more than 1.7 billion of them. Coupons can promote early trial of a new brand or stimulate sales of a mature brand. However, to combat the increase in coupon clutter, most major consumer goods companies are issuing fewer coupons and targeting them more carefully. For example, the number of coupons issued dropped a stunning 11.7 percent last year.[20]

● **Consumer samples can be a powerful tool. 7-Eleven's Free Slurpee Day celebration pulls new customers into the stores but also rewards loyal customers and encourages them to "maybe try something they haven't."**

7-Eleven, Inc.

Digital and mobile coupons represent today's fastest-growing coupon segment. Digital coupons can be individually targeted and personalized in ways that print coupons can't. Whether printed at home, loaded to a card, or redeemed via smartphone or other mobile device, digital coupons claim much higher redemptions rates than traditional newspaper insert coupons. Whereas consumers redeem only 0.28 percent of traditional insert coupons, they redeem almost 8 percent of digital and print-at-home coupons. That fact explains the drop in overall coupons—marketers can obtain the same levels of redemption with far fewer coupons issued.[21]

Rebates (or *cash refunds*) are like coupons except that the price reduction occurs after the purchase rather than at the retail outlet. The customer sends proof of purchase to the manufacturer, which then refunds part of the purchase price by mail. For example, Toro ran a clever preseason promotion on some of its snowblower models, offering a rebate if the snowfall in the buyer's market area turned out to be below average. Competitors were not able to match this offer on such short notice, and the promotion was very successful.

Price packs (also called *cents-off deals*) offer consumers savings off the regular price of a product. The producer marks the reduced prices directly on the label or package. Price packs can be single packages sold at a reduced price (such as two for the price of one) or two related products banded together (such as a toothbrush and toothpaste). Price packs are very effective—even more so than coupons—in stimulating short-term sales.

Premiums are goods offered either free or at low cost as an incentive to buy a product, ranging from toys included with kids' products to a free micro memory card with the purchase of a phone. A premium may come inside the package (in-pack), outside the package (on-pack), as a credit at point of purchase, or through the mail. For example, over the years, McDonald's has offered a variety of premiums in its Happy Meals—from Shopkins to Pokémon characters. Customers can visit www.happymeal.com to play games, read e-books, and watch commercials associated with the current Happy Meal sponsor.[22]

Advertising specialties, also called *promotional products*, are useful articles imprinted with an advertiser's name, logo, or message that are given as gifts to consumers. Typical items include T-shirts and other apparel, pens, coffee mugs, calendars, key rings, tote bags, coolers, golf balls, and caps. U.S. marketers spent more than $23 billion on advertising specialties last year. Such items can be very effective. Many of them stick around for months or even longer, subtly imprinting a brand name in the user's mind.[23]

Point-of-purchase (POP) promotions include displays and demonstrations that take place at the point of sale. Think of your last visit to the local Costco, Walmart, or Bed Bath & Beyond. Chances are good that you were tripping over aisle displays, promotional signs, "shelf talkers," or demonstrators offering free tastes of featured food products. Unfortunately, many retailers do not like to handle the hundreds of displays, signs, and posters they receive from manufacturers each year. Manufacturers have therefore responded by offering better POP materials, offering to set them up, and tying them in with television, print, or online messages.

Contests, sweepstakes, and *games* give consumers the chance to win something, such as cash, trips, or goods, by luck or through extra effort. A *contest* calls for consumers to submit an entry—a jingle, guess, suggestion—to be judged by a panel that will select the best entries. A *sweepstakes* calls for consumers to submit their names for a drawing. A *game* presents consumers with something—bingo numbers, missing letters—every time they buy, which may or may not help them win a prize.

All kinds of companies use sweepstakes and contests to create brand attention and boost consumer involvement. For example, furniture retailer West Elm ran a "$5,000 Room Redo Contest" inviting entrants to send short videos showcasing themselves and their spaces with a chance to win a complete one-room makeover valued up to $5,000. And for the past several years, Google's "Doodle for Google" contest has invited kids to design a Google logo based on themes such as "When I grow up, I hope" or "What inspires me," with prizes ranging from T-shirts and tablets to a $30,000 college scholarship or $50,000 for the technology program at the winner's school or organization.[24]

Event marketing (or event sponsorships)

Creating a brand-marketing event or serving as a sole or participating sponsor of events created by others.

Finally, marketers can promote their brands through **event marketing (or event sponsorships)**. They can create their own brand-marketing events or serve as sole or participating sponsors of events created by others. The events might include anything from mobile brand tours to festivals, reunions, marathons, concerts, or other sponsored gatherings. Event marketing is huge, and it may be the fastest-growing area of promotion.

Effective event marketing links events and sponsorships to a brand's value proposition. And with the social sharing power of today's digital media, even local events can have far-reaching impact. For example, Delta Faucet used an imaginative event to promote its H2Okinetic low-flow showerheads—which use 40 percent less water but work just as well as competing higher-flow models—to its fitness and family-oriented target audience.[25]

● Event marketing: As part of its #HappiMess campaign, Delta Faucet used an imaginative event to show target consumers firsthand how well its low-flow showerheads worked under really tough conditions—following a 5K mud run race.

Steven Mitchell/AP Images for Delta Faucet Company

Delta's #HappiMess promotion campaign is based on the insight that some of its customers' happiest moments came from making and overcoming big messes. To show target consumers firsthand how well its low-flow showerheads work under really tough conditions, Delta partnered with Warrior Dash, which sponsored several 5K mud run races around the country over the summer. ● At each event, Delta built a huge custom shower station, complete with 184 Delta showerheads, where mud-soaked competitors could meet and wash off after the race. "Warrior Dash is a great example of a place where people are having fun getting messy," says a senior Delta Faucet senior brand manager. "We want people to celebrate those fun moments having confidence that we have products that will help transform them back to clean." At one event in Indiana, 331 people gathered to shower, setting a Guinness World Record for most people showering simultaneously. After experiencing the showerheads, 75 percent of runners surveyed said they'd consider buying one. The shower stations also included a selfie station. As a result, the event boosted social media activity around Delta's #HappiMess campaign by 85 percent and gave the brand a 50 percent sales lift.

All kinds of brands now hold events. But one-time events are rarely as effective as well-planned event campaigns that tie into a brand's broader promotions and positioning. Consider energy drink maker Red Bull. Called by one business reporter the "mother of all event marketers," Red Bull holds hundreds of events around the globe each year designed to bring the high-octane world of Red Bull to its community of enthusiasts (see Real Marketing 16.2).

Trade Promotions

Trade promotions
Sales promotion tools used to persuade resellers to carry a brand, give it shelf space, and promote it in advertising.

Consumer package goods manufacturers spend nearly four times as much on trade sales promotion as on consumer sales promotion.[26] **Trade promotions** can persuade resellers to carry a brand, give it shelf space, promote it in advertising, and push it to consumers. Shelf space is so scarce these days that manufacturers often have to offer price-offs, allowances, buy-back guarantees, or free goods to retailers and wholesalers to get products on the shelf and, once there, to keep them on it.

Manufacturers use several trade promotion tools. Many of the tools used for consumer promotions—contests, premiums, displays—can also be used as trade promotions. Or the manufacturer may offer a straight *discount* off the list price on each case purchased during a stated period of time (also called a *price-off, off-invoice,* or *off-list*). Manufacturers also may offer an *allowance* (usually so much off per case) in return for the retailer's agreement to feature the manufacturer's products in some way. For example, an advertising allowance compensates retailers for advertising the product, whereas a display allowance compensates them for using special displays.

Manufacturers may offer *free goods*, which are extra cases of merchandise, to resellers who buy a certain quantity or who feature a certain flavor or size. They may also offer *push money*—cash or gifts to dealers or their sales forces to "push" the manufacturer's goods. Manufacturers may give retailers free *specialty advertising items* that carry the company's name, such as pens, calendars, memo pads, flashlights, and tote bags.

Business Promotions

Business promotions
Sales promotion tools used to generate business leads, stimulate purchases, reward customers, and motivate salespeople.

Companies spend billions of dollars each year on promotion geared toward industrial customers. **Business promotions** are used to generate business leads, stimulate purchases, reward customers, and motivate salespeople. Business promotions include many of the same tools used for consumer or trade promotions. Here, we focus on two additional major business promotion tools: conventions and trade shows and sales contests.

Real Marketing 16.2 | Red Bull: The Mother of All Event Marketers

There's no question: Coca-Cola and PepsiCo dominate the global beverage industry. Each boasts leading brands in almost every category, from carbonated soft drinks to enhanced juice drinks to bottled waters. Last year, Coca-Cola sold nearly $32 billion worth of beverages worldwide; PepsiCo was a solid runner-up at nearly $30 billion. Both companies spend hundreds of millions of dollars annually on sophisticated marketing and advertising programs. So how does a smaller company compete effectively with such global powerhouses? The best answer: It doesn't—at least not directly. Instead, it uses a unique marketing approach and runs where the big dogs don't.

That's what Red Bull does. When Red Bull first introduced its energy drink more than 30 years ago, few imagined that it would become the $6.3 billion-a-year success that it is today. Red Bull has succeeded by avoiding head-to-head promotional battles with giants like Coca-Cola and Pepsi. Instead, it has energized brand fans with a unique product, brand personality, and event-marketing approach.

Back in 1987, energy drinks simply didn't exist. If you wanted a quick pick-me-up, about the only options were caffeinated soft drinks or a good old cup of coffee. But Red Bull formulated a new beverage containing a hefty dose of caffeine along with little-known ingredients such as taurine and glucuronolactone. It tasted terrible. But it packed the right punch, producing unique physical-energy and mental-clarity benefits. To make the new beverage even more distinctive, the founders gave it a unique name (Red Bull) and packaged it in a slim 8.3-ounce blue-and-silver can with a distinct red-and-yellow logo. Thus was born a whole new beverage category—energy drinks—with Red Bull as its only player.

The unique Red Bull product demanded equally unique brand positioning and personality, a declaration that this was no ordinary beverage. Red Bull's marketing didn't disappoint. The brand's first and still-only slogan—"Red Bull Gives You Wings"—communicated the product's energy-inducing benefits. More important, it tapped into the forces that moved the brand's narrow target segment—customers seeking to live life in the adrenaline-stoked fast lane.

To reinforce the "Gives You Wings" brand promise and in line with the new brand's meager early finances, Red Bull shunned the big-budget, mass-media advertising common in the beverage industry at the time. Instead, it relied on grassroots, high-octane sports and event marketing. It sponsored extreme sports events and athletes who were overlooked by big beverage competitors but were spiking in popularity with Red Bull's target customers, events such as snowboarding and freestyle motocross and athletes like Shaun White and Travis Pastrana.

In the years since, Red Bull has turned event marketing into a science. Today, the brand holds hundreds of events each year in dozens of sports around the world. Each event features off-the-grid experiences designed to bring the high-octane world of Red Bull to its impassioned community of enthusiasts. Red Bull owns Formula 1 car racing teams and soccer clubs. Its name is plastered all over events such as the Red Bull Crashed Ice World Championship and the annual Red Bull Rampage freeride mountain bike competition. Beyond sports, the company also sponsors lifestyle events in music, dance, fashion, and art.

Red Bull is perhaps best known by some for its massive, highly promoted events intended to reach as many viewers as possible. A classic example was the Red Bull Stratos project, in which extreme skydiver Felix Baumgartner jumped from a helium balloon 128,000 feet (more than 24 miles) above the earth, breaking the sound barrier and numerous other records in the process. The jump also set records for consumer brand engagement. Baumgartner diving into space fit perfectly with Red Bull's "Gives You Wings" brand message. And both Baumgartner's capsule and his space-age jumpsuit were emblazoned with the Red Bull name and logo. More than 8 million people watched the event live on 40 TV stations and 130 digital channels. For months before and after the event, you couldn't see or hear anything about Baumgartner without thinking about Red Bull. And by one estimate, 90 million people worldwide followed the campaign on social media, creating 60 million trusted brand impressions. You just can't buy that kind of consumer engagement in traditional media.

Although Red Bull is known for such massive viral hits, the real bread and butter comes from its constant menu of smaller events. And the bigger purpose of behind Red Bull's non-stop event machine is to create action-filled fodder for its massive video library. Visitors to the brand's www.redbull.com website won't find so much as a single picture of a Red Bull beverage. Instead, they'll find a cleanly designed, carefully curated video showcase with a seemingly unending selection of video clips organized by events, athletes, moods, and seasons. With a little browsing, they can view videos of everything from 27-meter ocean cliff dives at its Red Bull's Cliff Diving Series event in Grimstad, Norway, to daredevil freeskiing feats at its Red Bull Cold Rush event in the Colorado mountain peaks to video documentaries on their extreme sports heroes to absolutely breathtaking wing suit flights at Red Bull events staged in exotic locations from Monterrey, Mexico, to Hunan Province, China.

Individually, the smaller events and videos don't pack the wallop of the Red Bull Stratos project. The average Red Bull video gets a modest 500,000 views in its first 30 days. But the torrent of events adds up to massive impact. During a recent one-year period, Red Bull uploaded 4,331 videos to 23 channels.

Event marketing: Red Bull has turned event marketing into a science. It hosts hundreds of events each year designed to bring the high-octane world of Red Bull to its community of enthusiasts.

Mi Pan/Shutterstock

Combined, these videos generated more than 2.5 billion views and over 50 million engagements. That's equivalent to more than 60 space jumps every year. That made Red Bull the nation's most-viewed brand for nine of the year's 12 months.

More than just a beverage company, Red Bull today has become a close-knit brand community. Red Bull's event marketing has produced a steady stream of absorbing brand content that engages and entertains brand fans in relevant ways. During the past few years, Red Bull's Media House unit has filmed movies, signed a deal with NBC for a show called *Red Bull Signature Series*, developed reality-TV ideas with big-name producers, become one of the biggest producers of

original content on YouTube and Facebook, and loaded its own web and mobile sites with unique content features. "Whenever we [have done] any event, or signed an athlete or executed a project, everything has been put on film or photographed. Stories have been told," says the head of the Red Bull Media House unit. "It's part of the DNA of the brand."

Thus, Red Bull can't compete directly across the board with big-budget brands like Coca-Cola and PepsiCo—it doesn't even try. Then again, given the depth of consumer engagement and loyalty that Red Bull engenders in its own corner of the beverage world, Coke and Pepsi have found it even more difficult to compete with Red Bull in the energy drink segment. Red Bull still owns around

40 percent of the global energy drink category it created, with Coke and Pepsi also-rans.

In the end, although Red Bull events draw large crowds and plenty of media coverage, it's about more than just the events—it's about customer engagement. Event marketing is about creating tactile engagements where people can feel, touch, taste, and experience the brand face-to-face rather than simply reading about or watching it. Red Bull doesn't just sponsor an event—it *is* the event. The brand experience is often as much of the story as the event itself. Through smart event marketing, Red Bull has given its customers—and itself—new wings and a big shot of energy. As one observer puts it, Red Bull is the "mother of all event marketers."[27]

Many companies and trade associations organize *conventions and trade shows* to promote their products. Firms selling to the industry show their products at the trade show. Vendors at these shows receive many benefits, such as opportunities to find new sales leads, contact customers, introduce new products, meet new customers, sell more to present customers, and educate customers with publications and audiovisual materials. Trade shows also help companies reach many prospects that are not reached through their sales forces.

Some trade shows are huge. For example, at this year's International Consumer Electronics Show, more than 4,400 exhibitors attracted some 182,000 professional visitors. ● Even more impressive, at the Bauma mining and construction equipment trade show in Munich, Germany, more than 3,400 exhibitors from 58 countries presented their latest product innovations to over 583,000 attendees from more than 210 countries. Total exhibition space equaled about 6.5 million square feet (more than 112 football fields).[28]

A *sales contest* is a contest for salespeople or dealers to motivate them to increase their sales performance over a given period. Sales contests motivate and recognize good company performers, who may receive trips, cash prizes, or other gifts. Some companies award points for performance, which the receiver can turn in for any of a variety of prizes. Sales contests work best when they are tied to measurable and achievable sales objectives (such as finding new accounts, reviving old accounts, or increasing account profitability).

● Some trade shows are huge. At this year's Bauma mining and construction equipment trade show, more than 3,400 exhibitors from 58 countries presented their latest product innovations to more than 583,000 attendees from more than 210 countries.

dpa picture alliance/Alamy Stock Photo

Developing the Sales Promotion Program

Beyond selecting the types of promotions to use, marketers must make several other decisions in designing the full sales promotion program. First, they must determine the *size of the incentive*. A certain minimum incentive is necessary if the promotion is to succeed; a larger incentive will produce more sales response. The marketer also must set *conditions for participation*. Incentives might be offered to everyone or only to select groups.

Marketers must determine how to promote and distribute the promotion program itself. For example, a $2-off coupon could be given out in a package, in an advertisement, at the store, via a website or social media, or in a mobile download. Each distribution method involves a different level of reach and cost. Increasingly, marketers are blending several media into a total campaign concept. The length of the promotion is also important. If the sales promotion period is too short, many prospects (who may not be buying during that time) will miss it. If the promotion runs too long, the deal will lose some of its "act now" force.

Evaluation is also very important. Marketers should work to measure the returns on their sales promotion investments, just as they should seek to assess the returns on other marketing activities. The most common evaluation method is to compare sales before, during, and after a promotion. Marketers should ask: Did the promotion attract new customers or more purchasing from current customers? Can we hold onto these new customers and purchases? Will the long-run customer relationship and sales gains from the promotion justify its costs?

Clearly, sales promotion plays an important role in the total promotion mix. To use it well, the marketer must define the sales promotion objectives, select the best tools, design the sales promotion program, implement the program, and evaluate the results. Moreover, sales promotion must be coordinated carefully with other promotion mix elements within the overall IMC program.

Reviewing and Extending the Concepts

Objectives Review

This chapter is the third of four chapters covering the final marketing mix element—promotion. The previous chapter dealt with overall integrated marketing communications and with advertising and public relations. This chapter investigated personal selling and sales promotion. Personal selling is the interpersonal arm of the communications mix. Sales promotion consists of short-term incentives to encourage the purchase or sale of a product or service.

OBJECTIVE 16-1 Discuss the role of a company's salespeople in engaging customers, creating customer value, and building customer relationships. (pp 464–466)

Most companies use salespeople, and many companies assign them an important role in the marketing mix. For companies selling business products, the firm's sales force works directly with customers. Often, the sales force is the customer's only direct contact with the company and therefore may be viewed by customers as representing the company itself. In contrast, for consumer product companies that sell through intermediaries, consumers usually do not meet salespeople or even know about them. The sales force works behind the scenes, dealing with wholesalers and retailers to obtain their support and helping them become more effective in selling the firm's products.

As an element of the promotion mix, the sales force is very effective in achieving certain marketing objectives and carrying out such activities as prospecting, communicating, selling and servicing, and information gathering. But with companies becoming more market oriented, a customer-focused sales force also works to produce both customer satisfaction and company profit. The sales force plays a key role in engaging customers and developing and managing profitable customer relationships.

OBJECTIVE 16-2 Identify and explain the six major sales force management steps. (pp 466–476)

High sales force costs necessitate an effective sales management process consisting of six steps: designing sales force strategy and structure, recruiting and selecting, training, compensating, supervising, and evaluating salespeople and sales force performance.

In designing a sales force, sales management must address various issues, including what type of sales force structure will work best (territorial, product, customer, or complex structure), sales force size, who will be involved in selling, and how various salespeople and sales-support people will work together (inside or outside sales forces and team selling).

Salespeople must be recruited and selected carefully. In recruiting salespeople, a company may look to the job duties and the characteristics of its most successful salespeople to suggest the traits it wants in new salespeople. It must then look for applicants through recommendations of current salespeople, ads, and the internet and social media as well as college recruitment/placement centers. After the selection process is complete, training programs familiarize new salespeople not only with the art of selling but also with the company's history, its products and policies, and the characteristics of its customers and competitors.

The sales force compensation system helps to reward, motivate, and direct salespeople. In addition to compensation, all salespeople need supervision, and many need continuous encouragement because they must make many decisions and face many frustrations. Periodically, the company must evaluate their performance to help them do a better job. In evaluating salespeople, the company relies on information gathered from sales reports, personal observations, customer surveys, and conversations with other salespeople.

The fastest-growing sales trend is the explosion in *social selling*—using online, mobile, and social media in selling. Digital technologies are providing salespeople with powerful tools for identifying and learning about prospects, engaging customers, creating customer value, closing sales, and nurturing customer relationships. Many of today's customers no longer rely as much on assistance provided by salespeople. Instead, increasingly, they use online and social media resources to analyze their own problems, research solutions, get advice from colleagues, and rank buying options before ever speaking to a salesperson. In response, sellers are reorienting their selling processes around the new customer buying process. They are using social media, mobile devices, web forums, online communities, blogs, and other digital tools to engage customers earlier and more fully. Ultimately, online, mobile, and social media technologies are helping to make sales forces more efficient, cost-effective, and productive.

OBJECTIVE 16-3 Discuss the personal selling process, distinguishing between transaction-oriented marketing and relationship marketing. *(pp 476–479)*

Selling involves a seven-step process: prospecting and qualifying, preapproach, approach, presentation and demonstration, handling objections, closing, and follow-up. These steps help marketers close a specific sale and, as such, are transaction oriented. However, a seller's dealings with customers should be guided by the larger concept of relationship marketing. The company's sales force should help to orchestrate a whole-company effort to develop profitable long-term relationships with key customers based on superior customer value and satisfaction.

OBJECTIVE 16-4 Explain how sales promotion campaigns are developed and implemented. *(pp 479–486)*

Sales promotion campaigns call for setting sales promotion objectives (in general, sales promotions should be *consumer relationship building*); selecting tools; and developing and implementing the sales promotion program by using *consumer promotion tools* (from coupons, refunds, premiums, and point-of-purchase promotions to contests, sweepstakes, and events), *trade promotion tools* (from discounts and allowances to free goods and push money), and *business promotion tools* (conventions, trade shows, and sales contests) as well as determining such things as the size of the incentive, the conditions for participation, how to promote and distribute the promotion package, and the length of the promotion. After this process is completed, the company must evaluate its sales promotion results.

Key Terms

OBJECTIVE 16-1

Personal selling (p 464)
Salesperson (p 465)

OBJECTIVE 16-2

Sales force management (p 466)
Territorial sales force structure (p 467)
Product sales force structure (p 467)
Customer (or market) sales force structure (p 467)
Outside sales force (or field sales force) (p 468)

Inside sales force (p 468)
Team selling (p 469)
Sales quota (p 472)
Social selling (p 473)

OBJECTIVE 16-3

Selling process (p 476)
Prospecting (p 476)
Preapproach (p 477)
Approach (p 477)
Presentation (p 477)
Handling objections (p 478)

Closing (p 478)
Follow-up (p 478)

OBJECTIVE 16-4

Sales promotion (p 479)
Consumer promotions (p 481)
Event marketing (or event sponsorships) (p 482)
Trade promotions (p 483)
Business promotions (p 483)

Discussion Questions

16-1 Define *personal selling* and discuss its role in a company's promotion mix. (AACSB: Written and Oral Communication; Reflective Thinking)

16-2 Name and explain the major steps in sales force management. (AACSB: Written and Oral Communication)

16-3 To what extent have online and social media resources replaced salespersons? (AACSB: Communication; Reflective Thinking)

16-4 What do you understand by the term "relationship marketing"? (AACSB: Communication)

16-5 What activities can be used in customer relationship building? (AACSB: Communication)

16-6 Discuss the differences among consumer promotions, trade promotions, and business promotions. Provide examples of the different sales promotion tools that could be used in each promotion campaign. (AACSB: Written and Oral Communication)

Critical Thinking Exercises

16-7 Write a job description for an order getter at Snap-on tools, a company that sells advanced tools to auto mechanics and technicians. (AACSB: Written and Oral Communication; Information Technology; Reflective Thinking)

16-8 A sales manager for a telecommunications company is trying to calculate the optimal number of salespeople. The company has 500 A-level accounts and 3,000 B-level accounts. A-level accounts require 20 calls per year; B-level accounts require 10 calls per year. The average salesperson can make 1,000 calls per year. What is the workload? How many salespeople should the sales manager hire? What other factors should he or she consider? (AACSB: Written and Oral Communication; Reflective Thinking)

16-9 Design a consumer promotion to increase brand awareness and trial of cricket flour–based Chirps Chips (www.eatchirps.com). (AACSB: Written and Oral Communication; Reflective Thinking)

APPLICATIONS AND CASES

Online, Mobile, and Social Media Marketing Innovation Lab at a Trade Show

Marriott set up a pop-up innovation lab at the Americas Lodging and Investment Summit (a hotel industry investment conference) to showcase its Aloft and Element hotel brands. Marriott wanted not only to get feedback from consumers (influencers) and industry professionals (potential investors and franchisees), who visited the conference on separate days and answered different questions, but also to create opportunities for both groups to share images of and reactions to their conference experiences via social media. The pop up innovation lab allowed participants to experience the two hotel properties using virtual reality. They could also interact with the Aloft's Botlr Bellhop Robot service; use eco-friendly Element's self-service wine tap, which can be accessed using an app or a keycard; and try the solar-powered umbrellas, which doubled as charging devices. Marriott brand ambassadors carrying iPads engaged attendees and asked them to take a survey about their perceptions and reactions to the space—or they texted people a link to take the survey later.

16-10 Marriott used the innovation lab as both a business promotion and a consumer promotion, which served different segments with different needs. Was that a wise strategy? Explain. (AACSB: Written and Oral Communication, Information Technology, Reflective Thinking)

16-11 An alternative, potentially lower-cost way to get consumers to interact with the Aloft and Element brands would be to offer deep promotional discounts to influencers and prospects so they stay at one of the properties. How would a price-only promotion compare to the trade show innovation lab? (AACSB: Written and Oral Communication; Information Technology; Reflective Thinking)

Marketing Ethics Using Pharmaceutical Sales Strategies to Promote Cost-Effective Drugs

One criticism of pharmaceutical sales is that it makes health care more expensive. Although pharmaceutical companies increasingly restrict entertainment gifts, meals, and other incentives that were once part of pharmaceutical salespeople's sales pitches, the reps still buy lunches for medical staffs, take doctors out to eat, and pay for doctors to attend informational presentations at physician conferences, sometimes in exotic destinations, as part of their efforts to promote expensive medications. They also pitch their branded drugs rather than less expensive generics. But now, health insurers are recruiting existing pharmaceutical salespeople away from big pharmaceutical companies to use the same relationship-building and creative selling skills, but without the expense accounts, to raise health-care provider awareness of generic drugs, which cost less and work as well as the expensive brands. The premise is that doctors are often unaware of the costs of drugs they prescribe and may not realize when pharmaceutical companies increase their prices. The insurance companies' pitch to the pharmaceutical salespeople is that they will get to use the skills they learned from pharmaceutical companies to do something meaningful: lower health-care costs. The goal is to save the insurance companies and the insured millions of dollars.

16-12 A recent analysis of top salespeople suggested salespeople who are driven by a strong sense of customer-related purpose outsell salespeople who are focused on sales and money goals. The insurance companies are using such purpose-related pitches in recruiting the pharmaceutical salespeople. What other characteristics should the insurance companies look for in their recruits? (AACSB: Written and Oral Communication; Reflective Thinking)

16-13 Why would the insurance companies recruit existing pharmaceutical salespeople instead of hiring and training their own sales forces? (AACSB: Written and Oral Communication; Ethical Understanding and Reasoning)

Marketing by the Numbers Buy One, Get Something Free!

Mountain Goat Cyclery is an independent bicycle retailer in Colorado specializing in mountain bikes. It offers a full line of mountain bikes for men, women, and children as well as accessories and bike repair services. Like many local retailers, it advertises in local media such as newspapers, radio, magazines, and local news programs. The owner is considering spending $500 to advertise a summer sales promotion premium offer. For every Diamondback Lux bicycle purchased, the retailer is offering a free Fox Flux mountain bike helmet. It sells the bike for $500, and the retail value of the helmet is $100.

16-14 If Mountain Goat's markup percentage on selling prices is 35 percent, what margin will the retailer realize for each bike purchased during the premium offer? How many additional bikes would Mountain Goat need to sell to break even on this premium offer? Refer to Break-Even and Margin Analysis in Appendix 2: Marketing by the Numbers to learn how to perform this analysis. (AACSB: Written and Oral Communication; Analytic Reasoning; Reflective Thinking)

16-15 Mountain Goat ran the promotion and sold 15 bikes during the promotional period. Assuming the $500 spent on advertising is the only marketing cost associated with this promotion, calculate the net marketing contribution of the promotion. Was the promotion successful? Refer to Net Marketing Contribution in Appendix 2: Marketing by the Numbers to learn how to do this analysis. (AACSB: Analytic Reasoning; Reflective Thinking)

Company Case Procter & Gamble: Selling through Customer Business Development

When it comes to personal selling, the term *win-win* gets thrown around so much that it has become a cliché. But at Procter & Gamble, the selling concept that the company benefits only if the customer benefits has long been a way of life. Since William Procter and James Gamble formed a family-operated soap and candle company in 1837, P&G has understood that if the customer doesn't do well, neither will the company.

So although P&G boasts a sales force of more than 3,000 employees in the United States alone, P&Gers rarely utter the term *sales*. Instead, at P&G, they call it *customer business development*, or CBD. The title pretty much says it all. Rather than just selling detergent or toothpaste, P&G's philosophy is to grow its own business by growing the business of its customers, the thousands of retailers and wholesalers that distribute P&G's brands throughout the world. To these customers, P&G isn't just a supplier. It's a strategic business partner. "We depend on them as much as they depend on us," says Jeff Weedman, a CBD manager.

The Core Competency of Customer Business Development

As today's big retailers get bigger and bigger, they also grow more complex. Take companies such as Walmart, Kroger, or Amazon. How can a vendor like P&G ever fully understand such giant customers? These complex organizations have so many arms and legs that it becomes nearly impossible to get a full and firm grasp on their operations and needs.

To deal with such customer complexities, P&G organizes its sales representatives into customer business development teams. Rather than assigning reps to specific geographic regions or products, it assigns each CBD team to a P&G customer. For the company's biggest customer, Walmart (which accounts for 16 percent of all P&G sales), the CBD team consists of more than 300 employees. For a customer such as Family Dollar, the nation's second-largest dollar store chain, the CBD team has a comparatively few 30 employees.

Regardless of the team's size, the strength of the CBD concept derives from the fact that each team, in and of itself, is a complete customer-service unit, containing at least one support specialist for every important business function. In addition to an overall CBD manager and several sales account executives (each responsible for a specific category of P&G products), each CBD team includes specialists in marketing strategy, operations, information systems, logistics, finance, and human resources. This multifunctional structure enables each team to meet the multiple and vast needs of its customer, whether the needs revolve around those of a chief finance officer or an entire IT department.

A real strength of the CBD teams is that team members function as a collaborative whole rather than as individuals performing their own tasks in isolation. Team members share information, organizational capabilities, and technologies. "I have all the resources I need right here," says Amy Fuschino, a HealthCare and Cosmetics account executive. "If I need to, I can go right down the hall and talk with someone in marketing about doing some kind of promotional deal. It's that simple."

But the multifunctional nature of the CBD team also means that collaboration extends far beyond internal interactions. Each time a CBD team member contacts the customer, he or she represents the entire team. For example, if during a customer call a CBD account executive receives a question about a promotional, logistical, or financial matter, the account executive acts as the liaison with the appropriate CBD specialist. So, although not each CBD member has specialized knowledge in every area, the CBD team as a unit does.

Competitors have attempted to implement some aspects of P&G's multifunctional approach. However, P&G pioneered the CBD structure. And it has built in some unique characteristics that have allowed it to leverage more power from its team structure than its rivals can.

The True Advantage

For starters, P&G's CBD structure is broader and more comprehensive, making it more multifunctional than similar team structures employed by other companies. But perhaps more important, P&G's structure is designed to accomplish four key objectives. So important are these objectives that they are referred to internally as the "core work" of CBD. These four objectives are:

- *Align strategy:* To create opportunities for both P&G and the customer to benefit by collaborating in strategy development.
- *Create demand:* To build profitable sales volume for P&G and the customer through consumer value and shopper satisfaction.
- *Optimize supply:* To maximize the efficiency of the supply chain from P&G to the point of purchase to optimize cost and responsiveness.
- *Enable the organization:* To develop capabilities to maximize business results by creating the capacity for frequent breakthrough.

More than just corporate catchphrases jotted down in an employee handbook, these are words to live by for CBD employees. P&G trains sales employees in methods of achieving each objective and evaluates their effectiveness in meeting the objectives. In fact, the CBD concept came about through the recognition that, in order to develop true win-win relationships with each customer, P&G would need to accomplish the first objective. According to Bill Warren, a CBD senior account executive, "The true competitive advantage is achieved by taking a multifunctional approach from basic selling to strategic customer collaboration!"

Strategic collaboration starts with annual joint business planning. Both the P&G team and the customer come to the table focused on the most important thing: How can each best provide value for the final consumer? The team and customer give much attention during this planning phase to how products can best be presented and placed in the retail setting. This is because P&G and its customers know that the end consumer assesses value within the first three to seven seconds of seeing that product on the shelf. At P&G, this is known as "winning the first moment of truth." If customers quickly perceive that a product will meet their needs, they will likely purchase it.

CBD team members are very good at demonstrating to the retailer that the best way to win the first moment of truth is most often with a P&G product. But P&G is so committed to developing the *customer's* business as a means of developing its own that it is open to the possibility that the best way to serve the customer may be through a competitor's product. The CBD team's primary goal is to help the customer win in each product category. Sometimes, analysis shows that the best solution for the customer is "the other guy's product." For P&G, that's OK. P&G knows that creating the best situation for the retailer ultimately brings in more customer traffic, which in turn will likely result in increased sales for other P&G products in the same category. Because most of P&G's brands are market leaders, P&G stands to benefit more from the increased traffic than competitors. Again, it's a win-win situation. This type of honesty also helps to build trust and strengthen the company/customer relationships.

The collaborative efforts between P&G and each of its customers often involve more than joint planning and the sharing of information. They may also involve cooperative efforts to share the costs of different activities. "We'll help customers run these commercials or do those merchandising events, but there has to be a return-on-investment," explains Amy Fuschino. "Maybe it's helping us with a new distribution or increasing space for fabric care. We're very willing if the effort creates value for us in addition to creating value for the customer and the consumer."

If the CBD team can effectively accomplish the first objective of aligning strategy and collaborating on strategic development, accomplishing the other three objectives will follow more easily. For example, if strategic planning leads to winning the first moment of truth, not only does the consumer benefit, but both the retailer and P&G achieve higher revenues and profits as well. Through proper strategic planning, it is also more likely that both P&G and the customer will create greater efficiencies in the supply chain.

It's Better to Give ... *Then* to Receive

By collaborating with customers, P&G receives as much as or more than it gives. Among other things, P&G receives information that helps in achieving the fourth CBD objective, enabling the organization to achieve innovation. So far as the research and development process is concerned, this means creating better products. This is one reason why, at the 2019 Product of the Year awards held in New York City, P&G cleaned up, winning four of the categories in which it competes.

In recent years, the consumer products industry has been hit hard by tough economic times and a rise in popularity of store brands. But P&G has weathered the storm. Over the past few years, P&G has divested many low-performing brands in order to strengthen its best brands. P&G remains the world's largest consumer products firm with $67 billion in revenues and more brands that bring in more than $1 billion every year than any other company. Last year, Pampers sales alone exceeded $8.5 billion, a figure that by itself would have made the leading diaper brand number 357 on the prestigious *Fortune* 500 list.

Many factors have contributed to P&G's growth and success. But the role that CBD plays can't be overestimated. And as P&G moves forward, Mr. Weedman's words that "We depend on them as much as they depend on us" ring ever more true. As P&G's mega-customers grow in size and power, developing P&G's business means first developing its customers' businesses. And the CBD sales organization lies at the heart of that effort.[29]

Questions for Discussion

16-16 Which of the sales force structures discussed in the text best describes P&G's CBD structure?

16-17 From the perspective of team selling, discuss the positive as well as possible negative aspects to the customer business development sales organization.

16-18 Discuss ways that the CBD structure may be more effective than a single sales rep for each step in the personal selling process.

16-19 It seems that P&G has the most effective sales force structure of any company in its industry. Why have competitors not been able to match it?

17

Direct, Online, Social Media, and Mobile Marketing

OBJECTIVES OUTLINE

OBJECTIVE 17-1 Define *direct and digital marketing* and discuss their rapid growth and benefits to customers and companies. **See: Direct and Digital Marketing** *(pp 494–497)*

OBJECTIVE 17-2 Identify and discuss the major forms of direct and digital marketing. **See: Forms of Direct and Digital Marketing** *(p 497)*

OBJECTIVE 17-3 Explain how companies have responded to the digital age with various online marketing strategies. **See: Marketing in the Digital Age** *(pp 498–503)*

OBJECTIVE 17-4 Discuss how companies use social media and mobile marketing to engage consumers and create brand community. **See: Social Media and Mobile Marketing** *(pp 503–510)*

OBJECTIVE 17-5 Identify and discuss the traditional direct marketing forms and overview public policy and ethical issues presented by direct marketing. **See: Traditional Direct Marketing Forms** *(pp 510–517)*

CHAPTER PREVIEW In the previous three chapters, you learned about engaging consumers and communicating customer value through integrated marketing communication and about four elements of the marketing communications mix: advertising, publicity, personal selling, and sales promotion. In this chapter, we examine direct marketing and its fastest-growing form: digital marketing (online, social media, and mobile marketing). Over the past decade, spurred by the surge in digital technologies—from smartphones, tablets, and IoT devices to the spate of online, mobile and social media—direct marketing has undergone a dramatic transformation. As you read this chapter, remember that although direct and digital marketing are presented as separate tools, they must be carefully integrated with each other and with other elements of the promotion and marketing mixes.

Let's start by looking at Coca-Cola, a company famous for its advertising. Its classic mass-media advertising campaigns have informed and entertained generations of consumers over many decades. But as the times have changed in this digital age, so has the way Coca-Cola communicates with and engages consumers. Although it still relies heavily on massive advertising campaigns to position the brand and tell the brand story, Coca-Cola has also mastered digital, social, and mobile media to engage consumers directly, spark brand conversations, and make the brand a part of consumers' lives.

COCA-COLA: Making the Brand a Part of the Customer's Story

Down through the decades, Coca-Cola has been an undisputed master of mass-media advertising and marketing. The company has produced an impressive string of big-budget campaigns built around classic slogans such as "The Pause That Refreshes," "Things Go Better with Coke," "I'd Like to Teach the World to Sing," "Have a Coke and a Smile," and the current "Taste the Feeling." The campaigns have featured memorable characters ranging from Michael Jordan to Santa Claus and the iconic Coca-Cola Polar Bears. Coca-Cola now spends an eye-popping $4 billion a year on advertising worldwide—10 percent of its revenues.

Its huge advertising presence has made Coca-Cola one of the world's best-known brands—according to one source, the word *Coca-Cola* is the second most recognized word in the world after *okay*. But you know all that. What you might not have realized is that, as the world has shifted massively toward digital, so has Coca-Cola. Although the brand is still the king of mass-media marketing, Coca-Cola has shifted with the times to become a leading-edge digital, social media, and mobile marketer as well.

In the old days, Coca-Cola's advertising objective was to build the brand's image and positioning through mass-media impressions. Brand messages flowed from the company to consumers. A single Super Bowl ad could create hundreds of millions of consumer impressions worldwide. That's still important. But today's digital media let the brand take consumer engagement a big step further. In addition to creating *impressions,* Coca-Cola now seeks to create consumer *"expressions,"* brand-related exchanges and responses such as comments, retweets, photo uploads, advocating the brand, and sharing brand content on social media.

Coca-Cola has learned that today's empowered consumers often generate more content about a brand than a company can. For example, Coca-Cola estimates that of the hundreds of millions of views of Coca-Cola-related content on YouTube each year, only about 18 percent are from content created by Coca-Cola. The other 82 percent are from content created by engaged consumers. So, many Coca-Cola marketing campaigns are aimed at sparking brand-related consumer expressions rather than just impressions.

For instance, the brand's "Share a Coke" campaign—in which it swaps out the company's iconic logo on 20-ounce Coke bottles for one of more than 1,000 of the nation's most popular names—encourages Coca-Cola fans to share the bottles with friends and family. Consumers can also go online and order multi-packs with custom labels or create virtual custom Coke bottles they can save, post, or share. They can also share their Coca-Cola photos, stories, and experiences online using the hashtag #ShareaCoke with selected posts featured on the brand's websites and across company billboards.

"Share a Coke" has become one of Coca-Cola's most successful campaigns ever. After only one year, it resulted in more than 500,000 photos and 6 million virtual Coke bottles shared online, along with a boost of nearly 25 million Coca-Cola Facebook followers. Now in its sixth year, the

Coca-Cola's digital, mobile, social media campaigns spark brand conversations, build brand community, and make the brand a part of consumers' lives.

Barry Tuck/Stockimo/Alamy Stock Photo

campaign has a new twist. The "Share a Coke" name labels on bottles are now stickers that customers can be peel off and stick to clothes, backpacks, phones, cars, or anywhere else, providing even more opportunities to share brand conversations and photos in social media.

In its efforts to create a "connected Coke" and spur consumer co-creation and sharing of brand content, Coca-Cola maintains a massive digital footprint. In addition to hundreds of websites around the world, the brand hosts 70 Facebook pages, 35 Twitter handles, 21 Instagram accounts, 10 YouTube channels, and 2 LinkedIn accounts. Its home Facebook page has 107 million fans. It draws 3.3 million Twitter followers, 2.6 million Instagram followers, 3 million YouTube subscribers, and 2 million LinkedIn followers. Coca-Cola fills its always-on, endlessly connected websites and social media pages with interactive content designed to connect consumers with the brand and get them to share their brand experiences.

For example, a few years ago, Coca-Cola transformed its corporate website into a dynamic digital magazine, called Coca-Cola Journey. The highly journalistic site contains magazine-style feature stories, brought to life with compelling photography, video and audio formats, and eye-catching graphics that are "Refreshing the

> Long known for its classic mass-media advertising campaigns, Coca-Cola has shifted its communications to fit the digital times. It has now also mastered digital, social media, and mobile content that engages consumers directly and interactively.

world, one story at a time." On any given day, you'll find real-time stories about company happenings, new products, and the company's views on key current issues. But you'll also find features written by staff, employees, and customers on topics ranging from the history of Coca-Cola advertising slogans and how to order a Coke bottle with your name on it to what it's like to work at Coca-Cola and even how to bake a Coca-Cola cake (complete with a video).

The site also invites visitors to "join the journey," to "share you're your Coke moments" and "spread happiness" by uploading photos or videos. "Puppy dog eyes … a walk in the woods … sharing ice cream and laughs with a friend—those are a few of our Journey staffers' favorite things," says the site. "So we'd like to know what makes you happy!" Selected fan submissions are featured on Coca-Cola Journey. Thus, anything but a typically staid and stale corporate website, Coca-Cola Journey brims with engaging and sharable brand content.

Coca-Cola also makes extensive use of mobile marketing. For example, it offers more than a dozen mobile apps of its own, from its mainstay Coca-Cola app to Coke Studio (streaming music), Coca-Cola Happy Shopmate (finding and redeeming exciting local Coke deals, perks, and freebies on mobile), Simply Tasty (providing everyday recipes and "food adventures"), and even Coca-Cola Freestyle (a mixology app that lets customers blend and save their own favorite Coke concoctions and then order them digitally at a local Coke Freestyle vending machine).

Coca-Cola also produces a steady stream of mobile campaigns, designed to deliver "snackable, portable content" for today's time-pressed, highly mobile consumers. An example is Coca-Cola's "The Ahh Effect" campaign, launched a few years ago as one of the brand's first digital-led efforts. Optimized for mobile, "The Ahh Effect" campaign provided easily digestible, mobile-friendly bits of content designed to engage the world's teens, an audience known for its short attention span. "Think amusing videos and GIFs that teens [could] choose to spend only a few seconds viewing to get the message and simple games that they [could] play for two or three minutes," says a digital marketing analyst. "They [could] dip in, dip out, and move on," says a senior Coca-Cola marketing executive, "and if you look at the way teens consume tweets and posts and texts, that's pretty much their behavior." The "Ahh Effect" content came not only from Coca-Cola but also from teens themselves. And it was updated regularly, "continuously tapping into a teen's desire for discovery, constant stimulation, and novelty," says the marketer.

Thus, Coca-Cola is still a prolific traditional mass-media advertiser; its massive advertising campaigns position the brand and tell the brand story. But Coca-Cola is also a leader in creating digital, social media, and mobile content. Digital content doesn't just *tell* the brand story, it makes the brand part of the *consumer's* story. It engages consumers directly and personally, fuels brand conversations, and makes the brand a part of consumers' lives.[1]

MANY OF THE MARKETING and promotion tools that we've examined in previous chapters were developed in the context of *mass marketing*: targeting broad markets with standardized messages and offers distributed through intermediaries. Today, however, with the trend toward narrower targeting and the surge in digital and social media technologies, many companies are shifting toward *direct marketing*, either as a primary marketing approach or as a supplement to other approaches. In this section, we explore the exploding world of direct marketing and its fastest-growing form—digital marketing using online, social media, and mobile marketing channels.

| Author Comment | For most companies, direct and digital marketing are supplemental channels or media. But for many other companies today—such as Amazon, GEICO, or Travelocity—direct marketing is a complete way of doing business. |

Direct and Digital Marketing

OBJECTIVE 17-1 Define *direct and digital marketing* and discuss their rapid growth and benefits to customers and companies.

Direct and digital marketing

Engaging directly with carefully targeted individual consumers and customer communities to both obtain an immediate response and build lasting customer relationships.

Direct and digital marketing involve engaging directly with carefully targeted individual consumers and customer communities to both obtain an immediate response and build lasting customer relationships. Companies use direct marketing to tailor their offers and content to the needs and interests of narrowly defined segments or individual buyers. In this way, they build customer engagement, brand community, brand advocacy, and sales.

For example, Amazon interacts directly with customers via its website or mobile app to help them discover and buy almost anything and everything online. Similarly,

GEICO interacts directly with customers—by phone, through its website or smartphone app, or on its Facebook, Twitter, Instagram, and YouTube pages—to build individual brand relationships, give insurance quotes, sell policies, or service customer accounts.

The New Direct Marketing Model

Early direct marketers—catalog companies, direct mailers, and telemarketers—gathered customer names and sold goods mainly by mail and telephone. During the past decade, however, spurred by the surge in internet usage and buying and by rapid advances in digital technologies—from smartphones, tablets, and other digital devices to the spate of online social and mobile media—direct marketing has undergone a dramatic transformation.

In previous chapters, we discussed direct marketing as direct distribution—as marketing channels that contain no intermediaries. We also included direct and digital marketing elements of the promotion mix—as an approach for engaging consumers directly and creating brand community. In actuality, direct marketing is both of these things and much more.

Most companies still use direct marketing as a supplementary channel or medium. Thus, most department stores, such as Macy's or Kohl's, sell the majority of their merchandise off their store shelves, but they also sell through websites and online catalogs, direct mail, and mobile and social media pages. Pepsi's Mountain Dew brand markets heavily through mass-media advertising and its retail partners' channels. However, it also supplements these channels with a heavy dose of direct marketing. For example, the brand aired blockbuster television ads during a recent Super Bowl. But it also spent heavily on digital media to engage its passionately loyal fan base in the weeks leading up to and following the big game. "Close to 40 percent of our investment [was] on digital because that's where consumers are having conversations," says Pepsi's chief marketer. We spent "big dollars on the Super Bowl game day. But that itself is not enough to have a two-way conversation with a consumer."[2] Mountain Dew also engages fans digitally though a heavy website and social media presence.

However, for many companies today, direct and digital marketing are more than just supplementary channels or advertising media—they constitute a complete model for doing business. Firms employing this direct model use it as the only approach. Online giants such as Amazon, Netflix, GEICO, and Expedia have successfully built their entire approaches to the marketplace around direct and digital marketing.

● **The new direct marketing model: Online travel company Expedia Group has successfully built its entire approach to the marketplace around direct and digital marketing. Its Travelocity.com unit and the famous Roaming Gnome make it easy for customer to "Wander Wisely."**

Travelocity

● For example, Expedia Group is a huge collection of online-only travel businesses, including such familiar brands as Expedia, Travelocity, Hotels.com, Hotwire, trivago, Orbitz, and HomeAway. With combined revenues of $11.2 billion in 2018, the company does business through more than 200 travel booking sites and over 150 mobile websites. Its Travelocity unit was one of the first online travel companies that let customers find and book travel arrangements without the help of travel agents or brokers. Now itself one of the world's largest travel brands, Travelocity and its famous Roaming Gnome help customers to "Wander Wisely," making their travel experiences both simple and memorable.[3]

The direct and digital marketing model also provides opportunities for new, smaller brands. Recent years have seen a rash of online-only startups—the so-called

Direct-to-consumer (DTC) brands
Brands that avoid direct competition with established traditional brands by selling and shipping directly to consumers only through online and mobile channels.

direct-to-consumer (DTC) brands—that avoid direct competition with established traditional brands by selling and shipping directly to consumers only through online and mobile channels. Just a few examples of successful DTC brands include Dollar Shave Club and Harry's (razors and shaving products), Peloton (fitness equipment and programs), and Casper (mattresses and bedding). By eliminating intermediaries, DTC companies can cut costs and lower prices, offer greater convenience, build direct relationships with customers, and deliver more personalized offerings. Interestingly, just as traditional sellers have added digital channels, the DTC brands are adding traditional channels. For example, consumers can now buy Harry's razors and Casper mattress products at most Target stores, and Casper is opening its own Casper Sleep Shop locations.

Rapid Growth of Direct and Digital Marketing

Direct and digital marketing are the fastest-growing form of marketing. And as direct marketing continues to shift toward digital, digital direct marketing is claiming a surging share of marketing spending and sales. Total digital advertising spending—spending for advertising that appears on computers, mobile phones, tablets, and other internet-connected devices—now grabs about 54 percent of all U.S. advertising spending. Growing at more than 20 percent per year, digital will claim an estimated two-thirds of all ad spending by 2023. And as consumers spend more and more time on their tablets and smartphones, ad spending on mobile media is exploding. By itself, mobile ad spending now accounts for 34 percent of all U.S. ad spending, a 2 percent-greater share than the amount spent on television advertising.[4]

Benefits of Direct and Digital Marketing to Buyers and Sellers

For buyers, direct and digital marketing are convenient, easy, and private. They give buyers anywhere, anytime access to an almost unlimited assortment of goods and a wealth of product and buying information. For example, on its website and mobile app, Amazon.com offers more information than most consumers can digest, ranging from top 10 product lists, extensive product descriptions, and expert and user product reviews to recommendations based on customers' previous searches and purchases.

Through direct marketing, buyers can interact with sellers by phone or on the seller's website or mobile app to create exactly the configuration of information, products, or services they want and then order them on the spot and have them delivered days or even hours later. Finally, for consumers who want it, digital marketing through online, mobile, and social media provides a sense of brand engagement and community—a place to share brand information and experiences with other brand fans.

For sellers, direct marketing often provides a low-cost, efficient, speedy alternative for reaching their markets. Today's direct marketers can target small groups or individual customers. Because of the one-to-one nature of direct marketing, companies can interact with customers by phone or online, learn more about their needs, and personalize products and services to specific customer tastes. In turn, customers can ask questions and volunteer feedback.

Direct and digital marketing also offer sellers greater flexibility. They let marketers make ongoing adjustments to prices and programs or to create immediate, timely, and personal engagement and offers. For example, home-improvement retailer Lowe's online "How-Tos Library" links consumers to hundreds of in-depth how-to videos, project planning guides, cost calculators, and other helpful information on almost any project, from building a backyard patio or installing a lawn sprinkler system to hanging drywall or even getting rid of mice. The guides are available whenever projects pop up and, of course, provide detailed lists of supplies available at a nearby Lowe's store.[5]

● **Direct and digital marketing:** Snack brand MoonPie is known for its skillful use of real-time social media marketing to create a fresh, relevant brand personality and spark ongoing real-time engagement with the brand's fans.
Moonpie

Especially in today's digital environment, direct marketing provides opportunities for *real-time marketing* that links brands to important moments in customers' lives. It is a powerful tool for moving customers through the buying process or for simply building ongoing customer engagement, community, and personalized relationships. Online and social media offer an ideal platform for engaging consumers in the moment by linking brands to important trending topics, real-world events, causes, personal occasions, or other happenings. They provide exciting opportunities to extend customer engagement and get people talking about a brand. ● For example, snack brand MoonPie is known for its skillful use of real-time social media to spark an ongoing dialogue with the brand's fans about anything or nothing at all:[6]

> "Baby boomers and other older generations remember the 100-year-old company fondly for combining graham crackers, marshmallows, and chocolate-flavored coating together as the perfect treat," says a digital analyst. "Millennials and Gen Z, on the other hand, know it for having one of the snarkiest Twitter handles this side of Wendy's and Denny's." MoonPie's quirky posts on Twitter, Instagram, and Facebook have taught followers to expect the unexpected, and that's just what they get. "Back in the day 'mooning' meant 'the giving of a MoonPie to a friend,'" quips one tweet, "and then someone went and ruined the whole thing >:(." Says another tweet, "You wanna throw a MoonPie at my face I say go for it buddy that's where I was gonna put it anyway." Still another tweet, showing a takeoff of the cover of classic children's bedtime story *Goodnight Moon* but with the title *Goodnight MoonPie* read, "Every morning my boss reads this book to us which is weird because 1) it's morning and 2) I don't even think this is a real book." Real-time social media success gives MoonPie a fresh, relevant personality and creates an engaged and active community that helps spread the brand's message. It also gives the social brand continuous national reach without big-budget ad spending, boosting sales not only in retail stores but also though its own brand site and Amazon.

> **Author Comment** | Direct marketing is rich in tools, from traditional favorites such as direct mail and catalogs to newer digital tools such as online, mobile, and social media.

Forms of Direct and Digital Marketing

OBJECTIVE 17-2 Identify and discuss the major forms of direct and digital marketing.

The major forms of direct and digital marketing are shown in ● **Figure 17.1**. Traditional direct marketing tools include face-to-face selling, direct-mail marketing, catalog marketing, telemarketing, direct-response television marketing, and kiosk marketing. In recent years, however, newer digital direct marketing tools have burst onto the marketing scene, including online marketing (websites, online ads and promotions, email, online videos, and blogs), social media marketing, and mobile marketing.

We'll begin by examining direct digital and social media marketing tools that now receive so much attention. Then we'll look at the still heavily used and very important traditional direct marketing tools. As always, however, it's important to remember that all of these tools—both the new digital and the more traditional forms—must be blended into a fully integrated marketing communications program.

As noted earlier, **digital and social media marketing** is the fastest-growing form of direct marketing. It uses digital marketing tools such as websites, online video, email, blogs, social media, mobile ads and apps, and other digital platforms to directly engage consumers anywhere, anytime via their computers, smartphones, tablets, internet-ready TVs, and other digital devices. The widespread use of the internet and digital technologies has had a dramatic impact on both buyers and the marketers who serve them.

Digital and social media marketing
Using digital marketing tools such as websites, social media, mobile apps and ads, online video, email, and blogs that engage consumers anywhere, anytime via their digital devices.

● **FIGURE 17.1**
Forms of Direct and Digital Marketing

Marketing in the Digital Age

OBJECTIVE 17-3 Explain how companies have responded to the digital age with various online marketing strategies.

These days, people connect digitally with information, brands, and each other at almost any time and from almost anywhere. In the age of the "Internet of Things" (IoT), it seems that everything and everyone will soon be connected digitally to everything and everyone else. The digital age has fundamentally changed customers' notions of convenience, speed, price, product information, service, and brand interactions. As a result, it has given marketers a whole new way to create customer value, engage customers, and build customer relationships.

Digital usage and impact continues to grow steadily. More than 90 percent of all U.S. adults use the internet, and the average U.S. internet user spends four hours a day consuming digital media, primarily via mobile devices. Worldwide, more than 55 percent of the population has internet access, and one-third has access to the mobile internet.[7]

As a result, more than half of all U.S. households now regularly shop online, and digital buying continues to grow at a healthy double-digit rate. U.S. online retail sales were an estimated $517 billion last year, a 15 percent one-year increase and 15 percent of total retail sales. By 2027, as consumers continue to shift their spending from physical to digital stores, online sales are expected to grow to more than $1 trillion. Perhaps even more important, an estimated more than one-half of all U.S. retail sales were either transacted directly online or influenced by internet research.[8] As today's omni-channel consumers become more and more adept at blending online, mobile, and in-store shopping, digital channels will come into play for an ever-larger proportion of their purchases.

To reach this burgeoning market, most companies now market online. Some companies operate *only* online. They include a wide array of firms, from *e-tailers* such as Amazon, Quicken Loans, and Expedia.com that sell products and services directly to final buyers via the internet to *search engines and portals* (such as Google, Bing, and Yahoo!), *transaction sites* (eBay, Craigslist), *content sites* (*The New York Times*, ESPN.com, and Wikipedia), and *online social media* (Facebook, Twitter, Instagram, YouTube, and Snapchat).

Omni-channel retailing
Creating a seamless cross-channel buying experience that integrates in-store, online, and mobile shopping.

Today, however, it's hard to find a company that doesn't have a substantial online presence. Even companies that have traditionally operated offline have now created their own online sales, marketing, and brand community channels. Traditional store retailers are reaping increasingly larger proportions of their sales online. For example, Walmart's is now the nation's fourth-largest e-tailer, with nearly $16 billion in annual online revenues. Even uber-store retailer Nordstrom captures 30 percent of its sales online.[9]

In fact, **omni-channel retailing** companies are having as much online success as their online-only competitors. For example, home-improvement retailer Home Depot has nearly 2,300 stores in North America.[10]

Omni-channel retailing: Home Depot's goal is to provide "a seamless and frictionless experience no matter where our customers shop, be it in the digital world, our brick and mortar stores, at home, or on the job site. Anywhere the customer is, we need to be there."

THE HOME DEPOT name and logo are trademarks of Home Depot Product Authority, LLC, used under license.

While sheets of plywood and nails are hardly items you might imagine a company selling online, online sales are Home Depot's hottest growth area, growing at a rate of nearly 40 percent annually over the past 5 years. Home Depot is now one of the world's top 10 online merchants with an online inventory exceeding 1 million products, compared with the 40,000 or so products available in a typical Home Depot store.

The home-improvement retailer offers multiple contact points and delivery modes. Customers can buy products off the shelf in any Home Depot store or can buy products online from the virtual shelves of Home Depot's website. Products ordered online can still be delivered but more than 40 percent of online orders are now picked up in-store. ● Retailers around the world are recognizing that customers are changing how they shop. Australian department store Myer and clothing retailer Sportscraft offer their customers the option to purchase products in-store or online with traditional postal delivery. Both retailers also offer a "click and collect" option. With "click and collect," customers can select products off each retailers' virtual shelves and then check to see if they are available at a retail outlet of their choosing anywhere in Australia. If their product selection is available, transactions are completed online and products are ready for collection at the selected outlet at the customer's convenience, saving customers additional delivery charges. Products not available at local retail outlets can, of course, still be home delivered. Australian consumers can even "click and collect" their groceries, including fresh produce and frozen foods, by placing their orders online at Australia's two major supermarkets, Woolworth's and Coles, for pick-up later; they effectively have their own personal grocery shopper!

Direct digital and social media marketing takes any of the several forms shown in Figure 17.1. These forms include online marketing, social media marketing, and mobile marketing. We discuss each in turn, starting with online marketing.

Online Marketing

Online marketing
Marketing via the internet using company websites, online ads and promotions, email, online video, and blogs.

Online marketing refers to marketing via the internet using company websites, online advertising and promotions, email marketing, online video, and blogs. Social media and mobile marketing also take place online and must be closely coordinated with other forms of digital marketing. However, because of their special characteristics, we discuss social media and mobile marketing approaches in separate sections.

Websites and Branded Web Communities

Marketing website
A website that engages consumers to move them closer to a direct purchase or other marketing outcome.

For most companies, the first step in conducting online marketing is to create a website. Websites vary greatly in purpose and content. Some websites are primarily **marketing websites**, designed to engage customers and move them closer to a direct purchase or other marketing outcome.

For example, GEICO operates a marketing website at www.geico.com. Once a potential customer clicks in, GEICO wastes no time trying to turn the inquiry into a sale and then into a long-term relationship. A bold headline urges potential customers to "Steer your way to savings. Get a quote," and the site provides all the information and tools needed to do just that, complete with an auto insurance calculator to help buyers estimate the right insurance coverage, rates, and savings. The straight-forward site also makes it easy for current customers to manage their accounts and policies, add or replace vehicles, and make and view claims, all under the watchful eye of the familiar GEICO Gecko. Customers can also use GEICO's mobile app to pay bills, get account and coverage information, or connect by chat.

Brand community website
A website that presents brand content that engages consumers and creates customer community around a brand.

In contrast, **brand community websites** do much more than just sell products. Instead, their primary purpose is to present brand content that engages consumers and creates customer-brand community. Such sites typically offer a rich variety of brand information, videos, blogs, activities, and other features that build closer customer relationships and generate engagement with and between the brand and its customers. ● For example, you can't buy anything at Sony's PlayStation Forums site. Instead it serves as a social hub for PlayStation PS4 game enthusiasts. A place where PS4 fans can follow game trends, share content, and interact with other fans—all in real time.[11]

Similarly, you can't buy diapers at Pampers.com. Instead, it's an online community that's rich in resources for expectant parents and parents of newborns, babies, and toddlers. The site offers everything from a baby name generator, pregnancy calendar, baby shower planner, and hospital bag checklist for parents-to-be to articles by experts on topics ranging from caring for newborns and dealing with teething babies to eliminating toddler tantrums. At Pampers.com, parents can explore and discuss almost any conceivable baby care or young child parenting topic, get advice and tips from experts, and download guides and other handy resources.[12]

Creating a website is one thing; getting people to *visit* the site is another. To attract visitors, companies aggressively promote their websites in offline print and broadcast advertising and through ads and links on other sites. But today's web users are quick to abandon any website that doesn't measure up. The key is to create enough

● **Branded community websites: The Sony's PlayStation Forums site serves as a social hub where PlayStation PS4 enthusiasts can share content and interact with other fans—all in real time.**

Christian Bertrand/Shutterstock

engaging and valued content to get consumers to come to the site, stick around, and come back again.

At the very least, a website should be easy to use and visually appealing. Ultimately, however, websites must also be *useful*. When it comes to online browsing and shopping, most people prefer substance over style and function over flash. For example, the Pampers.com website isn't all that flashy, and it's pretty heavily packed and congested. But it connects customers quickly and effectively to all the baby care information and involvement they are seeking. Thus, effective websites contain deep and useful information, interactive tools that help find and evaluate content of interest, links to other related sites, changing promotional offers, and entertaining features that lend relevant excitement.

Online Advertising

Online advertising

Advertising that appears while consumers are browsing online, including display ads and search-related ads.

As consumers spend more and more time online, companies are shifting more of their marketing dollars to **online advertising** to build brand sales or attract visitors to their internet, mobile, and social media sites. Online advertising has become a major promotional medium. The main forms of online advertising are display ads and search-related ads.

Online display ads might appear anywhere on an internet user's screen and are often related to the information being viewed. For example, while browsing espn.com on a warm summer day, users might see the web content wrapped at the top and both sides by a large banner ad for RTIC Coolers, touting the product's durability and ice-keeping prowess. Clicking on the banner or on an inset display ad nearby takes them to brand's website.

● **Online display advertising: To create anticipation for a summer promotion, Sonic paired a real-time countdown clock with an interactive quiz that "made it easy to say 'yes!' to half-price summer treats from Sonic."**

Courtesy SONIC Drive-In

Display ads have come a long way in recent years in terms of engaging consumers and moving them along the path to purchase. Today's rich media ads incorporate animation, video, sound, and interactivity. For example, Boeing recently ran a display ad featuring a breathtaking, rotating 3D view of the International Space Station. ● At the other extreme, when Sonic restaurants wanted to create awareness and anticipation for a summer promotion making its shakes and ice cream slushes half price after 8 p.m., it created an online display ad featuring a real-time daily countdown clock. The ad paired the clock with an interactive quiz to help customers decide in advance their perfect flavor, and a store locator helped them find the nearest Sonic restaurant. "In other words," says a Sonic marketer, "we made it easy to say 'yes!' to half-price summer treats from Sonic."[13]

Using *search-related ads* (or *contextual advertising*), text- and image-based ads and links appear atop or alongside search engine results on sites such as Google, Yahoo!, and Bing. For example, search Google for "LED TVs." At the top and side of the resulting search list, you'll see ads for 10 or more advertisers, ranging from Samsung and Visio to Best Buy, Amazon.com, Walmart.com, and Crutchfield. Eighty-five percent of Google's $137 billion in revenues last year came from ad sales. Search is an always-on kind of medium, and the results are easily measured.[14]

A search advertiser buys search terms or keywords from the search site and pays only if consumers click through to its site. The average cost per click-through for Google Search Network keywords is between $1 and $2. The most expensive and competitive keywords can cost $50 or more per click. Search advertising is a large component in the digital advertising mix of most brands. Large retailers might easily spend $50 million or more per year on paid search advertising. In all, search advertising accounts for 45 percent of all digital advertising spending.[15]

Email Marketing

Email marketing remains an important and growing digital marketing tool. Around the world, people send out more than 406 million emails every minute of every day. According to one survey, 50 percent of consumers prefer to engage with brands via email versus direct mail, phone, text, or social media. And 76 percent of consumers agree that retail brands send relevant emails that accurately reflect their shopping preferences, locations, or purchase histories. Email is an important business-to-business tool—86 percent of business professionals prefer to use email when communicating for business purposes, and email rates as the third most influential source of information for B-to-B audiences. What's more, email is now an on-the-go medium—55 percent of all emails are now opened on mobile devices. Not surprisingly, given its low costs and targetability, email can yield a very high return on investment.[16]

When used properly, email can be the ultimate direct marketing medium. Today's emails are anything but the staid, text-only messages of the past. Instead, they are colorful, inviting, and interactive. Email lets marketers send highly targeted, tightly personalized, relationship-building messages. For example, eyewear brand Warby Parker sends a sequence of nine informational and promotional emails to home try-on customers. Each is personally addressed and keyed to steps in the trial process, from initial registration and order confirmation to offers of selection assistance and instructions for returning frames. "The magical part was feeling like Warby Parker was right there with me throughout the process," says one customer. Warby Parker also sends cheerful after-purchase follow-up, announcement, and promotional emails. ● For example, it sends personalized emails to customers on the first anniversary of their purchase, with the message "You've had your Warby Parker frames for one year now. Tell 'em we said Happy Birthday! We hope the first 365 days have been joyful." And just in case the customer wants "to start more traditions," the email also includes a link to Warby Parker's web and social media sites.[17]

But there's a dark side to the use of email marketing. The explosion of **spam**—unsolicited, unwanted commercial email messages that clog up our email boxes—has produced consumer irritation and frustration. According to one source, spam now accounts for 55 percent of the billions of emails sent worldwide each day. American office workers receive an average of 200 emails per day and spend nearly two and a half hours reading and replying to them. As a result, according to one recent study, more than half of consumers say they delete at least 50 percent of brand emails without opening them.[18] Email marketers walk a fine line between adding value for consumers and being intrusive and annoying.

To address these concerns, most legitimate marketers now practice *permission-based email marketing*, sending email pitches only to customers who "opt in." Many companies use configurable email systems that let customers choose what they want to get. For example, Amazon targets opt-in customers with a limited number of helpful "we thought you'd like to know" messages based on their expressed preferences and previous purchases. Few customers object, and many actually welcome such promotional messages. Amazon benefits through higher return rates and by avoiding alienating customers with emails they don't want.

Online Videos

Another form of online marketing is posting digital video content on brand websites or on social media. Some videos are ads that a company makes primarily for TV or other media but posts online before or after an advertising campaign to extend their reach and impact. Other videos are made specifically for the web and social media. Such videos range from "how-to" instructional videos and public relations pieces to brand promotions and brand-related entertainment.

Good online videos can engage consumers by the tens of millions. The online video audience is soaring. Almost 72 percent of the U.S. population has viewed online videos. YouTube users now upload more than 300 hours of video every minute. Facebook alone generates and estimated more than 60 billion video views per day worldwide. By one estimate, video will account for 82 percent of all internet traffic by 2022. "Over the past few years," notes one analyst, "the internet has evolved from a text-based medium to the new TV."[19]

Email marketing
Sending highly targeted, highly personalized, relationship-building marketing messages via email.

● Email marketing: Eyewear brand Warby Parker sends personalized emails to home try-on customers throughout the purchase and after-purchase process. "You've had your Warby Parker frames for one year now. Tell 'em we said Happy Birthday!"

Courtesy of Warby Parker

Spam
Unsolicited, unwanted commercial email messages.

Many brands produce multi-platform video campaigns that bridge traditional TV, online, and mobile media. For example, video versions of and promotions for most Super Bowl ads attract huge audiences before and after the big game airs. Consider Amazon's humorous "Alexa loses her voice" ad shown during Super Bowl LII. In the ad, a host of big-name celebrities filled in when the tech-giant's AI assistant lost her voice and couldn't fulfill requests. The 90-second ad ranked number one in the *USA Today* ad meter ratings, making more than 81 million TV ad impressions and earning more than 8 million online views on game day. But short-form teaser videos and prerelease versions of the ad grabbed more than 20 million online views in the days leading up to the game and tens of millions more views in the days following. By one account, the Amazon ad and related videos ranked number four in online "digital buzz" prior to the game.[20]

Viral marketing

The digital version of word-of-mouth marketing: videos, ads, and other marketing content that is so infectious that customers will seek it out or pass it along to friends.

Like Amazon, marketers hope that some of their videos will go viral. **Viral marketing**, the digital version of word-of-mouth marketing, involves creating videos, ads, and other marketing content that are so infectious that customers will seek them out or pass them along to their friends. Because customers find and pass along the content, viral marketing can be very inexpensive. And when content comes from a friend, the recipient is much more likely to view or read it.

Brands often use videos for engaging consumers beyond promoting products, giving brands a voice and creating positive brand associations. Consider this this video campaign from Gatorade:[21]

> After learning that girls abandon sports 50 percent more than boys by their teenage years, Gatorade created a six-episode video series called "Versus." The 21-minute episodes, starring female high school lacrosse players, were designed to "candidly spark a conversation on the importance of keeping girls in the game," says a Gatorade marketer. "We wanted to find something that would encourage girls who had a love for sports to stay motivated." The video series ran alongside Gatorade's "Sisters in Sweat" campaign featuring professional athletes like Serena William and other famous women for whom sports had been a positive influence. The "Versus" video series quickly earned more than 1 million views, creating a "double-digit lift" in girls' sports participation confidence and boosting positive brand associations for Gatorade. "We knew we had something special, emotional, and thought-provoking on our hands right away," says another Gatorade marketer.

Despite the many viral successes, it's important to note that marketers usually have little control over where their viral messages end up. They can seed content online, but that does little good unless the message itself strikes a chord with consumers. Says one creative director, "You hope that the creative is at a high enough mark where the seeds grow into mighty oaks. If they don't like it, it ain't gonna move. If they like it, it'll move a little bit; and if they love it, it's gonna move like a fast-burning fire through the Hollywood hills."[22]

Blogs and Other Online Forums

Brands also conduct online marketing through various digital forums that appeal to specific special-interest groups and brand communities. **Blogs** are online forums where people and companies post their thoughts and other content, usually related to narrowly defined topics. Blogs can be about anything, from politics or baseball to haiku, car repair, brands, or the latest television series. Many bloggers use social networks such as Twitter, Facebook, Tumblr, and Instagram to promote their blogs, giving them huge reach. Such reach can give blogs—especially those with large and devoted followings—substantial influence.

Blogs

Online forums where people and companies post their thoughts and other content, usually related to narrowly defined topics.

These days, almost every company has its own brand-related blog that reaches out to customer communities. ● For example, the *Oh My Disney* blog gives Disney buffs an "official destination for Disney quizzes, nostalgia, news, and other Disney magic." Starbucks's *1912 Pike* blog, named after the address of the first Starbucks location, is a "coffee education blog" that offers caffeine junkies and Starbucks brand fans an interesting mix of coffee-related articles and industry news, plus recipes and how-to guides. Chase bank's *Chase News & Stories* blog focuses on "helping you make the most of your money" with useful articles and stories on financial topics such as buying your first home, planning ahead for college education expenses, or saving money when buying groceries. And Patagonia's blog, *The Cleanest Line*, shares stories about the environment, tells where the company stands on key issues, and spreads the brand's "save our home planet" message rather than promoting sales. Patagonia uses its popular social

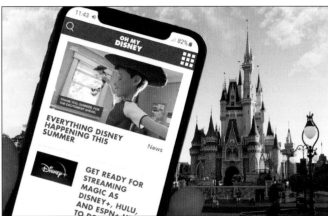

● **Company blogs:** The *Oh My Disney* blog gives Disney buffs an "official destination for Disney quizzes, nostalgia, news, and other Disney magic."

Eyal Dayan Photography

media sites, especially Instagram (with more than 3.8 million followers), to steer fans to the blog's longer-form stories and videos.[23]

Beyond their own brand blogs, many marketers use third-party blogs to help get their messages out. For example, some fashion bloggers have amassed millions of followers, with fan bases larger even than the blogs and social media accounts of major fashion magazines. For example, 27-year-old Danielle Bernstein started the We Wore What fashion blog as an undergraduate at the Fashion Institute of Technology in New York City. The blog and Instagram account are now a source of daily outfit inspiration to a fan base of more than 2 million. Because of such large followings, brands flock to Bernstein and other fashion blog influencers such as BryanBoy, The Blonde Salad, Song of Style, and Gal Meets Glam, paying them $15,000 or more to post and tag product images in their blog, Facebook, and Instagram sites. Bernstein posts images that contain sponsored products from small brands such as Schultz Shoes and Revolve Clothing to large brands such as Nike, Lancôme, and Nordstrom.[24]

As a marketing tool, blogs offer some advantages. They can offer a fresh, original, personal, and cheap way to enter into consumer online and social media conversations. However, the blogosphere is cluttered and difficult to control. And although companies can sometimes leverage blogs to engage customers in meaningful relationships, blogs remain largely a consumer-controlled medium. Whether or not they actively participate in the blogs, companies should monitor and listen to them. Marketers can use insights from consumer online conversations to improve their marketing programs.

Author Comment | As in about every other area of our lives, digital media and mobile technologies have taken the marketing world by storm. They offer some amazing marketing possibilities. But truth be told, many marketers are still sweating over how to use them most effectively.

Social Media and Mobile Marketing

OBJECTIVE 17-4 Discuss how companies use social media and mobile marketing to engage consumers and create brand community.

Social Media Marketing

Social media

Independent and commercial online social networks where people congregate to socialize and share messages, opinions, pictures, videos, and other content.

The surge in internet usage and digital technologies and devices has spawned a dazzling array of online **social media** and other digital communities. Countless independent and commercial social networks have arisen where people congregate to socialize and share messages, opinions, pictures, videos, and other content. These days, it seems, almost everyone is buddying up on Facebook, checking in with Twitter, tuning into the day's hottest videos at YouTube, pinning images on social scrapbooking site Pinterest, or sharing photos with Instagram, Snapchat, and TikTok. And, of course, wherever consumers congregate, marketers will surely follow.

Marketers are now riding the huge social media wave. Almost all businesses large and small use one or more social media channels. Large brands usually have a huge social media presence. For example, according to one source, Nike maintains at least 108 Facebook pages, 104 Twitter handles, 16 Instagram accounts, and 41 YouTube channels.[25]

Interestingly, just as marketers are mastering the use of social media to engage customers, the social media themselves are learning how to make their communities a suitable platform for marketing content, in a way that benefits both social media users and brands. Most social media, even the most successful ones, still face a monetization issue: how they can profitably tap the marketing potential of their massive communities to make money without driving off loyal users. Exceptions are Facebook and massively successful Facebook-owned Instagram (see Real Marketing 17.1).

Using Social Media

Marketers can engage in social media in two ways: They can use existing social media, or they can set up their own. Using existing social media seems the easiest. Thus, most

Real Marketing 17.1

Instagram: A Win-Win-Win for the Company, Advertisers, and Instagrammers

Social media giant Facebook acquired a young startup called Instagram seven years ago for the then-mind-blowing sum of $1 billion—a record price paid for any app and far more than Facebook had ever spent on an acquisition. Experts were shocked, and some critics mocked Facebook's sanity. At the time, Instagram had zero revenue, only 30 million users, and no idea how it would make money. But Facebook saw big potential in the fledgling Instagram.

As the world has rapidly gone social and mobile, social networks have played a huge role. Whether it's on massive social media platforms or lesser-known niche sites, it's common to see people everywhere these days, heads down with devices in hand, connecting, posting, messaging, and sharing. On Facebook alone, every day, 1.6 billion of the network's 2.4 billion monthly active users worldwide watch 8 billion videos, generate 5.7 billion Likes, and share 4.8 billion pieces of content.

However, even as social media networks have achieved incredible success in terms of numbers of users and sheer content volume, a nagging problem still plagues them. It's called monetization. How can social media profitably tap the marketing potential of their massive communities to make money without driving off their legions of loyal users? Most social media still struggle to make a profit. Last year, Twitter made a profit for the first time ever; Snapchat lost nearly $1.3 billion.

Facebook was the first social medium to solve the profitability issue, and it's the only one yet to do that on a large scale. Last year, Facebook netted $22 billion in profits on revenues of just over $56 billion—an amazing 39 percent margin. And although Facebook began making money only seven years ago, its revenues have grown by an average of nearly 50 percent annually and profits by 80 percent a year. How does Facebook succeed where so many other social media still wrestle with monetization? It's all about advertising. Facebook rakes in money by providing effective ways for companies to target and engage its gigantic user community with relevant ads and other brand content.

Perhaps nowhere is this monetization success more apparent than at massively successful Instagram. Launched as a private startup in 2010, Instagram differentiated itself from other apps in two ways: It was mobile-only, and it was designed with a single simple function in mind—sharing photos. Instagram's simplicity and the wide appeal of communicating through images made it an instant hit. The photo-sharing app quickly became the preferred social network for then-young millennials to communicate with their friends, out of the sight of their parents' watchful eyes.

The Facebook acquisition came less than two years after Instagram's launch. Although small at the time, Instagram's youthful audience complemented Facebook's aging one. A year later, Instagram introduced paid advertising. The decision was controversial. Like most social media users, Instagrammers cherished the free (and commercial-free) sharing culture of their digital community. If not well conceived, commercial content would be an unwelcome intrusion that could alienate users and drive them away. The challenge for Instagram, as for all social media, was to inject brand content alongside user content without upsetting the community dynamic.

But even as more and more advertisers have jumped aboard Instagram—first hundreds, then thousands, then millions—Instagram's user base has continued to explode. In fact, although still much smaller than Facebook, Instagram's growth rates rival those of its parent. Every day, 1.1 billion Instagrammers now share more than 100 million photos and videos and hit the Like button more than 4.2 billion times. And Instagram's advertiser base has grown in harmony with its user base. Instagram is one of the world's premier digital, social media, and mobile advertising channels, now attracting 2 million monthly advertisers, ranging from marketing heavyweights like Nike, Disney, and P&G to your local restaurant or fitness center.

Instagram's unique user base makes it an ideal fit for the content strategies of many brands. The Instagram community is big and youngish—71 percent of U.S. 18- to 29-year-olds—but spans a wide demographic range that allows for precision targeting. Instagram's audience is also brand loyal: 80 percent of users follow one or more brands on the app, and 60 percent say they discover new products there. What's more, some 75 percent of Instagram users take action after looking at an advertising post, such as visiting a website or checking out an offer.

Instagram's design makes it easy for advertisers to blend their brand content naturally with the flow of user content. As a result, rather than disrupting the Instagrammer experience, brand content often enhances it. Beyond their own

Hugely successful Instagram has figured out how to integrate advertising with consumer content in a way that satisfies users, advertisers, and its own bottom line.
ELF

Instagram feeds, advertisers can choose from several content formats. Using photo ads—Instagram's most basic ad format—advertisers can post high-impact images on the app's "clean, simple, and beautiful creative canvas." Video ads inject the power of sound and motion in brand videos up to 60 seconds long. Carousel ads bring more depth, letting users swipe to view additional photos or videos in a single ad. And with Stories ads, advertisers can present brand content in the same way that Instagrammers use the Stories feature—weaving photos and videos together, enhancing them with text and doodles, and presenting them in full-screen slideshows that stay around for 24 hours.

Designed for sharing photos and videos, Instagram's presentation formats let users process the visual content quickly and efficiently, with more emotional impact, befitting today's in-the-moment mobile generation. Instagram ad content creates high levels of consumer engagement compared with other social media. For example, whereas as closest competitor Snapchat's disappearing content makes brand-consumer connections fleeting, Instagram's format lets consumers scroll through, linger over, and share content on their own time terms.

Beyond Snapchat comparisons, one recent study revealed that brands get as much as 30 times more engagement on Instagram than on Twitter and three times more engagement than on Facebook. In one example, Mercedes recently posted social media teasers for the world premiere of its new A-Class hatchback. On Facebook, the post racked up a respectable 10,000 Likes. By comparison, however, the very same image on Instagram generated 150,000 Likes. Thus, Instagram reaps engagement levels that older, more text-based social media often can't match.

Beyond its ability to engage consumers with impactful brand content, Instagram has now set its sights on the next step of the customer journey—purchase. Brands can now create storefronts on Instagram, where users can click through to a company's web or mobile site to place orders. Instagram's recently launched Collection ads let users purchase a brand's products directly from the ad. And Instagram now accepts payments, letting users pay for purchases without having to leave the network.

Thus, it didn't take long for Facebook to turn Instagram into a moneymaker. Although Facebook doesn't report Instagram financial information separately, by one estimate, Instagram will generate $14 billion in advertising revenue this year—double that of last year. Instagram Stories ads alone generate more revenue than all of rival Snapchat. Another analysis values Instagram at more than $100 billion as a standalone company—100 times what Facebook paid for it just seven years ago. In short, no one is mocking Facebook's Instagram purchase anymore.

Instagram is soaring because it has figured out how to integrate advertising with consumer content in a way that satisfies everyone. Far from resenting brand content as intrusive, many Instagrammers appear to welcome it, making social media advertising a win-win-win for Instagram, its advertisers, and its user community.[26]

brands—large and small—have set up shop on a host of social media sites. Check the websites of brands ranging from Coca-Cola, Nike, and Chick-fil-A to the Chicago Bulls or even the U.S. Forest Service, and you'll find links to each brand's Facebook, Twitter, Instagram, YouTube, LinkedIn, or other social media pages. Such social media can create substantial brand communities. For example, the Chicago Bulls have more the 18 million Facebook fans; Coca-Cola has an eye-popping 108 million Facebook fans.

Some of the major social networks are huge. Facebook has 2.4 billion monthly active users, more than seven times the population of the United States. Twitter has more than 326 million monthly active users, and YouTube's more than 1.3 billion users upload 300 hours of video every minute of every day. The list goes on: Instagram has 186 million active users, LinkedIn 500 million, TikTok 500 million, Pinterest 250 million, Snapchat 186 million.[27]

Although these large, general-interest social media networks grab most of the headlines, countless niche and interest-based social media have also emerged. These online social networks cater to the needs of smaller communities of like-minded people, making them ideal vehicles for marketers who want to target special-interest groups. There's at least one social media network for just about every interest, hobby, or group. ● Goodreads is a social network where 65 million avid readers can "Meet your next favorite book" and discuss it with friends, whereas moms share advice and commiseration at CafeMom. com. At Doximity, more than 1 million medical professionals—doctors, nurse practitioners, pharmacists, and others—network with colleagues, catch up on medical news, and research employment opportunities. PURRsonals is where "cat lovers meet and greet." FarmersOnly.com provides online dating for

● **Countless niche and special-interest social media have emerged, catering to communities of like-minded people. Goodreads is a place where you can "Meet your next favorite book" and discuss it with others.**

Sharaf Maksumov/Shutterstock

down-to-earth "country folks" who enjoy "blue skies, living free and at peace in wide open spaces, raising animals, and appreciating nature"—"because city folks just don't get it."[28]

Social Media Marketing Advantages and Challenges

Using social media presents both advantages and challenges. On the plus side, social media are *targeted* and *personal*—they allow marketers to create and share tailored brand content with individual consumers and customer communities. Social media are *interactive*, making them ideal for starting and participating in customer conversations and listening to customer feedback. Social media are also *immediate* and *timely*. They can be used to reach customers anytime, anywhere with timely and relevant marketing content regarding brand happenings and activities. As discussed earlier in the chapter, the rapid growth in social media usage has caused a surge in *real-time marketing*, allowing marketers to create and join consumer conversations around situations and events as they occur. Consider JetBlue:[29]

● **JetBlue is legendary for the speed and quality of its social media responses. For example, the JetBlue social media team responds to every single Twitter mention it receives, with an impressive average response time of 10 minutes.**

JetBlue

A man once tweeted JetBlue while waiting at the airport to ask why he was charged $50 for taking an earlier flight. JetBlue responded to his Tweet within several minutes, and the customer seemed satisfied. But the JetBlue social media crew didn't stop there. Instead, it forwarded the exchange to the JetBlue staff at the airport. The airport staff studied the man's Twitter profile picture and then walked around the terminal until they found him so they could follow up in person. In another case, one JetBlue customer jokingly tweeted that she expected a "welcome parade" at the gate when she arrived in Boston. Much to the delighted customer's surprise, when she arrived at her destination, the JetBlue airport staff welcomed her with fanfare, including marching band music and handmade signs.

Of course, JetBlue can't surprise every customer in this way. ● However, the airline is legendary for the speed and quality of its social media interactions. It receives 2,500 to 2,600 Twitter mentions every day, and the JetBlue social media team reads and responds to every single one, with an impressive average response time of 10 minutes. Beyond engaging customers and keeping them happy, such social media interactions provide valuable customer feedback. "We're all about people," says JetBlue's Manager of Customer Commitment, "and being on social media is just a natural extension of that."

Social media can be very *cost-effective*. Although creating and administering social media content can be costly, many social media are free or inexpensive to use. Thus, returns on social media investments are often high compared with those of expensive traditional media such as television or print. The low cost of social media puts them within easy reach of even small businesses and brands that can't afford the high costs of big-budget marketing campaigns.

Perhaps the biggest advantage of social media is their *engagement and social sharing capabilities*. Social media are especially well suited to creating customer engagement and community—for getting customers involved with the brand and with each other. More than any other channels, social media can involve customers in shaping and sharing brand content, experiences, information, and ideas.

For example, consider Etsy—the online craft marketplace that's "Your place to buy and sell all things handmade." Etsy uses its web and mobile sites and a host of social media to create an Etsy lifestyle community, where buyers congregate to learn about, explore, exchange, and share ideas about handmade and vintage products and related topics. In addition to its active Facebook, Twitter, and YouTube pages, Etsy engages 2 million brand followers on photo-sharing site Instagram, where the Etsy community shares photos of creative ideas and projects. It also engages some 1.2 million followers on social scrapbooking site Pinterest, with boards on topics ranging from "DIY Projects," "Entertaining," and "Stuff We Love" to "Etsy Weddings" and even "Yum! Recipes to Share," where the community posts favorite recipes. Etsy sells few of the ingredients that go into the recipes, but it's all part of the Etsy lifestyle. Through its extensive online and social media presence, Etsy has created an active and engaged worldwide community of 39.4 million shoppers and 2.1 million sellers worldwide in what it calls "The marketplace we make together."[30]

Social media marketing also presents challenges. For example, such social networks are largely user controlled. The company's goal in using social media is to make the brand a part of consumers' conversations and their lives. However, marketers can't simply muscle their way into consumers' digital interactions—they need to earn the right to be there. Rather than intruding, marketers must become a valued part of the online experience by developing a steady flow of engaging content.

Also, because consumers have so much control over social media content, even a seemingly harmless social media campaign can backfire. All Coca-Cola wanted to do at the start of 2016 was wish its customers Happy New Year on VK, Russia's most popular social media platform. Unfortunately, the cartoon map posted omitted Crimea, angering Russian customers. Coke replaced the map with one including Crimea, but this offended customers in Ukraine, which still disputes Russia's annexation. If this wasn't bad enough, the second map also included the Kuril Islands, offending customers in Japan, which still lays claim to the islands. The online firestorm finally ended when Coke pulled the message, with apologies. In 2016, Aldi Australia asked Twitter users to #tellus "I became an ALDI lover when I tasted _____ for the first time." However, the campaign didn't just generate the expected list of customers' favorite Aldi brands. The hashtag also turned into a revenge hashtag–bashtag, with unexpectedly rude, often sexually themed mocking of the supermarket chain by disgruntled customers.

There's a clear message. With social media, "you're going into the consumer's backyard. This is their place," warns one social marketer. "Social media is a pressure cooker," says another. "The hundreds of thousands, or millions, of people out there are going to take your idea, and they're going to try to shred it or tear it apart and find what's weak or stupid in it."[31]

Integrated Social Media Marketing

Using social media might be as simple as posting some messages and promotions on a brand's Facebook or Twitter pages or creating brand buzz with videos or images on YouTube, Instagram, or Pinterest. However, most large companies are now designing full-scale social media efforts that blend with and support other elements of a brand's marketing content strategy and tactics. More than making scattered efforts and chasing Likes and retweets, companies that use social media successfully are integrating a broad range of diverse media to create brand-related social sharing, engagement, and customer community.

Managing a brand's social media efforts can be a major undertaking. For example, Starbucks is one of the world's most successful social media marketers. Its core social media team connects with its fans through 87 accounts on five different social platforms. Frappuccino drinks alone have more than 14 million followers on Facebook, Twitter, and Instagram. Managing and integrating all that social media content is challenging, but the results are worth the investment. Customers can and do engage with Starbucks by the tens of millions digitally, without ever setting foot in a store. One recent study found that Starbucks tallied 17 times the Facebook and Instagram engagement of nearest competitor Dunkin'.[32]

But more than just creating online engagement and community, Starbucks' social media presence also drives customers into its stores. For example, in its first big social media promotion several years ago, Starbucks offered a free pastry with a morning drink purchase. A million people showed up. A more recent "Tweet-a-Coffee" promotion, which let customers give a $5 gift card to a friend by putting both #tweetacoffee and the friend's handle in a tweet, resulted in $180,000 in purchases within little more than one month. And when Starbucks introduced the Unicorn Frappuccino—a limited-time drink that changed colors when swirled—it was perfectly crafted to catch the attention of Instagrammers, who posted some 180,000 Instagram photos of the drink in only a week. Although offered for one week, many Starbucks locations ran out of supplies sooner. Social media "are not just about engaging and telling a story and connecting," says Starbucks's head of global digital marketing. "They can have a material impact on the business."[33]

Mobile Marketing

Mobile marketing
Marketing messages, promotions, and other content delivered to on-the-go consumers through their mobile devices.

Mobile marketing features marketing messages, promotions, and other marketing content delivered to on-the-go consumers through their mobile devices. Marketers use mobile marketing to engage customers anywhere, anytime during the buying and relationship-building processes. The widespread adoption of mobile devices and the surge in mobile web traffic have made mobile marketing a must for every brand.

With the recent proliferation of smartphones and tablets, mobile device penetration is now greater than 100 percent in the United States (many people possess more than one mobile device). More than 75 percent of people in the United States own a smartphone, and more than half of all U.S. households are currently mobile-only households with no landline phone. The mobile apps market, little more than a decade old, has exploded globally: There are millions of apps available, and the average smartphone owner uses nine apps a day.[34]

Most people love their phones and rely heavily on them. According to one study, nearly 90 percent of consumers who own smartphones, tablets, computers, and TVs would give up all of those other screens before giving up their phones. On average, Americans check their smartphones 80 times a day and spend five hours a day on their mobile devices using apps, talking, texting, and browsing the web. Thus, although TV is still a big part of people's lives, mobile is rapidly becoming their "first screen." Away from home, it's their only screen.[35]

● For consumers, a smartphone or tablet can be a handy shopping companion. It can provide on-the-go product information, price comparisons, advice and reviews from other consumers, access to instant deals, and fast and convenient avenues to purchase. One recent study found that more than 90 percent of smartphone-toting shoppers have used their phone while shopping and 51 percent have made a purchase using a mobile device. Among 18- to 34-year-olds, 61 percent had made a mobile purchase within the past month. Mobile buying now accounts for more than one-third of all e-commerce sales.[36]

Mobile provides a rich platform for engaging consumers more deeply as they move through the buying process with tools ranging from mobile ads, coupons, and texts to apps and mobile websites. As a result, mobile advertising spending in the United States is surging. Mobile devices now account for about two-thirds of all digital ad spending. Mobile ad spending alone now exceeds TV ad spending and is expected to double TV ad spending by 2022.[37] Almost every major marketer—from Nike, P&G, and Nordstrom to your local supermarket to nonprofits such as the Red Cross—is now integrating mobile marketing into its direct marketing programs.

● For consumers, a smartphone or tablet can be a handy shopping companion. As a result, mobile advertising spending is surging.

George Rudy/Shutterstock

Companies use mobile marketing to stimulate immediate buying, make shopping easier, enrich the brand experience, or all of these. It lets marketers provide consumers with information, incentives, and choices at the moment they are expressing an interest or when they are most likely to make a buying choice (see Real Marketing 17.2). Today's rich-media mobile ads can create substantial engagement and impact. For example, Gatorade put mobile marketing's timely engagement potential to good use during a recent Super Bowl:[38]

Gatorade wanted to re-create the iconic Gatorade dunk moment—the tradition of dousing a sports coach with a cooler of ice-cold Gatorade after a big win—but make it a personal moment, one that individual fans could enjoy and share during and after the game. So it worked with Snapchat to create a Snapchat filter that made it look like a cooler of the sports drink was spilling over users' heads while fans cheered in the background. The result? Fans created more than 8.2 million videos of themselves getting virtually dunked with more than 165 million views in 48 hours. Although it never appeared on TV, it was the most viewed and interacted-with ad of the

Real Marketing 17.2 | Mobile Marketing: Engaging Consumers in Moments That Matter

It seems like whatever you want to do these days, "there's an app for that." The mobile app market has exploded in recent years. Apple's App Store now boasts 1.8 million apps; the Google Play Store leads with more than 2.1 million apps. Mobile has become today's brave new marketing frontier, especially for brands courting younger consumers. Mobile devices are very personal, ever-present, and always on. That makes them an ideal medium for obtaining quick responses to individualized, time-sensitive offers. Mobile marketing lets brands engage consumers in moments that matter.

Some mobile apps are brand-specific—they help consumers navigate the brand's products, services, special offers, and community. For example, the Sephora app "Makes Beauty Mobile," providing "instant, on-the-go access to daily inspiration, exclusive offers, and more." The Chick-fil-A app gives customers "Endless Awesome"—it makes ordering easier, lets them bypass lines and scan to pay, remembers menu preferences, and rewards them with special treats. Is that Redbox kiosk too slow? Download the Redbox app—it lets you find and reserve a DVD using your mobile device and have it waiting for you at the kiosk.

Other apps help consumers navigate the marketplace and access other companies' offers. The Angie's List app provides on-the-go access to lists, ratings, and reviews of best local services providers, from roofers, plumbers, and mechanics to doctors and dentists. The coupon organizing Flipp app delivers weekly store flyer deals to consumers' phones even as they shop; the AwardWallet app helps users track and manage points and awards from all their rewards accounts in one place.

In today's cluttered mobile environment, successful mobile marketing goes well beyond just texting out a coupon or a link to buy. Instead, it engages customers in the moment with relevant features and offers that enhance brand relationships and buying experiences. Google's Waze app does more than just help users navigate from point A to point B and find local stops along way. The "community-driven" navigation app also pinpoints traffic jams, accidents, speed traps, and fuel prices in real time, faithfully updated by Waze's 110 million active users in 185 countries. REI has a full suite of apps covering a range of mountain sports including hiking, climbing, mountain biking, trail running, and skiing and snowboarding. Each app provides maps,

GPS routing, real-time weather and terrain conditions, reviews, tips, and forums. And for times you decide you can't live without a pair of Darn Tough hiking socks or a two-man Hubba Hubba tent, REI has a shopping app as well.

Consumers have come to expect frictionless mobile buying experiences from marketing giants like Amazon. But with rapid advances in mobile capabilities, more and more companies are becoming the Amazons of their industries. Consider travel company TripAdvisor. What started mostly as a hotel and restaurant review website has now become the "ultimate travel companion." TripAdvisor's mobile apps give users "the wisdom of the crowds" with anytime, anywhere, as-they-travel access to comprehensive reviews, photos and videos, maps, and descriptive information about hotels, restaurants, air travel options, places to go, and things to see worldwide. The easy-to-use apps include lots of useful features, such as smartphone lock screen notifications that call out nearby points of interest as you travel. And booking options for hotels, restaurants, and flights are always just a tap away.

One user likens the TripAdvisor app to a best friend who's an endlessly knowledgeable travel expert and helps you make all your vacation travel arrangements. And then she goes along with you on your vacation as your own personal travel guide, sharing just the right information about local points of

interest, finding and reviewing good places to eat, and providing digital maps to help you get where you're going. In turn, TripAdvisor is a great place for travel- and hospitality-related brands to link up with 490 million engaged and connected travelers a month who are actively traveling or planning trips. TripAdvisor took in $1.6 billion in revenues from mobile advertising and bookings last year.

Mobile marketing lets brands personalize promotions and weave them into relevant everyday customer experiences. For example, Kiip (pronounced "keep") is a mobile rewards network that specializes in helping brands provide customers with just the right rewards at just the right times based on their everyday activities. Kiip started by embedding its technology into video-game apps, rewarding gamers who reached new game levels or met other goals with coupons for one of their favorite brands, such as Coca-Cola. It now helps brands across a range of categories to use mobile rewards to engage customers at key brand-related moments. Kiip has worked with hundreds of brands—including Coca-Cola, Kraft, Johnson & Johnson, McDonald's, BMW, and General Mills—and is now embedded in thousands of mobile apps.

Kiip works with brands to help them map out "demand moments"—times when consumers might be most receptive to brand engagement and messages. It then uses the here-and-now power of mobile to let brands be right there when the behavior is occurring.

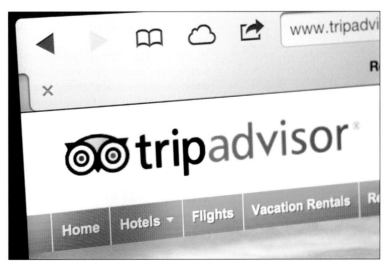

Mobile marketing: TripAdvisor's mobile app—"your ultimate travel companion"—gives users as-they-travel access to crowd-sourced information about hotels, restaurants, places to go, and things to see worldwide. And booking options are always just a tap away.

Ian Dagnall/Alamy Stock Photo

For fitness apps like MapMyRun and productivity apps like Any.do, Kiip ties rewards to real-life achievements. When users cross things off their to-do lists or achieve a running goal, they get a reward from a relevant brand. PepsiCo uses Kiip to map out app-related demand moments for all its brands— such as moments when using an app for fitness activities, listening to music, or watching a movie—to figure out when someone might thirst for Gatorade or hunger for Doritos. At appropriate times, it offers brand-related messages, rewards, and promotions via the apps.

Kiip helped spirits company Campari America with a corporate responsibility campaign designed to connect consumers with the brand while promoting responsible drinking. Kiip identified probable drinking occasions—as when customers were doing mobile searches for happy hours, consulting cocktail recipes, or checking game scores while at sports bars during the wee hours. Campari then offered users coupons for discounted or even free rides from ride-hailing service Lyft to help them return home safely.

Unlike typical banner ads, pop-ups, or emails, Kiip's offers enhance a user's regular activities rather than interrupt them. According to Kiip's founder, Kiip "is less about real-time marketing and more about real-time-needs addressing." In fact, he asserts, Kiip isn't really in the mobile ad business at all—it's in the happiness business. "We want to capitalize on happiness," he says. "Everything's better when you're happy." Mobile timeliness, relevance, and happiness pay off in terms of consumer response. Across its entire network, Kiip's average engagement rate—people claiming a reward, clicking on it, or watching a video related to it—is 10 percent but can reach as high as 50 percent. That's impressive given that engagement rates for typical app ads run below one percent.

Many consumers are still initially skeptical about mobile marketing. But they often change their minds if mobile offers deliver useful, in-the-moment brand and shopping information, entertaining content, or timely coupons and discounted prices. Most mobile efforts target only consumers who voluntarily opt in or download apps. But in today's cluttered mobile marketing space, customers just won't do that unless they see real value in it. The challenge for marketers: develop valued mobile offers, ads, and apps that make customers want to come calling.[39]

Super Bowl. "We've always been a little hesitant to activate against the dunk because it's such a natural moment that happens in the game," says a Gatorade marketer. But "this ended up feeling like the right opportunity because it's not about what happens on the field—it's about the fans being able to participate."

Most marketers have created their own mobile online sites. Others have created useful or entertaining mobile apps to engage customers with their brands and help them shop. For example, the Benjamin Moore Color Capture app lets customers take photos of colorful objects and then match them to any of 3,500 Benjamin Moore paint colors. Starbucks's mobile app lets customers use their phones as a Starbucks card to make fast and easy purchases. Fitbit's mobile app lets users use their smartphones to count steps, log fitness activities, and connect with and compete against friends. And Charles Schwab's mobile apps let customers get up-to-the-minute investment news, monitor their accounts, and make trades at any time from any location—it helps you "stay connected with your money."

As with other forms of direct marketing, however, companies must use mobile marketing responsibly or risk angering already ad-weary consumers. Most people don't want to be interrupted regularly by advertising, so marketers must be smart about how they engage people on mobile devices. The key is to provide genuinely useful information and offers that will make consumers want to engage. Thus, many marketers target mobile ads on an opt-in-only basis.

In all, digital direct marketing—online, social media, and mobile marketing—offers both great promise and many challenges. Its most ardent apostles still envision a time when the internet and digital marketing will replace magazines, newspapers, and even stores as sources for information, engagement, and buying. Most marketers, however, hold a more realistic view. For most companies, digital, mobile, and social media marketing will remain important approaches to the marketplace that work alongside other approaches in a fully integrated marketing mix.

Author | Although online, social
Comment | media, and mobile direct
marketing get much of the attention
these days, traditional direct media
still carry a lot of the direct marketing
freight. Just think about your often-
overstuffed mailbox.

Traditional Direct Marketing Forms

OBJECTIVE 17-5 Identify and discuss the traditional direct marketing forms and overview public policy and ethical issues presented by direct marketing.

Although the fast-growing digital, social, and mobile marketing tools have grabbed most of the headlines lately, traditional direct marketing tools are very much alive and still heavily used. We now examine the traditional approaches shown on the right side of Figure 17.1.

The major traditional forms of direct marketing are face-to-face or personal selling, direct-mail marketing, catalog marketing, telemarketing, direct-response television (DRTV) marketing, and kiosk marketing. We examined personal selling in depth in Chapter 16. Here, we look into the other forms of traditional direct marketing other than personal selling.

Direct-Mail Marketing

Direct-mail marketing

Marketing that occurs by sending an offer, announcement, reminder, or other item directly to a person at a particular address.

Direct-mail marketing involves sending an offer, announcement, reminder, or other item to a person at a particular address. Using highly selective mailing lists, direct marketers send out millions of mail pieces each year—letters, catalogs, ads, brochures, samples, videos, and other "salespeople with wings." U.S. marketers spend an estimated $44 billion annually on direct mail (including both catalog and noncatalog mail), which accounts for 12 percent of all marketing spending in the United States.[40]

Direct mail is well suited to direct, one-to-one communication. It permits high target market selectivity, can be personalized, is flexible, and allows the easy measurement of results. Although direct mail costs more per thousand people reached than mass media such as television or magazines, the people it reaches are much better prospects. Direct mail has proved successful in promoting all kinds of products, from books, insurance, travel, gift items, gourmet foods, clothing, and other consumer goods to industrial products of all kinds. Charities also use direct mail heavily to raise billions of dollars each year.

Some analysts have predicted the eventual demise of traditional forms of direct mail in the coming years as marketers switch to newer digital forms, such as email and online, social media, and mobile marketing. The newer digital direct marketing approaches deliver messages at incredible speeds and lower costs compared to the U.S. Post Office's "snail mail" pace.

However, although the volume of traditional direct mail has decreased during the past decade, it is still heavily used by most marketers. Mail marketing offers some distinct advantages over digital forms. It provides something tangible for people to hold and keep, and it can be used to send samples. "Mail makes it real," says one analyst. It "creates an emotional connection with customers that digital cannot. They hold it, view it, and engage with it in a manner entirely different from their [digital] experiences." In contrast, email and other digital forms are easily ignored, filtered, or trashed. With spam filters and ad blockers filtering out email and mobile ads these days, says a direct marketer, "sometimes you have to lick a few stamps."[41]

● **Direct-mail marketing: GEICO uses lots of good old direct mail to break through the glut of insurance advertising clutter.**

All text and images are copywritten with permission from GEICO.

Traditional direct mail can be an effective component of a broader integrated marketing campaign. For example, GEICO relies heavily on TV advertising to establish broad customer awareness and positioning. However, it also uses lots of good old direct mail to break through the glut of insurance advertising clutter on TV. GEICO uses direct mail offers that invite carefully targeted customers act immediately to save money on their auto insurance by visiting geico.com, calling 1-800-947-AUTO, or contacting a local GEICO agent. GEICO makes its direct mailers as unskippable as its TV and digital ads. ● For example, potential customers might receive a personally addressed mail piece with a "save money" message and scannable code on the front of the envelope, inviting them to look inside or simply scan the code with their smartphone. Scanning the code takes them directly to GEICO's mobile site where they receive additional information and calls to action.

Direct mail may be resented as *junk mail* if sent to people who have no interest in it. For this reason, smart marketers are targeting their direct mail carefully so as not to waste their money and recipients' time. They are designing permission-based programs that send direct mail only to those who want to receive it.

Catalog Marketing

Catalog marketing

Direct marketing through print, video, or digital catalogs that are mailed to select customers, made available in stores, or presented online.

Advances in technology, along with the move toward personalized, one-to-one marketing, have resulted in exciting changes in **catalog marketing**. *Catalog Age* magazine used to define a *catalog* as "a printed, bound piece of at least eight pages, selling multiple products, and offering a direct ordering mechanism." That definition has now be revamped to meet changing times.

With the stampede to the internet and digital marketing, more and more catalogs are going digital and mobile. A variety of online-only catalogers have emerged, and most print catalogers have added web-based catalogs and mobile catalog apps to their marketing mixes. For example, catalogs from retailers such as Macy's, Anthropologie, L.L. Bean, Williams-Sonoma, Restoration Hardware, J. Crew, and West Elm are only a finger swipe away on a mobile device.

Digital catalogs eliminate printing and mailing costs. They also allow real-time merchandising. Whereas printed catalogs are frozen in time, digital catalogs let sellers add or remove products and features as needed and adjust prices instantly to match demand. And whereas space is limited in a print catalog, online catalogs can offer an almost unlimited amount of merchandise.

Customers can carry digital catalogs anywhere they go, even when shopping in stores. Digital catalogs can be interactive, and they can offer a broader assortment of presentation formats, including search, video, and augmented reality (AR). For example, IKEA's catalog app contains 3D and AR features that let customers experiment with room designs and colors schemes and even virtually place furniture and other IKEA products in their homes to see how they might look or to share them with others via social media.

Despite the advantages of digital catalogs, however, as your overstuffed mailbox may suggest, printed catalogs are still thriving. U.S. direct marketers mailed out almost 10 billion catalogs last year.[42] Although that's less than half the number mailed out a decade ago, it's still a lot of catalogs.

● Despite the rapid growth of digital catalogs, printed catalogs are still thriving. Somehow, turning actual catalog pages engages consumers in a way that digital images simply can't.

Hadrian/Shutterstock

Beyond their ability to drive immediate sales, paper catalogs create emotional connections with customers. ● Somehow, turning actual catalog pages engages consumers in a way that digital images simply can't. For example, despite IKEA's high-tech digital catalogs, many of its customers would likely revolt if the retailer stopped sending them the annual print version that it's been producing for more than six decades. Most of today's print catalogs are much more than just big books full of product pictures and prices. Anthropologie calls its catalogs "journals" and fills them with lifestyle images. Although the retailer has been expanding its digital marketing, it realizes that "there is something special about holding a beautiful book of imagery in your hands," says an Anthropologie marketer. "Years ago, [a catalog] was a selling tool, and now it's become an inspirational source," says another direct marketer. "We know our customers love a tactile experience."[43]

Importantly, printed catalogs are one of the best ways to drive in-store, online, and mobile sales. For example, furniture retailer Restoration Hardware says that its catalogs, which it calls "source books," are "a key driver of sales through both our websites and retail stores." "I think their catalog is a work of art," says a retail consultant. "It's very, very high end. People end up wanting to see the products [in stores] because of how beautiful they look on the page." Catalogs and online sales together make up 45 percent of Restoration Hardware's revenues. And just as store retailers are turning to digital catalogs, some digital marketers are adding printed catalogs. For example, even oh-so-digital Amazon sent out its first-ever printed catalog before the past holiday season—a holiday toy catalog with QR codes to help customers find items at its online site. Thus, the key to catalog marketing today is to carefully integrate catalogs with online and store marketing efforts.[44]

Telemarketing

Telemarketing
Using the telephone to sell directly to customers.

Telemarketing involves using the telephone to sell directly to consumers and business customers. We're all familiar with telephone marketing directed toward consumers, but business-to-business marketers also use telemarketing extensively. Marketers use *outbound* telephone marketing to sell directly to consumers and businesses. They also use *inbound* toll-free numbers to receive orders referred from television and print ads, direct mail, catalogs, websites, and phone apps.

Properly designed and targeted telemarketing provides many benefits, including purchasing convenience and increased product and service information. However, the explosion in unsolicited outbound telephone marketing over the years annoyed many consumers, who objected to the almost daily "junk phone calls." In 2003, U.S. lawmakers responded with the National Do Not Call Registry, which is managed by the Federal Trade Commission (FTC). The legislation bans most telemarketing calls to registered phone numbers (although people can still receive calls from nonprofit groups, politicians, and companies with which they have recently done business). Consumers responded enthusiastically. To date, more than 235 million home and mobile phone numbers have been registered at www.donotcall.gov or by calling 888-382-1222.[45] Businesses that break do-not-call laws can be fined more than $40,000 per violation. As a result, the program has been very successful.

Despite do-not-call laws, consumers still face an epidemic of illegal spam robocalls for everything from lower credit card interest rates and debt-relief services to auto warranties and home security systems. Last year, U.S. consumers received an estimated 26.3 billion unwanted calls, up 46 percent over the previous year.[46] Such abuses, along with do-not-call laws and the more-prevalent use of caller ID to screen calls, have done substantial damage to the legitimate consumer outbound telemarketing industry.

However, two major forms of telemarketing—inbound consumer telemarketing and outbound B-to-B telemarketing—remain strong and growing. Interestingly, do-not-call regulations appear to be helping some direct marketers more than hurting them. Rather than making unwanted calls, many of these marketers are developing "opt-in" calling systems, in which they provide useful information and offers to customers who have invited the company to contact them by phone or email. The opt-in model provides better returns for marketers than the formerly invasive one.

Direct-Response Television Marketing

Direct-response television (DRTV) marketing

Direct marketing via television that persuasively describes a product and give customers a toll-free number or an online site for ordering.

Using **direct-response television (DRTV) marketing**, direct marketers air television spots, often 60 or 120 seconds in length, which persuasively describe a product and give customers a toll-free number or an online site for ordering. It also includes full 30-minute or longer advertising programs, called *infomercials*, for a single product.

Successful direct-response television advertising campaigns can ring up big sales. For example, little-known infomercial maker Guthy-Renker has helped propel Proactiv acne treatment, Crepe Erase, Meaningful Beauty, and other "transformational" beauty products into multimillion-dollar power brands. Guthy-Renker combines DRTV with social media campaigns using Facebook, Pinterest, Twitter, and YouTube to create a powerful integrated direct marketing channel that builds consumer involvement and buying.

DRTV ads are sometimes associated with somewhat loud or questionable pitches for cleaners, stain removers, kitchen gadgets, and nifty ways to stay in shape without working very hard at it. For example, over the past few years "yell and sell" TV pitchmen like Anthony Sullivan (Swivel Sweeper, Awesome Auger) and Vince Offer (ShamWow, SlapChop) have racked up billions of dollars in sales of "As Seen on TV" products. Brands like OxiClean, ShamWow, and the Snuggie (a blanket with sleeves) have become DRTV cult classics. And direct marketer Beachbody brings in more than $1 billion annually via an army of shakes and workout videos—from P90X and T-25 to Insanity and Hip Hop Abs—that it advertises on TV using before-and-after stories, clips of the workout, and words of encouragement from the creators.[47]

In recent years, however, a number of large companies—from P&G, AT&T, and GEICO to L'Oreal—have used infomercials to sell their wares, refer customers to retailers, recruit members, or attract buyers to their online, mobile, and social media sites. DRTV can also be effective in launching new brands or in building brands that are trying to move beyond digital and social media channels. Many direct-to-consumer brands—such as Peloton, Dollar Shave Club, and Chewy (pet supplies)—have successfully used the power of mass-reach DRTV to fuel rapid growth.[48]

Increasingly, as the lines continue to blur between TV and other screens, direct response ads and infomercials are appearing not just on TV but also on mobile, online, and social media platforms, adding even more TV-like interactive direct marketing venues.

Also, most TV ads these days routinely feature web, mobile, and social media links that let multiscreen consumers connect in real time to obtain and share more information about advertised brands.

Kiosk Marketing

As consumers become more and more comfortable with digital and touchscreen technologies, many companies are placing information and ordering machines—called *kiosks* (good old-fashioned vending machines but so much more)—in stores, airports, hotels, college campuses, and other locations. Kiosks are everywhere these days, from self-service hotel and airline check-in devices, to unmanned product and information kiosks in malls, to in-store ordering devices that let you order merchandise not carried in the store. Many modern "smart kiosks" are now wireless-enabled. And some machines can even use facial recognition software that lets them guess gender and age and make product recommendations based on those data.

In Japan, everything—from flying fish soup and self-freezing bottled Coke to underwear and live puppies—is available via kiosks. Consumers can expand their Lego collections at German train stations, get the latest trainers from London's Carnaby Street, drink freshly ground coffee in the United States, eat hot mashed potatoes in Singapore, and purchase live crabs in subway stations in China, all from kiosks open 24/7. Even gold is available in kiosks; Gold to Go, a company operating ATM machines that dispense gold coins and bars, started in Germany and has now expanded throughout the Middle East.

Retailers can also use kiosks inside their stores to improve the customer shopping experience or assist their salespeople. ● An example is Home Depot's in-store Appliance Finder virtual inventory kiosk. Because appliances are a big purchase, customers often do online research to determine their brand and feature preferences but then come to Home Depot to make the purchase. However, the Home Depot stores can stock only about 5 percent of the appliances available for sale, so customers may browse the store and not find what they want. The Home Depot Appliance Finder kiosk helps such customers find and buy the products they want on the spot. On their own, customers can digitally navigate Home Depot's entire catalog, view informative content including photos and videos, narrow in a product that's right for them, and then pay for and set up delivery of their selection. Sales associates can also use the kiosk as a sales tool. The Home Depot stores featuring the Appliance Finder have seen a 10 to 12 percent increase in appliance sales.[49]

● **Kiosk marketing: The in-store Home Depot Appliance Finder kiosk helps customers find and buy the products they want on the spot. Sales associates can also use the kiosk as a sales tool.**

Image Manufacturing Group

Public Policy Issues in Direct and Digital Marketing

Direct marketers and their customers usually enjoy mutually rewarding relationships. Occasionally, however, a darker side emerges. The aggressive and sometimes shady tactics of a few direct marketers can bother or harm consumers, giving the entire industry a black eye. Abuses range from simple excesses that irritate consumers to instances of unfair practices or even outright deception and fraud. The direct marketing industry has also faced growing privacy concerns, and online marketers must deal with internet and mobile security issues.

Irritation, Unfairness, Deception, and Fraud

Direct marketing excesses sometimes annoy or offend consumers. For example, most of us dislike direct-response TV commercials that are too loud, long, and insistent. Our mailboxes fill up with unwanted junk mail, our email inboxes bulge with unwanted spam, and our computer, phone, and tablet screens flash with unwanted online or mobile display ads, pop-ups, or pop-unders.

Beyond irritating consumers, some direct marketers have been accused of taking unfair advantage of impulsive or less-sophisticated buyers. Television shopping channels, enticing websites, and program-long infomercials targeting television-addicted shoppers seem to be the worst culprits. They feature smooth-talking hosts, elaborately staged demonstrations, claims of drastic price reductions, flash sales, "while they last" time limitations, and unequaled ease of purchase to inflame buyers who have low sales resistance.

Fraudulent schemes, such as investment scams or phony collections for charity, have also multiplied in recent years. *Internet fraud*, including identity theft and financial scams, has become a serious problem. ● According to the Internet Crime Complaint Center, since 2005, internet scam complaints have more than tripled to more than 300,000 per year. Last year, the monetary loss of scam complaints exceeded $1.4 billion.[50]

● **Internet fraud has multiplied in recent years. The FBI's Internet Crime Complaint Center provides consumers with a convenient way to alert authorities to suspected violations.**

FBI

One common form of internet fraud is *phishing*, a type of identity theft that uses deceptive emails and fraudulent web and online mobile sites to fool users into divulging their personal data. For example, consumers may receive an email, supposedly from their bank or credit card company, saying that their account's security has been compromised. The sender asks them to log on to a provided web address and confirm their account number, password, and perhaps even their Social Security number. By following the instructions, users are actually turning this sensitive information over to scam artists. Although most consumers are now aware of such schemes, phishing can be extremely costly to those caught in the net. It also damages the brand identities of legitimate online marketers who have worked to build user confidence in digital interactions.

Many consumers also worry about *online and digital security*. They fear that unscrupulous snoopers will eavesdrop on their online transactions and social media postings, picking up personal or financial information. Although online and mobile shopping are now commonplace, one recent study indicated that more than 70 percent of participants were still concerned about identity theft. Such concerns are often justified in this age of massive consumer data breaches by organizations ranging from retailers, social media, telecommunications services, and banks to health-care providers and the government. According to one source, there were more than 1,200 major data security breaches in the United States last year alone.[51]

Another internet marketing concern is that of *access by vulnerable or unauthorized groups*. For example, marketers of adult-oriented materials and sites have found it difficult to restrict access by minors. Although Facebook, Twitter, Instagram, and other social networks allow no children under age 13 to have profiles, all have significant numbers of underage users. Young social media users can be especially vulnerable to identity theft schemes, revealing personal information, negative experiences, and other online dangers. Concerned state and national lawmakers are currently debating bills that would help better protect children online. Unfortunately, this requires the development of technology solutions, and as Facebook puts it, "That's not so easy."[52]

Consumer Privacy

Invasion of privacy is perhaps the toughest public policy issue now confronting the direct marketing industry. Consumers often benefit from database marketing; they receive more offers that are closely matched to their interests. However, many critics worry that marketers know *too* much about consumers' lives and that they may use this knowledge to take unfair advantage of consumers. At some point, they claim, the extensive use of databases intrudes on consumer privacy. Consumers, too, worry about their privacy. Although they are now much more willing to share personal information and preferences with marketers via digital and social media, they are still nervous about it. One recent survey found that 77 percent of U.S. consumers are very concerned about data privacy. Another found that 68 percent of Americans think government should do more to protect data privacy.[53]

In these days of "big data," it seems that almost every time consumers post something on social media or send a tweet, visit a website, enter a sweepstakes, apply for a credit card, or order products by phone or online, their names, profiles, and behaviors are entered into some company's already bulging database. Using sophisticated big data analytics, direct marketers can mine these databases to "microtarget" their selling efforts. For example, using mobile phone usage data supplied by mobile operators, SAP's Consumer Insight 365 unit gleans and sells customer insights from up to 300 mobile call, web surfing, and text messaging events per day for each of 20 million to 25 million mobile subscribers.[54]

Most marketers have become highly skilled at collecting and analyzing detailed consumer information both online and offline. Even the experts are sometimes surprised by how much marketers can learn. For example, got a Google account? Consider what Google alone likely knows about you:[55]

> Google knows everything you've ever searched, across all your devices. It knows where you've been—it stores your location every time you turn on your phone. It knows what apps you use, when, and how often. And it stores your YouTube history, from which it can likely glean your family status, religion, favorite sports, political leanings, and the fact, say, that you recently sought instructions on fixing your dishwasher. Google creates an advertising profile of you based on things like your location, age, gender, interests, career, income, and a host of other variables.
>
> Google lets you download all the data it stores about you at google.com/takeout; one reporter was stunned to learn that his download file was 5.5GB big (roughly 3 million Word documents). "This link includes your bookmarks, emails, contacts, your Google Drive files, your YouTube videos, the photos you've taken on your phone, the businesses you've bought from, [and] the products you've bought through Google," says the reporter. Google also has "data from your calendar, your Google hangout sessions, your location history, the music you listen to, the Google books you've purchased, the Google groups you're in, the websites you've created, the phones you've owned, the pages you've shared, how many steps you walk in a day…" He concludes, "Manage to gain access to someone's Google account? Perfect, you have a diary of everything that person has done."

Facebook, which has been breached often in the past few year, can construct similar profiles. And then there's Amazon and most other sellers who track details of consumer online browsing and purchase transactions. Add the data held by credit reporting agencies such as Equifax, also recently breached, and the potential for consumer abuse can be frightening.

A Need for Action

To curb direct marketing excesses, various government agencies are investigating not only do-not-call lists but also do-not-mail lists, do-not-track-online lists, and can-spam legislation. In response to online privacy and security concerns, the federal government has considered numerous legislative actions to regulate how online, social media, and mobile operators obtain and use consumer information. The European Union recently passed a tough new privacy law—the General Data Protection Regulation (GDPR)—designed to protect the privacy rights of Europeans in this age of big data. The GDPR sets strict requirements for collecting and protecting personal information about people who live in the European Union and gives European consumers more control over what is collected and how it is used. Many American lawmakers and consumer privacy advocates are calling for similar legislation in the United States.[56] In addition, the FTC is taking a more active role in policing online privacy.

All of these concerns call for strong actions by marketers to monitor and prevent privacy abuses before legislators step in to do it for them. For example, to head off increased government regulation, six advertiser groups—the American Association of Advertising Agencies, the American Advertising Federation, the Association of National Advertisers, the Data & Marketing Association, the Interactive Advertising Bureau, and the Network Advertising Initiative—issued a set of online advertising principles through the Digital Advertising Alliance. Among other measures, the self-regulatory principles call for online and mobile marketers to provide transparency and choice to consumers if online data are collected or used for targeting interest-based advertising.

The ad industry uses an *advertising option icon*—a little "i" inside a triangle—that it adds to behaviorally targeted online ads to tell consumers why they are seeing a particular ad and allowing them to opt out.

Of special concern are the privacy rights of children. In 1998, Congress passed the Children's Online Privacy Protection Act (COPPA), which requires online operators targeting children to post privacy policies on their sites. They must also notify parents about any information they're gathering and obtain parental consent before collecting personal information from children under age 13. With the subsequent advent of online social media, mobile phones, and other digital technologies, Congress in 2013 extended COPPA to include "identifiers such as cookies that track a child's activity online, as well as geolocation information, photos, videos, and audio recordings." The main concern is the amount of data mined by third parties from social media as well as social media's own hazy privacy policies.[57]

Many companies have responded to consumer privacy and security concerns with actions of their own. Still others are taking an industry-wide approach. For example, TrustArc, a nonprofit self-regulatory organization, works with many large corporate sponsors, including Microsoft, Yahoo!, AT&T, Facebook, Disney, and Apple, to audit privacy and security measures and help consumers navigate the internet safely. To reassure consumers, the company lends its TRUSTe privacy seal to websites, mobile apps, email marketing, and other online and social media channels that meet its privacy and security standards.[58]

Direct marketers know that, if left untended, direct marketing abuses will lead to increasingly negative consumer attitudes, lower response and engagement rates, and calls for more restrictive state and federal legislation. Most direct marketers want the same things that consumers want: honest and well-designed marketing offers targeted only toward consumers who will appreciate and respond to them. Direct marketing is just too expensive to waste on consumers who don't want it.

Reviewing and Extending the Concepts

Objectives Review

This chapter is the last of four chapters covering the final marketing mix element—promotion. The previous chapters dealt with integrated marketing communications, advertising, public relations, personal selling, and sales promotion. This one investigates the burgeoning field of direct and digital marketing, including online, social media, and mobile marketing.

OBJECTIVE 17-1 Define *direct and digital marketing* and discuss their rapid growth and benefits to customers and companies. (pp 494–497)

Direct and digital marketing involve engaging directly with carefully targeted individual consumers and customer communities to both obtain an immediate response and build lasting customer relationships. Companies use direct marketing to tailor their offers and content to the needs and interests of narrowly defined segments or individual buyers to build direct customer engagement, brand community, and sales. Today, spurred by the surge in internet usage and buying and by rapid advances in digital technologies—from smartphones, tablets, and other digital devices to the spate of online social and mobile media—direct marketing has undergone a dramatic transformation.

For buyers, direct and digital marketing are convenient, easy to use, and private. They give buyers anywhere, anytime access to an almost unlimited assortment of products and buying information. Direct marketing is also immediate and interactive, allowing buyers to create exactly the configuration of information, products, or services they desire and then order them on the spot. Finally, for consumers who want it, digital marketing through online, mobile, and social media provides a sense of brand engagement and community—a place to share brand information and experiences with other brand fans. For sellers, direct and digital marketing are powerful tools for building customer engagement and close, personalized, interactive customer relationships. They also offer greater flexibility, letting marketers make ongoing adjustments to prices and programs or make immediate, timely, and personal announcements and offers.

OBJECTIVE 17-2 Identify and discuss the major forms of direct and digital marketing. (p 497)

The main forms of direct and digital marketing include traditional direct marketing tools and the more recent digital marketing tools. Traditional direct approaches are face-to-face personal selling, direct-mail marketing, catalog marketing, telemarketing, direct response TV marketing, and kiosk marketing. These traditional tools are still heavily used and very important in most firms' direct marketing efforts. In recent years, however, direct digital marketing tools have burst onto the marketing scene, including online marketing (websites, online ads and promotions, email, online videos, and blogs), social media marketing, and mobile marketing. The chapter first discusses the fast-growing digital direct marketing tools and then examines the traditional tools.

OBJECTIVE 17-3 Explain how companies have responded to the digital age with various online marketing strategies. (pp 498–503)

The digital age has fundamentally changed customers' notions of convenience, speed, price, product information, service, and brand interactions. As a result, they have given marketers a whole new way to create customer value, engage customers, and build customer relationships. The internet now influences a large proportion of total sales—including sales transacted online plus those made in stores but encouraged by online research. To reach this burgeoning market, most companies now market heavily online.

Online marketing takes several forms, including company websites, online advertising and promotions, email marketing, online video, and blogs. Social media and mobile marketing also take place online. But because of their special characteristics, we discuss these fast-growing digital marketing approaches in separate sections. For most companies, the first step in conducting online marketing is to create a website. The key to a successful website is to create enough value and engagement to get consumers to come to the site, stick around, and come back again.

Online advertising has become a major promotional medium. The main forms of online advertising are display ads and search-related ads. Email marketing is also an important form of digital marketing. Used properly, email lets marketers send highly targeted, tightly personalized, relationship-building messages. Another important form of online marketing is posting digital video content on brand websites or social media. Marketers hope that some of their videos will go viral, engaging consumers by the tens of millions. Finally, companies can use blogs as effective means of reaching customer communities. They can create their own blogs and advertise on existing blogs or influence content there.

OBJECTIVE 17-4 Discuss how companies use social media and mobile marketing to engage consumers and create brand community. (pp 503–510)

Countless independent and commercial social media have arisen that give consumers online places to congregate, socialize, and exchange views and information. Most marketers are now riding this huge social media wave. Brands can use existing social media or they can set up their own. Using existing social media seems the easiest. Thus, most brands—large and small—have set up shop on a host of social media sites. Some of the major social networks are huge; other niche social media cater to the needs of smaller communities of like-minded people. Beyond these independent social media, many companies have created their own online brand communities. More than making just scattered efforts and chasing Likes and tweets, most companies are integrating a broad range of diverse media to create brand-related social sharing, engagement, and customer community.

Using social media presents both advantages and challenges. On the plus side, social media are targeted and personal, interactive, immediate and timely, and cost-effective. Perhaps the biggest advantage is their engagement and social sharing capabilities, making them ideal for creating customer community. On the down side, consumers' control over social media content makes social media difficult to control.

Mobile marketing features marketing messages, promotions, and other content delivered to on-the-go consumers through their mobile devices. Marketers use mobile marketing to engage customers anywhere, anytime during the buying and relationship-building processes. The widespread adoption of mobile devices and the surge in mobile web traffic have made mobile marketing a must for most brands, and almost every major marketer is now integrating mobile marketing into its direct marketing programs. Many marketers have created their own mobile online sites. Others have created useful or entertaining mobile apps to engage customers with their brands and help them shop.

OBJECTIVE 17-5 Identify and discuss the traditional direct marketing forms and overview public policy and ethical issues presented by direct marketing. *(pp 510–517)*

Although the fast-growing digital marketing tools have grabbed most of the headlines lately, traditional direct marketing tools are very much alive and still heavily used. The major forms are face-to-face or personal selling, direct-mail marketing, catalog marketing, telemarketing, direct-response television (DRTV) marketing, and kiosk marketing.

Direct-mail marketing consists of the company sending an offer, announcement, reminder, or other item to a person at a specific address. Some marketers rely on catalog marketing—selling through catalogs mailed to a select list of customers, made available in stores, or accessed online. Telemarketing consists of using the telephone to sell directly to consumers. DRTV marketing involves television advertising that persuasively describes a product and gives customers a toll-free number or an online site for ordering. Kiosks are information and ordering machines that direct marketers place in stores, airports, hotels, and other locations.

Direct marketers and their customers usually enjoy mutually rewarding relationships. Sometimes, however, direct marketing presents a darker side. The aggressive and sometimes shady tactics of a few direct marketers can bother or harm consumers, giving the entire industry a black eye. Abuses range from simple excesses that irritate consumers to instances of unfair practices or even outright deception and fraud. The direct marketing industry has also faced growing concerns about invasion-of-privacy and internet security issues. Such concerns call for strong action by marketers and public policy makers to curb direct marketing abuses. In the end, most direct marketers want the same things that consumers want: honest and well-designed marketing offers targeted only toward consumers who will appreciate and respond to them.

Key Terms

OBJECTIVE 17-1
Direct and digital marketing (p 494)
Direct-to-consumer (DTC) brands (p 496)

OBJECTIVE 17-2
Digital and social media marketing (p 497)

OBJECTIVE 17-3
Omni-channel retailing (p 498)

Online marketing (p 499)
Marketing website (p 499)
Branded community website (p 499)
Online advertising (p 500)
Email marketing (p 501)
Spam (p 501)
Viral marketing (p 502)
Blogs (p 502)

OBJECTIVE 17-4
Social media (p 503)

Mobile marketing (p 508)

OBJECTIVE 17-5
Direct-mail marketing (p 511)
Catalog marketing (p 511)
Telemarketing (p 512)
Direct-response television (DRTV) marketing (p 513)

Discussion Questions

17-1 Compare and contrast the new direct marketing model with the traditional direct marketing model. (AACSB: Written and Oral Communication)

17-2 What are the main purposes of a marketing website? (AACSB: Communication)

17-3 How does viral marketing work? Is it effective? Are there aspects of it that make it uncontrollable by a business? (AACSB: Communication)

17-4 With a dominant Internet presence, is there still a place for catalog marketing? (AACSB: Communication)

17-5 Discuss how the traditional forms of direct marketing continue to be important promotion tools. (AACSB: Written and Oral Communication)

17-6 How does the General Data Protections Regulation (GDPR) act affect data collection and protection? (AACSB: Written and Oral Communication)

Critical Thinking Exercises

17-7 In a small group, search the internet to locate a controversial or failed social media campaign. Present an analysis of the failed campaign. Make a recommendation on how to address the controversy. (AACSB: Information Technology; Written and Oral Communication; Reflective Thinking)

17-8 Taco Bell uses social media to engage consumers around marketing stunts targeting its millennial and Gen Z segments. For example, it has hosted Airbnb sleepovers in its restaurants and once erected a billboard that dispensed hot nacho cheese. Recently, Taco Bell created a slide-thru window through which 125 snow-tubers and Taco Bell fans bused to a resort outside Toronto could reach out and grab a Cheetos Crunchwrap Slider in a to-go bag as they tubed past. The goal was to generate social media engagement that would raise awareness of the return of the Cheetos Crunchwrap Slider. Fans ordered their food at the top of the hill. The food was prepared in a kitchen and taken to the booth below by snowmobile. The snow tubers were then given a Taco Bell–branded tube to slide by and grab their food before heading to the lounge to enjoy the meal. How can Taco Bell's marketers evaluate the success of this promotion event? (AACSB: Written and Oral Communication; Information Technology; Reflective Thinking)

17-9 Thanks to the Internet of Things, marketers can now add value to the shopping experience by using digital displays. They can use the displays to gather data about consumers, send advertising messages to their mobile phones as they pass, and use their mobile phones or facial recognition to personalize the marketing messages that appear on the displays. However, in response to technology advancements and heighted sensitivity to privacy, several policies have been introduced to limit the collection and resharing of data. Is it a wise strategy for retailers to use digital displays to market directly to consumers? Why or why not? (AACSB: Written and Oral Communication; Information Technology; Reflective Thinking)

APPLICATIONS AND CASES

Online, Mobile, and Social Media Marketing On the Move

According to Google's Consumer Barometer, an interactive digital consumer insights tool, some 35 percent of UAE and Saudi Arabian under-35s go online using either smartphones or tablets. The 2016 data suggests that 30 percent of UAE residents preferred mobile devices compared to traditional desktops; in Saudi Arabia, this was 32 percent. In both countries, over 70 percent of smartphone owners preferred to carry out tasks, including product searches and purchases, using their smartphones. Despite some continued reluctance over online security and product quality, 24 percent of the population of the United Arab Emirates have recently made a purchase online. In Saudi Arabia, this figure was 33 percent. Consumers in both countries use mobile Internet connections to search for information and reviews of local businesses in addition to making enquiries and purchases abroad. In the United Arab Emirates, 54 percent of users searched for prices of local products online, in Saudi Arabia this was lower, at 45 percent. It does mean that local as well as international businesses have potential opportunities in the United Arab Emirates and Saudi Arabia. Typically, consumers were interested in contact information, location, and business hours. For businesses, there are encouraging signs in the younger generations. Some 85 percent of under-25s in Saudi Arabia researched a recent purchase using their smartphone. In the United Arab Emirates, this figure was 57 percent but showed all signs of future growth.

17-10 What local businesses in your community are using online, social media, or mobile marketing? Interview the owner or manager of one of these businesses to learn how they use these marketing activities and how satisfied they are with the activities. (AACSB: Communication; Reflective Thinking)

17-11 Mobile marketing can be confusing for a small business owner. Develop a presentation for small business owners that describes mobile marketing, its advantages and disadvantages, and examples of how small businesses are using mobile marketing. (AACSB: Communication; Reflective Thinking)

Marketing Ethics Home Hub Paranoia

Home hubs that contain voice technologies and microphones, such as Amazon's Echo with Alexa and Google's Nest Hub with Google Assistant, are popular devices that continuously listen in for commands. Many consumers like the convenience that comes with the home hubs but worry about their privacy. In response, people often place the devices in common areas but not in bedrooms or other more private areas. Wherever the devices are located, marketers could conceivably use them to collect information that could be used to microtarget selling efforts to consumers. This possibility along with recent revelations about other devices, such as the unadvertised, on-device microphone included in Amazon's Nest Guard that lets Amazon collect information in order to provide future features and reports of Amazon employees listening in on Alexa conversations, have made some consumers paranoid about who is listening.

17-12 How should companies that offer home hubs address consumer concerns about privacy violations? (AACSB: Written and Oral Communication; Reflective Thinking)

17-13 Is it ethical for marketers to gather and use data from inside the home to improve the value proposition to consumers? Explain. (AACSB: Written and Oral Communication; Information Technology; Reflective Thinking)

Marketing by the Numbers Uniqlo's Digital Marketing Campaigns

Uniqlo is a Japanese retail brand that has grown into a global brand in 15 countries thanks to digital marketing campaigns. Founder Tadashi Yamai inherited a chain of men's tailoring retail stores, so he was no stranger to fashion retailing. But he wanted to bring affordable, fashionable, casual clothing to all people, so he created Uniqlo in 1984 to offer casual clothing for all. The philosophy of the brand is "UNIQLO clothes are MADE FOR ALL." The company focuses on its signature innovative clothing lines that have names like HeatTech, UV Cut, LifeWear, and AIRism. In 2007, its pioneering "Uniqlock" viral marketing campaign won dozens of advertising awards, including the coveted Grand Prix award at Cannes. The company continues to run digital marketing campaigns, and while awards are nice, results are better. Marketers measure all sorts of metrics related to digital campaigns, from impressions and click-throughs to purchases.

Consider one of its most recent digital campaigns running in the United States to increase brand awareness and sales of its LifeWear line of clothing:

Measures	Value
Impressions	4,000,000
Click-through to site	150,000
Cost of campaign	$45,000
Number of orders	10,250
Revenue generated	$750,000
Abandoned shopping cart	650
Average cost of goods sold (%)	45%
Shipping and handling costs (per order)	$8.50

Performance Metric	Equation
Click-through rate (CTR)	(Click-throughs ÷ Impressions) × 100
Cost-per-click (CPC)	Cost of campaign ÷ Click-throughs
Conversion ratio	(Number of orders ÷ Click-throughs) × 100
Cost per conversion	Cost of campaign ÷ Number of orders
Average-order-value (AOV)	Revenue generated ÷ Number of orders
Shopping cart abandonment rate	(Abandoned shopping cart ÷ Click-throughs) × 100

17-14 Calculate the performance metrics listed in the preceding table. Based on these metrics, evaluate the campaign. (AACSB: Communication; Analytic Reasoning; Reflective Thinking)

17-15 Calculate the net marketing contribution (NMC), marketing return on sales marketing ROS), and marketing return on investment (marketing ROI). Was the campaign successful? Refer to Marketing Profitability Metrics in Appendix 2: Marketing by the Numbers to learn how to do this analysis. (AACSB: Communication; Reflective Thinking; Analytic Reasoning)

Company Case OfferUp: A Mobile Solution for the Mobile Era

When people think of buying and selling things online locally, most think automatically of Craigslist, the classified ad marketplace that has dominated that business for the past two decades. But as the rest of the world has gone mobile, Craigslist has not. In fact, the familiar but cluttered collection of blue hyperlinks has changed very little over the years. Some critics suggest that Craigslist has taken its monopoly for granted. One industry observer refers to Craigslist as "the cockroach of the internet age—an ugly but effective e-commerce platform that...emerged unscathed from technology shifts that crippled mightier contemporaries like Netscape and Yahoo."

In the new landscape of digital disruption, one thing seems certain: What dominates today could be under threat tomorrow. That tomorrow may already be here for Craigslist as numerous, more user-friendly competitors have emerged to challenge the classified ad champ. Enter OfferUp—a relatively new mobile app for buying and selling items that is taking the digital marketplace by storm. OfferUp is not only challenging Craigslist as the go-to platform by which individuals and businesses sell goods and services in local markets, it's also starting to challenge the likes

of eBay and even Amazon by flexing its muscles beyond local market boundaries. Unexpectedly, OfferUp now rivals the most popular social media apps in terms of time spent by users.

About a decade ago, as the mobile device revolution began to explode, Seattle resident Nick Huzar was frustrated as he tried to unload unwanted household items in preparation for his soon-to-be-born daughter's nursery. He didn't have time to post all these items on Craigslist, which required multiple steps that pretty much required a desktop or laptop to complete. Instead, he went to Goodwill, where he always found a line to drop donations. With a smartphone in his hand, he recognized the potential for an online marketplace that made posting, monitoring, and browsing items for sale in a local market as simple as social media interactions. That led to a partnership with friend Arean van Veelen and the ultimate launch of OfferUp in 2011.

A Different Kind of Marketplace

The main thing that differentiates OfferUp from Craigslist and other traditional online marketplace platforms is that it's designed exclusively for mobile channels. For sellers, that means that posting an item is as simple as posting a photo to Facebook—point, shoot, add a description, and click. Each local ad defaults to a 30-mile radius, and standard ads are free. OfferUp's goal is to have the process take no more than 30 seconds. For sellers, it's painless with little risk.

For shoppers, the interface is also very appealing, with a Pinterest-like vibe that is primarily visual. The bottomless scroll entices users, luring them in to a virtual treasure hunt. People typically access the OfferUp app looking for one thing but discover a trove of unexpected goodies. This element of surprise has users spending an average of 25 minutes a day on OfferUp, the same as Snapchat and Instagram. "It's not like Amazon where it's very intent-based—where you know what you want," says Huzar. "OfferUp is more discovery-based. You go in there and you kind of look around and you find that thing you didn't think you wanted that you end up buying."

Beyond the Pinterest-like feel, OfferUp also boasts the strong sense of community that is normally reserved for dedicated social media sites. Core to its mission, OfferUp aims to "connect people and empower them to live locally." The foundation of this community is trust and reputation. Take the user profile and rating system for example. Users are not random, anonymous users but *community* members. A user can create a profile and upload a photo. What's more, users can take it a step further and apply for TruYou verification, submitting a mobile phone number, a picture, and a state-issued ID. Once verified, a Trubadge is displayed as part of the user's profile.

Beyond TruYou, a user's status can be enhanced through various achievements—positive reviews, average response time, and trusted connections, to name a few. Users can also personalize their background images and profile descriptions, just as they can on social media sites. And when it comes to communicating, OfferUp includes a chat-like message function that lets users communicate with each other without revealing personal contact information. If that isn't enough, OfferUp facilitates Community MeetUp Spots for users to make their exchanges. Partnering with local businesses and police forces, OfferUp's more than 1,900 Community MeetUp Spots provide well-lit, video-monitored places that are safe for buyers and sellers to make exchanges—a stark contrast to Craigslist's traditional and laissez-faire approach.

All this does more than just help people feel connected or even develop social networks within OfferUp. It eliminates some of Craiglist's biggest security issues. For starters, because phone numbers and email addresses are typically shared on Craigslist, users are commonly targeted by scam artists. What's more, meeting someone in person for a transaction has led to robberies, assaults, and even murders. That's right. Dozens of people have suffered death at the hands of the person they were meeting to conduct a Craigslist transaction.

During its first five years, OfferUp focused on building its user base while putting little effort into generating revenue, a typical strategy for online marketplaces. In fact, with 18

million downloads and fifth-year transactions totaling more than $14 billion, OfferUp hadn't made a dime for itself. With very little marketing expense and a growth rate that exceeded Craigslist and eBay in their early years, OfferUp was able to raise money through investors—first in the tens of millions of dollars and then in the hundreds of millions.

From Mobile App to Mobile Marketer

But OfferUp eventually began addressing the issue of how to make money off all those users and transactions. Like Craigslist, OfferUp developed naturally as a platform for consumer-to-consumer transactions as well as business-to-consumer and even business-to-business transactions. Although there were various options for starting a revenue stream, OfferUp first focused on businesses. For starters, it designed two optional premium features to facilitate targeting customers—"Bump" and "Feature." With Bump, a seller can put an item at the top of browsing and search results for new items. Feature, on the other hand, allows sellers to promote items and makes them appear in special promotional spots within the top 50 search, browse, and category results. Both of these features can be purchased for runs of 3, 7, or 14 days. While these features appeal primarily to business sellers, they can be selected by anyone.

Not one to rest on its momentum, OfferUp made two big moves to increase its value to national brands and to increase the company's income base. First, it introduced paid advertising. Marketers can now target specific users based on their network, browsing, and posting activities. So when a user searches for a home theater system among the local offerings by individuals and businesses, for example, that shopper will likely see ads for relevant offerings by online retailers such as eBay, Amazon, and Walmart as well as by marketers such as Sony or Samsung that sell their products directly.

To complement paid advertising, OfferUp expanded its marketplace beyond local boundaries by adding a shipping option. When an item is sold through this new nationwide shipping feature, the seller is charged a 7.9 percent fee—lower than eBay or Amazon. The buyer pays between $5 and $20 for shipping, depending on the size of the product. This new transaction fee offers far more value to companies and brands of all sizes and locations while also increasing the utility of the platform for shoppers. For OfferUp, advertising and transaction fees represent substantial new revenue streams over the paid tools for promoting items for sale.

OfferUp's strategies appear to be working. It now boasts over 40 million downloads. And while Craigslist still grabs a huge audience, its traffic has been on the decline. That isn't entirely due to OfferUp. There are at least a dozen other viable rivals, not the least of which is LetGo—the similar mobile marketplace that is doing just about as much business as OfferUp in the United States. And while OfferUp plans to eventually take its app international, LetGo is already doing business in multiple countries. LetGo has also raised nearly double the amount of venture capital as OfferUp and is spending aggressively on advertising, whereas OfferUp has relied more on word-of-mouth. In addition to LetGo and other dedicated marketplace apps, Facebook Marketplace has rapidly increased its presence as an avenue for local buying and selling. And based on its size, Facebook needs only to engage a fraction of its user base to make a large dent in the market.

Although Huzar recognizes the competition posed by LetGo, Facebook, Craigslist, and others, he has a different perspective than most. He doesn't view the business of online marketplaces—whether local, national, or global—as a zero-sum game. In his view, OfferUp doesn't need to take business from Craigslist in order to thrive. Instead, along with LetGo and other entrants, OfferUp needs to attract a new generation of mobile device users that never even considered Craigslist as a shopping or selling platform.

Huzar may be right. It's nearly impossible to calculate the sales volume that flows through Craigslist—the company leaves all money-changing to the buyers and sellers. But OfferUp and LetGo combined last year for an estimated $40 billion worth of goods and services sales in the United States. Compare that to eBay's total global volume of $95 billion or even Amazon's North American e-commerce sales of approximately $125 billion. The new entrants are having a substantial impact.

Ultimately, although OfferUp faces some stiff challenges ahead, its future looks bright. With its focus on an easy-to-use interface made for today's mobile users as well as a growing and safe community, OfferUp will continue disrupt the world of digital marketplaces. Huzar takes the challenges seriously but tries not to let it bother him too much. "I don't lose much sleep at night over it," referring to the competition. Indeed, Huzar is counting on OfferUp being around in a decade when it's time to buy his daughter her first car.[59]

Questions for Discussion

17-16 As a mobile marketplace, how does OfferUp provide value to shoppers? Sellers?

17-17 Analyze OfferUp's business model relative to the different forms of digital and online marketing covered in this chapter.

17-18 Describe the value of OfferUp to national brands and retailers as a channel for mobile marketing. Does OfferUp also pose a threat to these companies?

17-19 Compare the competitive relationship between OfferUp and LetGo with that of Uber and Lyft. Based on this comparison, what does the future hold for OfferUp?

17-20 Do you agree with Nick Huzar that OfferUp can succeed without taking business away from Craigslist? Explain.

18 | Creating Competitive Advantage

OBJECTIVES OUTLINE

OBJECTIVE 18-1 Discuss the need to understand competitors as well as customers through competitor analysis. **See: Competitor Analysis** *(pp 526–533)*

OBJECTIVE 18-2 Explain the fundamentals of competitive marketing strategies based on creating value for customers. **See: Competitive Strategies** *(pp 533–543)*

OBJECTIVE 18-3 Illustrate the need for balancing customer and competitor orientations in becoming a truly market-centered organization. **See: Balancing Customer and Competitor Orientations** *(pp 543–544)*

CHAPTER PREVIEW In previous chapters, you explored the basics of marketing. You learned that the aim of marketing is to engage customers and to create value *for* them in order to capture value *from* them in return. Good marketing companies win, keep, and grow customers by understanding customer needs, designing customer value–driven marketing strategies, constructing value-delivering marketing programs, engaging customers, and building customer and marketing partner relationships. In the final three chapters, we'll extend this concept to three special areas: creating competitive advantage, global marketing, and social and environmental marketing sustainability.

To start, let's look at the competitive marketing strategy of Nordstrom, the upscale department store retailer known for creating unparalleled customer experiences. To its core, Nordstrom practices a "customer intimacy" strategy—pampering customers to keep them coming back (more on this competitive strategy later in the chapter). From its very beginnings as a Seattle shoe store nearly 120 years ago, Nordstrom has been obsessed with "Taking care of customers no matter what it takes."

NORDSTROM: Taking Care of Customers No Matter What It Takes

Nordstrom is legendary for outstanding customer service. The upscale department store chain thrives on stories about its service heroics, such as employees dropping off orders at customers' homes or warming up their cars on a cold day while customers spend a little more time shopping. Then there's the one about the Nordstrom employee who split pairs of shoes in order to fit a man with different-sized feet or the sales clerk who ironed a new shirt for a customer who needed it for a meeting that afternoon. In another case, a man reportedly walked into Nordstrom to return a set of tires that he insisted he'd bought there. Nordstrom doesn't sell tires. But without hesitation, even though his receipt clearly indicated a different store, the Nordstrom clerk refunded the man's money out of her own pocket. Later, on her lunch hour, she took the tires and receipt to the store where they'd been purchased and got her money back.

Whether factual or fictional, such stories are rooted in actual customer experiences at Nordstrom. It seems that almost everyone who shops regularly at Nordstrom has a favorite story to tell. As one journalist noted after seeing the chain near the top of yet another Customer Service Hall of Fame list, "It almost gets old: Nordstrom and its legendarily good customer service." But such stories never get old at Nordstrom. "Nordstrom just goes above and beyond in a way that customers never forget," says a retailing expert.

Superb customer service is deeply rooted in the nearly 120-year-old Nordstrom's DNA, as summarized in its staunchly held mantra: Take care of customers no matter what it takes. Although many companies pay homage to similar pronouncements hidden away in their mission statements, Nordstrom really means it—and really makes it happen. Consider these customer delight–inducing stories:

- One man tells a story about his wife, a loyal Nordstrom customer, who died with $1,000 owing on her Nordstrom account. Not only did Nordstrom settle the account, it also sent flowers to the funeral.

- A woman had been shopping with her daughter at San Diego's ritzy Horton Plaza. After browsing in Nordstrom for a while and believing nobody was around, she said with an exhausted sigh, as if thinking out loud to herself, "I could sure use a Dr Pepper." Sure enough, within only a few short minutes, a Nordstrom employee appeared out of nowhere with an ice-cold can of Dr Pepper.

- One late November, a woman buying a sweater as a Christmas present for her husband found just the one she wanted at Nordstrom, but not in the right color or size. No worries, said the Nordstrom manager. He'd find her one in plenty of time for the holidays. A week before Christmas, just as the woman was beginning to worry, the manager called ahead and personally delivered the sweater to her home, already beautifully gift-wrapped. That's amazing enough, but here's the back story: The manager hadn't been able to find the right sweater after all. But while discussing the problem with his wife, he learned that she'd already bought that very sweater for *him* for Christmas and that it was already wrapped and under their tree. The manager and his wife quickly agreed to pass his sweater along to the customer.

How does Nordstrom consistently exceed customer expectations? For starters, it hires people who truly enjoy serving other people. Then it trains them thoroughly on the intricacies of providing customer care and turns them loose. Nordstrom trusts its employees to make the right judgments without bogging them down with procedures and policies. The famous Nordstrom employee "handbook" consists of a single two-sided card containing only 74 words, among them: "Our one rule: Use good judgment in all situations. There will be no additional rules." As a result, at Nordstrom, customer service doesn't come across as sales clerks reciting rehearsed scripts. Rather, it's about Nordstrom people genuinely connecting with and serving customers. "What it boils down to is we give employees complete freedom to take care of the customer," says a Nordstrom executive. "And we

A competitive marketing strategy of "Taking care of customers no matter what it takes" is deeply rooted in Nordstrom's DNA. "We have only one rule: Use good judgment in all situations."

Michael Gordon/Shutterstock

say, if you're going to make a mistake, let's make sure you make it in the customer's favor."

To motivate its employees even more, Nordstrom collects and recycles stories of customer service heroics. Every Nordstrom register supplies pens and paper with which customers can share their good experiences. Every morning, in the main lobby of each store, managers share some of the best customer stories from the previous day and reward the employees involved for their good deeds. In turn, the feel-good stories inspire everyone in the store to continue the cycle of pampering customers and making them feel special.

Founded in 1901 by Swedish immigrant John W. Nordstrom, the company is now run by the fourth generation of Nordstroms—brothers Pete and Erik (co-presidents)—in a way that would make their great-great-grandfather proud. This latest generation of leadership has given Nordstrom's ageless philosophy a dose of modern technology. For example, they completely restructured the chain's entire purchasing and inventory management system, making it easier for tablet-toting front-line employees to quickly find and obtain items that customers want. When the system went live, sales immediately surged. But more important, customer service improved dramatically.

Nordstrom is also blurring the line between the digital world and its brick-and-mortar stores. For example, shoppers can buy items they see on Instagram or Pinterest with just a couple of taps on their smartphones. The Nordstrom TextStyle app even lets customers chat with associates and stylists, get product recommendations, and purchase items on the go. And Nordstrom has invested heavily in its own online shopping platforms, updating its web and mobile sites, and offering faster delivery. Thirty

> Nordstrom's legendary customer service gives it a strong competitive advantage. The upscale retailer is obsessed with "Taking care of customers no matter what it takes."

percent of Nordstrom's sales are now digital. The chain's innovative use of customer data helps it understand customers better and provide even more personalized omni-channel experiences. "Our goal is to build a seamless 'One Nordstrom' customer experience ... no matter how they choose to shop," says Nordstrom. Each contact—in-store or online—"represents an opportunity for us to connect with customers on their terms, which means an experience that is increasingly relevant, convenient, and personalized."

Creating customer delight has been good for Nordstrom's top and bottom lines over the years. During just the past five years, despite the depths of the retail apocalypse that threw numerous major retailers into bankruptcy, Nordstrom's sales have grown more than 27 percent to a record $15.5 billion. And whereas many rival department stores have grown little or not at all, Nordstrom has continued to gain market share with 10 straight years of growth.

As Erik Nordstrom shared these and other good tidings with shareholders at a Nordstrom annual meeting, he also shared yet another story of customer delight. He told of a woman in North Carolina who recently lost the diamond from her wedding ring while trying on clothes at a Nordstrom store. A store security worker saw her crawling on the sales floor under the racks and joined the search. When they came up empty, the security employee enlisted the help of two building-services workers, who vacuumed the area and then opened the vacuum cleaner bags and painstakingly searched the contents, where they recovered the sparkling gem.

After showing a video clip featuring the delighted shopper, to thunderous applause, Erik Nordstrom introduced the three employees to the shareholders. Extending his hand to the three, Nordstrom proclaimed that when it comes to taking care of customers no matter what it takes, "this raises the bar."[1]

TODAY'S COMPANIES FACE their toughest competition ever. In previous chapters, we argued that to succeed in today's fiercely competitive marketplace, companies must move from a product-and-selling philosophy to a customer-and-marketing philosophy.

This chapter spells out in more detail how companies can outperform competitors to win, keep, and grow customers. To win in today's marketplace, companies must become adept not only in managing products but also in managing customer relationships in the face of determined competition and a difficult marketing environment. Understanding customers is crucial, but it's not enough. Building profitable customer relationships and gaining **competitive advantage** require delivering more value and satisfaction to target customers than competitors do. Customers will see competitive advantages as customer advantages, giving the company an edge over its competitors.

In this chapter, we examine competitive marketing strategies—how companies analyze their competitors and develop successful, customer value–based strategies for engaging customers and building profitable customer relationships. The first step is **competitor analysis**, the process of identifying, assessing, and selecting key competitors. The second step is developing **competitive marketing strategies** that strongly position the company against competitors and give the company the strongest possible strategic advantage.

Competitive advantage
An advantage over competitors gained by offering consumers greater value.

Competitor analysis
Identifying key competitors; assessing their objectives, strategies, strengths and weaknesses, and reaction patterns; and selecting which competitors to attack or avoid.

Competitive marketing strategies
Strategies that strongly position the company against competitors and give it the greatest possible competitive advantage.

Author | Creating competitive
Comment | advantage begins
with a thorough understanding of
competitors' strategies. But before a
company can analyze its competitors,
it must first identify them—a task
that's not as simple as it seems.

Competitor Analysis

OBJECTIVE 18-1 Discuss the need to understand competitors as well as customers through competitor analysis.

To plan effective marketing strategies, a company needs to find out all it can about its competitors. It must constantly compare its marketing strategies, products, prices, channels, and promotions with those of close competitors. In this way, the company can find areas of potential competitive advantage and disadvantage. As shown in ● **Figure 18.1**, competitor analysis involves first identifying and assessing competitors and then selecting which competitors to attack or avoid.

Identifying Competitors

Normally, identifying competitors would seem to be a simple task. At the narrowest level, a company can define its competitors as other companies offering similar products and services to the same customers at similar prices. Thus, Zara might see H&M as a major

Identifying competitors isn't as easy as it seems. For example, Kodak saw other camera film makers as its major competitors. But its real competitors turned out to be the makers of digital cameras that used no film at all. Kodak fell behind in digital technologies and ended up declaring bankruptcy.

Identifying the company's competitors → **Assessing** competitors' objectives, strategies, strengths and weaknesses, and reaction patterns → **Selecting** which competitors to attack or avoid

● **FIGURE 18.1**

Steps in Analyzing Competitors

competitor but not Nordstrom or Target. The Ritz-Carlton might see the Four Seasons hotels as a major competitor, but not Holiday Inn, Hampton Inn, or any of the thousands of bed-and-breakfasts that dot the nation.

However, companies actually face a much wider range of competitors. The company might define its competitors as all firms with the same product or class of products. Thus, Ritz-Carlton would see itself as competing against all other hotels. Even more broadly, competitors might include all companies making products that supply the same service. Here Ritz-Carlton would see itself competing not only against other hotels but also against businesses large and small that supply rooms for busy travelers, from Airbnb to private bed-and-breakfasts. Finally, and still more broadly, competitors might include all companies that compete for the same consumer dollars. Here Ritz-Carlton would see itself competing with travel and leisure products and services, from cruises and summer homes to vacations abroad.

Companies must avoid "competitor myopia." A company is more likely to be "buried" by its latent competitors than its current ones. For example, Kodak didn't lose out to competing film makers such as Fuji; it fell to the makers of digital cameras that use no film at all (see Real Marketing 18.1). And once-blazing-hot video-rental superstore Blockbuster didn't go bankrupt at the hands of other traditional brick-and-mortar retailers. It fell victim first to unexpected competitors such as direct marketer Netflix and kiosk marketer Redbox and then to a host of new digital video streaming services and technologies. By the time Blockbuster recognized and reacted to these unforeseen competitors, it was too late.

● **Market-based competitive definition: By changing to a market concept of competition—selling "irresistible indulgence"—Cinnabon has grown into a much broader competitive arena. While the global brick and mortar bakery business remains at its core, some 72 percent of total consumer sales now come from licensed food service and consumer packaged goods.**

FOCUS Brands

Companies can identify their competitors from an *industry* point of view. They might see themselves as being in the oil industry, the pharmaceutical industry, or the beverage industry. A company must understand the competitive patterns in its industry if it hopes to be an effective player in that industry. Companies can also identify competitors from a *market* point of view. Here they define competitors as companies that are trying to satisfy the same customer need or build relationships with the same customer group.

From an industry point of view, Google once defined its competitors as other search engine providers such as Yahoo! or Microsoft's Bing. Now, Google takes a broader view of serving market needs for online and mobile access to the digital world. Under this market definition, Google squares off against once-unlikely competitors such as Apple, Samsung, Microsoft, Amazon, and Facebook.

In general, the market concept of competition opens the company's eyes to a broader set of actual and potential competitors. ● For example, from an industry view, Cinnabon long defined itself as a mall- and airport-based fresh baked goods chain. Adopting a market view, however, let the brand grow into a much broader competitive arena against consumer packaged goods competitors:[2]

Cinnabon has long been known for its ginormous "World Famous Cinnamon Rolls," creations that radiate that enticing Cinnabon aroma at your local mall or airport. But from a broader market view, Cinnabon realized that it doesn't just sell cinnamon rolls in malls. Instead, it sells "irresistible indulgence," with attributes such as "aroma," "soft," and "indulgent." Cinnabon fans "wanted the flavors of Cinnabon in

Real Marketing 18.1 | Kodak: The Competitor It Didn't See Soon Enough—No Film

Kodak. That venerable brand name was a household word for generations worldwide. For more than a century, people relied on Kodak for products to help them capture "Kodak moments"—important personal and family events to be shared and recorded for posterity. The Hollywood movie industry evolved around Kodak technology. In 1972, Paul Simon even had a number-two hit single called "Kodachrome," a song that put into words the emotional role that Kodak products played in people's lives.

In 2012, however, Kodak fell into bankruptcy. Today, the brand that once monopolized the consumer photography industry, capturing 85 percent of all camera sales and 90 percent of a huge film market, doesn't even sell consumer cameras and film anymore. Once among the bluest of blue chips and rolling in cash, a completely transformed Kodak now struggles with dwindled sales and year-after-year losses.

How could such a storied brand—as mighty in its day as Apple or Microsoft today—fall so far so fast? Kodak fell victim to marketing and competitor myopia—focusing on a narrow set of current products and competitors rather than on underlying customer needs and emerging market dynamics. It wasn't competing film makers that brought Kodak down. It was the competitor Kodak didn't see soon enough—digital photography and cameras that used no film at all. All along, Kodak continued to make the very best film.

But in an increasingly digital world, customers no longer needed film. Clinging to its legacy products, Kodak lagged behind competitors in making the shift to digital.

In 1880, George Eastman founded Kodak based on a method for dry-plate photography. In 1888, he introduced the Kodak camera, which used glass plates for capturing images. Looking to expand the market, Eastman next developed film and the innovative little Kodak Brownie film camera. He sold the camera for only $1 but reaped massive profits from the sale of film, along with the chemicals and paper required to produce photographs. Although Kodak also developed innovative imaging technologies for industries ranging from health care to publishing, throughout the twentieth century, cameras and film remained the company's massive cash cow.

Interestingly, way back in 1975, Kodak engineers invented the first digital camera— a toaster-sized image sensor that captured rough hues of black and white. However, failing to recognize the mass-market potential of digital photography and fearing that digital technology would cannibalize its precious film business, Kodak shelved the digital project. Company managers simply could not envision a filmless world. So Kodak held fast to film and focused its innovation and competitive energies on making better film and out-innovating other film producers. When the company later realized its mistake, it was too late.

Blinded by its film fixation, Kodak failed to see emerging competitive trends associated with capturing and sharing images. Kodak's culture became bound up in its history and the nostalgia that accompanied it. "They were a company stuck in time," says one analyst. "Their history was so important to them—this rich century-old history when they made a lot of amazing things and a lot of money along the way. [Then,] their history [became] a liability."

By the time Kodak finally introduced a line of pocket-sized digital cameras in the late 1990s, the market was already crowded with digital products from Sony, Canon, Nikon, Samsung, and a dozen other camera makers. That was soon followed by a completely new category of competitors, as more and more people began pointing and clicking their phones and other mobile devices and sharing photos instantly via texting, messaging, email, and online photo-sharing social networks. Late to the digital game, Kodak became a relic of the past and an also-ran to a host of new-age digital competitors that hadn't even existed a decade or two earlier.

Somewhere along the way, swelled with success, once-mighty Kodak lost sight of founder George Eastman's visionary knack for defining customer needs and competitor dynamics. According to one biographer, Eastman's legacy was not film; it was innovation. "George Eastman never looked back. He always looked forward to doing something better than what he had done, even if he had the best on the market at the time." If it had retained Eastman's philosophy, Kodak might well have been the market leader in digital technologies. We might all still be capturing "Kodak moments" on Kodak digital cameras and smartphones and sharing them on social media and Kodak-run online sites.

As Kodak emerged from bankruptcy, it stopped making cameras and discontinued its famous Kodachrome color film. Instead, it now licenses its name to other manufacturers that make devices ranging from instant print cameras and digital photo frames to baby monitors under the Kodak brand. Almost all of its revenues now come from commercial imaging and printing products and services for business customers in graphic arts, commercial print, publishing, packaging, electronic displays, and entertainment and commercial films. So, along with Kodak's illustrious fortunes, it looks as though the famed "Kodak moment" has now passed into history.[3]

Competitor myopia: It wasn't competing film makers that brought Kodak down. It was the competitor Kodak didn't see soon enough—digital photography and cameras that used no film at all.

© Finnbarr Webster/Alamy

other sorts of occasions where they indulge," says the brand's CEO. This realization led to an expansion into consumer products through licensing partnerships with companies ranging from Pillsbury and Green Mountain Coffee to Taco Bell, Air Wick, and even Pinnacle vodka. Each partner now makes products that capture the irresistible Cinnabon taste and smell. As a result, although the global brick and mortar bakery business remains at its core, some 72 percent of total consumer sales now come from licensed food service and consumer packaged goods.

Assessing Competitors

Having identified the main competitors, marketing management now asks: What are the competitors' objectives? What does each seek in the marketplace? What is each competitor's strategy? What are various competitors' strengths and weaknesses, and how will each react to actions the company might take?

Determining Competitors' Objectives

Each competitor has a mix of objectives. The company wants to know the relative importance that a competitor places on current profitability, market share growth, cash flow, technological leadership, service leadership, and other goals. Knowing a competitor's mix of objectives reveals whether the competitor is satisfied with its current situation and how it might react to different competitive actions. For example, a company that pursues low-cost leadership will react much more strongly to a competitor's cost-reducing manufacturing breakthrough than to the same competitor's increase in advertising.

A company also must monitor its competitors' objectives for various segments. If the company finds that a competitor has discovered a new segment, this might be an opportunity. If it finds that competitors plan new moves into segments now served by the company, it will be forewarned and, hopefully, forearmed.

Strategic group
A group of firms in an industry following the same or a similar strategy.

Identifying Competitors' Strategies

The more that one firm's strategy resembles another firm's strategy, the more the two firms compete. In most industries, the competitors can be sorted into groups that pursue different strategies. A **strategic group** is a group of firms in an industry following the same or a similar strategy in a given target market. For example, in the major home appliance industry, Whirlpool, Maytag, and LG belong to the same strategic group. Each produces a full line of medium-price appliances supported by good service. ● In contrast, Sub-Zero and Viking belong to a different strategic group. They produce a narrower line of higher-quality appliances, offer a higher level of service, and charge a premium price. "We're as passionate about building Viking products as chefs are about cooking with them," says Viking. "We innovate. We over-engineer. And then we use high-grade, heavy-duty materials to create the most powerful products available. At Viking, it's more than just steel on the line. It's our pride."[4]

Some important insights emerge from identifying strategic groups. For example, if a company enters a strategic group, the members of that group become its key competitors. Thus, if the company enters a group against Whirlpool, Maytag, and LG, it can succeed only if it develops strategic advantages over these three brands.

Although competition is most intense within a strategic group, there is also rivalry among groups. First, some strategic groups may appeal to overlapping customer segments. For example, no matter what their strategy, all major appliance manufacturers will go after the apartment and homebuilders segment. Second, customers may not see much difference in the offers of different groups; they

● **Strategic groups: Viking belongs to the appliance industry strategic group offering a narrow line of higher quality appliances supported by good service.**

Viking Corporate Offices Location

may see little difference in quality between LG and Whirlpool. Finally, members of one strategic group might expand into new strategy segments. Thus, LG's Signature line of appliances competes in the premium-quality, premium-price category with Viking and Sub-Zero. LG Signature let you "Experience the Art of Essence."[5]

The company needs to look at all the dimensions that identify strategic groups within the industry. It must understand how each competitor delivers value to its customers. It needs to know each competitor's product quality, features, and mix; customer services; pricing policy; distribution coverage; sales force strategy; and advertising, digital, mobile, and social media content programs. And it must study the details of each competitor's research and development (R&D), manufacturing, purchasing, financial, and other strategies.

Assessing Competitors' Strengths and Weaknesses

Marketers need to carefully assess each competitor's strengths and weaknesses to answer a critical question: What *can* our competitors do? As a first step, companies can gather data on each competitor's goals, strategies, and performance over the past few years. Admittedly, some of this information will be hard to obtain. For example, business-to-business (B-to-B) marketers find it hard to estimate competitors' market shares because they do not have the same syndicated data services that are available to consumer packaged-goods companies.

Companies normally learn about their competitors' strengths and weaknesses through secondary data, personal experience, and word of mouth. They can also conduct primary marketing research with customers, suppliers, and dealers. They can check competitors' online and social media sites. Or they can try **benchmarking** themselves against other firms, comparing the company's products and processes to those of competitors or leading firms in other industries to identify best practices and find ways to improve quality and performance. Benchmarking is a powerful tool for increasing a company's competitiveness.

Benchmarking
Comparing the company's products and processes to those of competitors or leading firms in other industries to identify best practices and find ways to improve quality and performance.

Estimating Competitors' Reactions

Next, the company wants to know: What *will* our competitors do? A competitor's objectives, strategies, and strengths and weaknesses go a long way toward explaining its likely actions. They also suggest its likely reactions to company moves, such as price cuts, promotion increases, or new product introductions. In addition, each competitor has a certain philosophy of doing business, a certain internal culture and guiding beliefs. Marketing managers need a deep understanding of a competitor's mentality if they want to anticipate how that competitor will act or react.

Each competitor reacts differently. Some do not react quickly or strongly to a competitor's move. They may feel their customers are loyal, they may be slow in noticing the move, or they may lack the funds to react. Some competitors react only to certain types of moves and not to others. Other competitors react swiftly and strongly to any action. Thus, P&G does not allow a competitor's new product to come easily into the market. Many firms avoid direct competition with P&G and look for easier prey, knowing that P&G will react fiercely if it is challenged. Knowing how major competitors react gives the company clues on how best to attack competitors or how best to defend its current positions.

In some industries, competitors live in relative harmony; in others, competitors are more openly combative. ● For example, rivals Pepsi and Coca-Cola have for years aggressively attacked each other with advertising, usually in good fun but sometimes in more heated ways:[6]

It began years ago with the long-running "Pepsi Challenge" campaign, where Pepsi ads showed blind taste tests in shopping malls and other public places in which consumers invariably preferred the taste of Pepsi to that of Coca-Cola. Since then, Pepsi has run regular comparative ads tweaking its larger competitor, ranging from an ad showing Santa Claus (long associated with Coca-Cola advertising) choosing a Pepsi over a Coke to one in which a Pepsi delivery driver snaps a candid photo of a Coke driver covertly draining a cold can of Pepsi.

● **Competitor reactions: Pepsi and Coca-Cola have for years aggressively attacked each other with advertising. When Coca-Cola's hometown Atlanta hosted Super Bowl LIII, Pepsi blanketed the town with large, snarky Pepsi ads.**

David J Phillip/AP/Shutterstock.

More recently, when Coca-Cola's hometown Atlanta hosted Super Bowl LIII, Pepsi blanketed the town with more than 350 large ads placed on everything from billboards and recycling bins to the walls of train stations. "The ads are not only huge, they're snarky too," reported one analyst. One billboard down the street from The World of Coca-Cola museum read "Pepsi in Atlanta. How Refreshing." Another said, "Hey Atlanta, Thanks for Hosting. We'll Bring the Drinks." Such advertising has been popular with Pepsi fans. "There are few things that grab our fans' attention as much as seeing our beloved blue and that red next to each other," says Pepsi's brand marketing and digital director. "It's done well for us in the past, and it's just something that we know works and that they love to see."

In some cases, competitive exchanges can provide useful information to consumers and advantages for brands. In other cases, they can reflect unfavorably on the entire industry.

Selecting Competitors to Attack and Avoid

A company has already largely selected its major competitors through prior decisions on customer targets, positioning, and its marketing mix strategy. Management now must decide which competitors to compete against most vigorously.

Strong or Weak Competitors

A company can focus on one of several classes of competitors. Most companies prefer to compete against weak competitors. This requires fewer resources and less time. But in the process, the firm may gain little. You could argue that a firm also should compete with strong competitors to sharpen its abilities. And sometimes, a company can't avoid its largest competitors. But even strong competitors have some weaknesses, and succeeding against them often provides greater returns.

Customer value analysis

An analysis conducted to determine what benefits target customers value and how they rate the relative values of various competitors' offers.

A useful tool for assessing competitor strengths and weaknesses is **customer value analysis**. The aim of customer value analysis is to determine the benefits that target customers value and how customers rate the relative values of various competitors' offers. In conducting a customer value analysis, the company first identifies the major attributes that customers value and the importance customers place on these attributes. Next, it assesses its performance against competitors on those valued attributes.

The key to gaining competitive advantage is to examine how a company's offer compares to that of its major competitors in each customer segment. The company wants to find the place in the market where it meets customers' needs in a way rivals can't. If the company's offer delivers greater value than the competitor's offer on important attributes, it can charge a higher price and earn higher profits, or it can charge the same price and gain more market share. But if the company is seen as performing at a lower level than its major competitors on some important attributes, it must invest in strengthening those attributes or find other important attributes where it can build a lead.

Good or Bad Competitors

A company really needs and benefits from competitors. The existence of competitors results in several strategic benefits. Competitors may share the costs of market and product development and help legitimize new technologies. They may serve less-attractive segments or lead to more product differentiation. Finally, competitors may help increase total demand.

For example, you might think that having the world's major automakers move full-tilt into all-electric cars might spell trouble for electric car pioneer Tesla. ● Industry leader Volkswagen, for instance, plans to introduce 70 new electric models and sell 28 million electric cars across its Volkswagen, Audi, Porsche, Bentley, Skoda, and other brands by 2028. As the major car brands jump in massively, Tesla will have to keep innovating and improving its cars to compete well. However, Tesla welcomes the increased competition. More competitors will help Tesla move electric cars into the mainstream, increasing demand it its own models. "You need

● **Good competition: Rather than spelling trouble for electric car pioneer Tesla, the more that major competitors like Volkswagen buy into electric cars, the better it is for Tesla.**

Kyodo/AP Images

some critical mass to legitimize what you're doing," says one analyst. "It can be lonely at the top," says another. "The more companies that buy into electric cars, the better it is."[7]

However, a company may not view all its competitors as beneficial. An industry often contains *good competitors* and *bad competitors*. Good competitors play by the rules of the industry. Bad competitors, in contrast, break the rules. They try to buy share rather than earn it, take large risks, and play by their own rules. For example, many airlines view ultra-low-cost carrier Spirit Airlines as a bad competitor. Rather than competing on standard industry measures such as comfort, service, amenities, and on-time departures, Spirit competes strictly on rock-bottom prices, even if that means sacrificing service and extras. Its "Bare Fare" prices run as much as 90 percent lower than those of competing airlines. Slashing prices makes sense for Spirit Airlines—thanks to its industry-lowest cost per seat-mile, Spirit still reaps industry-leading profit margins. But Spirits rebellious pricing causes headaches for competitors that can't match its low fares and still make decent margins.

Finding Uncontested Market Spaces

Rather than competing head-to-head with established competitors, many companies seek out unoccupied positions in uncontested market spaces. They try to create products and services for which there are no direct competitors. Called a "blue-ocean strategy," the goal is to make competition irrelevant.[8]

Companies have long engaged in head-to-head competition in search of profitable growth. They have fought for competitive advantage, battled over market share, and struggled for differentiation. Yet in today's overcrowded industries, competing head-on results in nothing but a bloody "red ocean" of rivals fighting over a shrinking profit pool. In their book *Blue Ocean Strategy*, two strategy professors contend that although most companies compete within such red oceans, the strategy isn't likely to create profitable growth in the future. Tomorrow's leading companies will succeed not by battling competitors but by creating "blue oceans" of uncontested market space. Such strategic moves—termed *value innovation*—create powerful leaps in value for both the firm and its buyers, creating all-new demand and rendering rivals obsolete. By creating and capturing blue oceans, companies can largely take rivals out of the picture.

Apple has long practiced this strategy, introducing product firsts such as the iPod, iPhone, App Store, iPad, and iTunes that created whole new categories. Similarly, Redbox reinvented the DVD-rental category via kiosks in convenient locations. And rather than competing against traditional coffee maker brands such as Hamilton Beach and Mr. Coffee that brew coffee by the pot, Keurig reinvented the process with innovative cup-at-a-time, pod-based coffee makers. As a result, Keurig has achieved annual sales of coffee makers and pods exceeding $4 billion and captures 30 percent of the U.S. single-serve market. Including licensing and manufacturing partnerships with brands such as Starbucks, Dunkin', Caribou Coffee, Eight O'Clock, Folgers, Maxwell House, and others, Keurig owns an 80 percent share of the K-Cup pod market.[9]

● Blue-ocean strategy: Direct-to-consumer (DTC) brands like Casper have staked out new competitive space by selling and shipping directly to consumers through online and mobile channels.

Yana Paskova/For The Washington Post via Getty Images

Another example of blue ocean competitors is the recent surge of direct-to-consumer (DTC) brands. Rather than competing head-to-head with established competitors in retail stores, DTC brands have staked out new competitive space by selling and shipping directly to consumers through online and mobile channels. DTC brands have found success in categories ranging from beauty and personal care, apparel, and food to home furnishings and fitness. Just a few examples include Dollar Shave Club and Harry's (razors and shaving products), Peloton (fitness equipment and programs), Casper (mattresses and bedding), Bonobos (men's apparel), Allbirds (environmentally friendly footwear), and BarkBox (dog toys, treats, and goodies). By bypassing intermediaries, DTC companies can cut costs and lower prices, offer greater convenience, build closer direct customer relationships, and deliver hyper-focused offerings.

Many DTC brands have been highly successful in carving out new market spaces. ● For example, after only five years, Casper now sells close to $500 million worth of mattresses and bedding products direct to consumers annually, and the company is worth an estimated $1.1 billion. Footwear company Allbirds, whose shoes give you "Comfort that Comes Naturally," is valued at $1.4 billion after only two years. Responding to the DTC surge, established brands have acquired or set up their own DTC operations. For example, Walmart bought up Bonobos, Unilever acquired Dollar Shave Club, and P&G set up its own Gillette on Demand DTC site.[10]

Designing a Competitive Intelligence System

We have described the main types of information that companies need about their competitors. This information must be collected, interpreted, distributed, and used. Gathering competitive intelligence can cost much money and time, so the company must design a cost-effective competitive intelligence system.

The competitive intelligence system first identifies the vital types of competitive information needed and the best sources of this information. Then the system continuously collects information from the field (sales force, channels, suppliers, market research firms, internet and social media sites, online monitoring, and trade associations) and published data (government publications, speeches, and online databases). Next the system checks the information for validity and reliability, interprets it, and organizes it in an appropriate way. Finally, it sends relevant information to decision makers and responds to inquiries from managers about competitors.

With this system, company managers receive timely intelligence about competitors in the form of reports and assessments, posted bulletins, newsletters, and email and mobile alerts. Managers can also connect when they need to interpret a competitor's sudden move, know a competitor's weaknesses and strengths, or assess how a competitor will respond to a planned company move.

> Author | Now that we've identified
> Comment | competitors and know
> all about them, it's time to design
> a strategy for gaining competitive
> advantage.

Competitive Strategies

OBJECTIVE 18-2 Explain the fundamentals of competitive marketing strategies based on creating value for customers.

Having identified and evaluated its major competitors, a company now must design broad marketing strategies by which it can gain competitive advantage. But what broad competitive marketing strategies might the company use? Which ones are best for a particular company or for the company's different divisions and products?

Approaches to Marketing Strategy

No one strategy is best for all companies. Each company must determine what makes the most sense given its position in the industry and its objectives, opportunities, and resources. Even within a company, different strategies may be required for different businesses or products. Johnson & Johnson uses one marketing strategy for its leading brands in stable consumer markets, such as BAND-AID, Tylenol, Listerine, or J&J's baby products, and a different marketing strategy for its high-tech health-care businesses and products, such as Monocryl surgical sutures or NeuFlex finger joint implants.

Companies also differ in how they approach the strategy-planning process. Many large firms develop formal competitive marketing strategies and implement them religiously. However, other companies develop strategy in a less formal and orderly fashion. Some companies, such as Red Bull, Shinola, and Spanx, have succeeded by breaking many of the rules of marketing strategy. Such companies start with large marketing departments, conduct expensive marketing research, spell out elaborate competitive strategies, and spend huge sums on advertising. Instead, they sketched out strategies on the fly, stretched their limited resources, lived close to their customers, and created more satisfying solutions to customer needs. They formed buyers' clubs, used buzz marketing, engaged customers up close, and focused on winning customer loyalty. It seems that not all marketing must follow in the footsteps of marketing giants such as P&G, McDonald's, and Microsoft.

In fact, approaches to marketing strategy and practice often pass through three stages—entrepreneurial marketing, formulated marketing, and intrapreneurial marketing:

● **Entrepreneurial marketing: Boston Beer Company founder Jim Koch first marketed his Samuel Adams beer by carrying bottles in a suitcase from bar to bar, telling his story, educating consumers, getting people to taste the beer, and persuading bartenders to carry it. The company is now the leading craft brewery in America.**

Kelvin Ma/Bloomberg via Getty Images

- *Entrepreneurial marketing.* Most companies are started by individuals who live by their wits. They visualize an opportunity, construct flexible strategies on the backs of envelopes, and knock on every door to gain attention. ● Jim Koch, founder of Boston Beer Company, whose Samuel Adams Boston Lager beer has become the top-selling craft beer in America, started out in 1984 brewing a cherished family beer recipe in his kitchen. For marketing, Koch carried bottles of Samuel Adams in a suitcase from bar to bar, telling his story, educating consumers about brewing quality and ingredients, getting people to taste the beer, and persuading bartenders to carry it. For 10 years, he couldn't afford advertising; he sold his beer through direct selling and grassroots public relations. "It was all guerrilla marketing," says Koch. "The big guys were so big, we had to do innovative things like that." Today, however, his business pulls in nearly $1 billion a year, making it the leader over more than 1,000 competitors in the craft brewery market.[11]

- *Formulated marketing.* As small companies achieve success, they inevitably move toward more-formulated marketing. They develop formal marketing strategies and adhere to them closely. Boston Beer Company now employs a large sales force and has a marketing department that carries out market research and plans strategy. Although Boston Beer Company is far less formal and sophisticated in its strategy than $55-billion mega-competitor Anheuser-Busch Inbev, it has adopted some of the tools used in professionally run marketing companies.

- *Intrapreneurial marketing.* Many large and mature companies get stuck in formulated marketing. They pore over the latest Nielsen numbers, scan market research reports, and try to fine-tune their competitive strategies and programs. These companies sometimes lose the marketing creativity and passion they had at the start. They now need to build more marketing initiative and "intrapreneurship"—encouraging employees to be more entrepreneurial within the larger corporation—recapturing some of the spirit and action that made them successful in the first place. Some companies build intrapreneurship into their core marketing operations. For example, IBM encourages employees at all levels to interact on their own with customers through blogs, social media, and other platforms. Google's Innovation Time-Off program encourages all of its engineers and developers to spend 20 percent of their time developing "cool and wacky" new product ideas—blockbusters such as Google News, Gmail, Google Maps, and AdSense are just a few of the resulting products. And Facebook sponsors regular "hackathons," during which it encourages internal teams to come up with and present intrapreneurial ideas. One of the most important innovations in the company's history—the "Like" button—resulted from such a hackathon.[12]

The bottom line is that there are many approaches to developing effective competitive marketing strategies. There will be a constant tension between the formulated side of marketing and the creative side. It is easier to learn the formulated side of marketing, which has occupied most of our attention in this book. But we have also seen how marketing creativity and passion in the strategies of many of the companies studied—whether small or large, new or mature—have helped to build and maintain success in the marketplace. With this in mind, we now look at the broad competitive marketing strategies companies can use.

Basic Competitive Strategies

More than three decades ago, Michael Porter suggested four basic competitive positioning strategies that companies can follow—three winning strategies and one losing one.[13] The three winning strategies are as follows:

- *Overall cost leadership.* Here the company works hard to achieve the lowest production and distribution costs. Low costs let the company price lower than its competitors and win a large market share. Walmart, Lenovo, and Spirit Airlines are leading practitioners of this strategy.

- *Differentiation.* Here the company concentrates on creating a highly differentiated product line and marketing program so that it comes across as the class leader in the industry. Most customers would prefer to own this brand if its price is not too high. Nike and Caterpillar follow this strategy in apparel and heavy construction equipment, respectively.

- *Focus.* Here the company focuses its effort on serving a few market segments well rather than going after the whole market. For example, Ritz-Carlton focuses on the top 5 percent of corporate and leisure travelers. Bose concentrates on very high-quality electronics products that produce better sound. And search engine DuckDuckGo focuses on a segment of users who are especially concerned about internet tracking and privacy.

Companies that pursue a clear strategy—one of the above—will likely perform well. The firm that carries out that strategy best will make the most profits. But firms that do not pursue a clear strategy—*middle-of-the-roaders*—do the worst. Sears, Levi-Strauss, and Holiday Inn encountered difficult times because they did not stand out as the lowest in cost, highest in perceived value, or best in serving some market segment. Middle-of-the-roaders try to be good on all strategic counts but end up being not very good at anything.

Two marketing consultants, Michael Treacy and Fred Wiersema, offer a more customer-centered classification of competitive marketing strategies.[14] They suggest that companies gain leadership positions by delivering superior value to their customers. Companies can pursue any of three strategies—called *value disciplines*—for delivering superior customer value:

- *Operational excellence.* The company provides superior value by leading its industry in price and convenience. It works to reduce costs and create a lean and efficient value delivery system. It serves customers who want reliable, good-quality products or services but want them cheaply and easily. Examples include Walmart, IKEA, Zara, Southwest Airlines, and Trader Joe's. For example, through operational excellence, Trader Joe's offers a price-value equation that has made it one of the nation's best performing and most popular grocery store chains (see Real Marketing 18.2).

- *Customer intimacy.* The company provides superior value by precisely segmenting its markets and tailoring its products or services to exactly match the needs of targeted customers. It specializes in satisfying unique customer needs through a close relationship with and intimate knowledge of the customer. It empowers its people to respond quickly to customer needs. Customer-intimate companies serve customers who are willing to pay a premium to get precisely what they want. They will do almost anything to build long-term customer loyalty and to capture customer lifetime value. Examples include Nordstrom, Amazon, Salesforce, Lexus, and Ritz-Carlton hotels.

- *Product leadership.* The company provides superior value by offering a continuous stream of leading-edge products or services. It aims to make its own and competing products obsolete. Product leaders are open to new ideas, relentlessly pursue new solutions, and work to get new products to market quickly. They serve customers who want state-of-the-art products and services regardless of the costs in terms of price or inconvenience. One example of a product leader is Apple:[15]

From the very beginning, Apple has churned out one cutting-edge product after another. It all started with the sleek, affordable Apple Macintosh, the first personal computer ever to feature a graphic user interface and mouse. That was followed by an Apple-led revolution in which groundbreaking Apple products such as the iPod, iTunes, the iPhone, and the iPad all created whole new categories where none previously existed. More recently, the latest iPhone models continue to wow users, Apple's wireless AirPods have become fixtures around the globe, and the Apple Watch Series 3 fitness watch is a best-seller. At Apple, innovation is more than skin deep.

Product leadership: From the very beginning, Apple has churned out one cutting-edge product after another, creating a consumer love affair that has made Apple one of the world's most valuable companies.

Malcolm Haines/Alamy Stock Photo.

Real Marketing 18.2 | Operational Excellence: Trader Joe's Unique "Cheap Gourmet" Value Positioning

On an early July morning, a large and enthusiastic crowd has already gathered. The occasion: Trader Joe's is opening a new store, and waiting shoppers are sharing their joy over the arrival of the trendy retailer in their neighborhood. Trader Joe's is more than a grocery store, it's a cultural experience. Its shelves are packed with goods that are at the same time both exotic luxuries and affordable. Whether it's organic creamy Valencia peanut butter or cage-free eggs, Thai lime-and-chili cashews or Belgian butter waffle cookies, you'll find them only at Trader Joe's.

Within moments of the new store's opening, the deluge of customers makes it almost impossible to navigate the aisles. They line up 10 deep at checkouts with carts full of Trader Joe's exclusive $2.99 Charles Shaw wine—aka "Two-Buck Chuck"—and an assortment of other exclusive gourmet products at impossibly low prices. All of this has made Trader Joe's one of the nation's hottest retailers.

Trader Joe's isn't really a gourmet food store. Then again, it's not a discount food store either. It's actually a bit of both. Though operational excellence, Trader Joe's has put its own special twist on the food price-value equation—call it "cheap gourmet." It offers gourmet-caliber, one-of-a-kind products at bargain prices, all served up in a festive, vacation-like atmosphere that makes shopping fun. However you define it, Trader Joe's inventive price-value positioning has earned it an almost cult-like following of devoted customers who love what they get from Trader Joe's for the prices they pay.

Trader Joe's describes itself as an "island paradise" where "value, adventure, and tasty treasures are discovered, every day." Shoppers bustle and buzz amid cedar-plank-lined walls and fake palm trees as a ship's bell rings out occasionally at checkout, alerting them to special announcements. Unfailingly helpful and cheery associates chat with customers about everything from the weather to menu suggestions for dinner parties. At the recent store opening, workers greeted customers with high-fives and free cookies. Customers don't just shop at Trader Joe's; they experience it.

Shelves bristle with an eclectic assortment of gourmet-quality grocery items. Trader Joe's stocks only a limited assortment of about 4,000 products (compared with the 45,000 items found in a typical grocery store). However, the assortment is uniquely Trader Joe's, including special concoctions of gourmet packaged foods and sauces, ready-to-eat soups, fresh and frozen entrees, snacks, and desserts—all free of artificial colors, flavors, and preservatives.

Trader Joe's is a gourmet foodie's delight, featuring everything from organic broccoli slaw, creamy Valencia peanut butter, and fair trade coffees to corn and chile tomato-less salsa and triple-ginger ginger snaps. Another thing that makes Trader Joe's products so special is that you just can't get most of them elsewhere. For example, try finding Ginger Cats cookies, quinoa and black bean tortilla chips, or mango coconut popcorn at

some other store. More than 80 percent of the store's brands are private label goods, sold exclusively by Trader Joe's. If asked, almost any customer can tick off a ready list of Trader Joe's favorites that they just can't live without—a list that quickly grows. People come in intending to buy a few favorites and quickly fill a cart.

A special store atmosphere, exclusive gourmet products, helpful and attentive associates—this all sounds like a recipe for high prices. Not so at Trader Joe's. Whereas upscale competitors such as Whole Foods Market charge upscale prices to match their wares ("Whole Foods, Whole Paycheck"), Trader Joe's amazes customers with its relatively frugal prices. The prices aren't all that low in absolute terms, but they're a real bargain compared with what you'd pay for the same quality and coolness elsewhere. "At Trader Joe's, we're as much about value as we are about great food," says the company. "So you can afford to be adventurous without breaking the bank."

How does Trader Joe's keep its gourmet prices so low? Through operational excellence. It carefully shapes non-price elements to support its overall price-value strategy. For starters, Trader Joe's has lean operations and a near-fanatical focus on saving money. To keep costs down, Trader Joe's typically locates its stores in low-rent, out-of-the-way locations, such as suburban strip malls. Notorious for small, always-packed parking lots, Trader Joe's points out that spacious parking lots require more real estate and that costs money. The chain's small-sized stores, with small back rooms and limited product assortments, result in reduced facilities and inventory costs. Trader Joe's stores save money by eliminating large produce sections and expensive on-site bakery, butcher, deli, and seafood shops. And for its private label brands, Trader Joe's buys directly from suppliers and negotiates hard on price.

Finally, the frugal, operationally excellent retailer saves money by spending almost nothing on advertising, and it offers no coupons, discount cards, or special promotions. Trader Joe's unique combination of quirky products and low prices produces so much word-of-mouth promotion and buying urgency that the company doesn't really need to advertise or price promote. The closest things to official promotion are the company's website, mobile app, and *The Fearless Flyer* monthly e-newsletter. Trader Joe's most potent promotional weapon is its army of faithful followers. Trader Joe's customers have even started

Trader Joe's has put its own special twist of the food price-value equation— call it "cheap gourmet."

their own fan web and social media sites, such as www.traderjoesfan.com, where they discuss new products and stores, trade recipes, and swap their favorite Trader Joe's stories.

Thus, building the right price-value formula has made Trader Joe's one of the nation's best performing and most popular food stores. Its more than 504 stores in 48 states now reap annual sales of an estimated $13.3 billion, more than quadruple its sales a decade ago. Trader Joe's stores pull in sales per square foot at more than twice the supermarket industry average. And year after year, you'll find Trader Joe's at or near the top of almost every list of best-performing grocery retailers, both for financial performance and customer preference.

It's all about value and price—what you get for what you pay. Just ask Trader Joe's regular Chrissi Wright, found early one morning browsing her local Trader Joe's in Bend, Oregon.

Chrissi expects she'll leave Trader Joe's with eight bottles of the popular Charles Shaw wine priced at $2.99 each tucked under her arms. "I love Trader Joe's because they let me eat like a yuppie without taking all my money," says Wright. "Their products are gourmet, often environmentally conscientious and beautiful ... and, of course, there's Two-Buck Chuck—possibly the greatest innovation of our time."[16]

For example, the company designs its own sophisticated processor chips, specifically optimized for its Apple's operating system, display, camera, and apps.

Apple's product leadership results from understanding what makes its customers tick and then creating ahead-of-the-curve products that put customers at the front of the crowd. Many tech companies make products that just occupy space and do work. By contrast, Apple has a genius for sparking consumer imaginations and creating "life-feels-good" products that customers want—often before consumers themselves even know what they want. Such product leadership has produced a consumer love affair with Apple. In turn, Apple has produced stunning sales and profit results over the years, placing Apple in a tight race with innovation all-stars Microsoft and Amazon for the title of world's most valuable company.

Some companies successfully pursue more than one value discipline at the same time. For example, FedEx excels at both operational excellence and customer intimacy. However, such companies are rare; few firms can be the best at more than one of these disciplines. By trying to be good at all value disciplines, a company usually ends up being best at none.

Thus, most excellent companies focus on and excel at a single value discipline while meeting industry standards on the other two. Such companies design their entire value delivery network to single-mindedly support the chosen discipline. For example, Walmart knows that customer intimacy and product leadership are important. Compared with other discounters, it offers good customer service and an excellent product assortment. Still, it purposely offers less customer service and less product depth than does Nordstrom or Williams-Sonoma, which pursue customer intimacy. Instead, Walmart focuses obsessively on operational excellence—on reducing costs and streamlining its order-to-delivery process to make it convenient for customers to buy just the right products at the lowest prices.

Classifying competitive strategies as value disciplines is appealing. It defines marketing strategy in terms of the single-minded pursuit of delivering superior value to customers. Each value discipline defines a specific way to build lasting customer relationships.

Competitive Positions

Firms competing in a given target market at any point differ in their objectives and resources. Some firms are large; others are small. Some have many resources; others are strapped for funds. Some are mature and established; others new and fresh. Some strive for rapid market share growth; others for long-term profits. And these firms occupy different competitive positions in the target market.

We now examine competitive strategies based on the roles firms play in the target market—leader, challenger, follower, or nicher. Suppose that an industry contains the firms shown in ● **Figure 18.2**. As you can see, 40 percent of the market is in the hands of the

● FIGURE 18.2
Competitive Market Positions and Roles

Each market position calls for a different competitive strategy. For example, the market leader wants to expand total demand and protect or expand its share. Market nichers seek market segments that are big enough to be profitable but small enough to be of little interest to major competitors.

Market leader	Market challengers	Market followers	Market nichers
40%	30%	20%	10%

Market leader
The firm in an industry with the largest market share.

Market challenger
A runner-up firm that is fighting hard to increase its market share in an industry.

Market follower
A runner-up firm that wants to hold its share in an industry without rocking the boat.

Market nicher
A firm that serves small segments that the other firms in an industry overlook or ignore.

market leader, the firm with the largest market share. Another 30 percent is in the hands of **market challengers**, runner-up firms that are fighting hard to increase their market share. Another 20 percent is in the hands of **market followers**, other runner-up firms that want to hold their share without rocking the boat. The remaining 10 percent is in the hands of **market nichers**, firms that serve small segments not being pursued by other firms.

● **Table 18.1** shows specific marketing strategies that are available to market leaders, challengers, followers, and nichers.[17] Remember, however, that these classifications often do not apply to a whole company but only to its position in a specific industry. Large companies such as Amazon, Microsoft, Google, P&G, or Disney might be leaders in some markets and nichers in others. For example, Amazon leads the online retailing market but challenges Apple and Samsung in smartphones and tablets. P&G leads in many segments, such as laundry detergents and shampoo, but it challenges Unilever in hand soaps and Kimberly-Clark in facial tissues. Such companies often use different strategies for different business units or products, depending on the competitive situations of each.

Market Leader Strategies

Most industries contain an acknowledged market leader. The leader has the largest market share and usually leads the other firms in price changes, new product introductions, distribution coverage, and promotion spending. The leader may or may not be admired or respected, but other firms concede its dominance. Competitors focus on the leader as a company to challenge, imitate, or avoid. Some of the best-known market leaders are Walmart (retailing), Amazon (online retailing), McDonald's (fast food), AT&T (telecommunications), Coca-Cola (beverages), Boeing (aerospace), Nike (athletic footwear and apparel), Marriott (hotels and resorts), and Google (internet search).

A leader's life is not easy. It must maintain a constant watch. Other firms keep challenging its strengths or trying to take advantage of its weaknesses. The market leader can easily miss a turn in the market and plunge into second or third place. A product innovation may come along and hurt the leader (as when Netflix's direct marketing and video streaming unseated then-market leader Blockbuster or when Apple developed the iPod and iTunes and took the market lead from Sony's Walkman portable audio devices). The leader might grow arrogant or complacent and misjudge the competition (as when Sears lost its lead to Walmart). Or the leader might look old-fashioned against new and peppier rivals (as when Abercrombie & Fitch lost ground to stylish or lower-cost brands such as Zara, H&M, and Forever 21).

To remain number one, leading firms can take any of three actions. First, they can find ways to expand total demand. Second, they can protect their current market share through good defensive and offensive actions. Third, they can try to expand their market share further, even if market size remains constant.

Expanding Total Demand

The leading firm normally gains the most when the total market expands. If Americans eat more fast food, McDonald's stands to gain the most because it holds a much larger fast-food market share than competitors such as Subway, Burger King, or Taco Bell. If McDonald's can convince more Americans that fast food is the best eating-out choice, it will benefit more than its competitors.

Market leaders can expand the market by developing new users, new uses, and more usage of its products. They usually can find *new users* or untapped market segments in

● **Table 18.1 Strategies for Market Leaders, Challengers, Followers, and Nichers**

Market Leader Strategies	Market Challenger Strategies	Market Follower Strategies	Market Nicher Strategies
Expand total market	Full frontal attack	Follow closely	By customer, market, quality, price, service
Protect market share	Indirect attack	Follow at a distance	Multiple niching
Expand market share			

● **Attracting new users: To attract new customers, IKEA is setting up small-format stores—called IKEA Planning Studios—that serve the special needs of consumers who live in tiny apartments in densely populated city centers such as New York City.**

Associated Press

many places. ● For example, IKEA is setting up special small-format stores—called IKEA Planning Studios—to attract new customers in densely populated city centers such as New York City, London, Paris, and Moscow:[18]

> The first U.S. IKEA Planning Studio, located in Manhattan, is about one-twentieth the size of a regular IKEA superstore. It's designed to serve the unique needs of many New Yorkers living in tiny apartments. Often without cars, these consumers are looking to buy furniture on a budget but find it difficult to get to a larger IKEA superstore or to haul furniture back to their apartments ("Because sometimes your ideas are bigger than the 6 train," says a sign near the store's entryway). Customers can't take anything home from the planning center. Instead, they can view carefully designed room setups based on real-life New York apartments—one 333-square-foot floor plan even has a bathtub in the living room. Or they can consult with an iPad-toting IKEA associate to create custom configurations of IKEA furniture, fixtures, and accessories to fit their own small spaces. Purchases are shipped directly to customers' homes. "This planning studio is set up and designed specifically for the New Yorker's way of living and what works in their space, their needs," says an IKEA marketer. "The city center stores could give IKEA access to a new set of customers," adds a retailing analyst.

Marketers can expand markets by discovering and promoting *new uses* for the product. For example, The WD-40 Company's knack for finding new uses has made the product one of the truly essential survival items in most American homes. Some years ago, WD-40 polled users to discover unique uses and posted the best 2,000-plus suggestions on the company website.[19] Some consumers suggested simple and practical uses, such as keeping wicker chairs from squeaking, freeing stuck LEGO bricks, or cleaning crayon marks from just about anywhere. Others, however, reported some pretty unusual applications. Lots of people, it seems, use WD-40 to make squirrels slide off birdfeeder poles. One man uses WD-40 to polish his glass eye; another uses it to remove a prosthetic leg. And did you hear about the nude burglary suspect who had wedged himself in a vent at a café in Denver? The fire department extracted him with a large dose of WD-40. Or how about the Mississippi naval officer who used WD-40 to repel an angry bear? As the company concludes: "You only need two things in life: duct tape and WD-40. If it moves and shouldn't, use duct tape. If it doesn't move and should, use WD-40."

Finally, market leaders can encourage *more usage* by convincing people to use the product more often or use more per occasion. For example, Campbell's urges people to eat soup and other Campbell's products more often by running ads containing new recipes. At the Campbell's Kitchen website (www.campbellskitchen.com), visitors can search for or exchange recipes, create their own personal recipe box, learn ways to eat healthier, and sign up for a daily or weekly Meal Mail program. At the Campbell's Facebook, Pinterest, and Twitter sites, consumers can join in and share on Campbell's Kitchen Community conversations.

Protecting Market Share

While trying to expand total market size, the leading firm also must protect its current business against competitors' attacks. Walmart must constantly guard against Amazon, Target, and Costco; McDonald's against Wendy's and Burger King; and Nike against adidas.

What can the market leader do to protect its position? First, it must prevent or fix weaknesses that provide opportunities for competitors. It must always fulfill its value promise and work tirelessly to engage valued customers in strong relationships. Its prices must remain consistent with the value that customers see in the brand. The leader should "plug holes" so that competitors do not jump in.

But the best defense is a good offense, and the best response is continuous innovation. The market leader refuses to be content with the way things are and leads the industry

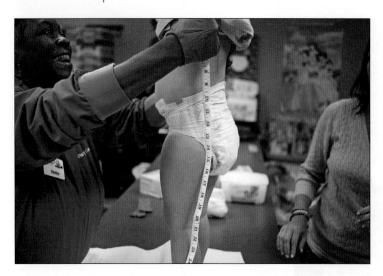

● **Protecting market share: P&G's researchers push the boundaries of science and style to keep a technological edge over disposable diaper challengers. Thanks to relentless innovation and brand building, P&G maintains a commanding market share lead.**

Luke Sharrett/Bloomberg/Getty Images

in new products, customer services, distribution effectiveness, promotion, and cost cutting. It keeps increasing its competitive effectiveness and value to customers. And when attacked by challengers, the market leader reacts decisively. ● For example, in the $58 billion global disposable diaper market, market leader P&G—with its Pampers and Luvs brands—has been relentless in its offense against challengers such as Kimberly-Clark's Huggies:[20]

> Disposable diapers make up about 14 percent of P&G's sales. So the company invests huge resources in disposable diaper and baby-care R&D, seeking to build the ultimate diaper that yields "zero leakage, ultimate dryness, ultimate comfort, with an underwear-like fit," says a P&G baby-care research manager. At five baby-care centers around the globe, P&G's researchers push the boundaries of science and style to keep a technological edge over challengers. P&G's baby-care division now has more than 5,000 diaper patents granted or pending. For instance, it introduced Pamper Premium Care Pants, diapers with all-around elastic that can be pulled on like underwear, now the most popular diaper variety in China. It recently introduced Pampers Pure, now the top-selling natural diaper. Next up in diaper innovation: smart diapers with imbedded sensors that alert parents through smartphone apps when their babies wet a diaper or even notify parents if they detect the wearer catching a disease. Beyond its push for technological superiority, P&G employs its hefty marketing clout to engage consumers and persuade them that its diapers are best for their babies. In all, thanks to its relentless innovation and brand building, in the United States P&G holds a 43-percent-and-growing market share versus challenger Kimberly-Clark's 35 percent. In the huge Chinese diaper market, it holds a 27 percent share to Kimberly-Clark's 22 percent.

Expanding Market Share

Market leaders also can grow by increasing their market shares further. In many markets, small market share increases mean very large sales increases. For example, in the U.S. hair care market, a 1 percent increase in market share is worth $128 million in annual sales; in carbonated soft drinks, almost $1.9 billion![21]

Studies have shown that, on average, profitability rises with increasing market share. Because of these findings, many companies have sought expanded market shares to improve profitability. In recent years, for example, P&G has shed dozens of smaller, low-share brands in order to focus its resources on fewer but larger-share billion-dollar-plus brands. More than one-third of the company's brands now fall into this mega-brand category.

However, some studies have found that many industries contain one or a few highly profitable large firms, several profitable and more focused firms, and a large number of medium-sized firms with poorer profit performance. It appears that profitability increases as a business gains share relative to competitors in its served market. For example, Lexus holds only a small share of the total car market, but it earns a high profit because it is a leading brand in the luxury-performance car segment. And it has achieved this high share in its served market because it does other things right, such as producing high-quality products, creating outstanding service experiences, and building close customer relationships.

Companies must not think, however, that gaining increased market share will automatically improve profitability. Much depends on their strategy for gaining increased share. There are many high-share companies with low profitability and many low-share companies with high profitability. The cost of buying higher market share may far exceed the returns. Higher shares tend to produce higher profits only when unit costs fall with increased market share or when the company offers a superior-quality product and charges a premium price that more than covers the cost of offering higher quality.

Market Challenger Strategies

Firms that are second, third, or lower in an industry are sometimes quite large, such as PepsiCo, Ford, Lowe's, Hertz, and Target. These runner-up firms can adopt one of two competitive strategies: They can challenge the market leader and other competitors in an aggressive bid for more market share (market challengers), or they can play along with competitors and not rock the boat (market followers).

A market challenger must first define which competitors to challenge and its strategic objective. The challenger can attack the market leader, a high-risk but potentially high-gain strategy. Its goal might be to take over market leadership. Or the challenger's objective may simply be to wrest more market share.

Although it might seem that the market leader has the most going for it, challengers often have what some strategists call a "second-mover advantage." The challenger observes what has made the market leader successful and improves on it. For example, Home Depot invented the home-improvement superstore. However, after observing Home Depot's success, number-two Lowe's, with its brighter stores, wider aisles, and arguably more helpful salespeople, has positioned itself as the friendly alternative to Big Bad Orange. Over the past decade, follower Lowe's has substantially closed the gap in sales and market share with Home Depot.

In fact, challengers often become market leaders by imitating and improving on the ideas of pioneering processors. For example, McDonald's first imitated and then mastered the fast-food system first pioneered by White Castle. And founder Sam Walton admitted that Walmart borrowed most of its practices from discount pioneer Sol Price's FedMart and Price Club chains and then perfected them to become today's dominant retailer.

Alternatively, the challenger can avoid the leader and instead challenge firms its own size or smaller local and regional firms. These smaller firms may be underfinanced and not serving their customers well. If the challenger goes after a small local company, its objective may be to put that company out of business. The important point remains: The challenger must choose its opponents carefully and have a clearly defined and attainable objective.

How can the market challenger best attack the chosen competitor and achieve its strategic objectives? It may launch a full *frontal attack*, matching the competitor's product, advertising, price, and distribution efforts. It attacks the competitor's strengths rather than its weaknesses. The outcome depends on who has the greater strength and endurance. PepsiCo challenges Coca-Cola in this way, Ford challenges Toyota frontally, and Sprint goes directly at AT&T.

If the market challenger has fewer resources than the competitor, however, a frontal attack makes little sense. Thus, many new market entrants avoid frontal attacks, knowing that market leaders can head them off with ad blitzes, price wars, and other retaliations. Rather than challenging head-on, the challenger can make an indirect attack on the competitor's weaknesses or on gaps in the competitor's market coverage. It can carve out toeholds using tactics that established leaders have trouble responding to or choose to ignore.

● **Market challenger strategies: When it entered the U.S. market, rather than attacking market leaders Coca-Cola and Pepsi directly, Red Bull used indirect, unconventional marketing approaches.**

Eyal Dayan Photography

● For example, consider how challenger Red Bull first entered the U.S. soft drink market against market leaders Coca-Cola and PepsiCo. Red Bull tackled the leaders indirectly by selling a high-priced niche product in nontraditional distribution points. It began by selling Red Bull via unconventional outlets that were under the radar of the market leaders, such as nightclubs and bars where young revelers gulped down their caffeine fix so they could go all night. Once it had built a core customer base, the brand expanded into more traditional outlets, where it now sits within arm's length of Coke and Pepsi. Finally, Red Bull used a collection of guerilla marketing tactics rather than the high-cost traditional media used by the market leaders. The indirect approach worked for Red Bull. Despite ever-intensifying competition in the United States, Red Bull is now a $7.3 billion brand that captures a 42 percent share of the energy drink market, with Coca-Cola and PepsiCo holding only minor market shares.[22]

Market Follower Strategies

Not all runner-up companies want to challenge the market leader. The leader never takes challenges lightly. If the challenger's lure is lower prices, improved service, or additional product features, the market leader can quickly match these to defuse the attack.

The leader probably has more staying power in an all-out battle for customers. For example, a few years ago, when Sears-owned Kmart renewed its once-successful low-price "bluelight special" campaign, directly challenging Walmart's everyday low prices, it started a price war that it couldn't win. Walmart had little trouble fending off Kmart's challenge, leaving Kmart worse off for the attempt. With no competitive strategy to effectively challenge retailing leaders like Walmart and Amazon, Kmart now teeters on the verge of extinction. Thus, many firms prefer to follow rather than challenge the market leader.

A follower can gain many advantages. The market leader often bears the huge expenses of developing new products and markets, expanding distribution, and educating the market. By contrast, as with challengers, the market follower can learn from the market leader's experience. It can copy or improve on the leader's products and programs, usually with much less investment. Although the follower will probably not overtake the leader, it often can be as profitable.

Following is not the same as being passive or a carbon copy of the market leader. A follower must know how to hold current customers and win a fair share of new ones. It must find the right balance between following closely enough to win customers from the market leader and following at enough of a distance to avoid retaliation. Each follower tries to bring distinctive advantages to its target market—location, services, financing. A follower is often a major target of attack by challengers. Therefore, the market follower must maintain customer value, through either lower costs and prices or higher quality and better services that justify higher prices. It must also enter new markets as they open.

Market Nicher Strategies

Almost every industry includes firms that specialize in serving market niches. Instead of pursuing the whole market or even large segments, these firms target subsegments. Nichers are often smaller firms with limited resources. But smaller divisions of larger firms also may pursue niching strategies. Firms with low shares of the total market can be highly successful and profitable through smart niching.

Why is niching profitable? The main reason is that the market nicher ends up knowing the target customer group so well that it meets their needs better than other firms that casually sell to that niche. As a result, the nicher can charge a substantial markup over costs because of the added value. Whereas the mass marketer achieves high volume, the nicher achieves high margins.

Nichers try to find one or more market niches that are safe and profitable. An ideal market niche is big enough to be profitable and has growth potential. It is one that the firm can serve effectively. Perhaps most important, the niche is of little interest to major competitors. And the firm can build the skills and customer goodwill to defend itself against a major competitor as the niche grows and becomes more attractive.

The key idea in niching is specialization. Nichers thrive by meeting in depth the special needs of well-targeted customer groups. For example, Google dominates U.S. online search with its massive 63 percent market share. Two other giants—Microsoft's Bing and Yahoo!—combine for another 34 percent. That leaves a precious 3 percent sliver for dozens of other search engines trying to get a foothold. So how does a small search engine wannabe compete against global powerhouses? It doesn't—at least not directly. Instead, it finds a unique market niche and runs where the big dogs don't. That's the strategy of DuckDuckGo, a plucky search engine startup that's carving out its own special market niche:[23]

> Instead of battling Google and other giants head-on, DuckDuckGo positions itself strongly on a key differentiating feature that the Googles of the world simply can't mimic—real privacy. Then it energizes its unique niche with brand personality and user community, personified by DuckDuckGo's icon—a quirky bow-tied duck. Google's entire model is built around personalization for customers and behaviorally targeted marketing for advertisers. That requires collecting and sharing data about users and their searches. When you search on Google, the company knows and retains in detail who you are, what you've searched for, and when you've searched.
>
> By contrast, DuckDuckGo is less invasive and less creepy. It doesn't know who you are. It doesn't log user IP addresses. use cookies to track users, or even save user search histories. Perhaps most important, when users click on DuckDuckGo's search results links, the linked websites don't receive any information generated by the search engine. "No tracking, no ad targeting, just searching," promises DuckDuckGo. Thus, DuckDuckGo has become a preferred search engine for people who prize online privacy, and that's a fast-growing group.

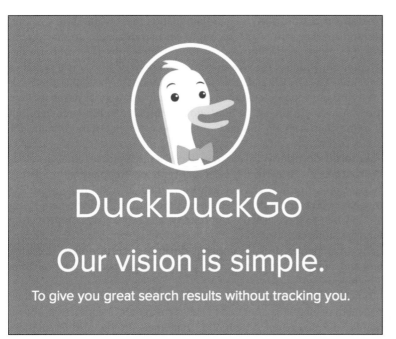

Niche marketing: DuckDuckGo thrives in the shadows of giant search engine competitors by giving its user community something the Googles of the world can't mimic—real privacy.

Duck Duck Go, Inc.

DuckDuckGo isn't just surviving in its niche, it's exploding. The company is still comparatively tiny—it averages about 12 billion searches a year versus Google's nearly 2 trillion. But DuckDuckGo's daily search volume has surged nearly fourfold in just the past three years, whereas Google's volume growth has lagged a bit. In many ways, DuckDuckGo is David to Google's Goliath. But unlike David, DuckDuckGo isn't out to slay the giant. It knows that it can't compete head-on with Google. Then again, given the depth of consumer engagement and loyalty that DuckDuckGo engenders in its own small corner of the online search market, Google and the other giants may find it difficult to compete with DuckDuckGo for privacy-minded users.

A market nicher can specialize along any of several market, customer, product, or marketing mix lines. For example, it can specialize in serving one type of *end user*, as when a law firm specializes in the criminal, civil, or business law markets. The nicher can specialize in serving a given *customer-size* group. Many nichers specialize in serving small and midsize customers who are neglected by the majors.

Some nichers focus on one or a few *specific customers*, selling their entire output to a single company, such as Walmart or General Motors. Still other nichers specialize by *geographic market*, selling only in a certain locality, region, or area of the world. For example, Vegemite is primarily sold and consumed in Australia. *Quality-price* nichers operate at the low or high end of the market. For example, Manolo Blahnik specializes in the high-quality, high-priced women's shoes. Finally, *service nichers* offer services not available from other firms. For example, LendingTree provides online lending and realty services, connecting homebuyers and sellers with national networks of mortgage lenders and realtors who compete for the customers' business. "When lenders compete," it proclaims, "you win."

Niching carries some major risks. For example, the market niche may dry up, or it might grow to the point that it attracts larger competitors. That is why many companies practice *multiple niching*. By developing two or more niches, a company increases its chances for survival. Even some larger firms prefer a multiple niche strategy to serving the total market. For example, footwear maker Wolverine World Wide markets a dozen lifestyle brands ranging from kids, casual, and athletic footwear to work shoes. For example, its age-old Stride Rite brand features durable footwear for kids. The Saucony brand offers athletic footwear for runners. The Keds brand targets women with a casual sneakers and leather shoes, whereas the Hush Puppies brand offers timeless comfort in casual shoes, boots, and sandals. In contrast, Wolverine's Bates and CAT brands target the construction, police, and military markets with durable footwear for work. Altogether, its separate niche brands combine to make Wolverine a $2.4-billion footwear company that "has the world at its feet, both literally and figuratively."[24]

Balancing Customer and Competitor Orientations

OBJECTIVE 18-3 Illustrate the need for balancing customer and competitor orientations in becoming a truly market-centered organization.

Whether a company is the market leader, challenger, follower, or nicher, it must watch its competitors closely and find the competitive marketing strategy that positions it most effectively. And it must continually adapt its strategies to the fast-changing competitive environment. This question now arises: Can the company spend *too* much time and energy tracking competitors, damaging its customer orientation? The answer is yes. A company can become so competitor centered that it loses its even more important focus on maintaining profitable customer relationships.

Competitor-centered company

A company whose moves are mainly based on competitors' actions and reactions.

Customer-centered company

A company that focuses on customer developments in designing its marketing strategies and delivering superior value to its target customers.

Market-centered company

A company that pays balanced attention to both customers and competitors in designing its marketing strategies.

A **competitor-centered company** is one that spends most of its time tracking competitors' moves and market shares and trying to find strategies to counter them. This approach has some pluses and minuses. On the positive side, the company develops a fighter orientation, watches for weaknesses in its own position, and searches out competitors' weaknesses. On the negative side, the company becomes too reactive. Rather than carrying out its own customer relationship strategy, it bases its own moves on competitors' moves. As a result, it may end up simply matching or extending industry practices rather than seeking innovative new ways to create more value for customers.

A **customer-centered company**, by contrast, focuses more on customer developments in designing its strategies. Clearly, the customer-centered company is in a better position to identify new opportunities and set long-run strategies that make sense. By watching customer needs evolve, it can decide what customer groups and what emerging needs are the most important to serve. Then it can concentrate its resources on delivering superior value to target customers.

In practice, today's companies must be **market-centered companies**, watching both their customers and their competitors. But they must not let competitor watching blind them to customer focusing.

● **Figure 18.3** shows that companies might have any of four orientations. First, they might be product oriented, paying little attention to either customers or competitors. Next, they might be customer oriented, paying attention to customers. In the third orientation, when a company starts to pay attention to competitors, it becomes competitor oriented. Today, however, companies need to be market oriented, paying balanced attention to both customers and competitors. Rather than simply watching competitors and trying to beat them on current ways of doing business, they need to watch customers and find innovative ways to build profitable customer relationships by delivering more customer value than competitors do.

● FIGURE 18.3
Evolving Company Orientations

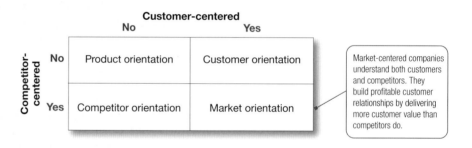

Market-centered companies understand both customers and competitors. They build profitable customer relationships by delivering more customer value than competitors do.

Reviewing and Extending the Concepts

Objectives Review

Today's companies face their toughest competition ever. Understanding customers is an important first step in developing strong customer relationships, but it's not enough. To gain competitive advantage, companies must use this understanding to design market offerings that deliver more value than the offers of competitors seeking to win over the same customers. This chapter examines how firms analyze their competitors and design effective competitive marketing strategies.

OBJECTIVE 18-1 Discuss the need to understand competitors as well as customers through competitor analysis. *(pp 526–533)*

To prepare an effective marketing strategy, a company must consider its competitors as well as its customers. Building profitable customer relationships requires satisfying target consumer needs better than competitors do. A company must continuously analyze competitors and develop competitive marketing strategies that position it effectively against competitors and give it the strongest possible competitive advantage.

Competitor analysis first involves identifying the company's major competitors, using both an industry-based and a market-based analysis. The company then gathers information on competitors' objectives, strategies, strengths and weaknesses, and reaction patterns. With this information in hand, it can select competitors to attack or avoid. Competitive intelligence must be collected, interpreted, and distributed continuously. Company marketing managers should be able to obtain full and reliable information about any competitor affecting their decisions.

OBJECTIVE 18-2 Explain the fundamentals of competitive marketing strategies based on creating value for customers. *(pp 533–543)*

Which competitive marketing strategy makes the most sense depends on the company's industry and on whether it is the market leader, challenger, follower, or nicher. The market leader has to mount strategies to expand the total market, protect market share, and expand market share. A market challenger is a firm that tries aggressively to expand its market share by attacking the leader, other runner-up companies, or smaller firms in the industry. The challenger can select from a variety of direct or indirect attack strategies.

A market follower is a runner-up firm that chooses not to rock the boat, usually from fear that it stands to lose more than it might gain. But the follower is not without a strategy and seeks to use its particular skills to gain market growth. Some followers enjoy a higher rate of return than the leaders in their industry. A market nicher is a smaller firm that is unlikely to attract the attention of larger firms. Market nichers often become specialists in some end use, customer size category, specific customer group, geographic area, or service.

OBJECTIVE 18-3 Illustrate the need for balancing customer and competitor orientations in becoming a truly market-centered organization. *(pp 543–544)*

A competitive orientation is important in today's markets, but companies should not overdo their focus on competitors. Companies are more likely to be hurt by emerging consumer needs and new competitors than by existing competitors. Market-centered companies that balance customer and competitor considerations are practicing a true market orientation.

Key Terms

Competitive advantage (p 526)
Competitor analysis (p 526)
Competitive marketing strategies (p 526)

OBJECTIVE 18-1

Strategic group (p 529)
Benchmarking (p 530)

Customer value analysis (p 531)

OBJECTIVE 18-2

Market leader (p 538)
Market challenger (p 538)
Market follower (p 538)
Market nicher (p 538)

OBJECTIVE 18-3

Competitor-centered company (p 544)
Customer-centered company (p 544)
Market-centered company (p 544)

Discussion Questions

18-1 Define *competitive advantage*. How do companies go about finding their competitive advantage? (AASCB: Written and Oral Communication; Reflective Thinking)

18-2 What questions should marketing managers ask after they identify the firm's main competitors? (AACSB: Written and Oral Communication; Reflective Thinking)

18-3 Describe the strategies that a market follower might adopt, and explain why they might never challenge the market leader. (AACSB: Communication)

18-4 How can a market leader retain their position against competition? (AACSB: Communication)

18-5 Provide examples of alternatives to market orientation and explain why they are followed. (AACSB: Communication; Reflective Thinking)

Critical Thinking Exercises

18-6 The multibillion-dollar pet care market is growing thanks to market factors including the increased availability of technology products for pets, the use of the internet to feature pets, the rise in pet adoptions, and growing demand for premium pet care products and services. Provide one example of a pet care provider that uses entrepreneurial marketing, one that uses formulated marketing, and one that uses intrapreneurial marketing. Compare and contrast each approach. (AACSB: Written and Oral Communication; Reflective Thinking)

18-7 Walmart, a market leader and the nation's biggest private employer, recently implemented a "Great Workplace" model that increases wages and responsibilities for some employees and emphasizes teamwork, accountability, and skill improvement for all frontline employees. The model aims to improve Walmart's reputation as an employer and its customer services, as it includes an attitude report card system that encourages all employees to "Be bold, be an owner, be open, and be kind." Walmart is also adding robots to clean floors, sort deliveries, and complete other repetitive tasks that were previously done by humans. How does the Great Workplace model relate to Walmart's competitive positioning strategy? How does it relate to Walmart's value discipline? (AACSB: Written and Oral Communication; Reflective Thinking)

18-8 Using the internet, find one market nicher in each of three different industries. Identify the competitive strategy each one uses. (AACSB: Written and Oral Communication; Reflective Thinking)

APPLICATIONS AND CASES

Online, Mobile, and Social Media Marketing Can Social Media Raise Awareness of Uniqlo in the United States?

Uniqlo targets young, urban, professional, and practical American shoppers with fashions that are not unique and bear no labels. It offers low prices (for example, jeans for $40), so it is sometimes grouped with other big brands in the fast-fashion category: Zara and H&M. However, unlike Zara and H&M, Uniqlo does not chase trends. It offers staples, the way the Gap did when it made basics cool in the 1990s—before it lost its edge by being in every mall and becoming the uniform of suburban moms and dads. Uniqlo offers basics with clean lines and positions itself as affordable fashion that is not disposable. It offers free tailoring and built a reputation for durability. It also uses a number of signature technologies in its clothing, including ultralight down, HEATTECH insulating system, and AIRism moisture-wicking. Madewell and Everlane offer similar products at a higher price. Although Uniqlo is owned by Fast Retailing, one of the five largest clothing retailers in the world, only a small percentage of Uniqlo's 2,000 stores are located in the United States, where it lacks brand awareness. Uniqlo fell short of the expected 200 stores in the United States by 2020; it operates 50 U.S. stores at a loss.

18-9 Compare Uniqlo's approach on Instagram (www.instagram.com/uniqlousa) to Madewell's approach (www.instagram.com/madewell). Based on your comparison, is Uniqlo a market challenger, market follower, or niche marketer? Explain your response. (AACSB: Written and Oral Communication; Reflective Thinking)

18-10 In a small group, design a social media approach that would help increase brand awareness and communicate the value proposition of Uniqlo relative to its competitors. (AACSB: Written and Oral Communication; Reflective Thinking)

Marketing Ethics Is Ugly Produce a True Food Waste Solution?

Following a USDA report that nearly one-third of food is wasted at the retail and consumer levels, "ugly produce" innovators began receiving millions of dollars in private funding to address food waste. However, some people question whether for-profit, U.S.-based ugly produce companies such as Hungry Harvest and Imperfect Produce actually help solve food waste challenges. For example, non-profit Phat Beets, which experienced a 30 percent drop in subscriptions, accused venture capital–backed Imperfect Produce of commodifying need, undercutting prices, and undermining community-supported agriculture efforts. An agricultural scientist noted that most waste comes from consumers, restaurants, and grocery stores, which are not affected by taking ugly produce from farmers. A related argument is that farmers would otherwise use the ugly produce to feed the hungry, feed animals, or fertilize the soil, so it is not clear if selling it to consumers would limit food waste. However, others argue that ugly produce companies can help address food loss, which, like waste, affects the environment and the economy. Further, marketing ugly produce may start a conversation that raises awareness about food waste.

18-11 Phat Beets and Imperfect Produce are in different categories but serve similar target markets with similar products. How should Phat Beets differentiate itself from Imperfect Produce, if at all? (AACSB: Written and Oral Communication; Reflective Thinking)

18-12 Is it ethical for ugly produce companies to position themselves as social enterprises or as solutions to the food waste challenge? Why or why not? (AACSB: Ethical Reasoning; Written and Oral Communication)

Marketing by the Numbers Changing Numbers in the Smartphone Market

Greek philosopher Heraclitus certainly understood modern-day markets when he said, "The only thing that is constant is change." The smartphone market has changed considerably since its inception just over 25 years ago. According to the Pew Research Center, 77 percent of Americans now own a smartphone. But today's smartphone market is not like it was when IBM introduced the first smart mobile device, called the Simon Personal Communicator, in 1994. Although before its time, it could perform many of today's smartphone functions. However, it was much bulkier, had a battery life of only one hour, had a small monochrome LCD screen, and could be plugged into a regular phone jack to make lower-cost calls over a landline. The next market leader was RIM's BlackBerry mobile device, which enjoyed market leadership for many years. Then along came Apple, which revolutionized the smartphone market in 2007 by introducing the iPhone. Sales of the iPhone jumped from 1.4 million units that year to almost 12 million in 2008 to more than 200 million in 2018. Apple enjoyed market leadership for many years, but new competitors entered the market, eating away at Apple's market share. Below is worldwide unit shipment data for the top smartphone companies in 2017 and 2018:

Company	Units Shipped (in millions)	
	2017	2018
Samsung	317.7	292.3
Apple	215.8	208.8
Huawei	154.2	206.0
Xiaomi	92.7	122.6
OPPO	111.7	113.1
Others	573.4	462.0

18-13 Refer to the Marketing Performance Measures section of Appendix 2: Marketing by the Numbers and calculate market shares for each company for both years. Calculate the percentage change in year-over-year unit sales for each company. What can you conclude from the market shares and year-over-year changes that you calculated? (AACSB: Analytical Reasoning; Reflective Thinking)

18-14 Find market data for previous years and analyze how the smartphone market has changed over time. (AACSB: Use of IT; Communication; Reflective Thinking)

Company Case TikTok: A Chinese Social Media App to Watch

TikTok is a social media app that allows users to upload 15-second videos, similar to the now-defunct video-hosting service Vine or, to some users, a more video-focused Instagram or Snapchat. The videos can be created with simple tools that allow users to add special effects and music before posting them on the app. TikTok's virtually endless store of videos show its users lip-syncing, dancing, and performing comedy skits, showcasing its immense popularity among youngsters, but its pure entertainment value has won it a large number of older fans as well. TikTok is available in 150 markets and 75 languages, and the company has offices in Beijing, Berlin, Jakarta, London, Los Angles, Moscow, Mumbai, Sao Paulo, Seoul, Shanghai, Singapore, and Tokyo. In June 2018, there were 500 million active users of TikTok worldwide.

Beating Local Companies in Global Markets

TikTok was originally launched by Chinese entrepreneurs Alex Zhu and Luyu Yang in 2014, but it was taken over in 2016 by ByteDance, a Beijing-based tech company traditionally focused on news. Despite heavy investments in social video-making apps and platforms, none of the big Chinese tech giants like Alibaba, Tencent, or Baidu has had anything like the success of TikTok, which seems to has had an early mover's advantage over them. TikTok is known as Douyin in China and enjoys huge popularity there as well. In November 2017, ByteDance acquired Musical.ly, a karaoke-style, short-form video app that became very popular after its launch in 2014 and had over 100 million active monthly users (by August 2018, all of its accounts were absorbed into TikTok). Although Musical.ly was also a Chinese company, most of its user accounts, the majority of which belonged to teenage girls, were based in the United States. By taking over Musical.ly, TikTok had acquired the relatively uncontested short-video-hosting market and avoided head-to-head competition. With a worth of $75 billion, ByteDance has become one of the most valuable private technology firms in the world. For its news app Toutiao, ByteDance uses advanced AI algorithms that provide customized news feeds to its users by learning about their preferences; it is using similar technology to suggest relevant video feeds for its TikTok user base.

Taking On Other Foreign Giants

Despite a competitive dominance worldwide in the hardware market, Chinese firms had been unable to replicate that success in the software market until Byte Dance's TikTok. In 2018, TikTok became one of the most downloaded mobile apps in the U.S. and European markets for Apple and Android devices, displacing traditional market leaders like Snapchat, Instagram, and YouTube. In October 2018, TikTok logged more than 4 million downloads from the App Store in the United States alone, reaching a total of 80 million. It is also one of the most popular apps on Google Play. By the end of 2018, TikTok had more than half a billion active users, more than Twitter, and around 40 percent of them were from outside China.

What makes TikTok different from the competition? From the looks of it, there is little to distinguish it from other social media video-sharing apps like Dubsmash or Snapchat, down to their shortcomings (privacy issues). Nor does TikTok set itself apart with its reaction features and mirror camera. Where it differs is the algorithms and sound and visual effects. A key selling point is simplicity of use: TikTok has made video editing extremely easy and simple. In some ways, it is like Instagram for mobile video without the excessive number of influencers and advertisers.

What Makes TikTok's Users Tick?

TikTok's technology enables users to be creative and develop videos that are more fun and engaging. TikTok won popularity for its pleasant social experience, fun features, and ad-free interface (though it did start including advertisements, like other apps, in 2019). Comedy creator Drea Knows Best, who has more than 1.8 million followers, has said that the main difference between TikTok and other social media apps is a very active and loyal user base. Comparing her videos on Musical.ly and Vine with TikTok, she found that user engagement and activity is much superior and just more fun on the latter app. She also noted that TikTok offers opportunities for creators and companies to collaborate; for example, she makes most of her TikTok earnings through her partnerships with brands like Netflix.

Here are some of the other factors that have driven TikTok's popularity:

1. *Viral Trends*: Lip-synced music videos became very popular very quickly and developed into one of the app's main performing features.
2. *Celebrities and Opinion Leaders*: To increase its user base, TikTok has leveraged internet celebrities and key opinion leaders like Cardi B and Loren Gray.
3. *Integrated Marketing Channels*: TikTok has tied up with other popular social media apps, like China's Weibo, to share their videos with the TikTok logo. These apps have become stepping stones for TikTok to penetrate their market.
4. *AI Technology*: TikTok's AI learns what its users want to see every time they click on a video, and it customizes their feed and page with similar suggestions.
5. *Producing Local Content and Contests*: TikTok began to promote localized content when it took over Musical.ly. TikTok encouraged localization of content by running contests in the countries it had a presence in, with specific localized hashtags to increase user engagement.
6. *Users as Broadcasters*: Users sharing their TikTok videos on other social media platforms, like Facebook and Instagram, worked like a catalyst to increase TikTok's popularity.

The kind of success TikTok has enjoyed was bound to attract competition locally as well as globally. Features that have worked well for TikTok include the simplicity of its design, dynamic integrated promotion, adaptability to different local markets, focused acquisition, and the ability to come up with a winning formula for different global markets. Other Chinese giants are closely observing TikTok's model and strategies. Tencent, an internet-based technology and cultural giant in China, was already looking to enter the short-video streaming industry by investing in Kuaishou, TikTok's main local competitor, boasting more than 200 million daily active users. Kuaishou is reportedly giving out subsidies worth nearly $500 million to promote its own platform, Weishi. The popular instant messaging and social entertainment platform WeChat is part of Tencent's huge portfolio, which includes with some of the world's leading apps under two main business operations: social platforms and digital content.

The Future of Competition in Social Media

Competition for TikTok is also heating up internationally. In November 2018, Facebook quietly launched Lasso, an app that enables users to create fun, short videos in much the same way as TikTok. This has widely been regarded as Facebook's latest effort to win back the younger users it had lost to other, newer apps. By February 2019, three months after its launch, Lasso was downloaded by an estimated 70,000 users in the United States, but TikTok has been downloaded by 39.6 million Americans in the same time frame. Typically, Facebook's competitive strategy has been to remove its potential competition by copying its popular features, as it did with Snapchat, but this shown little success against TikTok. TikTok was also recently quoted as a competitor by both Snap and Twitter in their financial reports.

To build on the success of the first-ever globally successful "made in China" app, ByteDance will have to be proactive, innovative, and open to collaborations. TikTok will need to massively expand from its base while countering challenges from well-funded and ambitious Chinese and global competitors. TikTok and ByteDance need to come up with good defense mechanisms in different markets. However, to defend its current position and expand its market share, ByteDance has many potential avenues through which TikTok can maintain its dominance.

Among the possible routes open to TikTok to maintain and build on its success are the music industry, upcoming artists, and collaborations with well-established brands. The music industry and TikTok seem to be developing a mutually beneficial relationship; many artists' songs have become hits after they were used by millions of TikTok users, and the TikTok creators have managed to produce their own original videos with fun and entertaining songs. In fact, many new artists have started to use the platform to release their music.

Similarly, many brands and marketers have realized the potential reach of TikTok. Some have used TikTok features, such as its challenges and contests, to create brand-specific content. Many have leveraged their hashtags to promote their messages on the TikTok platform. For example, Guess in the United States partnered with TikTok to run the #InMyDenim campaign, inviting users to create video content wearing denim. Brands can also collaborate with TikTok's celebrities to create brand-specific content.

To remain attractive and fun, TikTok will have to innovate continuously and keep its user base engaged. As more brands to look to collaborate with TikTok and leverage its reach, the company should be ready to capitalize on those brand engagements as well and grow through them. ByteDance continues to grow its social media empire, which will give TikTok a strong backing. ByteDance recently launched another app, Feilio (FLipchat in English), that allows users to create interest-based chat groups. With TikTok popularity's and its introduction of new apps, ByteDance looks set to continue its expansion and increase its local and global dominance.[25]

Questions for Discussion

18-15 Define TikTok in terms of competitive advantage.

18-16 What basic competitive strategy does ByteDance follow?

18-17 What market challenger strategies can Tencent use to enter the social media video app segment?

18-18 What kind of market leader strategies can TikTok use to defend its position in the social media video-sharing segment against local and global competition?

18-19 What kind of customer- and competitor-based orientation should TikTok adopt to continue growing?

19

The Global Marketplace

OBJECTIVES OUTLINE

OBJECTIVE 19-1 Discuss how the international trade system and the economic, political-legal, and cultural environments affect a company's international marketing decisions. **See: Global Marketing Today** *(pp 552–563)*

OBJECTIVE 19-2 Describe three key approaches to entering international markets. **See: Deciding How to Enter the Market** *(pp 564–566)*

OBJECTIVE 19-3 Explain how companies adapt their marketing strategies and mixes for international markets. **See: Deciding on the Global Marketing Program** *(pp 566–572)*

OBJECTIVE 19-4 Identify the three major forms of international marketing organization. **See: Deciding on the Global Marketing Organization** *(p 573)*

CHAPTER PREVIEW You've now learned the fundamentals of how companies develop competitive marketing strategies to engage customers, create customer value, and build lasting customer relationships. In this chapter, we extend these fundamentals to global marketing. Although we've discussed global topics in each previous chapter—it's difficult to find an area of marketing that doesn't contain at least some international elements—here we'll focus on special considerations that companies face when they market brands globally. Advances in communication, transportation, and digital technologies have made the world a much smaller place. Today, almost every firm, large or small, faces international marketing issues.

In this chapter, we will examine six major decisions marketers make in going global.

To start our exploration of global marketing, let's look at L'Oréal, the French cosmetics and beauty care giant. L'Oréal and its brands are truly global in scope and appeal. But the company's outstanding international success comes from achieving a global–local balance, one that adapts and differentiates L'Oréal's well-known brands to meet local needs while also integrating them across world markets to optimize their global impact. This global–local balance lies at the roots of the organization whose mission is to offer "beauty for all" by providing "beauty for each individual."

L'ORÉAL: "Beauty for All. Beauty for Each Individual."

How does a French company successfully market an American version of a Korean skin beautifier under a French brand name in Australia? Ask L'Oréal, which sells more than $30 billion worth of cosmetics, hair care products, skin care concoctions, and fragrances each year in 150 countries, making it the world's biggest cosmetics marketer. L'Oréal sells its brands globally by understanding how they appeal to varied cultural nuances of beauty in specific local markets. Then it finds the best balance between standardizing its brands for global impact and adapting them to meet local needs and desires.

L'Oréal is as global as a company gets, with offices spread throughout the world and more than half of its sales coming from markets outside Europe and North America. L'Oréal's 34 well-known brands originated in different cultures, including French (L'Oréal Paris, Garnier, Lancôme), American (Maybelline, Kiehl's, SoftSheen-Carson, Ralph Lauren, Urban Decay, Clarisonic, Redken), Italian (Giorgio Armani), and

Japanese (Shu Uemura). With these and many other well-known brands, the master global marketer is the uncontested world leader in makeup, skin care, and hair coloring and second only to P&G in hair care.

L'Oréal's global mastery starts with a corps of highly multicultural managers. The company is famous for building global brand teams around managers who have deep backgrounds in several cultures. L'Oréal managers around the world bring diverse cultural perspectives to their brands as if they were, say, German or American or Chinese—or all three at once. As explained by one Indian-American-French manager of a team that launched a men's skin care line in Southeast Asia: "I cannot think about things one way. I have a stock of references in different languages: English, Hindi, and French. I read books in three different languages, meet people from different countries, eat food from different [cultures], and so on."

For example, a French-Irish-Cambodian skin care manager noticed that, in Europe, face creams tended to be either "tinted" (and considered makeup) or "lifting" (considered skin care). In Asia, however, many face creams combine both traits. Recognizing the growing popularity of Asian beauty trends in Europe, the manager and his team developed a tinted lifting cream for the French market, a product that proved highly successful.

With its global presence, L'Oréal's vision is to universalize beauty—to offer "beauty for all" around the world. But universalization doesn't mean uniformity. To the contrary, says the company: "At L'Oréal, we are convinced that no single and unique model of beauty exists, but an infinite diversity, changing with the times, through cultures, histories, individuals." Thus, to achieve "beauty for all," L'Oréal seeks to provide "beauty for each individual."

To that end, L'Oréal digs deep to understand what beauty means to consumers in different parts of the world. It outspends all major competitors on R&D, painstakingly researching beauty and personal care behaviors unique to specific locales. L'Oréal has set up R&D centers all over the world, perfecting a local observation approach it calls "geocosmetics." This science is fueled with insights gained through everything from in-home visits to observations made in "bathroom laboratories" equipped with high-tech gadgetry. L'Oréal's research produces precise information about regional beauty and hygiene rituals and about local conditions and constraints that affect the use of its products, such as humidity and temperature.

L'Oréal uses such detailed insights to create products and positioning for brands in local markets. "Beauty is less and less one size fits all," says a L'Oréal executive in China. "You have to

Global–local balance: Cosmetics and beauty care giant L'Oréal balances local brand responsiveness and global brand impact, offering "beauty for all" by providing "beauty for each individual."
TY Lim/Shutterstock

have an answer for very different needs." For example, more than 260 scientists now work in L'Oréal's Shanghai research center, tailoring products ranging from lipstick to herbal cleaners to cucumber toners for Chinese tastes.

At the same time that understanding of the minute details of local customer behavior helps L'Oréal be responsive to specific market needs, it also lets the company achieve global scale by integrating brands across world cultures. For example, consider Elséve Total Reparação, a hair care line initially developed at L'Oréal's labs in Rio de Janeiro to address specific hair problems described by Brazilian women. In Brazil, more than half of all women have long, dry, dull, and very curly hair, resulting from the humid Brazilian climate, exposure to the sun, frequent washing, and smoothing and straightening treatments. Elséve Total Reparação was an immediate hit in Brazil, and L'Oréal quickly rolled it out to other South American and Latin American markets. The company then tracked down other global locales with climate characteristics and hair care rituals similar to those faced by Brazilian women. Subsequently, L'Oréal launched the brand as Elséve Total Repair in numerous European, Indian, and other South East Asian markets, where consumers greeted it with similar enthusiasm.

Such adaptation often plays out across multiple L'Oréal brands—which takes us back to that Korean skin beautifier sold under a French brand in Australia mentioned in the opening paragraph. Blemish Balm Cream (BB Cream) was originally created by L'Oréal dermatologists in Korea to soothe skin and hide minor blemishes. It quickly became a high-flying Korean brand. However, applying its

> Cosmetic and beauty care giant L'Oréal and its brands are truly global. But the company's huge international success comes from a global–local balance that adapts brands to local markets while optimizing their impact globally.

deep knowledge of skin colors, treatments, and makeup worldwide, L'Oréal developed a successful new-generation BB Cream adapted to conditions and skin colors in U.S. markets (where BB stands for "beauty balm") and launched it under the Maybelline New York brand. Still not finished, L'Oréal created yet another local version for Europe under the Garnier brand, which it also introduced in other world markets, including Australia.

L'Oréal doesn't adapt just its product formulations globally. It also adapts brand positioning and marketing to international needs and expectations. For example, more than 25 years ago, the company bought stodgy American makeup producer Maybelline. To reinvigorate and globalize the brand, it moved the unit's headquarters from Tennessee to New York City and added "New York" to the label. The resulting urban, street-smart, Big Apple image played well with the midprice positioning of the workaday makeup brand globally. The makeover quickly earned Maybelline a 20 percent market share in its category in Western Europe. The young urban positioning also hit the mark in Asia, where few women realized that the trendy "New York" Maybelline brand belonged to French cosmetics giant L'Oréal.

In its latest effort to bring beauty to each individual, L'Oréal recently launched Color&Co, a direct-to-consumer brand that aims to give dye-at-home users their own personal hair color. The experience begins at the brand's website, where a customer takes a quiz and has a real-time video consultation with a professional hair colorist. The colorist applies an algorithm that comes up with a personalized formula to achieve the perfect hair shade based on each customer's hair type, ethnicity, natural undertones, preferences, and other factors. Within days, the customer receives a Color&Co Colorbox with the custom-blended formula, personalized instructions, and a how-to video. Going forward, Color&Co gives L'Oréal the beginnings of what might be the ultimate technology platform for delivering individualized beauty solutions across its wide range of products anywhere in the world.

Thus, L'Oréal and its brands are truly global, capturing nearly 30 percent of the worldwide cosmetics market. But L'Oréal's huge international success comes from achieving a global–local balance that adapts and differentiates brands in local markets while optimizing their impact across global markets. L'Oréal is one of few companies that have achieved both local brand responsiveness and global brand integration. "We respect the differences among our consumers around the world," says L'Oréal's CEO. "We have global brands, but we need to adapt them to local [and even individual] needs."[1]

IN THE PAST, U.S. COMPANIES paid little attention to international trade. If they could pick up some extra sales via exports, that was fine. But the big market was at home, and it teemed with opportunities. The home market was also much safer. Managers did not need to learn other languages, deal with strange and changing currencies, face political and legal uncertainties, or adapt their products to different customer needs and expectations. Today, however, the situation is much different. Organizations of all kinds, from Coca-Cola, Apple, and Nike to Google, Airbnb, and even the NBA, have gone global.

Author | The rapidly changing
Comment | global environment
provides both opportunities and threats. It's difficult to find a marketer today that isn't affected in some way by global developments.

Global Marketing Today

OBJECTIVE 19-1 Discuss how the international trade system and the economic, political-legal, and cultural environments affect a company's international marketing decisions.

The world is shrinking rapidly with the advent of faster digital communication, transportation, and financial flows. Products and services developed in one country—McDonald's hamburgers, Netflix video service, Samsung electronics, Zara fashions, Caterpillar construction equipment, German BMWs, Facebook social networking—have found enthusiastic acceptance in other countries. It would not be surprising to hear about a German businessman wearing an Italian suit meeting an English friend at a Japanese restaurant who later returns home to drink Russian vodka while steaming the latest episode of *This Is Us* and checking Facebook posts from friends around the world.

International trade has boomed over the past three decades. Since 1990, the number of multinational corporations in the world has soared, and many multinationals are true giants. In fact, of the largest 150 economies in the world, only about half are countries.

● Many American companies have now made the world their market. KFC's Colonel Sanders is almost as familiar in Shanghai, China (above), or Tokyo, Japan, as he is in Boise, Idaho.

Gary Armstrong

The rest are multinational corporations. Walmart, the world's largest company (based on a weighted average of sales, profits, assets, and market value) has annual revenues greater than the gross domestic product (GDP) of all but the world's 25 largest countries.[2] The global trade of products and services last year was valued at more than $23 trillion, about 27 percent of GDP worldwide.[3]

● Many U.S. companies are successful international marketers: Coca-Cola, McDonald's, Starbucks, Nike, Netflix, Amazon, Google, Caterpillar, Boeing, and dozens of other American firms have the world their market. In the United States, non-American brands such as Toyota, Samsung, Nestlé, IKEA, and adidas have become household words. Other products and services that appear to be American are, in fact, produced or owned by foreign companies, such as Ben & Jerry's ice cream, Budweiser beer, Purina pet foods, 7-Eleven, Universal Studios, and Motel 6. Michelin, the oh-so-French tire manufacturer, now does 36 percent of its business in North America; J&J, the maker of quintessentially all-American products such as BAND-AIDs and Johnson's Baby Shampoo, does almost half of its business abroad. Once all-American KFC's Colonel Sanders is almost as familiar in Shanghai, China (above), or Tokyo, Japan, as he is in Boise, Idaho. And with more than 500 brands worldwide, American favorite Coca-Cola now lets consumers "taste the feeling" more than 1.9 billion times a day in over 200 countries.[4]

But as global trade grows, global competition is also intensifying. Foreign firms are expanding aggressively into new international markets, and home markets are no longer as rich in opportunity. Few industries are currently safe from foreign competition. If companies delay taking steps toward internationalizing, they risk being shut out of growing markets in Western and Eastern Europe, China and Southeast Asia, Russia, India, Brazil, and elsewhere. Firms that stay at home to play it safe might not only lose their chances to enter other markets but also risk losing their home markets. Domestic companies that never thought about foreign competitors suddenly find these competitors in their own backyards.

Ironically, although the need for companies to go abroad is greater today than in the past, so are the risks. Companies that go global may face highly unstable governments and currencies, restrictive government policies and regulations, and high trade barriers. The recently dampened global economic environment has also created big global challenges. In addition, corruption is an increasing problem; officials in several countries often award business not to the best bidder but to the highest briber.

Global firm

A firm that, by operating in more than one country, gains R&D, production, marketing, and financial advantages in its costs and reputation that are not available to purely domestic competitors.

A **global firm** is one that, by operating in more than one country, gains marketing, production, research and development (R&D), and financial advantages that are not available to purely domestic competitors. Because the global company sees the world as one market, it minimizes the importance of national boundaries and develops global brands. The global company raises capital, obtains materials and components, and manufactures and markets its goods wherever it can do the best job.

For example, U.S.-based Otis Elevator, the world's largest elevator maker, is headquartered in Farmington, Connecticut. However, it sells and maintains elevators and escalators in more than 200 countries and achieves 73 percent of its sales from outside the United States. It gets elevator door systems from France, small-geared parts from Spain, electronics from Germany, and special motor drives from Japan. It operates manufacturing facilities in the Americas, Europe, and Asia and engineering and test centers in the United States, Austria, Brazil, China, Czech Republic, France, Germany, India, Italy, Japan, Korea, and Spain. In turn, Otis Elevator is a wholly owned subsidiary of global commercial and aerospace giant United Technologies Corporation.[5] Many of today's global corporations—both large and small—have become truly borderless.

● **FIGURE 19.1**
Major International Marketing Decisions

It's a big and beautiful but threatening world out there for marketers! Most large American firms have made the world their market. For example, once all-American McDonald's now captures two-thirds of its sales from outside the United States.

This does not mean, however, that every firm must operate in dozens of countries to succeed. Smaller firms can practice global niching. But the world is becoming smaller, and every company operating in a global industry—whether large or small—must assess and establish its place in world markets.

The rapid move toward globalization means that all companies will have to answer some basic questions: What market position should we try to establish in our country, in our economic region, and globally? Who will our global competitors be, and what are their strategies and resources? Where should we produce or source our products? What strategic alliances should we form with other firms around the world?

As shown in ● **Figure 19.1**, a company faces six major decisions in international marketing. We discuss each decision in detail in this chapter.

Elements of the Global Marketing Environment

Author | As if operating within a
Comment | company's own borders wasn't difficult enough, going global adds many layers of complexities. For example, Coca-Cola markets its products in 200 countries around the globe. It must understand the varying trade, economic, cultural, and political environments in each market.

Before deciding whether to operate internationally, a company must understand the international marketing environment. That environment has changed a great deal in recent decades, creating both new opportunities and new problems.

The International Trade System

U.S. companies looking abroad must start by understanding the international *trade system*. When selling to another country, a firm may face restrictions on trade between nations. Governments may charge *tariffs* or *duties*, taxes on certain imported products designed to raise revenue or protect domestic firms. Tariffs and duties are often used to force favorable trade behaviors from other nations.

For example, in efforts to negotiate more favorable trade terms that would rein in its large and growing annual trade deficit with China, the United States recently began charging tariffs on Chinese imports ranging from pork, soybeans, and wine to steel, aluminum, and a breadth of industrial, technology, transport, medical, textile, and fashion products. China retaliated with its own tariffs on U.S. goods, setting off several rounds of heated trade negotiations. Such trade disputes between nations are part of wider international dynamics. However, they can cause major difficulties for companies trying to market their goods across international borders.[6]

Countries may set quotas, limits on the amount of imports that they will accept in certain product categories. The purpose of a quota is to conserve on foreign exchange and protect local industry and employment. Firms may also encounter exchange controls, which limit the amount of foreign exchange and the exchange rate against other currencies.

A company also may face nontariff trade barriers, such as biases against its bids, restrictive product standards, or excessive host-country regulations or enforcement. ● For example, India is notorious for throwing up nontariff obstacles to protect the nation's own predominately mom-and-pop retailers, which control 88 percent of India's $1.1 trillion in retail sales.[7] The country recently laid down new e-commerce restrictions that prohibit foreign-owned online companies, such as Amazon or Walmart's Flipkart unit, from selling their own products directly to consumers on their sites. For Amazon, that includes products such as Amazon's Echo, Kindle, and Fire TV devices and a growing list of private-branded products ranging from batteries and fashions to home goods. Under the new rules, Amazon and Flipkart can serve only as marketplaces that connect independent

● Nontariff trade barriers: New restrictions on foreign-owned online sellers caused major obstacles for Amazon in India's huge e-commerce market.

REBECCA CONWAY/The New York Times/Redux

buyers with sellers. The new rules also ban forming exclusive deals with major sellers and offering deep discounts. Designed to protect local Indian stores and online retailers from the inventory and pricing power of large foreign-owned businesses, such regulations have caused major obstacles for Amazon and Walmart, which have both invested heavily in recent years to develop a presence in India's huge $100 billion e-commence market.[8]

At the same time, certain other forces can *help* trade between nations. Examples include the World Trade Organization (WTO) and various regional free trade agreements.

The World Trade Organization. The General Agreement on Tariffs and Trade (GATT), established in 1947 and modified in 1994, was designed to promote world trade by reducing tariffs and other international trade barriers. It established the World Trade Organization (WTO), which replaced GATT in 1995 and now oversees the original GATT provisions. WTO and GATT member nations (currently numbering 164) have met in eight rounds of negotiations to reassess trade barriers and establish new rules for international trade. The WTO also imposes international trade sanctions and mediates global trade disputes. Its actions have been productive. The first seven rounds of negotiations reduced the average worldwide tariffs on manufactured goods from 45 percent to just 5 percent. And the WTO's trade dispute mechanism has been used extensively. Over the past two decades, members have filed more than 500 disputes, most of which were settled within the WTO framework.[9]

Economic community

A group of nations organized to work toward common goals in the regulation of international trade.

Regional Free Trade Zones. Certain countries have formed *free trade zones* or **economic communities**. These are groups of nations organized to work toward common goals in the regulation of international trade. One such community is the *European Union (EU)*. Formed in 1957, the EU set out to create a single European market by reducing barriers to the free flow of products, services, finances, and labor among member countries and developing policies on trade with nonmember nations. Today, the EU represents one of the world's largest single markets. ● Currently, it has 28 member countries containing 513 million consumers and accounting for more than 20 percent of the world's imports and exports.[10] The EU offers tremendous trade opportunities for U.S. and other non-European firms.

For 20 years, 19 EU member nations have adopted the euro as a common currency. Widespread adoption of the euro decreased much of the currency risk associated with doing business in Europe, making member countries with previously weak currencies more attractive markets. However, the adoption of a common currency has also caused problems, as European economic powers such as Germany and France have had to step in recently to prop up weaker economies such as those of Greece, Portugal, and Cyprus. This ongoing "euro crisis" has led some analysts to predict the possible breakup of the euro zone as it is now set up. However, the euro has survived many similar previous predictions.[11]

It is unlikely that the EU will ever go against 2,000 years of tradition and become the "United States of Europe." A community with more than two dozen different languages and cultures and a history of sometimes strained relationships will always have difficulty coming together and acting

● Economic communities: The European Union represents one of the world's largest single markets. It contains more than half a billion consumers and accounts for almost 20 percent of the world's imports and exports.

Paul Grecaud/123RF

as a single entity. For example, in a 2016 national referendum, the people of the United Kingdom voted to exit the European Union—the so-called "Brexit." The UK is set to depart the EU in 2019 with a "transition period" to smooth the way to post-Brexit relations with the remaining EU countries. However, negotiations have continued, and the exact nature and timing of Brexit remain uncertain. Brexit has sent aftershocks across Europe and the world, raising concerns about the future of European economic and political unity. Still, with a post-Brexit combined annual GDP of more than $17 trillion, whatever the outcome, the EU will remain a potent economic force.[12]

In 1994, the North American Free Trade Agreement (NAFTA) established a free trade zone among the United States, Mexico, and Canada. The agreement created a single market of 450 million people who produce and consume $24 trillion worth of goods and services annually. Over the past 25 years, NAFTA has eliminated trade barriers and investment restrictions among the three countries. Total trade among the NAFTA countries nearly tripled from $288 billion in 1993 to more than $1.3 trillion a year.[13]

Another major world trade agreement is the Comprehensive and Progressive Agreement for Trans-Pacific Partnership (CPTPP). The recently signed CPTPP promises to lower trade barriers and increase economic cooperation among 11 Pacific Rim countries: Australia, Brunei, Canada, Chile, Japan, Malaysia, Mexico, New Zealand, Peru, Singapore, and Vietnam. This major trade agreement will have a significant and sometimes controversial economic and political impact. The 11 CPTPP countries have a collective population of 495 million people, more than NAFTA, and account for 13.5 percent of the world's GDP.[14]

Each nation has unique features that must be understood. A nation's readiness for different products and services and its attractiveness as a market to foreign firms depend on its economic, political-legal, and cultural environments.

Economic Environment

The international marketer must study each country's economy. Two economic factors reflect the country's attractiveness as a market: its industrial structure and its income distribution.

The country's industrial structure shapes its product and service needs, income levels, and employment levels. For example, in subsistence economies, most people engage in simple agriculture, consume most of their output, and barter the rest for simple goods and services. These economies offer fewer market opportunities and require special marketing efforts. Many African countries fall into this category. At the other extreme, industrial economies are major importers and exporters of manufactured goods and services. Their varied manufacturing activities and large middle classes make them rich markets for all sorts of goods. The United States, Japan, and the Western European countries are examples.

Emerging economies are those experiencing rapid economic growth and industrialization. Examples include the BRICS countries—Brazil, Russia, India, China, and South Africa—and MENA countries (the Middle East and North Africa region). Industrialization typically creates a new rich class and a growing middle class, both demanding new types of goods and services. As more-developed markets stagnate and become increasingly competitive, many marketers are now targeting growth opportunities in emerging markets.

The second economic factor is the country's income distribution. Industrialized nations may have low-, medium-, and high-income households. In contrast, countries with subsistence economies consist mostly of households with very low family incomes. Still other countries may have households with either very low or very high incomes. Even poor or emerging economies may be attractive markets for all kinds of goods. In recent years, as growth has slowed in both domestic and emerging markets, many companies have shifted their sights to the so-called "bottom of the economic pyramid," the vast untapped market consisting of the world's poorest consumers.

These days, companies in a wide range of industries—from cars to computers to soft drinks—are increasingly targeting middle-income or low-income consumers in subsistence and emerging economies. For example, as soft drink sales growth has lost its fizz in North America and Europe, Coca-Cola has looked elsewhere to meet its ambitious growth goals. So the company has set its sights on Africa, with its promising though challenging long-term growth opportunities. Many Western companies view Africa as an untamed final frontier, plagued by poverty, political instability, unreliable transportation, and shortages of fresh water and other essential resources. But Coca-Cola sees

Real Marketing 19.1 | Tata Steel: Entering High-Potential International Markets

Tata Steel, part of the Tata Group, is one of the largest steel manufacturers in the world. The company was founded 1907 in India, and today its key operations have spread to The Netherlands and United Kingdom. Across manufacturing operations spread over Europe, Australia, South Africa, Asia, and the Middle East, the company reached a turnover of over $9.8 billion in 2018, mainly from working with other businesses. Responding to a weakened global economy that has slowed growth in both domestic and emerging markets, Tata Steel approaches the "bottom of the pyramid" (BoP) markets: India, Nigeria, China, Indonesia, and South Africa. These countries offer diverse spending patterns and market potential, and are lucrative destinations for a steel-making business.

When approaching new targets and entering new markets, Tata Steel must navigate various legal, political, and economic challenges. For instance, the international trading system comprises thousands of unilateral, bilateral, regional, and multilateral rules and agreements among more than two hundred nations. By operating in more than 175 countries with more than 50 production sites on three different continents, the company must consider import and export restrictions, tariffs, quotas, and non-tariff barriers. Furthermore, some BoP countries are far less receptive to advertisements and personal selling than Europe. As a multinational company, Tata Steel needs to consider all of this when making decisions about BoP markets.

In 2013, as part of an agreement with UK India Business Council (UKIBC), Tata Steel committed to an initiative to educate 500 million skilled people by the year 2022 and to support growth, investment, jobs creation, and an improved demand supply. This was an attractive investment for the company as it could now determine what features help in the sustainability of its products in the long run and how such products could help in reverse innovation. As part of the UKIBC agreement, Tata Steel has developed products with a low price and adapted its marketing approach to BoP consumers, which includes finding ingenious ways to use local commodities and local production techniques to compete with the more technologically advanced producers in the West. Tata Steel invested over $ 3.4 billion in a greenfield steel project in Kalinganagar, Odisha, with plans for further expansion.

However, the project was met with some hostility from local villagers, and the company was forced to acknowledge the importance of building relationships with locals, even those in its home country.

Tata Steel currently operates in four markets: packaging, automobiles, construction, and engineering. Ownership of mineral reserves and raw materials puts Tata Steel in a very strong position within the markets it operates in; it can produce steel at lower costs than nearly any other steelmaker in the world. The possibilities of entering a whole new international market are huge. However, a much-sought-after merger with Thyssenkrupp was blocked by the EU's antitrust enforcer in 2019 on the grounds that it would disrupt perfect competition within the EU and reduce competition in the supply of special steel for car-makers and packaging; additionally, the two companies had failed to propose sufficient remedies to address the EU's concerns. Political and economic conditions like this have put a dent in company's ambitions to become the biggest steel business in the world.

Despite such difficulties in responding adequately to complex new environments, Tata Steel offers several good examples of how acquiring another multinational opens new markets. For example, the acquisition of Corus in 2007 made Tata Steel the fifth-largest global steel producer, with an annual production capacity of 25 million tons of steel a year. In addition, the company gained access to European markets and was able to profit from newly acquired technologies. In fact, Tata Steel was sufficiently impressed by the favorable strategic and financial outcomes that it paid more for Corus than its original bid.

Another positive outcome from the merger is that the combination of low-cost upstream production in India and Corus's high-end downstream processing facilities in Europe offered synergies in manufacturing, procurement, R&D, logistics, and back-office operations that would improve the competitiveness of European operations. Thanks to the acquisition, Tata Steel has gained access to raw materials at low cost and exposure to high-growth emerging markets while confirming price stability in developed markets. Tata Steel decided to retain Corus's top management and consider a restructuring at a later date, after any integration issues had been resolved.

Tata Steel's continued acquisitions, such as Usha Martin in April 2019 and Bhushan Steel in May 2018, show that it has found a proven way to strengthen its market position and global presence. These are not the only reasons that Tata Steel acquires companies; for one thing, it is easier to buy into a company that has debt but is a big name in the market that Tata Steel wants to enter. Purchasing a company in a new market lowers the risk and cost of failure and bypasses barriers to entry. However, the company must already be fully functioning for Tata Steel to truly benefit from it.

Mergers and acquisitions in other countries may bring huge opportunities, but there are often cultural challenges to contend with as well—in fact, by some estimates, they have contributed to the failure of nearly 70 percent of all mergers and acquisitions. For example, in 2007, the credit rating agency Standard & Poor declared a "negative implications" watch in India due the fact that Indian companies often lack experience in international acquisitions, especially with regard to corporate culture and employment rules (the rating meant that the agency was

Tata Steel has encountered various legal, political, and economic challenges while entering international markets.

Volodymyr Plysiuk/Shutterstock

looking to lower the company's credit score based on its performance or international market trends). Indeed, in 2000, the acquisition of Tetley, a UK beverage company, ran into cultural obstacles between the British employees and the Indian managers. This issue also arose during the 2007 merger with Corus, an Anglo-Dutch steel firm. In addition, while analyzing the possibility of moving production from the United Kingdom to the lower-cost India markets, Tata Steel's management had to respond to the uncertainty of their European employees with regard to the newly created entity. Left unchecked, such situations have the potential of creating low morale, resulting in decreased productivity.

To help mitigate such difficulties in a broader sense, Tata Steel has declared that in global operating locations it is an equal-opportunity employer and does not tolerate discrimination based on race, caste, religion, color, ancestry, gender, marital status, sexual orientation, age, nationality, ethnic origin, or disability. Moreover, Tata Steel ensures that employee policies and practices are administered in a manner which ensures that all decisions relating to promotion, compensation, and any other form of reward and recognition are based entirely on merit.[15]

plenty of opportunity to justify the risks. The African continent has a growing population of more than 1.3 billion people, a just-emerging middle class, and $5 trillion of GDP and spending power. And about half of the world's fastest-growing markets are in Africa:[16]

Coca-Cola has operated in Africa since 1929 and holds a dominant market share over Pepsi in Africa and the Middle East. However, there's still plenty of room for Coca-Cola to grow there. For example, annual per capita consumption of Coke and other soft drinks is about 13 times less in Africa than in North America. Still, marketing in Africa is very different from marketing in more developed regions. Beyond just marketing through traditional channels in larger African cities, Coca-Cola has invaded smaller communities with more grassroots tactics.

● With sales stagnating in its mature markets, Coca-Cola is looking to emerging markets—such as Africa—to meet its ambitious growth goals. Its African distribution network is rudimentary but effective.

John Wollwerth/Shutterstock

● Small stores play a big role in helping Coca-Cola to grow in Africa. In countless poor neighborhoods across the continent, crowded streets are lined with shops painted Coke red, selling low-priced Coca-Cola products by the bottle out of Coke-provided, refrigerated coolers. Such shops are supplied by a rudimentary but effective network of Coca-Cola distributors, whose crews often deliver crates of Coke products by hand-pulled trolleys or even a crate at a time carried on their heads. Because of the poor roads crowded with traffic, moving drinks by hand is often the best method. The company's first rule is to get its products "cold and close." "If they don't have roads to move products long distances on trucks, we will use boats, canoes, or trolleys," says the president of Coca-Cola South Africa. For example, in Nigeria's Makako district—a maze of stilt houses on the Lagos lagoon—women crisscross the waterways in canoes selling Coca-Cola directly to residents.

Political-Legal Environment

Nations differ greatly in their political-legal environments. In considering whether to do business in a given country, a company should consider factors such as the country's attitudes toward international buying, government bureaucracy, political stability, and monetary regulations.

Some nations are very receptive to foreign firms; others are less accommodating. For example, India has tended to bother foreign businesses with import quotas, currency restrictions, foreign investment limits, and other limitations that make operating there a challenge. In contrast, neighboring Asian countries such as Singapore, Vietnam, and Thailand court foreign investors and shower them with incentives and favorable operating conditions. Political and regulatory stability is another issue. For example, Russia is consumed by corruption and governmental red tape, which the government finds difficult to control. The country's recent geopolitical conflicts with Europe, the United States, and other countries have made doing business in Russia difficult and risky.[17]

Companies must also consider a country's monetary regulations. Sellers want to take their profits in a currency of value to them. Ideally, the buyer can pay in the seller's currency or in other world currencies. Short of this, sellers might accept a blocked currency—one whose removal from the country is restricted by the buyer's government—if they can buy other goods in that country that they need or can sell elsewhere for a needed currency. In addition to currency limits, a changing exchange rate also creates high risks for the seller.

Most international trade involves cash transactions. Yet many nations have too little hard currency to pay for their purchases from other countries. They may want to pay with other items instead of cash. *Barter* involves the direct exchange of goods or services. For example, Indonesia recently bartered coffee, tea, rubber, and palm oil for military aircraft from Russia. And South Korea bartered apples for coffee from Vietnam to help balance an apple surplus against a burgeoning coffee demand.[18]

Cultural Environment

Each country has its own folkways, norms, and taboos. When designing global marketing strategies, companies must understand how culture affects consumer reactions in each of its world markets. In turn, they must also understand how their strategies affect local cultures.

The Impact of Culture on Marketing Strategy. Sellers must understand the ways that consumers in different countries think about and use certain products before planning a marketing program. There are often surprises. For example, the average French man uses almost twice as many cosmetics and grooming aids as his wife. The Germans and the French eat more packaged, branded spaghetti than Italians do. A clock makes a nice gift in Western countries but is inappropriate in China, where such a gift is associated with death and funerals. Most American women let down their hair and take off makeup at bedtime, whereas some Chinese women style their hair at bedtime and even put *on* makeup.[19]

Companies that violate cultural norms and differences can make some very expensive and embarrassing mistakes. Here are just two examples:[20]

> Nike inadvertently offended Chinese officials when it ran an ad featuring LeBron James crushing a number of culturally revered Chinese figures in a kung fu–themed television ad. The Chinese government found that the ad violated regulations to uphold national dignity and respect the "motherland's culture" and yanked the multimillion-dollar campaign. With egg on its face, Nike released a formal apology.
>
> ● Marriott International recently stumbled in China when its website listed Tibet, Hong Kong, Macau, and Taiwan as "countries." Officially, the first three locations are "autonomous regions" of China; Hong Kong and Macau are "special administrative regions." And China considers Taiwan to be a "breakaway province" controlled by an illegitimate government. What seemed like an innocent mistake led to harsh penalties in China, where Marriott operates 124 large properties. Although Marriott apologized and corrected the error, the Chinese government shut down Marriott's Chinese website and app for more than a week, preventing online sales and bookings in China.

Business norms and behaviors also vary from country to country. For example, American executives like to get right down to business and engage in fast and tough face-to-face bargaining. However, Japanese and other Asian businesspeople often find this behavior offensive. They prefer to start with polite conversation, and they rarely say no in face-to-face conversations.

As another example, firm handshakes are a common and expected greeting in most Western countries; in some Middle Eastern countries, however, handshakes might be refused if offered. Microsoft founder Bill Gates once set off a flurry of international controversy when he shook the hand of South Korea's president with his right hand while keeping his left hand in his pocket, something that Koreans consider highly disrespectful. In some countries, when being entertained at a meal, not finishing all the food implies that it was somehow substandard. In other countries, in contrast, wolfing down every last bite might be taken as a mild insult, suggesting that

● **Culture and marketing strategy: Marriott International recently stumbled in China when its website listed Tibet, Hong Kong, Macau, and Taiwan as "countries." The Chinese government shut down Marriott's Chinese website and app for more than a week.**

Imagine China/Newscom

the host didn't supply enough quantity. And in most places, smiling during a business meeting sets a congenial tone; in Russia, it suggests insecurity.[21] American business executives need to understand these kinds of cultural nuances before conducting business in another country.

By the same token, companies that understand cultural nuances can use them to their advantage in global markets. For example, when British clothing retailer Marks & Spencer decided to open its first standalone lingerie and beauty store, to the surprise of many it bypassed Paris, London, and New York and instead chose Saudi Arabia. Operating in Saudi Arabia requires some significant but worthwhile cultural adjustments:[22]

> The Saudi retail market is booming, and the country has a fast-growing and affluent consumer class. However, the conservative Islamic kingdom has no end of restrictive cultural and religious rules, especially when it involves retailing to women. In Saudi Arabia, women cover themselves in full-length black cloaks—called *abaya*—when they go out in public and must have a male chaperone, usually a relative. However, because they typically wear Western clothes at home or when traveling abroad, Western-style fashion stores are still very popular.
>
> When selling to Saudi women, Marks & Spencer must adhere to rigorously enforced religious and cultural strictures. For example, by government decree, its lingerie stores must employ an exclusively female sales staff. Because women's faces can't be shown and certain public dress is prohibited, Marks & Spencer uses tamer in-store marketing photos and video displays requiring separate photo shoots. Music is forbidden in Saudi malls and stores, so Marks & Spencer has eliminated the usual background compositions. Thanks to these and many other cultural adaptations, Saudi Arabia has become one of Marks & Spencer's highest-grossing emerging markets, well worth the additional costs of operating there. Marks & Spencer now has six lingerie and beauty stores in Saudi Arabia along with 16 full department stores. It has even gone so far as to use headless or faceless female mannequins to display its lingerie. "Unfortunately," says one Marks & Spencer marketer, "even the mannequins are not allowed to show faces."

Thus, understanding cultural traditions, preferences, and behaviors can help companies not only avoid embarrassing mistakes but also take advantage of cross-cultural opportunities.

The Impact of Marketing Strategy on Cultures. Whereas marketers worry about the impact of global cultures on their marketing strategies, others may worry about the impact of marketing strategies on global cultures. For example, social critics contend that large American multinationals, such as McDonald's, Coca-Cola, Starbucks, Nike, Google, Disney, and Facebook, aren't just globalizing their brands; they are Americanizing the world's cultures.

Other elements of American culture have become pervasive worldwide. For instance, more people now study English in China than speak it in the United States. If you assemble businesspeople from Brazil, Germany, and China, they'll likely transact in English. And the thing that binds the world's teens together in a kind of global community, notes one observer, "is American culture—the music, the Hollywood fare, the electronic games, Google, Facebook, American consumer brands. The … rest of the world is becoming [evermore] like us—in ways good and bad."[23]

Critics worry that, under such "McDomination," countries around the globe are losing their individual cultural identities. Teens in Turkey stream American movies, connect with others globally through Facebook and Twitter, and ask their parents for more Westernized clothes and other symbols of American pop culture and values. Grandmothers in small European villas no longer spend each morning visiting local meat, bread, and produce markets to gather the ingredients for dinner. Instead, they now shop at Walmart. Women in Saudi Arabia see American films, question their societal roles, and shop at any of the country's growing number of Victoria's Secret boutiques. In China, most people never drank coffee before Starbucks entered the market. Now Chinese consumers rush to Starbucks stores because it symbolizes a new kind of lifestyle. Similarly, in China, where McDonald's plans to expand from 2,500 to 4,500 locations by 2022, nearly half of all children identify the chain as a domestic brand.[24]

Such concerns have sometimes led to a backlash against American globalization. Well-known U.S. brands have become the targets of boycotts and protests in some international markets. As symbols of American capitalism, companies such as Coca-Cola, McDonald's,

Nike, and KFC have been singled out by protestors and governments in hot spots around the world, especially when anti-American sentiment peaks. For example, following Russia's annexation of Crimea and the resulting sanctions by the West, Russian authorities initiated a crackdown on McDonald's franchises (even though most were Russian-owned), forcing some to close for uncertain reasons. McDonald's flagship store in Moscow was shut down for several weeks by the Russian Food Safety Authority. And the three McDonald's in Crimea were permanently shuttered, with at least one becoming a nationalist chain outlet called Rusburger, serving "Czar Cheeseburgers" where Quarter Pounders once flowed.[25]

Despite such problems, defenders of globalization argue that concerns of Americanization and the potential damage to American brands are overblown. U.S. brands are doing very well internationally. In the most recent Millward Brown BrandZ brand value survey of global consumer brands, 19 of the top 25 global brands were American owned, including megabrands such as Google, Apple, IBM, Microsoft, McDonald's, Coca-Cola, and Amazon.[26]

Many iconic American brands are soaring globally. For example, most international markets covet American fast food. Consider KFC in Japan. On the day that KFC introduced its outrageous Double Down sandwich—bacon, melted cheese, and a "secret sauce" between two deep-fried chicken patties—in one of its restaurants in Japan, fans formed long lines and slept on the sidewalks outside to get a taste. "It was like the iPhone," says the CMO of KFC International, "people [were] crazy." The U.S. limited-time item has since become a runaway success worldwide, from Canada to Australia, the Philippines, and Malaysia. ● More broadly, KFC has become its own cultural institution in Japan. For instance, the brand has long been one of Japan's leading Christmas dining traditions, with the iconic Colonel Sanders standing in as a kind of Japanese Father Christmas:[27]

● **American brands in other cultures: KFC has become one of Japan's leading Christmas dining traditions, with the iconic Colonel Sanders standing in as a kind of Japanese Father Christmas.**

Anthea Freshwater

> Japan's KFC Christmas tradition began more than 40 years ago when the company unleashed a "Kentucky for Christmas" advertising campaign in Japan to help the brand get off the ground. Now, eating Kentucky Fried Chicken has become one of the country's most popular holiday traditions. Each KFC store displays a life-size Colonel Sanders statue, adorned in a traditional fur-trimmed red suit and Santa hat. A month in advance, Japanese customers order their special Christmas meal—a special bucket of fried chicken with wine and cake for about $40. Some 3.6 million Japanese households have a KFC Christmas feast each year. Those who don't preorder risk standing in lines that snake around the block or having to go without KFC's coveted blend of 11 herbs and spices altogether. Christmas Eve is KFC's most successful sales day of the year in Japan, and December monthly sales run as much as 10 times greater than sales in other months.

More fundamentally, the cultural exchange goes both ways: America gets as well as gives cultural influence. True, Hollywood dominates the global movie market, but British TV originated the programming that was Americanized into such hits as *American Idol, Dancing with the Stars,* and *Hell's Kitchen.* Although Chinese and Russian youth are donning NBA superstar jerseys, the increasing popularity of soccer in America has deep international roots.

Even American childhood has been increasingly influenced by European and Asian cultural imports. Most kids know all about imports such as Hello Kitty, Pokémon, or any of a host of Nintendo or Sega game characters. And J. K. Rowling's so-very-British Harry Potter books shaped the thinking of a generation of American youngsters, not to mention the millions of American oldsters who fell under their spell as well. For the moment, English remains the dominant language of the internet, and having web and mobile access often means that third-world youth have greater exposure to American popular culture. Yet these same technologies let Eastern European students studying in the United States hear webcast news and music from Poland, Romania, or Belarus.

Thus, globalization is a two-way street. If the world is eating Big Macs and drinking Coca-Cola, it is also talking on Samsung smartphones, buying furniture at IKEA, driving Toyota Camrys, and watching British-inspired shows on an LG OLED televisions.

Deciding Whether to Go Global

Not all companies need to venture into international markets to survive. For example, most local businesses need to market well only in their local marketplaces. Operating domestically is easier and safer. Managers don't need to learn another country's language and laws. They don't have to deal with unstable currencies, face political and legal uncertainties, or redesign their products to suit different customer expectations. However, companies that operate in global industries, where their strategic positions in specific markets are affected strongly by their overall global positions, must compete on a regional or worldwide basis to succeed.

Any of several factors might draw a company into the international arena. For example, global competitors might attack the company's home market by offering better products or lower prices. The company might want to counterattack these competitors in their home markets to tie up their resources. The company's customers might be expanding abroad and require international servicing. Or, most likely, international markets might simply provide better opportunities for growth. For example, as noted previously, Coca-Cola has emphasized international growth in recent years to offset stagnant or declining U.S. soft drink sales. Today, non–North America markets account for 80 percent of Coca-Cola's unit case volume, and the company is making major pushes into dozens of emerging markets, such as China, India, and the entire African continent.[28]

Before going abroad, the company must weigh several risks and answer many questions about its ability to operate globally. Can the company learn to understand the preferences and buyer behavior of consumers in other countries? Can it offer competitively attractive products? Will it be able to adapt to other countries' business cultures and deal effectively with foreign nationals? Do the company's managers have the necessary international experience? Has management considered the impact of regulations and the political environments of other countries?

Deciding Which Markets to Enter

Before going abroad, a company should try to define its international *marketing objectives and policies*. It should decide what *volume* of foreign sales it wants. Most companies start small when they go abroad. Some plan to stay small, seeing international sales as a small part of their business. Other companies have bigger plans, however, seeing international business as equal to—or even more important than—their domestic business.

The company also needs to choose in *how many* countries it wants to market. Companies must be careful not to spread themselves too thin or expand beyond their capabilities by operating in too many countries too soon. Next, the company needs to decide on the *types* of countries to enter. A country's attractiveness depends on the product, geographical factors, income and population, political climate, and other considerations. In recent years, many major new markets have emerged, offering both substantial opportunities and daunting challenges.

After listing possible international markets, the company must carefully evaluate each one. It must consider many factors. ● For example, Netflix's decision to expand into India seems like a no-brainer. The video streaming giant is already doing well in Europe, South America, and other global markets, which now account for more than half of its total streaming revenues. And as the U.S. market becomes saturated, Netflix is looking to international

● **Entering new global markets:** Netflix's decision to enter India seems like a no-brainer. But it's also a very large and complex undertaking.

ABHISHEK CHINNAPPA/REUTERS/Newscom

markets for growth. India offers huge potential, with a population of 1.4 billion people, more than four times the U.S. population and almost 2 times Europe's. Now the world's second-largest internet market, India's online video market is expected to triple in just the next four years.[29]

However, as Netflix considers expanding into new markets such as India, it must ask some important questions. Can it compete effectively with local competitors? Can it master the varied cultural and buying differences of Indian consumers? Will it be able to meet environmental and regulatory hurdles in each country? Can it overcome some daunting infrastructure problems?

In entering India, Netflix faces many challenges. For example, India is crowded with formidable competitors, including Amazon Prime Video and Indian digital and mobile entertainment platform Hotstar (owned by Disney India). And some 35 local online streaming services have sprung up in India during the past few years. Hotstar, with 150 million monthly active users, claims about 70 percent of India's on-demand local streaming services market. By contrast, Netflix currently has fewer than one million Indian subscribers.

Netflix also faces pricing challenges. As a premium pricer, it's cheapest monthly plan costs about 500 rupees (about $8), roughly twice as much as Hotstar or a local cable TV subscription, putting it out of reach to many low-income India households. Netflix is currently testing a $4 monthly mobile-only plan. Content is another major consideration. Netflix has a huge inventory of international content. But a large majority of titles on Netflix's service in India are in English, whereas the market prefers films in Hindi or Tamil. So Netflix is pouring money into developing original content by local producers, with Netflix India originals such as *Sacred Games, Delhi Crime*, and *Love Per Square Foot*, which have helped boost subscriber numbers in the country. Superior and locally relevant Netflix content is a key to charging premium prices.

Thus, Netflix's decision to enter India is, in fact, a no-brainer. It's also a very large and complex undertaking. But despite the challenges, Netflix CEO Reed Hastings predicts that the company's next 100 million customers will come from India. "It's the most phenomenal [opportunity] anywhere in the world," he says.

Possible global markets should be ranked on several factors, including market size, market growth, the cost of doing business, competitive advantage, and risk level. The goal is to determine the potential of each market, using indicators such as those shown in ● **Table 19.1**. Then the marketer must decide which markets offer the greatest long-run return on investment.

● Table 19.1 | Indicators of Market Potential

Demographic Characteristics	Sociocultural Factors
Education	Consumer lifestyles, beliefs, and values
Population size and growth	Business norms and approaches
Population age composition	Cultural and social norms
	Languages

Geographic Characteristics	Political and Legal Factors
Climate	National priorities
Country size	Political stability and compatibility
Population density—urban, rural	Government attitudes toward global trade
Transportation structure and market accessibility	Government bureaucracy
	Monetary and trade regulations

Economic Factors

GDP size and growth
Income distribution
Industrial infrastructure
Natural resources
Financial and human resources

Deciding How to Enter the Market

OBJECTIVE 19-2 Describe three key approaches to entering international markets.

Once a company has decided to sell in a foreign country, it must determine the best mode of entry. Its choices are *exporting, joint venturing*, and *direct investment*. ● **Figure 19.2** shows the three market entry strategies along with the options each one offers. As the figure shows, each succeeding strategy involves more commitment and risk but also more control and potential profits.

Exporting

Exporting
Entering foreign markets by selling goods produced in the company's home country, often with little modification.

The simplest way to enter a foreign market is through **exporting**. The company may passively export its surpluses from time to time, or it may make an active commitment to expand exports to a particular market. In either case, the company produces all its goods in its home country. It may or may not modify them for the export market. Exporting involves the least change in the company's product lines, organization, investments, or mission.

Companies typically start with *indirect exporting*, working through independent international marketing intermediaries. Indirect exporting involves less investment because the firm does not require an overseas marketing organization or network. It also involves less risk. International marketing intermediaries bring know-how and services to the relationship, so the seller normally makes fewer mistakes. Sellers may eventually move into *direct exporting*, whereby they handle their own exports. The investment and risk are somewhat greater in this strategy, but so is the potential return.

Joint Venturing

Joint venturing
Entering foreign markets by joining with foreign companies to produce or market a product or service.

A second method of entering a foreign market is by **joint venturing**—joining with foreign companies to produce or market products or services. Joint venturing differs from exporting in that the company joins with a host country partner to sell or market abroad. It differs from direct investment in that an association is formed with someone in the foreign country. There are four types of joint ventures: *licensing, contract manufacturing, management contracting*, and *joint ownership*.

Licensing

Licensing
Entering foreign markets through developing an agreement with a licensee in the foreign market.

Licensing is a simple way for a manufacturer to enter international marketing. The company enters into an agreement with a licensee in the foreign market. For a fee or royalty payments, the licensee buys the right to use the company's manufacturing process, trademark, patent, trade secret, or other item of value. The company thus gains entry into a foreign market at little risk; at the same time, the licensee gains production expertise or a well-known product or name without having to start from scratch.

In Japan, Budweiser beer flows from Kirin breweries, and Mizkan produces Sunkist lemon juice, drinks, and dessert items. Coca-Cola markets internationally by licensing bottlers around the world and supplying them with the syrup needed to produce the

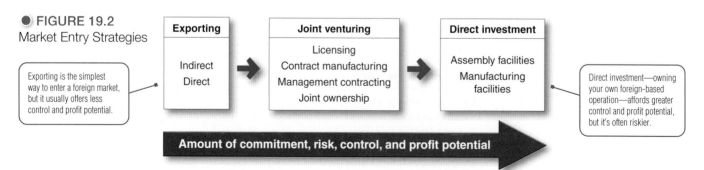

● FIGURE 19.2
Market Entry Strategies

Exporting is the simplest way to enter a foreign market, but it usually offers less control and profit potential.

Exporting	Joint venturing	Direct investment
Indirect Direct	Licensing Contract manufacturing Management contracting Joint ownership	Assembly facilities Manufacturing facilities

Direct investment—owning your own foreign-based operation—affords greater control and profit potential, but it's often riskier.

Amount of commitment, risk, control, and profit potential

product. Its global bottling partners range from the Coca-Cola Bottling Company of Saudi Arabia Europe-based Coca-Cola Hellenic, which bottles and markets 197 Coca-Cola brands to 605 million people in 28 countries, from Italy and Greece to Nigeria and Russia.[30] ● And Tokyo Disney Resort is owned and operated by Oriental Land Company under license from The Walt Disney Company. The 45-year license gives Disney licensing fees plus a percentage of admissions and food and merchandise sales.

Licensing has potential disadvantages, however. The firm has less control over the licensee than it would over its own operations. Furthermore, if the licensee is very successful, the firm has given up these profits, and if and when the contract ends, it may find it has created a competitor.

Contract Manufacturing

Another option is **contract manufacturing**, in which the company makes agreements with manufacturers in the foreign market to produce its product or provide its service. For example, P&G serves 650 million consumers across India with the help of nine contract manufacturing sites there. And Volkswagen contracts with Russia's largest auto manufacturer, GAZ Group, to make Volkswagen Jettas for the Russian market as well as its Škoda (VW's Czech Republic subsidiary) Octavia and Yeti models sold there.[31] The drawbacks of contract manufacturing are decreased control over the manufacturing process and loss of potential profits on manufacturing. The benefits are the chance to start faster with less risk and the later opportunity either to form a partnership with or buy out the local manufacturer. Contract manufacturing can also reduce plant investment, transportation, and tariff costs while at the same time helping to meet the host country's local manufacturing requirements.

Management Contracting

Under **management contracting**, the domestic firm provides the management know-how to a foreign company that supplies the capital. In other words, the domestic firm exports management services rather than products. Hilton uses this arrangement in managing hotels around the world. For example, the hotel chain operates DoubleTree by Hilton hotels in countries ranging from the UK and Italy to Peru and Costa Rica to China, Russia, and Tanzania. The properties are locally owned, but Hilton manages the hotels with its world-renowned hospitality expertise.[32]

Management contracting is a low-risk method of getting into a foreign market, and it yields income from the beginning. The arrangement is even more attractive if the contracting firm has an option to buy some share in the managed company later on. The arrangement is not sensible, however, if the company can put its scarce management talent to better uses or if it can make greater profits by undertaking the whole venture. Management contracting also prevents the company from setting up its own operations for a period of time.

Joint Ownership

Joint ownership ventures consist of one company joining forces with foreign investors to create a local business in which they share possession and control. A company may buy an interest in a local firm, or the two parties may form a new business venture. Joint ownership may be needed for economic or political reasons. For example, the firm may lack the financial, physical, or managerial resources to undertake the venture alone. Alternatively, a foreign government may require joint ownership as a condition for entry. Disney's Hong Kong Disneyland and Shanghai Disneyland are both joint ownership ventures with the Chinese government-owned Shanghai Shendi Group. Disney owns 43 percent of the Shanghai resort; the Shanghai Shendi Group owns 57 percent.[33]

● **International licensing: The Tokyo Disney Resort is owned and operated by Oriental Land Company (a Japanese development company) under license from The Walt Disney Company.**

David Harding/Alamy Stock Photo

Contract manufacturing

A joint venture in which a company contracts with manufacturers in a foreign market to produce its product or provide its service.

Management contracting

A joint venture in which the domestic firm supplies the management know-how to a foreign company that supplies the capital; the domestic firm exports management services rather than products.

Joint ownership

A cooperative venture in which a company creates a local business with investors in a foreign market who share ownership and control.

● **Joint ownership:** Walmart's joint ownership stake in Flipkart, India's leading online marketplace, helps the retailer to navigate India's strict foreign investment restrictions.

grzegorz knec/Alamy Stock Photo (Walmart); Farbentek/123RF (Flipkart)

Often, companies form joint ownership ventures to merge their complementary strengths in developing a global marketing opportunity. ● For example, Walmart's 81 percent ownership stake in Flipkart, India's leading online marketplace, has helped the U.S.-based retailer navigate India's strict foreign investment restrictions. The arrangement also gave Walmart a big head start over Amazon in market share and online retailing expertise in India. In turn, Flipkart benefits from Walmart's deep pockets and distribution experience. Similarly, joint ownership ventures have helped Kellogg move quickly and strongly into emerging markets in West Africa. For instance, Kellogg purchased 50-percent stakes in Tolaram Africa Foods, a leading manufacturer of packaged foods in Nigeria and Ghana, and Multipro, the largest foods distributor in those countries. The joint ownership investments will help Kellogg to better understand West African consumers and to master the region's complex distribution environment.[34]

Joint ownership has certain drawbacks, however. The partners may disagree over investment, marketing, or other policies. Whereas many U.S. firms like to reinvest earnings for growth, local firms often prefer to take out these earnings; whereas U.S. firms emphasize the role of marketing, local investors may rely on selling.

Direct Investment

Direct investment

Entering a foreign market by developing foreign-based assembly or manufacturing facilities.

The biggest involvement in a foreign market comes through **direct investment**—the development of foreign-based assembly or manufacturing facilities. For example, U.S. chipmaker Intel has made substantial investments in its own manufacturing and research facilities in Israeli. It recently spent $5 billion to expand capacity in its Kiryat Gat plant in southern Israeli and another $15 billion to purchase Israeli auto-focused chip and technology firm Mobileye. And it has announced plans to invest yet another $11 million in a new southern Israeli plant. A significant share of Intel Israel's chip exports goes to China. Thus, in the face of sometimes strained trade relations between the United States and China in recent years, increased direct investment in Israeli lets Intel better serve the large and growing Chinese chip market.[35]

If a company has gained experience in exporting and if the foreign market is large enough, foreign production facilities offer many advantages. The firm may have lower costs in the form of cheaper labor or raw materials, foreign government investment incentives, and freight savings. The firm may also improve its image in the host country because it creates jobs. Generally, a firm develops a deeper relationship with the government, customers, local suppliers, and distributors, allowing it to adapt its products to the local market better. Finally, the firm keeps full control over the investment and therefore can develop manufacturing and marketing policies that serve its long-term international objectives.

The main disadvantage of direct investment is that the firm faces many risks, such as restricted or devalued currencies, falling markets, or government changes. In some cases, a firm has no choice but to accept these risks if it wants to operate in the host country.

> **Author** | The major global **Comment** | marketing decision usually boils down to this: How much, if at all, should a company adapt its marketing strategy and programs to local markets? How might the answer differ for Boeing versus McDonald's?

Deciding on the Global Marketing Program

OBJECTIVE 19-3 Explain how companies adapt their marketing strategies and mixes for international markets.

Companies that operate in one or more foreign markets must decide how much, if at all, to adapt their marketing strategies and programs to local conditions. At one extreme are global companies that use **standardized global marketing**, essentially using the same marketing strategy approaches and marketing mix worldwide. At the other extreme is **adapted global marketing**. In this case, the producer adjusts the marketing strategy and mix elements to each target market, resulting in more costs but hopefully producing a larger market share and return.

Standardized global marketing

A global marketing strategy that basically uses the same marketing strategy and mix in all of the company's international markets.

Adapted global marketing
A global marketing approach that adjusts the marketing strategy and mix elements to each international target market, which creates more costs but hopefully produces a larger market share and return.

The question of whether to adapt or standardize the marketing strategy and program has been much debated over the years. On the one hand, some global marketers believe that technology is making the world a smaller place, and consumer needs around the world are becoming more similar. This paves the way for global brands and standardized global marketing. Global branding and standardization, in turn, result in greater brand power and reduced costs from economies of scale.

On the other hand, the marketing concept holds that marketing programs will be more engaging if tailored to the unique needs of each targeted customer group. If this concept applies within a country, it should apply even more across international markets. Despite global convergence, consumers in different countries still have widely varied cultural backgrounds. They still differ significantly in their needs and wants, spending power, product preferences, and shopping patterns. Because these differences are hard to change, most marketers today adapt their products, prices, channels, and promotions to fit consumer desires in each country.

However, global standardization is not an all-or-nothing proposition. It's a matter of degree. Most international marketers suggest that companies should "think globally but act locally." They should seek a balance between standardization and adaptation, leveraging global brand recognition but adapting their marketing, products, and operations to specific markets.

Consider Scandinavian furniture and housewares retailer IKEA. Giant IKEA successfully operates 420-plus locations in more than 52 countries, engaging consumers across vastly different means, languages, and cultures. IKEA follows a highly standardized international operating model designed to create good-quality, functional furniture at low prices that everyday people can afford. No matter where in the world you shop at IKEA, you'll find huge stores, the familiar blue-and-yellow brand logo and signage, large selections of contemporary Scandinavian-design furnishings, and affordable prices. At the same time, IKEA carefully adapts its merchandise assortments, store operations, and marketing to cater to the unique needs of customers in different global markets:[36]

IKEA routinely adjusts its product designs and assortments worldwide to meet the distinct needs and tastes of local consumers. ● For example, although IKEA stores in China carry many of the same items found in other parts of the world, they also heavy up on rice cookers and chopsticks. The Chinese love a good, hard mattress, so IKEA sells mostly firmer ones there. And because the average living space in China's crowded cities is much smaller than in Europe and the United States, Chinese IKEAs stock smaller appliances and products geared toward saving space and organizing a household.

But there are limits to how much IKEA can adapt product designs and assortments without increasing costs. So the retailer often simply adapts its marketing and merchandising to show locals how its standard products fit with their lives and cultures. For example, IKEA's websites and its heavily circulated IKEA print catalog (more than 200 million printed each year) are customized to show standard IKEA products in localized settings.

IKEA also adjusts its basic store operations to turn local cultural nuances into competitive advantages. In Chinese, for example, IKEA is known as Yi Jia. Translated, it means "comfortable home," a concept taken literally by the millions of consumers who visit one of IKEA's 20 huge Chinese stores each year. "Customers come on family outings, hop into display beds and nap, pose for snapshots with the décor, and hang out for hours to enjoy the air conditioning and free soda refills," notes one observer. On a typical Saturday afternoon, display beds and other furniture in a huge Chinese IKEA store are occupied, with customers of all ages lounging or even fast asleep. Whereas this might be considered unwanted loitering in the United States or other Western markets, IKEA managers in China encourage such behavior, figuring that familiarity with the store will result in later purchasing.

● **No matter where in the world you shop at IKEA, you'll find the huge and familiar blue-and-yellow stores and large selections of Scandinavian-design furnishings at affordable prices. At the same time, IKEA carefully adapts its merchandise and marketing to the unique needs of customers in specific global markets.**

Lou Linwei/Alamy Stock Photo

Collectively, local brands still account for the overwhelming majority of consumer purchases. Most consumers, wherever they live, lead very local lives. So a global brand must engage consumers at a local level, respecting the culture and becoming a part of it.

● FIGURE 19.3
Five Global Product and
Communications Strategies

The real question buried in this figure is this: How much should a company standardize or adapt its products and marketing across global markets?

Product

Communications	Don't change product	Adapt product	Develop new product
Don't change communications	Straight extension	Product adaptation	Product invention
Adapt communications	Communication adaptation	Dual adaptation	

Product

Five strategies are used for adapting product and marketing communication strategies to a global market (see ● **Figure 19.3**).[37] We first discuss the three product strategies and then turn to the two communication strategies.

Straight product extension

Marketing a product in a foreign market without making any changes to the product.

Straight product extension means marketing a product in a foreign market without making significant changes to the product. Top management tells its marketing people, "Take the product as is and find customers for it." The first step, however, should be to find out whether foreign consumers use that product and what form they prefer.

Straight extension has been successful in some cases and disastrous in others. Apple iPads, Gillette razors, and Black & Decker tools are all sold successfully in about the same form around the world. But when General Foods introduced its standard powdered JELL-O in the British market, it discovered that British consumers prefer a solid wafer or cake form. Likewise, Philips began to make a profit in Japan only after it reduced the size of its coffeemakers to fit into smaller Japanese kitchens and its shavers to fit smaller Japanese hands. And Panasonic's refrigerator sales in China surged tenfold in a single year after it shaved the width of its appliances by 15 percent to fit smaller Chinese kitchens.[38] Straight extension is tempting because it involves no additional product development costs, manufacturing changes, or new promotion. But it can be costly in the long run if products fail to satisfy consumers in specific global markets.

Product adaptation

Adapting a product to meet local conditions or wants in foreign markets.

Product adaptation involves changing the product to meet local requirements, conditions, or wants. ● For example, in the United States, Amazon's Echo-based virtual voice assistant Alexa speaks a soft but precise version of American English. Alexa knows that Independence Day falls on July 4 and that Americans love turkey with all the fixings at Thanksgiving. But what happens when Alexa goes global? Amazon's Echo speakers and Alexa must be carefully adapted to the particulars of each new global culture. Consider Echo in India:[39]

Before introducing Alexa in India, teams of linguists, speech scientists, and developers gave her a decidedly local makeover. In India, Alexa speaks Hinglish—a blend of Hindi and English—with an unmistakable Indian accent. "She knows Independence Day is August 15, not July 4, and wishes listeners 'Happy Diwali and a prosperous New Year!'" says one business reporter. "She also refers to the living room as 'drawing room' and can add jeera (cumin), haldi (turmeric) and atta (flour) to your shopping list." Alexa's many "skills" cover a wide range of Indian interests, notes another reporter—"chants for cricket enthusiasts, recitations of the Gayatri Mantra, . . . daily horoscopes, Bollywood quizzes, Indian flute music, and even cooking instructions based on late celebrity chef Tarla Dalal's recipes."

Mastering Hinglish is critical. Although many Indians understand both English and Hindi, they feel more comfortable with an Alexa who sounds like them. Having Alexa understand the nuances of Hinglish and local subcultures is especially important as Amazon expands beyond India's big cities. A greater proportion of rural Indians speaks only Hindi or another local language, and lower literacy rates mean more people prefer voice controls to typing. "Alexa is not going to be a visiting American who is going to come to India for a few days and go back," says Amazon's country manager, Alexa Skills, India. "She is as Indian as it gets."

● **Product adaptation: Amazon carefully adapts its Echo-based virtual voice assistant Alexa to each new global culture. In India, Alexa speaks Hinglish—a blend of Hindi and English—with an unmistakable Indian accent.**

Zapp2Photo/Shutterstock

Product invention

Creating new products or services for foreign markets.

Product invention consists of creating something new to meet the needs of consumers in a given country. As markets have gone global, companies ranging from appliance manufacturers and carmakers to candy and soft drink producers have developed products that meet the special purchasing needs of low-income consumers in developing economies.

For example, Chinese appliance producer Haier developed sturdier washing machines for rural users Africa, India, and other emerging markets, where it found that lighter-duty machines often became clogged with mud when farmers used them to clean vegetables as well as clothes. P&G developed a Waterless line of shampoos and other hair care products that require no water for South African consumers facing severe water shortages. And solar lighting manufacturer d.light Solar has developed affordable solar-powered home lighting systems for the hundreds of millions of people in the developing world who don't have access to reliable power. d.light's hanging lamps and portable lanterns require no energy source other than the sun and can last up to 15 hours on one charge. The company has already sold close to 20 million solar light and power products in 62 countries, reaching 82 million users.[40]

Promotion

Companies can either adopt the same communication strategy they use in the home market or change it for each local market. Consider advertising messages. Some global companies use a standardized advertising theme around the world. For example, Coca-Cola unifies its global advertising around a "Taste the Feeling" theme. Of course, even in highly standardized communications campaigns, some adjustments might be required for language and cultural differences. Ads for Coca-Cola's "Taste the Feeling" campaign have a similar look worldwide but are adapted in different global markets to feature local consumers, languages, celebrities, and events.

Global companies often have difficulty crossing the language barrier, with results ranging from mild embarrassment to outright failure. Seemingly innocuous brand names and advertising phrases can take on unintended or hidden meanings when translated into other languages. For example, Interbrand of London, the firm that created household names such as Prozac and Acura, developed a brand name "hall of shame" list, which contained these and other foreign brand names you're never likely to see inside the local Kroger supermarket: Krapp toilet paper (Denmark), Plopp chocolate (Scandinavia), Crapsy Fruit cereal (France), Poo curry powder (Argentina), and Pschitt lemonade (France).

Communication adaptation

A global communication strategy of fully adapting advertising messages to local markets.

Similarly, advertising themes often lose—or gain—something in the translation. In Chinese, the KFC slogan "finger-lickin' good" came out as "eat your fingers off." And Motorola's Hellomoto ringtone sounds like "Hello, Fatty" in India. Marketers must be watchful to avoid such mistakes, taking great care when localizing their brand names and messages to specific global markets. In important but culturally different markets such as China, finding just the right name can make or break a brand (see Real Marketing 19.2).

Rather than standardizing their advertising globally, other companies follow a strategy of **communication adaptation**, adapting their advertising messages to local markets. For example, in the United States and most Western countries, parents view play as beneficial to child development and creativity. However, Chinese parents tend view play negatively, as a distraction from schoolwork that doesn't contribute to learning and development. As a result, although China has almost five times the population of the United States, Chinese parents spend less than half of what U.S. parents spend on toys.

To meet this challenge, U.S. toymakers adapt their Chinese communications campaigns to emphasize how play helps children to succeed in life by boosting their knowledge, skills, and creativity. ● For example, an Asian video for Mattel's Barbie, based on the brand's "You can be anything" theme, countered Chinese stereotypes about play being a waste of time by showing how playing with Barbie made girls more self-confident, creative, and emotionally

● **Communication adaptation: To counter negative Chinese stereotypes about play, Mattel created a campaign showing how playing with Barbie made girls more self-confident, creative, and emotionally intelligent.**

Eugene Hoshiko/AP Photo

Real Marketing 19.2 | Localizing Chinese Brand Names: Very Important but Notoriously Tricky

After a long day's work, an average upscale Beijinger can't wait to dash home, lace on a comfortable pair of Enduring and Persevering, pop the top on a refreshing can of Tasty Fun, and then hop into his Galloping Fast and head to the local tavern for a frosty glass of Happiness Power with friends. Translation? In China, those are the brand name meanings for Nike, Coca-Cola, Mercedes, and Heineken, respectively.

To Westerners, such names sound pretty silly, but to brands doing business in China, the world's biggest and fastest-growing consumer market, they are no laughing matter. Perhaps more than anywhere else in the world, brand names in China take on deep significance. Finding just the right name can make or break a brand. "Often, a company's most important marketing decision in China is localizing its name," asserts one global branding analyst. "It's also a notoriously tricky one."

Developing the right brand name, logo, and symbol is challenging, even in a company's home market. But it's especially difficult in China because of the complexity of the written and spoken language. Brand name development in China has become more of a science than an art, involving global branding consultants, computer software, linguistic analysis, and extensive consumer testing. "In most naming projects," says one branding consultant, "the final name is chosen out of several hundred possible candidates that all require careful pruning to single out the best."

Ideally, to maintain global consistency, the Chinese name should sound similar to the original while at the same time conveying the brand's benefits in meaningful symbolic terms. Nike's Chinese brand name, Nai ke, does this well. Not only does it sound the same when pronounced in Chinese, its "Enduring and Persevering" meaning powerfully encapsulates the "Just Do It" essence of the Nike brand the world over. Similarly, P&G's Tide is Taizi in China, which translates to "gets out the dirt," a perfect moniker for a tough-acting detergent. Coca-Cola's Chinese name—Ke kou ke le—dates all the way back to 1928. It not only sounds much like the English name, the Chinese symbols convey happiness in the mouth, a close fit to Coca-Cola's current "Taste the Feeling" positioning. Other names that wear well on Chinese ears while also conveying a brand's essence include Lay's snack foods—Le shi ("happy things"); Reebok—Rui bu ("quick steps");

and Colgate—Gau lu jie ("revealing superior cleanliness").

There was a time when Western companies entering China simply created a brand name that was phonetically similar to the domestic name, even if it had no meaning in the Chinese language. For example, Cadillac went with Ka di la ke—a meaningless group of sounds that gave status to the luxury brand. But names that lack meaning often fail to spark the Chinese imagination. Worse, phonetic names can take on unintended meanings. For example, when Coca-Cola first took its iconic beverage to China, it settled on the name ko kä kö la. That sounds like Coca-Cola but translates roughly in Chinese to "bit a wax tadpole."

Some brand names translate naturally. For example, when Garnier introduced its Clear shampoo in China, it lucked out. The Chinese word for "clear"—Qing—is one of a select few Chinese words with unusually positive associations that are used in many brand names. Garnier added the word yang, which means "flying" or "scattering to the wind." According to the director of Garnier's brand consultancy, the Qing Yang brand name connotes "very light, healthy, and happy—think of hair in the air," just what the brand intends. Other universally positive Chinese words commonly found in brand names include le and xi (happy), li (strength or power), ma (horse), and fu (lucky). Thus, Kia sells one model in China named Qian li ma, or "thousand kilometer horse," suggesting unusual strength.

Chinese brand names can convey subtle meanings that might not be apparent to Western sensibilities. For example, "Dashing Speed" seems appropriate enough for an upscale automobile brand like Mercedes. So does BMW's name—Bao Ma—which translates to "Precious Horse." However, in China, "precious" has a feminine connotation, whereas "Dashing Speed" is more masculine. This works out well for both car makers, which target different genders

among China's upper crust. For instance, BMW is a market leader among affluent Chinese women.

Many global brand names require careful recrafting. For example, Microsoft had to rethink the introduction of its Bing search engine in China, where the most common translations of the character pronounced "bing" are words like defect or virus, not good associations for a digital product. Microsoft changed the name in China to Bi ying, which means "very certain to respond." Even so, the brand is having difficulty shaking the resemblance to the original name.

Branding in China gets even more complicated when it involves visual associations of Mandarin characters with those of a brand mark or logo. Take TripAdvisor and its familiar owl logo, for example. When the leading travel website entered the Chinese market, it settled on dào dào ("arrive arrive"), a catchy name thought to capture the brand's core. But Chinese travelers just didn't make the connection. So TripAdvisor enlisted a branding agency to rework the Chinese brand name. After exhaustive development, the team discovered māo tóu yīng—or 猫头鹰—a group of characters that literally mean "cat head eagle" but that commonly translate as "the owl." To make the brand name more playful and to better align it with TripAdvisor's brand attributes, the company changed the set of characters to 猫途鹰, replacing the

Brand names in China take on deep significance. Coca-Cola's Chinese name sounds much like the English name, and the Chinese symbols convey" happiness in the mouth," a close fit to Coca-Cola's current "Taste the Feeling" positioning.
Sumeth Anu/Shutterstock

"head" character (头, *tóu*) with one meaning "journey" (途, *tú*). Both characters share a very close pronunciation, giving the new name a play on words that captures both the visual identity of TripAdvisor's iconic owl logo and the brand's association with travel planning.

Today, with so many foreign brands entering a growing Chinese market already crowded with local brands, selecting the right brand name is crucial. If Chinese consumers can't pronounce a name or don't know what it stands for, they are much less likely to buy it or talk about it with others, in person or in social media. Instead, with some work, companies can come up with names that will engage and inspire buyers. In China, it's not Subway, it's Sai bai wei—"better than 100 tastes." It's not Revlon but Lu hua nong, a phrase borrowed from a famous Tang Dynasty romantic poem, meaning, "blossoming flowers nourished by the morning dew." In any part of the world, branding is a matter of creating meaningful and positive associations between the brand and the value it brings to consumers. In China, that's especially important but also notoriously tricky.[41]

intelligent. The video drew 7.5 million views. Similarly, LEGO shared a WeChat post showing a father who is a Silicon Valley engineer using LEGO bricks to teach his son math skills. A Crayola campaign featured a virtual children's art gallery showing how children will grow up "creating not just art, but also ideas, products, and scientific progress." And a Mattel campaign reframed the value of play by, for example, showing how Hot Wheels can teach children about physics.[42]

Media also need to be adapted internationally because media availability and regulations vary from country to country. While TV advertising has few regulations in the United States, TV advertising time is very limited in Europe. For instance, France has banned retailers from advertising on TV, and Sweden forbids TV advertising to children. However, mobile phone ads are much more widely accepted in Europe and Asia than in the United States. Newspapers are national in the United Kingdom, only local in Spain, and the leading advertising medium in Germany. India has nearly 300 newspapers, but because of paper shortages, ads must be booked up to six months in advance.[43]

Price

Companies also face many considerations in setting their international prices. For example, how might Makita price its power tools globally? It could set a uniform price globally, but this amount would be too high a price in poor countries and not high enough in rich ones. It could charge what consumers in each country would bear, but this strategy ignores differences in the actual costs from country to country. Finally, the company could use a standard markup of its costs everywhere, but this approach might price Makita out of the market in some countries where costs are high.

Regardless of how companies go about pricing their products, their foreign prices probably will be higher than their domestic prices for comparable products. An Apple 11" iPad Pro that sells for $799 in the United States goes for $995 in the United Kingdom. Why? Apple faces a *price escalation* problem. It must add the cost of transportation, tariffs, importer margin, wholesaler margin, and retailer margin to its factory price. Depending on these added costs, a product may have to sell for two to five times as much in another country to make the same profit.

To overcome this problem when selling to less-affluent consumers in emerging markets, many companies make simpler or smaller versions of their products available that can be sold at lower prices. ● For example, to compete with low-end competitors in Indonesia, India, Pakistan, and other emerging economies, Samsung developed its low-priced Galaxy J line. The J models, priced under $150, carry the Galaxy name and style but with few high-end features. Or companies can reduce prices by manufacturing their products locally. For example, Motorola and Xiaomi serve the Indian market with phones they produce in India. Producing phones locally lets them avoid high import tariffs, and they can pass lower manufacturing costs along to customers in the form of lower prices. The two brands now account for one of every two smartphones sold in India.[44]

● **International pricing:** To compete with low-end competitors in emerging economies, Samsung developed its low-priced Galaxy J line, which carries the Galaxy name and style but with few high-end features.

rawpixel/123RF

● **FIGURE 19.4**
Whole-Channel Concept for
International Marketing

Distribution channels can vary dramatically
around the world. For example, in the U.S.,
Coca-Cola distributes products through
sophisticated retail channels. In less-developed
countries, it delivers Coca-Cola products using
everything from push carts to delivery donkeys.

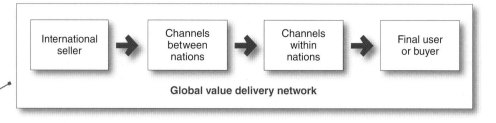

Global value delivery network

Recent economic and technological forces have had an impact on global pricing. For example, the internet is making global price differences more obvious. When firms sell their wares over the internet, customers can see how much products sell for in different countries. They can even order a given product directly from the company location or dealer offering the lowest price. This is forcing companies toward more standardized international pricing.

Distribution Channels

Whole-channel view

Designing international channels that take into account the entire global supply chain and marketing channel, forging an effective global value delivery network.

An international company must take a **whole-channel view** of the problem of distributing products to final consumers. ● **Figure 19.4** shows the two major links between the seller and the final buyer. The first link, *channels between nations*, moves company products from points of production to the borders of countries within which they are sold. The second link, *channels within nations*, moves products from their market entry points to the final consumers. The whole-channel view takes into account the entire global supply chain and marketing channel. It recognizes that to compete well internationally, the company must effectively design and manage an entire *global value delivery network*.

In some markets, the distribution system is complex, competitive, and hard to penetrate. For example, many Western companies find India's distribution system difficult to navigate. Large discount, department store, and supermarket retailers still account for only a small portion of the huge Indian market. Instead, most shopping is done in small neighborhood stores called *kirana* shops, run by their owners and popular because they offer personal service and credit. In addition, large Western retailers have difficulty dealing with India's complex government regulations and poor infrastructure.

Distribution systems in developing countries may be scattered, inefficient, or altogether lacking. For example, China's rural markets are highly decentralized, made of many distinct submarkets, each with its own subculture. And, because of inadequate distribution systems, most companies can profitably access only a small portion of China's massive population located in affluent cities. China's distribution system is so fragmented that logistics costs to wrap, bundle, load, unload, sort, reload, and transport goods amount nearly 15 percent of the nation's GDP, far higher than in most other countries. (In comparison, U.S. logistics costs account for about 7.5 percent of the nation's GDP.)[45]

Sometimes local conditions can greatly influence how a company distributes products in global markets. For example, in low-income neighborhoods in Brazil where consumers have limited access to supermarkets, Nestlé supplements its distribution with an army of self-employed salespeople who sell Nestlé products from refrigerated carts door to door. ● And in big cities in Asia and Africa, where crowded streets and high real estate costs make drive-thrus impractical, fast-food restaurants such as McDonald's and KFC offer delivery. Legions of motorbike delivery drivers in colorful uniforms dispense Big Macs and buckets of chicken to customers who call in. McDonald's reaped more than $1 billion in delivery sales worldwide last year.[46]

Thus, international marketers face a wide range of channel alternatives. Designing efficient and effective channel systems between and within various country markets poses a difficult challenge.

● **McDelivery: In big cities in Asia and Africa, where crowded streets and high real estate costs make drive-thrus impractical, legions of McDonald's motorbike delivery drivers dispense Big Macs and fries to customers who call in.**

Sorbis/Shutterstock

Author | Many large companies,
Comment | regardless of their "home
country," now think of themselves as
truly global organizations. They view
the entire world as a single borderless
market. For example, although
headquartered in Chicago, Boeing
is as comfortable selling planes to
Lufthansa or Air China as to American
Airlines.

Deciding on the Global Marketing Organization

OBJECTIVE 19-4 Identify the three major forms of international marketing organization.

Companies manage their international marketing activities in at least three different ways: Most companies first organize an export department, then create an international division, and finally become a global organization.

A firm normally gets into international marketing by simply shipping out its goods. If its international sales expand, the company will establish an *export department* with a sales manager and a few assistants. As sales increase, the export department can expand to include various marketing services so that it can actively go after business. If the firm moves into joint ventures or direct investment, the export department will no longer be adequate.

Many companies get involved in several international markets and ventures. A company may export to one country, license to another, have a joint ownership venture in a third, and own a subsidiary in a fourth. Sooner or later it will create *international divisions* or subsidiaries to handle all its international activity.

International divisions are organized in a variety of ways. An international division's corporate staff consists of marketing, manufacturing, research, finance, planning, and personnel specialists. It plans for and provides services to various operating units, which can be organized in one of three ways. They can be *geographical organizations*, with country managers who are responsible for salespeople, sales branches, distributors, and licensees in their respective countries. Or the operating units can be *world product groups*, each responsible for worldwide sales of different product groups. Finally, operating units can be *international subsidiaries*, each responsible for their own sales and profits.

Many firms have passed beyond the international division stage and are truly global organizations. For example, as discussed previously, despite its French origins, L'Oréal no longer has a clearly defined home market. Nor does it have a home-office staff. Instead, the company is famous for building global brand teams around managers who have deep backgrounds in several cultures. L'Oréal managers around the world bring diverse cultural perspectives to their brands.

Global organizations don't think of themselves as national marketers that sell abroad but as global marketers. The top corporate management and staff plan worldwide manufacturing facilities, marketing policies, financial flows, and logistical systems. The global operating units report directly to the chief executive or the executive committee of the organization, not to the head of an international division. Executives are trained in worldwide operations, not just domestic *or* international operations. Global companies recruit management from many countries, buy components and supplies where they cost the least, and invest where the expected returns are greatest.

Today, major companies must become more global if they hope to compete. As foreign companies successfully invade their domestic markets, companies must move more aggressively into foreign markets. They will have to change from companies that treat their international operations as secondary to companies that view the entire world as a single borderless market.

Reviewing and Extending the Concepts

CHAPTER REVIEW AND CRITICAL THINKING

Objectives Review

Companies today can no longer afford to pay attention only to their domestic market, regardless of its size. Many industries are global industries, and firms that operate globally achieve lower costs and higher brand awareness. At the same time, global marketing is risky because of variable exchange rates, unstable governments, tariffs and trade barriers, and several other factors. Given the potential gains and risks of international marketing, companies need a systematic way to make their global marketing decisions.

OBJECTIVE 19-1 Discuss how the international trade system and the economic, political-legal, and cultural environments affect a company's international marketing decisions. *(pp 552–563)*

A company must understand the *global marketing environment*, especially the international trade system. It should assess each foreign market's *economic, political-legal*, and *cultural characteristics*. The company can then decide whether it wants to go abroad and consider the potential risks and benefits. It must decide on the volume of international sales it wants, how many countries it wants to market in, and which specific markets it wants to enter. These decisions call for weighing the probable returns against the level of risk.

OBJECTIVE 19-2 Describe three key approaches to entering international markets. *(pp 564–566)*

The company must decide how to enter each chosen market—whether through *exporting, joint venturing*, or *direct investment*. Many companies start as exporters, move to joint ventures, and finally make a direct investment in foreign markets. In *exporting*, the company enters a foreign market by sending and selling products through international marketing intermediaries (indirect exporting) or the company's own department, branch, or sales representatives or agents (direct exporting). When establishing a *joint venture*, a company enters foreign markets by joining with foreign companies to produce or market a product or service. In *licensing*, the company enters a foreign market by contracting with a licensee in the foreign market and offering the right to use a manufacturing process, trademark, patent, trade secret, or other item of value for a fee or royalty.

OBJECTIVE 19-3 Explain how companies adapt their marketing strategies and mixes for international markets. *(pp 566–572)*

Companies must also decide how much their marketing strategies and their products, promotion, price, and channels should be adapted for each foreign market. At one extreme, global companies use *standardized global marketing* worldwide. Others use *adapted global marketing*, in which they adjust the marketing strategy and mix to each target market, bearing more costs but hoping for a larger market share and return. However, global standardization is not an all-or-nothing proposition. It's a matter of degree. Most international marketers suggest that companies should "think globally but act locally"—that they should seek a balance between globally standardized strategies and locally adapted marketing mix tactics.

OBJECTIVE 19-4 Identify the three major forms of international marketing organization. *(p 573)*

The company must develop an effective organization for international marketing. Most firms start with an *export department* and graduate to an *international division*. Large companies eventually become *global organizations*, with worldwide marketing planned and managed by the top officers of the company. Global organizations view the entire world as a single, borderless market.

Key Terms

OBJECTIVE 19-1

Global firm (p 553)
Economic community (p 555)

OBJECTIVE 19-2

Exporting (p 564)
Joint venturing (p 564)
Licensing (p 564)

Contract manufacturing (p 565)
Management contracting (p 565)
Joint ownership (p 565)
Direct investment (p 566)

OBJECTIVE 19-3

Standardized global marketing (p 566)
Adapted global marketing (p 567)

Straight product extension (p 568)
Product adaptation (p 568)
Product invention (p 569)
Communication adaptation (p 569)
Whole-channel view (p 572)

Discussion Questions

19-1 Briefly describe the World Trade Organization and its role in world trade. (AACSB: Written and Oral Communication)

19-2 What environmental factors must international marketers consider when entering foreign markets? (AACSB: Written and Oral Communication)

19-3 Explain how licensing might work for a business wanting to break into a new global market. How does licensing differ from other types of joint venture? (AACSB: Communication; Reflective Thinking)

19-4 When should a business use a standardized or an adapted marketing strategy in an overseas market? (AASCB: Communication)

19-5 Outline the key challenges a global business faces in establishing itself in an emerging market. (AACSB: Communication; Reflective Thinking)

19-6 Should Unilever utilize standardized international pricing for its Sunsilk hair care products? Why or why not? (AACSB: Written and Oral Communication; Reflective Thinking)

Critical Thinking Exercises

19-7 Based on national security concerns, the United States and several U.S. allies have chosen to limit market access for Huawei, a Chinese telecommunications company that is neck and neck with Apple as the world's number-two smartphone maker behind Samsung. Critics of the ban argue that it limits competition and innovation—Huawei is the fifth-largest investor in R&D worldwide. Rather than commenting on national security fears driving the bans, Huawei responded with ads that align with local cultures and promote Huawei's technological prowess, hoping to get consumers to demand that Huawei gain market access. Which part of the marketing environment is having the greatest impact on Huawei's expansion into other countries: economic, political-legal, or cultural? In your response, explain why you selected this factor and also why you ruled out the other two factors. (AACSB: Written and Oral Communication; Information Technology; Reflective Thinking)

19-8 Lush is a quintessentially British brand. Formed in 1994, it has a revolutionary approach to the creation and ethical sourcing of fresh beauty products, all made by hand. Lush could not be more different than the mass-produced cosmetics most consumers buy today. Lush is enjoying rapid global expansion. Research how this is being achieved and how they go about adapting their key messages to each new market while retaining their core message. (AACSB: Communication; Use of IT; Reflective Thinking)

19-9 You have been asked to consult with a small business owner who wants to expand her company overseas. She has asked you to develop a global marketing strategy. You are not certain if the owner thoroughly understands the international expansion process and the challenges involved. Prior to meeting with the owner next week, create a presentation listing the factors she will need to consider prior to her company going global. (AACSB: Written and Oral Communication; Reflective Thinking)

APPLICATIONS AND CASES

Online, Mobile, and Social Media Marketing Tinder Is an International Sensation

Match Group's biggest brand, Tinder, is a location-based, social search mobile app that is often used to set up dates. Launched in 2010, the dating app now accounts for 55 percent of total subscribers across all of Match Group's brands, which include Match.com, Hinge, and OkCupid. Tinder has had double-digit revenue growth year over year fueled, in part, by its expansion into emerging markets like India, where it is the nation's top-grossing dating app. The app's growth in India is attributed to India's urbanization and the decline of arranged marriages.

19-10 Which marketing environment factors may be having an impact on Tinder's growth in India? (AACSB: Written and Oral Communication; Reflective Thinking)

19-11 Develop a relevant profile of India that informs Match Group management about the country's demographics, competitors, and market potential. (AACSB: Written and Oral Communication; Reflective Thinking)

Marketing Ethics Cleaning Up the Chinese Pharmaceutical Market

By 2020, the Chinese pharmaceutical market will be worth $1.3 trillion per year. Pharmaceutical businesses from around the world have recognized the potential of the market and, at the same time, existing Chinese businesses have realized the potential threats to their market share. In order to grab some market share and profit, some pharmaceutical companies have been less than honest in their dealings and have subsequently found themselves under intense scrutiny from China's National Development and Reform Commission (NDRC). In 2016, the NDRC fined five domestic pharmaceutical companies over $600,000 for fixing their prices. This was part of the continuing battle to keep medicine prices at affordable levels. The five companies had colluded between April 2014 and September 2015 to raise the price of a drug used to treat kidney diseases. China has 1.4 billion potential customers, and the drug market was growing at 20 percent a year; it has now slowed to 5 percent.

The Chinese government is keen to stamp out corruption, but corruption is ingrained and persistent. China ranks 79th out of 175 countries on the Transparency International Index 2016, which tracks corruption across a variety of business markets. In one corruption case, the corruption took place outside of the normal parameters of business dealings; the individuals made deals outside the company's systems. In this particular case, there was a 30 percent drop in sales as the company scaled back in order to ensure it had oversight of all aspects of business operations in China. If foreign companies are found by the NDRC to be giving out bribes, then it will no longer be just "business as usual" after paying the fine; they must also repair their reputations.

19-12 Should pharmaceutical companies learn to adapt to bribery in China? Debate both sides of this issue. (AACSB: Communication; Ethical Reasoning)

19-13 Discuss whether multinational companies have difficulties breaking into the market in your country.

Marketing by the Numbers Peloton Pedals to the UK

The word *peloton* means "the main group of cyclists in a race." But Peloton means something different to the million or so fanatics in the United States who've shelled out $1,995 for an internet-connected indoor exercise bike and who pay $39 a month to stream live and on-demand classes from Peloton's New York City studio to the tablet connected to the bike. Peloton streams 12 hours of live content every day and offers more than 8,000 on-demand cycling classes and other "Beyond the Ride" classes such as yoga, arms, legs, and core strengthening. Riders can select their favorite instructor, class length, class type, and even music genre, and they can follow and compete with others. Peloton's success comes from being more than an exercise bike, studio, or cycling class—it's an experience that has created a cult-like following among its subscribers. Peloton's closed Facebook group boasts more than 90,000 members. More than 3,000 of those members descended on New York City during Peloton's Home Rider Invasion weekend, where they eagerly paid $50 to attend a cocktail party and two studio classes with Peloton's celebrity-like instructors. Now Peloton is expanding globally, beginning with the United Kingdom, the world's second-largest fitness market. With today's technologies, Peloton could distribute the service to consumers worldwide from its New York studio. But instead, the company re-created the entire experience in the United Kingdom, with a studio in London, British instructors, and retail showrooms just like in the United States. Bikes are priced at £1,995, and class subscriptions run £39.50 per month. Peloton sells the bikes at cost because it knows that the real money comes from selling the associated services.

19-14 How many bikes must Peloton sell to break even on this international expansion if total fixed costs are £30 million per year, variable costs are £1,995 per bike (Peloton sells them at cost), and monthly service variable costs are £5? Assume that a consumer purchasing a bike at the price of £1,995 will also subscribe for 12 months of the streaming service at £39.50 per month. Refer to Break-Even and Margin Analysis in Appendix 2: Marketing by the Numbers to learn how to perform this analysis. (AACSB: Analytic Reasoning)

19-15 What U.S. dollar sales does your answer to the previous question represent? Use a currency exchange calculator, such as the one at www.xe.com/currency-converter/, to convert from British pounds to U.S. dollars. (AACSB: Analytic Reasoning; Use of IT)

Company Case Huawei: Running the Global Telecommunications Race

Huawei has to be the poster child for Chinese tech firms that have become internationally successful. In a remarkably short time, Huawei has expanded phenomenally from a small electronics manufacturer to a global tech leader that is instantly associated with innovative high-tech products. Although Huawei as a brand is more popular because of its mobile phones, it has a major presence in cloud services and AI. Today, Huawei's products and solutions are installed in more than 170 countries around the world, and it serves more than a third of the world's population. Employing more than 180,000 people around the world, Huawei is the third-biggest global manufacturer of routers, switches, and other telecommunications equipment based on market share. In the super-competitive smartphone race where it is more popularly known, it has become a dominant player, taking on the big global giants like Apple and Samsung: according to an International Data Corporation report, in the third quarter of 2018, Samsung's global market share was 18.9 percent, Huawei's was 13.4 percent, and Apple was 11.8 percent. Additionally, the International Data Corporation reported that although the worldwide smartphone market showed a continued decline in the first quarter of 2019, Huawei was the only one of the top three manufacturers to increase its sales volume.

From a Rural Component Provider to a Tech Giant
Huawei Technologies was established in 1987 in Shenzhen, China, as a suburban/rural marketing agent for a Hong Kong–based phone company. Between 1996 and 1998, Huawei expanded into the metropolitan areas of China as the urban city population grew. The country's increasing global dominance and its emergence as the world's second-largest economy provided Huawei with a solid platform to launch into international markets. As Huawei started off primarily as a business-to-business (B2B) company, many of its achievements were not visible to the public; many of its business customers were telephone and internet operators that used Huawei's technology under their brand. Some estimates say that by 2030 China's urban population alone will be around one billion and its cities will have over one million inhabitants each by 2025. Large cities require hi-tech communication networks, and Huawei has grown tremendously

by serving this need in China. This allowed the company to harness the lessons it has learned and scale economies in preparation for a successful global entry.

Huawei has three core distinct business groups:
1. The Carrier Network Business Group, which provides wireless networks fixed networks, global services, and carrier software
2. The Enterprise Business Group, which provides services related to data centers and storage products (a perfect complement of the first group)
3. The Consumer Business Group, which looks after the company's mobile phone and smartphone segments

Building a Brand with a Global Mindset

Huawei's personal handset business has steadily built its expertise and brand image to become one of the top global mobile phone manufacturers. In 2008, it was already reported to be the third highest manufacturer of phone sets, yet its brand was still not well known. However, since then, Huawei has started to move up the value chain. By 2012, Huawei was manufacturing and shipping more than 90 percent of its consumer mobile phone devices under its own brand. This created conflicts with some business partners—telephone and internet operators—and they stopped doing business with Huawei, but this did not deter the company from branding its own phones. The decision to promote its own brand proved good for Huawei, for consumer popularity of other brands like Sony, Nokia, BlackBerry, and HTC was declining, which opened up new opportunities in the consumer retail market. Huawei's more affordable smartphones quickly became popular in markets like India, Indonesia, Taiwan, and many countries in Africa. Huawei is looking to strengthen its position in the European markets by introducing a smartphone with new camera features and a lower price than those from Samsung and Apple.

Huawei's Consumer Business Group became the third-largest smartphone manufacturer by market share in 2017, commanding 10 percent of the total global market. Soon after, Huawei displaced Apple to become the world's second-largest smartphone manufacturer and further cemented its place in the first quarter of 2019. According to the International Data Corporation's Worldwide Quarterly Mobile Phone Tracker report, Huawei's shipment increased from 39.3 million phones in Q1 of 2018 to 59.1 million shipments in Q1 of 2019.

Huawei has taken a people-led approach to its international marketing organization and global expansion efforts, encouraging a culture of global outlook. A key belief of the company's founder, Ren Zhengfei, is that if a company has global ambitions, it needs to ensure that its people can think with a global mindset. The company is known for creating an integrative work culture by bringing different parts and cultures of the world together, giving its employees increased global awareness and enhancing cross-cultural sensitivity. The tech giant believes that, for a truly global orientation, it must employ global procedures and strategies that focus on achieving the highest international levels, not just those suitable for a Chinese market. Huawei thus trains its employees in the highest international standards in terms of customs, procedures, laws, health and safety, language, local norms, and etiquette.

Challenges in Key Markets

Despite being hugely popular worldwide, Huawei's presence in the United States is limited. Although the reasons for this are largely political, there were preexisting market conditions that made the U.S. smartphone market a tough one to break into compared to other global markets. The main reason is that a large majority of Americans buy smartphones from network carriers, so a smartphone manufacturer must make a deal with one of the big carriers to feature their phones. Consumers in other parts of the world are more open to buying their phones directly from a store and the company itself, which exposes them to a greater number of brands.

The rise to global dominance has brought challenges for Huawei, especially with regards to its relations with the governments of some of the biggest markets. In 2018, the company faced political controversies rising out of concerns by some governments that Huawei telecom devices pose a potential security risk, which even led to banning of Huawei's business deals in some countries. For Huawei, the major impact comes from restrictions on the sales of its telecom network equipment; many countries, including the United States, New Zealand, Australia, and Japan have banned Huawei's network communication equipment.

Beyond Political Challenges

These political issues have not hindered Huawei's smartphone growth, thanks to a strong domestic market and demands from other international markets. But the path of expansion may not be as easy and smooth for Huawei as it used to be, given the tense political situation with some influential countries.

Huawei's global expansion is not dependent only on the political attitudes of these countries; the competitiveness of its products is of vital importance too, and its sustained growth will also depend on how well its products compare with that of its competitors. In the past, Huawei—along with other Chinese companies—has been under fire for copying competitors' technology and selling at lower prices. Huawei is thus investing a lot in developing innovative technologies and currently has one of the largest R&D budgets in the industry to develop a sustainable competitive advantage. It should also be noted that the security concerns that are raised by countries like the United States and Australia may not be shared by the other countries, like Thailand and Indonesia, who regard the need for affordable and reliable telecommunications and technology equipment as more important.

Global Competition and Technological Power Balance

The telecommunications sector, and the smartphone market space particularly, is dynamic and extremely competitive. In the span of a decade, we have seen the fortunes of the leading companies change with the pace of innovation. Apple emerged as the leader by displacing the established players like Nokia, Blackberry, and Sony Ericsson, but it in turn was toppled by Samsung, moving it to the second spot, and more recently, Huawei took over the second spot and shifted Apple down to third position—yet five years ago, many consumers would not have even heard of Huawei. The new shift in the global telecommunications race is 5G technology, the next generation of wireless networks. This technology will allow faster data speeds and will be used by self-driving cars and smart cities, which use the internet as the basic mode of functioning. Huawei, along with Ericsson and Nokia, is aiming to be among the principle suppliers of this technology. Upgrading to 5G will require telecommunication firms around the world to spend a significant amount of money on updating their equipment, but telecommunication vendors are trying to make an early start. According to Huawei, its 5G equipment is already being used by two-thirds of the commercially launched 5G networks outside China; the company has booked 50 commercial 5G contracts outside of China in markets like the United Kingdom, Switzerland, Finland, and South Korea. According to CEO Ren Zhengfei, no other provider of 5G technology will match Huawei for the next two to three years. In June 2019, the company announced that it has increased its investment into the 5G technology and that cybersecurity and privacy are its top priorities.

Huawei's growth and international expansion have been impressive and bold. Major factors that have contributed to its success are a strong commitment to R&D, a global philosophy and outlook, focus on building a corporate brand, effective pricing strategies, and market-targeting strategies. However, Huawei still has a relatively weak presence in the South Asian and North American markets, which puts its current number two position in the smartphone market (behind Samsung) into question. As consumer needs and product technology evolve, Huawei will have to work continuously to satisfy and create future consumer needs rather than merely meet their current ones. And with regard to the commercialization of 5G technology, Huawei will have to continue spearheading innovation and spreading the adoption of the technology in different world markets.[47]

Questions for Discussion

19-16 Discuss Huawei's transformation into a global brand.

19-17 Comment on the global marketing environment for Huawei.

19-18 For technology-based firms like Huawei, what global product and communication strategies work best? Do think Huawei has adopted the right strategy?

19-19 Do you think Huawei can lead the global smartphone race? Why or why not?

19-20 How important are political factors with regard to Huawei's ambition to be the leading provider of 5G technology globally?

20 Sustainable Marketing
Social Responsibility and Ethics

OBJECTIVES OUTLINE

OBJECTIVE 20-1 Define *sustainable marketing* and discuss its importance. **See: Sustainable Marketing** *(pp 582–584)*

OBJECTIVE 20-2 Identify the major social criticisms of marketing. **See: Social Criticisms of Marketing** *(pp 584–592)*

OBJECTIVE 20-3 Define *consumerism* and *environmentalism* and explain how they affect marketing strategies. **See: Consumer Actions to Promote Sustainable Marketing** *(pp 592–596)*

OBJECTIVE 20-4 Describe the principles of sustainable marketing. **See: Business Actions toward Sustainable Marketing** *(pp 596–600)*

OBJECTIVE 20-5 Explain the role of ethics in marketing. **See: Marketing Ethics and the Sustainable Company** *(pp 600–603)*

CHAPTER PREVIEW

In this final chapter, we'll examine the concept of sustainable marketing, meeting the needs of consumers, businesses, and society—now and in the future—through socially and environmentally responsible marketing actions. We'll start by defining sustainable marketing and then look at some common criticisms of marketing as it affects individual consumers as well as public actions that promote sustainable marketing. Finally, we'll see how companies themselves can benefit from proactively pursuing sustainable marketing practices that bring value to not only individual customers but also society as a whole. Sustainable marketing actions are more than just the right thing to do; they're also good for business.

First, let's look at an example of sustainable marketing in action at Unilever, the world's third-largest consumer products company. For 20 years running, Unilever has been named a sustainability leader in the food and beverage industry by the Dow Jones Sustainability Indexes. Nearly a decade ago, the company launched its 10-year Sustainable Living Plan, by which it intended to double its size while at the same time reducing its impact on the planet and increasing the social benefits arising from its activities. That's an ambitious goal.

UNILEVER: Creating a Better Future Every Day

When Paul Polman took over as CEO of Unilever a decade ago, the foods, home, and personal care products company was a slumbering giant. Despite its stable of star-studded brands—including the likes of Dove, Axe, Noxzema, Sunsilk, OMO, Hellmann's, Knorr, Lipton, and Ben & Jerry's—Unilever had experienced a decade of stagnant sales and profits. The company needed renewed energy and purpose. "To drag the world back to sanity, we need to know why we are here," said Polman.

To answer the "why are we here" question and find a more energizing mission, Polman looked beyond the usual corporate goals of growing sales, profits, and shareholder value. Instead, he asserted, growth results from accomplishing a broader social and environmental mission. Unilever exists "for consumers, not shareholders," he said. "If we are in sync with consumer needs and the environment in which we operate, and take responsibility for our [societal impact], then the shareholder will also be rewarded."

Evaluating and working on sustainability impact is nothing new at Unilever. Prior to Polman taking the reins, the company already had multiple programs in place to manage the impact of its products and operations. But the existing programs and results—while good—simply didn't go far enough. So in 2010 Unilever launched its Sustainable Living Plan—an aggressive long-term plan that takes capitalism to the next level. Under the plan, the company set out to "help create a world where everyone can live well within the natural limits of the planet [by] putting sustainable living at the heart of everything we do." According to Polman, Unilever's long-run commercial success depends on how well it manages the social and environmental impact of its actions.

The Sustainable Living Plan set out three major social and environmental objectives: "(1) To help more than one billion people take action to improve their health and well-being; (2) to halve the environmental footprint of the making and use of our products; and (3) to enhance the livelihoods of millions of people as we grow our business." The Sustainable Living Plan pulled together all of the work Unilever had already been doing and set ambitious new sustainability goals. These goals span the entire value chain, from how the company sources raw materials to how consumers use and dispose of its products. "Our aim is to make our activities more sustainable and also encourage our customers, suppliers, and others to do the same," says the company.

On the "upstream supply side," more than half of Unilever's raw materials come from agriculture, so the company is helping suppliers develop sustainable farming practices that meet its own high expectations for environmental and social impact. Unilever assesses suppliers against two sets of standards. The first is the Unilever Supplier Code, which calls for socially responsible actions regarding human rights, labor practices, product safety, and care for the environment. Second, specifically for agricultural suppliers, the Unilever Sustainable Agriculture Code details Unilever's expectations for sustainable agriculture practices so that it and its suppliers "can commit to the sustainability journey together."

But Unilever's Sustainable Living Plan goes far beyond simply creating more responsible supply and distribution chains. Approximately 68 percent of the total greenhouse gas footprint of Unilever's products and 50 percent of the water footprint occur during post-purchase consumer use. So Unilever is also working with its

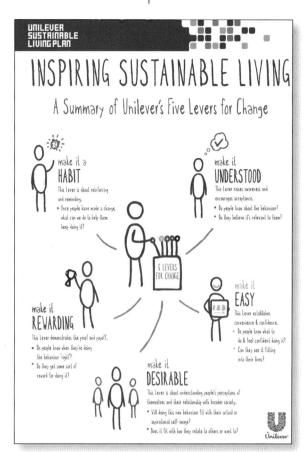

Under its Sustainable Living Plan, Unilever is working with billions of customers worldwide to improve the social and environmental impact of its products. "Small actions. Big difference."

Reproduced with kind permission of Unilever PLC and group companies

customers to improve the environmental impact of its products in use. On any given day, about 2.5 billion people in 190 global markets use a product from one of Unilever's more than 400 brands. Therefore, small everyday consumer actions can add up to a big difference. Unilever sums it up with this equation: "Unilever brands × small everyday actions × billions of consumers = big difference."

For example, almost one-third of households worldwide use Unilever laundry products to do their washing—approximately 125 billion washes every year. Therefore, under its Sustainable Living Plan, Unilever is both creating more eco-friendly laundry products and motivating consumers to improve their laundry habits.

Around the world, for instance, Unilever is encouraging consumers to wash clothes at lower temperatures and use the correct dosage of detergent. Unilever products such as OMO and Persil Small & Mighty concentrated laundry detergents

> **Under Unilever's Sustainable Living Plan, the consumer goods giant has set out to "create a better future every day for people around the world." Unilever's long-run commercial success depends on how well it manages the social and environmental impact of its actions.**

use less packaging, making them cheaper and less polluting to transport. More important, they've been reformulated to wash efficiently at lower temperatures, using less energy and water. Unilever estimates that these changes have achieved a 15 percent reduction in greenhouse gas emissions. Another Unilever product, Comfort One Rinse fabric conditioner, was created for hand-washing clothes in developing and emerging markets where water is often in short supply. The innovative product requires only one bucket of water for rinsing rather than three, saving consumers time, effort, and 30 liters of water per wash.

Such energy and water savings don't show up on Unilever's income statement, but they are extremely important to the people and the planet. "Ultimately," says the company, "we will only succeed if we inspire people around the world to take small, everyday actions that can add up to a big difference for the world." To meet this objective, Unilever has identified "Five Levers for Change"—things that its marketers can do to inspire people to adopt specific sustainable behaviors. The model helps marketers identify the barriers and triggers for change. The levers for change are: make it understood, make it easy, make it desirable, make it rewarding, and make it a habit.

Will Unilever's Sustainable Living Plan produce results for the company? So far, so good. Unilever is making excellent progress on its overall mission of "making sustainable living commonplace" and on its 79 aggressive Sustainable Living Plan goals. The company has already achieved 26 specific targets and is on track with 52 more. And despite volatility in its global markets, Unilever's profits continue to grow. In the past three years alone, although revenues dipped slightly, profits nearly doubled. Even more telling, Sustainable Living Brands now make up 26 of Unilever top 40 brands. And those brands grew 46 percent faster than the rest of Unilever's business, accounting for 70 percent of its growth.

Polman has always maintained that the sustainability plan is not just the right thing to do for people and the environment, it's also right for Unilever. The quest for sustainability saves money by reducing energy use and minimizing waste. It fuels innovation, resulting in new products and new consumer benefits. And it creates new market opportunities: More than half of Unilever's sales are from developing countries, the very places that face the greatest sustainability challenges.

After 10 years at the helm, Polman recently stepped down as Unilever's CEO. But his sustainability legacy remains. Under his leadership, profits doubled and the company delivered a total shareholder return of 290 percent. Prior to retiring, Polman reaffirmed that the sustainability plan is helping Unilever grow while also creating a better future for billions of people without increasing the environmental footprint. "We do not believe there is a conflict between sustainability and profitable growth," he concluded. "The daily act of making and selling consumer goods drives economic and social progress. There are billions of people around the world who deserve the better quality of life that everyday products like soap, shampoo, and tea can provide. Sustainable living is not a pipedream. It can be done, and there is very little downside."[1]

· ·

RESPONSIBLE MARKETERS DISCOVER what consumers want and respond with market offerings that create value for buyers and capture value in return. The *marketing concept* is a philosophy of customer value and mutual gain. Its practice leads the economy by an invisible hand to satisfy the many and changing needs of consumers.

Not all marketers follow the marketing concept, however. In fact, some companies use questionable marketing practices that serve their own rather than consumers' interests. Moreover, even well-intentioned marketing actions that meet the current needs of some consumers may cause immediate or future harm to other consumers or the larger society. Responsible marketers must consider whether their actions are sustainable in the longer run.

This chapter examines sustainable marketing and the social and environmental effects of private marketing practices. First, we address the question: What is sustainable marketing, and why is it important?

> Author Comment | Marketers must think beyond immediate customer satisfaction and business performance toward sustainable strategies that preserve the world for future generations.

Sustainable Marketing

OBJECTIVE 20-1 Define *sustainable marketing* and discuss its importance.

Sustainable marketing calls for socially and environmentally responsible actions that meet the present needs of consumers and businesses while also preserving or enhancing the ability of future generations to meet their needs. ● **Figure 20.1** compares the sustainable marketing concept with other marketing concepts we studied in earlier chapters.

The *marketing concept* recognizes that organizations thrive by determining the current needs and wants of target customers and fulfilling them more effectively and efficiently than competitors do. It focuses on meeting the company's short-term sales, growth, and

Sustainable marketing
Socially and environmentally responsible marketing that meets the present needs of consumers and businesses while also preserving or enhancing the ability of future generations to meet their needs.

● FIGURE 20.1
Sustainable Marketing

The marketing concept means meeting the current needs of both customers and the company. But that can sometimes mean compromising the future of both.

Needs of Consumers

	Now	Future
Now	Marketing concept	Societal marketing concept
Future	Strategic planning concept	**Sustainable marketing concept**

Needs of Business

Sustainable marketing means meeting current needs in a way that preserves the rights and options of future generations of consumers and businesses.

profit needs by engaging customers and giving them what they want now. However, satisfying consumers' immediate needs and desires doesn't always serve the future best interests of either customers or the business.

For example, McDonald's early decisions to market tasty but fat- and salt-laden fast foods created immediate satisfaction for customers as well as sales and profits for the company. However, critics assert that McDonald's and other fast-food chains contributed to a longer-term national obesity epidemic, damaging consumer health and burdening the national health system. They worried that McDonald's Happy Meals created poor eating habits in children that carried forward into their later years. In turn, many consumers began looking for healthier eating options, causing a slump in the sales and profits of the fast-food industry.

Beyond issues of ethical behavior and social welfare, McDonald's was also criticized for the sizable environmental footprint of its vast global operations, everything from wasteful packaging and solid waste creation to inefficient energy use in its stores. Thus, McDonald's strategy was not sustainable in the long run in terms of either consumer or company benefit.

Whereas the *societal marketing concept* identified in Figure 20.1 considers the future welfare of consumers and the *strategic planning concept* considers future company needs, the *sustainable marketing concept* considers both. Sustainable marketing calls for socially and environmentally responsible actions that meet both the immediate and future needs of customers and the company.

For example, for more than a decade, McDonald's has responded to these challenges with a more sustainable strategy of diversifying into salads, fruits, grilled chicken, low-fat milk, and other healthy fare. The company has also sponsored major education campaigns to help consumers better understand the keys to living balanced, active lifestyles. ● It announced a list of "Commitments to Offer Improved Nutrition Choices" and has been working with the Alliance for a Healthier Generation to make improvements to the Happy Meal, offering more balanced meals with simpler, healthier ingredients. McDonald's points out that 80 percent of the items on its national menu fall are under 400 calories—from a basic cheeseburger to products such as the Fruit & Maple Oatmeal, Egg White Delight McMuffin, and Iced Caramel Macchiato.[2]

McDonald's sustainability initiatives also address environmental issues. It calls for food-supply sustainability, reduced and environmentally sustainable packaging, reuse and recycling, and more responsible store designs. For example, McDonald's has made the commitment to source all packaging from renewable, recycled, or certified resources and make recycling an option at all locations by 2025.[3] Thus, McDonald's is now well positioned for a sustainably profitable future.

Truly sustainable marketing requires a smooth-functioning marketing system in which consumers, companies, public policy makers, and others work together to ensure socially and environmentally responsible marketing actions. Unfortunately, however, the marketing system doesn't always work smoothly. The following sections examine several sustainability questions: What are the most

● **Sustainability: McDonald's has responded to sustainability challenges by diversifying into salads, fruits, grilled chicken, low-fat milk, and other healthy fare, including Happy Meals offering more balanced meals with simpler ingredients.**

Michael Neelon(misc)/Alamy Stock Photo

frequent social criticisms of marketing? What steps have private citizens taken to curb marketing ills? What steps have legislators and government agencies taken to promote sustainable marketing? What steps have enlightened companies taken to carry out socially responsible and ethical marketing that creates sustainable value for both individual customers and society as a whole?

> **Author Comment** | In most ways, we all benefit greatly from marketing activities. However, like most other human endeavors, marketing has its flaws. Here we present both sides of some of the most common criticisms of marketing.

Social Criticisms of Marketing

OBJECTIVE 20-2 Identify the major social criticisms of marketing.

Marketing receives much criticism. Some of this criticism is justified; much is not. Social critics claim that certain marketing practices hurt individual consumers, society as a whole, and other business firms.

Marketing's Impact on Individual Consumers

Consumers have many concerns about how well the American marketing system serves their interests. Surveys usually show that consumers hold mixed or even slightly unfavorable attitudes toward marketing practices. Consumer advocates, government agencies, and other critics have accused marketing of harming consumers through high prices, deceptive practices, high-pressure selling, shoddy or unsafe products, planned obsolescence, and poor service to disadvantaged consumers. Such questionable marketing practices are not sustainable in terms of long-term consumer or business welfare.

High Prices

Many critics charge that the American marketing system causes prices to be higher than they would be under more "sensible" systems. Such high prices are hard to swallow, especially when the economy gets tight. Critics point to three factors—high costs of distribution, high advertising and promotion costs, and excessive markups.

A long-standing charge is that greedy marketing channel members mark up prices beyond the value of their services. As a result, distribution costs too much and consumers pay for these excessive costs in the form of higher prices. Resellers respond that intermediaries do work that would otherwise have to be done by manufacturers or consumers. Their prices reflect services that consumers want—more convenience, larger stores and assortments, more service, longer store hours, return privileges, and others. In fact, they argue, retail competition is so intense that margins are actually quite low. And resellers such as Walmart, Costco, Amazon, and others pressure their competitors to operate efficiently and keep their prices down.

Modern marketing is also accused of pushing up prices to finance unneeded advertising, sales promotion, and packaging.  For example, a heavily promoted national brand sells for much more than a virtually identical store-branded product. Critics charge that much of this promotion and packaging adds only psychological, not functional, value. Marketers respond that although advertising adds to product costs, it also adds value by informing potential buyers of the availability and merits of a brand. Brand name products may cost more, but branding assures buyers of consistent quality. Moreover, although consumers can usually buy functional versions of products at lower prices, they *want* and are willing to pay more for products that also provide psychological benefits—that make them feel wealthy, attractive, or special.

Critics also charge that some companies mark up goods excessively. They point to the drug industry, where a pill costing five cents to make may cost the consumer $2 to buy, and to the high charges for auto repairs and other services. Marketers respond that most businesses try to price

● **A heavily promoted national brand sells for much more than a virtually identical non-branded or store-branded product. Critics charge that promotion adds only psychological value to the product rather than functional value.**

Keri Miksza

fairly to consumers because they want to build customer relationships and repeat business. Also, they assert, consumers often don't understand the reasons for high markups. For example, pharmaceutical markups help cover the costs of making and distributing existing medicines plus the high costs of developing and testing new medicines. As pharmaceuticals company GlaxoSmithKline has stated in its ads, "Today's medicines finance tomorrow's miracles."

Deceptive Practices

Marketers are sometimes accused of deceptive practices that lead consumers to believe they will get more value than they actually do. Deceptive practices fall into three groups: promotion, packaging, and pricing. *Deceptive promotion* includes practices such as misrepresenting the product's features or performance or luring customers to the store for a bargain that is out of stock. *Deceptive packaging* includes exaggerating package contents through subtle design, using misleading labeling, or describing size in misleading terms.

Deceptive pricing includes practices such as falsely advertising "factory" or "wholesale" prices or a large price reduction from a phony high retail "list price." For example, retailers from JCPenney and Kohl's to Neiman Marcus and Nordstrom were hit with lawsuits alleging that they used inflated original prices. A class action suit against Ross Stores accused the retailer of duping customers with "false and/or misleading comparative prices which purport to be charged by other merchants for the same products." Ross Stores paid a $4.9 million settlement. And Overstock.com was recently fined $6.8 million by a California court as a result of a fraudulent pricing lawsuit filed by the attorneys general of eight California counties. The suit charged that the online giant routinely advertised its prices as lower than fabricated "list prices." It recites one example in which Overstock sold a patio set for $449 while claiming that the list price was $999. When the item was delivered, the customer found that it had a Walmart sticker stating a price of $247.[4]

Deceptive practices have led to legislation and other consumer protection actions. For example, in 1938 Congress enacted the Wheeler-Lea Act, which gave the Federal Trade Commission (FTC) power to regulate "unfair or deceptive acts or practices." The FTC has since published several guidelines listing deceptive practices.

Despite regulations, however, some critics argue that deceptive claims are still common, even for well-known brands. ● For example, identity theft protection company LifeLock recently paid a record $100 million relating to FTC charges of deceptive advertising. The FTC accused LifeLock—which claims that it is "relentlessly protecting your identity"—of falsely advertising that it protected consumers' sensitive data with the same high-level safeguards as financial institutions and of falsely claiming it protected consumers' identity around the clock by providing alerts "as soon as" it received any indication there was a problem. Said one reporter, "It's bad enough that people have to worry about their personal data getting stolen. Now they have to worry about the companies responsible for protecting their data not doing their job."[5]

The toughest problem often is defining what is "deceptive." For instance, an advertiser's claim that its chewing gum will "rock your world" isn't intended to be taken literally. Instead, the advertiser might claim, it is "puffery"—innocent exaggeration for effect. However, others claim that puffery and alluring imagery can harm consumers in subtle ways. Think about the popular and long-running Mastercard "Priceless" commercials that once painted pictures of consumers fulfilling their priceless dreams despite the costs. The ads suggested that your credit card could make it happen. But critics charge that such imagery by credit card companies encourages a spend-now-pay-later attitude that causes many consumers to *over*use their cards.

Marketers argue that most companies avoid deceptive practices. Because such practices harm a company's business in the long run, they simply aren't sustainable. Profitable customer relationships are built on a foundation

● **Deceptive advertising: The FTC accused LifeLock—which claims that it is "relentlessly protecting your identity"—of making false advertising claims.**

FOOTAGE VECTOR PHOTO/Shutterstock

of value and trust. If consumers do not get what they expect, they will switch to more reliable products. In addition, consumers usually protect themselves from deception. Most consumers recognize a marketer's selling intent and are careful when they buy, sometimes even to the point of not believing completely true product claims.

High-Pressure Selling

Salespeople are sometimes accused of high-pressure selling that persuades people to buy goods they had no thought of buying. It is often said that insurance, real estate, and used cars are *sold*, not *bought*. Salespeople are trained to deliver smooth, canned talks to entice purchases. They sell hard because sales contests promise big prizes to those who sell the most. Similarly, TV infomercial pitchmen use "yell and sell" presentations that create a sense of consumer urgency that only those with strong willpower can resist.

But in most cases, marketers have little to gain from high-pressure selling. Although such tactics may work in one-time selling situations for short-term gain, most selling involves building long-term relationships with valued customers. High-pressure or deceptive selling can seriously damage such relationships. For example, imagine a P&G account manager trying to pressure a Walmart buyer or an IBM salesperson trying to browbeat an information technology manager at GE. It simply wouldn't work.

Shoddy, Harmful, or Unsafe Products

Another criticism concerns poor product quality or function. One complaint is that, too often, products and services are not made well or do not perform well. A second complaint concerns product safety. Product safety has been a problem for several reasons, including company indifference, increased product complexity, and poor quality control. A third complaint is that many products deliver little benefit or may even be harmful.

For example, think about the soft drink industry. For years, industry critics have blamed the plentiful supply of sugar-laden, high-calorie soft drinks for the obesity epidemic and other health issues in the United States. They are quick to fault what they see

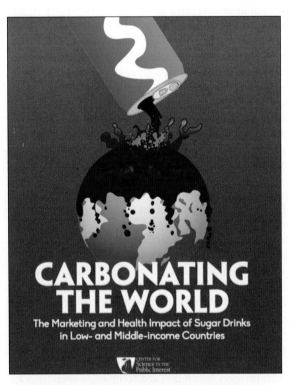

● **Harmful products: Is the soft drink industry being irresponsible by promoting harmful products in emerging markets, or is it simply serving the wants of consumers while letting them make their own consumption choices?**

Center for Science in the Public Interest

as greedy beverage marketers for cashing in on vulnerable consumers, turning us into a nation of Big Gulpers. Although U.S. consumption of soft drinks has dropped in recent years, beverage companies are now looking to emerging markets for growth. ● According to a report by the Center for Science in the Public Interest (CSPI) titled "Carbonating the World," in 2008 emerging markets such as China, India, and Mexico accounted for just over half of global soft drink consumption. Now, however, nearly 70 percent of soft drinks are sold in such markets. The CPSI accuses beverage companies of behaving much like the tobacco industry, marketing their harmful products to countries already struggling to provide health care to their citizens.[6]

Is the soft drink industry being socially irresponsible by aggressively promoting overindulgence to ill-informed or unwary consumers in emerging markets? Or is it simply serving the wants of customers by offering products that ping consumer taste buds while letting consumers make their own consumption choices? Is it the industry's job to police public tastes? As in many matters of social responsibility, what's right and wrong may be a matter of opinion. Whereas some analysts criticize the industry, others suggest that responsibility lies with consumers. Maybe companies shouldn't sell Big Gulps. Then again, nobody is forced to buy and drink one.

Most manufacturers *want* to produce quality goods. After all, the way a company deals with product quality and safety problems can harm or help its reputation. Companies selling poor-quality or unsafe products risk damaging conflicts with consumer groups and regulators. Unsafe products can result in product liability suits and large awards for damages. More fundamentally, consumers who are unhappy with a firm's products may avoid future purchases and talk other consumers into doing the same. In today's social media and online review environment, word of poor quality can spread like wildfire. Thus, quality missteps are not consistent with sustainable marketing. Today's marketers know that good quality results in customer value and satisfaction, which in turn create sustainable customer relationships.

Planned Obsolescence

Critics also have charged that some companies practice *planned obsolescence*, causing their products to become obsolete before they actually should need replacement. They accuse some producers of using materials and components that will break, wear, rust, or rot sooner than they should. And if the products themselves don't wear out fast enough, other companies are charged with *perceived obsolescence*—continually changing consumer concepts of acceptable styles to encourage more and earlier buying. An obvious example is the fast-fashion industry with its constantly changing clothing fashions, which some critics claim creates a wasteful disposable clothing culture. "Too many garments end up in landfill sites," bemoans one designer. "They are deemed aesthetically redundant and get discarded at the end of the season when there are often years of wear left."[7]

● Planned obsolescence: Apple was accused recently of deliberately slowing down older iPhones through software updates to encourage customers to upgrade to newer models.

Neil Godwin/Future Publishing/Shutterstock

Still others are accused of introducing planned streams of new products that make older models obsolete, turning consumers into "serial replacers." Critics claim that this occurs in the consumer electronics industries. If you're like most people, you probably have a drawer full of yesterday's hottest technological gadgets—from mobile phones and cameras to iPods and flash drives—now reduced to the status of fossils. It seems that anything more than a year or two old is hopelessly out of date. ● Apple was even accused recently of deliberately slowing down older iPhones through software updates to encourage customers to upgrade to newer models. Apple admitted slowing some phones but said it was doing so to "prolong the life" of the devices with aging batteries.[8]

Marketers respond that consumers *like* style changes; they get tired of the old goods and want a new look in fashion. Or they *want* the latest high-tech innovations, even if older models still work. No one has to buy a new product, and if too few people like it, it will simply fail. Finally, most companies do not design their products to break down earlier because they do not want to lose customers to other brands. Instead, they seek constant improvement to ensure that products will consistently meet or exceed customer expectations.

Much of the so-called planned obsolescence is the working of the competitive and technological forces in a free society—forces that lead to ever-improving goods and services. For example, if Samsung produced a new Galaxy phone or tablet that would last 10 years, few consumers would want it. Instead, buyers want the latest technological innovations. From that view, obsolescence isn't something brands are forcing on consumers. It's something that consumers are demanding.

Poor Service to Disadvantaged Consumers

Finally, the American marketing system has been accused of poorly serving disadvantaged consumers. For example, critics claim that the urban poor often have to shop in smaller stores that carry inferior goods and charge higher prices. The presence of large national chain stores in low-income neighborhoods would help to keep prices down. However, the critics accuse major chain retailers of *redlining*, drawing a red line around disadvantaged neighborhoods and avoiding placing stores there.

For example, the nation's poor areas have 30 percent fewer supermarkets than affluent areas do. As a result, many low-income consumers find themselves in "food deserts," which are awash with small markets offering frozen pizzas, Cheetos, Moon Pies, and Cokes but where fruits and vegetables or fresh fish and chicken are out of reach. The U.S. Department of Agriculture (USDA) has identified more than 6,500 food deserts in rural and urban areas of the United States. Currently, more than 17 million Americans—5.6 percent of the population—live in low-income areas where a supermarket is over a mile away

● **Serving underserved consumers: The USDA recently launched a pilot program that lets low-income SNAP consumers order online, giving them vastly broader food options at competitive prices.**

Food & Nutrition Service; Ronstik/123RF

in an urban area and 20 miles away in a rural area. In turn, the lack of access to healthy, affordable fresh foods has a negative impact on the health of underserved consumers in these areas.[9]

Many national chains, such as Walmart, Walgreens, SuperValu, and even Whole Foods Market, have recently agreed to open or expand more stores that bring nutritious and fresh foods to underserved communities. Other retailers have found that they can act responsibly and even operate profitably by focusing on low-income areas ignored by other companies. For example, Starbucks is now opening stores in low-income urban areas (see Real Marketing 20.1).

● To help alleviate the food desert problem, the USDA recently launched a pilot program in New York State that allows Supplemental Nutrition Assistance Program (SNAP) participants—people who receive government vouchers to buy groceries at supermarkets and farmers' markets—to use their benefits to buy food online. Under the program, designed to "put healthy food within reach," Amazon and ShopRite will serve SNAP shoppers in New York City; Walmart will serve upstate New York shoppers. The online buying program would give low-income SNAP participants who don't have access to supermarkets vastly broader food options at competitive prices from their living rooms. If the pilot program succeeds, the USDA plans to extend it to retailers nationwide, covering 40 million Americans who receive $60 billion in SNAP benefits annually.[10]

Clearly, better marketing systems must be built to service disadvantaged consumers. In fact, marketers in many industries profitably target such consumers with legitimate goods and services that create real value. In cases where marketers do not step in to fill the void, the government likely will. For example, the FTC has taken action against sellers that advertise false values, wrongfully deny services, or charge disadvantaged customers too much.

Marketing's Impact on Society as a Whole

The American marketing system has been accused of adding to several "evils" in American society at large, such as creating too much materialism, too few social goods, and a glut of cultural pollution.

False Wants and Too Much Materialism

Critics have charged that the marketing system urges too much interest in material possessions and that America's love affair with worldly possessions is not sustainable. Too often, people are judged by what they *own* rather than by who they *are*. The critics view this interest in material things not as a natural state of mind but rather as a matter of false wants created by marketing. Marketers, they claim, stimulate people's desires for goods and create materialistic models of the good life. Thus, marketers have created an endless cycle of mass consumption based on a distorted interpretation of the "American dream."

In this view, marketing's purpose is to promote consumption, and the inevitable outcome of successful marketing is unsustainable *over*consumption. According to the critics, more is not always better. Some groups have taken their concerns straight to the public. For example, New Dream is a nonprofit organization founded on a mission to empower individuals, communities, and organizations to change the ways they consume for the benefit of people and the planet. Through educational videos, services, and marketing campaigns such as "More fun! Less stuff!" the organization works to counter the commercialization of culture and promote positive changes in the way goods are produced and consumed.[11]

Marketers respond that such criticisms overstate the power of business to create needs. They claim people have strong defenses against advertising and other marketing tools. Marketers are most effective when they appeal to existing wants rather than when

Real Marketing 20.1 | Starbucks: Serving the Underserved—Doing Good *and* Doing Well

Starbucks has long been famous for its pricey premium coffee and upscale "Starbucks Experience," targeted largely toward well-off professionals. More than 80 percent of Starbucks's U.S. stores are located in predominately white middle-class or higher-than-middle-class communities. There's been a distinct underrepresentation of Starbucks stores in the nation's lowest-income areas populated by minorities. In recent years, however, Starbucks has been experimenting with stores in such underserved communities. In part, this initiative stems from Starbucks's long-held social responsibility mission. But beyond doing good, Starbucks believes that such stores also provide good opportunities for growth and profits.

Starbucks's move into underserved communities began in the mid-1990s when the company hooked up with retired Los Angeles Lakers basketball superstar Earvin "Magic" Johnson. Johnson was on a mission to take big business into depressed urban areas. More than just a philanthropic attempt to "give back," Johnson saw genuine marketing opportunities in inner-city "commerce deserts" largely ignored by big brands. He started with a few Pepsi bottling plants and then expanded into shopping centers and movie theater complexes.

Johnson soon found a kindred spirit in Starbucks founder and chairman emeritus Howard Schultz. "I said, 'Look Howard, Latinos and black folks. We like coffee too,'" Johnson later revealed. After seeing the success of Johnson's urban theaters, Schultz agreed that putting Starbucks in underserved low-income communities made good business sense. The two struck a deal for a 50-50 Starbucks–Johnson venture to build Starbucks shops in urban neighborhoods.

Targeting urban consumers required adapting the Starbucks model, everything from the menu to the music. "I had to take the scones out of my Starbucks and put in things like sweet potato pie and sock-it-to-me cake," Johnson said. Over the next 12 years, Starbucks built 105 Magic Johnson Enterprises stores. The stores were an unqualified success. When Johnson liquidated his business holdings a few years ago, Starbucks paid handsomely for full ownership of all 105 stores.

The Starbucks–Johnson stores were no big stretch for Starbucks. From its earliest days, the chain maintained a strong corporate culture of social responsibility. Schultz saw "doing good" as an essential prerequisite to "doing well." There is a great need "to achieve the fragile balance between profit, social impact, and a moral obligation," said Schultz. Companies must "enhance the lives of our employees and the communities we serve." And the best way to have strong social impact is to achieve strong financial performance.

To further serve the underserved, Starbucks committed to opening 15 "community stores" in low-income urban areas such as East Baltimore; the Jamaica neighborhood of Queens, NY; and Englewood on Chicago's South Side. The Starbucks Community Store initiative began after the 2014 riots in Ferguson, Missouri, part of greater metropolitan St. Louis. Schultz led a team of Starbucks executives on a tour of Ferguson, an urban community with a population that is 70 percent African American, where 22 percent of residents live below the poverty line and unemployment among young black males nears 50 percent. Schultz told the executives, "We're absent from this community...but we have a responsibility and an opportunity to be here."

Opening a store in Ferguson made sense from a social responsibility perspective. But from a business point of view, most analysts were skeptical. They viewed Ferguson as an urban economic dead zone. The riots had only made things worse, leaving behind 37 damaged businesses, 17 of which were completely destroyed. Increasing the risk, Starbucks met with substantial resistance locally. "Many people told us, 'You do not have a role here,'" says Starbucks's global responsibility chief. As it turned out, the Ferguson store was among the top performers of the hundreds of new stores opened by Starbucks that year, and it had 15 percent sales growth in the second year. Today, Starbucks considers the Ferguson store "a blueprint for the future" of its community stores.

How has a store that most businesses would never have opened been successful? A visit to the store tells the story. On the wall hangs a framed photo of a yard sign that reads, "WE LOVE ALL OF FERGUSON." A homeless woman who routinely parks her shopping cart outside sleeps at a table. Diedric Cook—a 21-year-old barista who was living out of his car before being hired a year ago—places a cup of tea on her table for when she wakes up. Around lunchtime, a dozen men and women gather in the shop's designated community room for a free job-skills training class led by members of the Urban League. The room serves as a community center, hosting job fairs, school board meetings, and poetry readings. Young, green apron–clad employees combine bright and hopeful personalities with hard knowledge of life on the street, creating an environment where they interact naturally among themselves and with customers.

Although employees in the Ferguson store appear carefree, a deeper look reveals how they struggle to keep things together. Cordell Lewis—the tattooed, mohawk-shorn manager who was recruited from the video game store across the street—will tell you

Serving the underserved: Starbucks is opening new stores in low-income urban areas often overlooked by other big companies. "There's a bigger purpose here than just coffee."

Jahi Chikwendiu/The Washington Post via Getty Image

that Cook isn't the only employee who's lived out of his car. Lewis himself had done that as a child. Referring to another young employee who had slept in her car in a Walmart parking lot the night before, Lewis says, "How am I ever going to get on that person and say, 'You're late, you're not in dress code'?" He continues, "If [such employees] were in a bad spot I would take care of it. Starbucks would take care of it."

Ironically, the situations that render these employees "unemployable" to most other companies are key ingredients in the mix that makes inner-city Starbucks locations work. "Seeing your manager care about you that much makes it where you like coming to work," Cook points out.

"He's like a dad around here," says another employee of Lewis. "This is our home away from home." That kind of employee commitment creates a place where local customers also feel at home.

By being one of the first to set up shop in underserved communities, Starbucks has inspired other businesses to follow suit. After Starbucks opened the Ferguson store, 41 other new businesses followed, creating a stronger economic base. "When one person steps out from the crowd, others will follow," says a local city council member. "Starbucks said, 'We are going to Ferguson. We are going to help this community recover.' Once Starbucks stepped out of the crowd, everybody began to follow."

Fifteen Starbucks community stores hardly make a dent in the massive network of Starbucks locations in well-heeled communities around the world. Nor do 105 former Magic Johnson shops. But it's a start. And Starbucks's rapid expansion has led to saturation in many markets. With a 7 percent annual new store growth goal, Starbucks must find new pockets of opportunity. As it ponders where to place the 10,000 new stores it plans to open in the next five years, Starbucks's community store successes suggest that it can both do good *and* do well by serving underserved communities. Says the manager of the new community store in the Bedford–Stuyvesant area of Brooklyn, NY, "There's a bigger purpose here than just coffee."[12]

---

they attempt to create new ones. Furthermore, people seek information when making important purchases and often do not rely on single sources. Even minor purchases that may be affected by advertising messages lead to repeat purchases only if the product delivers the promised customer value. Finally, the high failure rate of new products shows that companies are not able to control demand.

On a deeper level, our wants and values are influenced not only by marketers but also by family, peer groups, religion, cultural background, and education. If Americans are highly materialistic, these values arose out of basic socialization processes that go much deeper than business and marketing could produce alone. Consumption patterns and attitudes are also subject to larger forces, such as the economy.

These days consumers are also more supportive of environmental and social sustainability efforts by companies. As a result, instead of encouraging today's more sensible and conscientious consumers to overspend or spend wastefully, many marketers are working to help them find greater value with less. For example, Patagonia's "conscious consumption" campaigns actually urge its customers to buy less, telling them, "Don't buy what you don't need." and "Think twice before you buy anything." ● Similarly, for several years REI has closed its stores on Black Friday while its #OptOutside campaign urges customers to enjoy the outdoors instead of shopping. And L.L.Bean's "When" campaign encourages customers to buy and hang onto products that last rather than always buying new ones. It asks, "When did disposable become our default?" The answer: "At L.L.Bean, it never did. When you buy something from us, we want you to like it for a long time #llasting."[13]

● **Materialism: Some marketers are urging "conscious consumption." REI closes its stores on Black Friday and encourages customers to #OptOutside.**

Alex Milan Tracy/Sipa USA/NEWscom

Too Few Social Goods

Business has been accused of overselling private goods at the expense of public goods. As private goods increase, they require more public services that are usually not forthcoming. For example, private automobile ownership (private good) requires highways, traffic control, parking spaces, and police services (public goods). The overselling of private goods results in social costs. For cars, some of the social costs include traffic congestion, gasoline shortages, and air pollution. For example, American commuters lose, on average, 97 hours a year in traffic jams, costing the United States more than $87 billion a year—$1,348 per commuter. American commuters waste 3.1 billion gallons of fuel in traffic per year (enough to fill the New Orleans Superdome more than four times).[14]

A way must be found to restore a balance between private and public goods. One option is to make producers bear the full social costs of their operations. For example, the government is requiring automobile manufacturers to build cars with more efficient engines and better pollution-control systems. Automakers will then raise their prices to cover the extra costs. If buyers find the price of some car models too high, these models will disappear. Demand will then move to those producers that can support the sum of the private and social costs.

A second option is to make consumers pay the social costs. For example, many cities around the world are now levying congestion tolls and other charges in an effort to reduce traffic congestion. New York City recently implemented "Central Business District tolling," by which it charges motorists extra to enter Manhattan's busiest areas. Beyond reducing traffic and congestion, the toll is expected to raise more than $1 billion a year for improving the city's decrepit public transit systems.[15]

Cultural Pollution

Critics charge the marketing system with creating *cultural pollution*. They feel our senses are being constantly assaulted by marketing and advertising. Commercials interrupt serious programs; pages of ads obscure magazines; billboards mar beautiful scenery; spam fills our email inboxes; display and banner ads intrude on our online and mobile screens. What's more, the critics claim, these interruptions continually pollute people's minds with messages of materialism, sex, power, or status. Some critics call for sweeping changes.

Marketers answer the charges of commercial noise with these arguments: First, they hope that their ads primarily reach the target audience. But because of mass-communication channels, some ads are bound to reach people who have no interest in the product and are therefore bored or annoyed. People who buy magazines they like or who opt in to email, social media, or mobile marketing programs rarely complain about the ads because they involve products and services of interest.

Second, because of ads, many television, online, and social media sites are free to users. Ads also help keep down the costs of magazines and newspapers. Many people think viewing ads is a small price to pay for these benefits. In addition, consumers find many television commercials entertaining and seek them out; for example, ad viewership during the Super Bowl usually equals or exceeds game viewership. Finally, today's consumers have alternatives. For example, they can zip or zap TV commercials on recorded programs or avoid them altogether on many paid cable, satellite, and online streaming channels. Thus, to hold consumer attention, advertisers are making their ads more entertaining and informative.

Marketing's Impact on Other Businesses

Critics also charge that a company's marketing practices can harm other companies and reduce competition. They identify three problems: acquisitions of competitors, marketing practices that create barriers to entry, and unfair competitive marketing practices.

Critics claim that firms are harmed and competition is reduced when companies expand by acquiring competitors rather than by developing their own new products. The large number of acquisitions and the rapid pace of industry consolidation over the past several decades have caused concern that vigorous young competitors will be absorbed, thereby reducing competition. In virtually every major industry—store and online retailing, entertainment, financial services, utilities, transportation, automobiles, telecommunications, health care—the number of major competitors is shrinking.

Acquisition is a complex subject. In some cases, acquisitions can be good for society. The acquiring company may gain economies of scale that lead to lower costs and lower prices. In addition, a well-managed company may take over a poorly managed company and improve its efficiency. An industry that was not very competitive might become more competitive after the acquisition. But acquisitions can also be harmful and therefore are closely regulated by the government.

Critics have also charged that marketing practices bar new companies from entering an industry. Large marketing companies can use patents and heavy promotion spending or tie up suppliers or dealers to keep out or drive out competitors. Those concerned with antitrust regulation recognize that some barriers are the natural result of the economic advantages of doing business on a large scale. Existing and new laws can challenge other

● **Competitive marketing practices:** The European Commission recently fined Google heavily for illegally using its search dominance to manipulate the results of its Google Shopping search comparison services to favor its own shopping services at the expense of rivals.

Alexandros Michailidis/Shutterstock

barriers. For example, some critics have proposed a progressive tax on advertising spending to reduce the role of selling costs as a major barrier to entry.

Finally, some firms have, in fact, used unfair competitive marketing practices with the intention of hurting or destroying other firms. They may set their prices below costs, threaten to cut off business with suppliers, discourage the buying of a competitor's products, or use their size and market dominance to unfairly damage rivals. Although various laws work to prevent such predatory competition, it is often difficult to prove that the intent or action was really predatory. It's often difficult to differentiate predatory practices from effective competitive strategy and tactics.

In recent years, search giant Google has been accused of using predatory practices at the expense of smaller competitors. ● For example, the European Commission found Google of guilty of using its search dominance to manipulate the results of its Google Shopping search comparison services to favor its own shopping services at the expense of rivals. The commission fined Google $2.7 billion for the violations. "Google has come up with many innovative products and services that have made a difference to our lives. That's a good thing," said the EU's competition commissioner. "But Google's strategy for its comparison shopping service wasn't just about attracting customers by making its product better than those of its rivals. Instead, Google abused its market dominance as a search engine by promoting its own comparison shopping service in its search results and demoting those of competitors. ...That's illegal under EU antitrust rules." Google has appealed the decision, contending that its web-search and mobile operations constitute fair and effective competition that serves the best interests of consumers.[16]

> **Author Comment** | Sustainable marketing isn't something that only businesses and governments do. Through consumerism and environmentalism, consumers themselves can play an important role.

Consumer Actions to Promote Sustainable Marketing

OBJECTIVE 20-3 Define *consumerism* and *environmentalism* and explain how they affect marketing strategies.

Sustainable marketing calls for more responsible actions by both businesses and consumers. Because some people view businesses as the cause of many economic and social ills, grassroots movements have arisen from time to time to keep businesses in line. Two major movements have been *consumerism* and *environmentalism*.

Consumerism

Consumerism
An organized movement of citizens and government agencies designed to improve the rights and power of buyers in relation to sellers.

Consumerism is an organized movement of citizens and government agencies to improve the rights and power of buyers in relation to sellers. Traditional *sellers' rights* include the following:

- The right to introduce any product in any size and style, provided it is not hazardous to personal health or safety, or, if it is, to include proper warnings and controls
- The right to charge any price for the product, provided no discrimination exists among similar kinds of buyers
- The right to spend any amount to promote the product, provided it is not defined as unfair competition
- The right to use any product message, provided it is not misleading or dishonest in content or execution
- The right to use buying incentive programs, provided they are not unfair or misleading

Traditional *buyers' rights* include the following:

- The right not to buy a product that is offered for sale

Environmentalism

An organized movement of concerned citizens, businesses, and government agencies designed to protect and improve people's current and future living environment.

- The right to expect the product to be safe
- The right to expect the product to perform as claimed

In comparing these rights, many believe that the balance of power lies on the seller's side. True, the buyer can refuse to buy. But critics feel that the buyer has too little information, education, and protection to make wise decisions when facing sophisticated sellers. Consumer advocates call for the following additional consumer rights:

- The right to be well informed about important aspects of the product
- The right to be protected against questionable products and marketing practices
- The right to influence products and marketing practices in ways that will improve "quality of life"
- The right to consume now in a way that will preserve the world for future generations of consumers

Each proposed right has led to more specific proposals by consumerists and consumer protection actions by the government. ● The right to be informed includes the right to know the true interest on a loan (truth in lending), the true cost per unit of a brand (unit pricing), the ingredients in a product (ingredient labeling), the nutritional value of foods (nutritional labeling), product freshness (open dating), and the true benefits of a product (truth in advertising).

Proposals related to consumer protection include strengthening consumer rights in cases of business fraud and financial protection, requiring greater product safety, ensuring information privacy, and giving more power to government agencies. Proposals relating to quality of life include controlling the ingredients that go into certain products and packaging and reducing the level of advertising "noise." Proposals for preserving the world for future consumption include promoting the use of sustainable ingredients, recycling and reducing solid wastes, and managing energy consumption.

Sustainable marketing applies not only to businesses and governments but also to consumers. Consumers have not only the right but also the responsibility to protect themselves instead of leaving this function to the government or someone else. Consumers who believe they got a bad deal have several remedies available, including contacting the company; making their case through the media or social media; contacting federal, state, or local agencies; and going to small-claims courts. Consumers should also make good consumption choices, rewarding companies that act responsibly while punishing those that don't. Ultimately, the move from irresponsible consumption to sustainable consumption is in the hands of consumers.

Environmentalism

Whereas consumerists consider whether the marketing system is efficiently serving consumer wants, environmentalists are concerned with marketing's effects on the environment and the environmental costs of serving consumer needs and wants. **Environmentalism** is an organized movement of concerned citizens, businesses, and government agencies designed to protect and improve people's current and future living environment.

Environmentalists are not against marketing and consumption; they simply want people and organizations to operate with more care for the environment. They call for doing away with what sustainability advocate and former Unilever CEO Paul Polman calls "mindless consumption." According to Polman, "The road to well-being doesn't go via reduced consumption. It has to be done via more responsible consumption."[17] The marketing system's goal, environmentalists assert, should not be to maximize consumption, consumer choice, or consumer satisfaction but rather to maximize life quality. Life quality means not only the quantity and quality of consumer goods and services but also the quality of the environment, now and for future generations.

Environmentalism is concerned with humanity's damage to the ecosystem caused by global warming, resource depletion, toxic and solid wastes, the availability of fresh water, and other problems. Other issues include the loss of recreational areas and the increase in health problems caused by polluted air and water and chemically treated food.

Over the past several decades, such concerns have resulted in federal and state laws and regulations governing industrial commercial practices affecting the environment.

●FIGURE 20.2
Environmental Sustainability
and Sustainable Value

Source: Based on Stuart L. Hart,
"Sustainable Value," www.stuartlhart.
com/sustainablevalue.html, October
2016.

	Today: **Greening**	**Tomorrow:** **Beyond Greening**
Internal	**Pollution prevention** Eliminating or reducing waste before it is created	**New clean technology** Developing new sets of environmental skills and capabilities
External	**Product stewardship** Minimizing environmental impact throughout the entire product life cycle	**Sustainability vision** Developing a strategy framework for creating sustainable value

This framework addresses more than just natural environmental challenges. It also points to opportunities for creating sustainable value for markets and the firm through environmentally sustainable strategies and practices.

Some companies have strongly resented and resisted such environmental regulations, claiming that they are too costly and have made their industries less competitive. These companies responded to consumer environmental concerns by doing only what was required to avert new regulations or keep environmentalists quiet.

In recent years, however, most companies have accepted responsibility for doing no harm to the environment. They have shifted from protest to prevention and from regulation to responsibility. More and more companies are now adopting policies of environmental sustainability. Simply put, **environmental sustainability** is about generating profits while helping to save the planet. Today's enlightened companies are taking action not because someone is forcing them to or to reap short-run profits but because it's the right thing to do—because it's for their customers' well-being, the company's well-being, and the planet's environmental future.

●**Figure 20.2** shows a grid that companies can use to gauge their progress toward environmental sustainability. It includes both internal and external *greening* activities that will pay off for the firm and environment in the short run and *beyond greening* activities that will pay off in the longer term.

At the most basic level, a company can practice *pollution prevention*. This involves more than pollution control—cleaning up waste after it has been created. Pollution prevention means eliminating or minimizing waste *before* it is created. Companies emphasizing prevention have responded with internal green marketing programs—designing and developing ecologically safer products, recyclable and biodegradable packaging, better pollution controls, and more energy-efficient operations.

Environmental sustainability

A management approach that involves developing strategies that both sustain the environment and produce profits for the company.

●For example, in creating new products, athletic shoe and apparel maker adidas considers their environmental impact before ever producing them. This results in low-waste footwear and apparel, such as Duramo shoes, which yield both performance and sustainability benefits. With their simplified design—the upper is made of only four pieces—the lightweight shoes give athletes a more natural run while at the same time cutting down on materials, waste, and energy use in production. On a broader scale, adidas has developed a restricted substances list for product design and manufacturing: no PVCs, no materials from endangered or threatened species, and fewer materials from non-sustainable sources. And it recently introduced its Parley lines of shoes and apparel, created with yarn made in collaboration with Parley for the Oceans from recycled plastic waste intercepted from the world's beaches and coastal communities before it reaches the ocean. adidas has also set ambitious internal goals for reducing greenhouse emissions and energy, water, and paper consumption in its operations.[18]

●Environmental sustainability: adidas sets ambitious goals for
sustainable products and operations. Its Parley shoes and apparel
are created with yarn made from recycled plastic waste intercepted
from the world's beaches and coastal communities before it reaches
the ocean.

adidas

At the next level, companies can practice *product stewardship*—minimizing not only pollution from production and product design but also all environmental impacts throughout the full product life cycle while at the same time reducing costs. Many companies have adopted *design for environment (DFE)* and *cradle-to-cradle* practices. This involves thinking ahead to design products that are easier to recover, reuse, recycle, or safely return to nature after usage, thus becoming part of the ecological cycle. DFE and cradle-to-cradle practices not only help to sustain the environment, but they can also be highly profitable for the company.

For example, IBM started a business—IBM Global Asset Recovery Services—designed to reuse and recycle parts from returned mainframe computers and other equipment. Last year, IBM processed more than 58.5 million pounds of end-of-life products and product waste worldwide, stripping down old equipment to recover chips and valuable metals. Since 1995 it has processed more than 2.3 billion tons. IBM Global Asset Recovery Services finds uses for more than 99 percent of what it takes in, sending less than 1 percent to landfills and incineration facilities. What started out as an environmental effort has now grown into a multibillion-dollar IBM business that profitably recycles electronic equipment at 22 sites worldwide.[19]

Today's *greening* activities focus on improving what companies already do to protect the environment. The *beyond greening* activities identified in Figure 20.2 look to the future. First, internally, companies can plan for *new clean technology*. Many organizations that have made good sustainability headway are still limited by existing technologies. To create fully sustainable strategies, they will need to develop and employ innovative new technologies. For example, energy technology giant Siemens has committed to becoming fully carbon neutral by 2030. Making that happen requires lots of innovation:[20]

> With more than 379,000 employees in 200 countries, 150-year-old Siemens is reducing its carbon footprint by transferring from "combustification" to "electrification." As just one example, it's 50-year-old production facility in Kalawa, India, now uses 6,000 solar panels to supply 25 percent of its electricity use—the equivalent of 62,000 newly planted trees. To cut employee bottled water consumption, the plant installed a high-tech water-treatment facility that further cleans city water to make it drinkable and dispenses it to employees at 50 locations around the plant, saving more than 2 million single-use plastic water bottles per year. The water facility also treats all industrial water used at the plant and recycles it for everything from cleaning streets and flushing toilets to watering green areas. Finally, the plant's state-of-the-art waste segregation depot separates waste into 45 categories and readies it to be processed by recyclers. Siemens's carbon neutrality innovations will not only help save the environment, they will also save the company money. The technology project will pay for itself in just five years and will generate $20 million in annual savings thereafter.

Finally, companies can develop a *sustainability vision*, which serves as a guide to the future. It shows how the company's products and services, processes, and policies must evolve and what new technologies must be developed to get there. This vision of sustainability provides a framework for pollution control, product stewardship, and new environmental technology for the company and others to follow. It addresses not just challenges in the natural environment but also strategic opportunities for using environmental strategies to create sustainable value for the firm and its markets.

Most companies today focus on the upper-left quadrant of the grid in Figure 20.2, investing most heavily in pollution prevention. Some forward-looking companies practice product stewardship and are developing new environmental technologies. However, emphasizing only one or two quadrants in the environmental sustainability grid can be shortsighted. Investing only in the left half of the grid puts a company in a good position today but leaves it vulnerable in the future. In contrast, a heavy emphasis on the right half suggests that a company has good environmental vision but lacks the skills needed to implement it. Thus, companies should work at developing all four dimensions of environmental sustainability.

The North Face, for example, is doing just that through its own environmental sustainability actions and its impact on the actions of suppliers and consumers:[21]

> The North Face's headquarters building in Alameda, California, comes complete with solar panels and wind turbines that generate more electricity than the building uses. The building employs an evaporating cooling system that eliminates the need for emissions-heavy coolants. The company's other regional headquarters and distribution centers also incorporate solar or water-saving features. In manufacturing, The North Face works closely with

PROTECT OUR — PLAYGROUND

CLOTHES THE LOOP

THE NORTH FACE

RECYCLE RENEW REWARD

Recycle your used apparel and footwear at any The North Face retail store or outlet. Receive a reward for your efforts and help preserve our outdoor playground.

● **Sustainability vision: At The North Face, sustainability is about more than just doing the right thing—it also makes good business sense. Sustainability efforts such as its "Clothes the Loop" program are good for the company, its customers, *and* the planet.**

VF Corporation

suppliers to achieve its goal to use polyester—which makes up 80 percent of its clothing lines—from 100 percent recycled content. The North Face also partners with suppliers to reduce waste and chemical, water, and energy usage in their mills. Since 2010, The North Face's suppliers have removed more than 212 tanker trucks of chemicals and more than 470 Olympic swimming pools of water from their manufacturing processes.

In addition, The North Face has dedicated itself to inspiring customers to reduce the waste generated by today's fast-fashion era. The company's lifetime apparel and gear warranty results in the return and repair of more than 90,000 products annually. ● The North Face also runs a program called "Clothes the Loop," by which it collects worn-out or unwanted used clothing of any brand from customers for recycling or renewal. Items dropped in its collection bins are sent to a recycling center where they are carefully sorted, then repurposed for reuse to extend their life or recycled into raw materials for use in making other products. Proceeds from the program benefit the Conservation Alliance, which funds community-based campaigns to protect shared wilderness and recreation areas.

For The North Face, being environmentally sustainable is about more than just doing the right thing. It also makes good business sense. More efficient operations and less wasteful products not only are good for the environment but also save The North Face money, helping it to deliver more value to customers. It's a winning combination. "At the heart of The North Face is a mission to inspire a global movement of outdoor exploration and conservation," says the brand. "We believe the success of our business is fundamentally linked to having a healthy planet."[22]

Public Actions to Regulate Marketing

Citizen concerns about marketing practices will usually lead to public attention and legislative proposals. Legislation affecting business around the world has increased steadily over the years. The United States and many other countries have many laws covering issues such as competition, fair-trade practices, environmental protection, product safety, truth in advertising, consumer privacy, packaging and labeling, pricing, selling, and other important areas.

Understanding the public policy implications of various marketing activities is no easy matter. In the United States, there are many complex laws created at the national, state, and local levels, and these regulations often overlap. Many of the laws that affect marketing were identified in Chapter 3. The task is to translate these laws into a language that marketing executives understand as they make decisions about marketing strategy, competitive relations, marketing research, products, price, promotion, and distribution channels.

Author Comment | In the end, marketers themselves must take responsibility for sustainable marketing. That means operating in a responsible and ethical way to bring both immediate and future value to customers.

Business Actions toward Sustainable Marketing

OBJECTIVE 20-4 Describe the principles of sustainable marketing.

At first, many companies opposed consumerism, environmentalism, and other elements of sustainable marketing. They thought the criticisms were either unfair or unimportant. But by now, most companies have grown to embrace sustainability principles as a way to create both immediate and future customer value and strengthen customer relationships.

Sustainable Marketing Principles

Under the sustainable marketing concept, a company's marketing should support the best long-run performance of the marketing system. It should be guided by five sustainable marketing principles: *consumer-oriented marketing, customer value marketing, innovative marketing, sense-of-mission marketing,* and *societal marketing.*

Consumer-Oriented Marketing

Consumer-oriented marketing Consumer-oriented marketing
A company should view and organize its marketing activities from the consumer's point of view.

Consumer-oriented marketing means that the company should view and organize its marketing activities from the consumer's point of view. It should work hard to sense, serve, and satisfy the needs of a defined group of customers—both now and in the future. The good marketing companies that we've discussed throughout this text have had this in common: an all-consuming passion for delivering superior value to carefully chosen customers. Only by seeing the world through its customers' eyes can the company build sustainable and profitable customer relationships.

Customer Value Marketing

Customer value marketing
A company should put most of its resources into customer value–building marketing investments.

According to the principle of **customer value marketing**, the company should put most of its resources into customer value-building marketing investments. Many things marketers do—one-shot sales promotions, cosmetic product changes, direct-response advertising—may raise sales in the short run but add less *value* than would actual improvements in the product's quality, features, or convenience. Enlightened marketing calls for building long-run consumer engagement, loyalty, and relationships by continually improving the value consumers receive from the firm's market offering. By creating value *for* consumers, the company can capture value *from* consumers in return.

Innovative Marketing

Innovative marketing
A company should seek real product and marketing improvements.

The principle of **innovative marketing** requires that the company continuously seek real product and marketing improvements. The company that overlooks new and better ways to do things will eventually lose customers to another company that has found a better way.

Innovative marketers never stop looking for new and better ways to create customer value. For example, fast and dependable delivery is highly important to online shoppers. So Amazon delighted customers by being the first to innovate with free shipping on orders over $50. But Amazon didn't stop there. It next introduced Amazon Prime, by which customers could receive their packages within only two days for no extra charge or in one day for a small additional fee. ● Still not satisfied, Amazon innovated with Amazon Prime Now, which offers superfast same-day delivery—or even one-hour delivery—on tens of thousands of items in major metropolitan areas. In its never-ending quest to shorten delivery times, Amazon has even invested heavily in research on drones, driverless vehicles, and robots. This and a seemingly endless list of other innovations over the years—from Recommendations for You, Customer Reviews, and 1-Click Ordering features to the Amazon Marketplace, Kindle e-readers, and Amazon Cloud services—have helped Amazon to enhance the shopping customer experience and dominate online retailing.

● Innovative marketing: Amazon never stops looking for new ways to create customer value, such as Amazon Prime Now, which gives same-day—or even one-hour—delivery of customer orders.
creativep/Alamy Stock Photo

Sense-of-Mission Marketing

Sense-of-mission marketing
A company should define its mission in broad social terms rather than narrow product terms.

Sense-of-mission marketing means that the company should define its mission in broad *social* terms rather than narrow *product* terms. When a company defines a social mission, employees feel better about their work and have a clearer sense of direction. Brands linked with broader missions can serve the best long-run interests of both the brand and consumers.

For example, Pedigree makes good dog food, but that's not what the brand is really all about. Instead, at its core, the brand is about loving and caring for dogs. Dogs bring out the good in people and have a profound impact on the world, Pedigree reasons. So the brand wants to feed dogs well and bring out the good in them. In line with this sweeping brand philosophy, beyond making nutritious dog food, Pedigree backs a substantial effort to support dogs in need. Through its "You buy. We give." program, for every customer purchase, the brand donates healthy meals to shelter dogs. And to further fulfill its brand promise, the company created the Pedigree Foundation, which declares, "We see a day when all dogs are safe, secure, cared for, fed well, and loved." The Pedigree Foundation has raised millions of dollars for helping "shelter dogs" find homes. Sense-of-mission marketing has made Pedigree the world's number-one dog food brand.[23]

Some companies define their overall corporate missions in broad societal terms. For example, under its buy-one-give-one model, shoemaker TOMS seeks both profits and to make the world a better place. Thus, at TOMS, "doing good" and "doing well" go hand in hand. To achieve its social-change mission, TOMS has to make money. At the same time, the brand's social mission gives customers a powerful reason to buy.

However, having a *double bottom line* of values and profits isn't easy. Over the years, brands such as Ben & Jerry's, Timberland, The Body Shop, and Burt's Bees—all known and respected for putting "principles before profits"—have at times struggled with less-than-stellar financial returns. In recent years, however, a new generation of social entrepreneurs has emerged, well-trained business managers who know that to *do good*, they must first *do well* in terms of profitable business operations.

Moreover, today, socially responsible business is no longer the sole province of small, socially conscious entrepreneurs. Many large, established companies and brands—from Walmart and Nike to Starbucks and Coca-Cola—have adopted substantial social and environmental responsibility missions. Rather than being at odds with revenues and profits, purpose-driven missions can drive them.

Societal Marketing

Following the principle of **societal marketing**, a company makes marketing decisions by considering consumers' wants, the company's requirements, consumers' long-run interests, and society's long-run interests. Companies should be aware that neglecting consumer and societal long-run interests is a disservice to consumers and society. Alert companies view societal problems as opportunities.

Sustainable marketing calls for products that are not only pleasing but also beneficial. The difference is shown in ● **Figure 20.3**. Products can be classified according to their degree of immediate consumer satisfaction and long-run consumer benefit.

Deficient products, such as bad-tasting and ineffective medicine, have neither immediate appeal nor long-run benefits. **Pleasing products** give high immediate satisfaction but may hurt consumers in the long run. Examples include cigarettes and junk food. **Salutary products** have low immediate appeal but may benefit consumers in the long run, for instance, bicycle helmets or some insurance products. **Desirable products** give both high immediate satisfaction and high long-run benefits, such as a tasty *and* nutritious fast-casual food.

Companies should try to turn all of their products into desirable products. The challenge posed by pleasing products is that they sell very well but may end up hurting the consumer. The product opportunity, therefore, is to add long-run benefits without reducing

Societal marketing
A company should make marketing decisions by considering consumers' wants, the company's requirements, consumers' long-run interests, and society's long-run interests.

Deficient products
Products that have neither immediate appeal nor long-run benefits.

Pleasing products
Products that give high immediate satisfaction but may hurt consumers in the long run.

Salutary products
Products that have low immediate appeal but may benefit consumers in the long run.

Desirable products
Products that give both high immediate satisfaction and high long-run benefits.

● **FIGURE 20.3**
Societal Classification of Products

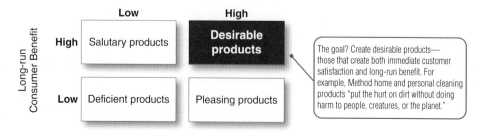

Immediate Satisfaction

The goal? Create desirable products—those that create both immediate customer satisfaction and long-run benefit. For example, Method home and personal cleaning products "put the hurt on dirt without doing harm to people, creatures, or the planet."

Real Marketing 20.2 | Waitrose: Bring Your Own Bag

At the World Economic Forum in Davos in January 2019, the supermarket giants Tesco and Carrefour announced a trial for an online shopping service based on refillable rather than recyclable containers. The trial was limited to items such as toiletries, ice cream, and breakfast cereals, but the British supermarket chain Waitrose went further. It soon announced a pilot for a service where customers who brought their own containers could buy and refill produce such as pasta, cereals, and rice, and the range was soon extended to include coffee and wine. Waitrose also offered "pick and mix" frozen fruit—a first, according to the company. Such initiatives not only position the company as sustainable, but potentially influence shopping behavior toward a more sustainable future.

The aim was to get shoppers to use less plastic packaging, and in some ways, this was a counterpart to Waitrose's own "Bag for Life" project, in which customers were encouraged to purchase a reusable woven shopping bag. To date, own-brand product packaging at Waitrose has included 18,400 tons of plastic, but 70 percent of this packaging is widely recyclable, and the company aims to increase this to 80 percent by 2020 and 100 percent by 2023. and the company has set a target for all own-brand packaging to be widely recycled, reusable, or home compostable by 2023. Meanwhile, products at Waitrose's unpacked refill stations are up to 15 percent cheaper, and consumers will be encouraged to use their own containers apart from for beer and wine or Ecover products made from plant-based and mineral ingredients.

Waitrose & Partners has more than three hundred shops across the United Kingdom, exports products to more than fifty countries, and has a royal warrant to supply groceries, wine, and spirits to Queen Elizabeth II and Prince Charles. In this market segment, customers tend to buy food at the most convenient location and at the lowest price possible as the products are the same at each store. Waitrose targets higher-income customers, so its market share cannot be enlarged significantly by catering to a broader demographic. Nevertheless, the company has enjoyed growth and ranks 8th in its market, with a share of 5.1 percent, as of May 2019. Waitrose's online store saw growth of over 10 percent during 2018, which significantly contributed to the company's revenue of €6.4 billion that year. Its grocery market share has been stable at just over 5 percent for a number of years now as compared to other market players, which include Sainsbury's, Tesco, and particularly Marks and Spencer, which also targets higher-income customers. Where most retail stores compete on pricing and try to gain a competitive edge through loyalty schemes, Waitrose instead focuses on increasing brand loyalty by offering differentiated, high-quality products.

Environmentalism is a clear and essential part of Waitrose's strategy, and the company positions itself as part of an organized movement of concerned citizens, businesses, and government agencies that work toward protecting and improving the environment. Consumers have become more conscious about their purchasing choices regarding the sustainability of products desired, and Waitrose's higher-income customers are very much concerned with environmentalism as well. Waitrose understands the importance of sustainable marketing for retaining existing customers and getting new ones, and its products reflect this. For example, a fish product will include labeling about the way the fish was caught so that consumers recognize that it has been done responsibly and in line with a responsible fishing policy.

Waitrose focuses on British-made products and supplies goods through joint ventures with local farms; this not only supports local business and locally grown products but also lowers the impact on the environment. The annual Waitrose Corporate Social Responsibility Report presents the company's sustainability efforts and achievements to the public in terms of supply chains, raw materials, farming, reuse policies, and carbon reduction. Waitrose has set a target for 100 percent of confectionery cocoa to be Fairtrade by the end of 2019; enrolled UK factories in Better Jobs Programs; and expanded the Waitrose & Partners Foundation to Senegal and Gambia. The company has Tier 1 status in the business benchmark on farm and animal welfare and increased third-party verified responsible fish sourcing to 91.2 percent. The company has made a new market-leading chicken welfare commitment as well as a pledge for cattle in its dairy farms to spend at least 100 days grazing in open pastures.

Waitrose also committed to better management of raw materials; for example, it has ensured that 100 percent of its palm oil comes from sustainable sources and is a signatory of the Better Cotton Initiative, which works toward more sustainable cotton farming. Waitrose aims for 100 percent of the timber and paper in its own-brand products to come from trusted sources by 2020–2021. Other initiatives include a supply chain mapping exercise on over 500 different timber sources, 38 percent of which are responsible and sustainable.

Sustainability is essential to Waitrose's marketing strategy, and the company positions itself as part of the larger movement working toward a better future.

Kumar Sriskandan/Alamy Stock Photo

According to the "Waitrose and Partners Food and Drink Report 2018/19," we live in a "vegan revolution," with 60 percent of vegans and 40 percent of vegetarians having adopted their lifestyles within the past five years. The company is responding to the rising demand for healthy and green products by offering sustainable, healthy, and environmentally friendly products, such as a wide assortment of vegan and vegetarian items for the convenience of those customers who follow this lifestyle.

Waitrose increased its procurement of renewable electricity in 2016 and became the first UK retailer to use "dedicated gas" trucks that run purely on biomethane. Transport contributes over 40 percent of Waitrose's operational carbon emissions, so it has plans to have a zero-carbon transport fleet by 2045, with an investment in biomethane trucks across the entire heavy vehicle fleet by 2028, bridging the transition to a fully electric one.

In terms of health and wellbeing, the company has achieved a 15 percent reduction in sugar content in 22 of its 27 own-brand cereals. It signed the "Time to Change" pledge as part of its commitment to supporting mental health, trained over 30 partners as dementia-friendly champions, ran awareness sessions for colleagues and local communities, and invested £11.5 million in community organizations. On the human rights side, the retailer has been reviewing its supply chain in compliance with the Modern Slavery Act 2015 in the United Kingdom, which requires supply chain transparency and a slavery and human trafficking statement from businesses.

Despite the challenges facing the retail sector as a whole, Waitrose has intensified company's efforts toward greater corporate responsibility. To realize its sustainability goals, the company must respond to environmental trends that span the globe, which require constant changes to the marketing strategy. To keep pace, the company regularly updates its Responsible Sourcing Code of Practice, which is aligned with revisions to the Ethical Trading Initiative Base Code. Waitrose's goal is not merely to meet standards but to be better positioned among its customers as a brand committed to a better world.[24]

---

the product's pleasing qualities. The challenge posed by salutary products is to add some pleasing qualities so that they will become more desirable in consumers' minds.

Consider Method, the "people against dirty" brand of household and personal cleaning products. Many effective household cleaning products contain chemicals or even toxic ingredients that can be harmful to people and the environment. But Method products are formulated with naturally derived, biodegradable, nontoxic ingredients. "We prefer ingredients that come from plants, not chemical plants," says the brand. Method also uses recycled and recyclable packaging, and it works with suppliers to reduce the carbon intensity of producing its products. Method uses renewable energy sources such as wind turbines and solar trees to help power its Chicago manufacturing facility. In all, "Method cleaners put the hurt on dirt without doing harm to people, creatures, or the planet," says the company. As Method's cofounder and "chief greenskeeper" puts it: "Beautiful design and environmental responsibility are equally important when creating a product and we shouldn't have to trade functionality for sustainability."[25]

Marketing Ethics and the Sustainable Company

OBJECTIVE 20-5 Explain the role of ethics in marketing.

Marketing Ethics

Good ethics are a cornerstone of sustainable marketing. In the long run, unethical marketing harms customers and society as a whole. Further, it eventually damages a company's reputation and effectiveness, jeopardizing its very survival. Thus, the sustainable marketing goals of long-term consumer and business welfare can be achieved only through ethical marketing conduct.

Conscientious marketers face many moral dilemmas. The best thing to do is often unclear. Because not all managers have fine moral sensitivity, companies need to develop *corporate marketing ethics policies*—broad guidelines that everyone in the organization must follow. These policies should cover distributor relations, advertising standards, customer service, pricing, product development, and general ethical standards.

The finest guidelines cannot resolve all the difficult ethical situations the marketer faces. ● **Table 20.1** lists some difficult ethical issues marketers could face during their careers. If marketers choose immediate-sales-producing actions in all of these cases, their marketing behavior might well be described as immoral or even amoral. If they refuse to

● Table 20.1 | **Some Morally Difficult Situations in Marketing**

1. Your R&D department has changed one of your company's products slightly. It is not really "new and improved," but you know that putting this statement on the package and in advertising will increase sales. What would you do?

2. You have been asked to add a stripped-down model to your line that could be advertised to pull customers into the store. The product won't be very good, but salespeople will be able to switch buyers who come into the store up to higher-priced units. You are asked to give the green light for the stripped-down version. What would you do?

3. You are thinking of hiring a product manager who has just left a competitor's company. She would be more than happy to tell you all the competitor's plans for the coming year. What would you do?

4. One of your top dealers in an important territory recently has had family troubles, and his sales have slipped. It looks like it will take him a while to straighten out his family problems. Meanwhile, you are losing many sales. Legally, on performance grounds, you can terminate the dealer's franchise and replace him. What would you do?

5. You have a chance to win a big account in another country that will mean a lot to you and your company. The purchasing agent hints that a "gift" would influence the decision. Such gifts are common in that country, and some of your competitors will probably make one. What would you do?

6. You have heard that a competitor has a new product feature that will make a big difference in sales. The competitor will demonstrate the feature in a private dealer meeting at the annual trade show. You can easily send a snooper to this meeting to learn about the new feature. What would you do?

7. You have to choose between three advertising and social media campaigns outlined by your agency. The first (a) is a soft-sell, honest, straight-information campaign. The second (b) uses emotion-loaded appeals that exaggerate the product's benefits. The third (c) involves a noisy, somewhat irritating commercial and pop-ups that are sure to gain audience attention. Pretests show that the campaigns are effective in the following order: c, b, and a. What would you do?

8. You are interviewing a capable female applicant for a job as salesperson. She is better qualified than the men who have been interviewed. Nevertheless, you know that in your industry some important customers prefer dealing with men and you will lose some sales if you hire her. What would you do?

go along with any of the actions, they might be ineffective as marketing managers and unhappy because of the constant moral tension. Managers need a set of principles that will help them figure out the moral importance of each situation and decide how far they can go in good conscience.

But *what* principle should guide companies and marketing managers on issues of ethics and social responsibility? One philosophy is that the free market and the legal system should decide such issues. Under this principle, companies and their managers are not responsible for making moral judgments. Companies can in good conscience do whatever the market and legal systems allow. However, history provides a long list of examples of company actions that were legal but highly irresponsible.

A second philosophy puts responsibility not on the system but in the hands of individual companies and managers. This more enlightened philosophy suggests that a company should have a social conscience. Companies and managers should apply high standards of ethics and morality when making corporate decisions, regardless of "what the system allows."

Each company and marketing manager must work out a philosophy of socially responsible and ethical behavior. Under the societal marketing concept, each manager must look beyond what is legal and allowed and develop standards based on personal integrity, corporate conscience, and long-run consumer welfare.

Dealing with issues of ethics and social responsibility in a proactive, open, and forthright way helps to build and maintain strong customer relationships based on integrity and trust. For example, consider CVS:[26]

● In 2014, CVS made the bold decision to stop selling cigarettes and other tobacco products. It was a risky decision. Stubbing out cigarettes resulted in the immediate loss of $2 billion in annual tobacco sales, and it risked driving a significant portion of CVS's smoking customers to competitors such as Walgreens, Walmart, or Kroger, all of which continued to

CVSquitsforgood

This is the right thing to do.

● Marketing ethics and social responsibility: CVS is on a mission of helping people on their path to better health. It succeeds by "delivering what's right for people every day in a way that creates economic value for the business."

CVS Caremark Corporation

sell cigarettes. But to CVS, dropping tobacco was pretty much a no-brainer. CVS is on an important mission of "helping people on their path to better health." Selling cigarettes *and* helping people on their path to better health? The two simply didn't jibe with one another. So CVS pulled tobacco products from its shelves. "CVS quits for good," the company announced. "This is the right thing to do." Stopping tobacco sales was a landmark moment for CVS. But it was only one step in a more sweeping purpose-driven transformation. At the same time that the company suspended tobacco sales, it changed its name to CVS Health. It now offers a full range of products and services that help people lead healthier lives.

So how is sense-of-mission marketing working for CVS Health? Although front-of-store sales dropped the year after it stopped selling tobacco products, overall CVS revenues increased by nearly 10 percent. And in the following year, revenues jumped another 10 percent. In turns out that the loss of tobacco revenues has been more than offset by revenues from new sources, including those resulting from the decision to quit selling cigarettes. New sales came both from new nonsmoking customers impressed by the decision and from smokers themselves. When CVS Health dropped cigarettes, it also launched a "Let's Quit Together" assistance program to help smokers kick the habit. By the end of the first year, CVS prescriptions for smoking cessation products grew by 63 percent.

In all, balancing purpose with profits has been good for both CVS's reputation and its bottom line. "I cannot think of another example in corporate America where a company sacrificed $2 billion of revenue for what they felt was the right thing to do," says CVS's chief marketer. "It's a stunning thing, [and] it proved out for us in [so may] ways." For CVS Health, he says, success means "delivering what's right for people every day in a way that creates economic value for the business."

As with environmentalism, the issue of ethics presents special challenges for international marketers. Business standards and practices vary a great deal from one country to the next. For example, bribes and kickbacks are illegal for U.S. firms, and various treaties against bribery and corruption have been signed and ratified by more than 60 countries. Yet these are still standard business practices in many countries. The International Monetary Fund estimates that bribes totaling more than $2 trillion per year are paid out worldwide.[27] The question arises as to whether a company must lower its ethical standards to compete effectively in countries with lower standards. The answer is no. Companies should make a commitment to a common set of shared standards worldwide.

Many industrial and professional associations have suggested codes of ethics, and many companies are now adopting their own codes. For example, the American Marketing Association, an international association of marketing managers and scholars, developed a code of ethics that calls on marketers to adopt the following ethical norms:[28]

- *Do no harm.* This means consciously avoiding harmful actions or omissions by embodying high ethical standards and adhering to all applicable laws and regulations in the choices we make.
- *Foster trust in the marketing system.* This means striving for good faith and fair dealing so as to contribute toward the efficacy of the exchange process as well as avoiding deception in product design, pricing, communication, and delivery or distribution.
- *Embrace ethical values.* This means building relationships and enhancing consumer confidence in the integrity of marketing by affirming these core values: honesty, responsibility, fairness, respect, transparency, and citizenship.

Companies are also developing programs to teach managers about important ethical issues and help them find the proper responses. They hold ethics workshops and seminars and create ethics committees. Furthermore, most major U.S. companies have appointed

● Marketing ethics: Under Armour's Code of Conduct urges all employees to "Protect this house—Make the right call." regarding issues of ethics and social responsibility. "It's as simple as it sounds."

IgorGolovniov/Shutterstock

high-level ethics officers to champion ethical issues and help resolve ethics problems and concerns facing employees. And most companies have established their own codes of ethical conduct.

● For example, Under Armour's Code of Conduct urges all employees ("teammates") to "Protect this house—Make the right call." regarding issues of ethics and social responsibility. All Under Armour teammates make decisions daily that can affect the brand's well-being. The detailed code's core message: "It's as simple as it sounds," states the code. "Whenever you're faced with a decision—big or small—always do what you know is ethically right, and, of course, always follow the law."

The Under Armour Code of Conduct covers in detail a wide range of topics, from gifts and bribery to honest and fair dealing. But it stresses that it can't cover *every* issue, so teammates "should be sensitive to situations and activities and know that if something looks wrong and feels wrong, it's probably wrong." If employees see or hear about any situation that might violate the ethics code, they are urged to report it to their management, to senior leaders in the human resources organization, or directly to anyone on Under Armour's Global Ethics & Compliance team. Or they can report issues on Under Armour's phone hotline or hotline website, both monitored 24 hours a day, seven days a week, with an option to report anonymously. "We're an aggressive brand, and we're going to stay that way," concludes Under Armour CEO and founder Kevin Plank in the code's introduction. "We all want to win—it's why we're here. [But] we're committed to winning the right way. Period."[29]

Still, written codes and ethics programs do not ensure ethical behavior. Ethics and social responsibility require a total corporate commitment. They must be a component of the overall corporate culture.

The Sustainable Company

At the foundation of marketing is the belief that companies that fulfill the needs and wants of customers will thrive. Companies that fail to meet customer needs or that intentionally or unintentionally harm customers, others in society, or future generations will decline.

Says one observer, "Sustainability is an emerging business megatrend, like electrification and mass production, that will profoundly affect companies' competitiveness and even their survival." Says another, "increasingly, companies and leaders will be assessed not only on immediate results but also on ... the ultimate effects their actions have on societal well-being. This trend has been coming in small ways for years but now is surging. So pick up your recycled cup of fair-trade coffee, and get ready."[30]

Sustainable companies are those that create value for customers through socially, environmentally, and ethically responsible actions. Sustainable marketing goes beyond caring for the needs and wants of today's customers. It means having concern for tomorrow's customers in ensuring the survival and success of the business, shareholders, employees, and the broader world in which they all live. It means pursuing the mission of shared value and a triple bottom line: people, planet, profits. Sustainable marketing provides the context in which companies can engage customers and build profitable relationships with them by creating value *for* customers in order to capture value *from* customers in return—now and in the future.

Reviewing and Extending the Concepts

Chapter Review and Critical Thinking

Objectives Review

In this chapter, we addressed many of the important *sustainable marketing* concepts related to marketing's sweeping impact on individual consumers, other businesses, and society as a whole. Sustainable marketing requires socially, environmentally, and ethically responsible actions that bring value to not only present-day consumers and businesses but also future generations and society as a whole. Sustainable companies are those that act responsibly to create value for customers in order to capture value from customers in return—now and in the future.

OBJECTIVE 20-1 Define *sustainable marketing* and discuss its importance. *(pp 582–584)*

Sustainable marketing calls for meeting the present needs of consumers and businesses while preserving or enhancing the ability of future generations to meet their needs. Whereas the marketing concept recognizes that companies thrive by fulfilling the day-to-day needs of customers, sustainable marketing calls for socially and environmentally responsible actions that meet both the immediate and future needs of customers and the company. Truly sustainable marketing requires a smooth-functioning marketing system in which consumers, companies, public policy makers, and others work together to ensure responsible marketing actions.

OBJECTIVE 20-2 Identify the major social criticisms of marketing. *(pp 584–592)*

Marketing's *impact on individual consumer welfare* has been criticized for its high prices, deceptive practices, high-pressure selling, shoddy or unsafe products, planned obsolescence, and poor service to disadvantaged consumers. Marketing's *impact on society* has been criticized for creating false wants and too much materialism, too few social goods, and cultural pollution. Critics have also denounced marketing's *impact on other businesses* for harming competitors and reducing competition through acquisitions, practices that create barriers to entry, and unfair competitive marketing practices. Some of these concerns are justified; some are not.

OBJECTIVE 20-3 Define *consumerism* and *environmentalism* and explain how they affect marketing strategies. *(pp 592–596)*

Concerns about the marketing system have led to citizen action movements. *Consumerism* is an organized social movement intended to strengthen the rights and power of consumers relative to sellers. Alert marketers view it as an opportunity to serve consumers better by providing more consumer information, education, and protection. *Environmentalism* is an organized social movement seeking to minimize the harm done to the environment and quality of life by marketing practices. Most companies are now accepting responsibility for doing no environmental harm. They are adopting policies of *environmental sustainability*—developing strategies that both sustain the environment and produce profits for the company. Both consumerism and environmentalism are important components of sustainable marketing.

OBJECTIVE 20-4 Describe the principles of sustainable marketing. *(pp 596–600)*

Many companies originally resisted these social movements and laws, but most now recognize a need for positive consumer information, education, and protection. Under the sustainable marketing concept, a company's marketing should support the best long-run performance of the marketing system. It should be guided by five sustainable marketing principles: *consumer-oriented marketing, customer value marketing, innovative marketing, sense-of-mission marketing*, and *societal marketing*.

OBJECTIVE 20-5 Explain the role of ethics in marketing. *(pp 600–603)*

Increasingly, companies are responding to the need to provide company policies and guidelines to help their managers deal with questions of *marketing ethics*. Of course, even the best guidelines cannot resolve all the difficult ethical decisions that individuals and firms must make. But there are some principles from which marketers can choose. One principle states that the free market and the legal system should decide such issues. A second and more enlightened principle puts responsibility not on the system but in the hands of individual companies and managers. Each firm and marketing manager must work out a philosophy of socially responsible and ethical behavior. Under the sustainable marketing concept, managers must look beyond what is legal and allowable and develop standards based on personal integrity, corporate conscience, and long-term consumer welfare.

Key Terms

OBJECTIVE 20-1

Sustainable marketing (p 582)

OBJECTIVE 20-3

Consumerism (p 592)
Environmentalism (p 593)
Environmental sustainability (p 594)

OBJECTIVE 20-4

Consumer-oriented marketing (p 597)
Customer value marketing (p 597)
Innovative marketing (p 597)
Sense-of-mission marketing (p 597)
Societal marketing (p 598)

Deficient products (p 598)
Pleasing products (p 598)
Salutary products (p 598)
Desirable products (p 598)

Discussion Questions

20-1 What is sustainable marketing, and why is it important? (AACSB: Written and Oral Communication)

20-2 Explain how marketing can be perceived as having a negative impact on the consumer. (AACSB: Communication)

20-3 How would you distinguish between consumerism and environmentalism in terms of scope and influence? (AACSB: Communication)

20-4 Identify a company that is engaged in product stewardship and explain how its practices differentiate it from companies that merely practice pollution prevention. (AACSB: Written and Oral Communication)

20-5 What is sense-of-mission marketing, and how does it impact on a business? (AACSB: Communication)

20-6 What guidelines should firms follow when developing corporate marketing ethics policies? (AACSB: Written and Oral Communication)

Critical Thinking Exercises

20-7 Assume that you are the marketing director of a new retail chain. From the outset, you want to be environmentally sustainable. Research how other retailers achieve this, and create a checklist. (AACSB: Communication; Use of IT; Reflective Thinking)

20-8 Suppose that you are leading PepsiCo's environmental sustainability efforts. How would you gauge the effectiveness of these programs? How would you communicate your efforts to loyal consumers of your brand? (AACSB: Written and Oral Communication; Information Technology; Reflective Thinking)

20-9 "Greenwashing" is the practice of promoting a product by misleading consumers about its environmentally beneficial aspects. Products might be labeled as "natural," "green," "environmentally friendly," or biodegradable" but have little or no environmental benefits. Go to www.truthinadvertising.org/six-companies-accused-greenwashing/ and choose one of the 10 examples of companies that are not as environmentally friendly as they would like to appear. In your opinion, is the company's product or business practice sustainable, or is the company engaging in greenwashing? Explain your answer. (AACSB: Written and Oral Communication; Information Technology; Ethical Reasoning)

APPLICATIONS AND CASES

Online, Mobile, and Social Media Marketing Politically Neutral Social Media

During a time when Starbucks was vowing to hire 10,000 refugees and Burger King UK social media posts seemed to encourage leftist activists who were throwing milkshakes at political opponents, Dunkin' Brands took a stand against politicizing its businesses, including Dunkin' and Baskin Robbins. A Dunkin' spokesperson noted that its stores aim for efficient customer service—getting satisfied customers in and out of its stores quickly—rather than trying to engage customers in political conversations. He also noted pointedly that the Dunkin' brand was not political like Starbucks. Conservative social media followers reacted favorably to Dunkin's choice to remain politically neutral.

20-10 Analyze recent Twitter posts from Starbucks and Dunkin'. Based on posts that are not related to the products—and customer responses to those posts—do you agree or disagree with Dunkin's decision to remain politically neutral? Explain. (AACSB: Written and Oral Communication; Ethical Reasoning)

20-11 How do Starbucks's decision to get political and Dunkin's decision to remain politically neutral relate to the five sustainable marketing principles? (AACSB: Written and Oral Communication; Reflective Thinking)

Marketing Ethics Patagonia Rethinks Fleeces for Banker Bros

Fleece vests from Patagonia, the outdoor clothing and gear company, have been popular among venture capitalists. They may be perceived as a visual statement that the wearer has elite status and can get things done. However, Patagonia recently announced that it would no longer do co-branded fleece vests for new financial services businesses. Instead, it would only do co-branded vests for B corporations (companies certified for meeting certain environmental and social standards), companies that are members of One Percent for the Planet, and existing B-to-B companies and nonprofits who were short- or long-term loyal customers. The idea is that Patagonia will do more to support companies that share the brand's value system and avoid pairing its brand name with brand names from companies with different philosophical approaches.

20-12 In a small group, research how Patagonia's previous societally oriented marketing decisions impacted its sales and profits. Then discuss how Patagonia's decision about who to target for co-branded merchandise could affect its profitability. Present your conclusions. (AACSB: Written and Oral Communication; Use of IT; Ethical Reasoning)

20-13 Is it wrong for Patagonia to exclude customers from firms that have different philosophies? Support your answer. (AACSB: Written and Oral Communication; Ethical Reasoning)

Marketing by the Numbers Gouging Their Eyes Out

MyEye 2.0 is a thumb drive–sized device that weighs less than an ounce and attaches magnetically to the stem of almost any pair of glasses. It helps people with impaired vision to "see." It recognizes paper money dominations, faces based on stored images, surroundings, and almost anything else to which the user points a finger. MyEye 2.0 can read a menu or package label and softly tell the wearer what's for dinner via a small speaker near the user's ear. To almost 8 million visually impaired Americans and 253 million visually impaired people worldwide, this could be a game-changer. However, for many, the $4,500 price tag is a game-stopper. Many smartphones equipped with AI technology have apps that can do many of the same things as MyEye 2.0, although they are not wearable. Some analysts believe this wearability does not add enough value to justify MyEye 2.0's outrageous price, especially considering that some 58 percent of U.S. adults with significant vision impairment are unemployed

and that percentage is likely higher worldwide. Apple's iPhone X series—with Face ID, Siri, and its other AI sensors, camera, speaker, and app capabilities—can do many of the things the MyEye 2.0 can do. It carries a price tag of $999 with the estimated cost of goods sold (COGS) of $360. In contrast, MyEye 2.0's COGS is estimated at $200 per device.

20-14 Calculate the gross margin dollars and percentage for the MyEye 2.0 and the iPhone X. Refer to The Profit-and-Loss Statement and Marketing Budget in Appendix 2: Marketing by the Numbers to learn how to calculate gross margins. (AACSB: Analytic Reasoning)

20-15 Discuss the pros and cons of the company's decision to price the MyEye 2.0 so high. Is the company following the principle of societal marketing? Should it? (AACSB: Communication; Reflective Thinking)

Company Case H&M: Offering Sustainable Fashion and Quality at the Best Price

Swedish retailer H&M is one of the world's most recognizable fast-fashion brands. Headquartered in Stockholm, the company is the second-largest retailer in the world, just trailing behind Inditex, the owner of Zara. Founded in 1947, the H&M group now has more than 4,700 stores in 69 markets and a strong digital presence.

H&M has accelerated the fast-fashion cycle to its current frenetic pace, driven by lower prices and increasing pressure within the clothing industry to produce more and quicker. In order to meet ever more sophisticated customer expectations, H&M launches a new collection every two weeks. The concept of fast-fashion serves consumerism very well; customers can always find something they have not purchased yet at H&M. However, this causes incredible amounts of waste. The fast-fashion industry has a particularly large impact on the environment due to overconsumption; according to waste statistics in 2018, textile accounted for 20 percent of wasted water worldwide. As much as 20,000 liters of water is used to produce one kilogram of cotton, the equivalent of one T-shirt, and so are several dangerous chemicals—24 percent of all insecticides and 11 percent of all pesticides worldwide used are in cotton-farming alone.

According to the 2017 "Pulse of the Fashion Industry" report, put together by Global Fashion Agenda and the Boston Consulting Group, in 2015, the clothing industry's impact on the environment amounted to 79 billion cubic meters of water, 1.715 million tons of CO_2 emissions, and 92 million tons of waste. Based on the reports' forecast, by 2030 these numbers will increase by at least 50 percent if no action is taken. The challenge for H&M is to embrace sustainability while producing clothing for a world where tastes seem to change every minute. Responding to these challenges, H&M has made several

commitments to sustainability that have redefined its marketing strategy.

Meeting Customers' Expectations
In its 2018 Sustainability Report, H&M declared the following "rights" of customers to protect their interests:

1. **The right to be well-informed about important aspects of the product**. Customers no longer demand only quality and design from H&M products; they also demand more information about the supply chain. H&M wants to be a leader in sustainability, from the materials used to the transport of products to the store, and to inform customers about its actions toward that goal.

2. **The right to be protected against questionable products and marketing practices**. To reach customers, H&M uses a mix of external media, which includes its stores, both online and physical. Its marketing campaigns need to be simple, keep the customer up-to-date on its activities, and be part of the shopping experience. All marketing activities must comply with the Advertising and Marketing Communications Code of the International Chamber of Commerce.

3. **The right to influence products and marketing practices in ways that will improve "quality of life."** H&M marketing and advertisement campaigns should convey a positive image that represents a range of styles, attitudes, and ethnic backgrounds.

   The right to consume now in a way that will preserve the world for future generations of consumers. H&M seeks to ensure respect for human rights and the least possible negative impact on the environment in its operations, and its products should be of high quality but also safe and free from harmful chemicals.

In order to serve all the customers' rights H&M integrates physical stores and digital channels to give them an easy, inspiring, and convenient shopping experience no matter where, when, and how they shop, giving unique proximity to customers.

Covering Media Concerns

The major clothing retailers have long been the target of widespread concern about labor working conditions. Among the alarming incidents that have made headlines over the past decade are a series of mass fainting incidents at Cambodian partner factories; criminally abusive working conditions in Myanmar; and most infamously, the collapse of the Rana Plaza complex in Bangladesh in 2013, which killed 1,136 garment workers. Greenpeace also alleges that H&M-affiliated factories has discharged hazardous chemicals into rivers in China and Indonesia.

Acknowledging the individuals involved in the company's global supply chain, H&M has teamed up with worker's organizations, governments, trade unions, factory owners, and NGOs to improve laborers' conditions and tackle various media issues. For example, in 2014, the company joined its peers in advocating for the Cambodian government's Trade Union Law. H&M has refined its Fair Living Wage Strategy, launched in 2013, after the discriminatory and exploitative labor conditions, such as short-term contracts or poor government labor inspection and enforcement, were revealed by Human Rights Watch in 2015. This strategy is based on its involvement in various collaborative initiatives, such as training on workplace cooperation, negotiation skills, collective bargaining, and labor law. Systems embracing the Fair Wage Method were being implemented in a total of 336 factories by the end of 2018, superseding H&M's goal of 50 percent of the total product volume by the end of 2019.

Sustainability Strategy

The company introduced its Sustainability Reports in 2002, making its sustainability strategy more comprehensive and ambitious than ever before. Published every year, each report regularly reveals sustainability efforts and key achievements to its customers. According to the 2018 report, by 2040 the company believes it can become 100 percent "climate positive" by using energy more efficiently or by using renewable energy. Fifty-seven percent of the materials H&M uses to make clothing originate from recycled clothing, and by 2030 all products will be 100 percent recycled or sustainable. H&M also aims to eliminate hazardous chemicals and solvent-based glues in the manufacturing of its products by 2020.

The Four Ps of Sustainability

To translate sustainability aims into action, H&M frames and reviews its sustainability goals and performance within the context of four pillars: people, product, planet, and partnership.

People: H&M's sustainability efforts are also oriented toward value for society. The company uses a percentage of the purchase price of its clothing to donate to good causes. H&M's All for Children is an initiative with UNICEF to help youngsters in nations where the company operates. It has raised around $12.5 million every year through deals and extra gifts from H&M. In addition, since 2009, H&M has made attempts to improve conditions in Tamil Nadu, India, one of the world's biggest suppliers of cotton.

Sustainable production within H&M is achieved through a long-term approach that involves creating jobs and driving prosperity in its markets. H&M has made some commendable improvements in their labor policies in recent years. Based on the 2018 Ethical Fashion Report, H&M received the top score of A+ for its Supplier Code of Conduct, though the code only applies to part of its supply chain. It also received an A+ for its transparency and ability to trace most of its suppliers. H&M audits most of the facilities in its supply chain over a two-year period.

However, only 1 to 25 percent of traced facilities across H&M's supply chain pay a living wage to their workers, and the company only implements some of the available worker empowerment initiatives at the final manufacturing stage, and even fewer at the raw materials and inputs stages of production, meaning that not enough of its facilities have collective bargaining or empower workers with the right to make a complaint. Another report by the Clean Clothes Campaign found out that H&M has not fulfilled its promise to pay 850,000 workers a living wage from 2013 through to 2018, so there is still a lot of work to do.

Product: H&M is one of the first companies to stock a "Conscious" sustainable fashion collection in its stores. Introduced in 2011, the collection includes clothing made from organic and recycled textiles. The 2018 Conscious collection focuses on using only ecofriendly and recycled materials, such as bio cotton, silk, Tencel, and recycled polyester. Furthermore H&M introduced two new materials: reused silver and Econyl, a 100 percent recovered nylon fiber produced using fishnets.

H&M also launched the Fair Living Wage Strategy Update to improve working conditions for the people making its products. The company has introduced a transparency tool to their online shop, enabling customers to trace the products all the way back to the factories where they were produced. H&M is also using AI to make it easier to ensure a good match between production and demand, thus saving energy, transport, and resources.

Planet: H&M is a large company—recently, H&M surpassed Walmart as the world's largest buyer of organic cotton, consuming more than 15,000 tons in 2010, an increase of 77 percent since the previous year. The company is also a founding member of the Better Cotton Initiative, which introduces more sustainable practices at every step of the cotton production supply chain, and experiments with eco-fibers, including recycled polyester, recycled polyamide, recycled plastic, organic linen, recycled cotton, recycled wool, and Tencel®. For animal welfare, H&M is using wool from non-mulesed sheep and banning the use of fur, angora, and exotic animal and skins; when it uses leather, it specifies where it is sourced.

Partnership: H&M's drive toward greater sustainability is dependent on partnerships with experts from other fields in technology and innovation, so it seeks out suitable suppliers and distributors, and builds relationships with other organizations that are trying to achieve the same sustainability goals as H&M. Examples of such relationships including work with the WWF on responsible use of water in the value chain; investments in companies that are developing technologies for textile recycling; partnership with the Ellen MacArthur Foundation to drive the development of a circular economy; and collaboration with the UN and textile workers' global trade union to tackle the issue of wages in the textile industry. The company is also an active participant of the Sustainable Apparel Coalition, a trade association that has worked to develop an index for measuring and tracking the comprehensive environmental and social impact of products across the value chain.

H&M is being recognized for the positive steps it has taken toward implementing sustainable concepts and its very tangible results. It was named one of the most ethical companies in the world by the Ethisphere Institute in 2019, and the "Ethical Fashion Report 2018" singled out H&M for its outstanding environmental management and for transparent and consistent reporting on sustainability manners, such as in its H&M Sustainability Report.[31]

Questions for Discussion

20-16 Explain the principles of environmentalism and elaborate what H&M does in order to balance it with consumerism.

20-17 Do recent marketing activities need to always be sustainable? Is it becoming a new standard?

20-18 Explain the importance of sustainable marketing for gaining new customers and retaining existing ones based on the H&M activities described in this case.

20-19 How does H&M try to improve the working conditions of cheap labor?

20-20 Elaborate on what H&M does for society using examples in this case.

Marketing Plan

The Marketing Plan: An Introduction

As a marketer, you will need a good marketing plan to provide direction and focus for your brand, product, or company. With a detailed plan, any business will be better prepared to launch a new product or build sales for existing products. Nonprofit organizations also use marketing plans to guide their fund-raising and outreach efforts. Even government agencies put together marketing plans for initiatives such as building public awareness of proper nutrition and stimulating area tourism.

The Purpose and Content of a Marketing Plan

Unlike a business plan, which offers a broad overview of the entire organization's mission, objectives, strategy, and resource allocation, a marketing plan has a more limited scope. It serves to document how the organization's strategic objectives will be achieved through specific marketing strategies and tactics, with the customer as the starting point. It is also linked to the plans of other departments within the organization. Suppose, for example, a marketing plan calls for selling 200,000 units annually. The production department must gear up to make that many units, the finance department must arrange funding to cover the expenses, the human resources department must be ready to hire and train staff, and so on. Without the appropriate level of organizational support and resources, no marketing plan can succeed.

Although the exact length and layout will vary from company to company, a marketing plan usually contains the sections described in Chapter 2. Smaller businesses may create shorter or less formal marketing plans whereas corporations frequently require highly structured marketing plans. To guide implementation effectively, every part of the plan must be described in considerable detail. Sometimes a company will post its marketing plans on an intranet site, which allows managers and employees in different locations to consult specific sections and collaborate on additions or changes.

The Role of Research

Marketing plans are not created in a vacuum. To develop successful strategies and action programs, marketers need up-to-date information about the environment, the competition, and the market segments to be served. Often, analysis of internal data is the starting point for assessing the current marketing situation, supplemented by marketing intelligence and research investigating the overall market, the competition, key issues, and threats and opportunities. As the plan is put into effect, marketers use a variety of research techniques to measure progress toward objectives and identify areas for improvement if results fall short of projections.

Finally, marketing research helps marketers learn more about their customers' requirements, expectations, perceptions, and satisfaction levels. This deeper understanding provides a foundation for building competitive advantage through well-informed segmenting, targeting, differentiating, and positioning decisions. Thus, the marketing plan should outline what marketing research will be conducted and how the findings will be applied.

The Role of Customer Involvement and Relationships

The marketing plan shows how the company will establish and maintain profitable customer engagement and relationships. In the process, however, it also shapes a number of internal and external relationships. First, it affects how marketing personnel work with each other and with other departments to deliver value and satisfy customers. Second, it affects how the company works with suppliers, distributors, and strategic alliance partners to achieve the objectives listed in the plan. Third, it influences the company's dealings with other stakeholders, including government regulators, the media, and the community at large. All of these relationships are important to the organization's success, so they should be considered when a marketing plan is being developed.

From Marketing Plan to Marketing Action

Companies generally create yearly marketing plans, although some plans cover a longer period. Marketers start planning well in advance of the implementation date to allow time for marketing research, thorough analysis, management review, and coordination between departments. Then, after each action program begins, marketers monitor ongoing results, compare them with projections, analyze any differences, and take corrective steps as needed. Some marketers also prepare contingency plans for implementation if certain conditions emerge. Because of inevitable and sometimes unpredictable environmental changes, marketers must be ready to update and adapt marketing plans at any time.

For effective implementation and control, the marketing plan should define how progress toward objectives will be measured. Managers typically use budgets, schedules, and performance standards for monitoring and evaluating results. With budgets, they can compare planned expenditures with actual expenditures for a given week, month, or other period. Schedules allow management to see when tasks were supposed to be completed— and when they were actually completed. Performance standards track the outcomes of marketing programs to see whether the company is moving toward its objectives. Some examples of performance standards are market share, sales volume, product profitability, and customer satisfaction.

Sample Marketing Plan: Chill Beverage Company

Executive Summary

The Chill Beverage Company is preparing to launch a new line of vitamin-enhanced water called NutriWater. Although the bottled water market is maturing, the functional water category—and more specifically the vitamin-enhanced water category—is still growing. NutriWater will be positioned by the slogan "Expect more"—indicating that the brand offers more in the way of desirable product features and benefits at a competitive price. Chill Beverage is taking advantage of its existing experience and brand equity among its loyal current customer base of millennials who consume its Chill Soda soft drink. NutriWater will target similar millennials who are maturing and looking for an alternative to soft drinks and high-calorie sugared beverages.

The primary marketing objective is to achieve first-year U.S. sales of $50 million, roughly 2 percent of the functional water market. Based on this market share goal, the company expects to sell more than 26 million units the first year and break even in the final quarter of the year.

Current Marketing Situation

The Chill Beverage Company—founded in 2010—markets niche and emerging products in the beverage industry. Rather than directly challenging established beverage giants like the Coca-Cola Company and PepsiCo, the Chill Beverage Company has focused on the fringes of the industry. Its Chill Soda soft drink brand hit the market with six unique flavors in glass bottles. The company now markets dozens of Chill Soda flavors, many unique to the brand. Over the past few years, Chill has successfully introduced new lines including natural juice drinks and iced teas. Chill Beverage has grown its business every year since it was founded. In the most recent year, it achieved $230 million in revenue and net profits of $18.6 million. As part of its future growth strategy, Chill Beverage plans to introduce new lines of beverages to continue to take advantage of emerging trends in the industry. Currently, it is preparing to launch a line of vitamin-enhanced waters.

For years, U.S. consumers have imbibed more carbonated soft drinks than any other bottled beverage. But concerns over health and obesity have taken the fizz out of the soda market—sales have declined for the past 13 years in a row. Meanwhile, bottled water consumption is on a growth trajectory that shows no sign of slowing down. In fact, bottled water passed carbonated soft drinks as the number one beverage by volume two years ago. People in the United States now consumer more bottled water than any other beverage, including carbonated soft drinks, coffee, beer, and milk.

Currently, the average person in the United States consumes more than 42 gallons of bottled water every year and experts expect that volume to rise to 50 gallons by 2020. In contrast, per capita consumption of carbonated soft drinks is down to 37.5 gallons and will continue to decline. Supporting bottled water's new position as the market leader, a recent study found that among U.S. consumers, bottled water is their most preferred beverage. An $18.5 billion market, bottled water revenues in the United States are expected to increase by more than 40 percent during the next four years.

Competition is more intense now than ever as the industry consolidates and new types of bottled water emerge. The U.S. market is dominated by three global corporations. With a global portfolio of more than 50 brands (including Poland Spring, Nestlé Pure Life, Arrowhead, Deer Park, and Ice Mountain), Nestlé leads the market for with a 28 share of all water sales (sparkling, functional water, flavored water, and so on). Coca-Cola is number two with more than 24 percent and PepsiCo follows at a distant third with approximately 13 percent. Private labels account for 22 percent of the market.

While bottled water as a whole is strong, the market for the sub-category of functional waters is even stronger, growing by 11 percent for the most recent year. In the current market environment, functional waters have thrived based on the promise of incremental benefits for health-conscious consumers based on the infusion of ingredients such as vitamins, minerals (including electrolytes), herbs, and other additives. Functional waters, therefore, carry the standard benefits of taste and convenience with an increased appeal to lifestyle and wellbeing. Most functional waters are sweetened and flavored and are distinguished from sports drinks that have the primary purpose of maximizing hydration by replenishing electrolytes.

To break into this market dominated by huge global corporations and littered with dozens of other small players, Chill Beverage must carefully target specific segments with features and benefits valued by those segments.

Market Description

The bottled water market consists of many different types of water. Varieties of plain water include spring, purified, mineral, and distilled. Although these different types of water are sold as consumer products, they also serve as the core ingredient for the various types of functional waters. The flexibility of bottled water as a category seems to be endless.

Although some consumers may not perceive much of a difference between brands, others are drawn to specific product features and benefits provided by different brands. For example, some consumers may perceive spring water as healthier than other types of water. Some may look for water that is optimized for hydration. Others seek additional nutritional benefits claimed by bottlers that enhance their brands with vitamins, minerals, herbs, and other additives. Still other consumers make selections based on flavor. A recent study revealed that the most important attribute driving the choice of bottled water is *all natural ingredients* (57 percent) followed by *vitamin-enhanced* (33 percent), *antioxidants* (31 percent), and *flavors* (31 percent).

The industry as a whole has positioned bottled water of all kinds as a low-calorie, healthy alternative to soft drinks, sports drinks, energy drinks, and other types of beverages. This positioning is working—94 percent of Americans believe bottled water is healthier than soda. Bottled water brands also distinguish themselves by size and type of container, multipacks, and refrigeration at point-of-sale.

Chill Beverage's market for NutriWater consists of consumers of single-serving-sized bottled beverages who are looking for a healthy yet flavorful alternative. *Healthy* in this context means natural ingredients, enhanced nutritional content, and low calories. This market includes traditional soft drink consumers who want to improve their health as well as non–soft drink consumers who want an option other than plain bottled water. Specific segments that Chill Beverage will target during the first year include athletes, the health conscious, the socially responsible, and millennials who favor independent corporations. The Chill Soda brand has established a strong base of loyal customers, primarily among millennials. This generational segment is becoming a prime target as it matures and seeks alternatives to full-calorie soft drinks. ● **Table A1.1** shows how NutriWater addresses the needs of targeted consumer segments.

● **Table A1.1** | Segment Needs and Corresponding Features/Benefits of NutriWater

Targeted Segment	Customer Need	Corresponding Features/Benefits
Athletes	• Hydration and replenishment of essential minerals • Energy to maximize performance	• Electrolytes and carbohydrates • B vitamins, carbohydrates
Health conscious	• Maintain optimum weight • Optimize nutrition levels • Avoid harmful chemicals and additives • Desire to consume a tastier beverage than water	• Half the calories of fully sugared beverages • Higher levels of vitamins A, B, C, E, zinc, chromium, and folic acid than other products; vitamins unavailable in other products • All natural ingredients • Six new-age flavors
Socially conscious	• Support causes that help solve world's social problems	• 25-cent donation from each purchase to Vitamin Angels
Millennials	• Aversion to mass-media advertising/technologically savvy • Counter-culture attitude • Diet enhancement due to fast-paced lifestyle	• Less-invasive online and social networking promotional tactics • Small, privately held company • Full RDA levels of essential vitamins and minerals

Product Review

Chill Beverage's new line of NutriWater vitamin-enhanced water offers the following features:

- Six new-age flavors including Peach Mango, Berry Pomegranate, Kiwi Dragonfruit, Mandarin Orange, Blueberry Grape, and Key Lime.
- Single-serving size, 20-ounce, PET recyclable bottles.
- Formulated for wellness, replenishment, and optimum energy.
- Full recommended daily allowance (RDA) of essential vitamins and minerals (including electrolytes).
- Higher vitamin concentration—vitamin levels are two to ten times higher than market-leading products, with more vitamins and minerals than any other brand.
- Additional vitamins—vitamins include A, E, and B2 as well as folic acid—none of which are contained in the market-leading products.
- All natural—no artificial flavors, colors, or preservatives.
- Sweetened with pure cane sugar and Stevia, a natural zero-calorie sweetener.
- Twenty-five cents from each purchase will be donated to Vitamin Angels, a nonprofit organization with a mission to prevent vitamin deficiency in at-risk children.

Competitive Review

More than a decade before Chill launched its first product, bottled water entered a strong growth phase. New types of plain water emerged, followed by new subcategories. These included flavored waters—such as Aquafina's Flavorsplash—as well as functional waters. Functional waters emerged to bridge the gap between soft drinks and waters, appealing to people who knew they should drink more water and less soft drinks but still wanted flavor. Initially, development of brands for this product variation occurred in startup and boutique beverage companies such as SoBe and Glacéau, creator of Vitaminwater. In the 2000s, major beverage corporations acquired the most successful smaller brands, providing the bigger firms with a solid market position in this category and diversification in bottled waters in general. Backed by the marketing expertise and budgets of the leading beverage companies, functional water grew at a rate exceeding that of plain water.

At one point, Coca-Cola's Vitaminwater was the fourth-largest bottled water brand, behind Nestlé Pure Life, Coca-Cola's Dasani, and Pepsi's Aquafina. After taking a hit in the press for the low amount of vitamins and high amount of sugar contained in most brands of vitamin-enhanced waters, sales for Vitaminwater temporarily slipped. But Coca-Cola lost no ground as sales for Smartwater—Vitaminwater's non-flavored sibling—filled the void, rising to the fourth largest brand. Industry insiders expect growth of functional waters to outpace non-functional waters in the coming years.

The fragmentation of this category, combined with domination by the market leaders, has created a severely competitive environment. Although there is indirect competition posed by all types of bottled waters and even other types of beverages (soft drinks, energy drinks, juices, teas, and flavor drops), this competitive analysis focuses on direct competition from leading functional water brands. Functional water brands are either sweetened and flavored, just flavored, or neither sweetened nor flavored. Sweetened varieties use blend traditional sugars with zero-calorie sweeteners. The types of sweeteners used create a point of differentiation. The result is a range of sugar content, carbohydrates, and calories as high as half that of regular soft drinks and other sweetened beverages and as low as zero.

Pricing for this product is consistent across brands and varies by type of retail outlet, with convenience stores typically charging more than grocery stores. The price for a 20-ounce bottle ranges from $1.00 to $1.99, with some niche brands costing slightly more. Smartwater—a plain still water enhanced with electrolytes—is the leading functional water brand. Chill Beverage's NutriWater will focus on competition posed by flavored and enhanced water brands, include the following:

- *Vitaminwater:* Created in 2000 as a new product for Energy Brands' Glacéau, which was also the developer of Smartwater (distilled water with electrolytes). Coca-Cola purchased Energy Brands for $4.1 billion in 2007. Vitaminwater is sold in regular, zero-calorie, and active varieties. With 22 bottled varieties—10 regular, 9 zero-calorie, and 3 active—as well as availability in fountain form, Vitaminwater offers more options than any brand on the market. Whereas Vitaminwater varieties are distinguished by flavor, they are named to invoke perceptions of benefits such as Refresh, Power-C, Focus, and Revive. The brand's current slogan is "Drink Outside the Lines." Vitaminwater is vapor distilled, de-ionized, and/or filtered and is sweetened with crystalline fructose (corn syrup) and cane sugar or erythritol and stevia. Vitaminwater exceeds $700 million in annual sales and commands approximately one-third of the functional water market.

- *Propel:* Gatorade created Propel in 2000, just one year prior to PepsiCo's purchase of this leading sports drink marketer. It marketed Propel as "Hydration for Your Workout," PepsiCo recently tied its fitness water brand to its market-leading sports drink brand with the tagline, "How Gatorade Does Water." Propel was originally available in regular and zero-calorie varieties. However, it is now available only as a zero-calorie beverage. Propel comes in nine flavored varieties as well as in unflavored form. Each variety of Propel contains the same blend of B vitamins, vitamin C, vitamin E, antioxidants, and electrolytes. Flavored versions are sweetened with sucralose. Propel is available in a wide variety of sizes, with 16.9 and 24-ounce PET bottles and multipacks. Propel is also marketed in powder form to be added to bottled water. With more than $200 million in revenues and double-digit growth during the past three years, Propel is the number three functional water brand behind Smartwater and Vitaminwater.

- *SoBewater:* PepsiCo bought SoBe in 2000 and introduced Lifewater in 2008 as an answer to Coca-Cola's Vitaminwater. Now rebranded as SoBewater, the brand includes multiple zero-calorie varieties. Each variety is infused with a formulation of vitamins, minerals, and herbs designed to provide a claimed benefit. Sweetened with Steviabased PureVia, SoBewater contains no artificial flavors or colors. SoBewater is sold in 20-ounce PET bottles and multipacks. With more than $150 million in annual revenues, SoBewater is the fourth-largest functional water brand with a 7 percent share.

- *Niche brands:* The market for functional waters includes companies that market their wares on a small scale through independent retailers: Assure, Zico, Ayala Herbal Water, and Skinny Water. Some brands feature exotic additives and/or artistic glass bottles.

Despite the strong competition, NutriWater believes it can create a relevant brand image and gain recognition among the targeted segments. The brand offers strong points of differentiation with higher and unique vitamin content, all-natural ingredients, and support for a relevant social cause. With other strategic assets, Chill Beverage is confident that it can establish a competitive advantage that will allow NutriWater to grow in the market. **Table A1.2** shows a sample of competing products.

● **Table A1.2** | Sample of Competitive Products

Competitor	Brand	Features
Coca-Cola	Vitaminwater	Regular and zero-calorie versions; 22 varieties; each flavor provides a different function based on blend of vitamins and minerals; vapor distilled, de-ionized, and/or filtered; sweetened with crystalline fructose and cane sugar; 20-ounce single-serve or multi-pack, fountain, and drops.
PepsiCo	Propel	Zero-calorie only; ten flavors; fitness positioning based on "Hydration for Your Workout"; B vitamins, vitamin C, vitamin E, antioxidants, and electrolytes; sweetened with sucralose; 16.9-ounce and 24-ounce PET bottles and multipacks; powdered packets; liquid enhancer.
PepsiCo	SoBewater	Zero calories, vitamins, minerals, and herbs; Pure—mildly flavored, sweetened with Stevia; 20-ounce single-serve and multi-packs.

Channels and Logistics Review

With the three main brands now owned by Coca-Cola and PepsiCo, there is a huge hole in the independent distributor system. NutriWater will be distributed through an independent distributor to a network of retailers in the United States. This strategy will avoid some of the head-on competition for shelf space with the Coca-Cola and PepsiCo brands and will also directly target likely NutriWater customers. As with the rollout of the core Chill Soda brand, this strategy will focus on placing coolers in retail locations that will exclusively hold NutriWater. These retailers include:

- *Grocery chains:* Regional grocery chains such as HyVee in the Midwest, Wegman's in the east, and WinCo in the west.
- *Health and natural food stores*: Chains such as Whole Foods as well as local health food co-ops.
- *Fitness centers:* National fitness center chains such as 24-Hour Fitness, Gold's Gym, and other regional chains.

As the brand gains acceptance, channels will expand into larger grocery chains, convenience stores, and unique locations relevant to the target customer segment.

Strengths, Weaknesses, Opportunities, and Threats Analysis

NutriWater has several powerful strengths on which to build, but its major weakness is lack of brand awareness and image. Major opportunities include a growing market and consumer trends targeted by NutriWater's product traits. Threats include barriers to entry posed by limited retail space as well as image issues for the bottled water industry. ● **Table A1.3** summarizes NutriWater's main strengths, weaknesses, opportunities, and threats.

● **Table A1.3** | NutriWater's Strengths, Weaknesses, Opportunities, and Threats

Strengths	Weaknesses
• Superior quality	• Lack of brand awareness
• Expertise in alternative beverage marketing	• Limited budget
• Social responsibility	
• Anti-establishment image	

Opportunities	Threats
• Market growth	• Limited shelf space
• Gap in the distribution network	• Image of enhanced waters
• Health trends	• Environmental issues
• Anti-establishment image	

Strengths

NutriWater can rely on the following important strengths:

1. *Superior quality:* NutriWater boasts the highest levels of added vitamins of any enhanced water, including full RDA levels of many vitamins. It is all natural with no artificial flavors, colors, or preservatives. It is sweetened with both pure cane sugar and the natural zero-calorie sweetener Stevia.
2. *Expertise in alternative beverage marketing:* The Chill Soda brand went from nothing to a successful and rapidly growing soft drink brand with fiercely loyal customers in a matter of only one decade. This success was achieved by starting small and focusing on gaps in the marketplace.
3. *Social responsibility:* Every customer will have the added benefit of helping malnourished children throughout the world. Although the price of NutriWater is in line with other competitors, low promotional costs allow for the substantial charitable donation of 25 cents per bottle while maintaining profitability.
4. *Anti-establishment image:* The big brands have decent products and strong distribution relationships. But they also carry the image of the large, corporate establishments. Chill Beverage has achieved success with an underdog image while remaining privately held. Vitaminwater, Propel, and SoBe were built on this same image but are now owned by major multinational corporations.

Weaknesses

1. *Lack of brand awareness:* As an entirely new brand, NutriWater will enter the market with limited or no brand awareness. The affiliation with Chill Soda will be kept at a minimum in order to prevent associations between NutriWater and soft drinks. This issue will be addressed through promotion and distribution strategies.
2. *Limited budget:* As a smaller company, Chill Beverage has much smaller funds available for promotional and research activities.

Opportunities

1. *Market growth:* Functional water as a category is growing at a rate of about 12 percent annually. Of the top six beverage categories, soft drinks, beer, milk, and fruit drinks experienced declines. The growth for coffee was less than 1 percent.
2. *Gap in the distribution network:* The market leaders distribute directly to retailers. This gives them an advantage in large national chains. However, no major enhanced water brands are currently being sold through independent distributors.
3. *Health trends:* Weight and nutrition continue to be issues for consumers in the United States. The country has the highest obesity rate for developed countries at 34 percent, with well over 60 percent of the population officially "overweight." Those numbers continue to rise. Additionally, Americans get 21 percent of their daily calories from beverages, a number that has tripled in the last three decades. Consumers still desire flavored beverages but look for lower calorie alternatives.
4. *Anti-establishment image:* Millennials (born between 1981 and 1997) maintain a higher aversion to mass marketing messages and global corporations than do Gen Xers and baby boomers.

Threats

1. *Limited shelf space:* Whereas competition is generally a threat for any type of product, competition in retail beverages is particularly high because of limited retail space. Carrying a new beverage product requires retailers to reduce shelf or cooler space already occupied by other brands.
2. *Image of enhanced waters:* The image of enhanced waters took a hit as Coca-Cola recently fought a class-action lawsuit accusing it of violating FDA regulations by promoting the health benefits of Vitaminwater. The lawsuit exposed the number one functional water brand as basically sugar water with minimal nutritional value. Each of the major brands is strengthening its zero-calorie lines. They no longer promote health benefits on the labels. Although this is potentially a threat, it is also an opportunity for Chill to exploit.

3. *Environmental issues:* Environmental groups continue to educate the public on the environmental costs of bottled water, including landfill waste, carbon emissions from production and transportation, and harmful effects of chemicals in plastics.

Objectives and Issues

Chill Beverage has set aggressive but achievable objectives for NutriWater for the first and second years of market entry.

First-year Objectives

During the first year on the market, Chill Beverage aims for NutriWater to achieve a 2 percent share of the functional water market, or approximately $50 million in sales, with break-even achieved in the final quarter of the year. With an average retail price of $1.89, that equates with a sales goal of 26,455,026 bottles.

Second-year Objectives

During the second year, Chill Beverage will unveil additional NutriWater flavors, including zero-calorie varieties. The second-year objective is to double sales from the first year, to $100 million.

Issues

In launching this new brand, the main issue is the ability to establish brand awareness and a meaningful brand image based on positioning that is relevant to target customer segments. Chill Beverage will invest in nontraditional means of promotion to accomplish these goals and to spark word-of-mouth. Establishing distributor and retailer relationships will also be critical in order to make the product available and provide point-of-purchase communications. Brand awareness and knowledge will be measured in order to adjust marketing efforts as necessary.

Marketing Strategy

NutriWater's marketing strategy will involve developing a "more for the same" positioning based on extra benefits for the price. The brand will also establish channel differentiation, as it will be available in locations where major competing brands are not. The primary target segments are millennials—born between 1981 and 1997. NutriWater will focus specifically on the young adult market. Subsets of this generational segment include athletes, the health conscious, and the socially responsible.

Positioning

NutriWater will be positioned on an "Expect more" value proposition. This will allow for differentiating the brand based on product features (expect more vitamin content and all-natural ingredients), desirable benefits (expect greater nutritional benefits), and values (do more for a social cause). Marketing will focus on conveying that NutriWater is more than just a beverage: It gives customers much more for their money in a variety of ways.

Product Strategy

NutriWater will be sold with all the features described in the Product Review section. As awareness takes hold and retail availability increases, more varieties will be made available. A zero-calorie version will be added to the product line, providing a solid fit with the health benefits sought by consumers. Chill Beverage's considerable experience in brand-building will be applied as an integral part of the product strategy for NutriWater. All aspects of the marketing mix will be consistent with the brand.

Pricing

There is little price variation in the enhanced waters category, particularly among leading brands. For this reason, NutriWater will follow a competition-based pricing strategy. Given that NutriWater claims superior quality, it must be careful not to position itself as a lower-cost alternative. Manufacturers do not quote list prices on this type of beverage, and prices vary considerably based on type of retail outlet and whether or not the product is refrigerated. Regular prices for single 20-ounce bottles of competing products are as low as $1.00 in discount-retailer stores and as high as $1.99 in convenience stores. Because NutriWater will not be targeting discount retailers and convenience stores initially, this will allow Chill Beverage to set prices at the average to higher end of the range for similar products in the same outlets. For grocery chains, this should be approximately $1.69 per bottle, with that price rising to $1.99 at health food stores and fitness centers, where prices tend to be higher.

Distribution Strategy

NutriWater will employ a selective distribution strategy with well-known regional grocers, health and natural food stores, and fitness centers. This distribution strategy will be executed through a network of independent beverage distributors, as there are no other major brands of enhanced water following this strategy. Chill Beverage gained success for its core Chill Soda soft drink line using this method. It also placed coolers with the brand logo in truly unique venues such as skate, surf, and snowboarding shops; tattoo and piercing parlors; fashion stores; and music stores—places that would expose the brand to target customers. Then, the soft drink brand expanded by getting contracts with retailers such as Panera, Barnes & Noble, Target, and Starbucks. This same approach will be taken with NutriWater by starting small, then expanding into larger chains. NutriWater will not target all the same stores used originally by Chill Soda, as many of those outlets were unique to the positioning and target customer for the Chill Soda soft drink brand.

Marketing Communication Strategy

As with the core Chill Soda brand, the marketing communication strategy for NutriWater will not follow a strategy based on traditional mass-communication advertising. Initially, there will be no broadcast or print advertising. Promotional resources for NutriWater will focus on three areas:

- *Online and mobile marketing:* The typical target customer for NutriWater spends more time online than with traditional media channels. A core component for this strategy will be building web and mobile brand sites and driving traffic to those sites by creating a presence on social networks, including Facebook, Twitter, Instagram, and Snapchat. The NutriWater brand will also incorporate location-based services by Foursquare and Facebook to help drive traffic to retail locations. A mobile phone ad campaign will provide additional support to the online efforts.
- *Trade promotions:* Like the core Chill Soda brand, NutriWater's success will rely on relationships with retailers to create product availability. Primary incentives to retailers will include point-of-purchase displays, branded coolers, and volume incentives and contests. This push marketing strategy will combine with the other pull strategies.
- *Event marketing:* NutriWater will deploy teams in brand-labeled RVs to distribute product samples at events such as skiing and snowboarding competitions, golf tournaments, and concerts.

Marketing Research

To remain consistent with the online promotional approach as well as using research methods that will effectively reach target customers, Chill Beverage will monitor online discussions. In this manner, the company will gauge customer perceptions of the brand, the products, and general satisfaction. For future development of the product and new distribution outlets, crowdsourcing methods will be utilized.

Action Programs

NutriWater will be introduced in February. The following are summaries of action programs that will be used during the first six months of the year to achieve the stated objectives.

January: Chill Beverage representatives will work with both independent distributors and retailers to educate them on the trade promotional campaign, incentives, and advantages for selling NutriWater. Representatives will also ensure that distributors and retailers are educated on product features and benefits as well as instructions for displaying point-of-purchase materials and coolers. The brand website and other sites such as Facebook will present teaser information about the product as well as availability dates and locations. Buzz will be enhanced by providing product samples to selected product reviewers, opinion leaders, influential bloggers, and celebrities.

February: On the date of availability, product coolers and point-of-purchase displays will be placed in retail locations. The full brand website and social network campaign will launch with full efforts on Facebook, Twitter, Instagram, and Snapchat. This campaign will drive the "Expect more" slogan as well as illustrate the ways that NutriWater delivers more than expected on product features, desirable benefits, and values by donating to Vitamin Angels and the social cause of battling vitamin deficiency in children.

March: To enhance the online and social marketing campaign, location-based services Foursquare and Facebook Location Services will be employed to drive traffic to retailers. Point-of-purchase displays and signage will be updated to support these efforts and to continue supporting retailers. The message of this campaign will focus on all aspects of "Expect more."

April: A mobile ad campaign will provide additional support, driving traffic to the brand website and social network sites as well as driving traffic to retailers.

May: A trade sales contest will offer additional incentives and prizes to the distributors and retailers that sell the most NutriWater during a four-week period.

June: An event marketing campaign will mobilize a team of NutriWater representatives in NutriWater RVs to concerts and sports events. This will provide additional visibility for the brand as well as giving customers and potential customers the opportunity to sample products.

Budgets

Chill Beverage has set a first-year retail sales goal of $50 million with a projected average retail price of $1.89 per unit for a total of 26,455,026 units sold. With an average wholesale price of 95 cents per unit, this provides revenues of $25.1 million. Chill Beverage expects to break even during the final quarter of the first year. A break-even analysis assumes per-unit wholesale revenue of 95 cents per unit, a variable cost per unit of 22 cents, and estimated first-year fixed costs of $12,500,000. Based on these assumptions, the break-even calculation is:

$$\frac{\$12,500,000}{\$0.95/\text{unit} \; - \; \$0.22/\text{unit}} = 17,123,287$$

Controls

Chill Beverage is planning tight control measures to closely monitor product quality, brand awareness, brand image, and customer satisfaction. This will enable the company to react quickly in correcting any problems that may occur. Other early warning signals that will be monitored for signs of deviation from the plan include monthly sales (by segment and channel) and monthly expenses. Given the market's volatility, contingency plans are also in place to address fast-moving environmental changes such as shifting consumer preferences, new products, and new competition.[i]

Marketing by the Numbers

Marketing managers are facing increased accountability for the financial implications of their actions. This appendix provides a basic introduction to measuring marketing financial performance. Such financial analysis guides marketers in making sound marketing decisions and in assessing the outcomes of those decisions.

The appendix is built around a hypothetical manufacturer of home automation products—Wise Domotics (*domotics* refers to information technology in the home). The company is introducing a device that allows users to control all internet-connected smart devices in their homes. Users will be able to control lighting, temperature, multimedia, security systems, appliances, windows and doors, phones, and any other smart devices in their homes that are connected to the internet. In this appendix, we will analyze the various decisions Wise Domotics's marketing managers must make before and after the new product launch.

The appendix is organized into *three sections*. The *first section* introduces pricing, break-even, and margin analysis assessments that will guide the introduction of Wise Domotics's new product. The *second section* discusses demand estimates, the marketing budget, and marketing performance measures. It begins with a discussion of estimating market potential and company sales. It then introduces the marketing budget, as illustrated through a *pro forma* profit-and-loss statement followed by the actual profit-and-loss statement. Next, we discuss marketing performance measures with a focus on helping marketing managers to better defend their decisions from a financial perspective. In the *third section,* we analyze the financial implications of various marketing tactics.

Each of the three sections ends with a set of quantitative exercises that provide you with an opportunity to apply the concepts you learned to situations beyond Wise Domotics.

Pricing, Break-Even, and Margin Analysis

Pricing Considerations

Determining price is one of the most important marketing mix decisions. The limiting factors are demand and costs. Demand factors, such as buyer-perceived value, set the price ceiling. The company's costs set the price floor. In between these two factors, marketers must consider competitors' prices and other factors such as reseller requirements, government regulations, and company objectives.

Most current competing home automation products sell at retail prices between $100 and $500. We first consider Wise Domotics's pricing decision from a cost perspective. Then we consider consumer value, the competitive environment, and reseller requirements.

Determining Costs

Fixed costs

Costs that do not vary with production or sales level.

Variable costs

Costs that vary directly with the level of production.

Total costs

The sum of the fixed and variable costs for any given level of production.

Recall from Chapter 10 that there are different types of costs. **Fixed costs** do not vary with production or sales levels and include costs such as rent, interest, depreciation, and clerical and management salaries. Regardless of the level of output, the company must pay these costs. Whereas total fixed costs remain constant as output increases, the fixed cost per unit (or average fixed cost) will decrease as output increases because the total fixed costs are spread across more units of output. **Variable costs** vary directly with the level of production and include costs related to the direct production of the product (such as costs of goods sold—COGS) and many of the marketing costs associated with selling it. Although these costs tend to be uniform for each unit produced, they are called variable because their total varies with the number of units produced. **Total costs** are the sum of the fixed and variable costs for any given level of production.

Wise Domotics has invested $10 million in refurbishing an existing facility to manufacture the new home automation product. Once production begins, the company estimates that it will incur fixed costs of $20 million per year. The variable cost to produce each device is estimated to be $125 and is expected to remain at that level for the output capacity of the facility.

Setting Price Based on Costs

Cost-plus pricing (or markup pricing)
A standard markup to the cost of the product.

Wise Domotics starts with the cost-based approach to pricing discussed in Chapter 10. Recall that the simplest method, **cost-plus pricing (or markup pricing)**, simply adds a standard markup to the cost of the product. To use this method, however, Wise Domotics must specify expected unit sales so that total unit costs can be determined. Unit variable costs will remain constant regardless of the output, but *average unit fixed costs* will decrease as output increases.

To illustrate this method, suppose Wise Domotics has fixed costs of $20 million, variable costs of $125 per unit, and expects unit sales of 1 million devices. Thus, the cost per unit is given by:

$$\text{Unit cost} = \text{variable cost} + \frac{\text{fixed costs}}{\text{unit sales}} = \$125 + \frac{\$20,000,000}{1,000,000} = \$145$$

Relevant costs
Costs that will occur in the future and that will vary across the alternatives being considered.

Note that we do *not* include the initial investment of $10 million in the total fixed cost figure. It is not considered a fixed cost because it is not a *relevant cost*. **Relevant costs** are those that will occur in the future and that will vary across the alternatives being considered. Wise Domotics's investment to refurbish the manufacturing facility was a one-time cost that will not reoccur in the future. Such past costs are *sunk costs* and should not be considered in future analyses.

Break-even price
The price at which total revenue equals total cost and profit is zero.

Also notice that if Wise Domotics sells its product for $145, the price is equal to the total cost per unit. This is the **break-even price**—the price at which total revenue equals total cost and profit is zero.

Suppose Wise Domotics does not want to merely break even but rather wants to earn a 25% markup on sales. Wise Domotics's markup price is:[i]

$$\text{Markup price} = \frac{\text{unit cost}}{(1 - \text{desired return on sales})} = \frac{\$145}{1 - .25} = \$193.33$$

This is the price at which Wise Domotics would sell the product to resellers such as wholesalers or retailers to earn a 25% profit on sales.

Return on investment (ROI) pricing (or target-return pricing)
A cost-based pricing method that determines price based on a specified rate of return on investment.

Another approach Wise Domotics could use is called **return on investment (ROI) pricing (or target-return pricing)**. In this case, the company *would* consider the initial $10 million investment, but only to determine the dollar profit goal. Suppose the company wants a 30% return on its investment. The price necessary to satisfy this requirement can be determined by:

$$\text{ROI price} = \text{unit cost} + \frac{\text{ROI} \times \text{investment}}{\text{unit sales}} = \$145 + \frac{0.3 \times \$10,000,000}{1,000,000} = \$148$$

That is, if Wise Domotics sells its product for $148, it will realize a 30% return on its initial investment of $10 million.

In these pricing calculations, unit cost is a function of the expected sales, which were estimated to be 1 million units. But what if actual sales were lower? Then the unit cost would be higher because the fixed costs would be spread over fewer units, and the realized percentage markup on sales or ROI would be lower. Alternatively, if sales are higher than the estimated 1 million units, unit cost would be lower than $145, so a lower price would produce the desired markup on sales or ROI. It's important to note that these cost-based pricing methods are *internally* focused and do not consider demand, competitors' prices, or reseller requirements. Because Wise Domotics will be selling this product to consumers through wholesalers and retailers offering competing brands, the company must consider markup pricing from this perspective.

Setting Price Based on External Factors

Whereas costs determine the price floor, Wise Domotics also must consider external factors when setting price. Wise Domotics does not have the final say concerning the final price of its product to consumers—retailers do. So it must start with its suggested retail price and

Markup

The difference between a company's selling price for a product and its cost to manufacture or purchase it.

work back. In doing so, Wise Domotics must consider the markups required by resellers that sell the product to consumers.

In general, a dollar **markup** is the difference between a company's selling price for a product and its cost to manufacture or purchase it. For a retailer, then, the markup is the difference between the price it charges consumers and the cost the retailer must pay for the product. Thus, for any level of reseller:

$$\text{Dollar markup} = \text{selling price} - \text{cost}$$

Markups are usually expressed as a percentage, and there are two different ways to compute markups—on *cost* or on *selling price*:

$$\text{Markup percentage on cost} = \frac{\text{dollar markup}}{\text{cost}}$$

$$\text{Markup percentage on selling price} = \frac{\text{dollar markup}}{\text{selling price}}$$

To apply reseller margin analysis, Wise Domotics must first set the suggested retail price and then work back to the price at which it must sell the product to a wholesaler. Suppose retailers expect a 30% margin and wholesalers want a 20% margin based on their respective selling prices. And suppose that Wise Domotics sets a manufacturer's suggested retail price (MSRP) of $299.99 for its product.

Wise Domotics selected the $299.99 MSRP because it is lower than most competitors' prices but is not so low that consumers might perceive it to be of poor quality. And the company's research shows that it is below the threshold at which more consumers are willing to purchase the product. By using buyers' perceptions of value and not the seller's cost to determine the MSRP, Wise Domotics is using **value-based pricing**. For simplicity, we will use an MSRP of $300 in further analyses.

Value-based pricing

Offering just the right combination of quality and good service at a fair price.

To determine the price Wise Domotics will charge wholesalers, we must first subtract the retailer's margin from the retail price to determine the retailer's cost ($300 − ($300 × 0.30) = $210). The retailer's cost is the wholesaler's price, so Wise Domotics next subtracts the wholesaler's margin ($210 − ($210 × 0.20) = $168). Thus, the **markup chain** representing the sequence of markups used by firms at each level in a channel for Wise Domotics's new product is:

Markup chain

The sequence of markups used by firms at each level in a channel.

Suggested retail price:	$300
minus retail margin (30%):	−$90
Retailer's cost/wholesaler's price:	$210
minus wholesaler's margin (20%):	−$42
Wholesaler's cost/Wise Domotics's price:	$168

By deducting the markups for each level in the markup chain, Wise Domotics arrives at a price for the product to wholesalers of $168.

Break-Even and Margin Analysis

The previous analyses derived a value-based price of $168 for Wise Domotics's product. Although this price is higher than the break-even price of $145 and covers costs, that price assumed a demand of 1 million units. But how many units and what level of dollar sales must Wise Domotics achieve to break even at the $168 price? And what level of sales must be achieved to realize various profit goals? These questions can be answered through break-even and margin analysis.

Determining Break-Even Unit Volume and Dollar Sales

Break-even analysis

Analysis to determine the unit volume and dollar sales needed to be profitable given a particular price and cost structure.

Based on an understanding of costs, consumer value, the competitive environment, and reseller requirements, Wise Domotics has decided to set its price to wholesalers at $168. At that price, what sales level will be needed for Wise Domotics to break even or make a profit on its product? **Break-even analysis** determines the unit volume and dollar sales needed to be profitable given a particular price and cost structure. At the break-even point, total revenue equals total costs and profit is zero. Above this point, the company will make a profit; below it, the company will lose money. Wise Domotics can calculate break-even volume using the following formula:

$$\text{Break-even volume} = \frac{\text{fixed costs}}{\text{price} - \text{unit variable cost}}$$

Unit contribution

The amount that each unit contributes to covering fixed costs—the difference between price and variable costs.

The denominator (price − unit variable cost) is called **unit contribution** (sometimes called contribution margin). It represents the amount that each unit contributes to covering fixed costs. Break-even volume represents the level of output at which all (variable and fixed) costs are covered. In Wise Domotics's case, break-even unit volume is:

$$\text{Break-even volume} = \frac{\text{fixed cost}}{\text{price} - \text{variable cost}} = \frac{\$20,000,000}{\$168 - \$125} = 465,116.2 \text{ units}$$

Thus, at the given cost and pricing structure, Wise Domotics will break even at 465,117 units.

To determine the break-even dollar sales, simply multiply unit break-even volume by the selling price:

$$\text{BE sales} = \text{BE}_{\text{vol}} \times \text{price} = 465,117 \times \$168 = \$78,139,656$$

Contribution margin

The unit contribution divided by the selling price.

Another way to calculate dollar break-even sales is to use the percentage contribution margin (hereafter referred to as **contribution margin**), which is the unit contribution divided by the selling price:

$$\text{Contribution margin} = \frac{\text{price} - \text{variable cost}}{\text{price}} = \frac{\$168 - \$125}{\$168} = 0.256 \text{ or } 25.6\%$$

Then

$$\text{Break-even sales} = \frac{\text{fixed costs}}{\text{contribution margin}} = \frac{\$20,000,000}{0.256} = \$78,125,000$$

Note that the difference between the two break-even sales calculations is due to rounding.

Such break-even analysis helps Wise Domotics by showing the unit volume needed to cover costs. If production capacity cannot attain this level of output, then the company should not launch this product. However, the unit break-even volume is well within Wise Domotics's capacity. Of course, the bigger question concerns whether Wise Domotics can sell this volume at the $168 price. We'll address that issue a little later.

Understanding contribution margin is useful in other types of analyses as well, particularly if unit prices and unit variable costs are unknown or if a company (say, a retailer) sells many products at different prices and knows the percentage of total sales variable costs represent. Whereas unit contribution is the difference between unit price and unit variable costs, total contribution is the difference between total sales and total variable costs. The overall contribution margin can be calculated by:

$$\text{Contribution margin} = \frac{\text{total sales} - \text{total variable costs}}{\text{total sales}}$$

Regardless of the actual level of sales, if the company knows what percentage of sales is represented by variable costs, it can calculate contribution margin. For example, Wise Domotics's unit variable cost is $125, or 74% of the selling price ($125 ÷ $168 = 0.74). That means for every $1 of sales revenue for Wise Domotics, $0.74 represents variable costs, and the difference ($0.26) represents contribution to fixed costs. But even if the company doesn't know its unit price and unit variable cost, it can calculate the contribution margin from total sales and total variable costs or from knowledge of the total cost structure. It can set total sales equal to 100% regardless of the actual absolute amount and determine the contribution margin:

$$\text{Contribution margin} = \frac{100\% - 74\%}{100\%} = \frac{1 - 0.74}{1} = 1 - 0.74 = 0.26 \text{ or } 26\%$$

Note that this matches the percentage calculated from the unit price and unit variable cost information. This alternative calculation will be very useful later when analyzing various marketing decisions.

Determining "Break-Even" for Profit Goals

Although it is useful to know the break-even point, most companies are more interested in making a profit. Assume Wise Domotics would like to realize a $5 million profit in the first year. How many units must it sell at the $168 price to cover fixed costs and produce this profit? To determine this, Wise Domotics can simply add the profit figure to fixed costs and again divide by the unit contribution to determine unit sales:

$$\text{Unit volume} = \frac{\text{fixed cost} + \text{profit goal}}{\text{price} - \text{variable cost}} = \frac{\$20,000,000 + \$5,000,000}{\$168 - \$125} = 581,395.3 \text{ units}$$

Thus, to earn a $5 million profit, Wise Domotics must sell 581,396 units. Multiply by price to determine dollar sales needed to achieve a $5 million profit:

$$\text{Dollar sales} = 581,396 \text{ units} \times \$168 = \$97,674,528$$

Or use the contribution margin:

$$\text{Sales} = \frac{\text{fixed cost} + \text{profit goal}}{\text{contribution margin}} = \frac{\$20,000,000 + \$5,000,000}{0.256} = \$97,656,250$$

Again, note that the difference between the two break-even sales calculations is due to rounding.

As we saw previously, a profit goal can also be stated as a return on investment goal. For example, recall that Wise Domotics wants a 30% return on its $10 million investment. Thus, its absolute profit goal is $3 million ($10,000,000 × 0.30). This profit goal is treated the same way as in the previous example:[ii]

$$\text{Unit volume} = \frac{\text{fixed cost} + \text{profit goal}}{\text{price} - \text{variable cost}} = \frac{\$20,000,000 + \$3,000,000}{\$168 - \$125} = 534,884 \text{ units}$$

$$\text{Dollar sales} = 534,884 \text{ units} \times \$168 = \$89,860,512$$

Or

$$\text{Dollar sales} = \frac{\text{fixed cost} + \text{profit goal}}{\text{contribution margin}} = \frac{\$20,000,000 + \$3,000,000}{0.256} = \$89,843,750$$

Finally, Wise Domotics can express its profit goal as a percentage of sales, which we also saw in previous pricing analyses. Assume Wise Domotics desires a 25% return on sales. To determine the unit and sales volume necessary to achieve this goal, the calculation is a little different from the previous two examples. In this case, we incorporate the profit goal into the unit contribution as an additional variable cost. Look at it this way: If 25% of each sale must go toward profits, that leaves only 75% of the selling price to cover fixed costs. Thus, the equation becomes:

$$\text{Unit volume} = \frac{\text{fixed cost}}{\text{price} - \text{variable cost} - (0.25 \times \text{price})} \text{ or } \frac{\text{fixed cost}}{(0.75 \times \text{price}) - \text{variable cost}}$$

So,

$$\text{Unit volume} = \frac{\$20,000,000}{(0.75 \times \$168) - \$125} = 20,000,000 \text{ units}$$

$$\text{Dollar sales necessary} = 20,000,000 \text{ units} \times \$168 = \$3,360,000,000$$

Thus, Wise Domotics would need more than $3 billion in sales to realize a 25% return on sales given its current price and cost structure! Could it possibly achieve this level of sales? The major point is this: Although break-even analysis can be useful in determining the level of sales needed to cover costs or to achieve a stated profit goal, it does not tell the company whether it is *possible* to achieve that level of sales at the specified price. To address this issue, Wise Domotics needs to estimate demand for this product.

Before moving on, however, let's stop here and practice applying the concepts covered so far. Now that you have seen pricing and break-even concepts in action as they relate to Wise Domotics's new product, here are several exercises for you to apply what you have learned in other contexts.

Marketing by the Numbers Exercise Set One

Now that you've studied pricing, break-even, and margin analysis as they relate to Wise Domotics's new product launch, use the following exercises to apply these concepts in other contexts.

1.1 Lawn King, a manufacturer of riding lawn mowers, realizes a cost of $450 for every unit it produces. Its total fixed costs equal $6 million. If the company manufactures 1 million units, compute the following:
   a. unit cost
   b. markup price if the company desires a 30% return on sales
   c. ROI price if the company desires a 60% return on an investment of $2 million

1.2 A sporting goods retailer purchases items to sell in his store. He purchases a kayak for $250 and sells it for $625. Determine the following:
   a. dollar markup
   b. markup percentage on cost
   c. markup percentage on selling price

1.3 A consumer purchases a bicycle from a retailer for $150. The retailer's markup is 40% and the wholesaler's markup is 15%, both based on selling price. For what price does the manufacturer sell the product to the wholesaler?

1.4 A furniture manufacturer has a unit cost of $100 on an end table and wishes to achieve a margin of 60% based on selling price. If the manufacturer sells directly to a retailer who then adds a set margin of 50% based on selling price, determine the retail price charged to consumers.

1.5 Home Solutions manufactures internet-connected doorbells and sells them to intermediaries in the channel of distribution for $55. Each doorbell costs Home Solutions $15 to manufacture in addition to $550,000 in fixed costs. Calculate the following:
   a. contribution per unit and contribution margin percentage
   b. break-even volume in units and dollars
   c. unit volume and dollar sales necessary if Home Solution's profit goal is $3 million
   d. unit volume and dollar sales necessary if Home Solution's profit goal is 10% profit on sales

Demand Estimates, the Marketing Budget, and Marketing Performance Measures

Market Potential and Sales Estimates

Wise Domotics has now calculated the sales needed to break even and to attain various profit goals on its new product. However, the company needs more information regarding demand in order to assess the feasibility of attaining the needed sales levels. This information is also needed for production and other decisions. For example, production schedules need to be developed, and marketing tactics need to be planned.

The **total market demand** for a product or service is the total volume that would be bought by a defined consumer group in a defined geographic area in a defined time period in a defined marketing environment under a defined level and mix of industry marketing effort. Total market demand is not a fixed number but a function of the stated conditions. For example, next year's total market demand for this type of product will depend on how much other producers spend on marketing their brands. It also depends on many environmental factors, such as government regulations, economic conditions, and the level of consumer confidence in a given market. The upper limit of market demand is called **market potential**.

One general but practical method that Wise Domotics might use for estimating total market demand uses three variables: (1) the number of prospective buyers, (2) the quantity purchased by an average buyer per year, and (3) the price of an average unit. Using these numbers, Wise Domotics can estimate total market demand as follows:

$$Q = n \times q \times p$$

Total market demand

The total volume that would be bought by a defined consumer group in a defined geographic area in a defined time period in a defined marketing environment under a defined level and mix of industry marketing effort.

Market potential

The upper limit of market demand.

where

Q = total market demand
n = number of buyers in the market
q = quantity purchased by an average buyer per year
p = price of an average unit

Chain ratio method

Estimating market demand by multiplying a base number by a chain of adjusting percentages.

A variation of this approach is the **chain ratio method**. This method involves multiplying a base number by a chain of adjusting percentages. For example, Wise Domotics's product is designed to automate operation of multiple internet-connected smart devices in a home. Thus, only consumers who have broadband internet access and Wi-Fi in their homes will be able to use the product. Finally, not all Wi-Fi internet households will be willing and able to purchase this product. Wise Domotics can estimate U.S. demand using a chain of calculations like the following:

Total number of U.S. households

$\times$ The percentage of U.S. households with broadband internet
$\times$ The percentage of internet households with Wi-Fi
$\times$ The percentage of these households willing and able to buy this device

The U.S. Census Bureau estimates that there are approximately 120 million households in the United States, and other research indicates that 70 percent of U.S. households have broadband internet and 71 percent of those have Wi-Fi in their homes.[iii] Finally, the company's research also reveals that 35 percent of households possess the discretionary income needed and are willing to buy a product such as this. Then the total number of households willing and able to purchase this product is:

120 million households $\times$ 0.70 $\times$ 0.71 $\times$ 0.35 = 20.9 million households

Households need to purchase only one device to control all other smart devices throughout the household. Assuming the average retail price across all brands is $350 for this type of product, the estimate of total market demand is as follows:

20.9 million households $\times$ 1 device per household $\times$ $350 = $7,315,000,000

This simple chain of calculations gives Wise Domotics only a rough estimate of potential demand. However, more detailed chains involving additional segments and other qualifying factors would yield more accurate and refined estimates. Still, these are only *estimates* of market potential. They rely heavily on assumptions regarding adjusting percentages, average quantity, and average price. Thus, Wise Domotics must make certain that its assumptions are reasonable and defendable. As can be seen, the overall market potential in dollar sales can vary widely given the average price used. For this reason, Wise Domotics will use unit sales potential to determine its sales estimate for next year. Market potential in terms of units is 20.9 million (20.9 million households $\times$ 1 device per household).

Assuming that Wise Domotics forecasts it will have a 3.56% market share in the first year after launching this product, then it can forecast unit sales at 20.9 million units $\times$ 0.0356 = 744,040 units. At a selling price of $168 per unit, this translates into sales of $124,998,720 (744,040 units $\times$ $168 per unit). For simplicity, further analyses will use forecasted sales of $125 million.

This unit volume estimate is well within Wise Domotics's production capacity and exceeds not only the break-even estimate (465,117 units) calculated earlier but also the volume necessary to realize a $5 million profit (581,396 units) or a 30% return on investment (534,884 units). However, this forecast falls well short of the volume necessary to realize a 25% return on sales (20 million units!) and may require that Wise Domotics revise expectations.

To assess expected profits, we must now look at the budgeted expenses for launching this product. To do this, we will construct a pro forma profit-and-loss statement.

The Profit-and-Loss Statement and Marketing Budget

(Pro forma or projected) profit-and-loss statement (or income statement or operating statement)

A statement that shows projected revenues less budgeted expenses and estimates the projected net profit for an organization, product, or brand during a specific planning period, typically a year.

All marketing managers must account for the profit impact of their marketing strategies. A major tool for projecting such profit impact is a **pro forma** (or projected) **profit-and-loss statement** (also called an **income statement** or **operating statement**). A pro forma statement shows projected revenues less budgeted expenses and estimates the projected net profit for an organization, product, or brand during a specific planning period, typically a year. It includes direct product production costs, marketing expenses budgeted to attain a given

● **Table A2.1** | Pro Forma Profit-and-Loss Statement for the 12-Month Period Ended December 31, 2020

			Percent of Sales
Net Sales		$125,000,000	100%
Cost of Goods Sold		62,500,000	50%
Gross Margin		$ 62,500,000	50%
Marketing Expenses			
Sales expenses	$17,500,000		
Promotion expenses	15,000,000		
Freight	12,500,000	45,000,000	36%
General and Administrative Expenses			
Managerial salaries and expenses	$2,000,000		
Indirect overhead	3,000,000	5,000,000	4%
Net Profit before Income Tax		$12,500,000	10%

sales forecast, and overhead expenses assigned to the organization or product. A profit-and-loss statement typically consists of several major components (see ● **Table A2.1**):

- *Net sales*—gross sales revenue minus returns and allowances (for example, trade, cash, quantity, and promotion allowances). Wise Domotics's net sales for 2020 are estimated to be $125 million, as determined in the previous analysis.
- *Cost of goods sold*—(sometimes called *cost of sales*)—the actual cost of the merchandise sold by a manufacturer or reseller. It includes the cost of inventory, purchases, and other costs associated with making the goods. Wise Domotics's cost of goods sold is estimated to be 50% of net sales, or $62.5 million.
- *Gross margin (or gross profit)*—the difference between net sales and cost of goods sold. Wise Domotics's gross margin is estimated to be $62.5 million.
- *Operating expenses*—the expenses incurred while doing business. These include all other expenses beyond the cost of goods sold that are necessary to conduct business. Operating expenses can be presented in total or broken down in detail. Here, Wise Domotics's estimated operating expenses include *marketing expenses* and *general and administrative expenses*.

Marketing expenses include sales expenses, promotion expenses, and distribution expenses. The new product will be sold through Wise Domotics's sales force, so the company budgets $5 million for sales salaries. However, because sales representatives earn a 10% commission on sales, Wise Domotics must also add a variable component to sales expenses of $12.5 million (10% of $125 million net sales), for a total budgeted sales expense of $17.5 million. Wise Domotics sets its advertising and promotion to launch this product at $10 million. However, the company also budgets 4% of sales, or $5 million, for cooperative advertising allowances to retailers who promote Wise Domotics's new product in their advertising. Thus, the total budgeted advertising and promotion expenses are $15 million ($10 million for advertising plus $5 million in co-op allowances). Finally, Wise Domotics budgets 10% of net sales, or $12.5 million, for freight and delivery charges. In all, total marketing expenses are estimated to be $17.5 million + $15 million + $12.5 million = $45 million.

General and administrative expenses are estimated at $5 million, broken down into $2 million for managerial salaries and expenses for the marketing function and $3 million of indirect overhead allocated to this product by the corporate accountants (such as depreciation, interest, maintenance, and insurance). Total expenses for the year, then, are estimated to be $50 million ($45 million marketing expenses + $5 million in general and administrative expenses).

- *Net profit before taxes*—profit earned after all costs are deducted. Wise Domotics's estimated net profit before taxes is $12.5 million.

In all, as Table A2.1 shows, Wise Domotics expects to earn a profit on its new product of $12.5 million in 2020. Also note that the percentage of sales that each component of the profit-and-loss statement represents is given in the right-hand column. These percentages are determined by dividing the cost figure by net sales (that is, marketing expenses represent 36% of net sales determined by $45 million ÷ $125 million). As can be seen, Wise Domotics projects a net profit return on sales of 10% in the first year after launching this product.

Marketing Performance Measures

Profit-and-loss statement (or income statement or operating statement)

A statement that shows actual revenues less expenses and net profit for an organization, product, or brand during a specific planning period, typically a year.

Now let's fast-forward a year. Wise Domotics's product has been on the market for one year, and management wants to assess its sales and profit performance. One way to assess this performance is to compute performance ratios derived from Wise Domotics's **profit-and-loss statement** (or **income statement** or **operating statement**).

Whereas the pro forma profit-and-loss statement shows *projected* financial performance, the statement given in ● **Table A2.2** shows Wise Domotics's *actual* financial performance based on actual sales, cost of goods sold, and expenses during the past year. By comparing the profit-and-loss statement from one period to the next, Wise Domotics can gauge performance against goals, spot favorable or unfavorable trends, and take appropriate corrective action.

The profit-and-loss statement shows that Wise Domotics lost $1 million rather than making the $12.5 million profit projected in the pro forma statement. Why? One obvious reason is that net sales fell $25 million short of estimated sales. Lower sales translated into lower variable costs associated with marketing the product. However, both fixed costs and the cost of goods sold as a percentage of sales exceeded expectations. Hence, the product's contribution margin was 21% rather than the estimated 26%. That is, variable costs represented 79% of sales (55% for cost of goods sold, 10% for sales commissions, 10% for freight, and 4% for co-op allowances). Recall that contribution margin can be calculated by subtracting that fraction from one $(1 - 0.79 = 0.21)$. Total fixed costs were $22 million, $2 million more than estimated. Thus, the sales that Wise Domotics needed to break even given this cost structure can be calculated as:

$$\text{Break-even sales} = \frac{\text{fixed costs}}{\text{contribution margin}} = \frac{\$22,000,000}{0.21} = \$104,761,905$$

If Wise Domotics had achieved another $5 million in sales, it would have earned a profit.

● **Table A2.2** | Profit-and-Loss Statement for the 12-Month Period Ended December 31, 2020

			Percent of Sales
Net Sales		$100,000,000	100%
Cost of Goods Sold		55,000,000	55%
Gross Margin		$ 45,000,000	45%
Marketing Expenses			
Sales expenses	$15,000,000		
Promotion expenses	14,000,000		
Freight	10,000,000	39,000,000	39%
General and Administrative Expenses			
Managerial salaries and expenses	$2,000,000		
Indirect overhead	5,000,000	7,000,000	7%
Net Profit before Income Tax		−$1,000,000	−1%

Market share

Company sales divided by market sales.

Although Wise Domotics's sales fell short of the forecasted sales, so did overall industry sales for this product. Overall industry sales were only $2.5 billion. That means that Wise Domotics's **market share** was 4% ($100 million ÷ $2.5 billion = 0.04 = 4%), which was higher than forecasted. Thus, Wise Domotics attained a higher-than-expected market share, but the overall market sales were not as high as estimated.

Analytic Ratios

Operating ratios

The ratios of selected operating statement items to net sales.

The profit-and-loss statement provides the figures needed to compute some crucial **operating ratios**—the ratios of selected operating statement items to net sales. These ratios let marketers compare the firm's performance in one year to that in previous years (or with industry standards and competitors' performance in that year). The most commonly used operating ratios are the gross margin percentage, the net profit percentage, and the operating expense percentage. The inventory turnover rate and return on investment (ROI) are often used to measure managerial effectiveness and efficiency.

Gross margin percentage

The percentage of net sales remaining after cost of goods sold—calculated by dividing gross margin by net sales.

The **gross margin percentage** indicates the percentage of net sales remaining after cost of goods sold that can contribute to operating expenses and net profit before taxes. The higher this ratio, the more a firm has left to cover expenses and generate profit. Wise Domotics's gross margin ratio was 45%:

$$\text{Gross margin percentage} = \frac{\text{gross margin}}{\text{net sales}} = \frac{\$45,000,000}{\$100,000,000} = 0.45 = 45\%$$

Note that this percentage is lower than estimated, and this ratio is seen easily in the percentage of sales column in Table A2.2. Stating items in the profit-and-loss statement as a percent of sales allows managers to quickly spot abnormal changes in costs over time. If there was previous history for this product and this ratio was declining, management should examine it more closely to determine why it has decreased (that is, because of a decrease in sales volume or price, an increase in costs, or a combination of these). In Wise Domotics's case, net sales were $25 million lower than estimated, and cost of goods sold was higher than estimated (55% rather than the estimated 50%).

Net profit percentage

The percentage of each sales dollar going to profit—calculated by dividing net profits by net sales.

The **net profit percentage** shows the percentage of each sales dollar going to profit. It is calculated by dividing net profits by net sales:

$$\text{Net profit percentage} = \frac{\text{net profit}}{\text{net sales}} = \frac{-\$1,000,000}{\$100,000,000} = -0.01 = -1.0\%$$

This ratio is easily seen in the percent of sales column. Wise Domotics's new product generated negative profits in the first year, not a good situation given that before the product launch net profits before taxes were estimated at more than $12 million. Later in this appendix, we will discuss further analyses the marketing manager should conduct to defend the product.

Operating expense percentage

The portion of net sales going to operating expenses—calculated by dividing total expenses by net sales.

The **operating expense percentage** indicates the portion of net sales going to operating expenses. Operating expenses include marketing and other expenses not directly related to marketing the product, such as indirect overhead assigned to this product. It is calculated by:

$$\text{Operating expense percentage} = \frac{\text{total expenses}}{\text{net sales}} = \frac{\$46,000,000}{\$100,000,000} = 0.46 = 46\%$$

This ratio can also be quickly determined from the percent of sales column in the profit-and-loss statement by adding the percentages for marketing expenses and general and administrative expenses (39% + 7%). Thus, 46 cents of every sales dollar went for operations. Although Wise Domotics wants this ratio to be as low as possible and 46% is not an alarming amount, it is of concern if it is increasing over time or if a loss is realized.

Inventory turnover rate (or stock-turn rate)

The number of times an inventory turns over or is sold during a specified time period (often one year)—calculated based on costs, selling price, or units.

Another useful ratio is the **inventory turnover rate** (also called **stockturn rate** for resellers). The inventory turnover rate is the number of times an inventory turns over or is sold during a specified time period (often one year). This rate tells how quickly a business is moving inventory through the organization. Higher rates indicate that lower investments in inventory are made, thus freeing up funds for other investments. It may be computed on a cost, selling price, or unit basis. The formula based on cost is:

$$\text{Inventory turnover rate} = \frac{\text{cost of goods sold}}{\text{average inventory at cost}}$$

Assuming Wise Domotics's beginning and ending inventories were $30 million and $20 million, respectively, the inventory turnover rate is:

$$\text{Inventory turnover rate} = \frac{\$55,000,000}{(\$30,000,000 + \$20,000,000)/2} = \frac{\$55,000,000}{\$25,000,000} = 2.2$$

That is, Wise Domotics's inventory turned over 2.2 times in 2020. Normally, the higher the turnover rate, the higher the management efficiency and company profitability. However, this rate should be compared with industry averages, competitors' rates, and past performance to determine if Wise Domotics is doing well. A competitor with similar sales but a higher inventory turnover rate will have fewer resources tied up in inventory, allowing it to invest in other areas of the business.

Return on investment (ROI)
A measure of managerial effectiveness and efficiency—net profit before taxes divided by total investment.

Companies frequently use **return on investment (ROI)** to measure managerial effectiveness and efficiency. For Wise Demotics, ROI is the ratio of net profits to total investment required to manufacture the new product. This investment includes capital investments in land, buildings, and equipment (here, the initial $10 million to refurbish the manufacturing facility) plus inventory costs (Wise Domotics's average inventory totaled $25 million), for a total of $35 million. Thus, Wise Domotics's ROI for this product is:

$$\text{Return on investment} = \frac{\text{net profit before taxes}}{\text{investment}} = \frac{-\$1,000,000}{\$35,000,000} = -.0286 = -2.86\%$$

ROI is often used to compare alternatives, and a positive ROI is desired. The alternative with the highest ROI is preferred to other alternatives. Wise Domotics needs to be concerned with the ROI realized. One obvious way Wise Domotics can increase ROI is to increase net profit by reducing expenses. Another way is to reduce its investment, perhaps by investing less in inventory and turning it over more frequently.

Marketing Profitability Metrics

Given the preceding financial results, you may be thinking that Wise Domotics should drop this new product. But what arguments can marketers make for keeping or dropping this product? The obvious arguments for dropping the product are that first-year sales were well below expected levels and the product lost money, resulting in a negative return on investment.

So what would happen if Wise Domotics did drop this product? Surprisingly, if the company drops the product, the profits for the total organization will decrease by $4 million! How can that be? Marketing managers need to look closely at the numbers in the profit-and-loss statement to determine the *net marketing contribution* for this product. In Wise Domotics's case, the net marketing contribution for the product is $4 million, and if the company drops this product, that contribution will disappear as well. Let's look more closely at this concept to illustrate how marketing managers can better assess and defend their marketing strategies and programs.

Net Marketing Contribution

Net marketing contribution (NMC)
A measure of marketing profitability that includes only components of profitability controlled by marketing.

Net marketing contribution (NMC), along with other marketing metrics derived from it, measures *marketing* profitability. It includes only components of profitability that are controlled by marketing. Whereas the previous calculation of net profit before taxes from the profit-and-loss statement includes operating expenses not under marketing's control, NMC does not. Referring back to Wise Domotics's profit-and-loss statement given in Table A2.2, we can calculate net marketing contribution for the product as:

$$\text{NMC} = \text{net sales} - \text{cost of goods sold} - \text{marketing expenses}$$

$$= \$100 \text{ million} - \$55 \text{ million} - \$41 \text{ million} = \$4 \text{ million}$$

The marketing expenses include sales expenses ($15 million), promotion expenses ($14 million), freight expenses ($10 million), and the managerial salaries and expenses of the marketing function ($2 million), which total $41 million.

Thus, the product actually contributed $4 million to Wise Domotics's profits. It was the $5 million of indirect overhead allocated to this product that caused the negative profit. Further, the amount allocated was $2 million more than estimated in the pro forma profit-and-loss statement. Indeed, if only the estimated amount had been allocated, the product would have earned a *profit* of $1 million rather than losing $1 million. If Wise Domotics drops the product, the $5 million in fixed overhead expense will not disappear—it will simply have to be allocated elsewhere. However, the $4 million in net marketing contribution *will* disappear.

Marketing Return on Sales and Investment

To get an even deeper understanding of the profit impact of marketing strategy, we'll now examine two measures of marketing efficiency—*marketing return on sales* (marketing ROS) and *marketing return on investment* (marketing ROI).[iv]

Marketing return on sales (or **marketing ROS**) shows the percent of net sales attributable to the net marketing contribution. For our product, ROS is:

Marketing return on sales (or marketing ROS)

The percent of net sales attributable to the net marketing contribution—calculated by dividing net marketing contribution by net sales.

$$\text{Marketing ROS} = \frac{\text{net marketing contribution}}{\text{net sales}} = \frac{\$4,000,000}{\$100,000,000} = 0.04 = 4\%$$

Thus, out of every $100 of sales, the product returns $4 to Wise Domotics's bottom line. A high marketing ROS is desirable. But to assess whether this is a good level of performance, Wise Domotics must compare this figure to previous marketing ROS levels for the product, the ROSs of other products in the company's portfolio, and the ROSs of competing products.

Marketing return on investment (or **marketing ROI**) measures the marketing productivity of a marketing investment. In Wise Domotics's case, the marketing investment is represented by $41 million of the total expenses. Thus, marketing ROI is:

Marketing return on investment (or marketing ROI)

A measure of the marketing productivity of a marketing investment—calculated by dividing net marketing contribution by marketing expenses.

$$\text{Marketing ROI} = \frac{\text{net marketing contribution}}{\text{marketing expenses}} = \frac{\$4,000,000}{\$41,000,000} = 0.0976 = 9.76\%$$

As with marketing ROS, a high value is desirable, but this figure should be compared with previous levels for the given product and with the marketing ROIs of competitors' products. Note from this equation that marketing ROI could be greater than 100%. This can be achieved by attaining a higher net marketing contribution and/or a lower total marketing expense.

In this section, we estimated market potential and sales, developed profit-and-loss statements, and examined financial measures of performance. In the next section, we discuss methods for analyzing the impact of various marketing tactics. However, before moving on to those analyses, here's another set of quantitative exercises to help you apply what you've learned to other situations.

Marketing by the Numbers Exercise Set Two

2.1 Determine the market potential for a product that has 10 million prospective buyers who purchase an average of five per year and price averages $5.

2.2 Develop a profit-and-loss statement for a company that had $50 million in net sales last year. Cost of goods sold represents 45% of net sales. Marketing expenses include selling expenses, promotion expenses, and freight. Selling expenses include sales salaries totaling $2 million per year and sales commissions (10% of sales). The company spent $2 million on advertising last year, and freight costs were 5% of sales. Other costs include $500,000 for managerial salaries and expenses for the marketing function and another $2 million for indirect overhead allocated to the division.

2.3 Using the profit-and-loss statement you developed in question 2.2 and assuming that the company's beginning inventory was $15 million, ending inventory was $6 million, and total investment was $30 million including inventory, determine the following:
a. gross margin percentage
b. net profit percentage
c. operating expense percentage
d. inventory turnover rate
e. return on investment (ROI)
f. net marketing contribution
g. marketing return on sales (marketing ROS)
h. marketing return on investment (marketing ROI)
i. Is the company doing well? Explain your answer.

Financial Analysis of Marketing Tactics

Although the first-year profit performance for Wise Domotics's new product was less than desired, management feels that this attractive market has excellent growth opportunities. Although the sales of Wise Domotics's product were lower than initially projected, they were not unreasonable given the size of the current market. Thus, Wise Domotics wants to explore new marketing tactics to help grow the market for this product and increase sales for the company.

For example, the company could increase advertising to promote more awareness of the new product and its category. It could add salespeople to secure greater product distribution. Wise Domotics could decrease prices so that more consumers could afford its product. Finally, to expand the market, Wise Domotics could introduce a lower-priced model in addition to the higher-priced original offering. Before pursuing any of these tactics, Wise Domotics must analyze the financial implications of each.

Increase Advertising Expenditures

Wise Domotics is considering boosting its advertising to make more people aware of the benefits of this device in general and of its own brand in particular. What if Wise Domotics's marketers recommend increasing national advertising by 50% to $15 million (assume no change in the variable cooperative component of promotional expenditures)? This represents an increase in fixed costs of $5 million. What increase in sales will be needed to break even on this $5 million increase in fixed costs?

A quick way to answer this question is to divide the increase in fixed cost by the contribution margin, which we found in a previous analysis to be 21%:

$$\text{Increase in sales} = \frac{\text{increase in fixed cost}}{\text{contribution margin}} = \frac{\$5,000,000}{0.21} = \$23,809,524$$

Thus, a 50% increase in advertising expenditures must produce a sales increase of almost $24 million to just break even. That $24 million sales increase translates into an almost 1 percentage point increase in market share (1% of the $2.5 billion overall market equals $25 million). That is, to break even on the increased advertising expenditure, Wise Domotics would have to increase its market share from 4% to 4.95% ($123,809,524 ÷ $2.5 billion = 0.0495, or 4.95% market share). All of this assumes that the total market will not grow, which might or might not be a reasonable assumption.

Increase Distribution Coverage

Wise Domotics also wants to consider hiring more salespeople in order to call on new retailer accounts and increase distribution through more outlets. Even though Wise Domotics sells directly to wholesalers, its sales representatives call on retail accounts to perform other functions in addition to selling, such as training retail salespeople. Currently, Wise Domotics employs 70 sales reps who earn an average of $60,000 in salary plus 10% commission on sales. The product is currently sold to consumers through 1,875 retail outlets. Suppose Wise Domotics wants to increase that number of outlets to 2,500, an increase of 625 retail outlets. How many additional salespeople will Wise Domotics need, and what sales will be necessary to break even on the increased cost?

One method for determining what size sales force Wise Domotics will need is the **workload method**. The workload method uses the following formula to determine the salesforce size:

Workload method
An approach to determining sales force size based on the workload required and the time available for selling.

$$NS = \frac{NC \times FC \times LC}{TA}$$

where

NS = number of salespeople
NC = number of customers
FC = average frequency of customer calls per customer
LC = average length of customer call
TA = time an average salesperson has available for selling per year

Wise Domotics's sales reps typically call on accounts an average of 20 times per year for about two hours per call. Although sales reps work 2,000 hours per year (50 weeks per year × 40 hours per week), they spent about 15 hours per week on nonselling activities such as administrative duties and travel. Thus, the average annual available selling time per sales rep per year is 1,250 hours (50 weeks × 25 hours per week). We can now calculate how many sales reps Wise Domotics will need to cover the anticipated 2,500 retail outlets:

$$NS = \frac{2,500 \times 20 \times 2}{1,250} = 80 \text{ sales people}$$

Therefore, Wise Domotics will need to hire 10 more salespeople. The cost to hire these reps will be $600,000 (10 salespeople × $60,000 salary per salesperson).

What increase in sales will be required to break even on this increase in fixed costs? The 10% commission is already accounted for in the contribution margin, so the contribution margin remains unchanged at 21%. Thus, the increase in sales needed to cover this increase in fixed costs can be calculated by:

$$\text{Increase in sales} = \frac{\text{increase in fixed cost}}{\text{contribution margin}} = \frac{\$600,000}{0.21} = \$2,857,142$$

That is, Wise Domotics's sales must increase by almost $3 million to break even on this tactic. So, how many new retail outlets will the company need to secure to achieve this sales increase? The average revenue generated per current outlet is $53,333 ($100 million in sales divided by 1,875 outlets). Wise Domotics would need about 54 new outlets to break even on this tactic ($2,857,142 ÷ $53,333 = 53.6 outlets), or about 5 or 6 outlets per new rep. Given that current reps cover about 27 outlets apiece (1,875 outlets ÷ 70 reps), it seems very reasonable that Wise Domotics can break even on this tactic.

Decrease Price

Wise Domotics is also considering lowering its price to increase sales revenue through increased volume. The company's research has shown that demand for most types of consumer electronics products is elastic—that is, the percentage increase in the quantity demanded is greater than the percentage decrease in price.

What increase in sales would be necessary to break even on a 10% decrease in price? That is, what increase in sales will be needed to maintain the total contribution that Wise Domotics realized at the higher price? The current total contribution can be determined by multiplying the contribution margin by total sales:[v]

$$\text{Current total contribution} = \text{contribution margin} \times \text{sales} = 0.21 \times \$100 \text{ million}$$
$$= \$21 \text{ million}$$

Price changes result in changes in unit contribution and contribution margin. Recall that the contribution margin of 21% was based on variable costs representing 79% of sales. Therefore, unit variable costs can be determined by multiplying the original price by this percentage: $168 × 0.79 = $132.72 per unit. If price is decreased by 10%, the new price is $151.20. However, variable costs do not change just because price decreased, so the contribution and contribution margin decrease as follows:

	Old	**New (Reduced 10%)**
Price	$168	$151.20
− Unit variable cost	$132.72	$132.72
= Unit contribution	$35.28	$18.48
Contribution margin	$35.28/$168 = 0.21 or 21%	$18.48/$151.20 = 0.12 or 12%

So a 10% reduction in price results in a decrease in the contribution margin from 21% to 12%. Oftentimes, we may not be conducting this analysis on the unit level. Recall that the contribution margin of 21% was based on variable costs representing 79% of sales.

Therefore, if we do not know unit price, we can set it equal to $1.00. If price equals $1.00, 79 cents represents variable costs and 21 cents represents unit contribution. If price is decreased by 10%, the new price is 90 cents. However, variable costs do not change just because price decreased, so the unit contribution and contribution margin decrease as follows:

	Old	**New (Reduced 10%)**
Price	$1.00	$0.90
−Unit variable cost	$0.79	$0.79
=Unit contribution	$0.21	$0.11
Contribution margin	$0.21/$1.00 = 0.21 or 21%	$0.11/$0.90 = 0.12 or 12%

Notice that the new contribution margin (12%) is the same as found when working from the actual unit price.

To determine the sales level needed to break even on this price reduction, we calculate the level of sales that must be attained at the new contribution margin to achieve the original total contribution of $21 million:

$$\text{New contribution margin} \times \text{new sales level} = \text{original total contribution}$$

So,

$$\text{New sales level} = \frac{\text{original contribution}}{\text{new contribution margin}} = \frac{\$21{,}000{,}000}{0.12} = \$175{,}000{,}000$$

Thus, sales must increase by $75 million ($175 million − $100 million) just to break even on a 10% price reduction. This means that Wise Domotics must increase market share to 7% ($175 million ÷ $2.5 billion) to achieve the current level of profits (assuming no increase in the total market sales). The marketing manager must assess whether or not this is a reasonable goal.

Extend the Product Line

Cannibalization

The situation in which one product sold by a company takes a portion of its sales from other company products.

As a final option, Wise Domotics is considering extending its product line by offering a lower-priced model. Of course, the new, lower-priced product would steal some sales from the higher-priced model. This is called **cannibalization**—the situation in which one product sold by a company takes a portion of its sales from other company products. If the new product has a lower contribution than the original product, the company's total contribution will decrease on the cannibalized sales. However, if the new product can generate enough new volume, it is worth considering.

To assess cannibalization, Wise Domotics must look at the incremental contribution gained by having both products available. Recall that in the previous analysis we determined that unit variable costs were $132.72 and unit contribution was just over $35. Assuming costs remain the same next year, Wise Domotics can expect to realize a contribution per unit of approximately $35 for every unit of the original product sold.

Assume that the first model offered by Wise Domotics is called Wise Domotics1 and the new, lower-priced model is called Wise Domotics2. Wise Domotics2 will retail for $250, and resellers will take the same markup percentages on price as they do with the higher-priced model. Therefore, Wise Domotics2's price to wholesalers will be $140 as follows:

Retail price:	$250
minus retail margin (30%):	−$ 75
Retailer's cost/wholesaler's price:	$175
minus wholesaler's margin (20%):	−$ 35
Wholesaler's cost/Wise Domotics's price	$140

If Wise Domotics2's variable costs are estimated to be $120, then its contribution per unit will equal $20 ($140 − $120 = $20). That means for every unit that Wise Domotics2 cannibalizes from Wise Domotics1, Wise Domotics will *lose* $15 in contribution toward fixed costs and profit (that is, contribution$_{\text{Wise Domotics2}}$ − contribution$_{\text{Wise Domotics1}}$ = $20 − $35 = −$15). You might conclude that Wise Domotics should not pursue this tactic because it appears as though the company will be worse off if it introduces the lower-priced model. However, if Wise Domotics2 captures enough *additional* sales, Wise Domotics will be better off even though some Wise Domotics1 sales are cannibalized. The company must examine what will happen to *total* contribution, which requires estimates of unit volume for both products.

Originally, Wise Domotics estimated that next year's sales of Wise Domotics1 would be 600,000 units. However, with the introduction of Wise Domotics2, it now estimates that 200,000 of those sales will be cannibalized by the new model. If Wise Domotics sells only 200,000 units of the new Wise Domotics2 model (all cannibalized from Wise Domotics1), the company would lose $3 million in total contribution (200,000 units × −$15 per cannibalized unit = −$3 million)—not a good outcome. However, Wise Domotics estimates that Wise Domotics2 will generate the 200,000 of cannibalized sales plus an *additional* 500,000 unit sales. Thus, the contribution on these additional Wise Domotics2 units will be $10 million (i.e., 500,000 units × $20 per unit = $10 million). The net effect is that Wise Domotics will gain $7 million in total contribution by introducing Wise Domotics2.

The following table compares Wise Demotics' total contribution with and without the introduction of Wise Domotics2:

	Wise Domotics1 only	Wise Domotics1 and Wise Domotics2
Wise Domotics1 contribution	600,000 units × $35 =$21,000,000	400,000 units × $35 =$14,000,000
Wise Domotics2 contribution	0	700,000 units × $20 =$14,000,000
Total contribution	$21,000,000	$28,000,000

The difference in the total contribution is a net gain of $7 million ($28 million − $21 million). Based on this analysis, Wise Domotics should introduce the Wise Domotics2 model because it results in a positive incremental contribution. However, if fixed costs will increase by more than $7 million as a result of adding this model, then the net effect will be negative and Wise Domotics should not pursue this tactic.

Now that you have seen these marketing tactic analysis concepts in action as they relate to Wise Domotics's new product, here are several exercises for you to apply what you have learned in this section in other contexts.

Marketing by the Numbers Exercise Set Three

3.1 Synegys, Inc. manufactures accent lighting that is sold to consumers through retail outlets in the southern United States. The company's sales are $1 million and contribution margin is 30%. The company is considering options to increase sales.

  a. The marketing manager has suggested increasing consumer advertising by $50,000. By how much would dollar sales need to increase to break even on this expenditure? What percentage increase in sales does this represent?

  b. Another suggestion is to make a 5% across-the-board price reduction. By how much would dollar sales need to increase to maintain Synegys's current contribution? What percentage increase in sales does this represent?

3.2 A company currently has 2,000 industrial customer accounts and wants to expand to another geographic market to acquire 3,000 more. It currently has 10 sales representatives who earn $60,000 per year and 5% commission on sales. Each customer account is visited six times per year, and sales reps spend an hour and a half on each call (that is, 1.5 hours). An average salesperson works 2,000 hours per year (50 weeks per year × 40 hours per week), but each will spend 10 hours a week on nonselling activities, such as administrative tasks and travel. The company's contribution margin is 40%, and each customer generates an average $50,000 in sales for the company.

a. How many salespeople will the company need to hire?
b. What increase in sales is needed to cover the increased cost of an additional sales representative? How much must sales increase to break even on the number of sales representatives the company needs to hire?
c. How many customers must the company acquire to break even on this tactic?

3.3 BriteSmile brand of teeth whitening products is considering adding a modified version of the product—a gel product in addition to its regular paste product. Variable costs and prices to wholesalers are:

	Current paste product	**New gel product**
Unit selling price	$4.00	$4.50
Unit variable costs	$1.70	$2.50

BriteSmile expects to sell 1 million units of the new gel product in the first year after introduction, but it estimates that only 45% of those sales will come from buyers who do not already purchase the company's paste product (that is, new customers). BriteSmile estimates that it would sell 1.5 million units of the current paste product if it did not introduce the gel. If the fixed costs of launching the new gel product will be $250,000 during the first year, should BriteSmile add the new gel product to its line? Why or why not?

Careers in Marketing

You may have decided you want to pursue a marketing career because it offers constant challenge, stimulating problems, the opportunity to work with people, and excellent advancement opportunities. But you still may not know which part of marketing best suits you—marketing is a very broad field offering a wide variety of career options.

This appendix helps you discover what types of marketing jobs best match your special skills and interests, shows you how to conduct the kind of job search that will get you the position you want, describes marketing career paths open to you, and suggests other information resources.

Marketing Careers Today

The marketing field is booming, with nearly a third of all working Americans now employed in marketing-related positions. Marketing salaries may vary by company, position, and region, and salary figures change constantly. In general, entry-level marketing salaries usually are only slightly below those for engineering and chemistry but equal or exceed starting salaries in economics, finance, accounting, general business, and the liberal arts. Moreover, if you succeed in an entry-level marketing position, it's likely that you will be promoted quickly to higher levels of responsibility and salary. In addition, because of the consumer and product knowledge you will gain in these jobs, marketing positions provide excellent training for the highest levels in an organization.

Overall Marketing Facts and Trends

In conducting your job search, consider the following facts and trends that are changing the world of marketing:

Focus on customers. More and more, companies are realizing that they win in the marketplace only engaging customers and creating superior value for them. To capture value from customers, they must first find new and better ways to engage customers, solve customer problems, and improve customer brand experiences. This increasing focus on the customer puts marketers at the forefront in many of today's companies. As the primary customer-facing function, marketing's mission is to get all company departments to "think customer."

Technology. Technology is changing the way marketers work. For example, internet, social media, mobile, and other digital technologies are rapidly changing the ways marketers interact with and serve customers. They are also changing everything from the ways marketers create new products and advertise them to how marketers access information and recruit personnel. Whereas advertising firms have traditionally recruited "generalists" in account management, *generalist* has now taken on a whole new meaning—advertising account executives must now have both broad and specialized knowledge.

Diversity. The number of women and minorities in marketing continues to grow, and women and minorities also are advancing rapidly into marketing management. For example, women now outnumber men as advertising account executives. As marketing becomes more global, the need for diversity in marketing positions will continue to increase, opening new opportunities.

Global. Companies such as Coca-Cola, McDonald's, Google, Walmart, IBM, Facebook, and P&G have become multinational with manufacturing and marketing operations in hundreds of countries. Indeed, such companies often make more profit from sales outside the United States than from within. And it's not just the big companies that are involved in international marketing. Organizations of all sizes have moved into the global arena. Many new marketing opportunities and careers will be directly linked to the expanding global marketplace. The globalization of business also means that you will need more cultural, language, and people skills in the marketing world of the twenty-first century.

Not-for-profit organizations. Increasingly, colleges, arts organizations, libraries, hospitals, and other not-for-profit organizations are recognizing the need for effectively marketing their "products" and services to various publics. This awareness has led to new marketing positions—with these organizations hiring their own marketing directors and marketing vice presidents or using outside marketing specialists.

Looking for a Job in Today's Marketing World

To choose and find the right job, you will need to apply the marketing skills you've learned in this course, especially marketing analysis and planning. Follow these eight steps for marketing yourself: (1) Conduct a self-assessment and seek career counseling; (2) examine job descriptions; (3) explore the job market, follow up, and assess opportunities; (4) develop search strategies; (5) prepare résumés; (6) write a cover letter and assemble supporting documents; (7) interview for jobs; and (8) take a follow-up interview.

Conduct a Self-Assessment and Seek Career Counseling

If you're having difficulty deciding what kind of marketing position is the best fit for you, start out by doing some self-testing or seeking career counseling. Self-assessments require that you honestly and thoroughly evaluate your interests, strengths, and weaknesses. What do you do well (your best and favorite skills) and not so well? What are your favorite interests? What are your career goals? What makes you stand out from other job seekers?

The answers to such questions may suggest which marketing careers you should seek or avoid. For help in completing an effective self-assessment, look for the following books in your local bookstore or online: Nicholas Lore, *The Pathfinder: How to Choose or Change Your Career for a Lifetime of Satisfaction and Success* (Touchstone, 2012) and Richard Bolles, *What Color Is Your Parachute? 2019* (Ten Speed Press, 2018; also see www.eparachute.com). Many online sites also offer self-assessment tools, such as the Keirsey Temperament Theory and the Temperament Sorter, a free but broad assessment available at Keirsey.com. For a more specific evaluation, CareerLeader.com offers a complete online business career self-assessment program designed by the Directors of MBA Career Development at Harvard Business School. You can use this for a fee.

For help in finding a career counselor to guide you in making a career assessment, Richard Bolles's *What Color Is Your Parachute? 2019* contains a useful state-by-state sampling. CareerLeader.com also offers personal career counseling. (Some counselors can help you in your actual job search, too.) You can also consult the career counseling, testing, and placement services at your college or university.

Examine Job Descriptions

After you have identified your skills, interests, and desires, you need to see which marketing positions are the best match for them. Two U.S. Labor Department publications available in your local library or online—the *Occupation Outlook Handbook* (www.bls.gov/ooh) and the *Dictionary of Occupational Titles* (www.occupationalinfo.org)—describe the duties involved in various occupations, the specific training and education needed, the availability of jobs in each field, possibilities for advancement, and probable earnings.

Your initial career shopping list should be broad and flexible. Look for different ways to achieve your objectives. For example, if you want a career in marketing management, consider the public as well as the private sector and local and regional as well as national and international firms. Be open initially to exploring many options, and then focus on specific industries and jobs, listing your basic goals as a way to guide your choices. Your list might include "a job in a startup company, near a big city on the West Coast, doing new product planning with a computer software firm."

Explore the Job Market and Assess Opportunities

At this stage, you need to look at the market and see what positions are actually available. You do not have to do this alone. Any of the following may assist you.

Career Development Centers

Your college's career development center and its website are excellent places to start. For example, the websites of the undergraduate career services center provide lists of career links that can help to focus your job search. Most schools also provide career coaches and career education courses. Also check the National Association of Colleges and Employers website (www.naceweb.org). It publishes a national forecast of hiring intentions of employers as they relate to new college graduates (search: "Job Outlook").

In addition, find out everything you can about the companies that interest you by consulting company websites, business magazine articles and online sites, annual reports, business reference books, faculty, career counselors, and others. Try to analyze the industry's and the company's future growth and profit potential, advancement opportunities, salary levels, entry positions, travel time, and other factors of significance to you.

Job Fairs

Career development centers often work with corporate recruiters to organize on-campus job fairs. You might also use the internet to check on upcoming career fairs in your region. For example, visit National Career Fairs at www.nationalcareerfairs.com or Choice Career Fairs listings at https://choicecareerfairs.com.

Networking

Networking—asking for job leads from friends, family, people in your community, and career centers—is one of the best ways to find a marketing job. Studies estimate that 60 to 90 percent of jobs are found through networking. The idea is to spread your net wide, contacting anybody and everybody.

Internships

An internship is filled with many benefits, such as gaining experience in a specific field of interest and building up a network of contacts. The biggest benefit: the potential of being offered a job shortly before or soon after graduation. According to a recent survey by the National Association of Colleges and Employers, employers converted more than 45 percent of last year's interns into full-time hires. In addition, 62 percent of the seniors who had paid internship experience and applied for a job received at least one job offer. Conversely, only 43 percent of seniors without internship experience who applied for a job received an offer. In addition, survey results show that the median accepted salary offer for seniors with a paid internship was 27 percent higher than the median accepted salary offered to non-intern seniors.

Many company internet sites have separate internship areas. For example, check out Internships.com, InternshipPrograms.com, CampusCareerCenter.com, InternJobs.com, and GoAbroad.com (www.goabroad.com/intern-abroad). If you know of a company for which you wish to work, go to that company's corporate website, enter the human resources area, and check for internships. If none are listed, try emailing the human resources department, asking if internships are offered.

Job Hunting on the Internet

A constantly increasing number of sites on the internet deal with job hunting. You can also use the internet to make contacts with people who can help you gain information on and research companies that interest you. CareerBuilder, Indeed, Monster, and ZipRecruiter are good general sites for seeking job listings. Other helpful sites are Disability.gov and Diversity.com, which contain information on opportunities for individuals with disabilities and minorities, respectively.

Most companies have their own online sites on which they post job listings. This may be helpful if you have a specific and fairly limited number of companies that you are keeping your eye on for job opportunities. But if this is not the case, remember that to find out what interesting marketing jobs the companies themselves are posting, you may have to visit hundreds of corporate sites.

Professional Networking Sites

Many companies have now begun to take advantage of social networking sites to find talented applicants. From LinkedIn to Facebook to Google+, social networking has become professional networking. For example, companies ranging from P&G to BASF have jobs pages on LinkedIn (www.linkedin.com/company/procter-and-gamble/jobs/and www.linkedin.com/company/basf/jobs/) to find potential candidates for entry-level positions. And professional organizations, such as the Public Relations Society of America and the American Advertising Federation, have job listings on their websites. For job seekers, online professional networking offers more efficient job targeting and reduces associated costs as compared with traditional interaction methods such as traveling to job fairs and interviews, printing résumés, and other expenses.

However, although the internet offers a wealth of resources for searching for the perfect job, be aware that it's a two-way street. Just as job seekers can search the internet to find job opportunities, employers can search for information on job candidates. Jobs searches can sometimes be derailed by information mined by potential employers from online social networking sites that reveals unintended or embarrassing anecdotes and photos. Internet searches can sometimes also reveal inconsistencies and résumé inflation. A recent study found that more than half of recruiters surveyed have reconsidered a candidate based on their social profile.

Develop Search Strategies

Once you've decided which companies you are interested in, you need to contact them. One of the best ways is through on-campus interviews. However, not every company you are interested in will visit your school. In such instances, you can write, email, or phone the company directly or ask marketing professors or school alumni for contacts.

Prepare Résumés

A résumé is a concise yet comprehensive written summary of your qualifications, including your academic, personal, and professional achievements, that showcases why you are the best candidate for the job. Because an employer will spend on average only 15 to 20 seconds reviewing your résumé, you want to be sure that you prepare a good one.

In preparing your résumé, remember that all information on it must be accurate and complete. Résumés typically begin with the applicant's full name, telephone number, and mail and email addresses. A simple and direct statement of career objectives generally appears next, followed by work history and academic data (including awards and internships) and then by personal activities and experiences applicable to the job sought.

The résumé sometimes ends with a list of references the employer may contact (at other times, references may be listed separately). If your work or internship experience is limited, nonexistent, or irrelevant, then it is a good idea to emphasize your academic and nonacademic achievements, showing skills related to those required for excellent job performance.

There are three main types of résumés. Reverse *chronological* résumés, which emphasize career growth, are organized in reverse chronological order, starting with your most recent job. They focus on job titles within organizations, describing the responsibilities and accomplishments for each job. *Functional* résumés focus less on job titles and work history and more on assets and achievements. This format works best if your job history is scanty or discontinuous. *Mixed,* or *combination,* résumés take from each of the other two formats. First, the skills used for a specific job are listed, and then the job title is stated. This format works best for applicants whose past jobs are in other fields or seemingly unrelated to the position. For further explanation and examples of these types of résumés, see the Which Résumé Format to Use page at www.zipjob.com/blog/resume-format-types/.

Many books can assist you in developing your résumé. A popular guide is Dan Clay, *How to Write the Perfect Resume* (Dan Clay, 2018). Websites such as MyPerfectResume (www.myperfectresume.com) provide sample résumés and ready-to-use phrases while guiding you through the résumé preparation process. CareerOneStop (www.careeronestop.org/resumeguide/introduction.aspx) offers a step-by-step résumé tutorial, and Monster (www.

monster.com/career-advice) offers résumé advice and writing services. Finally, you can even create your own personalized online résumé at sites such as optimalresume.com.

Online Résumés

The internet is now a widely used job-search environment, so it's a good idea to have your résumé ready for the online environment. You can forward it to networking contacts or recruiting professionals through email. You can also post it in online databases with the hope that employers and recruiters will find it.

Successful internet-ready résumés require a different strategy than that for paper résumés. For instance, when companies search résumé banks, they search key words and industry buzz words that describe a skill or the core work required for each job, so nouns are much more important than verbs. Two good resources for preparing internet-ready résumés are GCF (www.gcflearnfree.org/resumewriting/9/print) and LiveCareer (www. livecareer.com/career/advice/resume/e-resumes).

After you have written your internet-ready résumé, you need to post it. Indeed and LinkedIn are good locations to star. However, use caution when posting your résumé on various sites. In this era of identity theft, you need to select sites with care so as to protect your privacy. Limit access to your personal contact information, and don't use sites that offer to "blast" your résumé into cyberspace.

Résumé Tips

- Communicate your worth to potential employers in a concrete manner, citing examples whenever possible.
- Be concise and direct.
- Use active verbs to show you are a doer.
- Do not skimp on quality or use gimmicks. Spare no expense in presenting a professional résumé.
- Have someone critique your work. A single typo can eliminate you from being considered.
- Customize your résumé for specific employers. Emphasize your strengths as they pertain to your targeted job.
- Keep your résumé compact, usually one page.
- Format the text to be attractive, professional, and readable. Times New Roman is often the font of choice. Avoid too much "design" or gimmicky flourishes.

Write Cover Letter, Follow Up, and Assemble Supporting Documents

Cover Letter

You should include a cover letter informing the employer that a résumé is enclosed. But a cover letter does more than this. It also serves to summarize in one or two paragraphs the contents of the résumé and explains why you think you are the right person for the position. The goal is to persuade the employer to look at the more detailed résumé. A typical cover letter is organized as follows: (1) the name and position of the person you are contacting; (2) a statement identifying the position you are applying for, how you heard of the vacancy, and the reasons for your interest; (3) a summary of your qualifications for the job; (4) a description of what follow ups you intend to make, such as phoning in two weeks to see if the résumé has been received; and (5) an expression of gratitude for the opportunity of being a candidate for the job.

CareerOneStop (www.careeronestop.org/ResumeGuide/Writeeffectivecoverletters.aspx) offers a step-by-step tutorial on how to create a cover letter, and Cover Letter Now contains more than 50 cover letter samples (www.cover-letter-now.com). Another popular site, Resume Genius, can build a cover letter for you (https://resumegenius.com/cover-letter-builder). A popular guide to check out is Jeremy Schifeling, *Get It Done: Write a Cover Letter* (Jeremy Schifeling, 2018).

Follow Up

Once you send your cover letter and résumé to prospective employers via the method they prefer—email, their website, or regular mail—it's often a good idea to follow up. In today's market, job seekers can't afford to wait for interviews to find them.

A quality résumé and an attractive cover letter are crucial, but a proper follow-up may be the key to landing an interview. However, before you engage your potential employer, be sure to research the company. Knowing about the company and understanding its place in the industry will help you shine. When you place a call, send an email, or mail a letter to a company contact, be sure to restate your interest in the position, check on the status of your résumé, and ask employers about any questions they may have.

Letters of Recommendation

Letters of recommendation are written references by professors, former and current employers, and others that testify to your character, skills, and abilities. Some companies may request letters of recommendation, to be submitted either with the résumé or at the interview. Even if letters of recommendation aren't requested, it's a good idea to bring them with you to the interview. A good reference letter tells why you would be an excellent candidate for the position. In choosing someone to write a letter of recommendation, be confident that the person will give you a good reference. In addition, do not assume the person knows everything about you or the position you are seeking. Rather, provide the person with your résumé and other relevant data. As a courtesy, allow the reference writer at least a month to complete the letter and enclose a stamped, addressed envelope with your materials.

In the packet containing your résumé, cover letter, and letters of recommendation, you may also want to attach other relevant documents that support your candidacy, such as academic transcripts, graphics, portfolios, and samples of writing.

Interview for Jobs

As the old saying goes, "The résumé gets you the interview; the interview gets you the job." The job interview offers you an opportunity to gather more information about the organization, while at the same time allowing the organization to gather more information about you. You'll want to present your best self. The interview process consists of three parts: before the interview, the interview itself, and after the interview. If you pass through these stages successfully, you will be called back for the follow-up interview.

Before the Interview

In preparing for your interview, do the following:

1. Understand that interviewers have diverse styles, including the "chitchat," let's-get-to-know-each-other style; the interrogation style of question after question; and the tough-probing "why, why, why" style, among others. So be ready for anything.
2. With a friend, practice being interviewed and then ask for a critique. Or video yourself in a practice interview so that you can critique your own performance. Your college placement service may also offer "mock" interviews to help you.
3. Prepare at least five good questions whose answers are not easily found in the company literature, such as "What is the future direction of the firm?" "How does the firm differentiate itself from competitors?" or "Do you have a new-media division?"
4. Anticipate possible interview questions, such as "Why do you want to work for this company?" or "Why should we hire you?" Prepare solid answers before the interview. Have a clear idea of why you are interested in joining the company and the industry to which it belongs.
5. Avoid back-to-back interviews—they can be exhausting, and it is unpredictable how long each will last.
6. Prepare relevant documents that support your candidacy, such as academic transcripts, letters of recommendation, graphics, portfolios, and samples of writing. Bring multiple copies to the interview.
7. Dress conservatively and professionally. Be neat and clean.
8. Arrive 10 minutes early to collect your thoughts and review the major points you intend to cover. Check your name on the interview schedule, noting the name of the interviewer and the room number. Be courteous and polite to office staff.
9. Approach the interview enthusiastically. Let your personality shine through.

During the Interview

During the interview, do the following:

1. Shake hands firmly in greeting the interviewer. Introduce yourself, using the same form of address that the interviewer uses. Focus on creating a good initial impression.
2. Keep your poise. Relax, smile when appropriate, and be upbeat throughout.
3. Maintain eye contact and good posture and speak distinctly. Don't clasp your hands or fiddle with jewelry, hair, or clothing. Sit comfortably in your chair.
4. Along with the copies of relevant documents that support your candidacy, carry extra copies of your résumé with you.
5. Have your story down pat. Present your selling points. Answer questions directly. Avoid either one-word or too-wordy answers.
6. Let the interviewer take the initiative but don't be passive. Find an opportunity to direct the conversation to things about yourself that you want the interviewer to hear.
7. To end on a high note, make your most important point or ask your most pertinent question during the last part of the interview.
8. Don't hesitate to "close." You might say, "I'm very interested in the position and I have enjoyed this interview."
9. Obtain the interviewer's business card or address, email address, and phone number so that you can follow up later.

A tip for acing the interview: Before you open your mouth, find out *what it's like* to be a brand manager, sales representative, market researcher, advertising account executive, social media analyst, or other position for which you're interviewing. See if you can find a "mentor"—someone in a position similar to the one you're seeking, perhaps with another company. Talk with this mentor about the ins and outs of the job and industry.

After the Interview

After the interview, do the following:

1. Record the key points that arose. Be sure to note who is to follow up and when a decision can be expected.
2. Analyze the interview objectively, including the questions asked, the answers to them, your overall interview presentation, and the interviewer's responses to specific points.
3. Immediately send a thank-you letter or email, mentioning any additional items and your willingness to supply further information.
4. If you do not hear from the employer within the specified time, call, email, or write the interviewer to determine your status.

Follow-Up Interview

If your first interview takes place off-site, such as at your college or at a job fair, and if you are successful with that initial interview, you will be invited to visit the organization. The in-company interview will probably run from several hours to an entire day. The organization will examine your interest, maturity, enthusiasm, assertiveness, logic, and company and functional knowledge. You should ask questions about issues of importance to you. Find out about the working environment, job role, responsibilities, opportunities for advancement, current industrial issues, and the company's personality. The company wants to discover if you are the right person for the job, whereas you want to find out if it is the right job for you. The key is to determine if the right *fit* exists between you and the company.

Marketing Jobs

This section describes some of the key marketing positions.

Advertising

Advertising is one of the most exciting fields in marketing, offering a wide range of career opportunities.

Job Descriptions

Key advertising positions include copywriter, art director, production manager, account executive, account planner, digital and social media content managers, and media planner/buyer.

- *Copywriters* write advertising copy and help find the concepts behind the written words and visual images of advertisements.
- *Art directors,* the other part of the creative team, help translate the copywriters' ideas into dramatic visuals called "layouts." Agency artists develop print layouts, package designs, television and video layouts (called "storyboards"), corporate logotypes, trademarks, and symbols.
- *Production managers* are responsible for physically creating ads, either in-house or by contracting through outside production houses.
- *Account development executives* research and understand clients' markets and customers and help develop marketing and advertising strategies to impact them.
- *Account executives* serve as liaisons between clients and agencies. They coordinate the planning, creation, production, and implementation of an advertising campaign for the account.
- *Account planners* serve as the voice of the consumer in the agency. They research consumers to understand their needs and motivations as a basis for developing effective ad campaigns.
- *Digital and social media content managers* plan and place digital and social media marketing and advertising content and coordinate it with traditional media content.
- *Media planners (or buyers)* determine the best mix of television, radio, newspaper, magazine, digital, and other media for the advertising campaign.

Skills Needed, Career Paths, and Typical Salaries

Work in advertising requires strong people skills in order to interact closely with an often-difficult and demanding client base. In addition, advertising attracts people with strong skills in planning, problem solving, creativity, communication, initiative, leadership, and presentation. Advertising involves working under high levels of stress and pressure created by unrelenting deadlines. Advertisers frequently have to work long hours to meet deadlines for a presentation. But work achievements are very apparent, with the results of creative strategies observed by thousands or even millions of people.

Positions in advertising sometimes require an MBA. But most jobs only require a business, graphic arts, or liberal arts degree. Advertising positions often serve as gateways to higher-level management. Moreover, with large advertising agencies opening offices all over the world, there is the possibility of eventually working on global campaigns.

Starting advertising salaries are relatively low compared to those of some other marketing jobs because of strong competition for entry-level advertising jobs. Compensation will increase quickly as you move into account executive or other management positions. For more facts and figures, see the online pages of *Advertising Age*, a key ad industry publication (www.adage.com, click on the Jobs link) and the American Association of Advertising Agencies (www.aaaa.org).

Brand and Product Management

Brand and product managers plan, direct, and control business and marketing efforts for their products. They are involved with research and development, packaging, manufacturing, sales and distribution, advertising, promotion, market research, digital marketing, and business analysis and forecasting.

Job Descriptions

A company's brand management team consists of people in several positions:

- *Brand managers* guide the development of marketing strategies for a specific brand.
- *Assistant brand managers* are responsible for certain strategic components of the brand.
- *Product managers* oversee several brands within a product line or product group.
- *Product category managers* direct multiple product lines in the product category.
- *Market analysts* research the market and provide important strategic information to the project managers.

- *Project directors* are responsible for collecting market information on a marketing or product project.
- *Research directors* oversee the planning, gathering, and analyzing of all organizational research.

Skills Needed, Career Paths, and Typical Salaries

Brand and product management requires high problem-solving, analytical, presentation, communication, and leadership skills as well as the ability to work well in a team. Product management requires long hours and involves the high pressure of running large projects. In consumer goods companies, the newcomer—who usually needs an MBA—joins a brand team as an assistant and learns the ropes by doing numerical analyses and assisting senior brand people. This person eventually heads the team and later moves on to manage a larger brand, then several brands.

Many industrial goods companies also have product managers. Product management is one of the best training grounds for future corporate officers. Product management also offers good opportunities to move into international marketing. Product managers command relatively high salaries. Because this job category encourages or requires a master's degree, starting pay tends to be higher than in other marketing categories such as advertising or retailing.

Sales and Sales Management

Sales and sales management opportunities exist in a wide range of profit and not-for-profit organizations and in product and service organizations, including financial, insurance, consulting, and government organizations.

Job Descriptions

Key jobs include consumer sales, industrial sales, national account managers, service support, sales trainers, and sales management:

- *Consumer sales* involves selling consumer products and services through retailers.
- *Industrial sales* involves selling products and services to other businesses.
- *National account managers (NAMs)* oversee a few very large accounts.
- *Service support* personnel support salespeople during and after the sale of a product.
- *Sales trainers* train new hires and provide refresher training for all sales personnel.
- *Sales management* includes a sequence of positions ranging from district manager to vice president of sales.

Salespeople enjoy active professional lives, working outside the office and interacting with others. They manage their own time and activities. And successful salespeople can be very well paid. Competition for top jobs can be intense. Every sales job is different, but some positions involve extensive travel, long workdays, and working under pressure. You can also expect to be transferred more than once between company headquarters and regional offices. However, most companies are now working to bring good work–life balance to their salespeople and sales managers.

Skills Needed, Career Paths, and Typical Salaries

Selling is a people profession in which you will work with people every day, all day long. In addition to people skills, sales professionals need sales and communication skills. Most sales positions also require strong problem-solving, analytical, presentation, and leadership abilities as well as creativity and initiative. Teamwork skills are increasingly important.

Career paths lead from salesperson to district, regional, and higher levels of sales management and, in many cases, to the top management of the firm. Today, most entry-level sales management positions require a college degree. Increasingly, people seeking selling jobs are acquiring sales experience in an internship capacity or from a part-time job before graduating. Sales positions are great springboards to leadership positions, with more CEOs starting in sales than in any other entry-level position. This might explain why competition for top sales jobs is intense.

Starting base salaries in sales may be moderate but compensation is often supplemented by significant commission, bonus, or other incentive plans. In addition, many sales jobs include a company car or car allowance. Successful salespeople are among most companies' highest paid employees.

Other Marketing Jobs

Marketing Research

Marketing researchers interact with managers to define problems and identify the information needed to resolve them. They design research projects, prepare questionnaires and samples, analyze data, prepare reports, and present their findings and recommendations to management. They must understand statistics, data analytics tools, consumer behavior, psychology, and sociology. As more and more marketing research goes digital, they must also understand the ins and outs of obtaining and managing online information. A master's degree helps. Career opportunities exist with manufacturers, retailers, some wholesalers, trade and industry associations, marketing research firms, advertising agencies, and governmental and private nonprofit agencies.

Marketing Data Science

A marketing data scientist's job is to analyze marketing data to gain actionable customer insights. Data scientists collect big data sets and apply marketing analytics to discover actionable insights and marketing solutions. They share these insights and solutions with marketing managers to help them make better marketing decisions. Being a marketing data scientist often requires math, statistics, analytical, and computer science skills, along with an understanding of marketing strategy. Most data scientists have at least a master's degree.

Digital and Social Media Management

The exploding use of digital and social media has created a wide range of marketing positions and careers, from digital and social media strategists and managers to social media planners, digital content producers, data scientists and big data analysts, and online community managers. These positions involve varying degrees of helping to develop digital and social media campaigns, developing and managing digital content across social media platforms, managing online brand communities, mining customer insights from social media data, and engaging and interacting with customers via websites, mobile, and social media. Such positions require a knowledge of digital technologies and social media platforms such as Twitter, Facebook, Instagram, YouTube, LinkedIn, Pinterest, and Snapchat.

Retailing

Retailing provides an early opportunity to assume marketing responsibilities. Key jobs include store manager, regional manager, buyer, department manager, and salesperson. *Store managers* direct the management and operation of an individual store. *Regional managers* manage groups of stores across several states and report performance to headquarters. *Buyers* select and buy the merchandise that the store carries. The *department manager* acts as store manager of a department, such as clothing, but on the department level. The *salesperson* sells merchandise to retail customers. Retailing can involve relocation, but generally there is little travel, unless you are a buyer. Retailing requires high people and sales skills because retailers are constantly in contact with customers. Enthusiasm, willingness, and communication skills are very helpful for retailers, too.

Retailers work long hours, but their daily activities are often more structured than in some types of marketing positions. Starting salaries in retailing tend to be low but pay increases as you move into management or a retailing specialty job.

New Product Planning

People interested in new product planning can find opportunities in many types of organizations. They usually need a good background in marketing, marketing research, and sales forecasting; they need organizational skills to motivate and coordinate others; and they may need a technical background. Usually, these people work first in other marketing positions before joining the new product department.

Marketing Logistics (Physical Distribution)

Marketing logistics, or physical distribution, is a large and dynamic field, with many career opportunities. Major transportation carriers, manufacturers, wholesalers, and retailers all employ logistics specialists. Increasingly, marketing teams include logistics specialists, and marketing managers' career paths include marketing logistics assignments. Coursework in quantitative methods, finance, accounting, and marketing will provide you with the necessary skills for entering the field.

Public Relations

Most organizations have a public relations staff to anticipate problems with various publics, handle complaints, deal with media, and build the corporate image. People interested in public relations should be able to speak and write clearly and persuasively, and they should have a background in journalism, communications, or the liberal arts. The challenges in this job are highly varied and very people-oriented.

Not-for-Profit Services

The key jobs in not-for-profits include marketing director, director of development, event coordinator, publication specialist, and intern/volunteer. The *marketing director* is in charge of all marketing activities for the organization. The *director of development* organizes, manages, and directs the fundraising campaigns that keep a not-for-profit in existence. An *event coordinator* directs all aspects of fundraising events, from initial planning through implementation. The *publication specialist* oversees publications designed to promote awareness of the organization. Although typically an unpaid position, the *intern/volunteer* performs various marketing functions, and this work can be an important step to gaining a full-time position.

The not-for-profit sector is typically not for someone who is money-driven. Rather, most not-for-profits look for people with a strong sense of community spirit and the desire to help others. Therefore, starting pay is usually lower than in other marketing fields. However, the bigger the not-for-profit, the better your chance of rapidly increasing your income when moving into upper management.

Other Resources

Professional marketing associations and organizations are another source of information about careers. Marketers belong to many such societies. You may want to contact some of the following in your job search:

American Advertising Federation, 1101 Vermont Avenue NW, 5th Floor, Washington, DC 20005. (202) 898-0089 (www.aaf.org)

American Marketing Association, 130 E Randolph Street, 22nd Floor, Chicago, IL 60601. (800) AMA-1150 (www.ama.org)

The Association of Women in Communications, 1717 E Republic Road, Suite A, Springfield, MO 65804. (417) 886-8606 (www.womcom.org)

The Insights Association, 1156 15th Street NW, Suite 700, Washington, DC 20005. (202) 800-2545 (www.insightsassociation.org)

National Association of Sales Professionals, 2121 Lohmans Crossing Rd, Ste 504579, Austin, TX 78734. (866) 365-1520 (www.nasp.com)

National Management Association, 2210 Arbor Boulevard, Dayton, OH 45439. (937) 294-0421 (www.nma1.org)

National Retail Federation, 1101 New York Avenue NW, Suite 1200, Washington, DC 20005. (800) 673-4692 (www.nrf.com)

Product Development and Management Association, 1000 Westgate Drive, Suite 252, St. Paul, MN 55114. (651) 290-6280 (www.pdma.org)

Public Relations Society of America, 120 Wall St, 21st Floor, New York, NY 10005. (212) 460-1400 (www.prsa.org)

Sales and Marketing Executives International, PO Box 1390, Sumas, WA, 98295. (312) 893-0751 (www.smei.org)

She Runs It, 1460 Broadway, New York, NY 10036. (212) 221-7969 (https://sherunsit.org)

Glossary

Adapted global marketing A global marketing approach that adjusts the marketing strategy and mix elements to each international target market, which creates more costs but hopefully produces a larger market share and return.

Administered VMS A vertical marketing system that coordinates successive stages of production and distribution through the size and power of one of the parties.

Adoption process The mental process through which an individual passes from first hearing about an innovation to final adoption.

Advertising Any paid form of nonpersonal presentation and promotion of ideas, goods, or services by an identified sponsor.

Advertising agency A marketing services firm that assists companies in planning, preparing, implementing, and evaluating all or portions of their advertising programs.

Advertising budget The dollars and other resources allocated to a product or a company advertising program.

Advertising media The vehicles through which advertising messages are delivered to their intended audiences.

Advertising objective A specific communication task to be accomplished with a specific target audience during a specific period of time.

Advertising strategy The strategy by which the company accomplishes its advertising objectives. It consists of two major elements: creating advertising messages and selecting advertising media.

Affordable method Setting the promotion budget at the level management thinks the company can afford.

Agent A wholesaler who represents buyers or sellers on a relatively permanent basis, performs only a few functions, and does not take title to goods.

Age and life-cycle segmentation Dividing a market into different age and life-cycle groups.

Allowance Promotional money paid by manufacturers to retailers in return for an agreement to feature the manufacturer's products in some way.

Alternative evaluation The stage of the buyer decision process in which the consumer uses information to evaluate alternative brands in the choice set.

Approach The sales step in which a salesperson meets the customer for the first time.

Artificial intelligence (AI) Technology by which machines think and learn in a way that looks and feels human but with a lot more analytical capacity.

Attitude A person's consistently favorable or unfavorable evaluations, feelings, and tendencies toward an object or idea.

B-to-B digital and social media marketing Using digital and social media marketing approaches to engage business customers and manage customer relationships anywhere, any time.

Baby boomers The 72 million people born during the years following World War II and lasting until 1964.

Basing-point pricing Pricing in which the seller designates some city as a basing point and charges all customers the freight cost from that city to the customer.

Behavioral segmentation Dividing a market into segments based on consumer knowledge, attitudes, uses of a product, or responses to a product.

Behavioral targeting Using online consumer tracking data and analytics to target advertisements and marketing offers to specific consumers.

Belief A descriptive thought that a person holds about something.

Benchmarking Comparing the company's products and processes to those of competitors or leading firms in other industries to identify best practices and find ways to improve quality and performance.

Benefit segmentation Dividing the market into segments according to the different benefits that consumers seek from the product.

Big data The huge and complex data sets generated by today's sophisticated information generation, collection, storage, and analysis technologies.

Blogs Online forums where people and companies post their thoughts and other content, usually related to narrowly defined topics.

Brand A name, term, sign, symbol, or design or a combination of these that identifies the products or services of one seller or group of sellers and differentiates them from those of competitors.

Brand community website A website that presents brand content that engages consumers and creates customer community around a brand.

Brand equity The differential effect that knowing the brand name has on customer response to the product or its marketing.

Brand extension Extending an existing brand name to new product categories.

Brand value The total financial value of a brand.

Break-even pricing (target return pricing) Setting price to break even on the costs of making and marketing a product, or setting price to make a target return.

Broker A wholesaler who does not take title to goods and whose function is to bring buyers and sellers together and assist in negotiation.

Business analysis A review of the sales, costs, and profit projections for a new product to find out whether these factors satisfy the company's objectives.

Business buyer behavior The buying behavior of organizations that buy goods and services for use in the production of other products and services that are sold, rented, or supplied to others.

Business buying process The decision process by which business buyers determine which products and services their organizations need to purchase and then find, evaluate, and choose among alternative suppliers and brands.

Business portfolio The collection of businesses and products that make up the company.

Business promotions Sales promotion tools used to generate business leads, stimulate purchases, reward customers, and motivate salespeople.

Buyers People in an organization's buying center who make an actual purchase.

Buying center All the individuals and units that play a role in the purchase decision-making process.

Buzz marketing Cultivating opinion leaders and getting them to spread information about a product or a service to others in their communities.

By-product pricing Setting a price for by-products to help offset the costs of disposing of them and help make the main product's price more competitive.

Captive-product pricing Setting a price for products that must be used along with a main product, such as blades for a razor and games for a video-game console.

Catalog marketing Direct marketing through print, video, or digital catalogs that are mailed to select customers, made available in stores, or presented online.

Category killer A giant specialty store that carries a very deep assortment of a particular line.

Causal research Marketing research to test hypotheses about cause-and-effect relationships.

Channel conflict Disagreements among marketing channel members on goals, roles, and rewards—who should do what and for what rewards.

Channel level A layer of intermediaries that performs some work in bringing the product and its ownership closer to the final buyer.

Closing The sales step in which a salesperson asks the customer for an order.

Co-branding The practice of using the established brand names of two different companies on the same product.

Cognitive dissonance Buyer discomfort caused by postpurchase conflict.

Commercialization Introducing a new product into the market.

Communication adaptation A global communication strategy of fully adapting advertising messages to local markets.

Competition-based pricing Setting prices based on competitors' strategies, prices, costs, and market offerings.

Competitive advantage An advantage over competitors gained by offering greater customer value either by having lower prices or providing more benefits that justify higher prices.

Competitive marketing intelligence The systematic monitoring, collection, and analysis of publicly available information about consumers, competitors, and developments in the marketing environment.

Competitive marketing strategies Strategies that strongly position the company against competitors and give it the greatest possible competitive advantage.

Competitive-parity method Setting the promotion budget to match competitors' outlays.

Competitor analysis Identifying key competitors; assessing their objectives, strategies, strengths and weaknesses, and reaction patterns; and selecting which competitors to attack or avoid.

Competitor-centered company A company whose moves are mainly based on competitors' actions and reactions.

Complex buying behavior Consumer buying behavior in situations characterized by high consumer involvement in a purchase and significant perceived differences among brands.

Concentrated (niche) marketing A market-coverage strategy in which a firm goes after a large share of one or a few segments or niches.

Concept testing Testing new product concepts with a group of target consumers to find out if the concepts have strong consumer appeal.

Consumer buyer behavior The buying behavior of final consumers—individuals and households that buy goods and services for personal consumption.

Consumer market All the individuals and households that buy or acquire goods and services for personal consumption.

Consumer product A product bought by final consumers for personal consumption.

Consumer promotions Sales promotion tools used to boost short-term customer buying and engagement or enhance long-term customer relationships.

Consumer-generated marketing Brand exchanges created by consumers themselves—both invited and uninvited—by which consumers are playing an increasing role in shaping their own brand experiences and those of other consumers.

Consumer-oriented marketing A company should view and organize its marketing activities from the consumer's point of view.

Consumerism An organized movement of citizens and government agencies designed to improve the rights and power of buyers in relation to sellers.

Content marketing Creating, inspiring, and sharing brand messages and conversations with and among consumers across a fluid mix of paid, owned, earned, and shared channels.

Contract manufacturing A joint venture in which a company contracts with manufacturers in a foreign market to produce its product or provide its service.

Contractual VMS A vertical marketing system in which independent firms at different levels of production and distribution join together through contracts.

Convenience product A consumer product that customers usually buy frequently, immediately, and with minimal comparison and buying effort.

Convenience store A small store, located near a residential area, that is open long hours seven days a week and carries a limited line of high-turnover convenience goods.

Conventional distribution channel A channel consisting of one or more independent producers, wholesalers, and retailers, each a separate business seeking to maximize its own profits, perhaps even at the expense of profits for the system as a whole.

Corporate chains Two or more outlets that are commonly owned and controlled.

Corporate VMS A vertical marketing system that combines successive stages of production and distribution under single ownership—channel leadership is established through common ownership.

Cost-based pricing Setting prices based on the costs of producing, distributing, and selling the product plus a fair rate of return for effort and risk.

Cost-plus pricing (markup pricing) Adding a standard markup to the cost of the product.

Creative concept The compelling "big idea" that will bring an advertising message strategy to life in a distinctive and memorable way.

Crowdsourcing Inviting broad communities of people—customers, employees, independent scientists and researchers, and even the public at large—into the new product innovation process.

Cultural environment Institutions and other forces that affect society's basic values, perceptions, preferences, and behaviors.

Culture The set of basic values, perceptions, wants, and behaviors learned by a member of society from family and other important institutions.

Customer (or market) sales force structure A sales force organization in which salespeople specialize in selling only to certain customers or industries.

Customer brand advocacy Actions by which satisfied customers initiate favorable interactions with others about a brand.

Customer equity The total combined customer lifetime values of all of the company's customers.

Customer insights Fresh marketing information-based understandings of customers and the marketplace that become the basis for creating customer value, engagement, and relationships.

Customer journey The sum of the ongoing experiences consumers have with a brand that affect their buying behavior, engagement, and brand advocacy over time.

Customer lifetime value The value of the entire stream of purchases a customer makes over a lifetime of patronage.

Customer relationship management (CRM) Managing detailed information about individual customers and carefully managing customer touch points to maximize customer loyalty.

Customer relationship management The overall process of building and maintaining profitable customer relationships by delivering superior customer value and satisfaction.

Customer satisfaction The extent to which a product's perceived performance matches a buyer's expectations.

Customer value analysis An analysis conducted to determine what benefits target customers value and how they rate the relative values of various competitors' offers.

Customer value marketing A company should put most of its resources into customer value–building marketing investments.

Customer value–based pricing Setting price based on buyers' perceptions of value rather than on the seller's cost.

Customer-centered company A company that focuses on customer developments in designing its marketing strategies and delivering superior value to its target customers.

Customer-centered new product development New product development that focuses on finding new ways to solve customer problems and create more customer-satisfying experiences.

Customer-engagement marketing Making the brand a meaningful part of consumers' conversations and lives by fostering direct and continuous customer involvement in shaping brand conversations, experiences, and community.

Customer-perceived value The customer's evaluation of the difference between all the benefits and all the costs of a marketing offer relative to those of competing offers.

Deciders People in an organization's buying center who have formal or informal power to select or approve the final suppliers.

Decline stage The PLC stage in which a product's sales fade away.

Deficient products Products that have neither immediate appeal nor long-run benefits.

Demand curve A curve that shows the number of units the market will buy in a given time period at different prices that might be charged.

Demands Human wants that are backed by buying power.

Demographic segmentation Dividing the market into segments based on variables such as age, life-cycle stage, gender, income, occupation, education, religion, ethnicity, and generation.

Demography The study of human populations in terms of size, density, location, age, gender, race, occupation, and other statistics.

Department store A retail store that carries a wide variety of product lines, each operated as a separate department managed by specialist buyers or merchandisers.

Derived demand Business demand that ultimately comes from (derives from) the demand for consumer goods.

Descriptive research Marketing research to better describe marketing problems, situations, or markets, such as the market potential for a product or the demographics and attitudes of consumers.

Desirable products Products that give both high immediate satisfaction and high long-run benefits.

Differentiated (segmented) marketing A market-coverage strategy in which a firm targets several market segments and designs separate offers for each.

Differentiation Actually differentiating the market offering to create superior customer value.

Digital and social media marketing Using digital marketing tools such as websites, social media, mobile apps and ads, online video, email, and blogs to engage consumers anywhere, at any time, via their digital devices.

Direct and digital marketing Engaging directly with carefully targeted individual consumers and customer communities to both obtain an immediate response and build lasting customer relationships.

Direct investment Entering a foreign market by developing foreign-based assembly or manufacturing facilities.

Direct marketing channel A marketing channel that has no intermediary levels.

Direct-mail marketing Marketing that occurs by sending an offer, announcement, reminder, or other item directly to a person at a particular address.

Direct-response television (DRTV) marketing Direct marketing via television that persuasively describes a product and give customers a toll-free number or an online site for ordering.

Direct-to-consumer (DTC) brands Brands that avoid direct competition with established traditional brands by selling and shipping directly to consumers only through online and mobile channels.

Discount A straight reduction in price on purchases during a stated period of time or of larger quantities.

Discount store A retail operation that sells standard merchandise at lower prices by accepting lower margins and selling at higher volume.

Disintermediation The cutting out of marketing channel intermediaries by product or service producers or the displacement of traditional resellers by radical new types of intermediaries.

Dissonance-reducing buying behavior Consumer buying behavior in situations characterized by high involvement but few perceived differences among brands.

Distribution center A large, highly automated warehouse designed to receive goods from various plants and suppliers, take orders, fill them efficiently, and deliver goods to customers as quickly as possible.

Diversification Company growth through starting up or acquiring businesses outside the company's current products and markets.

Dynamic pricing Adjusting prices continually to meet changing conditions and situations in the marketplace.

E-procurement Purchasing through electronic connections between buyers and sellers—usually online.

Economic community A group of nations organized to work toward common goals in the regulation of international trade.

Economic environment Economic factors that affect consumer purchasing power and spending patterns.

Email marketing Sending highly targeted, highly personalized, relationship-building marketing messages via email.

Environmental sustainability A management approach that involves developing strategies that both sustain the environment and produce profits for the company.

Environmental sustainability Developing strategies and practices that create a world economy that the planet can support indefinitely.

Environmentalism An organized movement of concerned citizens, businesses, and government agencies designed to protect and improve people's current and future living environment.

Ethnographic research A form of observational research that involves sending trained observers to watch and interact with consumers in their "natural environments."

Event marketing (or event sponsorships) Creating a brand-marketing event or serving as a sole or participating sponsor of events created by others.

Exchange The act of obtaining a desired object from someone by offering something in return.

Exclusive distribution Giving a limited number of dealers the exclusive right to distribute the company's products in their territories.

Execution style The approach, style, tone, words, and format used for executing an advertising message.

Experience curve (learning curve) The drop in the average per-unit production cost that comes with accumulated production experience.

Experimental research Gathering primary data by selecting matched groups of subjects, giving them different treatments, controlling related factors, and checking for differences in group responses.

Exploratory research Marketing research to gather preliminary information that will help define problems and suggest hypotheses.

Exporting Entering foreign markets by selling goods produced in the company's home country, often with little modification.

Factory outlet An off-price retailing operation that is owned and operated by a manufacturer and normally carries the manufacturer's surplus, discontinued, or irregular goods.

Fad A temporary period of unusually high sales driven by consumer enthusiasm and immediate product or brand popularity.

Fashion A currently accepted or popular style in a given field.

Five As The five customer journey stages on the path from awareness of a brand to advocating it to others: awareness, appeal, ask, act, and advocacy.

Fixed costs (overhead) Costs that do not vary with production or sales level.

FOB-origin pricing Pricing in which goods are placed free on board a carrier; the customer pays the freight from the factory to the destination.

Focus group interviewing Personal interviewing that involves inviting small groups of people to gather for a few hours with a trained interviewer to talk about a product, service, or organization. The interviewer "focuses" the group discussion on important issues.

Follow-up The sales step in which a salesperson follows up after the sale to ensure customer satisfaction and repeat business.

Franchise A contractual association between a manufacturer, wholesaler, or service organization (a franchisor) and independent businesspeople (franchisees) who buy the right to own and operate one or more units in the franchise system.

Franchise organization A contractual vertical marketing system in which a channel member, called a franchisor, links several stages in the production-distribution process.

Freight-absorption pricing Pricing in which the seller absorbs all or part of the freight charges in order to get the desired business.

Gatekeepers People in an organization's buying center who control the flow of information to others.

Gender segmentation Dividing a market into different segments based on gender.

General need description The stage in the business buying process in which a buyer describes the general characteristics and quantity of a needed item.

Generation Alpha Kids born after 2012, largely the children of the millennials.

Generation X The 55 million people born between 1965 and 1980 in the "birth dearth" following the baby boom.

Generation Z People born between 1997 and 2012 who make up the tweens to twenty-something markets.

Geographic segmentation Dividing a market into different geographical units, such as nations, states, regions, counties, cities, or even neighborhoods.

Geographical pricing Setting prices for customers located in different parts of the country or world.

Global firm A firm that, by operating in more than one country, gains R&D, production, marketing, and financial advantages in its costs and reputation that are not available to purely domestic competitors.

Good-value pricing Offering just the right combination of quality and good service at a fair price.

Government market Governmental units—federal, state, and local—that purchase or rent goods and services for carrying out the main functions of government.

Growth stage The PLC stage in which a product's sales start climbing quickly.

Growth-share matrix A portfolio-planning method that evaluates a company's SBUs in terms of market growth rate and relative market share.

Habitual buying behavior Consumer buying behavior in situations characterized by low consumer involvement and few significant perceived brand differences.

Handling objections The sales step in which a salesperson seeks out, clarifies, and overcomes any customer objections to buying.

Horizontal marketing system A channel arrangement in which two or more companies at one level join together to follow a new marketing opportunity.

Hyperlocal social marketing Location-based targeting to consumers in local communities or neighborhoods using digital and social media.

Idea generation The systematic search for new product ideas.

Idea screening Screening new product ideas to spot good ones and drop poor ones as soon as possible.

Income segmentation Dividing a market into different income segments.

Independent off-price retailer An off-price retailer that is independently owned and operated or a division of a larger retail corporation.

Indirect marketing channel A marketing channel containing one or more intermediary levels.

Individual marketing Tailoring products and marketing programs to the needs and preferences of individual customers.

Industrial product A product bought by individuals and organizations for further processing or for use in conducting a business.

Influencer marketing Enlisting established influencers or creating new influencers to spread the word about a company's brands.

Influencers People in an organization's buying center who affect the buying decision; they often help define specifications and also provide information for evaluating alternatives.

Information search The stage of the buyer decision process in which the consumer is motivated to search for more information.

Innovative marketing A company should seek real product and marketing improvements.

Inside sales force Salespeople who conduct business from their offices via telephone, online and social media interactions, or visits from prospective buyers.

Institutional market Schools, hospitals, nursing homes, prisons, and other institutions that provide goods and services to people in their care.

Integrated logistics management The logistics concept that emphasizes teamwork—both inside the company and among all the marketing channel organizations—to maximize the performance of the entire distribution system.

Integrated marketing communications (IMC) Carefully integrating and coordinating the company's many communications channels to deliver a clear, consistent, and compelling message about the organization and its products.

Intensive distribution Stocking the product in as many outlets as possible.

Interactive marketing Training service employees in the fine art of interacting with customers to satisfy their needs.

Intermarket (cross-market) segmentation Forming segments of consumers who have similar needs and buying behaviors even though they are located in different countries.

Internal databases Collections of consumer and market information obtained from data sources within the company network.

Internal marketing Orienting and motivating customer-contact employees and supporting service employees to work as a team to provide customer satisfaction.

Internet of Things (IoT) A global environment where everything and everyone is digitally connected to everything and everyone else.

Introduction stage The PLC stage in which a new product is first distributed and made available for purchase.

Joint ownership A cooperative venture in which a company creates a local business with investors in a foreign market who share ownership and control.

Joint venturing Entering foreign markets by joining with foreign companies to produce or market a product or service.

Learning Changes in an individual's behavior arising from experience.

Licensing Entering foreign markets through developing an agreement with a licensee in the foreign market.

Lifestyle A person's pattern of living as expressed in his or her activities, interests, and opinions.

Line extension Extending an existing brand name to new forms, colors, sizes, ingredients, or flavors of an existing product category.

Local marketing Tailoring brands and marketing to the needs and wants of local customer segments—cities, neighborhoods, and even specific stores.

Macroenvironment The larger societal forces that affect the microenvironment—demographic, economic, natural, technological, political, and cultural forces.

Management contracting A joint venture in which the domestic firm supplies the management know-how to a foreign company that supplies the capital; the domestic firm exports management services rather than products.

Manufacturers' and retailers' branches and offices Wholesaling by sellers or buyers themselves rather than through independent wholesalers.

Market The set of all actual and potential buyers of a product or service.

Market challenger A runner-up firm that is fighting hard to increase its market share in an industry.

Market development Company growth by identifying and developing new market segments for current company products.

Market follower A runner-up firm that wants to hold its share in an industry without rocking the boat.

Market leader The firm in an industry with the largest market share.

Market nicher A firm that serves small segments that the other firms in an industry overlook or ignore.

Market offerings Some combination of products, services, information, or experiences offered to a market to satisfy a need or want.

Market penetration Company growth by increasing sales of current products to current market segments without changing the product.

Market segment A group of consumers who respond in a similar way to a given set of marketing efforts.

Market segmentation Dividing a market into distinct groups of buyers who have different needs, characteristics, or behaviors and who might require separate marketing strategies or mixes.

Market targeting (targeting) Evaluating each market segment's attractiveness and selecting one or more segments to serve.

Market-centered company A company that pays balanced attention to both customers and competitors in designing its marketing strategies.

Market-penetration pricing Setting a low price for a new product in order to attract a large number of buyers and a large market share.

Market-skimming pricing (price skimming) Setting a high price for a new product to skim maximum revenues layer by layer from the segments willing to pay the high price; the company makes fewer but more profitable sales.

Marketing The process by which companies engage customers, build strong customer relationships, and create customer value in order to capture value from customers in return.

Marketing analytics The analysis tools, technologies, and processes by which marketers dig out meaningful patterns in big data to gain customer insights and gauge marketing performance.

Marketing channel (distribution channel) A set of interdependent organizations that help make a product or service available for use or consumption by the consumer or business user.

Marketing channel design Designing effective marketing channels by analyzing customer needs, setting channel objectives, identifying major channel alternatives, and evaluating those alternatives.

Marketing channel management Selecting, managing, and motivating individual channel members and evaluating their performance over time.

Marketing concept A philosophy in which achieving organizational goals depends on knowing the needs and wants of target markets and delivering the desired satisfactions better than competitors do.

Marketing control Measuring and evaluating the results of marketing strategies and plans and taking corrective action to ensure that the objectives are achieved.

Marketing environment The actors and forces outside marketing that affect marketing management's ability to build and maintain successful relationships with target customers.

Marketing implementation Turning marketing strategies and plans into marketing actions to accomplish strategic marketing objectives.

Marketing information system (MIS) People and procedures dedicated to assessing information needs, developing the needed information, and helping decision makers to use the information to generate and validate actionable customer and market insights.

Marketing intermediaries Firms that help the company to promote, sell, and distribute its goods to final buyers.

Marketing logistics (physical distribution) Planning, implementing, and controlling the physical flow of materials, final goods, and related information from points of origin to points of consumption to meet customer requirements at a profit.

Marketing management The art and science of choosing target markets and building profitable relationships with them.

Marketing mix The set of tactical marketing tools—product, price, place, and promotion—that the firm blends to produce the response it wants in the target market.

Marketing myopia The mistake of paying more attention to the specific products a company offers than to the benefits and experiences produced by these products.

Marketing research The systematic design, collection, analysis, and reporting of data relevant to a specific marketing situation facing an organization.

Marketing return on investment (marketing ROI) The net return from a marketing investment divided by the costs of the marketing investment.

Marketing strategy The marketing logic by which the company hopes to create customer value and achieve profitable customer relationships.

Marketing strategy development Designing an initial marketing strategy for a new product based on the product concept.

Marketing website A website that engages consumers to move them closer to a direct purchase or other marketing outcome.

Maturity stage The PLC stage in which a product's sales growth slows or levels off.

Merchant wholesaler An independently owned wholesale business that takes title to the merchandise it handles.

Microenvironment The actors close to the company that affect its ability to serve its customers—the company, suppliers, marketing intermediaries, customer markets, competitors, and publics.

Micromarketing Tailoring products and marketing programs to the needs and wants of specific individuals and local customer segments; it includes local marketing and individual marketing.

Millennials (or Generation Y) The 75 million children of the baby boomers born between 1981 and 1996.

Mission statement A statement of the organization's purpose—what it wants to accomplish in the larger environment.

Mobile marketing Marketing messages, promotions, and other content delivered to on-the-go consumers through their mobile devices.

Modified rebuy A business buying situation in which the buyer wants to modify product specifications, prices, terms, or suppliers.

Motive (drive) A need that is sufficiently pressing to direct the person to seek satisfaction of the need.

Multichannel distribution system A distribution system in which a single firm sets up two or more marketing channels to reach one or more customer segments.

Multimodal transportation Combining two or more modes of transportation.

Native advertising Advertising or other brand-produced online content that looks in form and function like the other natural content surrounding it on a web or social media platform.

Natural environment The physical environment and the natural resources that are needed as inputs by marketers or that are affected by marketing activities.

Need recognition The first stage of the buyer decision process, in which the consumer recognizes a problem or need.

Needs States of felt deprivation.

New product A good, service, or idea that is perceived by some potential customers as new.

New product development The development of original products, product improvements, product modifications, and new brands through the firm's own product development efforts.

New task A business buying situation in which the buyer purchases a product or service for the first time.

Nonpersonal communication channels Media that carry messages without personal contact or feedback, including major media, atmospheres, and events.

Objective-and-task method Developing the promotion budget by (1) defining specific promotion objectives, (2) determining the tasks needed to achieve these objectives, and (3) estimating the costs of performing these tasks. The sum of these costs is the proposed promotion budget.

Observational research Gathering primary data by observing relevant people, actions, and situations.

Occasion segmentation Dividing the market into segments according to occasions when buyers get the idea to buy, actually make their purchase, or use the purchased item.

Off-price retailer A retailer that buys at less-than-regular wholesale prices and sells at less than retail.

Omni-channel retailing Creating a seamless cross-channel buying experience that integrates instore, online, and mobile shopping.

Online advertising Advertising that appears while consumers are browsing online, including display ads and search-related ads.

Online focus groups Gathering a small group of people online with a trained moderator to chat about a product, service, or organization and gain qualitative insights about consumer attitudes and behavior.

Online marketing Marketing via the internet using company websites, online ads and promotions, email, online video, and blogs.

Online marketing research Collecting primary data through internet and mobile surveys, online focus groups, consumer tracking, experiments, and online panels and brand communities.

Online social networks Online social communities—blogs, online social media, brand communities, and other online forums—where people socialize or exchange information and opinions.

Opinion leader A person within a reference group who, because of special skills, knowledge, personality, or other characteristics, exerts social influence on others.

Optional-product pricing The pricing of optional or accessory products along with a main product.

Order-routine specification The stage of the business buying process in which the buyer writes the final order with the chosen supplier(s), listing the technical specifications, quantity needed, expected time of delivery, return policies, and warranties.

Outside sales force (or field sales force) Salespeople who travel to call on customers in the field.

Packaging The activities of designing and producing the container or wrapper for a product.

Partner relationship management Working closely with partners in other company departments and outside the company to jointly bring greater value to customers.

Percentage-of-sales method Setting the promotion budget at a certain percentage of current or forecasted sales or as a percentage of the unit sales price.

Perception The process by which people select, organize, and interpret information to form a meaningful picture of the world.

Performance review The stage of the business buying process in which the buyer assesses the performance of the supplier and decides to continue, modify, or drop the arrangement.

Personal communication channels Channels through which two or more people communicate directly with each other, including face-to-face, on the phone, via mail or email, or even through an internet "chat."

Personal selling Personal presentation by the firm's sales force for the purpose of engaging customers, making sales, and building customer relationships.

Personality The unique psychological characteristics that distinguish a person or group.

Personalized pricing Adjusting prices in real time to fit individual customer needs, situations, locations, and buying behaviors.

Pleasing products Products that give high immediate satisfaction but may hurt consumers in the long run.

Political environment Laws, government agencies, and pressure groups that influence and limit various organizations and individuals in a given society.

Portfolio analysis The process by which management evaluates the products and businesses that make up the company.

Positioning Arranging for a market offering to occupy a clear, distinctive, and desirable place relative to competing products in the minds of target consumers.

Positioning statement A statement that summarizes company or brand positioning using this form: To (target segment and need) our (brand) is (concept) that (point of difference).

Postpurchase behavior The stage of the buyer decision process in which consumers take further action after purchase, based on their satisfaction or dissatisfaction.

Preapproach The sales step in which a salesperson learns as much as possible about a prospective customer before making a sales call.

Presentation The sales step in which a salesperson tells the "value story" to the buyer, showing how the company's offer solves the customer's problems.

Price The amount of money charged for a product or service, or the sum of the values that customers exchange for the benefits of having or using the product or service.

Price elasticity A measure of the sensitivity of demand to changes in price.

Primary data Information collected for the specific purpose at hand.

Problem recognition The first stage of the business buying process in which someone in the company recognizes a problem or need that can be met by acquiring a good or a service.

Product Anything that can be offered to a market for attention, acquisition, use, or consumption that might satisfy a want or need.

Product adaptation Adapting a product to meet local conditions or wants in foreign markets.

Product bundle pricing Combining several products and offering the bundle at a reduced price.

Product concept A detailed version of the new product idea stated in meaningful consumer terms.

Product concept The idea that consumers will favor products that offer the most quality, performance, and features; therefore, the organization should devote its energy to making continuous product improvements.

Product development Company growth by offering modified or new products to current market segments.

Product development Developing the product concept into a physical product to ensure that the product idea can be turned into a workable market offering.

Product invention Creating new products or services for foreign markets.

Product life cycle (PLC) The course of a product's sales and profits over its lifetime.

Product line A group of products that are closely related because they function in a similar manner, are sold to the same customer groups, are marketed through the same types of outlets, or fall within given price ranges.

Product line pricing Setting the price steps between various products in a product line based on cost differences between the products, customer evaluations of different features, and competitors' prices.

Product mix (or product portfolio) The set of all product lines and items that a particular seller offers for sale.

Product position The way a product is defined by consumers on important attributes—the place it occupies in consumers' minds relative to competing products.

Product quality The characteristics of a product or service that bear on its ability to satisfy stated or implied customer needs.

Product sales force structure A sales force organization in which salespeople specialize in selling only a portion of the company's products or lines.

Product specification The stage of the business buying process in which the buying organization decides on and specifies the best technical product characteristics for a needed item.

Product/market expansion grid A portfolio-planning tool for identifying company growth opportunities through market penetration, market development, product development, or diversification.

Production concept The idea that consumers will favor products that are available and highly affordable; therefore, the organization should focus on improving production and distribution efficiency.

Promotion mix (marketing communications mix) The specific blend of promotion tools that the company uses to persuasively communicate customer value and build customer relationships.

Promotional pricing Temporarily pricing products below the list price, and sometimes even below cost, to increase short-run sales.

Proposal solicitation The stage of the business buying process in which the buyer invites qualified suppliers to submit proposals.

Prospecting The sales step in which a salesperson or company identifies qualified potential customers.

Psychographic segmentation Dividing a market into different segments based on lifestyle or personality characteristics.

Psychological pricing Pricing that considers the psychology of prices and not simply the economics; the price is used to say something about the product.

Public Any group that has an actual or potential interest in or impact on an organization's ability to achieve its objectives.

Public relations (PR) Building good relations with the company's various publics by obtaining favorable publicity, building a good corporate image, and creating favorable events, stories, and other marketing content.

Pull strategy A promotion strategy that calls for spending a lot on consumer advertising, promotion, and other content to induce final consumers to engage with and buy the product, creating a demand vacuum that "pulls" the product through the channel.

Purchase decision The buyer's decision about which brand to purchase.

Push strategy A promotion strategy that calls for using the sales force and trade promotion to push the product through channels. The producer promotes the product to channel members who in turn promote it to final consumers.

Reference group A group that serves as direct or indirect point of comparison or reference in forming a person's attitudes or behavior.

Reference prices Prices that buyers carry in their minds and refer to when they look at a given product.

Retailer A business whose sales come primarily from retailing.

Retailing All the activities involved in selling goods or services directly to final consumers for their personal, nonbusiness use.

Return on advertising investment The net return on advertising investment divided by the costs of the advertising investment.

Sales force management Analyzing, planning, implementing, and controlling sales force activities.

Sales promotion Short-term incentives to encourage the purchase or sale of a product or a service.

Sales quota A standard that states the amount a salesperson should sell and how sales should be divided among the company's products.

Salesperson An individual who represents a company to customers by performing one or more of the following activities: prospecting, communicating, selling, servicing, information gathering, and relationship building.

Salutary products Products that have low immediate appeal but may benefit consumers in the long run.

Sample A segment of the population selected for marketing research to represent the population as a whole.

Secondary data Information that already exists somewhere, having been collected for another purpose.

Segmented pricing Selling a product or service at two or more prices, where the difference in prices is not based on differences in costs.

Selective distribution The use of more than one but fewer than all of the intermediaries that are willing to carry the company's products.

Selling concept The idea that consumers will not buy enough of the firm's products unless the firm undertakes a large-scale selling and promotion effort.

Selling process The steps that salespeople follow when selling, which include prospecting and qualifying, preapproach, approach, presentation and demonstration, handling objections, closing, and follow-up.

Sense-of-mission marketing A company should define its mission in broad social terms rather than narrow product terms.

Service An activity, benefit, or satisfaction offered for sale that is essentially intangible and does not result in the ownership of anything.

Service inseparability Services are produced and consumed at the same time and cannot be separated from their providers.

Service intangibility Services cannot be seen, tasted, felt, heard, or smelled before they are bought.

Service perishability Services cannot be stored for later sale or use.

Service profit chain The chain that links service firm profits with employee and customer satisfaction.

Service retailer A retailer whose product line is actually a service; examples include hotels, airlines, banks, colleges, and many others.

Service variability The quality of services may vary greatly depending on who provides them and when, where, and how they are provided.

Share of customer The portion of the customer's purchasing that a company gets in its product categories.

Shopper marketing Focusing the entire marketing process on turning shoppers into buyers as they move along toward the point of sale, whether during in-store, online, or mobile shopping.

Shopping center A group of retail businesses built on a site that is planned, developed, owned, and managed as a unit.

Shopping product A consumer product that the customer, in the process of selecting and purchasing, usually compares on such attributes as suitability, quality, price, and style.

Social class Relatively permanent and ordered divisions in a society whose members share similar values, interests, and behaviors.

Social marketing The use of traditional business marketing concepts and tools to encourage behaviors that will create individual and societal well-being.

Social media Independent and commercial online social networks where people congregate to socialize and share messages, opinions, pictures, videos, and other content.

Social selling Using online, mobile, and social media to engage customers, build stronger customer relationships, and augment sales performance.

Societal marketing A company should make marketing decisions by considering consumers' wants, the company's requirements, consumers' long-run interests, and society's long-run interests.

Societal marketing concept The idea that a company's marketing decisions should consider consumers' wants, the company's requirements, consumers' long-run interests, and society's long-run interests.

Spam Unsolicited, unwanted commercial email messages.

Specialty product A consumer product with unique characteristics or brand identification for which a significant group of buyers is willing to make a special purchase effort.

Specialty store A retail store that carries a narrow product line with a deep assortment within that line.

Standardized global marketing A global marketing strategy that basically uses the same marketing strategy and mix in all of the company's international markets.

Store brand (or private brand) A brand created and owned by a reseller of a product or service.

Straight product extension Marketing a product in a foreign market without making any changes to the product.

Straight rebuy A business buying situation in which the buyer routinely reorders something without modifications.

Strategic group A group of firms in an industry following the same or a similar strategy.

Strategic planning The process of developing and maintaining a strategic fit between the organization's goals and capabilities and its changing marketing opportunities.

Style A basic and distinctive mode of expression.

Subculture A group of people with shared value systems based on common life experiences and situations.

Supermarket A large, low-cost, low-margin, high-volume, self-service store that carries a wide variety of grocery and household products.

Superstore A store much larger than a regular supermarket that offers a large assortment of routinely purchased food products, nonfood items, and services.

Supplier development Systematic development of networks of supplier-partners to ensure an appropriate and dependable supply of products and materials for use in making products or reselling them to others.

Supplier search The stage of the business buying process in which the buyer tries to find the best vendors.

Supplier selection The stage of the business buying process in which the buyer reviews proposals and selects a supplier or suppliers.

Supply chain management Managing upstream and downstream value-added flows of materials, final goods, and related information among suppliers, the company, resellers, and final consumers.

Survey research Gathering primary data by asking people questions about their knowledge, attitudes, preferences, and buying behavior.

Sustainable marketing Socially and environmentally responsible marketing that meets the present needs of consumers and businesses while also preserving or enhancing the ability of future generations to meet their needs.

SWOT analysis An overall evaluation of the company's strengths (S), weaknesses (W), opportunities (O), and threats (T).

Systems selling (or solutions selling) Buying a packaged solution to a problem from a single seller, thus avoiding all the separate decisions involved in a complex buying situation.

Target costing Pricing that starts with an ideal selling price and then targets costs that will ensure that the price is met.

Target market A set of buyers who share common needs or characteristics that a company decides to serve.

Team selling Using teams of people from sales, marketing, engineering, finance, technical support, and even upper management to service large, complex accounts.

Team-based new product development New product development in which various company departments work closely together, overlapping the steps in the product development process to save time and increase effectiveness.

Technological environment Forces that create new technologies, creating new product and market opportunities.

Telemarketing Using the telephone to sell directly to customers.

Territorial sales force structure A sales force organization that assigns each salesperson to an exclusive geographic territory in which that salesperson sells the company's full line.

Test marketing The stage of new product development in which the product and its proposed marketing program are tested in realistic market settings.

Third-party logistics (3PL) provider An independent logistics provider that performs any or all of the functions required to get a client's product to market.

Total costs The sum of the fixed and variable costs for any given level of production.

Total market strategy Integrating ethnic themes and cross-cultural perspectives within a brand's mainstream marketing, appealing to consumer similarities across subcultural segments rather than differences.

Trade promotions Sales promotion tools used to persuade resellers to carry a brand, give it shelf space, and promote it in advertising.

Undifferentiated (mass) marketing A market-coverage strategy in which a firm decides to ignore market segment differences and go after the whole market with one offer.

Uniform-delivered pricing Pricing in which the company charges the same price plus freight to all customers, regardless of their location.

Unsought product A consumer product that the consumer either does not know about or knows about but does not normally consider buying.

Users Members of the buying organization who will actually use the purchased product or service.

Value chain The series of internal departments that carry out value-creating activities to design, produce, market, deliver, and support a firm's products.

Value delivery network A network composed of the company, suppliers, distributors, and, ultimately, customers who partner with each other to improve the performance of the entire system in delivering customer value.

Value proposition The full positioning of a brand—the full mix of benefits on which it is positioned.

Value-added pricing Attaching value-added features and services to differentiate a company's offers and charging higher prices.

Variable costs Costs that vary directly with the level of production.

Variety-seeking buying behavior Consumer buying behavior in situations characterized by low consumer involvement but significant perceived brand differences.

Vertical marketing system (VMS) A channel structure in which producers, wholesalers, and retailers act as a unified system. One channel member owns the others, has contracts with them, or has so much power that they all cooperate.

Viral marketing The digital version of word-of-mouth marketing: videos, ads, and other marketing content that is so infectious that customers will seek it out or pass it along to friends.

Wants The form human needs take as they are shaped by culture and individual personality.

Warehouse club An off-price retailer that sells a limited selection of brand name grocery items, appliances, clothing, and other goods at deep discounts to members who pay annual membership fees.

Whole-channel view Designing international channels that take into account the entire global supply chain and marketing channel, forging an effective global value delivery network.

Wholesaler A firm engaged primarily in wholesaling activities.

Wholesaling All the activities involved in selling goods and services to those buying for resale or business use.

Word-of-mouth influence The impact of the personal words and recommendations of trusted friends, family, associates, and other consumers on buying behavior.

Zone pricing Pricing in which the company sets up two or more zones. All customers within a zone pay the same total price; the more distant the zone, the higher the price.

References

Chapter 1

1. "Emirates Launches New Global Brand Platform—'Hello Tomorrow'," Emirates website, April 2, 2012, http://www.emirates.com/english/about/news/news_detail.aspx?article=839087, assessed August 18, 2015; "BBC Advertising Helps Emirates Take Off as a Lifestyle Brand," *BBC Worldwide*, http://advertising.bbcworldwide.com/home/casestudies/compendium/emirates; Joan Voight, Emirates Is the World's Most Glamorous Airline, *Adweek*, October 12, 2014, http://www.adweek.com/news/advertising-branding/emirates-worlds-most-glamorousairline-160714; "Case Study: Emirates Facebook Page Attracts More than 300,000 Fans within 3 Weeks of Launch," Digital Strategy Consulting, June 17, 2012, http://www.digitalstrategyconsulting.com/intelligence/2012/06/case_study_emirates_facebook_p.php; "Hello Tomorrow—Transforming Travel," Dubai Lynx 10, http://www.dubailynx.com/winners/2013/media/entry.cfm?entryid=647&award=101&keywords=&order=0&direction=1; "Annual Report 2014-15: Keeping a Steady Compass," downloaded from The Emirates Group website, http://www.theemiratesgroup.com/english/facts-figures/annual-report.aspx; Emirates Group website, https://www.emirates.com/media-centre/emirates-brand-value-grows-17-to-reachus77-billion#, accessed April 1, 2017; The Brand Finance Group, "Emirati Brands Are Jewel in the Crown of Middle East," January 22, 2019, https://brandfinance.com/news/press-releases/emirati-brands-are-jewel-in-the-crown-of-middle-east/.

2. See http://newsroom.fb.com/company-info/; www.facebook.com/pg/Amazon/about/; and www.starbucks.com/about-us/company-information/mission-statement, accessed August 2019.

3. See Philip Kotler and Kevin Lane Keller, *Marketing Management*, 15th ed. (Hoboken, NJ: Pearson Education, 2016), p. 5.

4. The American Marketing Association offers the following definition: "Marketing is the activity, set of institutions, and processes for creating, communicating, delivering, and exchanging offerings that have value for customers, clients, partners, and society at large." See https://marketing-dictionary.org/m/marketing/, accessed September 2019.

5. See Leah Fessler, "Airbnb Is Defined by Its CEO's Obsessive Perfection," *Quartz,* February 21, 2018, https://work.qz.com/1214411/airbnb-ceo-brian-chesky-wants-to-do-home-visits-to-check-your-wifi/; and Cahterine Clifford, "The Brilliant Business Lesson behind the Emails Jeff Bezos Sends to His Amazon Executives with a Single '?,'" *CNBC*, May 8, 2018, www.cnbc.com/2018/05/07/why-jeff-bezos-still-reads-the-emails-amazon-customers-send-him.html.

6. See and Tim Nudd, "The 10 Best Ads of 2017," *Adweek*, December 10, 2017, www.adweek.com/creativity/the-10-best-ads-of-2017.

7. See Theodore Levitt's classic article, "Marketing Myopia," *Harvard Business Review,* July–August 1960, pp. 45–56. For more recent discussions, see Roberto Friedmann, "What Business Are You In?" *Marketing Management*, Summer 2011, pp. 18–23; Al Ries, "'Marketing Myopia' Revisited: Perhaps a Narrow Vision Is Better Business," *Advertising Age*, December 4, 2013, http://adage.com/print/245511; and Amy Gallo, "A Refresher on Marketing Myopia," *Harvard Business Review*, August 22, 2016, https://hbr.org/2016/08/a-refresher-on-marketing-myopia.

8. See "Apple Stores: Keep Track of Apple's Retail Stores Worldwide," *MacRumors*, February 6, 2019, www.macrumors.com/roundup/apple-retail-stores/; "How Online Retailers Are Creating Immersive Brand Experiences in the Real World," *Advertising Age,* March 25, 2015, www.adage.com/print/297750; Barbara Farfan, "Apple's Retail Stores around the World," *The Balance Small Business,* December 27, 2018, www.thebalancesmb.com/apple-retail-stores-global-locations-2892925; and www.apple.com/retail/ and www.apple.com/retail/learn/, accessed September 2019.

9. Erin Ollila, "4 Brands That Mastered the Omnichannel Customer Experience," *SmarterCX*, March 13, 2019, https://smartercx.com/4-brands-that-mastered-the-omnichannel-customer-experience/; Nikki Gilliland, "How Disney World Has Mastered Customer Experience," *Econsultancy*, September 28, 2017, https://econsultancy.com/how-disney-world-has-mastered-customer-experience/; "Why I Love Walt Disney World," https://ithoughtyouwereshorter.wordpress.com/2012/11/15/why-i-love-walt-disney-world/, accessed July 2019; Bruce Jones, "3 Principles Disney Uses to Enhance Customer Experience," *Harvard Business Review*, February 28, 2018, https://hbr.org/sponsored/2018/02/3-principles-disney-uses-to-enhance-customer-experience; "Walt Disney World Statistics," https://magicguides.com/disney-world-statistics/, accessed July 2019, "Best Customer Service Moment at WDW," *WDWMagic*, https://forums.wdwmagic.com/threads/best-customer-service-moment-at-wdw.845821/, accessed September 2019; and www.disneyinstitute.com and https://disneyworld.disney.go.com, accessed September 2019.

10. "Steve Jobs: Quotable Quotes," *Goodreads,* www.goodreads.com/quotes/988332-some-people-say-give-the-customers-what-they-want-but, accessed September 2019.

11. See Michael E. Porter and Mark R. Kramer, "Creating Shared Value," *Harvard Business Review,* January–February 2011, pp. 63–77; Marc Pfitzer, Valerie Bockstette, and Mike Stamp, "Innovating for Shared Value," *Harvard Business Review,* September 2013, pp. 100–107; and "About Shared Value," Shared Value Initiative, http://sharedvalue.org/about-shared-value, accessed September 2019.

12. Julie Sygiel, "How the Visionary Founder behind Jeni's Splendid Churned Her Ice Cream Dreams into Reality," *Forbes*, February 28, 2018, www.forbes.com/sites/juliesygiel/2018/02/28/jenibrittonbauer/#79fc3eaa58bf; Kara Stiles, "How Jeni's Splendid Ice Creams Flavor-Finessed Its Way to the Top," *Forbes*, December 15, 2017, www.forbes.com/sites/karastiles/2017/12/15/how-jenis-splendid-ice-creams-flavor-finessed-its-way-to-the-top/#1c6472694807; Hanna Snyder, "Community, Quality and Creativity: Jeni's Splendid Ice Cream Founder Shares the Scoop on Her B-Corp Business," *Yellow/Co.*, December 29, 2017, https://yellowco.co/blog/2017/12/29/jenis-ice-cream-b-corp-business/; and https://jenis.com/about/, accessed September 2019.

13. See Megan Willett, "How Swiss Watchmaker Patek Philippe Handcrafts Its Famous $500,000 Watches," *Business Insider,* July 12, 2013, www.businessinsider.com/how-a-patek-philippe-watch-is-made-2013-7; Stacy Perman, "Patek Philippe Crafts Its Future," *Fortune*, June 16, 2014, pp. 37–44; and www.patek.com/contents/default/en/values.html, accessed September 2019.

14. Based on information from www.llbean.com/llb/shop/516917?lndrNbr=516884&nav=leftnav-cust and other pages at www.llbean.com, accessed September 2019. Also see "L.L. Bean Beats Amazon.com, Once Again, for Best Customer Service," *Forbes*, August 3, 2017, www.forbes.com/sites/forbesinsights/2017/08/03/l-l-bean-beats-amazon-com-once-again-for-best-customer-service/#7923b45050f6; and Shep Hyken, "L.L. Bean Discontinues Lifetime Guarantee," *Forbes*, February 18, 2018, www.forbes.com/sites/shephyken/2018/02/18/l-l-bean-discontinues-lifetime-guarantee/#5a149cd3714d.

15. Stephen Diorio, "How Leading Brands Are Winning the 'Direct-to-Customer' Conversation," *Forbes*, http://www.forbes.com/sites/forbesinsights/2016/06/07/how-leading-brands-are-winning-the-direct-to-customer-conversation/; Hilton, "Hilton Honors History," Honors Global Media Center, http://news.hiltonhhonors.com/index.cfm/page/9013; Hilton, "Hilton's Loyalty Program—Hilton HHonors—Again Achieves Top Ranking from J.D. Power for Excellence in Customer Satisfaction," Honors Global Media Center, http://news.hiltonworldwide.com/index.cfm/newsroom/detail/30410; Hilton, "Hilton Launches Its Largest Campaign Ever with Exclusive Room Rates Not Found Anywhere Else," Honors Global Media Center, http://news.hiltonworldwide.com/index.cfm/news/hilton-launches-its-largest-campaign-ever-with-exclusive-room-rates-not-found-anywhere-else; Hilton, "Hilton Honors Fact Sheet," Honors Global Media Center, http://news.hiltonhhonors.com/index.cfm/page/9001; Hilton, "Hilton Honors App," http://hhonors3.hilton.com/en/hhonors-mobile-app/index2.html?cid=OM,MB,CORE9974x_52c31.3658.c6cbdb0.6c3b88c8_All,MULTIPR,Interact, Multipage, SingleLink; https://www.accomnews.com.au/2016/09/program-retooling-focusses-on-personalisation/; BigDoor, "Top 5 Hotel Loyalty Programs," http://bigdoor.com/blog/2014/03/11/top-5-hotel-loyalty-programs/; "Kundenbindungsprogramme Hilton HHonors" Tophotel.de, http://www.tophotel.de/kundenbindung/5355-kundenbindungsprogramme-hilton-hhonors.html.

16. See https://www.innocentdrinks.co.uk/, accessed August 2019.

17. See https://mondelez.promo.eprize.com/myoreocreation/and https://ideas.starbucks.com/, accessed September 2019.

18. See Tim Nudd, "Tesla Crowned This Commercial as the Winner of Its Fan-Made Ad Contest," *Adweek*, July 31, 2017, www.adweek.com/brand-marketing/tesla-crowned-this-commercial-as-the-winner-of-its-fan-made-ad-contest/; Darrell Etherington, "Tesla's Top 10 Project Loveday Videos Reveal Truly Dedicated Fans," *Tech Crunch*, July 26, 2017, https://techcrunch.com/2017/07/26/teslas-top-10-project-loveday-videos-reveal-truly-dedicated-fans/; and www.youtube.com/watch?v=oSnoYEzZnUg and www.tesla.com/project-loveday, accessed September 2019.

19. See "#Bashtag: Avoiding User Outcry in Social Media," *WordStream*, March 8, 2013, www.wordstream.com/blog/ws/2013/03/07/bashtag-avoiding-social-media-backlash; "What Is Hashtag Hijacking?" *Small Business Trends*, August 18, 2013, http://smallbiztrends.com/2013/08/what-is-hashtag-hijacking-2.html; "HBD #Hashtag! What Brands Can Learn from a Decade of Hashtagging," *Social Media Week*, August 23, 2017, https://socialmediaweek.org/blog/2017/08/hashtag-ten-years-old/; and "Hashtags Turned Bashtags: When Marketing Goes Wrong," *Search Engine People*, January 27, 2017, www.searchenginepeople.com/blog/150240925-epic-hashtag-fails.html.

20. See www.stewleonards.com/how-it-all-began/, accessed September 2019.

21. See Mai Erne, "Calculating Customer Lifetime Value," HaraPartners, www.harapartners.com/blog/calculating-lifetime-value/, accessed September 2018. For more on calculating customer value, see V. Kumar, "A Theory of Customer Valuation: Concepts, Metrics, Strategy, and Implementation," *Journal of Marketing*, January 2018, pp. 1–19.

22. See Carl Richards, "4 Steps to Manage Your Desire for Instant Gratification," *The Motley Fool*, April 24, 2013, www.fool.com/investing/general/2013/04/24/4-steps-to-manage-your-desire-for-instant-gratific.aspx; Dennis Green, "Prime Members Spend Way More on Amazon Than Other Customers—and the Difference Is Growing," *Business Insider*, October 21, 2018, www.businessinsider.com/amazon-prime-customers-spend-more-than-others-2018-10; and www.amazon.com/prime, accessed September 2019.

23. For more discussions on customer equity, see Roland T. Rust, Valerie A. Zeithaml, and Katherine N. Lemon, *Driving Customer Equity* (New York: Free Press, 2000); Roland T. Rust, Katherine N. Lemon, and Valerie A. Zeithaml, "Return on Marketing: Using Customer Equity to Focus Marketing Strategy," *Journal of Marketing*, January 2004, pp. 109–127; Christian Gronroos and Pekka Helle, "Return on Relationships: Conceptual Understanding and Measurement of Mutual Gains from Relational Business Engagements," *Journal of Business & Industrial Marketing*, Vol. 27, No. 5, 2012, pp. 344–359; and V. Kumar, "A Theory of Customer Valuation: Concepts, Metrics, Strategy, and Implementation," *Journal of Marketing*, January 2018, pp. 1–19.

24. This example is based on one found in Rust, Lemon, and Zeithaml, "Where Should the Next Marketing Dollar Go?" *Marketing Management*, September–October 2001, pp. 24–28; with information from Grant McCracken, "Provocative Cadillac, Rescuing the Brand from Bland," *Harvard Business Review*, March 4, 2014, http://blogs.hbr.org/2014/03/provocative-cadillac-rescuing-the-brand-from-bland/; "Cadillac Is Reinventing Its Entire Lineup after Years of Losing US Market Share," *CNBC*, March 23, 2018, www.cnbc.com/2018/03/23/cadillac-is-reinventing-its-lineup-after-years-of-lost-us-market-share.html; "GM Reports Another Strong Year of Earnings," GM Media, February 2019, https://media.gm.com/content/dam/Media/gmcom/investor/2019/feb/GM-Q4-2018-Press-Release-PDF.pdf; and www.dare-greatly.com, accessed September 2019.

25. Based on Werner Reinartz and V. Kumar, "The Mismanagement of Customer Loyalty," *Harvard Business Review*, July 2002, pp. 86–94. Also see Chris Lema, "Not All Customers Are Equal—Butterflies & Barnacles," April 18, 2013, http://chrislema.com/not-all-customers-are-equal-butterflies-barnacles/; Jill Avery, Susan Fournier, and John Wittenbraker, "Unlock the Mysteries of Your Customer Relationships," *Harvard Business Review*, July–August 2014, pp. 72–81, "Telling Customers 'You're Fired,'" Sales and Marketing.com, September/October 2014, p. 8; and Michele McGovern, "6 Rules for Firing a Customer," *Customer Insight Experience*, January 6, 2016, www.customerexperienceinsight.com/6-rules-for-firing-a-customer/.

26. Khadeeja Sadar, "How Your Returns Are Used against You at Best Buy, Other Retailers," *Wall Street Journal*, March 13, 2018, www.wsj.com/articles/how-your-returns-are-used-against-you-at-best-buy-other-retailers-1520933400.

27. Pew Research Center, "Mobile Face Sheet," February 5, 2018, www.pewinternet.org/fact-sheet/mobile/; and "Internet Usage Statistics," *Internet World Stats*, www.internetworldstats.com/stats.htm; accessed September 2019.

28. Lee Raine, "About 6 in 10 Young Adults in U.S. Primarily Use Online Streaming to Watch TV," *Pew Research*, September 13, 2017, www.pewresearch.org/fact-tank/2017/09/13/about-6-in-10-young-adults-in-u-s-primarily-use-online-streaming-to-watch-tv/; Amanda Kooser, "Sleep with Your Smartphone in Hand? You're Not Alone," *CNET*, June 30, 2015, www.cnet.com/news/americans-like-to-snooze-with-their-smartphones-says-survey/; and Justin Smith, "Mobile eCommerce Stats in 2018 and the Future Online Shopping Trends of mCommerce," *Outerbox*, December 19, 2018, www.outerboxdesign.com/web-design-articles/mobile-ecommerce-statistics.

29. See "Fitbit Community Grows to More Than 25 Million Active Users," *BusinessWire*, January 8, 2018, www.businesswire.com/news/home/20180108005763/en/Fitbit-Community-Grows-25-Million-Active-Users; Danielle Kosecki, "New Fitbit Community Makes It Easier to Find Friends, Join Groups & Share Inspiration," *Fitbit Blog*, January 5, 2017, https://blog.fitbit.com/fitbit-community-announcement/; and https://community.fitbit.com and https://help.fitbit.com/articles/en_US/Help_article/2187, accessed September 2019.

30. See www.statista.com; https://newsroom.fb.com/company-info/, www.cafemom.com, www.newgrounds, and ravelry.com, accessed September 2019.

31. Andrew Martin, "Show Me the Data: 4 Ways You Can Win Customers with Data and Not Just Tell Stories," *EContent*, February 21, 2019,

www.econtentmag.com/Articles/Column/Marketing-Master-Class/Show-Me-the-Data-4-Ways-You-Can-Win-Customers-with-Data-and-Not-Just-Tell-Stories-130081.htm; Emily Abrams, "7 Surprising Facts Every Snickers Lover Should Know," *Swirled,* February 14, 2018, https://swirled.com/snickers-facts/; Erik Oster, "Clemenger BBDO Melbourne Programs 'Hungerithm' for Snickers," *Adweek,* May 26, 2016, www.adweek.com/agencyspy/clemenger-bbdo-melbourne-programshungerithm-for-snickers/110055; T. L. Stanley, "How Snickers Used Social Media Outrage to Fuel the Year's Most Innovative Media Plan," *Adweek,* September 17, 2017, p. 14; Karlene Lukovitz, "Snickers Brings 'Hungerithm' to the U.S.," *Mediapost,* November 27, 2017, www.mediapost.com/publications/article/310600/snickers-brings-hungerithm-to-the-us.html; "7-Eleven & Snickers Bring Back 'Hungerithm' Holiday Promotion," *Convenience Store News,* November 13, 2018, https://csnews.com/7-eleven-snickers-bring-back-hungerithm-holiday-promotion; and www.mediacom.com/en/work/hungerithm, accessed August 2019.

32. See www.redbull.com, https://twitter.com/redbull, and www.facebook.com/redbull, accessed September 2019.

33. John Koetsier, ""Mobile Advertising Will Drive 75% of All Digital Ad Spend in 2018: Here's What's Changing," *Forbes,* February 23, 2018, www.forbes.com/sites/johnkoetsier/2018/02/23/mobile-advertising-will-drive-75-of-all-digital-ad-spend-in-2018-heres-whats-changing/#b7eece4758be; and "U.S. Mobile Retail Commerce Sales as a Percentage of Retail E-commerce Sales from 2017 to 2021," *Statista,* www.statista.com/statistics/249863/us-mobile-retail-commerce-sales-as-percentage-of-e-commerce-sales/, accessed September 2019.

34. Lauren Johnson, "Taco Bell's Mobile Ads Are Highly Targeted to Make Users Crave Its Breakfast Menu," *Adweek,* March 14, 2016, www.adweek.com/print/170155; and Johnson, "Taco Bell Beefs Up Mobile Advertising Play to Drive In-Store Foot Traffic," *Mobile Marketer,* www.mobilemarketer.com/ex/mobilemarketer/cms/news/advertising/13229.html, accessed March 2019.

35. Information from www.stjude.org/media-resources/media-tools/facts.html, accessed September 2019; and various pages at www.stjude.org, accessed September 2019. Finding Cures. Saving Children®, Up 'Til Dawn®, St. Jude Dream Home® Giveaway, and St. Jude Thanks and Giving® are registered trademarks of St. Jude Children's Research Hospital.

36. See "United States Advertisers/Agencies," *Ad Brands,* www.adbrands.net/us/top-us-advertisers.htm, accessed September 2019.

37. See https://corporate.mcdonalds.com/corpmcd/about-us/our-business-model.html and www.nikeinc.com, accessed September 2019.

38. See Jason Del Rey, "Warby Parker Is Valued at $1,75 Billion after a Pre-IPO Investment of $75 Million," *Recode,* March 14, 2018, www.recode.net/2018/3/14/17115230/warby-parker-75-million-funding-t-rowe-price-ipo; Tom Foster, "Warby Parker Grew to $250 Million in Sales through Disciplined Growth. Now It's Time to Get Aggressive," *Inc.,* June 2017, www.inc.com/magazine/201706/tom-foster/warby-parker-eyewear.html; and www.warbyparker.com, www.warbyparker.com/history, and www.warbyparker.com/buy-a-pair-give-a-pair, accessed September 2019.

39. Argos "About Argos," Affiliate Program, http://www.argos-affiliates.co.uk/blog/resources/about-argos; Argos, "Finding Your Perfect Dog Breed," Argos Pet Insurance, https://www.argospetinsurance.co.uk/we-talk-pet/finding-perfect-dog-breed; Argos, "Welcome to Argos, Part of Home Retail Group", http://www.argos.co.uk/static/StaticDisplay/includeName/AboutArgos.htm; Argos, "Our History: A Major British Company," https://argosforbusiness.co.uk/about-us/story; S. Farrell, "Argos Owner Home Retail Backs Sainsbury's 1.4bn Takeover Bid," *The Guardian,* April 1, 2016, https://www.theguardian.com/business/2016/apr/01/home-retail-backs-sainsburys-argos-takeover-bid; A. Armstrong, "Argos Exec John Walden: 'When I First Joined, People Didn't Think Argos Had a Future At All'," *The Telegraph,* August 20, 2016, http://www.telegraph.co.uk/business/2016/08/20/sunday-interview-john-walden—when-i-first-joined-people-didnt; M. Price, "Further Argos Integration Promised by Sainsbury's", ShopSafe, November 11, 2016, http://www.shopsafe.co.uk/news/further-argos-integration-promised-by-sainsburys/11725; G. Bowden, "Sainsbury's Exec Appointed Commercial Bosses Following Argos Acquisition," *RetailWeek,* September 21, 2016, https://www.retail-week.com/topics/people/sainsburys-execs-appointed-commercial-bosses-following-argos-acquisition/7012309.article; J. Taylor, "Sainsbury's to Open Argos Branch inside Every One of Its Supermarkets," *The Mirror,* October 11, 2016, http://www.mirror.co.uk/news/uk-news/sainsburys-open-argos-branch-inside-9023091; J. Rodger, "Tesco to Take on Argos as Supermarket Vows to Price Match Best Selling Toys This Christmas," *Birmingham Mail,* October 21, 2016, http://www.birminghammail.co.uk/whats-on/shopping/tesco-take-argos-supermarket-vows-12055229; K. Hope, "Why Does Sainsbury's Want to Buy Argos?", *BBC News,* February 1, 2016, http://www.bbc.co.uk/news/business-35290161; J. Kollewe, "Argos Sales Boom Fuelled by Top-end TVs and Tablets," *The Guardian,* June 9, 2016, https://www.theguardian.com/business/2016/jun/09/argos-salesboom-fuelled-by-top-end-tvs-and-tablets; H. Crouch, "Early Christmas Present: Argos Creates 10,000 Jobs in Time for Christmas," *The Sun,* September 29, 2016, https://www.thesun.co.uk/news/1879858/argos-creates-10000-jobs-in-time-for-christmas; J. Easton, "What the Argos-Sainsbury's Deal Means for the Channel," PCR, September 12, 2016, http://www.pcr-online.biz/news/read/what-the-argos-sainsburys-deal-means-for-the-channel/038698; S. Butler, "Argos Boss Plans Whirlwind Shop Four to Boost Catalogue Retailer," *The Guardian,* November 13, 2016, https://www.theguardian.com/business/2016/nov/13/argos-boss-plans-whirlwind-shop-tour-to-boost-catalogueretailer; B. Stevens, "Mike Coupe Defends £1.4 Billion Argos Acquisition," *Retail Gazette,* October 18, 2016, http://www.retailgazette.co.uk/blog/2016/10/mike-coupe-defends-1-pounds-4-pence-billion-argosaquisition; Argos, "Argos Launches Same-day UK-wide Home Delivery Service," Post and Parcel, October 7, 2015, http://postandparcel.info/68489/news/argos-launches-same-day-uk-wide-home-deliveryservice.

Chapter 2

1. George Belch and Michael Belch, Advertising and Promotion: An Integrated Marketing Perspective (New York: McGraw Hill-Irwin, 2009); J. Dobrian, "A Century of Watches," *National Jeweler,* Vol. 100, No. 20, 2006, pp. 40–44; "The History of Rolex," 2009, in-terwatches.com, accessed October 2015; K. James, "Rolex Watch Company History," www.thewatchguy.com; K. Heine, "The Concept of Luxury Brands," 2011, www.conceptofluxurybrands.com; P. Kotler, "Distribution and Channels: Kotler on Marketing," Marketing Insights from A to Z: 80 Concepts Every Manager Needs to Know, 2003, http://www.wiley.com; Robert Klara, "How Rolex Runs on Autopilot," *Adweek,* April 3, 2013, http://www.adweek.com/news/advertising-branding/how-rolexruns-autopilot-148233; "The World's Most Valuable Brands: #65 Rolex," *Forbes,* http://www.forbes.com/companies/rolex/; "Brand Finance Best Retail Brands 2015," Ranking the Brands, http://www.rankingthebrands.com/The-Brand-Rankings.aspx?rankingID=236&year=917; "Branding Case Study: Purchasing a Rolex Sports Watch," *International Branding,* http://www.internationalbranding.org/en/branding-case-study; Stephen Pulvirent, "Rare Tiffany-Branded Rolexes to Be Sold at Sotheby's Bunny Mellon Auction," *Bloomberg,* November 20, 2014, http://www.bloomberg.com/news/articles/2014-11-19/rare-tiffany-branded-rolexes-to-be-sold-at-sotheby-s-bunny-mellon-auction; "Rolex Amplifies

30-Year Wimbledon Sponsorship with Digital Content," Digital Training Academy, http://www.digitaltrainingacademy.com/casestudies/2013/07/rolex_amplifies_30year_wimbledon_sponsorship_with_digital_content.php; Eli Epstein, "Rolex: How a 109-Year-Old Brand Thrives in the Digital Age," *Mashable*, April 18, 2014, http://mashable.com/2014/04/17/rolex-marketing-strategy/#O2FKcQHWRGqs; Hitesh Bhasin, "Marketing Mix of Rolex — Rolex Marketing Mix," *Marketing* 91, November 30, 2016, http://www.marketing91.com/marketing-mix-of-rolex/; "Rolex Branding Strategy," *Finance Maps of World*, http://finance.map-sofworld.com/brand/value/rolex.html; Tim Fleschner, "Rolex, Coca-Cola Use Content Marketing to Support Brand Legacy," *Content Standard*, June 11, 2014, http://www.skyword.com/contentstandard/enterprise-marketing/rolex-coca-cola-use-content-marketing-to-support-brandlegacy/; http://rolexpassionreport.com/5207/new-rolex-strategy-after-mr-heiningers-2009-departure-from-branding-manager-guru-daniel-gaujac/; all internet sources accessed October 2015.

2. See www.ritzcarlton.com/en/about/gold-standards, accessed September 2019. For more mission statement examples, see https://www.missionstatements.com/fortune_500_mission_statements.html, accessed September 2019.

3. Information about CVS Health and its mission and activities from www.cvshealth.com/about, www.cvshealth.com/about/our-story, www.cvs.com/minuteclinic/visit/about-us/history, and www.cvshealth.com/about/our-offerings, accessed September 2019.

4. Deanna Ting, "Airbnb's Response to Booking.com? We've Got More Listings," *Skift*, March 1, 2019, https://skift.com/2019/03/01/airbnbs-response-to-booking-com-weve-got-more-listings/; Leigh Gallagher, "How Airbnb Found a Mission and a Brand," *Fortune*, January 1, 2017, pp. 56–62; Max Chafkin, "Airbnb Opens Up the World?" *Fast Company*, February 2016, pp. 76–95; Leigh Gallagher, "Here's How 'Experiences' Are Doing So Far," *Fortune*, October 23, 2017, http://fortune.com/2017/10/23/airbnb-ceo-experiences-new-york/; Theodore Schleifer, "Airbnb Sold Some Common Stock at a $35 Billion Valuation, but What Is the Company Really Worth?" *Recode,* March 29, 2019, www.recode.net/2019/3/19/18272274/airbnb-valuation-common-stock-hoteltonight; and additional information from www.airbnb.com and https://blog.atairbnb.com/belong-anywhere/, accessed September 2019.

5. See www.mars.com/global, http://cis.mars.com/global/doing-our-part/principles-in-action/business-segment-highlights, www.mars.com/about/five-principles, and www.mars.com/global/about-us, accessed September 2019.

6. The following discussion is based in part on information found at www.bcg.com/documents/file13904.pdf, accessed September 2019.

7. See http://espnmediazone.com/us/espn-inc-fact-sheet/, www.espn.com, and www.thewaltdisneycompany.com/wp-content/uploads/2019/01/2018-Annual-Report.pdf, accessed July 2019.

8. H. Igor Ansoff, "Strategies for Diversification," *Harvard Business Review*, September–October 1957, pp. 113–124.

9. Information about Starbucks in this section is from "Starbucks CEP Kevin Johnson Unveils Innovative Growth Strategy at 2018 Annual Meeting," March 21, 2018, https://news.starbucks.com/press-releases/starbucks-unveils-innovative-growth-strategy-at-2018-annual-meeting; Sarah Whitten, "Starbucks Opens First Princi Location, Teases More to Come in 2018," *CNBC,* November 7, 2017, www.cnbc.com/2017/11/07/starbucks-opens-first-princi-location-teases-more-to-come-in-2018.html; Luis Sanchez, "Why Starbucks Is Betting Big on China," *The Motley Fool,* February 8, 2019, www.fool.com/investing/2019/02/08/why-starbucks-is-betting-big-on-china.aspx; and various pages at www.starbucks.com, accessed September 2019.

10. See Michael E. Porter, *Competitive Advantage: Creating and Sustaining Superior Performance* (New York: Free Press, 1985); and Michael E. Porter, "What Is Strategy?" *Harvard Business Review*, November–December 1996, pp. 61–78. Also see "The Value Chain," www.quickmba.com/strategy/value-chain, accessed September 2019; and Philip Kotler and Kevin Lane Keller, *Marketing Management*, 15th ed. (Hoboken, NJ: Pearson Education, 2016), Chapter 2.

11. Blake Morgan, "When the CMO Owns the Customer Experience: 10 Top CMOs Share Their POV," *Forbes,* August 29, 2017, www.forbes.com/sites/blakemorgan/2017/08/29/when-the-cmo-owns-customer-experience-10-top-cmos-share-their-pov/#65afabf469d2.

12. Seewww.gapinc.com/content/gapinc/html/aboutus/ourbrands/gap.html, accessed September 2019.

13. Minda Smiley, "Adidas's 'Impossible Is Nothing' Campaign Starring Muhammad Ali Wins Top Marketing Moment," *The Drum*, March 31, 2016, https://www.thedrum.com/news/2016/03/31/adidas-s-impossible-nothing-campaign-starring-muhammad-ali-wins-top-marketing-moment; "Huawei Makes It Possible through Innovation," *NetMag Pakistan*, June 13, 2016, https://netmag.pk/huawei-makes-it-possible-through-innovation/; BMW Group, "40 Years of Sheer Driving Pleasure—Anniversary Celebrations for the BMW and MINI Driving Experience," September 21, 2017, https://www.press.bmwgroup.com/global/article/detail/T0274648EN/40-years-of-sheer-driving-pleasure-%E2%80%93-anniversary-celebrations-for-the-bmw-and-mini-driving-experience?language=en.

14. Cathy Siegner "Consumers Reveal Why They Buy Plant-Based Dairy Alternatives," Food Dive, February 15, 2015; https://www.fooddive.com/news/consumers-reveal-why-they-buyplant-based-dairy-alternatives/516702/; Katarina Gustaffsson, "Oatly Riles Big Dairy," Bloomberg Business Week, May 14, 2015, https://www.bloomberg.com/news/articles/2015-05-14/swedishoat-milk-producer-benefits-from-dairy-industrylawsuit; Jaclyn London, "The Best Milk Alternatives to Pour in Your Coffee, Cereal, and Smoothies, According to a Dietitian," Good House Keeping, September 18, 2019, https://www.goodhousekeeping.com/health/diet-nutrition/g27128821/best-milk-alternative-substitutes/; Gillian Phair, "Europe and U.S. See Significant Rise in Non-Dairy Milk Substitutes," Futures Center, May 19, 2015, https://thefuturescentre.org/articles/3774/europe-and-us-see-significant-rise-non-dairymilksubstitutes; Innova Market Insights, "Global Plant Milk Market to Top US $16 Billion in 2018: Dairy Alternative Drinks Are Booming, Says Innova Market Insights," PR Newswire, June 13, 2017, https://www.prnewswire.com/newsreleases/global-plant-milk-market-to-top-us-16-billionin-2018—dairy-alternative-drinks-are-booming-says-innovamarket-insights-300472693.html; PBN Contributor, "EU Court Says Plant-Based Products Cannot Have 'Dairy-Style' Names," Plant Based News, June 15, 2017, https://www.plantbasednews.org/post/dairy-like-names-banned-for-veganproducts-within-eu; Katie Morley, "Is Carbonated Milk the Next Sparkling Water?", The Telegraph, September 23, 2017, https://www.telegraph.co.uk/news/2017/09/23/fizzy-milkcould-hit-supermarket-shelves-boost-milk-sales/.

15. Wayne Friedman, "TV Stations Hear the Ford Blues: Ad Cuts for Carts," *MediaPost*, September 13, 2018, www.mediapost.com/publications/article/325036/tv-stations-hear-the-ford-blues-ad-cuts-for-cars.html.

16. The four Ps classification was first suggested by E. Jerome McCarthy, *Basic Marketing: A Managerial Approach* (Homewood, IL: Irwin, 1960). The four As are discussed in Jagdish Sheth and Rajendra Sisodia, *The 4 A's of Marketing: Creating Value for Customer, Company and Society* (New York: Routledge, 2012); and Philip Kotler and Kevin Lane Keller,

Marketing Management, 15th ed. (Hoboken, NJ: Pearson Education, 2016), p. 26.

17. Blake Morgan, "When the CMO Owns the Customer Experience: 10 Top CMOs Share Their POV," *Forbes,* August 29, 2017, www.forbes.com/sites/blakemorgan/2017/08/29/when-the-cmo-owns-customer-experience-10-top-cmos-share-their-pov/#65afabf469d2. Also see Sonal Jaiswal, "Under the Microscope—Who Is a Chief Customer Officer?" *Customer Think,* September 5, 2018, http://customerthink.com/under-the-microscope-who-is-a-chief-customer-officer/.

18. For more on marketing dashboards and financial measures of marketing performance, see Jim Hopkins, "6 Sales Management Dashboards Every Leader Needs," *Salesforce Blog,* January 16, 2019, www.salesforce.com/blog/2019/01/sales-management-dashboards.html; and "Marketing Dashboard Examples," *Klipfolio,* www.klipfolio.com/resources/dashboard-examples, accessed September 2019.

19. For a full discussion of this model and details on customer-centered measures of marketing return on investment, see Roland T. Rust, Katherine N. Lemon, and Valerie A. Zeithaml, "Return on Marketing: Using Customer Equity to Focus Marketing Strategy," *Journal of Marketing*, January 2004, pp. 109–127; Roland T. Rust, Katherine N. Lemon, and Das Narayandas, *Customer Equity Management* (Upper Saddle River, NJ: Prentice Hall, 2005); Roland T. Rust, "Seeking Higher ROI? Base Strategy on Customer Equity," *Advertising Age,* September 10, 2007, pp. 26–27; Andreas Persson and Lynette Ryals, "Customer Assets and Customer Equity: Management and Measurement Issues," *Marketing Theory*, December 2010, pp. 417–436; and Kirsten Korosec, "'Tomato, Tomäto'? Not Exactly," *Marketing News*, January 13, 2012, p. 8.

20. Molly Soat, "More Companies Require Revenue-Focused Marketing ROI Measures, Study Finds," *Marketing News Weekly,* www.ama.org/publications/eNewsletters/Marketing-News-Weekly/Pages/more-companies-require-revenue-focused-marketing-roi-measures.aspx, accessed September 2019.

21. Steve Hanley, "Dyson Doubles Down on Plan to Build an Electric Car (That Doesn't Suck)," *Clean Technica,* August 31, 2018, www.cleantechnica.com/2018/08/31/dyson-doubles-down-on-plan-to-build-an-electric-car-that-doesnt-suck/; Paul Eisenstein, "Vacuum-Maker Dyson Releases Patents for New Electric Vehicle Line Set to Debut in 2021," *CNBC,* May 11, 2019, www.cnbc.com/2019/05/10/vacuum-maker-dyson-releases-patents-for-new-ev-line-to-debut-in-2021.html; Eamon Barrett, "Dyson Has Big Electric Car Plans. But Unlike Tesla, the Road Doesn't Go through China," *Fortune,* February 26, 2019, http://fortune.com/2019/02/26/singapore-shanghai-dyson-tesla/; Alicia Kirby, "A Day in the Life of James Dyson," *Wall Street Journal,* December 5, 2013, www.online.wsj.com/news/articles/SB10001424052702303914304579192123334228460; and information found at www.dyson.com, accessed September 2019.

Chapter 3

1. See Klint Finley, "Microsoft Wants Cortana to Play Nice with Amazon and Google," *Wired,* January 18, 2019, www.wired.com/story/microsoft-wants-cortana-play-nicely-amazon-and-google/; Bob Evans, "#1 Microsoft Beats Amazon in 12-Month Cloud Revenue," *Forbes,* October 29, 2018, www.forbes.com/sites/bobevans1/2018/10/29/1-microsoft-beats-amazon-in-12-month-cloud-revenue-26-7-billion-to-23-4-billion-ibm-third/#1d1709a52bf1; Matt Weinberger, "Microsoft CEO Satya Nadella's Genius Plan: To Swap One Monopoly for Another," *Business Insider,* August 29, 2015, www.businessinsider.com/microsoft-ceo-satya-nadella-focus-on-office-2015-8; Tom Vander Ark, "Hit Refresh: How a Growth Mindset Culture Tripled Microsoft's Value," *Forbes,* April 18, 2018, www.forbes.com/sites/tomvanderark/2018/04/18/hit-refresh-how-a-growth-mindset-culture-tripled-microsofts-value/#4904470652ad; and www.microsoft.com and www.microsoft.com/en-us/investor/, accessed September 2018.

2. See www.ikea.cn/ms/en_CN/about_ikea/the_ikea_way/our_business_idea/a_better_everyday_life.html, www.ikea.com/gb/en/this-is-ikea/people-planet/people-communities/suppliers/, and https://preview.thenewsmarket.com/Previews/IKEA/DocumentAssets/525318.pdf, accessed September 2019.

3. "Apple Authorized Service Provider Program," https://support.apple.com/en-lamr/aasp-program, accessed February 13, 2017; Dylan Love, "An Inside Look at Apple's Secret Weapon in Retail: Authorized Resellers," *Business Insider*, February 17, 2012, http://www.businessinsider.com/apple-reseller-asheville-citymac-2012-2?IR=T, accessed February 13, 2017; Negar Salek, "My Mac Pioneers Apple's Premium Reseller Program," Connecting the Australian Channel, October 8, 2010, https://www.crn.com.au/news/my-mac-pioneers-apples-premium-reseller-program-234602, accessed February 13, 2017.

4. Susannah Birkwood, "NatWest Sets Up £2.5m Fund to Give Grants to Charities, Social Enterprises and Community Groups," Third Sector, May 12, 2015, http://www.thirdsector.co.uk/natwest-sets-25m-fund-give-grants-charities-social-enterprises-community-groups/finance/article/1346687, accessed February 13, 2017; Graham Martin, "New £2.5 Million Fund for Charities," Third Force News, May 12, 2015, http://thirdforcenews.org.uk/tfn-news/new-2.5-million-fund-for-charities#xiA1ljGBlJerFHa2.99, accessed February 13, 2017; Natwest Bank, "About Us: Sustainability," http://jobs.natwest.com/pages/sustainability, accessed February 13, 2017; Prince's Trust, "Natwest," https://www.princes-trust.org.uk/about-the-trust/success-stories/natwest, accessed February 13, 2017.

5. U.S. and World POP Clock, U.S. Census Bureau, www.census.gov/popclock/, accessed September 2019. This website provides continuously updated projections of the U.S. and world populations.

6. See "Population Projections for the United States from 2015 to 2060," *Statista,* www.statista.com/statistics/183481/united-states-population-projection/, accessed September 2019.

7. "U.S. Population," *Worldometers,* www.worldometers.info/world-population/us-population/, accessed September 2019.

8. Population numbers in this section are based on "The Generations Defined," *Pew Research*, January 17, 2019, www.pewresearch.org/fact-tank/2018/03/01/millennials-overtake-baby-boomers. Financial numbers are based on Paul Davidson, "The Economy Is Still About—Who Else?—Boomers," *USA Today*, July 17, 2017, www.usatoday.com/story/money/2017/07/17/economy-still-all-who-else-boomers/476908001.

9. "Generational Marketing: Tips for Reaching Baby Boomers," July 16, 2015, www.mayecreate.com/2015/07/generational-marketing-tips-for-reaching-baby-boomers/; Janet Morrissey, "Baby Boomers to Advertisers: Don't Forget about Us," *New York Times*, October 15, 2017, www.nytimes.com/2017/10/15/business/media/baby-boomers-marketing.html?mtrref=undefined; Chloe Aiello, "Tech Companies Will Increasingly Look to Aging Baby Boomers for Growth, Says Evercore Analyst," *CNBC,* January 26, 2018, www.cnbc.com/2018/01/26/tech-companies-will-increasingly-look-to-aging-baby-boomers-for-growth.html; and Larissa Faw, "Report: Brands Need to Rethink Attitudes about Consumers and Aging," *MediaPost,* July 18, 2019, www.mediapost.com/publications/article/322391/report-brands-need-to-rethink-attitudes-about-con.html.

10. See Alexandra Jardine, "After the Rise of 'Femvertising,' Is 'Oldvertising' the Next Big Thing?" *Advertising Age,* April 5, 2017, http://adage.com/article/creativity/femvertising-vertising/308527/.

11. See Mark Bradbury, "The Tide of Boomer Marketing Continues to Turn," *MediaPost,* August 16, 2017; and www.youtube.com/watch?v=xVkv0NCHi5s and www.youtube.com/watch?v=xMj0w6r4GPA, accessed September 2019.

12. The specific date ranges for the generations varies by source. The ones used here are from the Pew Research Center. See www.pewresearch.org/fact-tank/2019/01/17/where-millennials-end-and-generation-z-begins/ft_19-01-17_generations_2019/.

13. Colby Graff, "Gen X: 'The Forgotten Generation' by Name, by Advertisers in Real Life," *Marketing Insider*, March 30, 2018, www.mediapost.com/publications/article/316885/gen-x-the-forgotten-generation-by-name-by-adve.html.

14. Robert Klara, "5 Reasons Marketers Have Largely Overlooked Generation X," *Adweek,* April 4, 2016, www.adweek.com/brand-marketing/5-reasons-marketers-have-largely-overlooked-generation-x-170539/; Richard Fry, "Millennials Projected to Overtake Baby Boomers as America's Largest Generation," *Pew Research,* March 1, 2018, www.pewresearch.org/fact-tank/2018/03/01/millennials-overtake-baby-boomers/; and Colby Graff, "Gen X: 'The Forgotten Generation' by Name, by Advertisers in Real Life," *Marketing Insider*, March 30, 2018, www.mediapost.com/publications/article/316885/gen-x-the-forgotten-generation-by-name-by-adve.html.

15. See Michelle Markelz, "Why You Should Be Marketing to Gen X," American Marketing Association, www.ama.org/publications/eNewsletters/Marketing-News-Weekly/Pages/why-you-should-be-marketing-to-gen-x.aspx, accessed September 2018; www.lowes.com/mobile, www.lowes.com, www.youtube.com/watch?v=zbFX7p6ZGTk, and www.pinterest.com/lowes/, accessed September 2019.

16. Carrie Cummings, "Blue Ribbon Millennials," *Adweek,* April 11, 2018, p. 13.

17. See Emma Brazilian, "Millennial Movers," *Adweek,* February 27, 2017, p. 9. Also see "Millennials," Pew Research Center, www.pewresearch.org/topics/millennials/, accessed September 2019.

18. See Fred Ulrich, "Venmo, Chime and the Adulting of Millennial Financial Apps," *Business 2 Community,* January 24, 2019, www.business2community.com/finance/venmo-chime-and-the-adulting-of-millennial-financial-apps-02161835; Tim Parker, *The Balance,* "Chime Bank Review: Everything You Need to Know," January 17, 2019, www.thebalance.com/chime-bank-review-4580300; and www.chimebank.com, accessed September 2019.

19. See Sarah Perez, "US Mobile Bank Chime Raises $200 Million, Valuing Its Business at $1.5 Billion." *TechCrunch,* March 5, 2019, https://techcrunch.com/2019/03/05/u-s-mobile-bank-chime-raises-200-million-valuing-at-1-5-billion/, accessed September 2019.

20. The specific date ranges for this generation vary by source. The one used here are from the Pew Research Center. See www.pewresearch.org/fact-tank/2019/01/17/where-millennials-end-and-generation-z-begins/ft_19-01-17_generations_2019. For other data listed, see Josh Perlstein, "Engaging Generation Z: Marketing to a New Brand of Consumer," *Adweek,* November 27, 2017, www.adweek.com/digital/josh-perlstein-response-media-guest-post-generation-z/; Libby Kane, "Meet Generation Z, the 'Millennials on Steroids' Who Could Lead the Change in the US," *Business Insider*, December 4, 2017, www.businessinsider.com/generation-z-profile-2017-9; and "The Power of Gen Z Influence," Barkley Report, January 2018, www.millennialmarketing.com/wp-content/uploads/2018/01/Barkley_WP_GenZMarketSpend_Final.pdf.

21. See "GenZ: Digital in Their DNA"; Shannon Bryant, "'Generation Z' Children More Tech-Savvy; Prefer Gadgets, Not Toys," *Marketing Forecast,* April 3, 2013, www.ad-ology.com/tag/tech-savvy-children/#.U5d9avldV8E; Brett Relander, "How to Market to Gen Z," *Entrepreneur,* November 4, 2014, www.entrepreneur.com/article/238998; Josh Perlstein, "Engaging Generation Z: Marketing to a New Brand of Consumer," *Adweek,* November 27, 2017, www.adweek.com/digital/josh-perlstein-response-media-guest-post-generation-z/; and "Redesigning Retail for the Next Generation," Accenture, www.accenture.com/us-en/insight-redesigning-retail-next-generation, accessed September 2019.

22. Carrie Cummings, "Infographic: Here's How Gen Z Girls Prefer to Shop and Socialize Online," *Adweek,* May 8, 2016, www.adweek.com/brand-marketing/infographic-heres-how-gen-z-girls-prefer-shop-and-socialize-online-171328/; and "13 Strategies for Marketing to Generation Z," *Forbes,* February 22, 2018, www.forbes.com/sites/forbesbusinessdevelopmentcouncil/2018/02/22/13-strategies-for-marketing-to-generation-z/#2f6cf90731c3.

23. Erica Sweeney, "American Eagle Hands Creative Control to Gen Zers for Spring Campaign," Marketing Dive, January 28, 2019, www.marketingdive.com/news/american-eagle-hands-creative-control-to-gen-zers-for-spring-campaign/546938/.

24. For this and other quotes, examples, and data in this section, see Adrianne Pasquarelli and E.J. Schultz, "Move Over Gen Z, Generation Alpha Is the One to Watch," *Advertising Age,* January 22, 2019, https://adage.com/article/cmo-strategy/move-gen-z-generation-alpha-watch/316314/; Daniel Lavell, "Move Over Millennials and Gen Z, Here Comes Generation Alpha," *The Guardian,* January 11, 2019, www.theguardian.com/society/shortcuts/2019/jan/04/move-over-millennials-and-gen-z-here-comes-generation-alpha; and Nina Lentini, "Crest's 'Chompers' Keeps Kids Attuned to Brushing," *Media Post,* January 24, 2019, www.mediapost.com/.../crests-chompers-keeps-kids-attuned-to-brushing.html.

25. For statistics on family composition, see U.S. Census Bureau, "Family by Presence of Own Children Under 18," Table FM1, www.census.gov/data/tables/time-series/demo/families/families.html, accessed September 2019; and U.S. Census Bureau, "Households by Type, Age of Members, Region of Residence, and Age of Householder: 2018," Table H2, www.census.gov/data/tables/2018/demo/families/cps-2018.html, accessed September 2019.

26. "Interracial Marriage across the U.S. by Metro Area," *Pew Research,* May 18, 2017, www.pewsocialtrends.org/interactives/intermarriage-across-the-u-s-by-metro-area/; Mona Chalabi, "What's Behind the Rise of Interracial Marriage in the US," *Guardian,* February 21, 2018, www.theguardian.com/lifeandstyle/2018/feb/21/whats-behind-the-rise-of-interracial-marriage-in-the-us; and U.S. Census Bureau, "Table 1. Household Characteristics of Opposite-Sex and Same-Sex Couple Households," www.census.gov/data/tables/time-ries/demo/same-sex-couples/ssc-house-characteristics.html, accessed September 2019.

27. See Department of Labor, "Facts over Time: Women in the Labor Force," www.dol.gov/wb/stats/newstats/facts.htm, accessed September 2019; Katica Roy, "Breadwinner Moms Are the New Norm," *Medium,* June 28, 2018, https://medium.com/@katicaroy/breadwinner-moms-are-the-new-norm-heres-what-you-should-know-d992e1cc7386; U.S. Census Bureau, "America's Families and Living Arrangements: 2016," Table FG1, www.census.gov/hhes/families/data/cps2015FG.html, accessed September 2019; and U.S. Census Bureau, "Parents and Children in Stay at Home Parent Family Groups: 1994 to Present," Table SHP-1, www.census.gov/hhes/families/data/families.html, accessed September 2019.

28. See T.L. Stanley, "Angel Soft Continues to Build Ads around Quiet, Relatable Moments in People's Lives," *Adweek,* January 11, 2017, www.adweek.com/creativity/angel-soft-continues-build-ads-around-quiet-relatable-moments-peoples-lives-175479/; "Best of Dad Ads," *Ad Forum,* www.adforum.com/creative-work/best-of/13299/best-of-dad-ads/

play#34540302, accessed September 2019; and www.youtube.com/watch?v=nKXYc7lHs3s, accessed September 2019.

29. See Cord Jefferson, "Cheerios Ad Starring Interracial Family Predictably Summons Bigot Wave," *Gawker,* May 30, 2013, http://gawker.com/cheerios-ad-starring-interracial-family-predictably-sum-510591871; Jessica Wohl, "Campbell Soup Shows 'Real, Real Life' in New Brand Campaign," *Advertising Age,* October 5, 2016, http://adage.com/print/300750; and www.youtube.com/watch?v=yNkCp5vjYzs and www.youtube.com/watch?v=5qkJHgkUzDA, accessed September 2019.

30. Tim Henderson, "Americans Are Moving South, West Again," Pew Charitable Trusts, January 8, 2016, www.pewtrusts.org/en/research-and-analysis/blogs/stateline/2016/01/08/americans-are-moving-south-west-again; U.S. Census Bureau, "Declining Mover Rate Drive by Renters, Census Bureau Reports," November 15, 2017, www.census.gov/newsroom/press-releases/2017/mover-rates.html; and U.S. Census Bureau, "Migration/Geographical Mobility," www.census.gov/topics/population/migration/data.html, accessed September 2019.

31. See U.S. Census Bureau, "Metropolitan and Micropolitan Statistical Areas," www.census.gov/programs-surveys/metro-micro.html, accessed September 2019; William H. Frey, "US Population Disperses to Suburbs, Exurbs, Rural Areas, and 'Middle of the Country' Metros," *Brookings,* March 26, 2018, www.brookings.edu/blog/the-avenue/2018/03/26/us-population-disperses-to-suburbs-exurbs-rural-areas-and-middle-of-the-country-metros/; and "List of Micropolitan Statistical Areas," *Wikipedia,* http://en.wikipedia.org/wiki/List_of_Micropolitan_Statistical_Areas, accessed September 2019.

32. Niraj Chokshi, "Out of the Office: More People Are Working Remotely, Survey Finds." *New York Times,* February 15, 2017, www.nytimes.com/2017/02/15/us/remote-workers-work-from-home.html.

33. See www.slack.com, accessed September 2019.

34. Erik Schmidt, "For the First Time, 90 Percent Completed High School More," July 31, 2018, www.census.gov/library/stories/2018/07/educational-attainment.html; and U.S. Census Bureau, "Educational Attainment," www.census.gov/data/tables/2017/demo/education-attainment/cps-detailed-tables.html, accessed June 2019.

35. See U.S. Department of Labor, "Employment Projections: 2016–2026 Summary," www.bls.gov/news.release/ecopro.nr0.htm, accessed September 2019.

36. See U.S. Census Bureau, "Projections of the Size and Composition of the U.S. Population: 2017 to 2060," www.census.gov/data/tables/2017/demo/popproj/2017-summary-tables.html, accessed September 2019; "Multicultural Consumers by the Numbers," *Advertising Age,* April 6, 2015, p. 20; U.S. Census Bureau, "The Nation's Older Population Is Still Growing, Census Bureau Reports," June 22, 2017, www.census.gov/newsroom/press-releases/2017/cb17-100.html; and Census Quick Facts, www.census.gov/quickfacts/fact/table/US/PST045217, accessed September 2019.

37. See Brielle Jaekel, "Marriott Celebrates Latino Love of Travel in Social Media Campaign," *Mobile Marketer,* www.mobilemarketer.com/ex/mobilemarketer/cms/news/advertising/21118.html, accessed September 2018; Parker Morse, "3 Hispanic Marketing Campaigns That Are Awesome," *Media Post,"* December 6, 2017, https://www.mediapost.com/publications/article/311189/3-hispanic-marketing-campaigns-that-are-awesome.html; and http://lovetravelswithme.com/, accessed September 2019.

38. Jeff Green, "LGBT Purchasing Power Near $1 Trillion Rivals other Minorities," *Bloomberg,* July 20, 2016, www.bloomberg.com/news/articles/2016-07-20/lgbt-purchasing-power-near-1-trillion-rivals-other-minorities; and Tim Fitzsimons, "A Record 4.5 Percent of U.S. Adults Identify as LGBT, Gallup Estimates," *NBC News,* May 25, 2018, www.nbcnews.com/feature/nbc-out/record-4-5-percent-u-s-adults-identify-lgbt-gallup-n877486.

39. For more discussion, see Jacob Passy, "Wells Fargo: Ad with Gay Couple Reflects 'Demographic Reality,'" *American Banker,* June 23, 2015, www.americanbanker.com/news/consumer-finance/wells-fargo-ad-with-gay-couple-reflects-demographic-reality-1075043-1.html; Kristina Monllos, "Doritos Has Launched Limited-Time Rainbow Chips in Support of the LGBT Community," *Adweek,* September 17, 2015, www.adweek.com/brand-marketing/doritos-has-launched-limited-time-rainbow-chips-support-lgbt-community-166983/; and https://www.youtube.com/watch?v=DxDsx8HfXEk, accessed September 2019.

40. Ashley Welch, "1 in 4 U.S. Adults Has a Disability, CDC Says," *CBS News,* August 16, 2018, www.cbsnews.com/news/1-in-4-u-s-adults-has-a-disability-cdc-says/; "What Is the Disability Market," http://returnondisability.com/disability-market/, accessed September 2018; and "Disability Travel Generates $17.3 Billion in Annual Spending," *PR Newswire,* July 31, 2015, www.prnewswire.com/news-releases/disability-travel-generates-173-billion-in-annual-spending-300121930.html; and Michelle Yin, Dahlia Shewitz, Cynthia Overton, and Deeze-Mae Smith, "A Hidden Market: The Purchasing Power of Working-Age Adults with Disabilities," American Institutes for Research, April 17, 2018, www.air.org/resource/hidden-market-purchasing-power-working-age-adults-disabilities.

41. See Michelle Diament, "Microsoft Spotlights Adaptive Device In Holiday TV Commercial," *Disability Scoop,* December 11, 2018, www.disabilityscoop.com/2018/12/11/microsoft-adaptive-commercial/25800/; and www.microsoft.com/en-us/accessibility and www.xbox.com/en-US/xbox-one/accessibility, accessed September 2019.

42. Katie Richards, "Toyota Is Betting on the Olympics with 7 New Pieces of Creative for Its First Global Campaign," *Adweek,* February 9, 2018, www.adweek.com/brand-marketing/toyota-is-betting-big-on-the-olympics-with-7-new-pieces-of-creative-for-its-first-global-campaign/; "Toyota Rolls Out 'Start Your Impossible' Global Campaign That Reflects the Olympic and Paralympic Spirit of Encouragement, Challenge and Progress," Toyota Newsroom, February 9, 2018, https://newsroom.toyota.co.jp/en/corporate/21064838.html; and www.youtube.com/watch?v=38PMmAbR_e4, accessed September 2019.

43. See "Purpose & Beliefs," https://corporate.target.com/about/purpose-beliefs, accessed September 2019.

44. Drew Harwell, "Meet the Secret Army of Meteorologists Who Keep Your Holiday Deliveries on Time," *The Washington Post,"* December 8, 2014, www.washingtonpost.com/business/economy/meet-the-secret-army-of-meteorologists-who-keep-your-holiday-deliveries-on-time/2014/12/08/2d9d3c82-759d-11e4-9d9b-86d397daad27_story.html; and Steve Banker, "Using Weather Data to Improve Supply Chain Resiliency," *Forbes,* June 29, 2016, www.forbes.com/sites/stevebanker/2016/06/29/using-weather-to-improve-supply-chain-resiliency/#5da581be23f2.

45. See Joel Makower, "Walmart Sustainability at 10: An Assessment," *GreenBiz,* November 17, 2016, www.greenbiz.com/article/walmart-sustainability-10-assessment; Luna Atamian, "Why Is Walmart a Sustainability Leader?" *Huffington Post,* December 14, 2017, www.huffingtonpost.com/entry/why-is-walmart-a-sustainability-leader_us_5a329da5e4b00caf3d59eae8; and http://corporate.walmart.com/global-responsibility/sustainability/and https://corporate.walmart.com/global-responsibility/global-responsibility-report, accessed September 2019.

46. See "A $1 Billion Project to Remake the Disney World Experience, Using RFID," www.fastcodesign.com/1671616/a-1-billion-project-to-remake-the-disney-world-experience-using-rfid#1; and Arthur Levine, "Disney Park Upgrades Make Visiting More Convenient," *USA Today,* February 27, 2018, www.usatoday.com/story/travel/experience/america/theme-parks/2018/02/27/disney-parks-magicbands-fastpasses-app/374588002/.

47. See, for example, Taylor Armerding, "The 17 Biggest Data Breaches of the 21st Century," *CSO,* January 26, 2018, www.csoonline.com/article/2130877/data-breach/the-biggest-data-breaches-of-the-21st-century.html; Sarah Frier, "Facebook Just Doubled the Number of People Exposed in Data Breach," *Time,* April 4, 2018, time.com/money/5228277/facebook-cambridge-analytica-data-breach-numbers/; Kate O'Flaherty, "Breaking Down Five 2018 Breaches—and What They Mean for Security in 2019," *Forbes,* December 19, 2018, www.forbes.com/sites/kateoflahertyuk/2018/12/19/breaking-down-five-2018-breaches-and-what-they-mean-for-security-in-2019/; and Gavin O'Malley, "Facebook Faces New Accusations of Data, Privacy Breaches," *MediaPost,* January 2, 2019, www.mediapost.com/publications/article/329965/facebook-faces-new-accusations-of-data-privacy-br.html.

48. See Hal Conick, "How Brands and Nonprofits Can Work Together on a Cause," *Marketing News,* March 2019, pp. 16–17; and https://carecounts.whirlpool.com/, accessed September 2019.

49. See www.benjerry.com/values, www.benandjerrysfoundation.org, and www.unilever.co.uk/brands/food-and-drink/ben-and-jerrys.html, accessed September 2019.

50. See Larissa Faw, "Report: Majority of Global Consumers Are 'Belief-Drive' Buyers," *MediaPost,* October 2, 2018, www.mediapost.com/publications/article/325911/report-majority-of-global-consumers-are-belief-d.html; and Hal Conick, "How Brands and Nonprofits Can Work Together on a Cause," *Marketing News,* March 2019, pp. 16–17.

51. See David Gianatasio, "A New Cycle," *Adweek,* September 11, 2017, p. 13; and "Top Ice Cream Brands of the United States," *Statista,* www.statista.com/statistics/190426/top-ice-cream-brands-in-the-united-states/, accessed July 2019.

52. See "Social Impact Statistics You Should Know," http://engageforgood.com/guides/statistics-every-cause-marketer-should-know/, accessed September 2019.

53. "Sarah Jessica Parker Joins Stella Artois and Water.org to 'Pour it Forward®' and Help End the Global Water Crisis," *PR Newswire,* January 22, 2019, www.prnewswire.com/news-releases/sarah-jessica-parker-joins-stella-artois-and-waterorg-to-pour-it-forward-and-help-end-the-global-water-crisis-300782004.html; "Aerie Continues to Accelerate Growth, Expands #AerielReal Role Model Family," January 31, 2019, http://investors.ae.com/news-releases/news-releases-details/2019/Aerie-Continues-to-Accelerate-Growth-Expands-AerieREAL-Role-Model-Family/default.aspx; David Hessekiel, "Donating at Checkout Remains High amidst Retail Slump," *Forbes,* June 20, 2017, www.forbes.com/sites/davidhessekiel/2017/06/20/charity-checkout-champions/; Janet Freund, "A Stumbling Victoria's Secret Could Become the 'Sears of Brassieres,'" *Bloomberg,* May 10, 2018, www.bloomberg.com/news/articles/2018-05-10/victoria-s-secret-weak-pink-sales-has-l-brands-deeper-in-the-red; Elizabeth Segran, "Move Over, Victoria's Secret: Aerie Is Winning with Gen-Z," *Fast Company,* February 1, 2019, www.fastcompany.com/90300687/aeries-radically-diverse-campaign-gives-me-hope-for-genz; and information from www.water.org/partners/stella-artois/, www.water.org/stellaartois/, and www.stellaartois.com/en_us/water.html.

54. See Sherry Turkle, "The Flight from Conversation," *New York Times,* April 22, 2012, p. SR1; and Turkle, "Stop Googling. Let's Talk," *New York Times,* September 27, 2015, p. SR1; and Jenny Anderson, "In the Age of Screens, Families Are Spending More Time 'Alone-Together,'" *Quartz,* March 16, 2019, https://qz.com/1573329/are-families-spending-less-time-together-due-to-screens/.

55. See "Jeep Has One of the Most Patriotic Ads You'll Ever Watch," *Lifezette,* February 3, 2019, www.lifezette.com/2019/02/jeep-has-one-of-the-most-patriotic-ads-youll-ever-watch/; Erica Sweeney, "Jeep Racks Up 106M Online Views without Running Super Bowl Ad," *Marketing Dive,* February 6, 2019, www.marketingdive.com/news/jeeps-digital-only-super-bowl-spot-racks-up-106m-views-breaks-company-rec/547740/';

and www.youtube.com/watch?v=msllMWcmC08, accessed September 2019.

56. See U.S. Organic Food Market Size Worth $70.4 Billion by 2025," *PR Newswire,* July 18, 2018, www.prnewswire.com/news-releases/u-s-organic-food-market-size-worth-70-4-billion-by-2025-hexa-research-894007633.html; and "Natural and Organic Cosmetics 2019 Global Market Expected to Grow at CAGR 9.4 % and Forecast to 2025," *MarketWatch,* January 4, 2019, www.marketwatch.com/press-release/natural-and-organic-cosmetics-2019-global-market-expected-to-grow-at-cagr-94-and-forecast-to-2025-2019-01-04.

57. See www.lovebeautyandplanet.com and https://gillette.com/en-us/products/pre-and-post-shave/shaving-creams-gels-and-foams/pure-natural-shave-gel-shaving-cream, accessed September 2019.

58. "America's Changing Religious Landscape," May 12, 2015, www.pewforum.org/2015/05/12/americas-changing-religious-landscape/; Daniel Cox and Robert P. Jones, "America's Changing Religious Identity," PRRI, September 6, 2017, www.prri.org/research/american-religious-landscape-christian-religiously-unaffiliated/; Michael Sheremer, "The Number of Americans with No Religious Affiliation Is Rising," *Scientific American,* April 1, 2018, www.scientificamerican.com/article/the-number-of-americans-with-no-religious-affiliation-is-rising/; and www.pewforum.org/religious-landscape-study/, accessed July 2019.

59. For more discussion, see David Masci and Michael Lipka, "Americans May Be Getting Less Religious, but Feelings of Spirituality Are on the Rise," Pew Research Center, January 21, 2016, www.pewresearch.org/fact-tank/2016/01/21/americans-spirituality/; and "Rising Spirituality in America," Pew Research Center, March 7 2018, www.pewtrusts.org/en/research-and-analysis/articles/2018/rising-spirituality-in-america.

60. See Gini Dietrich, "5 Crisis Lessons from Crock-Pot and 'This Is Us,'" *PR Daily,* February 19, 2017, www.prdaily.com/mediarelations/Articles/5_crisis_lessons_from_CrockPot_and_This_Is_Us_23990.aspx; Amy George, "Crock-Pot's Response to Its Tragic Role in 'This Is Us' Is a Lesson in Smart PR," *Inc.,* January 29, 2018, www.inc.com/amy-george/crock-pots-response-to-angry-this-is-us-fans-shows-why-every-company-needs-a-pr-crisis-plan.html; and Dan Snierson, "One Year after Jack's Death on *This Is Us,* the Slow Cooker Defends Itself," *Entertainment Weekly,* February 4, 2019, https://ew.com/tv/2019/02/04/this-is-us-jack-death-anniversary-slow-cooker/.

61. David Kerley, "Behind the Scenes with Southwest Airlines' Social Media 'Listening Center,'" *ABC News,* November 21, 2017, http://abcnews.go.com/US/scenes-southwest-airlines-social-media-listening-center/story?id=51297908; Conor Shine, "Southwest's Heavy Heart: How the LUV Airline Is Responding to the Worst Accident in Its History," *Dallas News,* April 22, 2018, www.dallasnews.com/business/southwest-airlines/2018/04/22/southwests-heavy-heart-luv-airline-responded-worst-accident-history; Sherry Smith, "United Airlines and the 'Re-Accommodation' Debacle," *Clarity,* November 30, 2017, http://clarity.pr/best-worst-2017s-pr-disasters-2-united-airlines-re-accomodation-debacle/; David Angelo, "CMOs, Agencies: It's Time to Live Your Brands," *Advertising Age,* October 2, 2013, https://adage.com/article/agency-viewpoint/turn-consumers-social-media-advocates/244524; Alanna Petroff, "United Airlines Shows How to Make a PR Crisis a Total Disaster," *CNN Money,* April 11, 2017, http://money.cnn.com/2017/04/11/news/united-passenger-pr-disaster/index.html; Jennifer Earl, "Whole Foods Responds to $6 Pre-Peeled Orange Twitterstorm," *CBS News,* March 8, 2016, www.cbsnews.com/news/whole-foods-responds-to-6-pre-peeled-orange-twitterstorm/; Chris Matyszczyk, "Many KFCs Are Still Closed Because They Have No Chicken," *Inc.,* February 18, 2018, www.inc.com/chris-matyszczyk/kfc-is-still-short-of-chicken-one-customer-just-let-colonel-know-how-big-of-a-mistake-hes-made.html; Robbie Abed, "KFC Just Handled a Public Relations Crisis Perfectly

with a Single Picture," *Inc.*, February 23, 2018, www.inc.com/robbie-abed/kfc-just-handled-a-public-relations-crisis-perfectly-with-a-single-picture.html; and Hal Conick, "The Best Way to Respond to Social Fury? It's Still Up in the Air," *Marketing News,* October 2018, pp. 10–12.

62. Rupert Jones, "Insurance Body Calls for 'Easy Comparison' Renewal Quotes," *The Guardian*, July 10, 2014, http://www.theguardian.com/money/2014/jul/10/insurance-car-home-renewal-quotes-premium

63. Based on information from Harry McCracken, "Square Is One of the Most Innovative Companies in the World Because It Provides a More Elegant Way to Pay," *Fast Company*, February 19, 2019, www.fastcompany.com/90298939/squaremost-innovative-companies-2019; "Squaring the Circle That Is Square," PYMNTS, April 17, 2017, www.pymnts.com/mpostracker/2017/square-jack-dorsey-cash-capitalfirst-data-vantiv-paypal-uk-apples-pay-debit-pymntsmpos-tracker-mobile-payments-mobile-point-of-sale/; Harry McCracken, "Square Takes on the Clunky Old-SchoolPayment Terminal," *Fast Company*, October 18, 2018, www.fastcompany.com/90253151/square-takes-on-the-clunkyold-school-payment-terminal; and information from www.squareup.com/us/en, accessed May 2019.

Chapter 4

1. Klaus Kneale, "World's Most Reputable Companies," *Forbes*, May 6, 2009, http://www.forbes com; "Ferrero Financial Results 2014," Confectionerynews.com, http://www.confectionerynews.com/Manufacturers/Ferrero-financial-results-2014; "Research and Markets: India Chocolate Market Overview 2015–2021—Milk Chocolate Accounts for Majority of the Revenues," Morningstar, April 11, 2015, http://www.morningstar.com/news/business-wire/BWIPREM_20151104006553/research-and-markets-india-chocolate-market-overview-20152021-milk-chocolate-accounts-for-majority-of-the-revenues.html; "Tic Tac Goes Desi and Introduces 'Elaichi' Flavour," Media4Growth, December 23, 2014, http://www.media4growth.com/retail/article.html?aid=1907_Tic_Tac_goes_desi_and_introduces_%E2%80%98Elaichi%E2%80%99_flavour; Ajita Shashidhar, "Unwrapped," *Business Today*, March 30, 2014, http://www.businesstoday.in/magazine/features/confectionary-firm-ferrero-in-india-premium-chocolate-market/story/204086.html; Sohini Sen, "'We Have Faced More Difficult Marketing Challenges for Nutella Elsewhere Than in India': Emanuele Fiordalisi, Marketing Head, Ferrero India," Afaqs!, May 14, 2015, http://www.afaqs.com/interviews/in-dex.html?id=456_We-have-facedmore-difficult-marketing-challenges-for-Nutella-elsewhere-than-in-India-Emanuele-Fiordalisi-marketing-head-Ferrero-India; Oliver Nieburg, "Ferrero to Tap into Rapid Indian Chocolate Growth with New Production Site—Analysts," Confectionerynews.com, October 27, 2011, http://www.confectionerynews.com/Manufacturers/Ferrero-to-tap-into-rapid-Indian-chocolate-growth-with-new-production-site-analysts; http://www.ferrero.com.au; http://www.floweradvisor.com, all internet sites accessed November 2015; Reputation Institute, "2016 Global RepTrak®100 The World's Most Reputable Companies," March 22, 2016, https://www.rankingthebrands.com/PDF/Global%20RepTrak%20100%20Report%202016,%20Reputation%20Institute.pdf, accessed November 22, 2019; Ferrero website, "Key Figures: Group Growth in 2014/2015," http://www.ferrero.com/the-ferrero-group/business/business/key-figures, accessed April 1, 2017; "Chocolate Maker Ferrero Reports 1.5 Percent Rise in Revenue in 2017," *Reuters*, March 23, 2018, https://www.reuters.com/article/us-ferreroresults/chocolate-maker-ferrero-reports-1-5-percent-rise-in-revenue-in-2017-idUSKBN1GY2PM, accessed February 5, 2019.

2. See Bernard Marr, "How Much Data Do We Create Every Day? The Mind-Blowing Stats Everyone Should Read," *Forbes,* May 21, 2018, www.forbes.com/sites/bernardmarr/2018/05/21/how-much-data-do-we-create-every-day-the-mind-blowing-stats-everyone-should-read/#1ec7ce0760ba; and "Big Data," *Wikipedia,* http://en.wikipedia.org/wiki/Big_data, accessed September 2019.

3. See Jordan Bitterman, "Let's Clear Up the Data Forecast," *Adweek,* December 12, 2016, p. W1.

4. Based on information from Frank van den Driest, Stan Sthanunathan, and Keith Weed, "Building an Insights Engine," *Harvard Business Review,* September 2016, https://hbr.org/2016/09/building-an-insights-engine; "Unilever's PeopleWorld Case Study, July 15, 2017, www.marketlogicsoftware.com/unilevers-peopleworld-case-study/; and www.unilever.com, accessed September 2019.

5. See https://corporate.walmart.com/suppliers, accessed September 2019; and "What Is Retail Link For?" 8th & Walton, https://blog.8thandwalton.com/2015/08/what-is-retail-link-for//.

6. Katrina Lake, "Stitch Fix's CEO on Selling Personal Style to the Masses," *Harvard Business Review,* May-June 2018, https://hbr.org/2018/05/stitch-fixs-ceo-on-selling-personal-style-to-the-mass-market; Calvin Claveria, "3 Companies That Have Mastered the Art of Using Customer Data," *Vision Critical,* www.visioncritical.com/master-use-customer-data/, accessed September 2019, and https://investors.stitchfix.com/ and www.stitchfix.com, accessed September 2019.

7. See, "Mastercard Conversation Suite Video," http://newsroom.mastercard.com/videos/mastercard-conversation-suite-video/, accessed September 2019; Sheila Shayon, "Mastercard Harnesses the Power of Social with Innovative Conversation Suite," *brandchannel,* May 7, 2013, www.brandchannel.com/home/post/2013/05/07/Mastercard-Conversation-Suite-050713.aspx; "Mastercard's, Conversation Suite: Bringing Insights and Analytics to Social," http://shortyawards.com/7th/mastercards-conversation-suite-bringing-insights-and-analytics-to-social, accessed September 2019; and "MasterCard Conversation Suite Video," https://newsroom.mastercard.com/videos/mastercard-conversation-suite-video/, accessed September 2019.

8. See "Samsung: Growing Up," www.theverge.com/2017/11/6/16611758/samsung-mocks-iphone-x-commercial, November 6, 2017; and Mike Murphy, "Samsung's Strategy for Keeping Up with Apple Is to Be Mean," *Quartz,* August 18, 2018, https://qz.com/1358333/samsungs-strategy-for-keeping-up-with-apple-is-to-be-mean/.

9. Michael Brereton and Diane Bowers, "The 2017 AMA Gold Global Top 25 Market Research Firms," *Marketing News,* October 1, 2017, www.ama.org/publications/MarketingNews/Pages/2017-ama-gold-global-report.aspx. Also see Zach Brooke, "The Market Research Arms Race," *Marketing News,* July 2018, pp. 79-85.

10. Patrick Young, "Embracing an Era of Just-in-Time Research," *Marketing,* October 19, 2017, www.marketing-interactive.com/embracing-an-era-of-just-in-time-research/. Also see Michael Beebe, "Disruption Is Coming to Marketing Research," *MTA Martech Advisor,* September 3, 2018, www.martechadvisor.com/articles/interactive-marketing/disruption-is-coming-to-marketing-research/.

11. Amanda Lacey, "The New Age of Market Research Is Here," *CMO Magazine,* May 4, 2016, www.theceomagazine.com/business/the-new-age-of-market-research-is-here/; and Kelvin Claveria, "5 Marketing Research Trends to Watch in 2018," *Vision Critical,* www.visioncritical.com/market-research-predictions-2018/.

12. Kristen Meyer, "Data Science and the Art of Persuasion," *Harvard Business Review,* January–February 2019, pp. 127–137; Dan Tynan, "Winners' Playbook," *Adweek,* December 2, 2018, pp. 21–22.

13. Stacy Roman, "7 European Fast-Food Chains to Check Out," Stripes Europe, March 22, 2018, https://europe.stripes.com/lifestyle/7-europeanfast-food-chains-check-out; "Vegan-Trend: Daten und Fakten zum Veggie-Boom," VEBU, https://vebu.de/veggie-fakten/entwicklung-in-zahlen/vegan-trend-fakten-zum-veggie-boom/; "Flensburg Holm," Nordsee website,

https://www.nordsee.com/de/filialen/detail/store/nordsee-flensburgholm-278/; "Nordsee Franchise," World Franchise, http://worldfranchise.eu/franchise/nordsee.

14. For more on research firms that supply marketing information, see Michael Brereton and Diane Bowers, "The 2018 AMA Gold Global Top 50 Report," *Marketing News*, May 31, 2018, www.ama.org/publications/MarketingNews/Pages/2018-ama-gold-top50-report.aspx. Other information from www.nielsen.com/us/en/solutions/measurement/retail-measurement.html and www.kantarfutures.com/products/us-monitor, accessed September 2019.

15. See www.iriworldwide.com, accessed September 2019.

16. Kai Ryssdal and Tommy Andres, "Domino's CEO Patrick Doyle: Tech with a Side of Pizza," *Marketplace*, September 24, 2015, www.marketplace.org/2015/09/24/business/corner-office/dominos-ceo-patrick-doyle-tech-side-pizza; and Nathaniel Meyersohn, "Why Domino's Is Winning the Pizza Wars," *CNN Business*, March 6, 2018, https://money.cnn.com/2018/03/06/news/companies/dominos-pizza-hut-papa-johns/index.html.

17. See Geoff Colvin, "How Intuit Reinvents Itself," *Fortune*, November 12, 2017, pp. 76–82.

18. Ron Kohavi and Stefan Thomke, "The Surprising Power of Experiments," *Harvard Business Review*, September-October 2017, pp. 74–82. Also see Daniel Burstein, "The Top 3 A/B Testing Challenges That Prevent Marketers from Getting Big Lifts," *Target Marketing*, September 19, 2018, www.targetmarketingmag.com/article/the-top-3-a-b-testing-challenges-that-prevent-marketers-from-getting-big-lifts/.

19. See Rebecca Greenfield, "How the Deepest, Darkest Secrets of Moms Shape the Products in Aisle 6," *Fast Company*, December 19, 2014, www.fastcompany.com/3039798/most-creative-people/how-the-deepest-darkest-secrets-of-moms-shape-the-products-in-aisle-6?utm_source; Christine Michel Carter, "Meet the Company Decoding How to Market to Millennial Moms," Forbes, May 1, 2017, www.forbes.com/sites/christinecarter/2017/05/01/marketing-to-millennial-moms-where-there-is-pain-there-is-profit/#2fc67df35201; and www.momcomplex.com, accessed September 2019.

20. See "Mobile Fact Sheet," Pew Research Center, February 5, 2018, www.pewinternet.org/fact-sheet/mobile/; "Internet World Stats," www.internetworldstats.com/stats14.htm#north, accessed September 2019.

21. For more information, see www.focusvision.com/products/intervu/, accessed September 2019.

22. See Giselle Tsirulnik, "ESPN Is Mobile Publisher of the Year," *Mobile Marketing*, www.mobilemarketer.com/ex/mobilemarketer/cms/news/media/7846.html, accessed September 2019; and Vision Critical, "ESPN: How the Sports Media Company Delivers What Fans Want—and Saves Resources," www.visioncritical.com/customer-stories/espn/, accessed September 2019.

23. For more discussion, see "S.2404 (114th): Do Not Track Online Act of 2015," January 17, 2018, www.govtrack.us/congress/bills/114/s2404; Jeff John Roberts, "The GDPR Is in Effect: Should U.S. Companies Be Afraid?" *Fortune*, May 25, 2018, http://fortune.com/2018/05/24/the-gdpr-is-in-effect-should-u-s-companies-be-afraid/; Nate Lord, "What Is GDPR (General Data Protection Regulation)? Understanding and Complying with GDPR Data Protection Requirements," *Digital Guardian*, September 19, 2018, https://digitalguardian.com/blog/what-gdpr-general-data-protection-regulation-understanding-and-complying-gdpr-data-protection; and "Do Not Track Legislation," http://en.wikipedia.org/wiki/Do_Not_Track_legislation, accessed September 2019.

24. See Hal Conick, "Where Does Convenience Turn Creepy?" *Marketing News*, April/May 2017, p. 10; Lara O'Reilly, "Snapchat Is About to Introduce Something Advertisers Have Been Wanting for Ages: Behavioral Targeting," *Business Insider*, August 26, 2016, www.businessinsider.com/snapchat-to-launch-behavioral-targeting-for-advertisers-2016-8; "Data Suggest

Surprising Shift: Duopoly Not-All-Powerful," *eMarkter*, March 19, 2018, www.emarketer.com/content/google-and-facebook-s-digital-dominance-fading-as-rivals-share-grows; and "Choose Your Audience," www.facebook.com/business/products/ads/ad-targeting, accessed September 2019.

25. Based on information from Drake Bennett, "Getting to Know You: Expedia Has Bet Everything on Understanding the Psyche of the Modern Traveler," *Bloomberg Businessweek*, February 29, 2016, pp. 45–49; Jeremy Kahn, "Expedia Reads Your Mind (and Face) to Beat Rivals," *Bloomberg Businessweek*, January 19, 2017, www.bloomberg.com/news/articles/2017-01-19/expedia-reads-your-mind-and-face-to-beat-rivals; Rob Loveitt, "Inside Expedia's Usability Lab, Consumer Behavior Provides Insights," *PhocusWire*, May 23, 2016, www.phocuswire.com/Inside-Expedia-s-Usability-Lab-consumer-behavior-provides-insights; and "This New Experiment by Expedia Might Give It a Significant Competitive Advantage," *Forbes*, February 1, 2017, www.forbes.com/sites/greatspeculations/2017/02/01/this-new-experiment-by-expedia-might-give-it-a-significant-competitive-advantage/#6ca49b821830.

26. "Internet of Things (IoT) Connected Devices Base Worldwide from 2015 to 2025 (in Billions)," *Statista*, www.statista.com/statistics/471264/iot-number-of-connected-devices-worldwide/, accessed September 2019.

27. For example, see Katie Baron, "Rewiring Storytelling: Neuroanalytic Brand Boosting from the Startup That Predicted the Trump Win," *Forbes*, October 22, 2018, www.forbes.com/sites/katiebaron/2018/10/22/rewiring-storytelling-neuro-brand-boosting-from-the-startup-that-predicted-the-trump-win/#2749e5c46625.

28. See Jennifer Alsever, "At MetLife, Technology Is the Best Policy," *Fortune*, November 18, 2013; "MetLife Wall—Customer Focus by Leveraging Big Data," KPMG, www.the-digital-insurer.com/dia/metlife-wall-customer-focus-by-leveraging-big-data/, accessed September 2019; and "Rethinking the Customer Experience at MetLife," MongoDB, www.mongodb.com/customers/metlife, accessed September 2019.

29. Andrew Nusca, "Despite High Tech, the Future of Marketing Is Exactly the Same: Focus on Customers," *Fortune*, July 15, 2014, http://fortune.com/2014/07/15/big-data-future-marketing-customer-focus; and Carl F. Mela and Christine Moorman, "Why Marketing Analytics Hasn't Lived Up to Its Promise," *Harvard Business Review*, May 30, 2018, https://hbr.org/2018/05/why-marketing-analytics-hasnt-lived-up-to-its-promise.

30. See Kate Jones, "What Can Associations Learn from Netflix about Member Analytics?" *Informz*, November 9, 2016, www.informz.com/blog/associations/associations-learn-member-analytics/; Danny Vena, "Netflix Subscribers Could More Than Double by 2023," *The Motley Fool*, September 24, 2018, www.fool.com/investing/2018/09/24/netflix-subscribers-could-more-than-double-by-2023.aspx; Craig Smith, "135 Amazing Netflix Statistics and Facts," *Expanded Ramblings*, accessed January 2019; and www.netflix.com, accessed September 2019.

31. "Google CEO: AI Is a Bigger Deal Than Fire or Electricity," *Fast Company*, January 19, 2018, www.fastcompany.com/40519204/google-sundar-pichai-ai-is-a-bigger-deal-than-fire-or-electricity; and Vijay Chittoor, "Five Predictions for AI in Marketing 2019," *Forbes*, January 15, 2019, www.forbes.com/sites/forbestechcouncil/2019/01/15/five-predictions-for-ai-in-marketing-in-2019/.

32. See Daryl Travis, "The Best Omni-Channel Brands Look More Like a Cause Than a Business," *The Hub*, August 2014, www.hubmagazine.com/the-hub-magazine/zappos-omnivalues-082014/; and https://zuul.zappos.com/zuul, accessed September 2019.

33. "Google CEO: AI Is a Bigger Deal Than Fire or Electricity," *Fast Company*, January 19, 2018, www.fastcompany.com/40519204/google-sundar-pichai-ai-is-a-bigger-deal-than-fire-or-electricity;

Hal Conick, Brian Dumaine, "It Might Get Loud," *Fortune,* November 2, 2018, pp. 113-128; "The Past, Present, and Future of AI in Marketing," *Marketing News,* December 29, 2016, pp. 27–35; Erik Wander, "Welcome to the Machine," *Adweek,* December 4, 2017, p. 16; Marty Swant, "As IBM Ramps Up Its AI-Powered Advertising, Can Watson Crack the Code of Digital Marketing," *Adweek,* September 25, 2017, pp. 19–23; Lauren Johnson, "5 Bleeding-Edge Brands That Are Infusing Retail with Artificial Intelligence," *Adweek,* January 2, 2017, www.adweek.com/digital/5-bleeding-edge-brands-are-infusing-retail-artificial-intelligence-175312/; "Software For Hardware: How Artificial Intelligence Is Helping Lowe's Customers," *Forbes,* July 17, 2018, https://www.forbes.com/sites/insights-intelai/2018/07/17/software-for-hardware-how-artificial-intelligence-is-helping-lowes-customers/#7901c4534286; "Artificial Intelligence Software Market to Reach $105.8 Billion in Annual Worldwide Revenue in 2025," *Tractica,* August 20, 2018, www.tractica.com/newsroom/press-releases/artificial-intelligence-software-market-to-reach-105-8-billion-in-annual-worldwide-revenue-by-2025/; and "AI for Advertising," www.ibm.com/watson-advertising, accessed September 2019.

34. John Simmons, "These Men Are Innocent . . . ," *The Guardian,* February 18, 2007, https://www.theguardian.com/business/2007/feb/18/theobserver.observerbusiness12; "Building England's Ethical, Healthy, and Slightly Cheeky Beverage Brand," Inc., https://www.inc.com/articles/2010/07/building-englands-favorite-smoothie-company.html; Richard Wray, "Peach of an Idea," *The Guardian,* August 7, 2004, https://www.theguardian.com/business/2004/aug/07/1.

35. For some good advice on conducting market research in a small business, search "conducting market research" at www.sba.gov or see "Researching Your Market," *Entrepreneur,* www.entrepreneur.com/article/43024-1, accessed September 2019.

36. See "The 2017 AMA Gold Global Top 25 Report," *Marketing News,* October 2017, pp. 36+; and www.nielsen.com/us/en/about-us.html and www.nielsen.com/us/en/about-us.html, accessed September 2019.

37. See Zach Brooke, "When Surveys Get Lost in Translation," *Marketing News,* October 2017, pp. 12-13; and "Why Mobile Is Great for Marketing Research," *MMRA,* www.mmra-global.org/, accessed September 2018.

38. Subhash C. Jain, *International Marketing Management,* 3rd ed. (Boston: PWS-Kent, 1990), p. 338. For more discussion on international marketing research issues and solutions, see Warren J. Keegan and Mark C. Green, *Global Marketing,* 8th ed. (Upper Saddle River, NJ: Pearson, 2015), pp. 170–201.

39. For more on problems and solutions in international marketing research, see Caitlin Sanford, "Tips for Market Research in Emerging Markets," *Medium,* August 1, 2017, https://medium.com/facebook-research/tips-for-market-research-in-emerging-markets-695bed660517; and Zack Brooke, "3 Common Pitfalls of International Market Research (and How to Avoid Them)," *Marketing News,* October 1, 2017, www.ama.org/publications/MarketingNews/Pages/3-common-pitfalls-of-international-market-research-and-how-to-avoid-them.aspx.

40. See Charles Duhigg, "Psst, You in Aisle 5," *New York Times,* February 19, 2012, p. MM30; Kashmir Hill, "How Target Figured Out a Teen Girl Was Pregnant before Her Father Did," *Forbes,* February 16, 2012, www.forbes.com/sites/kashmirhill/2012/02/16/how-target-figured-out-a-teen-girl-was-pregnant-before-her-father-did/; "7 Big Data Blunders You're Thankful Your Company Didn't Make," Umbel, October 22, 2014, www.umbel.com/blog/big-data/7-big-data-blunders/?utm_content=buffer6a719&utm_medium=social&utm_source=twitter.com&utm_campaign=buffer; and Leslie K. John, Tami Kim, and Kate Barasz, "Ads That Don't Overstep," *Harvard Business Review,* January–February 2018, pp. 62–69.

41. See Kate Kaye, "The $24 Billion Data Business That Telcos Don't Want to Talk About," *Advertising Age,* October 26, 2015, pp. 12–14; and "Mobile Data Analysis with SAP Consumer Insight 365," https://experience.sap.com/designservices/work/mobile-data-analysis-with-sap-consumer-insight-365, accessed September 2019.

42. See "Respondent Bill of Rights," www.marketingresearch.org/issues-policies/best-practice/respondent-bill-rights, accessed September 2019.

43. See Dennis Green and Mary Hanbury, "If You Shopped at These 16 Stores in the Last Year, Your Data Might Have Been Stolen," *Business Insider,* August 22, 2018, www.businessinsider.com/data-breaches-2018-4; Mike Isaac and Sheera Frenkel, "Facebook Security Breach Exposes Accounts of 50 Million Users," *New York Times,* September 28, 2018, www.nytimes.com/2018/09/28/technology/facebook-hack-data-breach.html; and "Learn More about the Latest Data Breaches," *Fraud!Org,* www.fraud.org/latest_breaches?page=1, accessed September 2018.

44. See Nicole Perlroth, Amie Tsang, and Adam Satariano, "Marriott Hacking Exposes Data of Up to 500 Million Guests," *New York Times,* November 30, 2018, www.nytimes.com/2018/11/30/business/marriott-data-breach.html; and Seena Gressin, "The Marriott Data Breach," *Federal Trade Commission: Consumer Information Blog,* December 6, 2018, www.consumer.ftc.gov/blog/2018/12/marriott-data-breach.

45. See www.insightsassociation.org/issues-policies/casro-code-standards-and-ethics, accessed September 2019.

46. Ben Goldacre, "When Data Gets Creepy: The Secrets We Don't Realise We're Giving Away," *The Guardian,* December 5, 2014, http://www.theguardian.com/technology/2014/dec/05/when-data-gets-creepysecrets-were-giving-away.

47. Oliver Maier, "Bayer AG Capital Markets Day," December 5, 2018, https://www.investor.bayer.com/securedl/16668 (accessed August 2019); Luis H. Tobler Garcia, "Big Data for Best Results," Bayer: Crop Science, https://www.cropscience.bayer.com/en/blogs/corporate-blog/2017/luis-tobler-garcia-big-data-for-best-results; Bayer, "Corporate Policy 'Responsible Marketing & Sales'," https://www.bayer.com/downloads/bayer-responsible-marketing-and-sales-policy.pdfx; Bayer AG, "Privacy Statement," November 26, 2019, https://www.bayer.com/en/privacy-statement.aspx; Bayer AG, "Bayer's Annual Report 2017: Marketing and Distribution," https://www.annualreport2017.bayer.com/management-report-annexes/about-the-group/sustainable-conduct/marketing-and-distribution.html; Ruth Bender, "How Bayer-Monsanto Became One of the Worst Corporate Deals—in 12 Charts," *Wall Street Journal,* August 28, 2019, https://www.wsj.com/articles/how-bayer-monsanto-became-one-of-the-worst-corporate-dealsin-12-charts-11567001577; T. Buck, "Bayer Keen to Shift Attention from Monsanto Woe to Tech Vision," *Financial Times,* 2019, https://www.ft.com/content/63942794-1b32-11e9-9e64-d150b3105d21; Business and Human Rights Resource Center, "Bayer: Business & Human Rights Resource Centre," n.d., https://www.business-humanrights.org/en/bayer-0; L. Chao, "Big Data Brings Relief to Allergy Medicine Supply Chains," *The Wall Street Journal,* May 26, 2015, https://www.wsj.com/articles/big-data-brings-relief-to-allergy-medicine-supply-chains-1432679948; J. Dye, "U.S. Set to Approve Bayer-Monsanto Deal with Divestitures," *Financial Times,* May 29, 2018, https://www.ft.com/content/8c3d51d0-6349-11e8-90c2-9563a0613e56; A. Green, "Sustainable Agriculture," *The Economist,* December 1, 2016, https://eiuperspectives.economist.com/sustainability/food-sustainability-index-2016/infographic/sustainable-agriculture; FAO, IFAD, UNICEF, WFP, and WHO, 2019, The State of Food Security and Nutrition in the World 2019, "Safeguarding against Economic Slowdowns and Downturns," Rome, FAO, https://www.unicef.org/reports/state-of-food-security-and-nutrition-2019; Life Sciences Trainers & Educators Network, "Training's Vital Role in the Patient-Focused Transformation of Customer Engagement

at Bayer Pharma," 2019, https://www.ltenconference. com/sessions/trainings-vital-role-in-the-patient-focused-transformation-of-customer-engagement-at-bayer-pharma/; National Health Policy Forum, *Pharmaceutical Marketplace Dynamics*, Issue Brief, 2000, Washington. https://www.nhpf. org/library/issue-briefs/IB755_RxMarketplace_5-31-00.pdf; PTI, Bayer Pharmaceuticals Committed to India Growth; to Push for More R&D, March 15, 2018, https://economictimes. indiatimes.com/industry/healthcare/biotech/pharmaceuticals/ bayer-pharmaceuticals-committed-to-india-growth-to-push-for-more-rd/articleshow/63317722.cms; Reuters, "Factbox: Challenges Facing German Pharmaceutical Company Bayer," September 4, 2018, https://www.reuters.com/article/us-bayer-development-factbox/factbox-challenges-facing-german-pharmaceutical-company-bayer-idUSKCN1LK171; E. Reuter, "Bayer Targets Animal Health Marketing in a World 'Awash' in Data," *Kansas City Business Journal*, https://www.bizjournals. com/kansascity/news/2016/12/08/bayer-animal-health-marketing-big-data-changes.html; Statista, "Bayer AG's Total Revenue from 1995 to 2018 (in Million Euros)," 2019, https:// www.statista.com/statistics/263778/revenue-of-bayer-ag-since-1995/; Matej Mikulic, "Bayer - Statistics & Facts," *Statista*, February 28, 2019, https://www.statista.com/topics/4292/ bayer-ag/; Martine Vesco, "How Bayer Pharmaceuticals Found the Right Prescription for Clinical Data Access," Talend, January 31, 2019, https://www.talend.com/blog/2019/01/31/how-bayer-pharmaceuticals-found-the-right-prescription-for-clinical-data-access/.

Chapter 5

1. Asiaweek, June 13, 1997; "High Scores for Lenovo for Business, Continues to Edge Competitors in TBR Study," FidelityIT, http:// fidelityit.com/lenovo-continues-to-impress-in-business-world-gets-highest-marks-in-tbr-study; "Lenovo Receives #1 Spot for Customer Satisfaction from TBR," Insight, https://au.insight. com/en_AU/learn/content/130646645/lenovo-receives-1-spot-for-customer-satisfaction-from-tbr/; Melissa Barker, Krista E. Neher, Nicholas F. Bormann, and Donald I. Barker, *Social Media Marketing: A Strategic Approach* (Cengage South-Western 2012); "Happy 1st Birthday Lenovo!," *Lenovo Blog*, December 1, 2008, http://blog.lenovo.com/en/blog/happy-1st-birthday-lenovo-forum, accessed September 8, 2015; "Lenovo: Behavioral Differences between Purchasers & Non-Purchasers," Clicktale, https://www.clicktale.com/casestudies/lenovobehavioral-differences-between-purchasers-non-purchasers; Lindsay Stein, "Lenovo to Build 'Brand Personality' in US," *PR Week*, January 30, 2012, http://www.prweek.com/article/1280283/lenovo-build-brand-personalityus; "4 Tips to Becoming '2015 Marketer of the Year'," *Marketing*, March 3, 2015, http://www.marketing-interac-tive.com/features/mmsg-jan-feb-futurist-2015-lenovo/; Lenovo forums, https://forums.lenovo.com/t5/General- Discussion/ Thinkpads-without-trackpoint-buttons/td-p/1007847 and https://forums.lenovo.com/t5/Welcome-FAQs/bd-p/Hello; all Internet sites accessed November 2015; Google Marketing Platform, "Google Surveys 360 Helps Lenovo Innovate by Understanding Their Customers," https://marketingplatform. google.com/about/resources/google-surveys-360-helps-lenovo-innovate-and-understand-customers/; "Creating Customer Value by Harnessing Data," *Harvard Business Publishing*, August 9, 2016, https://hbr.org/sponsored/2016/08/ creating-customer-value-by-harnessing-data.

2. Consumer expenditure figures from "United States Consumer Spending Forecast," *Trading Economics*, https:// tradingeconomics.com/united-states/consumer-spending/ forecast, accessed September 2019. Population figures from the World POPClock, U.S. Census Bureau, www.census.gov/ popclock, accessed September 2019. This website provides continuously updated projections of U.S. and world populations.

3. "Advertising Age Hispanic Fact Pack," August 13, 2018, https://adage.com/article/hispanic-marketing/hispanic-fact-pack-2018/314518/; Parker Morse, "Six Facts about the Hispanic Market that May Surprise You," *Forbes*, January 9, 2018, www. forbes.com/sites/forbesagencycouncil/2018/01/09/six-facts-about-the-hispanic-market-that-may-surprise-you/#51ddbf25f307; and "Buying Power of Hispanic Consumers in the United States," *Statista*, www.statista.com/statistics/251438/hispanics-buying-power-in-the-us/, accessed September 2018.

4. See Ilyse Liffreing, "Inside Twitter's Push to Connect Advertisers with Its Hispanic Audience," *Digiday*, October 12, 2018, https://digiday.com/marketing/inside-twitters-push-connect-hispanic-audience/.

5. See Alexandria Jardine, "Toyota Made a Super-Strong Coffee for Early-Rising Hispanic World Cup Fans," *Advertising Age*, June 28, 2018, https://adage.com/creativity/work/tundra-power-world-cup-coffee/54919; and "Tundra Power," www.ads oftheworld.com/media/film/toyota_tundra_power, accessed September 2019.

6. See Nielsen, "Black Impact: Consumer Categories Where African Americans Move Markets," February 15, 2018. www.nielsen. com/us/en/insights/news/2018/black-impact-consumer-categories-where-african-americans-move-markets.html; Bill Chappell, "Census Finds a More Diverse America, as Whites Lag Growth," *NPR*, June 22, 2017, www.npr.org/sections/thetwo-way/2017/06/22/533926978/census-finds-a-more-diverse-america-as-whites-lag-growth; and U.S. Census Bureau, "U.S. Population Projections," www.census.gov/topics/population. html, accessed September 2019.

7. See Charlotte McEleny, "P&G's 'The Talk' for My Black Is Beautiful Wins the Outstanding Commercial Emmy Award," *The Drum*, September 28, 2018, www.thedrum.com/ news/2018/09/18/pg-s-the-talk-my-black-beautiful-wins-the-outstanding-commercial-emmy-award; Ann-Christine Dias, "P&G's 'The Taslk' Wins Film Grand Prix at Cannes," *Advertising Age*, June 22, 2018, https://adage.com/creativity/ work/talk-full-length/52300; and www.pgeveryday.com/tag/ mbib-all-together-beautiful and www.pgeveryday.com/tag/ mbib-about-us, accessed September 2019.

8. See Nielsen, "Asian-America Consumers Are Predictive Adopters of New Media Platforms, Online Shopping and Smartphone Use," May 8, 2018, www.nielsen.com/us/en/press-room/2018/ asian-american-consumers-are-predictive-adopters-of-new-media-platforms.html; and Gustavo Lopez, Neil G. Ruiz, and Eileen Patten, "Key Facts about Asian Americans, a Diverse and Growing Population," Pew Research, September 8, 2017, www.pewresearch.org/fact-tank/2017/09/08/key-facts-about-asian-americans/.

9. See "State Farm Launches New Asian Creative Across Multiple Channels," August 1, 2018, https://newsroom.statefarm.com/ new-state-farm-asian-market-commercials/; Shannon Miller, "See a Smart Home Go Rogue in New State Farm Campaign," *Adweek*, August 2, 2018, www.adweek.com/creativity/see-a-smart-home-go-rogue-in-new-state-farm-campaign/; and www. youtube.com/watch?v=MS9Uz5iOkh8 and www.youtube.com/ watch?v=8Tgfl2A_42c, accessed September 2019.

10. See Yuriy Boykiv, "What Leaders Need to Know about the 'Total Market' Approach to Diverse Audiences," *Inc.*, November 10, 2014, www.inc.com/yuriy-boykiv/what-leaders-need-to-know-about-the-total-market-approach-to-diverse-audiences.html; Laurel Wentz, "Welcome to the Multicultural Mainstream," *Advertising Age*, April 6, 2015, pp. 18+; and "Total Market," Culture Marketing Council, http:// culturemarketingcouncil.org/Market-Research/Total-Market, accessed September 2019.

11. See ANA, "Totally Sold on Total Marketing?" 2017 ANA Multicultural Thought Leadership Supplement, www.portada-online.com/wp-content/uploads/2017/guides/2017-ANA-MULTICULTURAL/docs/17-POR-003_Issue_FINAL_singles. pdf; Sapna Maheshwari, "Different Ads, Different Ethnicities,

Same Car," *New York Times,* October 12, 2017, www.nytimes.com/interactive/2017/10/12/business/media/toyota-camry-ads-different-ethnicities.html; and "All-New Toyota Camry Ignites the Senses," September 1, 2017, http://toyotanews.pressroom.toyota.com/releases/all+new+toyota+camry+ignites+senses.htm.

12. Nicole Laporte, "How CoverGirl Built an Ad Campaign around Multicultural Badassness," *Fast Company,* October 30, 2017, www.fastcompany.com/40485716/how-covergirl-built-an-ad-campaign-around-multicultural-badassness; Kelsey Castanon, "CoverGirl Is Getting a Makeover—& These Women Are Leading the Charge," *Refinery29,* October 10, 2017, www.refinery29.com/2017/10/175599/covergirl-new-slogan-no-easy-breezy-beautiful; and Elana Gross, "CoverGirl Just Dropped Its 'Easy, Breezy, Beautiful, CoverGirl' Slogan," *Allure,* October 10, 2017, www.allure.com/story/covergirl-drops-easy-breezy-beautiful-covergirl-slogan; and Droga5, "CoverGirl: I Am What I Make Up," https://droga5.com/work/covergirl/, accessed September 2019.

13. Hal Conick, "How to Win Friends and Influence Millions: The Rules of Influencer Marketing," *Marketing News,* August 2018, pp. 36–45; Fabian Gorsler, "Here's How Much 10 of the World's Biggest Celebrities Make on Instagram per Post," *Business Insider,* July 26, 2018, www.businessinsider.com/how-much-celebrities-make-on-instagram-2018-7; Declan Eytan, "Kylie Jenner Joins Adidas as Latest Brand Ambassador," *Forbes,* August 29, 2018, www.forbes.com/sites/declaneytan/2018/08/29/kylie-jenner-joins-adidas-as-latest-brand-ambassador/#48cf96211e91; Lisa Richwine, "Disney's Powerful Marketing Force: Social Media Moms," *Reuters,* June 15, 2015, www.reuters.com/article/us-disney-moms-insight-idUSKBN0OV0DX20150615; Neil Patel, "9 Things We Can Learn from the Mom Blog Industry," *Forbes,* November 3, 2016, www.forbes.com/sites/neilpatel/2016/11/03/9-things-we-can-learn-from-the-mom-blog-industry/#1ac630062181; Jack Neff, "Clean Break: Why J&J Is Enlisting Teens with Modest Followings as Influencers," *Advertising Age,* October 1, 2018, pp. 30–32; and "Social Media Moms," https://twitter.com/disneymoms?lang=en, accessed September 2019.

14. Nielsen, "Females Are Queens of Clean, but Men Are Sharing Some of the Load," April 5, 2016, www.nielsen.com/us/en/insights/news/2016/females-are-queens-of-clean-but-men-are-sharing-some-of-the-load.html; "American Time Use Survey," December 20, 2016, www.bls.gov/tus/charts/household.htm; and Girl Power Marketing, "Statistics on the Purchasing Power of Women," https://girlpowermarketing.com/statistics-purchasing-power-women/, accessed September 2019.

15. See Alissa Fleck, "Infographic: What Marketers Should Know about Marketing to Fathers," *Adweek,* June 13, 2018, www.adweek.com/creativity/infographic-fathers-present-unique-targets-for-advertisers/; and www.youtube.com/watch?v=CsroaCfdiCY and www.youtube.com/watch?v=KgDT49BMBvA, accessed September 2019.

16. Anna Noel Taylor, "Around the World, Kids Exert a Powerful Influence on Household Decisions," October 18, 2017, https://insights.viacom.com/post/around-the-world-kids-exert-a-powerful-influence-on-household-decisions/.

17. Tanyua Gazdik, "Honda Odyssey Helps 'Keep the Peace,'" *Marketing Daily,* June 13, 2017, www.mediapost.com/publications/article/302750/honda-odyssey-helps-keep-the-peace.html.

18. Curtis Silver, "The CAT S61 Is Bold, Tough Proof That Phones Can Be True Tools of Any Trade," *Forbes,* July 10, 2018, https://www.forbes.com/sites/curtissilver/2018/07/10/cat-s61-review/#5485d6d436d2; additional information from http://www.catphones.com/, http://www.caterpillar.com/ and https://bullitt-group.com/.

19. For more on the Claritas PRIZM, visit https://claritas360.claritas.com/mybestsegments/?ID=0&menuOption=home&pageName=Home#, accessed September 2019.

20. Daniel B. Kline, "Are Whole Foods' Prices Really Lower under Amazon?" *The Motley Fool,* September 4, 2018, www.fool.com/investing/2018/09/14/are-whole-foods-prices-really-lower-under-amazon.aspx.

21. Sarah Lyall, "Anita Roddick, Body Shop Founder, Dies at 64," *The New York Times,* September 12, 2007, http://www.nytimes.com/2007/09/12/world/europe/12roddick.html; Michael McCarthy, "How Anita Changed the World," *The Independent,* September 12, 2007, http://www.independent.co.uk/news/people/profiles/how-anita-changed-the-world-402108.html; The Body Shop website, https://www.thebodyshop.com/en-gb/; Sarah Young, "The Body Shop buys 250 tonnes of recycled plastic in bid to tackle pollution," *The Independent,* May 10, 2019, https://www.independent.co.uk/life-style/body-shop-plastic-pollution-recycling-waste-india-a8907811.html.

22. See Jennifer Aaker, "Dimensions of Measuring Brand Personality," *Journal of Marketing Research,* August 1997, pp. 347–356; and Philip Kotler and Kevin Lane Keller, *Marketing Management,* 15th ed. (Upper Saddle River, New Jersey: Pearson Publishing, 2016), p. 163.

23. Deborah Malone, *The Reinvention of Marketing* (New York: The Internationalist Press, 2014), Kindle location 142; and "Which Mini Cooper Persona Are You?" June 9, 2016, www.schompmini.com/mini-cooper-persona/.

24. See Abraham H. Maslow, "A Theory of Human Motivation," *Psychological Review, 50* (1943), pp. 370–396. Also see Maslow, *Motivation and Personality,* 3rd ed. (New York: HarperCollins Publishers, 1987); Michael R. Solomon, *Consumer Behavior,* 12th ed. (Hoboken, NJ: Pearson Publishing, 2017), pp. 156–157; and Kendra Cherry, "The Five Levels of Maslow's Hierarchy of Needs," *Very Well Mind,* November 11, 2018, www.verywellmind.com/what-is-maslows-hierarchy-of-needs-4136760.

25. See Jon Simpson, "Finding Brand Success in the Digital World," *Forbes,* August 25, 2017, https://www.forbes.com/sites/forbesagencycouncil/2017/08/25/finding-brand-success-in-the-digital-world/#40ecfced626e; and Joshua Saxon, "Why Your Customers' Attention Is the Scarcest Resource in 2017," www.ama.org/partners/content/Pages/why-customers-attention-scarcest-resources-2017.aspx, accessed November 2017.

26. See Ian Zimmerman, "Subliminal Ads, Unconscious Influence, and Consumption," *Psychology Today,* June 2014, www.psychologytoday.com/blog/sold/201406/subliminal-ads-unconscious-influence-and-consumption and "Does Subliminal Advertising Actually Work?" *BBC,* January 20, 2015, www.bbc.com/news/magazine-30878843.

27. See Craig S. Smith, "Alexa and Siri Can Hear This Hidden Command. You Can't.," *New York Times,* May 10, 2018, www.nytimes.com/2018/05/10/technology/alexa-siri-hidden-command-audio-attacks.html.

28. See Larissa Zimberoff, "New-Wave Veggie Burgers," *Rachael Ray Every Day,* May 30, 2017, www.rachaelraymag.com/food/new-wave-veggie-burgers; Leanna Garfield, "Leonardo DiCaprio Just Invested in the Bill Gates-Backed Veggie Burger That 'Bleeds' Like Beef—Here's How It Tastes," *Business Insider,* October 17, 2017, www.businessinsider.com/review-leonardo-dicaprio-beyond-meat-veggie-plant-burger-2017-10; Sami Grover, "Beyond Meat's Veggie Burger Produces 90% Fewer Greenhouse Gas Emissions Than Cow-Based Burgers," *Treehugger,* October 16, 2018, www.treehugger.com/green-food/beyond-meats-veggie-burger-produces-90-fewer-greenhouse-gas-emissions-cow-based-burgers.html; Amanda Capritto, "Where to Get the Beyond Burger," *CNET,* July 24, 2019, www.cnet.com/news/where-to-get-the-beyond-burger/; and www.beyondmeat.com/products/view/beyond-burger, accessed September 2019.

29. Fiza Pirani, "Founder of Atlanta-Based SPANX Makes Forbes' America's Richest Self-Made Women 2018," *Atlanta Journal-Constitution,* July 12, 2018, www.ajc.com/blog/buzz/founder-atlanta-based-spanx-makes-forbes-america-richest-self-made-women-2018/WB1SWiafqAfBwZOWTWrQUK/; Danielle Wiener-Bronne, "She Was Too Short to Play Goofy. Then She Invented SPANX. Now She's a Billionaire," *CNN Money,* April 2, 2018, http://money.cnn.com/2018/04/02/news/companies/

sara-blakely-rebound/index.html; Guy Raz, "SPANX: Sara Blakely," *How I Built This*, September 11, 2016, https://one.npr.org/?sharedMediaId=493169696:493311384; Lynn Yaeger, "The Bottom Line: A Profile on SPANX Founder Sara Blakely," *Vogue*, March 19, 2012, www.vogue.com/article/the-bottom-line-spanx-founder-sara-blakely; Ali Montag, "How an Embarrassing Moment Led to SPANX Billionaire Sara Blakely's Huge Success," *CNBC*, August 15, 2017, www.cnbc.com/2017/08/15/billionaire-sarah-blakelys-embarrassing-moment-led-to-spanx-success.html; "Compression Wear and Shapewear Market to Reach $5,576 Million, Globally, by 2022," *Allied Market Research*, www.alliedmarketresearch.com/press-release/compression-wear-shapewear-market.html, accessed June 2019; and www.spanx.com, accessed September, 2019.

30. See Karlene Lukovitz, "Morton Salt Helps Home Chefs Open Pop-Up Restaurants," MediaPost, November 11, 2016, www.mediapost.com/publications/article/288870/morton-salt-helps-home-chefs-open-pop-up-restaurant.html; "Morton: Next Door Chef," and www.mortonsalt.com/nextdoorchef/, accessed September 2019.

31. See www.yelp.com, www.yelp.com/about, and www.yelp.com/factsheet, accessed September 2019.

32. Stuart Hogg, "Customer Journey Mapping: The Path to Loyalty," *Think with Google*, February 2018, www.thinkwithgoogle.com/marketing-resources/experience-design/customer-journey-mapping/. For more on the customer journey, see Adam Richardson, "Using Customer Journey Maps to Improve Customer Experience," *Harvard Business Review*, November 15, 2010, https://hbr.org/2010/11/using-customer-journey-maps-to; "Customer Journey Analysis," Bain & Company, April 2, 2018, www.bain.com/insights/management-tools-customer-journey-analysis/; and Paul Talbot, "Deciphering the Customer Journey," *Forbes*, July 30, 2018, www.forbes.com/sites/paultalbot/2018/07/30/deciphering-the-customer-journey/.

33. The following discussion draws from the work of Everett M. Rogers. See his *Diffusion of Innovations*, 5th ed. (New York: Free Press, 2003).

34. Based on Rogers, *Diffusion of Innovation*, p. 281. For more discussion, see http://en.wikipedia.org/wiki/Everett_Rogers, accessed September 2019.

35. See "EV Market Share," evadoption.com/ev-market-share/, accessed January 2019; *Bloomberg Businessweek*, June 7, 2017, www.bloomberg.com/ and "Plug-In Vehicle Tracker: What's Coming, When," www.pluginamerica.org/vehicles, accessed September 2019.

36. Avie Schneider, "Kraft, Oscar Mayer Brands Take a Massive Hit as Tastes Shift," *NPR*, February 22, 2019, www.npr.org/2019/02/22/696984494/kraft-heinz-stock-drops-after-announcement-of-big-loss-sec-probe; Paul La Monica, "What Went Wrong at Kraft," *CNN*, February 22, 2019, www.cnn.com/2019/02/22/investing/kraft-heinz-stock-strategy/index.html; Jessi Devenyns, "Food Companies Struggle to Adapt to Quickly Changing Consumer Tastes," *Grocery Dive*, June 7, 2019, www.grocerydive.com/news/grocery-food-companies-struggle-to-adapt-to-quickly-changing-consumer-tastes/533954/; Alina Selyukh, "From Campbell's to Kellogg's, Classic Brands Are Feeling the Crunch," *NPR*, January 1, 2019, www.npr.org/2019/01/01/677390110/from-campbells-to-kellogg-s-classic-brands-are-feeling-the-crunch.

Chapter 6

1. Yana Nirshberg, "How to Get the Most Out of LinkedIn for Middle-Market B2B Managers," *Forbes*, August 20, 2018, www.forbes.com/sites/forbesagencycouncil/2018/08/20/how-to-get-the-most-out-of-linkedin-for-middle-market-b2b-marketers/#737685011273; Jordan Novet, "Microsoft Is Now Tying Satya Nadella's Pay to LinkedIn's Performance," *CNBC*, October 19, 2018, www.cnbc.com/2018/10/19/microsoft-is-now-tying-satya-nadellas-pay-to-linkedins-performance.html; Mansoor Iqbal, "LinkedIn Usage and Revenue Statistics,"

Business of Apps, November 12, 2018, www.businessofapps.com/data/linkedin-statistics/; "Utah State University attracts quality graduate students with targeted LinkedIn campaign," https://business.linkedin.com/content/dam/me/business/en-us/marketing-solutions/resources/pdfs/linkedin-utah-state-university-case-study-en-us.pdf, accessed September 2019; "Adobe Raises Brand Awareness and Captures the Attention of Hard-to-Reach Marketers with LinkedIn Sponsored Content," https://business.linkedin.com/content/dam/me/business/en-us/marketing-solutions/case-studies/pdfs/LIAdobeCaseStudy5-19-16.pdf, accessed September 2019; and https://business.linkedin.com/ and https://business.linkedin.com/marketing-solutions, accessed September 2019.

2. See Scott Lanza, "Shine United, Gore-Tex Ads," January 24, 2017, www.scottlanza.com/posts/shine-united-gore-tex-ads/; and www.gore-tex.com, accessed September 2019.

3. See Chuck Robbins, "Why Cisco Is the Most Strategic Digital Partner," *Cisco Blogs*, October 5, 2015, https://blogs.cisco.com/news/why-cisco-is-the-most-strategic-digital-partner; and www.cisco.com/c/en/us/about.html, https://newsroom.cisco.com/overview, and www.cisco.com/c/dam/en_us/about/annual-report/2018-annual-report-full.pdf, accessed September 2019.

4. This classic categorization was first introduced in Patrick J. Robinson, Charles W. Faris, and Yoram Wind, *Industrial Buying Behavior and Creative Marketing* (Boston: Allyn & Bacon, 1967). Also see Philip Kotler and Kevin Lane Keller, *Marketing Management* (Hoboken, NJ: Pearson Publishing, 2016), pp. 192–193.

5. See "Moving Returns Forward with Overstock.com," www.ups-scs.com/solutions/case_studies/cs_Overstock.pdf, accessed September 2019; and http://investors.overstock.com/phoenix.zhtml?c=131091&p=irol-irhome, accessed September 2019.

6. See Frederick E. Webster Jr. and Yoram Wind, *Organizational Buying Behavior* (Upper Saddle River, NJ: Prentice Hall, 1972), pp. 78–80. Also see Philip Kotler and Kevin Lane Keller, *Marketing Management*, 15th ed. (Hoboken, NJ: Pearson Publishing, 2016), pp. 193-197.

7. See "USG Corporation: Structural Panels—Octopus," *Ads of the World*, Juley 18, 2017, www.adsoftheworld.com/media/print/usg_corporation_structural_panels_octopus; and USG Structural Solutions, "A New Level of Performance," http://info.usg.com/structuralpanels.html, accessed September 2019.

8. Portions adapted from Susan Harte, "When in Rome, You Should Learn to Do What the Romans Do," *The Atlanta Journal-Constitution*, January 22, 1990, pp. D1, D6. Additional information and examples can be found in Jeanette S. Martin and Lillian H. Cheney, *Global Business Etiquette* (Santa Barbara, CA: Praeger Publishers, 2013); "A Quick Guide to Business Etiquette around the World," *Business Insider*, May 12, 2015, www.businessinsider.com/a-guide-to-business-etiquette-around-the-world-2015-5; Adam C. Uzialco, "15 International Business Customs That Could Make or Break a Deal," *Business News Daily*, April 4, 2018, www.businessnewsdaily.com/5176-unusual-international-business-customs.html; and "International Business Etiquette, Manners, & Culture," www.cyborlink.com, accessed September 2019.

9. Robinson, Faris, and Wind, *Industrial Buying Behavior*, p. 14. Also see Kotler and Keller, *Marketing Management*, pp. 198–204.

10. See Simon Mulcahy, "Behind the Scenes: The Making of Salesforce's New Ad Campaign," *Salesforce Blog*, March 23, 2017, www.salesforce.com/blog/2017/05/behind-the-scenes-salesforce-new-ad-campaign; and www.salesforce.com/campaign/blaze-your-trail/, accessed September 2019.

11. See David Moth, "Q&A: How Maersk Line Created a Brilliant B2B Social Media Strategy," September 9, 2015, https://econsultancy.com/blog/66901-q-a-how-maersk-line-created-a-brilliant-b2b-social-media-strategy; Zsolt Katona and Miklos Katona Sarvary, "Maersk Line: B2B Social Media—It's Communication, Not Marketing," University of California Berkeley, Spring 2014; and www.maerskline.com/ar-sa/social/our-social-media, accessed September 2019.

12. "World's Top 20 B2B Brands Revealed," *B2B Marketing*, June 4, 2018, www.thinkmediaconsult.com/think-media-consulting-blog/social-media-case-study-series-ibm; Lydia Patton, "Social Media Case Study Series: IBM," *Think Media Consulting*, January 25, 2018, www.thinkmediaconsult.com/think-media-consulting-blog/social-media-case-study-series-ibm; Christopher Heine, "How IBM Got 1,000 Staffers to Become Brand Advocates on Social Media and Then Take Home a Big Award," *Adweek*, July 1, 2015, www.adweek.com/digital/how-ibm-got-1000-staffers-become-brand-advocates-social-media-165664/; Erin O'Gara, "Five B2B Brands That Are Taking Over Social Media," *Red Brand Media*, February 22, 2017; https://redbranchmedia.com/blog/5-b2b-brands-taking-social-media/; "Three Examples of Great B2B Social Media Campaigns," *Target Internet*, December 19, 2018, www.targetinternet.com/3-examples-of-great-b2b-social-media-campaigns/; and www.ibm.com, www.instagram.com/ibm, www.facebook.com/IBM/, www.twitter.com/IBM, and www.linkedin.com/company/ibm/, accessed September 2019.

13. Information from www.shrinershospitalsforchildren.org; and www.chs.net/investor-relations/annual-reports/, accessed September 2019.

14. See Aimee Picchi, "The High Price of Incarceration in the United States," *CBS News*, May 8, 2014, www.cbsnews.com/news/the-high-price-of-americas-incarceration-80-billion/; and "List of Countries by GDP," *Wikipedia*, https://en.wikipedia.org/wiki/List_of_countries_by_GDP_(nominal), accessed September 2019.

15. National Center for Education Statistics, https://nces.ed.gov/fastfacts/, accessed September 2019.

16. See www.pgpro.com and www.nestleprofessional.us, accessed September 2019.

17. Niraj Chokshi, "There's About One 'Government Unit' for Every 3,566 People in the U.S.," *Washington Post*, September 4, 2013, www.washingtonpost.com/blogs/govbeat/wp/2013/09/04/theres-about-one-governmental-unit-for-every-3566-people-in-the-u-s/; and "State & Local Government Finances," www.census.gov/programs-surveys/gov-finances.html, accessed September 2019.

18. See Lockheed Martin annual reports at www.lockheedmartin.com/en-us/news/annual-reports.html?_ga=2.5297339.963821565.1530553440-464839600.1498153874, accessed September 2019.

19. See "GSA Organization Overview," www.gsa.gov/portal/content/104438, accessed September 2019; "Defense Logistics Agency: Medical Supply Chain," www.dscp.dla.mil/sbo/medical.asp, accessed September 2019; and Department of Veterans Affairs Office of Acquisition & Material Management, www.va.gov/oal/business/dbwva.asp, accessed September 2019.

20. Megan Simpson, "Shopify Reaches Milestone, Surpassing $1 Billion in Total Revenue in 2018," *Betakit*, February 12, 2019, www.betakit.com/shopify-reaches-milestone-surpassing-1-billion-in-total-revenue-in-2018/; Amira Zubairi, "How Harley Finkelstein Went from Lawyer to COO of Shopify," *Betakit*, March 19, 2019, www.betakit.com/how-harley-finkelstein-went-from-lawyer-to-coo-of-shopify/; Shareen Pathak, "Network Effect: How Shopify Is the Platform Powering the DTC Brand Revolution," *Digiday*, September 24, 2018, www.digiday.com/marketing/network-effect-shopify-platform-powering-dtc-brand-revolution/; Natalie Robehmed, "How 20-Year-Old Kylie Jenner Built a $900 Million Fortune in Less Than 3 Years," *Forbes*, July 11, 2018, www.forbes.com/sites/forbesdigitalcovers/2018/07/11/how-20-year-old-kylie-jenner-built-a-900-million-fortune-in-less-than-3-years/#5a0b1824aa62; Stephen Baldwin, "The Invisible Selling Machine," *Fortune*, March 15, 2017, www.fortune.com/2017/03/15/shopify-ecommerce-revolution/; and information from www.shopify.com/about, www.fastcompany.com/most-innovative-companies/2019, accessed September 2019.

Chapter 7

1. http://mid-east.info/news/company-news/p/persil/, accessed September 2015; PRLOG, "Persil Abaya Shampoo Leaves Abayas as Black as New," February 21, 2013; www.prlog.org/12084469-persil-abaya-shampoo-leaves-abayas-as-black-as-new.html; PRLOG, "Henkel Launches Persil Abaya Shampoo Anaqa; Adds a Touch of Elegance to the World of Abayas," November 28, 2010, www.prlog.org/11106530-henkel-launches-persil-abaya-shampoo-anaqa-adds-touchof-elegance-to-the-world-of-abayas.html; PRLOG, "Persil Liquid Detergent Now with Oud Fragrance," May 20, 2012, http://www.prlog.org/11879511-persil-liquid-detergent-now-with-oud-fragrance.html; "Extend Lifespan of Your Abayas by Giving It the Persil Abaya Shampoo Wash," Mid East Information, September 24, 2014, http://mid-east.info/extend-lifespan-of-your-abayas-by-giving-it-thepersil-abaya-shampoo-wash-27772/; Vjmedia Work Team, "GLOCAL Shoppers' Perspective—Global Understanding with Local Implementation," Media4Growth, February 2, 2013, http://www.media4growth.com/retail/shopper-marketing-detail.html?id=1_GLOCAL_Shoppers%E2%80%99_Perspective_%E2%80%93_Global_Understanding_with_local_implementation and information from http://www.henkel.com and http://www.persil.com, accessed September 2015; Henkel website, "Investors & Analysts," http://www.henkel.com/investors-and-analysts/strategy-and-facts, accessed April 1, 2017; "World's Most Admired Companies," *Fortune*, http://fortune.com/worlds-most-admired-companies/henkel-100000/, accessed April 1, 2017; Henkel website, "Henkel Is the Only German Company in FMCG-Top 50," August 25, 2016, http://www.henkel.com/newsroom/2016-08-25-henkel-is-the-only-german-company-in-fmcgtop-50/705918, accessed April 1, 2017.

2. Corinne Ruff, "How Target Is Using Small-Format Stores to Score with Younger Shoppers," *Retail Dive*, August 24, 2017, www.retaildive.com/news/how-target-is-using-small-format-stores-to-score-with-younger-shoppers/503362/; Tonya Garcia, "Target's Small-Format Stores Are Turning into a Big Winner for the Retailer," August 19, 2017, www.marketwatch.com/story/targets-small-format-stores-are-turning-into-a-big-win-for-the-retailer-2017-08-16; "Here's What Makes Our Small-Format Stores Stand Out in a Big Way," *A Bullseye View*, July 20, 2018, https://corporate.target.com/article/2018/07/small-format-stores; and Bill Schiffner, "Target to Open Columbus Circle Small-Format Stored in 2019," *Chain Drug Review*, October 29, 2018, www.chaindrugreview.com/target-to-open-columbus-circle-small-format-store-in-2019/.

3. "Mazda Digital Certified Program," http://mazdadigitalcertified.com/DealerWebsite/DealerOn; Ben Grubb, "Geo-targeting: Hyundai Case Study of Targeted Advertising," *Crikey*, July 09, 2018, https://www.crikey.com.au/2018/07/09/youre-never-alone-no-matter-where-you-goor-what-you-do-there/; Mazda Marketing Targeting Maps, December 27, 2009, https://de.slideshare.net/CardinaleMazda/mazda-marketing-targeting-maps; Johnathan Dane, "7 Retargeting Case Studies That'll Boost Your Current Campaigns," CXL, February 7, 2019, https://conversionxl.com/blog/ppc-retargeting-case-studies/; Tracy Vides, "How Geographical Targeting Can Supercharge Your Marketing," UserTesting Blog, December 22, 2015, https://www.usertesting.com/blog/geographical-targeting/.

4. See www.dove.com/us/en/men-care.html, accessed September 2019.

5. Michael McCarthy, "Ad of the Day: Dick's Sporting Goods Goes the Extra Mile in Its First Campaign for Women," April 30, 2015, www.adweek.com/print/164418; Alana Vagianos, "'Who Will You Be?' Campaign Celebrates the Raw Strength of Women's Bodies," *Huffington Post*, May 8, 2015, www.huffingtonpost.com/2015/05/08/

who-will-you-be-campaign-dicks-sporting-goods_n_7242320.html; and www.youtube.com/watch?v=Mf0_G1FS0l4, accessed September 2019.

6. See "American Express Centurion Card Best 'Black Card' 2019," *Best Business Credit,* November 29, 2018, https://businesscreditcards0.wordpress.com/2018/11/29/american-express-centurion-card-best-black-card-2019/; Johnny Jet, "American Express Centurion Black Card Review," *Forbes,* July 28, 2017, www.forbes.com/sites/johnnyjet/2017/07/28/american-express-centurion-black-card-review/#2a3e997d7055; "What Super Rich People Do to Show Their Status in Style?" *LinkedIn,* November 4, 2017, www.linkedin.com/pulse/what-super-rich-people-do-show-status-style-property-find; and Bryan Kelly, "Travel Secrets of the World's Most Exclusive Travel Card," *Travel+Leisure,* www.travelandleisure.com/travel-tips/points-miles/american-express-black-card, accessed September 2019.

7. See Andrew McMains, "Ad of the Day: Panera Gets into Lifestyle Branding with Manifesto about Healthy Living," *Adweek,* June 15, 2015, and www.panerabread.com/en-us/our-beliefs/food-as-it-should-be-nopt.html; and www.panerabread.com/en-us/our-beliefs/our-food-policy/clean-ingredients.html, accessed September 2019.

8. "Loews, Elicit, Spotify Win People-Based Marketing Awards," *Media Daily News,* September 25, 2017, www.mediapost.com/publications/article/307818/loews-elicit-spotify-win-people-based-marketing.html.

9. Julia Glum, "People in This State Drink the Most Pumpkin Spice Lattes in the Country," *Money,* October 3, 2018, http://time.com/money/5412045/pumpkin-spice-latte-most-popular-state/

10. See "From Deviled to Divorciados—The Incredible Egg Asks How Do You Like Your Eggs?" *PRNewswire,* November 15, 2017, www.prnewswire.com/news-releases/from-deviled-to-divorciados-the-incredible-egg-asks-how-do-you-like-your-eggs-300556149.html; and http://energybbdo.com/en/work/5a846b16f1e61dfc7d2d9319, www.aeb.org, and www.aeb.org/about-aeb/about, accessed September 2019.

11. See www.schwinnbikes.com/usa/bikes/, accessed September 2019.

12. See www.pampers.com/Diapers/Swaddlers, accessed September 2019.

13. See Jeremy Markovich, "The Bo-lievers," *Our State,* April 2017, pp. 114-122; and http://investing.bojangles.com/financial-information/annual-reports and www.bojangles.com, accessed September 2019.

14. See www.patagonia.com/us/ambassadors, accessed September 2019.

15. Hal Conick, "A Night in the Life of the Chicago Bulls Digital Media Team," *Marketing News,* April 2018, pp. 24–35; Darren Heitner, "How the Chicago Bulls Are Making Digital Strategy a Priority for Growth," *Inc.,* April 4, 2018, www.inc.com/darren-heitner/how-chicago-bulls-are-making-digital-strategy-a-priority-for-growth.html; Bailey Knecht, "Chicago Bulls Strive to Digitally Innovate While Honoring Their Past," *Front Office Sports,* December 13, 2018, https://frntofficesport.com/chicago-bulls-digitally-innovate/; and https://twitter.com/chicagobulls, www.facebook.com/chicagobulls/, www.instagram.com/chicagobulls, and www.nba.com/bulls/, accessed September 2019.

16. Market Insight, "Emirati Telco Du Launches UAE's New Mobile Brand as Rival Etisalat Unveils Plans to Follow Suit," *IHS Markit,* September 13, 2017, https://technology.ihs.com/595430/emirati-telco-du-launches-uaes-new-mobile-brand-as-rival-etisalat-unveils-plans-to-follow-suit; Mike Priest, "There's Now a Fourth Mobile Provider in the UAE, but It Comes with a Catch," *What's On,* September 12, 2017; http://whatson.ae/dubai/2017/09/theres-now-fourth-mobile-provider-uae-comes-catch/; Ammara Rounaq, "How to Choose the Right Mobile and Data Plan in the UAE," *Techradar,* July 2, 2018; https://www.techradar.com/news/how-to-choose-the-right-mobile-plan-in-the-uae; "Etisalat Launches New SIM Aimed at Millennials," *Arabian Business,* September 10, 2017, http://www.dubaiweek.ae/families/30798/swyp-new-sim-card-phone-etisalat/; Vanisha Rajesh "There's a New SIM Card in Town but You Need to Be a Millennial to Use It," Dubaiweek.ae, September 16, 2017; http://www.dubaiweek.ae/families/30798/swyp-new-sim-card-phone-etisalat/.

17. See http://c.ymcdn.com/sites/dema.site-ym.com/resource/resmgr/Member_Resources/Lifestage_Clustering.pdf and https://isapps.acxiom.com/personicx/personicx.aspx, accessed September 2019.

18. See www.starbucks.com/business and https://solutions.starbucks.com, accessed September 2019.

19. For examples, see www.steelcase.com, www.steelcase.com/discover/information/government/, www.steelcase.com/discover/information/education/, www.steelcase.com/discover/information/health/, www.steelcase.com/discover/information/architects-and-designers/, www.steelcase.com/research/articles/topics/collaboration/a-new-legal-brief/, and www.steelcase.com/research/articles/topics/coworking/work-hospitality/, accessed September 2019.

20. See Pamela N. Danziger, "Why Zara Succeeds: It Focuses on Pulling People In, Not Pushing Product Out," Forbes, April 23, 2018, www.forbes.com/sites/pamdanziger/2018/04/23/zaras-difference-pull-people-in-not-push-product-out/#30b78b1723cb; and www.zara.com, www.instagram.com/zara, ans www.facebook.com/Zara, accessed September 2019.

21. See Michael Porter, *Competitive Advantage* (New York: Free Press, 1985), pp. 4–8, 234–236. For a more recent discussion, see Philip Kotler and Kevin Lane Keller, *Marketing Management,* 15th ed. (Hoboken, NJ: Pearson, 2016), pp. 263–264.

22. See "Marriott International Brand Fact Sheets," Marriott News Center, http://news.marriott.com/p/marriott-international-brand-fact-sheets-2/, accessed September 2019; Deanna Ting and Greg Oates, "Every One of Marriott's 30 Hotel Brands, Explained," Skift, September 21, 2016, https://skift.com/2016/09/21/every-one-of-marriotts-30-hotel-brands-explained/; and "Powerful Brand Advantage," Marriott, https://hotel-development.marriott.com/brands/, accessed September 2019.

23. See Halah Touryalai, "World's Largest Hotels 2018: Marriott Dominates, Hyatt & Accor Rise," *Forbes,* June 6, 2018, www.forbes.com/sites/halahtouryalai/2018/06/06/worlds-biggest-hotels-2018/#57f4715247c7.

24. See Dorothy Crouch, "American Giant Enters the Made-in-America Denim Segment," *Apparel News,* September 13, 2018, www.apparelnews.net/news/2018/sep/13/american-giant-enters-made-america-denim-segment/; Robert Klara, "American Giant, Maker of the Famous Hoodie, Is Getting into the Jeans Business," *Adweek,* September 6, 2018, www.adweek.com/brand-marketing/american-giant-maker-of-the-famous-hoodie-is-getting-into-the-jeans-business/; and www.american-giant.com, accessed September 2019.

25. Myelle Lansat and Richard Feloni, "A Startup CEO Who's Raised Nearly $500 Million Says Business Strategy Isn't What You Do—It's What You Don't," *Business Insider,* November 1, 2018, www.businessinsider.com/harrys-jeff-raider-business-strategy-2018-10; Burt Helm, "With Flamingo, Shaving Pioneer Harry's Branches into Women's Grooming," *Fast Company,* October 16, 2018, www.fastcompany.com/90244932/with-flamingo-shaving-pioneer-harrys-branches-into-womens-grooming; Kaitlyn Tiffany, "The Absurd Quest to Make the Best Razor," *Vox,* December 11, 2018, www.vox.com/the-goods/2018/12/11/18134456/best-razor-gillette-harrys-dollar-shave-club; Bernhard Warner, "The New Industrialists," *Inc.,* May 2016, pp. 46-56; "Startups Shook Up the Sleepy Razor Market. Here's What's Next," *CNBC,* September 26, 2018, www.cnbc.com/2018/09/26/startups-shook-up-the-sleepy-razor-market-whats-next.html; Alexandria Olson, "Schick Owner Buys Harry's in New Shaving Alliance," *Post Register,* www.postregister.com/

business/schick-owner-buys-harry-s-in-new-shaving-war-alliance/article_a5b5e5fd-7993-594a-bdab-43246e92a1bf.html; and www.harrys.com; https://ondemand.gillette.com/; www.dollarshaveclub.com, accessed September 2019.

26. David Turner, "How Fila Sneaked Back into Favor," *The New Yorker*, October 8, 2018, https://www.newyorker.com/culture/on-and-off-the-avenue/how-fila-snuck-back-into-favor; Brett Hershman, "How Changing Trends Resurrected FILA as a Fashion Brand," Benzinga, November 24, 2017, https://www.benzinga.com/news/17/11/10813099/how-changing-trends-resurrected-fila-as-a-fashion-brand; Jon Keehn, "Athletic Wear Is Leading the Pack in the Apparel Industry," *Quarterly Insights*, Spring 2017, https://www.capitalgroup.com/pcs/latest-perspectives/athletic-wear-leading-pack.html; Cam Wolf, "The Fila Disruptor 2 Is a Chunky High-Fashion Shoe for Everybody," *GQ*, November 14, 2018, https://www.gq.com/story/fila-disruptor-2-sneaker-of-the-week.

27. See https://renaissance-hotels.marriott.com/, http://renaissance-hotels.marriott.com/navigators, and www.marriott.com/renaissance-hotels/mobile-apps.mi, accessed September 2019.

28. Alanis King, "This Oddball Rolls-Royce Could Be the Most Expensive Ever," *Jalopnik*, May 27, 2017, https://jalopnik.com/this-oddball-rolls-royce-could-be-the-new-most-expensiv-1795605881, Harvey Briggs, "For Rolls-Royce the Future Is Bespoke," *Purist*, http://pursuitist.com/for-rolls-royce-the-future-is-bespoke/, accessed September 2018; and www.rolls-roycemotorcars.com/en-US/bespoke.html, accessed September 2019.

29. "YouTube Targets Young Kids with Ads, Say Privacy Advocates, Urging FTC to Investigate," *Los Angeles Times*, April 9, 2018, www.latimes.com/business/hollywood/la-fi-tn-youtube-kids-privacy-20180409-story.html.

30. See "2017 Internet Crime Report," May 7, 2018, www.fbi.gov/news/stories/2017-internet-crime-report-released-050718.

31. SUV sales data furnished by www.WardsAuto.com, accessed September 2019. Price data from www.edmunds.com, accessed September 2019.

32. Kyle O'Brien, See "Glad Touts Strength of New Trash Bag by Sending It Through Airline Luggage System," *The Drum*, February 26, 2018, www.thedrum.com/news/2018/02/26/glad-touts-strength-new-trash-bag-sending-it-through-airline-luggage-system; and www.youtube.com/watch?v=cHlOtiJnFsI, accessed September 2019.

33. "Apply Now: Wegmans Begins Hiring and Training Full-Time Employees for First North Carolina Store," Wegmans News & Media," January 8, 2019, www.wegmans.com/news-media/press-releases/2019/apply-now-wegmans-begins-hiring-and-training-full-time-employee.html; and www.wegmans.com and https://jobs.wegmans.com/diversity, accessed September 2019.

34. See www.toyota.com/landcruiser/, accessed September 2019.

35. See www.heartsonfire.com, accessed September 2019.

36. See Bobby J. Calder and Steven J. Reagan, "Brand Design," in Dawn Iacobucci, ed., *Kellogg on Marketing* (New York: John Wiley & Sons, 2001), p. 61. For more discussion, see Philip Kotler and Kevin Lane Keller, *Marketing Management*, 15th ed. (Hoboken, NJ: Pearson, 2016), Chapter 10.

37. See Joanna Fantozzi, "The New Website Where Everything Costs $3 Is Not Worth It—Here's Why," *Insider*, July 15, 2017, www.thisisinsider.com/new-website-where-everything-costs-3-not-worth-it-2017-7; Dennis Green, "Brandless, the Online Store that Sells Everything for $3, Just Got $2490 Million to Take on Amazon," *Business Insider*, July 321, 2018, www.businessinsider.com/review-brandless-store-sells-everything-for-3-dollars-2017-8; and https://brandless.com/about, accessed September 2019.

38. "Do 5-Hour Energy Shots Actually Work?", *Stack*, June 29, 2018, www.stack.com/a/do-5-hour-energy-shots-actually-work; Clare O'Connor, "The Mystery Monk Makes Billions with 5-Hour Energy," *Forbes*, February 8, 2012, www.forbes.com/sites/clareoconnor/2012/02/08/manoj-bhargava-the-mystery-monk-making-billions-with-5-hour-energy/#30b89c0927ae; Robert Klara, "How This Tiny, Caffeine-Packed Bottle Became the Boost of Choice for 7 Million Americans," *Adweek*, October 3, 2016, pp. v35-36; and information from https://5hourenergy.com, www.caffeineinformer.com/the-15-top-energy-drink-brands, and https://one.npr.org/?sharedMediaId=519514841:519712175, accessed March 2019.

Chapter 8

1. Maja Zuvela, "IKEA Mulls Joint Venture with Bosnia Furniture Maker," Reuters.com, January 8, 2008, http://www.reuters.com/article/2008/01/08/idUSL0861625720080108; Carsten Dierig: "IKEA baut Filialen im 'Mini'-Format," Die Welt, December 14, 2015, p. 21; Kerry Capell, "IKEA: How the Swedish Retailer Became a Global Cult Brand," *Business Week*, November 14, 2005, p. 96, "Need a Home to Go with That Sofa?" *Business Week*, November 14, 2005, p. 106; Ellen Ruppel Shell, "Buy to Last," *Atlantic*, July/August 2009; Jon Henley, "Do You Speak IKEA?" *The Guardian*, February 4, 2008; Laine Doss, "IKEA Miami Opens Today: Here's What to Expect (Photos)," *Miami New Times*, August 27, 2014, http://www.miaminewtimes.com/restaurants/ikea-miami-opens-todayheres-what-to-expect-photos-6570691; "IKEA Group Yearly Summary 2014," http://money.howstuffworks.com/ikea2.htm; "IKEA," *Bloomberg*, November 13, 2005, http://www.bloomberg.com/bw/stories/2005-11-13/ikea; Ken Bernhardt, "IKEA Crafted Itself into a Cult Brand," *Atlanta Business Chronicle*, November 23, 2005, http://www.bizjournals.com/atlanta/stories/2005/11/28/smallb2.html; "IKEA Reports Sales Development Financial Year 2014: Sales Up and Consumer Spending Continues to Increase," September 9, 2015, http://www.ikea.com/us/en/about_ikea/newsitem/090914-IKEA-sales-report-fy14; and information from www.Ikea.com; "IKEA India Launches First Online Store in Mumbai," *Business Today*, August 19, 2019, https://www.businesstoday.in/current/corporate/ikea-india-launches-first-online-store-in-mumbai/story/373679.html; "IKEA Is Now Open for Business in India: Here's What It Offers," *The Economic Times*, August 10, 2018, https://economictimes.indiatimes.com/industry/services/retail/ikea-opens-its-first-india-store-tomorrow-heres-what-it-offers/articleshow/65319086.cms; Michael Jarrett Quy and Nguyen Huy, "IKEA's Success Can't Be Attributed to One Charismatic Leader," *Harvard Business Review*, February 2, 2018, https://hbr.org/2018/02/ikeas-success-cant-be-attributed-to-one-charismatic-leader.

2. See www.22squared.com/work/project/buffalo-wild-wings; http://ir.buffalowildwings.com/financials.cfm, http://worldwidewingsus.com/default.aspx?Page=About, and www.buffalowildwings.com/en/, accessed September 2019.

3. See Rich Duprey, "12 Motorcycle Statistics That Will Floor You," *The Motley Fool*," March 5, 2017, Susanna Hamner, "Harley, You're Not Getting Any Younger," *New York Times*, March 22, 2009, p. BU1; www.fool.com/investing/2017/03/05/7-motorcycle-statistics-thatll-floor-you.aspx; Tim Clark, "Harley-Davidson Goes Whole Hog with Customer Insight," *Forbes*, www.forbes.com/sites/sap/2011/06/29/harley-davidson-goes-whole-hog-with-customer-insight/#3803c03250eb; and various pages at www.harley-davidson.com, accessed September 2019.

4. See Charlotte Rogers, "Patagonia on Why Brands Can't Reverse into Purpose through Marketing," Marketing Week, July 18, 2018, www.marketingweek.com/2018/07/18/patagonia-you-cant-reverse-into-values-through-marketing; and patagonia.com/save-our-public-lands.html?zoom=3&center=40.317756,-94.421097 and www.patagonia.com/environmentalism.html, accessed September 2019.

5. Ron Stodghill, "Brand Visionary: Serena Williams," *Adweek*, November 5, 2018, pp. 21-26.

6. See https://visitdetroit.com, www.ireland.com/en-us/, and www.idaireland.com, accessed September 2019.

7. See Lindsey Stein, "Microsoft's New 'Makes What's Next' Ad Shows Girls How to Pursue STEM Careers," *Advertising Age,* March 7, 2017, http://adage.com/article/cmo-strategy/microsoft-s-make-ad-shows-pursue-stem/308189/; and www.microsoft.com/en-us/philanthropies/make-whats-next, accessed September 2019.

8. For more on social marketing, see Nancy Lee and Philip Kotler, *Social Marketing: Changing Behaviors for Good*, 5th ed. (Thousand Oaks, CA: SAGE Publications, 2015); and www.adcouncil.org and www.i-socialmarketing.org, accessed September 2019.

9. Quotes and definitions from Philip Kotler, *Marketing Insights from A to Z* (Hoboken, NJ: Wiley, 2003), p. 148; and www.asq.org/glossary/q.html, accessed September 2019.

10. For more on TQM, see "What Is Total Quality Management?" *ASQ,* https://asq.org/quality-resources/total-quality-management, accessed September 2019.

11. See "Award Recipient: Americas Best Value Inn," J.D. Power, www.jdpower.com/ratings/study/North-America-Hotel-Guest-Satisfaction-Study/2572ENG/Economy/2672, accessed September 2018; and www.americasbestvalueinn.com, accessed September 2019.

12. See Christine Lagorio-Chafkin, "This Philosophy Professor Turned the Answer to One of Life's Big Questions into a $169 Million Business," *Inc.,* August 2018, www.inc.com/christine-lagorio/2018-inc5000-how-popsockets-became-a-169-million-dollar-business.html; and Amit Chowdhry, "PopSockets: The Story behind How It Went from a Simple Concept to Selling Tens of Millions of Units," *Forbes,* February 14, 2018, www.forbes.com/sites/amitchowdhry/2018/02/14/popsockets/.

13. Emily Dawling, "the Sports Hijab Dividing Opinions," January 10, 2018, *BBC,* http://www.bbc.com/culture/story/20180110-the-sports-hijab-dividing-opinions; Teresa Kerr, "Nike Pro Hijab: One of the World's Most Popular Clothing Item," *Morocco World News,* May 17, 2019, https://www.moroccoworldnews.com/2019/05/273344/nike-pro-hijab/amp/; Danielle Wightman-Stone, "Nike's Pro Hijab among Design of the Year Winners," *Fashion United,* January 29, 2018, https://fashionunited.uk/news/fashion/nike-s-pro-hijab-among-design-of-the-year-winners/2018012927882; "Nike Strengthens Ties with Muslim Market with New 'Pro Hijab' Line," Marketing-Interactive.com, August 3, 2017, https://www.marketing-interactive.com/nike-strengthens-ties-with-muslim-market-with-new-pro-hijab-line/; "What Will They Say about You?: Nike Releases Empowering Ad for the Pro Hijab Designed for Muslim Athletes," *DNA,* https://www.dnaindia.com/world/report-what-will-they-say-about-you-nike-releases-empowering-ad-for-the-pro-hijab-designed-for-muslim-athletes-2346398.

14. See Megan Cerullo, "Payless Sold Discount Shoes at Luxury Prices—and It Worked," *CBS News,* November 29, 2018, www.cbsnews.com/news/payless-sold-discount-shoes-at-luxury-prices-and-it-worked/; and T. L. Stanley, "Payless Opened a Fake Luxury Store, 'Palessi,' to See How Much People Would Pay for $20 Shoes," *Adweek,* November 28, 2018, www.adweek.com/brand-marketing/payless-opened-a-fake-luxury-store-palessi-to-see-how-much-people-would-pay-for-20-shoes/.

15. See Michael Castillo. "The Most Talked About Super Bowl Advertiser Online Was Avocados From Mexico," *CNBC,* February 5, 2018, www.cnbc.com/2018/02/05/the-most-talked-about-super-bowl-ad-online-was-about-avocados-.html; Patrick Coffee, "Avocados From Mexico Puts Its Account in Review Ahead of 4th Straight Super Bowl Campaign," *Adweek,* February 1, 2018, www.adweek.com/agencyspy/avocados-from-mexico-goes-into-review-ahead-of-4th-straight-super-bowl-campaign/142907; and https://avocadosfrommexico.com/, accessed September 2019.

16. See "FMI—Supermarket Facts," www.fmi.org/our-research/supermarket-facts, accessed September 2019; Christina Ng, "The Drivers behind Shoppers' Purchasing Decisions," *Project Nosh,* April 30, 2015, www.projectnosh.com/news/2015/the-drivers-behind-shoppers-

purchasing-decisions; "2018 Packaging Matters," Westrock, www.westrock.com/-/media/images/insights/packaging-matters-2018/westrock-packaging-matters-2018-whitepaper.pdf; and "Our Retail Divisions," http://news.walmart.com/news-archive/2005/01/07/our-retail-divisions, accessed September 2019.

17. See www.tiffany.com/WorldOfTiffany/TiffanyStory/Legacy/BlueBox.aspx, www.luxury24-7.com/blog/2016/08/the-historyof-tiffany-co/, www.luxury24-7.com/blog/2016/08/the-historyof-tiffany-co/accessed September 2019.

18. See "Keep Your Home and Loved Ones Safe," P&G, https://tide.com/en-us/safety, accessed September 2019.

19. Bennett Bennett, "Lexus Gets Conceptual, Create Perceptual Origami Art to Celebrate Customer Service," The Drum, March 8, 2018, www.thedrum.com/news/2018/03/08/lexus-gets-conceptual-createsperceptual-origami-art-celebrate-customer-service; and www.lexuslearn.com/covenant accessed September 2019.

20. See www.bmwgroup.com/com/en/brands/bmw.html and www.bmw.com/en, accessed September 2019.

21. Information on the Colgate-Palmolive product mix is from www.colgatepalmolive.com/en-us/brands, accessed September 2019.

22. See CIA World Fact Book, www.cia.gov/library/publications/the-world-factbook, accessed September 2019; and "List of Countries by GDP Sector Composition," https://en.wikipedia.org/wiki/List_of_countries_by_GDP_sector_composition, accessed September 2019.

23. See Bruce Japson, "Oscar Health's Obamacare Enrollment Surges Past 250K," *Forbes,* December 21, 2017, www.forbes.com/sites/brucejapsen/2017/12/21/oscar-healths-2018-obamacare-enrollment-surges-past-250k/#5ef8520b2fff; "10 Things to Know about Oscar Health Insurance: Will It Be the Uber of Health Plans," *Becker's Healthcare Review,* August 4, 2015, www.beckershospitalreview.com/payer-issues/10-things-to-know-about-oscar-health-insurance-will-it-be-the-uber-of-health-plans.html; Sarah Buhr, "Oscar Health Expects to Generate $1 Billion in Revenue and Sign Up 250,000 Members in 2018," *Tech Crunch,* December 21, 2017, https://techcrunch.com/2017/12/21/oscar-health-expects-to-generate-1-billion-in-revenue-and-sign-up-250000-members-in-2018/; Morgan Haefner, "Oscar Health Posts $5M Profit: 4 Things to Know," *Becker's Hospital Review,* August 25, 2018, www.beckershospitalreview.com/payer-issues/oscar-health-posts-5m-profit-4-things-to-know.html; and www.hioscar.com/about, accessed September 2019.

24. See James L. Heskett, W. Earl Sasser Jr., and Leonard A. Schlesinger, *The Service Profit Chain: How Leading Companies Link Profit and Growth to Loyalty, Satisfaction, and Value* (New York: Free Press, 1997); and Heskett, Sasser, and Schlesinger, *The Value Profit Chain: Treat Employees Like Customers and Customers Like Employees* (New York: Free Press, 2003). Also see Jay Doerksen, "How Employee Satisfaction Drives the Service-Profit Chain and Improves the Customer Experience," *Vision Critical,* May 11, 2017, www.visioncritical.com/employee-satisfaction-service-profit-chain/; and The Service-Profit Chain Institute, http://serviceprofitchain.com/, accessed September 2019.

25. See Pamela N. Danziger, "Why Wegmans Food Markets Gets the Love of Customers," *Forbes,* March 3, 2018, www.forbes.com/sites/pamdanziger/2018/03/03/why-wegmans-food-markets-gets-the-love-of-customers/; "Fortune 100 Best: Wegmans," http://fortune.com/best-companies/wegmans-food-markets/, accessed September 2019; and "It's the Actions That Count: Find Out Why Our Employees Enjoy Coming into Work Every Day," https://jobs.wegmans.com/employee-satisfaction-at-wegmans, accessed September 2019.

26. See IQVIA Institute for Data Science, "Medicine Use and Spending in the U.S.," www.iqvia.com/institute/reports/medicine-use-and-spending-in-the-us-review-of-2017-outlook-to-2022, April 19, 2018, chart 9, p. 13; and "Postal Facts," http://about.usps.com/who-we-are/postal-facts/welcome.htm, accessed September 2019.

27. Ira Kalb, "Corporate Image: The Foundation for Your Brand's Success," *Huffington Post,* September 3, 2017, www.

huffingtonpost.com/entry/corporate-image-the-foundation-for-your-brands-success_us_59ab8e09e4b0c50640cd600c.

28. Micah Solomon, "Thanks a Latte: How to Fix a Customer Service Failure, per Starbucks, Marriott, and Me," *Forbes*, November 29, 2017, www.forbes.com/sites/micahsolomon/2017/11/19/thanks-a-latte-how-to-fix-a-customer-service-failure-per-starbucks-marriott-and-me/#4a1a1873462a.

29. See Martha White, "Lost Bags, at 140 Characters, and Airlines Respond," *New York Times*, October 20, 2015, p. B6; and Leslie Josephs, "Between Five Minutes and Five Hours: How Long Airlines Take to Respond to Your Complaint on Twitter," *CNBC*, January 9, 2018, https://www.cnbc.com/2018/01/09/how-long-airlines-take-to-respond-to-your-complaints-on-twitter.html.

30. See Lulu Garcia-Navarro, "The Robots Are Coming to Las Vegas," NPR, October 7, 2018, www.npr.org/2018/10/07/652363255/the-robots-are-coming-to-las-vegas.

31. Garcia-Navarro, "The Robots Are Coming to Las Vegas," *NPR*.

32. See "McAtlas Shrugged," *Foreign Policy*, May–June 2001, pp. 26–37; and Philip Kotler and Kevin Lane Keller, *Marketing Management*, 15th ed. (Upper Saddle River, NJ: Pearson Publishing, 2016), p. 316.

33. See "For Sale: Hessian, a Brand without a Product," *Fast Company*, February 12, 2013, www.fastcodesign.com/1671819/for-sale-hessian-a-brand-without-a-product.

34. See Kevin Systrom, "On Instagram's Big Moves," *Fast Company*, March 3, 2018, www.fastcompany.com/3069066/kevin-systrom-on-instagrams-big-moves-its-almost-riskier-not-to-disrupt-yo; and www.instagram.com/about/us/, accessed September 2019.

35. For more on BrandAsset Valuator, see Kotler and Keller, *Marketing Management*, Chapter 11; and "BrandAsset Valuator," www.yr.com/BAV, accessed September 2019.

36. See Kantar Millward Brown, "BrandZ Top 100 Most Valuable U.S. Brands," http://www.millwardbrown.com/brandz, accessed September 2019; and "BrandZ Top 100 Most Valuable U.S. Brands 2019," http://online.pubhtml5.com/bydd/doqx/#p=102, accessed September 2019.

37. See Scott Davis, *Brand Asset Management*, 2nd ed. (San Francisco: Jossey-Bass, 2002). For more on brand positioning, see Kotler and Keller, *Marketing Management*, Chapter 10.

38. See Avi Dan, "FedEx's New Campaign Delivers," *Forbes*, November 5, 2018, www.forbes.com/sites/avidan/2018/11/05/fedex-new-campaign-delivers/; Katie Baron, "Rewiring Stroytelling," *Forbes*, October 22, 2018, www.forbes.com/sites/katiebaron/2018/10/22/rewiring-storytelling-neuro-brand-boosting-from-the-startup-that-predicted-the-trump-win/; and "What We Deliver By Delivering," www.fedex.com/en-us/possibilities.html, accessed September 2019.

39. "Why I Love Walt Disney World," https://ithoughtyouweresshorter.wordpress.com/2012/11/15/why-i-love-walt-disney-world/, accessed September 2019.

40. Leslie Scism, "Travelers Doesn't Want to Share Its Umbrella Logo," *Wall Street Journal*, May 25, 2015, www.wsj.com/articles/travelers-doesnt-want-to-share-its-umbrella-logo-1432598794.

41. See Alexander Coolidge, "The Simple Truth: Private Selection, and Other Kroger Brands Drive Sales," *Cincinnati Enquirer*, July 26, 2017, www.cincinnati.com/story/money/2017/07/27/kroger-gins-up-own-goods-win-thrifty-consumers/472740001/; "Courtney Regan, "Grocer Aldi Targets Nearby Rivals in Its Bid to Boost Its US Footprint," *CNBC*, August 9, 2018, www.cnbc.com/2018/08/08/grocer-aldi-targets-nearby-rivals-in-bid-to-its-boost-its-us-footprint.html.

42. See https://brandless.com/about, accessed September 2019.

43. Thomas Franck, "Amazon Will Dethrone Walmart as the No. 1 Retailer of Apparel This Year, Predicts Wells Fargo," *CNBC*, September 10, 2018, www.cnbc.com/2018/09/10/amazon-to-usurp-walmart-as-top-apparel-retailer-in-2018-wells-fargo.html; Nathaniel Meyersohn, "Who Needs Brand Names? Now Amazon Makes the Stuff It Sells," *CNNBusiness*, October 8, 2018, www.cnn.com/2018/10/08/business/amazon-private-label-brands/index.html; Tonya Garcia, "Amazon's Apparel Business Could Grow to as Much as $85 Billion in Sales by 2020," *Market Watch*, December 10, 2017, www.marketwatch.com/story/amazons-apparel-business-could-to-grow-to-as-much-as-85-billion-in-sales-by-2020-2017-12-05; Matthew Boyle, "How Private Labels Caught the Public Eye," *Bloomberg BusinessWeek*, December 18, 2017, pp. 13–14; Alex Moazed, "How Amazon's Marketplace Supercharged Its Private-Label Growth," *Inc.*, November 11, 2018, www.inc.com/alex-moazed/what-brands-need-to-know-about-amazons-private-label-growth-how-to-respond.html; Amanda Harding, "These Are the Real Brands behind Your Favorite Trader Joe's Snacks," *Cheatsheet*, June 16, 2018; www.cheatsheet.com/culture/these-are-the-real-brands-behind-your-favorite-trader-joes-snacks.html/; Phil Wahba, "How Target Keeps Its 'Tar-Zhay' Luster," *Fortune*, August 22, 2018, http://fortune.com/2018/08/22/target-private-label/; and www.amazon.com/stores/AmazonBasics/AmazonBasics/page/947C6949-CF8E-4BD3-914A-B411DD3E4433, www.amazon.com/Amazon-Elements-Premium-products-Transparent-origins-Exclusive-to-Prime/b?ie=UTF8&node=10166275011, and www.amazon.com/stores/AmazonEssentials/AmazonEssentials/page/F8FB6F3C-F896-455C-BC52-7879F4CEF0CF, accessed September 2019.

44. "Top 150 Global Licensors 2018," *Global License*, April 2018, www.licenseglobal.com/resource/top-150-global-licensors-2018.

45. See "Sector Trend Analysis–Savoury Snacks in the United States," Agriculture and Agri-Food Canada; October 2018, www5.agr.gc.ca/eng/industry-markets-and-trade/international-agri-food-market-intelligence/sector-trend-analysis-savoury-snacks-in-the-united-states/?id=1537469466763#e; and www.fritolay.com/our-snacks/doritos.html, accessed September 2019.

46. See www.birkenstock-group.com/de/en/products/bed-collection/, www.birkenstock-group.com/de/en/products/bed-collection/, www.birkenstock.com/gb/sleep-systems/, and www.birkenstock.com/us, accessed September 2019.

47. For interesting lists of good and bad brand extension candidates, see "12 Brand Extensions the World Would Like to See," *Attest*, November 13, 2017, http://insights.askattest.com/12-brand-extensions-consumers-would-love-to-see; and Geoffrey James, "18 Insane Brand Extensions (2 Were Huge Successes)," *Forbes*, December 5, 2018, www.inc.com/geoffrey-james/18-insane-brand-extensions-2-were-huge-successes.html.

48. "Ad Age World's Largest Advertisers," *Advertising Age*, December 3, 2018, p. 10.

49. Stephen Cole, "Value of the Brand," *CA Magazine*, May 2005, pp. 39–40. Also see "The Power of Customer Service," *Fortune*, December 3, 2012, www.timeincnewsgroupcustompub.com/sections/121203_Disney.pdf; and "Customer Engagement," http://thewaltdisneycompany.com/citizenship/community/consumer-engagement, accessed September 2019.

50. Minhea Radu, "306 HP 2020 Mini John Cooper Works Clubman, Countryman Revealed," *Autoevolution*, May 14, 2019, www.autoevolution.com/news/306-hp-2020-mini-john-cooper-works-clubman-countryman-revealed-134451.html; Kyle Hyatt, "Mini's Got a New Boss, and It's Barreling Towards a More Electric Future," *CNet*, April 19, 2019, www.cnet.com/roadshow/news/mini-new-boss-bmw-group-2019/; Jonathan Bacon, July 8, 2015, "Mini: Reinventing a Brand Icon," *Marketing Week*, July 8, 2015, www.marketingweek.com/2015/07/08/how-mini-is-reinventing-itself-to-remain-iconic/; Hannah Elliott, "Fifty Years of Mini Love," *Forbes*, July 29, 2009, www.forbes.com/2009/07/29/bmw-mini-cooper-lifestyle-vehicles-mini-car-50.html#2a21eb2ccb74; and information from www.miniusa.com/, accessed May 2019.

Chapter 9

1. See Nina Zipkin, "Eight of the Coolest Projects to Come Out of X, Google's Moonshot Factory," *Entrepreneur*, January 23, 2019, www.entrepreneur.com/article/326836; Alex Davies, "Inside X,

the Moonshot Factory Racing to Build the Next Google," *Wired,* January 11, 2018, www.wired.com/story/alphabet-google-x-innovation-loon-wing-graduation/; David Pierce, "One Man's Quest to Make Google's Gadgets Great," *Wired,* February 8, 2018, www.wired.com/story/one-mans-quest-to-make-googles-gadgets-great/; Chuck Salter, "Google: The Faces and Voices of the World's Most Innovative Company," *Fast Company,* March 2008, pp. 74–88; Jeff Desjardins, "How Google Retains More Than 90% of Market Share," *Business Insider,* April 23, 2018, www.businessinsider.com/how-google-retains-more-than-90-of-market-share-2018-4; and https://abc.xyz/and http://investor.google.com, accessed September 2019.

2. See "Apple 2018 10-K Filing," https://s22.q4cdn.com/396847794/files/doc_financials/quarterly/2018/Q4/10-K-2018-(As-Filed).pdf, accessed September 2019; and Todd Haselton, "Here's What We're Expecting Apple to Launch This Year," *CNBC,* January 2, 2019, www.cnbc.com/2019/01/02/apple-product-service-expectations-in-2019.html.

3. Marc Emmer, "95 Percent of the New Products Fail," *Inc.,* July 6, 2018, www.inc.com/marc-emmer/95-percent-of-new-products-fail-here-are-6-steps-to-make-sure-yours-dont.html.

4. See Michael Martinez, "Ford Opens Silicon Valley Innovation Center," *The Detroit News,* January 22, 2015, www.detroitnews.com/story/business/autos/ford/2015/01/22/ford-silicon-valley/22165837/; "Chick-fil-A Goes High Tech at Tech Square," March 8, 2017, https://thechickenwire.chick-fil-a.com/News/Chick-fil-A-Goes-High-Tech-at-Tech-Square; and http://corporate.ford.com/innovation/research-and-innovation-center.html, accessed September 2019.

5. See Harry McCracken, "Google's 100% Solution," *Fast Company,* December 2018/January 2019, pp. 22-26.

6. See "Dominic Powell, "Want to Run Your First Hackathon? Here Are Some Tips from KPMG," *Smart Company,* August 15, 2017, www.smartcompany.com.au/startupsmart/advice/want-run-first-internal-hackathon-tips-kpmg/; Matt Weinberger, "'There Are Only Two Rules'—Facebook Explains How 'Hackathons,' One of Its Oldest Traditions, Is Also One of Its Most Important," *Business Insider,* January 11, 2017, www.businessinsider.com/facebook-hackathons-2017-6; and www.facebook.com/hackathon/, accessed September 2019.

7. Blake Morgan, "Customer Collaboration with Salesforce's Mike Rosenbaum," *Forbes,* January 3, 2017, www.forbes.com/sites/blakemorgan/2017/01/03/customer-collaboration-with-salesforces-mike-rosenbaum/#464b47ce7403; Erica Kuhl, "4 Tips to Turn Customer Feedback into Action," *Salesforce Blog,* December 15, 2016, www.salesforce.com/blog/2016/12/4-tips-to-turn-customer-feedback-into-action.html; and Salesforce IdeaExchange, https://success.salesforce.com/ideaSearch, accessed September 2019.

8. See Bonnie Cad, "Ben & Jerry's Taste for Crowdsourcing," *Digital Initiative,* December 29, 2018, https://digital.hbs.edu/platforms-crowds/ben-jerrys-taste-crowdsourcing; Jeff Beer, "Why Under Armour's Future Show Is Key to Its Brand Innovation Strategy," *Fast Company,* October 14, 2015, www.fastcocreate.com/3052298/why-under-armours-future-show-is-key-to-its-brand-innovation-strategy#13; Michael Wolf, "With New Contest, Tupperware Looks to Discover the Future of Food Containers," *The Spoon,* December 7, 2018, https://thespoon.tech/with-new-contest-tupperware-looks-to-discover-the-future-of-food-containers/; Beau Muniz, "The Tupperware Clever Container Challenge," *Giddy Blog,* December 6, 2018, https://blog.giddy.io/2018/12/06/the-tupperware-clever-container-challenge/; and http://ideahouse.ua.com/shows#future-show, accessed September 2019.

9. See George S. Day, "Is It Real? Can We Win? Is It Worth Doing?" *Harvard Business Review,* December 2007, pp. 110–120.

10. This example is based on Tesla Motors and information obtained from www.teslamotors.com and www.tesla.com/model3, accessed September 2018; and "Electric Car," *Wikipedia,* http://en.wikipedia.org/wiki/Electric_car, accessed September 2019.

11. See www.brooksrunning.com/en_us/programs/beta-runners, accessed September 2019.

12. See Maureen Morrison, "Marketer of the Year: Taco Bell," *Advertising Age,* September 2, 2013, pp. 15–16; Susan Berfield, "Baristas, Patrons Steaming over Starbucks VIA," *Bloomberg BusinessWeek,* November 13, 2009; and Tamara Walsh, "Starbucks Makes a Big Bet on New Product Mix in 2014," *The Motley Fool,* January 8, 2014, www.fool.com/investing/general/2014/01/08/starbucks-makes-a-big-bet-on-new-product-mix-in-20.aspx.

13. See Alex Samuely, "Mobile Ordering, Payments Responsible for 20pc of Starbucks' October Transactions," *Retail Dive,* www.retaildive.com/ex/mobilecommercedaily/mobile-ordering-payments-made-up-20pc-of-october-transactions-starbucks, accessed February 2019; Austin Carr, "Starbucks Leap of Faith," *Fast Company,* June 2013, pp. 46–48; and www.starbucks.com/coffeehouse/mobile-apps, accessed September 2019.

14. See Jack Neff, "P&G Reinvents Laundry with $150 Million Tide Pods Launch," *Advertising Age,* April 26, 2011, www.adage.com/print/227208/; Sheila Shayon, "Microsoft Unleashes Global Marketing Blitz for Windows 8, New Devices," *BrandChannel,* October 25, 2012, www.brandchannel.com/home/post/2012/10/25/Microsoft-Global-Windows-8-Launch-102512.aspx; and Thomas Whitehead, "Nintendo of America Spent Big on Switch Advertising in March," *Nintendo Life,* May 2, 2017, www.nintendolife.com/news/2017/05/nintendo_of_america_spent_big_on_switch_tv_advertising_in_march.

15. "iPhone X Available for Pre-Order on Friday, October 27," October 24, 2017, www.apple.com/newsroom/2017/10/iphone-x-available-for-pre-order-on-friday-october-27/; and Daniel Eran Dilger, "Apple and the Aggressive Rollout of Its iPhone XS Vision for the Future," *Apple Insider,* September 13, 2018, https://appleinsider.com/articles/18/09/13/apple-and-the-aggressive-rollout-of-its-iphone-xs-vision-for-the-future.

16. Jonathon Ringen, "When It Clicks, It Clicks," *Fast Company,* February 2015, pp. 72–78+; Andrew Jack, "How LEGO Took to Anthropology," *Financial Times,* February 26, 2014, www.ft.com/cms/s/0/b071990c-9d4c-11e3-a599-00144feab7de.html#axzz3N8u6XIPH; Christian Madsbjerg and Mikkel B. Rasmussen, "An Anthropologist Walks into a Bar...," *Harvard Business Review,* March, 2014, pp. 80–88; Jeff Beer, "The Secret of Lego's Social Media Success Is in the Creative Power of Crowds," *Fast Company,* June 20, 2017, www.fastcompany.com/40432685/the-secret-to-legos-social-media-success-is-in-the-creative-power-of-crowds; and https://ideas.lego.com/dashboard and www.lego.com/en-us, accessed September 2019.

17. "Nestlé Toque d'Or: Top Students Line Up for Culinary Battle," NZ Chefs, http://www.nzchefs.org.nz/NewsEvents/Nestl+Toque+dOr.html; Nestlé UK and Ireland, http://www.nestle.co.uk/csv2013/nhw/consumersandourproducts; "Competition and Prize 2016," Nestlé Toque d'Or, https://www.nestle-toquedor.co.uk/Home/Competition; "Nestle, or How Consumer Insights Can Lead Product Development," Instantly Blog, https://blog.instant.ly/blog/2012/07/nestle-or-how-consumer-insights-can-leadproduct-development/; "Company Scorecard," Behind the Brands, http://www.behindthebrands.org/en/company-scorecard; "Nutrition, Health & Wellness—New Product Development at Nestlé," Business Case Studies, http://businesscasestudies.co.uk/nestle/nutrition-health-wellnessnewproduct-development-at-nestle/introduction.html#axzz3qcCRzjad; "Final Design of Consistent Nutritional Labelling System Given Green Light," GOV.UK, https://www.gov.uk/government/news/final-design-of-consistent-nutritional-labelling-system-given-green-light; and information from http://www.nestle.com, all Internet sites accessed November 2015; "Nestlé Financials and News Global 500," *Fortune,* http://beta.fortune.com/global500/nestle-66, accessed April 1, 2017; Behind the Brands, "Company Scorecard," http://www.behindthebrands.org/en/companyscorecard, accessed April 1, 2017.

18. See Lisa Fu, "The Fidget Spinner Trend Is Ending and You Missed It," *Fortune,* June 13, 2017, http://fortune.com/2017/06/13/the-fidget-spinner-trend-is-ending-and-you-missed-it/; and www.crazyfads.com, accessed September 2019.

19. "Euromonitor Makeup Sell-in CA Net 2012 vs 2003," www.euromonitor.com; "Worldwide Value Market Shares Full Year 2014," www.euromonitor.com; www.loreal.com, accessed October 2015; the authors would like to thank Moïra Taillefer and the L'Oréal Paris International Development Makeup team for their contribution to this case.

20. See www.lorealparisusa.com/products/skin-care/brand/men-expert.aspx, accessed September 2019.

21. See Erin DeJesus, "CES's Kitchen of the Future Is Sort of a Nightmare," *Eater,* January 8, 2019, www.eater.com/2019/1/8/18173843/ces-2019-kitchen-tech-ge-samsung-whirlpool; and www.samsung.com/us/explore/chef-collection/features/, accessed September 2019.

22. See www.quakeroats.com and www.quaker.com.my, accessed September 2018.

23. See Andrea Darlas, "A Look Inside Radio Flyer's Chicago Headquarters," *WGN TV,* November 17, 2018, https://wgntv.com/2018/11/17/a-look-inside-radio-flyers-chicago-headquarters/; Sheila Marikar, "How One Iconic American Brand Got Back on a Roll," *Inc.,* March 2016, p. 32; Robert Klara, "How an Immigrant Cabinetmaker Accidentally Invented the Toy That Defined America," *Adweek,* March 21, 2017, www.adweek.com/brand-marketing/how-an-immigrant-cabinetmaker-accidentally-invented-the-toy-that-defined-american-childhood/; and www.radioflyer.com/content/about-us/, accessed September 2019.

24. For more discussion of marketing strategies over the course of the PLC, see Philip Kotler and Kevin Lane Keller, *Marketing Management*, 15th ed. (Hoboken, NJ: Pearson Education, 2016), pp. 358.

25. See Andrew J. Hawkins, "Volkswagen Settles Diesel Emissions Lawsuit Right before Trial Set to Begin," *The Verge,* February 26, 2018, www.theverge.com/2018/2/26/17053928/volkswagen-diesel-emissions-lawsuit-settled; "$10.4-Billion Lawsuit over Diesel Emissions Scandal Opens against Volkswagen," *Los Angeles Times,* September 10, 2018, www.latimes.com/business/la-fi-volkswagen-trial-20180910-story.html; and Neal E. Boudette, "Fiat Chrysler Is Expected to Pay Nearly $650 Million in Emissions Case," *New York Times,* January 9, 2019, www.nytimes.com/2019/01/09/business/fiat-chrysler-justice-settlement-emissions.html.

26. See "McDonald's Food You Can't Get Here," *Chicago Tribune,* www.chicagotribune.com/business/ct-biz-mcdonalds-food-around-the-world,0,5168632.photogallery, accessed September 2019.

27. Henry Samuel, "French Island Loses High 'Steaks' Fight to Keep McDonald's off Its Shores," *The Telegraph,* October 12, 2018, www.telegraph.co.uk/news/2018/10/12/french-island-loses-high-steaks-fight-keep-mcdonalds-shores/; and www.mcdonalds.fr/#happymeal, accessed September 2019.

28. Information from www.db.com, accessed September 2019.

29. See "Global Powers of Retailing 2018," https://www2.deloitte.com/content/dam/Deloitte/at/Documents/about-deloitte/global-powers-of-retailing-2018.pdf; "Walmart Corporate International," http://corporate.walmart.com/our-story/locations, accessed September 2019; and information from www.walmart.com and www.carrefour.com, accessed September 2019.

30. N. E. Boudette, "Can Prius Set The Pace Again?", *Automotive News,* September 21, 2014, https://www.autonews.com/article/20140921/RETAIL03/309229993/can-prius-set-the-pace-again; Toyota Motor Corporation, "75 Years of TOYOTA: Total Quality Management (TQM): Changes and Innovations," 2012, https://www.toyota-global.com/company/history_of_toyota/75years/data/company_information/management_and_finances/management/tqm/change.html;

Campaign, "A Collection of Toyota's Best Ads," https://www.campaignlive.co.uk/the-work/advertiser/toyota/7997; Toyota Motor Corporation, "Electric Vehicles," https://global.toyota/en/mobility/toyota-brand/toyota-design/gallery/ev/; Rudi Halbright, "Case Study: The Toyota Prius Lessons in Marketing Eco-Friendly Products," Max Dunn's Website, March 3, 2010, https://www.maxdunn.com/storage/www.maxdunn.com/PMBA:%20Presidio%20MBA%20Home/Prius_Marketing_Case_Study.pdf; Zack Hicks, "Steal This Idea: Toyota's Secret to Innovation,"' CIO, February 8, 2016, https://www.cio.com/article/3030990/steal-this-idea-toyota-s-secret-to-innovation.html; Fred Lambert, "Toyota Unveils Images of Upcoming All-electric Cars, Accelerates EV Plans by 5 Years," June 7, 2019, https://electrek.co/2019/06/07/toyota-electric-car-images-accelerate-plan/; M. May, *The Elegant Solution. Toyota's Formula for Mastering Innovation* (New York: The Free Press, 2007); James Morgan and Jeffrey K. Liker, *The Toyota Product Development System: Integrating People, Process and Technology* (New York: Productivity Press, 2006); James M. Morgan and Jeffrey K. Liker, "The Toyota Product Development System: Integrating People, Process and Technology" *Journal of Product Innovation Management*, 24(3) (2007): 276–278, https://doi-org.nlhhg.idm.oclc.org/10.1111/j.1540-5885.2007.00250_1.x; Anmol Rajpurohit, "Interview: Brian Kursar, Toyota on Big Data & Advanced Analytics—Cornerstones of Innovation," https://www.kdnuggets.com/2015/07/interview-brian-kursar-toyota-big-data-advanced-analytics.html; Shmula.com, "The Toyota Product Development System Principles" (2007), https://www.shmula.com/the-toyota-product-development-system/344/; "History of the Toyota Prius," The Official Blog of Toyota GB, February 10, 2015, https://blog.toyota.co.uk/history-toyota-prius; The Official Blog of Toyota GB, "The Five Processes of Toyota Design," May 7, 2014, https://blog.toyota.co.uk/history-toyota-prius; Toyota Europe, "An Electrified Route to Cleaner City Mobility," 2019, https://www.toyota-europe.com/world-of-toyota/feel/environment/better-air/electric-vehicle; Toyota Global, "Toyota Develops New Magnet for Electric Motors Aiming to Reduce Use of Critical Rare-Earth Element by up to 50%," https://global.toyota/en/newsroom/corporate/21139684.html; Toyota Global, "Guiding Principles at Toyota," 2019, https://www.toyota-global.com/company/history_of_toyota/75years/data/conditions/philosophy/guiding_principles.html; Toyota UK, "About. History of Toyota," 2019, https://www.toyotauk.com/about-toyota/history-of-toyota.html; Toyota Press Room, "2010 Third-Generation Prius Marketing Campaign," https://pressroom.toyota.com/album/2010-third-generation-prius-marketing-campaign/; "Toyota's Mobility Arm to Ease Bengaluru's Traffic Woes," *The Hindu Business Line,* January 16, 2018, https://www.thehindubusinessline.com/specials/auto-focus/toyotas-mobility-arm-to-ease-bengalurus-traffic-woes/article9440679.ece; J. Voelker, "Toyota Prius Hybrid Sales Have Tanked: Here Are 4 Reasons Why," Green Car Reports, February 9, 2018, https://www.greencarreports.com/news/1115184_toyota-prius-hybrid-sales-have-tanked-here-are-4-reasons-why; Durward K. Sobek, IIJeffrey Liker, and Allen C. Ward, "Another Look at How Toyota Integrates Product Development," *Harvard Business Review,* July–August 1998, https://hbr.org/1998/07/another-look-at-how-toyota-integrates-product-development.

Chapter 10

1. See Tripp Mickle, "Apple May Need New Plan for China," *Wall Street Journal,* January 31, 2019, p. B3; Dave Smith, "Apple Should Give the iPhone XS and iPhone XR a Permanent Price Cut," *Business Insider,* January 21, 2019, www.businessinsider.com/apple-should-give-iphone-xs-xr-permanent-price-cut-2019-1; Manish Singh, "Apple Says It's Struggling to Sell iPhones in India, but It's Really Not Trying," *VentureBeat,* November 3, 2018, http://venturebeat.com/2018/11/03/apple-says-its-struggling-to-sell-iphones-in-india-but-its-really-not-trying/; Daisuke Wakabayashi,

"Can Apple's Tim Cook Keep the iPhone Buzzing in China?" *Wall Street Journal*, January 25, 2016, www.wsj.com/articles/can-apples-tim-cook-keep-the-iphone-buzzing-in-china-1453775120; Chuck Jones, "No Surprise That Apple's iPhone Dominates Smartphone Profits," *Forbes*, November 20, 2017, www.forbes.com/sites/chuckjones/2017/11/20/no-surprise-that-apples-iphone-dominates-smartphone-profits/#5c9bd1ecbf8c; Mike Wuerthele, "Apple Grabs 86% of Global Smartphone Profits, iPhone Alone Seizes 35%," *Apple Insider*, April 17, 2018, https://appleinsider.com/articles/18/04/17/apple-grabs-86-of-smartphone-profits-globally-iphone-x-alone-seizes-35; "Apple to Cut iPhone Prices Outside the U.S. for Second Time in 12 Years," *The Economic Times*, January 30, 2019, economictimes.indiatimes.com/magazines/panache/apple-to-cut-iphone-prices-outside-u-s-for-the-second-time-in-12-years/articleshow/67749333.cms; and www.apple.com and http://investor.apple.com/financials.cfm, accessed September 2019.

2. For more on the importance of sound pricing strategy, see Thomas T. Nagle and Georg Muller, *The Strategy and Tactics of Pricing: A Guide to Growing More Profitably*, 6th ed. (New York: Routledge, 2018), Chapter 1.

3. See "Bear-Resistant Products," Interagency Grizzly Bear Committee, http://igbconline.org/bear-resistant-products/, accessed September 2019; "YETI," Scales, www.scalesadvertising.com/work.html, accessed September 2019; and https://stories.yeti.com/story/our-story and www.yeti.com/en_US/hard-coolers#, accessed September 2019.

4. See "Bear-Resistant Products," Interagency Grizzly Bear Committee, http://igbconline.org/bear-resistant-products/, accessed September 2019; "YETI," Scales, www.scalesadvertising.com/work.html, accessed September 2019; and https://stories.yeti.com/story/our-story and www.yeti.com/en_US/hard-coolers#, accessed September 2019.

5. See www.mbusa.com/mercedes/vehicles/class/class-CLA/bodystyle-CPE, accessed October 2019.

6. Marianne Wilson, "Study: ALDI a Growing Competitive Force," *Chain Store Age*, January 30, 2019, www.chainstoreage.com/news/study-aldi-a-growing-competitive-force/; Russell Redman, "ALDI Set to Kick Off National Ad Campaign," *Supermarket News*, September 13, 2018, www.supermarketnews.com/marketing/aldi-set-kick-national-ad-campaign; "Top 250 Global Powers of Retailing 2018," Deloitte, p. 16, www2.deloitte.com/content/dam/Deloitte/at/Documents/about-deloitte/global-powers-of-retailing-2018.pdf; Jessica Tyler, "Here's How ALDI's Explosive Growth Transformed It from a Corner Store in Germany to One of the Biggest Supermarket Chains in the World," *Business Insider*, August 12, 2018, www.businessinsider.com/aldi-store-growth-history-2018-8; Courtney Reagan, "Grocer ALDI Targets Nearby Rivals in Its Bid to Boost Its U.S. Footprint," *CNBC*, August 9, 2018, www.cnbc.com/2018/08/08/grocer-aldi-targets-nearby-rivals-in-bid-to-its-boost-its-us-footprint.html; and www.aldi.us/en/, accessed September 2019.

7. "Royal Philips," http://www.philips.com/a-w/about/company/our-heritage.html"; Borderless Brand Management by Ciarlone and Dalrymple, http://gilbane.com/case_studies_pdf/Case-Study-Philips-6-1-09.pdf; Philips Lighting, http://www.lighting.philips.nl/home; Philips Healthcare, http://www.usa.philips.com/healthcare/country-selector; Philips Annual Report 2015; http://www.philips.com/corporate/resources/annualresults/2015/PhilipsFullAnnualReport2015_English.pdf.

8. Accumulated production is drawn on a semilog scale so that equal distances represent the same percentage increase in output.

9. The arithmetic of markups and margins is discussed in Appendix 2: Marketing by the Numbers.

10. See "Caterpillar Looks to 'Rewrite the Rules'," *Demolition and Recycling International*, February 5, 2019, www.khl.com/demolition-and-recycling-international/caterpillar-looks-to-rewrite-the-rules/136845. article; Donald V. Fites, "Make Your Dealers Your Partners," *Harvard Business Review*, March–April 1996, pp. 84–95; "Caterpillar Grows Service and Repair Choices," *Lift and Access*, December 12, 2017, www.liftandaccess.com/article/caterpillar-grows-service-and-repair-choices-including-launch-yellowmark%E2%84%A2-parts; Jon Markman, "This Is What You Should Know about Caterpillar," *Fortune*, April 26, 2018, www.forbes.com/sites/jonmarkman/2018/04/26/this-is-what-you-should-know-about-caterpillar/#50b9c4d93e43; "Caterpillar Continues Margin Expansion in 2018; FVE Reduced on Less Ebullient Outlook for 2019," *Morningstar*, January 30, 2019, http://analysisreport.morningstar.com/stock/research; and www.statista.com and www.caterpillar.com, accessed September 2019.

11. See Kim Renfro, "I Finally Caved and Flew on the 'Worst Airline in America'—Here's What It Was Like," *Business Insider*, December 6, 2019, www.thisisinsider.com/spirit-airlines-flight-review-food-photos-2018-6; Adam Levine, "Could Rising Fuel Prices Lift Spirit Airlines in 2018?" *The Motley Fool*, January 2, 2018, www.fool.com/investing/2018/01/02/could-rising-fuel-prices-lift-spirit-airlines-2018.aspx; and www.spirit.com, accessed September 2019.

12. See www.sleepnumber.com, accessed September 2019.

13. "Watch the Newest Ads on TV from Amazon, Honda, Google, and More," *Advertising Age*, December 12, 2017, http://adage.com/article/media/watch-newest-tv-ads-amazon-honda-google/311610/; and https://store.google.com/us/product/pixel_2?hl=en-US, accessed September 2019.

14. See Jessica Wohl, "ConAgra's Banquet Raises Prices, Brings Back Commercials," *Advertising Age*, December 9, 2015, www.adage.com/print/301684. Joseph Weber, "Over a Buck for Dinner? Outrageous," *BusinessWeek*, March 9, 2009, p. 57; Tom Mulier and Matthew Boyle, "Dollar Dinners from ConAgra's Threatened by Costs," *Bloomberg Businessweek*, August 19, 2010, www.businessweek.com; and Angelica LaVito, "ConAgra's Bet on Frozen Foods Appears to Be Paying Off," *CNBC*, November 15, 2017, www.cnbc.com/2017/11/15/conagras-bet-on-frozen-food-appears-to-be-paying-off.html.

15. Nathaniel Meyersohn, "Gillette Is Selling a $200 Luxury Razor That Heats Up to 122 Degrees," *CNN*, May 2, 2019, www.cnn.com/2019/05/02/tech/gillette-heated-razor/index.html; Tiffany Kary, "Edgewell Deal for Harry's Razors Will Only Nick Gillette—At First," *Bloomberg*, May 9, 2019, www.bloomberg.com/news/articles/2019-05-09/edgewell-and-harry-s-deal-will-only-nick-gillette-at-first; Barrett Brunsman, "Should P&G Exit the Shaving Business?" *Cincinnati Business Courier*, April 23, 2019, www.bizjournals.com/cincinnati/news/2019/04/23/should-p-g-exit-the-shaving-business.html; and information from www.gillette.com/en-us/our-history, accessed September 2019.

Chapter 11

1. See Bethany Biron, "Competition Has Flywheel and SoulCycle Spiraling into an Identity Crisis," *Vox*, January 11, 2019, www.vox.com/the-goods/2019/1/11/18176929/flywheel-soulcycle-peloton-spinning-bubble-cycling-class; Sara Ivry, "The Cult of Peloton," *Adweek*, May 28, 2018, www.adweek.com/brand-marketing/peloton/; JP Mangalindan, "Peloton CEO: Sales Increased after We Raised Prices to $2,245 per Bike," *Yahoo! Finance*, September 12, 2018, https://finance.yahoo.com/news/peloton-ceo-says-sales-increased-raised-prices-2245-exercise-bike-132256225.html?guccounter=1; Alexandra Bruell, "How Peloton Is Marketing a $2,000 Bike beyond the Rich," *Wall Street Journal*, January 19, 2019, www.wsj.com/articles/peloton-shifts-gears-with-more-attainable-marketing-plan-1508959554; and www.onepeloton.com, accessed September 2019.

2. See Mike Wuerthele, "Apple Grabs 86% of Global Smartphone Profits, iPhone Alone Seizes 35%," *Apple Insider*, April 17, 2018, https://appleinsider.com/

articles/18/04/17/apple-grabs-86-of-smartphone-profits-globally-iphone-x-alone-seizes-35; and Daniel Morial, "Apple Leads Global Smartphone Profits for Q2 2018," *Gadget Match,* September 20, 2018, www.gadgetmatch.com/apple-samsung-huawei-global-smartphone-profits-q2-2018/.

3. See Jacob Passy, "Amazon Rolls Out More Echo Devices, but They Could Make You Spend More Money," *Marketing Watch,* September 23, 2018, www.marketwatch.com/story/your-amazon-echo-could-be-making-you-spend-more-money-2018-01-03; "Amazon Is Extending Prime Video's Introductory, Discounted Pricing Globally," *Gadgets 360,* June 28, 2017, https://gadgets.ndtv.com/entertainment/news/amazon-prime-video-introductory-price-offer-extended-1717819; and www.amazon.com/All-new-Echo-Dot-3rd-Gen/dp/B0792KTHKJ, accessed July 2019.

4. See Charlie Hall, "Japanese Site Estimates Nintendo Spends $257 to Make One Switch," *Polygon,* April 5, 2107, www.polygon.com/2017/4/5/15195638/nintendo-switch-component-cost-estimate; and "Dedicated Video Game Sales Units," www.nintendo.co.jp/ir/en/finance/hard_soft/index.html, accessed September 2019.

5. "Harry's Shaving Club Shook Up the Razor Market. What's Next?" *Trib Live,* September 26, 2018, https://triblive.com/business/headlines/14118900-74/harrys-shaving-club-shook-up-the-razor-market-whats-next; and "Sales of the Leading Cartridge Razor Blade Brands in the United States," *Statista,* www.statista.com/statistics/276535/leading-men-s-cartridge-razor-blade-brands-sales/, accessed September 2019.

6. See Lucy Hornsby, "China's Love of U.S. Chicken Feet Proves a Recipe for Perfect Trade," *Financial Times,* August 14, 2017, www.ft.com/content/90ebf59a-80bb-11e7-a4ce-15b2513cb3ff; Matthew Philips, "The Economics of Chicken Feet… and Other Parts," *Freakonomics,* December 9, 2011, http://freakonomics.com/2011/12/09/the-economics-of-chicken-feet-and-other-parts/; and Pan Demetrakakes, "The Rib Bone Connects to the Foot Bone," *Food Processing,* November 20, 2018, www.foodprocessing.com/blogs/thescoop/the-rib-bone-connects-to-the-foot-bone/.

7. See Anne-Marcelle Ngabirano, "'Pink Tax' Forces Women to Pay More Than Men," *USA Today,* March 27, 2017, www.usatoday.com/story/money/business/2017/03/27/pink-tax-forces-women-pay-more-than-men/99462846/; and Karen Duffin, "The Problem with the Pink Tax," *NPR,* November 13, 2018, www.npr.org/sections/money/2018/11/13/667539767/the-problem-with-the-pink-tax.

8. See Alexandra Jardin, "Dunkin' Fooled Portland Foodies with an Espresso Pop-Up," *Advertising Age,* December 6, 2018, https://adage.com/creativity/work/dunkin-espresso-popup/962656; and "How We Fooled Portland Foodies into Trying a New Espresso," Dunkin' Newsroom, December 4, 2018, https://news.dunkindonuts.com/blog/how-we-fooled-portland-foodies-into-trying-a-new-espresso.

9. For this and other examples and explanations, see Peter Coy, "Why the Price Is Rarely Right," *Bloomberg Businessweek,* February 1 & 8, 2010, pp. 77–78; and Utpal Dholakia, "What Shoppers Should Know about Reference Prices," *Psychology Today,* September 8, 2015, www.psychologytoday.com/blog/the-science-behind-behavior/201509/what-shoppers-should-know-about-reference-prices.

10. See Emmie Martin, "There's a Sneaky Reason Why the New iPhone X Costs $999 Instead of $1,000," *CNBC,* September 13, 2017, www.cnbc.com/2017/09/13/why-iphone-x-costs-999-instead-of-1000.html; and "Subdued Sales May Force Apple to Call Time on the iPhone X," *The Times,* January 24, 2018, www.thetimes.co.uk/article/subdued-sales-may-force-apple-to-call-time-on-the-iphone-x-3wzbtxd2d.

11. See Anthony Allred, E. K. Valentin, and Goutam Chakraborty, "Pricing Risky Services: Preference and Quality Considerations," *Journal of Product and Brand Management*, Vol. 19, No. 1, 2010, p. 54; Kenneth C. Manning and David E. Sprott, "Price Endings, Left-Digit Effects, and Choice," *Journal of Consumer Research*, August 2009, pp. 328–336; Bouree Lam, "The Psychological Difference between $12.00 and $11.67," *The Atlantic,* January 30, 2015, www.theatlantic.com/business/archive/2015/01/the-psychological-difference-between-1200-and-1167/384993/; and Darian Kovacs, "4 Psychological Techniques That Can Improve Your Product Pricing," *Entrepreneur,* November 15, 2017, www.entrepreneur.com/article/304687.

12. Sarah Halzack, "The Trouble with Those 20 Percent Off Coupons from Bed Bath & Beyond," *Washington Post,* September 30, 2015, www.washingtonpost.com/news/business/wp/2015/09/30/the-trouble-with-those-20-percent-off-coupons-from-bed-bath-beyond/; and Wayne Duggan, "Bed Bath & Beyond Struggles to Adapt," *US News,* December 21, 2017, https://money.usnews.com/investing/stock-market-news/articles/2017-12-21/bed-bath-beyond-inc-bbby.

13. Alex Samuels, "Texans Drive Mad as Tolls Burn Holes in Their Wallets," *Texas Tribune,* November 17, 2017, www.texastribune.org/2017/11/17/texans-driven-mad-tolls-burn-holes-their-wallets/; David Schaper, "Are $40 Toll Roads the Future?" *NPR,* December 12, 2017, www.npr.org/2017/12/12/570248568/are-40-toll-roads-the-future; and Lori Aratani, "Dulles Toll Road Upgrade Could Foreshadow Congestion-Priced Tolling," *Washington Post,* March 31, 2018, www.washingtonpost.com/local/trafficandcommuting/dulles-toll-road-upgrade-could-foreshadow-congestion-priced-tolling/2018/03/31/2f07cbe2-329f-11e8-8bdd-cdb33a5eef83_story.html?noredirect=on&utm_term=.df7b0527a53f.

14. Dennis Green, "Target Changed Its App after an Investigation Found Prices Went Up for Shoppers Using It in Stores—but It Hasn't Changed the Practice," *Business Insider*, February 9, 2019, www.businessinsider.com/target-app-prices-different-in-stores-2019-2; "How Far Can Dynamic Prices Go in 2019," *PYMNTS.com,* December 20, 2018, www.pymnts.com/news/ecommerce/2018/dynamic-pricing-holiday-shopping-amazon/; Laura Gunderson, "Amazon's 'Dynamic' Prices Get Some Static," *The Oregonian,* May 5, 2012, http://blog.oregonlive.com/complaintdesk/2012/05/amazons_dynamic_prices_get_som.html; Kathy Kristof, "How Amazon Uses Surge Pricing Just Like Uber," *CBS News,* July 24, 2017, www.cbsnews.com/news/a; Chris Hrapsky, "Target Changes App after KARE 11 Investigation," *KARE11,* February 7, 2019, www.kare11.com/article/money/consumer/target-changes-app-after-kare-11-investigation/89-40ee0e76-9a0f-425d-93b0-b0eb89150f6c; and "About Shopping Cart Prices," www.amazon.com/gp/help/customer/display.html?nodeId=201895490, accessed September 2019.

15. Ralph Jennings, "Why Apple Will Lose China Marketing Share in 2018, despite the Success of the iPhone X," *Forbes,* February 25, 2018, www.forbes.com/sites/ralphjennings/2018/02/25/why-apple-despite-the-iphone-x-will-lose-china-market-share-in-2018/#7a927675462e; and Benjamin Mayo, "iPhone Prices Discounted by Up to 20% at Chinese Retailers," *9TO5Mac,* January 11, 2019, https://9to5mac.com/2019/01/11/iphone-prices-discounted-by-up-to-20-at-chinese-retailers/.

16. See "International Trade Policy," The Wine Institute, accessed at www.wineinstitute.org/international_trade_policy, September 2019.

17. See Peter Sarnoff, "Samsung Is Shifting Its Focus to Mid-Range Smartphones," *Business Insider,* September 5, 20918, www.businessinsider.com/samsung-strategy-mid-range-smartphones-2018-9; and Panos Mourdoukoutas, "Samsung Beats Apple in the Global Smartphone Market as Chinese Brands Close In," *Forbes,* September 13, 2018, www.forbes.com/sites/panosmourdoukoutas/2018/09/13/samsung-beats-apple-in-the-global-smartphone-market-as-chinese-brands-close-in/.

18. See David Sax, "Hang $99.99," *Bloomberg Businessweek,* November 2–8, 2015, pp. 43–44; Chris Ahrens, "The Advantage

of a Custom Board," *San Diego Reader,* January 2, 2018, www.sandiegoreader.com/news/2018/jan/02/waterfront-advantage-custom-board/#; "The 7 Best Beginner Surfboards Reviewed & Rated [2018]," *Outside Pursuits,* accessed March 2018; and www.wavestormboards.com/about-us/, accessed July 2019.

19. See Katy Allen, "Shrinking Sweets? 'You're Not Imagining It,' ONS Tells Shopper," *The Guardian,"* July 24, 2017, www.theguardian.com/business/2017/jul/24/sweets-are-shrinking-youre-not-imagining-it-ons-tells-shoppers; and David Brown, Daniele Palumbo, Mark Bryson, and Luke Keast, "Biscuits and Chocolates Take the 'Shrinkflation' Test," *BBC News,* February 1, 2018, www.bbc.com/news/uk-42864685.

20. Joshua Cohen, "Pouring Billions of Dollars into Marketing of Drugs," *Forbes,* February 7, 2019, www.forbes.com/sites/joshuacohen/2019/02/07/pouring-billions-of-dollars-into-marketing-of-drugs/#39eb2c2e3282; "Trends in Retail Prices of Brand Name Prescription Drugs," *AARP Bulletin,* September 2018, www.aarp.org/content/dam/aarp/ppi/2018/09/trends-in-retail-prices-of-brand-name-prescription-drugs-year-end-update.pdf; Joyce Frieden, "Senator's Probe 'Enormous' Insulin Price Spikes," *MedPage Today,* May 8, 2018, www.medpagetoday.com/endocrinology/type1diabetes/72771; Benjamin Siegel and Mary Bruce, "Former Pharma Big Martin Shkreli Boasted '$1 Bn Here We Come,' Documents Say," *ABC News,* February 2, 2016, http://abcnews.go.com/Politics/pharmabig-martin-shkreli-boasted-bn-documents/story?id=36671216; "Fact Check: Trump's 2019 State of the Union Address," *ABC News,* February 6, 2019, www.abc7chicago.com/politics/fact-check-2019-state-of-the-union-address/5122821/; Tori Marsh, "Generic EpiPen Is Still Expensive," *GoodRx,* December 13, 2018, www.goodrx.com/blog/generic-epipen-is-still-expensive-heres-how-you-can-save/; Joshua Cohen, "The Curious Case of Gleevec Pricing," *Forbes,* September 12, 2018, www.forbes.com/sites/joshuacohen/2018/09/12/the-curious-case-of-gleevec-pricing/#4bcd73b254a3; facts and statistics from www.statista.com, accessed February 2019; and "Our Mission and Strategy," www.gsk.com/en-gb/about-us/our-mission-and-strategy/, accessed September 2019. For more on the biopharmaceutical industry viewpoint, see www.goboldly.com, accessed September 2019.

21. For discussions of these issues, see Dhruv Grewal and Larry D. Compeau, "Pricing and Public Policy: A Research Agenda and Overview of the Special Issue," *Journal of Public Policy and Marketing,* Spring 1999, pp. 3–10; Walter L. Baker, Michael V. Marn, and Craig C. Zawada, *The Price Advantage* (Hoboken, NJ: John Wiley & Sons, 2010), Appendix 2; and Thomas T. Nagle, and Georg Muller, *The Strategy and Tactics of Pricing: A Guide to Growing More Profitably,* 6th ed. (New York, NY: Routledge, 2017), chapter 12.

22. See "Visa and Mastercard Will Pay $6 Billion to End a Massive Price-Fixing Lawsuit," *Fortune,* September 18, 2018; http://fortune.com/2018/09/18/visa-mastercard-6-billion-price-fixing-lawsuit/; and Russel Lee, "Southwest, American Agree to Pay $60M in Price-Fixing Lawsuit," *Aerotime News,* October 24, 2018, www.aerotime.aero/ruta.burbaite/22016-southwest-american-agree-to-pay-60m-in-price-fixing-lawsuit.

23. Roger Lowenstein, "Why Amazon Monopoly Accusations Deserve a Closer Look," *Fortune,* July 23, 2015, http://fortune.com/2015/07/23/why-amazon-monopoly-accusations-deserve-a-closer-look/; and Emily Stewart, "Happy Prime Day! Experts Worry Amazon Is Building a Dangerous Monopoly," *Vox,* July 17, 2018, www.vox.com/2018/7/17/17583070/amazon-prime-day-monopoly-antitrust.

24. Jonathan Stempel, "Michael Kors Settles U.S. Lawsuit Alleging Deceptive Price Tags," *Reuters,* June 12, 2015, www.reuters.com/article/us-michaelkors-settlement-idUSKBN0OS2AU20150612; and Daphne Howland, "Ross to Settle $4.9 Million Lawsuit Over 'Deceptive' Price Tags," *Retail Dive,* October 3, 2018, www.retaildive.com/news/ross-to-settle-49m-lawsuit-over-deceptive-price-tags/538768/.

25. "FTC Guides against Deceptive Pricing," www.ecfr.gov/cgi-bin/text-idx?c=ecfr&sid=dfafb89837c306cf5b010b5bde15f041&rgn=div5&view=text&node=16:1.0.1.2.16&idno=16, accessed September 2019.

26. Amy Feldman, "Dozens of Upstart Companies Are Upending the $15-Billion Mattress Market," *Forbes,* May 2, 2017, www.forbes.com/sites/amyfeldman/2017/05/02/dozens-of-upstart-companies-are-upending-the-15-billion-mattress-market/#1f08c3e07da3; Jeff Andrews, "Why There Are So Many Mattress-in-a-Box Companies," *Curbed,* March 28, 2018, www.curbed.com/2018/3/28/17164898/bed-in-a-box-online-mattress-brands-why-so-many; Noah Higgins-Dunn, "Billion-Dollar Mattress Start-Up Casper Could Prove to Be a Hot IPO," *CNBC,* May 26, 2019, www.cnbc.com/2019/05/24/why-casper-kylie-jenners-mattress-could-be-an-ipo-market-sleeper.html; Andria Chang, "Casper, with Competition Growing, Wants to Be More Than a Mattress Company," *Forbes,* May 7, 2019, www.forbes.com/sites/andriacheng/2019/05/07/casper-facing-growing-competition-wants-to-take-care-of-your-entire-sleep-business/#4050129afb11; Jonathan Ringen, "Why Casper Is the $750 Million Startup That Just Can't Rest," *Fast Company,* August 7, 2017, www.fastcompany.com/40438355/why-casper-is-the-750-million-startup-that-just-cant-rest; Tom Huddleston Jr., "How Casper's Founders Built a Billion-Dollar Mattress Start-up," *CNBC,* April 5, 2019, www.cnbc.com/2019/04/05/how-caspers-founders-built-a-billion-dollar-mattress-start-up.html.

Chapter 12

1. Kamila Rivero, "How Many People Use Netflix," *CheatSheet,* February 8, 2019, www.cheatsheet.com/entertainment/how-many-people-use-netflix.html/; Josef Adalian, "How Netflix Broke HBO's 17-Year Emmy's Streak," *Vulture,* July 12, 2018, www.vulture.com/2018/07/emmys-2018-nominations-netflix-hbo.html; Rian Barrett, "Netflix Is Turning 20—but Its Birthday Doesn't Matter," *Wired,* August 29, 2017, www.wired.com/story/netflix-20th-anniversary/; "The World's Most Innovative Companies—2018," *Fast Company,* February 21, 2018, www.fastcompany.com/most-innovative-companies/2018; Dana Feldman, "Netflix's Content Budget Is Updated to $13B for 2018," *Forbes,* July 9, 2018, www.forbes.com/sites/danafeldman/2018/07/09/netflixs-content-budget-is-updated-to-13b-in-2018/#4613a36e2b8c; Ronald Grover and Cliff Edwards, "Can Netflix Find Its Future by Abandoning the Past?" *Bloomberg Businessweek,* September 22, 2011, www.bloomberg.com/news/articles/2011-09-22/can-netflix-find-its-future-by-abandoning-the-past; Ashley Rodriguez, "Keeping Up with Netflix Originals Is Basically a Part-Time Job Now," *Quartz,* January 1, 2019, https://qz.com/1505030/keeping-up-with-netflix-originals-is-basically-a-part-time-job-now/; Sara Salinas, "Netflix Beats on Subscriber Growth but Misses Slightly on Revenue," *CNBC,* January 17, 2019, www.cnbc.com/2019/01/16/netflix-earnings-q4-2018.html; and www.netflix.com, accessed September 2019.

2. See Sarah Whitten, "Owners of McDonalds Aren't Happy with Headquarters as Promotions Pick Up and Remodeling Costs Rise," *CNBC,* January 23, 2018, www.cnbc.com/2018/01/23/owners-of-mcdonalds-arent-happy-with-headquarters.html; Nancy Luna, "Tension Escalates between McDonald's and Franchisees over Remodels," *Nation's Restaurant News,* January 9, 2019, www.nrn.com/franchising/tension-escalates-between-mcdonald-s-and-franchisees-over-remodels; and "McDonald's Reports

Good Results, to Continue Growth in 2019," *Forbes*, February 4, 2019, www.forbes.com/sites/greatspeculations/2019/02/04/mcdonalds-reports-good-results-to-continue-growth-in-2019/.

3. See Sam Knight, "The Spectacular Power of Big Lens," *Guardian*, May 10, 2018, www.theguardian.com/news/2018/may/10/the-invisible-power-of-big-glasses-eyewear-industry-essilor-luxottica; and www.luxottica.com/en/company/quick_view, September 2019.

4. See Joseph Pisani, "Amazon Orders 20,000 Vans to Build Delivery Fleet, Quadrupling Its Original Purchase," *USA Today*, September 5, 20-18, www.usatoday.com/story/tech/news/2018/09/05/amazon-quadruples-order-vans-new-delivery-fleet-now-20-000/1204619002/; and "Forget Drones, Amazon Needs People," *Bloomberg Businessweek*, December 24, 2018, pp. 245-26.

5. "Franchise Business Economic Outlook for 2018," January 2018, www.franchise.org/sites/default/files/Franchise_Business_Outlook_Jan_2018.pdf.

6. See "2019 Franchise 500 Ranking," *Entrepreneur*, www.entrepreneur.com/franchise500/2019, accessed September 2019; and www.sportclipsfranchise.com/facts-stats/no1-haircare-franchise/ and https://sportclips.com/about-us/our-story, accessed September 2019.

7. See "Stores Top Retailers 2018," *Stores*, https://stores.org/stores-top-retailers-2018/; and www.rpminc.com/leading-brands/consumer-brands, www.rpminc.com/reports-and-filings/financial-reports/, http://ir.homedepot.com/financial-reports/annual-reports/recent, accessed September 2019.

8. Daphne Howland, "Why Target Sold Out to CVS," *Retail Dive*, February 11, 2016, www.retaildive.com/news/why-target-sold-out-to-cvs/413432/; and www.cvs.com/target-pharmacy, accessed September 2019.

9. See www.staralliance.com, www.oneworld.com, and www.skyteam.com, accessed September 2019.

10. Amy X. Wang, "Album Sales Are Dying as Fast as Streaming Services Are Rising," *Rolling Stone*, January 3, 2019, https://www.rollingstone.com/music/music-news/album-sales-dying-as-fast-as-streaming-services-rising-774563/.

11. See Dennis Green and Mike Nudelman, "Why Amazon Is Still Such a Threat to Toys R Us, in One Chart," *Business Insider*, September 20, 2017, www.businessinsider.com/amazon-beat-toys-r-us-online-sales-2017-9; Joan Verdon, "Toys R Us Said to Be Preparing for Liquidation," March 9, 2018, www.usatoday.com/story/money/business/2018/03/08/toys-r-us-preparing-liquidation-sources-say/408975002/; and Lauren Hirsch, "Toys R Us Tries for a Comeback Year after Going Out of Business," *CNBC*, February 11, 2019, www.cnbc.com/2019/02/11/toys-r-us-executives-plot-retailers-comeback-with-tru-kids.html.

12. "Zara," *Intidex*, http://www.inditex.com/en/brands/zara; Rupal Parekh, "How Zara Ballooned into a Multi-Billion Dollar Brand without Advertising," *Advertising Age*, August 19, 2013, http://adage.com/article/cmo-strategy/zara-grew-a-multi-billion-dollar-brand-sans-ads/243730/; Kevin O'Marah, "Zara Uses Supply Chain to Win Again," March 9, 2016, https://www.forbes.com/sites/kevinomarah/2016/03/09/zara-uses-supply-chain-to-win-again/#1f7de0411256; "Zara on the World's Most Valuable Brands," *Forbes*, May 2015, http://www.forbes.com/companies/zara/; Walter Loeb, "Zara Leads in Fast Fashion," *Forbes*, March 30, 2015, http://www.forbes.com/sites/walterloeb/2015/03/30/zara-leads-in-fast-fashion/; Svend Hollensen and Marc Opresnik, *Marketing: A Relationship Perspective*, 2nd ed. (Vahlen 2015); "The Best 100 Brands," Interbrand, http://www.bestglo-balbrands.com/2014/zara/; Graham Ruddick, "How Zara Became the World's Biggest Fashion Retailer," *The Telegraph*, October 20, 2014, http://www.telegraph.co.uk/finance/newsbysector/retailandconsumer/11172562/How-Inditex-became-the-worlds-biggest-fashion-retailer.html; "Zara: Managing Chain of Value and Driving CSR with Consumers," *JL Nueno*, http://www.jlnueno.com/wordpress/index.php/2011/07/29/gestionando-la-cadena-de-valor-y-accionando-la-rsc-con-los-consumidores/?lang=en;

The Economist, "Chain Reaction," February 2, 2002, pp. 1–3; C. Roux, "The Reign of Spain," *The Guardian*, October 28, 2002, pp. 6–7; "Store Wars: Fast Fashion, The Monet," *The Money Programme*, BBC, February19, 2003, television; A. Mitthell, "When Push Comes to Shove, It's All about Pull," *Marketing Week*, January 9, 2003, pp. 26–27; K. Capell, "Zara Thrives by Breaking All the Rules," *Business Week*, October 20, 2008, p. 66; M. Johnson and A. Falstead, "Inditex Breaks New Ground for Season in the South," *Financial Times*, May 2011, p. 17; http://www.inditex.com/en/investors/investors_relations/finan-cial_data, accessed April 1, 2017.

13. Adam Levy, "Walmart's Lead in Groceries Could Get Even Bigger," *Motley Fool*, October 11, 2018, https://www.fool.com/investing/2018/10/11/walmarts-lead-in-groceries-could-get-even-bigger.aspx; and "Benchmarks by Industry: Supermarkets," *ACSI*, www.theacsi.org/index.php?option=com_content&view=article&id=147&catid=&Itemid=212&i=Supermarkets, accessed September 2019.

14. "Four Seasons Hotels and Resorts Receives Record Number of Forbes Travel Guide Five-Star Awards for Fourth Year Running," Four Seasons Press Room, February 20, 2019, https://press.fourseasons.com/news-releases/2019/record-number-of-forbes-five-star-hotels/; Jeffrey O'Brien, "A Perfect Season," *Fortune*, February 1, 2008, http://archive.fortune.com/2008/01/18/news/companies/fourseasons.fortune/index.htm; and www.fourseasons.com/about_us/, accessed September 2019.

15. See "Subway Franchise Cost & Fees," www.franchisedirect.com/directory/subway/ufoc/915/, accessed September 2019.

16. Anita Chang Beattie, "Catching the Eye of a Chinese Shopper," *Advertising Age*, December 10, 2012, pp. 20–21.

17. Drew Hinshaw, "Burgers Face a Tough Slog in Africa," *Wall Street Journal*, December 10, 2013, www.wsj.com/articles/SB10001424052702304607104579214133498585594.

18. See Leanna Garfield, "Nestle Sponsored a River Barge to Create a 'Floating Supermarket' That Sold Candy and Chocolate Pudding to the Backwoods of Brazil," *Business Insider*, September 17, 2017, www.businessinsider.com/nestl-expands-brazil-river-barge-2017-9.

19. Richard Nieva, "Nest's Hello Doorbell, Other New Devices, Won't Be Sold on Amazon," *CNET*, March 14, 2018, www.cnet.com/news/nests-hello-doorbell-other-new-products-wont-be-sold-on-amazon/.

20. "Five Out of Six N.A. Automakers' Scores Drop in Annual Supplier Working Relations Study," *PRNewswire*, May 14, 2018, www.prnewswire.com/news-releases/five-out-of-six-na-automakers-scores-drop-in-annual-supplier-working-relations-study-300647418.html; and www.toyotasupplier.com, https://toyotasupplierdiversity.com/, and www.loreal.com/_en/_ww/html/suppliers/, accessed September 2019.

21. See Julie Bort, "Amazon Web Services Is Bigger Than Its Next 4 Competitors Combined," *Business Insider*, February 6, 2019, www.businessinsider.com/aws-market-share-dominates-70-billion-cloud-market-2019-2; "Microsoft Narrows Amazon's Lead in the Cloud, but the Gap Remains Large," *CNBC*, April 27, 2018, www.cnbc.com/2018/04/27/microsoft-gains-cloud-market-share-in-q1-but-aws-still-dominates.html; Dina Bass, "Google May Have to Get Used to Third Place in the Cloud," *Bloomberg Businessweek*, November 13, 2018, www.bloomberg.com/news/articles/2018-11-13/google-may-have-to-get-used-to-third-place-in-the-cloud; Dina Bass, "The Cloud: How to Catch Amazon," *Bloomberg Businessweek*, November 13, 2017, pp. 45–46; "Albertsons Companies to Transform Experiences for Shoppers with Microsoft Cloud and AI," *PR Newswire*, February 22, 2019, www.prnewswire.com/news-releases/albertsons-companies-to-transform-experiences-for-shoppers-with-microsoft-cloud-and-ai-300800184.html; Rosalie Chan, "Google Ventures-Backed Cloud Storage Company Egnyte Explains Why It's Betting Big on Microsoft, 'The Best Partner There Is,'" *Business Insider*, February 21, 2019, www.businessinsider.com/egnyte-microsoft-azure-2019-2?IR=T&_ga=2.245147975.334175892.1550861913-

507802238.1550861913; and https://azure.microsoft.com/en-us/, accessed September 2019.

22. See Marcus Williams, "Cutting Logistics Costs Key to GM Profit Targets," *Automotive Logistics,* October 2014, http://automotivelogistics.media/news/cutting-logistics-costs-key-to-gm-profit-targets; and "29th Annual State of Logistics Report: Carriers Take the Wheel," July 9, 2018, https://www.logisticsmgmt.com/article/29th_annual_state_of_logistics_report_carriers_take_the_wheel.

23. Andy Brack, "Piggly Wiggly Center Offers Info-Packed Field Trip," *Charleston Currents,* January 4, 2010, www.charlestoncurrents.com/issue/10_issues/10.0104.htm; "How Many Products Does Amazon Carry?" *Retail Touch Points,* www.retailtouchpoints.com/resources/type/infographics/how-many-products-does-amazon-carry, accessed March 2019; and information from http://en.wikipedia.org/wiki/Piggly_wiggly and http://corporate.walmart.com/_news_/news-archive/2005/01/07/our-retail-divisions, accessed September 2019.

24. Sarah Landrum, "Millennials Driving Brands to Practice Socially Responsible Marketing," *Forbes,* March 17, 2017, www.forbes.com/sites/sarahlandrum/2017/03/17/millennials-driving-brands-to-practice-socially-responsible-marketing/#2c2d4dc94990. See also Nielsen, "Sustainability Sells: Linking Sustainability Claims to Sales," October 16, 2018, https://www.nielsen.com/us/en/insights/news/2018/sustainability-sells-linking-sustainability-claims-to-sales.html.

25. "Levi's How Can 'Clean' Begin with 'Design?'" IPE, August 16, 2017, http://wwwen.ipe.org.cn/GreenSupplyChain/BrandStoryDetail.aspx?id=20; Gaylen Davenport, "Levi's Water Conservation Efforts Actually Save the Company Money," *Worldwide Energy,* February 24, 2015, www.worldwideenergy.com/levis-water-conservation-efforts-actually-save-company-money/; Anna Sanina, "Levi's Asks People Not to Wash Their Jeans," *Popsop,* March 22, 2012, http://popsop.com/2012/03/levis-asks-people-not-to-wash-their-jeans/; and www.levistrauss.com/sustainability/products/waterless/, http://store.levi.com/waterless/index.html; and www.levi.com/US/en_US/features/sustainability#process, accessed September 2019.

26. Lydia DePillis, "Watch How Amazon Spread Across the US," *CNN,* October 4, 2018, www.cnn.com/interactive/2018/10/business/amazon-distribution-map/index.html; "Inside a Tracy Amazon Fulfillment Center on Cyber Monday," *KCRA3,* November 26, 2018 www.kcra.com/article/inside-a-tracy-amazon-fulfillment-center-on-cyber-monday/25312342; and "Tour an Amazon Fulfillment Center," http://amazonfctours.com/, accessed October 2019.

27. See Nick Wingfield, "As Amazon Pushes Forward with Robots, Workers Find New Roles," September 10, 2017, www.nytimes.com/2017/09/10/technology/amazon-robots-workers.html; Andrea Cheng, "Amazon's Robot-Filled New York Fulfillment Center Gives Rivals Another Reason to Worry," *Forbes,* December 10, 2018, www.forbes.com/sites/andriacheng/2018/12/10/amazons-first-new-york-fulfillment-center-should-give-rival-retailers-another-cause-for-worry/#378cfe2a614c; and www.amazonrobotics.com, accessed September 2019.

28. Matthew Boyle, "Walmart Cracks the Whip on Suppliers," *Bloomberg Businessweek,* July 24, 2017, pp. 14-15.

29. Bureau of Transportation Statistics, "Pocket Guide to Transportation," https://s3-us-west-2.amazonaws.com/dot-concept-menus/menu/accordion.html, accessed September 2019.

30. See Walmart's supplier requirements at http://corporate.walmart.com/suppliers, accessed September 2019.

31. www.oracle.com/webfolder/assets/infographics/value-chain/index.html, accessed September 2019.

32. For this and other UPS examples and information, see "Moving Returns Forward with Overstock.com," www.ups-scs.com/solutions/case_studies/cs_Overstock.pdf, accessed October 2018; Daniel Goure, "United Parcel Service Is on the Forefront of the Revolution in Healthcare," Lexington Institute, September 14, 2017, www.lexingtoninstitute.org/united-parcel-service-forefront-revolution-healthcare/; and www.ups-scs.com/solutions/and https://solvers.ups.com/, accessed September 2019.

33. Jennifer McKevitt, "Fortune 500 Companies Are Using 3PLs More, Study Finds," *Supply Chain Dive,* May 30, 2017, www.supplychaindive.com/news/third-party-logistics-3pl-increase-large-companies-2017/443710/; and Adam Robinson, "Trends Driving Growth of 3PL in 2019," *Cerasis,* February 6, 2019, https://cerasis.com/growth-of-3pl.

34. "In Grocery Delivery Apps Market, Instacart Continues to Experience Strongest Growth Trajectory," *Edison,* February 14, 2019, www.medium.com/edison-discovers/in-grocery-delivery-apps-market-instacart-continues-to-experience-strongest-growth-trajectory-58702e41f87a; "Walmart Expands Its Grocery Delivery Service Providers," January 17, 2019, www.news.walmart.com/2019/01/17/walmart-expands-its-grocery-delivery-service-providers; Anne D'Innocenzio, "Walmart Prepares to Roll Out Online Same-Day Grocery Delivery to 100 Cities," *Chicago Tribune,* March 14, 2018, www.chicagotribune.com/business/ct-walmart-online-same-day-grocery-delivery-20180314-story.html; Sarah Berger, "How This 32-Year-Old High School Dropout Built a Business That Sold to Target For $550 Million," *CNBC,* March 29, 2018, www.cnbc.com/2018/03/29/how-bill-smith-founded-shipt-and-sold-it-to-target.html; Dennis Green, "Amazon's Struggles with Its Fresh Grocery Service Show a Huge Liability for Prime," *Business Insider*, July 1, 2018, www.businessinsider.com/amazon-fresh-struggles-show-a-huge-liability-in-prime-2018-7; and information from www.shipt.com/about/, accessed September 2019.

Chapter 13

1. Chloe Halley, "UNIQLO: On a Global Expansion Spree," Chloe's Portfolio, http://chloehalley.com/2014/01/20/case-study-onuniqlo-on-a-global-expansion-spree/; Chauncey Zalkin, "Made in Japan: The Culture behind the Brand," http://www.brandchannel.com; Andrea Graelis, "Japan Clothes Giant Uniqlo Takes On World's Fashion Capital," Agence France Presse, September 30, 2009, accessed at http://www.factiva.com, Kana Inagaki, "Uniqlo Aims 7-Fold Rise in Group Sales to 5 Trillion Yen by 2020," *Kyodo News,* September 2, 2009, accessed at http://www.factiva.com; Kim Yoon-mi, "Asian Market Is Uniqlo's No. 1 Priority," *The Korea Herald,* September 24, 2009, accessed at http://www.factiva.com; Stuart Elliott, "Retailers Summon Optimism as They Enter a Critical Season," *The New York Times,* September 5, 2011; and Michiyo Nakamoto, "Japanese Shoppers Break with Tradition," *Financial Times,* September 9, 2009, accessed at http://www.factiva.com; Tara Shen, "Fashion Retailers Leverage Technology to Maintain Lead in the Market: Case Studies of Uniqlo and Topshop," February 6, 2014, http://tarashen.com/fashion-retailers-leverage-technology-tomaintain-lead-in-the-market-case-studies-of-uniqlo-and-topshop/; Annual Report 2014, http://www.fastretailing.com/eng/ir/library/pdf/ar2014_en.pdf; and information from http://www.uniqlo.com and http://www.fastretailing.com, accessed October 2019; http://www.fastretailing.com/eng/ir/financial/past_5yrs.html, accessed April 1, 2017; http://www.uniqlo.com/uk/corp/corp_about.html, accessed April 1, 2017.

2. See "Monthly and Annual Retail Trade," U.S. Census Bureau, www.census.gov/retail/, accessed September 2019.

3. See Chris Chang, "5 Reasons We're Seeing a Resurgence of Google's Zero Moment of Truth," *Adweek,* February 6, 2019, www.adweek.com/digital/5-reasons-were-seeing-a-resurgence-of-googles-zero-moment-of-truth/; and *Think with Google,* www.thinkwithgoogle.com/marketing-resources/micro-moments/zero-moment-truth/and www.thinkwithgoogle.com/

marketing-resources/micro-moments/, accessed September 2019.

4. Hal Conick, "The End of Retail (as We Knew It)," *Marketing News,* September 27, 2017, pp. 38–47; and Dan Alaimo, "Mobile to Drive 60% of Holiday e-Commerce Traffic," *Retail Dive,* September 17, 2018, www.retaildive.com/news/mobile-to-drive-68-of-holiday-e-commerce-traffic/532468/.

5. For more on the current struggles of traditional retailers, Phil Wahba, "The Death of Retail Is Greatly Exaggerated," *Fortune,* June 25, 2017, pp. 33–34; Steve Dennis, "Retail 2018: Now Comes the Real Reckoning," *Forbes,* January 12, 2018, www.forbes.com/sites/stevendennis/2018/01/12/retail-2018-now-comes-the-real-reckoning/#46bed5a55f54; and Steve Dennis, "Out on a Limb: 14 Predictions for Retail in 2010," *Forbes,* January 10, 2019, www.forbes.com/sites/stevendennis/2019/01/10/out-on-a-limb-my-14-predictions-for-retail-in-2019/.

6. Phil Wahba, "Everything Must Go," *Fortune,* March 1, 2017, pp. 95–100; Lauren Thomas, "Another Wave of Retail Store Closures Coming. 'No light at the End of the Tunnel,'" *CNBC,* February 13, 2019, www.cnbc.com/2019/02/13/another-wave-of-retail-store-closures-coming-no-light-at-the-end-of-the-tunnel.html; and Doug Whiteman, "These Chains Are Closing Tons More Stores in 2019," *MoneyWise,* February 19, 2019, https://moneywise.com/a/retailers-closing-stores-in-2019.

7. Daniel B. Kline, "Grocery Stores Are Facing a New Challenge and It's Not Just Amazon," *Business Insider,* September 14, 2017, www.businessinsider.com/grocery-stores-are-facing-a-new-challenge-and-its-not-just-amazon-2017-9; Pamela Danziger, "Online Grocery Sale to Reach $100 Billion in 2025; Amazon Is Current and Future Leader," *Forbes,* January 18, 2018, www.forbes.com/sites/pamdanziger/2018/01/18/online-grocery-sales-to-reach-100-billion-in-2025-amazon-set-to-be-market-share-leader/#683ed44462f3; and Jessica Dumont, "Report: Online Grocery Reaches 5.5% of Total Sales," *Grocery Dive,* August 1, 2018, www.grocerydive.com/news/grocery-report-online-grocery-reaches-55-of-total-sales/533805/.

8. Russell Redmon, "H-E-B to Build New Tech Innovation Lab," *Supermarket News,* February 22, 2019, www.supermarketnews.com/online-retail/h-e-b-build-new-tech-innovation-lab; "H-E-B and Favor Delivery to Join Forces," H-E-B, February 15, 2018, www.heb.com/static-page/article-template/heb-and-favor-delivery-to-join-forces; and www.heb.com, accessed September 2019.

9. Mike Tighe, "Kwik Trip Aims to Fill Grills with Fresh Meat Offerings," *LaCrosse Tribune,* May 16, 2014, http://lacrossetribune.com/news/local/kwik-trip-aims-to-fill-grills-with-fresh-meat-offerings/article_0d23f455-1c56-5b94-884f-013d22b78fa9.html; Amanda Baltazar, "C-Stores Challenge Perceptions about Grocery," *CSP Magazine,* October 2017, www.cspdailynews.com/print/csp-magazine/article/c-stores-challenge-consumer-perceptions-about-grocery; "Kwik Trip Named Convenience Store Decisions' 2018 Chain of the Year," *Convenience Store Decisions,* June 27, 2018, https://cstoredecisions.com/2018/06/27/kwik-trip-named-convenience-store-decisions-2018-chain-of-the-year/; and www.kwiktrip.com, accessed September 2019.

10. "Store Productivity—Walmart US," *eMarketer,* https://retail-index.emarketer.com/company/data/5374f24d4d4afd2bb4446614/5374f3094d4afd2bb444a93c/lfy/false/wal-mart-stores-inc-walmart-us, accessed September 2019; and "Supermarket Facts," www.fmi.org/research-resources/supermarket-facts, accessed September 2019.

11. See www.realogy.com/news/company-facts, www.realogy.com/assets/docs/Fact-Sheets/CB_Facts_FINAL.pdf, and www.realogy.com/assets/docs/Fact-Sheets/C21_Facts_FINAL.pdf, accessed September 2019.

12. Company and franchising information from "Top 200 Franchise Systems," *Franchise Times,* September 26, 2018, www.franchisetimes.com/October-2018/Newcomers-Heavy weights-Ranking-franchisings-biggest-500/; www.azfranchises.com/quick-franchise-facts, accessed September 2019; and www.aboutmcdonalds.com/mcd/our_company.html, accessed October 2019.

13. See Marsha Kaplan, "Ecommerce Briefs: Holiday Sales, Retail Chains, 2019 Predictions," *Practical Ecommerce,* January 17, 2019, www.practicalecommerce.com/ecommerce-briefs-holiday-sales-retail-chains-2019-predictions.

14. Dan O'Shea, "Shopping Is Going Mobile, In-Store and Out," *Retail Dive,* March 13, 2018, https://www.retaildive.com/news/shopping-is-going-mobile-in-store-and-out/518876/.

15. See Sameer Sarnat, "The 3 New Realities of Local Retail," *Think with Google,* October 2014, www.thinkwithgoogle.com/marketing-resources/3-new-realities-of-local-retail/; and Nicole Genchur, "Five Consumer Trends to Watch in 2019," *GroundTruth,* January 1, 2019, www.groundtruth.com/insight/consumer-trends-to-watch/.

16. Erik Wander, "Meet the Omnishopper," *Adweek,* September 12, 2017, p. 10.

17. "Online or In-Store? How about a Little of Both?" *Washington Post,* November 28, 2014, p. A01; and "Social Media 2018: It's Influence in the Path to Purchase," *eMarketer,* December 18, 2017, www.emarketer.com/Report/Social-Commerce-2018-Its-Influence-Path-Purchase/2002175; and "SUMO Heavy's Retail Consumer Survey Reveals Shoppers Have Mixed Views on Social Commerce," *PR Newswire,* September 20, 2018, www.prnewswire.com/news-releases/sumo-heavys-retail-consumer-survey-reveals-shoppers-have-mixed-views-on-social-commerce-300716292.html.

18. See Dan Tynan, "Meet the New Chief Collaboration Officer: The CMO," Adweek, October 7, 2018, www.adweek.com/digital/meet-the-new-chief-collaboration-officer-the-cmo/; and www.carmax.com and http://investors.carmax.com/financial-reports/annual-reports-and-other-financial-information/default.aspx, accessed September 2019.

19. Susan Berfield and Matthew Boyle, "Best Buy Should Be Dead, but It's Thriving in the Age of Amazon," *Bloomberg Businessweek,* July 19, 2018, www.bloomberg.com/news/features/2018-07-19/best-buy-should-be-dead-but-it-s-thriving-in-the-age-of-amazon; Adrianne Pasquarelli, "Best Buy Unveils Rebranding that Was a Year in the Making," *Advertising Age,* May 9, 2018, https://adage.com/article/cmo-strategy/buy-rebrands-plans-hire-house-creative-team/313425/; Panos Mourdoukoutas, "Best Buy Is Still in Business—and Thriving," *Forbes,* March 2, 2019, www.forbes.com/sites/panosmourdoukoutas/2019/03/02/best-buy-is-still-in-business-and-thriving/#46eb55fc6774; and information from www.bestbuy.com, accessed September 2019.

20. Se Josh Morris, "Lush Made Up after Posting Record Results," *Insider Media Limited,* April 12, 2018, www.insidermedia.com/insider/southwest/Lush-hails-record-turnover; and www.loreal-finance.com/eng, www.lushusa.com, and https://uk.lush.com/article/lush-life-we-believe, accessed September 2019.

21. Austin Carr, "The Future of Retailing in the Age of Amazon," *Fast Company,* December 2017–January 2018, pp. 84–101.

22. See Jean E. Palmieri, "Adidas Fifth Avenue Flagship Centered Around Experiences," *WWD,* November 30, 2016, https://wwd.com/business-news/retail/adidas-fifth-avenue-flagship-claire-midwood-10714929/; Corinne Ruff and Cara Salpini, "22 Experiential Stores NYC Has to Offer," *Retail Dive,* June 21, 2018, www.retaildive.com/news/22-experiential-stores-nyc-has-to-offer/525669/; and "The Adidas Store," www.nycgo.com/shopping/the-adidas-store, accessed September 2019.

23. See Alexandra Maryanne Wilson, "Study: Music, Visuals and Scent Critical to In-Store Experience," *Chain Store Age,* January 15, 2019, www.chainstoreage.com/store-spaces/study-music-visuals-and-scent-critical-to-in-store-experience/; Sifferlin, "My Nose Made Me Buy It," *Time,* December 16, 2013, http://healthland.time.com/2013/12/16/my-nose-made-

me-buy-it-how-retailers-use-smell-and-other-tricks-to-get-you-to-spend-spend-spend/; Kimberly Mas, "How Marketers Target Your Nose," *Vox*, September 2018, www.vox.com/the-goods/2018/9/26/17907002/scent-marketing-branding-nose; and www.scentair.com, accessed September 2019.

24. "How We Do It," http://tjmaxx.tjx.com/store/jump/topic/how-we-do-it/2400087, accessed September 2019.

25. Elyse Dupre, "Personalization at the Heart of CVS's ExtraCare Loyalty Program," *DMN*, May 9, 2017, www.dmnews.com/multichannel-marketing/personalization-is-at-the-heart-of-cvss-extracare-loyalty-program/article/656057/; and www.cvs.com, accessed September 2019.

26. For definitions of these and other types of shopping centers, see "Dictionary," *American Marketing Association*, www.ama.org/resources/Pages/Marketing-Dictionary.aspx, accessed September 2019.

27. Kate Taylor, "These Haunting Photos of the Retail Apocalypse Reveal a New Normal in America as Sears Clings On after Closing Hundreds of Stores," *Business Insider*, January 16, 2019, www.businessinsider.com/the-american-retail-apocalypse-in-photos-2017-3; and Sarah Mulholland, "Why Some Shopping Malls May Be in Deeper Trouble Than You Think," *Bloomberg*, January 8, 2018, www.bloomberg.com/news/articles/2018-01-08/why-some-shopping-malls-may-be-in-deeper-trouble-than-you-think.

28. Jennifer Reingold and Phil Wahba, "Where Have All the Shopper Gone?" *Fortune*, September 3, 2014, http://fortune.com/2014/09/03/where-have-all-the-shoppers-gone/.

29. See Mary Hanbury, "Macy's Is Clsoing Eight Stores Early This Years—Here's a Full List," *Business Insider*, January 10, 2019, www.businessinsider.com/macys-stores-closing-list-2019-1; Susan Berfield, "Shop Today," *Bloomberg Businessweek*, November 27, 2017, pp. 46–51, Phil Wahba, "Macy's Make-or-Break Christmas," *Fortune*, December 1, 2017, pp. 79–84; Marshall Fisher, Santiago Gallino, and Serguei Netessine, "Retailers Are Squandering Their Most Potent Weapons," *Harvard Business Review*, January-February 2019, pp. 73-80; and http://investors.macysinc.com/phoenix.zhtml?c=84477&p=irol-reportsannual, accessed September 2019.

30. See Laia Garcia, "The Edit at Roosevelt Field Mall Brings Your URL Favs IRL," *Refinery*, November 30, 2017, www.refinery29.com/the-edit-store-experience-roosevelt-field-mall; Daniel Keyes, "Malls Look to Pop-Up Shops to Boost Their Appeal," *Business Insider*, December 1, 2017, www.businessinsider.com/malls-look-to-pop-up-shops-to-boost-their-appeal-2017-12; and www.simon.com/the-edit, accessed September 2019.

31. See www.gilt.com, www.zulily.com, www.target.com, and www.amazon.com/gp/help/customer/display.html?nodeId=201134080, accessed September 2019.

32. See Barrett J. Brunsman, "P&G Brand Director of Walmart Joins C-Suite of E-commerce Strategy Firm," *Cincinnati Business Courier*, January 3, 2019, www.bizjournals.com/cincinnati/news/2019/01/03/p-g-brand-director-for-walmart-joins-c-suite-of-e.html; Eric Platt, "22 Companies That Are Addicted to Walmart," *Business Insider*, June 13, 2012, www.businessinsider.com/22-companies-who-are-completely-addicted-to-walmart-2012-6#; Ben Levisohn, "Colgate, Clorox & Procter: The Uninvestable," *Barron's*, April 19, 2017, www.barrons.com/articles/colgate-clorox-procter-the-uninvestable-1492615711; Adam Levy, "Walmart's Lead in Groceries Could Get Even Bigger," *Motley Fool*, October 11, 2018, www.fool.com/investing/2018/10/11/walmarts-lead-in-groceries-could-get-even-bigger.aspx; Cal-Maine Foods Annual Reports, http://calmainefoods.com/investors/financial-reports/, accessed September 2019.

33. See Andria Cheng, "Why Amazon Go May Soon Change the Way We Shop," *Forbes*, January 13, 2019, www.forbes.com/sites/andriacheng/2019/01/13/why-amazon-go-may-soon-change-the-way-we-want-to-shop/; and Russell Redman, "Report: Amazon Go Could Become $4 Billion Business," *Supermarket News*, January 7, 2019, www.supermarketnews.com/retail-financial/report-amazon-go-could-become-4-billion-business.

34. Sarah Perez, "Target Rolls Out Bluetooth Beacon Technology in Stores to Power New Indoor Maps in Its App," *Tech Crunch*, September 20, 2017, https://techcrunch.com/2017/09/20/target-rolls-out-bluetooth-beacon-technology-in-stores-to-power-new-indoor-maps-in-its-app/; Keith Wright, "Say Hello to Our Little Friends: How New Beacons May Save Old Retail," *Marketing Insider*, January 3, 2018, www.mediapost.com/publications/article/312422/say-hello-to-our-little-friends-how-new-beacons-m.html; and Chantal Tode, "Target Innovates In-Store Beacon Marketing with Newsfeed-Like Content Stream," *Retail Dive*, August 5, 2018, www.retaildive.com/ex/mobilecommercedaily/target-innovates-in-store-beacon-marketing-with-newsfeed-like-content-stream.

35. See Nikki Baird, "In Retail, AR Is for Shoppers and VR Is for Business," *Forbes*, April 26, 2017, www.forbes.com/sites/nikkibaird/2017/04/26/in-retail-ar-is-for-shoppers-and-vr-is-for-business/#2197c621618f; and Carolanne Mangies, "Is Marketing Ready for VR/AR in 2018?" *Smart Insights*, January 11, 2018, www.smartinsights.com/digital-marketing-platforms/video-marketing/is-marketing-ready-for-vr-ar-in-2018/.

36. "Green MashUP: 7 Trends Transforming Retail Sustainability," *The Fifth Estate*, February 17, 2015, www.thefifthestate.com.au/business/trends/green-mashup-7-trends-transforming-retail-sustainability/71455; "The IKEA Group Yearly Summary FY2017 Report," www.ikea.com/ms/en_US/pdf/yearly_summary/IKEA_Group_Yearly_Summary_2017.pdf, accessed October 2018; and "The IKEA Group Approach to Sustainability," www.ikea.com/ms/en_US/pdf/sustainability_report/group_approach_sustainability_fy11.pdf, accessed September 2019.

37. See Dennis O'Shea, "Virtual Reality for Retail Marketing Could Hit $1.8 Billion in 2022," *Retail Dive*, January 28, 2019, www.retaildive.com/news/virtual-reality-for-retail-marketing-could-hit-18b-in-2022/546962/; Nick Carvell, "The New Nike iD Direct Studio Is the Future of Customized Kicks," *GQ*, February 1, 2018, www.gq-magazine.co.uk/article/nike-id-london; Ben Lang, "Audi Has Deployed 1,000 VR Showrooms in Dealerships Worldwide," *Road to VR*, December 9, 2018, www.roadtovr.com/audi-has-deployed-1000-vr-showrooms-in-dealerships-worldwide/; Dan Tynan, "Find Your Virtual Intelligence," *Adweek*, December 4, 2017, pp. 18–19; Carolanne Mangies, "Is Marketing Ready for VR/AR in 2018?" *Smart Insights*, January 11, 2018, www.smartinsights.com/digital-marketing-platforms/video-marketing/is-marketing-ready-for-vr-ar-in-2018/; Suman Bhattacharyya, "Lowe's Is Using VR and AR to Get People into Stores," *DigiDay*, July 25, 2018, https://digiday.com/retail/lowes-using-vr-ar-get-people-stores/; and Sangeeta Singh-Kurtz, "Brands from Warby Parker to Sephora Have Actually Found Sensible Uses for AR," *Quartz*, February 5, 2019, https://qz.com/quartzy/1541585/warby-parkers-virtual-try-on-app-could-change-the-way-people-buy-glasses/.

38. See www.staples.com/sbd/cre/marketing/sustainability-center/, accessed September 2019.

39. See www.walmartsustainabilityhub.com/sustainability-index, accessed September 2019.

40. See "Global Powers of Retailing 2019," *Deloitte*, January 2019, accessed at www2.deloitte.com/global/en/pages/consumer-business/articles/global-powers-of-retailing.html.

41. Grainger facts and other information are from the http://pressroom.grainger.com/phoenix.zhtml?c=194987&p=irol-mediakit and www.grainger.com, accessed September 2019.

42. Bill Briggs, "E-commerce Accounts for 56% of 2017 Revenue for Grainger," *Digital Commerce 360*, January 24, 2018; and www.grainger.com, accessed September 2019.

43. See http://investors.sysco.com/~/media/Files/S/Sysco-IR/documents/quarterly-results/1q18-factsheet.pdf and www.sysco.com/, accessed September 2019.

44. See www.supervalu.com, accessed September 2019.

45. Walter Loeb, "Why Ulta Beauty Is Winning Customers and Keeps Growing Rapidly," *Forbes*, March 18, 2019, www.forbes.com/sites/walterloeb/2019/03/18/why-ulta-beauty-wins-customers-and-keeps-growing-rapidly/#3f962f82664a; Jennifer Braunschweiger, "How Mary Dillon Turned Ulta Beauty into the Leading Cosmetics Retailer," *Fast Company*, March 20, 2017, www.fastcompany.com/3068653/how-mary-dillon-turned-ulta-beauty-into-the-leading-cosmetics-retailer; Bethany Biron, "How Ulta Overhauled Its Business to Edge Out Sephora," *Digiday*, August 17, 2017, https://digiday.com/marketing/ulta-overhauled-business-edge-sephora/; Helen Edwards and Dave Edwards, "The One Retailer that Amazon Can't Seem to Destroy Is in Cosmetics," *Quartz*, May 28, 2018, https://qz.com/1282750/ulta-beauty-is-proving-that-amazon-isnt-destroying-all-brick-and-mortar/; Pamela Danziger, "In the Battle for Beauty Shoppers, Ulta Is Pulling Ahead of Sephora and Amazon," *Forbes*, March 19, 2019, www.forbes.com/sites/pamdanziger/2019/03/19/ulta-puts-more-distance-from-sephora-and-amazon-in-the-number-of-people-who-prefer-to-shop-there/#4aabe2836f45; and information from www.ulta.com/company/about-us/#ourStory, accessed June 2019.

Chapter 14

1. See Jessica Wohl, "Burger King Has It Its Way," *Advertising Age*, February 18, 2019, p. 7; Tim Nudd, "Burger King Staged a Car Fire on a Highway, and Surprised Those Who Stopped to Help," *Adweek*, March 13, 2018, www.adweek.com/brand-marketing/burger-king-staged-a-car-fire-on-a-highway-and-surprised-those-who-stopped-to-help/; Tim Nudd, "Why Burger King's 'Burning Stores' Are the Perfect Print Ads for the Social Media Age," *Adweek*, June 19, 2017, www.adweek.com/creativity/why-burger-kings-burning-stores-are-the-perfect-print-ads-for-the-social-media-age/; "Integrated Campaigns," *Advertising Annual 2008*, Communication Arts, pp. 72–73; Emily Bryson, "Whopper Freakout Wins Grand Effie," *Advertising Age*, June 4, 2009, https://adage.com/article/news/whopper-freakout-wins-grand-effie-burger-king-crispin/137066; Peter Adams, "Campaign of the Year: Burger King's 'Google Home of the Whopper,'" *Marketing Dive*, December 4, 2017, www.marketingdive.com/news/campaign-of-the-year-burger-kings-google-home-of-the-whopper/510770/; Hal Conick, "OK, Google, How Did Burger King Create the Longest 15-Second Ad in History?" *Marketing News*, February 2018, pp. 12-13; and www.youtube.com/watch?v=pcOh161hpn4, www.youtube.com/watch?v=8fIfPKpY7HQ, www.rbi.com/AnnualReports, and www.bk.com/about-bk, accessed September 2019.

2. For other definitions, see https://marketing-dictionary.org, accessed October 2019.

3. See Greg Sterling, "Report: Digital Now Makes Up 51% of US Ad Spending," *Marketing Land*, September 20, 2018, https://marketingland.com/report-digital-now-makes-up-51-of-us-ad-spending-248617; and Jasmine Enberg, "Digital Ad Spending 2019: U.S.," *eMarketer*, March 28, 2019, www.emarketer.com/content/us-digital-ad-spending-2019.

4. Julia Kollewe, "Marmite Maker Unilever Threatens to Pull Ads from Facebook and Google," *The Guardian*, February 12, 2018, www.theguardian.com/media/2018/feb/12/marmite-unilever-ads-facebook-google.

5. Karen Gilchrist, "Adidas Steps Away from TV Advertising as It Targets $4 Billion Growth," *CNBC*, March 15, 2017, www.cnbc.com/2017/03/15/adidas-steps-away-from-tv-advertising-as-it-targets-4-billion-growth.html; Daphne Howland, "Adidas Ditching TV Ads to Reach Generation Z on Mobile," *Marketing Dive*, March 16, 2017, www.marketingdive.com/news/adidas-ditching-tv-ads-to-reach-generation-z-on-mobile/438291; and "Adidas Goes All In on Digital Advertising," *Digital Stand*, November 28, 2018, https://digitalstand.com/digital-advertising.

6. See Lesley Bielby, "The 'A' Word—Does Advertising Still Exist?" *Advertising Age*, April 22, 2016, www.adage.com/print/303678; Michael Strober, "We Interrupt This Interruption for an Important Message," *Advertising Age*, September 25, 2018, pp. 62–63; and Lilach Bullock, "2019 Content Marketing Strategy: Here Are 5 Content Marketing Trends That You Can't Ignore This Year," *Forbes*, January 30, 2019, www.forbes.com/sites/lilachbullock/2019/01/30/2019-content-marketing-strategy-here-are-5-content-marketing-trends-that-you-cant-ignore-this-year/#69ae11105618.

7. See Kerry Flynn, "Inside Intuit's First Ad Campaign," *Digiday*, May 29, www.digiday.com/marketing/inside-intuits-first-ever-ad-campaign/; Evelyn Timson, "Understanding Paid, Owned, Earned and Shared Media," *Business West*, February 7, 2018, www.businesswest.co.uk/blog/understanding-paid-owned-earned-and-shared-media; Randall Rothenberg, "What Is Advertising Anyway?" *Adweek*, September 16, 2013, p. 15; Gini Dietrich, "Why and How PR Pros Should Adopt the PESO Model," *PR Daily*, January 23, 2018, www.prdaily.com/mediarelations/Articles/Why_and_how_PR_pros_should_adopt_the_PESO_model_23870.aspx; Kyle O'Brien, "Intuit Promotes Its Suite of Products with Engaging Entrepreneurial Animation," *The Drum*, February 8, 2019, www.thedrum.com/news/2019/02/08/intuit-promotes-its-suite-products-with-engaging-entrepreneurial-animation; and www.youtube.com/watch?v=ktafrbsKeZw, www.youtube.com/watch?v=jUPGpJ4NRkg, and www.youtube.com/watch?v=Irpdx1gRhe0, accessed October 2019.

8. See "The NewsCred Top 50 Awards," *NewsCred*, https://insights.newscred.com/best-content-marketing-brands/#about, accessed October 2018; and www.landroverusa.com/experiences/stories/index.html, www.instagram.com/landrover/, www.youtube.com/user/landrover, www.facebook.com/landrover/, and https://twitter.com/LandRover?ref_src=twsrc%5Egoogle%7Ctwcamp%5Eserp%7Ctwgr%5Eauthor, accessed October 2019.

9. See Philip Kotler, Hermawan Kartajaya, and Iwan Setiawan, *Marketing 4.0: Moving from Traditional to Digital* ((Hoboken, NJ: Wiley, 2016); and Michael Krauss, "Marketing 4.0 Argues the Marketplace Has Changed, and the Customer Is in Control," *Marketing News*, April/May 2017, pp. 26–27.

10. See Maxx Hall, "Planters' Social Media Brings Mr. Peanut to New Audience," *Medium*, February 15, 2019, https://medium.com/@zoomph.inc/planters-social-media-brings-mr-peanut-to-new-audience-e6d0bb00f42e; Erica Sweeney, "Planters Boosts Ad Awareness, Purchase Consideration Ahead of the Holidays, Analysis Finds," *Marketing Dive*, December 19, 2018, www.marketingdive.com/news/planters-boosts-ad-awareness-purchase-consideration-ahead-of-the-holidays/544712/; Lindsay Stein, "Planters' Super Bowl Ad Get Nuttier with Charlie Sheen," *Campaign*, January 29, 2019, www.campaignlive.com/article/planters-super-bowl-spot-gets-nuttier-charlie-sheen/1524212?dcmp=emc-conthecampaignfix&bulletin=the-campaign-fix; and www.youtube.com/watch?v=0BTYEXLlFdQ, accessed September 2019.

11. See "Sprint Launches New Advertising Campaign," Sprint Newsroom, https://newsroom.sprint.com/presskits/sprint-launches-new-advertising-campaign.htm, accessed April 2019.

12. See Patrick Coffee, "Google Translate's Emotional Super Bowl Ad Focuses on the Unifying Power of Language," *Adweek*, February 3, 2019, www.adweek.com/brand-marketing/google-translates-emotional-super-bowl-ad-focuses-on-the-unifying-power-of-language/; and www.youtube.com/watch?v=Vq7tHjEXTJg, accessed September, 2019.

13. See Convince and Convert, "Chatter Matters: The 2018 Word of Mouth Report," http://partners.convinceandconvert.com/i/1014284-chatter-matters-research-fall2018/0?, accessed October 2019; and Sammy Nickalls, "Talking Heads," *Adweek*, September 24, 2018, p. 14.

14. See "5 Successful Brand Ambassador Program Examples," Duel, November 22, 2018, https://duel.tech/5-successful-ambassador-programs/; and https://jobs.redbull.com/za/en-GB/wings, accessed September 2019.

15. See https://shop.lululemon.com/story/ambassador-program, accessed September 2019.

16. See T. L. Stanley, "Dancing with the Stars," *Brandweek*, March 8, 2010, pp. 10–12; Chris Isidore, "Lance Armstrong: How He'll Make Money Now," *CNNMoney*, January 18, 2013, http://money.cnn.com/2013/01/16/news/companies/armstrong-endorsements/; and Alissa Fleck, "8 High-Profile Celebrity Endorsements that Backfired," *Adweek*, August 23, 2018, www.adweek.com/brand-marketing/8-high-profile-celebrity-endorsements-that-backfired/. Also see "Topic: Celebrity Endorsements," *Adweek*, www.adweek.com/?s=celebrity+endorsements&orderby=date, accessed October 2019.

17. For more on advertising spending by company and industry, see "200 Leading National Advertisers 2018 Fact Pack," *Advertising Age*, June 25, 2018.

18. See Don Reisinger, "Super Bowl LIII Was a Disappointment for TV Ratings," *Fortune*, February 5, 2019, http://fortune.com/2019/02/05/super-bowl-ratings/; and Joe Otterson, "Oscars 2019 Ratings Rise From Last Year to 29.6 Million Viewers," *Variety*, February 25, 2019, https://variety.com/2019/tv/news/oscars-ratings-2019-1203144417/.

19. See Marty Swant, "These Were the Most Viewed and Searched Super Bowl Ads and Moments on YouTube," *Adweek*, February 4, 2019, www.adweek.com/digital/these-were-the-most-viewed-and-searched-super-bowl-ads-and-moments-on-youtube/; Nelson Granados, "2019 Super Bowl Ads Were Viewed Massively Online before and after the Game," *Forbes*, www.forbes.com/sites/nelsongranados/2019/02/08/2019-super-bowl-ads-were-viewed-massively-online-before-and-after-the-game/; and www.youtube.com/watch?v=j5MQUWRXTRE, accessed September 2019.

20. Joe McGauley, "How Much Do Super Bowl Commercials Cost in 2019?" *Thrillist*, February 3, 2019, www.thrillist.com/news/nation/super-bowl-commercials-cost-2019.

21. "Marketing Fact Pack 2019," *Advertising Age*, December 2018, p. 8.

22. Jacqueline Fernandez, "Gillette Generates 1.5 Million Mentions from New Campaign," *a.list*, January 16, 2019, www.alistdaily.com/lifestyle/gillettes-new-campaign/; Broede Carmody, "Gillette Defends Controversial Short Film 'The Best Men Can Be,'" *Sydney Morning Herald*, January 16, 2019, www.smh.com.au/entertainment/tv-and-radio/gillette-defends-controversial-short-film-the-best-men-can-be-20190116-p50rrl.html; Andrew Cave, "Gillette's Close Shave: A Victory for #MeToo or Toxic Masculinity," *Forbes*, January 22, 2019, www.forbes.com/sites/andrewcave/2019/01/22/gillettes-close-shave-a-victory-for-metoo-or-toxic-masculinity/#2d4030f077f5; Tanya Dua, "Here's the Full List of All the Super Bowl Commercials That Ran This Year," *Business Insider*, February 4, 2019, www.businessinsider.com/super-bowl-commercials-2019-list-2019-1; Tim Johnson, "Google Event Encourages Girls to Look at Computer Science Careers," *Daily Nonpareil*, December 7, 2018, www.nonpareilonline.com/news/education/google-event-encourages-girls-to-look-at-computer-science-careers/article_2a08d2dd-b48d-54cf-8c41-c5c91a8ade7e.html; "Noses On! Walgreens Welcomes Red Nose Day Back to America as the Exclusive Retailer of the New Sparkle Red Nose," Walgreens Newsroom, April 2, 2018, https://news.walgreens.com/press-releases/general-news/noses-on-walgreens-welcomes-red-nose-day-back-to-america-as-the-exclusive-retailer-of-the-new-sparkle-red-nose.htm; "Red Nose Day Campaign Returns to NBC on May 23, 2019," December 13, 2018, rednoseday.org/news/red-nose-day-campaign-returns-nbc-on-may-23-2019; and www.madewithcode.com/about/, https://shortyawards.com/2nd-socialgood/rednose-day-at-walgreens, gillette.com/en-us/the-best-men-can-be, and www.walgreens.com/topic/promotion/rednoseday.jsp, accessed October 2019.

23. See "Dove Ads with 'Real' Women Get Attention," *NBC News*, August 3, 2005, http://www.nbcnews.com/id/8757597/ns/business-us_business/t/dove-ads-real-women-get-attention/#.XLTPiehKiw4; and www.dove.com/us/en/stories/campaigns.html and www.dove.com/us/en/stories/about-dove/our-vision.html, accessed October 2019.

24. Adsoftheworld, "Kit Kat: Free No-WiFi Zone," December 1, 2012, https://www.adsoftheworld.com/media/ambient/kit_kat_free_nowifi_zone; Blue Star Direct, "10 Awesome Direct Marketing Examples," August 7, 2019, https://www.bluestardirect.com.au/10-awesome-direct-marketing-examples/; H. Bhasin, "Marketing Mix of Nestlé—4 Ps of Nestlé—Nestlé Product Marketing Mix," August 1, 2019, https://www.marketing91.com/marketing-mix-nestle/; Ellen Milligan, "Nestle's Japanese Green Tea KitKats Are Finally Coming to Europe," *Bloomberg*, February 19, 2019, https://www.bloomberg.com/news/articles/2019-02-19/nestle-s-taste-of-japan-is-coming-to-europe-with-kitkat-launch; M. Adelere, "Planning Process of Nestle PLC as a Tool for Strategic Decision Making," https://www.academia.edu/28789815/PLANNING_PROCESS_OF_NESTLE_PLC_AS_A_TOOL_FOR_STATEGIC_DECISION_MAKING; N. Cameron, "CMO Interview: 5 Learnings from Nestlé on Modern Marketing and Communications," CMO, September 5, 2016, https://www.cmo.com.au/article/606255/cmo-interview-how-marketing-communications-changing-Nestlé/?pp=2; Ricki Green, "KitKat Launches New 'Snap Out of It' Creative Campaign via J. Walter Thompson, Sydney," Campaign Brief, August 1, 2019, https://campaignbrief.com/kitkat-launches-new-snap-out-o/?fbclid=IwAR33avFb0aKxjm1l94dU6TFEA9C49eSHfHoqSjLp_whVlD2NwVLIbz4Rl4; Consumer Goods, "Nestlé Brand Launches Integrated Marketing Campaign," May 18, 2017, https://consumergoods.com/Nestle-brand-launches-integrated-marketing-campaign; J. Conway, "Nestlé Group's Sales Worldwide in 2018, by Product Category," https://www.statista.com/statistics/413559/global-sales-of-Nestle-by-product-category/; Curve Interactive, "Kit Kat's Latest Integrated Marketing Campaign," November 2, 2012, http://curve-interactive.com/kit-kats-latest-integrated-marketing-campaign/; A.-C. Diaz, "These KitKat Billboards Will Give You a Massage," October 27, 2015, https://adage.com/creativity/work/massage-billboard/43936; Digital Training Academy (n.d.), "Kitkat Boosts Local Audience in India with Instagram Campaign," http://www.digitaltrainingacademy.com/casestudies/2016/09/kitkat_boosts_local_audience_in_india_with_instagram_campaign.php; "Digital Acceleration Team | The European Commission's Digital Cities Challenge," August 1, 2019, https://www.digitallytransformyourregion.eu/good-practices/digital-acceleration-team; Douglas Yu, "Nestlé Brings Green Tea-Flavored KitKat to Europe," February 25, 2019, https://www.forbes.com/sites/douglasyu/2019/02/25/nestle-brings-green-tea-flavored-kitkat-to-europe/?fbclid=IwAR0TV0j7Z4oEbw7MsxuKjUzW9B4DaabsqjoOoxzvLaALqfg53Wn9J_cTBqw#6997f2ab692f; "Häagen-Dazs® Brand Captures the Essence of 'La Dolce Vita' with Integrated Marketing Campaign for New Häagen-Dazs Gelato," April 18, 2013, https://www.nestleusa.com/media/pressreleases/hdladolcevita; Leonie Roderick, "KitKat Talks Up 'Moment Marketing' Drive as It Celebrates Growing Sales," *Marketing Week*, December 2, 2015, https://www.marketingweek.com/kit-kat-talks-up-moment-marketing-drive-as-it-celebrates-growing-sales/; Ellen Milligan, "Nestle's Japanese Green Tea KitKats Are Finally Coming to Europe," February 19, 2019, https://www.bloomberg.com/news/articles/2019-02-19/nestle-s-taste-of-japan-is-coming-to-europe-with-kitkat-launch; "Nestlé Digital and Social Media Marketing Strategies—Branding & Targeting Strategy, May, 2015, https://www.marketresearch.com/Socintel360-v4016/Nestl%C3%A9-Digital-Social-Media-Strategies-9013827/; "Nestlé Deals with Public Concerns Using Effective Social Media Engagement—Social Media for Business Performance,"

October 24, 2014, http://smbp.uwaterloo.ca/2014/10/Nestle-deals-with-public-concerns-using-effective-social-media-engagement/; Tim Nudd, "KitKat's Christmas Commercial Is 30 Seconds of Blankness, the Ultimate Ad Break," *Adweek*, December 4, 2015, https://www.adweek.com/creativity/kitkats-christmas-commercial-30-seconds-blankness-ultimate-ad-break-168459/; Tejal Rao, "In Japan, the Kit Kat Isn't Just a Chocolate. It's an Obsession," *The New York Times*, October 24, 2018, https://www.nytimes.com/interactive/2018/10/24/magazine/candy-kit-kat-japan.html; David Court, Dave Elzinga, Susan Mulder, and Ole Jørgen Vetvik, "The Consumer Decision Journey," McKinsey Quarterly, June 2009, https://www.mckinsey.com/business-functions/marketing-and-sales/our-insights/the-consumer-decision-journey; D. Seifert, "Nestle and Google Rebrand KitKat to YouTube Break in the UK because Everything Is Terrible," *The Verge*, May 12, 2015, https://www.theverge.com/2015/5/12/8592067/nestle-google-kitkat-youtube-break-packaging-rebrand-uk.

Chapter 15

1. See Gianfranco Arena and Peter Kain, "How Snickers Transformed a Basic Biological Need into Super Bowl Success," *Adweek*, January 27, 2019, www.adweek.com/brand-marketing/how-snickers-transformed-a-basic-biological-need-into-super-bowl-success/; Robert Williams, "Snickers Preps #SmoothItOver Campaign for After Valentine's Day," *Mobile Marketer*, February 7, 2019, www.mobilemarketer.com/news/snickers-preps-smoothitover-campaign-for-after-valentines-day/547872/; Robert Klara, "How Snickers Fired a Quarterback, Hired a Zebra, and Tweaked One of Advertising's Most Famous Tag Lines," *Adweek*, February 27, 2014, www.adweek.com/print/155873; and www.candyindustry.com/2018-Global-Top-100-candy-companies-Part-4, and www.mars.com, www.youtube.com/channel/UCDviI62w0VbD_9oRNkV1Uig; https://www.youtube.com/watch?v=SycY-XjZmG8; and www.snickers.tumblr.com/, accessed October 2019.

2. For these and other advertising spending facts, see "Marketing Fact Pack 2019," *Advertising Age,* December 17, 2018, p. 4.

3. See "200 Leading National Advertisers 2018 Fact Pack," *Advertising Age,* June 25, 2018, p. 7; Patrick Coffee, "U.S. Army Audit Claims 'Ineffective Marketing Programs' Have Wasted Millions in Taxpayer Dollars Each Year," *Adweek,* January 3, 2018, www.adweek.com/agencies/u-s-army-audit-claims-ineffective-marketing-programs-have-wasted-millions-in-taxpayer-dollars-each-year/.

4. See Mike Murphy, "Samsung's Strategy for Keeping Up with Apple Is to Be Mean," *Quartz,* August 18, 2018, https://qz.com/1358333/samsungs-strategy-for-keeping-up-with-apple-is-to-be-mean/; and Malcolm Owen, "Samsung Continues Attacking iPhone and Apple Stores in Ad Campaign," *Apple Insider,* July 20, 2018, https://appleinsider.com/articles/18/07/20/samsung-continues-attacking-iphone-and-apple-stores-in-ad-campaign.

5. See Minda Smiley, "Wendy's Calls Out McDonald's Frozen Beef in Super Bowl Ad," *The Drum*, January 31, 2018, www.thedrum.com/news/2018/01/31/wendy-s-calls-out-mcdonald-s-frozen-beef-super-bowl-ad; Jessica Wohl, "Why Wendy's Is Lovin' Its Attack Ads on McDonald's," *Advertising Age*, September 10, 2018, p. 5; Kristina Monllos, "How Wendy's Cooked Up Its Killer Frozen Beef Tweet to McDonald's," *Adweek*, March 31, 2017, www.adweek.com/brand-marketing/how-wendys-cooked-up-its-killer-frozen-beef-tweet-to-mcdonalds/; and www.nfl.com/videos/nfl-super-bowl-commercials/0ap3000000913990/Wendy-s-fresh-beef-burgers, accessed September 2019.

6. See Michael Addady, "General Mills Sues Chobani for Advertising That Yoplait Contains 'Bug Spray,'" *Fortune,* January 12, 2016, http://fortune.com/2016/01/12/general-mills-sues-chobani/; Christine Birkner, "'Scare Tactics' Used in Its Ads: Spots Imply Yoplait and Dannon Contain Pesticides,

Chlorine," *Advertising Age*, January 20, 2016, www.adweek.com/print/169107; "United States Courts Opinions: United States District Court Eastern District of New York: Chobani, LLC, Plaintiff, v The Dannon Company, Inc., Defendant," April 25, 2016; Graig Giammona, "Why Big Brands Couldn't Stop Chobani from Winning the Yogurt War," *Bloomberg*, March 9, 2017, www.bloomberg.com/news/articles/2017-03-09/yogurt-war-exposes-big-food-s-flaws-as-chobani-overtakes-yoplait; and "Comparative Advertising Pitfalls—Consumers Shouldn't Have to Do the Math," *JD Supra*, February 12, 2019, www.jdsupra.com/legalnews/comparative-advertising-pitfalls-61692/.

7. Nicole Ortiz, "Super Bowl Stardom Requires an Endless Well of Creativity and an Understanding of What You're Getting Yourself Into," *Adweek*, February 1, 2019, www.adweek.com/brand-marketing/super-bowl-stardom-requires-an-endless-well-of-creativity-and-an-understanding-of-what-youre-getting-yourself-into/; Aaron Lewis, "Beyond the Buzz: Online Anthropology Reveals the True Post-Super Bowl Brand Winners," *LRW Online*, February 15, 2019, https://lrwonline.com/perspective/beyond-the-buzz-online-anthropology-reveals-the-true-post-super-bowl-brand-winners/; Stuart Elliott, "Super Bowl Ads Get Their Own Pregame Show," *New York Times*, January 17, 2014; Amy Gesenhues, "Which Super Bowl Advertisers Won the Digital Game?" *Marketing Land*, February 4, 2019, https://marketingland.com/which-super-bowl-advertisers-won-the-digital-game-verizon-bud-light-pepsi-256377; Delaney Strunk, "The Biggest Rivalry in Atlanta on Super Bowl Weekend, Has Nothing to Do with Football," *CNN*, January 29, 2019, www.cnn.com/2019/01/29/media/super-bowl-2019-coke-pepsi-trnd/index.html; and Rob Salkowitz, "These Are the Ads Everyone Is Talking About Ahead of Super Bowl LIII," *Forbes*, February 1, 2019, www.forbes.com/sites/robsalkowitz/2019/02/01/these-are-the-ads-everyone-is-talking-about-ahead-of-super-bowl-liii/#20856315235e.

8. See Jean Halliday, "Thinking Big Takes Audi from Obscure to Awesome," *Advertising Age*, February 2, 2009, http://adage.com/print/134234; "Luxury Vehicles Market 2019 Share, Size, Business Growth, Opportunities, Worldwide Trends, Regional Demand, Vehicle Type, Services and Industry Overview, Statistics 2024," *Reuters,* March 13, 2019, www.reuters.com/brandfeatures/venture-capital/article?id=90486.

9. "Who's Watching How Many TV Channels?" *Marketing Charts,* October 3, 2018, www.marketingcharts.com/television-71258; and "Number of Magazines in the United States from 2002 to 2017," *Statista,* www.statista.com/statistics/238589/number-of-magazines-in-the-united-states/, accessed October 2019.

10. Kelsey Libert and Kristen Tynski, "Research: The Emotions That Make Marketing Campaigns Go Viral," *HBR Blog Network,* October 24, 2013, http://blogs.hbr.org/2013/10/research-the-emotions-that-make-marketing-campaigns-go-viral/; and data from YouTube, Facebook, Instagram, and Twitter, accessed October 2019.

11. "Figuring Out a Production Budget These Days Is Complicated," *Advertising Age,* May 1, 2015, http://adage.com/lookbook/article/production-companies/figuring-a-production-budget-days-complicated/298390/; Maggie Aland, "TV Advertising Costs and How to Advertise on a Budget," *FitSmallBusiness.com,* November 28, 2017, https://fitsmallbusiness.com/tv-advertising/; and "Cost for a 30-Second Commercial," Marketing Fact Pack 2019, *Advertising Age,* December 17, 2018, p. 18.

12. See "Pizza Hut Hometown Heroes," Shorty Awards, https://shortyawards.com/11th/marketing-director-2, accessed April 2019; and www.facebook.com/YahooSports/videos/122530858663651/, accessed October 2019.

13. See Lindsay Kolowich, "Funny Tweets and Social Media Examples from 17 Real Brands," Hubspot, February 4, 2016, http://blog.hubspot.com/blog/tabid/6307/bid/33488/14-Funny-Brands-You-Can-t-Help-But-Follow-in-Social-Media.aspx; and https://twitter.com/hashtag/tweetfromtheseat?src=hash, accessed September 2019.

14. "Why *The Lego Movie* Is the Perfect Piece of Product Placement," *A.V. Club*, February 11, 2014, www.avclub.com/article/why-the-lego-movie-is-the-perfect-piece-of-product-201102; Katarina Gustafsson, "LEGO Movie Helps Full-Year Revenue Growth Beat Rivals," *Bloomberg Business*, February 25, 2015, www.bloomberg.com/news/articles/2015-02-25/lego-movie-helps-toymaker-s-full-year-sales-growth-beat-rivals; and E. J. Schultz, "Chevy Has Product Placement Deal with New LEGO Movie," *Advertising Age*, January 28, 2019, https://adage.com/article/cmo-strategy/chevy-product-placement-deal-lego-movie/316402.

15. See Timothy Nichols, "How to Get the Best Visibility with Native Ads," *Forbes*, February 8, 2018, www.forbes.com/sites/forbesagencycouncil/2018/02/08/how-to-get-the-best-visibility-with-native-ads/#1db31d54766f; Joshua Keller, "Native Advertising: The New Pillar of Digital," *Forbes*, January 24, 2019, www.forbes.com/sites/forbesagencycouncil/2019/01/24/native-advertising-the-new-pillar-of-digital/#74eeba115e0e; and Nicole Perrin, "US Native Advertising 2019," *eMarketer*, March 20, 2019, www.emarketer.com/content/us-native-advertising-2019.

16. See www.adsoftheworld.com/media/print/cat_footwear_go_ahead_look_up and www.wolverineworldwide.com/our-brands/cat/, accessed October 2019.

17. See Nikki Gilliland, "Six New and Creative Examples of User-Generated Content," Econsultancy, February 7, 2019, https://econsultancy.com/creative-examples-user-generated-content-marketing/; and www.instagram.com/aerie/?hl=en, accessed September 2019.

18. Christopher Heine, "West Elm Is Lifting Sales by Using Customer's Instagram Photos in Facebook Carousel Ads," *Adweek*, June 17, 2016, www.adweek.com/digital/west-elm-lifting-sales-using-customers-instagram-photos-facebook-carousel-ads-172076/; Daniela Forte, "West Elm's Pinterest Style Finder Lets Customers Aid in Design," *Multichannel Merchant*, August 25, 2017, http://multichannelmerchant.com/marketing/west-elms-pinterest-style-finder-lets-customers-aid-design/; and www.instagram.com/explore/tags/mywestelm/, accessed September 2019.

19. See Peter Adams, "Technology of the Year: Adidas' 'Here to Create Legend,'" *Marketing Dive*, December 3, 2018, www.marketingdive.com/news/technology-of-the-year-adidas-here-to-create-legend/541534/.

20. See "Multitasking Is Changing Media Consumption Habits," *Screen Media Daily*, April 8, 2016, http://screenmediadaily.com/multitasking-is-changing-media-consumption-habits; and "Juggling Act: Audiences Have More Media at Their Disposal and Are Using Them Simultaneously," *Nielsen*, December 12, 2018, www.nielsen.com/us/en/insights/news/2018/juggling-act-audiences-have-more-media-at-their-disposal-and-are-using-them-simultaneously.html.

21. *Forbes* and *People* cost and circulation data found online at www.forbes.com/forbes-media/advertising/and https://static.people.com/media-kit/assets/peop2019_ratecard.pdf, accessed October 2019.

22. Natalie Tadena, "With the New Year Approaching, Weight Loss Ad Barrage Has Commenced," *Wall Street Journal*, December 30, 2014, http://blogs.wsj.com/cmo/2014/12/30/with-the-new-year-approaching-weight-loss-ad-barrage-has-commenced/; and T. L. Stanley, "Popular at Easter, Peeps Candy Extends to the Quirky Holidays," *New York Times*, June 18, 2014, www.nytimes.com/2014/06/19/business/media/popular-at-easter-peeps-candy-extends-to-the-quirky-holidays.html.

23. For these and other examples, see "Marketing in the Moments, to Reach Customers Online," *New York Times*, January 18, 2016, p. B5; and Tanya Dua, "You Can Still Dunk in the Dark, but You Don't Need a War Room," *Digiday*, February 4, 2016, http://digiday.com/agencies/super-bowl-war-room-rip/.

24. Diana Bradley, "The Thrill Is Gone from Real-Time Marketing," *PRWeek*, March 1, 2019, www.prweek.com/article/1577621/thrill-gone-real-time-marketing; Mick Jacobs, "20 Savage Tweets that Prove Wendy's Twitter Is the Best Twitter," *Ranker*, www.ranker.com/list/the-best-of-wendys-twitter/mick-jacobs?page=4, accessed April 2019; Tanya Dua, "You Can Still Dunk in the Dark, but You Don't Need a War Room," *Digiday*, February 4, 2016, http://digiday.com/agencies/super-bowl-war-room-rip/; Lauren Johnson, "Tide's Spotless Super Bowl Campaign, as Seen from Inside the Brand's War Room," *Adweek*, February 5, 2018, www.adweek.com/digital/tides-spotless-super-bowl-campaign-as-seen-from-inside-the-brands-war-room/; and www.youtube.com/watch?v=IIW3l-ENHdA, www.youtube.com/watch?v=M4VKspkvWlU, and https://twitter.com/Wendys/, accessed October 2019.

25. See "Marketing Fact Pack 2019," *Advertising Age*, December 17, 2018, pp. 24-25.

26. E. J. Schultz, "Marketing A-List 2018: Coca-Cola," *Advertising Age*, December 28, 2018, https://adage.com/article/cmo-strategy/marketer-a-list-coca-cola/315796; Jeffrey N. Ross, "Chevrolet Will 'Find New Roads' as Brand Grows Globally: Aligns around the World behind Singular Vision," January 8, 2013, http://media.gm.com/media/us/en/gm/news.detail.html/content/Pages/news/us/en/2013/Jan/0107-find-new-roads.html; and Dale Buss, "Chevy Wins at Sochi by Giving Dimension to 'Find New Roads,'" *Forbes*, February 24, 2014, www.forbes.com/sites/dalebuss/2014/02/24/chevrolet-wins-at-sochi-as-find-new-roads-theme-gets-traction/.

27. Based on Glen Broom and Bey-Ling Sha, *Cutlip & Center's Effective Public Relations*, 11th ed. (Upper Saddle River, NJ: Prentice Hall, 2013), Chapter 1.

28. See "Healthcare Campaign of the Year 2015," *PR Week*, March 20, 2015, www.prweek.com/article/1337832; "CVS Health: CVS Quits for Good Campaign," *(add)ventures*, www.addventures.com/cvs-quits-good-campaign, accessed October 2018; and www.cvs.com/quit-smoking/, accessed October 2019.

29. See "Fearless Girl," State Street Global Advisors, March 6, 2019, www.ssga.com/content/ssga/pages/en/articles/investment-topics/environmental-social-governance/2018/03/wall-street-meet-fearless-girl.html; "PRWeek U.S. Awards 2018: The Winners," *PRWEEK*, March 16, 2019, www.prweek.com/article/1458806/prweek-us-awards-2018-winners; and www.ssga.com/global/en/about-us/who-we-are/fearless-girl.html, accessed September 2019.

30. Quotes from Sarah Skerik, "An Emerging PR Trend: Content PR Strategy and Tactics," January 15, 2013, http://blog.prnewswire.com/2013/01/15/an-emerging-pr-trend-content-pr-strategy-tactics/; Mary Teresa Bitti, "The New Mad Men: How Publics Relations Firms Have Emerged from the Shadows," *Financial Post*, December 28, 2014, http://business.financialpost.com/entrepreneur/the-changing-role-of-public-relations-firms; and Nelson Granados, "How Public Relations Agencies Are Becoming Top Creators of Digital Video Content," *Forbes*, January 9, 2018, www.forbes.com/sites/nelsongranados/2018/01/09/how-public-relations-agencies-are-becoming-top-creators-of-digital-video-content/#540e1b986626.

31. Lisa Green, "The Top 10 Largest Auto Insurance Companies in 2019," *NerdWallet*, March 15, 2019, www.nerdwallet.com/blog/insurance/car-insurance-basics/largest-auto-insurance-companies/; David Griner, "How GEICO Became the One Advertiser It's OK to Love," *Adweek*, February 5, 2019, www.adweek.com/agencies/how-geico-became-the-one-advertiser-its-ok-to-love/; Charles Taylor, "What Makes Flo from Progressive Effective? Lessons for Using Humor in Advertising," *Forbes*, March 15, 2019, www.forbes.com/sites/charlesrtaylor/2019/03/15/what-makes-flo-from-progressive-effective-lessons-for-using-humor-in-advertising/#165f53f65216; Patty Odell, "The Amazing Brands That Rank Tops in Viral Sharing," *Chief Marketer*, May 7, 2019, www.chiefmarketer.com/the-amazing-brands-that-rank-tops-in-viral-sharing/; Victoria Moran, "Leo Burnett Chicago Wins Best of Show Gold ADDY Award for Allstate's #MayhemSale Campaign,"

Advertising Age, June 8, 2016, www.adage.com/print/304370; Ashley Rodriguez, "How Allstate's Mayhem Disrupted the Chatter Around Insurance," *Advertising Age*, June 10, 2015, www.adage.com/print/298779; E.J. Schultz, "Allstate's Mayhem Joins Twitter…Now What," *Advertising Age*, October 14, 2013, p. 28; and advertisements and other information accessed at www.allstatenewsroom.com and www.youtube.com/user/Allstate, September 2019.

Chapter 16

1. Based on information from Ron Miller, "Salesforce at 20 Offers Lessons for Startup Success," *Tech Crunch*, March 8, 2019, https://techcrunch.com/2019/03/08/salesforce-at-20-offers-lessons-for-startup-success/; Bob Evans, "Why Salesforce Is Soaring in the Cloud," *Forbes*, March 5, 2018, www.forbes.com/sites/bobevans1/2018/03/05/20-eye-popping-stats-from-salesforce-com-as-it-soars-on-digital-transformation-boom/#554a7baf1412; David Whitford, "Salesforce.com: The Software and the Story," *Inc.*, September 2014, pp. 113–117; Whitford, "Selling, the Story: Four Strategies Salesforce.com Uses to Stay on Top," *Inc.*, September 2014, p. 116; Dan Gallagher, "Salesforce Won't Let Age Slow It Down," *Wall Street Journal*, November 9, 2017, www.wsj.com/articles/salesforce-wont-let-age-slow-it-down-1510240677; George P. Siefo, "Salesforce," *Advertising Age*, December 8, 2018, p. 26; The World's Most Innovative Companies," *Forbes*, www.forbes.com/innovative-companies/list/, accessed October 2019; and information from www.statista.com and www.salesforce.com, accessed October 2019.

2. See www.pg.com/vn/careers/our_functions/customer_business_development.shtml, accessed October 2019.

3. "Selling Power 500 Largest Sales Forces (2018)," *Selling Power*, www.sellingpower.com/resources/2018/selling-power-500, accessed October 2019.

4. See Gabe Larsen, "Inside vs. Outside Sales: How to Structure a Sales Team for Success," *HubSpot*, March 21, 2018, https://blog.hubspot.com/sales/inside-vs-outside-sales; Dan McDade, "How Much Leads Cost," Pointclear, January 4, 2018, www.pointclear.com/blog/how-much-leads-cost; and "What Is the Real Cost of a B2B Sales Call?" www.marketing-playbook.com/sales-marketing-strategy/what-is-the-real-cost-of-a-b2b-sales-call, accessed October 2019.

5. See "Virtual Sales Is on the Rise. Research Tells Us Why," *Salesforce Blog*, October 6, 2018, www.salesforce.com/blog/2018/10/virtual-sales-research.html; and "The State of Sales, 3rd Edition," Salesforce, pp. 20–21, www.salesforce.com/form/pdf/state-of-sales-3rd-edition?d=7010M000000ucatQAA&nc=7010M000001yovqQAA, accessed October 2019.

6. James Meincke, "The True Cost of a Bad Sales Hire and How to Avoid It," *CloserIQ*, February 13, 2019, https://blog.closeriq.com/2019/02/cost-bad-sales-hire/.

7. For this and more information and discussion, see www.gallupaustralia.com.au/consulting/118729/sales-force-effectiveness.aspx, accessed October 2012; Heather R. Morgan, "The Most Successful Salespeople All Have This One Thing in Common," *Forbes*, January 26, 2018,www.forbes.com/sites/heathermorgan/2018/01/16/the-most-successful-salespeople-all-have-this-one-thing-in-common/#bb4b8256d221; and Lisa Stancu, "Salesperson Skills of Top Performers," *Inside Sales*, January 17, 2019, https://blog.insidesales.com/sales-management/sales-skills-best-performers/.

8. See Steve Denning, "The One Thing the Greatest Salespeople All Have," *Forbes*, November 29, 2012, www.forbes.com/sites/stevedenning/2012/11/29/the-one-thing-the-greatest-sales-people-all-have/; and Lisa Stancu, "Salesperson Skills of Top Performers," *Inside Sales*, January 17, 2019, https://blog.insidesales.com/sales-management/sales-skills-best-performers/.

9. "Strengths Based Selling," www.gallup.com/press/176651/strengths-based-selling.aspx, accessed October 2019.

10. "2018 Training Industry Report," *Training Magazine*, https://trainingmag.com/sites/default/files/trn-2018-industry-report.pdf, accessed October 2019.

11. See "The State of Sales, 3rd Edition," Salesforce, p. 9, www.salesforce.com/form/pdf/state-of-sales-3rd-edition?d=7010M000000ucatQAA&nc=7010M000001yovqQAA, accessed October 2019.

12. See Lori Wizdo, "The Ways and Means of B2B Buyer Journey Maps," Forrester, August 21, 2017, https://go.forrester.com/blogs/the-ways-and-means-of-b2b-buyer-journey-maps-were-going-deep-at-forresters-b2b-forum/.

13. Regis Crawford, "What Is Social Selling and How Does It Work?" *Salesforce*, April 2, 2019, www.salesforce.com/blog/2017/08/guide-to-social-selling.html; Shelley Cernel, "5 Ways B2B Sales Reps Should Be Using Social Selling," *Salesforce.com*, March 29, 2017, www.salesforce.com/blog/2017/03/b2b-sales-reps-using-social-selling.html; Ian Altman, "Are Salespeople Becoming Obsolete," *Forbes*, May 16, 2017, www.forbes.com/sites/ianaltman/2017/05/16/are-sales-people-becoming-obsolete/#198567e03e93; Andy Hoar, "The Death of a (B2B) Salesman," Forrester, May 11, 2017, https://go.forrester.com/what-it-means/ep12-death-b2b-salesman/; Robert McGarvey, "All About Us," *SellingPower*, March 7, 2011, p. 48; Lain Chroust Ehmann, "Sales Up!" *SellingPower*, January/February, 2011, p. 40; Shep Hykin, "57% of Sales Reps Missed Their Quotas Last Year," *Forbes*, September 2, 2019, www.forbes.com/sites/shephyken/2018/09/02/77-of-sales-reps-missed-their-quotas-last-year/#5fe3705952e4; and www.bls.gov/ooh/sales/wholesale-and-manufacturing-sales-representatives.htm, accessed October 2019.

14. See "The Secret of Creating Effective Sales Content vs. Influential Marketing Content," *Sales for Life*, February 2, 2018, www.salesforlife.com/blog/the-secret-of-creating-effective-sales-content-vs.-influential-marketing-content; and Neil Davey, "Using Social Media Marketing in B2B Markets," *Smart Insights*, February 16, 2015, www.smartinsights.com/b2b-digital-marketing/b2b-social-media-marketing/b2bsocialmediamarketing/. For more on Makino's social networking efforts, see www.facebook.com/MakinoMachine, www.youtube.com/user/MakinoMachineTools, and http://twitter.com/#!/makinomachine, accessed October 2019.

15. See William Flaiz, "How to Leverage AI to Aid Prospecting and Sales," *Forbes*, November 5, 2019, www.forbes.com/sites/forbescommunicationscouncil/2018/11/05/how-to-leverage-ai-to-aid-prospecting-and-sales/; and Ron Miller, "AI Has Become Table Stakes in Sales, Customer Service, and Marketing," *Tech Crunch*, March 19, 2019, https://techcrunch.com/2019/03/19/ai-has-become-table-stakes-in-sales-customer-service-and-marketing-software/.

16. Example based on information from James C. Anderson, Nirmalya Kumar, and James A. Narus, "Become a Value Merchant," *Sales & Marketing Management*, May 6, 2008, pp. 20–23; and "Business Market Value Merchants," *Marketing Management*, March/April 2008, pp. 31+. For more discussion and examples, Larry Myler, "B2B Sales Insights for Commoditized Markets," *Forbes*, November 7, 2017, www.forbes.com/sites/larrymyler/2017/11/07/b2b-sales-insights-for-commoditized-markets/#7d74b1d8b63d; and Eric Almquist, Jamie Cleghorn, and Lori Sherer, "The B@B Elements of Value," *Harvard Business Review*, April 2018, https://hbr.org/2018/03/the-b2b-elements-of-value.

17. "200 Leading National Advertisers 2018 Fact Pack," *Advertising Age*, June 2018, p. 18, https://adage.com/article/datacenter/200-leading-national-advertisers-2018-index/313794/.

18. See "Welcome to IKEA Family!" https://info.ikea-usa.com/family/en-us/aboutfamily, accessed October 2019.

19. See "It's 7-Eleven Day!" 7-Eleven press release, July 10, 2018, https://corp.7-eleven.com/corp-press-releases/07-10-2018-it-s-7-eleven-day; and Stacy Fisher, "Free Slurpee Day at 7-Eleven,"

The Spruce Eats, March 17, 2019, www.thespruceeats.com/free-slurpee-day-at-7-eleven-1357341.

20. "Couponing in Crisis? Companies and Consumers Both Lose Interest in Coupons," *Coupons in the News,* February 11, 2019, http://couponsinthenews.com/2019/02/11/couponing-in-crisis-companies-and-consumers-both-lose-interest-in-coupons/.

21. "Digital Coupons Continue to be the Fastest Growing Method of Redemption Due to Shoppers' Increased Demand for Convenience," Inmar Press Release, February 13, 2019, www.globenewswire.com/news-release/2019/02/13/1724510/0/en/Digital-Coupons-Continue-to-be-the-Fastest-Growing-Method-of-Redemption-Due-to-Shoppers-Increased-Demand-for-Convenience.html.

22. See www.happymeal.com, accessed October 2019.

23. See "2017 a Huge Year for Promo Sales," *PPAI,* https://pubs.ppai.org/ppb-magazine/2017-a-huge-year-for-promo-sales.

24. See www.infinitesweeps.com/sweepstake/155913-West-Elm-The-5000-Room.html and https://doodles.google.com/d4g/, accessed October 2019.

25. Rachael Kirkpatrick, "Delta Sets Record with Mass Shower at Warrior Dash," *Event Marketer,* July 10, 2015, www.eventmarketer.com/-article/delta-sets-new-world-record-331-person-shower-warrior-dash/; "Mud Shower Station," *Adweek,* September 7, 2015, p. 38; and "Delta Faucet Embraces Muddy Mess Makers, Celebrates Shower Singers," *PR Newswire,* August 2, 2017, www.prnewswire.com/news-releases/delta-faucet-embraces-muddy-mess-makers-celebrates-shower-singers-300303609.html.

26. Cadent Consulting Group, "2017 Marketing Spending Industry Study," http://cadentcg.com/wp-content/uploads/2017-Marketing-Spending-Study.pdf.

27. Mack Collier, "The Power of Being Second: How Red Bull Is Winning the (Content) Marketing Wars," *MackCollier.com,* February 1, 2018, www.mackcollier.com/red-bull-content-marketing/; Greg Jarboe, "How Red Bull Quietly Changed Its Video Marketing Strategy," *Tubular Insights,* January 13, 2017, http://tubularinsights.com/red-bull-video-marketing-strategy/; Richard Parket, "Storytelling Is So Passé – Welcome to the Age of Story-Making," *B&T Magazine,* March 15, 2017, www.bandt.com.au/opinion/storytelling-passe-welcome-age-story-making; Bruce Weinstein, "Do Not Dump: Make Your Marketing Strategy Story-Based, Not Fact-Based," *Forbes,* April 4, 2018, www.forbes.com/sites/bruceweinstein/2018/04/04/do-not-dump-make-your-marketing-strategy-story-based-not-fact-based/#2bef49bd5427; and www.coca-colacompany.com/investors, www.pepsico.com/investors, www.redbullmediahouse.com, and www.redbull.com, accessed October 2019.

28. See "CES Attendee Audit Summary Results," https://www.ces.tech/About-CES/CES-by-the-Numbers.aspx, accessed October 2019; "The Greatest and Most Fascinating Show on Earth," www.bauma.de/trade-fair/information/about-bauma/index.html, accessed October 2019.

29. Based on information from numerous P&G managers; Erin Caproni, "P&G Products Named Best in Nation," *Cincinnati Business Courier,* February 8, 2019, www.bizjournals.com/cincinnati/news/2019/02/08/p-g-products-named-best-in-nation.html; with additional information from "Selling Power 500 Largest Sales Forces (2018)," *Selling Power,* www.sellingpower.com/resources/2018/selling-power-500, www.pginvestor.com/CustomPage/Index?keyGenPage=1073748359, and www.pg.com/vn/careers/our_functions/customer_business_development.shtml, accessed October 2019.

Chapter 17

1. See Alex Samuely, "Coca-Cola Uses Snackable Mobile Content for Refreshing Marketing Approach," *Mobile Marketer,* www.mobilemarketer.com/ex/mobilemarketer/cms/news/content/22824.html, accessed October 2019; David Feinleib, "Coca-Cola's Digital Transformation: How eCommerce Is Shaping the Future of this Iconic Brand," *The Drum,* September 14, 2019, www.thedrum.com/opinion/2018/09/14/coca-cola-s-digital-transformation-how-e-commerce-shaping-the-future-iconic-brand; Christine Champagne, "Coca-Cola Goes Full Digital in Multisite Campaign to Reach Teens," *Fast Company,* April 23, 2013, www.fastcompany.com/1682843/coca-cola-goes-full-digital-in-multi-site-campaign-to-reach-teens; Joe Tripodi, "Coca-Cola Marketing Shifts from Impressions to Expressions," *Harvard Business Review,* April 27, 2011, https://hbr.org/2011/04/coca-colas-marketing-shift-fro; "A Deep Dive into the Social Media Habits and Performance of Coca-Cola," *Unmetric,* https://unmetric.com/brands/coca-cola, accessed October 2018; Larissa Faw, "Coca-Cola Adds New Features to 'Share a Coke' Campaign," *MediaPost,* May 10, 2018, www.mediapost.com/publications/article/319083/coca-cola-adds-new-features-to-share-a-coke-camp.html?edition=108997; "Marketing Fact Pack 2019," *Advertising Age,* December 17, 2018, p. 9; and www.coca-colacompany.com, http://uploader.coca-colacompany.com/jump-in-ugc-image-uploader, www.coca-colacompany.com/our-company/about-coca-cola-journey, and www.coca-colacompany.com/tags/share-a-coke, https://buy.shareacoke.com/, accessed October 2019.

2. Lauren Johnson, "Q&A: PepsiCo's CMOs on Why 40% of Its Super Bowl Budget Is Going to Digital," *Adweek,* January 28, 2018, www.adweek.com/digital/qa-pepsicos-cmos-why-40-its-super-bowl-budget-going-digital-169270/.

3. See www.expediagroup.com, www.expediagroup.com/about, www.expediagroup.com/brands/travelocity/, and www.travelocity.com/inspire/, accessed October 2019.

4. See Greg Sterling, "Report: Digital Now Makes Up 51% of US Ad Spending," *Marketing Land,* September 20, 2018, https://marketingland.com/report-digital-now-makes-up-51-of-us-ad-spending-248617; and Jasmine Enberg, "Digital Ad Spending 2019," *eMarketer,* March 28, 2019, www.emarketer.com/content/us-digital-ad-spending-2019.

5. See www.lowes.com/how-to-library, accessed October 2019.

6. See Deborah Sweeney, "What MoonPie's Social Strategies Can Teach Brands about Engaging with Fans," Social Media Today, January 13, 2018, www.socialmediatoday.com/news/what-moonpies-social-strategies-can-teach-brands-about-engaging-with-fans/514645/; David Griner, "MoonPie Followed Up Its Bizarre, Fake Super Bowl Ad Scripts by Actually Filming Them," Adweek, February 4, 2019, www.adweek.com/agencies/moonpie-followed-up-its-bizarre-fake-super-bowl-ad-scripts-by-actually-filming-them/; and https://twitter.com/MoonPie, accessed October 2019.

7. See "Time Flies: U.S. Adults Now Spend Nearly Half a Day Interacting with Media," *Nielsen,* July 31, 2018, www.nielsen.com/us/en/insights/news/2018/time-flies-us-adults-now-spend-nearly-half-a-day-interacting-with-media.print.html; "Internet Usage Statistics," *Internet World Stats,* www.internetworldstats.com/stats.htm; accessed October 2019; "Mobile Phone Users Worldwide," *Statista,* www.statista.com/statistics/330695/number-of-smartphone-users-worldwide/, accessed October 2019.

8. See "U.S. Online Retail Sales Likely to Surpass $1 Trillion by 2027," *Reuters,* October 17, 2017, www.reuters.com/article/us-usa-retail-internet/u-s-online-retail-sales-likely-to-surpass-1-trillion-by-2027-fti-idUSKBN1CM1LW; and U.S. E-commerce Sales Grow 15.0% in 2018," *Internet Retailer,* February 28, 2019, www.digitalcommerce360.com/article/us-ecommerce-sales/.

9. See "Amazon Now Has Nearly 50% of US Ecommerce Market," *eMarketer,* July 16, 2018, www.emarketer.com/content/amazon-now-has-nearly-50-of-us-ecommerce-market; Phil Wahba, "Inside Nordstrom's Laboratory," *Fortune,* June 3, 2018, pp. 195-199; and John Ballard, "Walmart Is Making Big Strides in E-Commerce," *The Motley Fool,* January 10, 2019, www.fool.

com/investing/2019/01/10/walmart-is-making-big-strides-in-e-commerce.aspx.

10. James Risley, "Internet Retailer: The Home Depot," *Digital Commerce 360,* February 27, 2019, www.digitalcommerce360.com/2019/02/27/half-of-home-depots-online-orders-are-picked-up-in-stores/; "Amazon Now Has Nearly 50% of US Ecommerce Market," *eMarketer*, July 16, 2018, www.emarketer.com/content/amazon-now-has-nearly-50-of-us-ecommerce-market; Demitrios Kalogeropoulos, "Call It Reverse Showrooming: These Companies Are Cashing In on Their Physical Stores," *Motley Fool,* March 19, 2019, www.fool.com/investing/2019/03/19/call-it-reverse-showrooming-these-companies-are-ca.aspx; and Home Depot annual reports and other information found at http://ir.homedepot.com/financial-reports/annual-reports/recent, accessed October 2019.

11. See https://community.playstation.com/, accessed October 2019.

12. See www.pampers.com, accessed October 2019.

13. See "IAC Internet Advertising Competition," www.iacaward.org/iac/winner/17152/21st-century-fox-truex-sonic-wins-2018-iac-award-for-sonic.html, accessed October 2019.

14. Alphabet annual reports, https://abc.xyz/investor/, accessed October 2019.

15. Greg Sterling, "Report: Digital Now Makes Up 51% of U.S. Ad Spending," *Marketing Land*, September 20, 2018, https://marketingland.com/report-digital-now-makes-up-51-of-us-ad-spending-248617; Dan Shewan, "How Much Does Google Ads Cost," *Word Stream*, November 8, 2018, www.wordstream.com/blog/ws/2015/05/21/how-much-does-adwords-cost.

16. See Allen Finn, "35 Face-Melting Email Marketing Stats for 2018," *WordStream,* November 13, 2018, www.wordstream.com/blog/ws/2017/06/29/email-marketing-statistics; Jess Nelson, "Majority of Emails Read on Mobile Devices," *MediaPost,* July 21, 2017, www.mediapost.com/publications/article/304735/majority-of-emails-read-on-mobile-devices.html; Michael Guta, "Consumer Email Use Up 17% over Last Year, Is Your Business Engaging?" *Small Biz Trends,* August 30, 2018, https://smallbiztrends.com/2018/08/consumer-email-statistics.html; "2017 Consumer Email Habits Report: What Do Your Customers Really Want?" *Campaign Monitor,* www.campaignmonitor.com/resources/guides/insights-research-report/, accessed October 2019; and The Radicati Group, "Email Statistics Report 2019–2023," https://www.radicati.com/wp/wp-content/uploads/2018/12/Email-Statistics-Report-2019-2023-Executive-Summary.pdf, accessed October 2019.

17. See Joe Putnam, "How Warby Parker Creates Magical Moments with Email," Rejoiner, http://rejoiner.com/resources/case-study/warby-parker-magical-moments-email/, accessed October 2019; Grace Miller, "Positively Good Marketing: Warby Parker," December 12, 2018, www.campaignmonitor.com/blog/email-marketing/2018/12/positively-good-marketing-warby-parker/; and "Really Good Emails: Warby Parker," Really Good Emails, accessed October 2019.

18. Anabel Acton, "How to Stop Wasting 2.5 Hours on Email Every Day," *Forbes,* July 13, 2017, www.forbes.com/sites/annabelacton/2017/07/13/innovators-challenge-how-to-stop-wasting-time-on-emails/#7ca30e049788; Symantec Security Response Publications, www.symantec.com/security-response/publications/monthlythreatreport.jsp, accessed October 2019; and Sammy Nickalls, "Cutting Through the Clutter," *Adweek,* March 43, 2019, p. 10.

19. James G. Brooks, "Here's How Social Video Will Evolve in 2018," *Venture Beat,* November 19, 2017, https://mashable.com/2017/12/05/how-facebook-watch-will-overtake-youtube-as-biggest-video-platform/#CkdhCWfv35qG; Brendan Gahan, "Facebook Watch Will Overtake YouTube as the Biggest Video Platform." *Mashable,* December 5, 2017, https://mashable.com/2017/12/05/how-facebook-watch-will-overtake-youtube-as-biggest-video-platform/#CkdhCWfv35qG; Salman Aslam,

"Snapchat by the Numbers," Omnicore Agency, February 13, 2018, www.omnicoreagency.com/snapchat-statistics/; Aaron Smith and Monica Anderson, "Social Media Use in 2018," Pew Research, March 1, 2018, www.pewinternet.org/2018/03/01/social-media-use-in-2018/; and "Cisco Visual Networking Index: Forecast and Trends, 2017-2022," Cisco White Paper, February 27, 2019, www.cisco.com/c/en/us/solutions/collateral/service-provider/visual-networking-index-vni/white-paper-c11-741490.html.

20. "Being Heard: The Top 10 Super Bowl Ads by Digital Share of Voice," *Advertising Age,* February 5, 2018, http://adage.com/article/special-report-super-bowl/top-10-super-bowl-ads-digital-share-voice/312257/; "Amazon Rolls Out Celebs for 90-Seconde Alexa Super Bowl Commercial," *Seattle Times,* February 2, 2018, www.seattletimes.com/business/amazon/amazon-rolls-out-celebs-for-90-second-alexa-super-bowl-commercial/; and "2018 Ad Meter Results," http://admeter.usatoday.com/results/2018.

21. See "The Year's 23 Best Media Plans Sparked Conversation with Next-Level Innovation and Creativity," *Adweek,* September 16, 2018, www.adweek.com/brand-marketing/2018s-23-most-effective-media-plans-used-next-level-innovation-and-creativity-to-reach-consumers/8/; and www.youtube.com/watch?v=4ea59Myyjr4, accessed October 2019.

22. Troy Dreier, "The Force Was Strong with This One," *Streaming Media Magazine,* April/May 2011, pp. 66–68. Also see "Why Certain Things Go Viral," *HBR Video,* January 2016, https://hbr.org/video/4698519638001/why-certain-things-go-viral; and Christine DesMarais, "Want Your Video to Go Viral? The Rules Have All Changed," *Inc,* February 5, 2018, www.inc.com/christina-desmarais/5-steps-to-a-viral-video-according-to-a-guy-behind-youtubes-number-one-ad-of-decade.html.

23. For these and other examples, see Megan Hendrickson, "Blog Your Way to an Awesome Reputation: The 10 Best Company Blogs," *DreamHost,* January 16, 2019, www.dreamhost.com/blog/best-company-blogs/; and https://ohmy.disney.com/, www.blog.google, https://flipboard.com/@starbucks/1912-pike-blog-cndc4g24z; www.chase.com/news, and www.patagonia.com/blog/, accessed October 2019.

24. Claire Coghlan, "How 'We Wore What' Blogger Danielle Bernstein Went from Sophomore to 6 Figures in Under 6 Years," *Forbes,* August 23, 2017, www.forbes.com/sites/clairecoghlan/2017/08/23/how-we-wore-what-blogger-danielle-bernstein-went-from-sophomore-to-seven-figures-in-under-6-years/#415d42275843; Eddie Roche, "Danielle Bernstein Gets Real About Money and the Power of Influence," *The Daily Front Row,"* February 11, 2019, https://fashionweekdaily.com/danielle-bernstein-fashion-influencer/; and http://weworewhat.com/, accessed October 2019.

25. "A Deep Dive into the Social Media Habits and Performance of Nike," *Unmetric,* https://unmetric.com/brands/nike, accessed October 2019.

26. Ryan Holmes, "As Facebook Shifts, Instagram Emerges as a New Home for Brands," *Forbes,* February 1, 2018, www.forbes.com/sites/ryanholmes/2018/02/01/as-facebook-shifts-instagram-emerges-as-a-new-home-for-brands/#567780a37834; Todd Clarke, "22+ Instagram Stats That Marketers Can't Ignore This Year," *Hootsuite,* March 5, 2019, https://blog.hootsuite.com/instagram-statistics/; Tony Tran, "How To Advertise on Instagram: A 6 Step Guide to Using Instagram Ads," *Hootsuite,* April 24, 2019, https://blog.hootsuite.com/instagram-ads-guide/#types; Mary Lister, "Instagram Is Worth Over $100 Billion," Mediakix, http://mediakix.com/2017/12/how-much-is-instagramworth-market-cap/#gs.unG4ykE; Peter Jackson, "Instagram Engagement Is Killing It—20X More Than Twitter!" *Foreign Policy*, December 20, 2018, https://foreignpolicyi.org/instagram-engagement-is-killing-it-20x-more-than-twitter/; Adam Levy, "Instagram Stories Will Generate More Ad Revenue Than All of Snap This Year," *Motley Fool*, March 17, 2019, www.fool.com/investing/2019/03/17/

instagram-stories-more-ad-revenue-than-snap-2019.aspx; Evan Niu, "Instagram Could Bring In $14 Billion in Revenue This Year," *Motley Fool*, January 22, 2019, www.fool.com/investing/2019/01/22/instagram-could-bring-in-14-billion-in-revenue-thi.aspx; Sara Salinas, "Instagram Now Lets You Store Payment Info and Buy Products Directly in the App," *CNBC*, May 3, 2018, www.cnbc.com/2018/05/03/instagram-launches-payments-allowing-users-to-buy-products-in-the-app.html; and https://investor.fb.com/financials/default.aspx, accessed October 2019.

27. See David Cohen, "Controversies Galore Didn't Impact Facebook's Revenue in Q1 2019," *Adweek*, April 26, 2019, www.adweek.com/digital/controversies-galore-didnt-impact-facebooks-revenue-in-q1-2019/; and http://newsroom.fb.com/company-info, www.youtube.com/yt/press/statistics.html, and www.statista.com/statistics/282087/number-of-monthly-active-twitter-users/, accessed October 2019.

28. For these and other examples, see www.goodreads.com, www.farmersonly.com, www.birdpost.com, and www.cafemom.com, accessed October 2018.

29. See Mary Blacklston, "Why JetBlue Is the Best Example of Customer Service," *Success Agency Growth HQ Blog*, October 18, 2017, www.successagency.com/growth/2017/10/18/jetblue-best-customer-service/; and Lindsay Kolowich, "Delighting People in 140 Characters: An Inside Look at JetBlue's Customer Service Success," *Hubspot*, https://blog.hubspot.com/marketing/jetblue-customer-service-twitter, accessed October 2019.

30. See www.instagram.com/etsy/, www.pinterest.com/etsy/, https://investors.etsy.com/financials/annual-reports-and-proxy/default.aspx; and www.etsy.com/about, accessed October 2019.

31. Michael Bourne, "Sailing of 14 Social Cs," *Mullen Advertising*, February 13, 2012.

32. David Cohen, "What Dunkin' Donuts Can Learn from Starbucks' Social Strategy," *Adweek*, April 3, 2018, www.adweek.com/digital/what-dunkin-donuts-can-learn-from-starbucks-social-strategy/; and https://unmetric.com/brands/starbucks, accessed October 2019.

33. Kate Taylor, "The Unicorn Frappuccino Completely Revolutionized How Starbucks Invents New Drinks," *Business Insider*, July 2, 2017, www.businessinsider.com/starbucks-new-unicorn-frappuccino-inspired-era-2017-6; Todd Wassermann, "Starbucks 'Tweet-a-Coffee' Campaign Prompted $180,000 in Purchases," *Mashable*, December 13, 2013, http://mashable.com/2013/12/05/starbuckss-tweet-a-coffee-180000/; and www.facebook.com/Starbucks and https://twitter.com/Starbucks, accessed October 2019.

34. Facts in this paragraph are from "Why Nearly 46 Percent of Households Still Have Landlines," *Associated Press*, May 4, 2017, https://nypost.com/2017/05/04/why-nearly-46-percent-of-household-still-have-landlines/; Sara Perez, "Report: Smartphone Owners Are Using 9 Apps per Day, 30 per Month," *Tech Crunch*, May 4, 2017, https://techcrunch.com/2017/05/04/report-smartphone-owners-are-using-9-apps-per-day-30-per-month/; and "Mobile Fact Sheet," *Pew Research Center*, February 5, 2018, www.pewinternet.org/fact-sheet/mobile/.

35. Sarah Perez, "U.S. Consumers Now Spend More Time in Apps Than Watching TV," *Tech Crunch*, September 10, 2015, http://techcrunch.com/2015/09/10/u-s-consumers-now-spend-more-time-in-apps-than-watching-tv/; "Americans Check Their Phones 80 Times a Day," *New York Post*, November 8, 2017, https://nypost.com/2017/11/08/americans-check-their-phones-80-times-a-day-study/; and Chris Klotzbach and Lali Kesiraju, "Flurry State of Mobile 2017: With Captive Mobile Audiences, New App Growth Stagnates," *Flurry Blog*, January 10, 2018, http://flurrymobile.tumblr.com/post/169545749110/state-of-mobile-2017-mobile-stagnates.

36. Justin Smith, "Mobile eCommerce Stats in 2018 and the Future Trends of mCommerce," *OuterBox Blog*, January 11, 2018, www.outerboxdesign.com/web-design-articles/mobile-ecommerce-statistics; and Drake Droesch, "Smartphones Will Account for More than One-Third of Ecommerce Sales in 2019," *eMarketer*, April 4, 2019, www.emarketer.com/content/smartphones-will-account-for-more-than-one-third-of-ecommerce-sales-in-2019.

37. See "Mobile Ad Spending to Surpass All Traditional Media Combined by 2020," *eMarketer*, October 16, 2018, www.emarketer.com/content/mobile-ad-spending-to-surpass-all-traditional-media-combined-by-2020; Greg Sterling, "Report: Digital Now Makes Up 51% of U.S. Ad Spending," *Marketing Land*, September 20, 2018, https://marketingland.com/report-digital-now-makes-up-51-of-us-ad-spending-248617; and Jasmine Enberg, "Digital Ad Spending 2019," *eMarketer*, March 28, 2019, www.emarketer.com/content/us-digital-ad-spending-2019.

38. See "Check Out the 26 Boldly Inventive Campaigns That Won This Year's Project Isaac Awards," *Adweek*, August 21, 2016, www.adweek.com/brand-marketing/check-out-26-boldly-inventive-campaigns-won-years-project-isaac-awards-173060/; Lauren Johnson, "How Brands Are Using Instagram and Snapchat for Their Super Bowl Campaigns," *Adweek*, February 5, 2017, www.adweek.com/digital/how-brands-are-using-instagram-and-snapchat-for-their-super-bowl-campaigns/; and "Gatorade Super Bowl Dunk," www.jeffschroer.com/filter/Cannes/Gatorade-Super-Bowl-Dunk, accessed October 2019.

39. See Ameya Dusane, "Kiip Partners with Purchase Decision Network, Provides Mobile Targeting Across Shopping Apps," *Martech Advisor*, January 15, 2019, www.martechadvisor.com/news/interactive-marketing/kiip-partners-with-purchase-decision-network-provides-mobile-targeting-across-shopping-apps/; "Kiip CEO: Engage Consumers in the Moments that Matter," *Wall Street Journal*, January 9, 2018, http://deloitte.wsj.com/cmo/2018/01/09/kiip-ceo-engage-consumers-in-the-moments-that-matter/; and information from www.statista.com/statistics/276623/number-of-apps-available-in-leading-app-stores/, www.rei.com/mobile; www.kiip.me/brands/#, and www.tripadvisor.mediaroom.com/us-about-us, accessed October 2019.

40. See Bruce Biegel, "Outlook for Data Drive Marketing: First Look 2019," Winterberry Group, January 17, 2019, https://www.winterberrygroup.com/our-insights.

41. See Julie Liesse, "When Times Are Hard, Mail Works," *Advertising Age*, March 30, 2009, p. 14; and Steve Olenski, "An Appreciation for an Old Friend: Direct Mail," *Forbes*, August 17, 2018, www.forbes.com/sites/steveolenski/2018/08/17/an-appreciation-for-an-old-friend-direct-mail/#267212322c94.

42. Joseph Myers, "Amazon Is Mailing a Print Catalog, Are You?" *Promo Marketing*, November 8, 2018, https://magazine.promomarketing.com/article/amazon-is-mailing-a-print-catalog-are-you/.

43. Molly Soat, "In the Mood to Peruse," *Marketing News*, July 2015, pp. 41–49; and Ronald D. White, "The Old-Fashioned Mail-Order Catalog Is Making a Comeback," *Los Angeles Times*, November 23, 2017, www.latimes.com/business/la-fi-catalogs-return-20171123-story.html.

44. Ronald White, "The Old-Fashioned Mail-Order Catalog Is Making a Comeback," *Los Angeles Times*, November 23, 2017, www.latimes.com/business/la-fi-catalogs-return-20171123-story.html; Joseph Myers, "Amazon Is Mailing a Print Catalog—Are You?" *Promo Magazine*, November 8, 2018, https://magazine.promomarketing.com/article/amazon-is-mailing-a-print-catalog-are-you/; and "Data & Marketing Association Direct Mail Statistics," https://thedma.org/marketing-insights/marketing-statistics/direct-mail-statistics/, accessed October 2019.

45. See Federal Trade Commission, "FTC Release FY 2018 National Do Not Call Registry Data Book and Mini Site," December 6, 2018, www.ftc.gov/news-events/press-releases/2018/12/ftc-releases-fy-2018-national-do-not-call-registry-data-book-mini.

46. See Corky Siemaszko, "In an Era of Endless Robocalls, Why Telemarketers Persist," *NBC News*, December 9, 2018, www.nbcnews.com/news/us-news/era-endless-robocalls-why-telemarketers-persist-n943831; and Stephanie Mlot, "FTC Shutters

Four Groups Responsible for Billions of Illegal Robocalls," *Geek,* March 28, 2018, www.geek.com/tech/ftc-shutters-four-groups-responsible-for-billions-of-illegal-robocalls-1780462/.

47. Lauren Debter, "Inside Beachbody's Billion Dollar Fat Burning Empire," *Forbes,* April 30, 2018, www.forbes.com/sites/laurengensler/2018/04/10/beachbody-carl-daikeler-shakeology/#65277ad47960.

48. Bill Cogar, "Why Direct Response TV Marketing Is Still Effective," *Smart Brief,* October 23, 2018, www.smartbrief.com/original/2018/10/why-direct-response-tv-marketing-still-effective.

49. See "The Home Depot Appliance Finder," Image Manufacturing Group, http://imgarchitectural.com/case-studies/2014/3/26/the-home-depot-appliance-finder; and "Customer Experience Is the New Marketing," August 21, 2017, Momentum Worldwide, www.momentumww.com/news/2017/8/16/customer-experience-is-the-new-marketing.

50. See Internet Crime Complaint Center, www.ic3.gov, accessed October 2019.

51. See Generali Global Assistance, "Three-Quarters of Americans Concerned about Identity Theft During Holiday Shopping Season," November 28, 2018, www.prnewswire.com/news-releases/nearly-three-quarters-of-americans-concerned-about-identity-theft-during-holiday-shopping-season-300756518.html; and "2018 Date Breach Report," *Identity Theft Resource Center,* https://www.idtheftcenter.org/surveys-studys/, accessed October 2019.

52. See Jenny Anderson, "When Will Social Media Companies Get Serious about Their Effect on Young Kids," *Quartz,* January 15, 2018, https://qz.com/1179894/when-will-social-media-companies-like-facebook-and-snapchat-get-serious-about-their-effect-on-young-kids/; and "21 Completely Insane Social Media Statistics," *Content Factory,* www.contentfac.com/more-people-own-cell-phone-than-toothbrush-10-crazy-social-media-statistics/, accessed October 2019.

53. See "Consumer Privacy Survey Shows 70% Want Personal Data to Stay on Mobile Phones," *BusinessWire,* November 13, 2018, www.businesswire.com/news/home/20181113005171/en/Consumer-Privacy-Survey-Shows-70-Personal-Data; and "SAS Survey: 67 Percent of US Consumers Think Government Should Do More to Protect Data Privacy," December 10, 2018, www.sas.com/en_us/news/press-releases/2018/december/data-management-data-privacy-survey.html.

54. See https://experience.sap.com/designservices/work/project/mobile-data-analysis-with-sap-consumer-insight-365, accessed October 2019.

55. Dylan Currin, "Are You Ready? Here Is All the Data Facebook and Google Have on You," *The Guardian,* March 28, 2018, www.theguardian.com/commentisfree/2018/mar/28/all-the-data-facebook-google-has-on-you-privacy; and Ben Popken, "Google Sells the Future, Powered by Your Personal Data," *NBC News,* May 10, 2018, www.nbcnews.com/tech/tech-news/google-sells-future-powered-your-personal-data-n870501.

56. See Kelsey Sutton, "The Age of Consent," *Adweek,* January 7, 2019, p. 8; and David Meyer, "In Privacy We Trust," *Fortune,* December 1, 2018, pp. 38–39.

57. See Richard Byrne Reilly, "Feds to Mobile Marketers: Stop Targeting Kids, or Else," *Venture Beat,* March 27, 2014, http://venturebeat.com/2014/03/27/feds-to-mobile-marketers-stop-targeting-kids-or-else-exclusive/; and www.business.ftc.gov/privacy-and-security/childrens-privacy, accessed October 2019.

58. Information on TrustArc and Truste at www.trustarc.com/products/enterprise-privacy-certification, accessed October 2019.

59. "Average Time Spent per Day with Facebook, Instagram and Snapchat by US Adult Users of Each Platform, 2014–2019 (minutes)," *eMarketer,* March 29, 2019, www.emarketer.com/Chart/Average-Time-Spent-per-Day-with-Facebook-Instagram-and-Snapchat-by-US-Adult-Users-of-Each-Platform-2014-2019-minutes/211521; Sarah Perez. "Local Marketplace OfferUp Takes on EBay with Launch of Nationwide Shipping," *TechCrunch,* May 1, 2018, techcrunch.com/2018/05/01/local-marketplace-offerup-takes-on-ebay-with-launch-of-nationwide-

shipping/; Jason Del Rey, "OfferUp Went Head to Head with Craigslist to Build a Following. Now It's Going After Ebay to Build a Business," *Recode,* May 1, 2018, www.recode.net/2018/5/1/17305648/offerup-shipping-feature-ebay-letgo-facebook-marketplace; and Ryan Mac, "Can Craigslist Be Killed? These Startups Are Taking Aim," *Forbes,* May 2, 2017, www.forbes.com/sites/ryanmac/2017/05/02/offerup-letgo-killing-craigslist/#5ed619256ff7, and information from https://about.offerup.com/ and https://we.letgo.com/, accessed September 2019.

Chapter 18

1. See Jennifer Overstreet, "Nordstrom Sets the Standard for Customer Service. Again and Again," RTF, March 4, 2019, https://nrf.com/blog/nordstrom-sets-standard-customer-experience-again-and-again; Stacy Conradt, "21 of the Best Customer Service Stories Ever," *Mental Floss,* January 12, 2016, http://mentalfloss.com/article/73540/21-best-customer-service-stories-ever; Amy Martinez, "Tale of Lost Diamond Adds Glitter to Nordstrom's Customer Service," Seattle Times, May 11, 2011; Garrett Pierson and Scott Brandley, The Trust Factor (eBookit.com, 2013), Chapter 7; Carol Toller, "How Nordstrom Built the World's Best Customer-Service Machine," *Canadian Business,* March 5, 2015, www.canadianbusiness.com/innovation/secrets-of-nordstrom-customer-service/; Blake Morgan, "The 10 Keys to Nordstrom's Digital Transformation," *Forbes,* March 26, 2019, www.forbes.com/sites/blakemorgan/2019/03/26/the-10-keys-to-nordstroms-digital-transformation/; and http://shop.nordstrom.com/c/company-history and www.investor.nordstrom.com, accessed October 2019.

2. Maureen Morrison, "Cinnabon's Recipe for Expansion: Licensing and Co-branding," *Advertising Age,* February 19, 2014, http://adage.com/article/news/cinnabon-expands-licensing-vodka-air-fresheners/291726/; and "New Tricks: How Old Brands Can Still Surprise Customers," *Knowledge@Wharton,* May 5, 2015, http://knowledge.wharton.upenn.edu/article/new-tricks-how-old-brands-can-still-surprise-consumers/; Allecia Vermillion, "Scents from a Mall: The Sticky, Untold Story of Cinnabon," *Seattle Met,* October 23, 2017, www.seattlemet.com/articles/2017/10/23/scents-from-a-mall-the-sticky-untold-story-of-cinnabon; and www.cinnabon.com, accessed October 2019.

3. "Eastman Kodak Company Earnings: KODK Stock Sinks as 2018 Sales Down 4%," *NASDAQ,* April 1, 2019, www.nasdaq.com/article/eastman-kodak-company-earnings-kodk-stock-sinks-as-2018-sales-down-4-cm1123113; Ernest Scheyder, "Focus on Past Glory Kept Kodak from Digital Win," *Reuters,* January 19, 2012, www.reuters.com/article/2012/01/19/us-kodak-bankruptcy-idUSTRE80I1N020120119; Dawn McCarty and Beth Jink, "Kodak Files for Bankruptcy as Digital Era Spells End to Film," *Bloomberg Businessweek,* January 25, 2012, www.-businessweek.com/news/2012-01-25/kodak-files-for-bankruptcy-as-digital-era-spells-end-to-film.html; Kyle O'Brien, "Kodak Captures Special Moments in Its Latest Campaign," *The Drum,* September 21, 2017, www.thedrum.com/news/2017/09/21/kodak-captures-special-moments-its-latest-campaign; and www.kodak.com/ek/us/en/corp/aboutus/heritage/milestones/default.htm, http://investor.kodak.com/investor-relations, and www.kodak.com, accessed October 2019.

4. See www.masterchefappliancecenter.com/manufacturers/viking/, accessed October 2019.

5. See www.lg.com/us/lg-signature, accessed October 2019.

6. See Brian Steinberg, "Coke, Pepsi Go to Super Bowl Battle Armed with Similar Pitches," *Variety,* February 1, 2018, http://variety.com/2018/tv/news/super-bowl-commercials-coca-cola-pepsi-advertising-1202684017/; E. J. Schultz, "Pepsi Ads Take Shot at Share-A-Coke, Polar Bears," *Advertising Age,* June 15, 2015, www.adage.com/print/298985; and Delaney Strunk, "The Biggest Rivalry in Atlanta on Super Bowl Weekend Has Nothing to Do with Football," *CNN Business,* January 29, 2019, www.cnn.

com/2019/01/29/media/super-bowl-2019-coke-pepsi-trnd/index.html.

7. See Jill Kransy, "Why Competition May Be the Best Thing for Your Business," *Inc.,* November 13, 2013, www.inc.com/magazine/201311/jill-krasny/more-competition-is-better-for-start-ups.html; and Charles Riley, "Volkswagen Is Betting Its Future on Electric Cars," *CNN Business,* March 12, 2019, www.cnn.com/2019/03/12/business/volkswagen-electric-cars/index.html.

8. Adapted from information found in W. Chan Kim and Renée Mauborgne, *Blue Ocean Strategy, Expanded Edition: How to Create Uncontested Market Space and Make Competition Irrelevant* (Boston: Harvard Business Press, 2015). For other discussion, see Kim and Mauborgne, "Red Ocean Traps," *Harvard Business Review,* March 2015, pp. 68–73; and "Blue Ocean Strategy," www.blueoceanstrategy.com, accessed October 2019.

9. See "Market Share of the Leading Single-Cup Coffee Vendors in the United States in 2017," www.statista.com/statistics/586731/market-share-single-cup-coffee-vendors-in-the-united-states/, accessed October 2019; and https://investors.keurigdrpepper.com/ and www.keurig.com/, accessed October 2019.

10. See Steve Olenski, "Why Traditional Brands Are Moving to DTC Model," *MediaPost,* February 27, 2019, www.mediapost.com/publications/article/332494/why-traditional-brands-are-moving-to-dtc-model.html; Kate Clark, "Mattress Startup Casper Valued at $1.1B with New Funding," *Tech Crunch,* March 27, 2019, https://techcrunch.com/2019/03/27/mattress-startup-casper-said-to-be-valued-at-1-1b-with-new-funding/; Cameron Albert-Deitch, "Comfy Shoes Helped Allbirds Become a $1.4 Billion Company, but It's Never Been Just about Shoes," *Inc.,* December 4, 2018, www.inc.com/cameron-albert-deitch/allbirds-2018-company-of-the-year-nominee.html, and www.casper.com, accessed September 2019.

11. See Dinah Eng, "Samuel Adams's Beer Revolution," *Fortune,* April 8, 2013, pp. 23–26; and www.bostonbeer.com/overview and www.bostonbeer.com/investor-relations/earnings-releases, accessed October 2019.

12. For these and other examples, see Harry McCracken, "Google's 100% Solution," *Fast Company,* December 2018/January 2019, pp. 22–26; Dominic Powell, "Want to Run Your First Hackathon? Here Are Some Tips from KPMG," *Smart Company,* August 15, 2017, www.smartcompany.com.au/startupsmart/advice/want-run-first-internal-hackathon-tips-kpmg/; Matt Weinberger, "'There Are Only Two Rules'—Facebook Explains How 'Hackathons,' One of Its Oldest Traditions, Is Also One of Its Most Important," *Business Insider,* January 11, 2017, www.businessinsider.com/facebook-hackathons-2017-6; and www.facebook.com/hackathon/, accessed October 2019.

13. Michael E. Porter, *Competitive Strategy: Techniques for Analyzing Industries and Competitors* (New York: Free Press, 1980), Chapter 2; and Porter, "What Is Strategy?" *Harvard Business Review,* November–December 1996, pp. 61–78. Also see "Porter's Generic Strategies," www.quickmba.com/strategy/generic.shtml, accessed October 2019.

14. See Michael Treacy and Fred Wiersema, "Customer Intimacy and Other Value Disciplines," *Harvard Business Review,* January–February 1993, pp. 84–93; Treacy and Wiersema, *The Discipline of Market Leaders: Choose Your Customers, Narrow Your Focus, Dominate Your Market* (New York: Perseus Press, 1997); and Wiersema, *Double-Digit Growth: How Great Companies Achieve It—No Matter What* (New York: Portfolio, 2003). Also see Elaine Cascio, "Fast, Cheap, or Good—Pick Two," *Inter@ction Solutions,* January/February 2012, p. 8; Joe Weinman, "How Customer Intimacy Is Evolving to Collective Intimacy, Thanks to Big Data," *Forbes,* June 4, 2013, www.forbes.com/sites/joeweinman/2013/06/04/how-customer-intimacy-is-evolving-to-collective-intimacy-thanks-to-big-data/; and "Value Disciplines: Customer Intimacy, Product Leadership and Operational Excellence," *Business-to-You,* October 23, 2018, www.business-to-you.com/value-disciplines-customer-intimacy/.

15. See "Most Innovative Companies 2019," *Fast Company,* www.fastcompany.com/most-innovative-companies/2019/sectors/consumer-electronics, accessed October 2019; and Lauren Feiner, "Apple Is Once Again the Most Valuable Company in the World," *CNBC,* February 6, 2019, www.cnbc.com/2019/02/06/apple-is-once-again-the-most-valuable-public-company-in-the-world.html.

16. See "Trader Joe's Repeats as Top U.S. Grocery Retailer in the Dunnhumby Retailer Preference Index," *Business Wire,* January 9, 2019, www.businesswire.com/news/home/20190109005221/en/Trader-Joe's-Repeats-Top-U.S.-Grocery-Retailer; Jack Houston, "A Psychologist Explains How Trader Joe's Gets You to Spend More Money," *Business Insider,* February 19, 2019, www.businessinsider.com/trader-joes-how-gets-you-spend-money-psychologist-2019-1; Anna Sowa, "Trader Joe's: Why the Hype?" *McClatchy-Tribune Business News,* March 27, 2008; Megan McArdle, "What's Not to Love About Trader Joe's," *Washington Post,* March 30, 2018, www.washingtonpost.com/blogs/post-partisan/wp/2018/03/30/whats-not-to-love-about-trader-joes/?noredirect=on&utm_term=.cd7f8ae8939d; Alan Liddle, "2019 Top 75—Sales Overview," *Supermarket News,* February 19, 2019, supermarketnews.com/rankings-research/top-75-retailers-wholesalers; and www.traderjoes.com, accessed October 2019.

17. For more discussion, see Philip Kotler and Kevin Lane Keller, *Marketing Management,* 15th ed. (Hoboken, NJ: Prentice Hall, 2016), Chapter 12.

18. See Katharine Schwab, "You Can't Take Anything Home from IKEA's New Store," *Fast Company,* April 10, 2019, www.fastcompany.com/90332083/i-went-to-ikeas-first-small-store-and-it-answered-all-my-prayers; Aine Cain, "I Visited IKEA's New Manhattan Location—and It Was Like Nothing Else I've Seen from a Retailer," *Business Insider,* April 10, 2019, www.businessinsider.com/ikea-nyc-store-planning-studio-tour-2019-4; and www.ikea.com/ms/en_US/expansion/planning-studio/upper-east-side-nyc/, accessed October 2019.

19. See "2000+ Uses," www.wd40.com/uses-tips/ and www.wd40.com/img/WD-40_2000_uses.pdf, accessed October 2019.

20. Tamara Walsh, "Is This Procter & Gamble's Secret Weapon?" *The Motley Fool,* July 7, 2015, www.fool.com/investing/general/2015/07/07/is-this-procter-gambles-secret-weapon.aspx; "Race to Win Over a New Generation of Consumers in Asia," *Nonwoven Industries,* February 18, 2016, www.nonwovens-industry.com/issues/2016-02-08/view_features/race-to-win-over-a-new-generation-of-consumers-in-asia; Lauren Coleman-Lochner, "P&G Studies 'Pee Points' to Maintain Edge in Diaper Wars," *Bloomberg,* March 24, 2014, www.bloomberg.com/news/articles/2014-03-04/p-g-studies-pee-points-to-maintain-edge-in-diaper-wars; "Pampers vs Huggies: Innovations in Diaper Technology Creates Fierce Competition," *Technavio,* March 5, 2018, www.technavio.com/blog/pampers-or-huggies-innovations-in-diaper-technology-creates-fierce-competition; Nathaniel Meyersohn, "Why Diapers Are in Trouble: Americans Are Having Fewer Babies," *CNN,* June 14, 2018, https://money.cnn.com/2018/06/14/news/companies/pampers-huggies-diapers/index.html; and "Global Diaper Market Is Projected to Reach $84,317.6 Million by 2023, According to P&S Intelligence," September 2018, https://www.psmarketresearch.com/press-release/diaper-market.

21. See "Hair Care—United States," *Statista,* www.statista.com/outlook/70040000/109/hair-care/united-states, accessed October 2019; and "Marketing Size of Soft Drinks in the United States," *Statista,* www.statista.com/statistics/422532/united-states-soft-drink-market-size/, accessed October 2019.

22. "Top Selling Energy Drink Brands," *Caffeine Informer,* www.caffeineinformer.com/the-15-top-energy-drink-brands, accessed October 2019; and www.redbull.com/us/en, accessed October 2019.

23. See Matt Southern, "DuckDuckGo Hits a Record 1 Billion Monthly Searches in January 2019," *Search Engine Journal,* February 4, 2019, www.searchenginejournal.com/duckduckgo-hits-a-record-1-billion-monthly-searches-in-january-2019/291609/#close; and https://duckduckgo.com, accessed October 2019.

24. See www.wolverineworldwide.com and www.wolverine worldwide.com/about-us/, accessed October 2019.

25. Rebecca Jennings, "TikTok, Explained," *Vox,* July 12, 2019, https://www.vox.com/culture/2018/12/10/18129126/tiktok-app-musically-meme-cringe; Michael Wade and Jialu Shan, "TikTok: The World's Most Valuable Startup That You've Never Heard of," *The Conversation,* January 8, 2019, http://theconversation.com/tiktok-the-worlds-most-valuable-startup-that-youve-never-heard-of-109302; Arjun Kharpa, "TikTok Owner ByteDance Is a $75 billion Chinese Tech Giant—Here's What You Need to Know about It," *CNBC,* May 29, 2019, https://www.cnbc.com/2019/05/30/tiktok-owner-bytedance-what-to-know-about-the-chinese-tech-giant.html; Mansoor Iqbal, "TikTok Revenue and Usage Statistics (2019)," Business of Apps, February 27, 2019, https://www.businessofapps.com/data/tik-tok-statistics/; Sarah Perez, "It's Time to Pay Serious Attention to TikTok," *The Tech Crunch,* January 30, 2019, https://techcrunch.com/2019/01/29/its-time-to-pay-serious-attention-to-tiktok/; Shannon Liao, "Facebook Quietly Launches a TikTok Competitor App Called Lasso," *The Verge,* November 9, 2018, https://www.theverge.com/2018/11/9/18080280/facebook-lasso-tiktok-competitor-app; Salvador Rodriguez, "TikTok Is Showing That It's Possible to Beat Facebook with Hot App Teens Love," CNBC, February 27, 2019, https://www.cnbc.com/2019/02/27/tiktok-is-staying-way-ahead-of-facebooks-lasso.html; Alyssa Bereznak, "Memes Are the New Pop Stars: How TikTok Became the Future of the Music Industry," *The Ringer,* June 27, 2019, https://www.theringer.com/tech/2019/6/27/18760004/tiktok-old-town-road-memes-music-industry.

Chapter 19

1. See Ann-Marie Alcántara, "L'Oréal Debuts a Personalized Direct-to-Consumer Hair Color Brand," *Adweek,* May 8, 2019, www.adweek.com/brand-marketing/loreal-debuts-a-personalized-direct-to-consumer-hair-color-brand; "Our Mission Is 'Beauty for All,' Says L'Oréal Global CEO Jean-Paul," *The Economic Times,* January 30, 2015, www.articles.economictimes.indiatimes.com/2015-01-30/news/58625572_1_l-oreal-loreal-jean-paul-agon; Hae-Jung Hong and Yves Doz, "L'Oréal Masters Multiculturalism," *Harvard Business Review,* June, 2013, pp. 114-119; "A Worldwide Approach to Beauty Rituals," www.loreal.com/research-innovation/when-the-diversity-of-types-of-beauty-inspires-science/a-world-wide-approach-to-beauty-rituals.aspx, accessed October 2019; and www.loreal.com/group/who-we-are/our-mission, www.lorealusa.com/research-and-innovation/when-the-diversity-of-types-of-beauty-inspires-science/stories-of-multicultural-innovations, www.lorealusa.com/group/who-we-are/our-ambition, and www.loreal-finance.com/eng/annual-report, accessed October 2019.

2. Data from www.walmart.com, accessed October 2019; United Nations Conference on Trade and Development, "World Investment Report 2018: Key Messages and Overview," https://unctad.org/en/PublicationsLibrary/wir2018_overview_en.pdf, accessed April 2018; and "List of Countries by GDP: List by the CIA World Factbook," *Wikipedia,* http://en.wikipedia.org/wiki/List_of_countries_by_GDP_(nominal), accessed October 2019.

3. See "World Trade Statistical Review 2018," *WTO,* https://www.wto.org/english/res_e/statis_e/wts2018_e/wts18_toc_e.htm; and "Gross Domestic Product (GDP) at Current Prices from 2012 to 2022," *Statista,* www.statista.com/statistics/268750/global-gross-domestic-product-gdp/, accessed October 2019.

4. Information from www.michelin.com/eng/finance/financial-results/2017-annual-results, www.jnj.com, www.coca-colacompany.com, and www.coca-colacompany.com/our-company/infographic-coca-cola-at-a-glance, accessed October 2019.

5. See https://www.otis.com/en/us/about/ and UTC Annual Report, www.utc.com/Investors/Pages/Annual-Reports-and-Proxy-Statements.aspx, accessed October 2019.

6. Max Bouchet and Joseph Parilla, "How Trump's Steel and Aluminum Tariffs Could Affect State Economies," *Brookings,* March 6, 2018, www.brookings.edu/blog/the-avenue/2018/03/06/how-trumps-steel-and-aluminum-tariffs-could-affect-state-economies/; Rishi Iyengar, "US-China Trade Battle: How We Got Here," *CNN,* April 4, 2018, http://money.cnn.com/2018/04/04/news/economy/trump-china-us-tariffs-trade-timeline/index.html; "China Hits Back at Trump with Tariffs on $60bn US Goods," *BBC News,* September 18, 2018, www.bbc.com/news/business-45555749; and Natashe Bach, "Trump's Plan to Reduce Trade Deficit Falters as It Hits an All-Time High Instead," *Fortune,* March 6, 2019, http://fortune.com/2019/03/06/us-trade-deficit-record-high/.

7. "Retail Industry in India," India Brand Equity Foundation, www.ibef.org/industry/retail-india.aspx, accessed October 2019.

8. See Saritha Rai, "India's E-commerce Crackdown," *Bloomberg Businessweek,* February 11, 2019, pp. 17–19; and Saheli Roy Choudhury, "If You Own Amazon Shares, Here's What You Need to Know about India's E-commerce Law," *CNBC,* February 4, 2019, www.cnbc.com/2019/02/05/amazon-how-india-ecommerce-law-will-affect-the-retailer.html;

9. See James McBride, "What's Next for the WTO?" Council on Foreign Relations, March 23, 2018, www.cfr.org/backgrounder/whats-next-wto; and "What Is the WTO?" www.wto.org/english/thewto_e/whatis_e/whatis_e.htm, accessed October 2019.

10. "The EU at a Glance," http://europa.eu/about-eu/index_en.htm; "EU Statistics and Opinion Polls," http://europa.eu/documentation/statistics-polls/index_en.htm; and "EU Position in World Trade," http://ec.europa.eu/trade/policy/eu-position-in-world-trade/, all accessed October 2019.

11. See Alan Crawford, "The EU and Euro Keep Defying the Doomsayers," *Bloomberg Businessweek,* January 3, 2019, www.bloomberg.com/news/articles/2019-01-03/the-eu-and-euro-keep-defying-the-doomsayers; and "European Union: The Euro," http://europa.eu/about-eu/basic-information/money/euro/, accessed October 2019.

12. "Brexit Timeline: Key Dates in the Divorce from the EU," *Financial Times,* April 12, 2019, www.ft.com/content/64e7f218-4ad4-11e7-919a-1e14ce4af89b; CIA, *The World Factbook,* www.cia.gov/library/publications/resources/the-world-factbook/index.html, and "The Economy," https://europa.eu/european-union/about-eu/figures/economy_en, accessed October 2019.

13. Statistics and other information from "How NAFTA Changed U.S. Trade with Canada and Mexico," *New York Times,* August 15, 2017, www.nytimes.com/interactive/2017/business/nafta-canada-mexico.html; and CIA, *The World Factbook;* and "NAFTA's Economic Impact," www.cfr.org/backgrounder/naftas-economic-impact, accessed October 2019.

14. "Eleven Asia-Pacific Countries Signed a Trans-Pacific Partnership in Chile," *Merco Press,* March 9, 2018, http://en.mercopress.com/2018/03/09/eleven-asia-pacific-countries-signed-a-trans-pacific-partnership-in-chile; and Government of Canada, "Comprehensive and Progressive Agreement for Trans-Pacific Partnership (CPTPP)," https://international.gc.ca/trade-commerce/trade-agreements-accords-commerciaux/agr-acc/cptpp-ptpgp/index.aspx?lang=eng, accessed October 2019.

15. Euromonitor, "Top 5 Bottom of the Pyramid Markets: Diverse Spending Patterns and Future Potential," https://blog.euromonitor.com/top-5-bottom-pyramid-markets-diverse-spending-patterns-future-potential/; Kimberly Freeman, Suresh Gopalan, and Jessica Bailey, "Achieving Global Growth through Acquisition: Tata's Takeover of Corus," *Journal of Case Research in Business and Economics,* https://www.aabri.com/

manuscripts/09198.pdf; Prashant Kale, Harbir Singh, and Anand Raman, "Don't Integrate Your Acquisitions, Partner with Them," *Harvard Business Review*, December 2009, https://hbr.org/2009/12/dont-integrate-your-acquisitions-partner-with-them; P. R. Sanjai, "Tata Steel to Further Expand Kalinganagar Steel Plant in Odisha," *Mint*, July 13, 2016, https://www.livemint.com/Industry/H4LsIlKuXXaIM0qFF2fHAL/Tata-Steel-to-further-expand-Kalinganagar-steel-plant-in-Odi.html; Valentina Pop, "EU Blocks Merger of Steelmaking Units of Tata, Thyssenkrupp," *The Wall Street Journal*, June 11, 2019, https://www.wsj.com/articles/eu-blocks-merger-of-steelmaking-units-of-tata-thyssenkrupp-11560251203; "Tata Steel Business Model & Corporate Strategy for Business Growth," https://www.tatasteel.com/corporate/our-value-chain/business-model-strategy/; "Tata Steel—Financial Capital," August 2, 2019, https://www.tatasteel.com/investors/integrated-report-2018-19/financial-capital.html; Tata Steel Europe, "Our Strategy," https://www.tatasteeleurope.com/en/about%E2%80%93us/strategy; Tata Steel Europe, "Markets," https://www.tatasteeleurope.com/en/markets; Tata Steel, "Our Work Culture | Tata Steel Careers," https://www.tatasteel.com/careers/culture-at-tata-steel/culture-tata/; "Tata Steel to Focus on India as Global Markets Face Headwinds," *The Hindu Business Line*, July 29, 2017, https://www.thehindubusinessline.com/companies/tata-steel-to-focus-on-india-as-global-markets-face-headwinds/article9793630.ece; TNN, "Tata Steel to Adopt Corus Technology for New Units," *The Economic Times*, September 8, 2007, https://m.economictimes.com/industry/indl-goods/svs/steel/tata-steel-to-adopt-corus-technology-for-new-units/articleshow/2349060.cms; PTI, "Tata Steel to Focus on Turning around European Operations and Not to Raise More Debt This Fiscal," *The Economic Times*, July 19, 2019, https://economictimes.indiatimes.com/industry/indl-goods/svs/steel/tata-steel-to-focus-on-turning-around-european-operations-and-not-to-raise-more-debt-this-fiscal/articleshow/70297685.cms; PTI Washington, "Tata Steel, Shining Example of Job Creation in USA through FDI," *The Hindu BusinessLine*, November 12, 2017, from https://www.thehindubusinessline.com/companies/%60Tata-Steel-shining-example-of-job-creation-in-USA-through-FDI%E2%80%99/article20327774.ece; D. V. R. Seshadri and Arabinda Tripathy, "'Reinventing a Giant Corporation: The Case of Tata Steel," *Vikalpa: The Journal for Decision Makers*, 31(3) (2006): 131–46, https://doi.org/10.1177/0256090920060309; "UNCTAD | The International Trading System and Trade Negotiations," https://unctad.org/en/Pages/DITC/TNCD/International-trading-system.aspx.

16. See Zeenat Moorad, "The Coca-Cola Company: Tapping Africa's Fizz," *Financial Mail*, May 4, 2015, www.financialmail.co.za/coverstory/2015/04/30/the-coca-cola-company-tapping-africas-fizz; Annaleigh Vallie, "Coke Turns 125 and Has Much Life Ahead," *Business Day*, May 16, 2011, www.bdlive.co.za/articles/2011/05/16/coke-turns-125-and-has-much-more-life-ahead; Kate Taylor, "Coca-Cola Has Discovered an Untapped Market to Save the Soda Business," *Business Insider*, February 7, 2016, www.businessinsider.com/africa-is-the-future-of-coca-cola-2016-2; Yinka Adegoke, "Africa Will Have Some of the World's Fastest-Growing Economies in 2019—and a Looming Debt Crisis," *Quartz*, January 13 2019, https://qz.com/africa/1522126/african-economies-to-watch-in-2019-and-looming-debt; and www.imf.org/external/datamapper/PPPSH@WEO/OEMDC/ADVEC/WEOWORLD/AFQ/WEQ and Coca-Cola annual reports and other information from www.thecoca-colacompany.com, accessed October 2019.

17. See "2018 Investment Climate Statement—Russia," U.S. Bureau of Economic and Business Affairs, May 2018, www.state.gov/e/eb/rls/othr/ics/investmentclimatestatements/index.htm?year=2018&dlid=281629; and "Russia County Commercial Guide," www.export.gov/article?series=a0pt0000000PAulAAG&type=Country_Commercial__kav, accessed October 2019.

18. See "Indonesia Barters Coffee and Palm Oil for Russian Fighter Jets," *Bloomberg*, August 7, 2017, www.bloomberg.com/news/articles/2017-08-07/indonesia-barters-coffee-palm-oil-for-russian-fighter-jets; "South Korean Organization Proposes Coffee-Barter Trade with Vietnam," *International Comunicaffe*, March 14, 2018, www.comunicaffe.com/south-korean-organisation-proposes-coffee-barter-trade-with-vietnam/; and Nick Fouriezos, "To Avoid Trump's Sanctions, Countries Turn to Stone Age Bartering," *Ozy*, January 9, 2019, www.ozy.com/politics-and-power/to-avoid-trumps-sanctions-countries-turn-to-stone-age-bartering/91467.

19. For these and other examples, see Emma Hall, "Do You Know Your Rites? BBDO Does," *Advertising Age*, May 21, 2007, p. 22; Michael R. Czinkota and Ilkka A. Ronkainen, *International Marketing* (Cincinnati, OH: South-Western College Publishing, 2013), Chapter 3; and "13 Unusual International Customs You Never Knew Existed," *Reader's Digest*, www.readersdigest.ca/travel/travel-tips/13-unusual-international-customs-you-never-knew-existed/, accessed October 2019.

20. Mason Hinsdale, "International Brands," *Jing Daily*, January 13, 2018, https://jingdaily.com/marriotts-blunder-a-warning-in-dealing-with-beijings-understanding-of-history/; Jamie Bryan, "The Mintz Dynasty," *Fast Company*, April 2006, pp. 56–61; Sui-Lee Wee, "Marriott to China: We Do Not Support Separatists," *New York Times*, January 11, 2018, www.nytimes.com/2018/01/11/business/china-marriott-tibet-taiwan.html; and Britt Morse, "The 7 Most Embarrassing Branding Mistakes of 2018," *Inc.*, January 9, 2019, www.inc.com/brit-morse/2018-biggest-marketing-branding-fails.html.

21. For these and other examples, see Bill Chappell, "Bill Gates' Handshake with South Korea's Park Sparks Debate," *NPR*, April 23, 2013, www.npr.org/blogs/thetwo-way/2013/04/23/178650537/bill-gates-handshake-with-south-koreas-park-sparks-debate; and "Worst Mistakes You Can Make during Overseas Business Meeting," *smallbusiness.co.uk*, October 5, 2017, https://smallbusiness.co.uk/worst-mistakes-overseas-business-meeting-2540989/.

22. See Rory Jones, "Foreign Retailers Bend to Conform to Saudi Religious Rules," *Wall Street Journal*, June 16, 2015, www.wsj.com/articles/foreign-retailers-bend-to-conform-to-saudi-religious-rules-1434421369; and www.marksandspencer.com, accessed October 2019.

23. Andres Martinez, "The Next American Century," *Time*, March 22, 2010, p. 1.

24. Emily Feng, "McDonald's to Double Number of China Restaurants," *Financial Times*, August 8, 2017, www.ft.com/content/ae5b2e96-7c1c-11e7-9108-edda0bcbc928; and Clarissa Wei, "Why China Loves American Chain Restaurants So Much," *Eater*, March 20, 2018, www.eater.com/2018/3/20/16973532/mcdonalds-starbucks-kfc-china-pizza-hut-growth-sales.

25. See Ben Miller, "McDonald's Is Succeeding in Russia by Going Local," *Chicago Business Journal*, November 9, 2018, www.bizjournals.com/chicago/news/2018/11/09/mcdonalds-is-succeeding-in-russia-by-going-local.html; Adam Chandler, "How McDonald's Became a Target for Protest," *The Atlantic*, April 16, 2015, www.theatlantic.com/business/archive/2015/04/setting-the-symbolic-golden-arches-aflame/390708/; "McDonald's Set for Russia Expansion," *New Europe Investor*, August 26, 2015, www.neweuropeinvestor.com/news/mcdonalds-set-for-russia-expansion10522/. Also see "Russia Could Ban US Imports," *Reuters*, April 4, 2018, www.newshub.co.nz/home/world/2018/04/russia-could-ban-us-imports.html.

26. "2018 BrandZ Top 100 Global Brands," Millward Brown, https://brandz.com/report/global/2018.

27. See Rachael Tepper, "Yum! Brands' International Product Strategy: How the Double Down Went Global," *Huffington Post*, March 11, 2013, www.huffingtonpost.com/2013/03/11/yum-brands-international-product-strategy_n_2814360.html; Molly

Osberg, "How Colonel Sanders Became Father Christmas in Japan," *TPM,* December 23, 2014, http://talkingpointsmemo.com/theslice/kfc-christmas-in-japan-colonel-sanders-history-12-23-2014; Kate Taylor, "How KFC Made Christmas All about Fried Chicken—in Japan," *Business Insider,* December 25, 2017, www.businessinsider.com/how-kfc-became-a-christmas-tradition-in-japan-2016-12?r=UK&IR=T; and "Episode 19: Kentucky Fried Christmas," *Household Name,* December 19, 2018 https://podcasts.apple.com/us/podcast/19-kentucky-fried-christmas/id1413374332?i=1000426105857.

28. See annual reports and other financial and review data from www.coca-colacompany.com/our-company/ and www.coca-colacompany.com/our-company/infographic-coca-cola-at-a-glance/, accessed October 2019.

29. For this and other information in this section on Netflix in India, see Lucas Shaw, "Can Netflix Beat Bollywood?" *Bloomberg Businessweek,* July 2, 2018, pp. 16–18; Manish Singh, "Netflix and Amazon Are Struggling to Win Over the World's Second-Largest Internet Market, *CNBC,* July 5, 2018, www.cnbc.com/2018/07/05/netflix-and-amazon-are-struggling-to-win-over-indian-viewers.html; Ananya Bhattacharya, "Netflix Dangles a $4 Bait to Tap New Users in India," *Quartz,* March 27, 2019, https://qz.com/india/1581601/netflixs-4-plan-to-rival-amazon-hotstar-eros-zee5-in-india/; Noah Higgins-Dunn, "Netflix Isn't Concerned about Lower Prices as Disney Streaming Starts, Except in One Huge Market," *CNBC,* April 17, 2019, www.cnbc.com/2019/04/17/netflix-not-concerned-about-lower-prices-except-in-one-huge-market.html; and www.netflixinvestor.com/financials/annual-reports-and-proxies/default.aspx, accessed October 2019.

30. See Kate Taylor, "Coca-Cola Has Discovered an Untapped Market to Save the Soda Business," *Business Insider,* February 7, 2016, www.businessinsider.com/africa-is-the-future-of-coca-cola-2016-2; and https://coca-colahellenic.com/en/about-us/coca-cola-hbc-at-a-glance/, accessed October 2019.

31. See "Volkswagen Group Rus and GAZ Group Extend Their Cooperation in Russia," June 15, 2017, www.volkswagen-media-services.com/en/detailpage/-/detail/Volkswagen-Group-Rus-and-GAZ-Group-extend-their-cooperation-in-Russia/view/5145928/7a5bbec13158edd433c6630f5ac445da?p_p_auth=kiEFZdL3; and www.pg.com/en_IN/company/pg-india.shtml, accessed October 2019.

32. See "HOTEL Announces the Signing of the Management Contract for the DoubleTree by Hilton Toluca," *MarketWatch,* September 10, 2018, www.marketwatch.com/press-release/hotel-announces-the-signing-of-the-management-contract-for-the-doubletree-by-hilton-toluca-2018-09-10; and http://en.wikipedia.org/wiki/Doubletree, accessed October 2019.

33. Rick Munarriz, "Shanghai Disney Hits a Few Hiccups," *The Motley Fool,* March 28, 2016, www.fool.com/investing/general/2016/03/28/shanghai-disney-hits-a-few-hiccups.aspx; and Seth Kubersky, "Who Owns the Disney Parks around the World," *Attractions Magazine,* February 12, 2017, http://attractionsmagazine.com/owns-disney-parks-around-world/; and www.shanghaidisneyresort.com/en/, accessed September 2019.

34. See Adam Levy, "3 Reasons Walmart's Flipkart Acquisition Is Its Most Important Yet," *The Motley Fool,* May 15, 2018, www.fool.com/investing/2018/05/15/3-reasons-walmarts-flipkart-acquisition-is-its-mos.aspx; "Walmart Raises Stake in Flipkart to 81.3%," *Hindu BusinessLine,* November 20, 2018, www.thehindubusinessline.com/companies/walmart-raises-stake-in-flipkart-to-813/article25550934.ece; "Kellogg Tops Profit Estimates, Makes West Africa Investment," *Reuters,* May 3, 2018, www.reuters.com/article/us-kellogg-results/kellogg-tops-profit-estimates-makes-west-africa-investment-idUSKBN1I41E9; and Steve Symington, "Why Kellogg Just Sold a Smorgasbord of Beloved Brands," *The Motley Fool,* April 3, 2019, www.fool.com/investing/2019/04/03/why-kellogg-just-sold-a-smorgasbord-of-beloved-bra.aspx.

35. See Erik Sherman, "Intel Plans an $11 Billion Expansion in Israel," *Fortune,* January 29, 2019; http://fortune.com/2019/01/29/intel-11-billion-expansion-israel/; and Tova Cohen and Steven Scheer, "Exclusive: Israel's Chip Sales to China Jump as Intel Expands," *Reuters,* March 19, 2019, www.reuters.com/article/us-israel-china-tech-exclusive/exclusive-israels-chip-sales-to-china-jump-as-intel-expands-idUSKCN1R00DF.

36. See Anna Molin, "Ikea Plans to Expand to a Dozen New Markets in Coming Years," *Bloomberg Businessweek,* October 10, 2018, www.bloomberg.com/news/articles/2018-10-10/ikea-plans-to-expand-to-a-dozen-new-markets-in-coming-years; Tim Nudd, "11 Ikea Ads That Show What a Brilliant Year the Brand Had Creatively," *Adweek,* December 8, 2017, www.adweek.com/creativity/11-ikea-ads-that-show-what-a-brilliant-year-the-brand-had-creatively/; Beth Kowitt, "It's IKEA's World," *Fortune,* March 15, 2015, pp. 166-175; Michael Wei, "In IKEA's China Stores, Loitering Is Encouraged," *Bloomberg Businessweek,* November 1, 2010, pp. 22–23; David Pierson, "A Beijing Theme Park with Futons," *Los Angeles Times*, August 25, 2009, p. A1; Emily Raulhala, "No, IKEA Hasn't Banned Customers from Sleeping in Its Chinese Stores," *Time,* April 10, 2015, http://time.com/3814935/ikea-china-customers-sleeping/; Anne Quinto, "How the IKEA Catalogue Cracked What 'Domestic Bliss' Means in Different Cultures," *Quartzy,* July 25, 2017, https://quartzy.qz.com/1036380/ikea-catalogue-2017-defining-domestic-bliss-in-different-cultures; and https://highlights.ikea.com/2017/facts-and-figures, accessed October, 2019.

37. See Warren J. Keegan and Mark C. Green, *Global Marketing*, 9th ed. (Hoboken, NJ: Pearson, 2017), pp. 322–329.

38. Toshiro Wakayama, Junjiro Shintaku, and Tomofumi Amano, "What Panasonic Learned in China," *Harvard Business Review,* December 2012, pp. 109–113.

39. See Saritha Rai, "Amazon Teaches Alexa to Speak Hinglish. Apple's Siri Is Next," *Bloomberg Businessweek,* October 30, 2017, www.bloomberg.com/news/articles/2017-10-30/amazon-teaches-alexa-to-speak-hinglish-apple-s-siri-is-next; J. Vignesh, "Amazon Intent on Making Alexa 'As Indian as It Gets,'" *Economic Times,* March 29, 2018, https://economictimes.indiatimes.com/small-biz/startups/newsbuzz/for-amazon-alexa-shines-new-light-on-india/articleshow/63525866.cms; and Astha Viaywargiya, "Smart-Speaker Must Get the Local Tongue," *Hindu BusinessLine,* April 21, 2019, www.thehindubusinessline.com/news/smart-speakers-must-get-the-local-tongue/article26904627.ece.

40. See Barrett J. Brunsman, "P&G Launches First New Hair Care Brand in Four Years," *Cincinnati Business Courier,* March 4, 2019, www.bizjournals.com/cincinnati/news/2019/03/04/p-g-launches-first-new-hair-care-collection-in.html; and www.dlight.com/and www.dlight.com/about-us, accessed October 2019.

41. See Arnold Ma, "The Importance of Having a Chinese Version of Your Brand: It's Much More Than Just a Name," *The Drum*, October 11, 2018, www.thedrum.com/opinion/2018/10/11/the-importance-having-chinese-version-your-brand-it-s-much-more-just-name; Benjamin Cost, "Lost in Translation? Pick Your Chinese Brand Name Carefully," *Shanghaiist*, May 5, 2018, www.shanghaiist.com/2014/03/28/hutong-school-pick-your-chinese-brand-name-carefully.php; Michael Wines, "Picking Brand Names in China Is a Business Itself," *New York Times*, November 12, 2011, p. A4; Carly Chalmers, "12 Amazing Translations of Chinese Brand Names," *todaytranslations*, August 27, 2013, www.todaytranslations.com/blog/12-amazing-translations-of-chinese-brand-names/; Arnold Ma, "Why Choosing a Chinese Name for Your Western Brand Will Increase Sales in China," *The Drum*, October 16, 2018, www.thedrum.com/opinion/2018/10/16/why-choosing-chinese-name-your-western-brand-will-increase-sales-china-0; and Thomas O'Neill, "From Biting the Wax Tadpole to Rushing towards Death, Why

It's Important to Get Your Chinese Name Right," *The Drum*, February 9, 2019, www.thedrum.com/news/2019/02/09/biting-the-wax-tadpole-rushing-towards-death-why-its-important-get-your-chinese-name.

42. For these and other examples, see "How Crayola Used WeChat and Alibaba to Grow Sales in China," *Advertising Age*, May 30, 2016, p. 27; and Angela Doland, "How to Sell Toys in a Culture Where Play Is Viewed Negatively," *Advertising Age*, March 20, 2017, http://adage.com/article/cmo-strategy/sell-toys-a-culture-parents-playtime/308340/.

43. See Warren J. Keegan and Mark C. Green, *Global Marketing*, 9th ed. (Hoboken, NJ: Pearson Publishing, 2017), pp. 423–424.

44. See Gordon Gottsegen, "Samsung Makes the Cheap Galaxy J5 and J7 Official," CNET, June 6, 2017, www.cnet.com/news/samsung-unveils-galaxy-j5-j7-2017/; Rishi Iyengar, "How China's Xiaomi Took India's Smartphone Market by Storm," *CNN Business*, May 1, 2018, https://money.cnn.com/2018/04/30/technology/xiaomi-india-smartphone-manu-jain/index.html; and Rishi Iyengar, "Apple Needs a Cheap iPhone to Crack India," *CNN Business*, January 4, 2019, www.cnn.com/2019/01/04/tech/india-smartphone-market-iphone-apple/index.html.

45. See "China's Logistics Sector Continues to Grow in 2016," *Xinhuanet.com*, March 9, 2017, http://news.xinhuanet.com/english/2017-03/09/c_136115835.htm; and "Total US Logistics Spend Dipped in 2016, Says CSCMP," *Transport Topics*, June 20, 2017, http://www.ttnews.com/articles/total-us-logistics-spend-dipped-2016-says-cscmp.

46. See http://corporate.mcdonalds.com/mcd/investors/financial-information/annual-report.html, accessed October 2019.

47. Vlad Savov, "Huawei's Phone Sales Are Ballooning While Apple and Samsung's Slump," *The Verge*, May 1, 2019, https://www.theverge.com/circuitbreaker/2019/5/1/18525034/huawei-apple-samsung-smartphone-market-share-idc-2019; Lucy Hooker and Danile Palumbo, "Huawei: The Rapid Growth of a Chinese Champion in Five Charts," *BBC News*, May 20, 2019, https://www.bbc.com/news/business-46480208; Martin Roll, "Huawei—Transforming a Chinese Technology Business to A Global Brand," *Business and Brand Leadership*, February 2018, https://martinroll.com/resources/articles/strategy/huawei-transforming-chinese-technology-business-global-brand/; Christian Edwards, "A Timid Huawei Has Emerged from Its Global PR Storm to See What's Left to Salvage," *Business Insider*, December 18, 2018, https://www.businessinsider.com/huawei-whats-next-after-global-public-relations-storm-us-china-2018-12; "Huawei Is Ready to Meet Challenges Ahead: CEO, *Gulf Times*, May 23, 2019, https://www.gulf-times.com/story/632213/Huawei-is-ready-to-meet-challenges-ahead-CEO; Mathieu Rosemain, "Huawei Targets the European Market with Lower-Priced Smartphone," January 22, 2019, https://www.theglobeandmail.com/business/technology/article-huawei-targets-european-market-with-lower-priced-honor-view2/; David de Cremer, "Lessons from Huawei: When Chinese Companies Go Global," *London Business School*, April 16, 2018, https://www.london.edu/lbsr/lessons-from-huawei-when-chinese-companies-go-global; Ashish Kumar Sen, "The Huawei Challenge," *The Atlantic*, May 1, 2019, https://www.atlanticcouncil.org/blogs/new-atlanticist/huawei-china-technology.

Chapter 20

1. See Jeff Beer, "Why Brand Purpose Marketing Isn't Working with Young People," *Fast Company*, May 10, 2019, www.fastcompany.com/90347311/why-brand-purpose-marketing-isnt-working-with-young-people; "Unilever Named Industry Leader in Dow Jones Sustainability Index," September 13, 2018, www.unilever.com/news/press-releases/2018/unilever-named-as-an-industry-leader-in-djsi.html; Andrew Saunders, "Paul Polman of Unilever," *Management Today*, March 2011, pp. 42–47; Adi Ignatius, "Captain Planet," *Harvard Business Review*, June 2012, pp. 2–8; Dale Buss, "Unilever's Sustainable Living Brands," *Brand Channel*, May 10, 2018, www.brandchannel.com/2018/05/10/unilever_sustainable_living_brands_good_business/; Sarah George, "Unilever Reveals Mixed Progress towards Sustainable Living Plan Goals," *Edie.net*, April 17, 2019, www.edie.net/news/7/Unilever-reveals-mixed-progress-towards-Sustainable-Living-Plan-goals/; and www.unilever.com/sustainable-living/; www.unilever.com/investor-relations/annual-report-and-accounts/; and www.unilever.com/about/who-we-are/about-Unilever/, accessed October 2019.

2. See "McDonald's Announces Global Commitment to Support Families with Increased Focus on Happy Meals," February 18, 2018, http://news.mcdonalds.com/news-releases/news-release-details/mcdonalds-announces-global-commitment-support-families-0; and www.mcdonalds.com/us/en-us/about-our-food/quality-food.html; https://corporate.mcdonalds.com/corpmcd/scale-for-good/using-our-scale-for-good.html; and www.mcdonalds.com/us/en-us/about-our-food/nutrition-calculator.html, accessed October 2019.

3. Melissa Locker, "If McDonald's Keeps Its Promise, Your Happy Meal Could Be Green within Seven Years," *Fast Company*, January 16, 2017, www.fastcompany.com/40517145/mcdonalds-promises-to-start-recycling-its-packaging-by-2025; and https://corporate.mcdonalds.com/corpmcd/scale-for-good/packaging-and-recycling.html#goals, accessed October 2019.

4. David Streitfeld, "It's Discounted, but Is It a Deal? How List Prices Lost Their Meaning," *New York Times*, March 6, 2016, p. A1; and Paul Tassin, "Overstock Must Pay $6.8 Million Penalty in 'Compare At' Pricing Lawsuit," Top Class Actions, June 7, 2017, https://topclassactions.com/lawsuit-settlements/lawsuit-news/722412-overstock-must-pay-6-8m-penalty-compare-pricing-lawsuit/, and Daphne Howland, "Ross to Settle $4.9M Lawsuit over 'Deceptive' Price Tags," *Retail Dive*, October 3, 2018, www.retaildive.com/news/ross-to-settle-49m-lawsuit-over-deceptive-price-tags/538768/.

5. Jonathan Vanian, "LifeLock Pays Big to Settle FTC Suit over Weak Data Security," *Fortune*, December 17, 2015; and "LifeLock to Pay $100 Million in FTC Settlement," *Practical Law*, January 21, 2016, https://content.next.westlaw.com/Document/I02f47330a46e11e598dc8b09b4f043e0/View/FullText.html?originationContext=document&transitionType=DocumentItem&contextData=(sc.Default).

6. Dan Mitchell, "Americans Don't Buy Enough Soda—Here's the New Targets," *Fortune*, February 19, 2016, http://fortune.com/2016/02/19/soda-emerging-nations-sales/; Trefis Team, "How Coca-Cola Plans to Make India Its Third Largest Market," *Forbes*, September 7, 2017, www.forbes.com/sites/greatspeculations/2017/09/07/how-coca-cola-plans-to-make-india-its-third-largest-market/#5114de2e848b; "Cola-Cola Faces Shareholder Activism on Sugar's Health Risks," *Bloomberg LP*, February 11, 2019, https://news.bloomberglaw.com/corporate-law/cola-cola-faces-shareholder-activism-on-sugars-health-risks-7; and Center for Science in the Public Interest, "Carbonating the World," www.cspinet.org/carbonating/, accessed October 2019.

7. Brian Clark Howard, "Planned Obsolescence: 8 Products Designed to Fail," *Popular Mechanics*, www.popularmechanics.com/technology/planned-obsolescence-460210#slide-5, accessed September 2015. Also see Linda Simpson, "Is There a Cure for Society's Affluenza?" *Huffington Post*, January 10, 2018, www.huffingtonpost.ca/linda-simpson/is-there-a-cure-for-our-societys-affluenza_a_23329763/.

8. "Apple Apologizes for Slowing Older iPhones Dawn," *Reuters*, December 29, 2018, www.bbc.com/news/technology-42508300; "Apple Investigated by France for 'Planned Obsolescence,'"

BBC, January 8, 2018, www.bbc.com/news/world-europe-42615378; and Chance Miller, "Apple Filing Shows Company Plans to Pay for iPhone Throttling Issues," *9TO5Mac,* February 4, 2019, https://9to5mac.com/2019/02/04/iphone-throttling-lawsuits-apple/.

9. See Alana Rhone, Michele Ver Ploeg, Chris Dicken, Ryan Williams, and Vince Breneman, "Low-Income and Low-Supermarket-Access Census Tracts, 2010–2015," *Economic Information Bulletin,* January 2017, p. 12, www.ers.usda.gov/webdocs/publications/82101/eib-165.pdf?v=0; and U.S. Department of Agriculture, "Food Access Research Atlas: Documentation," www.ers.usda.gov/data-products/food-access-research-atlas/documentation/, accessed October 2019.

10. See Nevin Cohen, "SNAP is Going Online. Will the Term 'Food Desert' Soon Be Obsolete?" *Civil Eats,* May 19, 2019, https://civileats.com/2019/05/01/snap-is-going-online-will-the-term-food-desert-soon-be-obsolete/; and Emily Moon, "SNAP Participants Can Buy Groceries Online for the First Time," *Pacific Standard,* April 19, 2019, https://psmag.com/news/snap-participants-can-buy-groceries-online-for-the-first-time.

11. See www.newdream.org/ and www.newdream.org/about/mission, accessed October 2019.

12. Michaela Winberg, "The Year in Starbucks: How the Coffee Giant Has Remained in the Local Spotlight," *Billy Penn,* April 12, 2019, www.billypenn.com/2019/04/12/the-year-in-starbucks-how-the-coffee-giant-has-remained-in-the-local-spotlight/; Tanya Mohn, "Howard Schultz, Starbucks, and a History of Corporate Responsibility," *New York Times,* November 15, 2017, www.nytimes.com/2017/11/15/business/dealbook/howard-schultz-starbucks-corporate-responsibility.html; Biz Carson, "The Vital Lesson Magic Johnson Taught Starbucks CEO Howard Schultz," *Business Insider,* February 9, 2016, www.businessinsider.com/magic-johnson-nba-star-to-businessman-2016-2; Kate Taylor, "As the American Middle Class Shrinks, Starbucks Sees Ferguson Store as a Blueprint for the Future," *Business Insider,* April 27, 2017, www.businessinsider.com/starbucks-in-ferguson-is-a-blueprint-for-the-future-2017-4; Chris Isidore, "Starbucks Says Ferguson Store Is One of Its Top New Locations," *Money,* September 7, 2016, www.money.cnn.com/2016/09/07/news/companies/ferguson-starbucks-schultz/index.html; Karen Valby, "Starbucks Is Bringing Hope—and Profit—to the Communities America's Forgotten," *Fast Company,* July 31, 2017, www.fastcompany.com/40438365/starbucks-is-bringing-hope-and-profit-to-the-communities-americas-forgotten; Marianne Wilson, "Starbucks Hits Milestone," *Chain Store Age,* March 18, 2019, www.chainstoreage.com/store-spaces/starbucks-hits-milestone/; www.starbucks.com/responsibility/community; and www.starbucks.com/responsibility, accessed October 2019.

13. See "How REI Is Keeping the #OptOutside Magic Alive on Black Friday," *Fast Company,* November 11, 2018, www.fastcompany.com/90271139/how-rei-is-keeping-the-optoutside-magic-alive-on-black-friday; Kevin Moss, "Don't Read This Article: How Ads against Consumerism Help Sustainability," *World Resources Institute,* February 5, 2018, www.wri.org/blog/2018/02/dont-read-article-how-ads-against-consumerism-help-sustainability; and www.facebook.com/llbean/videos/when-did-disposable-become-our/10153921325967415/ and www.rei.com/opt-outside, accessed October 2019.

14. See "INRIX: Congestion Costs Each American 97 House, $1,348 a Year," February 11, 2019, http://inrix.com/press-releases/scorecard-2018-us/; and Texas Transportation Institute, "Urban Mobility Scorecard," https://mobility.tamu.edu/ums/, accessed October 2019.

15. Allison Griswold, "New York Will Be the First U.S. City to Charge Drivers to Enter Its Busiest Areas," *Quartz,* March 31, 2019.

16. See Natasha Lomas, "Google Fined $2.7BN for EU Antitrust Violations over Shopping Searches," *Tech Crunch,* June 27, 2017, https://techcrunch.com/2017/06/27/google-fined-e2-42bn-for-eu-antitrust-violations-over-shopping-searches/; Terry Collins, "Google Appeals Record $2.7 Billion EU Antitrust Fine," *CNET,* September 11, 2017, www.cnet.com/news/google-is-appealing-record-2-7-billion-eu-antitrust-fine/; and James Vincent, "Google Hit with 1.5 Euro Billion Anti-Trust Fine by EU," *The Verge,* March 20, 2019, www.theverge.com/2019/3/20/18270891/google-eu-antitrust-fine-adsense-advertising.

17. See Philip Kotler, "Reinventing Marketing to Manage the Environmental Imperative," *Journal of Marketing,* July 2011, pp. 132–135; and Kai Ryssdal, "Unilever CEO: For Sustainable Business, Go against 'Mindless Consumption,'" *Marketplace,* June 11, 2013, www.marketplace.org/topics/sustainability/consumed/unilever-ceo-paul-polman-sustainble-business.

18. "Adidas Group Sustainable Materials," www.adidas-group.com/en/sustainability/products/materials/#/recyceltes-polystrol/sustainable-better-cotton/pvc-and-phthalates/, accessed October 2018; Sarah Mahoney, "Adidas Steps Up Ocean-Trash Efforts, Aims to Make 22M Shoes," *MediaPost,* January 22, 2019, www.mediapost.com/publications/article/330911/adidas-steps-up-ocean-trash-efforts-aims-to-make.html; and www.adidas-group.com/en/sustainability/managing-sustainability/general-approach/ and www.adidas-group.com/en/sustainability/products/sustainability-innovation/, accessed October 2019.

19. See Alan S. Brown, "The Many Shades of Green," *Mechanical Engineering,* January 2009, http://memagazine.asme.org/Articles/2009/January/Many_Shades_Green.cfm; www.ibm.com/ibm/environment/products/recycling.shtml, accessed October 2019.

20. See "Decarbonization," www.siemens.com/global/en/home/company/sustainability/decarbonization.html, and "Green, Greener Kalwa," www.siemens.com/global/en/home/company/about/businesses/real-estate/green-greener-kalwa.html, accessed October 2019.

21. Information from "Sustainability Is Opportunity for the North Face," *Clean Technica,* August 27, 2018, https://cleantechnica.com/2018/08/27/sustainability-is-opportunity-for-the-north-face-an-interview-with-james-rogers-director-of-sustainability; and www.thenorthface.com/about-us/responsibility.html, accessed October 2019.

22. See www.thenorthface.com/about-us/responsibility.html, accessed October 2019.

23. See www.pedigree.com/why-pedigree/about-us and www.pedigreefoundation.org/about-us-2/, accessed October 2019.

24. S. Butler, "Appetite Grows for Vegan Products at UK Supermarkets," *The Guardian,* June 8, 2018, https://www.theguardian.com/business/2018/jun/08/appetite-grows-vegan-products-uk-supermarkets-waitrose-iceland; "Bring Your Own Containers, Says Waitrose," *BBC,* June 4, 2019, https://www.bbc.com/news/business-48498346; Government UK, Modern Slavery Act 2015, The National Archives, http://www.legislation.gov.uk/ukpga/2015/30/section/54/enacted; John Lewis Partnership, "Corporate Responsibility Report 2018/19," https://www.johnlewispartnership.co.uk/content/dam/cws/pdfs/Juniper/jlp_cr_report_1819.pdf; lovemoney.com, "Waitrose: The Story of How It Started and Why It's Become a British High Street Favourite," https://www.lovemoney.com/gallerylist/80196/waitrose-the-story-of-how-it-started-and-why-its-become-a-british-high-st; F. McKevitt, "Supermarket Sales Suffer by Comparison with Last Year's Summer Highs," https://uk.kantar.com/consumer/shoppers/2019/supermarket-sales-suffer-by-comparison-with-last-year%E2%80%99s-summer-highs/; "UK's Waitrose Plans 1 Billion Pound Online Grocery Business," *Reuters,* May 16, 2019, https://www.reuters.com/article/us-waitrose-internet/uks-waitrose-plans-1-billion-pound-online-grocery-business-idUSKCN1SM1TT; A. Voinea, "John Lewis Report Highlights Corporate Responsibility Achievements," *Co-operative News,* May 17, 2017, https://www.thenews.coop/118274/sector/john-lewis-report-highlights-corporate-responsibility-achievements/; Waitrose & Partners,

"The Waitrose Food & Drink Report," https://www.waitrose.com/home/about_waitrose/the-waitrose-fooddrinkreport.html; Waitrose & Partners, "We're Fishing Responsibly," https://www.waitrose.com/home/inspiration/about_waitrose/the_waitrose_way/responsible_fishing.html; Waitrose & Partners, "We're Backing British," https://www.waitrose.com/home/inspiration/about_waitrose/the_waitrose_way/the_origin_of_our_food.html; Waitrose & Partners, "The Corporate Responsibility Report 2018/19," https://www.johnlewispartnership.co.uk/content/dam/cws/pdfs/Juniper/jlp_cr_report_1819.pdf; Waitrose & Partners, "Sustainability," https://www.waitrose.com/ecom/shop/featured/groceries/sustainability.

25. See "Leading Cleaning Products Company Method Commits Majority of Its Product Lineup to Cradle to Cradle Product Certification," April 9, 2014, www.c2ccertified.org/news/article/leading_cleaning_products_company_method_commits_majority_of_its_product_li; and https://methodhome.com/ and https://methodhome.com/about-us/our-story/ accessed October 2019.

26. See Bruce Japsen, "CVS Kicks In Another $50 Million for Anti-Tobacco Push," *Forbes*, March 10, 2016, www.forbes.com/sites/brucejapsen/2016/03/10/cvs-kicks-in-another-50m-to-anti-tobacco-push/#41c6eb5f11f3; Phil Wahba, "She Thanks You for Not Smoking," *Fortune*, September 11, 2015, http://fortune.com/2015/09/11/cvs-health-helena-foulkes/; Kristina Monllos, "CVS Health's Marketing Chief on Turning the Pharmacy Brand into a Healthcare Player," *Adweek*, March 28, 2016, www.adweek.com/print/170437; and information from www.cvs.com/shop/health-medicine/stop-smoking, www.cvs.com/minuteclinic/resources/smoking-cessation, cvshealth.com/about/facts-and-company-information, http://investors.cvshealth.com, and https://cvshealth.com/about/purpose-statement, accessed October 2019.

27. See International Monetary Fund Staff Team from the Fiscal Affairs Department the Legal Department, "Corruption: Costs and Mitigating Strategies," May 2016, www.imf.org/external/pubs/ft/sdn/2016/sdn1605.pdf; and Rhoda Weeks-Brown, "Corruption Disintegration," International Monetary Fund, November 29, 2018, www.imf.org/en/News/Articles/2018/12/04/sp112918-corruption-disintegration#_ftn1, Also see Michael Montgomery, "The Cost of Corruption," *American RadioWorks*, http://americanradioworks.publicradio.org/features/corruption/, accessed October 2019.

28. See www.ama.org/codes-of-conduct/, accessed October 2019.

29. See "Protect This House: The Under Armour Code of Conduct. Make the Right Call," www.uabiz.com/static-files/fdd4d03e-a31e-49a4-9500-88c4a0abcb80, accessed October 2019.

30. David A. Lubin and Daniel C. Esty, "The Sustainability Imperative," *Harvard Business Review*, May 2010, pp. 41–50; and Roasbeth Moss Kanter, "It's Time to Take Full Responsibility," *Harvard Business Review*, October 2010, p. 42.

31. Better Cotton Initiative, "H&M 'Making Sustainability Fashionable'," April 16, 2015, https://bettercotton.org/hm-making-sustainability-fashionable/; Nitin Bhalla, "H&M Says Working to Improve Labor Conditions in India, Cambodia Factories," May 21, 2016, https://www.reuters.com/article/us-india-cambodia-hennes-mauritz-idUSKCN0YC0SD; Hayley Peterson, "How H&M Churns Out New Styles in Just 2 Weeks," *Business Insider*, September 13, 2014, https://www.businessinsider.com/hm-produces-new-fashions-in-two-weeks-2014-9?international=true&r=US&IR=T; Kelly-Leigh Cooper, "Fast Fashion: Inside the Fight to End the Silence on Waste," *BBC News*, July 31, 2018, https://www.bbc.com/news/world-44968561; Edge, "Fashion Industry Waste Statistics," https://edgexpo.com/fashion-industry-waste-statistics/; Ethisphere, "Ethisphere Recognizes 128 World's Most Ethical Companies for 2019," February 26, 2019, https://ethisphere.com/128-worlds-most-ethical-companies-for-2019/; European Union (2019), Nikolina Šajn, "Environmental Impact of the Textile and Clothing Industry What Consumers Need to Know," European Parliamentary Research Service, https://www.europarl.europa.eu/RegData/etudes/BRIE/2019/633143/EPRS_BRI(2019)633143_EN.pdf; R. L. Ferla, "'Cheap Chic' Draws Crowds on 5th Ave.," *The New York Times*, April 11, 2000, https://www.nytimes.com/2000/04/11/style/cheap-chic-draws-crowds-on-5th-ave.html; James Hitchings-Hales, "Hundreds of H&M and Gap Factory Workers Abused Daily, Report Says," Global Citizen, https://www.globalcitizen.org/en/content/hm-gap-factory-abuse-fast-fashion-workers/; H&M, *The H&M Way*, Sustainability Reports (2018), https://sustainability.hm.com/en/sustainability/downloads-resources/reports/sustainability-reports.html; H&M, "How H&M Gives Back to the Community," http://sites.mediaplanet.com/holidayshoppingguide/winterfashion/how-hm-gives-back-to-the-communityHitchings-Hales; Human Rights Watch, "'Work Faster or Get Out': Labor Rights Abuses in Cambodia's Garment Industry," August 17, 2018, https://www.hrw.org/report/2015/03/11/work-faster-or-get-out/labor-rights-abuses-cambodias-garment-industry; J. M. Radparvar and J. M. Radparvar, "Behind the Label: H&M's Conscious Collection," December 7, 2017, https://www.huffpost.com/entry/h-and-m-conscious-collection_b_1261082; Reuters, "H&M Says Working to Improve Labour Conditions in India, Cambodia Factories after Reports of Forced Overtime and Loss of Job If Pregnant," *South China Morning Post*, July 20, 2018, https://www.scmp.com/news/asia/southeast-asia/article/1950478/hm-says-working-improve-labour-conditions-india-cambodia; Lara Robertson, "How Ethical Is H&M?", September 4, 2019, https://goodonyou.eco/how-ethical-is-hm/; S. Young, "H&M Launches Conscious Exclusive 2018 Collection," *The Independent*, April 28, 2018, https://www.independent.co.uk/life-style/fashion/hm-conscious-exclusive-2018-collection-sustainable-organic-a8322011.html.

Appendix 1

i. "Bottled Water Holds Steady at No. 1," *Beverage Industry*, July 2018, p. SOI 15; "Global Flavored and Functional Water Market: Growing Incidence of Obesity to Stimulate Growth," *Transparency Market Research*, June 2017, www.transparencymarketresearch.com/pressrelease/flavored-functional-water.htm; Jeff Beer, "Propel Water's New Brand Strategy Is Hyping Its Gatorade Roots," *Fast Company*, March 29, 2018, www.fastcompany.com/40551566/propel-watersnew-brand-strategy-is-hyping-its-gatorade-roots; and product and market information obtained from http://vitaminwater.com, http://propelwater.com, and http://nestle-watersna.com, July 2019.

Appendix 2

i. This is derived by rearranging the following equation and solving for price: Percentage markup = (price − cost) ÷ price.

ii. Using the basic profit equation, we set profit equal to ROI × I: ROI × I = (P × Q) − TFC − (Q × UVC). Solving for Q gives Q = (TFC + (ROI × I)) ÷ (P − UVC).

iii. YCharts (2018), "US Households," available at ycharts.com/indicators/us_households; Pew Research Center (2018), "US Households," available at www.pewinternet.org/fact-sheet/internet-broadband/; and Parks Associates (2017), "Internet/Broadband Fact Sheet," available at www.parksassociates.com/blog/article/pr-01102017).

iv. See Roger J. Best, *Market-Based Management*, 6th ed. (Upper Saddle River, NJ: Prentice Hall, 2013).

v. Total contribution can also be determined from the unit contribution and unit volume: Total contribution = unit contribution × unit sales. Total units sold in 2020 were 595,238 units, which can be determined by dividing total sales by price per unit ($100 million ÷ $168). Total contribution = $35.28 contribution per unit × 595,238 units = $20,999,996.64 (difference due to rounding).

Index

Subject Index

Figures and tables are indicated by page numbers in italics.